Oxford
School
SPANISH
Dictionary

Editoria'
New
with the assista

OXFORD
UNIVERSITY PRESS

...n Street,

Oxford University Press is a d...........................ord.
It furthers the University's objective of excellence in research,
scholarship, and education by publishing worldwide in

Oxford   New York

Auckland   Cape Town   Dar es Salaam   Hong Kong   Karachi
Kuala Lumpur   Madrid   Melbourne   Mexico City   Nairobi
New Delhi   Shanghai   Taipei   Toronto

With offices in

Argentina   Austria   Brazil   Chile   Czech Republic   France   Greece
Guatemala   Hungary   Italy   Japan   Poland   Portugal   Singapore
South Korea   Switzerland   Thailand   Turkey   Ukraine   Vietnam

Oxford is a registered trade mark of Oxford University Press
in the UK and in certain other countries

British Library Cataloguing in Publication Data
Data available

ISBN: 978 0 19 275706 7

10 9 8 7 6 5 4 3 2 1

Printed in Malaysia

Paper used in the production of this book is a natural, recyclable product made
from wood grown in sustainable forests. The manufacturing process conforms to
the environmental regulations of the country of origin.

INTRODUCTION

This dictionary has been specially written for students who are in their first years of learning Spanish all the way through to preparing for exams. We have paid particular attention to making the dictionary user-friendly. With the help of colour headwords, alphabet tabs, easy-to-follow signposts, and examples, the right translation can quickly be found. Spanish verbs on both sides of the dictionary are numbered to direct the student to the appropriate table in the centre pages.

Throughout the writing of this dictionary we have worked in close consultation with students, teachers, inspectors, and examining boards. We gratefully acknowledge the examining boards AQA (formerly NEAB and SEG), OCR, and EDEXCEL, who have read and commented on the dictionary text.

Since the first edition of this dictionary there have been many changes in Spanish life. Not least has been the introduction of the euro. This new edition takes full account of these changes and many new words and examples have been included in order to provide the best possible learner's dictionary of Spanish at this level.

HOW A BILINGUAL DICTIONARY WORKS

A bilingual dictionary contains two languages. When you look up a word in one of the languages, it gives the translation for that word in the other language. This dictionary is divided into two halves separated by a section of blue-edged pages. In the first half you look up Spanish words, which are in alphabetical order, to find out what they mean in English and in the second half you look up English words, also in alphabetical order, to find out how to say them in Spanish. The blue-edged pages are verb tables and you can see how to use them further on in this section.

At each entry you will find not only translations but also other information that will help you get the right translation and use the word correctly. Here is a guide to the different things you will find printed in an entry:

headword	a word you look up in the dictionary
translation	translations are the only things that are in 'ordinary' type in the dictionary. They are *always* typed like this, and something which is typed in a different way can *never* be a translation
noun	word class (part of speech): tells you whether the word you are looking up is a noun, a verb, an adjective, or some other part of speech. A headword can be more than one part of speech. For instance, book can be a noun *(she was reading a book)* or a verb *(I've booked the seats)*
(signpost)	helpful information: to guide you to the right translation, to show you how to use the translation, or to give you extra information
example	a phrase or sentence using the word you have looked up. You should read through them carefully to see if they are close to what you want to understand or say
Masc.	gender: after a Spanish noun, to tell you that it is masculine
Fem.	gender: after a Spanish noun, to tell you that it is feminine. *Fem.* also shows the feminine form of some adjectives
●	indicates a phrasal verb such as *to carry on*
★	shows an idiomatic expression such as *over the moon*
[27]	verb number – tells you which verb table to look up in the blue-edged centre pages of the dictionary

You can think of a dictionary entry as being made out of different sorts of building bricks. In the entries below you can see how they fit together to help you find what you need. The more you use your dictionary, the more confident you will feel about finding your way around it.

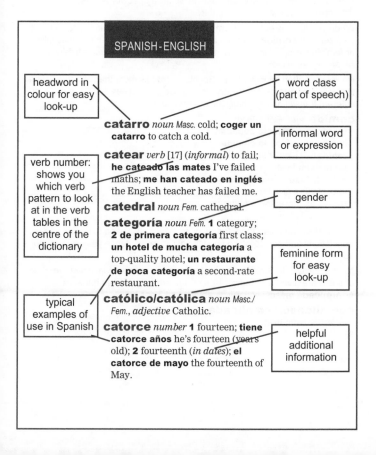

SPANISH-ENGLISH

headword in colour for easy look-up

word class (part of speech)

catarro *noun Masc.* cold; **coger un catarro** to catch a cold.

informal word or expression

catear *verb* [17] (*informal*) to fail; **he cateado las mates** I've failed maths; **me han cateado en inglés** the English teacher has failed me.

verb number: shows you which verb pattern to look at in the verb tables in the centre of the dictionary

catedral *noun Fem.* cathedral.

gender

categoría *noun Fem.* **1** category; **2 de primera categoría** first class; **un hotel de mucha categoría** a top-quality hotel; **un restaurante de poca categoría** a second-rate restaurant.

feminine form for easy look-up

typical examples of use in Spanish

católico/católica *noun Masc./ Fem.*, *adjective* Catholic.

catorce *number* **1** fourteen; **tiene catorce años** he's fourteen (years old); **2** fourteenth (*in dates*); **el catorce de mayo** the fourteenth of May.

helpful additional information

USING THE DICTIONARY

To find out what a Spanish word means

Suppose you want to find out what the Spanish word **comida** means. You need to use the first half of the dictionary to find the Spanish word that you are looking for. To help you do this, the guide words at the top of each page show the alphabetical range of words on the pages you have open. Notice that hyphens and spaces between words in Spanish headwords make no difference to their alphabetical order.

When you find the entry for **comida** you will find the translation. But you will also see that **comida** is a noun and because all nouns are either masculine or feminine in Spanish, you are given the gender *Fem.* (*Fem.* = feminine, *Masc.* = masculine).

However, it often happens that a Spanish word has more than one translation in English. If you look at the entry for **comida** you can see that there are three different translations, each of which is numbered:

comida *noun Fem.* **1** food;
   tenemos suficiente comida we
   have enough food; **la comida
   rápida** fast food; **2** lunch; **a la hora
   de la comida** at lunch time;
   3 meal; **cuatro comidas al día**
   four meals a day; **mi comida
   fuerte es a mediodía** I have my
   main meal at midday.

So **comida** can mean *food*, *lunch*, or *meal*. You will need to look at all the translations and decide which one fits best in the sentence you are trying to understand.

Most adjectives in Spanish have a masculine form and a feminine form. Both of these are given as headwords, so if you are trying to find out what **complicada** means, you will be able to find it easily:

complicado/complicada
   adjective complicated.

To find an English word and how to say it in Spanish

You can see that it is quite easy, once you know how the dictionary works, to look up a Spanish word and find out what it means. Students usually find it harder to use the dictionary to find out how to say something in Spanish. This dictionary is written specially to help you do this and to make it easy to find the right way of saying things in Spanish.

Suppose you want to know how to say **garden** in Spanish. Look up the word in the second part of the dictionary. If you follow the same method of looking through the alphabetical order of the headwords as you did when you were looking up a Spanish word, you will find the entry **garden** on page 427.

garden *noun* jardín *Masc*.

Now you can see that the Spanish word for garden is *jardín*. But if you want to make a sentence using a noun such as jardín you need to know whether it is masculine or feminine. The *Masc*. after jardín tells you that it is masculine so *in the garden* is **en el jardín**.

It is not always easy to work out which Spanish word you need. When the dictionary gives you more than one translation, it is very important to take the time to read through the whole entry. If you look up **hall** the entry looks like this:

hall *noun* **1** (*in a house*) entrada *Fem*.; **2** (*public*) salón *Masc*.; **the village hall** el salón de actos del pueblo; **3 a concert hall** una sala de conciertos.

You can see that **1** tells you that the Spanish word for a hall in your house is **entrada**, **2** that the word for a public place like a village hall or a school hall is **salón**, and **3** that the phrase for a concert hall is **sala de conciertos**.

Remember that the information which is in brackets and italics, or both, is there to guide you to the right translation but *will never be* the translation itself. Often it is not enough to find the translation of one single word. In the case of frequently used words, the dictionary also gives you a selection of common phrases you will want to use. In the entry **hair** you can see how the translation works in different expressions:

hair *noun* **1** pelo *Masc*.; **to have short hair** tener [9] el pelo corto; **to brush your hair** cepillarse [17] el pelo; **to wash your hair** lavarse [17] el pelo; **to have your hair cut** cortarse [17] el pelo; **she's had her hair cut** se ha cortado el pelo; **2 a hair** (*from the head*) un pelo; (*from the body*) un vello.

HOW TO USE THE VERB TABLES

On the Spanish side of the dictionary all the headwords which are verbs look like this: **cerrar** *verb* [29]. On the English side of the dictionary all the verbs given as translations of English verbs look like this: **frighten** *verb* asustar [17].

If you look at the pages edged in blue in the centre of the dictionary, you will find tables showing you how to use the different types of Spanish verbs.

The verb **cerrar** above has the number 29. If you look up number 29 in the verb tables you will find the tense patterns for this verb. The same is true for verb numbers after Spanish verbs in the English-Spanish side of the dictionary.

With practice you will soon be able to find your way easily around the dictionary and identify what you are looking for in each entry. Some entries may seem long and complicated at first glance. Reading carefully through the signposts and examples will lead you to the translation you need.

Aa

a. de C. *abbreviation* (*short for: antes de Cristo*) BC, before Christ.

a *preposition* (*note that 'a + el' becomes 'al'*) **1** to; **iremos a Italia** we'll go to Italy; **tuerce a la derecha** turn right; **voy a casa** I'm going home; **2 está a la izquierda** it's on the left; **sentados a la mesa** sitting at the table; **siéntate al sol** sit in the sun; **estaban a mi lado** they were by my side; **3** at; **a las diez** at ten o'clock; **a medianoche** at midnight; **se casó a los treinta años** she married at thirty; **¿a qué hora termina?** what time does it finish?; **4 hoy estamos a dos de enero** it's the second of January today; **5 está a diez kilómetros de aquí** it's ten kilometres from here; **la vi a lo lejos** I saw her in the distance; **6 dos veces al día** twice a day; **están a tres euros el kilo** they're three euros a kilo; **a ochenta kilómetros por hora** at eighty kilometres an hour; **7 ir a pie** to go on foot; **hecho a mano** handmade; **escrito a mano** handwritten; **a lápiz** in pencil; **8** to; **se lo di a Laura** I gave it to Laura; **le mandé un regalo a mi madre** I sent a present to my mother; **le da clases de piano a mi hermana** he gives my sister piano lessons; **9** (*not translated after certain verbs when followed by a person*) **no se lo dije a Mar** I didn't tell Mar; **vi a tu madre** I saw your mother; **10 voy a hacer los deberes** I'm going to do my homework; **nos fuimos a dormir** we went to sleep; **se han ido a nadar** they've gone swimming; **salimos a pasear** we went out for a walk; **11** (*in commands*) **¡a dormir!** go to sleep!; **¡a callar!** shut up!; **¡a comer!** food's ready!

abadía *noun Fem.* abbey.

abajo *adverb* **1 aquí abajo** down here; **allí abajo** down there; **2** downstairs; **hay otro piso abajo** there's another flat downstairs; **los vecinos de abajo** the downstairs neighbours; **3 el piso de abajo** the flat below, the bottom flat.

abalanzarse *reflexive verb* [22] **abalanzarse sobre alguien/algo** to leap on somebody/something; **se abalanzaron hacia la ventana** they rushed towards the window.

abandonado/abandonada *adjective* **1** deserted; **2** abandoned; **sentirse abandonado** to feel abandoned; **3** neglected.

abandonar *verb* [17] **1** to leave; **abandonó a su familia** he left his family; **2** to abandon; **abandonar el barco** to abandon ship.

abanico *noun Masc.* fan.

abarrotado/abarrotada *adjective* packed; **un bar abarrotado de gente** a bar packed with people.

abecedario *noun Masc.* alphabet.

abedul *noun Masc.* birch.

abeja *noun Fem.* bee.

abejón, abejorro *noun Masc.* bumble-bee.

abertura *noun Fem.* opening.

a b c d e f g h i j k l m n ñ o p q r s t u v w x y z

abeto noun Masc. fir.

abierto/abierta adjective
1 open; **la puerta está abierta** the door's open; **abierto al público** open to the public; **abierto de par en par** wide open; **siempre dejas el grifo abierto** you always leave the tap running; **2** open-minded; **mis padres son muy abiertos** my parents are very open-minded.

abochornado/ abochornada adjective embarrassed.

abogado/abogada noun Masc./ Fem. **1** lawyer; **2** solicitor.

abolir verb [19] to abolish.

abolladura noun Fem. dent.

abollar verb [17] to dent.
abollarse reflexive verb [17] to get dented.

abonar verb [17] **1** to pay (a bill); **2** to fertilize (a field or plant).
abonarse reflexive verb [17] **1** to subscribe; **abonarse a una revista** to subscribe to a magazine; **2** to buy a season ticket.

abono noun Masc. **1** fertilizer; **2** a season ticket.

abordar verb [17] **1** to tackle (a problem); **2** to raise (a subject).

aborrecer verb [35] to detest.

aborto noun Masc. **1** abortion; **2** miscarriage.

abotonarse reflexive verb [17] to do your buttons up; **me abotoné la chaqueta** I buttoned my jacket up.

abrasado/abrasada adjective **1** burnt; **murieron abrasados** they

burned to death; **2 estoy abrasada** I'm boiling.

abrasador/abrasadora adjective burning.

abrasar verb [17] to burn.

abrazar verb [22] to hug.
abrazarse reflexive verb [22] to hug each other.

abrazo noun Masc. hug.

abrebotellas noun Masc. (does not change in the plural) bottle opener.

abrelatas noun Masc. (does not change in the plural) tin opener.

abreviatura noun Fem. abbreviation.

abridor noun Masc. **1** bottle opener; **2** tin opener.

abrigar verb [28] to be warm (a jumper or coat).
abrigarse reflexive verb [28] to wrap up warmly.

abrigo noun Masc. **1** coat; **2 ropa de abrigo** warm clothes.

abril noun Masc. April.

abrir verb [46] **1** to open; **abre la ventana** open the window; **abrió la boca para hablar** he opened his mouth to speak; **no abrió la boca en toda la tarde** she didn't say a word all afternoon; **abrir algo de par en par** to open something wide; **2** to turn on (a tap); **abrir el agua** to turn the water on; **3 ¡abran paso!** make way!
abrirse reflexive verb [46] to open; **la puerta se abrió** the door opened.

abrocharse reflexive verb [17] **1** to do up your buttons; **abróchate la**

chaqueta do your jacket up; **2** to fasten (*a seat belt*); **abróchense los cinturones** fasten your seat belts.

absoluto/absoluta *adjective* **1** absolute; **2 en absoluto** not at all; **'¿te importa?'** – **'en absoluto'** 'do you mind?' – 'not at all'.

absorbente *adjective* absorbent.

absorber *verb* [18] to absorb.

abstracto/abstracta *adjective* abstract.

absurdo/absurda *adjective* absurd.

abuchear *verb* [17] to boo; **the crowd booed the referee** el público abucheó al árbitro.

abuelo/abuela *noun Masc./Fem.* **1** grandfather/grandmother; **2 mis abuelos** my grandparents.

aburrido/aburrida *adjective* **1** boring; **ser aburrido/aburrida** to be boring; **2** bored; **estar aburrido/aburrida** to be bored.

aburrimiento *noun Masc.* boredom; **¡qué aburrimiento!** how boring!

aburrirse *reflexive verb* [19] to get bored.

abusar *verb* [17] **1 abusar (de)** to take too much/many (*alcohol or pills, for example*); **2 abusar de** to take advantage of; **están abusando de tu amabilidad** they are taking advantage of your kindness.

abusivo/abusiva *adjective* **1** excessive (*price*); **2** unfair (*a law or rule, for example*).

abuso *noun Masc.* **1** abuse; **el abuso del alcohol** alcohol abuse; **2** outrage; **¡esto es un verdadero abuso!** this is really outrageous!

aC *abbreviation* (*short for: antes de Cristo*) BC, before Christ.

acá *adverb* here; **¡ven acá!** come here!

acabado/acabada *adjective* finished.

acabar *verb* [17] **1** to finish; **aún no he acabado de leer el libro** I haven't finished reading the book yet; **¿has acabado con el lápiz?** have you finished with the pencil?; **2** to be over; **cuando acabó la fiesta** when the party was over; **3** to end; **la palabra acaba en 'r'** the word ends in 'r'; **la historia acaba bien** the story has a happy ending; **4 acabar de hacer** to have just done; **acabo de hablar con él** I've just spoken to him; **acaban de llegar** they've just arrived; **acabábamos** we had just finished. **acabarse** *reflexive verb* [17] **1** to be over (*a party or film, for example*); **cuando se acabó la clase** when the class was over; **2** to run out (*money or food, for example*); **se ha acabado el pan** we've run out of bread; **se me acabó el dinero** I ran out of money.

academia *noun Fem.* school; **academia de idiomas** language school.

académico/académica *adjective* academic.

acampada *noun Fem.* camping; **ir de acampada** to go camping.

a
b
c
d
e
f
g
h
i
j
k
l
m
n
ñ
o
p
q
r
s
t
u
v
w
x
y
z

3

acampar *verb* [17] to camp.

acantilado *noun Masc.* cliff.

acariciar *verb* [17] **1** to caress (*a person*); **2** to stroke (*a cat or dog*).

acaso *adverb* **por si acaso** just in case.

acatarrado/acatarrada *adjective* **estar acatarrado/ acatarrada** to have a cold.

acatarrarse *reflexive verb* [17] to catch a cold.

acceder *verb* [18] **1** **acceder a algo** to agree to something; **2** to access (*information or a file*).

accesible *adjective* **1** accessible (*a place, for example*); **2** affordable.

accesorios *plural noun Masc.* accessories.

accidental *adjective* accidental.

accidente *noun Masc.* accident; **tener un accidente/sufrir un accidente** to have an accident; **un accidente de circulación** a road accident.

acción *noun Fem.* **1** act; **una buena acción** a good deed; **2** share (*in a company*).

acebo *noun* holly.

aceite *noun Masc.* oil; **aceite de oliva** olive oil.

aceitoso/aceitosa *adjective* oily.

aceituna *noun Fem.* olive.

acelerador *noun Masc.* accelerator; **pisar el acelerador** to put your foot down (*accelerate*).

acelerar *verb* [17] to accelerate.

acento *noun Masc.* **1** accent; **tener acento andaluz** to have an Andalusian accent; **casi no tienes acento** you have hardly any accent; **2** accent (*on a letter in written Spanish*); **un acento agudo** an acute accent.

acentuarse *reflexive verb* [20] to have an accent; **se acentúa en la última sílaba** it has an accent on the last syllable.

aceptable *adjective* acceptable.

aceptar *verb* [17] **1** to accept (*an invitation or apology, for example*); **2** **aceptar hacer** to agree to do; **aceptaron dejármelo** they agreed to lend it to me.

acera *noun Fem.* pavement.

acerca de *preposition* about.

acercar *verb* [31] **1** **acerqué la silla a la ventana** I moved the chair nearer the window; **acércame un poco la lámpara** bring the lamp closer to me; **2** to pass; **acércame ese libro** pass me that book; **3** **acercar a alguien a** to give somebody a lift to; **me acercó a la oficina** she gave me a lift to the office.

acercarse *reflexive verb* [31] to come/go near; **acércate más** come/ get closer; **se acercó a la ventana** she went over to the window.

acero *noun Masc.* steel.

acertado/acertada *adjective* right (*decision or answer*).

acertar *verb* [29] **1** to be right; **¡has acertado!** you've got it right!; **2** **acertar algo** to get something

4

right; **3 acertar en el blanco** to hit the target.

ácido *noun Masc.* acid.

acierto *noun Masc.* **1** correct answer; **2** good decision; **ese regalo ha sido un acierto** that present was a good idea.

aclaración *noun Fem.* explanation.

aclarar *verb* [17] to make clear. **aclararse** *reflexive verb* [17] (*informal*) to understand; **aún no me aclaro** I still don't understand.

acné *noun Masc.* acne.

acoger *verb* [3] **1** to receive (*news or a proposal*); **2** to take in (*refuge*).

acompañar *verb* [17] **1** to go with; **la acompañé al dentista** I went with her to the dentist's; **te acompaño a tu casa** I'll see you home; **2** to keep company; **el perro me acompaña mucho** the dog keeps me company.

aconsejar *verb* [17] to advise.

acordarse *reflexive verb* [24] to remember; **no me acuerdo** I don't remember; **acordarse de algo** to remember something.

acorde *noun Masc.* chord.

acordeón *noun Masc.* accordion.

acortar *verb* [17] to shorten.

acostarse *reflexive verb* [24] **1** to go to bed; **¿a qué hora te acuestas?** what time do you go to bed?; **2 acostarse con alguien** to sleep with somebody.

acostumbrado/ acostumbrada *adjective* estar

acostumbrado/acostumbrada a algo to be used to something; **está acostumbrada a tener muchos deberes** she's used to having lots of homework.

acostumbrarse *reflexive verb* [17] **acostumbrarse a algo** to get used to something.

acróbata *noun Masc./Fem.* acrobat.

actitud *noun Fem.* attitude.

actividad *noun Fem.* activity.

activo/activa *adjective* active.

acto *noun Masc.* **1** act; **2 en el acto** immediately.

actor *noun Masc.* actor.

actriz *noun Fem.* actress; **quiere ser actriz** she wants to be an actress.

actuación *noun Fem.* performance (*in a play or film*).

actual *adjective* present, current; **la situación actual** the present situation; **el actual presidente** the current president.

actualidad *noun Fem.* **1 en la actualidad** at present, at the moment; **en la actualidad viven en Madrid** at present they're living in Madrid; **2** nowadays; **en la actualidad es más fácil viajar** nowadays it's easier to travel.

actualmente *adverb* **1** at present; **actualmente trabaja en un banco** at present he's working in a bank; **2** nowadays; **actualmente se fabrica con máquinas** nowadays it's made by machine.

actuar *verb* [20] to act.

a
b
c
d
e
f
g
h
i
j
k
l
m
n
ñ
o
p
q
r
s
t
u
v
w
x
y
z

a
b
c
d
e
f
g
h
i
j
k
l
m
n
ñ
o
p
q
r
s
t
u
v
w
x
y
z

acuarela *noun Fem.* watercolour.

acuario¹ *noun Masc.* aquarium.

acuario² *noun Masc./Fem.* Aquarius; **soy acuario** I'm an Aquarius.

Acuario *noun Masc.* Aquarius.

acudir *verb* [19] **acudir a** to attend.

acuerdo *noun Masc.* **1** agreement; **llegaron a un acuerdo** they reached an agreement; **2 estar de acuerdo (en algo)** to agree (on something); **están de acuerdo en la fecha** they agree on the date; **no estoy de acuerdo** I don't agree; **ponerse de acuerdo** to come to an agreement; **3 ¡de acuerdo!** okay!

acusación *noun Fem.* accusation.

acusar *verb* [17] to accuse; **acusar a alguien de algo** to accuse somebody of something; **me acusó de mentir** he accused me of lying.

acústica *noun Fem.* acoustics.

adaptador *noun Masc.* adaptor (*electrical*).

adaptar *verb* [17] to adapt. **adaptarse** *reflexive verb* [17] **adaptarse a** to adapt to.

adecuado/adecuada *adjective* **1 adecuado/adecuada para** suitable for; **2 el momento adecuado** the right moment.

adelantado/adelantada *adjective* **1** advanced; **2** fast (*a clock or watch*); **tu reloj va adelantado** your watch is fast; **3 pagar por adelantado** to pay in advance.

adelantamiento *noun Masc.* overtaking.

adelantar *verb* [17] **1** to bring forward (*a date or trip*); **2** to overtake (*when driving*); **3 adelantar el reloj** to put the clock forward.

adelante *adverb* **1** forward; **ir hacia adelante** to go forward; **2 seguir adelante** to go on; **3 más adelante** further on; **4** later; **5 ¡adelante!** come in!

adelgazar *verb* [22] to lose weight; **he adelgazado tres kilos** I've lost three kilos.

además *adverb* **1** besides; **además, no es mi problema** besides, it's not my problem; **no ayuda y además se queja** he doesn't help and on top of that he complains; **2 además de** apart from; **además de eso, no sabes conducir** apart from that, you can't drive; **además de estos tres, tengo cinco más** besides these three, I've got five more; **son tres, además de la madre** there are three, not counting the mother.

adentro *adverb* inside, in; **vete adentro** go inside.

adicto/adicta *adjective* **adicto/ adicta a** addicted to.

adiós *exclamation* **1** bye!; **2** hello! (*when passing somebody in the street*).

aditivo *noun Masc.* additive.

adivinanza *noun Fem.* riddle.

adivinar *verb* [17] to guess.

adivino/adivina *noun Masc./Fem.* fortune-teller.

adjetivo *noun Masc.* adjective.

adjuntar *verb* [17] **1** to enclose; **2** to attach.

adjunto/adjunta *adjective* enclosed.

administración *noun Fem.* administration; **la administración pública** the civil service.

admirable *adjective* admirable.

admiración *noun Fem.* **1** admiration; **sentir admiración por alguien** to admire someone; **2 signo de admiración** exclamation mark.

admirador/admiradora *noun Masc./Fem.* admirer.

admirar *verb* [17] to admire.

admitir *verb* [19] **1** to admit; **admitió su responsabilidad** she admitted her responsibility; **2 'no se admiten perros'** 'no dogs'; **'no se admiten devoluciones'** 'goods cannot be returned'.

adolescente *noun Masc./Fem.* adolescent.

adónde *adverb* where; **¿adónde vas?** where are you going?

adonde *adverb* where; **la ciudad adonde iban** the city where they were going.

adoptar *verb* [17] to adopt.

adoptivo/adoptiva *adjective* **1** adoptive (*parents*); **2** adopted (*child*).

adorar *verb* [17] to adore.

adorno *noun Masc.* ornament; **los adornos de Navidad** Christmas decorations.

adquirir *verb* [47] to acquire.

adrede *adverb* on purpose.

aduana *noun Fem.* customs; **libre de derechos de aduana** duty-free.

adulto/adulta *noun Masc./Fem.*, **adulto** *adjective* adult.

adverbio *noun Masc.* adverb.

advertencia *noun Fem.* warning.

advertir *verb* [14] to warn; **quedas/ estás advertido** you've been warned; **le advertí que no llegase tarde otra vez** I warned him not to be late again.

aéreo/aérea *adjective* air (*traffic*); **el puente aéreo** the shuttle.

aerobic *noun* (*plural* **aerobics**) *Masc.* aerobics.

aeropuerto *noun Masc.* airport.

aerosol *noun Masc.* aerosol.

afán *noun Masc.* eagerness; **tienen afán de aprender** they are eager to learn.

afectar *verb* [17] to affect.

afecto *noun Masc.* affection; **tenerle afecto a alguien/sentir afecto por alguien** to be fond of somebody.

afectuoso/afectuosa *adjective* affectionate (*person*); **recibe un afectuoso saludo** kind regards (*in a letter*).

afeitarse *reflexive verb* [17] **1** to shave; **hoy no me he afeitado** I haven't shaved today; **2** to shave off (*a beard or moustache*).

afición *noun Fem.* interest, hobby; **¿qué aficiones tienes?** what are your interests?; **por afición** as a hobby.

aficionado/aficionada
adjective ser aficionado/
aficionada a algo to be fond of
something.

aficionado/aficionada *noun*
Masc./Fem. **1** fan; **un aficionado al
jazz** a jazz fan; **un aficionado al
rugby** a rugby fan; **para los
aficionados a la cocina** for those
who like cooking; **2** amateur; **un
grupo de aficionados** a group of
amateurs.

aficionarse *reflexive verb* [17]
aficionarse a algo to become fond
of something.

afilar *verb* [17] to sharpen.

afinar *verb* [17] to tune (*an
instrument*).

afirmación *noun Fem.*
1 statement; **2** yes answer.

afirmar *verb* [17] **1** to state; **afirmó
que era de su familia** he stated that
it belonged to his family; **2** afirmar
con la cabeza to nod.

afirmativo/afirmativa
adjective affirmative.

aflojar *verb* [17] **1** to loosen;
2 aflojar la marcha to slow down.

afónico/afónica *adjective* estar
afónico/afónica to have lost your
voice.

afortunadamente *adverb*
fortunately.

afortunado/afortunada
adjective fortunate.

África *noun Fem.* Africa.

africano/africana *noun Masc./
Fem.*, *adjective* African.

afuera *adverb* outside, out; **salimos
afuera** we went outside.

afueras *plural noun Fem.* **las
afueras** the outskirts.

agachar *verb* [17] **agachar la
cabeza** to lower your head.
agacharse *reflexive verb* [17] **1** to
bend down; **2** to duck.

agarrar *verb* [17] to grab.
agarrarse *reflexive verb* [17] to
hold on; **se agarró a la barandilla**
she held on to the handrail.

agencia *noun Fem.* agency;
agencia inmobiliaria estate agent's
office; **agencia de viajes** travel
agency.

agenda *noun Fem.* diary.

agente *noun Masc./Fem.* **1** agent;
agente inmobiliario estate agent;
2 agente de policía police officer.

agitar *verb* [17] to shake.

agosto *noun Masc.* August.

agotado/agotada *adjective*
1 worn out; **estoy agotado** I'm
worn out; **2** sold out; **3** flat (*a
battery*).

agotador/agotadora *adjective*
exhausting.

agotarse *reflexive verb* [17] **1** to
wear yourself out; **2** to sell out
(*goods*); **3** to go flat (*a battery*); **4** to
run out (*reserves or supplies*); **5** se
me está agotando la paciencia my
patience is running out.

agradable *adjective* pleasant.

agradecer *verb* [35]
1 agradecerle algo a alguien to be
grateful to somebody for something;

te agradezco tu ayuda I'm grateful for your help; **2** to thank; **te lo agradezco** thank you; **¡y así nos lo agradeces!** and that's all the thanks we get from you!

agradecido/agradecida *adjective* grateful; **le estoy muy agradecido** I'm very grateful to you.

agradecimiento *noun Masc.* gratitude.

agresión *noun Fem.* aggression.

agresivo/agresiva *adjective* aggressive.

agricultor/agricultora *noun Masc./Fem.* farmer.

agricultura *noun Fem.* **1** agriculture; **2** farming; **agricultura biológica** organic farming.

agrio/agria *adjective* sour.

agua *noun Fem.* water (*even though 'agua' is feminine, it is takes 'el' or 'un' in the singular*) **el agua está fría** the water is cold; **agua mineral con gas** sparkling mineral water; **agua mineral sin gas** still mineral water; **agua potable** drinking water; **agua corriente** running water; **agua de colonia** eau de cologne; ★ **estar más claro que el agua** to be crystal clear (*literally: to be clearer than water*).

aguacate *noun Masc.* avocado.

aguacero *noun Masc.* downpour.

aguafiestas *noun Masc./Fem.* (*does not change in the plural*) spoilsport.

aguanieve *noun Fem.* sleet.

aguantar *verb* [17] **1** to bear (*pain or heat*); **no aguanto este calor** I can't bear this heat; **2** to take; **no aguanto más** I can't take any more; **3 aguantar la respiración** to hold your breath; **aguantar la risa** to stop yourself laughing; **4** to hold (*an object*) **aguanta esta caja un momento** hold this box for a minute.

aguantarse *reflexive verb* [17] **tendrás que aguantarte** you'll have to put up with it.

agudo/aguda *adjective* **1** acute (*pain*); **2** acute (*an accent*); **3** high-pitched (*a voice or sound*); **4** stressed on the last syllable (*a word*).

aguijón *noun Masc.* sting.

águila *noun Fem.* eagle (*even though 'águila' is feminine, it takes 'el' or 'un' in the singular*) **vimos un águila** we saw an eagle.

aguja *noun Fem.* **1** needle (*for sewing or knitting*); **2** hand (*of a watch or clock*).

agujero *noun Masc.* hole.

agujetas *plural noun Fem.* stiffness; **tengo muchas agujetas** I'm really stiff.

ahí *adverb* **1** there; **ahí están** there they are; **ponlo ahí** put it there; **2 tenemos que ir por ahí** we have to go that way; **dejó las llaves por ahí** she left the keys somewhere.

ahijado/ahijada *noun Masc./Fem.* **1** godson/goddaughter; **2 mis ahijados** my godchildren.

a
b
c
d
e
f
g
h
i
j
k
l
m
n
ñ
o
p
q
r
s
t
u
v
w
x
y
z

9

a **b** **c** **d** **e** **f** **g** **h** **i** **j** **k** **l** **m** **n** **ñ** **o** **p** **q** **r** **s** **t** **u** **v** **w** **x** **y** **z**

ahogado/ahogada *adjective*
1 morir ahogado to drown; **2** morir
ahogado to suffocate.

ahogarse *reflexive verb* [28] **1** to
drown; **se ahogó en el río** he
drowned in the river; **2** to suffocate.

ahora *adverb* **1** now; ¿**qué vas a
hacer ahora?** what are you going to
do now?; **de ahora en adelante**
from now on; **ahora mismo** right
now; **2** nowadays; **3** in a moment;
ahora vuelvo I'll be back in a
moment; **ahora lo hago** I'll do it in a
moment; **ahora viene** he's coming;
4 por ahora for the time being.

ahorcar *verb* [31] to hang (*execute*).
ahorcarse *reflexive verb* [31] to
hang yourself.

ahorrar *verb* [17] to save.

ahorros *plural noun Masc.* savings;
todos mis ahorros all my savings.

ahumado/ahumada *adjective*
smoked.

aire *noun Masc.* **1** air; **al aire libre** in
the open air; **teatro al aire libre**
open-air theatre; **mis hijos
disfrutan jugando al aire libre** my
children enjoy playing outdoors;
aire acondicionado air
conditioning; **salir a tomar el aire**
to go out for some fresh air; **2** wind;
hace mucho aire it's very windy;
3 tiene un aire interesante he
looks interesting; **llegó con aire
preocupado** she arrived looking
worried.

aislado/aislada *adjective*
isolated.

ajedrez *noun Masc.* chess; **jugar al
ajedrez** to play chess.

ajillo *noun Masc.* **al ajillo** with garlic;
gambas al ajillo garlic prawns.

ajo *noun Masc.* garlic; **un diente de
ajo** a clove of garlic; **una cabeza de
ajo** a head of garlic.

ajustar *verb* [17] **1** to adjust (*a seat
or safety belt*); **2** to fit.

al (*formed by 'a + el'; look under 'a' for
more examples*) **1 fuimos al colegio**
we went to school; **se lo di al
camarero** I gave it to the waiter;
2 (*with infinitive*) when; **al salir nos
encontramos con Marta** when we
were leaving we met Marta; **tengan
cuidado al bajar del autobús** be
careful when leaving the bus.

ala¹ *noun Fem.* (*even though 'ala' is
feminine, it takes 'el' or 'un' in the
singular*) **1** wing; **el ala del avión**
the wing of the plane; **el pájaro
batió las alas** the bird beat its
wings; **el hospital tiene dos alas**
the hospital has two wings; **2** brim
(*of a hat*).

ala² *noun Masc./Fem.* winger.

alabanza *noun Fem.* praise.

alabar *verb* [17] to praise.

alambre *noun Masc.* wire; **alambre
de púas** barbed wire.

alargador *noun Masc.* extension
lead.

alargar *verb* [28] **1** to lengthen; **voy
a alargar esta falda un poco** I'm
going to lengthen this skirt a bit;
2 to extend (*a visit or holiday, for
example*); **el presidente ha
alargado su visita** the president

has extended his visit; **3** to stretch out (*an arm*); **alargué el brazo para alcanzarlo** I stretched out my arm to reach it.

alargarse *reflexive verb* [28] **1** to get longer; **los días se van alargando** the days are getting longer; **2** to go on; **la conferencia se alargó mucho** the conference went on for a long time.

alarma *noun Fem.* alarm; **alarma contra incendios** fire alarm.

alarmante *adjective* alarming.

albañil *noun Masc.* **1** builder; **2** bricklayer.

albaricoque *noun Masc.* apricot.

albergue *noun Masc.* **1** hostel; **albergue juvenil** youth hostel; **2** refuge (*in the mountains*).

albóndiga *noun Fem.* meatball.

albornoz *noun Masc.* bathrobe.

alborotar *verb* [17] **alborotar a los niños** to get the children excited. **alborotarse** *reflexive verb* [17] to get excited.

alboroto *noun Masc.* racket; **¡qué alboroto!** what a racket!

álbum *noun Masc.* album; **un álbum de fotografías** a photograph album; **el mejor álbum del grupo** the group's best album.

alcachofa *noun Fem.* artichoke.

alcalde *noun Masc.* mayor.

alcaldesa *noun Fem.* mayoress, mayor (*woman*).

alcanzar *verb* [22] **1** to reach; **la temperatura alcanzó los cuarenta grados** the temperature reached

forty; **no alcanzo a la ventana** I can't reach the window; **2** to catch up with; **no pude alcanzar al resto del grupo** I couldn't catch up with the rest of the group; **3 alcanzarle algo a alguien** to pass somebody something; **¿me alcanzas las tijeras?** can you pass me the scissors?

alcohol *noun Masc.* alcohol.

alcohólico/alcohólica *noun Masc./Fem.*, *adjective* alcoholic.

alcoholismo *noun Masc.* alcoholism.

aldaba *noun Fem.* knocker.

aldea *noun Fem.* village.

aldeano/aldeana *noun Masc./Fem.* villager.

alegrar *verb* [17] to cheer up; **verla les alegró un poco** seeing her cheered them up a bit; **me alegra saberlo** I'm glad to hear it. **alegrarse** *reflexive verb* [17] to be happy; **me alegro mucho por ellos** I'm very happy for them; **¡cuánto me alegro!** I'm so happy!; **se alegró de venir** he was glad to come; **me alegro de haberte llamado** I'm glad I phoned you; **me alegro de verte** it's nice to see you.

alegre *adjective* **1** happy; **una cara alegre** a happy face; **2** cheerful; **soy una persona muy alegre** I'm a cheerful kind of person; **3** bright (*a colour*).

alegría *noun Fem.* happiness; **¡qué alegría veros!** it's great to see you!; **¡qué alegría me das!** that makes

11

me really happy!; **saltar de alegría** to jump for joy.

alejar *verb* [17] **alejar algo de alguien** to move something away from somebody.

alejarse *reflexive verb* [17] to move away; **¡aléjate del fuego!** move away from the fire!.

alemán¹ *noun Masc.* German (*the language*).

alemán²/alemana *noun Masc./ Fem., adjective* German.

Alemania *noun Fem.* Germany.

alergia *noun Fem.* allergy; **tener alergia a algo** to be allergic to something; **alergia al polen** hayfever.

alerta *adjective* **1** alert.
alerta *noun Fem.* **estar al alerta por algo** to be on the alert for something; **hay que estar al alerta por los carteristas** be on the alert for pickpockets.

alfabético/alfabética *adjective* alphabetical; **por orden alfabético** in alphabetical order.

alfabeto *noun Masc.* alphabet.

alfarería *noun Fem.* pottery.

alféizar *noun Masc.* sill; **el alféizar de la ventana** the windowsill.

alfiler *noun Masc.* pin.

alfombra *noun Fem.* **1** rug;
2 carpet.

alfombrilla *noun Fem.* mat;
alfombrilla de baño bath mat.

alga *noun Fem.* seaweed.

algo *pronoun* **1** something; **algo así** something like that; **¿te pasa algo?**

is there something wrong?;
2 anything; **¿has cogido algo de aquí?** have you taken anything from here?; **3** some; **algo de leche** some milk; **4** any; **¿tienes algo de leche?** do you have any milk?
algo *adverb* a bit; **estoy algo cansado** I'm a bit tired.

algodón *noun Masc.* cotton; **una camisa de algodón** a cotton shirt.

alguien *pronoun* **1** somebody, someone; **vino alguien preguntando por ti** somebody came asking for you; **2** anybody, anyone; **¿has hablado con alguien?** have you talked to anybody?

algún SEE **alguno/alguna**.

alguno/alguna *pronoun*
1 **alguno/alguna** one; **alguno de vosotros** one of you; **tiene que haber alguno aquí** there must be one here; **para alguna de sus hijas** for one of her daughters; **2** **algunos/ algunas** some; **faltan algunos** there are some missing; **3** (*in questions*) any; **tengo demasiadas plantas, ¿quieres alguna?** I've got too many plants, do you want any?
alguno *adjective* ('*alguno*' *becomes* '*algún*' *before a masculine singular noun*) **1** some; **compré algunos libros** I bought some books; **algún día iré** I'll go some day; **2** (*in questions*) any; **¿tienes alguna razón para no ir?** do you have any reason for not going?; **¿tienes algún problema?** do you have any problems?; **3** **en algún lugar** somewhere; **en algún momento** sometime; **4** **alguna vez lo he**

pensado I've thought about it sometimes; **¿has estado alguna vez en España?** have you ever been to Spain?

aliado/aliada noun Masc./Fem. ally.
aliado adjective allied.

alianza noun Fem. alliance.

aliarse reflexive verb [32] **aliarse con alguien** to form an alliance with somebody.

alicates plural noun Masc. **1** pliers; **unos alicates** a pair of pliers; **2** nail clippers.

aliento noun Masc. breath; **mal aliento** bad breath; **estar sin aliento** to be breathless; **recuperar el aliento** to get your breath back.

alimentar verb [17] **1** to feed; **2** to be nutritious; **las lentejas alimentan mucho** lentils are very nutritious.
alimentarse reflexive verb [17] to feed; **se alimentan de insectos** they feed on insects.

alimenticio/alimenticia adjective **productos alimenticios** foodstuffs; **valor alimenticio** nutritional value.

alimento noun Masc. **1** food; **el arroz es su alimento básico** rice is their staple food; **buenos alimentos** good food; **2 tiene mucho alimento** it's very nutritious.

aliñar verb [17] **1** to dress (salad); **2** to season.

aliño noun Masc. **1** salad dressing; **2** seasoning.

alioli noun Masc. garlic mayonnaise.

alistarse reflexive verb [17] to join up; **alistarse en el ejército** to join the army.

aliviar verb [17] to relieve (pain).

allá adverb **1** there; **allá abajo** down there; **¡allá voy!** here I come/go!; **ahora vamos para allá** we're on our way; **2 más allá** further away; **no lo pongas muy allá** don't put it too far away; **3 allá tú** that's your lookout.

allí adverb there; **allí arriba** up there; **lo puso por allí** she put it somewhere around there; **se fueron por allí** they went that way.

alma noun Fem. (even though 'alma' is feminine, it takes 'el' or 'un' in the singular) soul.

almacén noun Masc. warehouse.

almacenar verb [17] to store (goods).

almacenes plural noun Masc. **unos (grandes) almacenes** a department store.

almeja noun Fem. clam (shellfish).

almendra noun Fem. almond.

almíbar noun Masc. syrup; **peras en almíbar** pears in syrup.

almidón noun Masc. starch.

almohada noun Fem. pillow; **una almohada de plumas** a feather pillow; **una funda de almohada** a pillowcase; ★**consultarlo con la almohada** to sleep on it (a decision).

almohadón noun Masc. cushion.

almorzar verb [26] **1** to have a mid-morning snack; **2** to have lunch (in some areas of Spain).

a
b
c
d
e
f
g
h
i
j
k
l
m
n
ñ
o
p
q
r
s
t
u
v
w
x
y
z

almuerzo noun Masc. **1** mid-morning snack; **2** lunch (*in some areas of Spain*).

alojamiento noun Masc. accommodation, lodgings.

alojarse reflexive verb [17] to stay; **se alojaron en un hotel** they stayed in a hotel.

alondra noun Fem. lark (*bird*).

Alpes plural noun Masc. **los Alpes** the Alps.

alpinismo noun Masc. mountaineering.

alpinista noun Masc./Fem. mountaineer.

alquilar verb [17] **1** to rent; **hemos alquilado un apartamento en la playa** we've rented an apartment at the seaside; **2** to hire (*a car or equipment, for example*); **alquilar una bicicleta** to hire a bike; **3** to let (*a house, flat, or room*); **se aquila esa casa** that house is to let; **4** to hire out (*equipment*); **allí alquilan botas de esquiar** they hire out ski boots there.

alquilarse reflexive verb [17] **se alquila local** premises to let; **se alquilan coches** cars for hire.

alquiler noun Masc. **1** rent (*for a flat or premises*); **2** hire charge (*for cars or equipment*); **3** **una casa de alquiler** a rented house; **una casa en alquiler** a house to let; **coches de alquiler** hire cars.

alquitrán noun Masc. tar.

alrededor adverb **1** around; **a nuestro alrededor** around us; **mirar alrededor** to look around;

2 **alrededor de algo** around something; **se sentaron alrededor de la mesa** they sat around the table; **3** **de alrededor** surrounding; **los campos de alrededor** the surrounding fields.

alrededores plural noun Masc. **1** outskirts (*of a town or city*); **2** surrounding area (*of an airport or building*).

altavoz noun Masc. **1** loudspeaker; **2** megaphone.

alternar verb [17] to alternate. **alternarse** reflexive verb [17] to take turns; **nos alternábamos para hacer la comida** we took turns to cook.

alternativa¹ noun Fem. alternative; **no tenemos otra alternativa** we have no alternative.

alternativo/alternativa² adjective alternative.

altitud noun Fem. altitude.

altivo/altiva adjective arrogant.

alto¹**/alta** adjective **1** high; **la montaña más alta de España** the highest mountain in Spain; **habitaciones de techo alto** rooms with high ceilings; **los precios están muy altos** prices are very high; **en lo alto de la torre** at the top of the tower; **tiene la tensión alta** he has high blood pressure; **2** tall; **todos sus hijos son muy altos** all their children are very tall; **¡qué alta está!** hasn't she grown!; **3** loud; **en voz alta** in a loud voice; **no pongas la radio tan alta** don't have the radio on so loud.

alto[2] *noun Masc.* de alto high; **un muro de dos metros de alto** a two-metre high wall.
alto *adverb* **1** loud; **habla un poco más alto, por favor** speak a little louder, please; **2** high; **volar alto** to fly high.

altura *noun Fem.* **1** height; **a la misma altura** at the same height; **¿qué altura tiene?** how high is it?; **2** altitude; **volar a una altura de 10.000m** to fly at an altitude of 10,000 metres; **3 a estas alturas** at this stage; **a estas alturas no importa** it doesn't matter at this stage.

alubia *noun Fem.* haricot bean.

alucinación *noun Fem.* hallucination.

alucinado/alucinada *adjective* (*informal*) **estar alucinado/alucinada** to be stunned; **nos quedamos alucinados** we were stunned.

alucinante *adjective* (*informal*) amazing; **es un espectáculo alucinante** it's an amazing spectacle.

alucinar *verb* [17] (*informal*) **1** to amaze; **me alucina** it amazes me; **2** to be amazed; **con este disco es que alucinas** this record's amazing.

alud *noun Masc.* **1** avalanche; **2** landslide.

aluminio *noun Masc.* aluminium.

alumno/alumna *noun Masc./Fem.* pupil, student.

alusión *noun Fem.* allusion.

ama de casa *noun Fem.* (*even though 'ama de casa' is feminine, it takes 'el' or 'un' in the singular*) housewife; **un ama de casa** a housewife.

amabilidad *noun Fem.* kindness; **tuvieron la amabilidad de ayudarme** they were kind enough to help me.

amable *adjective* kind; **¿sería tan amable de sujetar esto?** would you be so kind as to hold this?

amado/amada *adjective* beloved; **mi amado** my beloved.

amaestrar *verb* [17] to train (*an animal*).

amanecer *noun Masc.* dawn; **al amanecer** at dawn.
amanecer *verb* [35] to get light; **¿a qué hora amanece?** what time does it get light?

amante *noun Masc./Fem.* lover.
amante *adjective* **ser amante de algo** to be fond of something; **son grandes amantes del cine** they're great film-lovers.

amapola *noun Fem.* poppy.

amar *verb* [17] to love.

amargo/amarga *adjective* bitter.

amarillo[1] *noun Masc.* yellow.

amarillo[2]**/amarilla** *adjective* yellow.

amasar *verb* [17] to knead (*dough*).

Amazonas *noun Masc.* **el Amazonas** the Amazon.

ambición *noun Fem.* ambition.

a
b
c
d
e
f
g
h
i
j
k
l
m
n
ñ
o
p
q
r
s
t
u
v
w
x
y
z

ambicioso/ambiciosa *adjective* ambitious.

ambientador *noun Masc.* air freshener.

ambiental *adjective* environmental.

ambiente *noun Masc.*
1 environment; **la contaminación del ambiente** the pollution of the environment; **2** atmosphere (*at a party, for example*); **había muy buen ambiente** there was a good atmosphere.

ambiguo/ambigua *adjective* ambiguous.

ambos/ambas *plural pronoun, plural adjective* both; **se lo dije a ambos** I told both of them; **ambas ciudades** both cities.

ambulancia *noun Fem.* ambulance.

ambulante *adjective* travelling; **un grupo de teatro ambulante** a travelling theatre group; **una biblioteca ambulante** a mobile library.

ambulatorio *noun Masc.* outpatients department.

amén *noun Masc.* amen.

amenaza *noun Fem.* threat.

amenazador/amenazadora *adjective* threatening.

amenazar *verb* [22] to threaten; **amenazó con despedirme** he threatened to fire me; **amenazar de muerte a alguien** to threaten to kill somebody.

América *noun Fem.* America; **América Central** Central America; **América del Sur** South America; **América Latina** Latin America.

americana *noun Fem.* jacket.

americano/americana *noun Masc./Fem.*, *adjective* American.

ametralladora *noun Fem.* machine gun.

amigo/amiga *noun Masc./Fem.* friend; **amigo/amiga por correspondencia** penfriend; **un amigo nuestro** a friend of ours; **un amigo de Carmen** a friend of Carmen's; **son amigos íntimos** they are very close friends; **mi amigo del alma** my best friend. **amigo** *adjective* **son muy amigos** they are very good friends; **hacerse amigos** to become friends.

amistad *noun Fem.* friendship.

amistades *plural noun Fem.* friends; **mis amistades** my friends.

amistoso/amistosa *adjective* friendly.

amo/amo *noun Fem.* (*even though 'ama' is feminine, it takes 'el' or 'un' in the singular*) owner (*of an animal*); **el ama del perro** the owner of the dog.

amontonar *verb* [17] to pile up. **amontonarse** *reflexive verb* [17] to pile up.

amor *noun Masc.* **1** love; **amor mío** my love; **amor a primera vista** love at first sight; **2 amor propio** self esteem; ★ **por amor al arte** for the sake of it.

amoroso/amorosa *adjective*
las relaciones amorosas love
relationships.

ampliar *verb* [32] **1** to enlarge (*a
photograph*); **2** to extend (*a road or
building*); **3** to increase (*vocabulary
or knowledge*).

amplificador *noun Masc.*
amplifier.

amplio/amplia *adjective* **1** wide
(*a road*); **2** spacious (*a room*);
3 loose-fitting (*a garment*).

amplitud *noun Fem.* **1** width (*of a
road*); **2** spaciousness (*of a room*).

ampolla *noun Fem.* blister; **me han
salido ampollas en las manos** I've
got blisters on my hands.

amueblar *verb* [17] to furnish (*a
house or room*).

analfabeto/analfabeta
adjective illiterate.

analgésico *noun Masc.* painkiller.

análisis *noun Masc.* analysis.

analizar *verb* [22] to analyse.

anatomía *noun Fem.* anatomy.

ancho¹ *noun Masc.* width; **¿cuánto
tiene de ancho?/¿qué ancho
tiene?** how wide is it?; **mide/tiene
dos metros de ancho** it's two
metres wide.

ancho²/ancha *adjective* **1** wide;
una carretera muy ancha a very
wide road; **2** broad; **ser ancho de
espaldas** to have broad shoulders;
3 loose-fitting (*a garment*); **te está
muy ancho** it's too loose for you.

anchoa *noun Fem.* anchovy.

anchura *noun Fem.* width; **tiene
una anchura de cinco metros** it's
five metres wide; **¿qué anchura
tiene?** how wide is it?

anciano/anciana *noun* old
man/old woman.
anciano *adjective* elderly; **un
hombre muy anciano** a very
elderly man.

ancla *noun Fem.* (*even though 'ancla'
is feminine noun, it takes 'el' or 'un'
in the singular*) anchor; **el ancla** the
anchor; **echar (las) anclas** to drop
anchor.

Andalucía *noun Fem.* Andalusia.

andamio *noun Masc.* scaffolding.

andar *verb* [21] **1** to walk; **¿has
venido andando?** did you walk
here?; **casi no podía andar** I could
hardly walk; **2 ¿cómo andas?** how
are you?; **¿cómo andas de dinero?**
how are you doing for money?; **3** to
work; **mi coche no anda** my car's
not working; **4** (*expressing surprise*)
¡anda! si es Pedro well, if it isn't
Pedro!; **5** (*urging somebody to do
something*) **anda, date prisa** come
on, hurry up.

andén *noun Masc.* platform.

Andes *plural noun Masc.* **los Andes**
the Andes.

Andorra *noun Fem.* Andorra.

andrajo *noun Masc.* rag; **iba vestido
de andrajos** he was dressed in rags.

anécdota *noun Fem.* anecdote.

anestesia *noun Fem.*
1 anaesthesia; **2** anaesthetic.

anfitrión *noun Masc.* host.

anfitriona *noun Fem.* hostess.

ángel *noun Masc.* angel; **no es ningún angelito** he's no angel; ⋆ **que sueñes con los angelitos** sweet dreams (*literally: dream with the angels*).

angelical *adjective* angelic.

anginas *plural noun Fem.* throat infection; **tener anginas** to have a throat infection.

anglicano/anglicana *noun Masc./Fem.* Anglican.

anguila *noun Fem.* eel.

angustiado/angustiada *adjective* worried; **sus padres están angustiados porque no saben nada de él** his parents are really worried because they haven't heard from him.

angustiarse *reflexive verb* [17] to get worried; **no hay por qué angustiarse** there's no reason to get worried.

angustioso/angustiosa *adjective* worrying.

anillo *noun Masc.* ring; **anillo de boda** wedding ring.

animado/animada *adjective* **1** lively (*a bar or party, for example*); **2** in good spirits; **muy animada** she was in high spirits.

animal¹ *noun Masc.* animal; **animal doméstico** pet, domestic animal.

animal² *noun Masc./Fem.* brute; **es un animal** he's a brute. **animal** *adjective* stupid; **¡qué animal eres!** you're so stupid!

animar *verb* [17] **1** to liven up (*a party, for example*); **2** to cheer up (*a person*); **3** to cheer on. **animarse** *reflexive verb* [17] to cheer up; **¡anímate!** cheer up!

ánimo *noun Masc.* **1** **no tengo ánimo para nada** I don't feel in the mood for anything; **se la ve con mucho ánimo** she's in high spirits; **con el ánimo por los suelos** feeling really low; **2** **¡ánimo!** cheer up!

anís *noun Masc.* anisette.

aniversario *noun Masc.* anniversary.

anoche *adverb* last night; **anoche no dormí bien** I didn't sleep well last night; **antes de anoche** the night before last.

anochecer *noun Masc.* nightfall; **al anochecer** at nightfall. **anochecer** *verb* [35] to get dark; **está anocheciendo** it's getting dark.

anónimo¹/**anónima** *adjective* anonymous.

anónimo² *noun Masc.* anonymous letter.

anormal *adjective* abnormal.

anotar *verb* [17] to write down.

ansiedad *noun Fem.* anxiety.

ante¹ *noun Masc.* suede.

ante² *preposition* before; **ante el juez** before the judge.

anteanoche *adverb* the night before last.

anteayer *adverb* the day before yesterday.

antemano *in phrase* **de antemano** in advance.

antena *noun Fem.* **1** aerial; **2** antenna.

antepasados *plural noun Masc.* ancestors.

anterior *adjective* previous; **la noche anterior** the previous night; **anterior a algo** prior to something.

antes *adverb* **1** before; **la noche antes** the night before; **deberías haberlo dicho antes** you should have said it before; **2 antes de** before; **antes del viernes** before Friday; **piénsalo antes de comprarlo** think about it before you buy it; **3** earlier; **este año la primavera ha llegado antes** this year spring has come earlier; **a las cinco está bien, no hace falta que vengas antes** five is fine, you don't need to come any earlier; **4** first; **ésta va antes** this goes first; **5 lo antes posible** as soon as possible.

antibiótico *noun Masc.* antibiotic.

anticipación *noun Fem.* **con mucha anticipación** well in advance; **con dos días de anticipación** two days in advance.

anticipo *noun Masc.* advance.

anticoncepción *noun* contraception.

anticonceptivo *noun Masc.* contraceptive.

anticuado/anticuada *adjective* old-fashioned.

antídoto *noun Masc.* antidote.

antigüedad *noun Fem.* **1** antique; **tienda de antigüedades** antique

shop; **2** seniority (*at work*); **3 en la antigüedad** in the old days.

antiguamente *adverb* in the old days.

antiguo/antigua *adjective* **1** old; **una costumbre muy antigua** a very old tradition; **2** former; **el antiguo presidente** the former president; **3** ancient; **una civilización antigua** an ancient civilization.

Antillas *plural noun Fem.* **las Antillas** the West Indies.

antipático/antipática *adjective* unpleasant; **es muy antipático** he's very unpleasant; **¡qué mujer más antipática!** what a horrible woman!

antojarse *reflexive verb* [17] **se le antojó un helado** he fancied an ice-cream; **se me antojó comprar el jarrón** I felt like buying the vase.

antropología *noun Fem.* anthropology.

anual *adjective* annual.

anualmente *adverb* yearly.

anunciar *verb* [17] **1** to announce (*news or a decision*); **2** to advertise (*a product, for example*).

anuncio *noun Masc.* **1** announcement; **2** advertisement.

anzuelo *noun Masc.* hook.

añadidura *in phrase* **por añadidura** in addition.

añadir *verb* [19] to add.

año *noun Masc.* **1** year; **el año pasado** last year; **los años cincuenta** the 50s; **el Año Nuevo**

a
b
c
d
e
f
g
h
i
j
k
l
m
n
ñ
o
p
q
r
s
t
u
v
w
x
y
z

the New Year; **año bisiesto** leap year; **2** (*talking about age*) **mi madre tiene cincuenta años** my mother is fifty; **¿cuántos años tienes?** how old are you?

apagado/apagada *adjective*
1 off; **con la luz apagada** with the light off; **¿está la televisión apagada?** is the television off?; **2** out; **el fuego estaba casi apagado** the fire was almost out.

apagar *verb* [28] **1** to switch off (*the television or a light*); **2** to put out (*a fire or cigarette*).

apagón *noun Masc.* power cut.

aparato *noun Masc.* **1** appliance; **aparatos eléctricos** electrical appliances; **2 los aparatos de laboratorio** laboratory equipment; **3** piece of apparatus (*in the gym*).

aparcamiento *noun Masc.* car park.

aparcar *verb* [31] to park.

aparecer *verb* [35] **1** to appear (*a person or symptom*); **2** to turn up (*a lost object*).

aparente *adjective* apparent.

apariencia *noun Fem.*
1 appearance; **a juzgar por las apariencias** judging by appearances; **en apariencia no estaba roto** it appeared not to be broken; **2 un niño de apariencia delicada** a delicate-looking child.

apartado/apartada *adjective* isolated.

apartamento *noun Masc.* flat, apartment.

apartar *verb* [17] **1** to move away; **aparta la manta del fuego** move the blanket away from the fire; **2** to move out of the way; **aparta la planta para que pueda ver** move the plant out of the way so that I can see.
apartarse *reflexive verb* [17] to move away; **se apartó de la ventana** she moved away from the window.

aparte *adverb* **1** aside; **poner algo aparte** to put something aside; **llamar a alguien aparte** to call somebody aside; **2** separately; **esto lo pago aparte** I'll pay for this separately; **3 aparte de eso** apart from that.

apasionado/apasionada *adjective* passionate.

apasionar *verb* [17] **el deporte me apasiona** I have a passion for sports; **la ópera no me apasiona** I'm not wild about opera.

apearse *reflexive verb* [17] **apearse de** to get off (*a bus or train*), to get out of (*a car*), to dismount from (*a horse*).

apellidarse *reflexive verb* [17] **me apellido Alejos** my surname is Alejos.

apellido *noun Masc.* surname; **¿qué apellido tienes?/¿cuál es tu apellido?** what's your surname?; **apellido de soltera** maiden name.

apenas *adverb* **1** hardly; **apenas hay suficiente** there's hardly enough; **2** hardly ever; **ahora apenas nos vemos** we hardly ever see each other now; **3** scarcely; **hace apenas tres horas que se fueron** it's scarcely three hours since they went; **apenas lo veo** I can scarcely see it; **4 apenas me había sentado, cuando sonó el teléfono** no sooner had I sat down than the telephone rang.

apéndice *noun Masc.* appendix.

apendicitis *noun Fem.* appendicitis.

aperitivo *noun Masc.* **1** aperitif (*before a meal*); **2** nibbles (*food*).

apetecer *verb* [35] **no me apetece** I don't feel like it; **¿te apetece ir a cenar fuera?** do you fancy going out for dinner?; **haz lo que te apetezca** do whatever you feel like.

apetito *noun Masc.* appetite; **no tengo apetito** I don't feel hungry; **para abrir el apetito** to give you an appetite.

apio *noun Masc.* celery.

aplastar *verb* [17] to squash.

aplaudir *verb* [19] to applaud.

aplauso *noun Masc.* round of applause; **los aplausos del público** the applause of the audience.

aplazamiento *noun Masc.* postponement.

aplazar *verb* [22] to postpone.

aplicado/aplicada *adjective* hard-working.

aplicar *verb* [31] to apply.

apodo *noun Masc.* nickname.

apostar *verb* [24] to bet; **te apuesto cincuenta euros** I bet you fifty euros; **te apuesto a que no viene** I bet she won't come; **apostar a las carreras** to bet on horses;

apostaron por el favorito they bet on the favourite.

apóstrofo *noun Masc.* apostrophe.

apoyar *verb* [17] **1** to support (*a candidate or plan, for instance*); **2** to lean; **apoyé la bicicleta en la pared** I leaned the bicycle against the wall; **3** to rest; **apoya la cabeza en este cojín** rest your head on this cushion.

apoyarse *reflexive verb* [17] **apoyarse en** to lean on; **me apoyé en la puerta** I leaned against the door.

apoyo *noun Masc.* support.

apreciar *verb* [17] **1** to appreciate; **2 apreciar a alguien** to be fond of somebody; **la aprecio mucho** I'm very fond of her.

aprecio *noun Masc.* **sentir aprecio por alguien** to be fond of somebody.

aprender *verb* [18] to learn; **aprender español** to learn Spanish; **aprender a conducir** to learn to drive; **aprender algo de memoria** to learn something by heart.

aprendiz/aprendiza *noun Masc./Fem.* apprentice.

aprendizaje *noun Masc.* apprenticeship.

apretado/apretada *adjective* tight.

apretar *verb* [29] **1** to press (*a button*); **2** to tighten (*a bolt or knot*); **3 apretar el acelerador** to put your foot on the accelerator; **4** to be too tight (*shoes*); **5** to squeeze; **me apretó el brazo** she squeezed my arm.

a
b
c
d
e
f
g
h
i
j
k
l
m
n
ñ
o
p
q
r
s
t
u
v
w
x
y
z

a
b
c
d
e
f
g
h
i
j
k
l
m
n
ñ
o
p
q
r
s
t
u
v
w
x
y
z

apretón *noun* Masc. **un apretón de manos** a handshake.

aprieto *noun* Masc. predicament; **meterse en un aprieto** to get into a predicament; **poner a alguien en un aprieto** to put somebody in an awkward situation.

aprisa *adverb* quickly.

aprobar *verb* [24] **1** to approve (*a plan or decision, for example*); **2** to approve of (*behaviour or an idea*); **3** to pass; **aprobar un examen** to pass an exam.

aprovechado/aprovechada *adjective* **es un aprovechado** he takes advantage of people.

aprovechar *verb* [17] **1** to use; **podemos aprovechar estos trozos de madera** we can use these pieces of wood; **2** to make the most of (*time or resources*); **3** to take advantage of (*an opportunity or offer*); **4 aproveché para decírselo** I took the chance to tell him; **quiero aprovechar esta oportunidad para** ... I want to take this opportunity to ...; **5 ¡que aproveche!** enjoy your meal!

aproximadamente *adverb* approximately, roughly.

aproximado/aproximada *adjective* approximate, rough.

aproximar *verb* [17] to bring nearer.

aproximarse *reflexive verb* [17] **1** to go/come up to; **se aproximó a la ventana** she went/came up to the window; **2** to approach; **se aproximaba el momento** the moment was approaching; **se me**

aproximó un hombre a man approached me.

apto/apta *adjective* **apto para algo** suitable for something.

apuesta *noun* Fem. bet; **hacerle una apuesta a alguien** to make a bet with somebody; **me hicieron una apuesta** they made a bet with me.

apuntar *verb* [17] **1** to write down (*telephone number or address, for example*); **2** to point out; **apuntó con el dedo hacia la torre** she pointed out the tower; **3** to aim; **me apuntó con la pistola** he aimed the gun at me; **4 me apuntaron las respuestas** they whispered the answers to me.

apuntarse *reflexive verb* [17] **apuntarse a algo** to enrol on something, to put your name down for something.

apuntes *plural noun* Masc. notes; **tomar apuntes** to take notes.

apuro *noun* Masc. **estar en un apuro** to be in a tight spot; **pasar apuros** to go through a lot.

aquel/aquella *adjective* **1** that; **en aquel momento** at that moment; **2 aquellos/aquellas** those. **aquel/aquella** *pronoun* **1** that one; **quiero aquel** I want that one; **2 aquellos/aquellas** those; **estas no, dame aquellas** not these, give me those.

aquél/aquélla *pronoun* SEE **aquel/aquella**.

aquello *pronoun* that; **¿qué es aquello?** what's that?; **aquello que vimos** what we saw.

22

aquí *adverb* here; **lo puse aquí abajo** I put it down here; **aquí llegan** here they are; **debe estar por aquí** it must be around here; **el vino es de aquí** the wine is from here.

árabe[1] *noun Masc.* Arabic (*the language*).

árabe[2] *noun Masc./Fem., adjective* Arab.

Aragón *noun Masc.* Aragon.

aragonés/aragonesa *noun Masc./Fem., adjective* Aragonese.

araña *noun Fem.* spider.

arañar *verb* [17] to scratch.

arañazo *noun Masc.* scratch.

árbitro/árbitra *noun Masc./Fem.* **1** referee; **2** umpire.

árbol *noun Masc.* tree; **un árbol de Navidad** a Christmas tree.

arbusto *noun Masc.* shrub.

arcén *noun Masc.* hard shoulder (*on the motorway*).

archivador *noun Masc.* **1** filing cabinet; **2** ring binder.

archivar *verb* [17] to file.

archivo *noun Masc.* **1** archive; **2** file (*on a computer*).

arcilla *noun Fem.* clay.

arco *noun Masc.* **1** arch; **2** bow (*for firing arrows or playing the violin*); **3 arco iris** rainbow.

arder *verb* [18] to burn; **el bosque estaba ardiendo** the forest was burning.

ardiente *adjective* burning.

ardilla *noun Fem.* squirrel.

área *noun Fem.* area (*even though 'área' is feminine, it takes 'el' or 'un' in the singular*) **el área de penalty** the penalty area; **las áreas más peligrosas** the most dangerous areas.

arena *noun Fem.* sand.

Argentina *noun Fem.* Argentina.

argentino/argentina *noun Masc./Fem., adjective* Argentinian.

argot *noun Masc.* slang; **el argot juvenil** youth slang.

argumento *noun Masc.* **1** argument; **2** plot (*of a film, for example*).

aries *noun Masc./Fem.* Aries; **soy aries** I'm Aries.

Aries *noun Masc.* Aries.

aritmética *noun Fem.* arithmetic.

arma *noun Fem.* weapon (*even though 'arma' is a feminine noun, it takes 'el' or 'un' in the singular*) **un arma de fuego** a fire arm; **armas nucleares** nuclear weapons; **un arma blanca** a knife (*as a weapon*).

armado/armada *adjective* armed.

armar *verb* [17] **1** to arm; **2** to assemble (*a piece of furniture*); **3** to pitch (*a tent*); **4** (*informal*) **armar ruido** to make a noise; **armar jaleo** to make a racket; **armar un escándalo** to cause a scene. **armarse** *reflexive verb* [17] **1 armarse un lío** to get confused; **me armé un lío con las fechas** I got confused with the dates; **2 armarse de paciencia** to be patient.

a
b
c
d
e
f
g
h
i
j
k
l
m
n
ñ
o
p
q
r
s
t
u
v
w
x
y
z

a

armario *noun Masc.* wardrobe.

b

armonía *noun Fem.* harmony.

c

armónica *noun Fem.* harmonica.

d

armonioso/armoniosa
adjective harmonious.

e

aro *noun Masc.* **1** hoop; **2** hoop
earring.

f

g

aroma *noun Masc.* **1** scent; **2** aroma.

aromático/aromática
adjective aromatic.

h

i

arpa *noun Fem.* harp (*even though
'arpa' is feminine, it takes 'el' or 'un'
in the singular*).

j

k

arqueología *noun Fem.*
archaeology.

l

arqueólogo/arqueóloga
noun Masc./Fem. archaeologist.

m

n

arquitecto/arquitecta *noun*
Masc./Fem. architect.

ñ

o

arquitectura *noun Fem.*
architecture.

p

arrancar *verb* [31] **1** to tear out;
arrancar una hoja del cuaderno to
tear out a sheet from the notebook;
2 to tear off; **arrancar una etiqueta**
to tear off a label; **3** to pull up (*a
plant*); **4** to pull off (*a button*); **5** to
snatch; **me arrancó el libro de las
manos** she snatched the book from
my hands; **6** to start (*a car or
engine*).

q

r

s

t

u

v

arrastrar *verb* [17] to drag (*an
object*).
arrastrarse *reflexive verb* [17] to
crawl.

w

x

y

z

arrebatar *verb* [17] to snatch.

arreglado/arreglada *adjective*
1 tidy; **deja tu habitación
arreglada** leave your room tidy;
2 well dressed; **siempre va muy
arreglado** he's always very well
dressed.

arreglar *verb* [17] **1** to fix; **2** to
mend; **3** to tidy (*a room or house*);
4 to sort out (*a problem, for
example*); **no te preocupes, yo lo
arreglaré** don't worry, I'll sort it out.
arreglarse *reflexive verb* [17] **1** to
get ready; **me arreglo enseguida y
salimos** I'll get ready straight away
and we can go out; **2** to dress up; **mi
hermana siempre se arregla
mucho** my sister always dresses up
a lot; **3** **arreglárselas** to manage; **se
las arregla muy bien sola** she
manages very well on her own.

arrepentirse *reflexive verb* [14]
arrepentirse de algo to regret
something; **no me arrepiento** I
don't regret it.

arrestar *verb* [17] to arrest; **queda
usted arrestado** you're under
arrest.

arresto *noun Masc.* arrest.

arriba *adverb* **1** up; **aquí arriba** up
here; **lo puse más arriba** I put it a
bit higher up; **2** **de arriba** (*next up*)
above, (*highest*) top; **el cajón de
arriba** (*the next up*) the drawer
above, (*highest*) the top drawer;
3 upstairs; **ha ido arriba** he's gone
upstairs; **viven en el piso de arriba**
they live upstairs; **4** **arriba de todo**
at the very top; **de arriba abajo**
from top to bottom.

arriesgado/arriesgada *adjective* risky.

arriesgar *verb* [28] to risk.
arriesgarse *reflexive verb* [28] to take a risk.

arroba *noun Fem.* **1** @, at (*in email addresses; punto = dot*);
juanrobledoARROBAeasycomPU NTOcom
juanrobledo@easycomDOTcom;
2 *former measurement of weight*

arrodillarse *reflexive verb* [17] to kneel down; **estaba arrodillado** he was on his knees.

arrogante *adjective* arrogant.

arrojar *verb* [17] to throw.

arropar *verb* [17] **1** to wrap up (*a child or sick person*); **2** to tuck in (*in bed*).
arroparse *reflexive verb* [17] to wrap up; **arrópate bien** wrap up well.

arroyo *noun Masc.* stream.

arroz *noun Masc.* rice.

arruga *noun Fem.* wrinkle.

arrugar *verb* [28] **1** to wrinkle; **2** to crease; **3** to crumple up.

arruinar *verb* [17] to ruin.
arruinarse *reflexive verb* [17] to go bankrupt.

arte *noun Masc.* art (*'arte' is masculine in the singular and feminine in the plural*) **el arte moderno** modern art; **las artes gráficas** graphic arts; ★ **por arte de magia** as if by magic.

artesanía *noun Fem.* crafts; **objetos de artesanía** handicrafts.

artesanía *noun Masc.*
1 craftsmanship; **2** craftwork.

artesano/artesana *noun Masc./ Fem.* craftsman/craftswoman.

ártico/ártica *adjective* Arctic.

Ártico *noun Masc.* **el Ártico** the Arctic.

articulación *noun Fem.* joint (*in arm, etc.*).

artículo *noun Masc.* article; **el artículo definido** the definite article; **artículos de papelería** stationery.

artificial *adjective* artificial.

artista *noun Masc./Fem.* artist.

artístico/artística *adjective* artistic.

arzobispo *noun Masc.* archbishop.

asa *noun Fem.* handle (*even though 'asa' is feminine, it takes 'el' or 'un' in the singular*) **cógelo por el asa** take it by the handle.

asado *noun Masc.* roast.

asamblea *noun Fem.* meeting.

asar *verb* [17] **1** to roast (*meat*); **2** to bake (*vegetables*).

ascender *verb* [36] **1** to be promoted; **ha ascendido** he's been promoted; **2** to promote; **3** to rise (*temperature, prices or a balloon*); **ascender a** to amount to; **la cuenta asciende a quinientos euros** the bill amounts to five hundred euros.

ascenso *noun Masc.* promotion.

ascensor *noun Masc.* lift.

asco *noun Masc.* **le dio asco** it made him feel sick; **¡qué asco!** how disgusting!

a b c d e f g h i j k l m n ñ o p q r s t u v w x y z

25

a
b
c
d
e
f
g
h
i
j
k
l
m
n
ñ
o
p
q
r
s
t
u
v
w
x
y
z

asegurar *verb* [17] **1** to insure; **2** to secure; **3** to assure; **te aseguro que** ... I can assure you that ....
asegurarse *reflexive verb* [17] to make sure; **asegúrate de que cierras el grifo** make sure you turn the tap off.

asentir *verb* [14] **asentir con la cabeza** to nod (*in agreement*).

aseo *noun Masc.* toilet; **los aseos de señoras** the Ladies.

asesinar *verb* [17] to murder.

asesinato *noun Masc.* murder.

asesino/asesina *noun Masc./ Fem.* murderer.

asesor/asesora *noun Masc./Fem.* adviser.

asfixia *noun Fem.* **1** asphyxia; **2** suffocation; **tenía sensación de asfixia** I felt I was suffocating.

asfixiante *adjective* **1** asphyxiating (*air or fumes*); **2** suffocating (*heat*).

asfixiarse *reflexive verb* [17] **1** to suffocate; **2** to choke to death.

así *adverb* **1** like this; **hazlo así** do it like this; **2** like that; **el pueblo se llama Robellón, o algo así** the village is called Robellón, or something like that; **3** that way; **me llevaré el coche, así podremos volver pronto** I'll take the car, that way we can come back early; **4** **así que** so; **así que te vas de vacaciones** so you're going on holiday; **5** **así es** that's right; **6** **así, así** so, so; **'¿te gusta?'** – **'así, así'** 'do you like it?' – 'so-so'; **7** **¡así me**

gusta! that's what I like to see!; **¡así se hace!** well done!

Asia *noun Fem.* Asia.

asiático/asiática *noun Masc./ Fem., adjective* Asian.

asiento *noun Masc.* seat; **asiento delantero** front seat; **asiento trasero** back seat.

asignatura *noun Fem.* subject.

asilo político *noun Masc.* political asylum.

asistenta *noun Fem.* cleaning lady; **¿hay servicio de asistenta?** is there a maid service?

asistente social *noun Masc./ Fem.* social worker.

asistente *noun Masc./Fem.* assistant.

asma *noun Fem.* asthma (*even though 'asma' is feminine, it takes 'el' or 'un' in the singular*).

asmático/asmática *adjective* asthmatic.

asociación *noun Fem.* association.

asociar *verb* [17] to associate (*two ideas or words, for example*).
asociarse *reflexive verb* [17] to go into partnership (*in business*).

asomar *verb* [17] **asomar la cabeza** to stick your head out/in; **'no asomar la cabeza por la ventana'** 'do not lean out of the window'.
asomarse *reflexive verb* [17] **se asomó a la ventana** he had a look out of the window; **'prohibido**

asomarse por la ventana' 'do not lean out of the window'.

asombrar *verb* [17] to amaze; **me asombra su actitud** I'm amazed by her attitude.
asombrarse *reflexive verb* [17] to be amazed; **ya no me asombro con/de nada** nothing amazes me any more.

asombro *noun Masc.* surprise; **con cara de asombro** with a look of surprise on her face.

asombroso/asombrosa *adjective* amazing.

aspecto *noun Masc.* look; **tiene aspecto de policía** he looks like a policeman; **una mujer de aspecto elegante** an elegant-looking woman; **¿qué aspecto tenían?** what did they look like?; **tienes muy buen aspecto** you look very well.

áspero/áspera *adjective* rough.

aspirador *noun Masc.* SEE **aspiradora**.

aspiradora *noun Fem.* vacuum cleaner; **pasar la aspiradora por el salón** to vacuum the living room.

aspirina *noun Fem.* aspirin.

asterisco *noun Masc.* asterisk.

astilla *noun Fem.* splinter.

astrología *noun Fem.* astrology.

astrólogo/astróloga *noun Masc./Fem.* astrologer.

astronauta *noun Masc./Fem.* astronaut.

astronomía *noun Fem.* astronomy.

astrónomo/astrónoma *noun* astronomer.

astuto/astuta *adjective*
1 shrewd; **2** crafty; **eso fue muy astuto por su parte** that was very crafty of her.

asunto *noun Masc.* **1** matter; **asuntos de negocios** business matters; **un asunto complicado** a complicated matter; **2** business; **no quiero saber nada de este asunto** I don't want to know anything about this business; **no es asunto tuyo** mind your own business.

asustar *verb* [17] to frighten.
asustarse *reflexive verb* [17] to get frightened; **me asusté al oír un ruido** I got frightened when I heard a noise.

atacar *verb* [31] to attack.

atajo *noun Masc.* shortcut.

ataque *noun Masc.* **1** attack; **un ataque cardíaco/un ataque al corazón** a heart attack; **2** fit; **un ataque de celos** a fit of jealousy; **me dio un ataque de risa** I got a fit of the giggles.

atar *verb* [17] to tie (up).

atardecer *noun Masc.* dusk; **al atardecer** at dusk.
atardecer *verb* [35] to get dark; **estaba atardeciendo** it was getting dark.

atascar *verb* [31] to block (*a pipe*).
atascarse *reflexive verb* [31] to get blocked.

atasco *noun Masc.* **1** traffic jam; **2** blockage.

ataúd *noun Masc.* coffin.

atención *noun Fem.* attention; **presta atención** pay attention; **no**

pones atención en lo que haces
you don't concentrate on what you
are doing; ¡atención, por favor!
your attention, please!

atender *verb* [36] **1** to pay
attention; **atiende a la profesora**
pay attention to your teacher; **2 ¿la
atiende alguien?** are you being
served?

atentado *noun Masc.* **un atentado
terrorista** a terrorist attack.

atentado *noun Masc.* attack; **un
atentado terrorista** a terrorist
attack; **un atentado contra el
presidente** an attempted
assassination of the president.

atentamente *adverb*
1 attentively; **2 le saluda
atentamente** yours faithfully,
yours sincerely.

atento/atenta *adjective* attentive.

ateo/atea *noun Masc./Fem.* atheist.

aterrizaje *noun Masc.* landing (*of a
plane*).

aterrizar *verb* [22] to land (*a plane*).

aterrorizar *verb* [22] to terrify.

ático *noun Masc.* **1** top-floor
apartment; **2** loft.

atizador *noun Masc.* poker (*for fire*).

atlántico/atlántica *adjective*
Atlantic.

Atlántico *noun Masc.* **el Atlántico**
the Atlantic.

atlas *noun Masc.* atlas.

atleta *noun Masc./Fem.* athlete.

atlético/atlética *adjective*
1 athletic (*person*); **2 competición
atlética** athletics competition.

atletismo *noun Masc.* athletics.

atómico/atómica *adjective*
atomic.

átomo *noun Masc.* atom.

atracador/atracadora *noun
Masc./Fem.* **1** robber; **2** mugger.

atracar *verb* [31] **1** to hold up (*a
bank or shop*); **2** to mug (*a person*).

atracción *noun Fem.* attraction.

atraco *noun Masc.* **1** hold-up (*of a
bank or shop*); **2** mugging.

atractivo/atractiva *adjective*
attractive.

atraer *verb* [42] to attract.

atragantarse *reflexive verb* [17]
atragantarse con algo to choke on
something.

atrapar *verb* [17] to catch.

atrás *adverb* **1** back; **nos sentamos
demasiado atrás** we sat too far
back; **hacia atrás** backwards; **la
parte de atrás** the back; **2** at the
back; **esto va atrás** this goes at the
back; **3 quedarse atrás** to be left
behind.

atrasado/atrasada *adjective*
1 slow (*a watch or clock*); **llevo el
reloj atrasado** my watch is slow;
2 backward (*a country*); **3** old-
fashioned (*ideas or a person*);
4 behind; **voy atrasado en los
estudios** I'm behind at school; **van
muy atrasados con los ensayos**
they're very behind with the
rehearsals; **5 pagos atrasados**
outstanding payments.

atrasar *verb* [17] **1** to put back (*a
watch or clock*); **hay que atrasar los**

relojes una hora we have to put the clocks back an hour; **2** to lose time (*a watch or clock*); **este reloj atrasa** this watch loses time; **3** to postpone.

atrasarse *reflexive verb* [17] to lose time (*a watch or clock*).

atravesar *verb* [29] to cross.

atrayente *adjective* appealing.

atreverse *reflexive verb* [18] to dare; **no me atrevo a preguntarle** I don't dare ask him.

atrevido/atrevida *adjective* **1** daring; **2** cheeky; **¡qué niño más atrevido!** what a cheeky child!

atropellar *verb* [17] to run over, to knock down; **lo atropelló un coche** he was run over by a car.

atún *noun Masc.* tuna.

au pair (*plural* **au pairs**) *noun Masc./Fem.* au pair.

audífono *noun Masc.* hearing aid.

aula *noun Fem.* (*even though 'aula' is feminine, it takes 'el' or "un" in the singular*) **1** classroom; **2** lecture theatre.

aullido *noun Masc.* howl.

aumentar *verb* [17] **1** to increase; **aumentar el suelo** to give/get a rise; **2** to rise (*temperature or pressure*).

aumento *noun Masc.* **1** increase; **2** rise.

aún *adverb* **1** still; **aún estoy esperando** I'm still waiting; **2** yet; **aún no se lo he dicho a ellos** I haven't told them yet; **3** even; **este es aún mejor** this one is even better.

aun *adverb* even; **aun así** even so; **ni aun con tu ayuda** not even with your help.

aunque *conjunction* **1** although; **aunque estaba cansada, la ayudé** although I was tired, I helped her; **2** even though; **3** even if; **aunque llegues tarde, llámame** even if you arrive late, give me a ring; **aunque no lo parezca** even if it doesn't look like it.

auricular *noun Masc.* **1** receiver (*of a phone*); **2 auriculares** headphones.

ausente *adjective* **estar ausente** to be absent, to be away.

Australia *noun Fem.* Australia.

australiano/australiana *noun Masc./Fem., adjective* Australian.

Austria *noun Fem.* Austria.

austriaco/austriaca *noun Masc./Fem., adjective* Austrian.

auténtico/auténtica *adjective* authentic.

auto *noun Masc.* car.

autoadhesivo *adjective* self-adhesive.

autobiografía *noun Fem.* autobiography.

autobús *noun* bus; **coger el autobús** to take the bus; **perder el autobús** to miss the bus.

autocar *noun Masc.* coach.

autoescuela *noun Fem.* driving school.

a b c d e f g h i j k l m n ñ o p q r s t u v w x y z

autógrafo *noun Masc.* autograph.

automático/automática *adjective* automatic.

automóvil *noun Masc.* car.

automovilismo *noun Masc.* motor racing.

automovilista *noun Masc./Fem.* motorist.

autonomía *noun Fem.*
1 autonomy; **2** autonomous region (*of Spain*).

autonómico/autonómica *adjective* regional (*elections or a candidate*).

autopista *noun Fem.* motorway.

autor/autora *noun Masc./Fem.* author.

autoridad *noun Fem.* authority.

autoritario/autoritaria *adjective* authoritarian.

autorización *noun Fem.* authorization.

autorizar *verb* [22] to authorize.

autoservicio *noun Masc.* **1** self-service restaurant; **2** supermarket.

autostop *noun Masc.* hitch-hiking; **hacer autostop** to hitch-hike.

autostop *noun Masc.* hitchhiking; **hacer autostop** to hitchhike.

autostopista *noun Masc./Fem.* hitch-hiker.

autovía *noun Fem.* dual carriageway.

auxiliar *noun Masc./Fem.* assistant; **auxiliar de vuelo** flight attendant.

auxilio *noun Masc.* aid; **acudir en auxilio de alguien** to go to the aid of somebody; **primeros auxilios** first aid.

avalancha *noun Fem.* avalanche.

avanzar *verb* [22] **1** to move forward (*traffic or a person*); **2** to make progress (*a student or researcher*); **3** to wind on (*a tape*).

avaricia *noun Fem.* greed.

avaricioso/avariciosa *adjective* greedy.

Avda. *abbreviation* (*short for: avenida*) Ave., Avenue.

ave *noun Fem.* bird (*even though 'ave' is feminine, it takes 'el' or 'un' in the singular*) **un ave** a bird; **las aves** the birds.

avellana *noun Fem.* hazelnut.

avenida *noun Fem.* avenue.

aventura *noun Fem.* adventure.

aventurero/aventurera *adjective* adventurous.

avergonzado/avergonzada *adjective* **1** ashamed; **2** embarrassed.

avería *noun Fem.* breakdown (*of a car, for example*); **sufrir una avería** to break down.

averiado/averiada *adjective* **1** broken down; **2** out of order.

avestruz *noun Masc.* ostrich.

avión *noun Masc.* aeroplane; **avión a reacción** jet (*plane*).

avisar *verb* [17] **1 avisar a alguien de algo** to let somebody know about something; **le avisé del problema** I let him know about the problem; **me avisaron que llegarían tarde** they told me they would be late; **2** to

a b c d e f g h i j k l m n ñ o p q r s t u v w x y z

warn; **avisar a alguien del peligro** to warn somebody about the danger; **3 avisar al médico** to call the doctor.

aviso *noun Masc.* **1** warning; **el profesor ya le ha dado tres avisos** the teacher has already given him three warnings; **sin previo aviso** without prior warning; **2** notice; **hasta nuevo aviso** until further notice; **3 último aviso para los pasajeros del vuelo** ... last call for passengers on flight ....

avispa *noun Fem.* wasp.

axila *noun Fem.* armpit.

ayer *adverb* yesterday; **antes de ayer** the day before yesterday.

ayuda *noun Fem.* **1** help; **ir en ayuda de alguien** to go to somebody's assistance; **2** aid.

ayudante *noun Masc./Fem.* helper, assistant.

ayudar *verb* [17] to help; **¿en qué puedo ayudarle?** how can I help you?

ayuntamiento *noun Masc.* **1** town council, city council; **2** town hall.

azafata *noun Fem.* **1** flight attendant; **2** trade fair attendant.

azar *noun Masc.* **1** chance; **por azar** by chance; **2 al azar** at random.

azote *noun Masc.* smack.

azotea *noun Fem.* (flat) roof.

azúcar *noun Masc. or Fem.* sugar (*'azúcar' always takes 'el', but it can take an adjective in the feminine form*) **el azúcar blanca/blanco** white sugar; **el azúcar de caña**

cane sugar; **azúcar glas/glaseado** icing; **el azúcar morena/moreno** brown sugar; **un terrón de azúcar** a sugar lump.

azucarero *noun Masc.* sugar bowl.

azul *noun Masc.* blue; **azul claro** light blue; **azul marino** navy blue; **azul celeste** sky blue.
azul *adjective* blue; **ojos azules** blue eyes.

azulejo *noun Masc.* tile.

Bb

baca *noun Fem.* luggage-rack.

bacalao *noun Masc.* cod.

bachillerato *noun Masc.*
1 secondary education;
2 Bachillerato *the two-year course leading to university entrance in Spain.*

baguette *noun Fem.* baguette, French stick.

Bahamas *noun Fem.* (*plural*) **las Bahamas** the Bahamas; **las islas Bahamas** the Bahama Islands.

bahameño/bahameña *adjective, noun* Bahamian.

bahía *noun Fem.* bay.

bailar *verb* [17] to dance.

bailarín/bailarina *noun Masc./Fem.* dancer.

baile *noun Masc.* **1** dance; **2** dancing; **una clase de baile** a dancing class.

bajar *verb* [17] **1** to bring down; **¿puedes bajarme el abrigo?** could

a
b
c
d
e
f
g
h
i
j
k
l
m
n
ñ
o
p
q
r
s
t
u
v
w
x
y
z

a

b

c

d

e

f

g

h

i

j

k

l

m

n

ñ

o

p

q

r

s

t

u

v

w

x

y

z

you bring down my coat?; **2** to take down; **baja las maletas a recepción** take the suitcases down to reception; **3** to go down; **el ascensor está bajando** the lift's going down; **bajamos por las escaleras** we went down the stairs; **bajar la calle** to go down the street; **4** to come down; **¡ya bajo!** I'm coming down!; **creo que ya bajan** I think they're coming down now; **5** to fall (*the temperature or prices*); **6** to turn down (*volume*); **baja un poco la tele** turn the television down a bit; **7** to lower (*a blind or prices*).
  bajarse *reflexive verb* [17] **bajarse de un coche** to get out of a car; **se bajó de la bicicleta** he got off the bike.

bajo¹ *noun Masc.* ground floor.
  bajo *preposition* **1** under; **bajo los árboles** under the trees; **2 bajo cero** below zero.
  bajo *adverb* **1** low; **volar bajo** to fly low; **2** quietly; **hablar bajo** to speak quietly.

bajo²/**baja** *adjective* **1** short (*a person*); **soy bastante baja** I'm quite short; **2** low; **pon la música baja** put the music on low; **los precios están bajos** prices are low.

bala *noun Fem.* bullet.

balancín *noun Masc.* **1** swing seat; **2** seesaw; **3** rocking chair.

balanza *noun Fem.* scales.

balbucear, balbucir *verb* [17] to stammer.

balcón *noun Masc.* balcony.

baldosa *noun Fem.* tile.

Baleares *plural noun Fem.* **las islas Baleares** the Balearic Islands.

ballena *noun Fem.* whale.

ballet *noun Masc.* ballet.

balón *noun Masc.* ball; **un balón de fútbol** a football.

baloncesto *noun Masc.* basketball.

balonmano *noun Masc.* handball.

balonvolea *noun Masc.* volleyball.

balsa *noun Fem.* **1** raft; **2** pond.

banca *noun* banking *Fem.*

banco *noun Masc.* **1** bench (*in a park*); **2** pew (*in church*); **3** bank; **trabaja en un banco** she works in a bank.

banda *noun Fem.* **1** band (*of musicians*); **2** gang (*of criminals*); **3 banda sonora** soundtrack.

bandeja *noun Fem.* tray.

bandera *noun Fem.* flag.

banderilla *noun Fem.* banderilla (*a decorated dart used in bullfighting*).

bandido/bandida *noun Masc./Fem.* bandit.

banqueta *noun Fem.* stool.

banquete *noun Masc.* banquet; **un banquete de bodas** a wedding banquet.

bañador *noun Masc.* **1** swimming trunks; **2** swimming costume.

bañar *verb* [17] **bañar a** to bath (*a baby*).
  bañarse *reflexive verb* [17] **1** to have a bath; **voy a bañarme esta noche** I'm going to have a bath

tonight; **2** to have a swim; **¿te apetece bañarte?** do you fancy going for a swim?

bañera *noun Fem.* bath (*bathtub*).

baño *noun Masc.* **1** bath; **darse un baño** to have a bath; **voy a darme un baño** I'm going to have a bath; **2** swim; **darse un baño** to go for a swim; **¿te apetece darte un baño?** do you fancy going for a swim?; **3** bathroom; **¿dónde está el baño?** where's the bathroom?

bar *noun Masc.* bar.

baraja *noun Fem.* pack of cards.

barajar *verb* [17] to shuffle (*cards*).

barandilla *noun Fem.* rail.

baratija *noun Fem.* knick-knack.

barato/barata *adjective* cheap.

barba *noun Fem.* beard; **afeitarse la barba** to shave off your beard; **dejarse barba** to grow a beard; **voy a dejarme barba** I'm going to grow a beard.

barbacoa *noun Fem.* barbecue.

barbadense *adjective, noun* Barbadian.

Barbados *noun Masc.* Barbados.

barbaridad *noun Fem.* **1** fortune; **nos cobraron una barbaridad** they charged us a fortune; **2** eso es una barbaridad that's far too much; **3** deja de decir barbaridades stop talking nonsense; **4** ¡qué barbaridad! my God!

barbero *noun Masc.* barber.

barbilla *noun Fem.* chin.

barca *noun Fem.* boat; **una barca de pesca** a fishing boat; **una barca de remos** a rowing boat.

Barcelona *noun Fem.* Barcelona.

barco *noun Masc.* **1** boat; **viajar en barco** to travel by boat; **un barco de pesca** a fishing boat; **2** ship; **un barco de guerra** a warship.

barniz *noun Masc.* **1** varnish; **2** barniz de uñas nail varnish.

barómetro *noun Masc.* barometer.

barra *noun Fem.* **1** rail (*for clothes*); **2** bar; **una barra de jabón** a bar of soap; **nos sirvieron en la barra** they served us at the bar; **3** una barra de pan a baguette; **4** una barra de labios a lipstick.

barrer *verb* [18] to sweep.

barrera *noun Fem.* barrier.

barriga *noun Fem.* stomach, tummy; **tener dolor de barriga** to have a stomachache.

barril *noun Masc.* barrel.

barrio *noun Masc.* area (*of a town*); **los barrios bajos** the slums.

barro *noun Masc.* **1** mud; **lleno de barro** covered in mud; **2** clay (*for making pots*).

bártulos *plural noun Masc.* (*informal*) stuff, things; **coge todos tus bártulos** take all your stuff.

basar *verb* [17] to base; **basar algo en algo** to base something on something.
basarse *reflexive verb* [17] **¿en qué te basas para decir eso?** what basis do you have for saying that?

a
b
c
d
e
f
g
h
i
j
k
l
m
n
ñ
o
p
q
r
s
t
u
v
w
x
y
z

base *noun Fem.* **1** base; **2 base de datos** database; **3 base de maquillaje** foundation (*make-up*); **4 a base de** by; **lo aprendió a base de repetirlo** he learnt it by repeating it; ★ **a base de bien** (*informal*) a lot; **nos divertimos a base de bien** we enjoyed ourselves a lot.

básico/básica *adjective* basic.

bastante *adjective* **1** enough; **no tenemos bastante pan** we don't have enough bread; **ya tenemos bastantes sillas** we've got enough chairs now; **2** quite a lot of; **bastante gente** quite a lot of people; **bebimos bastante café** we drank quite a lot of coffee.

bastante *pronoun* enough; **con esto ya hay bastante** there's enough with this.

bastante *adverb* **1** enough; **¿has comido bastante?** have you eaten enough?; **2** (*before an adjective or adverb*) quite; **se puso bastante contenta** she was quite happy; **3** quite a lot; **ha mejorado bastante** he's improved quite a lot.

bastar *verb* [17] **1** to be enough; **con esto basta** this is enough; **¡ya basta!** that's enough!; **2 basta con preguntarle** you just need to ask him.

bastón *noun Masc.* walking stick.

bastoncillo *noun Masc.* cotton bud.

basura *noun Fem.* **1** rubbish; **hay que sacar la basura** we have to put the rubbish out; **2** dustbin, bin; **tirar**

algo a la basura** to throw something in the bin.

basurero¹ *noun Masc.* rubbish tip.

basurero²**/basurera** *noun Masc./Fem.* refuse collector.

bata *noun Fem.* **1** dressing gown; **2 una bata de médico** a white coat (*doctor's*).

batalla *noun Fem.* battle.

bate *noun Masc.* bat.

batería¹ *noun Fem.* **1** battery (*for a car*); **2** drum kit; **tocar la batería** to play the drums.

batería² *noun Masc./Fem.* drummer.

batido *noun Masc.* milkshake; **un batido de fresa** a strawberry milkshake.

batidora *noun Fem.* food mixer.

batir *verb* [19] **1** to beat; **batir las claras a punto de nieve** beat the egg whites until stiff; **2** to whip (*cream*); **3 batir un récord** to break a record.

baúl *noun Masc.* trunk (*for clothes*).

bautismo *noun Masc.* christening.

bautizar *verb* [22] to christen.

baya *noun Fem.* berry.

bayeta *noun Fem.* cloth (*for wiping*).

bebé *noun Masc.* baby.

beber *verb* [18] to drink; **¿quieres beber algo?** do you want something to drink?

bebida *noun Fem.* drink; **una bebida caliente** a hot drink.

beca *noun Fem.* **1** grant; **2** scholarship.

béisbol *noun Masc.* baseball.

billar

belén *noun Masc.* nativity scene, crib.

belga *noun Masc./Fem.*, *adjective* Belgian.

Bélgica *noun Fem.* Belgium.

belleza *noun Fem.* beauty.

bello/bella *adjective* beautiful.

bendito/bendita *adjective* **1** blessed; **2** holy (*water or bread*).

beneficiar *verb* [17] to benefit.

beneficio *noun Masc.* benefit.

benéfico/benéfica *adjective* charity; **una organización benéfica** a charity.

berenjena *noun Fem.* aubergine.

berro *noun Masc.* watercress.

besamel *noun Fem.* white sauce.

besar *verb* [17] to kiss.

beso *noun Masc.* kiss; **dame un beso** give me a kiss; **me dio un beso en la mejilla** he gave me a kiss on the cheek.

bestia *noun Fem.* **1** beast (*animal*); **2** ignorant person; **es un bestia, no sabe nada** he's so ignorant, he doesn't know a thing; **3** brute. **bestia** *adjective* **1** ignorant; **2 no seas bestia y habla bien** don't be so rude, mind your language.

betún *noun Masc.* shoe polish.

Biblia *noun Fem.* Bible.

biblioteca *noun Fem.* library.

bibliotecario/bibliotecaria *noun Masc./Fem.* librarian.

bicho *noun Masc.* creepy-crawly.

bici *noun Fem.* (*informal*) bike; **montar en bici** to ride a bike.

bicicleta *noun Fem.* bicycle; **montar en bicicleta** to ride a bicycle; **¿sabes montar en bicicleta?** can you ride a bicycle?.

bien *noun Masc.* good; **la diferencia entre el bien y el mal** the difference between good and evil.
bien *adverb*, *adjective* **1** well; **lo has hecho muy bien** you've done it very well; **no me siento bien** I don't feel well; **'¿cómo están tus padres?' – 'muy bien, gracias'** 'how are your parents?' –'very well, thank you'; **¡bien hecho!** well done!; **¡muy bien!** (*expressing approval*) well done!; **2** all right; **¿estás bien en esa silla?** are you all right in that chair?; **así está bien** it's all right like this; **¡está bien!** (*expressing agreement*) all right!, okay!; **3 huele bien** it smells nice; **sabe bien** it tastes nice; **4 hablas muy bien español** you speak very good Spanish; **5** properly; **no funciona bien** it doesn't work properly; **6 ¡bien!** hoorray!

bienestar *noun Masc.* welfare.

bienvenida[1] *noun Fem.* welcome; **dar la bienvenida a alguien** to welcome somebody.

bienvenido/bienvenida[2] *adjective* welcome; **¡bienvenido!** welcome!; **aquí siempre sois bienvenidos** you're always welcome here.

bigote *noun Masc.* moustache.

bikini *noun Masc.* bikini.

bilingüe *adjective* bilingual.

billar *noun Masc.* **1** billiards; **2** pool; **3** snooker.

35

a
b
c
d
e
f
g
h
i
j
k
l
m
n
ñ
o
p
q
r
s
t
u
v
w
x
y
z

billares plural noun Masc. amusement arcade.

billete noun Masc. **1** note (money); **un billete de cincuenta euros** a fifty euro note; **2** ticket; **un billete de tren** a train ticket; **un billete sencillo/un billete de ida** a single ticket; **un billete de ida y vuelta** a return ticket.

billetera noun Masc./Fem. wallet.

billetero noun SEE **billetera**.

biografía noun Fem. biography.

biología noun Fem. biology.

biólogo/bióloga noun Masc./Fem. biologist.

biquini noun Masc. bikini.

bisabuela noun Fem. great-grandmother.

bisabuelo noun Masc. **1** great-grandfather; **2 mis bisabuelos** my great-grandparents.

bisnieta noun Fem. great-granddaughter.

bisnieto noun Masc. **1** great-grandson; **2 mis bisnietos** my great-grandchildren.

bistec noun Masc. steak.

bizcocho noun Masc. sponge cake.

blanco¹ noun Masc. **1** white; **2** target; **dar en el blanco** to hit the target.

blanco²/**blanca** adjective white.

blando/blanda adjective **1** soft; **un colchón blando** a soft mattress; **la mantequilla se ha puesto blanda** the butter's gone soft; **2** tender (meat); **3** soft (person).

bloc noun Masc. writing pad.

bloque noun Masc. block; **un bloque de pisos** a block of flats.

bloquear verb [17] to block; **una muchedumbre nos bloqueaba el camino** a crowd was blocking our way.

blusa noun Fem. blouse.

bobo/boba adjective (informal) silly; **eres bobo** you are silly.

boca noun Fem. **1** mouth; **no abrió la boca en toda la tarde** he didn't say a word all afternoon; **2 una boca de metro** an entrance to the underground; **una boca de incendios** a fire hydrant; **una boca de riego** an irrigation hydrant; **3 boca arriba** face up (card or photograph); **pon el vaso boca arriba** put the glass the right way up; **túmbate boca arriba** lie on your back; **4 boca abajo** (card or photograph) face down; upside down; **estaba tumbado boca abajo** he was lying face down; ★ **quedarse con la boca abierta** to be flabbergasted.

bocacalle noun Fem. side street; **es la segunda bocacalle a la derecha** it's the second turning on the right.

bocadillo noun Masc. **1** baguette sandwich; **un bocadillo de queso** a cheese baguette; **2** speech bubble.

bocado noun Masc. **1** mouthful (of food); **2** bite to eat.

bocata noun Fem. sandwich.

bocatería noun Fem. sandwich bar.

bochorno *noun Masc.* **1 hoy hace bochorno** it's really muggy today; **2** embarrassment; **¡qué bochorno pasamos!** we were so embarrassed!; **fue un bochorno** it was really embarrassing.

bocina *noun Fem.* horn (*of a car*).

boda *noun Fem.* wedding; **bodas de plata** silver wedding; **bodas de oro** golden wedding.

bodega *noun Fem.* **1** wine merchant's; **2** cellar; **3** wine bar.

bofetada *noun Fem.* slap.

bofetón *noun Masc.* slap.

boina *noun Fem.* beret.

bola *noun Fem.* **1** ball; **una bola de nieve** a snowball; **una bola de billar** a billiard ball; **2** scoop (*of ice cream*); **3** (*informal*) fib; **contar bolas** to tell fibs.

bolera *noun Fem.* bowling alley.

boletín *noun Masc.* **1** bulletin; **boletín informativo** news bulletin; **boletín meteorológico** weather report; **2** school report.

boleto *noun Masc.* **1** ticket (*for a raffle or lottery*); **2** coupon (*football pools*).

boli *noun Masc.* (*informal*) (ballpoint) pen.

bolígrafo *noun Masc.* ballpoint pen.

Bolivia *noun Fem.* Bolivia. **boliviano/boliviana** *noun Masc., Fem., adjective* Bolivian.

bollo *noun Masc.* bun.

bolsa *noun Fem.* **1** bag; **una bolsa de palomitas** a bag of popcorn; **una bolsa de plástico** a plastic bag; **una bolsa de viaje** a travel bag; **una bolsa de la basura** a bin liner; **mi bolsa de la compra** my shopping bag; **2 la bolsa (de valores)** the stock exchange.

bolsillo *noun Masc.* pocket; **un diccionario de bolsillo** a pocket dictionary; **libro de bolsillo** paperback book.

bolso *noun Masc.* handbag; **me robaron el bolso** they stole my handbag; **bolso de mano/bolso de viaje** overnight bag.

bomba *noun Fem.* **1** bomb; **pusieron una bomba en un restaurante** they planted a bomb in a restaurant; **lanzar una bomba** to drop a bomb; **la bomba atómica** the atomic bomb; ★ **pasarlo bomba** to have a terrific time; **2** pump; **una bomba de bicicleta** a bicycle pump; **una bomba de agua** a water pump.

bombero/bombera *noun Masc./ Fem.* firefighter.

bombilla *noun Fem.* light bulb; **se ha fundido la bombilla** the bulb's gone.

bombón *noun Masc.* chocolate; **una caja de bombones** a box of chocolates.

bonachón/bonachona *adjective* (*informal*) kind.

bondad *noun Fem.* kindness.

bonito/bonita *adjective* **1** pretty; **es una chica muy bonita** she's a very pretty girl; **un pueblo muy bonito** a very pretty village; **2** nice; **ropa bonita** nice clothes.

bono *noun Masc.* voucher.

boquiabierto/boquiabierta
adjective astonished; **me quedé
boquiabierto** I was astonished.

bordado *noun Masc.* embroidery.

bordar *verb* [17] to embroider.

borde *noun Masc.* **1** edge; **me di con
el borde de la mesa** I bumped
myself on the edge of the table; **se
acercó al borde del andén** he went
up to the edge of the platform; **2** rim
(*of a glass or cup*); **3 llenar algo
hasta el borde** to fill something to
the brim; **4 el borde del río** the
river bank; **5 al borde de la guerra**
on the brink of war; **al borde de las
lágrimas** on the verge of tears.
borde *adjective* (*informal*) stroppy;
se puso muy borde conmigo he got
very stroppy with me.

bordear *verb* [17] to go round (*the
edge of something*); **bordeamos el
lago** we went round the lake.

bordillo *noun Masc.* kerb.

bordo *noun Masc.* **a bordo** on board;
subimos a bordo we went on board.

borrachera *noun Fem.* **cogerse
una borrachera** to get drunk.

borracho/borracha *noun Masc./
Fem.* drunk.
borracho *adjective* drunk;
estaban borrachos they were
drunk.

borrador *noun Masc.* **1** rough draft;
hacedlo primero en borrador do it
in rough first; **papel de borrador**
rough paper; **2** board rubber
(*eraser*).

borrar *verb* [17] **1** to rub out (*a
pencil mark or word*); **2** to erase (*a
track or tape*); **3** to clean (*the
blackboard*).
borrarse *reflexive verb* [17] to fade;
se ha borrado el nombre the name
has faded.

borrasca *noun Fem.* **1** area of low
pressure; **2** storm.

borrón *noun* blot.

borroso/borrosa *adjective*
1 blurred (*image or photograph*);
2 vague (*memory*).

bosque *noun Masc.* **1** wood;
2 forest; **el bosque ecuatorial** the
tropical rainforest.

bostezar *verb* [22] to yawn.

bota *noun Fem.* boot; **botas de
esquiar** ski boots; **botas de agua**
wellingtons.

botadura *noun Fem.* launch (*of
ship*).

botánica¹ *noun Fem.* botany.

botánico/botánica² *adjective
Masc./Fem.* botanical.

botar *verb* [17] to launch (*a ship*).

botavara *noun Fem.* (*of boat*) boom.

bote *noun Masc.* **1** boat; **un bote de
pesca** a fishing boat; **un bote de
remos** a rowing boat; **un bote
salvavidas** a lifeboat; **2** jar; **un bote
de aceitunas** a jar of olives; **3** can;
un bote de barniz a can of varnish;
4 jump; **pegar un bote** to jump;
pegué un bote de alegría I jumped
for joy.

botella *noun Fem.* bottle.

botijo *noun Masc.* drinking jug (*with
a long spout: with practice you can*

drink the water as it spurts out in an arc).

botiquín *noun Masc.* medicine cabinet; **botiquín de primeros auxilios** first aid kit.

botón *noun Masc.* button (*on a garment or a machine*); **se me ha caído un botón** I've lost a button; **coser un botón** to sew on a button; **para encender la tele tienes que apretar este botón** to switch on the television you have to press this button; **el botón de grabar** the record button.

boxeador/boxeadora *noun Masc./Fem.* boxer.

boxear *verb* [17] to box.

boxeo *noun Masc.* boxing; **un combate de boxeo** a boxing match.

bragas *plural noun Fem.* knickers, panties; **un par de bragas** a pair of knickers.

bragueta *noun Fem.* flies (*in trousers*).

brasileño/brasileña *noun Masc./Fem., adjective* Brazilian.

bravo/brava *adjective* fierce (*animal*).
bravo *exclamation* ¡bravo! well done!, bravo!

brazo *noun Masc.* arm; **me cogió del brazo** he took me by the arm; **iban del brazo** they were arm in arm; **cruzar los brazos** to cross your arms; **cogió al niño en brazos** he picked the child up in his arms; **yo llevaba al bebé en brazos** I was carrying the baby in my arms; **el brazo del sofá** the arm of the sofa;

★ **con los brazos abiertos** with open arms; ★ **ser el brazo derecho de alguien** to be somebody's right-hand man/woman.

brécol *noun Masc.* broccoli.

breve *adjective* short; **una pausa breve** a short pause.

brevemente *adective* briefly.

brezo *noun Masc.* heather.

bribón/bribona *noun Masc./Fem.* rascal.

bricolaje *noun Masc.* DIY.

brillante *noun Masc.* diamond.
brillante *adjective* **1** shiny; **2** bright (*light or colour*).

brillar *verb* [17] **1** to shine; **2** to sparkle.

brindar *verb* [17] to toast.

brindis *noun Masc.* toast; **hacer un brindis por alguien** to drink a toast to somebody.

brisa *noun Fem.* breeze.

británico/británica *noun Masc./Fem.* British man/woman; **los británicos** the British.
británico *adjective* British.

brocha *noun Fem.* **1** paintbrush; **2 brocha de afeitar** shaving brush.

broche *noun Masc.* brooch.

broma *noun Fem.* joke; **hacerle/gastarle una broma a alguien** to play a joke on somebody; **lo he dicho en broma** I was joking; **bromas aparte** joking apart; **¡ni en broma!** no way!

bromear *verb* [17] to joke.

bromista *noun Masc./Fem., bromista* *adjective* **es un**

a
b
c
d
e
f
g
h
i
j
k
l
m
n
ñ
o
p
q
r
s
t
u
v
w
x
y
z

39

a

b

c

d

e

f

g

h

i

j

k

l

m

n

ñ

o

p

q

r

s

t

u

v

w

x

y

z

bromista/es muy bromista he's always joking.

bronca *noun Fem.* (*informal*)
1 armar una bronca to kick up a fuss; **si no me devuelven el dinero, voy a armar una bronca** if they don't give me the money back I'm going to kick up a fuss; **2** telling-off; **echar una bronca a alguien** to tell somebody off; **tu madre te va a echar una buena bronca** your mum's going to give you a good telling-off.

bronceado/bronceada *adjective* suntanned.

bronceador *noun Masc.* suntan lotion.

broncearse *reflexive verb* [17] to get a suntan.

bronquitis *noun Fem.* bronchitis.

brote *noun* bud *Masc.*.

bruja *noun Fem.* witch.

brujo *noun Masc.* wizard.

brújula *noun Fem.* compass.

bruma *noun Fem.* mist.

bruto/bruta *adjective* **1** ignorant; **2** rude; **es muy bruto, ¡dice unas cosas!** he's very rude, he says such things!; **3 ¡qué bruto! ¡cómo trata a su hijo!** what a brute! what a way to treat his child!.

buceador/buceadora *noun Masc./Fem.* diver.

bucear *verb* [17] to dive.

buen *adjective* SEE **bueno/buena**.

bueno¹ *adverb* **1** okay; **'¿quieres venir?' – 'bueno'** 'do you want to come?' – 'okay'; **2 bueno, no**

importa well, it doesn't matter; **bueno, no estoy segura** well, I'm not sure; **bueno, ya basta** right, that's enough.

bueno²**/buena** *adjective* (*'bueno' becomes 'buen' before a masculine singular noun*) **1** good; **es muy buena persona** she's a very good person; **de buena calidad** good quality; **ser bueno para algo** to be good at something; **es muy buena para las matemáticas** she's very good at maths; **es muy buen amigo mío** he's a very good friend of mine; **¡buen viaje!** have a good journey!; **2 buenos días** good morning; **buenas tardes** good afternoon, good evening; **buenas noches** good evening, goodnight; **3** nice; **hace buen tiempo** the weather is nice; **el pastel estaba muy bueno** the cake was very nice; **¡está buenísimo!** it's delicious!

bufanda *noun Fem.* scarf.

bufar *verb* [17] to snort.

bufet *noun Masc.* buffet.

bufón *noun Masc.* clown (*silly person*).

buhardilla *noun Fem.* attic.

búho *noun Masc.* owl.

bujía *noun Fem.* spark plug.

bulto *noun Masc.* **1** shape; **vi un bulto en la oscuridad** I saw a shape in the darkness; **2** piece of luggage; **¿cuántos bultos llevas?** how many pieces of luggage do you have?; **3** bag; **yo te llevos los bultos** I'll carry your bags for you; **iba cargada de bultos** she was

carrying lots of bags; **4** bulk;
5 lump, swelling (*on the body*).

bungalow *noun Masc.* cabin, chalet
(*in holiday resorts*).

buñuelo *noun Masc.* fritter.

buque *noun Masc.* ship; **buque de
guerra** warship.

burbuja *noun Fem.* **1** bubble; **2 una
bebida sin burbujas** a still drink;
una bebida con burbujas a fizzy
drink.

burdo/burda *adjective* coarse.

burlarse *reflexive verb* [17]
burlarse de alguien to make fun of
somebody; **¡deja de burlarte de mí!**
stop making fun of me!

burocracia *noun Fem.*
bureaucracy.

burrada *noun Fem.* **¡vaya burrada
has dicho!** what a stupid thing to
say; **¡no hagas esa burrada!** don't
do such a stupid thing; **sólo dijo
burradas** he just talked rubbish.

burro¹ *noun Masc.* **1** donkey; **2 es un
burro** he's really stupid.

burro²/**burra** *noun Masc./Fem.* **es
un burro** he's really stupid.
burro *adjective* stupid.

bus *noun Masc.* (*informal*) bus.

busca *noun Fem.* search; **ir en
busca de algo** to go in search of
something.

buscar *verb* [31] **1** to look for; **¿qué
buscas?** what are you looking for?;
**mi hermana está buscando
trabajo** my sister's looking for a job;
estoy buscando un ayudante I'm
looking for an assistant; **2** to look; **si**
**no lo encuentras aquí busca en la
oficina** if you don't find it here look
in the office; **3 ir a buscar algo** to go
to to pick up something; **mañana iré a
buscar mis cosas** I'll go and pick
up my things tomorrow; **4 ir a
buscar a alguien** to pick somebody
up; **yo te iré a buscar al
aeropuerto** I'll pick you up at the
airport; **5 ir a buscar a alguien** to
go to get someone (*the police or a
doctor, for example*); **fueron a
buscar a un médico enseguida**
they went to get a doctor straight
away.

búsqueda *noun Fem.* search.

butaca *noun Fem.* **1** armchair;
2 seat (*in a cinema or theatre*); **una
butaca de patio** a seat in the stalls.

butano *noun Masc.* butane gas; **una
bombona de butano** a bottle of
butane gas.

buzo *noun Masc.* diver.

buzón *noun Masc.* **1** letterbox;
2 postbox.

Cc

caballa *noun Fem.* mackerel.

caballero *noun Masc.* **1** gentleman;
es un verdadero caballero he's a
real gentleman; **2** sir; **caballero,
¿me deja pasar?** could you let me
through, sir?; **3 caballeros** Gents
(*toilets*), men's department (*in a
store*).

a
b
c
d
e
f
g
h
i
j
k
l
m
n
ñ
o
p
q
r
s
t
u
v
w
x
y
z

a
b
c
d
e
f
g
h
i
j
k
l
m
n
ñ
o
p
q
r
s
t
u
v
w
x
y
z

caballo noun Masc. **1** horse;
montar a caballo to ride a horse; **un
caballo de carreras** a racehorse;
2 knight (in chess); **3** horse (in
Spanish cards: equivalent to the
queen).

cabaña noun Fem. cabin.

cabecear verb [17] to head (a ball).

cabecera noun Fem. **1** headboard;
2 head (of table); **se sentó a la
cabecera de la mesa** he sat at the
head of the table.

cabello noun Masc. hair; **tener el
cabello rubio** to have blond hair;
cabello rizado curly hair; **cabello
liso** straight hair.

caber verb [33] **1 caber en** to fit
into; **es demasiado grande, no
cabe en la caja** it's too big, it
doesn't fit into the box; **no vamos a
caber en el coche** we won't all fit in
the car; **2 aquí ya no cabe nada
más** there's no room for anything
else in here; **¿caben estos libros
en la maleta?** is there room for
these books in the suitcase?;
3 caber por algo to fit through
something; **no cabía por la puerta**
it wouldn't fit through the door.

cabeza rapada noun Masc./Fem.
skinhead.

cabeza noun Fem. **1** head; **me
duele la cabeza** I've got a headache;
asentir con la cabeza to nod;
2 lavarse la cabeza to wash your
hair; **tengo que lavarme la cabeza**
I've got to wash my hair; **3 una
cabeza de ajo** a bulb of garlic;
4 tirarse al agua de cabeza to dive;
5 cabeza abajo upside down; **el**

cuadro está cabeza abajo the
picture's upside down; **6 a la
cabeza de** at the head of; **iban a la
cabeza de la manifestación** they
were at the head of the
demonstration; ★ **está mal de la
cabeza** he's not right in the head.

cabina noun Fem. **1** cab (of a lorry);
2 cockpit (of a plane); **3** cabin (on a
plane or boat); **4** booth (in a
language lab); **5 cabina de
teléfonos** telephone box.

cabo noun Masc. **1** corporal; **2** cape;
cabo de Buena Esperanza Cape of
Good Hope; **3 al cabo de** after; **al
cabo de tres semanas** after three
weeks; **4** end (of a length of rope or
piece of string); ★ **atar cabos** to put
two and two together.

cabra noun Fem. goat.

cabré, cabría, etc. verb SEE
caber.

cacahuete noun Masc. peanut.

cacao noun Masc. **1** cocoa (drink);
2 lipsalve.

cacerola noun Fem. saucepan.

cachete noun Masc. slap.

cachorro/cachorra noun Masc./
Fem. puppy.

cada adjective **1** each; **un alumno
de cada clase** a pupil from each
class; **hay diez para cada uno** there
are ten each; **2** every; **me llaman
cada día** they phone me every day;
cada tres días every three days;
3 cada vez más more and more; **se
parecen cada vez más** they look
more and more alike; **cada vez
menos** less and less; **cada vez**

mejor better and better; **lo hace cada vez mejor** she's getting better and better all the time; **cada vez peor** worse and worse.

cadena *noun Fem.* **1** chain; **una cadena de hierro** an iron chain; **una cadena antirrobo** a bicycle lock; **una cadena de supermercados** a supermarket chain; **2** channel (*on the TV*); **lo ponen en la segunda cadena** they're showing it on Channel Two; **3** station (*on the radio*); **4 cadena musical** hi-fi system; **5 cadenas** snow chains; **6 tirar de la cadena** to flush the toilet; **7 condenar a alguien a cadena perpetua** sentence somebody to life imprisonment.

cadera *noun Fem.* hip.

caer *verb* [34] **1** to fall; **el jarrón cayó al suelo** the vase fell to the ground; **2 dejar caer algo** to drop something (*on purpose*); **dejé caer la bandeja** I dropped the tray; **3 se dejó caer en el sofá** he flopped into the sofa; **4** (*informal*) **tu hermano me cae bien** I like your brother; **Ana me cae fatal** I can't stand Ana. **caerse** *reflexive verb* [34] **1** to fall over; **tropecé y me caí** I tripped and fell over; **2** to fall; **casi se cayó del tejado** he almost fell from the roof; **me caí por las escaleras** I fell down the stairs; **se cayó de la bici** he fell off his bike; **3 se me cayó el plato** I dropped the plate (*accidentally*); **4 se le ha caído un diente** he's lost a tooth; **se me está cayendo el pelo** I'm losing my hair.

café *noun Masc.* **1** coffee; **¿quieres un café?** do you want a cup of coffee?; **un café solo** a black coffee; **un café con leche** a white coffee; **un café cortado** a coffee with a dash of milk; **café descafeinado** decaffeinated coffee; **2** (*place*) cafe.

cafetera *noun Fem.* coffee maker.

cafetería *noun Fem.* café.

caído/caída *adjective* fallen.

caiga, caigo, etc. *verb* SEE **caer**.

caimán *noun* alligator *Masc.*.

caja *noun Fem.* **1** box; **una caja de cartón** a cardboard box; **caja de las herramientas** toolbox; **caja de cambios** gearbox; **2** crate; **una caja de naranjas** a crate of oranges; **3** checkout (*in a supermarket*); **pague en caja** pay at the checkout; **4** till (*in a shop*); **5 una caja fuerte** a safe; **6 caja de ahorros** savings bank.

cajero/cajera *noun Masc./Fem.* **1** cashier; **2** checkout operator; **3 cajero automático** cash dispenser.

cajón *noun Masc.* drawer.

calabacín *noun Masc.* courgette.

calamar *noun Masc.* squid; **calamares a la romana** squid rings in batter.

calambre *noun Masc.* **1** cramp; **me dio un calambre** I got cramp; **2** electric shock; **la lámpara me ha dado calambre** the lamp gave me an electric shock.

calamidad *noun Fem.* disaster.

calavera *noun Fem.* skull.

a
b
c
d
e
f
g
h
i
j
k
l
m
n
ñ
o
p
q
r
s
t
u
v
w
x
y
z

calcetín *noun Masc.* sock; **unos calcetines** a pair of socks.

calcomanía *noun Fem.* transfer (*sticker*)

calculadora *noun Fem.* calculator.

calcular *verb* [17] to calculate, to work out.

caldo *noun Masc.* **1** stock; **caldo de verdura** vegetable stock; **2** broth.

calefacción *noun Fem.* heating; **calefacción central** central heating; **calefacción de gas** gas heating.

calendario *noun Masc.* calendar.

calentador *noun Masc.* **1** boiler; **2** water heater.

calentar *verb* [29] **1** to heat (up); **voy a calentar la sopa** I'm going to heat up the soup; **2** to give off heat; **esta estufa calienta mucho** this heater gives off a lot of heat; **3 calentar los músculos** to warm up (*before sport or dancing*). **calentarse** *reflexive verb* [29] to heat up.

calidad *noun Fem.* quality; **materiales de calidad** high quality materials; **productos de mala calidad** poor quality products.

calienta, caliento, etc. *verb* SEE **calentar**.

caliente *adjective* **1** hot; **los platos están muy calientes** the plates are very hot; **2** warm; **un baño caliente** a hot bath; **en el salón se está más caliente** it's warmer in the living-room.

calificación *noun Fem.* mark; **obtuvo buenas calificaciónes** he got good marks.

callado/callada *adjective* quiet; **¡estate callado!** be quiet!

callar *verb* [17] to be quiet; **calla, no oigo** be quiet, I can't hear; **¡calla ya!** shut up! **callarse** *reflexive verb* [17] to go quiet; **al verla todos se callaron** everybody went quiet when they saw her; **¡cállate!** shut up!

calle *noun Fem.* street; **una calle cortada** a cul-de-sac; **una calle de sentido único** a one way street (*when writing an address, the word 'calle' is abbreviated to 'C/'*).

callejón *noun Masc.* alley; **un callejón sin salida** a blind alley.

calma *noun Fem.* calm; **hazlo con calma** do it calmly; **mantener la calma** to keep calm; **la ciudad está en calma** the city is calm.

calmar *verb* [17] to calm down. **calmarse** *reflexive verb* [17] to calm down; **después de un rato me calmé** I calmed down after a while.

calor *noun Masc.* **1** heat; **el calor de la estufa** the heat of the stove; **2** hoy hace mucho calor it's very hot today; **¡qué calor hace!** it's so hot!; **3 tener calor** to be hot; **tengo mucho calor** I'm very hot.

caluroso/calurosa *adjective* hot (*a day or place*).

calvo/calva *adjective* bald; **quedarse calvo** to go bald.

calzado *noun Masc.* footwear.

calzar *verb* [22] ¿qué número calzas? what shoe size do you take?

calzoncillos *plural noun Masc.* underpants; unos calzoncillos a pair of underpants.

cama *noun Fem.* bed; una cama individual a single bed; una cama doble/una cama de matrimonio a double bed; camas gemelas twin beds; una cama elástica a trampoline; hacer la cama to make the bed; ¡a la cama! off to bed!

cámara *noun Fem.* camera; una cámara de fotos a camera; una cámara de vídeo a video camera.

camarera *noun Fem.* **1** waitress; **2** camarera de habitación chambermaid.

camarero *noun Masc.* waiter.

camarón *noun Masc.* shrimp.

cambiar *verb* [17] **1** to change; no has cambiado you haven't changed; cambiar libras a euros to change pounds into euros; **2** cambiar de to change; ha cambiado de trabajo he's changed his job; cambiar de idea to change your mind; cambiar de canal to change channels; **3** to exchange; quiero cambiar estos zapatos I want to exchange these shoes; **4** cambiar de casa to move house; **5** to swap; te cambio mi pluma por esa cinta I'll swap my pen for that tape.

cambiarse *reflexive verb* [17] **1** to get changed; voy a cambiarme y ahora vuelvo I'm going to get changed, I'll be back in a minute; voy a cambiarme de ropa I'm going to change my clothes; **2** cambiarse de sitio to change places.

cambio *noun Masc.* **1** change; un cambio a mejor a change for the better; ha habido un cambio de planes there's been a change of plan; **2** exchange; no se admiten cambios goods will not be exchanged; **3** change; ¿tienes cambio? do you have any change?; me dieron mal el cambio they gave me the wrong change; 'cambio' 'bureau de change'; **4** a cambio de in return for; a cambio de información in return for information.

camello *noun Masc.* camel.

caminar *verb* [17] to walk; me gusta caminar I like walking.

caminata *noun Fem.* long walk.

camino *noun Masc.* **1** road; todos los caminos están cortados all the roads are closed; el camino al éxito the road to success; **2** path; un camino por el bosque a path through the forest; **3** way; ¿puede indicarme el camino a la estación? could you tell me the way to the station?; yo sé el camino I know the way.

camión *noun Masc.* lorry; el camión de la mudanza the removal van; un camión cisterna a petrol tanker.

camionero/camionera *noun Masc./Fem.* lorry driver.

camioneta *noun Fem.* van.

camisa *noun Fem.* shirt.

a
b
c
d
e
f
g
h
i
j
k
l
m
n
ñ
o
p
q
r
s
t
u
v
w
x
y
z

a
b
c
d
e
f
g
h
i
j
k
l
m
n
ñ
o
p
q
r
s
t
u
v
w
x
y
z

camiseta *noun Fem.* **1** T-shirt;
2 vest.

camisón *noun Masc.* nightdress.

campamento *noun Masc.* camp;
se han ido de campamento
they've gone camping.

campana *noun Fem.* bell; **tocar la
campana** to ring the bell.

campaña *noun Fem.* campaign;
campaña electoral electoral
campaign.

campeón/campeona *noun
Masc./Fem.* champion.

campeonato *noun Masc.*
championship.

campesino/campesina *noun
Masc./Fem.* **1** country person;
2 peasant.

camping *noun Masc.* campsite; **ir
de camping** to go camping.

campista *noun Masc./Fem.* camper.

campo *noun Masc.* **1** country; **una
casa en el campo** a house in the
country; **2** countryside; **el campo
está muy bonito** the countryside
looks very beautiful; **3** field; **un
campo de trigo** a field of wheat;
4 un campo de fútbol a football
pitch.

cana *noun Fem.* white hair; **le están
saliendo canas** he's going grey.

Canadá *noun Masc.* Canada.

canadiense *noun Masc./Fem.,
adjective* Canadian.

canal *noun Masc.* **1** channel (*on the
TV*); **no cambies de canal** don't
change channels; **2** channel (*water*);
el canal de la Mancha the English

Channel; **3** canal; **el canal de
Panamá** the Panama Canal.

canario[1] *noun Masc.* canary.

canario[2]**/canaria** *adjective* of/
from the Canary Islands.
canario *noun Masc./Fem.* Canary
Islander.

canasta *noun Fem.* basket.

canasto *noun Masc.* basket (*usually
with a lid*).

cancelar *verb* [17] to cancel.

cáncer[1] *noun Masc.* cancer; **tiene
cáncer** he's got cancer; **cáncer de
mama** breast cancer; **cáncer de
piel** skin cancer.

cáncer[2] *noun Masc./Fem.* Cancer;
soy Cáncer I'm Cancer.

Cáncer *noun Masc.* Cancer.

cancha *noun Fem.* court; **una
cancha de baloncesto** a basketball
court.

canción *noun Fem.* song; **canción
de cuna** lullaby.

candelabro *noun Masc.*
candlestick; **un candelabro dorado**
a brass candlestick.

candidato/candidata *noun
Masc./Fem.* candidate.

canela *noun Fem.* cinnamon;
canela en rama stick cinnamon;
canela en polvo ground cinnamon.

cangrejo *noun Masc.* **1** crab;
2 crayfish.

canguro[1] *noun Masc.* kangaroo.

canguro[2] *noun Masc./Fem.*
babysitter.

canica *noun Fem.* marble; **jugar a
las canicas** to play marbles.

46

canoa *noun Fem.* canoe.

cansado/cansada *adjective*
1 tired; **estoy muy cansado** I'm very tired; **2** tiring; **esperar es muy cansado** waiting's very tiring.

cansar *verb* [17] **1** to make tired; **le cansa andar** walking makes him tired; **2** to be tiring; **es un trabajo que cansa mucho** it's a very tiring job; **3** to be boring; **esta música cansa un poco** this music's a bit boring.
cansarse *reflexive verb* [17] **1** to get tired; **se cansa muy fácilmente** he gets tired very easily; **se me cansa la vista** my eyes get tired; **2** to get bored; **me canso de repetir siempre lo mismo** I get bored always repeating the same thing.

Cantábrico *noun Masc.* **el mar Cantábrico** the Bay of Biscay.

cantante *noun Masc./Fem.* singer.

cantar *verb* [17] to sing.

cantera *noun Fem.* quarry.

cantidad *noun Fem.* **1** amount; **una enorme cantidad de nieve** a huge amount of snow; **2** ¿qué cantidad de vasos necesitamos? how many glasses do we need?; **es increíble la cantidad de aceite gastas** it's incredible how much oil you use; **3** **tanta cantidad** so much; **no pongas tanta cantidad de leche** don't put so much milk in; **4** **cantidad de/cantidades de** lots of; **había cantidad de gente** there were lots of people; **con grandes cantidades de flores** with lots of flowers; **5** sum; **una cantidad importante de dinero** a considerable sum of money.

cantina *noun Fem.* **1** cafeteria; **2** canteen.

caña *noun Fem.* **1** cane; **caña de azúcar** sugar cane; **2** **caña de pescar** fishing rod.

cañería *noun Fem.* pipe.

cañón *noun* cannon.

capa *noun Fem.* **1** layer; **la capa de ozono** the ozone layer; **2** cape, cloak.

capacidad *noun Fem.* capacity.

capaz *adjective* **1** capable; **es capaz de cualquier cosa** he's capable of anything; **soy capaz de no ir** I'm quite capable of not going; **2** able; **no fueron capaces de darme una respuesta** they weren't able to give me an answer.

capital *noun Fem.* **1** capital; **la capital de España** the capital of Spain; **2** **Valencia capital** the city of Valencia (*as opposed to the province*).

capitán/capitana *noun Masc./ Fem.* captain (*in sports*).

capítulo *noun Masc.* **1** chapter; **2** episode (*of a TV series*).

capó *noun Masc.* bonnet (*of a car*).

capricornio *noun Masc./Fem.* Capricorn; **es capricornio** he's Capricorn.

Capricornio *noun Masc.* Capricorn.

cara *noun Fem.* **1** face; **tiene una cara bonita** she has a pretty face; **tienes cara de cansada** you look tired; **al oírlo puso cara de**

a
b
c
d
e
f
g
h
i
j
k
l
m
n
ñ
o
p
q
r
s
t
u
v
w
x
y
z

sorpresa he looked surprised when he heard it; **tu hermana tenía mala cara** your sister looked ill; ★ **¡qué cara más dura tienes!** (*informal*) you've got some nerve! (*literally: what a hard face you have!*); **2** side; **la otra cara del disco** the other side of the record; **3** ¿**cara o cruz?** heads or tails?

caracol *noun Masc.* **1** snail; **2** winkle.

carácter *noun Masc.* **1** character; **el carácter Latino** the Latin character; **2 tiene muy mal carácter** he's got a very bad temper; **es una persona de buen carácter** she's a good-natured person; **3 no tiene mucho carácter** he doesn't have much personality.

caramba *exclamation* **1** good heavens!; **2** damn it!.

caramelo *noun Masc.* **1** sweet; **un caramelo de menta** a mint; **2** caramel.

caravana *noun Fem.* **1** tailback; **hay caravana para entrar en Sevilla** there's a tailback into Seville; **una caravana de diez kilómetros** a ten-kilometre tailback; **2** caravan.

carbón *noun Masc.* coal; **carbón vegetal** charcoal.

cárcel *noun Fem.* jail; **meter a alguien en la cárcel** to put somebody in jail.

cardíaco/cardíaca *adjective* heart; **un ataque cardíaco** a heart attack.

careta *noun Fem.* mask.

carga *noun Fem.* **1** burden; **no quiero ser una carga para nadie** I don't want to be a burden on anybody; **2** freight, cargo; **3** load; **carga máxima** maximum load; **4** refill (*for a pen*); **5** ¡**a la carga!** charge!

cargado/cargada *adjective* **1** loaded; **la pistola estaba cargada** the gun was loaded; **vas muy cargada** you're loaded down; **iba cargado de paquetes** he was loaded down with parcels; **2 un café cargado** a strong coffee.

cargar *verb* [28] **1** to load (*a lorry or weapon*); **2** to fill (*a pen*).

cargo *noun Masc.* **1** position; **un cargo de responsabilidad** a position of responsibility; **2 a cargo de** in charge of; **estoy a cargo del departamento** I'm in charge of the department; **dejó los niños a mi cargo** she left the children in my care.

Caribe *noun Masc.* **el Caribe** the Caribbean; **el mar Caribe** the Caribbean Sea.

caribeño/caribeña *noun Masc., Fem., adjective* Caribbean.

cariño *noun Masc.* **1** affection; **tenerle cariño a** to be fond of; **les tengo cariño** I'm fond of them; **tomarle cariño a** to become fond of; **les tomó cariño** he became fond of them; **2 con cariño, Maya** love, Maya (*in letters*); **3** dear; **ven, cariño** come here, dear.

cariñoso/cariñosa *adjective* **1** affectionate, loving (*a person*);

2 warm; **un cariñoso saludo** warm regards (*in a letter*).

carmín *noun Masc.* lipstick.

carnaval *noun Masc.* carnival.

carné, carnet *noun Masc.* card; **carné de identidad** identity card; **carné de estudiante** student card; **carné de conducir** driving licence.

carne *noun Fem.* **1** meat; **carne de vaca** beef; **carne de cerdo** pork; **carne de cordero** lamb; **carne de ternera** veal; **2** flesh.

carnicería *noun Fem.* butcher's.

carnicero/carnicera *noun Masc./Fem.* butcher.

carnívoro/carnívora *adjective* carnivorous.

caro/cara *adjective* expensive; **cuesta muy caro** it's very expensive; **eso lo vas a pagar caro** you're going to pay dearly for this.

carpeta *noun Fem.* folder; **carpeta de anillas** ring binder.

carpintero/carpintera *noun Masc./Fem.* carpenter.

carrera *noun Fem.* **1** race; **una carrera automovilística** a car race; **las carreras de caballos** the races; **una carrera de obstáculos** a steeplechase; **una carrera de relevos** a relay race; **2** echar una carrera to have a race (*against somebody*); **echamos una carrera** let's have a race; **te echo una carrera** I'll race you; **3** echar una carrera to run; **eché una carrera y alcancé el autobús** I ran and got the bus; **4** degree course; **hacer una carrera** to study for a

degree; **no quiero hacer una carrera** I don't want to go to university; **está haciendo la carrera de medicina** she's studying medicine.

carreta *noun Fem.* cart.

carretera *noun Fem.* road; **carretera nacional** A-road; **carretera comarcal** B-road; **carretera de circunvalación** ringroad.

carretilla *noun Fem.* wheelbarrow.

carril *noun Masc.* lane; **carril bus** bus lane.

carrito *noun Masc.* trolley.

carro *noun Masc.* cart.

carta *noun Fem.* **1** letter; **mandar una carta** to send a letter; **echar una carta al correo** to post a letter; **una carta certificada** a registered letter; **2** menu; **¿nos puede traer la carta, por favor?** could you bring us the menu, please?; **3** card (*in a pack*); **jugar a las cartas** to play cards.

cartel *noun Masc.* **1** poster (*for publicity*); **2** sign; **¿qué dice el cartel?** what does the sign say?

cartelera *noun Fem.* **la cartelera de cine** 'what's on' at the cinema; **la obra lleva tres años en cartelera** the play has been running for three years; **la película sigue en cartelera** the film is still showing.

cartera *noun Fem.* **1** wallet; **2** briefcase; **3** satchel.

carterista *noun Masc./Fem.* pickpocket.

a
b
c
d
e
f
g
h
i
j
k
l
m
n
ñ
o
p
q
r
s
t
u
v
w
x
y
z

a
b
c
d
e
f
g
h
i
j
k
l
m
n
ñ
o
p
q
r
s
t
u
v
w
x
y
z

cartero/cartera *noun Masc./Fem.* postman/postwoman.

cartón *noun Masc.* cardboard.

casa *noun Fem.* **1** house; **una casa adosada** a semi-detached house; **una casa de campo** a country house; **una casa de huéspedes** guesthouse; **2** flat; **su casa está en la quinta planta** her flat's on the fifth floor; **3** home; **no están en casa** they're not at home; **estoy pasando unos días en casa de Juan** I'm staying at Juan's for a few days.

casado/casada *adjective* married; **estar casado/ser casado** to be married.

casarse *reflexive verb* [17] to get married; **se casó con mi primo** she married my cousin.

cascar *verb* [31] to crack.

cáscara *noun Fem.* **1** peel; **2** shell.

casco *noun Masc.* **1** helmet; **un casco protector** a safety helmet, crash helmet; **2** hoof (*of a horse*); **3** empty bottle; **guardo los cascos para reciclarlos** I keep the empty bottles for recycling; **4 cascos** headphones.

caserío *noun Masc.* **1** farmhouse; **2** hamlet.

casero/casera *noun Masc./Fem.* landlord/landlady.
casero *adjective* homemade.

caseta *noun Fem.* **1** hut (*for a watchman or guard*); **2** stand (*in an exhibition*); **3** kennel.

casete¹ *noun Masc.* cassette recorder.

casete² *noun Masc. or Fem.* cassette.

casi *adverb* **1** almost; **casi me pierdo** I almost got lost; **¡casi, casi!** almost!; **2** hardly; **casi no había gente** there was hardly anybody there; **casi nunca** hardly ever.

casilla *noun Fem.* **1** square (*in a crossword*); **2** box (*on a form*).

caso *noun Masc.* **1** case; **en ese caso** in that case; **en caso de accidente** in case of accident; **en todo caso/en cualquier caso** in any case; **en el peor de los casos** if the worst comes to the worst; **2 el caso es que** ... the thing is ...; **3 hacer caso de** to pay attention to; **haz caso de las señales** pay attention to the signs; **no me hace caso** he pays no attention to me.

cassette *noun Masc. or Fem.* cassette.

castaña¹ *noun Fem.* chestnut.

castaño/castaña² *adjective* chestnut brown.

castañuelas *plural noun Fem.* castanets.

castellano¹ *noun Masc.* **1** Castilian; **2** Castilian Spanish (*as opposed to other varieties of Spanish, particularly those of Spanish-speaking America; Castilian Spanish generally means the Spanish spoken in Spain*).

castellano²/**castellana** *noun Masc./Fem., adjective* Castilian.

castigar *verb* [28] **1** to punish; **2 castigar a alguien sin salir** to ground somebody; **3** to give a detention (*at school*); **la profesora**

me dejó castigado the teacher gave me a detention.

castigo *noun Masc.* punishment.

Castilla *noun Fem.* Castile.

castillo *noun Masc.* castle; **castillo de arena** sandcastle.

casualidad *noun Fem.* **1** chance; **de casualidad** by chance; **lo vi por casualidad** I saw it by chance; **2 da la casualidad de que** ... it so happens that ...; **dio la casualidad de que llevaba las señas en mi bolso** it so happened that I had the address in my bag; **3 ¡qué casualidad!** what a coincidence!.

catalán¹ *noun Masc.* Catalan (*the language*).

catalán²/catalana *noun Masc./ Fem., adjective* Catalan.

Cataluña *noun Fem.* Catalonia.

catarata *noun Fem.* **1** waterfall; **2** cataract (*of the eye*).

catarro *noun Masc.* cold; **coger un catarro** to catch a cold.

catear *verb* [17] (*informal*) to fail; **he cateado las mates** I've failed maths; **me han cateado en inglés** the English teacher has failed me.

catedral *noun Fem.* cathedral.

categoría *noun Fem.* **1** category; **2 de primera categoría** first class; **un hotel de mucha categoría** a top-quality hotel; **un restaurante de poca categoría** a second-rate restaurant.

católico/católica *noun Masc./ Fem., adjective* Catholic.

catorce *number* **1** fourteen; **tiene catorce años** he's fourteen (years old); **2** fourteenth (*in dates*); **el catorce de mayo** the fourteenth of May.

caucho *noun Masc.* rubber.

causa *noun Fem.* **1** cause; **sin causa** without cause; **2 a causa de** because of; **a causa de esto lo despidieron** they sacked him because of it.

causar *verb* [17] to cause.

cautiverio *noun Masc.* captivity; **mantener a alguien en cautiverio** to keep someone in captivity .

cautivo/cautiva *noun* prisoner.

cava *noun Masc.* cava (*sparkling wine*).

cavar *verb* [17] to dig.

caverna *noun Fem.* cave.

cayendo SEE **caer**.

caza *noun Fem.* hunting; **ir de caza** to go hunting.

cazar *verb* [22] to hunt.

cazuela *noun Fem.* casserole.

cebada *noun* barley *Fem.*

cebolla *noun Fem.* onion.

cebolleta *noun Fem.* spring onion.

cebollino *noun Masc.* chives.

ceder *verb* [18] **1** to give in; **finalmente cedí** I finally gave in; **2 ceder el paso** to give way; **3 le cedí mi asiento a un anciano** I gave up my seat to an elderly man.

ceguera *noun Fem.* blindness.

ceja *noun Fem.* eyebrow.

celda *noun Fem.* cell (*in a prison*).

a
b
c
d
e
f
g
h
i
j
k
l
m
n
ñ
o
p
q
r
s
t
u
v
w
x
y
z

a
b
c
d
e
f
g
h
i
j
k
l
m
n
ñ
o
p
q
r
s
t
u
v
w
x
y
z

celebración *noun Fem.*
celebration.

celebrar *verb* [17] **1** to celebrate;
2 to hold (*a meeting*).

celebrarse *reflexive verb* [17] to
take place; **la boda se celebró el
sábado pasado** the wedding took
place last Saturday.

célebre *adjective* famous.

celo *noun Masc.* Sellotape™.

celos *plural noun Masc.* **1** jealousy;
2 tener celos de alguien to be
jealous of somebody; **tiene celos de
su hermana pequeña** she's jealous
of her little sister; **3 darle celos a
alguien** to make somebody feel
jealous; **lo hace para darte celos**
he does it to make you feel jealous.

celoso/celosa *adjective* jealous.

cementerio *noun Masc.* cemetery.

cemento *noun Masc.* cement.

cena *noun Fem.* **1** dinner (*evening
meal*); **2** supper; **¿qué hay de
cena?** what's for supper?

cenar *verb* [17] to have dinner;
**normalmente cenamos a las
nueve** we normally have dinner at
nine; **salimos a cenar fuera** we
went out for dinner.

cenicero *noun Masc.* ashtray.

ceñido/ceñida *adjective* tight;
una camiseta muy ceñida a very
tight T-shirt.

ceniza *noun Fem.* ash.

ceño *noun Masc.* **fruncir el ceño** to
frown.

centavo *noun Masc.* **1** one
hundredth; **2** cent (*in the dollar
system*).

centenar *noun Masc.* hundred; **un
centenar de libros** (about) a
hundred books; **centenares de
cartas** hundreds of letters.

centenario *noun Masc.* centenary.

centeno *noun Masc.* rye.

centésima *noun Fem.* hundredth;
una centésima de segundo a
hundredth of a second.

centésimo/centésima²
adjective hundredth.

centígrado *adjective* centigrade.

centímetro *noun Masc.* centimetre.

céntimo *noun* **1** cent (*in the euro
system*); **el euro se divide en cien
céntimos** the euro is divided into a
hundred cents; **2** penny; **no tengo
ni un céntimo** I am penniless.

central *noun Fem.* **1** head office;
2 central telefónica telephone
exchange; **central de correos**
general post office; **3** power station;
central nuclear nuclear power
station.
central *adjective* central.

céntrico/céntrica *adjective*
central; **un barrio céntrico** an area
in the centre of town.

centrifugar *verb* [28] to spin-dry.

centro *noun Masc.* **1** centre; **el
centro de la ciudad** the town/city
centre; **un centro cultural** a
cultural centre; **estaba justo en el
centro** it was right in the middle;
2 un centro comercial a shopping
mall.

cepillar *verb* [17] to brush.
cepillarse *reflexive verb* [17] to brush; **cepillarse los dientes** to brush your teeth; **cepillarse el pelo** to brush your hair.

cepillo *noun Masc.* brush; **un cepillo de dientes** a toothbrush; **un cepillo del pelo** a hairbrush.

cera *noun Fem.* wax.

cerámica *noun Fem.* pottery.

cerca *adverb* **1** near, close; **viven aguí cerca** they live near here; **ponlos cerca el uno del otro** put them close to each other; **2** nearby; **mi casa está cerca** my house is nearby; **3 cerca de** near; **se sentó cerca de mí** he sat near me; **está cerca de la estación** it's near the station; **vive muy cerca de mí** she lives very near me; **4 cerca de** almost; **cerca de diez mil personas** almost ten thousand people.

cercanía *noun Fem.* proximity.

cercanías *plural noun Fem.*
1 surrounding area; **Barcelona y sus cercanías** Barcelona and the surrounding area; **en las cercanías del aeropuerto** in the area around the airport; **2** vicinity; **en las cercanías del bar** in the vicinity of the bar.

cercano/cercana *adjective*
1 nearby; **las casas cercanas** the nearby houses; **2 cercano a algo** near something; **los pueblos cercanos al aeropuerto** the villages near the airport; **3** near; **en un futuro cercano** in the near future.

cerdo¹ *noun Masc.* pork; **no como cerdo** I don't eat pork.

cerdo²**/cerda** *noun Masc./Fem.* pig.

cereales *plural noun Masc.* cereals.

ceremonia *noun Fem.* ceremony.

cereza *noun Fem.* cherry.

cerilla *noun Fem.* match.

cero *noun Masc.* **1** zero; **tres grados bajo cero** three degrees below zero; **mi prefijo en Londres es cero, dos, cero** my dialling code in London is 020; **2** love (*in tennis*); **3** nil (*in football*).

cerrado/cerrada *adjective*
1 closed; **la ventana está cerrada** the window's closed; **2 cerrado con llave** locked; **cerrado con cerrojo** bolted; **3 el grifo está cerrado** the tap's turned off.

cerradura *noun Fem.* **1** lock; **2 el ojo de la cerradura** the keyhole.

cerrar *verb* [29] **1** to close; **cierrra la puerta** close the door; **cerramos a las ocho** we close at eight; **han cerrado la fábrica** the factory has been closed; **2 cerrar algo de un portazo** to slam something; **cerró la puerta de un portazo** he slammed the door shut; **3 cerrar con llave** to lock; **no te olvides de cerrar con llave** don't forget to lock up; **4 cerrar con cerrojo** to bolt; **5 cerrar el grifo** to turn off the tap; **6 cierra la botella** put the top on the bottle; **¿has cerrado el frasco?** have you put the lid on the jar?; **7 cerrar una carta** to seal a letter.

cerrarse *reflexive verb* [29] to

a b c d e f g h i j k l m n ñ o p q r s t u v w x y z

53

a
b
c
d
e
f
g
h
i
j
k
l
m
n
ñ
o
p
q
r
s
t
u
v
w
x
y
z

close; **la puerta se cerró** the door closed; **cerrarse de un portazo** to slam shut.

certificado¹ *noun Masc.* certificate.

certificado²/certificada *adjective* registered (*a letter or parcel*).

certificar *verb* [31] to certify.

cervecería *noun Fem.* **1** brewery; **2** bar (*selling lots of different beers*).

cerveza *noun Fem.* beer; **¿quieres una cerveza?** do you want a beer?; **cerveza de barril** draught beer; **cerveza negra** stout; **cerveza rubia** lager.

césped *noun Masc.* lawn; **'prohibido pisar el césped'** 'keep off the grass'.

cesta *noun Fem.* **1** basket; **una cesta de mimbre** a wicker basket; **2 una cesta de Navidad** a Christmas hamper.

cesto *noun Masc.* basket.

chalado/chalada *adjective* (*informal*) crazy.

chalé, **chalet** *noun Masc.* **1** villa; **2** detached house (*on estate*); **3** semi-detached house (*on estate*).

chaleco *noun Masc.* waistcoast; **un chaleco de punto** a sleeveless sweater.

champán *noun Masc.* champagne.

champaña *noun m or Fem.* champagne.

champiñón *noun Masc.* mushroom.

champú *noun Masc.* shampoo.

chanclas *noun Fem.* (*plural*) flip-flops.

chándal *noun Masc.* tracksuit.

chapa *noun Fem.* **1** top (*of a bottle*); **2** badge; **una chapa de policía** a police badge.

chapapote *noun Masc.* oil (*washed up on a beach*).

chaparrón *noun Masc.* downpour.

chaqueta *noun Fem.* jacket; **chaqueta de punto** cardigan.

charca *noun Fem.* pond.

charco *noun Masc.* puddle; **no pises los charcos** don't walk in the puddles.

charcutería *noun Fem.* delicatessen (*specializing in pork products*).

charlar *verb* [17] to chat.

chasco *noun Masc.* disappointment; **me llevé un chasco** I felt really disappointed.

chat *noun Masc.* chatroom.

cheque *noun Masc.* cheque; **extender un cheque** to write out a cheque; **me puedes extender un cheque a mi nombre** you can make out a cheque to me; **un cheque a nombre de Alberto López** a cheque payable to Alberto López; **cobrar un cheque** to cash a cheque; **un cheque de viaje/un cheque de viajero** a traveller's cheque.

chequeo *noun Masc.* checkup; **hacerse un chequeo** to have a checkup.

chica *noun Fem.* girl.

chichón *noun Masc.* bump; **me di un golpe en la frente y me ha salido un chichón** I banged my forehead and now I've got a bump.

chicle *noun Masc.* chewing gum; **¿quieres un chicle?** do you want some chewing gum?

chico *noun Masc.* **1** boy; **2 unos chicos** some children; **había unos chicos jugando en la calle** there were some children playing in the street; **3** guy; **sale con un chico** she's going out with a guy.

chiflado/chiflada *adjective* (*informal*) crazy.

Chile *noun Masc.* Chile.

chile *noun Masc.* chilli.

chileno/chilena *noun Masc./Fem.*, *adjective* Chilean.

chillar *verb* [17] to shout.

chimenea *noun Fem.* **1** chimney; **2** fireplace.

China *noun Fem.* **(la) China** China.

chincheta *noun Fem.* drawing pin.

chino¹ *noun Masc.* Chinese (*the language*).

chino²/china *noun Masc./Fem.* Chinese man/Chinese woman. **chino** *adjective* Chinese.

Chipre *noun Fem.* Cyprus.

chirriar *verb* [32] to squeak (*a door*).

chis *exclamation* **1** shush!; **2 ¡chis, chis!** hey! (*calling somebody in the street, for example*).

chisme *noun Masc.* **1** piece of gossip; **siempre está contando chismes** he's always gossiping; **2** thing; **¿para qué sirve este chisme?** what's this thing for?; **tiene un montón de chismes que no sirven para nada** he's got all sorts of useless stuff.

chispa *noun Fem.* **1** spark; **saltaron chispas del fuego** sparks flew out of the fire; **2 una chispa de** (*informal*) a drop of; **una chispa de ginebra** a drop of gin; **pon una chispa de sal** add a tiny bit of salt. **chispa** *adjective* (*informal*) tipsy; **estaba un poco chispa** she was a bit tipsy.

chiste *noun Masc.* joke; **contar un chiste** to tell a joke; **un chiste verde** a dirty joke.

chocar *verb* [31] **1** to crash; **dos coches chocaron en la autopista** two cars crashed on the motorway; **2 chocar con** to run into; **chocaron con una farola** they ran into a lamppost; **me choqué con ella** I bumped into her.

chocolate *noun Masc.* chocolate; **chocolate con leche** milk chocolate; **chocolate negro** dark chocolate; **una barra de chocolate** a bar of chocolate.

chocolatina *noun Fem.* chocolate bar.

chollo *noun Masc.* (*informal*) **1** cushy job; **2 este chico es un chollo, sabe hacer de todo** this guy's a real find, he can do anything.

choque *noun Masc.* **1** crash; **un choque frontal** a head-on collision; **2** clash; **choques entre los manifestantes y la policía** clashes between demonstrators and police.

a
b
c
d
e
f
g
h
i
j
k
l
m
n
ñ
o
p
q
r
s
t
u
v
w
x
y
z

chorizo *noun Masc.* chorizo (*spicy salami-shaped sausage*).

chorrada *noun Fem.* (*informal*) **eso es una chorrada** that's nonsense; **decir chorradas** to talk nonsense; **se enfada por cualquier chorrada** he gets upset over the smallest thing.

chubasco *noun Masc.* **1** shower; **2** downpour.

chuchería *noun Fem.* trinket.

chuleta *noun Fem.* chop; **una chuleta de cerdo** a pork chop.

chupar *verb* [17] **1** to suck; **2** to absorb; **este papel chupa la tinta** this paper absorbs ink.
chuparse *reflexive verb* [17] to suck; **chuparse el dedo** to suck your thumb.

churro *noun Masc.* **1** fritter; **2** (*informal*) botched job; **¡vaya churro ha salido!** it's turned out a real mess!.

chutar *verb* [17] to shoot (*at goal*).

cibercafé *noun Masc.* Internet cafe; **¿dónde hay un cibercafé?** where is there an Internet cafe?

cibernauta *noun Masc./Fem.* surfer.

cicatriz *noun Fem.* scar.

ciclismo *noun Masc.* cycling.

ciclista *noun Masc./Fem.* cyclist.

ciego/ciega *noun Masc./Fem.* blind person; **los ciegos** the blind.
ciego *adjective* blind; **quedarse ciego** to go blind.

cielo *noun Masc.* **1** sky; **2** heaven; **ir al cielo** to go to heaven; **¡cielos!** good heavens!

cien *number* hundred (*see also 'ciento'*); **cien personas** a hundred people; **el cien por cien** a hundred per cent; **cien mil euros** a hundred thousand euros.

ciencia *noun Fem.* **1** science; **ciencia ficción** science fiction; **2 ciencias** science (*subject at school*); **ciencias naturales** natural science; **Ciencias Económicas** Economic Sciences; **Ciencias Empresariales** Business Studies; **Ciencias de la Información** Media Studies.

cieno *noun Masc.* silt.

científico/científica *noun Masc./Fem.* scientist.
científico *adjective* scientific.

ciento *number* **1** hundred; **ciento cinco** one hundred and five; **dos cientos diez** two hundred and ten; **cientos de cartas** hundreds of letters; **2 por ciento** per cent; **cinco por ciento** five per cent; **tanto por ciento** percentage.

cierra, cierro, etc. *verb* SEE **cerrar**.

cierto/cierta *adjective* **1** true; **eso no es cierto** that's not true; **2** certain; **cierta clase de negocios** certain types of business; **en cierta ocasión** on a certain occasion; **3 en cierto modo** in a way; **en cierto modo, lo entiendo** in a way, I understand; **4 hasta cierto punto** up to a point; **5 por cierto** by the way; **por cierto, ¿se lo**

has preguntado? by the way, did you ask him?.

ciervo *noun Masc.* **1** deer; **2** stag.

cifra *noun Fem.* figure; **una cifra muy alta** a very high figure.

cigarrillo *noun Masc.* cigarrette.

cigüeña *noun Fem.* stork.

cilindro *noun Masc.* cylinder.

cima *noun Fem.* top (*of a mountain*).

cinco *number* **1** five; **Julia tiene cinco años** Julia's five (years old); **2** fifth (*in dates*); **hoy es día cinco** today is the fifth; **3** five (*in clock time*); **son las cinco** it's five o'clock; **a las dos y cinco** at five past two.

cincuenta *number* fifty; **mi madre tiene cincuenta años** my mum's fifty (years old); **cincuenta y ocho** fifty-eight; **los años cincuenta** the fifties.

cine *noun Masc.* cinema; **ir al cine** to go to the cinema; **¿qué ponen en el cine?** what's on at the cinema?; **cine de barrio** local cinema; **la cartelera de cine** 'what's on' at the cinemas.

cineasta *noun Masc./Fem.* film-maker.

cinta *noun Fem.* **1** ribbon; **una cinta para el pelo** a hair ribbon; **2** tape; **una cinta de vídeo** a video tape; **grabar una cinta** to record a tape; **una cinta virgen** a blank tape; **cinta magnetofónica** magnetic tape; **cinta adhesiva** adhesive tape; **cinta métrica** tape measure.

cintura *noun Fem.* waist; **¿cuánto tienes de cintura?** what's your waist measurement?

cinturón *noun Masc.* belt; **cinturón de seguridad** seatbelt; **es cinturón negro de karate** he's a karate black belt; ★ **apretarse el cinturón** to tighten one's belt.

circo *noun Masc.* circus.

circulación *noun Fem.* **1** circulation; **2** traffic.

circular *noun Fem.*, **circular** *adjective* circular. **circular** *verb* [17] **1** to flow (*blood or water*); **2** to drive; **circulen por la derecha** drive on the right; **el coche circulaba a mucha velocidad** the car was travelling very fast.

círculo *noun Masc.* circle.

circunferencia *noun Fem.* circumference.

circunstancia *noun Fem.* **1** reason; **por alguna circunstancia no pudo hacerlo** he couldn't do it for some reason; **2** circumstances; **bajo ninguna circunstancia** under no circumstances; **en estas circunstancias** in these circumstances; **dadas las circunstancias** given the circumstances.

cirio *noun Masc.* candle.

ciruela *noun Fem.* plum; **ciruela pasa** prune.

cirugía *noun Fem.* surgery; **cirugía estética** plastic surgery; **cirugía láser** laser surgery.

cirujano/cirujana *noun Masc./Fem.* surgeon.

cisne *noun Masc.* swan.

a
b
c
d
e
f
g
h
i
j
k
l
m
n
ñ
o
p
q
r
s
t
u
v
w
x
y
z

a
b
c
d
e
f
g
h
i
j
k
l
m
n
ñ
o
p
q
r
s
t
u
v
w
x
y
z

cita noun Fem. **1** appointment;
tengo cita con el médico I've got
an appointment to see the doctor; **el
dentista me ha dado cita para el
jueves** the dentist has given me an
appointment for Thursday; **pedir
cita** to make an appointment; **llamé
al abogado para pedir cita** I
phoned the lawyer to make an
appointment; **2** date; **esta noche
tengo una cita** I've got a date
tonight, I'm meeting somebody
tonight; **3** quotation.

citar verb [17] **1** to quote (a writer or
book); **2** to mention; **citó algunos
casos** he mentioned a few cases;
3 to give an appointment; **el médico
me ha citado para esta tarde** the
doctor's given me an appointment
for this afternoon.

citarse reflexive verb [17] to
arrange to meet; **se citaron para
las cinco** they arranged to meet at
five.

ciudad noun Fem. **1** town; **ciudad
dormitorio** dormitory town; **2** city;
3 ciudad universitaria university
campus.

ciudadano/ciudadana noun
Masc./Fem. citizen.

civil adjective **1** civil; **un
matrimonio civil** a civil marriage;
2 civilian; **la población civil** the
civilian population.
civil noun Masc./Fem. civilian.

clarinete noun Masc. clarinet.

claro adjective **1** light; **un verde
claro** a light green; **un chico de
ojos claros** a guy with light-
coloured eyes (blue, green, or grey:

opposite of 'dark eyes'); **2** bright; **un
día claro** a bright, sunny day;
3 clear; **está muy claro** it's very
clear; **no lo tengo muy claro** I'm
not very clear about it.
claro adverb **1** clearly; **no habla
claro** he doesn't speak clearly; **lo
veo claro** I can see it clearly;
2 ¡claro! of course!; **claro que sí** of
course; **claro que no** of course not.

clase noun Fem. **1** kind, type; **¿qué
clase de material?** what kind of
material?; **2 de primera clase** top-
quality; **3** class; **la clase de
matemáticas** the maths class;
entro en clase a las nueve I start
my classes at nine; **toda la clase ha
ido al museo** the whole class has
gone to the museum; **4 dar clase de
algo** to teach something; **da clase
de física en un colegio** he teaches
physics in a school; **dar clase a
alguien** to give somebody lessons;
me da clases de inglés he gives me
English lessons; **5 dar clase de
algo** to have lessons in something;
**da clases de música por las
tardes** she has music lessons in the
evenings; **6** classroom; **¿en qué
clase están?** what classroom are
they in?; **7 clase social** social class;
un familia de clase media a
middle-class family; **8** class (of
travel); **viajar en primera clase** to
travel first class; **clase turista**
economy class; **clase ejecutiva/
clase preferente** business class;
9 class (elegance); **tener clase** to
have class.

clásico/clásica adjective
1 classical (decoration);

2 traditional (*method*); **3** classic; **la clásica broma** the classic joke.

clasificación *noun Fem.*
1 classification; **2** qualifying (*in sports*); **sin posibilidades de clasificación** with no chance of qualifying; **3** placings (*in sports*); **la clasificación es la siguiente** ... the placings are as follows ....

clasificar *verb* [31] to sort into order (*papers, for example*).
clasificarse *reflexive verb* [17] to qualify; **clasificarse para la final** to qualify for the final.

clavar *verb* [17] to hammer; **clavar un clavo en la pared** to hammer a nail into the wall.

clave *noun Fem.* **1** key (*to a mystery or problem*); **la clave es** ... the key to it is ...; **2** code; **mensaje en clave** coded message; **3** clef (*in music*); **clave de sol** treble clef.
clave *adjective* key; **un factor clave** a key factor.

clavija *noun Fem.* **1** peg; **2** plug (*for an electrical appliance*).

clavo *noun Masc.* **1** nail; **2** clove (*spice*).

claxon *noun Masc.* horn.

clic *noun Masc.* click; **un doble clic** a double click; **hacer doble clic** to double-click; **haz clic dos veces en el icono** click the icon twice.

cliente/clienta *noun Masc./Fem.*
1 customer; **2** client (*of a company or a lawyer*); **3** guest (*in a hotel*).

clima *noun Masc.* climate.

climatizado/climatizada *adjective* air-conditioned.

clínica *noun Fem.* private hospital.

clip *noun Masc.* **1** paper clip; **2 un clip para el pelo** a hairgrip; **3 de clip** clip-on.

club *noun Masc.* club; **club de jóvenes** youth club.

coartada *noun Fem.* alibi.

cobarde *noun Masc./Fem.* coward.
cobarde *adjective* cowardly.

cobrador/cobradora *noun Masc./Fem.* conductor.

cobrar *verb* [17] **1** to get paid; **cobro mil cuatro cientos euros al mes** I get paid one thousand four hundred euros a month; **cobramos a fin de mes** we get paid at the end of the month; **cobra el paro** he's on unemployment benefit; **cobra bastante de pensión** he gets a good pension; **2** to charge; **me cobraron sesenta euros por todo** they charged me sixty euros for everything; **cobrar de más** to overcharge; **cobrar de menos** to undercharge; **3** to collect; **han venido a cobrar la deuda** they've come to collect the money owing; **4** to draw; **cobrar un cheque** to draw a cheque; **cuando vengas a cobrar tu pensión** when you come to draw your pension.

cobre *noun Masc.* copper.

cocaína *noun Fem.* cocaine.

cocer *verb* [41] **1** to boil (*in water*); **cocer algo a fuego lento** to simmer something over a low heat; **2** to bake.

coche *noun Masc.* **1** car; **he venido en coche** I came by car; **coche**

a
b
c
d
e
f
g
h
i
j
k
l
m
n
ñ
o
p
q
r
s
t
u
v
w
x
y
z

bomba car bomb; **coche de alquiler** hire car; **coche de carreras** racing car; **coche patrulla** patrol car; **2** carriage, coach (*on a train*); **¿qué número de coche es?** what coach number is it?; **coche cama** sleeping car; **coche restaurante** restaurant car; **3 coche de bomberos** fire engine.

cochecito de bebé *noun Masc.* pram.

cochera *noun Fem.* bus depot.

cocido *noun Masc.* stew (*made with chickpeas*).

cocina *noun Fem.* **1** kitchen; **¿dónde está la cocina?** where's the kitchen?; **2** cooker; **cocina de gas** gas cooker; **cocina eléctrica** electric cooker; **3** cooking; **la cocina española** Spanish cooking; **un libro de cocina** a cookery book.

cocinar *verb* [17] to cook; **cocinar algo a fuego lento** to cook something on a low heat.

cocinero/cocinera *noun Masc./ Fem.* cook.

coco *noun Masc.* **1** coconut; **2** (*informal*) head; **me duele el coco** I've got a headache; ★ **darle al coco** (*informal*) to think; ★ **comerse el coco** (*informal*) to worry your head off;; **no te comas el coco** don't worry your head about it; ★ **comerle el coco a alguien** (*informal*) to try to convince somebody.

cocodrilo *noun Masc.* crocodile.

cóctel *noun Masc.* **1** cocktail; **2** cocktail party.

código *noun Masc.* code; **código de barras** bar code; **código postal** postcode.

codo *noun Masc.* elbow.

codorniz *noun Fem.* quail.

coger *verb* [3] **1** to take; **voy a coger el autobús** I'm going to take the bus; **¿has cogido los paquetes que había aquí?** have you taken the parcels that were here?; **la cogí del brazo** I took her by the arm; **2** to get; **cogió un resfriado** he got a cold; **coger una insolación** to get sunstroke; **voy a coger entradas para el teatro** I'll get tickets for the theatre; **3 coger el teléfono** to answer the phone; **4** to catch; **no pudo coger la pelota** he couldn't catch the ball; **¡a que no me coges!** I bet you can't catch me!; **cogieron al asesino** they caught the murderer; **no me dio tiempo a coger el tren** I didn't have time to catch the train; **5** to pick; **coger fresas** to pick strawberries; **coger algo del suelo** to pick something up from the floor.

cogerse *reflexive verb* [3] **1 cogerse de algo** to hold on to something; **cógete de la barra** hold on to the rail; **2 se cogieron de la mano** they held hands.

cogido/cogida *adjective* **1** taken; **esta silla ya está cogida** this chair is already taken; **2 ir cogidos de la mano** to walk hand in hand; **ir cogidos del brazo** to walk arm in arm.

cohibido/cohibida *adjective* **1** self-conscious; **2** shy.

coincidencia *noun Fem.*
coincidence; **¡qué coincidencia!**
what a coincidence!; **dio la
coincidencia de que** ... it so
happened that ....

coincidir *verb* [19] to coincide.

coja, cojo, etc. *verb* SEE **coger.**

cojín *noun Masc.* cushion.

cojo/coja *adjective* **1** lame; **es
cojo** he's lame; **2 está cojo** he has a
limp; **3 andar a la pata coja** to hop.

col *noun Fem.* cabbage; **coles de
Bruselas** Brussels sprouts.

cola *noun Fem.* **1** tail; **2** queue;
hacer cola to queue up; **saltarse la
cola** to jump the queue; **me puse a
la cola** I joined the queue; **3** glue;
cola de carpintero wood glue; **lo
pegué con cola** I glued it.

colada *noun Fem.* laundry; **hacer la
colada** to do the washing.

colador *noun Masc.* strainer.

colar *verb* [24] to strain (*vegetables*).
colarse *reflexive verb* [24] **1** to
jump the queue; **esa señora se ha
colado** that lady has jumped the
queue; **2 colarse en un sitio** to get
in somewhere without paying; **se
coló en el cine** he got into the
cinema without paying.

colcha *noun Fem.* bedspread.

colchón *noun Masc.* mattress.

colección *noun Fem.* collection.

coleccionar *verb* [17] to collect.

coleccionista *noun* collector.

colega *noun Masc./Fem.* colleague.

colegial/colegiala *noun Masc./
Fem.* schoolboy/schoolgirl.

colegio *noun Masc.* school; **colegio
público** state school; **colegio
privado** private school; **un colegio
de curas** a catholic boys' school.

coleta *noun Fem.* ponytail.

colgado/colgada *adjective*
1 colgado de algo hanging from
something; **2 el teléfono está mal
colgado** the phone's off the hook;
¿tienes el teléfono bien colgado?
have you put the phone down
properly?

colgar *verb* [23] **1** to hang; **2 colgar
la ropa** to hang out the washing;
3 colgar un cuadro to put up a
picture; **4** to put down (*telephone*);
cuelga el teléfono put the phone
down; **me ha colgado** she's hung up
on me; **no cuelgue, por favor** hold
the line, please.
colgarse *reflexive verb* [23]
colgarse de algo to hang from
something.

coliflor *noun Fem.* cauliflower.

colilla *noun Fem.* cigarette end.

colina *noun Fem.* hill.

collar *noun Masc.* **1** necklace; **un
collar de perlas** a string of pearls;
2 collar; **el collar del perro** the
dog's collar.

colmo *noun Masc.* **1 el colmo de la
incompetencia** the height of
incompetence; **2 ¡esto es el colmo!**
this is the limit!; **¡y para colmo** ... !
and to cap it all ... !; **sería el colmo
que no viniesen** it would be the
limit if they didn't come.

a
b
c
d
e
f
g
h
i
j
k
l
m
n
ñ
o
p
q
r
s
t
u
v
w
x
y
z

colocación *noun Fem.* job; **está buscando colocación** he's looking for a job.

colocar *verb* [31] **1** to put; **colócalo ahí** put it there; **¿dónde coloco esta silla?** where should I put this chair?; **2 aún tenemos que colocar los muebles** we still have to arrange the furniture; **3 colocar a alguien** to get somebody a job; **su tío lo ha colocado** his uncle's got him a job.
colocarse *reflexive verb* [31] to find a job; **se ha colocado muy bien** she's found a very good job.

Colombia *noun Fem.* Colombia.

colombiano/colombiana *noun Masc./Fem., adjective* Colombian.

colonia *noun Fem.* **1** (eau de) cologne; **2** colony; **3 una colonia de vacaciones** a summer camp.

coloquial *adjective* colloquial.

coloquio *noun Masc.* discussion.

color *noun Masc.* colour; **¿de qué color es?** what colour is it?; **colores claros** light colours; **es de color azul** it's blue; **telas de colores** coloured fabrics; **televisión en color** colour television.

colorado/colorada *adjective* red; **ponerse colorado** to go red; **¡te has puesto colorado!** you've gone red!

colorante *noun Masc.* colouring.

colorear *verb* [17] to colour; **colorear algo de rojo** to colour something red.

colorete *noun Masc.* blusher.

columna *noun Fem.* **1** column; **2** spine; **la columna vertebral** the spine.

columpiar *verb* [17] to push (*on a swing*).
columpiarse *reflexive verb* [17] to swing.

columpio *noun Masc.* swing.

coma *noun Fem.* **1** comma; **2** decimal point; **dos coma cinco** two point five.
coma *noun Masc.* coma; **entrar en coma** to go into a coma.

comadrona *noun Fem.* midwife.

comandante *noun Masc./Fem.* major.

comba *noun Fem.* skipping rope; **saltar a la comba** to skip; **jugar a la comba** to skip.

combate *noun Masc.* **1** combat; **2** fight.

combinación *noun Fem.* combination.

combinar *verb* [17] to combine.

comedia *noun Fem.* comedy; **una comedia musical** a musical.

comedor *noun Masc.* **1** dining-room; **2** dining hall; **3** canteen.

comentar *verb* [17] **1** to talk about; **comentamos un poco la noticia** we talked a bit about the news; **2** to mention; **me lo comentó de pasada** he mentioned it to me in passing; **3** to remark; **comentó que ...** he remarked that ....

comentario *noun Masc.* comment; **sin comentarios** no comment.

comenzar *verb* [25] to begin.

a
b
c
d
e
f
g
h
i
j
k
l
m
n
ñ
o
p
q
r
s
t
u
v
w
x
y
z

comer *verb* [18] **1** to eat; **2** to have lunch; **normalmente comemos a las dos** we normally have lunch at two; **¿qué había de comer?** what was for lunch?; **3** to take (*a piece in chess or draughts*); **te como el caballo** I take your knight.

comercial *adjective* commercial; **el centro comercial de la ciudad** the commercial centre of the town; **un centro comercial** a shopping centre.

comerciante *noun Masc./Fem.* **1** shopkeeper; **2** trader.

comercio *noun Masc.* **1** trade; **el comercio de animales exóticos** the trade in exotic animals; **2** shop; **un comercio pequeño** a small shop.

comestibles *plural noun Masc.* foodstuffs.

cometa *noun Fem.* **1** kite; **hacer volar una cometa** to fly a kite; **2** comet.

cometer *verb* [18] **1** to commit (*a crime*); **2** to make (*a mistake*); **he cometido un error** I've made a mistake.

cómic *noun Masc.* comic.

cómico/cómica *adjective* **1** funny (*a situation or face*); **2** comedy (*actor*).
cómico *noun Masc./Fem.* **1** comedian; **2** comedy actor/ comedy actress.

comida *noun Fem.* **1** food; **tenemos suficiente comida** we have enough food; **la comida rápida** fast food; **2** lunch; **a la hora de la comida** at lunch time; **3** meal; **cuatro comidas al día** four meals a day; **mi comida fuerte es a mediodía** I have my main meal at midday.

comienza, comienzo[1]**, etc.** *verb* SEE **comenzar**.

comienzo[2] *noun Masc.* beginning; **al comienzo** in the beginning.

comillas *plural noun Fem.* inverted commas; **poner algo entre comillas** to put something in inverted commas.

comino *noun Masc.* cumin; ★ **me importa un comino** (*informal*) I couldn't care less.

comisaría *noun Fem.* police station.

comisión *noun Fem.* commission.

cómo *adverb* **1** how; **¿cómo estás?** how are you?; **¿cómo se dice 'mesa' en francés?** how do you say 'table' in French?; **¿cómo se escribe tu nombre?** how do you write your name?; **no sé cómo se enteraron** I don't know how they found out; **2 ¿cómo es?** what's it like?; **¿cómo es tu casa?** what's your house like?; **3 ¿cómo?** pardon? (*when you haven't heard properly*); **4** (*in exclamations*) **¡cómo quema!** it's so hot!; **¡cómo se parecen!** they are so like each other!; **¡cómo no!** of course!; **¡cómo! ¿no la has visto aún?** what, you haven't seen her yet?

como *adverb* **1** like; **uno como éste** one like this; **ser como** to be like; **eres como tu padre** you're like your father; **pienso como tú** I agree with you; **2** as; **negro como el**

carbón as black as coal; **3** such as; **metales como el hierro** metals such as iron; **4** around; **eran como cincuenta personas** there were around fifty people; **como a las dos y media** around half past two; **5 como mucho** at the most; **como poco** at least; **serán como poco quince niños** there will be at least fifteen children.

como *conjunction* **1** since; **como estaba cerca de su casa, me pasé a verla** since I was near her house, I went to see her; **2** if; **como no tengas cuidado te vas a caer** if you're not careful you'll fall; **3 como si** as if; **como si no me importase** as if I didn't care; **4** the way; **así es como lo hizo** that's the way he did it; **5 como quieras** whatever you want, however you want; **hazlo como quieras** do it however you want.

cómoda¹ *noun Fem.* chest of drawers.

comodín *noun Masc.* joker (*in cards*).

cómodo/cómoda² *adjective* comfortable; **¿estás cómodo?** are you comfortable?; **un sillón muy cómodo** a very comfortable armchair; **ponerse cómodo** to make yourself comfortable.

compact disc, compacto *noun Masc.* **1** CD; **2** CD player.

compañero/compañera *noun Masc./Fem.* **1** colleague; **mis compañeros de trabajo** my colleagues at work; **2 un compañero de clase** a school mate;

su compañera de piso her flatmate; **3** partner (*in a relationship*).

compañía *noun Fem.* company; **hacerle compañía a alguien** to keep somebody company; **el director de la compañía** the company director.

comparación *noun Fem.* comparison; **hacer una comparación** to make a comparison; **en comparación con** in comparison with.

comparar *verb* [17] to compare.

compartir *verb* [19] to share; **compartir algo con alguien** to share something with somebody; **compartieron su comida conmigo** they shared their food with me.

compás *noun Masc.* **1** time, rhythm; **llevar el compás** to keep time; **2** pair of compasses.

compensar *verb* [29] to compensate.

competencia *noun Fem.* competition; **nos hacen la competencia** they're in competition with us.

competición *noun Fem.* competition (*in a magazine, for example*).

competir *verb* [57] to compete.

compita, compito, etc. *verb* SEE **competir**.

completar *verb* [17] to complete.

completo/completa *adjective* **1** complete; **2** full; **el hotel está completo** the hotel is full; **'completo'** 'no vacancies'.

complicado/complicada
adjective complicated.

complicar *verb* [31] to complicate.
complicarse *reflexive verb* [31] to
become complicated; **la situación
se ha complicado** the situation has
become complicated.

componer *verb* [11] **1** to make up;
**el equipo está compuesto de
once jugadores** the team is made
up of eleven players; **2** to compose
(*music or a poem*).
componerse *reflexive verb* [11]
componerse de to be made up of.

comportamiento *noun Masc.*
behaviour; **mal comportamiento**
bad behaviour.

comportarse *reflexive verb* [17]
to behave; **comportarse mal** to
misbehave.

composición *noun Fem.*
composition.

compositor/compositora
noun Masc./Fem. composer.

compra *noun Fem.* purchase; **fue
una buena compra** it was a good
buy; **ir de compras** to go shopping;
hacer la compra to do the
shopping.

comprador/compradora
noun Masc./Fem. buyer.

comprar *verb* [17] **1** to buy;
2 comprar algo a alguien to buy
something for somebody (*as a
present*); **le he comprado un jersey
por su cumpleaños** I've bought him
a jumper for his birthday;
3 comprar algo a alguien to buy
something from somebody; **voy a**

comprarle su bicicleta I'm going to
buy his bike from him.

comprender *verb* [18] to
understand; **no me comprenden**
they don't understand me; **no
comprendo su actitud** I don't
understand his attitude.

comprensión *noun Fem.*
comprehension; **un ejercicio de
comprensión** a comprehension
test.

compresa *noun Fem.* sanitary
towel.

comprimido *noun Masc.* pill.

comprobar *verb* [24] to check;
**creo que sí, pero voy a
comprobarlo** I think so, but I'm
going to check it.

compromiso *noun Masc.*
1 commitment; **compromiso
político** political commitment;
2 obligation; **sin compromiso**
without obligation; **3 poner a
alguien en un compromiso** to put
somebody in an awkward situation;
**ahora me has puesto en un
compromiso** now you've put me in
an awkward situation.

computador/computadora
noun Masc./Fem. computer (*large,
mainframe machine*).

común *adjective* common; **en
común** in common; **no tenemos
nada en común** we have nothing in
common; **trabajar en común** to
work together.

comunicación *noun Fem.*
1 communication; **2 ponerse en
comunicación con alguien** to get

a
b
c
d
e
f
g
h
i
j
k
l
m
n
ñ
o
p
q
r
s
t
u
v
w
x
y
z

in touch with someone; **3 cortarse la comunicación** to be cut off (*on the phone*); **se ha cortado la comunicación** I've been cut off; **4** (*in transport*) **las comunicaciones son buenas** the communications are good; **un barrio con buena comunicación** an area with good public transport services.

comunicar *verb* [31] **1** to inform; **debo comunicarles que ...** I must inform you that ...; **2** to be engaged (*a telephone*); **estaba comunicando** it was engaged.
comunicarse *reflexive verb* [31] **1** to communicate; **comunicarse por carta** to communicate by letter; **2** to be connected.

comunidad *noun Fem.* community; **la Comunidad Europea** the European Community.

comunión *noun Fem.* communion; **hacer la primera comunión** to take communion for the first time.

con *preposition* **1** with; **lo hice con un cuchillo** I did it with a knife; **2** to; **hablar con alguien** to speak to somebody; **estar casado con alguien** to be married to somebody; **3** and; **bistec con patatas** steak and chips; **pan con mantequilla** bread and butter; **4 con tal de que** as long as; **te lo dejo, con tal de que lo cuides** I'll lend it to you as long as you look after it.

concejal/concejala *noun Masc./Fem.* councillor; **su tío es concejal** her uncle is a councillor.

concentración *noun Fem.* concentration.

concentrar *verb* [17] to concentrate.
concentrarse *reflexive verb* [17] to concentrate; **me concentré en mi trabajo** I concentrated on my work.

concha *noun Fem.* shell.

concienzudo/concienzuda *adjective* conscientious.

concierto *noun Masc.* concert.

conclusión *noun Fem.* conclusion; **llegar a una conclusión** to reach a conclusion.

concurrido/concurrida *adjective* **1** busy (*bar or street*); **2** well-attended (*concert or exhibition*).

concurso *noun Masc.* competition; **concurso hípico** show-jumping competition; **programa concurso** quiz show.

conde *noun Masc.* count.

condesa *noun Fem.* countess.

condición *noun Fem.* condition; **a condición de que/con la condición de que** on condition that.

condón *noun Masc.* condom.

conducir *verb* [60] **1** to drive; **yo conduzco** I'll drive; **2** to lead; **el camino que conduce al pueblo** the road that leads to the village.

conductor/conductora *noun Masc./Fem.* driver.

conduje, **condujo** *verb* SEE **conducir**.

conduzca, conduzco, *etc. verb* SEE **conducir**.

conectar *verb* [17] to connect; **el teléfono aún no está conectado** the telephone's not connected yet.

conejillo de Indias *noun Masc.* guinea pig.

conejo/coneja *noun Masc./Fem.* rabbit.

conexión *noun Fem.* connection.

conferencia *noun Fem.* **1** lecture; **una conferencia de prensa** a press conference; **2** long-distance call; **poner una conferencia a alguien** to make a long distance call to somebody.

confesar *verb* [29] to confess.

confianza *noun Fem.* **1** trust; **una persona de confianza** a trustworthy person; **2 tener confianza en alguien** to have confidence in somebody; **tiene mucha confianza en sí mismo** he's very self-confident; **3 tener confianza con alguien** to know somebody very well; **tenemos mucha confianza** we know each other very well.

confiar *verb* [32] to trust; **confío en ti** I trust you.

confidencia *noun Fem.* confidence; **hacerle una confidencia a alguien** to tell somebody something in confidence.

confirmar *verb* [17] to confirm.

confitería *noun Fem.* patisserie.

confitura *noun Fem.* fruit preserve.

conforme *adjective* **1 estar conforme** to agree; **no estoy conforme** I don't agree; **¿conforme?** do you agree?; **2 ¡conforme!** ok!; **estar conforme con algo** to be happy with something.

confortable *adjective* comfortable.

confortar *verb* [17] to comfort.

confundir *verb* [19] **1** to confuse; **no me confundas** don't confuse me; **2** to get mixed up; **he confundido las fechas** I've got the dates mixed up; **3 confundir a alguien con alguien** to mistake somebody for somebody; **la confundí con Cristina** I mistook her for Cristina. **confundirse** *reflexive verb* [19] **1** to make a mistake; **creo que te has confundido con la cuenta** I think you've made a mistake with the bill; **2 se confundió de carpeta** he got the wrong folder.

confusión *noun Fem.* confusion.

confuso/confusa *adjective* **1** confused; **estaba confuso** he was confused; **2** confusing; **esto es muy confuso** this is very confusing.

congelado/congelada *adjective* **1** frozen; **¡estoy congelada!** I'm freezing!; **alimentos congelados** frozen food; **2 murió congelado** he died from exposure; **3 tenía un dedo congelado** he had frostbite in one finger.

congelador *noun Masc.* **1** freezer compartment; **2** deep freezer.

a
b
c
d
e
f
g
h
i
j
k
l
m
n
ñ
o
p
q
r
s
t
u
v
w
x
y
z

congelar *verb* [17] to freeze. **congelarse** *reflexive verb* [17] to freeze; ¡**me estoy congelando!** I'm freezing!.

conjugar *verb* [28] to conjugate.

conjunto ¹/**conjunta** *adjective* joint; **un esfuerzo conjunto** a joint effort.

conjunto ² *noun Masc.* **1** group; **un conjunto de personas** a group of people; **un conjunto de música** a pop group; **2** collection; **un conjunto de cosas** a collection of things; **3** outfit; ¡**qué conjunto más bonito!** what a nice outfit!; **un conjunto de falda y chaleco** a matching skirt and waistcoat; **hacer conjunto con algo** to match something; **4 en conjunto** as a whole.

conmigo *pronoun* **1** with me; **ven conmigo** come with me; **2** to me; **no habló conmigo** he didn't talk to me; **3 conmigo mismo/misma** with myself; **no estoy contento conmigo mismo** I'm not happy with myself.

conocer *verb* [35] **1** to know; **conozco la historia** I know that story; **los conozco de vista** I know them by sight; **se conocen bien** they know each other well; **2** to meet; ¿**conoces a su hermana?** have you met her sister?; **aún no conozco al nuevo profesor** I haven't met the new teacher yet; **3** ¿**conoces España?** have you been to Spain?; **4** to recognize; **te conocí por la forma de andar** I recognized you by the way you walk.

conocido/conocida *noun Masc./Fem.* acquaintance.
conocido *adjective* **1** well-known (*actor or song*); **2** familiar; **una cara conocida** a familiar face.

conocimiento *noun Masc.* knowledge.

conozca, **conozco**, **etc.** *verb* SEE **conocer**.

conque *conjunction* so; **conque esta es tu novia** so, this is your girlfriend.

conseguir *verb* [64] **1** to achieve; **han conseguido su objetivo** they've achieved their objective; **2** to get; **he conseguido un trabajo** I've got a job.

consejero/consejera *noun Masc./Fem.* **1** adviser; **2** minister (*in certain autonomous Spanish regions*); **3** board member (*of a company*); **consejero/consejera delegado/delegada** managing director.

consejo *noun Masc.* **1** piece of advice; **te voy a dar un consejo** I'm going to give you a piece of advice; **2 consejos** advice; **no hacen caso de mis consejos** they aren't following my advice; **3** board; **el consejo de administración** the board of directors; **consejo escolar** board of governors (*of a school*); **4** meeting; **un consejo de ministros** a cabinet meeting; **5** council; **el Consejo de Europa** the Council of Europe.

conserje *noun Masc./Fem.* **1** caretaker (*in a school or a public building*); **2** receptionist (*in a hotel*).

conservador/ conservadora *noun Masc./Fem.*, **conservador** *adjective* conservative.

conservar *verb* [17] **1** to preserve (*food*); **2** to keep up (*traditions*); **3** to keep; **conservo todas tus cartas** I keep all your letters; **intenta conservar la calma** try to keep calm.
conservarse *reflexive verb* [17] to keep (*food*); **las manzanas se conservan bien** apples keep well.

conservas *plural noun Fem.* tinned food.

considerable *adjective* considerable; **un número considerable de estudiantes** a considerable number of students.

consideración *noun Fem.* consideración; **tomar algo en consideración** to take something into consideration.

considerar *verb* [17] to consider.

consiga, consigo¹, consiguiendo, *etc. verb* SEE **conseguir.**

consigna *noun Fem.* left-luggage office.

consigo² *pronoun* **1** with him/her; **lo trae consigo** he's bringing it with him/she's bringing it with her; **2 consigo mismo** with himself; **consigo misma** with herself; **no está contento consigo mismo** he is not happy with himself; **3 consigo mismo** to himself; **consigo misma** to herself; **estaba hablando consigo misma** she was talking to herself; **4** with them; **el**

dinero que tenían consigo the money they had with them; **5** with you (*talking politely to somebody*); **si usted quiere lo puede traer consigo** if you wish, you can bring it with you.

consistir *verb* [19] **consistir en algo** to consist of something; **consiste en tres piezas de madera** it consists of three pieces of wood; **el trabajo consiste en ...** the job involves ....

consonante *noun Fem.* consonant.

constante *adjective* constant.

constipado¹/constipada *adjective* **estar constipado** to have a cold.

constipado² *noun Masc.* cold; **coger un constipado** to catch a cold.

constructor/constructora *noun Masc./Fem.* builder.

construir *verb* [54] to build.

construya, construyendo, construyo, etc. *verb* SEE **construir.**

cónsul *noun Masc.* consul.

consulado *noun Masc.* consulate.

consulta *noun Fem.* **1 hacer una consulta** to ask something; **2 de consulta** reference; **libro de consulta** reference book; **3** surgery; **tiene su consulta en esta calle** his surgery is in this street; **horas de consulta** surgery hours.

consultar *verb* [17] **1** to consult; **consultarle algo a alguien** to consult somebody about something;

a
b
c
d
e
f
g
h
i
j
k
l
m
n
ñ
o
p
q
r
s
t
u
v
w
x
y
z

2 tengo que consultarlo en diccionario I have to look it up in the dictionary.

consultorio *noun Masc.* surgery.

consumición *noun Fem.* drink (*in bar, café*); **consumición mínima cuatro euros** minimum charge four euros.

consumo *noun* consumption.

contable *noun Masc./Fem.* accountant.

contacto *noun Masc.* **1** contact; **estar en contacto** to be in contact; **2** ignition (*in a car*).

contado *noun Masc.* **al contado** cash; **pagar al contado** to pay cash; **lo compré al contado** I paid for it in cash.

contador *noun Masc.* meter.

contagiar *verb* [17] to pass on (*an illness*); **no me beses, no quiero contagiarte el resfriado** don't kiss me, I don't want to give you my cold. **contagiarse** *reflexive verb* [17] to become infected; **se ha contagiado de su hermana** she's got it from her sister.

contaminación *noun Fem.* **1** pollution; **2** contamination (*by radioactivity*).

contaminar *verb* [17] **1** to pollute (*air or water, for example*); **2** to contaminate (*with radioactivity*).

contar *verb* [24] **1** to count; **cuenta el dinero** count the money; **2 contar con alguien** to count on somebody; **nunca puedo contar contigo** I can never count on you; **3** to tell; **cuéntamelo** tell me about

it; **le conté el secreto** I told him the secret; **4** to count; **eso no cuenta** that doesn't count; **el trabajo cuenta para mi nota final** the essay counts towards my final mark.

contenedor *noun Masc.* **1** container; **2** skip; **3 un contenedor de vidrio** a bottle bank.

contener *verb* [9] **1** to contain; **no contiene conservantes** it does not contain preservatives; **2 contener las lágrimas** to hold back the tears; **contener la risa** to stop yourself laughing; **contener la respiración** to hold your breath.

contenido *noun Masc.* **1** contents; **el contenido de la botella** the contents of the bottle; **2** content; **el contenido del libro** the content of the book.

contento/contenta *adjective* **1** happy; **los niños estaban muy contentos** the children were very happy; **2** pleased; **estoy contento de verte** I'm pleased to see you.

contestación *noun Fem.* **1** answer; **no nos dio una contestación** he didn't give us an answer; **2** reply; **quedo a la espera de su contestación** looking forward to your reply.

contestador (automático) *noun Masc.* answering machine.

contestar *verb* [17] **1** answer; **contestar el teléfono** to answer the phone; **no contestó** he didn't answer; **2** reply; **no ha contestado a mi carta** he hasn't replied to my letter.

contexto *noun Masc.* context.

contigo *pronoun* **1** with you; **yo voy contigo** I'll go with you; **2** to you; **no estoy hablando contigo** I'm not talking to you; **3 contigo mismo/misma** with yourself; **¿estás contento contigo mismo?** are you pleased with yourself?

continente *noun Masc.* continent.

continuación *noun Fem.* continuation; **a continuación** ... next ....

continuar *verb* [20] to continue; **continuaron hablando** they went on talking; **continuará** to be continued.

continuo/continua *adjective* constant.

contra *preposition* **1** against; **se apoyó contra la pared** he leant against the wall; **son dos contra uno** it's two against one; **estar en contra de algo** to be against something; **2 chocar contra algo** to run into something.

contrabandista *noun Masc./Fem.* smuggler.

contrabando *noun Masc.* **1** smuggling; **pasar algo de contrabando** to smuggle something; **2** smuggled goods.

contrario¹/contraria *adjective* **1** opposite; **la dirección contraria** the opposite direction; **soy contrario a las reformas** I'm opposed to the reforms; **pasarse al bando contrario** to change sides; **todo lo contrario** quite the opposite; **2 de lo contrario** otherwise.

contrario² *noun Masc.* **1** opposite; **al contrario** on the contrary; **al contrario, me gusta mucho** on the contrary, I like it a lot; **es al contrario** it's the opposite way round; **2 por el contrario** on the other hand.

contrarreloj *adjective* **a contrarreloj** against the clock.

contrato *noun Masc.* contract.

contribución *noun Fem.* **1** contribution; **2** tax.

control *noun Masc.* **1** control; **bajo control** under control; **control de pasaportes** passport control; **control remoto** remote control; **2 llevar el control de algo** to keep a check on something; **3** test.

control *noun Masc.* **control de la natalidad** birth control.

controlar *verb* [17] **1** to control; **2** to keep a check on; **3 controlar la línea** to watch you weight.

controvertido/ controvertida *adjective* controversial; **una decisión controvertida** a controversial decision.

convencer *verb* [44] **1** to convince; **2** to persuade; **le convencimos para que fuera** we persuaded him to go; **3 no me convence mucho la idea** I'm not sure about the idea.

conveniente *adjective* **1** convenient; **2** advisable.

convenir *verb* [15] **1 te conviene preguntar** you should ask; **te conviene descansar** you should rest; **conviene informarse antes**

a
b
c
d
e
f
g
h
i
j
k
l
m
n
ñ
o
p
q
r
s
t
u
v
w
x
y
z

it's advisable to find out in advance;
2 (*in negative sentences*) **no te conviene cansarte** you should avoid tiring yourself out; **por ese sueldo no te conviene** for that salary it's not worth your while; **3 convenir en algo** to agree on something; **4 sueldo a convenir** salary negotiable.

convento *noun Masc.* convent.

convenza, convenzo, etc. *verb* SEE **convencer**.

conversación *noun Fem.* conversation.

convertir *verb* [14] **1 convertir algo en algo** to turn something into something; **convertir agua en vino** to turn water into wine; **convertir libras en euros** to convert pounds into euros; **2** to convert (*to a religion*).
convertirse *reflexive verb* [14] **1 convertirse en algo** to turn into something; **2** to convert; **convertirse al budismo** to convert to Buddhism.

convierta, convierto, etc. *verb* SEE **convertir**.

coñac *noun Masc.* brandy.

cooperar *verb* [17] to cooperate.

copa *noun Fem.* **1** wine glass; **una copa de vino** a glass of wine; **2** drink; **te invito a una copa** I'll buy you a drink; **tomar una copa** to have a drink.

copia *noun Fem.* copy; **copia de seguridad** back-up copy.

copiar *verb* [17] **1** to copy; **2** to make a copy of; **3** to copy down.

coraje *noun Masc.* courage.

corazón *noun Masc.* heart; **un ataque al corazón** a heart attack; **una persona de buen corazón** a kind-hearted person; **★ partirle el corazón a alguien** to break someone's heart.

corbata *noun Fem.* tie.

corcho *noun Masc.* cork.

cordero *noun Masc.* lamb; **una pierna de cordero** a leg of lamb; **una chuleta de cordero** a lamb chop.

cordón *noun Masc.* string; **un cordón de zapato** a shoelace.

coro *noun Masc.* choir; **a coro** in chorus.

corona *noun Fem.* **1** crown; **2** wreath; **una corona de flores** a wreath of flowers.

coronel *noun Masc.* colonel.

corral *noun Masc.* farmyard.

correa *noun Fem.* **1** strap; **correa de reloj** watchstrap; **2** lead (*for a dog*).

correctamente *adverb* **1** politely; **2** correctly; **¿has rellenado el formulario correctamente?** have you filled in the form correctly?

correcto/correcta *adjective* **1** correct; **la respuesta correcta** the correct answer; **2** polite; **siempre es muy correcto** he's always very polite.

corrector ortográfico *noun Masc.* spelling checker.

corredor/corredora *noun Masc./Fem.* **1** runner; **corredor de**

fondo long-distance runner;
2 corredor de coches racing
driver.

corregir *verb* [48] to correct.

correo *noun Masc.* post; **mandar
algo por correo** to send something
by post; **echar algo al correo** to
post something; **correo aéreo**
airmail; **correo electrónico**
electronic mail; **(la oficina de)
correos** the post office; **correo
urgente** special delivery.

correr *verb* [18] **1** to run; **crucé la
calle corriendo** I ran across the
street; **salió corriendo de la
habitación** she ran out of the room;
bajar las escaleras corriendo to
run down the stairs; **echar a correr**
to start running; **correr mucho** to
run very fast (*a person*), to drive
very fast (*a driver*), to go very fast (*a
car or bike*); **2 ¡corre, vístete!** hurry
up and get dressed!; **hice la comida
corriendo** I made dinner quickly;
vino corriendo a verme she rushed
to see me; **se tiene que marchar
corriendo** he has to rush off;
3 correr las cortinas to draw the
curtains; **4 no debemos correr
riesgos** we shouldn't take any risks;
5 correr peligro to be in danger.

correspondiente *adjective*
corresponding.

corresponsal *noun Masc./Fem.*
correspondent (*in journalism*).

corrida *noun Fem.* bullfight.

corrido/corrida *adjective*
embarrassed.

corriente *noun Fem.* **1** current
(*water or electricity*); **me ha dado la**
corriente I got an electric shock; **no
hay corriente** there's no electricity;
2 draught; **hace corriente** there's a
draught.

corriente *adjective* **1** common; **un
error muy corriente** a very
common mistake; **una chica
normal y corriente** an ordinary
kind of girl; **lo más corriente es ...**
the most usual thing is ...; **2 agua
corriente** running water; **3 estar al
corriente de algo** to be aware of
something; **mantener a alguien al
corriente de algo** to keep somebody
up to date about something.

corrija, **corrijo**, **etc.** *verb* SEE
corregir.

corrompido/corrompida
adjective corrupt.

corrupto/corrupta *adjective*
corrupt.

cortacésped *noun Masc.*
lawnmower.

cortado¹ *noun Masc.* small coffee
(*with a dash of milk*).

cortado²/cortada *adjective*
1 closed (*a road or street*); **2 la leche
está cortada** the milk is sour; **la
mayonesa está cortada** the
mayonnaise has separated; **3 ser
muy cortado** (*informal*) to be very
shy; **ser un poco cortado**
(*informal*) to be a bit shy; **4 estar
cortado** (*informal*) to be
embarrassed.

cortar *verb* [17] **1** to cut; **cortar un
pastel** to cut a cake; **cortar algo por
la mitad** to cut something in two;
cortar algo a rodajas to slice
something; **2 cortar el césped** to

a
b
c
d
e
f
g
h
i
j
k
l
m
n
ñ
o
p
q
r
s
t
u
v
w
x
y
z

mow the lawn; **3** to chop; **cortar leña** to chop wood; **cortar un árbol** to chop down a tree; **4** to cut off; **nos han cortado la luz** our electricity has been cut off; **corta esa punta** cut this end off.

cortarse *reflexive verb* [17] **1** to cut oneself; **me he cortado la mano** I've cut my hand; **2 cortarse el pelo** to have your hair cut; **mañana me voy a cortar el pelo** I'm going to have my hair cut tomorrow; **3 se ha cortado el agua** the water's been cut off; **4** to curdle; **5** (*informal*) to get embarrassed; **¡no te cortes!** don't get embarrassed.

cortaúñas *noun Masc.* nail clippers.

corte[1] *noun Masc.* **1** cut; **hacerse un corte** to cut yourself; **se hizo un corte en el dedo** he cut his finger; **un corte de pelo** a haircut; **ha habido un corte de agua** the water's been cut off; **2 corte y confección** dressmaking; **3** (*informal*) embarrassment; **me da corte preguntar** I'm embarrassed to ask; **¡qué corte!** how embarrassing!

corte[2] *noun Fem.* **1** court; **2 las Cortes** the Spanish Parliament.

cortés *adjective* polite.

corteza *noun Fem.* **1** bark (*of a tree*); **2** rind (*of cheese*); **3** crust (*of bread*); **4** peel (*of an orange or a lemon*).

cortina *noun Fem.* curtain.

corto/corta *adjective* short.

cosa *noun Fem.* **1** thing; **te he comprado una cosa** I've bought something for you; **¿qué tal van las cosas?** how are things going?; **se llevó todas sus cosas** he took all his things; **¡qué cosa más rara!** how strange!; **2 cualquier cosa** anything; **3 alguna cosa** something; **por si pasa alguna cosa** in case something happens; **4 alguna cosa** anything (*in questions*); **¿buscas alguna cosa en especial?** are you looking for anything in particular?; **¿quiere alguna otra cosa?** do you want anything else?

cosecha *noun Fem.* **1** harvest; **2** crop; **3** vintage.

cosechar *verb* [17] to harvest.

coser *verb* [18] to sew.

cosmético[1] *noun Masc.* cosmetic.

cosmético[2]**/cosmética** *adjective* cosmetic.

cosquillas *plural noun Fem.* **hacerle cosquillas a alguien** to tickle somebody; **tener cosquillas** to be ticklish.

Costa Rica *noun Fem.* Costa Rica.

costa *noun Fem.* coast.

costado *noun Masc.* side.

costar *verb* [24] **1** to cost; **¿cuánto cuesta?** how much is it?; **cuesta muy caro** it's very expensive; **la comida cuesta poco** food is cheap; **me costó barato** it didn't cost me very much; **2** to be hard; **cuesta mucho entenderlo** it's very hard to understand; **cuesta un poco acostumbrarse** it takes a bit of getting used to; **me costó hacerlo** I found it difficult to do.

costarricense *noun Masc., Fem.,* *adjective* Costa Rican.

coste *noun Masc.* cost.

costilla *noun Fem.* rib.

costoso/costosa *adjective* expensive.

costra *noun Fem.* scab.

costumbre *noun Fem.* **1** habit; **coger la costumbre de hacer algo** to get into the habit of doing something; **tengo la costumbre de leer un poco antes de dormir** I normally read for a bit before I go to sleep; **por costumbre** out of habit; **2 de costumbre** usual; **el lugar de costumbre** the usual place; **3** custom (*in a country or place*).

costura *noun Fem.* **1** needlework; **2** seam.

cotilla *noun Masc./Fem.,* *adjective* gossip; **es muy cotilla** he's such a gossip.

cotillear *verb* [17] to gossip.

cráneo *noun Fem.* skull.

creación *noun Fem.* creation.

creador/creadora *noun Masc./ Fem.* creator.
creador *adjective* creative.

crear *verb* [17] to create.

crecer *verb* [35] **1** to grow; **¡cuánto has crecido!** you've really grown!; **2** to grow up; **creció en Escocia** she grew up in Scotalnd.

crédito *noun Masc.* **1** credit (*in a shop, for example*); **tengo crédito aquí** they give me credit here; **2** loan; **me han concedido el** crédito they've granted me the loan; **crédito hipotecario** mortgage.

creer *verb* [37] **1** to think; **creo que se llama Nekane** I think she's called Nekane; **¿crees que me llamará?** do you think he'll phone me?; **creo que sí** I think so; **no creo** I don't think so; **2** to believe; **no creo en el destino** I don't believe in fate; **¡no lo puedo creer!** I don't believe it!

creíble *adjective* believable.

crema *noun Fem.* cream; **crema hidratante** moisturizer; **crema bronceadora** suntan lotion.

cremallera *noun Fem.* zip; **subirse la cremallera** to do up your zip.

crepúsculo *noun Masc.* twilight.

creyendo, creyó, etc. *verb* SEE **creer**.

crezca, crezco, etc. *verb* SEE **crecer**.

cría *noun Fem.* baby animal; **una cría de leopardo** a baby leopard.

criada *noun Fem.* maid.

criado *noun Masc.* servant.

criar *verb* [17] **1** to bring up; **lo crió su tía** he was brought up by his aunt; **2** to raise; **criar ganado** to raise cattle.
criarse *reflexive verb* [17] to grow up; **se crió en un pueblo** he grew up in a village.

crimen *noun Masc.* **1** crime; **cometer un crimen** to commit a crime; **2** murder.

criminal *noun Masc./Fem.* criminal.

a
b
c
d
e
f
g
h
i
j
k
l
m
n
ñ
o
p
q
r
s
t
u
v
w
x
y
z

crisis *noun Fém.* crisis; **estar en crisis** to be in crisis; **sufrir una crisis nerviosa** to have a nervous breakdown.

cristal *noun Masc.* 1 glass; **viene en botella de cristal** it comes in a glass bottle; 2 cristal; **cristal tallado** cut glass; 3 window pane; **tengo que limpiar los cristales del salón** I've got to clean the sitting-room windows; **la pelota rompió un cristal** the ball broke a window; 4 piece of broken glass; **el suelo estaba lleno de cristales** the floor was covered with broken glass.

cristianismo *noun* Christianity *Masc.*

cristiano/cristiana *noun Masc./ Fém., adjective* Christian.

Cristo *noun Masc.* Christ.

criterio *noun Masc.* 1 criterion; 2 judgement.

crítica *noun Fém.* 1 criticism; **recibió duras críticas** he's come in for a lot of harsh criticism; 2 review; **la película ha recibido muy buenas críticas** the film has had very good reviews.

criticar *verb* [31] 1 to criticize; 2 to review.

cromo *noun Masc.* sticker.

cruce *noun (plural cruces) Masc.* 1 crossroads; 2 'cruce peligroso' 'dangerous junction'; 3 crossing; **cruce de peatones** pedestrian crossing.

crucero *noun Masc.* cruise.

crucigrama *noun Masc.* crossword.

crudo/cruda *adjective* 1 raw; **una zanahoria cruda** a raw carrot; 2 **la verdura aún está cruda** the vegetables aren't cooked yet; 3 harsh; **la cruda realidad** the harsh reality.

cruel *adjective* cruel.

crueldad *noun* cruelty; **los trataron con gran crueldad** they were treated with great cruelty.

Cruz Roja *noun Fem.* Red Cross.

cruz *noun Fem.* 1 cross; 2 **¿cara o cruz?** heads or tails?

cruzar *verb* [22] to cross; **ten cuidado al cruzar** be careful when you cross the road; **crucé la calle corriendo** I ran across the road; **cruzar los brazos** to cross your arms.

cruzarse *reflexive verb* [22] 1 to intersect (*roads, for example*); 2 to pass each other; **los dos coches se cruzaron** the two cars passed each other; 3 **me crucé con ella en la calle** I met her in the street.

cuaderno *noun Masc.* 1 exercise book; 2 notebook.

cuadra *noun Fém.* stable.

cuadrado¹/cuadrada *adjective* square; **de forma cuadrada** square-shaped.

cuadrado² *noun Masc.* square.

cuadro *noun Masc.* 1 painting; 2 picture; 3 **a cuadros/de cuadros** checked; **una tela a cuadros** a piece of checked material.

cual *pronoun* 1 **el cual/la cual/los cuales/las cuales** who; **pregunté a mi hermano, el cual me dio las**

señas I asked my brother, who gave me the address; **2 el cual/la cual/los cuales/las cuales** whom; **los familiares a los cuales invité** the relatives whom he invited; **3 el cual/la cual/los cuales/las cuales** which; **los instrumentos con los cuales se hace la operación** the instruments with which the operation is carried out; **4 lo cual** which; **no ha llamado, lo cual es extraño** he hasn't rung, which is strange; **5 cada cual** everybody; **6 por lo cual** therefore.

cuál *pronoun* **1** which; **¿cuál te gusta?** which do you like?; **2** what; **¿cuál es el problema?** what's the problem?

cualesquiera *adjective, pronoun* SEE **cualquiera**.

cualidad *noun Fem.* quality.

cualquier *adjective* SEE **cualquiera**.

cualquiera (*plural* **cualesquiera**) *adjective* (*'cualquiera' becomes 'cualquier' before a singular noun*) any; **en un país cualquiera** in any country; **cualquier cosa** anything; **cualquier persona** anybody; **si por cualquier motivo** if for any reason. **cualquiera** *pronoun* **1** anybody, anyone; **cualquiera sabe algo así** anybody knows that sort of thing; **2** either, both; **'¿cuál de los dos quieres?' – 'cualquiera'** 'which of the two do you want?' – 'either'; **3** whichever (*when referring to more than two people or things*); **coge cualquiera de los que hay ahí** pick

whichever you want from the ones that are there.

cuando *conjunction* when; **cuando estuve en Barcelona** when I was in Barcelona; **cuando la vea la próxima semana** when I see her next week.

cuándo *adverb* when?; **¿cuándo la conociste?** when did you meet her?; **¿desde cuándo?** since when?

cuanto/**cuanta** *adjective* **1** as much as; **cuanta tela necesites** as much fabric as you need; **2 cuantos/cuantas** as many as; **compra cuantos libros necesites** buy as many books as you need; **3 unos cuantos** a few; **unos cuantos empleados** a few employees. **cuanto** *pronoun* **1 tengo cuanto necesito** I've got everything I need; **2 cuantos/cuantas** as many as; **coge cuantas quieras** take as many as you want; **3 unos cuantos** a few.

cuánto/**cuánta** *adjective* **1 cuánto/cuánta** how much; **¿cuánto café quieres?** how much coffee do you want?; **2 cuántos/cuántas** how many; **¿cuántas tazas saco?** how many cups should I put out?; **3** (*in exclamations*) **¡cuántas personas hay!** there are so many people!; **¡cuánta comida has hecho!** you've made so much food!; **4** (*in time*) **¿cuánto tiempo has tardado en hacerlo?** how long did you take to do it?; **¿cada cuánto tiempo la ves?** how often do you see her?

cuánto *pronoun* **1 cuánto/cuánta**

a
b
c
d
e
f
g
h
i
j
k
l
m
n
ñ
o
p
q
r
s
t
u
v
w
x
y
z

how much; **'pon agua' – '¿cuánta?'** 'add some water – 'how much?'; **2 cuántos/cuántas** how many; **dime cuántos necesitas** tell me how many you need; **3** how long (*in time*); **¿cuánto se tarda en llegar?** how long does it take to get there?; **¿cada cuánto la llamas?** how often do you call her?; **4** (*in exclamations*) **¡cuántas hay!** there are so many!; **¡cuánto ha quedado!** there's so much left!; **¡cuánto has tardado!** you've taken so long!

cuanto² *adverb* **1** as much as; **llama cuanto quieras** phone as much as you want; **2 cuanto más** the more; **cuanto más insiste, menos quiero** the more he insists, the less I want to; **cuanto menos ruido hagas mejor** the less noise you make, the better; **3 cuanto antes** as soon as possible; **4 en cuanto pueda** as soon as I can.

cuánto² *adverb* **1** how much; **¿cuánto cuesta?** how much is it?; **no sabes cuánto te he echado de menos** you don't know how much I've missed you; **2 ¿cuánto mide la mesa?** what's the size of the table?; **¿cuánto mide de ancho?** how wide is it?; **3** (*in exclamations*) **¡cuánto te quiero!** I love you so much!

cuarenta *number* forty; **mi madre tiene cuarenta años** my mum's forty; **cuarenta y siete** forty-seven.

cuaresma *noun Fem.* Lent.

cuarta *noun Fem.* fourth gear; **meter la cuarta** to change into fourth.

cuartel *noun* barracks; **el cuartel general** the headquarters.

cuarto¹ *noun Masc.* **1** room; **el cuarto de estar** the living room; **el cuarto de baño** the bathroom; **el cuarto de los niños** the children's bedroom; **2** quarter (*in clock time*); **son las dos y cuarto** it's quarter past two; **a las doce menos cuarto** at quarter to twelve; **3** quarter; **corté la tarta en cuatro cuartos** I cut the cake into four quarters; **un cuarto de kilo** a quarter of a kilo; **4 los cuartos de final** the quarter finals.

cuarto²/cuarta² *adjective* fourth; **en el cuarto piso** on the fourth floor; **llegar en cuarto lugar** to finish in fourth position.

cuatro *number* **1** four; **Juan tiene cuatro años** Juan's four (years old); **2** fourth (*in dates*); **el cuatro de mayo** the fourth of May; **3** four (*in clock time*); **son las cuatro** it's four o'clock.

cuatrocientos/ cuatrocientas *number* four hundred; **cuatrocientos quince** four hundred and fifteen.

Cuba *noun Fem.* Cuba.

cubano/cubana *noun Masc./Fem., adjective* Cuban.

cubierto¹/cubierta *adjective* covered.

cubierto² *noun Masc.* **1 los cubiertos** the cutlery; **pon los cubiertos en la mesa** put the knives and forks on the table; **cubiertos de plata** silver cutlery;

2 poner otro cubierto en la mesa
to lay another place at the table.

cubo *noun Masc.* **1** cube; **2** bucket;
un cubo de agua a bucket of water;
3 el cubo de la basura the bin.

cubrecama *noun Masc.* bedspread.

cubrir *verb* [46] to cover.
cubrirse *reflexive verb* [46] **1** to
cover yourself; **me cubrí las
rodillas** I covered my legs; **2** to cloud
over; **esta mañana hacía sol, pero
ahora se ha cubierto** this morning
it was sunny, but now it's clouded
over.

cucaracha *noun Fem.* cockroach.

cuchara *noun Fem.* spoon; **cuchara
de postre** dessert spoon; **cuchara
sopera** soup spoon.

cucharada *noun Fem.* spoonful.

cucharadita *noun Fem.*
teaspoonful.

cucharilla, **cucharita** *noun
Fem.* teaspoon; **una cucharilla de
café/una cucharita de café** a
coffee spoon.

cuchichear *verb* [17] to whisper.

cuchilla *noun Fem.* blade; **una
cuchilla de afeitar** a razor blade.

cuchillo *noun Masc.* knife.

cuelga, **cuelgo**, *etc. verb* SEE
colgar.

cuello *noun Masc.* **1** neck; **2** collar;
el cuello de la camisa the shirt
collar; **un jersey de cuello redondo**
a round-neck jumper; **un jersey de
cuello alto** a polo-neck jumper.

cuenco *noun Masc.* bowl.

cuenta¹, **cuento¹**, *etc. verb* SEE
contar.

cuenta² *noun Fem.* **1** bill; **¿nos
puede traer la cuenta, por favor?**
could you bring us the bill, please?;
2 sum; **hacer una cuenta** to do a
sum; **hacer cuentas** to work
something out; **haz las cuentas de
lo que te debo** work out how much
I owe you; **3 llevar la cuenta de
algo** to keep count of something;
perder la cuenta de algo to lose
count of something; **4** account;
cuenta corriente current account;
cuenta de ahorros savings
account; **abrir una cuenta** to open
an account; **5 tener algo en cuenta**
to bear something in mind; **6 darse
cuenta de algo** to realize
something; **me di cuenta de que
había perdido la cartera** I realized
I'd lost my wallet; **7 trabajar por su
cuenta** to be self-employed; **trabajo
por mi cuenta** I'm self-employed;
montar una tienda por su cuenta
to set up your own shop; **8 más de la
cuenta** too much; **bebieron más de
la cuenta** they drank too much;
9 cuenta atrás countdown; **10** bead
(*of necklace*).

cuento² *noun Masc.* **1** short story;
2 tale; **un cuento de hadas** a fairy
tale; **3 eso no viene a cuento** that
has nothing to do with it; ★ **¡eso es
un cuento chino!** (*informal*) that's
a load of rubbish!

cuerda *noun Fem.* **1** rope; **2 saltar a
la cuerda** to skip; **3 dar cuerda a
un juguete** to wind up a toy; **dar
cuerda a un reloj** to wind a watch.

a
b
c
d
e
f
g
h
i
j
k
l
m
n
ñ
o
p
q
r
s
t
u
v
w
x
y
z

cuerno *noun Masc.* **1** horn; **2** antler.

cuero *noun Masc.* leather; **un bolso de cuero** a leather bag; **el cuero cabelludo** the scalp.

cuerpo *noun Masc.* body.

cuervo *noun Masc.* crow.

cuesta¹, **cueste**, *etc. verb* SEE **costar**.

cuesta² *noun Fem.* **1** slope; **subir una cuesta** to go up a slope; **ir cuesta arriba** to go uphill; **ir cuesta abajo** to go downhill; **2 llevar algo a cuestas** to carry something on your back.

cuestión *noun Fem.* **1** matter; **en la reunión se hablará de esta cuestión** this matter will be discussed in the meeting; **2 la cuestión es ...** the thing is ....

cueva *noun Fem.* cave.

cueza, **cuezo**, **etc.** *verb* SEE **cocer**.

cuidado *noun Masc.* **1 tener cuidado con** to be careful with; **ten cuidado con los vasos** be careful with the glasses; **¡cuidado con el escalón!** mind the step!; **¡cuidado con el perro!** beware of the dog!; **2 hacer algo con cuidado** to do something carefully; **lo cogí con cuidado** I picked it up carefully; **3** care; **el cuidado de las manos es muy importante** hand care is very important; **4 cuidados intensivos** intensive care.

cuidado *exclamation* **¡cuidado!** watch out!

cuidadoso/cuidadosa *adjective* careful.

cuidar *verb* [17] **1** to look after; **yo me quedo cuidando a los niños** I'll stay and look after the children; **cuidan de su padre enfermo** they look after their sick father; **2** to take care of; **sé cuidar de mí misma** I can take care of myself.

culebra *noun Fem.* snake.

culebrón *noun Masc.* (*informal*) soap opera.

culo *noun Masc.* (*informal*) **1** bum; **2 el culo del vaso** the bottom of the glass.

culpa *noun Fem.* **1** fault; **no es mi culpa** it's not my fault; **es su culpa si se queda sin ir** it's his fault if he ends up not going; **no lo terminamos a tiempo por tu culpa** it's your fault we didn't finish it on time; **¿y qué culpa tengo yo?** and why is it my fault?; **2 echarle la culpa a alguien** to blame someone; **me echan la culpa de lo sucedido** they blame me for what happened; **3** guilt; **sentimiento de culpa** guilty feelings.

culpable *noun Masc./Fem.* **él es el único culpable de todo esto** he's the only one to blame for all this.
culpable *adjective* **1** guilty; **sentirse culpable de algo** to feel guilty about something; **2 ser culpable de algo** to be to blame for something; **yo no soy culpable de la situación** I'm not to blame for the situation; **3 ser culpable de algo** to be guilty of something (*a crime*).

culpar *verb* [17] to blame; **culpar a alguien de algo** to blame somebody for something.

cultivar *verb* [17] **1** to grow (*fruit or vegetables*); **2** to cultivate (*land*).

culto *noun Masc.* **1** cult; **2** worship; **la libertad de culto** the freedom of worship.

cultura *noun Fem.* **1** culture; **2** knowledge; **preguntas de cultura general** general knowledge questions.

culturismo *noun Masc.* bodybuilding.

cumpleaños *noun Masc.* birthday; **fiesta de cumpleaños** birthday party; **¿cuándo es tu cumpleaños?** when's your birthday?; **¡feliz cumpleaños!** Happy Birthday!

cumplir *verb* [19] **1** **¿cuándo cumples años?** when's your birthday?; **mañana cumplo quince años** I'll be fifteen tomorrow; **¡que cumplas muchos más!** many happy returns!; **2 cumplir una promesa** to keep a promise; **no has cumplido con tu palabra** you haven't kept your word; **3** to fulfil (*conditions*); **4** to carry out (*a task or an order*); **5 cumplir una condena** to serve a sentence.

cuna *noun Fem.* **1** cradle; **2** cot.

cuñada *noun Fem.* sister-in-law.

cuñado *noun Masc.* brother-in-law.

cupe, **cupiera**, **cupo**, **etc.** *verb* SEE **caber**.

cura¹ *noun Masc.* priest.

cura² *noun Fem.* cure.

curar *verb* [17] **1** to cure (*an illness or sick person*); **2** to dress (*a wound*).

curarse *reflexive verb* [17] to get better.

curioso/curiosa *noun Masc./Fem.* busybody.
curioso *adjective* **1** nosy; **¡qué curiosa eres!** you're so nosy!; **2 lo curioso es que** ... the funny thing is ...; **es curioso que** ... it's strange that ....

cursillo *noun Masc.* (short) course.

cursiva *noun Fem.* italics; **en cursiva** in italics.

curso *noun Masc.* **1** year; **¿en qué curso estás?** what year are you in?; **mi hermana está en el primer curso** my sister's in first year; **el curso escolar** the academic year; **2** course; **un curso intensivo** an intensive course.

cursor *noun Masc.* cursor.

curva¹ *noun Fem.* bend; **curva peligrosa** sharp bend; **tomar una curva** to take a bend.

curvo/curva² *adjective* curved.

cuyo/cuya *adjective* whose; **el amigo cuyo ordenador utilicé** the friend whose computer I used.

Dd

dabuten *adjective* (*informal*) fantastic, cool; **unos pantalones dabuten** a fantastic pair of trousers.
dabuten *adverb* **lo pasé dabuten** I had a fantastic time.

dabuti *adjective* (*informal*) SEE **dabuten**.

a
b
c
d
e
f
g
h
i
j
k
l
m
n
ñ
o
p
q
r
s
t
u
v
w
x
y
z

dado *noun Masc.* dice; **tirar los dados** to throw the dice.

dama *noun Fem.* lady; **damas y caballeros** ladies and gentlemen; **una dama de honor** a bridesmaid.

danés¹ *noun Masc.* Danish (*the language*).

danés²**/danesa** *noun Masc./Fem.* Dane.
danés/danesa *adjective* Danish.

danza *noun Fem.*,
danza *noun Fem.* dance; **estudiar danza** to study dance.

dañar *verb* [17] to damage.

dañino/dañina *adjective* harmful.

daño *noun Masc.* **1 hacerse daño** to hurt yourself; **te vas a hacer daño** you are going to hurt yourself; **¿se hizo daño al caer?** did she hurt herself when she fell?; **me hice daño en la pierna** I hurt my leg; **2 hacerle daño a alguien** to hurt someone; **no quiero hacerte daño** I don't want to hurt you; **3 daños y perjuicios** damages.

dar *verb* [4] **1** to give; **me dio su número de teléfono** he gave me his telephone number; **dale esta carta a María** give this letter to María; **dale recuerdos** give him my regards; **dame un beso** give me a kiss; **2 ¿me da un kilo de tomates?** can I have a kilo of tomatoes?; **3 me dieron un premio** I got a prize; **4** to turn on; **dar la luz** to turn on the light; **5 darle a un botón** to press a button; **darle a un interruptor** to flick a switch; **6 el reloj dio las doce** the clock struck twelve; **7 dar una fiesta** to have a party; **8** to say; **dar las gracias** to say thank you; **dar los buenos días** to say good morning; **darle la bienvenida a alguien** to welcome someone; **9 dar un grito** to shout; **10 darle la mano a alguien** to shake somebody's hand; **11 dar un paseo** to go for a walk; **fuimos a dar una vuelta** we went for a walk; **12 dar de comer a alguien** to feed somebody; **dar de beber a alguien** to give somebody something to drink; **13 me dio miedo** it scared me; **las patatas fritas le dieron sed** the crisps made him feel thirsty; **este jersey da mucho calor** this jumper is very warm; **14 da lo mismo** it doesn't matter; **da lo mismo si lo hacemos luego** it doesn't matter if we do it later; **15 me da lo mismo** I don't mind; **si te da lo mismo, te hago un cheque** if you don't mind, I'll write you a cheque; **16 el hotel da al mar** the hotel faces the sea; **la puerta da al salón** the door opens onto the living room.

darse *reflexive verb* [4] **1** to have; **darse un baño** to have a bath; **darse una ducha** to have a shower; **2 darse un golpe** to bump yourself; **me di con el pie en el bordillo** I hit my foot on the kerb; **3 darse prisa** to hurry up; **4 darse cuenta de algo** to realize something; **me di cuenta de que se me habían olvidado las llaves** I realized I'd forgotten my keys; **5 se le dan bien las matemáticas** she's good at maths; **no se me da bien pintar** I'm not good at painting.

dardo *noun Masc.* dart.

dársena *noun Fem.* **1** bay (*in bus station*); **2** (*for ships*) dry dock.

dC *abbreviation* (*short for: después de Cristo*) AD.

d. de J.C. *abbreviation* (*short for: después de Jesucristo*) AD.

de *preposition* (*note that 'de' + 'el' becomes 'del'*) **1 el coche de mis padres** my parent's car; **esto es de Juan** this is Juan's; **fuimos a casa de Isa** we went to Isa's; **2** of; **el nombre del libro** the name of the book; **el respaldo del asiento** the back of the chair; **3** from; **soy de Sevilla** I'm from Sevilla; **de Madrid a Bilbao** from Madrid to Bilbao; **de la cabeza a los pies** from head to toe; **no hemos tenido noticias de María** we haven't heard from María; **4 una silla de madera** a wooden chair; **flores de plástico** plastic flowers; **5** of (*in quantities*); **un vaso de leche** a glass of milk; **una caja de naranjas** a box of oranges; **6 una clase de conducir** a driving lesson; **los vasos del vino** the wine glasses; **una moneda de dos euros** a two-euro coin; **el cubo de la basura** the rubbish bin; **una película de miedo** a scary film; **7 la estación de Victoria** Victoria Station; **la ciudad de Barcelona** Barcelona; **el mes de marzo** the month of March; **8** (*describing people*) **un hombre de cincuenta años** a fifty-year-old man; **una niña de pelo corto** a gi'de' + 'el' becomes 'del'rl with short hair; **es la chica del jersey a rayas** it's the girl with a striped jumper; **yo iba vestida de rojo** I

was dressed in red; **9 el mejor de todos** the best of all; **el más bonito de los tres** the nicest of the three; **más de quince** more than fifteen; **el más inteligente de la clase** the cleverest in the class; **10 un tercio del total** a third of the total; **el doble de lo que yo gano** twice what I earn; **poco a poco** little by little; **de tres en tres** three at a time; **11 a las dos de la tarde** at two in the afternoon; **de noche** by night; **trabajan de noche** they work at night; **viajaron de día** they travelled by day; **12 trabajar de algo** to work as something; **trabajo de enfermera** I work as a nurse.

dé *verb* SEE **dar**.

debajo *adjective* (*note that*)
1 underneath; **pon un plato debajo** put a plate underneath; **2 el que está debajo** the one underneath; **el de debajo del todo** the one right at the bottom; **3 debajo de** under; **está debajo de la caja** it's under the box; **4 por debajo de** under; **pasé por debajo de la valla** I went under the fence; **por debajo de los diez grados** below ten degrees.

deber[1] *noun Masc.* **1** duty; **cumplir con tu deber** to do your duty; **2 deberes** homework; **hacer los deberes** to do your homework; **aún no he hecho los deberes** I haven't done my homework yet.

deber[2] *verb* [18] **1** to owe; **te debo veinte euros** I owe you twenty euros; **2** must; **debes intentarlo** you must try; **deberás estudiar mucho** you will have to study hard;

a
b
c
d
e
f
g
h
i
j
k
l
m
n
ñ
o
p
q
r
s
t
u
v
w
x
y
z

3 deberías descansar you should have a rest; **deberías haber seguido mis consejos** you should have followed my advice.

debido/debida *adjective* **1** due; **a su debido tiempo** in due course; **con el debido respeto** with due respect; **con el debido cuidado** with the necessary care; **2 como es debido** properly; **pórtate como es debido** behave properly; **3 debido a** due to; **debido al accidente** due to the accident.

débil *adjective* weak.

década *noun Fem.* decade; **la década de los sesenta** the sixties.

decena *noun Fem.* **una decena de libros** about ten books; **divídelos por decenas** divide them into tens.

decente *adjective* decent.

decepción *noun Fem.* disappointment.

decepcionar *verb* [17] to disappoint; **la película nos decepcionó** the film disappointed us.

decidir *verb* [19] to decide; **decidí quedarme** I decided to stay. **decidirse** *reflexive verb* [19] to make up your mind; **aún no se ha decidido del todo** she hasn't completely made up her mind.

décimo/décima *adjective* tenth; **el décimo piso** the tenth floor.

decir *verb* [5] **1** to say; **¿qué has dicho?** what did you say?; **aquí dice que ...** here it says that ...; **2** to tell; **me ha dicho que no viene** he's told me he's not coming; **dime lo que**

quieres tell me what you want; **3** to mean; **¿qué quieres decir?** what do you mean?; **¿qué quiere decir 'paloma'?** what does 'paloma' mean?; **4 no digas tonterías** don't talk nonsense; **5 ¿diga?** hello? (*on the phone*); **6 dime** yes? (*when somebody says your name*); **'¡mamá!' – '¿dime?'** 'Mum!' – 'yes?'.

decisión *noun Fem.* decision; **tomar una decisión** to make a decision.

declarar *verb* [17] **1** to declare; **declarar la guerra** to declare war; **¿algo que declarar?** anything to declare? (*at customs*); **2** to give evidence; **se ha negado a declarar** he's refused to give evidence. **declararse** *reflexive verb* [17] **declararse culpable** to plead guilty; **declararse inocente** to plead not guilty.

decorador/decoradora *noun Masc./Fem.* interior designer.

decorar *verb* [17] to decorate.

dedo *noun Masc.* **1** finger; **dedo índice** index finger; **dedo anular** ring finger; **dedo meñique** little finger; **dedo pulgar** thumb; **dedo corazón** middle finger; **2 dedo del pie** toe; **el dedo gordo del pie** the big toe; **3 hacer dedo** to hitchhike.

defecto *noun Masc.* flaw, defect.

defectuoso/defectuosa *adjective* faulty.

defender *verb* [36] to defend. **defenderse** *reflexive verb* [36] **1** to defend yourself; **2 me defiendo en inglés** I get by in English.

defensa *noun Fem.* **1** defence; **defensa personal** self-defence; **2** defender (*in sport*).

defensor/defensora *noun Masc./Fem.* defender; **el defensor del pueblo** the ombudsman.

deficiente *adjective* **1** deficient; **2** inadequate.

definición *noun Fem.* definition.

definitivo/definitiva *adjective* definitive.

dejar *verb* [17] **1** to leave; **quiere dejar el colegio** she wants to leave school; **ha dejado a su novia** he's left his girlfriend; **¡déjala en paz!** leave her alone!; **2** to let; **no la dejan salir los domingos** they don't let her go out on Sundays; **¡déjame entrar!** let me in!; **3** to lend; **le he dejado mis apuntes** I've lent him my notes; **¿me dejas un boli?** can you lend me a pen?; **4 dejar caer algo** to drop something; **5 dejar paso** to give way; **6 dejar de hacer algo** to stop doing something; **¡deja de molestar!** stop being a nuisance!; **dejar de fumar** to give up smoking; **7 no dejes de llamarme cuando llegues** make sure you phone me when you get there.

dejarse *reflexive verb* [17] **1** to leave; **me he dejado las gafas en el coche** I left my glasses in the car; **2 dejarse el pelo largo** to grow your hair long; **dejarse barba** to grow a beard.

del (*formed by 'de + el'; look under 'de' for more examples*) **el dedo gordo del pie** the big toe.

delantal *noun Masc.* apron.

delante *adverb* **1 delante de** in front of; **delante de la iglesia** in front of the church; **delante de mí** in front of me; **2 el asiento de delante** the front seat; **la parte de delante** the front; **3 ir delante** to go ahead; **4 lleva un bolsillo por delante** it has a pocket at the front; **entraron por delante** they came in through the front.

delantero/delantera *noun Masc./Fem.* forward (*in sport*). **delantero** *adjective* front; **la rueda delantera** the front wheel.

deletrear *verb* [17] to spell.

delfín *noun Masc.* dolphin.

delgado/delgada *adjective* thin.

delicado/delicada *adjective* **1** delicate; **una situación delicada** a delicate situation; **2** fragile (*a piece of china, etc.*); **3** sensitive (*skin*).

delicioso/deliciosa *adjective* delicious.

delincuente *noun Masc./Fem.* criminal.

delito *noun Masc.* crime; **cometer un delito** to commit a crime.

demás *adjective* **los demás alumnos** the rest of the pupils; **las demás cartas** the rest of the letters. **demás** *pronoun* **1 lo demás** the rest; **lo demás lo traigo mañana** I'll bring the rest tomorrow; **aquí está todo lo demás** here's everything else; **2 los/las demás** the rest, the others; **los demás pueden venir conmigo** the rest can come with me; **los problemas de los demás** other people's problems.

a
b
c
d
e
f
g
h
i
j
k
l
m
n
ñ
o
p
q
r
s
t
u
v
w
x
y
z

demasiado¹/demasiada
adjective, pronoun **1** too much;
gasta demasiado dinero he spends
too much money; **2** too many; **hay
demasiadas personas aquí** there
are too many people here;
3 demasiadas veces too often;
4 hacía demasiado calor it was too
hot.

demasiado² *adverb* **1** too much;
gasta demasiado he spends too
much; **no trabajes demasiado**
don't work too hard; **2** too; **los
billetes eran demasiado caro** the
tickets were too expensive.

democracia *noun Fem.*
democracy.

demoler *verb* [38] to demolish.

demolición *noun Fem.* demolition.

demonio *noun Masc.* devil.

demora *noun Fem.* delay; **sin
demora** without delay.

demos, **dan**, **den**, **etc.** *verb* SEE
dar.

densidad *noun Fem.* **1** density;
2 denseness.

dentado/dentada *adjective*
jagged.

dentífrico *noun Masc.* toothpaste.

dentista *noun Masc./Fem.* dentist.

dentro *adverb* **1** inside; **pasar
dentro** to go inside; **desde dentro**
from inside; **2 aquí dentro** in here;
allí dentro in there; **ponlo aquí
dentro** put it in here; **3 dentro de**
inside, in; **dentro del edificio**
inside the building; **dentro de la
caja** in the box; **4 por dentro** on the
inside; **por dentro es verde** it's

green on the inside; **lo limpié por
dentro** I've cleaned the inside.

denunciar *verb* [17] to report (*a
person or crime*).

departamento *noun Masc.*
department.

depender *verb* [18] to depend;
depender de algo to depend on
something; **depende del resultado**
it depends on the result; **'¿se lo vas
a decir?'** – **'depende'** 'are you
going to tell him?' – 'it depends'.

dependiente/dependienta
noun Masc./Fem. shop assistant.

deporte *noun Masc.* sport; **hacer
deporte** to play sports; **me gusta
hacer deporte** I like playing sports;
los deportes acuáticos water
sports; **los deportes de invierno**
winter sports.

deportista *noun Masc./Fem.*
sportsman/sportswoman.
deportista *adjective* sporty; **soy
muy deportista** I do a lot of sport;
Jack es muy buen deportista
Jack's very good at games.

deportivo¹ *noun Masc.* sports car.

deportivo²/deportiva *adjective*
sports; **club deportivo** sports club;
ropa deportiva sports clothes,
casual clothes.

depositar *verb* [17] **1** to place;
deposite su solicitud en esta caja
place your application in this box;
2 to deposit (*money in an account*).

depósito *noun Masc.* deposit.

deprimido/deprimida
adjective depressed.

a
b
c
d
e
f
g
h
i
j
k
l
m
n
ñ
o
p
q
r
s
t
u
v
w
x
y
z

deprimirse *reflexive verb* [19] to get depressed.

deprisa *adverb* fast, quickly; **no lo hagas tan deprisa** don't do it so quickly; **andaba muy deprisa** he was walking very fast; **¡deprisa, vístete!** hurry up and get dressed!

derecha [1] *noun Fem.* **1** right; **gira a la derecha** turn right; **conducir por la derecha** to drive on the right; **la segunda calle a la derecha** the second road on the right; **2** right hand; **escribo con la derecha** I write with my right hand; **3 la derecha** the right (*in politics*); **ser de derechas** to be right-wing.

derecho [1] *noun Masc.* **1** right; **tener derecho a** to have a right to; **tienes derecho a reclamar** you've got the right to claim; **los derechos humanos** human rights; **2** law; **estudiar derecho** to study law; **derecho penal** criminal law; **3 derechos de autor** royalties.

derecho [2] *adverb* straight; **ponlo derecho** put it straight; **siga todo derecho** go straight on; **siéntate derecho** sit up straight.

derecho [3]/**derecha** [2] *adjective* **1** right; **el guante derecho** the right glove; **en la esquina superior derecha** in the top right-hand corner; **2** straight; **no está derecho** it's not straight.

derramar *verb* [17] to spill; **he derramado el café en la alfombra** I've spilt the coffee on the carpet. **derramarse** *reflexive verb* [7] to spill; **se derramó la leche** the milk has spilt.

derribar *verb* [17] **1** to demolish (*a building or wall, for example*); **2** to break down (*a door*); **3** to shoot down (*a plane*).

derrotar *verb* [17] to defeat.

des *verb* SEE **dar**.

desabrochar *verb* [17] to undo (*a jacket or shirt*).
desabrocharse *reflexive verb* [17] to undo; **se desabrochó la chaqueta** he undid his jacket.

desafilado/desafilada *adjective* blunt.

desafortunadamente *adverb* unfortunately.

desafortunado/ desafortunada *adjective* **1** unlucky (*a person*); **2** unfortunate (*an event*).

desagradable *adjective* unpleasant.

desanimado/desanimada *adjective* discouraged.

desaparecer *verb* [35] **1** to disappear; **la tradición está desapareciendo** the tradition is dying out; **2** to go missing.

desaparición *noun Fem.* disappearance.

desaprovechar *verb* [17] to waste; **han desaprovechado mucho papel** they've wasted a lot of paper.

desarrollo *noun Masc.* development.

desastre *noun Masc.* disaster.

a b c d e f g h i j k l m n ñ o p q r s t u v w x y z

desatar *verb* [17] to untie.
desatarse *reflexive verb* [17] to come undone.

desatornillar *verb* [17] to unscrew.

desayunar *verb* [17] **1** to have breakfast; **desayuné muy temprano** I had breakfast very early; **2** to have for breakfast; **desayuno café y tostadas** I have coffee and toast for breakfast.

desayuno *noun Masc.* breakfast; **tomar el desayuno** to have breakfast.

desbordar *verb* [17] to exceed.
desbordarse *reflexive verb* [17] to overflow; **el río se desbordó** the river overflowed its banks.

descafeinado/descafeinada *adjective* decaffeinated.

descalificar *verb* [31] to disqualify.

descalzarse *reflexive verb* [22] to take your shoes off.

descalzo/descalza *adjective* barefoot.

descansado/descansada *adjective* rested.

descansar *verb* [17] **1** to rest; **necesitas descansar** you need to rest; **descansar la vista** to give your eyes a rest; **2 que descanses** sleep well; **3 ¡descansen!** at ease! (*in the army*).

descansillo *noun Masc.* landing (*on stairs*).

descanso *noun Masc.* **1** rest; **2** half-time.

descapotable *noun Masc.*, **descapotable** *adjective* convertible.

descargar *verb* [28] to unload.

descender *verb* [36] **1** to go down (*a mountaineer*); **2** to descend (*a plane*); **3** to fall (*prices or temperature, for example*).

descolgar *verb* [23] **1** to pick up (*the phone*); **2 han dejado el teléfono descolgado** they've left the phone off the hook; **3** to take down (*a picture, for example*).

desconectar *verb* [17] to disconnect; **¿has desconectado el ordenador?** have you disconnected the computer?

desconfiar *verb* [32] to mistrust; **desconfiar de alguien** to mistrust someone.

descongelar *verb* [17] to defrost (*the fridge or food*).
decongelarse *reflexive verb* [17] to defrost (*the fridge or food*).

desconocido/desconocida *noun Masc./Fem.* stranger.
desconocido *adjective* unknown.

descontento¹ *noun Masc.* dissatisfaction.

descontento²/descontenta *adjective* dissatisfied; **quedar descontento con algo** to be dissatisfied with something.

describir *verb* [52] to describe.

descripción *noun Fem.* description.

descrito *verb* SEE **describir**.

descubrir *verb* [53] **1** to discover; **2** to unveil (*a statue*).

descuento *noun* Masc. discount.

descuidado/descuidada *adjective* **1** careless (*a person*); **2** neglected; **el jardín está muy descuidado** the garden is very neglected.

desde *preposition* **1** since; **desde la semana pasada** since last week; **desde que nos conocimos** since we met; **2** from; **mídelo desde este extremo hasta el otro** measure it from this end to the other; **puedo mandarlo desde Madrid** I can send it from Madrid; **desde el principio** from the beginning; **desde el primer momento** right from the start; **3 desde hace** for; **no les veo desde hace años** I haven't seen them for years; **trabajo allí desde hace tres meses** I've been working there for three months; **4 desde luego** of course.

desear *verb* [17] **1** to wish; **te deseo lo mejor** I wish you all the best; **te deseo un feliz cumpleaños** wishing you a happy birthday (*in a card*); **2 ¿qué desea?** can I help you? (*in a shop, for example*); **3 estoy deseando verte** I'm looking forward to seeing you; **están deseando que llegue el verano** they can't wait for the summer to come.

desembarcar *verb* [31] **1** to unload; **2** to disembark.

desempleado/desempleada *noun* Masc./Fem. unemployed person.

desempleado *adjective* unemployed.

desempleo *noun* Masc. unemployment; **cobrar subsidio de desempleo** to get unemployment benefit.

desenchufar *verb* [17] to unplug.

desenvolver *verb* [45] to unwrap.

deseo *noun* Masc. **1** wish; **pedir un deseo** to make a wish; **se cumplió mi deseo** my wish came true; **2 con mis mejores deseos** best wishes; **3** desire.

desfavorable *adjective* unfavourable.

desfile *noun* Masc. **1** parade; **2 un desfile de modelos** a fashion show.

desgracia *noun* Fem. misfortune; **por desgracia** unfortunately; ★ **las desgracias nunca vienen solas** it never rains but pours.

desgraciado/desgraciada *adjective* **1** unhappy; **soy muy desgraciado** I'm very unhappy; **2** ill-fated; **aquel desgraciado día** that ill-fated day.

deshacer *verb* [7] **1** to undo (*a knot*); **2** to unwrap (*a parcel*); **3** to take apart (*a mechanism*); **4** to crumble (*a biscuit or stock cube, for example*); **5 deshacer las maletas** to unpack.
 deshacerse *reflexive verb* [7] **1** to come undone (*a knot or seam*); **2** to melt (*ice*); **3** to come apart; **se deshizo en mis manos** it came apart in my hands; **4 deshacerse de algo** to get rid of something; **voy**

a **a deshacerme de este sofá** I'm going to get rid of this sofa.

b **deshielo** *noun Masc.* thaw.

c **desierto**[1] *noun Masc.* desert.

desierto[2]**/desierta** *adjective* deserted.

e **designar** *verb* [17] to appoint.

f **desigual** *adjective* **1** uneven (*a surface or road*); **2** unequal (*a fight*).

g

h **desmaquillarse** *reflexive verb* [17] to remove your make-up.

i **desmayarse** *reflexive verb* [17] to faint.

j

k **desmontar** *verb* [17] **1** to take apart; **2** to take down (*a tent*).

l **desnudar** *verb* [17] to undress. **desnudarse** *reflexive verb* [17] to take your clothes off, to undress.

m

n **desnudo/desnuda** *adjective* **1** naked; **2** bare; **con los hombros desnudos** with bare shoulders.

ñ

o **desobedecer** *verb* [35] to disobey; **desobedeció el reglamento** she disobeyed the rules.

p

q

r **desobedezca**, **desobedezco**, *etc. verb* SEE **desobedecer**.

s

t **desobediente** *noun Masc./Fem.* **eres un desobediente** you are very disobedient. **desobediente** *adjective* disobedient.

u

v

w

x **desodorante** *noun Masc.* deodorant; **desodorante en barra** stick deodorant.

y

z **desorden** *noun Masc.* mess.

desorganizado/ desorganizada *adjective* disorganized.

despacho *noun Masc.* **1** office; **2** study (*at home*); **3 despacho de billetes** ticket office; **despacho de lotería** lottery agency.

despacio *adverb* slowly; **hazlo despacio** do it slowly; **¡más despacio!** slower!

despedida *noun Fem.* farewell; **una cena de despedida** a farewell dinner.

despedir *verb* [57] **1** to dismiss; **lo han despedido del trabajo** they've sacked him; **2** to lay off; **han tenido que despedir a algunos empleados** they've had to lay off some employees; **3** to say goodbye; **fuimos todos a despedirla** we all went to say goodbye to her; **¿vendrás a despedirme a la estación?** will you come to see me off at the station? **despedirse** *reflexive verb* [57] to say goodbye; **despedirse de alguien** to say goodbye to someone.

despegar *verb* [28] **1** to take off (*a plane*); **2** to peel off (*a label or a sticker*). **despegarse** *reflexive verb* [28] to come unstuck.

despegue *noun Masc.* takeoff (*of a plane*).

despejado/despejada *adjective* clear (*sky or a day, for example*).

despejar *verb* [17] to clear.

desperdiciar *verb* [17] to waste.

desperdicio noun Masc. **1** waste; **no tiene desperdicio** it's excellent; **2 desperdicios** scraps.

despertador noun Masc. alarm (clock); **poner el despertador** to set the alarm.

despertar verb [29] to wake up; **¿puedes despertarme a las siete?** can you wake me up at seven?. **despertarse** reflexive verb [29] to wake up; **me desperté a las diez** I woke up at ten.

despida, despido, etc. verb SEE **despedir.**

despierta¹, despierto¹, etc. verb SEE **despertar.**

despierto²/despierta² adjective awake.

despistado/despistada noun Masc./Fem. scatterbrain. **despistado** adjective absent-minded.

desplegar verb [30] to unfold.

despliega, despliego, etc. verb SEE **desplegar.**

después adverb **1** afterwards; **después me arrepentí** I regretted it afterwards; **poco después** shortly afterwards; **2** later; **lo haré después** I'll do it later; **se vieron mucho después** they saw each other much later; **3 después de** after; **después de las clases** after school; **4 después de todo** after all.

destino noun Masc. **1** destination; **¿qué destino tiene?** what's its destination?; **el vuelo con destino a Milán** the plane to Milan; **2** fate.

destornillador noun Masc. screwdriver.

destrucción noun Fem. destruction.

destruir verb [54] to destroy.

desván noun Masc. attic.

desventaja noun Fem. disadvantage; **estar en desventaja** to be at a disadvantage.

desvestirse reflexive verb [57] to undress.

desviar verb [32] to divert (a plane or traffic).

desvío noun Masc. diversion; **tomar un desvío** to make a detour.

detalle noun Masc. detail; **describir algo con todo detalle** to describe something in great detail.

detective noun Masc./Fem. detective; **detective privado** private detective.

detener verb [9] **1** to stop (traffic); **2** to arrest; **¡queda detenido!** you're under arrest! **detenerse** reflexive verb [9] to stop; **detenerse a hacer** to stop to do; **me detuve a descansar** I stopped to rest.

detergente noun Masc. **1** washing powder; **2** washing-up liquid.

detestar verb [17] to detest.

detrás adverb **1** behind; **creo que están detrás** I think they're behind; **2 detrás de** behind; **ponte detrás de mí** go behind me; **detrás de la estación** behind the station; **3 se abrocha por detrás** it buttons up at the back; **entraron por detrás** they got in through the back.

deuda *noun Fem.* debt; **tiene muchas deudas** he has a lot of debts.

devolver *verb* [45] **1** to bring back; **te devolveré el libro mañana** I'll bring you the book back tomorrow; **2** to take back; **he devuelto la camisa** I've taken the shirt back; **3** to return; **lo devolví a su dueño** I returned it to its owner; **4** to refund (*money*); **5** to be sick (*vomit*); **creo que voy a devolver** I think I'm going to be sick.

devuelto, devuelvo, etc. *verb* SEE **devolver**.

di *verb* SEE **dar**.

día *noun Masc.* **1** day; **el día siguiente** the following day; **el día anterior** the previous day; **el día tres de mayo** the third of May; **¿qué día es hoy?** what day is it today?; **todos los días** every day; **cada día** every day; **un día festivo** a public holiday; **se ha tomado el día libre** she's taken the day off; **día de Reyes** Twelfth Night (*the 6th of January, which is when people get Christmas presents in Spain*); **el día de los Inocentes** the 28th of December (*equivalent to April Fool's Day in Spain*); **el día de los enamorados** St Valentine's Day; **día del padre** Father's Day; **2 buenos días** good morning; **3 hacerse de día** to get light (*in the morning*); **aún no se ha hecho de día** it's not light yet; **en pleno día** in broad daylight; **4 estar al día** to be up to date; **poner a**

alguien al día to bring someone up to date.

diabético/diabética *noun Masc./Fem.*, **diabético** *adjective* diabetic.

diablo *noun Masc.* devil.

diagnóstico *noun Masc.* diagnosis; **emitir un diagnóstico** to make a diagnosis.

diagonal *noun Fem.*, **diagonal** *adjective* diagonal.

diagrama *noun Masc.* diagram.

dial *noun Masc.* dial.

diálogo *noun Masc.* **1** conversation; **2** dialogue.

diamante *noun Masc.* diamond.

diámetro *noun Masc.* diameter.

diapositiva *noun Fem.* slide.

diario[1] *noun Masc.* **1** diary; **llevar un diario** to keep a diary; **2** newspaper.

diario[2]/**diaria** *adjective* **1** daily; **la rutina diaria** the daily routine; **a diario** every day; **se escriben a diario** they write to each other every day; **2** a day; **ensayan dos horas diarias** they practise two hours a day; **3 de diario** everyday; **ropa de diario** everyday clothes.

diarrea *noun Fem.* diarrhoea.

dibujar *verb* [17] to draw.

dibujo *noun Masc.* **1** drawing; **hacer un dibujo** to do a drawing; **dibujo técnico** technical drawing; **2 dibujos animados** cartoons; **una película de dibujos animados** an animated cartoon film.

diccionario *noun Masc.* dictionary.

dice, **dicho**, **etc.** *verb* SEE **decir**.

diciembre *noun Masc.* December.

dictado *noun Masc.* dictation.

diecinueve *number* **1** nineteen; **tiene diecinueve años** she's nineteen (years old); **2** nineteenth (*in dates*); **el diecinueve de agosto** the nineteenth of August.

dieciocho *number* **1** eighteen; **tiene dieciocho años** she's eighteen (years old); **2** eighteenth (*in dates*); **el dieciocho de agosto** the eighteenth of August.

dieciséis *number* **1** sixteen; **tiene dieciséis años** she's sixteen (years old); **2** sixteenth (*in dates*); **el dieciséis de agosto** the sixteenth of August.

diecisiete *number* **1** seventeen; **tiene diecisiete años** she's seventeen (years old); **2** seventeenth (*in dates*); **el diecisiete de agosto** the seventeenth of August.

diente *noun Masc.* **1** tooth; **se le ha caído un diente** she's lost a tooth; **ya le están saliendo los dientes** he's already teething; **2 un diente de ajo** a clove of garlic.

diera, **dieras**, **etc.** *verb* SEE **dar**.

diesel *noun Masc.*, **diesel** *adjective* diesel.

dieta *noun Fem.* diet; **estar a dieta** to be on a diet; **ponerse a dieta** to go on a diet.

diez *number* **1** ten; **tiene diez años** she's ten (years old); **2** tenth (*in dates*); **el diez de agosto** the tenth of August; **3** ten (*in clock time*); **son**

las diez it's ten o'clock; **a las diez y cinco** at five past ten.

diferencia *noun Fem.* **1** difference; **hay poca diferencia de precio** there's not much difference in price; **2 a diferencia de** unlike; **a diferencia de su padre** unlike his father.

diferente *adjective* different; **ser diferente a/de** to be different from.

difícil *adjective* difficult.

dificultad *noun Fem.* difficulty; **con muchas dificultades** with great difficulty.

diga, **digo**, **etc.** *verb* SEE **decir**.

diluir *verb* [54] **1** to dilute; **2** to thin (*paint*).

dimensión *noun Fem.* dimension.

dimisión *noun Fem.* resignation; **presentar la dimisión** to hand in your resignation.

dimitir *verb* [19] to resign.

dimos *verb* SEE **dar**.

Dinamarca *noun Fem.* Denmark.

dinero *noun Masc.* money; **dinero de bolsillo** pocket money; **dinero en efectivo** cash; **dinero suelto** change; **no tengo dinero suelto** I haven't got any change.

dinosaurio *noun Masc.* dinosaur.

dio *verb* SEE **dar**.

dios *noun Masc.* god.

Dios *noun Masc.* God; **gracias a Dios** thank heavens; **¡por Dios!** for heaven's sake!; **¡Dios mío!** oh, my God!; **¡sabe Dios!** God knows!

diploma *noun Masc.* diploma.

a
b
c
d
e
f
g
h
i
j
k
l
m
n
ñ
o
p
q
r
s
t
u
v
w
x
y
z

diplomático/diplomática
noun Masc./Fem. diplomat.
diplomático *adjective* diplomatic.

diputado/diputada *noun Masc./
Fem.* member of parliament.

dirá, diré, etc. *verb* SEE **decir**.

dirección *noun Fem.* **1** address; **mi
dirección es** … my address is …;
2 direction; **¿en qué dirección se
fueron?** what direction did they go
in?; **venían en dirección contraria**
they were coming the other way;
3 'dirección prohibida' 'no entry';
'dirección obligatoria' 'one way';
4 management (*of a company*).

directo¹/directa *adjective*
1 direct; **¿hay un vuelo directo a
Santiago?** is there a direct flight to
Santiago?; **2 un tren directo** a
through train; **3 en directo** live;
retransmisión en directo live
broadcast.

directo² *adverb* direct; **el autobús
va directo al aeropuerto** the bus
goes direct to the airport.

director/directora *noun Masc./
Fem.* **1** headmaster/headmistress;
2 manager (*of a company*);
3 director (*of a film or play*);
4 conductor (*of an orchestra*);
5 editor (*of a newspaper*).

dirigir *verb* [49] **1** to manage (*a
company*); **2** to direct (*a film or
play*); **3** to conduct (*an orchestra*);
**4 no me dirigió la palabra en toda
la tarde** he didn't say a word to me
all afternoon.

dirigirse *reflexive verb* [49]
dirigirse a hacia algo to head
towards something; **se dirigió**

hacia la puerta he headed towards
the door.

discapacidad *noun Fem.*
disability; **¿tiene alguna
discapacidad?** does she have a
disability?

disciplina *noun Fem.* discipline.

disco *noun Masc.* **1** record; **grabar
un disco** to make a record; **disco
sencillo** single; **disco compacto**
compact disc; **disco compacto
interactivo** interactive compact
disc; **2** disk; **disco duro** hard disk;
disco flexible floppy disk; **3** traffic
light; **el disco se ha puesto rojo**
the lights are red.

discoteca *noun Fem.* disco.

disculpa *noun Fem.* apology; **pedir
disculpas a alguien por algo** to
apologize to someone for something.

disculparse *reflexive verb* [17] to
apologize.

discusión *noun Fem.* **1** argument;
2 discussion.

discutir *verb* [19] **1** to argue; **ha
discutido con su novio** she's had
an argument with her boyfriend;
2 to discuss.

diseñador/diseñadora *noun
Masc./Fem.* designer; **diseñador/
diseñadora gráfico/gráfica**
graphic designer.

diseñar *verb* [17] to design.

diseño *noun Masc.* design.

disfraz *noun Masc.* **1** disguise;
2 costume, fancy dress outfit; **un
disfraz de pirata** a pirate outfit; **una
fiesta de disfraces** a fancy dress
party.

disfrazarse *reflexive verb* [22] to dress up; **me disfracé de bruja** I dressed up as a witch.

disfrutar *verb* [17] to enjoy yourself; **disfrutar de algo** to enjoy something; **he disfrutado mucho de las vacaciones** I really enjoyed my holiday.

disgustar *verb* [17] to upset. **disgustarse** *reflexive verb* [17] to get upset.

disgusto *noun Masc.* **tengo un disgusto enorme** I'm very upset.

disminución *noun Fem.* decrease.

disminuir *verb* [54] **1** to decrease; **el número de visitantes ha diminuido** the number of visitors has decreased; **2** to reduce (*speed, costs*).

disolvente *noun Masc.* solvent.

disolver *verb* [45] to dissolve. **disolverse** *reflexive verb* [45] to dissolve.

disparar *verb* [17] **1** to fire; **2** to shoot.

disparo *noun Masc.* shot.

disposición *noun Fem.* **1** arrangement; **2** aptitude; **3 estoy a tu disposición** I'm at your disposal.

dispuesto/dispuesta *adjective* **1** arranged; **2** ready; **ya está todo dispuesto** everything's ready; **3 estar dispuesto a hacer** to be prepared to do; **no estoy dispuesto a esperar** I'm not prepared to wait.

disputa *noun Masc.* **1** dispute; **2** argument.

disputarse *reflexive verb* [17] **1** to compete for (*title, cup*); **2** to fight over (*inheritance*).

disquete *noun Masc.* diskette, floppy disk.

disquetera *noun Fem.* disk drive.

distancia *noun Fem.* distance; **¿a qué distancia está el colegio de tu casa?** how far is the school from your house?; **los dos postes están a una distancia de dos metros** the two posts are two metres apart; **está a poca distancia** it's quite near.

diste *verb* SEE **dar**.

distinguir *verb* [50] to distinguish. **distinguirse** *reflexive verb* [50] **1 distinguirse por algo** to distinguish yourself by something; **2 distinguirse de algo** to be different from something.

distintivo/distintiva *adjective* distinctive.

distinto *adjective* different; **ser distinto a** to be different from; **es distinto al resto** it's different from the rest.

distracción *noun Fem.* **1** entertainment; **es su distracción favorita** it's his favourite entertainment; **la tele le sirve de distracción** television is a way of passing the time for him; **2 se lo quitaron en un momento de distracción** they stole it from her when she wasn't paying attention.

distraer *verb* [42] **1** to distract; **distraer a alguien de algo** to distract somebody from something; **2 la costura me distrae** sewing

a
b
c
d
e
f
g
h
i
j
k
l
m
n
ñ
o
p
q
r
s
t
u
v
w
x
y
z

a
b
c
d
e
f
g
h
i
j
k
l
m
n
ñ
o
p
q
r
s
t
u
v
w
x
y
z

gives me somthing to do.
distraerse *reflexive verb* [42] **1** to get distracted; **2 se distrae con la jardinería** gardening gives him something to do.

distribuidor/distribuidora *noun Masc./Fem.* distributor.

distribuir *verb* [54] to distribute.

distrito *noun Masc.* district; **distrito postal** postal area.

diversión *noun Fem.* **1** fun; **por diversión** for fun; **2 un lugar lleno de diversiones** a place with plenty of things to do.

divertido/divertida *adjective* **1** funny; **es un chico muy divertido** he's really funny; **2 la fiesta fue muy divertida** the party was real fun.

divertir *verb* [14] to amuse.
divertirse *reflexive verb* [14] **1** to amuse yourself; **2** to have fun; **¡que te diviertas!** have fun!

dividir *verb* [19] to divide.

divisa *noun Fem.* currency; **divisas extranjeras** foreign currency.

división *noun Fem.* division.

divorciado/divorciada *noun Masc./Fem.* divorcee.
divorciado *adjective* divorced; **mis padres están divorciados** my parents are divorced.

divorciarse *reflexive verb* [17] to get divorced; **se divociaron en México** they got divorced in Mexico.

divorcio *noun Masc.* divorce.

DNI *abbreviation Masc.* (*short for: Documento Nacional de Identidad*) identity card.

doblar *verb* [17] **1** to fold (*a piece of paper or clothes*); **2** to bend (*a piece of metal or your leg*); **3** to double (*an offer or amount*); **4 doblar la esquina** to turn the corner.

doble *noun Masc.* **1 el doble de personas** twice as many people; **el doble de harina que de azúcar** twice as much flour as sugar; **el doble de peso** twice the weight; **el doble de largo** twice the length; **2 dobles** doubles (*in tennis*).
doble *adjective* double.

doce *number* **1** twelve; **tiene doce años** she's twelve (years old); **2** twelfth (*in dates*); **el doce de enero** the twelfth of January; **3** twelve (*in clock time*); **a las doce** at twelve o'clock; **son las doce del mediodía** it's twelve noon; **a las doce de la noche** at midnight.

doceavo/doceava *adjective* twelfth.

docena *noun Fem.* dozen; **una docena de huevos** a dozen eggs.

doctor/doctora *noun Masc./Fem.* doctor.

documentación *noun Fem.* **1** papers; **no llevaba mi documentación** I didn't have my papers on me; **2** documents (*for a car*).

documental *noun Masc.* documentary.
documental *adjective* **un programa documental** a documentary.

documento *noun Masc.* document; **mi documento de identidad** my identity card.

dólar *noun Masc.* dollar.

doler *verb* [38] **1** to hurt; **2 me duele el tobillo** my ankle hurts; **¿te duele mucho?** does it hurt a lot?; **me duele la cabeza** I've got a headache; **le dolía el estómago** he had stomachache.

dolor *noun Masc.* pain; **tengo dolor de garganta** I have a sore throat; **tengo dolor de muelas** I have toothache; **con dolor de estómago** with a stomachache.

doméstico/doméstica *adjective* domestic.

domicilio *noun Masc.* **¿cuál es su domicilio?** what's your address?; **en su domicilio particular** in his own home.

domingo *noun Masc.* Sunday; **domingo de Resurrección** Easter Sunday; **vienen el domingo** they're coming on Sunday; **el domingo pasado** last Sunday; **el domingo por la mañana** on Sunday morning; **un domingo sí y otro no** every other Sunday; **cierran los domingos** they close on Sundays.

dominical *noun Masc.* **1** Sunday newspaper; **2** Sunday supplement.

dominó *noun Masc.* dominoes; **jugar al dominó** to play dominoes.

don *noun Masc.* Mr; **Don Juan Pozo** Mr Juan Pozo.

doña *noun Fem.* Mrs, Ms; **Doña María del Valle** Mrs María del Valle.

donación *noun Fem.* donation.

donde *adverb* where; **el sitio donde nací** the place where I was born; **el lugar a donde nos dirigimos** the place we're going to; **iré a donde quiera** I'll go wherever I want; **ponlo donde sea** put it down anywhere.

dónde *adverb* where; **¿dónde está mi abrigo?** where's my coat?; **¿de dónde eres?** where are you from?; **no sé dónde lo guarda** I don't know where he keeps it; **¿por dónde se va a la oficina de correos?** what's the way to the post office?

donut™ *noun Masc.* doughnut.

dorado/dorada *adjective* gold, golden.

dormido/dormida *adjective* asleep; **estar dormido** to be asleep; **quedarse dormido** to fall asleep.

dormir *verb* [51] **1** to sleep; **¿has dormido bien?** did you sleep well?; **no he dormido nada** I couldn't sleep at all; **2 ¡a dormir!** time for bed!; **ya es hora de irse a dormir** it's time to go to bed; **3** to get to sleep; **no puedo dormir** I can't get to sleep; **4 estar durmiendo** to be asleep; **Juan está todavía durmiendo** Juan is still asleep; **5 dormir la siesta** to have a nap. **dormirse** *reflexive verb* [51] **1** to fall asleep; **no puedo dormirme** I can't get to sleep; **2** to oversleep; **me dormí y llegué tarde al trabajo** I overslept and was late for work.

a
b
c
d
e
f
g
h
i
j
k
l
m
n
ñ
o
p
q
r
s
t
u
v
w
x
y
z

a
b
c
d
e
f
g
h
i
j
k
l
m
n
ñ
o
p
q
r
s
t
u
v
w
x
y
z

dormitorio *noun Masc.* **1** bedroom; **2** dormitory.

dorso *noun Masc.* back; **el dorso de la mano** the back of the hand.

dos *number* **1** two; **tiene dos años** she's two (years old); **2** second (*in dates*); **el dos de enero** the second of January; **3** two (*in clock time*); **son las dos** it's two o'clock.

doscientos/doscientas *number* two hundred; **doscientos veinte** two hundred and twenty.

doy *verb* SEE **dar**.

dragón *noun Masc.* dragon.

drama *noun Masc.* drama.

dramático/dramática *adjective* dramatic.

droga *noun Fem.* drug.

drogadicto/drogadicta *noun Masc./Fem.* drug addict.

droguería *noun Fem.* **1** hardware shop (*specializing in household items*); **2** chemist's.

ducha *noun Fem.* shower; **pegarse una ducha** to have a shower.

ducharse *reflexive verb* [17] to have a shower.

duda *noun Fem.* **1** doubt; **sin duda es el mejor** it's undoubtedly the best; **no me queda la menor duda** I have no doubts whatsoever; **2** query; **¿tienes alguna duda?** do you have any queries?; **tengo algunas dudas** I have a few queries.

dudar *verb* [17] to doubt; **no lo dudo** I don't doubt it; **dudo que sepa hacerlo** I doubt he knows how to do it.

duela, **duelo**, **etc.** *verb* SEE **doler**.

dueño/dueña *noun Fem.* **1** owner; **¿quién es el dueño de este coche?** who's the owner of this car?; **se lo devolví a la dueña** I returned it to its owner; **2** landlord/landlady (*of a pub or a guesthouse*).

duerma, **duermo**, **etc.** *verb* SEE **dormir**.

dulce *noun Masc.* no me gustan los dulces I don't like sweet things. **dulce** *adjective* sweet.

duna *noun Fem.* dune.

duodécimo/duodécima *adjective* twelfth.

duque *noun Masc.* duke.

duquesa *noun Fem.* duchess.

duración *noun Fem.* **1** length; **la duración de la película** the length of the film; **2 disco de larga duración** LP.

durante *preposition* **1** during; **durante aquel tiempo** during that time; **lo haré durante las vacaciones** I'll do it during the holidays; **2** for; **no se vieron durante tres semanas** they didn't see each other for three weeks; **3** throughout; **durante todo el partido** throughout the match.

durar *verb* [17] to last; **la guerra duró tres años** the war lasted three years; **¿cuánto dura?** how long is it?; **no dura mucho** it's not very long.

dureza *noun Fem.* hardness.

duro¹/dura *adjective* **1** hard; **al secarse se pone duro** it goes hard when it dries; **fue un golpe muy duro para todos** it was a hard blow for all of us; **un profesor muy duro** a very strict teacher; **2** tough (*meat*); **3** stale (*bread*); **4 un huevo duro** a hard-boiled egg; **5 ser duro de oído** to be hard of hearing.

duro *adverb* hard; **estudiar duro** to study hard.

duro²/dura *noun Masc.* five-peseta coin.

Ee

e *conjunction* and ('*y*' becomes '*e*' before words beginning with '*i-*' or '*hi-*'); **padres e hijos** parents and children.

echar *verb* [17] **1** to put; **echa más sal a la sopa** put more salt in the soup; **eché el monedero en la bolsa** I put my purse in my bag; **tengo que echar gasolina al coche** I have to put some petrol in the car; **2** to give; **¿te echo un poco de salsa?** shall I give you some sauce?; **3** to throw; **eché agua al fuego** I threw water on the fire; **4 echar a alguien** to throw someone out; **los eché de mi casa** I threw them out of my house; **5 echar a alguien del trabajo** to sack someone; **lo han echado del trabajo** he's been sacked; **6** to show; **echan una película en la tele** they're showing a film on the television; **¿qué echan en el cine?** what's on at the cinema?; **7 echar una carta**

(**al correo**) to post a letter; **8 echar de menos a alguien** to miss somebody; **echo de menos a mi hermana** I miss my sister; **te echo mucho de menos** I miss you a lot.

echarse *verb reflexive* [17] **1 echarse al suelo** to throw yourself on the ground; **2 echarse a la derecha** to move to the right; **echarse para atrás** to move backwards; **me eché a un lado** I moved to one side; **3 echarse una siesta** to have a nap.

eclipse *noun Masc.* eclipse.

eco *noun Masc.* echo.

ecológico/ecológica *adjective* ecological.

ecologista *noun Masc./Fem.* ecologist.

economía *noun Fem.* economics.

económico/económica *adjective* **1** economic; **una crisis económica** an economic crisis; **2** financial; **los problemas económicos** financial problems; **3** cheap; **un hotel muy económico** a very cheap hotel; **4** thrifty (*person*).

ecuación *noun Fem.* equation.

ecuador *noun Masc.* equator.

Ecuador *noun Masc.* Equador.

ecuatoriano/ecuatoriana *noun, adjective* Ecuadorian.

edad *noun Fem.* age; **¿qué edad tienes?** how old are you?; **Carmen y yo tenemos la misma edad** Carmen and I are the same age; **tendrá tu edad más o menos** he must be around the same age as you; **una mujer de unos treinta años de**

a
b
c
d
e
f
g
h
i
j
k
l
m
n
ñ
o
p
q
r
s
t
u
v
w
x
y
z

a b c d e f g h i j k l m n ñ o p q r s t u v w x y z

edad a woman of about thirty; **la edad de piedra** the Stone Age; **la edad media** the Middle Ages; **está en la edad del pavo** he's at that awkward age.

edición *noun Fem.* **1** publication; **2** edition; **edición de bolsillo** pocket edition.

edificio *noun Masc.* building.

editar *verb* [17] **1** to publish; **2** to edit (*a text*).

edredón *noun Masc.* quilt; **un edredón nórdico** a duvet.

educación *noun Fem.* **1** education; **educación física** physical education; **educación secundaria** secondary education; **educación a distancia** distance learning; **2** upbringing; **3** manners; **tiene mucha educación** she's very polite; **eso es de mala educación** that's bad manners.

educado/educada *adjective* polite; **una persona mal educada** a rude person.

educar *verb* [31] **1** to educate; **2** to bring up.

EE.UU. *abbreviation* (*short for: Estados Unidos*) USA.

efectivo[1] *noun Masc.* cash; **un millón de euros en efectivo** a million euros in cash; **pagar en efectivo** to pay cash.

efectivo[2]**/efectiva** *adjective* effective (*remedy or method*).

efecto *noun Masc.* effect; **la pastilla no me hizo efecto** the pill didn't have any effect on me; **efectos secundarios** side effects; **efectos**

especiales special effects; **el efecto invernadero** the greenhouse effect.

efectuar *verb* [20] **1** to carry out; **efectuar un registro** to carry out a search; **2 efectuar un viaje** to go on a trip; **3 el tren efectuará su salida a las nueve treinta** the train will depart at 9:30; **4 efectuar un disparo** to fire a shot.

eficaz *adjective* effective.

egoísta *noun Masc./Fem.* **eres un egoísta** you're really selfish. **egoísta** *adjective* selfish.

ejecutar *verb* [17] to execute.

ejecutivo/ejecutiva *noun Masc./Fem., adjective* executive.

ejemplar *noun Masc.* **1** copy (*of a book*); **2** issue (*of a magazine*); **3** specimen (*of an animal or a plant*).

ejemplo *noun Masc.* example; **por ejemplo** for example; **no puedes poner ese caso como ejemplo** you can't take that case as an example; **dar buen ejemplo** to set a good example.

ejercicio *noun Masc.* exercise; **hacer ejercicio** to do exercise.

ejército *noun Masc.* army; **el ejército de tierra** the army; **el ejército de aire** the air force; **alistarse en el ejército** to join the army.

el *definite article* ('*el*' *is used before masculine singular nouns; see also* '*la*', '*los*' *and* '*las*') **1** the; **el libro blanco** the white book; **el sol** the sun; **2** ('*el*' *is also used before feminine nouns that start with* *stressed 'a' or 'ha')* **el águila** the eagle; **el hada** the fairy; **3** *('a' followed by 'el' becomes 'al')* **le llevaron al hospital** they took him to hospital; **4** *(sometimes 'el' is not translated)* **el caviar es muy caro** caviar is very dear; **éste es el señor Martínez** this is Mr Martínez; **el coche de Juan** Juan's car; **5** *(with parts of the body or personal belongings)* **se rompió el brazo** she broke her arm; **se afeitó el bigote** he shaved off his moustache; **me quité el abrigo** I took my coat off; **6** *(talking about dates and days of the week)* **el dos de mayo** the second of May; **iré el próximo lunes** I'll go next Monday; **el miércoles abren a las diez** they open at ten on Wednesdays; **7 me gustó el rojo** I liked the red one; **8 el mío es mejor** mine is better; **el suyo es más caro** his is more expensive; **9 el mío y el de usted** mine and yours; **éste es el de María** this one is María's; **me gusta más el de Toni** I like Toni's better; **10 el que** the one (that); **el que yo compré** the one I bought; **el que quieras** whichever you want.

él *pronoun* **1** he; **él no lo sabe** he doesn't know; **2** him; **estaba hablando con él** I was talking to him; **pregúntale a él** ask him; **iba detrás de él** I was behind him; **3 es de él** it's his; **4 él mismo** he himself.

elástico/elástica *adjective* elastic.

elección *noun Fem.* **1** choice; **no tener elección** to have no choice; **2 las elecciones** the election;

convocar elecciones to call an election.

electorado *noun Masc.* electorate.

electoral *adjective* **campaña electoral** election campaign.

electricidad *noun Fem.* electricity.

electricista *noun Masc./Fem.* electrician.

eléctrico/eléctrica *adjective* **1** electric; **2** electrical.

electrocutar *verb* [17] to electrocute.

electrodoméstico *noun Masc.* electrical appliance.

electrónico/electrónica *adjective* electronic.

elefante *noun Masc.* elephant.

elegante *adjective* **1** elegant; **2** smart; **siempre va muy elegante** he's always very smartly dressed.

elegir *verb* [48] to choose.

elemento *noun Masc.* element.

elepé *noun Masc.* LP.

elija, **elijo** *verb* SEE **elegir**.

eliminar *verb* [17] **1** to eliminate; **2** to remove.

eliminatorio/eliminatoria *adjective* qualifying (*round or match*).

ella *pronoun* **1** she; **ella no lo sabe** she doesn't know; **2** her; **estaba hablando con ella** I was talking to her; **pregúntale a ella** ask her; **yo iba detrás de ella** I was behind her; **3 es de ella** it's hers; **4 ella misma** she herself.

ellas *pronoun ('ellas' is the feminine plural form of the pronoun; it is used to refer to two or more females)* **1** they; **ellas no lo saben** they don't know; **2** them; **estaba hablando con ellas** I was talking to them; **pregúntales a ellas** ask them; **iba detrás de ellas** I was behind them; **3 es de ellas** it's theirs; **4 ellas mismas** they themselves.

ello *pronoun* **1** it; **se beneficiaron de ello** they benefited from it; **2** this; **para ello es necesario** ... for this, it is necessary ....

ellos *pronoun ('ellos' is the masculine plural form of the pronoun; it is used to refer to two or more males or a group of mixed sex)* **1** they; **ellos no lo saben** they don't know; **2** them; **estaba hablando con ellos** I was talking to them; **pregúntales a ellos** ask them; **iba detrás de ellos** I was behind them; **3 es de ellos** it's theirs; **4 ellos mismos** they themselves.

embajada *noun Fem.* embassy.

embajador/embajadora *noun Masc./Fem.* ambassador.

embalse *noun Masc.* reservoir.

embarazada *noun Fem.* pregnant woman.
embarazada *adjective* pregnant; **quedarse embarazada** to get pregnant; **estoy embarazada de tres meses** I'm three months pregnant.

embarazo *noun Masc.* **1** pregnancy; **2** embarrassment.

embarcación *noun Fem.* vessel (*boat*).

embarcadero *noun Masc.* wharf.

embarcar *verb* [31] **1** to board (*a plane*); **2** to embark (*on a boat*); **3** to load (*goods or luggage*).
embarcarse *reflexive verb* [31] **1** to board (*a plane*); **2** to embark (*on a boat*); **3 embarcarse en algo** to get involved in something.

emboscada *noun Fem.* ambush.

embotellamiento *noun Masc.* traffic jam.

embrague *noun Masc.* clutch.

embrujado/embrujada *adjective* **1** haunted; **2** bewitched.

emergencia *noun Fem.* emergency.

emigrar *verb* [17] to emigrate.

emisión *noun Fem.* emission.

emisora *noun Fem.* radio station.

emoción *noun Fem.* **1** emotion; **2** excitement; **¡qué emoción!** how exciting!; **un espectáculo lleno de emoción** a really exciting show.

emocionado/emocionada *adjective* **1** moved; **2** excited.

emocional *adjective* emotional.

emocionante *adjective* **1** moving; **2** exciting; **¡qué emocionante!** how exciting!

emoticón *noun Masc.* smiley, emoticon.

empacho *noun Masc.* (*informal*) **tener empacho** to have a stomach-ache (*from eating too much*); **se cogió un empacho de pasteles** he ate so many cakes he had a stomachache.

empalme noun Masc. junction (on railway).

empanada noun Fem. pie; **empanada de atún** tuna pie.

empapado/empapada adjective soaking wet; **venían empapados** they were soaking wet.

empaparse verb [17] to get soaking wet.

empastar verb [17] to fill (a tooth).

empaste noun Masc. filling (in a tooth).

empatar verb [17] to draw; **empataron a dos** they drew two all.

empate noun Masc. draw (in sports).

empecé verb SEE **empezar**.

empeorar verb [17] **1** to get worse; **la situación ha empeorado** things have got worse; **2** to make worse; **va a empeorar las cosas** it's going to make things worse.

emperador noun Masc. emperor.

emperatriz noun Fem. empress.

empezar verb [25] **1** to begin; **el colegio empieza el quince de septiembre** school begins on the fifteenth of September; **2** to start; **tendré que empezar otra vez** I'll have to start again; **empezó a llover** it started raining.

empiece, **empieza**, **empiezo**, **etc.** verb SEE **empezar**.

empinado/empinada adjective steep (a road or street).

empleado/empleada noun Masc./Fem. **1** employee; **2** clerk (in a bank or office); **3** shop assistant;

4 los empleados the staff (in a company); **todos los empleados se beneficiarán** all the staff will benefit.

emplear verb [17] **1** to employ; **2** to use; **emplearon materiales viejos** they used old materials.

empleo noun Masc. **1** employment; **2** job; **buscar empleo** to look for a job; **3 estar sin empleo** to be unemployed.

emprendedor/ emprendedora adjective enterprising.

empresa noun Fem. company.

empujar verb [17] to push.

en preposition **1** in; **ponlo en el cajón** put it in the drawer; **vivo en Londres** I live in London; **en español** in Spanish; **en invierno** in winter; **2** into; **entró en la casa** he went into the house; **3** on; **está en la mesa** it's on the table; **en el segundo piso** on the second floor; **4** at; **estaré en casa toda la tarde** I'll be at home all afternoon; **es muy buena en inglés** she's very good at English; **5** nunca he estado en **París** I've never been to Paris; **6** by; **ir en coche** to go by car.

enagua noun Fem. petticoat.

enaguas noun Fem. (plural) petticoat.

enamorado/enamorada adjective in love; **estar enamorado de alguien** to be in love with someone.

a

b

c

d

e

f

g

h

i

j

k

l

m

n

ñ

o

p

q

r

s

t

u

v

w

x

y

z

enamorarse *reflexive verb* [17] to fall in love; **enamorase de alguien** to fall in love with someone.

enano/enana *noun Masc./Fem.* dwarf.

encantado/encantada *adjective* **1** delighted; **están encantados con la casa** they're delighted with the house; **2** ¡**encantado de conocerte!** pleased to meet you!; **3** enchanted.

encantador/encantadora *noun Masc./Fem.* magician; **encantador de serpientes** snake-charmer.
encantador *adjective* **1** lovely (*thing*); **2** charming (*person*).

encantar *verb* [17] **me encantó el libro** I loved the book; **nos encantó el hotel** we loved the hotel; **le encantaría venir a verte** he'd love to come and see you.

encargado/encargada *noun Masc./Fem.* manager.
encargado *adjective* **encargado de algo** responsible for something; **la persona encargada del reparto** the person responsible for the delivery.

encendedor *noun Masc.* lighter.

encender *verb* [36] **1** to light; **2** to turn on.

encendido/encendida *adjective* **1** on; **2** alight.

encerado *noun Masc.* blackboard.

enchufar *verb* [17] **1** to plug in; **2** to turn on.

enchufe *noun Masc.* plug.

enciclopedia *noun Fem.* encyclopedia.

encienda, enciendo, etc. *verb* SEE **encender**.

encima *adverb* **1** on; **pon un plástico encima** put a piece of plastic on it; **ponlo ahí encima** put it on there; **el piso de encima** the flat above; **no llevaba el carnet de identidad encima** he didn't have his identity card on him; **2 encima de** on, on top of; **está encima de la cama** it's on the bed; **encima del armario** on top of the wardrobe; **llevaba una gabardina encima de la chaqueta** I was wearing a raincoat over my jacket; **el niño estaba sentado encima de su madre** the baby was sitting on his mother's lap; **3 el/la de encima** the top one; **4 por encima de** over; **5 encima de llegar tarde se queja** he arrives late and on top of that he complains; ¡**y encima no me lo devolvió!** and on top of that he didn't give it back to me!

encontrar *verb* [24] to find; **no he encontrado cerillas en ninguna parte** I couldn't find any matches anywhere.
encontrarse *reflexive verb* [24] **1** to meet; **me encontré con Carmen en la calle** I met Carmen in the street; **2** to find; **me encontré un billete de diez euros** I found a ten-euro note; **3** to be; **el pueblo se encuentra situado en la montaña** the village is situated in the mountains.

encuentra, encuentro, etc. *verb* SEE **encontrar**.

encuesta *noun Fem.* survey; **encuesta de opinión** opinion poll.

enemigo/enemiga *noun Masc./ Fem.* enemy.

energía *noun Fem.* energy.

enérgico/enérgica *adjective* energetic.

enero *noun Masc.* January.

enfadado/enfadada *adjective* **1** angry; **2** annoyed.

enfadar *verb* [17] **1** to make angry; **2** to annoy.
enfadarse *reflexive verb* [17] **1** to get angry; **se enfadó muchísimo** he got really angry; **2** to get annoyed; **se enfadó conmigo** he got annoyed with me; **3** to get cross; **mamá se va a enfadar** Mum's going to get cross.

énfasis *noun Masc.* emphasis.

enfermar *verb* [17] to get ill.

enfermedad *noun Fem.* illness.

enfermería *noun Fem.* **1** nursing; **2** infirmary.

enfermero/enfermera *noun Masc./Fem.* nurse.

enfermo/enferma *noun Masc./ Fem.* sick person; **los enfermos** sick people.
enfermo *adjective* ill; **está gravemente enferma** she's seriously ill; **caer enfermo** to fall ill.

enfrente *adverb* opposite; **la tienda está justo enfrente de la casa** the shop is just opposite the house.

engañar *verb* [17] **1** to deceive; **2** to cheat, swindle; **3** to be unfaithful to.
engañarse *reflexive verb* [17] to fool yourself.

engaño *noun Masc.* **1** deception; **2** swindle.

engordar *verb* [17] **1** to put on weight; **2** to be fattening.

enhorabuena *noun Fem.* **¡enhorabuena por tu trabajo nuevo!** congratulations on your new job!; **darle la enhorabuena a alguien** to congratulate someone.

enjuagar *verb* [28] to rinse.
enjuagarse *reflexive verb* [28] **enjuagarse el pelo** to rinse your hair.

enmohecerse *reflexive verb* [35] to go mouldy.

enojado/enojada *adjective* **1** angry; **2** annoyed.

enorme *adjective* huge.

enormemente *adverb* extremely, a lot; **enormemente preocupado** extremely worried.

enrollar *verb* [17] to roll up.

enroscar *verb* [31] **1** to wind; **2** to screw on.

ensaimada *noun Fem.* light round cake covered in icing sugar.

ensalada *noun Fem.* salad; **ensalada mixta** mixed salad; **ensalada de frutas** fruit salad.

ensaladera *noun Fem.* salad bowl.

ensaladilla, ensaladilla rusa *noun Fem.* potato salad.

ensanchar *verb* [17] to widen.

a
b
c
d
e
f
g
h
i
j
k
l
m
n
ñ
o
p
q
r
s
t
u
v
w
x
y
z

ensayo *noun Masc.* rehearsal;
ensayo general dress rehearsal.

enseguida *adverb* right away;
enseguida lo hago I'll do it right
away.

enseñanza *noun Fem.* **1** teaching;
me gusta la enseñanza I like
teaching; **2** education; **enseñanza
primaria** primary education;
enseñanza secundaria secondary
education; **enseñanza superior**
higher education.

enseñar *verb* [17] **1** to teach; **le
enseñé a montar en bicicleta** I
taught him to ride a bike; **2** to show;
nos enseñó la casa he showed us
the house.

ensuciar *verb* [17] to make dirty;
no ensucies la mesa don't make
the table dirty; **ensucié el mantel
de salsa de tomate** I got tomato
sauce on the tablecloth.

ensuciarse *reflexive verb* [17] to
get dirty; **te vas a ensuciar las
manos** you'll get your hands dirty;
**me he ensuciado las botas de
barro** I've got mud on my boots.

entender *verb* [36] **1** to
understand; **entiendo un poco de
español** I can understand a little bit
of Spanish; **entiendo lo que dices** I
understand what you are saying; **no
te entiendo** I can't understand you;
2 entender algo mal to
misunderstand something; **la
entendí mal** I misunderstood her;
3 dar a entender algo to imply
something; **4 entender de algo** to
know about something; **entiendo
un poco de fontanería** I know a bit

about plumbing.

entenderse *reflexive verb* [36]
1 entenderse con alguien to
communicate with someone; **nos
entendimos por señas** we
communicated with each other by
signs; **2 entenderse con alguien** to
get along with someone; **se
entiende muy bien con su
hermana** she gets along very well
with her sister.

entendido/entendida
adjective **1** understood; **queda bien
entendido** it's clearly understood;
¿entendido? is that clear?; **2 ser
entendido en algo** to know about
something.

entero/entera *adjective* **1** whole;
un día entero a whole day; **2 leche
entera** full-cream milk.

enterrar *verb* [29] to bury.

entienda, entiendo, etc. *verb*
SEE **entender**.

entonces *adverb* **1** then; **desde
entonces** since then; **entonces
llegó Carlos** then Carlos arrived;
2 so; **entonces nos vemos mañana**
so we'll see each other tomorrow.

entrada *noun Fem.* **1** entrance;
¿dónde está la entrada? where is
the entrance?; **2** ticket (*for the
cinema or theatre*); **ya he comprado
las entradas para el teatro** I've
already bought the tickets for the
theatre; **¿cuánto cuesta la
entrada?** how much is a ticket?; **los
niños pagan media entrada** it's
half-price for children; **3 'entrada
libre'** 'admission free'; **4** deposit;
pagué la entrada para el coche I

put down a deposit on the car;
5 tackle (*in football*).

entrar *verb* [17] **1** to get in; **no puedo entrar** I can't get in; **entraron por una ventana** they got in through a window; **2** to go in; **han entrado en esa tienda** they've gone into that shop; **entraron en la clase corriendo** they ran into the classroom; **3** to come in; **¡entra!** come in!; **4 dejar entrar a alguien** to let someone in; **5 hacer entrar a alguien** to show someone in; **6** to fit; **no entra por la puerta** it doesn't fit through the door; **7** to join; **entrar en la ONU** to join UN; **8 me entró hambre** I got hungry; **te va a entrar frío si te sientas ahí** you'll get cold if you sit there; **9** to be included; **el desayuno no entra en el precio** breakfast is not included in the price; **10 no me entra** (*informal*) I don't get it; **no le entran las matemáticas** (*informal*) he just can't get to grips with maths.

entre *preposition* **1** between; **estaba sentado entre Jaime y Margarita** I was sitting between Jaime and Margarita; **2** among; **lo encontré entre mis papeles** I found it among my papers; **3 lo hicimos entre todos** we did it all together; **4** by; **nueve dividido entre tres** nine divided by three; **5 entre paréntesis** in brackets; **6 cerrado entre semana** closed during the week.

entreabierto/entreabierta *adjective* half-open.

entreacto *noun Masc.* interval.

entrega *noun Fem.* **1** delivery (*of goods*); **2** presentation (*of a prize or award*); **3 la fecha límite para la entrega de formularios** the deadline for handing in the forms.

entregar *verb* [28] **1** to deliver; **vino a entregar una carta** he came to deliver a letter; **2** to give, to hand; **me entregó los documentos** he handed me the documents; **tenemos que entregar el trabajo el próximo lunes** we have to hand in the essay next Monday; **3** to present (*a prize or award*); **4** to surrender (*a town or weapons*); **5** to turn in (*a criminal*).
entregarse *reflexive verb* [28] to give yourself up; **se entregó a la policía** he gave himself up to the police.

entremés *noun Masc.* starter (*in a meal*).

entrenador/entrenadora *noun Masc./Fem.* trainer.

entrenamiento *noun Masc.* training.

entrenar *verb* [17] to train.
entrenarse *reflexive verb* [17] to train.

entretanto *adverb* in the meantime.

entretenido/entretenida *adjective* entertaining.

entrevista *noun Fem.* interview; **una entrevista de trabajo** a job interview.

entrevistar *verb* [17] to interview.

entumecido/entumecida *adjective* numb.

entusiasmar *verb* [17] **me entusiasmó la idea** I loved the idea; **le entusiasma el deporte** she's really keen on sports; **no me entusiasma viajar** I'm not very keen on travelling.
entusiasmarse *reflexive verb* [17] **entusiasmarse con algo/por algo** to get excited about something.

entusiasmo *noun Masc.* enthusiasm.

enviar *verb* [32] to send.

envidia *noun Fem.* **1** envy; **se muere de envidia** he's green with envy; **2** jealousy; **tenerle envidia a alguien** to be jealous of someone; **me tienen envidia** they're jealous of me; **le da envidia que yo tenga una bici mejor** she's jealous because I've got a better bike.

envidia *noun Fem.* envy; **tiene envidia de su hermana** she's envious of her sister.

envidiar *verb* [17] to be envious of; **me envidia el resultado de los exámenes** she's envious of my exam results.

envidioso/envidiosa *adjective* envious.

envolver *verb* [45] to wrap up.

envuelto¹/envuelta *adjective* **1** wrapped; **envuelto para regalo** gift-wrapped; **2** envuelto en algo involved in something.

envuelto² *verb* SEE **envolver**.

epidemia *noun Fem.* epidemic.

episodio *noun Masc.* episode.

época *noun Fem.* **1** age; **era otra época** it was a different age; **2** time;

en aquella época at that time; **3** times; **en la época de los romanos** in Roman times.

equilibrio *noun Masc.* balance; **estar en equilibrio** to be balanced; **perder el equilibrio** to lose your balance.

equipaje *noun Masc.* luggage; **equipaje de mano** hand luggage.

equipo *noun Masc.* **1** team; **formar un buen equipo** to make a good team; **el equipo visitante** the away team; **trabajo en equipo** team work; **2** equipment; **3** equipo de música sound system; **equipo de alta fidelidad** hi-fi system.

equis *noun Fem.* the Spanish name for the letter 'x'.

equitación *noun Fem.* horse riding.

equivaler *verb* [43] **equivaler a algo** to be equivalent to something.

equivocado/equivocada *adjective* wrong.

equivocarse *reflexive verb* [31] **1** to make a mistake; **creo que me he equivocado** I think I've made a mistake; **2** to be wrong; **te equivocas si piensas eso** you're wrong if you think like that; **3** me equivoqué de carpeta I picked up the wrong folder; **se equivocó de calle** he took the wrong street.

era, érais, eras, eres, etc. *verb* SEE **ser**.

error *noun Masc.* mistake; **cometer un error** to make a mistake; **un error tipográfico** a typing error; **un error de cálculo** a miscalculation.

eructar *verb* [17] to burp.

eructo *noun Masc.* burp.

es *verb* SEE **ser**.

esa¹ *adjective* that (*see 'ese*¹*/esa' for examples*).

esa², **ésa** *pronoun* that one (*see 'ese*²*/esa' for examples*).

esas¹ *adjective* those (*see 'esos*¹*/esas' for examples*).

esas², **ésas** *pronoun* those ones (*see 'esos*²*/esas' for examples*).

escala *noun Fem.* **1** stopover; **hacer escala en París** to stop over in Paris; **2** scale (*of a map or measurements*); **hacer algo a escala** to do something to scale; **a gran escala** on a large scale; **3** scale (*in music*).

escalada *noun Fem.* **1** (rock) climbing; **2** climb.

escalador/escaladora *noun Masc./Fem.* climber.

escalar *verb* [17] to climb.

escalera *noun Fem.* staircase; **subir las escaleras** to go up the stairs; **una escalera de caracol** a spiral staircase; **una escalera mecánica** an escalator; **una escalera de incendios** a fire escape; **una escalera de mano** a ladder.

escalofrío *noun Masc.* shiver; **tener escalofríos** to be shivering.

escalón *noun Masc.* step.

escalope *noun Masc.* escalope.

escándalo *noun Masc.* **1** scandal; **un escándalo político** a political scandal; **¡su comportamiento fue un escándalo!** his behaviour was really outrageous!; **2** racket; **armar un escándalo** to make a racket; **¡qué escándalo están armando!** what a racket they are making!.

escandaloso/escandalosa *adjective* **1** shocking (*behaviour or clothes*); **2** noisy (*people*).

Escandinavia *noun Fem.* Scandinavia.

escandinavo/escandinava *noun Masc./Fem.* Scandinavian; **los escandinavos** Scandinavians. **escandinavo** *adjective* Scandinavian.

escáner *noun Masc.* **1** scanner; **2** scan.

escapar *verb* [17] to escape; **escapar de algo** to escape from something.

escaparse *reflexive verb* [17] **1** to escape; **se ha escapado de la cárcel** he's escaped from prison; **2** to run away; **escaparse de casa** to run away from home; **3** to leak (*gas or water*).

escaparate *noun Masc.* shop window.

escarabajo *noun Masc.* beetle.

escarcha *noun Fem.* frost.

escasez *noun Fem.* shortage; **hay escasez de agua** there's a water shortage.

escena *noun Fem.* scene.

escenario *noun Masc.* stage.

esclavo/esclava *noun Masc./Fem.* slave.

esclusa *noun Fem.* lock (*on a canal*).

a
b
c
d
e
f
g
h
i
j
k
l
m
n
ñ
o
p
q
r
s
t
u
v
w
x
y
z

a **escoba** *noun Fem.* broom.

b **escocés/escocesa** *noun Masc./Fem.* Scot.

c **escocés/escocesa** *adjective* Scottish.

d **Escocia** *noun Fem.* Scotland.

e **escoger** *verb* [3] to choose.

f **escoja, escojo, etc.** *verb* SEE **escoger**.

g **escolar** *noun Masc./Fem.* schoolboy/schoolgirl.
escolar *adjective* school; **la vida escolar** school life.

h **esconder** *verb* [18] to hide.
esconderse *reflexive verb* [18] to hide; **esconderse de algo** to hide from something.

i

j

k **escondido/escondida** *adjective* hidden.

l **escorpión**¹, **escorpio** *noun Masc./Fem.* Scorpio; **soy escorpión** I'm Scorpio.

m

n **escorpión**² *noun Masc.* scorpion.

ñ **Escorpión, Escorpio** *noun Masc.* Scorpio.

o **escribir** *verb* [52] **1** to write; **escribir una novela** to write a novel; **le escribí una carta** I wrote a letter to him; **2 escribir a máquina** to type; **3** to spell; **¿cómo se escribe tu nombre?** how do you spell your name?

p

q

r

s

t

u **escrito** *verb* SEE **escribir**.

v **escritor/escritora** *noun Masc./Fem.* writer.

w **escritorio** *noun Masc.* desk.

x **escuchar** *verb* [17] **1** to listen; **escuchamos atentamente** we

y

z

listen carefully; **2** to listen to; **escucha bien lo que digo** listen carefully to what I say; **escúchame** listen to me.

escuela *noun Fem.* school; **escuela primaria** primary school; **escuela nocturna** night school.

escultor/escultora *noun Masc./Fem.* sculptor.

escultura *noun Fem.* sculpture.

escupir *verb* [19] **1** to spit; **escupir a alguien** to spit at someone; **2** to spit out; **escupió la comida** he spat out the food.

ese¹**/esa** *adjective* that; **ese libro** that book; **esa chica** that girl.

ese²**/esa, ése/ésa** *pronoun* that one; **ese es más bonito** that one is nicer; **esa es tu bolsa** that one is your bag.

esfuerzo *noun Masc.* effort; **hacer un esfuerzo** to make an effort.

esguince *noun Masc.* sprain.

eslogan *noun Masc.* slogan.

eslovaco/eslovaca *noun Masc./Fem., adjective* Slovak.

Eslovaquia *noun Fem.* Slovakia.

Eslovenia *noun Fem.* Slovenia.

esloveno/eslovena *noun Masc./Fem., adjective* Slovene.

eso *pronoun* that; **eso no importa** that doesn't matter; **por eso** that's why.

ESO *abbreviation Fem. (short for 'Educación Secundaria Obligatoria')* compulsory secondary education programme in Spain for the 12–16 age group.

esos¹/esas *adjective* those; **esos libros** those books; **esas chicas** those girls.

esos²/esas, ésos/ésas *pronoun* those ones; **esos son más bonitos** those ones are nicer.

espabilado/espabilada *adjective* alert.

espacio *noun Masc.* **1** space; **la conquista del espacio** the conquest of space; **dejar un espacio** leave a space; **2** room; **no tengo mucho espacio para ponerlo** I haven't got much room for it.

espaguetis *plural noun Masc.* spaghetti.

espalda *noun Fem.* back; **ser ancho de espaldas** to be broad-shouldered; **darle la espalda a alguien** to have your back to somebody, to turn your back on somebody; **nos daba la espalda** he had his back to us; **nadar de espaldas** to swim backstroke; **tumbarse de espaldas** to lie on your back.

España *noun Fem.* Spain.

español¹ *noun Masc.* Spanish (*the language*).

español²/española *noun Masc./Fem.* Spaniard; **los españoles** the Spanish.

español *adjective* Spanish.

espantapájaros *noun Masc.* scarecrow.

espantoso/espantosa *adjective* **1** horrific (*crime*); **2** horrible; **un vestido espantoso** a horrible dress; **tiene un gusto espantoso** he has a horrible sense

of taste; **3** hacía un frío espantoso it was terribly cold; **tengo un sueño espantoso** I'm terribly sleepy.

esparadrapo *noun Masc.* sticking plaster.

esparcimiento *noun Masc. Masc.* relaxation.

espárrago *noun Masc.* asparagus.

especia *noun Fem.* spice.

especial *adjective* special.

especialidad *noun Fem.* speciality.

espectáculo *noun Masc.* **1** sight; **era un espectáculo espantoso** it was a terrible sight; **2** show; **el mundo del espectáculo** show business.

espectador/espectadora *noun Masc./Fem.* spectator.

espejo *noun Masc.* mirror; **espejo retrovisor** rear-view mirror.

espera *noun Fem.* wait; **una corta espera** a short wait; **estar a la espera de algo** to be waiting for something.

esperanza *noun Fem.* hope; **darle esperanzas a alguien** to build up somebody's hopes; **hay pocas esperanzas de encontrarlos** there's little hope of finding them.

esperar *verb* [17] **1** to wait; **espera aquí** wait here; **2** to wait for; **te he estado esperando más de una hora** I've been waiting for you for more than an hour; **3** to hope; **espero que vengas** I hope you'll come; **espero que sí/eso espero** I hope so; **4** to expect; **no esperaba esa respuesta** I didn't expect that answer.

a b c d e f g h i j k l m n ñ o p q r s t u v w x y z

espeso/espesa *adjective* thick.

espesor *noun* Masc. thickness.

espesura *noun* Fem. thickness; **tiene diez centímetros de espesura** it's ten centimetres thick.

espía *noun* Masc./Fem. spy.

espiar *verb* [32] to spy on.

espina *noun* Fem. thorn.

espinaca *noun* Fem. spinach.

espionaje *noun* Masc. spying, espionage.

espléndido/espléndida *adjective* **1** splendid (*a party, day, or house*); **2** generous (*a person*).

espliego *noun* Masc. lavender.

esponja *noun* Fem. sponge.

esposa *noun* Fem. **1** wife; **la esposa de Juan** Juan's wife; **2 esposas** handcuffs.

esposo *noun* Masc. husband; **el esposo de mi hermana** my sister's husband.

espuma *noun* Fem. **1** foam; **espuma de afeitar** shaving foam; **2** lather (*of soap*); **3** froth (*of beer*); **4 espuma para el pelo** styling mousse.

espumoso/espumosa *adjective* **1** foaming; **2** frothy (*beer*); **3 vino espumoso** sparkling wine.

esqueleto *noun* Masc. skeleton; ★**estar hecho un esqueleto** to be all skin and bones.

esquí *noun* Masc. **1** ski; **2** skiing; **practicar el esquí** to go skiing; **esquí acuático** waterskiing; **esquí nórdico/esquí de fondo** cross-country skiing.

esquiador/esquiadora *noun* Masc./Fem. skier.

esquiar *verb* [32] to ski.

esquimal *noun* Masc./Fem., **esquimal** *adjective* Eskimo.

esquina *noun* Fem. corner; **doblar la esquina** to turn the corner; **vivo en la esquina de la calle León con la calle Viriato** I live on the corner of León Street and Viriato Street.

esta¹ *adjective* this (*see 'este/esta' for examples*).

esta², **ésta** *pronoun* this one (*see 'este³/esta' for examples*).

está *verb* SEE **estar**.

estación *noun* Fem. **1** station; **la estación de autobuses** the bus station; **una estación de servicio** a petrol station; **2** season; **el otoño es mi estación preferida** autumn is my favourite season; **la estación de las lluvias** the rainy season; **3 una estación de esquí** a ski resort.

estacionar *verb* [17] to park; **estacionar en doble fila** to double park.

estacionario/estacionaria *adjective* stationary.

estadio *noun* Masc. stadium; **el estadio de fútbol** the football stadium.

estado *noun* Masc. **1** state; **estado de guerra** state of war; **2 en buen estado** in good condition (*a picture, table, etc.*); **3 estado civil** marital status; **4 estar en estado** to be pregnant; **5 un estado de cuenta** a bank statement.

Estados Unidos *plural noun* Masc. United States.

estafa *noun Fem.* swindle; **¡qué estafa!** what rip-off!

estáis *verb* SEE **estar**.

estallar *verb* [17] **1** to explode (*a bomb*); **2** to burst (*a balloon*); **3** to blow out (*a tyre*).

estancia *noun Fem.* stay; **su estancia en Madrid durará tres días** his stay in Madrid will last three days.

estanco *noun Masc.* tobacconist's.

estanque *noun Masc.* pond.

estante *noun Masc.* shelf.

estantería *noun Fem.* **1** shelves; **2** bookcase.

estar *verb* [2] **1** (*location*) to be; **¿dónde está mi abrigo?** where's my coat?; **¿has estado en Buenos Aires?** have you been to Buenos Aires?; **estaré en Leeds un mes** I'll be in Leeds for a month; **2** (*state*) to be; **estoy contento** I'm happy; **está casado** he's married; **¿cómo estás?** how are you?; **desde que hablé con él está más simpático** he's nicer since I had a chat with him; **3** (*appearance, taste*) **esta paella está muy buena** this paella is very nice; **con ese vestido estás muy guapa** you look very nice in that dress; **4** (*with dates*) **estamos a tres de julio** it's the third of July today; **5 estar de** to be; **estar de viaje** to be away on a trip; **están de vacaciones** they're on holiday; **6** (*with a gerund or past participle*) to be; **están trabajando en Soria** they're working in Soria; **está**

nevando it's snowing; **estaban sentados allí** they were sitting over there; **aún no está terminado** it's not finished yet; **7** (*talking about how clothes fit*) **la chaqueta no me está bien** the jacket doesn't fit me; **esa falda te está corta** this skirt is too short for you; **me está grande** it's too big for me; **8 lo firmas y ya está** you sign it and that's that; **¿están ya las fotocopias?** are the photocopies ready?; **las patatas ya están** the potatoes are done.

estarse *reflexive verb* [2] **1** to be; **se estuvo sentado toda la tarde** he was sitting down all afternoon; **2** to stay; **se está horas mirando la tele** he stays in front of the TV for hours; **¡estate quieto!** keep still!

estatua *noun Fem.* statue.

estatus *noun Masc.* status.

este¹ *noun Masc.* east.

este²/esta *adjective* this; **este libro** this book; **esta chica** this girl.

este³/esta, **éste/ésta** *pronoun* this one; **este es más bonito** this one is nicer; **esta es tu bolsa** this one is your bag.

esté, **estén** *verb* SEE **estar**.

estera *noun Fem.* **1** rush matting; **2** rush mat; **3** beach mat.

estéreo *noun Masc.* stereo.

estés *verb* SEE **estar**.

esteticista *noun Masc./Fem.* beautician.

estilo *noun Masc.* **1** style; **2 ni nada por el estilo** or anything like that; **o algo por el estilo** or something of the kind.

a
b
c
d
e
f
g
h
i
j
k
l
m
n
ñ
o
p
q
r
s
t
u
v
w
x
y
z

a
b
c
d
e
f
g
h
i
j
k
l
m
n
ñ
o
p
q
r
s
t
u
v
w
x
y
z

estilográfica *noun Fem.* fountain pen.

estirar *verb* [17] to stretch.

esto *pronoun* this; **¿qué es esto?** what is this?; **esto es lo más importante** this is the most important thing.

estofado *noun Masc.* stew.

estómago *noun Masc.* stomach; **me duele el estómago** I've got stomachache.

Estonia *noun Fem.* Estonia.

estonio/estonia *noun Masc./ Fem., adjective* Estonian.

estornudar *verb* [17] to sneeze.

estornudo *noun Masc.* sneeze.

estoy *verb* SEE **estar.**

estrecho/estrecha *adjective* **1** narrow; **una calle estrecha** a narrow street; **2** tight; **me queda muy estrecho** it's too tight for me.

estrella *noun Fem.* star; **estrella fugaz** shooting star; **estrella de cine** film star.

estrellarse *reflexive verb* [17] to crash; **estrellarse contra algo** to crash into something.

estrenar *verb* [17] **1 la película se estrena el próximo lunes** the film comes out next Monday; **2 el domingo estrenaré los zapatos** I'll wear my new shoes on Sunday; **aún no he estrenado la bici** I haven't used the new bike yet.

estresado/estresada *adjective* stressed.

estricto/estricta *adjective* strict.

estropear *verb* [17] **1** to break; **vas a estropear la tele si sigues haciendo eso** you'll wreck the TV if you carry on doing that; **2** to spoil; **el tiempo nos estropeó las vacaciones** the weather spoiled our holidays; **3** to damage; **me estropeó el coche** he damaged my car; **4** to ruin (*a carpet or dress, for example*). **estropearse** *reflexive verb* [17] **1** to break down; **se ha estropeado el coche otra vez** the car's broken down again; **2** to go off (*fruit*); **3** to go bad (*milk or fish*); **4** to get ruined (*a carpet or dress, for example*).

estructura *noun Fem.* structure.

estuche *noun Masc.* case (*for glasses, pencils etc*).

estudiante *noun Masc./Fem.* student.

estudiar *verb* [17] **1** to study; **estudiar medicina** to study medicine; **2** to learn; **tenemos que estudiar dos tomas para mañana** we have to study two topics for tomorrow.

estudio *noun Masc.* **1** studio (*in a house*); **2** studio flat; **3** study; **el estudio de la naturaleza** the study of nature.

estudios *plural noun Masc.* studies; **estudios de medicina** medical studies; **estudios de mercado** market research.

estufa *noun Fem.* heater, fire.

estupendo/estupenda *adjective* great; **¿ganaste? ¡estupendo!** did you win? great!

estúpido/estúpida *noun Masc./Fem.* stupid person; **es un estúpido** he's really stupid.
estúpido *adjective* stupid.

estuve, **estuvo**, **etc.** *verb* SEE **estar**.

etapa *noun Fem.* stage; **por etapas** in stages.

etcétera *noun Masc.* etcetera.

eternidad *noun Fem.* eternity.

ética *noun Fem.* ethics.

etiqueta *noun Masc.* **1** label; **2** price tag.

euro *noun Masc.* euro; **el euro se divide en cien céntimos** the euro is divided into a hundred cents.

Europa *noun Fem.* Europe.

europeo/europea *noun Masc./Fem., adjective* European.

eurozona *noun Fem.* eurozone.

Euskadi *noun Fem.* the Basque Country.

euskera *noun Masc.* Basque (*the language*).
euskera *adjective* Basque.

evaluación *noun Fem.* assessment.

evaporarse *reflexive verb* [17] to evaporate.

evidencia *noun Fem.* evidence.

evidente *adjective* obvious.

evidentemente *adverb* obviously.

evitar *verb* [17] **1** to avoid; **evitan tomar la responsabilidad** they avoid taking responsibility; **2** to prevent; **evitar un accidente** to prevent an accident.

evolución *noun Fem.* evolution.

exactamente *adverb* exactly.

exacto/exacta *adjective* **1** exact; **2** accurate.

exagerar *verb* [17] to exaggerate.

examen *noun Masc.* exam; **hacer un examen** to take an exam; **presentarse a un examen** to sit an exam; **aprobar un examen** to pass an exam; **un examen oral** an oral exam.

examinar *verb* [17] to examine.
examinarse *reflexive verb* [17] to take an exam.

excelente *adjective* excellent.

excepción *noun Fem.* exception; **hacer una excepción** to make an exception; **a excepción de** with the exception of.

excepcional *adjective* exceptional.

excepcionalmente *adverb* exceptionally.

excepto *preposition* except for.

excursión *noun Fem.* trip; **ir de excursión al campo** to go on a trip to the countryside.

excusa *noun Fem.* excuse; **poner excusas** to make excuses.

exigente *adjective* demanding.

exigir *verb* [49] to demand.

a
b
c
d
e
f
g
h
i
j
k
l
m
n
ñ
o
p
q
r
s
t
u
v
w
x
y
z

existir *verb* [19] **1** to exist; **2 existen motivos para pensarlo** there are reasons to think that.

éxito *noun Masc.* success; **tener éxito** to be successful.

experiencia *noun Fem.* experience.

experimentado/ experimentada *adjective* experienced.

experimento *noun Masc.* experiment.

experto/experta *noun Masc./ Fem.* expert.

explicación *noun Fem.* explanation.

explicar *verb* [31] to explain.

explotar *verb* [17] explode.

exportación *noun Fem.* export; **la lana es la exportación más importante** wool is the most important export.

exportar *verb* [17] to export; **Rusia exporta mucha madera y petróleo** Russia exports a lot of oil and timber.

exposición *noun Fem.* exhibition.

expresar *verb* [17] to express.

expresión *noun Fem.* expression.

expreso¹ *noun Masc.* **1** express train; **2** espresso (*coffee*).

expreso²/expresa *adjective* express; **correo expreso** express mail.

exterior *noun Masc.* **1** exterior, outside; **el exterior de la casa** the outside of the house; **2** outward appearance; **en su exterior estaba tranquilo** his outward appearance was calm.

exterior *adjective* **1** outer (*layer*); **2** outside (*temperature*); **3 la parte exterior de la casa** the outside of the house; **4** foreign; **política exterior** foreign policy.

externo/externa *adjective* **1** outward (*appearance or signs*); **2** external.

extinción *noun Fem.* extinction; **una especie en en vías de extinción** an endangered species.

extincto *adjective* extinct.

extintor *noun Masc.* **extintor (de incendios)** fire extinguisher.

extrañar *verb* [17] **me extraña que no hayan llamado** I'm surprised they haven't phoned; **le extrañó verla allí** he was surprised to see her there.

extranjero¹ *noun Masc.* **vivir en el extranjero** to live abroad; **viaja mucho al extranjero** he travels abroad a lot.

extranjero²/extranjera *noun Masc./Fem.* foreigner. **extranjero** *adjective* foreign.

extraño/extraña *noun Masc./ Fem.* stranger. **extraño** *adjective* strange.

extraordinario/ extraordinaria *adjective* extraordinary.

extraterrestre *noun Masc./Fem.* alien (*from outer space*).

extremo¹ *noun Masc.* **1** extreme; **2** end.

extremo²/extrema *noun Masc./Fem.* winger (*in sports*).
extremo *adjective* extreme.

extrovertido/extrovertida *adjective* extrovert.

Ff

fábrica *noun Fem.* factory.

fabricar *verb* [31] to manufacture.

fácil *adjective* easy; **es un trabajo fácil** it's an easy job; **fácil de hacer** easy to do; **es fácil de entender** it's easy to understand.

facilidad *noun Fem.* **1** ease; **lo hice con facilidad** I did it with ease; **2 tener facilidad de palabra** to have a way with words.

fácilmente *adverb* easily.

factura *noun Fem.* **1** invoice; **2** bill.

facultad *noun Fem.* **1** faculty; **perder facultades** to lose your faculties; **2 ir a la facultad** to go to college; **la Facultad de Medicina** the Faculty of Medicine.

facultativo/facultativa *adjective* **1** optional; **2** medical.

faena *noun Fem.* task; **las faenas de la casa/domésticas** the housework.

faisán *noun Masc.* pheasant.

falda *noun Fem.* skirt; **una falda escocesa** a tartan skirt, a kilt; **una falda de tubo** a straight skirt.

falla *noun Fem.* flaw.

fallar *verb* [17] **1** to fail (*equipment or brakes, for example*); **2** to go wrong (*a plan*); **algo ha fallado** something's gone wrong; **3 me falló la puntería** I missed (*the target*).

fallo *noun Masc.* **1** fault; **el motor tiene un fallo** there's something wrong with the engine; **2** failure; **un fallo en el sistema** a failure in the system; **3 fallo humano** human error; **4** verdict (*in court or competition*).

falsificación *noun Fem.* forgery; **el cuadro es una falsificación** the picture is a forgery.

falso/falsa *adjective* **1** false; **2** fake (*a diamond or picture, for example*).

falta *noun Fem.* **1** lack; **falta de algo** lack of something; **por falta de dinero** due to lack of money; **falta de personal** staff shortage; **2 falta de educación** bad manners; **eso es una falta de educación** that's bad manners; **fue una falta de educación por su parte** it was really rude of him; **3** misdemeamour; **una falta grave** a serious misdemeanour; **4 falta de asistencia** absence (*from school*); **poner una falta a alguien** to mark someone absent; **ya tiene tres faltas** he's been absent three times already; **5 una falta de ortografía** a spelling mistake; **6** foul (*in sport*) **sacar la falta** to take the free kick; **7 hace falta lavarlo** it needs to be washed; **hace falta comprar pan** we need to buy bread; **no hace falta cambiarlo** it doesn't need to be

a
b
c
d
e
f
g
h
i
j
k
l
m
n
ñ
o
p
q
r
s
t
u
v
w
x
y
z

changed; **no hace falta que me esperes** you don't need to wait for me; **8 me hace falta un bolígrafo** I need a pen; **no me hace falta nada más, gracias** I don't need any more, thank you.

faltar *verb* [17] **1** to be missing; **¿quién falta?** who's missing?; **2 faltar al colegio** to be absent from school; **3 nos falta práctica** we need practice; **nos faltan mil euros para poder comprarlo** we need a thousand euros to buy it; **le falta interés** he lacks interest; **4 sólo faltan tres días** there are only three more days to go; **faltan diez días para mi cumpleaños** it's ten days to my birthday; **falta poco para el verano** it's almost summertime; **aún falta mucho para las doce** there's still a long way to go till twelve o'clock; **¿te falta mucho?** are you going to be long?; **no les falta mucho para terminar** they've almost finished; **nos faltó tiempo** we didn't have enough time.

fama *noun Fem.* **1** fame; **2** reputation; **tener buena fama** to have a good reputation; **tener fama de mentiroso** to have a reputation for being a liar.

familia *noun Fem.* family; **ser de familia numerosa** to be from a large family.

familiar *noun Masc./Fem.* relative. **familiar** *adjective* **1** family; **tuve problemas familiares** I had family problems; **2** familiar.

famoso/famosa *adjective* famous.

fantasía *noun Fem.* **1** fantasy; **un mundo de fantasía** a fantasy world; **2** imagination; **tener mucha fantasía** to have a lot of imagination; **3 joyas de fantasía** costume jewellery.

fantasma *noun Masc.* ghost.

fantástico/fantástica *adjective* fantastic.

farmacéutico/farmacéutica *noun Masc./Fem.* chemist, pharmacist.
farmacéutico *adjective* pharmaceutical.

farmacia *noun Fem.* chemist's, pharmacy; **farmacia de guardia/de turno** duty chemist.

farmacia *noun Fem.* chemist's; **farmacia de guardia/de turno** duty chemist.

faro *noun Masc.* **1** lighthouse; **2** headlamp.

farola *noun Fem.* **1** streetlight; **2** lamp post.

fascinar *verb* [17] to fascinate.

fastidiar *verb* [17] to annoy; **sólo lo hacen para fastidiar** they only do it to annoy; **¡deja de fastidiar!** stop being a pain!
fastidiarse *reflexive verb* [17] **¡que se fastidie!** he'll have to put up with it!; **¡te fastidias!** tough!

fastidio *noun Masc.* annoyance; **¡qué fastidio!** how annoying!

fatal *adjective* **1** (*informal*) awful; **sentirse fatal** to feel awful; **estar fatal** to be really ill, to be really badly done; **2** fatal (*an accident or illness*).

fatal *adverb* **canto fatal** I am hopeless at singing.

favor *noun Masc.* **1** favour; **hacerle un favor a alguien** to do someone a favour; **pedir un favor** to ask for a favour; **estar a favor de algo** to be in favour of something; **2 por favor** please.

favorito/favorita *adjective* favourite.

fax *noun Masc.* fax.

fe *noun Fem.* faith.

febrero *noun Masc.* February.

fecha *noun Fem.* date; **fecha de nacimiento** date of birth; **¿a qué fecha estamos hoy?** what's the date today?; **fecha de caducidad** expiry date (*for medicines*), use-by date (*for food*).

felicidad *noun Fem.* **1** happiness; **2 ¡felicidades!** happy birthday!, congratulations!.

felicitar *verb* [17] **felicitar a alguien** to wish someone happy birthday; to congratulate someone.

feliz *adjective* (*plural* **felices**) happy; **¡feliz Año Nuevo!** Happy New Year!; **¡feliz Navidad!** Merry Christmas!; **feliz cumpleaños** happy birthday; **felices Pascuas** Happy Easter.

felpudo *noun Masc.* doormat.

femenino ¹ *noun Masc.* feminine.

femenino ²**/femenina** *adjective* **1** woman's; **el equipo femenino** the women's team; **2** feminine (*style, manners, or noun*); **3** female; **el sexo femenino** the female sex.

fenomenal *adjective* (*informal*) great.
fenomenal *adverb* great; **pasarlo fenomenal** to have a great time.

feo/fea *adjective* ugly.

feria *noun Fem.* fair.

feroz *adjective* fierce.

ferretería *noun Fem.* ironmonger's.

ferrocarril *noun Masc.* railway.

ferry *noun Masc.* ferry.

festivo/festiva *adjective* **1** festive (*atmosphere*); **2 un día festivo** a public holiday.

fiable *adjective* reliable.

fiambre *noun Masc.* cold meats.

fiarse *reflexive verb* [32] **1 fiarse de** to believe; **no te fíes de los periódicos** don't believe what the newspapers say; **2 fiarse de alguien** to trust someone.

fibra *noun Fem.* fibre.

ficción *noun Fem.* fiction.

ficha *noun Fem.* **1** card; **2 ficha médica** medical card; **ficha policial** police records; **3** token (*for the telephone*); **4** counter (*in games*).

fideo *noun Masc.* noodle.

fiebre *noun Fem.* **1** temperature; **tener fiebre** to have a temperature; **le ha subido la fiebre** his temperature has gone up; **2** fever; **fiebre del heno** hay fever.

fiel *adjective* **1** faithful; **no le es fiel a su mujer** he's not faithful to his wife; **2** loyal; **3** accurate (*a translation or copy, for example*).

a
b
c
d
e
f
g
h
i
j
k
l
m
n
ñ
o
p
q
r
s
t
u
v
w
x
y
z

119

a
b
c
d
e
f
g
h
i
j
k
l
m
n
ñ
o
p
q
r
s
t
u
v
w
x
y
z

fiesta noun Fem. **1** party; **2** public holiday; **mañana es fiesta** tomorrow's a holiday.

figura noun Fem. figure.

figurar verb [17] to appear. **figurarse** reflexive verb [17] to imagine; **me figuro que sí** I imagine so.

fijar verb [17] to fix; **fijar una fecha** to fix a date. **fijarse** reflexive verb [17] **1 fijarse en algo** to look at something; **2** to notice; **se fija en todo** she notices everything.

fijo/fija adjective **1** fixed; **precios fijos** fixed prices; **está fijo a la pared** it's fixed to the wall; **2** permanent (a job); **3 ¿está la escalera bien fija?** is the ladder steady?

fila noun Fem. **1** line; **hacer fila** to form a line; **en fila india** in single line; **2** row (of seats in the theatre or cinema).

filete noun Masc. **1** steak; **2** fillet (of fish).

filmar verb [17] **1** to shoot (a film); **2** to film.

filosofía noun Fem. philosophy.

fin noun Masc. **1** end; **llegar al fin** to get to the end; **el fin de semana** the weekend; **a fin de mes** at the end of the month; **fin de año** New Year's Eve; **2 al fin/por fin** at last; **3 en fin, ya te llamaré** anyway, I'll give you a ring.

final noun Masc. **1** end; **el final de las vacaciones** the end of the holidays; **2** ending; **una película con final feliz** a film with a happy ending; **3 al final** at the end; **al final del libro** at the end of the book; **4 al final** in the end; **al final lo conseguí hacer** I managed to do it in the end. **final** noun Fem. final. **final** adjective final.

finca noun Fem. **1** plot of land; **2** farm.

finlandés¹ noun Masc. Finnish (the language).

finlandés²/**finlandesa** noun Masc./Fem. Finn. **finlandés/finlandesa** adjective Finnish.

Finlandia noun Fem. Finland.

fino¹ noun Masc. dry sherry.

fino²/**fina** adjective **1** fine (a line, for example); **2** thin (a layer or slice); **3** slender (waist or finger); **4** refined (a person); **5** subtle (sense of humour); **6 tener el oído muy fino** to have a very acute sense of hearing; **tener el olfato muy fino** to have a very acute sense of smell.

firma noun Fem. **1** signature; **2** company.

firmar verb [17] to sign.

firme adjective **1** steady (a ladder or chair, for example); **con pulso firme** with a steady hand; **2** firm; **3 estudiar de firme** to study hard.

física¹ noun Fem. physics.

físico¹ noun Masc. **1** physique; **2** appearance.

físico²/**física**² noun Masc./Fem. physicist. **físico** adjective physical.

fisioterapia *noun Fem.* physiotherapy.

fitness *noun Masc.* fitness training.

flaco/flaca *adjective* thin.

flamenco¹ *noun Masc.* flamenco.

flamenco²/flamenca *adjective* flamenco; **baile flamenco** flamenco dancing.

flan *noun Masc.* caramel custard.

flauta *noun Fem.* flute; **flauta dulce** recorder.

flecha *noun Fem.* arrow.

flequillo *noun Masc.* fringe.

flexible *adjective* flexible.

flojo/floja *adjective* **1** loose (*a knot or screw*); **2** slack (*rope*); **3** weak (*coffee or tea*); **4** poor (*piece of work*).

flor *noun Fem.* flower; **de flores** flower-patterned; **una falda de flores** a flower-patterned skirt; **estar en flor** to be in flower.

florero *noun Masc.* flowerpot.

florista *noun Masc./Fem.* florist.

floristería *noun Fem.* florist's.

flota *noun Fem.* fleet.

flotar *verb* [17] to float.

fluido¹/fluida *adj* fluid, freeflowing; **la circulación está fluida** the traffic is flowing freely.

fluido² *noun Masc.* fluid.

fluir *verb* [54] to flow.

flujo *noun Masc.* flow.

foca *noun Fem.* seal (*animal*).

foco *noun Masc.* **1** focus; **el foco de atención** the focus of attention; **2** spotlight.

folclórico/folclórica *adjective* folk; **musica folclórica** folk music.

folleto *noun Masc.* **1** leaflet; **2** brochure.

fondo *noun Masc.* **1** bottom; **el fondo del lago** the bottom of the lake; **al fondo del baúl** at the bottom of the trunk; **llegar al fondo de la cuestión** to get to the bottom of the matter; **sin fondo** bottomless; **2** back; **está al fondo de la sala** it's at the back of the room; **3** end; **al fondo del pasillo** at the end of the corridor; **4** kitty; **hacer un fondo común** to make a kitty; **5 fondos** funds (*money*); **6 estudiar algo a fondo** to study something in depth; **prepararse a fondo** to prepare thoroughly; **7 ruido de fondo** background noise; **música de fondo** background music.

fontanero/fontanera *noun Masc./Fem.* plumber.

footing *noun Masc.* jogging; **hacer footing** to go jogging.

forastero/forastera *noun Masc./Fem.* stranger.

forma *noun Fem.* **1** shape; **con la forma de una hoja** leaf-shaped; **tiene forma cuadrada** it's square; **2** way; **es mi forma de ser** it's the way I am; **3 en forma** fit; **mantenerse en forma** to keep fit; **4 de todas formas** anyway.

formación *noun Fem.* **1** education; **un chico con una buena formación** a well-educated boy; **2** training; **formación profesional** vocational training.

formal *adjective* **1** reliable (*person*); **2** formal (*dinner or invitation*); **3** firm (*offer*).

formar *verb* [17] **1** to form; **formar un grupo de música** to form a band; **2** to make up; **el equipo está formado por doce miembros** the team's made up of twelve members; **3** formar parejas to get into pairs (*in class or games*); **4** to educate (*a person*).

formarse *reflexive verb* [17] **1** to be educated; **2** to form; **formarse una opinión** to form an opinion; **se formó un atasco** a traffic jam formed.

formidable *adjective* formidable.

fórmula *noun Fem.* formula.

formulario *noun Masc.* form.

fortaleza *noun Fem.* fortress.

fortuna *noun Fem.* **1** fortune; **ganar una fortuna** to earn a fortune; **2 por fortuna** fortunately; **3 tener la buena fortuna de hacer** to have the good fortune of doing; **tuve la buena fortuna de conocerlos** I had the good fortune of meeting them; **4 probar fortuna** to try your luck.

forzar *verb* [26] **1** to force; **me forzaron a aceptar** they forced me to accept; **2 forzar la vista** to strain your eyes.

forzarse *reflexive verb* [26] **forzarse a hacer** to force yourself to do.

fosa *noun Fem.* pit; **las fosas nasales** the nostrils.

fósforo *noun Masc.* match (*that you strike*).

foto *noun Fem.* photo; **sacar/hacer una foto** to take a photo.

fotocopia *noun Fem.* photocopy.

fotocopiadora *noun Fem.* photocopier.

fotocopiar *verb* [17] to photocopy.

fotografía *noun Fem.* **1** photography; **2** photograph; **sacer una fotografía** to take a photograph.

fotógrafo/fotógrafa *noun Masc./Fem.* photographer.

fracasar *verb* [17] to fail.

fracaso *noun Masc.* failure.

fractura *noun Fem.* fracture.

frágil *adjective* fragile.

frambuesa *noun Fem.* raspberry; **mermelada de frambuesas** raspberry jam.

francés[1] *noun Masc.* French (*the language*).

francés[2]**/francesa** *noun Masc./Fem.* Frenchman/Frenchwoman. **francés/francesa** *adjective* French.

Francia *noun Fem.* France.

frasco *noun Masc.* **1** bottle; **2** jar; **un frasco de mermelada** a jar of jam.

frase *noun Fem.* **1** sentence; **2** phrase; **frase hecha** set phrase.

fraude *noun Masc.* fraud.

frecuencia *noun Fem.* frequency; **con frecuencia** often.

frecuente *adjective* frequent.

frecuentemente *adverb* often, frequently.

fregadero *noun Masc.* sink.

fregar *verb* [30] **1** to wash; **fregar los platos** to wash the dishes; **2 fregar el suelo** to mop the floor; **3** to scrub.

freír *verb* [53] to fry.

frenar *verb* [17] **1** to brake; **2** to slow down (*a process*); **3** to curb (*inflation*).

freno *noun Masc.* brake.

frente *noun Masc.* **1** front; **2 al frente de la manifestación** at the head of the demostration; **al frente de la patrulla** leading the patrol; **3 al frente del equipo** in charge of the team; **4 dar un paso al frente** to step forward; **5 hacer frente a** to face (*a problem or attacker*).
frente *noun Fem.* forehead.

fresa *noun Fem.* strawberry; **mermelada de fresas** strawberry jam.

fresco¹ *noun Masc.* **1** fresh air; **tomar el fresco** to get some fresh air; **estar al fresco** to be out in the fresh air; **2 hace fresco** it's chilly; **3** fresco (*painting*).

fresco²/fresca *adjective* **1** cool; **una bebida fresca** a cool drink; **una brisa fresca** a cool breeze; **2 hoy hace fresco** it's chilly today; **3** fresh; **pescado fresco** fresh fish; **4 pintura fresca** wet paint; **5 ¡qué fresco!** what a nerve!; **ser muy fresco** to have a nerve.

fría, frío, etc. *verb* SEE **freír.**

friega, friego, friegue, etc. *verb* SEE **fregar.**

frigorífico *noun Masc.* fridge.

frijol *noun Masc.* bean; **frijoles volteados** fried beans.

frío¹ *noun Masc.* cold; **hace frío** it's cold; **tengo frío** I'm cold; **un día frío** a cold day.

frío²/fría *adjective* cold.

frito/frita *adjective* **1** fried; **2 quedarse frito** (*informal*) to fall asleep.

frontera *noun* border *Fem.*; **cruzamos la frontera en Irún** we crossed the border at Irún.

frotar *verb* [17] to rub.
frotarse *reflexive verb* [17] to rub.

fruncir *verb* [66] **fruncir el ceño** to frown.

frustrante *adjective* frustrating.

frustrar *verb* [17] **1** to frustrate (*person*); **me frustra que ...** I find it frustrating that ...; **2** to thwart (*plans*).

fruta *noun Fem.* fruit.

frutería *noun Fem.* fruit shop.

frutero *noun Masc.* fruit bowl.

fruto *noun Masc.* fruit; **frutos secos** nuts and dried fruits.

fue *verb* SEE **ser, ir.**

fuego *noun Masc.* **1** fire; **encender el fuego** to light the fire; **prender fuego a algo** to set fire to something; **2 ¿tienes fuego?** have you got a light?; **3 a fuego lento** on a low heat.

fuegos artificiales *noun Masc.* (*plural*) fireworks.

fuente *noun Fem.* **1** spring; **2** fountain; **3** large dish; **una fuente**

a
b
c
d
e
f
g
h
i
j
k
l
m
n
ñ
o
p
q
r
s
t
u
v
w
x
y
z

a
b
c
d
e
f
g
h
i
j
k
l
m
n
ñ
o
p
q
r
s
t
u
v
w
x
y
z

de servir a serving dish; **una fuente de horno** an ovenproof dish.

fuera, **fuéramos**, **etc.** *verb* SEE **ser, ir**.

fuera *adverb* **1** out; **¡sal fuera!** go out!; **ahí fuera** out there; **salimos a cenar fuera** we went out for dinner; **2** outside; **están esperando fuera** they're waiting outside; **la parte de fuera de la maleta** the outside of the suitcase; **deja las cajas fuera** leave the boxes outside; **por fuera es plateado** it's silver on the outside; **3** away; **el jefe está fuera** the boss is away; **4** abroad; **están fuera del país** they're abroad; **5 fuera de peligro** out of danger; **fuera de lugar** out of place; **fuera de serie** exceptional; **6 fuera de juego** offside.

fueron *verb* SEE **ser, ir**.

fuerte *adjective* **1** strong; **ser fuerte** to be strong; **un olor fuerte** a strong smell; **2** loud; **no pongas la música tan fuerte** don't play the music so loud; **3** hard (*blow*); **4** big; **un beso fuerte** a big kiss; **5** substantial; **tomamos una comida fuerte al mediodía** we have a big meal at lunchtime; **6 un dolor fuerte** an intense pain.
fuerte *adverb* **1** hard; **pegar fuerte** hit it hard; **2** tight; **agárralo fuerte** hold it tight.

fuerza *noun Fem.* **1** strength; **tener fuerza** to be strong; **no tuvo fuerza para levantarlo** he wasn't strong enough to lift it; **2 hice fuerza y conseguí abrirlo** I used all my strength and I managed to open it;

3 empujar con fuerza to push hard; **4 por la fuerza** by force; **lo obligaron a entrar en el coche por la fuerza** they forced him to get into the car; **5 a fuerza de** by; **a fuerza de empujar** by pushing; **6** force; **fuerza aérea** air force; **fuerzas armadas** armed forces; **7 fuerza de voluntad** willpower.

fuga *noun Fem.* **1** leak; **una fuga de gas** a gas leak; **2 una fuga de prisioneros** a jailbreak; **3 darse a la fuga** to flee.

fui, **fuimos**, **fuiste**, **etc.** *verb* SEE **ser, ir**.

fumador/fumadora *noun Masc./ Fem.* smoker.

fumar *verb* [17] to smoke.

función *noun Fem.* **1** function; **2** performance; **función de noche** late-night performance; **función benéfica** charity performance.

funcionar *verb* [17] **1** to work; **¿cómo funciona?** how does it work?; **'no funciona'** 'out of order'; **2** to run; **funciona con electricidad** it runs on electricity.

funcionario/funcionaria *noun Masc./Fem.* government employee.

funda *noun Fem.* **1** cover (*for a cushion, pillow, etc.*); **2** sleeve (*of a record*); **3** pillow case.

fundamental *adjective* fundamental.

fundir *verb* [19] to melt.
fundirse *reflexive verb* [19] to melt.

funeral *noun Masc.* funeral.

funeraria *noun Fem.* funeral director's.

furgoneta *noun Fem.* van.

furia *noun Fem.* fury; **estar hecho una furia** (*informal*) to be furious.

furioso/furiosa *adjective* furious; **ponerse furioso** to get furious.

fusible *noun Masc.* fuse; **saltaron los fusibles** the fuses blew.

fusil *noun Masc.* rifle.

fusionar *verb* to merge.

futbito *noun Masc.* five-a-side football.

fútbol *noun Masc.* football; **jugar al fútbol** to play football.

futbolín *noun Masc.* **1** table football; **2 los futbolines** the amusement arcade.

futbolista *noun Masc./Fem.* footballer.

fútbol sala *noun Masc.* indoor-football.

futuro[1] *noun Masc.* future.

futuro[2]**/futura** *adjective* future.

Gg

gafas *plural noun Fem.* glasses; **gafas de sol** sunglasses; **llevar gafas** to wear glasses.

galápago *noun Masc.* **1** giant turtle; **2** terrapin.

galaxia *noun Fem.* galaxy.

galería *noun Fem.* **1** gallery; **galería de arte** art gallery; **2 galería comercial** shopping arcade.

galés[1] *noun Masc.* Welsh (*the language*).

galés[2]**/galesa** *noun Masc./Fem.* Welshman/Welshwoman. **galés/galesa** *adjective* Welsh.

Gales *noun Masc.* **el país de Gales** Wales.

gallego[1] *noun Masc.* Galician (*the language*).

gallego[2]**/gallega** *noun Masc./Fem.* Galician. **gallego** *adjective* Galician.

galleta *noun Fem.* biscuit.

gallina *noun Fem.* hen.

gallo *noun Masc.* cockerel.

galopar *verb* [17] to gallop.

gamba *noun Fem.* prawn.

gamberro/gamberra *noun Masc./Fem.* **1** rowdy; **2** hooligan. **gamberro** *adjective* **es muy gamberro** he's a real rowdy, he's a real hooligan.

gana *noun Fem.* **1 tener ganas de hacer algo** to feel like doing something; **no tengo ganas de ir al cine** I don't feel like going to the cinema; **2 tengo ganas de verlos** I'm looking forward to seeing them; **3** (*informal*) **no lo hace porque no le da la gana hacerlo** he doesn't do it because he doesn't want to; **voy porque me da la gana** I'm going because I feel like it; **hace siempre lo que le da la gana** she always does as she pleases; **4 hacer algo sin ganas** to do something halfheartedly; **hacer algo de buena gana** to do something willingly; **hacer algo de mala gana** to do something reluctantly.

ganador/ganadora noun Masc./Fem. winner.

ganador adjective winning (*number*).

ganancia noun Fem. profit.

ganar verb [17] **1** to win; **ganar una carrera** to win a race; **ganaron el primer premio** they won first prize; **2** to earn; **gano un buen sueldo** I earn a good salary.

ganarse reflexive verb [17] **1** to earn; **ganarse la vida** to earn your living; **se gana la vida pintando** he earns his living painting; **2** to win; **ganarse la confianza de alguien** to win someone's trust.

gancho noun Masc. hook.

ganga noun Fem. bargain.

ganso/gansa noun Masc./Fem. **1** goose; **2** (*informal*) **ser un ganso** to be a clown; **hacer el ganso** to clown around.

garaje noun Masc. garage.

garantía noun Fem. guarantee; **bajo garantía** under guarantee.

garantizar verb [22] to guarantee.

garbanzo noun Masc. chickpea.

garganta noun Fem. throat; **me duele la garganta** I have a sore throat.

gas noun Masc. **1** gas; **una cocina a gas** a gas cooker; **2** **gases tóxicos** toxic fumes.

gaseosa noun Fem. lemonade.

gasoil, gasóleo noun Masc. **1** heating oil; **2** diesel.

gasolina noun Fem. petrol; **voy a echar gasolina al coche** I'm going to put some petrol in the car; **gasolina sin plomo** unleaded petrol.

gasolinera noun Fem. petrol station.

gastar verb [17] **1** to spend; **gastan mucho en comida** they spend a lot of money on food; **2** to use; **mi coche gasta mucha gasolina** my car uses a lot of petrol; **me gastó todo el champú** she used up all my shampoo; **3** **¿qué número de pie gastas?** what shoe size do you take? **gastarse** reflexive verb [17] to run out; **se han gastado las pilas** the batteries have run out.

gasto noun Masc. expense; **tenemos muchos gastos** we have a lot of expenses; **gastos de desplazamiento** travel expenses; **gastos de envío** postage and packing.

gatear verb [17] to crawl.

gato/gata noun Masc./Fem. cat.

gaviota noun Fem. seagull.

gazpacho noun Masc. gazpacho (*a chilled soup made with tomatoes, cucumber, and other vegetables*).

gel noun Masc. gel.

gelatina noun Fem. jelly.

gemelo/gemela noun Masc./Fem., adjective twin.

gemelos plural noun Masc. binoculars.

a
b
c
d
e
f
g
h
i
j
k
l
m
n
ñ
o
p
q
r
s
t
u
v
w
x
y
z

géminis *noun Masc./Fem.* Gemini; **soy géminis** I'm Gemini.

Géminis *noun Masc.* Gemini.

gemir *verb* [57] to groan; **gemir de dolor** to groan with pain.

generación *noun Fem.* generation.

general *noun Masc./Fem.* general; **el general Serrano** General Serrano. **general** *adjective* general; **en general** in general; **por lo general** generally; **en líneas generales** broadly speaking.

generalmente *adverb* generally.

generoso/generosa *adjective* generous.

genética *noun Fem.* genetics.

genial *adjective* **1** brilliant; **una idea genial** a brilliant idea; **2** (*informal*) great, brilliant; **¡es genial!** it's great!

genio *noun Masc.* **1** genius; **Ana es un genio** Ana is a genius; **2** temper; **tener mal genio** to be bad-tempered; **¡vaya genio!** what a temper!

gente *noun Fem.* people; **vino mucha gente** a lot of people came; **la gente dice que** ... people say that ....

geografía *noun Fem.* geography.

geología *noun Fem.* geology.

geometría *noun Fem.* geometry.

gerente *noun Masc./Fem.* manager.

gestión *noun Fem.* **1** management; **la gestión de la empresa** the management of the company; **2 tengo que hacer una gestión en** el consulado I have to sort things out at the consulate.

gesto *noun Masc.* gesture; **me hizo un gesto para que me acercara** he gestured to me to come over; **hice un gesto de asentimiento** I nodded.

Gibraltar *noun Masc.* Gibraltar.

gigabyte *noun Masc.* gigabyte; **un disco duro de veinte gigabytes** a twenty gigabyte hard disk.

gigante/giganta *noun Masc./Fem.* giant.

gimnasia *noun Fem.* **1** gymnastics; **2** exercise; **es bueno hacer gimnasia** it's good to get exercise; **gimnasia de mantenimiento** keep-fit; **clase de gimnasia** PE class.

gimnasio *noun Masc.* gym.

gin tonic *noun Masc.* gin and tonic.

ginebra *noun Fem.* gin.

girar *verb* [17] **1** to turn; **gira a la derecha en el semáforo** turn right at the traffic lights; **girar la cabeza** to turn your head; **2** to go round; **la tierra gira alrededor del sol** the earth goes round the sun; **3** to spin; **4 girar un cheque** to draw a cheque; **5 girar dinero** to send money.

girasol *noun Masc.* sunflower.

gitano/gitana *noun Masc./Fem.* gypsy.

glaciar *noun Masc.* glacier.

globo *noun Masc.* **1** balloon; **2** lob (*in tennis*).

gloria *noun Fem.* glory.

glorieta *noun Fem.* **1** square (*in a town*); **2** roundabout (*on the road*).

a **glotón/glotona** *adjective* greedy.

b **gobernar** *verb* [17] **1** to rule; **2** to govern.

c **gobierno** *noun Masc.* government.

d **gol** *noun Masc.* goal; **marcar/meter un gol** to score a goal; **ganar/perder por tres goles a dos** to win/lose by three goals to two.

e

f

g **golf** *noun Masc.* golf; **jugar al golf** to play golf.

h **golfista** *noun Masc./Fem.* golfer.

i **golfo** *noun Masc.* **1** gulf (*in geography*); **2** scoundrel; **eres un golfo** you're a scoundrel; **3** little rascal (*to a child*).

j

k

l **golondrina** *noun Fem.* swallow.

golosina *noun Fem.* sweet; **no comas tantas golosinas** don't eat so many sweets.

m

n

ñ **golpe** *noun Masc.* **1** knock; **darse un golpe** to knock yourself; **se dió un golpe en la pierna** he knocked his leg; **2** blow; **fue un duro golpe** it was a hard blow; **3** **darle un golpe a alguien** to hit someone; **4** tap; **dar unos golpes en la mesa** to tap the table; **5** **la ventana se cerró de golpe** the window slammed shut; **cerré el baúl de golpe** I slammed the trunk shut.

o

p

q

r

s

t

u **golpear** *verb* [17] **1** to hit; **le golpeé el brazo con una revista** I hit him on the arm with a magazine; **2** bang; **la ventana golpeaba por el viento** the window was banging in the wind; **3** to beat; **golpear un tambor** to beat a drum; **4** to tap. **golpearse** *reflexive verb* [17] to bang; **se golpeó el brazo con la**

v

w

x

y

z

mesa he banged his arm on the table.

goma *noun Fem.* **1** rubber; **botas de goma** rubber boots; **goma espuma** foam rubber; **2** **una goma (de borrar)** a rubber; **3** **una goma (elástica)** a rubber band.

gorda¹ *noun Fem.* fat woman.

gordo¹ *noun Masc.* **1** fat man; **2** jackpot (*in the state lottery*).

gordo²**/gorda**² *adjective* **1** fat; **ponerse gordo** to get fat; **2** thick (*book or jumper*); **3** serious (*problem or mistake*); ★ **me cae gordo** (*informal*) I can't stand him.

gorila *noun Masc.* gorilla.

gorra *noun Fem.* cap.

gorro *noun Masc.* cap.

gota *noun Fem.* drop.

gotear *verb* [17] **1** to drip; **2** **una gota de** (*informal*) a drop of; **tomaré una gota de café** I'll have a drop of coffee; **no tiene ni una gota de paciencia** he hasn't got the slightest bit of patience.

gozar *verb* [22] to enjoy; **gozo mucho oyendo música** I enjoy listening to music a lot; **todos gozamos del espectáculo** we all enjoyed the show.

grabación *noun Fem.* recording.

grabador *noun Masc.* tape recorder.

grabadora *noun Fem.* tape recorder.

grabar *verb* [17] to record.

gracia *noun Fem.* **1** joke; **hacer una gracia** to make a joke; **2** **tener gracia** to be funny; **esa broma no**

tiene gracia that joke isn't funny; **tiene mucha gracia contando cosas** she's very good at telling funny stories; **3 me hace gracia verlo** seeing it makes me laugh; **4 no me hace ninguna gracia ir** I don't like the idea of going at all.

gracias *plural noun Fem.* thank you; **muchas gracias** thank you very much; **darle las gracias a alguien** to thank someone; **gracias a ellos** thanks to them.

gracioso/graciosa *adjective* funny.

grado *noun Masc.* degree; **veinte grados centígrados** twenty degrees centigrade; **cinco grados bajo cero** five degrees below zero.

gradual *adjective* gradual.

graduarse *reflexive verb* [20] to graduate.

gráfico *noun Masc.* graph; **gráficos** graphics (*in computing*).

gramática *noun Fem.* grammar.

gramo *noun Masc.* gram.

gran *adjective* SEE **grande**.

Gran Bretaña *noun Fem.* Great Britain.

grande, **gran** *adjective* ('*grande*' *becomes* '*gran*' *before a singular noun*) **1** big; **tienen una casa muy grande** they have a very big house; **la chaqueta me queda grande** the jacket's too big for me; **un gran número de personas** a great number of people; **2** great; **soy un gran admirador suyo** I'm a great admirer of hers; **es un gran actor** he's a great actor; **una gran**

oportunidad a great opportunity; **3** grown-up; **cuando sea grande** when I grow up; **ya eres muy grande para hacer eso** you're too grown-up to do that; **4 grandes almacenes** department store.

granizado *noun Masc.* crushed ice drink; **granizado de limón** iced lemon drink.

granizar *verb* [22] to hail.

granizo *noun Masc.* hail.

granja *noun Fem.* farm.

granjero/granjera *noun Masc./ Fem.* farmer; **es granjero** he's a farmer.

grano *noun Masc.* **1** grain; **un grano de arena** a grain of sand; **2** (coffee) bean; **3** spot, pimple; **me ha salido un grano** I've got a spot.

grapa *noun Fem.* staple.

grapadora *noun Fem.* stapler.

grapar *verb* [17] to staple.

grasa *noun Fem.* **1** fat; **el contenido de grasa** the fat content; **2** grease; **el horno estaba llena de grasa** the oven was covered in grease.

grasiento/grasienta *adjective* greasy.

gratis *adjective* free; **entrada gratis** free entry.
gratis *adverb* free; **los niños viajan gratis** children travel free.

gratuito/gratuita *adjective* free; **entrada gratuita** free entry.

grava *noun Fem.* gravel.

grave *adjective* serious; **está muy grave** he's seriously ill.

129

a
b
c
d
e
f
g
h
i
j
k
l
m
n
ñ
o
p
q
r
s
t
u
v
w
x
y
z

a
b
c
d
e
f

g

h
i
j
k
l
m
n
ñ
o
p
q
r
s
t
u
v
w
x
y
z

gravedad *noun Fem.* **1** gravity (*in physics*); **2** seriousness (*of problem*).

Grecia *noun Fem.* Greece.

griego[1] *noun Masc.* Greek (*the language*).

griego[2]/**griega** *noun Masc./Fem., adjective* Greek.

grifo *noun Masc.* tap; **abrir el grifo** to turn the tap on; **cerrar el grifo** to turn the tap off.

grillo *noun Masc.* cricket.

gripe *noun Fem.* flu; **tener (la) gripe/estar con gripe** to have flu.

gris *noun Masc., adjective* grey.

gritar *verb* [17] to shout; **gritar de alegría** to shout for joy; **gritar de dolor** to scream with pain.

grito *noun Masc.* **1** shout; **dar un grito** to shout; **2** cry; **un grito de protesta** a cry of protest; **3 un grito de dolor** a cry of pain; **un grito de horror** a scream of horror.

grosella *noun Fem.* redcurrant.

grosería *noun Fem.* **no digas groserías** don't be so rude; **¡qué grosería!** how rude!

grosero/grosera *adjective* rude.

grúa *noun Fem.* crane.

grueso/gruesa *adjective* **1** thick; **2** fat (*person*).

gruñón/gruñona *adjective* grumpy.

grupo *noun Masc.* group; **salir en grupo** to go out in a group; **un grupo musical** a group (*playing music*).

guante *noun Masc.* glove.

guapo/guapa *adjective* good-looking.

guarda *noun Masc./Fem.* **1** guard; **2** keeper (*in museum*).

guardabarros *noun Masc.* mudguard.

guardaespaldas *noun Masc./Fem.* bodyguard.

guardar *verb* [17] **1** to keep; **guardo todas sus cartas** I keep all his letters; **2** to put away; **guarda tus juguetes** put your toys away; **3 guardar cama** to stay in bed.

guardería infantil *noun Fem.* nursery.

guardia[1] *noun Masc./Fem.* **1** policeman/policewoman; **2 la Guardia Civil** the Civil Guard; **3 guardia jurado** security guard; **4 guardia urbano** police officer (*in local force*).

guardián/guardiana *noun Masc./Fem.* **1** guard; **2** guardian.

guarnición *noun Fem.* **1** side dish; **2** topping.

guarro/guarra *adjective* (*informal*) **1** filthy; **2** disgusting (*a person*).
guarro/guarra *noun Masc./Fem.* (*informal*) filthy pig.

guatemalteco/guatemalteca *noun Masc./Fem., adjective* Guatemalan.

guau *exclamation* wow!

guay *adjective* (*informal*) fantastic, cool; **¡qué música más guay!** what cool music!
guay *adverb* **lo pasé guay** I had a fantastic time.

guerra *noun Fem.* war.

guerrilla *noun Fem.* guerrilla unit.

guerrillero/guerrillera *noun Masc./Fem.* guerrilla, guerrilla fighter.

guía *noun Fem.* **1** guide; **guía de restaurantes** restaurant guide; **2** map (*of a city or town*); **3 guía telefónica** telephone directory. **guía** *noun Masc./Fem.* guide (*person*); **es guía turístico** he's a tourist guide.

guiar *verb* [32] to guide. **guiarse** *reflexive verb* [32] **guiarse por un mapa** to follow a map.

guijarro *noun Masc.* pebble.

guiñar *verb* [17] to wink.

guiño *noun Masc.* wink.

guión *noun Masc.* **1** dash; **2** hyphen; **una palabra con guión** a hyphenated word; **3** script (*of a film*).

guisante *noun Masc.* pea.

guisar *verb* [17] to cook; **guisa muy bien** he's a very good cook.

guitarra¹ *noun Fem.* guitar; **guitarra española** Spanish guitar.

guitarra² *noun Masc./Fem.* guitarist.

guitarrista *noun Masc./Fem.* guitarist.

gusano *noun Masc.* worm.

gustar *verb* [17] **me gusta mucho** I like it a lot; **me gustan los animales** I like animals; **no le gustó el libro** he didn't like the book; **a mi padre le gustan las fresas** my dad likes strawberries; **el que más me gusta** the one I like the best; **les gusta mirar la tele** they like watching telly; **¡así me gusta!** that's what I like to hear/see!

gusto *noun Masc.* **1** taste; **tiene gusto a menta** it tastes of mint; **tiene buen gusto** it tastes nice; **tengo mal gusto en la boca** I have a nasty taste in my mouth; **2 tiene muy buen gusto** she has very good taste; **3 mucho gusto en conocerle** pleased to meet you.

Hh

ha *verb* SEE **haber**.

haba *noun Fem.* **1** bean; **2** broad bean.

habéis *verb* SEE **haber**.

haber *verb* [6] **1** (*used with another verb in the same way as 'have' in English to form past tenses*); **he escrito a mi hermano** I have written to my brother; **él no lo ha cogido** he hasn't taken it; **aún no había comido** I hadn't eaten yet; **después de haberlo pensado bien** after having thought about it properly; **2** there is; **aquí no hay suficiente** there's not enough here; **había un paquete en recepción** there was a parcel in reception; **3** there are; **hay varios errores** there are various mistakes; **había más de treinta personas en la sala** there were more than thirty people in the room; **4 ¿qué hay que hacer?** what needs to be done?; **hay que limpiar la cocina** the kitchen

a
b
c
d
e
f
g
h
i
j
k
l
m
n
ñ
o
p
q
r
s
t
u
v
w
x
y
z

needs to be cleaned; **hay que sacar dinero** we need to take some money out; **ahora hay que pintarlo** it needs painting now; **5 hola, ¿qué hay?** hi, how are things?; **6 'muchas gracias' – 'no hay de qué'** 'thank you very much' – 'don't mention it'.

hábil *adjective* **1** skilful; **un jugador hábil** a skilful player; **2** clever; **es muy hábil para conseguir lo que quiere** he's very clever when it comes to getting what he wants.

habilidad *noun Fem.* skill.

habitación *noun Fem.* room; **una habitación sencilla/individual** a single room; **una habitación doble** a double room.

habitante *noun Masc./Fem.* inhabitant.

habla *noun Fem.* **1** speech; **se quedó sin habla** he was speechless; **2 un país de habla hispana** a Spanish-speaking country; **3 al habla** speaking (*on the phone*); **'¿el Señor López?' – 'al habla'** 'Mr López?' – 'speaking'.

hablador/habladora *noun Masc./Fem.* **1** chatterbox; **2** gossip. **hablador** *adjective* **1** talkative; **2** gossipy.

hablar *verb* [17] **1** to speak; **sabe hablar inglés** he speaks English; **¿hablas algún idioma?** do you speak any foreign languages?; **2** to talk; **no habla mucho** she doesn't talk very much; **hablar de** to talk about; **siempre habla mucho de ti** she's always talking about you; **me**

habló de sus proyectos he talked to me about his plans.

habrán, habré, etc. *verb* SEE **haber**.

hacer *verb* [7] **1** to make; **hacer un pastel** to make a cake; **hacer la cama** to make the bed; **2** to do; **no sé qué hacer** I don't know what to do; **hacer los deberes** to do your homework; **¿qué haces?** what are you doing?; **estoy haciendo derecho** I'm doing law; **3 hacer la comida** to cook lunch; **hacer la cena** to cook dinner; **4** to build (*a house or road, for example*); **5 hacer una visita** to pay a visit; **6 hacer un regalo a alguien** to give somebody a present; **7 hace (el papel) de Otelo** he plays Othello; **8** (*talking about the weather*) **hace frío** it's cold; **hacía mucho viento** it was very windy; **este verano ha hecho muy mal tiempo** the weather's been very bad this summer; **9** (*talking about time*) **hace tres días** three days ago; **hace tres días que se fueron** they left three days ago; **eso pasó hace mucho tiempo** that happened a long time ago; **¿cuánto tiempo hace que vives aquí?** how long have you been living here?; **hacía dos meses que no iba a verlos** I hadn't been to see them for two months; **trabaja aquí desde hace tres meses** she's been working here for three months now; **10 hacer a alguien hacer algo** to make someone do something; **le hice repetirlo** I made him do it again; **eso me hizo pensar** that made me think.

hacerse *reflexive verb* [7] **1** to become; **hacerse famoso** to become famous; **se hicieron amigos** they became friends; **2 se están haciendo viejos** they're getting old; **3 hacerse daño** to hurt yourself; **me he hecho un corte en el dedo** I've cut my finger; **4 me he hecho un vestido** I've made myself a dress; **se ha hecho una mesa para la cocina** she's made a table for her kitchen; **5 ¿cómo se hace?** how do you do it?

hacha *noun Fem.* axe (*even though 'hacha' is feminine, it takes 'el' or 'un' in the singular*).

hacia *preposition* **1** towards; **vinieron hacia mí** they came towards me; **hacia el norte** northwards; **muévelo hacia abajo** move it down; **2** (*with time*) about; **llamaré hacia las dos de la tarde** I'll call at about two o'clock; **te pagaré hacia final de mes** I'll pay you towards the end of the month.

hacienda *noun Fem.* estate, ranch.

hada *noun Fem.* fairy (*even though 'hada' is feminine, it takes 'el' or 'un' in the singular*).

haga, hago, etc. *verb* SEE **hacer**.

Haití *noun Masc.* Haiti.

haitiano/haitiana *noun Masc., Fem., adjective* Haitian.

halagar *verb* [28] to flatter.

halcón *noun Masc.* falcon.

hallar *verb* [17] to find; **no pudieron hallar una solución** they couldn't find a solution.
hallarse *reflexive verb* [17] **1** to be;

el pueblo se halla (situado) cerca del mar the village is (situated) near the sea; **2** to feel; **me hallaba tranquilo** I was feeling calm.

hamaca *noun Fem.* hammock.

hambre *noun Fem.* hunger (*even though 'hambre' is feminine, it takes 'el' or 'un'*); **tener hambre** to be hungry; **me muero de hambre** (*informal*) I'm starving; **el aire del mar me da hambre** the sea air makes me feel hungry.

hamburguesa *noun Fem.* hamburger.

hamburguesería *noun Fem.* hamburger bar.

hámster *noun Masc.* hamster.

han *verb* SEE **haber**.

harán, haré, etc. *verb* SEE **hacer**.

harina *noun Fem.* flour; **harina integral** wholemeal flour.

hartarse *reflexive verb* [17] to get fed up; **me estoy hartando de este color** I'm getting fed up with this colour; **se hartó de esperar** he got fed up of waiting.

harto/harta *adjective* **estar harto de** to be fed up of/with; **están hartos de comer siempre lo mismo** they're fed up of always eating the same thing; **estoy harta de tus excusas** I'm fed up with your excuses.

has *verb* SEE **haber**.

hasta *preposition* **1** until; **me quedaré hasta la semana que viene** I'll stay until next week; **hasta que** until; **no lo mandes hasta que yo lo diga** don't send it

until I tell you; **2 ¡hasta mañana!**
see you tomorrow!; **¡hasta luego!**
see you later!; **¡hasta pronto!** see
you soon!; **3** up to; **hasta ahora** up
to now; **hasta hace tres meses** up
to three months ago; **4 la falda me
llega hasta los tobillos** the skirt
goes down to my ankles; **5** as far as;
llegamos hasta Bilbao we went as
far as Bilbao.

hay *verb* SEE **haber**.

haz *verb* SEE **hacer**.

he *verb* SEE **haber**.

hechizo *noun Masc.* spell.

hecho¹ *noun Masc.* **1** fact; **el hecho
es que ...** the fact is ...; **¿cuáles son
los hechos?** what are the facts?;
**2 tenemos que pasar de las
palabras a los hechos** we must
stop talking and do something; **3 de
hecho** in fact.

hecho²/**hecha** *adjective* **1** made;
hecho a mano hand-made; **un
trabajo bien hecho** a job well done;
2 ¡bien hecho! well done!

helada¹ *noun Fem.* frost.

heladería *noun Fem.* ice-cream
parlour.

heladero/**heladera** *noun Masc./
Fem.* ice cream seller.

helado¹ *noun Masc.* ice cream; **un
helado de fresa** a strawberry ice
cream.

helado²/**helada**² *adjective*
1 frozen; **el río estaba helado** the
river was frozen; **la pobre chica
estaba helada** the poor girl was
frozen; **2** freezing; **tienes las
manos heladas** your hands are

freezing; **estoy helado** I'm freezing;
la casa está helada the house is
freezing.

helar *verb* [29] **esta noche va a
helar** there's going to be a frost
tonight.
helarse *reflexive verb* [29] to
freeze; **el río se ha helado** the river
has frozen over.

hélice *noun Fem.* propeller.

helicóptero *noun Masc.*
helicopter.

hemos *verb* SEE **haber**.

heno *noun Masc.* hay; **fiebre del
heno** hay fever.

heredar *verb* [17] **1** to inherit;
2 heredar el trono to succeed to the
throne.

heredero/**heredera** *noun Masc./
Fem.* heir.

herida¹ *noun Fem.* injury.

herido/**herida**² *adjective*
1 injured; **estar seriamente herido**
to be seriously injured; **2** wounded;
resultó herido en la pelea he was
wounded in the fight.

herir *verb* [14] **1** to wound; **2** to hurt;
hirieron mis sentimientos they
hurt my feelings.

hermana *noun Fem.* sister;
hermana gemela twin sister;
hermana política sister-in-law.

hermanastro/**hermanastra**
noun Masc./Fem. **1** stepbrother/
stepsister; **2** half-brother/half-
sister.

hermano *noun Masc.* **1** brother;
hermano gemelo twin brother;

hermano político brother-in-law;
2 hermanos brothers, brothers and
sisters; **¿tienes hermanos?** do you
have any brothers and sisters?

hermoso/hermosa *adjective*
beautiful.

héroe *noun Masc.* hero.

heroína *noun Fem.* **1** heroine;
2 heroin.

herramienta *noun Fem.* tool.

hervir *verb* [14] to boil; **hervir unas
patatas** to boil some potatoes.

hice *verb* SEE **hacer.**

hidratante *adjective*
moisturizing.

hiedra *noun Fem.* ivy.

hielo *noun Masc.* ice; **cubito de hielo**
ice cube.

hierba *noun Fem.* **1** grass; **'no pisar
la hierba'** 'do not walk on the grass';
2 herb; **hierbas de cocina**
(cooking) herbs; **3 una hierba mala**
a weed.

hierro *noun Masc.* iron.

hígado *noun Masc.* liver.

higiénico/higiénica *adjective*
hygienic.

higo *noun Masc.* fig.

hija *noun Fem.* daughter; **hija
política** daughter-in-law.

hijo *noun Masc.* **1** son; **su hijo se
llama Carlos** his son is called
Carlos; **hijo político** son-in-law;
2 hijos children; **tienen tres hijos**
they've got three children.

hilo *noun Masc.* thread.

himno *noun Masc.* hymn.

hincha *noun Masc./Fem.* supporter;
es hincha del Sevilla he's a Seville
supporter.

hinchado/hinchada *adjective*
swollen.

hinchar *verb* [17] **1** to blow up (*a
balloon*); **2** to pump up (*a tyre*).
hincharse *reflexive verb* [17] to
swell up; **se me ha hinchado el
tobillo** my ankle has swollen up.

hinchazón *noun Fem.* swelling.

hipermercado *noun Masc.*
hypermarket.

hipnotizar *verb* [25] hypnotize.

hipo *noun Masc.* hiccups; **tener hipo**
to have hiccups.

hipoteca *noun Fem.* mortgage.

hispano/hispana *noun Masc./
Fem.* Hispanic.
hispano *adjective* **1** Hispanic,
Spanish; **países de habla hispana**
Spanish-speaking countries;
2 Spanish American.

Hispanoamérica *noun Fem.*
Spanish America.

**hispanoamericano/
hispanoamericana** *noun
Masc./Fem., adjective* Spanish
American.

hispanohablante *noun Masc./
Fem.* Spanish-speaker.
hispanohablante *adjective*
Spanish-speaking.

historia *noun Fem.* **1** history; **la
historia de Chile** the history of
Chile; **2** story; **una historia de
miedo** a horror story.

a
b
c
d
e
f
g
h
i
j
k
l
m
n
ñ
o
p
q
r
s
t
u
v
w
x
y
z

histórico/histórica *adjective*
1 historical; **2** historic.

historieta *noun Fem.* cartoon.

hizo *verb* SEE **hacer**.

hogar *noun Masc.* home; **éste es mi hogar** this is my home; **labores del hogar** housework.

hoguera *noun Fem.* bonfire.

hoja *noun Fem.* **1** leaf (*of a tree or plant*); **2** sheet (*of paper or metal*); **3** page (*of a book*).

hola *exclamation* hello.

Holanda *noun Fem.* Holland.

holandés[1] *noun Masc.* Dutch (*the language*).

holandés[2]**/holandesa** *noun Masc./Fem.* Dutchman/Dutchwoman. **holandés/holandesa** *adjective* Dutch.

holgado/holgada *adjective* loose-fitting.

hombre *noun Masc.* **1** man; **un hombre de negocios** a businessman; **el hombre del tiempo** the weatherman; **un hombre rana** a frogman; **el hombre moderno es más alto que sus antepasados** modern man is taller than his ancestors; **2 ¡hombre! ¡tú por aquí!** hey! look who's here!; **¡no, hombre!** of course not!

hombro *noun Masc.* shoulder.

homenaje *noun Masc.* tribute; **un homenaje al autor** a ceremony to honour the author.

homosexual *noun Masc./Fem.*, *adjective* homosexual.

hondo[1] *adverb* **respirar hondo** to breathe deeply.

hondo[2]**/honda** *adjective* **1** deep; **un pozo hondo** a deep well; **2 en lo más hondo de mi corazón** deep in my heart.

hondureño/hondureña *noun Masc./Fem., adjective* Honduran.

honesto/honesta *adjective* honest.

hongo *noun Masc.* **1** fungus; **2 tener hongos** to have athlete's foot.

honor *noun Masc.* honour; **tener el honor de** to have the honour of; **en honor de** in honour of.

honra *noun Fem.* honour.

honradez *noun Fem.* honesty.

honrado/honrada *adjective* honest.

hora *noun Fem.* **1** hour; **la película dura dos horas** the film lasts two hours; **media hora** half an hour; **hora y media** an hour and a half; **a las quince horas** at fifteen hours; **la hora punta** the rush hour; **durante las horas de trabajo** during working hours; **horas de visita** visiting hours (*at the hospital*); **hay un bus que sale cada hora** there is an hourly bus; **2** time; **¿qué hora es?** what's the time?; **¿a qué hora empieza?** what time does it start?; **¿tiene hora?** have you got the time?; **¿me puede dar la hora?** could you tell me what time it is?; **a la hora de comer** at lunchtime; **es hora de ir a la cama** it's bedtime; **ya es hora de entrar** it's time to go in; **en mis horas libres** in my free time; **hacer**

horas extra to do overtime; **llegar a la hora** to arrive on time; **3 pedir hora** to make an appointment; **he pedido hora con el dentista** I made an appointment to see the dentist; **4 a primera hora de la mañana** first thing in the morning; **una noticia de última hora** a news flash.

horario *noun Masc.* **1** timetable; **el horario de clase** the school timetable; **2 horario de visitas** visiting hours (*at the hospital*).

horchata *noun Fem.* a cold drink made from tiger nuts.

horchatería *noun Fem.* refreshments stall (*selling horchata*).

horizontal *adjective* horizontal.

horizonte *noun Masc.* horizon.

hormiga *noun Fem.* ant.

hormigón *noun Masc.* concrete.

horno *noun Masc.* **1** oven; **verduras al horno** roast vegetables; **un horno microondas** a microwave oven; **2** kiln.

horóscopo *noun Masc.* horoscope.

horquilla *noun Fem.* hairpin.

horrible *adjective* horrible.

horror *noun Masc.* **1** horror; **2** (*informal*) **¡qué horror!** how awful!.

horrorizar *verb* [22] to horrify.

horroroso/horrorosa *adjective* **1** horrific (*crime*); **2** (*informal*) awful (*a dress, book or picture, for example*).

hospedar *verb* [17] to provide accommodation for.
  hospedarse *reflexive verb* [17] to stay; **nos hospedamos en una pensión** we stayed in a guesthouse.

hospital *noun Masc.* hospital.

hospitalidad *noun Fem.* hospitality.

hostal *noun Masc.* hotel (*small and not expensive*).

hotel *noun Masc.* hotel.

hotelero/hotelera *noun Masc./ Fem.* hotel manager.
  hotelero *adjective* hotel.

hoy *adverb* **1** today; **hoy es mi cumpleaños** it's my birthday today; **¿a qué estamos hoy?** what day is it today?; **2 hoy en día** nowadays; **hoy en día son bastante comunes** nowadays they are quite common.

hoyo *noun Masc.* hole.

hube, **hubo**, **etc.** *verb* SEE **haber**.

hucha *noun Fem.* moneybox.

hueco[1] *noun Masc.* **1** hollow; **suena a hueco** it sounds hollow; **2** space; **hazme un hueco** make some room for me; **un hueco para aparcar** a parking space; **3 el hueco de la escalera** the stairwell; **el hueco del ascensor** the lift shaft; **4** gap (*in timetable*).

hueco[2]**/hueca** *adjective* hollow.

huela, **huelo**, **etc.** *verb* SEE **oler**.

huelga *noun Fem.* strike; **hacer huelga** to strike; **estar en huelga** to be on strike; **huelga de celo** work-to-rule.

a
b
c
d
e
f
g
h
i
j
k
l
m
n
ñ
o
p
q
r
s
t
u
v
w
x
y
z

a

b

c

d

e

f

g

h

i

j

k

l

m

n

ñ

o

p

q

r

s

t

u

v

w

x

y

z

huella *noun Fem.* **1** footprint; **2** track (*of an animal or tyre, for example*); **3 huellas dactilares** fingerprints.

huérfano/huérfana *noun Masc./ Fem.* orphan.

huerto/huerta *noun Masc./Fem.* **1** vegetable garden; **2** orchard.

hueso *noun Masc.* **1** bone; **romperse un hueso** to break a bone; **2** stone (*in fruit*).

huésped *noun Masc./Fem.* guest.

huesudo *adjective* bony.

huevo *noun Masc.* egg; **huevo duro** hard-boiled egg; **huevo pasado por agua** soft-boiled egg; **huevo escalfado** poached egg; **huevo frito** fried egg; **huevos revueltos** scrambled eggs; **huevo de Pascua** Easter egg.

huir *verb* [54] to flee; **huir de la cárcel** to escape from prison.

humano/humana *noun Masc./ Fem.* human being.
humano *adjective* **1** human; **la naturaleza humana** human nature; **2** humane.

humedad *noun Fem.* **1** dampness; **la casa tiene humedad** the house is damp; **2** humidity.

húmedo/húmeda *adjective* **1** damp; **2** wet; **3** moist.

humillar *verb* [17] to humiliate.

humo *noun Masc.* smoke.

humor *noun Masc.* **1** humour; **tener sentido del humor** to have a sense of humour; **2** mood; **estar de buen humor** to be in a good mood; **estar de mal humor** to be in a bad mood; **no estoy de humor para verlos** I'm not in the mood to see them.

hundir *verb* [19] to sink.
hundirse *reflexive verb* [19] to sink.

húngaro¹ *noun Masc.* Hungarian (*the language*).

húngaro²/húngara *noun Masc./ Fem.*,
húngaro *adjective* Hungarian.

Hungría *noun Fem.* Hungary.

huracán *noun Masc.* hurricane.

hurra *exclamation* hurrah!

huyas, huyo, etc. *verb* SEE **huir**.

Ii

iba, iban, etc. *verb* SEE **ir**.

iceberg *noun Masc.* iceberg.

icono *noun Masc.* icon.

ida¹ *noun Fem.* departure; **un billete de ida** a single ticket; **un billete de ida y vuelta** a return ticket.

ida² *verb* SEE **ir**.

idea *noun Fem.* idea; **'¿a qué hora llegan?' – 'no tengo ni idea'** 'what time will they arrive?' – ' I haven't a clue'; **no tienen ni idea de cómo ir** they have no idea how to get there; **tengo una idea** I've got an idea.

ideal *adjective* ideal.

idéntico/idéntica *adjective* identical; **es idéntico a su padre** he's just like his father.

identidad *noun Fem.* identity; **un carné de identidad** an identity card.

identificación *noun Fem.* identification.

identificar *verb* [31] to identify. **identificarse** *reflexive verb* [31] **1** to identify yourself; **2 identificarse con** to identify with; **me identifico mucho con la protagonista del libro** I identify a lot with the heroine of the book.

idioma *noun Masc.* language; **hablar idiomas varios** to speak several foreign languages.

idiota *noun Masc./Fem.* idiot. **idiota** *adjective* stupid.

ido *verb* SEE **ir.**

iglesia *noun Fem.* church.

ignorante *adjective* ignorant.

ignorar *verb* [17] **1** to ignore; **no me gusta que me ignoren** I don't like being ignored; **2** not to know; **ignoro las razones** I don't know the reasons.

igual *adjective* **1** same; **uno de igual tamaño** one of the same size; **parecen todos iguales** they all look the same; **2 igual a/igual que** the same as; **era igual a éste** it was the same as this one; **no es igual que los demás** it's not the same as the others; **3 todo le da igual** he doesn't care about anything; **'¿quieres ir al cine o al teatro?' – 'me da igual'** 'do you want to go to the cinema or to the theatre?' – 'I don't mind'; **les da igual lo uno que lo otro** either way it makes no difference to them.

igual *adverb* **1** the same; **suenan igual** they sound the same; **2** equally; **los quiero a todos igual** I love them all equally; **los dos sistemas son igual de eficientes** both systems are equally efficient; **3** (*in comparisons*) **es igual de alto que su padre** he's as tall as his father; **es igual de ancho que la mesa** it's as wide as the table; **es Géminis, igual que yo** she's a Gemini, just like me; **4** maybe; **igual la vemos en la fiesta** maybe we'll see her at the party; **5 al igual que** just like.

igualdad *noun Fem.* equality; **igualdad de oportunidades** equal opportunities; **en igualdad de condiciones** on equal terms.

igualmente *adverb* **1** equally; **igualmente aburrido** equally boring; **2 'que pases una feliz Navidad' – 'igualmente'** 'have a good Christmas' – 'you too'.

ilegal *adjective* illegal.

ilegalmente *adverb* illegally.

ileso/ilesa *adjective* unhurt, uninjured.

ilimitado/ilimitada *adjective* unlimited.

iluminación *noun Fem.* **1** lighting (*in a room or theatre*); **2** illumination (*of a building or statue*).

iluminar *verb* [17] **1** to light (*a room or theatre*); **2** to illuminate (*a building or statue*).

a
b
c
d
e
f
g
h
i
j
k
l
m
n
ñ
o
p
q
r
s
t
u
v
w
x
y
z

ilusión *noun Fem.* **1** hope; **2 me hace ilusion ir** I'm excited about going; **3** illusion.

ilustración *noun Fem.* illustration.

ilustrar *verb* [17] to illustrate.

imagen *noun Fem.* **1** image; **es la viva imagen de su madre** she's the image of her mother; **2** picture (*on a TV screen*); **3** reflection (*in a mirror*).

imaginación *noun Fem.* imagination; **son imaginaciones suyas** he's just imagining things.

imaginar *verb* [17] to imagine. **imaginarse** *reflexive verb* [17] **1** to imagine; **me imaginaba que sería más grande** I imagined it would be bigger; **2 me imagino que no** I suppose not; **me imagino que sí** I imagine so.

imán *noun Masc.* magnet.

imbécil *noun Masc./Fem.* idiot. **imbécil** *adjective* stupid.

imitar *verb* [17] to imitate.

impacientar *verb* [17] to make impatient. **impacientarse** *reflexive verb* [17] to get impatient.

impaciente *adjective* impatient.

impacto *noun Masc.* impact.

impar *adjective* odd.

impecable *adjective* impeccable.

impedir *verb* [57] **1** to prevent; **impedirle a alguien hacer algo** to prevent someone from doing something; **2 impedir el paso** to block the way.

imperativo *noun Masc.* imperative.

imperdible *noun Masc.* safety pin.

imperfecto¹ *noun Masc.* imperfect.

imperfecto²**/imperfecta** *adjective* imperfect.

impermeable *noun Masc.* raincoat.

impersonal *adjective* impersonal.

implicar *verb* [31] to involve.

imponer *verb* [11] to impose (*a condition or punishment*).

importación *noun Fem.* import; **artículos de importación** imports.

importado/importada *adjective* imported.

importancia *noun Fem.* importance; **darle importancia a algo** to attach importance to something.

importante *adjective* **1** important; **lo importante es ...** the important thing is ...; **2** considerable; **una importante suma de dinero** a considerable sum of money.

importar *verb* [17] **1** to matter; **no importa, déjalo así** it doesn't matter, leave it like this; **no importa mucho el color** the colour doesn't matter very much; **2 no me importa ayudarles** I don't mind helping them; **¿te importa que use el teléfono?** do you mind if I use your phone?; **¿le importaría comprobarlo?** would you mind checking it?; **3 ¿y a ti que te importa?** it's none of your business; **no me importa lo que diga** I don't care what he says; **4** to import (*goods*); ★ **me importa un comino/**

un rábano (*informal*) I couldn't care less.

imposible *adjective* impossible.

impresión *noun Fem.* impression **1 causar una buena impresión** to make a good impression; **2 me da la impresión de que** ... I've got the feeling that...

impresionante *adjective* impressive.

impresionar *verb* [17] **1** to impress; **quiere impresionarte** she wants to impress you; **2** to affect; **me impresionó mucho verlos discutir** seeing them argue really affected me; **la violencia de la escena me impresionó mucho** the violence of the scene shocked me.

impreso[1] *noun Masc.* form; **impreso de solicitud** application form.

impreso[2]**/impresa** *adjective* printed.

impresora *noun Fem.* printer; **una impresora láser** a laser printer.

imprevisible *adjective* **1** unpredictable; **2** unforeseeable.

imprevisto[1] *noun Masc.* unforeseen event.

imprevisto[2]**/imprevista** *adjective* unforeseen, unexpected.

improvisado/improvisada *adjective* improvised.

improvisar *verb* [17] to improvise.

improviso *in phrase* **de improviso** unexpectedly, out of the blue.

imprudente *noun Masc./Fem.* **1** careless person; **2** reckless

person; **es un imprudente conduciendo** he's a reckless driver.

imprudente *adjective* **1** careless; **2** reckless.

impuesto *noun Masc.* tax.

impulsivo/impulsiva *adjective* impulsive.

inaccesible *adjective* inaccessible.

inaceptable *adjective* unacceptable.

inadecuado/inadecuada *adjective* **1** inappropriate; **2** inadequate.

inadmisible *adjective* unacceptable.

inadvertido/inadvertida *adjective* **pasar inadvertido** to go unnoticed.

inalámbrico/inalámbrica *adjective* cordless.

incapaz *adjective* **es incapaz de hacer daño a nadie** he's incapable of harming anyone; **fui incapaz de entenderlo** I was unable to understand it.

incendio *noun Masc.* fire.

incertidumbre *noun Fem.* uncertainty.

incierto/incierta *adjective* uncertain.

incitar *verb* [17] **incitar a alguien a hacer** to incite someone to do.

incluido/incluida *adjective* included; **dos mil euros, todo incluido** two thousand euros, everything included; **seremos diez personas, nosotros incluidos**

a
b
c
d
e
f
g
h
i
j
k
l
m
n
ñ
o
p
q
r
s
t
u
v
w
x
y
z

there will be ten people including us.

incluir *verb* [54] to include.

inclusive *adjective* inclusive; **los viernes inclusive** including Fridays.

incluso *adverb* even; **es incluso mejor** it's even better.

incluya, **incluyo**, **etc.** *verb* SEE **incluir**.

incoloro/incolora *adjective* colourless.

incómodo/incómoda *adjective* uncomfortable.

incompetente *adjective* incompetent.

incompleto/incompleta *adjective* incomplete.

incomprensible *adjective* incomprehensible.

incondicional *adjective* unconditional.

inconsciente *adjective* unconscious.

inconveniente *noun Masc.* drawback, disadvantage. **inconveniente** *adjective* inconvenient.

incorporar *verb* [17] to incorporate. **incorporarse** *reflexive verb* [17] to sit up.

incorrecto/incorrecta *adjective* incorrect.

increíble *adjective* unbelievable, incredible.

indecente *adjective* indecent.

indeciso/indecisa *adjective* 1 indecisive; 2 undecided; **están indecisos sobre la cantidad** they're undecided about the quantity.

indefenso/indefensa *adjective* defenceless.

indefinidamente *adverb* indefinitely, for good.

indefinido/indefinida *adjective* 1 indefinite; 2 vague (*outline, for example*).

indemnizar *verb* [22] to compensate; **los indemnizaron con veinte mil euros** they received twenty thousand euros in compensation.

indemnzación *noun Fem.* compensation; **le pagaron una indemnización** they paid her compensation.

independencia *noun Fem.* independence.

independiente *adjective* independent.

India *noun Fem.* **(la) India** India.

indicación *noun Fem.* 1 indication; 2 sign; **me hizo una indicación para que lo siguiese** he signalled to me to follow him; **hay una indicación en el camino** there's a sign on the road.

indicar *verb* [31] 1 to indicate; 2 to point to.

índice *noun Masc.* index.

indiferente *adjective* 1 indifferent; 2 **me es indiferente** it makes no difference to me.

indígena *adjective* native.

indigestión *noun Fem.* indigestion.

indigesto/indigesta *adjective* indigestible.

indignación *noun Fem.* **1** indignation; **2** outrage.

indignar *verb* [17] **1** to make angry; **2** to outrage.
indignarse *reflexive verb* [17] **1** to get angry; **2** to be outraged.

indio/india *noun Masc./Fem.*, *adjective* Indian.

indirecta¹ *noun Fem.* hint.

indirecto/indirecta² *adjective* indirect.

indiscreto/indiscreta *adjective* indiscreet.

indispensable *adjective* essential.

indispuesto/indispuesta *adjective* **estar indispuesto** to be unwell.

individual *adjective* individual.

individuo *noun Masc.* **1** person; **un individuo con pelo largo** a person with long hair; **2** (*pejorative*) character; **un individuo con muy mal aspecto** a nasty looking character.

industria *noun Fem.* industry.

industrial *adjective* industrial.

ineficaz *adjective* **1** ineffective (*remedy, measure*); **2** inefficient (*person*).

inepto/inepta *noun Masc./Fem.*, **inepto** *adjective* incompetent.

inesperado/inesperada *adjective* unexpected.

inevitable *adjective* unavoidable; **era inevitable que pasase** it was bound to happen.

inexperto/inexperta *adjective* inexperienced.

infancia *noun Fem.* childhood.

infantil *adjective* **1** childish; **eres muy infantil** you're so childish; **2** childlike; **3 literatura infantil** children's books.

infarto *noun Masc.* heart attack; **le dio un infarto** he had a heart attack.

infección *noun Fem.* infection.

infectado/infectada *adjective* infected.

infectar *verb* [17] to infect.
infectarse *reflexive verb* [17] to become infected.

infeliz *adjective* unhappy.

infiel *adjective* unfaithful; **serle infiel a alguien** to be unfaithful to someone.

infierno *noun Masc.* hell.

infinitivo *noun Masc.* infinitive.

infinito¹ *noun Masc.* infinity.

infinito²/infinita *adjective* infinite.

inflable *adjective* inflatable.

inflación *noun Fem.* inflation.

inflamable *adjective* flammable.

inflar *verb* [17] **1** to inflate (*a tyre, for example*); **2** to blow up (*a balloon, for example*).

influencia *noun Fem.* influence.

influir *verb* [54] to influence.

a
b
c
d
e
f
g
h
i
j
k
l
m
n
ñ
o
p
q
r
s
t
u
v
w
x
y
z

información *noun Fem.*
1 information; **'Información'**
'Information Desk' (*on a sign*);
2 news (*in newspaper or TV news*);
la información internacional the
foreign news; **3** directory enquiries
(*on the telephone*); **llamar a
información** to call directory
enquiries.

informal *adjective* **1** informal (*a
chat or meal, for example*); **2** casual
(*clothes*); **3** unreliable (*person*).

informar *verb* [17] to inform; **me
informaron mal** I was misinformed;
¿podría informarme sobre ... ?
could you give me information
about ... ?.
informarse *reflexive verb* [17] to
find out information; **me informaré
sobre el horario** I'll find out about
the timetable.

informática *noun Fem.* computer
science, IT.

informe *noun Masc.* report.

infracción *noun Fem.* offence;
cometer una infracción to commit
an offence; **una infracción de
tráfico** a traffic offence.

infusión *noun Fem.* herbal tea; **una
infusión de menta** a peppermint
tea.

ingeniero/ingeniera *noun
Masc./Fem.* engineer.

ingenuo/ingenua *noun Masc./
Fem.* **eres un ingenuo** you're so
naive.
ingenuo *adjective* naive.

Inglaterra *noun Fem.* England.

inglés[1] *noun Masc.* English (*the
language*).

inglés[2]**/inglesa** *noun Masc./Fem.*
Englishman/Englishwoman; **los
ingleses** the English, English
people.
inglés/inglesa *adjective* English.

ingrato/ingrata *adjective*
ungrateful.

ingrediente *noun Masc.*
ingredient.

inicial *noun Fem.* initial.
inicial *adjective* initial.

iniciativa *noun Fem.* initiative; **por
iniciativa propia** on her own
initiative.

injusto/injusta *adjective* unfair.

inmediatamente *adverb*
immediately.

inmediato/inmediata
adjective immediate; **de inmediato**
immediately.

inmenso/inmensa *adjective*
1 immense; **2** huge; **un salón
inmenso** a huge living room.

inmigración *noun Fem.*
immigration.

inmigrante *noun Masc./Fem.*
immigrant.

inmobiliaria *noun Fem.* estate
agent's.

inmoral *adjective* immoral.

inmueble *noun Masc.* property.

inmunizar *verb* [22] to immunize.

innecesario/innecesaria
adjective unnecessary.

innovación *noun Fem.* innovation.

innovar *verb* [17] to innovate.

innumerable *adjective* innumerable.

inocentada *noun Fem.* practical joke (*this is also used for a joke played on someone on 28 December, which is the Spanish equivalent of April Fool's Day*) **gastarle una inocentada a alguien** to play a practical joke on someone.

inocente *adjective* 1 innocent; 2 naive; SEE **día**.

inofensivo/inofensiva *adjective* harmless.

inolvidable *adjective* unforgettable.

inoxidable *adjective* **acero inoxidable** stainless steel.

inquieto/inquieta *adjective* 1 worried; 2 restless.

inquietud *noun Fem.* 1 uneasiness; 2 interest.

inquilino/inquilina *noun Masc./Fem.* tenant.

inscribir *verb* [52] 1 to register (*on a course, for example*); 2 to engrave. **inscribirse** *reflexive verb* [52] to register.

inscripción *noun Fem.* 1 registration (*on a course, for example*); 2 inscription.

insecto *noun Masc.* insect.

insertar *verb* [17] to insert.

insignificante *adjective* insignificant.

insistir *verb* [19] to insist; **insistir en algo** to insist on something.

insolación *noun Fem.* sunstroke; **coger una insolación** to get sunstroke.

insolente *adjective* rude.

insólito/insólita *adjective* unheard of.

insonorizado/insonorizada *adjective* soundproofed.

insoportable *adjective* unbearable.

inspección *noun Fem.* inspection.

inspeccionar *verb* [17] to inspect.

inspector/inspectora *noun Masc./Fem.* inspector.

inspiración *noun Fem.* inspiration.

inspirar *verb* [17] to inspire. **inspirarse** *reflexive verb* [17] **inspirarse en algo** to be inspired by something.

instalación *noun Fem.* installation.

instalar *verb* [17] to install (*a washing machine or a computer, for example*). **instalarse** *reflexive verb* [17] to install yourself.

instantáneo/instantánea *adjective* 1 instant; 2 immediate.

instante *noun Masc.* moment; **un instante, por favor** one moment, please.

instinto *noun Masc.* instinct; **instinto de conservación** survival instinct; **por instinto** instinctively.

instituto *noun Masc.* institute; **instituto de bachillerato** secondary school.

a
b
c
d
e
f
g
h
i
j
k
l
m
n
ñ
o
p
q
r
s
t
u
v
w
x
y
z

a
b
c
d
e
f
g
h
i
j
k
l
m
n
ñ
o
p
q
r
s
t
u
v
w
x
y
z

instrucción *noun Fem.*
1 education; **2** training;
instrucción militar military
training; **3 instrucciones**
instructions (*for a computer, for
example*).

instructor/instructora *noun
Masc./Fem.* instructor; **instructor de
autoescuela** driving instructor;
instructor de esquí ski instructor.

instruir *verb* [54] **1** to instruct; **2** to
educate.

instrumento *noun Masc.*
instrument; **tocar un instrumento**
to play an instrument.

insuficiente *noun Masc.* fail (*at
school*).
insuficiente *adjective* inadequate.

insultar *verb* [17] to insult.

insulto *noun Masc.* insult.

intacto/intacta *adjective* intact.

integral *adjective*
1 comprehensive; **2 pan integral**
wholemeal bread.

íntegro/íntegra *adjective* **la
versión íntegra de la película** the
full-length version of the film; **el
texto íntegro** the unabridged text.

intelectual *noun Masc./Fem.*,
intelectual *adjective* intellectual.

inteligencia *noun Fem.*
intelligence.

inteligente *adjective* intelligent.

intención *noun Fem.* intention; **no
fue mi intención** it wasn't my
intention; **no era mi intención
ofenderla** I didn't mean to offend
her; **tiene buenas intenciones** she

means well; **lo preguntó con mala
intención** he asked the question to
cause trouble.

intensivo/intensiva *adjective*
intensive.

intenso/intensa *adjective*
1 intense; **2** deep (*feeling*).

intentar *verb* [17] to try; **¡inténtalo
otra vez!** try again!; **intentar hacer**
to try to do; **intenté cerrarlo** I tried
to shut it; **intenta llegar temprano**
try to arrive early.

intercambiar *verb* [17] **1** to
exchange; **2** to swap.
intercambiarse *reflexive verb*
[17] to swap; **se intercambiaron las
revistas** they swapped their
magazines.

intercambio *noun Masc.*
1 exchange; **2** swap.

interés *noun Masc.* interest; **es de
gran interés para mí** it's of great
interest to me; **su interés por la
historia** her interest in history.

interesante *adjective* interesting;
un película interestante an
interesting film; **resulta
interesante que ...** it's interesting
that ....

interesar *verb* [17] **no me interesa
el deporte** I'm not interested in
sport; **¿te interesa la historia?** are
you interested in history?
interesarse *reflexive verb* [17]
**interesarse en algo/interesarse
por algo** to take an interest in
something.

interfono *noun Masc.*
1 entryphone; **2** intercom.

interior *noun Masc.* **1** inside; **el interior de la caja** the inside of the box; **2 en mi interior, tenía miedo** deep down inside, I was afraid. **interior** *adjective* **1** interior; **escalera interior** interior staircase; **2 un piso interior** a flat with windows facing into an inner courtyard; **3** inside; **en la parte interior** on the inside.

intermediario/ intermediaria *noun Masc./Fem.* intermediary.

intermedio¹ *noun Masc.* interval.

intermedio⁴/intermedia *adjective* **1** intermediate (*level or stage, for example*); **2** medium; **de tamaño intermedio** medium-sized.

intermitente *adjective* **1** flashing (*a light*); **2** intermittent.

internacional *adjective* international.

internado¹ *noun Masc.* boarding school.

internado⁴/internada *adjective* **está internado** he's been taken into hospital.

internauta *noun Masc./Fem.* surfer (*on the Internet*).

Internet *noun Masc.* Internet (*Spanish omits 'el' with Internet*); **en Internet** on the Internet.

interno/interna *noun Masc./Fem.* boarder (*in a school*). **interno** *adjective* internal.

interpretar *verb* [17] **1** to interpret; **2 interpretar un papel** to play a part (*in a play or film*); **interpretar una pieza de música** to perform a piece of music; **interpretar una canción** to sing a song.

intérprete *noun Masc./Fem.* **1** interpreter; **2** performer (*of a piece of music*); **3** singer (*of a song*).

interrogación *noun Fem.* interrogation.

interrogante *noun Masc. or Fem.* **1** question; **quedan muchos interrogantes sin responder** there are many questions left unanswered; **2** question mark; **pon un interrogante** write a question mark.

interrogar *verb* [28] to question (*a suspect*).

interrumpir *verb* [19] to interrupt.

interrupción *noun Fem.* interruption.

interruptor *noun Masc.* switch.

interurbano/interurbana *adjective* **1** long-distance; **una llamada interurbana** a long-distance call; **2 un tren interurbano** an intercity train.

intervalo *noun Masc.* interval.

intervención *noun Fem.* intervention.

intervenir *verb* [15] **1** to take part; **intervenir en las negociaciones** to take part in the negociations; **2** to intervene; **no quiero intervenir** I don't want to intervene; **3 intervenir a alguien** to operate on somebody.

interviú *noun Fem.* interview.

intimidar *verb* [17] to intimidate.

a
b
c
d
e
f
g
h
i
j
k
l
m
n
ñ
o
p
q
r
s
t
u
v
w
x
y
z

íntimo/íntima *adjective*
1 private; **mi vida íntima** my private life; **2** intimate; **un ambiente íntimo** an intimate atmosphere; **3 mis amigos íntimos** my close friends; **4 una cena íntima** a candlelit dinner.

intolerante *adjective* intolerant.

intoxicación *noun Fem.* poisoning; **intoxicación alimenticia** food poisoning.

intransitivo/intransitiva *adjective* intransitive.

intriga *noun Fem.* intrigue.

introducir *verb* [60] **1** to introduce; **introducir cambios** to introduce changes; **2** to insert; **introducir la moneda en la ranura** insert the coin in the slot.
introducirse *reflexive verb* [60] **1** to be introduced; **2** to get in; **el ladrón se introdujo por la ventana** the burglar got in through the window.

intruso/intrusa *noun Masc./Fem.* intruder.

intuitivo/intuitiva *adjective* intuitive.

inundación *noun Fem.* flooding; **ha habido inundaciones en Cataluña** there's been flooding in Catalonia.

inútil *noun Masc./Fem.* **es una inútil** she's useless.
inútil *adjective* **1** useless; **2 es inútil intentarlo** it's useless trying.

invadir *verb* [19] to invade.

inválido/inválida *noun Masc./Fem.* disabled person.

invasión *noun Fem.* invasion.

inventar *verb* [17] **1** to invent; **2** to make up (*a story or game*).
inventarse *reflexive verb* [17] to invent, to make up; **se inventó una excusa** he made up an excuse.

invento *noun Masc.* invention.

invernadero *noun Masc.* greenhouse.

inversión *noun Fem.* investment.

inverso/inversa *adjective* reverse.

investigación *noun Fem.* **1** investigation (*of a crime or accident, for example*); **2** research; **investigación de mercado** market research.

invierno *noun Masc.* winter; **en invierno** in winter; **el invierno pasado** last winter.

invisible *adjective* invisible.

invitación *noun Fem.* invitation.

invitado/invitada *noun Masc./Fem.* guest.

invitar *verb* [17] **1** to invite; **invitar a alguien a una fiesta** to invite someone to a party; **me han invitado a su casa** they've invited me to their house; **2 te invito a cenar** I'll take you out for dinner; **nos invitó a una copa** he bought us a drink; **¡yo invito!** it's on me!

involuntario/involuntaria *adjective* involuntary.

inyección *noun Fem.* injection.

ir *verb* [8] **1** to go; **van a casa de Alicia** they're going to Alicia's; **iremos al museo** we'll go to the museum; **¿adónde vas?** where are you going?; **¿dónde van los platos?** where do the plates go?; **aún no va al colegio** she doesn't go to school yet; **2** to come; **¡ya voy!** I'm coming!; **3** (*talking about how things are progressing*); **¿cómo van las cosas?** how are things?; **¿cómo te va?** how are you doing?; **¿cómo va el enfermo?** how is the patient doing?; **le va muy bien en el trabajo** he's doing very well at work; **me fue muy mal en la entrevista** I did very badly at the interview; **el proyecto va bien** the project is going well; **4** (*talking about how something works*) **la lavadora no va bien** the washing machine is not working properly; **5** to be; **iba solo** he was alone; **ellos iban en la parte de delante** they were at the front; **yo iba de pie** I was standing up; **6** (*referring to the way you dress*) **iba con un abrigo marrón** he was wearing a brown coat; **iban bien vestidos** they were well dressed; **7** (*talking about whether something suits you*) **el negro te va bien** black suits you; **8** (*talking about an activity*) **ir de vacaciones** to go on holiday; **voy a ir a España de vacaciones** I'm going to Spain for my holidays; **ir de compras** to go shopping; **ir a la compra** to do the shopping; **siempre tengo yo que ir a la compra** I'm always the one who does the shopping; **9** (*talking about transport*) **ir en coche** to go by car; **fueron en coche** they drove here; **ir en avión** to go by plane; **ir en bicicleta** to go by bike; **va en bicicleta a todas partes** she goes everywhere by bike; **ir a pie** to go on foot; **ir a caballo** to go on horseback; **10 ir a por algo/alguien** to go to get something/someone; **voy a por pan** I'm going to buy some bread; **fuimos a por ella** we went to fetch her; **vete a por el médico** go and get the doctor; **11 ir a hacer** to go to do; **fuimos a ver su casa nueva** we went to see their new house; **ve a recoger tu habitación** go and tidy up your room; **12** (*expressing the future*) **voy a comprar leche** I'm going to buy some milk; **voy a ser médico** I'm going to be a doctor; **iré a recogerla** I'll go to pick her up; **iba a mandártelo hoy** I was going to send it to you today; **13 su salud va mejorando** her health is getting better; **iban acercándose** they were getting closer; **14 ¡vamos!** come on!; **15** (*expressing surprise or annoyance*) **¡vaya hombre, un billete de cincuenta euros!** hey look, a fifty-euro note!; **¡vaya, si es Carlos!** what a surprise, it's Carlos!; **¡vaya, se ha fundido la luz!** oh dear, the light has gone!; **¡vaya, no lo encuentro!** bother, I can't find it!; **16 '¿lo ha hecho él solo?' – '¡qué va!'** 'did he do it on his own?' – 'not likely!'; **'¿te molesta?' – '¡qué va!'** 'do you mind?' – 'not at all!'.

irse *reflexive verb* [8] **1** to leave; **nos fuimos pronto** we left early; **bueno, me voy** well, I'm off; **2** to go; **se fueron a casa** they went home; **3 ¿cómo se va a la estación?** which is the way to the station?

a
b
c
d
e
f
g
h
i
j
k
l
m
n
ñ
o
p
q
r
s
t
u
v
w
x
y
z

a
b
c
d
e
f
g
h
i
j
k
l
m
n
ñ
o
p
q
r
s
t
u
v
w
x
y
z

ira *noun Fem.* rage; **en un arrebato de ira** in a fit of rage; ⋆ **ciego de ira** in a blind rage.

Irlanda *noun Fem.* Ireland.

irlandés¹ *noun Masc.* Irish (*the language*).

irlandés²/irlandesa *noun Masc./Fem.* Irishman/Irishwoman. **irlandés/irlandesa** *adjective* Irish.

ironía *noun Fem.* irony.

irónico/irónica *adjective* ironic.

irreal *adjective* unreal.

irresponsable *adjective* irresponsible.

irritación *noun Fem.* irritation.

irritar *verb* [17] to irritate. **irritarse** *reflexive verb* [17] **1** to get irritated (*a person*); **2** to become irritated.

isla *noun Fem.* island.

islámico/islámica *adjective* Islamic.

islandés/islandesa *noun Masc./Fem.* Icelander.

Islandia *noun Fem.* Iceland.

Israel *noun Masc.* Israel.

israelí *noun Masc./Fem., adjective* Israeli.

Italia *noun Fem.* Italy.

italiano¹ *noun Masc.* Italian (*the language*).

italiano²/italiana *noun Masc./Fem., adjective* Italian.

itinerario *noun Masc.* itinerary, route.

IVA *abbreviation Masc.* (*short for: Impuesto al Valor Agregado*) VAT.

izquierda¹ *noun Fem.* **1** left; **tuerce a la izquierda** turn left; **se sentaron a mi izquierda** they sat on my left; **2** **está a la izquierda** it's on the left-hand side; **3** **ser de izquierdas** to be left-wing (*in politics*).

izquierdo/izquierda² *adjective* left.

Jj

jabalí *noun Masc.* wild boar.

jabón *noun Masc.* soap; **una pastilla de jabón** a cake of soap.

jabonera *noun Fem.* soapdish.

Jamaica *noun Fem.* Jamaica.

jamaicano/jamaicana *noun Masc., Fem., adjective* Jamaican.

jamás *adverb* never; **no lo he visto jamás** I've never seen it; **nunca jamás volveré** I'll never ever go back again.

jamón *noun Masc.* ham; **jamón de York** cooked ham; **jamón serrano** cured raw ham.

Japón *noun Masc.* **(el) Japón** Japan.

jarabe *noun Masc.* syrup; **jarabe para la tos** cough mixture.

jardín *noun Masc.* **1** garden; **está en el jardín** she's in the garden; **2** **jardín de infancia** nursery (school).

jardinero/jardinera *noun Masc./ Fem.* gardener.

jarra *noun Fem.* SEE **jarro**.

jarro *noun Masc.* jug.

jarrón *noun Masc.* vase.

jaula *noun Fem.* cage.

jefe/jefa *noun Masc./Fem.* **1** boss (*at work*); **2** manager (*of a company*); **3** chief; **el jefe de policía** the chief of police; **el jefe de bomberos** the chief fire officer; **4** leader (*of a group*).

jengibre *noun Masc.* ginger.

jerez *noun Masc.* sherry.

jersey *noun Masc.* sweater.

Jesucristo *noun Masc.* Jesus Christ.

jinete *noun Masc.* **1** rider; **2** jockey.

JJ.OO. *abbreviation plural Masc.* (*short for: Juegos Olímpicos*) Olympic Games.

jornada *noun Fem.* day; **una jornada de trabajo** a working day; **trabajar media jornada** to work part time; **trabajar la jornada completa** to work full time.

joven *noun Masc./Fem.* **un joven** a young man; **una joven** a young woman.
joven *adjective* young; **moda joven** young fashion.

jovencito/jovencita *noun Masc./Fem.* young man/young woman.

joya *noun Fem.* **1** piece of jewellery; **no me gustan las joyas** I don't like jewellery; **2** **esa chica es una joya** that girl's a real gem.

joyería *noun Fem.* jeweller's.

jubilación *noun Fem.* retirement.

jubilado/jubilada *noun Masc./ Fem.* pensioner; **los jubilados** retired people.
jubilado *adjective* retired.

jubilarse *reflexive verb* [17] to retire.

judaísmo *noun Masc.* Judaism.

judía¹ *noun Fem.* bean; **judías blancas** haricot beans; **judías pintas** kidney beans; **judías verdes** green beans.

judío/judía² *noun Masc./Fem.* Jew. **judío** *adjective* Jewish.

judo *noun Masc.* judo.

juega, juego¹, **etc.** *verb* SEE **jugar**.

juego² *noun Masc.* **1** game; **juegos de mesa** board games; **un juego de azar** a game of chance; **los Juegos Olímpicos** the Olympic Games; **los Juegos Paralímpicos** the Paralympic Games; **a los diez minutos de juego** ten minutes into the game; **2** **un juego de manos** a conjuring trick; **3** gambling; **es aficionado al juego** he likes gambling; **4** play; **un juego de palabras** a play on words; **juego limpio** fair play; **5** set; **un juego de cacerolas** a set of pans; **un juego de llaves** a set of keys; **6** **hacer juego con algo** to match something; **no hace juego con los pantalones** it doesn't match the trousers; **7** **fuera de juego** offside; ★ **es un juego de niños** it's child's play.

juegue *verb* SEE **jugar**.

a
b
c
d
e
f
g
h
i
j
k
l
m
n
ñ
o
p
q
r
s
t
u
v
w
x
y
z

juerga *noun Fem.* **ir de juerga** (*informal*) to go out on the town.

juerguista *noun Masc./Fem.* (*informal*) raver.

jueves *noun Masc.* Thursday; **el jueves** on Thursday; **el jueves por la mañana** on Thursday morning; **los jueves** on Thursdays.

juez *noun Masc./Fem.* **1** judge; **2** referee.

jugador/jugadora *noun Masc./Fem.* **1** player; **2** gambler.

jugar *verb* [27] **1** to play; **jugar al fútbol** to play football; **jugar a la pelota** to play ball; **¿a qué quieres jugar?** what do you want to play?; **2** to gamble; **3** to move (*in board games*); **te toca jugar a ti** it's your turn (to move).

jugo *noun Masc.* juice.

jugoso/jugosa *adjective* juicy.

juguete *noun Masc.* toy; **un coche de juguete** a toy car.

juguetería *noun Fem.* toyshop.

juicio *noun Masc.* **1** trial; **llevar a alguien a juicio** to take someone to court; **2** sense; **no tiene ningún juicio** he's not very sensible; **3 no estar en su sano juicio** to be out of one's mind; **perder el juicio** to lose one's mind.

julio *noun Masc.* July; **en julio/en el mes de julio** in July.

jungla *noun Fem.* jungle.

junio *noun Masc.* June; **en junio/en el mes de junio** in June.

júnior *adjective* junior.

junta¹ *noun Fem.* **1** board, committee; **2** meeting.

juntar *verb* [17] **1** to put together; **2** to join.
juntarse *reflexive verb* [17] **1** to join; **2** to meet; **me junté con unos amigos** I met some friends; **3** to get closer; **juntaos más** come closer.

junto/junta² *adjective* **1** together; **ahora todos juntos** all together now; **no los pongas tan juntos** don't put them so close together; **2** junto a next to; **junto a la ventana** next to the window; **3** junto con with, together with.

jurado *noun Masc.* jury.

jurar *verb* [17] to swear; **te lo juro** I swear.

jurídico/jurídica *adjective* legal.

justamente *adverb* **1** fairly; **tratar a alguien justamente** to treat someone fairly; **2** exactly; **justamente eso es lo que yo quería decir** that's exactly what I meant; **¡justamente!** exactly!.

justicia *noun Fem.* justice.

justificar *verb* [31] to justify.

justo¹**/justa** *adjective* **1** fair; **no has sido justo con él** you haven't been fair with him; **una sociedad justa** a fair society; **2** exact; **la cantidad justa** the exact amount; **son ciento cincuenta euros justos** it's exactly one hundred and fifty euros; **3** just enough; **tengo lo justo para el autobús** I have just enough for my bus fare; **viven con lo justo** they have just enough to live on; **4** tight; **te está un poco justo** it's a

SPANISH-ENGLISH

la

bit tight on you; **los zapatos me quedan muy justos** the shoes are too tight on me.

justo² *adverb* **1** just; **justo a tiempo** just in time; **2 justo en el centro** right in the middle.

juvenil *adjective* **1** youthful (*appearance*); **2** young (*fashion*); **3** junior (*team or competition*).

juventud *noun Fem.* youth; **la juventud de hoy** today's youth.

juzgado *noun Masc.* court.

juzgar *verb* [28] **1** to judge (*people or behaviour*); **te he juzgado mal** I've misjudged you; **2** to try (*a case or person*).

Kk

kaki *adjective* khaki.

kárate *noun Masc.* karate.

karting *noun Masc.* karting.

ketchup *noun Masc.* ketchup *Masc.*

Kg. *abbreviation* (*short for: kilogramo*) kg.

kilo *noun Masc.* kilo.

kilogramo *noun Masc.* kilogram.

kilómetro *noun Masc.* kilometre.

kiosco *noun Masc.* **1** kiosk (*selling sweets, cigarrettes, etc*); **2** newspaper kiosk; **3** stand; **un kiosko de helados** an ice cream stand; **4 el kiosko de la orquesta** the bandstand.

kiwi *noun Masc.* **1** kiwifruit; **2** kiwi.

km. *abbreviation* (*short for: kilómetro*) km.

koala *noun Masc.* koala bear.

Ll

la¹ *definite article* ('*la*' is used before feminine singular nouns; see also '*el*', '*los*' and '*las*') **1** the; **la casa es grande** the house is big; **2** (*sometimes* '*la*' *is not translated*) **no me gusta la sandía** I don't like watermelon; **irse a la cama** to go to bed; **la maleta de Isabel** Isabel's suitcase; **esta es la señora Martínez** this is Mrs Martínez; **3** (*with parts of the body or personal belongings*) **se rompió la pierna** she broke her leg; **se afeitó la barba** he shaved his beard off; **me quité la chaqueta** I took my jacket off; **4** (*talking about time*) **iré la próxima semana** I'll go next week; **5 me gustó la verde** I liked the green one; **la mía es roja** mine is red; **esa es la tuya** that one is yours; **6 esta es la de Ana** this one is Ana's; **la mía y la de usted** mine and yours; **me gusta más la de Toni** I like Toni's better; **7 la que yo compré** the one I bought; **la que quieras** whichever you want.

la² *pronoun* **1** her; **la acompañé a casa** I took her home; **2** it (*referring to a Spanish feminine noun*); **compré una camiseta, pero la voy a cambiar** I bought a T-shirt, but I'm going to change it.

153

a **labio** *noun Masc.* lip.

b **laborable** *adjective* **día laborable** working day.

c **laboratorio** *noun Masc.* laboratory.

d **laca** *noun Fem.* **1** lacquer; **2** hairspray; **3** **laca de uñas** nail varnish.

e **ladera** *noun Fem.* slope.

g **lado** *noun Masc.* **1** side; **el otro lado** the other side; **hacerse a un lado** to move to the side; **al otro lado de la carretera** on the other side of the road; **2** **al lado de** next to; **al lado de Miguel** next to Miguel; **se sentó a mi lado** he sat next to me; **viven en la casa de al lado** they live next door; **3** **de lado** sideways; **ponlo de lado** put it sideways; **tumbarse de lado** to lie on your side; **4** **en todos lados/por todos lados** everywhere; **he buscado por todos lados** I've looked everywhere; **5** **en otro lado** somewhere else; **deben estar en otro lado** they must be somewhere else; **6** **en cualquier lado** anywhere; **deja siempre sus cosas en cualquier lado** he always leaves his things all over the place; **7** **en algún lado** somewhere; **debe estar en algún lado** it must be somewhere; **8** **en ningún lado/por ningún lado** nowhere, not anywhere; **no está por ningún lado** it's nowhere; **no lo encuentro en ningún lado** I can't find it anywhere; **9** **por un lado** ... **por otro** ... on the one hand ... on the other hand ....

z **ladrar** *verb* [17] to bark.

ladrillo *noun Masc.* brick.

ladrón/ladrona *noun Masc./Fem.* **1** thief, burglar; **2** robber.

lagarto *noun Masc.* lizard.

lago *noun Masc.* lake.

lágrima *noun Fem.* tear.

laguna *noun Fem.* **1** lake; **2** lagoon.

lamentar *verb* [17] **1** to regret; **lamento tener que informarle de** ... I regret to have to inform you that ...; **2** **lo lamento mucho** I'm very sorry; **lamento no poder ayudarle** I'm sorry I can't help you.

lamer *verb* [18] to lick.

lámpara *noun Fem.* lamp; **lámpara de pie** standard lamp.

lana *noun Fem.* wool; **una chaqueta de lana** a wool jacket; **pura lana virgen** pure new wool.

langosta *noun Fem.* lobster.

langostino *noun Masc.* king prawn.

lanza *noun Fem.* spear.

lanzamiento *noun Masc.* launch (*of rocket, product*).

lanzar *verb* [22] **1** to throw (*a ball or stone*); **2** to launch (*a product or an attack*).
lanzarse *reflexive verb* [22] **1** to throw yourself; **se lanzó al agua** he leapt into the water; **lanzarse en paracaídas** to parachute; **2** **lanzarse sobre alguien** to pounce on someone.

lápiz *noun Masc.* **1** pencil; **2** **un lápiz de color** a crayon; **3** **lápiz de ojos** eyeliner; **lápiz de labios** lipstick.

largo¹ *noun Masc.* length; **¿cuánto mide de largo?** how long is it?; **cinco metros de largo** five metres long.

largo²/larga *adjective* **1** long; **una falda larga** a long skirt; **te está muy largo** it's too long for you; **2 a lo largo de** along; **a lo largo de la costa** along the coast; **3 a lo largo de** throughout; **a lo largo del día** throughout the day.

las¹ *definite article ('las' is used before feminine plural nouns; see also 'el', 'la' and 'los')* **1** the; **deja las cajas ahí** leave the boxes there; **2** (*sometimes 'las' is not translated*) **no me gustan las naranjas** I don't like oranges; **las maletas de Isabel** Isabel's suitcases; **3** (*with parts of the body or personal belongings*) **se lavó las manos** she washed her hands; **me quité las botas** I took my boots off; **4 las mías son rojas** mine are red; **esas son las tuyas** those are yours; **me gustaron las verdes** I liked the green ones; **5 estas son las de Ana** these ones are Ana's; **las mías y las de usted** mine and yours; **me gustan más las de Toni** I like Toni's better; **6 las que yo compré** the ones I bought; **las que quieras** whichever you want.

las² *pronoun* them (*referring to a plural Spanish feminine noun*); **las vi ayer** I saw them yesterday; **te las puedes llevar** you can take them with you.

láser *noun Masc.* laser; **un rayo láser** a laser beam.

lástima *noun Fem.* **1** shame; **es una lástima que no puedas venir** it's a shame you can't come; **¡qué lástima!** what a shame!; **2 sentir lástima de alguien** to feel sorry for someone; **su madre me da lástima** I feel sorry for her mother; **3 estar hecho una lástima** to be in a pitiful state.

lata *noun Fem.* **1** tin; **una lata de tomates** a tin of tomatoes; **en lata** tinned; **sardinas en lata** tinned sardines; **2** (*informal*) nuisance; **¡qué lata!** what a nuisance!; **es una lata tener que esperar** it's a nuisance having to wait; **3 dar la lata** (*informal*) to be a nuisance; **¡deja de dar la lata!** stop being a nuisance!; **siempre están dando la lata** they're always such a nuisance.

latín *noun Masc.* Latin.

Latinoamérica *noun Fem.* Latin America.

latinoamericano/ latinoamericana *noun Masc./ Fem., adjective* Latin American.

latón *noun Masc.* brass.

laurel *noun Masc.* **1** laurel; **2 una hoja de laurel** a bayleaf.

lavabo *noun Masc.* **1** washbasin; **2** toilet; **¿dónde están los lavabos?** where are the toilets?

lavado *noun Masc.* wash; **lavado en seco** dry cleaning; **lavado a mano** handwashing.

lavadora *noun Fem.* washing machine.

lavanda *noun Fem.* lavender.

a
b

lavandería *noun Fem.* **1** laundry;
2 laundrette.

lavaplatos *noun Masc.* (*does not change in the plural*) dishwasher.

c

d
e
f
g

lavar *verb* [17] **1** to wash; **lavar la ropa** to wash the clothes; **lavar los platos** to wash the dishes; **2 lavar algo en seco** to dry-clean something; **3 lavar y marcar** wash and blow-dry.

h
i
j
k

lavarse *reflexive verb* [17] to wash; **lavarse las manos** to wash your hands; **lavarse la cabeza** to wash your hair; **me lavo la cabeza todos los días** I wash my hair everyday; **lavarse los dientes** to clean your teeth.

l

m

lavavajillas *noun Masc.* (*does not change in the plural*) dishwasher.

n

lazo *noun Masc.* ribbon.

ñ
o
p
q
r
s
t
u
v
w
x
y
z

le *pronoun* **1** him (*as indirect object*); **quedé con Carlos y le di las llaves** I met Carlos and gave him the keys; **le mandé el paquete el lunes** I sent him the parcel on Monday; **¿qué le quitaron?** what did they take from him?; **2** her (*as indirect object*); **quedé con Inés y le di las llaves** I met Inés and gave her the keys; **le mandé el paquete el lunes** I sent her the parcel on Monday; **¿qué le quitaron?** what did they take from her?; **3** you (*polite form: as indirect object*); **¿le llevo las maletas a su habitación?** shall I carry your suitcases to your room?; **le mandé el paquete el lunes** I sent you the parcel on Monday; **4** it (*as indirect object*); **le puse la tapa** I put the lid

on it; **le puse otra estantería** I added another shelf to it.

lección *noun Fem.* lesson.

leche *noun Fem.* milk; **leche desnatada/leche descremada** skimmed milk; **leche en polvo** powdered milk.

lechuga *noun Fem.* lettuce.

lectura *noun Fem.* reading.

leer *verb* [37] to read; **estoy leyendo una novela** I'm reading a novel; **¿has leído a Lorca?** have you read Lorca?

legal *adjective* legal.

legendario/legendaria *adjective* legendary.

lejano/lejana *adjective* distant; **son parientes lejanos** they are distant relatives; **el Lejano Oriente** the Far East.

lejía *noun Fem.* bleach.

lejos *adverb* **1** far; **no está muy lejos** it's not very far; **está demasiado lejos para ir andando** it's too far to walk; **2** a long way; **está lejos del centro** it's a long way from the centre; **viven lejos de aquí** they live a long way from here; **está muy lejos** it's a long way (away); **3 desde lejos** from a distance.

lengua *noun Fem.* **1** tongue; **morderse la lengua** to bite your tongue; **2** language; **una lengua muy difícil** a very difficult language; **mi lengua materna** my mother tongue.

lenguado *noun Masc.* sole.

lenguaje noun Masc. language;
lenguaje corporal body language.

lente noun Fem. lens; **lentes de contacto** contact lenses.

lenteja noun Fem. lentil.

lentilla noun Fem. contact lens.

lento/**lenta** adjective slow; **son muy lentos** they're very slow; **cocinar algo a fuego lento** to cook something over a low heat.

lento² adverb slowly; **caminan muy lento** they're walking very slowly.

leña noun Masc. firewood.

leño noun Masc. log.

leo noun Masc./Fem. Leo; **es leo** she's Leo.

Leo noun Masc. Leo.

león noun Masc. lion.

leopardo noun Masc. leopard.

leotardos plural noun Masc. woollen tights.

les pronoun **1** them (as indirect object); **les di las llaves** I gave them the keys; **les mandé el paquete el lunes** I sent them the parcel on Monday; **¿qué les quitaron?** what did they take from them?; **les puse la tapa** I put the lids on them; **2** you (polite form, talking to more than one person: as indirect object); **les mandé el paquete el lunes** I sent you the parcel on Monday.

lesión noun Fem. injury.

letón/letona noun Masc./Fem., adjective Latvian.

Letonia noun Fem. Latvia.

letra noun Fem. **1** letter; **letras mayúsculas** capital letters; **letras minúsculas** lower case letters; **2** handwriting; **tiene muy buena letra** she has very nice handwriting; **casi no se le entiende la letra** you can hardly read his handwriting; **3** lyrics (of a song); **4** instalment; **me quedan dos letras por pagar** I still have two instalments to pay.

letrero noun Masc. notice, sign.

levadura noun Fem. yeast.

levantar verb [17] **1** to lift; **levantar un peso** to lift a weight; **levantar la tapadera** to lift the lid; **2** to raise; **levantar la mano** to raise your hand; **3** to pick up; **levantamos a la niña del suelo** we picked the girl up from the floor; **4** ¡**levanta ese ánimo!** cheer up!

levantarse reflexive verb [17] **1** to get up; **levantarse de la cama** to get out of bed; **2** **levántate del suelo** get up off the floor; **3** **levantarse de la mesa** to leave the table.

ley noun Fem. law.

leyenda noun Fem. legend.

leyó verb SEE **leer**.

libanés/libanesa noun Masc./Fem., adjective Lebanese.

Líbano noun Masc. **(el) Líbano** Lebanon.

liberar verb [17] **1** to free; **2** to liberate.

libertad noun Fem. freedom; **libertad de expresión** freedom of speech; **libertad condicional** parole.

libra¹ noun Fem. pound; **diez libras esterlinas** ten pounds sterling.

157

a
b
c
d
e
f
g
h
i
j
k
l
m
n
ñ
o
p
q
r
s
t
u
v
w
x
y
z

libra² *noun Masc./Fem.* Libra; **Susana es libra** Susana's Libra.

Libra *noun Masc.* Libra.

librar *verb* [17] **librar a alguien de morir ahogado** to save someone from drowning.
librarse *reflexive verb* [17]
1 librarse de morir ahogado to save yourself from drowning; **me libré del castigo** I escaped punishment; **2 librarse de una obligación** to get out of an obligation; **se libró de lavar los platos** he got out of doing the dishes.

libre *adjective* **1** free; **dejar libre a alguien** to set someone free; **¿está libre este asiento?** is this seat free?; **quinientos metros libres** five hundred metres freestyle;
2 trabajar por libre to work freelance; **3 al aire libre** in the open air.

librería *noun Fem.* **1** bookshop; **2** bookcase.

libreta *noun Fem.* notebook.

libro *noun Masc.* book; **libro de texto** textbook; **libro de bolsillo** paperback; **libro de consulta** reference book.

licencia *noun Fem.* licence, permit.

licenciado/licenciada *noun Masc./Fem.* graduate.

licor *noun Masc.* liqueur.

licuadora *noun Fem.* liquidizer.

líder *noun Masc./Fem.* leader.

liebre *noun Fem.* hare.

liga *noun Fem.* league; **la liga de fútbol** the football league.

ligeramente *adverb* slightly.

ligero/ligera *adjective* **1** light; **un paquete ligero** a light parcel; **tener el sueño ligero** to be a light sleeper; **2** slight; **hay un ligero problema** there's a slight problem; **un ligero sabor a almendras** a slight taste of almonds; **3** thin (*fabric*); **4** fast; **un caballo muy ligero** a very fast horse; **5** agile.

lima *noun Fem.* **1** file; **una lima de uñas** a nailfile; **2** lime.

limitar *verb* [17] **1** to limit; **2 limitar con algo** to border on something; **España limita con Francia** Spain has a border with France.
limitarse *reflexive verb* [17] **1 el problema no se limita a eso** the problem is not just that; **2 me limité a ayudarlos con el ordenador** I just helped them with the computer.

límite *noun Masc.* **1** limit; **el límite de velocidad** the speed limit; **hay un tiempo límite** there's a time limit; **2 la fecha límite** the deadline; **3 ¡todo tiene un límite!** enough is enough!; **4** border (*of a country*).

limón *noun Masc.* lemon.

limonada *noun Fem.* lemonade.

limonero *noun Masc.* lemon tree.

limosna *noun Fem.* **pedir limosna** to beg; **dar limosna** to give money to beggars.

limpiaparabrisas *noun Masc.* (*does not change in the plural*) windscreen wiper.

limpiar *verb* [17] **1** to clean; **limpiar la casa** to clean the house; **2** to clean off; **limpiar una mancha de la mesa** to clean a dirty mark off the table; **3 limpiar algo con un trapo** to wipe something clean; **4 limpiar los zapatos** to polish the shoes; **5 limpiar algo en seco** to dry-clean something.

limpieza *noun Fem.* **1 hacer la limpieza** to do the cleaning; **hacer una limpieza general** to do a spring-clean; **2 limpieza en seco** dry-cleaning; **3 una limpieza de cutis** a facial.

limpio/limpia *adjective* **1** clean (*clothes, a house, or person, for example*); **2** fair (*a game or business deal, for example*).

lindo/linda *adjective* lovely.

línea *noun Fem.* **1** line; **línea de llegada** finishing line; **línea de meta** goal line; **2 línea aérea** airline; **línea regular** airline operating scheduled flights; **3 línea telefónica** telephone line; **no me da línea** the line is dead; **4 escribirle unas líneas a alguien** to drop someone a line; **leer entre líneas** to read between the lines; **5 un jugador de primera línea** a top player; **productos de primera línea** top-quality products; **6** figure; **mantener la línea** to watch your figure.

lino *noun Masc.* linen.

linterna *noun Fem.* torch.

lío *noun Masc.* (*informal*) **1** mess; **¡vaya lío!** what a mess!; **2 hacerse un lío** to get muddled up; **me hice un lío con las fechas** I got the dates all muddled up; **3 armar un lío** to

kick up a fuss; **4** trouble; **¡no te metas en líos!** keep out of trouble!

liquidación *noun Fem.* **1** sale; **liquidación por cierre** closing-down sale; **liquidación total** clearance sale; **2** liquidation (*of a business*); **3** settlement (*of a debt or an account*).

líquido[1] *noun Masc.* liquid.

líquido[2]**/líquida** *adjective* liquid.

liso/lisa *adjective* **1** smooth; **piel lisa** smooth skin; **2** straight; **tiene el pelo liso** she's got straight hair; **3** flat (*ground*).

lista[1] *noun Fem.* **1** list; **una lista de espera** a waiting list; **una lista de bodas** a wedding list; **una lista de precios** a price list; **la lista de vinos** the wine list; **2** (*at school*) register; **pasar lista** to take the register.

listín *noun Masc.* **listín telefónico/ listín de teléfonos** telephone directory.

listo/lista[2] *adjective* **1** clever; **2 estar listo** to be ready; **ya estamos listos para salir** we're ready to go now.

litera *noun Fem.* **1** bunk bed; **2** berth.

literatura *noun Fem.* literature.

litro *noun Masc.* litre.

Lituania *noun Fem.* Lithuania.

lituano/lituana *noun Masc./Fem.*, *adjective* Lithuanian.

llama *noun Fem.* **1** flame; **2** llama.

llamada *noun Fem.* call; **una llamada telefónica** a telephone

a
b
c
d
e
f
g
h
i
j
k
l
m
n
ñ
o
p
q
r
s
t
u
v
w
x
y
z

a
b
c
d
e
f
g
h
i
j
k
l
m
n
ñ
o
p
q
r
s
t
u
v
w
x
y
z

call; **una llamada interurbana** a long-distance call; **una llamada urbana** a local call; **una llamada a cobro revertido** a reverse-charge call.

llamar *verb* [17] **1** to call; **te llama tu madre** your mother is calling you; **llamar al médico** to call the doctor; **llamamos a un taxi** we called a taxi; **la llamamos Tintina** we call her Tintina; **2** to phone; **¿cuándo llamarás?** when will you phone?; **le llamé por teléfono** I phoned him.

llamarse *reflexive verb* [17] to be called; **se llama Ángeles** she's called Ángeles; **¿cómo te llamas?** what's your name?.

llano/llana *adjective* flat, level (*ground*).

llave *noun Fem.* **1** key; **una llave maestra** a master key; **la llave de contacto** the ignition key; **cerrar algo con llave** to lock something; **2 la llave del gas** the gas tap; **la llave del agua** the mains water tap; **3** switch (*for a light*); **4** spanner; **una llave inglesa** an adjustable spanner; **5** hold; **una llave de judo** a judo hold.

llavero *noun Masc.* keyring.

llegada *noun Fem.* arrival; **a su llegada al hotel** when he arrived at the hotel.

llegar *verb* [28] **1** to arrive; **llegan a las siete** they arrive at seven; **cuando lleguemos a casa** when we get home; **2** to come; **ya llega el invierno** winter is coming; **3 llegar pronto a un sitio** to get somewhere

early; **siempre llegas tarde** you're always late; **llegó justo a tiempo** he was just in time; **4** to reach; **no llego a la lámpara** I can't reach the lamp; **5 la hierba me llega hasta las rodillas** the grass comes up to my knees; **las cortinas llegan hasta el suelo** the curtains go down to the floor; **mi parte del jardín llega hasta la valla** my part of the garden goes up to the fence; **6** to be enough; **con tres litros de leche llega para todos** three litres of milk will be enough for everybody; **7 llegar a hacer** to get to do; **llegué a conocerlo** I got to meet him; **no llegué a verlo** I didn't get to see it; **8 llegar a ser** to become; **llegó a ser famoso** he became famous.

llenar *verb* [17] **1** to fill; **llenar la bañera** to fill the bath; **2** to fill up; **llene el depósito, por favor** fill up the tank, please; **3** fill in (*a form, for example*).

lleno/llena *adjective* **1** full; **la botella está llena de agua** the bottle is full of water; **2** covered; **el suelo estaba lleno de papeles** the floor was covered with papers.

llevar *verb* [17] **1** to take; **te lo puedes llevar** you can take it with you; **llevaré una botella de vino a la fiesta** I'll take a bottle of wine to the party; **yo te puedo llevar a la estación** I can take you to the station; **la llevé a comer a un restaurante** I took her for lunch to a restaurante; **2** to carry; **yo llevaba al niño en brazos** I was carrying the baby in my arms; **3 la llevé en coche a su casa** I drove her home;

4 to have; **¿qué llevas en el bolso?** what have you got in your bag?; **no llevo las llaves encima** I don't have the keys on me; **5** to wear; **llevaba un vestido verde** she was wearing a green dress; **6 lleva tiempo** it takes time; **me llevó dos semanas terminarlo** it took me two weeks to finish it; **le llevó mucho hacerlo** it took her a lot of time to do it; **lleva media hora hablando por teléfono** he's been on the phone for half an hour; **¿cuánto tiempo llevas trabajando aquí?** how long have you been working here?; **llevamos dos semanas en Londres** we've been in London for two weeks; **7 le llevo cuatro años** I'm four years older than him; **8** to lead; **el camino que lleva al río** the road that leads to the river.

llevarse *reflexive verb* [17] **1** to take (away); **se llevó los discos** he took the records; **ya puedes llevarte esto** you can take this away now; **2 llevarse bien con alguien** to get on with someone; **no se llevan bien** they don't get on.

llorar *verb* [17] to cry.

llover *verb* [38] to rain; **está lloviendo** it's raining; **★ está lloviendo a cántaros** it's pouring down (*literally: it's raining in jugfuls*).

llovizna *noun Fem.* drizzle.

llueva, llueve, etc. *verb* SEE **llover.**

lluvia *noun Fem.* rain.

lluvioso/lluviosa *adjective* rainy.

lo¹ *definite article* **1** the; **lo mejor es ...** the best thing is ...; **lo curioso es ...** the funny thing is ...; **prefiero lo salado a lo dulce** I prefer savoury things to sweet things; **2 lo mío** mine; **esto es lo tuyo** that's yours; **lo vuestro está en la habitación** your things are in the bedroom; **3 esto es lo de mi madre** this is my mother's; **lo de Marta lo he puesto en la mesa** I've put Marta's things on the table; **4 ¿sabes lo de Eva?** have you heard about Eva?; **lo de Pablo es muy raro** it's really strange this thing with Pablo; **lo del accidente fue horrible** that thing about the accident was horrible; **le conté lo tuyo** I told her about you; **5 lo que** what; **eso es lo que yo compré** that's what I bought; **coge lo que quieras** take whatever you want; **dime todo lo que sepas** tell me everything you know.

lo² *pronoun* **1** him; **lo vi ayer** I saw him yesterday; **2** it; **lo metí en tu bolso** I put it in your bag; **3 ya lo sé** I know.

lobo *noun Masc.* wolf.

local *noun Masc.* premises.

localidad *noun Fem.* **1** town; **una pequeña localidad** a small town; **2** ticket; **'no hay localidades'** 'sold out'.

loción *noun Fem.* lotion; **loción para después del afeitado** aftershave lotion; **loción bronceadora** suntan lotion.

loco/loca *noun Masc./Fem.* madman, madwoman.

loco *adjective* **1** mad; **¡tú estás**

a
b
c
d
e
f
g
h
i
j
k
l
m
n
ñ
o
p
q
r
s
t
u
v
w
x
y
z

loco! you're mad!; **2 estar loco por alguien** to be crazy about somebody; **3 ¡este niño me va a volver loco!** that child's going to drive me mad!; **las fresas la vuelven loca** she loves strawberries; ★**estar loco de remate** (*informal*) to be completely bonkers; ★**hacer algo a lo loco** to do something any old how.

locomotora *noun Fem.* engine (*of a train*).

locura *noun Fem.* **1** madness; **2 eso es una locura** that's crazy; **otra de sus locuras** another one of his crazy ideas.

locutor/locutora *noun Masc./ Fem.* **1** announcer; **2** newsreader; **3 locutor deportivo** sports commentator.

lógico/lógica *adjective* logical.

lograr *verb* [17] **1** to achieve; **lograr la victoria** to achieve victory; **2 lograr hacer** to manage to do; **lograr que alguien haga** to get someone to do.

lombriz *noun Fem.* worm.

lomo *noun Masc.* **1** back (*of an animal*); **2** spine (*of a book*); **3 lomo de cerdo** loin of pork; **4 filete de lomo** sirloin steak.

loncha *noun Fem.* slice; **una loncha de jamón** a slice of ham; **una loncha de bacon** a rasher of bacon.

londinense *noun Masc./Fem.* Londoner.

londinense *adjective* London.

Londres *noun Masc.* London.

longaniza *noun Fem.* spicy pork sausage.

longitud *noun Fem.* **1** length; **tiene doce metros de longitud** it's twelve metres long; **2** longitude; **3 longitud de onda** wavelength.

loro/lora *noun Masc./Fem.* parrot; ★**hablar como un loro** (*informal*) to be a chatterbox; ★**repetir algo como un loro** to repeat something parrot-fashion.

los¹ *definite article* ('*los*' *is used before masculine plural nouns; see also* '*el*', '*la*' *and* '*las*') **1** the; **deja los libros ahí** leave the books there; **2** (*sometimes* '*los*' *is not translated*) **no me gustan los tomates** I don't like tomatoes; **los discos de Isabel** Isabel's records; **3** (*with parts of the body or personal belongings*) **se frotó los ojos** she rubbed her eyes; **me quité los zapatos** I took my shoes off; **4 los míos son rojos** mine are red; **ésos son los tuyos** those are yours; **me gustaron los verdes** I liked the green ones; **5 éstos son los de Ana** these ones are Ana's; **los míos y los de usted** mine and yours; **me gustan más los de Toni** I like Toni's better; **6 los que yo compré** the ones I bought; **los que quieras** whichever you want.

los² *pronoun* them; **los vi ayer** I saw them yesterday; **te los puedes llevar** you can take them with you.

lote *noun Masc.* batch Masc.; **a batch of letters** un lote de cartas.

lotería *noun Fem.* lottery; **tocarle a alguien la lotería** to win the lottery.

luces *plural noun* SEE **luz**.

lucha *noun Fem.* fight.

luchar *verb* [17] **1** to fight; **luchar cuerpo a cuerpo** to fight hand to hand; **2** to struggle.

luego *adverb* **1** then; **luego vino su madre** then her mother came; **2** later; **luego te veo** I'll see you later; **¡hasta luego!** see you later!; **3** afterwards; **luego te arrepentirás** you'll be sorry afterwards; **luego podemos cenar** we can have dinner afterwards; **4** then; **primero está su casa y luego la mía** first comes her house and then mine; **primero iré al banco y luego a tu casa** I'll go to the bank first and then to your house; **5 desde luego** of course.

lugar *noun Masc.* **1** place; **un lugar precioso** a beautiful place; **lugar de nacimiento** place of birth; **me siento fuera de lugar** I feel out of place; **2 en cualquier lugar** anywhere; **por cualquier otro lugar** anywhere else; **3 en otro lugar** somewhere else; **4 yo en su lugar ...** if I were him ...; **5** position (*in a race or competition*); **en primer lugar** in first position; **llegó en último lugar** he finished in last place; **6 en primer lugar** first of all; **en segundo lugar ...** second ...; **en último lugar** last of all; **7 en lugar de** instead of.

lúgubre *adjective* gloomy.

lujo *noun Masc.* luxury; **apartamentos de lujo** luxury apartments.

lujoso/lujosa *adjective* luxurious.

luminoso/luminosa *adjective* **1** bright; **2** luminous.

luna *noun Fem.* **1** moon; **esta noche hay luna** the moon is out tonight; **luna llena** full moon; **luna creciente** waxing moon; **luna menguante** waning moon; **la luna de miel** the honeymoon; **2 una luna de espejo** a mirror; **la luna del escaparate** the shop window.

lunar *noun Masc.* **1** mole (*on your skin*); **2** polka-dot; **una camisa de lunares** a polka-dot shirt.

lunes *noun Masc.* Monday (*see 'domingo' for examples*).

lupa *noun Fem.* magnifying glass.

luto *noun Masc.* mourning; **ir de luto** to be in mourning; **ponerse de luto** to go into mourning.

Luxemburgo *noun Masc.* Luxembourg.

luz (*plural* **luces**) *noun Fem.* **1** light; **dar la luz** to switch on the light; **apagar la luz** to switch off the light; **la luz del sol** the sunlight; **2** electricity; **se ha ido la luz** the electricity's gone off; **3 luces de cruce/luces cortas** dipped headlights; **luces largas** full beam; **luces de freno** brake lights; **4 dar a luz** to give birth; ★ **tener pocas luces** to be a bit dim.

Mm

macarrones *plural noun Masc.* macaroni.

macedonia *noun Fem.* fruit salad.

maceta *noun Fem.* flowerpot.

a
b
c
d
e
f
g
h
i
j
k
l
m
n
ñ
o
p
q
r
s
t
u
v
w
x
y
z

a
b
c
d
e
f
g
h
i
j
k
l
m
n
ñ
o
p
q
r
s
t
u
v
w
x
y
z

machista *noun Masc./Fem.* male chauvinist.
machista *adjective* sexist.

macho *adjective* male.

madera *noun Fem.* **1** wood; **2** timber.

madrastra *noun Fem.* stepmother.

madre *noun Fem.* **1** mother; **ser madre soltera** to be a single mother; **madre política** mother-in-law; **2 ¡madre mía!** my goodness!.

Madrid *noun Fem.* Madrid.

madrileño/madrileña *noun Masc./Fem.* person from Madrid.
madrileño *adjective* of/from Madrid; **las iglesias madrileñas** the churches of Madrid.

madrina *noun Fem.* **1** godmother; **2** in Spanish weddings, the woman who accompanies the groom, usually his mother.

madrugada *noun Fem.* dawn; **de madrugada** at dawn; **nos levantamos de madrugada** we got up at dawn; **llegamos de madrugada** we arrived in the early hours of the morning; **a las cuatro de la madrugada** at four in the morning.

madurar *verb* [17] **1** to ripen; **2** to mature.

maduro/madura *adjective* **1** ripe; **2** mature; **es muy poco maduro** he's quite immature.

maestro/maestra *noun Masc./Fem.* **1** teacher (*primary school*); **2** master (*of a trade*).

magdalena *noun Fem.* fairycake.

magia *noun Fem.* magic.

mágico/mágica *adjective* magical.

magnético/magnética *adjective* magnetic.

magnetofón, magnetófono *noun Masc.* tape recorder.

magnífico/magnífica *adjective* **1** wonderful; **2** magnificent.

mago/maga *noun Masc./Fem.* **1** magician; **2** wizard.

mahonesa *noun Fem.* mayonnaise.

maíz *noun Masc.* **1** sweetcorn; **una mazorca de maíz** a corn on the cob; **2** maize.

mal *noun Masc.* evil; **el bien y el mal** good and evil.
mal *adjective* **1** bad; **es un mal amigo** he's a bad friend; **vinieron en mal momento** they came at a bad time; **2** wrong; **la respuesta está mal** the answer's wrong; **está mal criticar** it's wrong to criticize; **3** ill; **¿te sientes mal?** do you feel ill?; **su padre está muy mal** his father's very ill.
mal *adverb* **1** badly; **está muy mal pintado** it's really badly painted; **lo leyó muy mal** she read it very badly; **le va muy mal en el trabajo** he's doing very badly at work; **el país marcha mal** the country's not doing well; **2** wrong; **lo hizo mal** he did it wrong; **hace mal en no pedir perdón** he's wrong not to apologize; **3 contestar mal a alguien** to answer someone back; **4 te oigo mal** I can't hear you very well; **5 la comida sabe mal** the food tastes

manchar

horrible; **olía muy mal** there was a nasty smell; **6 portarse mal** to misbehave; **entender mal algo** to misunderstand something; **7 ¡menos mal!** thank goodness!

malabarismos *noun Masc.* (*plural*) **hacer malabarismos** to juggle.

malabarista *noun Masc./Fem.* juggler.

malcriado/malcriada *noun Masc./Fem.* **es un malcriado** he's really spoilt.
malcriado *adjective* **1** spoilt; **2** naughty

maldición *noun Fem.* **1** curse; **2 soltar una maldición** to swear; **3 ¡maldición!** damn!.

maleducado/maleducada *noun Masc./Fem.* **es una maleducada** she's really rude.
maleducado *adjective* rude.

malentendido *noun Masc.* misunderstanding.

maleta *noun Fem.* suitcase.

maletero *noun Masc.* boot (*of a car*).

maletín *noun Masc.* **1** briefcase; **2** overnight case; **3 el maletín del médico** the doctor's bag.

malhumor *noun Masc.* bad temper.

malla *noun Fem.* **1** mesh; **malla de alambre** wire mesh; **2** leotard; **3 mallas** leggings.

Mallorca *noun Fem.* Majorca.

mallorquín/mallorquina *noun Masc./Fem., adjective* Majorcan.

malo/mala *adjective* **1** bad; **una mala costumbre** a bad habit; **es**

malo para la salud it's bad for your health; **2** naughty; **¡qué niño más malo!** what a naughty child!; **3** nasty; **no seas mala y devuélveselo** don't be nasty and give it back to her; **4** poor; **de mala calidad** poor quality; **5 ayer hizo malo** the weather was bad yesterday; **nos hizo muy malo durante las vacaciones** we had horrible weather during the holidays; **6 estar malo** to be ill; **no puede venir porque está mala** she can't come because she's ill; **el pobre está muy malo** the poor thing is in a really bad way; **7 estar malo** to be off (*food*); **la leche está mala** the milk's gone off; **8 estar malo** to taste horrible; **la sopa estaba muy mala** the soup was horrible; **9 ser malo para** (*a person*) to be bad at; **soy malo para las matemáticas** I'm bad at maths; SEE **mal²**.

mamá *noun Fem.* (*informal*) Mum.

mamífero *noun Masc.* mammal.

manada *n Fem.* **1** herd (*of cattle*); **2** pack (*of dogs*); **3** gang (*of young people*)

mancha *noun Fem.* **1** stain; **una mancha de chocolate** a chocolate stain; **quitar una mancha** to remove a stain; **2** mark; **3 mancha de petróleo** oil slick.

manchar *verb* [17] **1** to get (something) dirty; **mancharon la alfombra de barro** they got mud all over the carpet; **2** to stain.
mancharse *reflexive verb* [17] to get yourself dirty; **cuidado, no te**

manches careful, don't get yourself dirty; **se manchó los pantalones de barro** he got mud all over his trousers.

manchón *noun Fem.* stain.

mandar *verb* [17] **1** to order; **2 le gusta mandar** she likes to give the orders; **3 mandar a alguien hacer** to tell somebody to do; **me mandó recoger la habitación** she told me to tidy my bedroom; **haz lo que te mandan** do as you're told; **4** to send; **mandar una carta a alguien** to send somebody a letter; **los mandé a comprar fruta** I sent them to buy some fruit; **5 mandar llamar a alguien** to send for someone.

mandarina *noun Fem.* mandarin, tangerine.

mando *noun Masc.* **1** command; **estar al mando de** to be in charge of; **2** control (*of a machine or a television, for example*); **mando a distancia** remote control.

manejar *verb* [17] **1** to use (*a computer, dictionary*); **2** to operate (*a machine*); **3** to manage (*a business*).

manera *noun Fem.* **1** way; **lo hice a mi manera** I did it my way; **no hubo manera de arreglarlo** there was no way of fixing it; **es su manera de ser** it's the way he is; **2 de alguna manera** somehow; **me las arreglaré de alguna manera** I'll do it somehow; **3 de cualquier manera**; any old how; **puedes decorarlo de cualquier manera** you can decorate it any way you want; **4 de una manera u otra** one way or another; **5 ¡de ninguna**

manera! no way!; **'¿me dejas el coche?'** – **'¡de ninguna manera!'** 'can I borrow your car?' – 'no way'; **6 de todas maneras** anyway; **de todas maneras no pensaba comprarlo** I wasn't thinking of buying it anyway; **7 de manera que** so; **de manera que al final no la vi** so I didn't see her in the end.

manga *noun Fem.* **1** sleeve; **una camisa de manga corta** a short-sleeved shirt; **sin mangas** sleeveless; **2** hose (*for watering*).

mango *noun Masc.* **1** handle (*of a knife or tool*); **2** mango.

manguera *noun Fem.* hosepipe.

manía *noun Fem.* **1 tiene la manía del orden** he's obsessed with tidiness; **es maja pero tiene sus manías** she's nice but she has her funny little ways; **2 tenerle manía a alguien** to have it in for somebody.

maniático/maniática *noun Masc./Fem.* **es una maniática de la limpieza** she's obsessed with cleanliness.
maniático *adjective* fussy.

manifestación *noun Fem.* **1** demonstration; **2** sign (*of disapproval, for instance*); **3 manifestaciones** statements.

manifestar *verb* [29] **1** to express (*disapproval or an opinion*); **2** to show (*emotions*).
manifestarse *reflexive verb* [29] **1** to demonstrate; **2** to become evident; **3 manifestarse en contra de algo** to come out against something.

manillar *noun Masc.* handlebars.

manipular *verb* [17] **1** to operate (*a machine*); **2** to manipulate (*data or information*).

maniquí *noun Masc.* mannequin.

manivela *noun Fem.* handle.

mano *noun Fem.* **1** hand; **levantar la mano** to raise your hand; **ir de la mano** to go hand in hand; **coger a alguien de la mano** to take somebody's hand; **2 darle la mano a alguien** to give somebody your hand, to shake somebody's hand; **3 decir adiós con la mano** to wave goodbye; **4** coat; **una mano de pintura** a coat of paint.

manómetro *noun Masc.* pressure gauge.

mansión *noun Fem.* mansion.

manso/mansa *adjective* **1** tame (*an animal*); **2** gentle (*a person*).

manta *noun Fem.* blanket.

manteca *noun Fem.* lard.

mantecado *noun Masc.* almond delicacy (*eaten at Christmas*).

mantel *noun Masc.* tablecloth.

mantendrá, **mantendría**, **etc.** *verb* SEE **mantener**.

mantener *verb* [9] **1** to keep; **mantener la calma** to keep calm; **mantener el equilibrio** to keep your balance; **2** to support (*a family, for example*).
mantenerse *reflexive verb* [9] to keep; **mantenerse en equilibrio** to keep your balance; **mantenerse en contacto con alguien** to keep in touch with somebody.

mantengo, **mantenga**, **etc.** *verb* SEE **mantener**.

mantenimiento *noun Masc.* **1** maintenance; **2 ejercicios de mantenimiento** keep-fit exercises.

mantequilla *noun Fem.* butter.

mantilla *noun Fem.* mantilla (*a lace headscarf*).

mantuve, **mantuvo**, **etc.** *verb* SEE **mantener**.

manual *adjective* manual.

manzana *noun Fem.* **1** apple; **2** block (*in a town*); **dar una vuelta a la manzana** to go round the block.

manzanilla *noun Fem.* **1** camomile tea; **2** dry sherry.

manzano *noun Masc.* apple tree.

mañana *noun Fem.* morning; **a la mañana siguiente** the next morning; **por la mañana** in the morning; **a las once de la mañana** at eleven o'clock in the morning.
mañana *adverb* tomorrow; **pasado mañana** the day after tomorrow; **hasta mañana** see you tomorrow; **mañana por la tarde** tomorrow afternoon.

mapa *noun Masc.* map; **un mapa de carreteras** a road map.

maquillaje *noun Masc.* make-up.

maquillar *verb* [17] to make up.
maquillarse *reflexive verb* [17] to put your make-up on; **apenas se maquilla** she hardly wears any make-up.

máquina *noun Fem.* **1** machine; **una máquina de escribir** a typewriter; **escribir a máquina** to

a b c d e f g h i j k l m n ñ o p q r s t u v w x y z

a b c d e f g h i j k l m n ñ o p q r s t u v w x y z

type; **una máquina de coser** a sewing machine; **2 una máquina de fotos** a camera; **3 una máquina de afeitar** an electric shaver.

maquinaria *noun Fem.* machinery.

maquinilla *noun Fem.* safety razor.

mar *noun Masc.* sea; **viajar por mar** to travel by sea; **el mar Cantábrico** the Bay of Biscay.

maratón *noun m or Fem.* marathon.

maravilla *noun Fem.* wonder; **es una maravilla de casa** it's a wonderful house; ★ **a las mil maravillas** (*informal*) wonderfully.

maravilloso/maravillosa *adjective* wonderful.

marca *noun Fem.* **1** mark; **el cuadro ha dejado una marca en la pared** the picture has left a mark on the wall; **2** brand; **artículos de marca** brand products; **ropa de marca** designer clothes; **3 marca registrada** registered trademark; **4** record (*in sports*); **establecer una nueva marca** to establish a new record; **batir una marca** to break a record.

marcador *noun Masc.* scoreboard.

marcar *verb* [31] **1** to mark; **la experiencia me marcó mucho** the experience really marked me; **2 mi reloj marca las nueve** my watch says nine o'clock; **el termómetro marcaba cinco grados** the thermometer was registering five degrees; **3 marcar un número** to dial a number; **marca 00 44 para Gran Bretaña** dial 00 44 for Britain; **4 marcar un gol** to score a goal;

5 marcar el ritmo/marcar el compás to beat time.

marcha *noun Fem.* **1** hike; **ir de marcha** to go hiking; **fuimos de marcha a la montaña** we went hiking in the mountains; **2** march (*a demonstration*); **3** gear (*in a car*); **marcha atrás** reverse; **meter la marcha atrás** to put the car into reverse; **4** speed; **disminuir la marcha** to reduce speed; **5 estar en marcha** to be running (*a car engine, for example*); **6 poner en marcha** to start (*a car, for example*); **7 ¡en marcha!** let's go!; **8** (*informal*) **una discoteca con mucha marcha** a really fun disco; **¡qué marcha tiene ese grupo!** this group's really wild!; **9** (*informal*) **ir de marcha** to go out partying.

marchar *verb* [17] **1** to work (*a machine or a company*); **esto no marcha** this isn't working; **2** to march; **3 ¡marchando dos cafés!** two coffees coming up!.

marcharse *reflexive verb* [17] to leave; **nos marchamos mañana** we're leaving tomorrow.

marco *noun Masc.* **1** frame; **2** framework; **3** goal (*in football*).

marea *noun Fem.* tide; **está subiendo la marea** the tide's coming in; **cuando baje la marea** when the tide goes out; **marea negra** oil slick.

mareado/mareada *adjective* **1 estar mareado** to feel dizzy, to feel queasy; **me siento mareado/mareada** I'm feeling dizzy/queasy; **2 estar mareado** (*informal*) to be muddled up; **estoy mareado con tantos números** I'm all muddled up with all these numbers.

marear *verb* [17] **1** to make (somebody) feel dizzy, to make (somebody) feel queasy; **2** (*informal*) to confuse; **me marearon a preguntas** they asked me so many questions my head was spinning.

mareo *noun Masc.* **1** sick feeling; **me dan mareos si viajo en coche** I get carsick; **2** seasickness; **3** dizziness.

marfil *noun Masc.* ivory.

margarina *noun Fem.* margarine.

margarita *noun Fem.* **1** daisy; **2** marguerite.

margen *noun Masc.* margin; **escribir algo en el margen** to write something in the margin.

marido *noun Masc.* husband.

marina *noun Fem.* navy.

marinero *noun Masc.* sailor.

marioneta *noun Fem.* puppet.

mariposa *noun Fem.* butterfly.

mariquita *noun Fem.* ladybird.

marisco *noun Masc.* shellfish; **me gusto el marisco** I like shellfish.

mármol *noun Masc.* marble.

marrón *noun Masc.* brown.
marrón *adjective* brown; **zapatos marrones** brown shoes; **unos pantalones marrón claro** a pair of light brown trousers (*note that 'marrón' does not change in the plural when used with another adjective*).

martes *noun Masc.* Tuesday (*see 'domingo' for examples*).

martillo *noun Masc.* hammer.

marzo *noun Masc.* March; **en marzo/ en el mes de marzo** in March.

más *adverb, adjective, pronoun*
1 more; **éste me gusta más** I like this one more; **pon más azúcar** add more sugar; **tres más** three more; **más o menos** more or less; **¿necesitas más?** do you need any more?; **no comas más** don't eat any more; **no lo hagas más** don't do it again; **es un poco más grande** it's a bit bigger; **tenemos que hacerlo más rápido** we have to do it faster; **3 es más interesante que su primer libro** it's more interesting than his first book; **más que nunca** more than ever; **me gusta más el de cuero que el de tela** I prefer the leather one to the cloth one; **más blanco que la nieve** as white as snow; **4 el de más peso** the heaviest one; **los de más prestigio** the most prestigious ones; **el libro con más páginas** the book with the most pages; **5 el que más me gusta** the one I like the most; **los que son más altos** the tallest ones; **6 más de** more than; **más de veinte kilos** more than twenty kilos; **vinieron más de veinte personas** more than twenty people came; **7 hay tres sillas de más** there are three chairs too many; **hay tres pasteles de más** there are three cakes left over; **si quieres venir, tengo un billete de más** I've got a spare ticket if you want to come; ★ **estar de más** to feel out of place;; **8** (*referring to time*) **no**

a b c d e f g h i j k l m n ñ o p q r s t u v w x y z

a

les he visto **más** I've never seen them again; **no me quedo más** I won't stay any longer; **9** else; **¿esperas a alguien más?** are you expecting anybody else?; **nadie más** nobody else; **no quiero nada más** I don't want anything else; **¿querías algo más?** did you want anything else?; **10** no ... **más** only; **no tardo más de diez minutos** I'll only take ten minutes; **no es más que un resfriado** it's only a cold; **11** (*in exclamations*) **¡es más bonito!** it's so beautiful!; **¡había más gente!** there were so many people!; **¡le gustó más!** he liked it a lot!
más *preposition* plus; **cinco más siete** five plus seven.

masa *noun Fem.* **1** dough; **masa de pan** bread dough; **2** pastry; **masa de hojaldre** puff pastry.

masaje *noun Masc.* massage.

máscara *noun Fem.* mask.

mascarilla *noun Fem.* mask.

masculino[1] *noun Masc.* masculine (*in grammar*).

masculino[2]/**masculina** *adjective* masculine.

masticar *verb* [31] to chew.

mástil *noun Masc.* **1** mast; **2** flagpole.

matador *noun Masc.* matador.

matanza *noun Fem.* **1** massacre (*of people*); **2** slaughter (*of animals*).

matar *verb* [17] to kill.
matarse *reflexive verb* [17] **1** to kill yourself; **2** to get killed; **si sigues conduciendo así, te vas a matar** if you carry on driving like that you're going to get killed.

mate *noun Masc.* **jaque mate** checkmate.
mate *adjective* matt.

matemáticas *plural noun Fem.* maths.

materia *noun Fem.* **1** material; **materia prima** raw material; **2 materia grasa** fat; **3** subject (*of study or of a book*).

material *noun Masc., adjective* material.

maternal *adjective* maternal.

materno/materna *adjective* **1** motherly; **2** mother; **lengua materna** mother tongue; **3 abuelos maternos** grandparents on the mother's side.

matiz *noun Masc.* shade (*of a colour*).

matrícula *noun Fem.*
1 registration; **hacer la matrícula** to register; **2** registration number (*of a car*); **un coche con matrícula de Sevilla** a car with a Seville number plate; **3 matrícula de honor** distinction; **sacar matrícula en física** to get a distinction in physics.

matrimonio *noun Masc.*
1 marriage; **matrimonio civil** civil wedding; **2** married couple; **son un matrimonio muy unido** they're a very close couple.

máximo/máxima *adjective*
1 maximum; **2** top (*speed*); **3** highest; **el punto máximo** the highest point.

170

mayo *noun* Masc. May; **en mayo/en el mes de mayo** in May.

mayonesa *noun* Fem. mayonnaise.

mayor *noun* Masc./Fem. adult.
mayor *adjective* **1** greater;
2 greatest; **3** higher; **un número mayor que cien** a number higher than one hundred; **a la mayor altura** at the maximum height;
4 bigger; **¿tienes una talla mayor?** do you have a bigger size?; **5** biggest; **el de mayor tamaño** the biggest one; **6** older; **es cinco años mayor que su mujer** he's five years older than his wife; **7** oldest; **mi hermana mayor** my oldest sister; **soy el mayor de todos mis hermanos** I'm the oldest of my brothers and sisters; **8 cuando seas mayor** when you grow up; **las personas mayores** the grown-ups; **ya son muy mayores** they're quite old now; **9 la mayor parte de** most of; **la mayor parte de los estudiantes** most of the students; **10 ser mayor de edad** to be of age.

mayores *plural noun* Masc. **los mayores** the grown-ups; the elderly.

mayoría *noun* Fem. majority; **la mayoría de** most of.

mayúscula¹ *noun* Fem. capital letter.

mayúsculo/mayúscula²
adjective **1** capital (*letter*);
2 (*informal*) terrible (*mistake or fright*).

mazapán *noun* Masc. marzipan.

me *pronoun* **1** me; **me invitaron a su fiesta** they invited me to their party; **no me han visto** they haven't seen me; **2** to me; **me lo dieron ellos** they gave it to me; **me mintió** he lied to me; **me lo ha comprado mi madre** my mother bought it for me;
3 myself; **me corté** I cut myself;
4 (*with reflexive verbs*) **me reí mucho** I laughed a lot; **voy a bañarme** I'm going for a swim; **me senté a la mesa** I sat at the table;
5 (*with parts of the body or clothes*) **me quité el abrigo** I took my coat off; **me limpié los pies al entrar** I wiped my feet at the door; **6** (*having things done*) **el sábado iré a cortarme el pelo** I'll go and have my hair cut on Saturday.

mecánico/mecánica² *noun* Masc./Fem. mechanic.
mecánico *adjective* mechanical.

mecanografía *noun* Fem. typing.

mecedora *noun* Fem. rocking chair.

mechero *noun* Masc. lighter.

medalla *noun* Fem. medal.

media¹ *noun* Fem. average; **la media de altura** the average height, average; **la media eúropea** the European average.

media² *noun* Fem. **1** stocking;
2 medias tights; **3** (*telling the time*) **las dos y media** half past two; **dos horas y media** two hours and a half;
4 hacer algo a medias to half-do something; **lo dejó a medias** he didn't finish it; **5 lo hicimos a medias** we did it between the two of us; **pagar a medias** to pay half each.

mediados *plural noun* Masc. **a mediados de semana** midweek; **a**

a

mediados de año halfway through the year.

b

mediano/mediana *adjective*
1 medium; **de peso mediano** medium weight; **2** average; **3 de mediana calidad** mediocre.

c

d

medianoche *noun Fem.* midnight; **a media noche** at midnight.

e

f

medicamento *noun Masc.* medicine.

g

h

medicina *noun Fem.* medicine; **estudiar medicina** to study medicine; **tomarse la medicina** to take your medicine.

i

j

médico/médica *noun Masc./Fem.* doctor; **médico de cabecera** family doctor.

k

l

médico *adjective* medical.

m

medida *noun Fem.* **1** measure; **tomar medidas a algo** to measure something; **2** measurement; **¿qué medidas tiene la mesa?** what are the measurements of the table?; **3 traje a medida** a made-to-measure suit; **4 a medida que** as; **a medida que pase el tiempo** as time goes by; **5 en gran medida** to a large extent; **en cierta medida** to a certain extent; **en la medida de lo posible** as far as possible.

n

ñ

o

p

q

r

s

medieval *adjective* medieval.

t

medio ambiente *noun Masc.* environment.

u

v

medio¹ *noun Masc.* **1** middle; **ponlo en el medio** put it in the middle; **la casa de en medio** the house in the middle; **2 quitarse de en medio** to get out of the way; **3** way; **es el mejor medio** it's the best way; **no**

w

x

y

z

hubo medio de localizarlo there was no way of finding him; **lo intenté por todos los medios** I tried every possible way; **4** means; **por cualquier medio** by any means; **por todos los medios** by any possible means; **medios de transporte** means of transport; **5 por medio de** through; **por medio de un amigo** through a friend; **6 en medio de todo aquel jaleo** amidst all that racket; **7 los medios de comunicación** the media.

medio² *adverb* half; **ya está medio convencido** he's half convinced now.

medio³/**media** *adjective* **1** half; **medio kilo** half a kilo; **media docena** half a dozen; **media pensión** half board; **2** average; **de estatura media** of average height; **3** (*in time expressions*) half; **media hora** half an hour.

mediodía *noun Masc.* midday; **al mediodía** at midday.

medir *verb* [57] **1** to measure; **¿cuánto mide de ancho?** how wide is it?; **mide sesenta centímetros de largo** it's sixty centimetres long; **2 ¿cuánto mides?** how tall are you?

mediterráneo/mediterránea *adjective* Mediterranean.

Mediterráneo *noun Masc.* Mediterranean.

mejicano/mejicana *noun Masc./Fem.*, *adjective* Mexican.

Méjico *noun Masc.* SEE **México**.

mejilla *noun Fem.* cheek.

mejillón *noun Masc.* mussel.

mejor *noun Masc./Fem.* **el/la mejor** the best one.

mejor *adjective* **1** better; **éste es de mejor calidad** this one is better quality; **cuanto antes mejor** the earlier the better; **es mejor que no vayamos** it's better if we don't go; **2** best; **la mejor forma es** ... the best way is ....

mejor *adverb* **1** better; **Isabel toca la guitarra mejor** Isabel plays the guitar better; **mejor que** better than; **mejor que el otro** better than the other one; **cada vez mejor** better and better; **2** best; **es la que mejor dibuja** she's the one that draws the best; **hazlo lo mejor que puedas** do your best; **3 a lo mejor** maybe; **a lo mejor es de Sara** maybe it's Sara's; **a lo mejor no voy** I might not go; **4 mejor no preguntes** it's better if you don't ask; **mejor déjalo así** it's better if you leave it like this; **mejor venid en tren** you'd be better coming by train.

mejora *noun Fem.* improvement.

mejorar *verb* [17] **1** to improve; **2** to get better; **ha mejorado del estómago** he's got over his stomach problems.

mejorarse *reflexive verb* [17] to get better; **¡que te mejores!** get well soon!.

mellizo/melliza *noun Masc./Fem.*, **mellizo** *adjective* twin.

melocotón *noun Masc.* peach.

melodía *noun Fem.* melody.

melón *noun Masc.* melon.

memoria *noun Fem.* **1** memory; **aprenderse algo de memoria** to learn something by heart; **2 memorias** memoirs.

mencionar *verb* [17] to mention.

mendigar *verb* [17] to beg.

mendigo/mendiga *noun Masc./Fem.* beggar.

menestra *noun Fem.* **menestra de verduras** vegetable stew.

meñique *noun Masc.* little finger.

menor *noun Masc./Fem.* **1** el/la menor the younger; **2** un/una menor a minor.

menor *adjective* **1** younger; **mi hermana menor** my younger sister; **soy menor que tú** I'm younger than you; **2** youngest; **el menor de la familia** the youngest of the family; **3** little; **con el menor esfuerzo posible** with as little effort as possible; **4** less; **su importancia es cada vez menor** it gets less and less important all the time; **en menor grado** to a lesser extent; **5** minor; **de menor importancia** of minor importance; **6** smaller; **un número menor de alumnos** a smaller number of pupils; **7** smallest; **hasta el menor detalle** even the smallest detail; **8 no tengo la menor idea** I haven't got the slightest idea.

menos *adjective (does not change in the plural)* **1** less; **de menos peso** of less weight; **2** few; **había menos de cien personas** there were fewer than a hundred people.

menos *adverb* **1** less; **ahora sale menos** he goes out less now; **cada vez menos** less and less; **2** least;

a
b
c
d
e
f
g
h
i
j
k
l
m
n
ñ
o
p
q
r
s
t
u
v
w
x
y
z

los menos informados the least well-informed; **es lo menos que esperaba** it's the least I expected; **3 el menos alto** the shortest one; **el que corre menos** the slowest of all; **4 menos que** less than, fewer than; **habla menos que yo** he speaks less than I do; **cuesta menos que el otro** it costs less than the other one; **había menos que ayer** there were fewer than yesterday; **5 menos de** less than; **cuesta menos de cien libras** it costs less than a hundred pounds; **adultos de menos de treinta años** adults under thirty; **6 ahora los veo menos** I don't see them as often now; **7 ahora sale menos** she doesn't go out as much now.

menos *pronoun* **1 ahora compramos menos** now we don't buy as much; **2 cobrar de menos** to undercharge; **hay diez tarjetas de menos** there are ten cards too few; **3 al menos/por lo menos** at least; **4 ¡menos mal!** thank goodness!

menos *preposition* except; **todos menos su madre** everybody except her mother.

mensaje *noun Masc.* message; **un mensaje de texto** a text message; **te mandaré un mensaje de texto mañana** I'll send you a text message tomorrow.

mensajero/mensajera *noun Masc./Fem.* **1** messenger; **2** courier; **servicio de mensajeros** courier service.

mensual *adjective* monthly; **dos cientos euros mensuales** two hundred euros a month.

mensualmente *adverb* monthly.

menta *noun Fem.* mint; **un caramelo de menta** a mint.

mental *adjective* mental.

mente *noun Fem.* mind; **se me quedó la mente en blanco** my mind went blank.

mentir *verb* [14] to lie.

mentira *noun Fem.* lie.

mentiroso/mentirosa *noun Masc./Fem.* liar.

mentón *noun Masc.* chin.

menú *noun Masc.* menu; **menú del día** set menu.

menudo/menuda *adjective* **1** small; **es muy menuda** she's quite small; **2 a menudo** often; **nos vemos a menudo** we see each other often; **3 ¡menudo problema!** what a problem!; **¡menuda moto!** what an incredible motorbike!

mercado *noun Masc.* market; **ir al mercado** to go to the market; **el Mercado Común** the Common Market.

mercancías *plural noun Fem.* goods.

mercería *noun Fem.* haberdashery.

merecer *verb* [35] **1** to deserve; **mereces un castigo** you deserve to be punished; **2 merecer la pena** to be worthwhile; **la película merece la pena** the film is worth seeing. **merecerse** *reflexive verb* [35] to deserve; **no me merezco que me traten así** I don't deserve to be treated like this.

merendar *verb* [29] to have a teatime snack; **siempre merienda pan y chocolate** he always has bread and chocolate in the afternoon; **¿quieres merendar algo?** do you want something to eat?; **¡a merendar!** teatime!

merezca, merezco, etc. *verb* SEE **merecer**.

meridional *adjective* southern.

merienda¹ *noun Fem.* **1** afternoon snack; **2 merienda campestre** picnic; **ir de merienda** to go for a picnic.

merienda², **meriendo, etc.** *verb* SEE **merendar**.

mérito *noun Masc.* merit.

mermelada *noun Fem.* jam.

mes *noun Masc.* month; **el mes que viene** next month; **mil euros al mes** a thousand euros a month; **un bebé de siete meses** a seven-month-old baby.

mesa *noun Fem.* table; **sentarse a la mesa** to sit at the table; **poner la mesa** to set the table; **quitar la mesa/recoger la mesa** to clear the table; **¡a la mesa!** food's ready!

mesita *noun Fem.* **mesita de noche** bedside table.

meta *noun Fem.* **1** finishing line; **2** aim; **tiene como meta ser actriz** her aim is to become an actress.

metal *noun Masc.* metal.

metálico/metálica *adjective* metallic.

meteorológico/ meteorológica *adjective* meteorological; **parte meteorológico** weather forecast.

meter *verb* [18] **1** to put (something) in; **metió la mano** he put his hand in; **métalo en la carpeta** put it in the folder; **2** to fit; **¿puedes meter algo más en la maleta?** can you fit anything else in the suitcase?; **3 meter la primera** to put the car in first gear; **meter la marcha atrás** to put the car into reverse; **4 meter un gol** to score a goal.

meterse *reflexive verb* [18] **1 meterse en** to get in(to); **meterse en la cama** to get into bed; **2 meterse en algo** to get involved in something; **no te metas en mis asuntos** mind your own business.

método *noun Masc.* method.

métrico *adjective* metric.

metro *noun Masc.* **1** underground; **2** metre; **los cien metros libres** the hundred metres freestyle.

mexicano/mexicana *noun Masc./Fem., adjective* Mexican.

México *noun Masc.* Mexico.

mezcla *noun Fem.* **1** mixture; **2** mix; **una mezcla de culturas** a mix of cultures.

mezclar *verb* [17] **1** to mix; **2** to mix up; **has mezclado todos los papeles** you've mixed up all the papers.

mezclarse *reflexive verb* [17] **mezclarse en algo** to get mixed up in something.

mezquita *noun Fem.* mosque.

mi *adjective* my; **mis amigos** my friends.

a
b
c
d
e
f
g
h
i
j
k
l
m
n
ñ
o
p
q
r
s
t
u
v
w
x
y
z

a
b
c
d
e
f
g
h
i
j
k
l
m
n
ñ
o
p
q
r
s
t
u
v
w
x
y
z

mí *pronoun* **1** me; **detrás de mí** behind me; **se olvidaron de mí** they forgot about me; **2** (*as indirect object*) **me lo dio a mí** he gave it to me; **3 a mí me gusta** I like it; **a mí me parece que ...** I think that ...; **4 mí mismo/misma** myself; **sé cuidar de mí misma** I can look after myself; **5 por mí ...** as far as I'm concerned.

micrófono *noun Masc.* microphone.

microondas *noun Masc.* (*does not change in the plural*) microwave (oven).

microscopio *noun Masc.* microscope.

mida, **midiendo**, **midió**, **mido**, **etc.** *verb* SEE **medir**.

miedo *noun Masc.* **1** fear; **tener miedo** to be scared; **tengo mucho miedo** I'm really scared; **tengo miedo de intentarlo** I'm afraid of trying; **¡qué miedo!** how frightening!; **miedo a algo** fear of something; **2 me da miedo la altura** I'm afraid of heights; **les da miedo ir solos** they are afraid of going on their own; **3 pasamos un rato de miedo** (*informal*) we had a great time.

miedoso/miedosa *adjective* **es muy miedoso** he's afraid of everything.

miel *noun Fem.* honey.

miembro *noun Masc.* **1** member; **2** limb.

mienta, **miento**, **etc.** *verb* SEE **mentir**.

mientras *adverb* meanwhile; **mientras tanto** in the meantime; **mientras tanto él estaba esperando en la estación** in the meantime he was waiting at the station.

mientras *conjunction* **1** while; **pon la mesa mientras yo hago la comida** lay the table while I cook the meal; **2** as long as; **mientras yo viva** as long as I'm alive.

miércoles *noun Masc.* Wednesday; **el miércoles** on Wednesday; **el miércoles por la mañana** on Wednesday morning; **los miércoles** on Wednesdays.

miga *noun Fem.* crumb.

mil *number* thousand; **mil doscientos** one thousand two hundred.

milagro *noun Masc.* miracle.

milenio *noun Masc.* millennium.

milésimo/milésima *adjective* thousandth.

mili *noun Fem.* (*informal*) military service.

milímetro *noun Masc.* milimetre.

militar *noun Masc./Fem.* soldier. **militar** *adjective* military.

millón *number* million; **un millón de euros** a million euros; **un millón de gracias** thank you ever so much.

millonario/millonaria *noun Masc./Fem.* millionaire.

mina *noun Fem.* mine; **una mina de carbón** a coalmine.

mineral *noun Masc., adjective* mineral.

minero/minera noun Masc./Fem. miner.

minero adjective mining.

mini noun Fem. (*informal*) mini.

minifalda noun Fem. miniskirt.

mínimo[1] noun Masc. minimum.

mínimo[2]/**mínima** adjective minimum; **no me importa lo más mínimo** I couldn't care less.

ministerio noun Masc. ministry.

ministro/ministra noun Masc./Fem. minister.

minoría noun Fem. minority.

mintamos, **mintió**, etc. verb SEE **mentir**.

minúscula[1] noun Fem. small letter (*not capital*).

minúsculo/minúscula[2] adjective tiny.

minusválido/minusválida noun Masc./Fem. disabled person.

minusválido adjective disabled.

minuto noun Masc. minute.

mío/mía adjective mine; **un amigo mío** a friend of mine.

mío pronoun mine; **el mío es verde** mine is green.

miope adjective shortsighted.

mirada noun Fem. look; **una mirada alegre** a happy look; **dirigir una mirada a** to look at; **me dirigió una mirada** she looked at me; **bajar la mirada** to look down.

mirar verb [17] **1** to look; **miré afuera** I looked outside; **mira en el cajón** look in the drawer; **2 mirar algo** to look at something; **miró el cuadro con interés** he looked at the picture with interest; **me miró** he looked at me; **3** to watch; **mirar la tele** to watch TV; **4 mirar fijamente** to stare.

mirarse reflexive verb [17] **mirarse en el espejo** to look at yourself in the mirror; **mirarse las manos** to look at your hands.

mirlo noun Masc. blackbird.

misa noun Fem. mass; **ir a misa** to go to mass.

miserable adjective **1** miserable; **2** stingy.

miseria noun Fem. **1** misery; **2** poverty; **3** pittance.

misil noun Masc. missile.

mismo[1] adverb **1** right; **ahora mismo** right now; **en ese mismo momento** right at that moment; **está ahí mismo** it's right there; **al lado mismo de casa** right next to the house; **2** just; **lo mismo que yo** just like me; **eso mismo dije yo** that's just what I said.

mismo[2]/**misma** adjective **1** same; **al mismo tiempo** at the same time; **llevan los mismos zapatos** they have the same shoes; **lo mismo** the same; **2** very; **en este mismo lugar** in this very spot; **3 yo mismo** I myself; **lo vi yo mismo** I saw it myself; **lo dijo ella misma** she said it herself.

mismo pronoun **1** el mismo the same one; **he usado la misma** I've used the same one; **Sara tiene los mismos** Sara has the same ones; **2 da lo mismo** it doesn't matter; **me da lo mismo el color** I don't mind which colour.

a

b

c

d

e

f

g

h

i

j

k

l

m

n

ñ

o

p

q

r

s

t

u

v

w

x

y

z

misterio *noun Masc.* mystery.

misterioso/misteriosa *adjective* mysterious.

mitad *noun Fem.* **1** half; **la mitad del pastel** half the cake; **a mitad de precio** half-price; **2** halfway; **a mitad de camino paramos a comer** we stopped halfway to eat; **llenar algo hasta la mitad** to half fill something; **lo he leído hasta la mitad** I'm halfway through reading it; **3 cortar algo por la mitad** to cut something in two.

mito *noun Masc.* myth.

mixto/mixta *adjective* mixed.

mobiliario *noun Masc.* furniture; **mobiliario de cocina** kitchen fittings.

mochila *noun Fem.* backpack.

mocos *plural noun Masc.* **tener mocos** to have a runny nose.

moda *noun Fem.* fashion; **la moda juvenil** young fashion; **estar de moda** to be in fashion; **pasarse de moda** to go out of fashion; **siempre va a la última moda** he's always wearing the latest fashion.

modales *plural noun Masc.* manners; **tener buenos modales** to have good manners.

modelo¹ *noun Masc.* model; **utilizar algo como modelo** to use something as a model.

modelo² *noun Masc./Fem.* model (*fashion*).

moderno/moderna *adjective* **1** modern; **2** trendy.

modesto/modesta *adjective* **1** modest; **2** humble.

modificar *verb* [31] to change.

modisto/modista *noun Masc./ Fem.* **1** dressmaker; **2** (fashion) designer.

modo *noun Masc.* **1** way; **lo haré a mi modo** I'll do it my way; **a mi modo de ver** to my way of thinking; **no hubo modo** there was no way (of doing it); **2 lo hizo de cualquier modo** he did it any old way; **3 de cualquier modo te llamaré antes** in any case, I'll phone you first; **4 ¡de ningún modo!** no way!; **5 de todos modos** anyway; **de todos modos no iba a comprarlo** I wasn't going to buy it anyway; **6 de modo que** so; **7 en cierto modo** somehow; **8 modo de empleo** instructions for use.

mohoso/mohosa *adjective* mouldy.

mojado/mojada *adjective* wet.

mojar *verb* [17] to wet.
mojarse *reflexive verb* [17] to get wet; **se me mojó el pelo** my hair got wet.

moler *verb* [38] to grind.

molestar *verb* [17] **1** to disturb; '**no molestar**' 'do not disturb'; **no molestes a tu madre, que está trabajando** don't disturb your mother, she's working; **2** to bother; **perdona que te moleste** sorry to bother you; **3 ¿te molesta que ponga la tele?** do you mind if I put the TV on?; **4** to annoy; **me molesta que no me hayan invitado** I'm annoyed that they haven't invited me.

molestarse *reflexive verb* [17] **1** to get upset; **se molestó porque fuimos sin ella** she got upset because we went without her; **2 molestarse en hacer algo** to bother to do something; **no se molestó en preguntar** she didn't bother to find out.

molestia *noun Fem.* **1** trouble; **no es ninguna molestia** it's no trouble at all; **causar molestias a alguien** to inconvenience someone; **2 tomarse la molestia de hacer algo** to take the trouble to do something; **3 perdone la molestia** sorry to bother you; **4 si no es molestia** … if you don't mind ….

molesto/molesta *adjective* **1** annoying; **2** uncomfortable; **3 estar molesto** to be upset; **sé que está molesto conmigo** I know he's upset with me.

momento *noun Masc.* moment; **justo en ese momento** right at that moment; **dentro de un momento** in a moment; **¡un momento!** just a moment!; **de momento** at the moment; **en cualquier momento** any moment now; **en este momento** right now.

monarquía *noun Fem.* monarchy.

monasterio *noun Masc.* monastery.

moneda *noun Fem.* **1** coin; **2** currency.

monedero *noun Masc.* purse.

monja *noun Fem.* nun.

monje *noun Masc.* monk.

mono/mona *noun Masc./Fem.* monkey.
mono *adjective* **1** cute (*a puppy or baby, for example*); **2** pretty (*person, garment*).

monopatín *noun Masc.* skateboard.

monstruo *noun Masc.* monster.

montaña *noun Fem.* **1** mountain; **en la montaña** in the mountains; **2 la montaña rusa** the roller coaster.

montar *verb* [17] **1** to get on; **montar en el avión** to get on the plane; **2** to get in; **montar en el coche** to get in the car; **3** to ride; **montar a caballo** to ride a horse; **montar en la moto** get on the motorbike; **montar en bicicleta** to ride a bike; **4** to mount (*a horse*); **5** to set up (*a business or an exhibition*); **6** to put up (*a tent*); **7 montar claras a punto de nieve** to whisk the egg whites until stiff; **8 montar un escándalo** (*informal*) to cause a scene.
montarse *reflexive verb* [17] **1** to get on; **se montó en el tren** he got on the train; **2** to get in; **montarse en un coche** to get in a car.

monte *noun Masc.* mountain; scrubland; **monte de piedad** pawnbroker's shop.

montón *noun Masc.* **1** pile; **puse todas las revistas en un montón** I put all the magazines in a pile; **2 un montón de** (*informal*) loads of; **había un montón de niños** there were loads of children; **montones de** (*informal*) loads of; **montones de**

dinero loads of money; **3 me gusta un montón** (*informal*) I like it a lot; **4 del montón** (*informal*) ordinary; **un cantante del montón** an ordinary singer.

monumento *noun Masc.* monument.

moqueta *noun Fem.* fitted carpet.

mora *noun Fem.* blackberry.

morado¹ *noun Masc.* purple.

morado²/morada *adjective* purple.

moral *noun Fem.* **1** morals; **no tienen ninguna moral** they have no morals; **2** morale; **estar bajo de moral** to feel low.
moral *adjective* moral.

morcilla *noun Fem.* black pudding.

morder *verb* [38] to bite.

mordisco *noun Masc.* bite; **darle un mordisco a algo** to bite (on) something.

moreno/morena *adjective* **1** dark (*hair*); **2 es morena** she's dark-haired; **3 estar moreno** to be tanned; **ponerse moreno** to get tanned.

morir *verb* [55] to die; **morir ahogado** to drown; **morir en un accidente** to be killed in an accident.
morirse *reflexive verb* [55] to die; **me muero de hambre** I'm starving; **se muere por ir a la playa** he's dying to go to the beach.

moro/mora *noun Masc./Fem.* **1** Moor; **2** North African.
moro *adjective* Moorish.

mortal *adjective* **1** deadly, lethal; **2** fatal.

mosca *noun Fem.* fly; ★ **por si las moscas** (*informal*) just in case; ★ **¿qué mosca le ha picado?** (*informal*) what's got into him? (*literally: 'what fly has bitten him?'*).

mosquito *noun Masc.* mosquito.

mostaza *noun Fem.* mustard.

mostrador *noun Masc.* **1** counter (*in a shop*); **2** bar (*in a pub*); **3** check-in desk.

mostrar *verb* [24] to show.
mostrarse *reflexive verb* [24] **mostrarse interesado** to show interest; **mostrarse amable** to be kind; **mostrarse contento** to be happy.

motivo *noun Masc.* **1** cause; **el motivo del accidente** the cause of the accident; **2** reason; **por motivos personales** for personal reasons.

moto *noun Fem.* motorbike; **montar en moto** to ride a motorbike; **montar en la moto** to get on the motorbike; **moto acuática** jetski.

motocicleta *noun Fem.* motorbike.

motociclista *noun Masc./Fem.* motorcyclist.

motor *noun Masc.* engine; **motor a reacción** jet engine.

motora *noun Fem.* motorboat.

motorista *noun Masc.* motorcyclist.

mover *verb* [38] to move.
moverse *reflexive verb* [38] to move; **no te muevas** don't move.

movimiento *noun Masc.*
movement.

moza *noun Fem.* young girl.

mozo *noun Masc.* **1** young boy;
2 mozo de estación porter.

muchacha *noun Fem.* girl.

muchacho *noun Masc.* boy.

muchedumbre *noun Fem.* crowd.

mucho[1] *adverb* **1** a lot; **lo usan mucho** they use it a lot; **eso es mucho mejor** that's a lot better; **salen mucho** they go out a lot; **2** very; **lo siento mucho** I'm very sorry; **'¿te interesa?' – 'mucho'** 'are you interested?' – 'very'; **trabajar mucho** to work very hard; **voy a estudiar mucho** I'm going to study very hard; **3 mucho antes** long before; **mucho después** long after; **4 como mucho** at the most; **5 ni mucho menos** far from it.

mucho[2] *pronoun* **1** a lot; **tienes mucho que aprender** you have a lot to learn; **2** much; **no tengo mucho** I haven't got much; **3** many; **no quedan muchas** there aren't many left; **muchos se sorprendieron** many were surprised; **4** (*talking about time*) **tardan mucho** they are taking a long time; **¿hace mucho que ha llamado?** did she call a long time ago?; **hace mucho que no sé nada de ella** it's a long time since I last heard from her; **ya no falta mucho para mi cumpleaños** it's not long to my birthday now.

mucho[3]/**mucha** *adjective* **1** a lot of; **mucho tiempo** a lot of time; **2** much; **no tienen mucho interés** they haven't got much interest;

3 many; **¿había muchos niños?** were there many children?; **muchas veces** many times; **4 hacía mucho frío** it was very cold; **tengo mucho sueño** I'm very sleepy; **5 tengo mucha prisa** I'm in a real hurry; **6 nos vimos hace mucho tiempo** we saw each other a long time ago; **7 muchas gracias** thanks a lot; **mucho gusto** nice to meet you; **lo haré con mucho gusto** I'd be very pleased to do it.

mudanza *noun Fem.* removal; **camión de mudanzas** removal van; **estar de mudanza** to be in the process of moving.

mudar *verb* [17] to move (*from one house to another*).
mudarse *reflexive verb* [17] **1** to change one's clothes; **2** to move; **mudarse de casa** to move house.

mueble *noun Masc.* piece of furniture; **muebles** furniture.

muela *noun Fem.* back tooth; **tener dolor de muelas** to have toothache.

muera, muero, etc. *verb* SEE **morir.**

muerda, muerdo, etc. *verb* SEE **morder.**

muerte *noun Fem.* death; **muerte repentina** sudden death; **estar condenado a muerte** to be sentenced to death.

muerto/muerta *noun Masc./Fem.* dead person; **no ha habido muertos** there were no casualties; **hubo un muerto** one person died.
muerto *adjective* dead; **muerto de sed** dying of thirst; **estoy muerto de frío** I'm freezing to death; **estoy**

muerto de hambre I'm starving; **estábamos muertos de cansancio** we were dead tired.

muestra, muestro, etc. *verb* SEE **mostrar**.

mueva, muevo, etc. *verb* SEE **mover**.

mujer *noun Fem.* **1** woman; **2** wife; **mi mujer** my wife.

muleta *noun Fem.* crutch.

mulo/mula *noun Masc./Fem.* mule.

multa *noun Fem.* fine; **me pusieron una multa** I was fined.

multicolor *adjective* multicoloured.

multiplicación *noun Fem.* multiplication.

multiplicar *verb* [31] to multiply.

mundial *noun Masc.* **el mundial de fútbol** the World Cup.
mundial *adjective* world; **un récord mundial** a world record; **la economía mundial** the world economy; **de fama mundial** world-famous.

mundo *noun Masc.* world.

municiones *noun Fem. (plural)* ammunition.

municipal *adjective* **1** local; **2** municipal.

muñeca *noun Fem.* **1** doll; **jugar a las muñecas** to play dolls; **muñeca de trapo** rag doll; **2** wrist.

muñeco *noun Masc.* **1** toy; **muñeco de peluche** soft toy; **2** puppet.

muralla *noun Fem.* wall (*fortified*); **the Great Wall of China** la Gran Muralla de China.

murciélago *noun Masc.* bat.

muriendo, murió, etc. *verb* SEE **morir**.

murmullo *noun Masc.*
1 whispering; **hablar en un murmullo** to whisper; **2** murmur.

murmurar *verb* [17] **1** to whisper; **2** to murmur; **3 murmurar sobre alguien** to gossip about someone; **se murmura que** ... the rumour is ....

muro *noun Masc.* wall.

músculo *noun Masc.* muscle.

museo *noun Masc.* museum; **un museo de pintura** a gallery; **un museo de arte moderno** a modern art museum.

música[1] *noun Fem.* music; **música en directo/música en vivo** live music; **música pop** pop music.

musical *adjective* musical.

músico/música[2] *noun Masc./Fem.*
1 musician; **2** composer.

muslo *noun Masc.* **1** thigh; **2** leg (*of a chicken*).

musulmán/musulmana *noun Masc./Fem., adjective* Muslim.

mutuo/mutua *adjective* mutual.

muy *adverb* **1** very; **es muy difícil** it's very difficult; **está muy bien** it's very good; **muy bien, sigamos** very good, let's continue; **2** too; **era muy pequeño para entenderlo** he was too small to understand it; **3 Muy señor mío** Dear sir (*in a letter*).

Nn

nabo *noun Masc.* turnip.

nácar *noun Masc.* mother-of-pearl.

nacer *verb* [35] to be born; **nací en Valencia** I was born in Valencia; **¿dónde has nacido?** where were you born?

nacido/nacida *adjective* born; **nacido en Sevilla** born in Seville; **un niño recién nacido** a new-born baby.

nacimiento *noun Masc.* **1** birth; **es ciego de nacimiento** he was born blind; **2** crib (*nativity scene*).

nación *noun Fem.* nation.

nacional *adjective* national.

nacionalidad *noun Fem.* nationality; **¿de qué nacionalidad eres?** what nationality are you?

nada *pronoun* **1** nothing; **no hay nada nuevo** there's nothing new; **no hay nada como …** there's nothing like …; **2** anything; **no me queda nada** I haven't got anything left; **yo no sé nada de eso** I don't know anything about that; **no me dijeron nada** they didn't say anything to me; **3** **no tengo nada de dinero** I have no money at all; **4** **nada más** nothing else; **sólo quiero hablar con ella, nada más** I only want to speak to her, nothing else; **nada más, gracias** that's all thank you; **5** **nada más** nothing else; **no quiero nada más** I don't want anything else; **6** **nada más que** only; **no quiero nada más que un kilo** I only

want one kilo; **7** **de nada** not at all (*to someone who has said thank you*); **8** love (*in tennis*); **treinta nada** thirty love.

nada *adverb* at all; **no me gusta nada** I don't like it at all; **no me ayudan nada** they don't help me at all.

nadar *verb* [17] to swim.

nadie *pronoun* **1** nobody; **al final nadie llamó** nobody phoned in the end; **2** **no se lo dije a nadie** I didn't tell anybody.

nailon *noun Masc.* nylon.

naipe *noun Masc.* card.

nana *noun Fem.* lullaby.

naranja *noun Fem.* orange; **zumo de naranja** orange juice.
naranja *noun Masc.* orange (*the colour*).
naranja *adjective* orange (*never changes*); **unos pantalones naranja** orange trousers.

naranjada *noun Fem.* orangeade.

naranjo *noun Masc.* orange tree.

narcotraficante *noun Masc./Fem.* drugs trafficker.

narcotráfico *noun Masc.* drugs trade.

nariz *noun Fem.* nose; **sonarse la nariz** to blow your nose; ⋆ **darse de narices con alguien** (*informal*) to bump into someone; ⋆ **en mis propias narices** (*informal*) right under my nose.

nata *noun Fem.* cream; **nata líquida** single cream; **nata para montar** double cream; **nata montada** whipped cream.

natación noun Fem. swimming.

natillas plural noun Fem. custard.

natural adjective natural.

naturaleza noun Fem. 1 nature; **respetar la naturaleza** to respect nature; **la naturaleza humana** human nature; 2 **naturaleza muerta** still life.

naturalmente adverb naturally.

náusea noun Fem. nausea; **tener náuseas** to feel sick; **el olor me daba náuseas** the smell was making me feel sick.

nauseabundo/nauseabunda adjective nauseating.

navaja noun Fem. 1 penknife; 2 **navaja de afeitar** razor.

nave noun Fem. 1 ship; **nave espacial** spaceship; 2 premises; **una nave industrial** industrial premises.

navegar verb [28] 1 to navigate; 2 to sail; **navegar en Internet** to surf the Internet.

navegar verb [28] to sail.

Navidad noun Fem. 1 Christmas; **el día de Navidad** Christmas Day; **feliz Navidad** Merry Christmas; 2 **Navidades** Christmas time; **pasaré las Navidades con mi hermana** I'll spend Christmas with my sister.

nazca, nazco, etc. verb SEE **nacer**.

neblina noun Fem. mist.

necesario/necesaria adjective necessary.

necesidad noun Fem. need; **no hay necesidad de llamarlos** there's no need to call them; **en caso de necesidad** ... if necessary ....

necesitar verb [17] 1 to need; **no necesitas llevar el pasaporte** you don't need to take your passport; 2 **'se necesitan camareros'** (on sign) 'waiters wanted'.

nectarina noun Fem. nectarine.

neerlandés¹ noun Masc. Dutch (the language).

neerlandés²/**neerlandesa** noun Masc./Fem. Dutchman/Dutchwoman.
neerlandés/neerlandesa adjective Dutch.

nefasto/nefasta adjective 1 disastrous (consequences); 2 awful (weather or taste in clothes).

negar verb [30] 1 to deny; **lo niega todo** he denies everything; 2 to refuse; **nos negaron su ayuda** they refused to help us.
negarse reflexive verb [30] to refuse; **se niega a colaborar** he refuses to colaborate.

negativo/negativa adjective negative.

negociación noun Fem. negotiation.

negociar verb [17] to negotiate.

negocio noun Masc. 1 business; **montar un negocio** to set up a business; **un viaje de negocios** a business trip; 2 **negocios** business; **dedicarse a los negocios** to be in business; 3 deal; **hacer un buen negocio** to make a good deal.

negro/negra *noun Masc./Fem.*
black man/black woman.
negro *adjective* black.

neozelandés/neozelandesa
noun New Zealander.
neozelandéneozlandesas
adjective (from) New Zealand.

nervio *noun Masc.* nerve; **tengo muchos nervios** I'm very nervous;
★**tener los nervios de punta** to be on edge.

nervioso/nerviosa *adjective*
nervous; **ponerse nervioso** to get nervous.

neumático *noun Masc.* tyre.

neumonía atípica *noun Fem.*
SARS (*the disease*).

neutro/neutra *adjective*
1 neutral; **2** neuter (*in grammar*).

nevada *noun Fem.* snowfall.

nevar *verb* [29] to snow; **está nevando** it's snowing.

nevasca *noun Fem.* snow storm.

nevera *noun Fem.* fridge.

nevisca *noun Fem.* snow flurry.

ni *conjunction* **1** not ... even; **ni lo he abierto** I haven't even opened it; **ni uno de ellos llamó** not even one of them called; **2** no ... **ni** ... neither ... nor; **no vino él ni su hermana** neither he nor his sister came; **no es mío ni suyo** it's not mine and it's not hers either; **una casa sin luz ni agua corriente** a house with neither water nor electricity; **ni uno ni otro** neither one nor the other; **3** **no es ni grande ni pequeño** it's neither big nor small; **4** ¡**ni hablar!** no way!

nicaragüense *noun Masc./Fem.*,
adjective Nicaraguan.

nido *noun Masc.* nest.

niebla *noun Fem.* fog; **había mucha niebla** it was very foggy.

nieta *noun Fem.* granddaughter.

nieto *noun Masc.* **1** grandson; **2 mis nietos** my grandchildren.

nieva, **nieve**¹, **etc.** *verb* SEE **nevar**.

nieve² *noun Fem.* **1** snow; **2 batir claras a punto de nieve** to beat eggwhites until stiff; ★**blanco como la nieve** as white as snow.

niña *noun Fem.* girl.

niñera *noun Fem.* nanny.

ningún *adjective* SEE **ninguno**.

ninguno/ninguna *adjective*
(*'ninguno' becomes 'ningún' before a masculine singular noun*) **1** any; **no trajeron ninguna caja** they didn't bring any boxes; **no he comprado ningún libro** I didn't buy any books; **no hay ninguna necesidad** there's no need; **2 en ningún momento** never; **en ningún lugar** nowhere; **no lo veo por ningún lado** I can't see it anywhere; **3 de ninguna manera** no way.

ninguno *pronoun* **1** neither; **ninguno de los dos vale** neither of them is suitable; **ninguno de los dos me gusta** I don't like either of them; **2** none; **ninguno de los que estaban allí** none of those who were there; **no compró ninguno** he didn't buy any of them; **3** nobody; **ninguno lo vio** nobody saw him.

a
b
c
d
e
f
g
h
i
j
k
l
m
n
ñ
o
p
q
r
s
t
u
v
w
x
y
z

niño *noun Masc.* **1** boy; **2** child; **van a tener un niño** they're going to have a baby; **3 niños** children; **ropa de niños** children's clothes.

nitrógeno *noun Masc.* nitrogen.

nivel *noun Masc.* **1** level; **el nivel del agua** the level of the water; **2** standard; **el nivel de vida** the standard of living.

no *adverb* **1** no; **'¿es tuyo?' – 'no'** 'is it yours?' – 'no'; **2** not; **no es mi amigo** he's not my friend; **no sabe nadar** he can't swim; **no se sabe** it's not known; **no mucho** not much; **ahí no** not there; **3 no comió nada** he didn't eat anything; **no voy nunca al cine** I never go to the cinema; **no se parecen en nada** they are not similar at all; **4 somos siete ¿no?** there are seven of us, aren't there?; **tú hablaste con ella, ¿no?** you spoke to her, didn't you?; **5 la no violencia** non-violence; **los nofumadores** non smokers; **6 ¡cómo no!** of course!

noche *noun Fem.* **1** evening, night; **a las ocho de la noche** at eight o'clock in the evening; **a las once de la noche** at eleven o'clock at night; **esta noche** this evening, tonight; **por la noche** in the evening, at night; **la noche anterior** the previous evening, the night before; **el lunes por la noche** Monday evening, Monday night; **de noche** in the evening, at night; **buenas noches** good evening, goodnight; **2 hacerse de noche** to get dark.

Nochebuena *noun Fem.* Christmas Eve.

Nochevieja *noun Fem.* New Year's Eve.

nocturno/nocturna *adjective* **1** nocturnal; **2** evening; **clases nocturnas** evening lessons.

nombrar *verb* [17] **1** to mention; **2** to appoint.

nombre *noun Masc.* **1** name; **¿qué nombre tiene el grupo?** what's the name of the group?; **¿qué nombre le van a poner al niño?** what are they going to call the baby?; **nombre de pila** first name; **2** (*on forms*) **'nombre'** 'first name'; **'nombre y apellidos'** 'full name'; **3** noun (*in grammar*).

nordeste, **noreste** *noun Masc.* northeast.

norma *noun Fem.* rule.

normal *adjective* **1** normal; **eso es normal** that's normal; **2 normal y corriente** ordinary.

normalmente *adverb* normally.

noroeste *noun Masc.* northwest.

norte *noun Masc.* north; **hacia el norte** northwards; **al norte del Madrid** to the north of Madrid.

norteamericano/ norteamericana *noun Masc./ Fem., adjective* North American.

Noruega *noun Fem.* Norway.

noruego¹ *noun Masc.* Norwegian (*the language*).

noruego²**/noruega** *noun Masc./ Fem., adjective* Norwegian.

nos *pronoun* **1** us; **nos invitaron a la fiesta** they invited us to the party; **2** to us; **nos mintió** he lied to us; **3** ourselves; **nos portamos bien** we behaved ourselves; **4** each other; **siempre nos ayudamos** we always help each other; **5** (*with reflexive verbs*) **nos reímos mucho** we laugh a lot; **vamos a bañarnos** let's go for a swim; **nos sentamos a la mesa** we sat at the table; **6** (*with parts of the body or clothes*) **nos quitamos los abrigos** we took our coats off; **nos limpiamos los pies al entrar** we wiped our feet at the door; **7** (*having something done*) **el sábado iremos a cortarnos el pelo** we'll go and get our hair cut on Saturday.

nosotros/nosotras *pronoun* **1** we; **lo hicimos nosotras** we did it; **2** us; **detrás de nosotros** behind us; **3** nosostros mismos ourselves.

nota *noun Fem.* **1** note; **tomar nota de algo** to write something down; **tomar notas** to take notes; **2** mark; **¿qué nota has sacado en física?** what did you get in physics?; **sacar buenas notas** to get good marks; **3 nota musical** note.

notable *adjective* noteworthy. **notable** *noun Masc.* mark between 70% and 85%.

notar *verb* [17] to notice; **te noto preocupado** you look worried; **se nota que** ... you can tell that ....

notario/notaria *noun Masc./Fem.* notary public.

noticia *noun Fem.* **1** (*noticia: singular*) **una noticia interesante**

an interesting piece of news; **la noticia me sorprendió** the news surprised me; **dar la noticia a alguien** to break the news to someone; **2** (*noticias: plural*) **tengo buenas noticias** I've got good news; **las noticias de las nueve** the nine o'clock news.

novecientos/novecientas *number* nine hundred; **novecientos veinte** nine hundred and twenty.

novela *noun Fem.* novel.

noveno/novena *adjective* ninth; **el noveno piso** the ninth floor.

noventa *number* ninety; **tiene noventa años** she's ninety (years old); **noventa y siete** ninety-seven; **los años noventa** the nineties.

novia *noun Fem.* **1** bride; **2** fiancée; **3** girlfriend.

noviembre *noun Masc.* November; **en noviembre/en el mes de noviembre** in November.

novillada *noun Fem.* bullfight for young bulls.

novillos *plural noun Masc.* **hacer novillos** to play truant.

novio *noun Masc.* **1** groom; **2** fiancé; **3** boyfriend.

nube *noun Fem.* cloud; **un cielo cubierto de nubes** a cloudy sky.

nublado/nublada *adjective* cloudy.

nublarse *reflexive verb* [17] to cloud over; **se nubló por la tarde** it clouded over in the afternoon.

a
b
c
d
e
f
g
h
i
j
k
l
m
n
ñ
o
p
q
r
s
t
u
v
w
x
y
z

nuclear *noun Fem.* nuclear power station.
nuclear *adjective* nuclear.

nudillo *noun Masc.* knuckle.

nudo *noun Masc.* knot.

nuera *noun Fem.* daughter-in-law.

nuestro/nuestra *adjective* our; **nuestra casa** our house; **un familiar nuestro** a relative of ours.
nuestro *pronoun* ours; **la nuestra es verde** ours is green; **los nuestros están en el salón** ours are in the living room; **aquél es el nuestro** that one is ours.

nueve *number* 1 nine; **Jaime tiene nueve años** Jaime's nine (years old); 2 ninth (*in dates*); **hoy estamos a nueve** it's the ninth today; 3 nine (*in clock time*).**son las nueve** it's nine o'clock.

nuevo/nueva *adjective* 1 new; **mis zapatos nuevos** my new shoes; 2 **de nuevo** once more; 3 **¿qué hay de nuevo?** (*informal*) what's new?

nuez *noun Fem.* 1 walnut; 2 Adam's apple; 3 **nuez moscada** nutmeg.

número *noun Masc.* 1 number; **mi número de teléfono** my telephone number; 2 issue (*of a magazine, for example*); 3 size; **¿qué número de zapatos calzas?** what size shoes do you take?

nunca *adverb* never; **nunca he estado en ese bar** I've never been to that bar; **nunca más** never again; **más que nunca** more than ever; **casi nunca** hardly ever.

nutritivo/nutritiva *adjective* nourishing.

Ññ

ñono/ñona *adjective* **no seas ñoño** don't be so wet.

Oo

o *conjunction* 1 or; **antes o después** sooner or later; (*note that before a word beginning with 'o', it becomes 'u'*) **plata u oro** silver or gold; (*note that when 'o' appears between numbers, it has an accent*) **11 ó 12** 11 or 12; 2 **o sea** so; **¿o sea que no te importa?** so you don't mind?

oasis *noun Masc.* oasis.

obedecer *verb* [35] to obey; **tienes que obedecerme** you must do as I say.

obedezca, obedezco, etc. *verb* SEE **obedecer**.

obediencia *noun Fem.* obedience.

obediente *adjective* obedient.

obispo *noun Masc.* bishop.

objetivo¹ *noun Masc.* objective.

objetivo²/objetiva *adjective* objective.

objeto *noun Masc.* object; **objetos de valor** valuables.

obligar *verb* [28] **obligar a alguien a hacer algo** to make somebody do something.
obligarse *reflexive verb* [28] **obligarse a hacer** to force yourself to do.

obligatorio/obligatoria *adjective* compulsory.

obra noun Fem. **1** deed; **una buena obra** a good deed; **2** play; **una obra de Shakespeare** a Shakespeare play; **3** work; **una obra de arte** a work of art; **4** **una obra maestra** a masterpiece; **5** building site; **estar en obras** to be having some building work done.

obrero/obrera noun Masc./Fem. **1** worker; **2** labourer.

obsceno/obscena adjective obscene.

obscuridad noun Fem. darkness.

obscuro/obscura adjective dark; **a obscuras** in the dark.

observación noun Fem. **1** observartion; **2** remark.

observador/observadora noun Masc./Fem. observer. **observador** adjective observant.

observar verb [17] **1** to observe; **2** to remark.

observatorio noun Masc. observatory.

obsesión noun Fem. obsession; **tiene una obsesión con la limpieza** he has an obsession with cleanliness; **tiene la obsesión de que la siguen** she's obsessed with the idea that she's being followed.

obstáculo noun Masc. obstacle; **superar un obstáculo** to overcome an obstacle.

obstante in phrase **no obstante** nevertheless.

obstinado/obstinada adjective obstinate.

obstinarse reflexive verb [17] **obstinarse en hacer** to insist on doing.

obtendré, obtendría, etc. verb SEE **obtener**.

obtener verb [9] **1** to obtain; **2** **obtener un premio** to win a prize.

obtenga, obtengo, obtuve, etc. verb SEE **obtener**.

obvio/obvia adjective obvious.

oca noun Fem. goose.

ocasión noun Fem. **1** occasion; **2** opportunity; **si hay ocasión** if there's an opportunity; **3** **precios de ocasión** bargain prices; **coches de ocasión** second-hand cars.

ocasionar verb [17] to cause.

occidental adjective Western.

Occidente noun Masc. the West.

océano noun Masc. ocean.

ochenta number eighty; **tiene ochenta años** she's eighty (years old); **ochenta y cinco** eighty-five; **los años ochenta** the eighties.

ocho number **1** eight; **tiene ocho años** she's eight (years old); **2** eighth (in dates); **estamos a ocho** it's the eighth today; **3** eight (in clock time); **son las ocho** it's eight o'clock.

ochocientos/ochocientas number eight hundred; **ochocientos siete** eight hundred and seven.

ocio noun Masc. spare time.

ocioso/ociosa adjective idle.

octavo/octava adjective eighth; **el octavo piso** the eighth floor.

a
b
c
d
e
f
g
h
i
j
k
l
m
n
ñ
o
p
q
r
s
t
u
v
w
x
y
z

a

b

octubre noun Masc. October; **en octubre/en el mes de octubre** in October.

c

ocupación noun Fem. occupation.

d

ocupado/ocupada adjective
1 busy; **está muy ocupado** he's very busy; 2 engaged; **la línea está ocupada** the line is engaged;
3 taken; **¿está ocupado este asiento?** is this seat taken?

e

f

g

h

ocupar verb [17] 1 **ocupar un asiento** to have a seat; **ocupa el asiento 11b** he's in seat 11b; **¿quién ocupa esa habitación?** who's in that room?; 2 to occupy (land or a building); 3 (talking about time) **ocupo mi tiempo libre leyendo** I spend my free time reading.
ocuparse reflexive verb [17] **ocuparse de algo** to take care of something.

i

j

k

l

m

n

ñ

ocurrir verb [19] to happen; **me ocurrió una cosa muy graciosa** something really funny happened to me; **¿qué le ocurre?** what's the matter with him?.
ocurrirse reflexive verb [19] **¿se te ocurre alguna idea?** can you think of anything?; **se me ocurrió que podríamos ...** I thought we could ....

o

p

q

r

s

odiar verb [17] to hate.

t

odio noun Masc. hate, hatred.

u

v

oeste noun Masc. west; **hacia el oeste** westwards; **al oeste de Madrid** to the west of Madrid.

w

x

ofender verb [18] to offend.
ofenderse reflexive verb [18] to take offence.

y

z

oferta noun Fem. offer; **estar de/en oferta** to be on offer.

oficial adjective official.
oficial noun Masc./Fem. officer.

oficina noun Fem. office; **oficina de cambio** bureau of change; **oficina de objetos perdidos** lost property (office); **oficina de (información y) turismo** tourist (information) office.

oficinista noun Masc./Fem. office worker.

oficio noun Masc. 1 trade; 2 service (in a church).

ofrecer verb [35] to offer.

ofrezca, **ofrezco**, **etc.** verb SEE **ofrecer**.

oído noun Masc. 1 ear; **tener dolor de oídos** to have earache; 2 **tener buen oído** to have a good ear.

oiga, **oigo**, **etc.** verb SEE **oir**.

oír verb [56] 1 to hear; **no oigo nada** I can't hear anything; 2 listen to; **oír las noticias** to listen to the news; **oír música** to listen to music; 3 **¡oye!** hey!

ojalá exclamation **¡ojalá me llame!** I hope he rings me!; **¡ojalá pudiera!** I wish I could!

ojo noun Masc. 1 eye; **tiene los ojos verdes** he's got green eyes; **ojos claros** light-coloured eyes (blue, green, or grey as opposed to brown); **con los ojos cerrados** with your eyes closed; 2 **el ojo de la cerradura** the keyhole; ★ **no pegué ojo en toda la noche** I didn't sleep a wink all night; ★ **salir por un ojo de la cara** (informal) to cost an arm and a leg.
ojo exclamation **¡ojo!** careful!

ola *noun Fem.* wave; **una ola de calor** a heatwave; **una ola de frío** a cold spell.

ole, **olé** *exclamation* olé.

oler *verb* [39] to smell; **oler una flor** to smell a flower; **oler a algo** to smell of something; **huele a lavanda** it smells of lavender.

olimpiadas *plural noun Fem.* Olympic Games.

olímpico/olímpica *adjective* Olympic.

oliva *noun Fem.* olive; **aceite de oliva** olive oil.

olivo *noun Masc.* olive tree.

olla *noun Fem.* pan; **olla a presión** pressure cooker.

olor *noun Masc.* smell; **tiene un olor raro** it has a funny smell; **tiene olor a almendras** it smells of almonds.

olvidar *verb* [17] to forget; **¡olvídalo!** forget it!
olvidarse *reflexive verb* [17] to forget; **se me olvidó llamarte** I forgot to ring you; **se me olvidó la cartera** I forgot my wallet.

ombligo *noun Masc.* navel.

omitir *verb* [19] to omit.

once *number* **1** eleven; **tiene once años** she's eleven (years old); **2** eleventh (*in dates*); **hoy estamos a once** it's the eleventh today; **3** eleven (*in clock time*); **son las once** it's eleven o'clock.

onceavo/onceava *adjective* eleventh.

onda *noun Fem.* wave; **onda larga** long wave; ★**estar en la onda** (*informal*) to be trendy.

ondulado/ondulada *adjective* wavy.

ONU *abbreviation Fem.* (*short for: Organización de las Naciones Unidas*) UN.

opcional *adjective* optional.

ópera *noun Fem.* opera.

operación *noun Fem.* operation; **ha sufrido una operación** he's had an operation.

operador/operadora *noun Masc./Fem.* operator.

operar *verb* [17] **1** to operate on (*a person*); **¿tendrán que operarlo?** will they have to operate on him?; **2** to produce (*a change*).
operarse *reflexive verb* [17] to have an operation; **se va a operar del corazón** she's going to have a heart operation.

opinar *verb* [17] **1** to think; **opino que** ... I think that ...; **¿qué opinas del diseño?** what do you think of the design?; **prefiero no opinar** I prefer not to say what I think; **2** to express an opinion.

opinión *noun Fem.* opinion; **¿cuál es vuestra opinión?** what do you think?; **cambiar de opinión** to change your mind.

oponer *verb* [11] **1** to raise (*an objection*); **2 oponer resistencia** to put up a fight.
oponerse *reflexive verb* [11] **oponerse a algo** to oppose something; **se oponen a cualquier cambio de las reglas** they are opposed to any change in the rules.

oporto *noun Masc.* port.

a
b
c
d
e
f
g
h
i
j
k
l
m
n
ñ
o
p
q
r
s
t
u
v
w
x
y
z

a
b
c
d
e
f
g
h
i
j
k
l
m
n
ñ
o
p
q
r
s
t
u
v
w
x
y
z

oportunidad *noun Fem.*
opportunity; **aprovechar una
oportunidad** to make the most of an
opportunity.

oposición *noun Fem.* **1** opposition;
2 oposiciones competitive public
exams for a government job.

optativo/optativa *adjective*
optional.

óptico/óptica *noun Masc./Fem.*
optician.

optimismo *noun Masc.* optimism.

optimista *noun Masc./Fem.*
optimist.
optimista *adjective* optimistic.

opuesto/opuesta *adjective*
1 conflicting (*views or opinions*);
2 opposite; **venían en dirección
opuesta** they were coming from the
opposite direction.

oral *noun Masc.*,
oral *adjective* oral.

orden¹ *noun Masc.* order; **en orden
alfabético** in alphabetical order; **en
orden de importancia** in order of
importance; **puestos en orden de
tamaño** arranged according to size;
ponlos en orden put them in order;
mantener el orden to keep order;
poner la habitación en orden to
tidy up the room; **¡orden!** order!

orden² *noun Fem.* order; **dar una
orden** to give an order.

ordenado/ordenada *adjective*
tidy; **es muy ordenado** he's very
tidy.

ordenador *noun Masc.* computer.

ordenar *verb* [17] **1** to tidy up (*a
room or house*); **2** to put in order;

ordenar algo alfabéticamente to
put something in alphabetical order;
3 to order; **nos ordenó seguir** he
ordered us to carry on.

ordinario/ordinaria *adjective*
1 vulgar; **2** rude (*a person*);
3 ordinary, normal (*a method or
system*).

oreja *noun Fem.* ear.

orgánico/orgánica *adjective*
organic.

organización *noun Fem.*
organization.

organizar *verb* [22] to organize.

órgano *noun Masc.* organ.

orgullo *noun Masc.* pride; **tiene
mucho orgullo** he's very proud.

orgulloso/orgullosa *adjective*
proud; **estar orgulloso de algo** to
be proud of something.

orientación *noun Fem.* **1** **¿qué
orientación tiene la casa?** which
way does the house face?;
2 orientation; **3** bearings;
4 orientación profesional careers
guidance.

oriental *noun Masc./Fem.* Oriental.
oriental *adjective* **1** Eastern;
2 Oriental.

orientar *verb* [17] **1** to guide; **2** to
give guidance to (*a young person or
student*).
orientarse *reflexive verb* [17] to
get your bearings.

Oriente *noun Masc.* East; **el Lejano
Oriente** the Far East.

original *noun Masc.*, *adjective*
original.

192

orilla *noun Fem.* **1** bank; **sentados a la orilla del río** sitting on the river bank; **2** shore; **una casa a orillas del mar** a house by the sea.

ornamental *adjective* ornamental.

oro *noun Masc.* gold; **un reloj de oro** a gold watch.

orquesta *noun Fem.* orchestra; **una orquesta de jazz** a jazz band.

ortiga *noun Fem.* nettle.

ortografía *noun Fem.* spelling.

oruga *noun Fem.* caterpillar.

os *pronoun* **1** you (*talking to more than one person*); **os vimos desde la ventana** we saw you from the window; **¿os dieron suficiente información?** did they give you enough information?; **2** to you; **os mintió** he lied to you; **3** yourselves; **os tenéis que portar bien** you must behave yourselves; **4** each other; **¿os conocéis?** do you know each other?; **5** (*with a reflexive verb*) **¿os divertisteis?** did you have a good time?; **iros a bañar** go for a swim; **6** (*with parts of the body or clothes*) **os podéis quitar los abrigos** you can take your coats off; **¿os habéis lavado las manos?** have you washed your hands?; **7** (*having something done*) **os tenéis que cortar el pelo** you have to have your hair cut.

osado/osada *adjective* bold.

oscuridad *noun Fem.* darkness.

oscuro/oscura *adjective* dark; **a oscuras** in the dark.

osito *noun Masc.* **un osito de peluche** a teddy bear.

oso/osa *noun Masc./Fem.* bear.

ostra *noun Fem.* oyster.

OTAN *abbreviation Fem.* (*short for: Organización del Tratado del Atlántico Norte*) NATO.

otoño *noun Masc.* autumn.

otro/otra *adjective* **1** another; **¿te has comprado otro casete?** did you buy another cassette?; **añade otros dos** add another two; **2** other; **en otros colores** in other colours; **la otra tarde le vi** I saw him the other evening; **¿no tienes ningún otro color?** don't you have any other colours?; **3 otra cosa** something else; **me gustaría comprarle otra cosa** I would like to buy her something else; **eso es otra cosa diferente** that's something different; **¿quieres alguna otra cosa?** do you want something else?; **no me gusta ninguna otra cosa** I don't like anything else; **4 otra vez** again; **hazlo otra vez** do it again.

otro *pronoun* **1** another one; **éste no, dame otro** not this one, give me another one; **2** other one; **el otro te queda mejor** the other one suits you better; **las otras están en el cajón** the other ones are in the drawer; **3** (*talking about people*) **los otros vendrán en coche** the others will come by car; **a otros les gustaría** other people would like it; **4** (*talking about time*) **un mes sí y otro no** every other month; **de un día para otro** from one day to the next.

oveja *noun Fem.* sheep.

OVNI *abbreviation Masc.* (*short for: objeto volante no identificado*) UFO.

a
b
c
d
e
f
g
h
i
j
k
l
m
n
ñ
o
p
q
r
s
t
u
v
w
x
y
z

a
b
c
d
e
f
g
h
i
j
k
l
m
n
ñ
o
p
q
r
s
t
u
v
w
x
y
z

oxidado/oxidada *adjective* rusty.

oxígeno *noun Masc.* oxygen.

oyendo, oyó *verb* SEE **oír**.

ozono *noun Masc.* ozone; **la capa de ozono** the ozone layer.

Pp

pabellón *noun Masc.* pavilion.

paciencia *noun Fem.* patience; **tener paciencia** to be patient.

paciente *noun Masc./Fem.*, **paciente** *adjective* patient.

padecer *verb* [35] to suffer; **padecer de algo** to suffer from something.

padrastro *noun Masc.* stepfather.

padre *noun Masc.* **1** father; **2 mis padres** my parents.

padrino *noun Masc.* **1** godfather; **2 mis padrinos** my godparents.

padrino de boda *noun Masc.* (*person who gives away the bride and carries out duties of the best man*).

paella *noun Fem.* paella.

paga *noun Fem.* **1** pay; **2** pocket money.

pagar *verb* [28] **1** to pay; **2** to pay off (*a debt*); **3** to pay for (*tickets, for example*); **4** to repay (*a favour*).

página *noun Fem.* page.

pago *noun Masc.* payment; **pago anticipado** payment in advance; **pago inicial** down payment; **pago al contado** payment in cash; **efectuar un pago** to make a payment.

país *noun Masc.* country.

paisaje *noun Masc.* landscape.

Países Bajos *plural noun Masc.* **los Países Bajos** the Netherlands.

País de Gales *noun Masc.* **el País de Gales** Wales.

País Vasco *noun Masc.* **el País Vasco** the Basque Country.

paja *noun Fem.* **1** straw; **2 pajita** drinking straw.

pajarita *noun Fem.* bow tie.

pájaro *noun Masc.* bird; ★ **matar dos pájaros de un tiro** to kill two birds with one stone.

pala *noun Fem.* **1** spade; **2** shovel; **3** bat (*for table tennis*); **4** slice (*in cooking*).

palabra *noun Fem.* **1** word; **palabra compuesta** compound word; **no cumplió con su palabra** he didn't keep his word; **2** speech; **el don de la palabra** the gift of speech; **3 pedir la palabra** to ask permission to speak.

palabrota *noun Fem.* swearword; **decir palabrotas** to swear.

palacio *noun Masc.* palace.

palanca *noun Fem.* **1** lever; **abrir algo haciendo palanca** to lever something open; **2** crowbar; **3 palanca de cambios** gearstick; **palanca de mando** joystick.

paleta *noun Fem.* **1** palette; **2** spatula (*for cooking*); **3** trowel; **4** bat (*in table tennis*).

palidecer *verb* [35] to go pale.

pálido/pálida *adjective* pale.

palillo *noun Masc.* **1** chopstick; **2** drumstick; **3 palillo de dientes** toothpick.

palma *noun Fem.* palm (*of hand*); **dar palmas** to clap your hands.

palmera *noun Fem.* palm tree.

palo *noun Masc.* **1** stick; **2** pole (*for a tent*); **3 palo de escoba** broomstick.

paloma *noun Fem.* **1** dove; **la paloma de la paz** the dove of peace; **2** pigeon.

palomitas *plural noun Fem.* popcorn.

pan *noun Masc.* bread; **un pan de molde** a loaf of bread; **una barra de pan** a French loaf; **pan integral** wholeheat bread; **pan tostado** toast; **pan rallado** breadcrumbs.

pana *noun Fem.* corduroy.

panadería *noun Fem.* bakery.

panadero/panadera *noun Masc./Fem.* baker.

Panamá *noun Masc.* Panama; **el Canal de Panamá** the Panama Canal.

panameño/panameña *noun Masc./Fem., adjective* Panamanian.

pancarta *noun Fem.* banner.

panceta *noun Fem.* belly pork.

pandereta *noun Fem.* tambourine.

panecillo *noun Masc.* bread roll.

pánico *noun Masc.* panic.

panorama *noun Masc.* **1** panorama; **2** view.

pantalla *noun Fem.* **1** screen; **la pantalla grande** the big screen; **2** shade (*of a lamp*).

pantalón *noun Masc.* trousers; **un pantalón** a pair of trousers.

pantalones *plural noun Masc.* trousers; **un par de pantalones/ unos pantalones** a pair of trousers; **pantalones vaqueros** jeans; **pantalones cortos** shorts; **pantalones de peto** dungarees.

pantano *noun Masc.* **1** swamp; **2** reservoir.

pantanoso/pantanosa *adjective* swampy, marshy.

pantorrilla *noun Fem.* calf.

panty, panti *noun Masc.* tights.

pañal *noun Masc.* nappy.

paño *noun Masc.* cloth; **un paño** a piece of cloth; **un paño de cocina** a dishcloth; ★**estar en paños menores** (*informal*) to be in your undies.

pañuelo *noun Masc.* **1** handkerchief; **2** headscarf; **3** scarf.

papá *noun Masc.* daddy; **mis papás** my mum and dad.

papagayo *noun Masc.* parrot.

papel *noun Masc.* paper; **un trozo de papel** a piece of paper; **se encontró un papel en la mesa** he found a piece of paper on the table; **papel aluminio** aluminium foil; **papel higiénico** toilet paper; **papel pintado** wallpaper; **papel de envolver** wrapping paper; **papel de lija** sandpaper.

papelera *noun Fem.* **1** paperbasket; **2** litter bin (*in the street*).

papelería *noun Fem.* stationer's.

paperas *plural noun Fem.* mumps.

paquete *noun Masc.* **1** parcel; **mandar un paquete** to send a parcel; **2** packet; **un paquete de cigarrillos** a packet of cigarettes.

par *noun Masc.* **1** pair; **un par de zapatos** a pair of shoes; **2** couple; **un par de veces** a couple of times; **3** **de par en par** wide open.
par *adjective* even; **un número par** an even number.

para *preposition* **1** for; **es para ti** it's for you; **sirve para limpiar** it's for cleaning; **¿para qué quieres la carpeta?** what do you want the folder for?; **hay suficiente para todos** there's enough for everybody; **estará terminado para el doce** it'll be finished for the twelfth; **2** to; **se dijo para sí** he said to himself; **es demasiado difícil para hacerlo** it's too difficult to do; **3** (*direction*) **me voy para casa** I'm going home; **iban para la estación** they were going to the station; **4** **para que** so that.

parabrisas *noun Masc.* (*does not change in the plural*) windscreen.

paracaídas *noun Masc.* (*does not change in the plural*) parachute.

parachoques *noun Masc.* (*does not change in the plural*) bumper.

parada¹ *noun Fem.* stop; **la parada del autobús** the bus stop; **parada de taxis** taxi rank.

parado/parada² *noun Masc./Fem.* unemployed person.
parado *adjective* unemployed.

parador *noun Masc.* state-owned hotel.

paraguas *noun Masc.* (*does not change in the plural*) umbrella.

Paraguay *noun Masc.* Paraguay.

paraguayo/paraguaya *noun Masc./Fem., adjective* Paraguayan.

paraíso *noun Masc.* paradise.

paralelo¹ *noun Masc.* parallel.

paralelo²**/paralela** *adjective* parallel; **paralelo a algo** parallel to something.

parapente *noun Masc.* hang gliding.

parar *verb* [17] **1** to stop; **parar de hablar** to stop talking; **bailamos sin parar toda la noche** we didn't stop dancing all night; **paré el coche** I stopped the car; **2** **para un momento** hang on a minute; **3** to save; **parar un gol** to make a save (*in football, hockey*); **4** **ir a parar** to end up; **fueron a parar al hospital** they ended up in hospital; **¡no sé a donde vamos a ir a parar!** I don't know what the world is coming to!
pararse *reflexive verb* [17] to stop; **no te pares en medio de la calle** don't stop in the middle of the road; **se paró a pensar** he stopped to think; **se me ha parado el reloj** my watch has stopped.

pararrayos *noun Masc.* (*does not change in the plural*) lightning conductor.

parasol *noun Masc.* parasol.

parcela *noun Fem.* plot of land.

parche *noun Masc.* patch.

parchís *noun Masc.* ludo.

parecer *verb* [35] **1** to seem; **no parece demasiado complicado** it doesn't seem too complicated; **parece que ya no vienen** it seems they're not coming any more; **2** to seem like, to look like; **parece de madera** it looks as if it's made of wood; **esa nube parece un pájaro** that cloud looks like a bird; **parece que está roto** it looks as though it's broken; **parece que va a llover** it looks like rain; **3 ¿qué te pareció la película?** what did you think of the film?; **me parece que llegan hoy** I think they arrive today; **me parece que no** I don't think so; **le pareció muy mal que no llamasen** he thought it was really bad of them not to call; **4 según parece/al parecer** apparently.

parecerse *reflexive verb* [35] **1** to look like; **se parece mucho a su padre** she looks very like her father; **nos parecemos mucho** we look very like each other; **2** to be like (*in character*); **se parece mucho a su madre** she is very like her mother.

parecido¹ *noun Masc.* **1** similarity; **el parecido era increíble** the similarity was incredible; **2 ser bien parecido** to be good-looking.

parecido²**/parecida** *adjective* similar.

pared *noun Fem.* wall.

pareja *noun Fem.* **1** pair; **trabajar en pareja** to work in pairs; **2** couple; **3 mi pareja** my partner.

paréntesis *noun Masc.* (*does not change in the plural*) brackets.

parezca, parezco, etc. *verb* SEE **parecer**.

pariente *noun Masc./Fem.* relative.

parking *noun Masc.* car park.

parlamento *noun Masc.* parliament.

paro *noun Masc.* **1** unemployment; **estar en paro** to be unemployed; **cobrar el paro** to receive unemployment benefit; **2** strike; **hicieron un paro de 24 horas** they went on a 24-hour strike; **3 un paro cardíaco** heart failure.

parpadear *verb* [17] to blink.

párpado *noun Masc.* eyelid.

parque *noun Masc.* **1** park; **parque nacional** national park; **parque infantil** play park; **2 parque de atracciones** amusement park; **parque temático** theme park; **parque zoológico** zoo; **3 parque de bomberos** fire station; **4 parque móvil** fleet (of cars, lorries etc); **5 parque eólico** wind farm.

parquímetro *noun Masc.* parking meter.

párrafo *noun Masc.* paragraph.

parrilla *noun Fem.* grill; **chuletas a la parrilla** barbecued chops.

parte¹ *noun Fem.* **1** part; **es parte de Asia** it's part of Asia; **una tercera parte de la herencia** a third of the inheritance; **la parte**

a
b
c
d
e
f
g
h
i
j
k
l
m
n
ñ
o
p
q
r
s
t
u
v
w
x
y
z

antigua de la ciudad the old part of town; **2** share; **mi parte del trabajo** my share of the work; **3 la mayor parte de** most of; **la mayor parte de los alumnos** most of the students; **4 en/por alguna parte** somewhere; **en/por cualquier parte** anywhere; **en/por todas partes** everywhere; **5 en parte** partly; **en parte tienen razón** they're partly right; **6 en gran parte** largely; **7 de un tiempo a esta parte** for some time now; **8 ¿de parte de quién?** who shall I say is calling? (on the phone); **saludos de parte de Juan** Juan says hello; **felicítalos de mi parte** give them my congratulations; **9 yo por mi parte** ... as far as I'm concerned ....

parte² noun Masc. report; **el parte meteorológico** the weather report.

partera noun Fem. midwife.

participación noun Fem. **1** participation; **2** share in lottery ticket.

participar verb [17] to participate.

participio noun Masc. participle; **participio pasado** past participle.

particular adjective **1** private (lesson or teacher); **2** particular (feature, for example); **3 un colegio particular** a fee-paying school; **4 mi teléfono particular** my home telephone number; **nuestro domicilio particular** our home address; **5 es muy particular** (informal) he's very peculiar.

partida noun Fem. game; **una partida de ajedrez** a game of chess.

partido noun Masc. **1** party (political); **2** game, match.

partir verb [19] **1** to cut; **partir algo por la mitad** to cut something in two; **2** to break (a branch, for example); **3** to crack (a nut); **4** to leave (a train or person); **5 a partir de ese momento** from that moment on; **a partir de ahora** from now on. **partirse** reflexive verb [19] to break (a branch, for example); **la rama se partió** the branch broke; **me partí un diente** I broke a tooth.

partitura noun Fem. score (music).

parto noun Masc. labour; **estar de parto** to be in labour.

pasa noun Fem. raisin.

pasado¹ noun Masc. past.

pasado²/**pasada** adjective **1** last; **el verano pasado** last summer; **2 pasados dos días, le llamé** after two days, I phoned him; **3 son las diez pasadas** it's past ten o'clock; **pasado mañana** the day after tomorrow; **4** off; **la leche está pasada** the milk is off; **5 quiero el filete muy pasado** I want my steak well done.

pasaje noun Masc. ticket.

pasajero/pasajera noun Masc./ Fem. passenger.

pasamanos noun Masc. (does not change in the plural) **1** banister; **2** handrail.

pasaporte noun Masc. passport.

pasar verb [17] **1** to go past; **pasaron por enfrente de mi casa** they went past my house; **pasar de largo** to go straight past; **me vió y**

pasó de largo he saw me and walked straight past me; **2** to come past; **pasaron por aquí** they came past here; **3** to get past; **no podíamos pasar** we couldn't get past; **4 pásate por mi casa por la tarde** call round at my house in the evening; **el cartero pasa a las diez** the postman comes at ten; **pasaré por el banco para recoger los impresos** I'll call in at the bank to collect the forms; **5** to go in; **pasaron todos al salón** they all went into the living room; **6** to come in; **pase, por favor** please come in; **7 pasar de un lado a otro** to go from one side to the other; **8 pasar por** to go through; **pasar por la aduana** to go through customs; **el tren no pasa por Talavera** the train does not go through Talavera; **9 pasar algo por algo** to put something through something; **10** to go by; **pasaron tres meses** three months went by; **11** to pass; **¿me pasas las tijeras?** could you pass me the scissors?; **me pasó el balón** he passed the ball to me; **12** to happen; **¿qué ha pasado?** what's happened?; **no le ha pasado nada** nothing has happened to him; **¿qué te ha pasado en la mano?** what's happened to your hand?; **¿qué te pasa?** what's the matter?; **13** to spend; **pasaremos las vacaciones en España** we'll spend our holidays in Spain; **pasé la noche en casa de un amigo** I spent the night at a friend's house; **14 pasarlo bien** to have a good time; **me lo pasé muy mal en las vacaciones** I didn't

enjoy myself at all during the holidays; **15 pasar con** to put through; **le paso con el Señor Muñoz** I'll put you through to Mr Muñoz.

pasarse *reflexive verb* [17] **1** to go off (*milk or fish*); **2** to go bad (*vegetables or fruit*); **3 pasarse de un lado a otro** to go from one side to the other; **4** to come (by); **pásate por la oficina cuando quieras** come by my office whenever you want; **me pasaré por correos antes de ir a trabajar** I'll stop by the post office before going to work; **5** to go past; **nos pasamos de parada** we missed our stop.

pasatiempo *noun Masc.* pastime.

Pascua *noun Fem.* **1** Easter; **2** Christmas; **¡felices Pascuas!** Merry Christmas!.

pasear *verb* [17] **1** to go for a walk; **me gusta pasear por la playa** I like walking on the beach; **sacar al perro a pasear** to take the dog for a walk; **2 pasear en coche** to go for a drive; **fuimos a pasear en bicicleta** we went for a bike ride.

pasearse *reflexive verb* [17] to go for a walk.

paseo *noun Masc.* **1** walk; **fuimos a dar un paseo** we went for a walk; **2** stroll; **3 ir a dar un paseo en coche** to go for a drive; **ir a dar un paseo en bicicleta** to go for a bike ride.

pasillo *noun Masc.* corridor.

pasión *noun Fem.* passion.

a
b
c
d
e
f
g
h
i
j
k
l
m
n
ñ
o
p
q
r
s
t
u
v
w
x
y
z

pasivo/pasiva *adjective* passive;
un fumador pasivo a passive
smoker.

paso *noun Masc.* **1** step; **dar un paso
adelante** to take a step forward;
paso a paso step by step; **2 oír
pasos** to hear footsteps; **3 un paso
a nivel** a level crossing; **un paso
elevado** a flyover; **un paso
subterráneo** a subway; **un paso de
peatones** a pedestrian crossing; **un
paso de cebra** a zebra crossing;
4 'ceda el paso' 'give way';
5 'prohibido el paso' 'no entry';
6 te viene de paso/te pilla de paso
it's on your way.

pasta *noun Fem.* **1** pasta; **prefiero el
arroz a la pasta** I prefer rice to
pasta; **2** paste; **3 pastas** biscuits;
4 pasta de dientes toothpaste.

pastel *noun Masc.* cake.

pastelería *noun Fem.* cake shop.

pastilla *noun Fem.* **1** pill; **2 una
pastilla de jabón** a bar of soap.

pastor/pastora *noun Masc./Fem.*
shepherd/shepherdess.

pata¹ *noun Fem.* **1** leg; **2** paw;
★ **meter la pata** (*informal*) to put
your foot in it.

patada *noun Fem.* kick; **dar una
patada a alguien** to kick someone.

patata *noun Fem.* potato; **patatas
fritas** chips, (potato) crisps.

paternal *adjective* paternal.

patín *noun Masc.* **1** roller skate; **2** ice
skate; **3** skateboard; **4** pedalo.

patinador/patinadora *noun*
skater.

patinaje *noun Masc.* **1** roller
skating; **2** ice skating; **patinaje
artístico** figure skating.

patinar *noun 17* **1** to roller skate;
2 to ice skate; **3** to slip; **patiné en
una mancha de aceite** I slipped on
a patch of oil; **4** to skid (*a car*).

patio *noun Masc.* **1** patio;
2 playground.

pato/pata² *noun Masc./Fem.* duck;
★ **ser un pato** (*informal*) to be very
clumsy.

patria *noun Fem.* homeland.

patrocinar *verb* [17] to sponsor.

patrón *noun Masc.* **1** boss;
2 landlord.

patrona *noun Fem.* landlady.

patrulla *noun Fem.* patrol; **patrulla
de rescate** rescue party.

patrullera *noun Fem.* patrol boat.

patrullero *noun Masc.* **1** patrol
boat; **2** patrol plane; **3** patrol car.

pausa *noun Fem.* pause; **hacer una
pausa** to have a break.

pavo/pava *noun Masc./Fem.*
1 turkey; **2 pavo real** peacock.

payaso/payasa *noun Masc./Fem.*
clown.

paz (*plural* **paces**) *noun Fem.*
1 peace; **2 hacer las paces** to make
up; **nos peleamos pero al final
hicimos las paces** we had a fight,
but we made up in the end; **3 dejar
en paz** to leave alone; **¡deja mi
calculadora en paz!** leave my
calculator alone!; **¡deja a tu
hermano en paz!** leave your
brother alone!; **¡estos niños nunca**

me dejan en paz! these children never give me a moment's peace!; **4 en paz descanse** rest in peace.

PD *abbreviation* P.S. (*at the end of a letter*).

peaje *noun Fem.* toll; **carretera de peaje** toll road.

peatón *noun Masc.* pedestrian.

peca *noun Fem.* freckle.

pecado *noun Masc.* sin.

pecho *noun Masc.* **1** breast; **dar el pecho a un bebé** to breastfeed a baby; **2** chest.

pechuga *noun Fem.* breast; **pechuga de pollo** chicken breast.

pedal *noun Masc.* pedal; **pedal de arranque** kickstart.

pedazo *noun Masc.* piece; **un pedazo de queso** a piece of cheese; **hacer pedazos** to smash to pieces; **hizo pedazos el vaso** he smashed the glass to pieces; **el jarrón se cayó y se hizo pedazos** the vase fell and smashed to pieces.

pedir *verb* [57] **1** to ask for; **pedir un favor** to ask for a favour; **pedir ayuda** to ask for help; **pedir consejo** to ask for advice; **2 pedir perdón** to apologize; **3 piden medio millón por el cuadro** they're asking half a million for the picture; **me pidió que le comprase un libro** he asked me to buy him a book; **4 pedir hora** to ask for an appointment; **5 pedir prestado** to ask to borrow; **me pidió prestada la moto** he asked to borrow my motorbike; **pedir dinero prestado** to ask to borrow some money, to ask for a loan; **6** to order (*in a restaurant*); **¿qué vas a pedir?** what are you going to order?

pegajoso/pegajosa *adjective* sticky.

pegamento *noun Masc.* glue.

pegar *verb* [28] **1** to hit; **me pegó** he hit me; **pegar una torta a alguien** to slap somebody; **pegar una patada a alguien** to kick somebody; **pegar una paliza a alguien** to give somebody a beating; **2 pegar un grito** to let out a yell; **3 pegar un salto** to jump; **pegar saltos de alegría** to jump for joy; **4 pegarle un susto a alguien** to give somebody a fright; **5** to stick; **he pegado una foto suya en la pared** I've stuck a picture of him on the wall; **6** to glue; **7** (*informal*) **me vas a pegar el resfriado** you're going to give me your cold.

pegarse *reflexive verb* [28] **1** to hit each other; **empezaron a pegarse** they started hitting each other; **2** to stick; **este sello no se pega** this stamp won't stick.

pegatina *noun Fem.* sticker.

peinado *noun Masc.* hairstyle.

peinar *verb* [17] **1** to comb; **2** to brush.

peinarse *reflexive verb* [17] **1** to comb your hair; **2** to brush your hair.

peine *noun Masc.* comb.

pela *noun Fem.* (*informal*) penny; **no me quedan pelas** I haven't got a penny.

pelar *verb* [17] **1** to peel (*a potato, for example*); **2 pelar a alguien al cero** to cut somebody's hair very short.
pelarse *reflexive verb* [17] **1** to peel (*from sunburn*); **se me está pelando la nariz** my nose is peeling; **2** (*informal*) to have your hair cut.

peldaño *noun Masc.* **1** step; **2** rung.

pelea *noun Fem.* **1** fight; **2** row; **tuvo una pelea con su novio** she had a row with her boyfriend.

pelear *verb* [17] **1** to fight; **2** to quarrel.
pelearse *reflexive verb* [17] **1** to fight; **había dos hombres peleándose** there were two men fighting; **2** to quarrel; **se pelearon por dinero** they quarrelled over money; **siempre se está peleando con sus padres** she's always quarrelling with her parents.

película *noun Fem.* **1** film; **¿qué película ponen hoy?** what film are they showing today?; **una película de terror** a horror film; **una película de risa** a comedy film; **una película de suspense** a thriller; **2** film (*for a camera*).

peligro *noun Masc.* danger; **estar en peligro/correr peligro** to be in danger; **poner a alguien en peligro** to put somebody at risk; **fuera de peligro** out of danger; **un peligro para la salud** a health risk; **peligro de incendio** a fire hazard.

peligroso/peligrosa *adjective* dangerous.

pelirrojo/pelirroja *adjective* **1** red-haired; **2 pelo pelirrojo** red hair.

pellizcar *verb* [31] to pinch.

pellizco *noun Masc.* pinch; **le di un pellizco en el brazo** I pinched her arm.

pelo *noun Masc.* **1** hair; **pelo liso/lacio** straight hair; **pelo rizado** curly hair; **tengo el pelo negro** I've got black hair; **2 un pelo de la barba** a whisker; **3** fur (*of an animal*); ★ **salvarse por los pelos** (*informal*) to escape by the skin of your teeth; ★ **no se cayó por los pelos** he very nearly fell; ★ **ponerle a alguien los pelos de punta** (*informal*) to make somebody's hair stand on end; ★ **tomarle el pelo a alguien** (*informal*) to pull somebody's leg (*literally: to take somebody's hair*).

pelota *noun Fem.* ball; **una pelota de fútbol** a football.

peluca *noun Fem.* wig.

peluche *noun Masc.* **un juguete de peluche** a cuddly toy; **un osito de peluche** a teddy bear.

peludo/peluda *adjective* hairy.

peluquería *noun Fem.* hairdresser's.

peluquero/peluquera *noun Masc./Fem.* hairdresser.

pena *noun Fem.* **1** shame; **¡qué pena!** what a shame; **es una pena que no puedas venir** it's a shame you can't come; **2** sadness; **me da pena verte llorar** it makes me sad to see you cry; **3 Sara me da mucha pena** I feel really sorry for Sara; **4** sentence; **pena de muerte** death penalty; **5 valer la pena** to be worth it; **no vale la pena** it's not worth it; **vale la pena ver la película** the film's worth seeing; **6 penas** problems; **cuéntame tus penas** tell me all your problems; ★**a duras penas** with great difficulty.

penalti *noun Masc.* penalty.

pendiente *noun Masc.* earring.
pendiente *noun Fem.* slope.
pendiente *adjective* unresolved.

pene *noun Masc.* penis.

penetrar *verb* [17] to penetrate.

península *noun Fem.* peninsula.

penique *noun Masc.* penny.

pensamiento *noun Masc.* thought.

pensar *verb* [29] to think; **piénsalo bien antes de decidir** think about it carefully before deciding anything; **pensándolo bien** ... on second thoughts ...; **pensar en** to think about; **estaba pensando en ti** I was thinking about you; **¿piensas llamarlo?** are you thinking of calling him?; **pensar mal de alguien** to think badly of someone; **¿qué piensas del nuevo entrenador?** what do you think of the new coach?.

pensión *noun Fem.* **1** pension; **cobrar la pensión** to draw your pension; **pensión de viudedad** widow's pension; **2** guesthouse; **3 pensión completa** full board; **media pensión** half board.

pensionista *noun Masc./Fem.* pensioner.

peor *noun Masc./Fem.* **el/la peor** the worst one; **los/las peores** the worst ones.

peor *adjective* **1** worse; **éstas son peores que las de la otra tienda** these are worse than the ones in the other shop; **mucho peor** much worse; **2** worst; **mi peor enemigo** my worst enemy; **en el peor de los casos** in the worst scenario; **3 peor para ti** it's your loss.

peor *adverb* worse; **es aún peor** it's even worse; **cada vez peor** worse and worse; **de mal en peor** from bad to worse; **yo bailo peor que tú** I'm a worse dancer than you.

pepinillo *noun Masc.* gherkin.

pepino *noun Masc.* cucumber.

pequeño/pequeña *noun Masc./ Fem.* small boy/small girl.
pequeño *adjective* **1** small; **una casa pequeña** a small house; **la chaqueta me está pequeña** the jacket's too small for me; **2** slight; **un pequeño esfuerzo** a slight effort; **3** young; **mi hermana pequeña** my little sister.

pera *noun Fem.* pear.

peral *noun Masc.* pear tree.

percha *noun Fem.* **1** hanger; **2** coat hook.

perder *verb* [36] **1** to lose; **he perdido la cartera** I've lost my wallet; **perder la paciencia** to lose patience; **perder el conocimiento** to lose consciousness; **2** to miss; **perder el tren** to miss the train; **has perdido una gran oportunidad** you've missed a great opportunity; **3 perder la costumbre** to get out of the habit; **4 perder el tiempo** to waste time.

a
b
c
d
e
f
g
h
i
j
k
l
m
n
ñ
o
p
q
r
s
t
u
v
w
x
y
z

a

b

perderse *reflexive verb* [36] to get lost; **me he perdido** I'm lost; **¿te has perdido?** are you lost?

c

d

pérdida *noun Fem.* **1** loss; **2 es una pérdida de tiempo** it's a waste of time.

e

perdiz *noun Fem.* partridge.

f

perdón *noun Masc.* pardon.
perdón *exclamation* excuse me.

g

h

i

perdonar *verb* [17] **1** to forgive; **no la he perdonado** I haven't forgiven her; **2 te perdono el castigo** I'll let you off (*without a punishment*);
3 ¡perdona!/¡perdone! sorry!, (*more formal*) excuse me!

j

k

l

peregrinación *noun Fem.* pilgrimage; **irse de pereginación** to go on a pilgrimage.

m

perejil *noun Masc.* parsley.

n

pereza *noun Fem.* laziness.

ñ

perezoso/perezosa *adjective* lazy.

o

p

perfeccionar *verb* [17] **1** to improve; **2** to perfect.

q

perfectamente *adverb* perfectly.

r

s

perfecto/perfecta *adjective* perfect.

t

perfil *noun Masc.* profile; **visto de perfil** from the side.

u

perfume *noun Masc.* perfume.

v

perfumería *noun Fem.* perfume shop.

w

periódico *noun Masc.* newspaper.

x

periodista *noun Masc./Fem.* journalist.

y

z

período, periodo *noun Masc.* period (*of time*).

periquito *noun Masc.* budgie.

perla *noun Fem.* pearl.

permanecer *verb* [35] **1** to stay (*in a place*); **2** to remain; **permanecer callado** to remain silent.

permanente *noun Fem.* perm; **hacerse la permanente** to have your hair permed.
permanente *adjective* permanent.

permanezca, permanezco, etc. *verb* SEE **permanecer**.

permiso *noun Masc.* **1** permission; **darle permiso a alguien para hacer** to give someone permission to do; **2 con permiso** may I come in?, excuse me (*to get past someone*); **3** permit; **permiso de trabajo** work permit; **4** leave; **estar de permiso** to be on leave; **un permiso de una semana** a week's leave; **5 permiso de conducir** driving licence.

permitir *verb* [19] **1** to allow; **no nos permitieron pasar** they didn't allow us in; **2 no te permito que me contestes** I won't have you answering me back; **3** (*when asking permission*) **¿me permite?** may I?; **¿me permite una sugerencia?** may I make a suggestion?; **4** to make possible; **este proceso permite ...** this process makes it possible to ....

pero *conjunction* but.

perrito *noun Masc.* **1** puppy; **2 perrito caliente** hot dog.

perro/perra *noun Masc./Fem.* dog; **perro callejero** stray dog; ★ **estar de un humor de perros** (*informal*) to be in a foul mood.

persecución *noun Fem.*
1 pursuit; **salir en persecución de alguien** to set off in pursuit of someone; **2** persecution.

perseguir *verb* [64] to pursue.

persiana *noun Fem.* blind.

persistir *verb* [19] to persist.

persona *noun Fem.* **1** person; **una persona importante** an important person; **2 personas** people; **en la sala había diez personas** there were ten people in the room.

personaje *noun Masc.* **1** character (*in a book, for example*); **2** important figure; **un personaje del mundo de la música** an important figure in the music world.

personal *noun Masc.* staff.
personal *adjective* personal.

personalidad *noun Fem.* personality.

perspectiva *noun Fem.*
1 perspective; **2** prospect; **hay buenas perspectivas** there are good prospects.

persuadir *verb* [19] to persuade.

pertenecer *verb* [35] to belong.

pertenezca, pertenezco, etc. *verb* SEE **pertenecer**.

Perú *noun Masc.* Peru.

peruano/peruana *noun Masc./ Fem., adjective* Peruvian.

pesa *noun Fem.* weight; **hacer pesas** to do weightlifting.

pesadilla *noun Fem.* nightmare.

pesado/pesada *noun Masc./Fem.*
¡eres un pesado! (*informal*) you're such a pain!

pesado *adjective* **1** heavy (*a box or piece of furniture, for example*); **2 ser muy pesado** (*informal*) to be a pain (*a person*); **3 ser muy pesado** to be boring (*a job or book, for example*).

pesar *verb* [17] **1** to weigh; **peso sesenta kilos** I weigh sixty kilos; **2 pesar mucho** to be very heavy; **puedo llevarlo, pesa poco** I can carry it, it's not very heavy; **¿te pesan mucho las bolsas?** are the bags too heavy for you?.

pesca *noun Fem.* fishing; **ir de pesca** to go fishing.

pescadería *noun Fem.* fishmonger's.

pescado *noun Masc.* fish.

pescador/pescadora *noun Masc./Fem.* fisherman/fisherwoman.

pescar *verb* [31] **1** to fish; **ir a pescar** to go fishing; **2** to catch; **no pescamos nada** we didn't catch anything.

peseta *noun Fem.* peseta (*former Spanish currency replaced by the euro; 500 pesetas = 3.00 euros*).

pesimista *noun Masc./Fem.* pessimist.
pesimista *adjective* pessimistic.

peso *noun Masc.* weight; **perder peso** to lose weight; **ganar peso** to put on weight; **peso bruto** gross weight; **vender al peso** to sell by weight.

pestaña *noun Fem.* eyelash.

pétalo *noun Masc.* petal.

petardo *noun Masc.* banger.

petróleo *noun Masc.* oil.

a
b
c
d
e
f
g
h
i
j
k
l
m
n
ñ
o
p
q
r
s
t
u
v
w
x
y
z

petrolero *noun Masc.* oil tanker (*ship*).

pez (*plural* **peces**) *noun Masc.* fish (*live*); **un pez espada** a swordfish.

piano *noun Masc.* piano; **tocar el piano** to play the piano.

picado/picada *adjective*
1 decayed (*tooth*); **tengo una muela picada** I have a cavity in one of my back teeth; **2 carne picada** mince; **3 el mar estaba picado** the sea was choppy; **4** (*informal*) **estar picado** to be miffed (*a person*); **está picada porque no la llamaste** she's a bit miffed that you didn't call her.

picadura *noun Fem.* bite, sting.

picante *adjective* hot (*spicy*).

picaporte *noun Masc.* door handle.

picar *verb* [31] **1** to bite, to sting; **2** to mince (*meat*); **3** to chop (*vegetables*); **4** to rot (*teeth*); **5** to be hot (*spicy*); **esta salsa pica mucho** this sauce is too hot; **6** to itch; **me pica la nariz** my nose is itching; **7 me pican los ojos** my eyes are stinging.

pico *noun Masc.* **1** beak; **2** pick; **3** peak (*of a mountain*); **4** corner (*of a table, for example*); **5 un cuello de pico** a V-neck; **6** **... y pico** ... and something; **fueron tres mil y pico** it was three thousand and something; **llegaron a las cinco y pico** they arrived after five.

pida, **pido**, **pidió**, **etc.** *verb* SEE **pedir**.

pie *noun Masc.* **1** foot; **ir a pie** to go on foot; **2 de pie** standing; **estaban de pie** they were standing; **ponerse de pie** to stand up; **3** base (*of a lamp or glass*).

piedra *noun Fem.* **1** stone; **una mesa de piedra** a stone table; **piedra preciosa** precious stone; **tener piedras en el riñón** to have kidney stones; **2** flint (*of a lighter*).

piel *noun Fem.* **1** skin; **tener la piel seca** to have dry skin; **2** peel; **3** fur; **un abrigo de pieles** a fur coat; **4** leather; **bolsos de piel** leather bags.

piensa, **pienso**, **etc.** *verb* SEE **pensar**.

pierna *noun Fem.* leg.

pieza *noun Fem.* **1** piece; **2 pieza de recambio** spare part.

pijama *noun Masc.* pyjamas.

pila *noun Fem.* **1** pile; **una pila de libros** a pile of books; **2** battery; **3** (*kitchen*) sink.

píldora *noun Fem.* pill.

piloto *noun Masc./Fem.* pilot.

pimentón *noun Masc.* **1** paprika; **2** cayenne pepper.

pimienta *noun Fem.* pepper.

pimiento *noun Masc.* pepper; **un pimiento rojo** a red pepper.

pimpón *noun Masc.* table tennis.

pincel *noun Masc.* **1** paintbrush; **2** make-up brush.

pinchadiscos *noun Masc./Fem.* (*informal*) disc jockey.

pinchar *verb* [17] **1** to prick; **2** to be prickly; **3** to burst; **4** to puncture; **creo que hemos pinchado** I think we've got a flat tyre; **5** (*informal*) to give an injection to.

pincharse *reflexive verb* [17] **1** to burst; **2** to puncture; **se me ha pinchado una rueda** I've got a flat tyre; **3** to get miffed.

pinchazo *noun Masc.* puncture; **tuvimos un pinchazo** we had a puncture.

pingüino *noun Masc.* penguin.

pino *noun Masc.* pine tree; **muebles de pino** pine furniture.

pinta *noun Fem.* **1 tiene pinta de oficinista** he looks like an office worker; **¡qué pinta más rara!** that looks very strange!; **la comida tiene muy buena pinta** the food looks delicious; **2** pint.

pintadas *plural noun Fem.* graffiti.

pintado/pintada *adjective* painted.

pintar *verb* [17] to paint.

pintor/pintora *noun Masc./Fem.* painter.

pintura *noun Fem.* **1** painting; **pintura al óleo** oil painting; **2 pinturas** crayons.

pinza *noun Fem.* **1** clothes peg; **2** hairgrip; **3** pincer; **4** dart; **pantalón con pinzas** trousers with pleats.

pinzas *plural noun Fem.* tweezers.

piña *noun Fem.* **1** pineapple; **2** pine cone.

pipa *noun Fem.* pipe; **fumar en pipa** to smoke a pipe.

piragua *noun Fem.* canoe.

piragüismo *noun Masc.* canoeing.

pirámide *noun Fem.* pyramid.

Pirineos *plural noun Masc.* **los Pirineos** the Pyrenees.

pisar *verb* [17] **1** to step; **pisar a alguien** to step on somebody's foot; **2** 'prohibido pisar el césped' 'keep off the grass'.

piscina *noun* swimming pool; **la parte honda de la piscina** the deep end of the pool; **la parte poco profunda de la piscina** the shallow end of the pool.

piscis *noun Masc./Fem.* Pisces; **soy piscis** I'm Pisces.

Piscis *noun Masc.* Pisces.

piso *noun Masc.* **1** floor; **vivo en el tercer piso** I live on the third floor; **2** storey; **un edificio de cinco pisos** a five-storey building; **3 un autobús de dos pisos** a double-decker bus; **4** flat; **se han comprado un piso** they've bought a flat.

pista *noun Fem.* **1** track; **seguirle la pista a alguien** to be on somebody's trail; **2** racecourse; **3** (tennis) court; **4 pista de hielo** ice rink; **pista de patinaje** skating rink; **5 pista de esquí** sky slope; **6 pista de despegue** runway.

pistacho *noun Masc.* pistachio.

pistola *noun Fem.* gun.

pitar *verb* [17] **1** to blow a whistle; **2** to sound the horn, to hoot (*in a car*).

pito *noun Masc.* **1** whistle; **tocar el pito** to blow the whistle; **2** horn; **tocar el pito** to sound the horn.

pizarra *noun Fem.* **1** blackboard; **2** slate.

placa *noun Fem.* **1** plate, sheet (*of metal, for example*); **2 placa de matrícula** number plate; **3** badge.

placer *noun Masc.* pleasure.

plan *noun Masc.* **1** plan; **hacer planes** to make plans; **¿qué planes tienes para las vacaciones?** what are your plans for the holidays?; **2** (*informal*) **está en plan tirano** he's behaving like a tyrant; **3** (*informal*) **viajar en plan económico** to travel on the cheap.

plancha *noun Fem.* **1** iron; **2 a la plancha** grilled; **3** sheet; **una plancha de plástico** a sheet of plastic.

planchar *verb* [17] to iron.

planear *verb* [17] **1** to plan; **2** to glide.

planeta *noun Masc.* planet.

plano[1] *noun Masc.* **1** street map; **un plano de Madrid** a street map of Madrid; **2** plan (*of a building*).

plano[2]**/plana** *adjective* flat.

planta *noun Fem.* **1** plant; **2** floor; **la planta baja** the ground floor; **la sexta planta** the sixth floor.

plantar *verb* [17] to plant.

plástico *noun Masc.* plastic.

plata *noun Fem.* silver; **cubiertos de plata** silver cutlery.

plataforma *noun Fem.* **1** platform; **2 plataforma de lanzamiento** launching pad.

plátano *noun Masc.* banana.

platillo *noun Masc.* saucer.

plato *noun Masc.* **1** plate; **plato llano** dinner plate; **plato de postre** dessert plate; **lavar los platos** to wash the dishes; **2** dish; **plato del día** dish of the day; **plato combinado** complete meal served on a plate; **3** course; **tomé pescado de primer/segundo plato** I had fish for the first/second course.

playa *noun Fem.* **1** beach; **2** seaside; **veranear en la playa** to spend your summer holidays at the seaside.

playera *noun Fem.* canvas shoe.

plaza *noun Fem.* **1** square; **plaza mayor** main square; **2** market; **los martes hay plaza** there's a market on Tuesdays; **3** seat (*in a bus or train*); **4** position (*at work*); **hay plazas vacantes** there are vacancies; **5 plaza de toros** bullring.

plazo *noun Masc.* **1** period; **el plazo de entrega acaba el once** the deadline is the eleventh; **2 plazo de vencimiento** expiry date (*of a passport, for example*); **3 a corto plazo** in the short term; **a largo plazo** in the long term; **4 pagar algo a plazos** to pay for something in instalments.

plegar *verb* [30] to fold.

pleno/plena *adjective* **1** full; **2 en pleno verano** in the middle of summer; **en pleno centro** right in the centre.

pliega, pliego, pliegue, etc. *verb* SEE **plegar**.

plomo *noun Masc.* **1** lead; **2** (*informal*) **ser un plomo** to be really boring; **3** fuse; **se han fundido los plomos** the fuses have blown.

pluma *noun Fem.* **1** pen; **2** feather.

plumier *noun Masc.* pencil case.

plural *noun Masc.* plural; **en plural** in the plural.
plural *adjective* plural.

población *noun Fem.* population.

pobre *noun Masc./Fem.* poor person; **los pobres** the poor; **¡la pobre!** poor thing!
pobre *adjective* poor; **¡pobre Jaime!** poor Jaime!

pobreza *noun Fem.* poverty.

pocilga *noun Fem.* pigsty; **tu habitación está hecha una pocilga** your room is a pigsty.

poco¹/poca *adjective* **1** little; **con poco esfuerzo** with little effort; **hay poco pan** there's not much bread; **es poca cosa** it's not much; **2** few; **había pocas personas** there were only a few people; **pocos días más tarde** a few days later.

poco²/poca *pronoun* **1** little; **basta con poco** a little is enough; **queda poco** there's not much left; **2** few; **vinieron pocos** only a few came; **pon unos pocos aquí** put a few here; **3** un poco a bit; **espera un poco** wait a bit; **me molesta un poco** it's a bit uncomfortable; **un poco de sal** a bit of salt; **4** (*referring to time*) **hace poco** not long ago; **hace poco que me escribió** he wrote to me not long ago; **aún voy a tardar un poco** it's going to take me a little while yet; **falta poco para las cinco** it's not long till five now; **dentro de poco** soon; **poco antes de comer** shortly before eating; **5 poco a poco** little by little.

poco³ *adverb* not very much; **habla poco** he doesn't talk very much; **soy muy poco paciente** I'm very impatient; **estaban poco interesados** they weren't very interested.

poder¹ *noun Masc.* power.

poder² *verb* [10] **1** to be able to (*but often translated as 'can' in sentences*); **no puedo levantarlo** I can't lift it; **no pude ir** I couldn't go; **pueden hacerlo solos** they can do it on their own; **lo mejor que puedas** the best you can; **¿podrás ayudarme?** will you be able to help me?; **¿pudiste encontrarlo?** were you able to find it?; **2** may (*asking permission*); **¿puedo abrir la ventana?** may I open the window?; **¿se puede?** may I come in?; **¿podría usar tu ordenador?** may I use your computer?; **3** (*possibility*) **puede que lleguen más tarde** they might come later; **puede que se haya roto** it might have got broken; **podía suceder** it could happen; **has podido romperlo** you could have broken it; **'¿crees que se habrán olvidado?' – 'puede ser'** 'do you think they might have forgotten?' – 'they might have'; **puede ser que no lo sepan** it might be that they don't know; **puede ser que se hayan perdido** they might have got lost; **4** (*suggesting*) **podrías preguntar** you could ask; **podríamos comer fuera** we could eat out; **5** (*reproaching*) **¡podrías haberlo dicho!** you could have said!; **6 no puedo con tanto trabajo** I can't cope with so much work; **7 ¡ya no puedo más!** I can't carry on!; **8 si puede ser** if possible.

poderoso/poderosa *adjective* powerful.

podrá, podré, podría, etc. *verb* SEE **poder**.

podrido/podrida *adjective* rotten.

poema *noun Masc.* poem.

poesía *noun Fem.* poetry.

poeta *noun Masc./Fem.* poet.

póker *noun Masc.* poker (*card game*).

polaco[1] *noun Masc.* Polish (*the language*).

polaco[2]**/polaca** *noun Masc./Fem.* Pole.
polaco *adjective* Polish.

polémico/polémica *adjective* controversial; **una decisión polémica** a controversial decision.

policía *noun Masc./Fem.* police officer.
policía *noun Fem.* police.

policíaco/policíaca *adjective* **novela policíaca** detective novel.

polideportivo *noun Masc.* sports centre.

polilla *noun Fem.* moth.

política *noun Fem.* **1** politics; **2** policy (*of a government*).

político/política *noun Masc./Fem.* politician.
político *adjective* political.

póliza *noun Fem.* policy (*insurance document*).

pollito/pollita *noun Masc./Fem.* chick.

pollo *noun Masc.* chicken; **pollo asado** roast chicken.

polo *noun Masc.* **1** pole; **el Polo Norte** the North Pole; **2** ice-lolly.

Polonia *noun Fem.* Poland.

polución *noun Fem.* pollution.

polvo *noun Masc.* **1** dust; **quitar el polvo a los muebles** to dust the furniture; **2 polvos** face powder; **polvos de talco** talcum powder; **3 estar hecho polvo** (*informal*) to be all in; **después de la excursión nos quedamos hechos polvo** we were worn out after the trip; **este sofá está hecho polvo** this sofa's a wreck.

polvorón *noun Masc.* pastry (*made with almonds; eaten at Christmas time*).

pomada *noun Fem.* ointment.

pomelo *noun Masc.* grapefruit.

pondría, pondrías, etc. *verb* SEE **poner**.

poner *verb* [11] **1** to put; **ponlo encima de la mesa** put it on the table; **lo puse en el armario** I put it in the wardrobe; **pusimos diez euros cada uno** we put in ten euros each; **2** (*with food*) **¿te pongo más sopa?** shall I serve you more soup?; **3** (*in a restaurant*) **¿qué les pongo?** what can I get you?; **¿me pone un café?** can I have a coffee please?; **4** to put on; **le puso la silla al caballo** she put the saddle on the horse; **no le he puesto camiseta al niño** I haven't put a vest on the baby; **5** to put on (*radio, hi-fi, etc.*); **poner la tele** to put on the telly; **poner**

música to put on some music; **pon el volumen más alto** turn the volume up; **6 poner el despertador** to set the alarm clock; **puse el despertador a las ocho** I set the alarm clock for eight; **7 poner la mesa** to lay the table; **8** to install; **9** to fit (*a carpet*); **10** (*with names*) **¿qué nombre le vais a poner al niño?** what are you going to call the baby?; **le pusieron el apodo de 'el Rubio'** they nicknamed him 'Blondy'; **11 poner una película** to show a film; **¿qué ponen en el 'Maxin'?** what's on at the 'Maxin'?; **poner una obra de teatro** to put on a play; **12 poner una tienda** to open a shop; **poner un negocio** to set up a business; **13 ¿me pone con el señor Sanz?** could you put me through to Mr Sanz? (*on the telephone*); **14 poner a alguien nervioso** to make somebody nervous; **poner a alguien triste** to make somebody sad; **poner a alguien de mal humor** to put somebody in a bad mood; **15 poner atención** to pay attention.

ponga, **pongo**, **etc.** *verb* SEE **poner**.

poni *noun Masc.* pony.

popular *adjective* popular.

por *preposition* **1** for; **por esa razón** for that reason; **por ejemplo** for example; **me ofrecieron dos mil euros por el coche viejo** they offered me two thousand euros for my old car; **lo hago por tu bien** I'm doing it for your own good; **2** through; **no entra por la ventana**

it won't go in through the window; **me enteré por mi hermana** I heard through my sister; **pasamos por Toledo** we went through Toledo; **3** by; **mandar algo por correo** to send something by post; **viajar por carretera** to travel by road; **4 mide tres metros por cuatro** it measures three metres by four; **cinco por tres son quince** five times three is fifteen; **5 por la mañana** in the morning; **6** (*place*) **lo dejé por aquí** I left it around here somewhere; **viven por la Avenida Mayor** they live somewhere around Mayor Avenue; **¿por dónde queda la estación?** whereabouts is the station?; **por todos lados** everywhere; **7** per; **treinta euros por persona** thirty euros per person; **a cien kilómetros por hora** at a hundred kilometres an hour; **8** in; **por escrito** in writing; **por adelantado** in advance; **9 preguntó por ti** he asked after you; **10 lo dijeron por la tele** they said so on the TV; **11 andar por la calle** to walk along the road; **caerse por la escalera** to fall down the stairs; **12 ¿por qué?** why?; **13 por supuesto** of course; **14 por eso no lo hice** that's why I didn't do it; **15 por cierto** by the way.

porcentaje *noun Masc.* percentage.

porche *noun Masc.* porch.

porción *noun Fem.* **1** portion; **una porción de tarta** a slice of cake; **2** share.

porque *conjunction* because.

a
b
c
d
e
f
g
h
i
j
k
l
m
n
ñ
o
p
q
r
s
t
u
v
w
x
y
z

porrón *noun Masc.* wine bottle (*with a long spout from which you drink, holding it as far away from your mouth as possible*).

portada *noun Fem.* **1** title page (*of a book*); **2** cover (*of a magazine*); **3** front page (*of a newspaper*).

portaequipajes *noun Masc.* (*does not change in the plural*) **1** roof rack; **2** luggage rack (*on a train*).

portarse *reflexive verb* [17] to behave; **portarse mal** to misbehave; **¡pórtate bien!** behave yourself!.

portátil *adjective* portable.
portátil *noun Masc.* laptop (computer).

portazo *noun Masc.* **dar un portazo** to slam the door.

portería *noun Fem.* goal.

portero/portera *noun Masc./Fem.* **1** goalkeeper; **2** caretaker; **3** porter; **4** **portero automático** entry-phone.

portorriqueño/ portorriqueña *noun Masc./Fem.*, *adjective* Puerto Rican.

Portugal *noun Masc.* Portugal.

portugués[1] *noun Masc.* Portuguese (*the language*).

portugués[2]**/portuguesa** *noun Masc./Fem.* Portuguese man/woman.
portugués/portuguesa *adjective* Portuguese.

porvenir *noun Masc.* future.

posar *verb* [17] **1** to pose; **2** to lay (*hand or object*).
posarse *reflexive verb* [17] to land.

poseer *verb* [37] **1** to own; **2** to hold (*a title or record*).

posibilidad *noun Fem.* **1** possibility; **es una posibilidad** it's a possibility; **2** **tener posibilidades de hacer** to have a good chance of doing; **no tienen muchas posibilidades de ganar** they don't have much chance of winning; **¿qué posibilidades tienen?** what are their chances?

posible *adjective* possible; **a ser posible** if possible; **no fue posible impedirlo** it was impossible to avoid it.
posible *adverb* **lo más tarde posible** as late as possible; **hazlo lo mejor posible** do the best you can.

posición *noun Fem.* **1** position; **en quinta posición** in fifth place; **2** **posición social** social status.

positivo/positiva *adjective* positive.

postal *noun Fem.* postcard.
postal *adjective* postal.

poste *noun Masc.* **1** post; **2** pole.

póster *noun Masc.* poster.

posterior *adjective* **1** back; **el asiento posterior** the back seat; **la parte posterior de la casa** the back of the house; **2** subsequent, later.

postilla *noun Fem.* scab.

postizo/postiza *adjective* false; **dentadura postiza** false teeth.

postre *noun Masc.* pudding, dessert; **¿qué hay de postre?** what's for pudding?

potable *adjective* **agua potable** drinking water.

potencial *adjective* potential.

práctica *noun Fem.* practice; **lo aprenderás con la práctica** you'll learn with practice; **tener mucha práctica** to have a lot of practice; **he perdido la práctica** I'm out of practice; **en la práctica** in practice.

practicar *verb* [31] **1** to practise; **practicar el violín** to practise the violin; **2 practicar deportes** to do sports.

práctico/práctica *adjective* practical.

pradera *noun Masc.* grassland.

prado *noun Masc.* meadow.

precaución *noun Fem.*
1 precaution; **tomar precauciones** to take precautions; **2** caution; **actuar con precaución** to act with caution.

precedente *adjective* previous.

precio *noun Masc.* price; **¿qué precio tiene?** how much is it?; **precio fijo** fixed price; **precios de saldo** bargain prices; **los precios han subido mucho** prices have gone up a lot.

precioso/preciosa *adjective*
1 beautiful; **2** precious; **piedras preciosas** precious stones.

precipicio *noun Masc.* precipice.

precipitación *noun Fem.* **1** rush; **hacer algo con mucha precipitación** to do something in a rush; **salió con mucha precipitación** he rushed out; **2 precipitaciones** rainfall; **habrá precipitaciones moderadas** there will be moderate rainfall.

precipitarse *reflexive verb* [17]
1 to rush; **no te precipites** don't rush into anything; **2 precipitarse hacia algo** to rush towards something.

precisamente *adverb* precisely.

precisión *noun Fem.* precision.

preciso/precisa *adjective*
1 precise; **2 llegaron en el momento preciso** they arrived just in time; **en este preciso momento no puedo** I can't right now;
3 necessary; **si es preciso** if necessary; **no es preciso pagar por adelantado** you don't have to pay in advance; **es preciso que nos aseguremos** we must make sure.

predilecto/predilecta
adjective favourite.

preescolar *adjective* preschool.

preferencia *noun Fem.*
1 preference; **2** right of way; **yo tenía preferencia** I had right of way; **3** priority; **tener preferencia** to have priority.

preferible *adjective* preferable; **ser preferible a algo** to be preferable to something.

preferido/preferida *adjective* favourite.

preferir *verb* [14] to prefer; **preferir algo a algo** to prefer something to something; **preferiría no tener que ir** I'd rather not have to go.

prefiera, **prefiero**, **etc.** *verb* SEE **preferir**.

prefijo *noun Masc.* **1** prefix; **2** dialling code; **el prefijo de España** the dialling code for Spain.

a
b
c
d
e
f
g
h
i
j
k
l
m
n
ñ
o
p
q
r
s
t
u
v
w
x
y
z

a
b

pregunta *noun Fem.* question; **hacer una pregunta** to ask a question.

c
d
e
f
g
h
i

preguntar *verb* [17] to ask; **preguntar acerca de/sobre algo** to ask about something; **preguntar por alguien** to ask about someone; **me preguntó por tus padres** he asked me about your parents.
preguntarse *reflexive verb* [17] to wonder; **me pregunto si dice la verdad** I wonder if he's telling the truth.

j
k

prejuicio *noun Masc.* prejudice; **tener prejuicios contra** to be prejudiced against.

l

prematuro/prematura *adjective* premature.

m
n

premiar *verb* [17] **premiar a alguien** to give somebody a prize.

ñ
o
p
q
r

premio *noun Masc.* prize; **dar un premio a alguien** to give someone a prize; **ganar un premio** to win a prize; **me tocó un premio en la rifa** I won a prize in the raffle; **¿qué dan de premio?** what's the prize?; **premio gordo** jackpot (*in the lottery*).

s
t
u

prender *verb* [18] **1** to catch (*a criminal*); **2** to light (*a cigarette or match*); **3 prenderle fuego a algo** to set something on fire.

v
w

prensa *noun Fem.* **la prensa** the press; **leer la prensa** to read the newspapers.

x
y
z

preocupado/preocupada *adjective* worried; **estar preocupado por algo** to be worried about something.

preocupar *verb* [17] to worry; **me preocupan los exámenes** I'm worried about the exams.
preocuparse *reflexive verb* [17] to get worried; **se preocupó porque no la llamé** she got worried because I didn't phone her.

preparación *noun Fem.*
1 preparation; **2** training (*in sport*); **3 un trabajador con muy buena preparación** a highly trained worker.

preparar *verb* [17] **1** to prepare; **preparar la cena** to prepare dinner; **preparar un examen** to prepare for an exam; **2** to train (*a player or athlete*); **3** to coach (*a student*); **4 preparar la cuenta** to draw up the bill.
prepararse *reflexive verb* [17] to get ready.

preparativos *plural noun Masc.* preparations.

preposición *noun Fem.* preposition.

presa *noun Fem.* **1** dam; **2** reservoir; **3** prey; **4 ser presa del terror** to be seized with panic.

presencia *noun Fem.* presence; **en presencia de sus padres** in front of his parents.

presentación *noun Fem.*
1 introduction; **hacer las presentaciones** to do the introductions; **2** presentation.

presentador/presentadora *noun Masc./Fem.* presenter.

presentar *verb* [17] **1** to introduce; **te presento a mi novio** this is my

boyfriend; **les presentó a su jefe** he introduced them to his boss; **2** to present (*a programme, for example*); **3** to submit (*an application*).
presentarse *reflexive verb* [17] **1** to introduce yourself; **2** to turn up; **se presentaron sin avisar a nadie** they turned up without letting anybody know;
3 presentarse voluntario to volunteer; **4 presentarse a un examen** to sit an exam;
5 presentarse a un concurso to enter a competition; **6 presentarse para un cargo** to apply for a post;
7 presentarse a la presidencia to run for the presidency.

presente *noun Masc.* present.

preservativo *noun Masc.* condom.

presidencia *noun Fem.* presidency.

presidente/presidenta *noun Masc./Fem.* president.

presión *noun Fem.* **1** pressure; **2 cerveza a presión** draught beer.

preso/presa *noun Masc./Fem.* prisoner.
preso *adjective* **estar preso** to be in prison; **meter preso a alguien** to send somebody to prison.

préstamo *noun Masc.* loan; **préstamo hipotecario** mortgage.

prestar *verb* [17] **1** to lend; **le presté dinero para el coche** I lent him money for the car; **2 ¿me prestas tu abrigo?** can I borrow your coat?; **3 prestar atención** to pay attention.

prestidigitador/ prestidigitadora *noun Masc./ Fem.* conjurer.

presumido/presumida *noun Masc./Fem.* **es un presumido** he's so conceited.
presumido *adjective* conceited.

presumir *verb* [19] to show off; **presumen de casa grande** they like to boast about how big their house is; **presume de guapa** she thinks she's very good-looking.

presupuesto *noun Masc.* budget.

pretender *verb* [18] **1** to try; **¿qué pretendes conseguir?** what are you trying to achieve?; **pretendía que pagase yo** he was trying to make me pay for it; **2 pretender que alguien haga** to expect somebody to do; **pretende que yo le ayude** he expects me to help him.

pretexto *noun Masc.* pretext, excuse; **siempre tiene algún pretexto para no hacerlo** he always has some excuse or other not to do it.

prevenir *verb* [15] **1** to prevent; **2** to warn.

prever *verb* [16] to forsee.

previsto/prevista *adjective* **está previsto que vengan mañana** they're due to come tomorrow; **a la hora prevista** at the scheduled time.

primavera *noun Fem.* spring.

primer *adjective* first SEE **primero/ primera**.

primero/primera *adjective, pronoun* first; **primera clase** first class; **el primero de mayo** the first of May; (*note that 'primero' becomes 'primer' before a masculine singular noun*) **primer piso** first floor; **llegar en primer lugar** to finish in first position; **en primer lugar, no me interesa** first of all, I'm not interested.

primero² *adverb* first; **yo estaba primero** I was here first; **primero vamos a informarnos** first of all, let's find out.

primicia *noun Fem.* **1** scoop (*news story*); **2** first showing (*of film*).

primo/prima *noun Masc./Fem.* cousin.

princesa *noun Fem.* princess.

principal *adjective* main.

príncipe *noun Masc.* prince.

principiante/principianta *noun Masc./Fem.* beginner.

principio *noun Masc.* beginning; **a principios de mes** at the beginning of the month; **al principio de la temporada** at the beginning of the season; **un buen principio** a good start.

prisa *noun Fem.* **1** hurry; **tener prisa** to be in a hurry; **date prisa, que llegamos tarde** hurry up or we'll be late; **2 de prisa** fast; **hacer algo de prisa** to do something fast; **a toda prisa** in a hurry; **3 correr prisa** to be urgent; **este trabajo corre prisa** this job is urgent.

prisión *noun Fem.* prison.

prisionero/prisionera *noun Masc./Fem.* prisoner.

prismáticos *plural noun Masc.* binoculars.

privado/privada *adjective* private.

privar *verb* [17] **privar a alguien de algo** to deprive somebody of something.
  privarse *reflexive verb* [17] **privarse de algo** to deprive yourself of something.

privilegiado/privilegiada *adjective* privileged.

privilegio *noun Masc.* privilege.

probable *adjective* probable.

probador *noun Masc.* changing room.

probar *verb* [24] **1** to try; **prueba a abrirlo con esta llave** try opening it with this key; **es la primera vez que pruebo la comida tailandesa** it's the first time I've tried Thai food; **probar no cuesta nada** there's no harm in trying; **2** to taste; **¿has probado la sopa?** have you tasted the soup?; **3** to test (*brakes, for example*); **4** to prove; **no pudo probar su inocencia** he could not prove his innocence.
  probarse *reflexive verb* [24] to try on; **¿quiere probárselo?** would you like to try it on?.

probeta *noun Fem.* test tube; **niño probeta** test-tube baby.

problema *noun Masc.* problem; **un problema muy importante** a major problem.

procedente *adjective* from; **el vuelo procedente de Londres** the flight from London.

proceder *verb* [18] **1 proceder de algo** to come from something; **2** to proceed; **procedieron con cautela** they proceeded with caution.

procesador *noun Masc.* **procesador de textos** word processor.

procesión *noun Fem.* procession.

proceso *noun Masc.* **1** process; **2** processing; **proceso de datos** data processing.

procurar *verb* [17] **procurar hacer** to try to do; **procura terminarlo para el viernes** try to finish it by Friday.

producción *noun Fem.* production.

producir *verb* [60] **1** to produce; **producir coches** to produce cars; **2** to cause; **la tormenta produjo daños** the storm caused damage.

producto *noun Masc.* **1** product; **2** production.

productor/productora *noun Masc./Fem.* producer. **productor** *adjective* producing; **países productores de petróleo** oil-producing countries.

produje, produzca, etc. *verb* SEE **producir**.

profe *noun Masc./Fem.* teacher (*informal*).

profesión *noun Fem.* profession.

profesional *adjective* professional.

profesor/profesora *noun Masc./Fem.* **1** professor, lecturer; **2** teacher (*in a secondary school*).

profundidad *noun Fem.* depth.

profundo/profunda *adjective* deep.

programa *noun Masc.* **1** programme; **2** program; **un programa informático** a computer program.

programador/programadora *noun Masc./Fem.* programmer.

programar *verb* [17] to program (*a computer*).

progresar *verb* [17] to progress.

progreso *noun Masc.* progress; **hacer progresos** to make progress.

prohibido/prohibida *adjective* forbidden; **está terminantemente prohibido** it's strictly forbidden; **'prohibido fumar'** 'no smoking'; **'prohibido el paso'/'prohibida la entrada'** 'no entry'; **'prohibido pisar el césped'** 'keep off the grass'.

prohibir *verb* [58] to prohibit; **se prohíbe la entrada a menores de dieciséis años** no admission to persons under 16.

prolongar *verb* [28] to prolong. **prolongarse** *reflexive verb* [28] to go on (*a meeting or party, for example*).

promedio *noun Masc.* average; **un promedio de quince libras por semana** an average of fifteen pounds a week.

promesa *noun Fem.* promise; **no cumplió con su promesa** he didn't keep his promise.

prometer *verb* [18] to promise; **te lo prometo** I promise.

a
b
c
d
e
f
g
h
i
j
k
l
m
n
ñ
o
p
q
r
s
t
u
v
w
x
y
z

a **prometida** *noun Fem.* fiancée.

b **prometido** *noun Masc.* fiancé.

c **promoción** *noun Fem.* promotion.

pronombre *noun Masc.* pronoun.

d **pronóstico** *noun Masc.* **1** forecast;
pronóstico del tiempo weather

e forecast; **2** prognosis.

f **pronto**[1] *adverb* **1** soon; **tan pronto
como sea posible** as soon as

g possible; **2** quickly; **respondieron
muy pronto** they answered very

h quickly; **3** early; **se marcharon
pronto** they left early; **4 de pronto**

i all of a sudden.

j **pronto**[2]**/pronta** *adjective* prompt;
una pronta respuesta a prompt

k reply.

l **pronunciación** *noun Fem.*

m pronunciation.

n **pronunciar** *verb* [17] to
pronounce.

ñ **propaganda** *noun Fem.*
1 advertising; **hacer propaganda**

o **de un producto** to advertise a
product; **2** propaganda.

p **propiedad** *noun Fem.* **1** property;
propiedad privada private

q property; **2 ser propiedad de
alguien** to belong to somebody.

r **propietario/propietaria** *noun
Masc./Fem.* owner.

s **propina** *noun Fem.* tip.

t **propio/propia** *adjective* **1** own;
mi propio hermano my own

u brother; **2 la propia Elena lo
admitió** Elena herself admitted it.

v **proponer** *verb* [11] **1** to suggest;
nos propuso ir a cenar fuera he

w suggested we went out for dinner;
2 to propose; **proponer una idea** to
propose an idea; **proponer un trato**
to make a proposition; **3** to put
forward (*a candidate*).

x **proponerse** *reflexive verb* [11] **1** to
set yourself a goal; **me propuse
encontrar un trabajo** I set myself
the goal of finding a job; **siempre
consigue lo que se propone** he
always achieves what he sets out to
do; **2** to decide; **me propuse ir a
verlos** I decided to go and see them.

proporción *noun Fem.*
1 proportion; **en proporción** in
proportion; **2 proporciones**
dimensions.

proposición *noun Fem.* proposal.

propósito *noun Masc.* intention.

prórroga *noun Fem.* **1** extension;
2 extra time (*in sports*).

prospecto *noun Masc.* **1** patient
information leaflet (*supplied with
medicine*); **2** advertising leaflet.

próspero/próspera *adjective*
1 prosperous; **2 ¡Próspero Año
Nuevo!** Happy New Year!

prostituta *noun Fem.* prostitute.

protagonista *noun Masc./Fem.*
1 leading player; **2** leading
character.

protección *noun Fem.* protection.

protector/protectora *noun
Masc./Fem.* protector.
protector *adjective* **1** protective;
**2 Sociedad Protectora de
Animales** Society for the
Prevention of Cruelty to Animals.

proteger *verb* [3] to protect.
protegerse *reflexive verb* [3] to protect yourself.

protesta *noun Fem.* protest; **en señal de protesta** in protest.

protestante *noun Masc./Fem.*, **protestante** *adjective* Protestant.

protestar *verb* [17] to protest.

provecho *noun Masc.* **1** benefit; **sacar provecho de algo** to benefit from something; **2 siempre piensa primero en su propio provecho** he always thinks of himself first; **3 ¡buen provecho!** enjoy your meal!

proveniente *adjective* **personas provenientes de otros países** people from other countries.

proverbio *noun Masc.* proverb.

provincia *noun Fem.* province.

provisional *adjective* provisional.

provocador/provocadora *noun Masc./Fem.* political agitator.
provocador *adjective* provocative.

provocar *verb* [31] **1** to provoke (*a person*); **2** to cause (*an explosion or fire*).

proximidad *noun Fem.* proximity.

próximo/próxima *adjective* **1** next; **la próxima semana** next week; **2 en fecha próxima** in the near future.

proyecto *noun Masc.* **1** project; **2** plan; **¿qué proyectos tienes para el verano?** what are your plans for the summer?; **3 tengo varios trabajos en proyecto** I've got a few jobs lined up.

proyector *noun Masc.* projector.

prudente *adjective* sensible; **sé prudente conduciendo** drive carefully.

prueba¹ *noun Fem.* **1** proof; **no tienen pruebas** they have no proof; **2** test; **3 hacer la prueba** to try; **hice la prueba y funcionó** I tried and it worked; **haz la prueba de limpiarlo con lejía** try cleaning it with bleach; **4 a prueba** on trial; **trabajadores a prueba** people working on a trial basis; **5 a prueba de balas** bullet-proof; **a prueba de agua** waterproof.

prueba², **pruebo**, **etc.** *verb* SEE **probar**.

psicólogo/psicóloga *noun Masc./Fem.* psychologist.

psiquiatra *noun Masc./Fem.* psychiatrist.

publicar *verb* [31] to publish.

publicidad *noun Fem.* **1** publicity; **2** advertising.

público¹ *noun Masc.* **1** public; **2** audience.

público²/**pública** *adjective* public.

pude, **pudo**, **etc.** *verb* SEE **poder**.

pudrir *verb* [59] to rot.
pudrirse *reflexive verb* [59] to rot.

pueblo *noun Masc.* **1** village; **2** small town; **3** people; **el pueblo español** the Spanish people.

puente *noun Masc.* **1** bridge; **2 puente aéreo** shuttle service; **3 hacer puente** take a long weekend (*usually when the Thursday before or the Tuesday after is a public holiday*).

a
b
c
d
e
f
g
h
i
j
k
l
m
n
ñ
o
p
q
r
s
t
u
v
w
x
y
z

a
b
c
d
e
f
g
h
i
j
k
l
m
n
ñ
o
p
q
r
s
t
u
v
w
x
y
z

puerco/puerca *noun Masc./Fem.* pig.

puerro *noun Masc.* leek.

puerta *noun Fem.* **1** door; **puerta principal** main door; **puerta giratoria** revolving door; **puerta trasera** back door; **quedamos en la puerta del cine** we arranged to meet outside the cinema; **2 puerta de embarque** gate (*in an airport*); **3 la puerta del jardín** the garden gate.

puerto *noun Masc.* **1** port; **un puerto pesquero** a fishing port; **2** harbour; **un puerto deportivo** a marina.

Puerto Rico *noun Masc.* Puerto Rico.

puertorriqueño/ puertorriqueña *noun Masc./ Fem., adjective* Puerto Rican.

pues *conjunction* **1 pues bien, como te iba diciendo** ... well, as I was telling you ...; **pues no estoy seguro** I'm not sure now; **pues mira, ahora no me acuerdo** well, look, I can't remember now; **2 ¡pues no vayas!** don't go then!; **pues si no te gusta el libro, no lo leas** if you don't like the book, don't read it then; **3 ¡pues claro!** of course!; **¡pues claro que no!** of course not!; **'¿lo querías tú?' – '¡pues sí!'** 'did you want it?' – 'yes, I did!'

puesto¹ *noun Masc.* **1** position; **llegar en primer puesto** to finish in first position; **sacar el primer puesto en un examen** to come top in an exam; **2** job; **puestos de trabajo** jobs; **perdió su puesto de trabajo** he lost his job; **puestos vacantes** vacancies; **un puesto fijo** a permanent job; **3** post; **un puesto de socorro** a first-aid post; **4** stall (*in a market*).

puesto *conjunction* **puesto que** since.

puesto²/puesta *adjective* **1 la mesa estaba puesta** the table was laid; **2 llevaba el abrigo puesto** I had my coat on.

pulga *noun Fem.* flea.

pulgada *noun Fem.* inch.

pulgar *noun Masc.* thumb.

pulir *verb* [19] to polish.

pulmón *noun Masc.* lung.

pulpo *noun Masc.* octopus.

pulsar *verb* [17] **1** to press (*a key or button*); **2** to pluck (*a string*).

pulsera *noun Fem.* **1** bracelet; **1** watchstrap.

pulso *noun Masc.* **1** pulse; **le tomó el pulso** he took his pulse; **2 tener buen pulso** to have a steady hand; **me temblaba el pulso** my hand was shaking; **3 levantar algo a pulso** to lift something with your bare hands; **dibujar algo a pulso** to draw something freehand; **4** arm-wrestling contest.

punta *noun Fem.* **1** point (*of a knife or needle, for example*); **acaba en punta** it's pointed; **2** tip (*of pencil, tongue, finger, etc.*); ★**tener algo en la punta de la lengua** (*informal*) to have something on the tip of your tongue; **3** end; **a la otra punta del pasillo** at the other end of the corridor; **4 las puntas: cortarse**

las puntas to have your hair trimmed; **tener las puntas abiertas** to have split ends; **5 sacar punta a un lápiz** to sharpen a pencil; **6 la hora punta** the rush hour.

puntada *noun Fem.* stitch.

puntapié *noun Masc.* kick; **darle un puntapié a algo** to kick something.

puntería *noun Fem.* aim; **tiene buena puntería** he's a good shot.

puntilla *noun Fem.* **1** lace edging; **2 ponerse de puntillas** to stand on tiptoe; **andar de puntillas** to walk on tiptoe.

punto *noun Masc.* **1** point; **un punto de vista** a point of view; **es mi punto débil** it's my weak point; **llevan tres puntos de ventaja** they're three points ahead; **hasta cierto punto** up to a point; **punto por punto** point by point; **2** dot; **el punto sobre la 'i'** the dot on the 'i'; **3** (*in punctuation*) **punto final** full stop; **punto y coma** semicolon; **4 en punto** on the dot; **las cinco en punto** five o'clock sharp; **a las dos en punto** at two on the dot; **llegar en punto** to arrive exactly on time; **5** stitch; **hacer punto** to knit; **de punto** knitted; **una falda de punto** a knitted skirt; **6 estar a punto de hacer** to be about to do; **7 estar algo en su punto** to be just right; **la carne está en su punto** the meat is just right; **8 batir las claras a punto de nieve** beat the egg whites until stiff; **9 punto muerto** neutral (*gear*); **10 punto negro** black spot (*for accidents*); black head (*on skin*).

puntocom *noun Fem.* una **puntocom** a dot-com company.

puntuación *noun Fem.* **1** punctuation; **2** score (*in sports*); **3** marks (*in an exam*).

puntual *adjective* punctual; **ser puntual** to be always on time; **llegaron puntuales** they arrived on time.

puñetazo *noun Masc.* punch; **me dio un puñetazo** he punched me; **di un puñetazo en la mesa** I banged the table with my fist.

puño *noun Masc.* **1** fist; **2** cuff; **3** handle (*of a tool*).

pupila *noun Fem.* pupil.

pupitre *noun Masc.* desk.

puré *noun Masc.* **1** purée; **2** thick soup; **puré de guisantes** pea soup; **3 puré de patatas** mashed potatoes.

puro¹ *noun Masc.* cigar.

puro²/pura *adjective* **1** pure; **2 la pura verdad** the simple truth; **3 de puro aburrimiento** out of sheer boredom.

púrpura *adjective* purple.

puse, puso, etc. *verb* SEE **poner**.

puzzle *noun Masc.* jigsaw puzzle.

Qq

que¹ *pronoun* **1** who; **el hombre que me lo dijo** the man who told me; **los que están interesados** those who are interested; **2** which, that; **el**

a
b
c
d
e
f
g
h
i
j
k
l
m
n
ñ
o
p
q
r
s
t
u
v
w
x
y
z

a
b
c
d
e
f
g
h
i
j
k
l
m
n
ñ
o
p
q
r
s
t
u
v
w
x
y
z

libro que recomendé the book which I recommended; **la marca que me gusta** the brand (that) I like; **3 el que prefiero** the one (that) I prefer.

que² *conjunction* **1** that; **dijo que no lo necesitaba** she said (that) she didn't need it; **sé que le gusta** I know (that) he likes it; **nos pidió que le ayudásemos** he asked us to help him (*'que' is followed by the subjunctive in certain constructions*); **2** (*in comparisons*) **es más alto que yo** he's taller than me; **3** (*for emphasis*) **¡que te he dicho que sí me gusta!** I've already told you that I like it!; **¡que es mío!** I'm telling you it's mine!; **'¿te importa?' – '¡que no!'** 'do you mind?' – 'I've already told you that I don't!'; **4** (*expressing surprise*) **¿que tiene veinte años?** she's twenty?; **5** (*expressing a wish*) **que te mejores pronto** get well soon; **que pases unas buenas vacaciones** have a nice holiday; **6** (*giving an order*) **¡que te calles!** shut up!; **que pasen** show them in; **7 yo que tú** if I were you.

qué¹ *pronoun* **1** what; **¿qué es eso?** what's that?; **¿a qué te refieres?** what are you referring to?; **2 ¿qué?** what?; **3 ¿qué tal?** how are you doing?; **¿qué tal va?** how's it going?; **¿qué hay de nuevo?** what's new?; **4 ¡qué va!** no way!

qué² *adjective* **1** which; **¿qué abrigo es el tuyo?** which coat is yours?; **2** what (*in exclamations*); **¡qué casa tan grande!** what a big house!

qué³ *adverb* **¡qué bonito!** how nice!; **¡qué egoísta eres!** you're so selfish!

quebradero *noun Fem.* worry.

quebrado *noun Masc.* fraction.

quebrar *verb* [29] to break.

quedar *verb* [17] **1** to be left; **quedan tres paquetes** there are three packets left; **¿te queda dinero?** do you have any money left?; **no queda leche** there's no milk; **2** (*in time expressions*) **aún quedan dos días** there are still two days to go; **quedaban quince minutos para el final de la clase** it was still fifteen minutes till the end of the class; **¿cuánto tiempo me queda?** how much time do I have left?; **aún queda tiempo** there's still time; **3** (*with distances*) **quedaban quince kilómetros** there were still fifteen kilometres to go; **4** (*expressing a person's situation*) **quedó viudo** he was widowed; **quedó ciego tras el accidente** he was left blind after the accident; **quedaron solos** they were left alone; **quedar en último lugar** to end up last; **5** (*talking about the appearance of something*) **así queda mejor** it's better like this; **queda muy feo con esa tela** it's horrible with that material; **6** (*arranging meetings*) **quedamos en la plaza** we arranged to meet in the square; **¿te apetece quedar?** would you like to meet?; **¿quedamos para el sábado?** shall we meet on Saturday?; **7** (*when talking about clothes, hairstyles, etc.*) **me queda apretado** it's too tight on me; **¿te**

queda bien? does it fit you?; **esos pantalones te quedan fenomenal** those trousers look great on you; **ese color te queda muy bien** that colour really suits you; **8** (*impressions*) **quiere quedar bien con mi familia** she wants to make a good impression on my family; **9 va a quedar mal si no lo hacemos** it will look bad if we don't do it; **quedamos muy mal con sus padres** we made a bad impression on her parents; **10 quedar en algo** to agree on something; **quedamos en vernos hoy** we agreed to see each other today; **11** (*talking about location*) to be; **queda cerca de mi casa** it's near my house; **queda bastante lejos** it's quite a long way away; **¿dónde queda la estación?** where is the station?

quedarse *reflexive verb* [17] **1** to stay; **prefiero quedarme en casa** I'd rather stay at home; **se quedó en la cama** he stayed in bed; **2** (*expressing somebody's situation or state*) **quedarse ciego** to go blind; **quedarse calvo** to lose your hair; **quedarse sin trabajo** to lose your job; **quedarse viudo** to be widowed; **quedarse soltero** to stay single; **quedarse dormido** to fall asleep; **quedarse callado** to remain silent; **3 quedarse con algo** to keep something.

queja *noun Fem.* complaint; **presentar una queja** to make a complaint; **presentó una queja al gerente por el mal servicio** she made a complaint to the manager about the bad service.

quejarse *reflexive verb* [17] to complain; **se quejan de la comida** they complain about the food; **se quejan de que tardamos mucho** they complain about how long we take.

quemado/quemada *adjective* burnt.

quemadura *noun Fem.* burn.

quemar *verb* [17] **1** to burn; **2** to scald; **3** to be very hot; **la sopa quema mucho** the soup's really hot; **4 quemar un motor** to burn out an engine; **5 quemar calorías** to burn up calories; **6 ¡cómo quema el sol!** the sun's scorching!
quemarse *reflexive verb* [17] **1** to burn yourself; **me quemé la mano** I burnt my hand; **2** to scald; **3** to get burned; **el mantel se quemó un poco** the tablecloth got slightly burnt; **¡cómo te has quemado!** you've really got burnt! (*in the sun*); **4** to burn down; **la casa se quemó toda** the house burned down.

querer *verb* [12] **1** to want; **¿qué quieres para tu cumpleaños?** what do you want for your birthday?; **no quiero ir al cine** I don't want to go to the cinema; **2** to love; **te quiero** I love you; **3** (*making an offer*) **¿quieres beber algo?** would you like something to drink?; **si quieres voy más tarde** if you like I'll go later; **4** (*asking for something in a shop, cafe, etc.*) **quisiera ver plumas** I would like to see some pens; **yo quiero un café** I'll have a coffee; **quisiera reservar una mesa para cuatro** I'd like to book a table

a
b
c
d
e
f
g
h
i
j
k
l
m
n
ñ
o
p
q
r
s
t
u
v
w
x
y
z

for four; **5** (*asking somebody to do something*) **¿quieres apagar la tele, por favor?** would you mind switching off the television, please?; **6 querer decir** to mean; **¿qué quieres decir?** what do you mean?.
quererse *reflexive verb* [17] to love each other.

querido/querida *adjective* dear; **Querido Pablo** Dear Pablo (*starting a letter*).

querrá, querré, querría, etc. *verb* SEE **querer**.

queso *noun Masc.* cheese; **queso rallado** grated cheese.

quiebra *noun Fem.* bankruptcy.

quien *pronoun* **1** who; **no fui yo quien lo dijo** it wasn't me who said it; **ellos son quienes no quisieron** they're the ones who didn't want to (*sometimes not translated*) **la persona con quien hablé** the person I spoke to; **2** whom, who; **Isabel, a quien vi ayer** Isabel, whom I saw yesterday.

quién *pronoun* **1** who; **¿quién es?** who is it?; **¡quién lo hubiese dicho!** who would have said!; **2** which; **¿quién de vostros es Carlos?** which of you is Carlos?; **3 ¿de quién?** whose?; **¿de quién es esta cartera?** whose is this wallet?

quienquiera *pronoun* whoever.

quiera, quiere, etc. *verb* SEE **querer**.

quieto/quieta *adjective* still; **¡estate quieto!** keep still!

química¹ *noun Fem.* chemistry.

químico/química² *noun Masc./ Fem.* chemist.
químico *adjective* chemical.

quince *number* **1** fifteen; **tiene quince años** he's fifteen (years old); **2 quince días** a fortnight; **3** fifteenth (*in dates*); **hoy estamos a quince** it's the fifteenth today.

quinceañero/quinceañera *noun Masc./Fem.* teenager.

quincena *noun Fem.* **una quincena** a fortnight; **la primera quincena de mayo** the first two weeks in May.

quiniela *noun Fem.* pools coupon; **rellenar una quiniela** to fill in a pools coupon; **jugar a las quinielas** to do the pools.

quinientos/quinientas *number* five hundred; **quinientos cinco** five hundred and five.

quinto/quinta *adjective* fifth; **el quinto piso** the fifth floor; **llegar en quinto lugar** to finish in fifth position.

quiosco *noun Masc.* **1** news-stand; **2 el quiosco de los helados** the ice cream stand; **3 el quiosco de bebidas** the drinks stand; **4** kiosk.

quiosquero/quiosquera *noun Masc./Fem.* **1** newspaper vendor; **2** kiosk vendor.

quirúrgico/quirúrgica *adjective* surgical.

quise, quisiera, quiso, etc. *verb* SEE **querer**.

quitaesmalte *noun Masc.* nail varnish remover.

quitanieves *noun Masc.* snowplough.

quitar *verb* [17] **1** to take off; **quita los pies de la mesa** take your feet off the table; **no puedo quitar la tapa** I can't get the lid off; **2 le quité los zapatos al niño** I took the child's shoes off; **3 quitarle algo a alguien** to take something from someone; **le quitaron la cartera** they took his wallet; **4** to take away; **le han quitado el carnet de conducir** they've taken his driving licence away; **quita esa silla de ahí** take that chair away from there; **5** to remove; **quitar la suciedad** to remove the dirt; **quitar el polvo** to dust.

quitarse *reflexive verb* [17] **1** to come out (*a stain, for example*); **2** to go away (*a pain*); **3 quitarse algo** to take something off; **se quitó el abrigo** he took his coat off.

quizá, **quizás** *adverb* perhaps.

Rr

rábano *noun Masc.* radish; ★ **me importa un rábano** (*informal*) I couldn't care less (*literally: it matters a radish to me*).

rabia *noun Fem.* **1** rabies; **2 me da mucha rabia** it really annoys me; **me da mucha rabia llegar tarde** I get very annoyed when I'm late; **le dio mucha rabia que no se lo dijeran** it really annoyed him that they didn't tell him; **3 tenerle rabia**

a alguien to have it in for someone; **4 con rabia** angrily.

rabo *noun Masc.* tail.

racha *noun Fem.* **1 una racha de mala suerte** a spell of bad luck; **pasar una mala racha** to go through a bad patch; **tener una buena racha** to be on a winning streak; **2** gust (*of wind*).

racimo *noun Masc.* bunch; **un racimo de uvas** a bunch of grapes.

ración *noun Fem.* portion; **una ración de gambas** a portion of prawns (*in a tapas bar*).

racionar *verb* [17] to ration.

racismo *noun Masc.* racism.

racista *noun Masc./Fem.*, **racista** *adjective* racist.

radar *noun Masc.* radar.

radiación *noun Fem.* radiation.

radiactivo/radiactiva *adjective* radioactive.

radiador *noun Masc.* radiator.

radio¹ *noun Fem.* radio; **escuchar la radio** to listen to the radio; **poner la radio** to switch on the radio.

radio² *noun Masc.* radius.

radiocassette *noun Masc.* radio cassette player.

radiografía *noun Fem.* X-ray; **hacerse una radiografía** to have an X-ray taken.

ráfaga *noun Fem.* **1** gust; **una ráfaga de viento** a gust of wind; **2 una ráfaga de ametralladora** a burst of machine-gun fire.

a
b
c
d
e
f
g
h
i
j
k
l
m
n
ñ
o
p
q
r
s
t
u
v
w
x
y
z

a
b
c
d
e
f
g
h
i
j
k
l
m
n
ñ
o
p
q
r
s
t
u
v
w
x
y
z

raíz *noun Fem.* **1** root; **echar raíces** to take root; **2 raíz cuadrada** square root; **3 a raíz de** as a result of.

rallado/rallada *adjective* **1** grated; **2 pan rallado** breadcrumbs.

rallador *noun Masc.* grater.

rallar *verb* [17] to grate.

rama *noun Fem.* branch; ★ **irse por las ramas** to beat about the bush.

ramo *noun Masc.* **1** bunch (*of flowers*); **2** bouquet.

rampa *noun Fem.* ramp; **rampa de lanzamiento** launch pad.

rana *noun Fem.* frog.

ranura *noun Fem.* coin slot.

rape *noun Masc.* **1** monkfish; **2 llevar el pelo cortado al rape** to have your hair closely cropped.

rápidamente *adverb* quickly.

rápido¹ *noun Masc.* express train. **rápido** *adverb* fast, quickly; **todo lo rápido que podía** as fast as I possibly could.

rápido²**/rápida** *adjective* **1** quick, fast; **comida rápida** fast food; **2** rapid.

raqueta *noun Fem.* **1** racket; **2** snowshoe.

raro/rara *adjective* **1** strange; **¡qué raro que no hayan llamado!** how strange they haven't called!; **2** rare; **es raro que llueva en esa zona** it's rare for it to rain in that area.

rascacielos *noun Masc.* (*does not change in the plural*) skyscraper.

rascar *verb* [31] to scratch.

rascarse *reflexive verb* [31] to scratch yourself; **se rascó la nariz** he scratched his nose.

rasgar *verb* [28] to tear.

rasguño *noun Masc.* scratch.

rastrillo *noun Masc.* rake.

rastro *noun Masc.* **1** trail; **sin dejar rastro** without a trace; **2** flea market.

rata *noun Fem.* rat.

ratero/ratera *noun Masc./Fem.* **1** pickpocket; **2** petty thief.

rato *noun Masc.* **1** while; **tardaré un rato en hacerlo** it will take me a while to do it; **después de un rato** after a while; **dentro de un rato** in a while; **ya hace rato que se han ido** they went a while ago; **al rato** after a while; **al poco rato** soon afterwards; **2 pasar el rato** to kill time; **3 pasar un buen rato** to have a good time; **4 ratos libres** spare time.

ratón *noun Masc.* mouse.

raya *noun Fem.* **1** line; **2** dash (*in punctuation*); **3** parting (*in your hair*); **hacerse la raya** to part your hair; **4 a rayas** striped, stripy (*a dress or material, for example*); **una falda a rayas** a stripy skirt; **5** skate (*fish*).

rayar *verb* [17] **1** to scratch; **2 rayar en** to border on; **raya en lo ridículo** it's bordering on the ridiculous.

rayo *noun Masc.* **1** ray; **un rayo de luz** a ray of light; **2** flash of lightning; **3 un rayo láser** a laser beam; **4 rayos X** X-rays.

raza *noun Fem.* **1** race; **2** breed; **un perro de raza** a pedigree dog.

razón *noun Fem.* **1** reason; **por alguna razón** for some reason; **¿por qué razón se enfadó?** why did he get cross?; **con razón** with good reason; **por razones de salud** for medical reasons; **2 tener razón** to be right; **tienes razón** you're right; **no tienes razón en eso** you're wrong about that; **darle la razón a alguien** to agree that somebody is right; **3** reason; **perder la razón** to lose your mind; **4 razón: 279452** call 279452 for information.

razonable *adjective* reasonable.

reacción *noun Fem.* reaction.

reacio/reacia *adjective* reluctant.

reactor *noun Masc.* **1** jet; **2** reactor.

real *adjective* **1** real; **2** true; **una historia real** a true story; **3** royal.

realidad *noun Fem.* **1** reality; **hacerse realidad** to become true; **2 en realidad** actually.

realista *adjective* **1** realistic; **es muy poco realista** he's very unrealistic; **2** royalist.

realizador/realizadora *noun Masc./Fem.* producer.

realizar *verb* [22] **1** to carry out (*a task*); **2** to make (*a visit or trip*); **3** to fulfil (*a dream*).
realizarse *reflexive verb* [22] **1** to come true (*a dream*); **2** to fulfil yourself.

rebaja *noun Fem.* **1** reduction; **hacer una rebaja** to give a reduction; **me hizo una rebaja de diez euros** he gave me a ten euro reduction; **lo rebajó a cuarenta euros** he reduced it to forty euros; **2 rebajas** sales; **esa tienda está de rebajas** this shop has a sale on.

rebajar *verb* [17] **1** to bring down (*prices*); **2** to reduce (*an article*); **todas las faldas están rebajadas** all the skirts are reduced; **3 rebajar peso** to lose weight.

rebanada *noun Fem.* slice.

rebaño *noun Masc.* **1** flock (*of sheep*); **2** herd (*of goats*).

rebeca *noun Fem.* cardigan.

rebelarse *reflexive verb* [17] to rebel.

rebelde *noun Masc./Fem.* rebel.
rebelde *adjective* **1** rebel; **2** unruly; **3 una tos rebelde** a persistent cough.

rebelión *noun Fem.* rebellion.

rebobinar *verb* [17] rewind.

rebotar *verb* [17] **1** to bounce; **la pelota rebotó en el poste** the ball bounced off the post; **2** to ricochet.

rebuznar *verb* [17] to bray.

recado *noun Masc.* **1** message; **no han dejado recado** they didn't leave a message; **2** errand; **hacer un recado** to run an errand.

recalentar *verb* [29] reheat.

recambio *noun Masc.* **1** spare part; **2** refill (*for a pen*).

recepción *noun Fem.* reception.

recepcionista *noun Masc./Fem.* receptionist.

receta *noun Fem.* **1** recipe; **2** prescription.

recetar *verb* [17] to prescribe.

a
b
c
d
e
f
g
h
i
j
k
l
m
n
ñ
o
p
q
r
s
t
u
v
w
x
y
z

227

a **recibidor** noun Masc. entrance hall.

b **recibir** verb [19] 1 to receive; **he recibido una carta de Lola** I've received a letter from Lola; 2 to get; **recibí una llamada del editor** I got a phone call from the editor; 3 **recibir a alguien con los brazos abiertos** to welcome somebody with open arms; 4 **ir a recibir a alguien** to go to meet somebody; **fuimos a recibirlos a la estación** we went to meet them at the station; 5 (ending a letter) **recibe un fuerte abrazo** best wishes; **reciba un cordial saludo** yours sincerely.

k **recibo** noun Masc. receipt.

reciclar verb [17] recycle.

recién adverb 1 **pasteles recién hechos** freshly baked cakes; **'recién pintado'** 'wet paint'; 2 **un recién nacido** a newborn baby; **los recién casados** the newly-weds; **los recién llegados** the newcomers.

reciente adjective recent.

recientemente adverb recently.

recipiente noun Masc. container.

recitar verb [17] to recite.

reclamación noun Fem. 1 complaint; **hacer una reclamación** to make a complaint; 2 reclamación Fem.; **hacer una reclamación al seguro** to make a claim on insurance.

reclamar verb [17] 1 to complain; 2 to demand (rights, money).

recoger verb [3] 1 to pick up; **recoge ese papel del suelo** pick up that piece of paper off the floor; **fui a recogerlos a la estación** I went to

pick them up from the station; 2 to tidy up; **tienes que recoger tu habitación** you have to tidy up your room; 3 **recoger la mesa** to clear the table; 4 to collect (money or signatures); 5 to pick (fruit or flowers).
recogerse reflexive verb [3] **recogerse el pelo** to tie your hair back.

recogida noun Fem. collection.

recomendación noun Fem. 1 recommendation; 2 reference (for a job).

recomendar verb [29] to recommend.

recompensa noun Fem. reward.

recompensar verb [17] to reward.

reconciliarse reflexive verb [17] **reconciliarse con alguien** to make it up with somebody.

reconocer verb [35] 1 to recognize; **al principio no la reconocí** I didn't recognize her to start with; 2 to admit (a mistake); 3 to examine (a patient).

reconocimiento noun Masc. 1 **reconocimiento médico** medical examination; 2 reconnaissance.

reconozca, etc. verb SEE **reconocer**.

récord noun Masc. record.

recordar verb [24] 1 to remember; **si mal no recuerdo** if I remember rightly; **recuerdo que terminamos a las tres** I remember that we finished at three; 2 to remind; **me recuerda mucho a ella** he reminds me of her a lot; **3 recordarle a alguien que haga algo** to remind somebody to do something; **recuérdale que traiga los papeles** remind him to bring the papers.

recreo noun Masc. break (at school).

recta¹ noun Fem. straight line.

rectángulo noun Masc. rectangle.

recto/recta² adjective **1** straight; **2** honest.
recto adverb **seguir todo recto** to carry straight on.

recuerda, recuerdo¹, **etc.** verb SEE **recordar**.

recuerdo² noun Masc. **1** memory; **tengo buenos recuerdos** I've got happy memories; **2** souvenir; **'recuerdo de España'** 'souvenir from Spain'; **3 recuerdos** regards; **dale recuerdos a tu hermana de mi parte** say hello to your sister from me.

recuperar verb [17] **1** to recover (money, strength); **2 recuperar tiempo** to make up for lost time.
recuperarse reflexive verb [17] **recuperarse de una enfermedad** to recover from an illness.

red noun Fem. **1** net; **2** network; **3 la Red** the Net (Internet); ★ **caer en las redes de alguien** to fall into sombody's clutches.

redacción noun Fem. **1** essay; **2** editorial team.

redactor/redactora noun Masc./Fem. editor.

redondo/redonda adjective round; **en números redondos** in round figures.

reducción noun Fem. reduction.

reducir verb [60] to reduce.

reduje, reduzca, reduzco, etc. verb SEE **reducir**.

reembolsar verb [17] to refund.

reembolso noun Masc. refund.

reemplazar verb [22] **reemplazar a alguien** to stand in for somebody.

reemplazo noun Masc. replacement.

referencia noun Fem. reference; **hacer referencia a** to refer to.

referirse reflexive verb [14] **referirse a** to refer to; **se refiere a ti** she's referring to you.

refiera, refiero, refiramos, refirió, etc. verb SEE **referirse**.

reflejar verb [17] to reflect.
reflejarse reflexive verb [17] to be reflected.

reflejo noun Masc. **1** reflection; **2 reflejos** highlights; **3 reflejos** reflexes.

reflexión noun Fem. reflection.

reflexionar verb [17] to reflect on; **después de reflexionarlo bien** after thinking it over.

reforestación Fem. reforestation.

refrán noun Masc. saying.

refrescante adjective refreshing.

refrescar verb [31] to refresh.

refresco noun Masc. soft drink.

refrigerio noun Masc. light refreshments.

refugiado/refugiada noun Masc./Fem. refugee.

a
b
c
d
e
f
g
h
i
j
k
l
m
n
ñ
o
p
q
r
s
t
u
v
w
x
y
z

refugiarse *reflexive verb* [17]
refugiarse de to take refuge from.

refugio *noun Masc.* shelter; **dar
refugio a alguien** to give somebody
shelter; **un refugio de montaña** a
mountain refuge.

regadera *noun Fem.* watering can;
★**estar como una regadera**
(*informal*) to be raving mad
(*literally: to be like a watering can*).

regalar *verb* [17] **1** to give (*as a
present*); **mis padrinos me han
regalado un reloj** my godparents
have bought me a watch; **¿qué vas a
regalarle por Navidad?** what are
you going to get her for Christmas?;
2 to give away; **me ha regalado su
abrigo** he's given his coat to me; **¿te
gusta? te lo regalo** do you like it?
you can have it.

regalo *noun Masc.* **1** present; **regalo
de cumpleaños** birthday present;
**2 compre dos y llévese uno de
regalo** buy two and get one free.

regañar *verb* [17] **1** to tell off; **mi
madre me regañó por llegar tarde**
my mother told me off because I got
home late; **2 regañar con alguien**
to quarrel with somebody; **ha
regañado con su hermano** he's
had an argument with his brother.

regar *verb* [30] to water.

régimen *noun Masc.* diet; **ponerse
a régimen** to go on a diet.

región *noun Fem.* region.

regional *adjective* regional.

registrar *verb* [17] **1** to search; **nos
registraron** we were searched; **la
policía registró la casa** the police

searched the house; **2** to go through;
me registró todos los papeles he
went through all my papers; **3** to
register (*a birth, for example*); **4** to
record (*temperature*).

registrarse *reflexive verb* [17] **1** to
register; **2** to check in; **she
checked in at five o'clock** se
registró a las cinco.

registro *noun Masc.* **1** register; **2 el
registro civil** the registry office;
3 search.

regla *noun Fem.* **1** ruler (*for
measuring*); **2** rule; **por regla
general** as a general rule; **3 estar
con la regla** to have your period.

reglamento *noun Masc.*
regulations.

regresar *verb* [17] to return.

regreso *noun Masc.* return.

regular *adjective* **1** regular; **2** poor
(*mark*); **3 de tamaño regular**
medium-sized; **4 por lo regular** as a
general rule.

regular *adverb* '**¿qué tal está tu
padre?' – 'regular'** 'how's your
father?' – 'so-so'.

regularidad *noun Fem.* regularity;
con regularidad regularly.

rehacer *verb* [7] **1 rehacer algo** to
do something again; **2 rehízo su
vida** she rebuilt her life.

reina *noun Fem.* queen.

reinado *noun Masc.* reign; **durante
el reinado del rey Juan Carlos**
during the reign of King Juan
Carlos.

reinar *verb* [17] to reign.

reino *noun Masc.* kingdom.

Reino Unido *noun Masc.* United Kingdom.

reír *verb* [61] to laugh; **echarse a reír** to start laughing.
reírse *reflexive verb* [61] **reírse de** to laugh about; **siempre se están riendo de mí** they're always laughing at me; **reírse a carcajadas** to roar with laughter.

reja *noun Fem.* **1** railing; **2** grille; **estar entre rejas** to be behind bars.

relación *noun Fem.* **1** relationship; **2 relaciones públicas** public relations; **3** connection; **en relación con** mix with (*people*).

relacionado/relacionada *adjective* related.

relacionar *verb* [17] to relate; **relacionar algo con algo** to relate something to something.
relacionarse *reflexive verb* [17] to be related (*facts, for example*); **relacionarse con** to mix with (*a person*).

relajar *verb* [17] to relax.
relajarse *reflexive verb* [17] to relax.

relámpago *noun Masc.* flash of lightning; ★ **como un relámpago** like greased lightning.

religión *noun Fem.* religion.

religioso/religiosa *adjective* religious.

rellenar *verb* [17] **1 rellenar un impreso** to fill in a form; **2** to fill up; **3** to stuff (*a chicken, for example*).

relleno¹ *noun Masc.* **1** filling; **2** stuffing.

relleno²/rellena *adjective* **1** filled; **2** stuffed (*peppers, for example*).

reloj *noun Masc.* **1** clock; **un reloj despertador** an alarm clock; **2** watch; **un reloj de pulsera** a wristwatch; **mi reloj va atrasado** my watch is slow.

relojería *noun Fem.* watchmaker's.

remar *verb* [17] to row.

remate *noun Masc.* **1** smash (*in tennis*); **2** finish (*in football*); **un remate de cabeza** a header; **3** end (*of a pole, for example*); **4** top (*of a tower, for example*); **5 y para remate** and to cap it all; ★ **loco de remate** (*informal*) completely nuts.

remediar *verb* [17] **1** to remedy; **2 no lo puede remediar** he can't help it; **no pudimos remediarlo** we couldn't do anything about it.

remedio *noun Masc.* **1** remedy; **remedios naturales** natural remedies; **2 si no queda más remedio** if there's no other alternative; **no queda más remedio que aguantarse** we had to put up with it, there was nothing else we could do; **no tuvimos más remedio que ir** we had no other option but to go; **¡qué remedio me queda!** what else can I do!; **eso ya no tiene remedio** there's nothing we can do about it now.

remendar *verb* [29] to mend.

remite *noun Masc.* return address.

remitente *noun Masc./Fem.* sender (*of a letter*).

remo *noun Masc.* oar.

a
b
c
d
e
f
g
h
i
j
k
l
m
n
ñ
o
p
q
r
s
t
u
v
w
x
y
z

a **remojar** *verb* [17] to soak.

b **remojo** *noun Masc.* **poner algo en remojo** to soak something.

c **remolacha** *noun Fem.* beetroot.

d **remolcar** *verb* [31] to tow.

e **remolino** *noun Masc.* whirlpool.

f **remolque** *noun Masc.* **1** trailer; **2 llevar algo a remolque** to tow something.

g
h **remorder** *verb* [38] **aún me remuerde la conciencia** I still feel guilty about it.

i **remoto/remota** *adjective* remote.

j
k **remover** *verb* [38] **1** to stir (*a sauce, for example*); **2** to toss (*a salad*); **3** to turn over (*soil*).

l
m **remueva, remuevo, etc.** *verb* SEE **remover**.

n **renacuajo** *noun Masc.* tadpole.

ñ **rencor** *noun Masc.* **guardarle rencor a alguien** to bear someone a grudge.

o **rendición** *noun Fem.* surrender.

p **rendir** *verb* [57] **1 rendirle homenaje a alguien** to pay tribute to someone; **2 ayer me rindió mucho en el trabajo** I managed to get a lot done yesterday at work. **rendirse** *reflexive verb* [57] to surrender.

q

r **RENFE** *abbreviation Fem.* (*short for: Red Nacional de Ferrocarriles Españoles*) the Spanish national rail network.

s
t **renglón** *noun Masc.* line.

u **renta** *noun Fem.* **1** rent; **2** income.

v **rentable** *adjective* profitable.

w
x
y
z

renunciar *verb* [17] **renunciar a** to renounce, to give up; **renunciar a un puesto** to resign from a job.

reparación *noun Fem.* repair; **taller de reparaciones** repair shop.

reparar *verb* [17] **1** to repair; **2** to mend.

repartir *verb* [19] **1** to deliver; **2** to hand out (*leaflets, for example*); **3** to distribute; **lo repartiremos entre todos nosotros** we'll share it between us.

reparto *noun Masc.* **1** delivery; **reparto a domicilio** home delivery service; **2** distribution; **hacer el reparto del dinero** to share out the money.

repasar *verb* [17] **1** to revise; **repasar los apuntes** to revise your notes; **2** to check through (*a list*).

repaso *noun Masc.* **1** revision; **dar un repaso a los apuntes** to revise your notes; **2** check (*for mistakes*).

repente *in phrase* **de repente** all of a sudden.

repentino/repentina *adjective* sudden.

repetición *noun Fem.* repetition.

repetición de la jugada *noun Fem.* action replay.

repetir *verb* [57] to repeat; **¿quieres repetir?** would you like a second helping?

repisa *noun Fem.* **1** ledge (*of window*); **2** mantelpiece (*of chimney*).

repita, repitió, repito, etc. *verb* SEE **repetir**.

repleto/repleta *adjective* full up; **estar repleto de algo** to be packed with something; **una sala repleta de gente** a room packed with people.

repollo *noun Masc.* cabbage.

reponer *verb* [11] **1** to replace; **2** to repay; **3 reponer fuerzas** to get your strength back.
reponerse *reflexive verb* [11] to recover; **cuando me repuse del susto** when I recovered from the shock.

reportaje *noun Masc.* **1** article (*in a newspaper*); **2** report (*on TV*).

reportero/reportera *noun Masc./Fem.* reporter.

reposar *verb* [17] **1** to rest; **2 dejar reposar** to leave to stand.

reposo *noun Masc.* rest.

repostería *noun Fem.* confectionery.

representante *noun Masc./Fem.* representative.

representar *verb* [17] **1** to represent; **2 representar una obra** to perform a play; **representar un papel** to play a part.

reproducción *noun Fem.* reproduction.

reproducir *verb* [60] to reproduce. **reproducirse** *reflexive verb* [60] to reproduce.

reptil *noun Masc.* reptile.

república *noun Fem.* republic.

República Checa *noun Fem.* **la República Checa** the Czech Republic.

repugnante *adjective* disgusting.

repulsivo/repulsiva *adjective* repulsive.

reputación *noun Fem.* reputation.

requisito *noun Masc.* requirement.

resaca *noun Fem.* hangover.

resbaladizo/resbaladiza *adjective* slippery.

resbalar *verb* [17] to slip. **resbalarse** *reflexive verb* [17] to slip.

rescatar *verb* [17] to rescue.

rescate *noun Masc.* rescue; **una operación de rescate** a rescue operation.

reserva *noun Fem.* **1** reservation; **hacer una reserva** to make a reservation; **2** reserve; **jugadores de reserva** reserve players; **una reserva natural** a nature reserve; **3 tengo otro de reserva** I have a spare one; **4 tengo mis reservas** I have my reservations.

reservado/reservada *adjective* reserved.

reservar *verb* [17] **1** to reserve; **2** to book.

resfriado *noun Masc.* cold; **tener un resfriado** to have a cold.

resfriarse *reflexive verb* [32] to catch a cold.

residencia *noun Fem.* **1** residence; **permiso de residencia** residence permit; **2** hall of residence; **3 residencia de ancianos** old people's home.

residir *verb* [19] **residir en** to live in.

a
b
c
d
e
f
g
h
i
j
k
l
m
n
ñ
o
p
q
r
s
t
u
v
w
x
y
z

a
b
c
d
e
f
g
h
i
j
k
l
m
n
ñ
o
p
q
r
s
t
u
v
w
x
y
z

resistencia *noun Fem.*
1 resistance; **2** element (*electrical*);
3 tener mucha resistencia to have
a lot of stamina.

resistir *verb* [19] **1** to resist; **2** to
stand (*pain or cold*); **¡no puedo
resistirlo!** I can't stand it!
resistirse *reflexive verb* [19] to
resist.

resolver *verb* [45] **1** to solve; **2** to
resolve.

resorte *noun Masc.* spring.

respaldo *noun Masc.* **1** back;
2 backing.

respecto *noun Masc.* **respecto a** ...
regarding ....

respetable *adjective* respectable.

respetar *verb* [17] to respect.

respeto *noun Masc.* respect.

respiración *noun Fem.* breathing;
contener la respiración to hold
your breath.

respirar *verb* [17] to breathe.

responder *verb* [18] **1** to answer;
responder a algo to answer
something; **2** to respond; **3** to
answer back; **¡a mí no me
respondas!** don't answer back!

responsabilidad *noun Fem.*
responsibility.

responsable *noun Masc./Fem.*
1 person in charge; **el responsable
de ventas** the person in charge of
sales; **2** person responsible.
responsable *adjective*
responsible.

respuesta *noun Fem.* **1** answer;
2 response.

restante *adjective* remaining; **lo
restante** the remainder.

restar *verb* [17] to subtract, to take
away.

restaurante *noun Masc.*
restaurant.

restaurar *verb* [17] to restore.

resto *noun Masc.* **1** rest; **el resto de
los libros** the rest of the books;
2 restos remains; **los restos del
castillo** the remains of the castle;
3 restos leftovers (*from a meal*).

restricción *noun Fem.* restriction.

restringir *verb* [49] to restrict.
restringirse *reflexive verb* [49] to
restrict yourself.

resultado *noun Masc.* **1** result;
2 outcome; **3 dar resultado** to work
(*a plan or an idea*).

resultar *verb* [17] **1** to work (*a plan
or an idea*); **2 así resulta más fácil**
it's easy this way; **resultó
imposible convencerlo** it was
impossible to convince him.

resumen *noun Masc.* summary.

resumir *verb* [19] **1** to summarize;
2 to sum up.

retener *verb* [9] **1** to retain; **2** to
keep back.

retirar *verb* [17] **1** to withdraw; **2** to
move back; **retira esa silla** move
that chair back.
retirarse *reflexive verb* [17] **1** to
withdraw; **2** to move back.

retrasado/retrasada *noun
Masc./Fem.* mentally handicapped.
retrasado *adjective* **1** mentally
handicapped; **2 vamos muy**

retrasados con el trabajo we're very late with the job; **3 me reloj va retrasado** my watch is slow.

retrasar *verb* [17] **1** to delay (*departure*); **2** to postpone; **3 retrasar un reloj** to put a clock back.

retrasarse *reflexive verb* [17] **1** to be late; **me retrasé diez minutos** I was ten minutes late; **2** to fall behind; **voy retrasado con mi trabajo** I'm behind with my work.

retraso *noun Masc.* **1** delay; **una media hora de retraso** a half-hour delay; **llevan retraso** they're late; **2 con retraso** late; **llegaron con retraso** they arrived late.

retrato *noun Masc.* portrait; ★ **ser el vivo retrato de alguien** to be the spitting image of somebody.

retrovisor *noun Masc.* **1** rear-view mirror; **2** wing mirror.

reuma, **reúma**, **reumatismo** *noun Masc.* rheumatism.

reunión *noun Fem.* **1** meeting; **2** gathering; **3** reunion; **una reunión de antiguos alumnos** a reunion of former pupils.

reunir *verb* [62] **1** to gather (*information, for example*); **2** to have; **reúne los elementos que busco** it has everything I'm looking for; **no reúne los requisitos necesarios** it doesn't satisfy the necessary requirements; **3 reunir dinero** to raise money.

reunirse *reflexive verb* [62] to meet.

revancha *noun Fem.* **1** return game; **jugar la revancha** to play a

rematch; **2 tomarse la revancha** to get your own back.

revelar *verb* [17] **1** to reveal; **2** to develop (*a film*).

reverencia *noun Fem.* bow, curtsey; **hacer una reverencia** to bow, to curtsey.

reverso *noun Masc.* back.

revés *noun Masc.* **1** back; **el revés de la página** the back of the page; **2** inside; **el revés del abrigo** the inside of the coat; **3 se puso el jersey al revés** he put his jumper on inside out, he put his jumper on back-to-front; **ese cuadro está al revés** that picture's upside down; **4 del revés** inside out.

revisar *verb* [17] **1** to check; **2** to revise; **3** to service.

revisión *noun Fem.* **1** (medical) checkup; **2** revision; **3** service (*for a car or a machine*).

revisor/revisora *noun Masc./Fem.* ticket inspector.

revista *noun Fem.* magazine.

revolución *noun Fem.* revolution.

revolver *verb* [45] **1** to stir (*soup or sauce*); **2 me revolvieron todos los cajones** they went through all my drawers; **le habían revuelto todos sus papeles** they'd left all his papers in a mess.

revólver *noun Masc.* gun.

revuelto/revuelta *adjective* **1** in a mess; **los papeles estaban todos revueltos** all the papers were in a mess; **2** rough (*sea*); **3** unsettled (*weather*).

rey *noun Masc.* **1** king; **2 los reyes** the king and queen.

rezar *verb* [22] to pray.

ría, rían, etc. *verb* SEE **reír.**

riada *noun Fem.* flood.

ribera *noun Fem.* riverbank.

rico/rica *noun Masc./Fem.* rich person; **los ricos** the rich. **rico** *adjective* rich.

ridículo[1] *noun Masc.* **hacer el ridículo** to make a fool of yourself; **dejar a alguien en ridículo** to make a fool of somebody.

ridículo[2]**/ridícula** *adjective* ridiculous.

ríe, ríen, etc. *verb* SEE **reír.**

riega, riego, riegue, etc. *verb* SEE **regar.**

rienda *noun Fem.* rein.

riesgo *noun Masc.* risk; **correr un riesgo** to run a risk; **voy a correr el riesgo** I'll take the risk; **un riesgo para la salud** a health hazard.

rifa *noun Fem.* raffle.

rímel *noun Masc.* mascara.

rincón *noun Masc.* **1** corner (*of a room*); **2 estará en algún rincón** it must be somewhere; **3 un rincón pintoresco** a lovely spot (*in the country*).

rinoceronte *noun Masc.* rhinoceros.

riña *noun Fem.* **1** fight; **una riña callejera** a street fight; **2** quarrel; **tuvo una riña con su novio** she had a quarrel with her boyfriend.

riñón *noun Masc.* **1** kidney; **2 tener dolor de riñones** to have backache.

río *noun Masc.* river; **ir río abajo** to go downstream.

rió *verb* SEE **reír.**

riqueza *noun Fem.* wealth.

risa *noun Fem.* **1** laugh; **una risa histérica** an hysterical laugh; **2 risas** laughter; **las risas del público** the laughter of the audience; **3 me dio risa verlo** seeing him made me laugh; **de repente le dio la risa** suddenly he got the giggles; **4 ¡qué risa!** how funny!; **5 morirse de risa** (*informal*) to die laughing.

ritmo *noun Masc.* rhythm; **llevar el ritmo** to keep time; **marcar el ritmo** to beat time.

rival *noun Masc./Fem.* rival.

rizado/rizada *adjective* curly.

rizo *noun Masc.* curl.

robar *verb* [17] **1** to steal; **robarle algo a alguien** to steal something from somebody; **2** to rob; **robar un banco** to rob a bank; **3 robar en una casa** to burgle a house; **les robaron mientras estaban de vacaciones** they were burgled while they were away; **4** to rip (somebody) off.

roble *noun Masc.* oak.

robo *noun Masc.* **1** theft; **2** robbery; **3** burglary; **4** break in; **5 ¡esto es un robo!** this is a rip-off!.

roca *noun Fem.* rock; ★**firme como una roca** solid as a rock.

rocío *noun Masc.* dew.

rodaja *noun Fem.* slice; **cortar en rodajas** to slice.

rodar verb [24] **1** to roll (a ball, for example); **2** to turn (a wheel); **3** to shoot (a film).

rodeado/rodeada adjective surrounded; **rodeado de** surrounded by.

rodear verb [17] to surround.

rodilla noun Fem. knee; **ponerse de rodillas** to kneel down.

rogar verb [24] **1** to beg; **te ruego que me perdones** I beg you to forgive me; **2** 'se ruega no fumar' 'no smoking'.

rojo¹ noun Masc. red.

rojo²**/roja** adjective red; **ponerse rojo** to turn red.

rollo noun Masc. **1** roll; **un rollo de tela** a roll of fabric; **un rollo de papel higiénico** a toilet roll; **2** coil (of rope, wire); **3** (informal) bore; **¡vaya rollo de película!** what a boring film!; **4** (informal) business.

romántico/romántica adjective romantic.

rompecabezas noun Masc. (does not change in the plural) puzzle.

romper verb [40] **1** to break; **vas a romper la silla** you're going to break the chair; **2** to tear; **rompió la carta en pedazos** he tore up the letter; **3** romper algo en mil pedazos to smash something to pieces.

romperse reflexive verb [40] to break; **la lámpara se ha roto** the lamp has broken; **romperse una pierna** to break your leg.

rompiente noun Masc. breaker (wave).

ron noun Masc. rum.

roncar verb [31] to snore.

ronco/ronca adjective hoarse; **quedarse ronco** to go hoarse.

ronda noun Fem. **1** round; **esta ronda la pago yo** it's my round; **2** patrol.

ronronear verb [31] to purr.

ropa noun Fem. **1** clothes; **tengo mucha ropa** I have a lot of clothes; **2** cambiarse de ropa to get changed; **3** la ropa sucia the dirty laundry; **4** ropa interior underwear.

ropero noun Masc. wardrobe.

rosa¹ noun Fem. rose.

rosa² noun Masc., adjective pink.

rosado¹**/rosada** adjective pink.

rosado² noun Masc. **1** rosé (wine); **2** pink.

rosario noun Masc. rosary.

rosbif noun Masc. roast beef.

rostro noun Masc. **1** face; **2** nerve; **¡vaya rostro que tiene!** (informal) he's got a nerve!.

roto/rota adjective **1** broken; **2** torn; **3** worn out (shoes).

rotulador noun Masc. felt-tip pen.

rubio/rubia adjective blonde.

ruborizarse reflexive verb [22] to blush.

rueda noun Fem. **1** wheel; **la rueda de repuesto** the spare wheel; **la rueda delantera** the front wheel; **2** una rueda de prensa a press conference.

rugir verb [49] to roar.

a
b
c
d
e
f
g
h
i
j
k
l
m
n
ñ
o
p
q
r
s
t
u
v
w
x
y
z

a
b
c
d
e
f
g
h
i
j
k
l
m
n
ñ
o
p
q
r
s
t
u
v
w
x
y
z

ruido *noun Masc.* noise; **hacer ruido** to make a noise.

ruidoso/ruidosa *adjective* noisy.

ruina *noun Fem.* **1** ruin; **dejar a alguien en la ruina** to ruin somebody; **la empresa está en la ruina** the company is in a terrible state; **2 ruinas** ruins; **las ruinas del castillo** the ruins of the castle; **estar en ruinas** to be in ruins; ★ **estar hecho una ruina** (*informal*) to be a wreck.

ruiseñor *noun Masc.* nightingale.

rulo *noun Masc.* roller (*curler*).

Rumania, Rumanía *noun Fem.* Romania.

rumano/rumana *noun Masc./ Fem., adjective* Romanian.

rumbo *noun Masc.* **1** course; **poner rumbo a** to set a course for; **el rumbo que tomaron los acontecimientos** the course of events; **2** direction; **3 ir con rumbo a** to be heading for; **4 sin rumbo fijo** aimlessly.

rumor *noun Masc.* **1** rumour; **2** murmur.

Rusia *noun Fem.* Russia.

ruso¹ *noun Masc.* Russian (*the language*).

ruso²/rusa *noun Masc./Fem., adjective* Russian.

ruta *noun Fem.* route.

rutina *noun Fem.* routine; **por rutina** out of habit.

Ss

sábado *noun Masc.* Saturday (*see 'domingo' for examples*).

sábana *noun Fem.* sheet (*for a bed*).

saber *noun Masc.* knowledge.
saber *verb* [13] **1** to know; **ya lo sé** I know; **no sabe** he doesn't know; **sabía que no iba a querer hacerlo** I knew he wouldn't want to do it; **2 saber algo de memoria** to know something by heart; **3 ¿sabes montar en bicicleta?** can you ride a bike?; **sabe hablar inglés muy bien** she can speak English very well; **no sé alemán** I can't speak German; **4** to find out; **lo supe por su hermana** I found out through her sister; **5** to taste; **la comida sabía muy rica** the food tasted very nice; **¡qué mal sabe!** it tastes disgusting!; **6 saber a** to taste of; **sabe a fresa** it tastes of strawberry.

sabiduría *noun Fem.* wisdom.

sabio/sabia *adjective* wise.

sabor *noun Masc.* taste; **sabor a fresa** strawberry-flavoured.

sabrá, sabré, sabría, etc. *verb* SEE **saber**.

sabroso/sabrosa *adjective* tasty.

sacacorchos *noun Masc.* (*does not change in the plural*) corkscrew.

sacapuntas *noun Masc.* (*does not change in the plural*) pencil sharpener.

sacar *verb* [31] **1** to take out; **sacó su monedero del bolso** she took

her purse out of her bag; **lo saqué de la caja** I took it out of the box; **sacar la basura** to take the rubbish out; **sacar al perro a pasear** to take the dog for a walk; **2 sacar la pistola** to draw a gun; **3** to get; **sacar entradas** to get tickets; **aún no he sacado los billetes** I haven't got the tickets yet; **4 sacar buenas notas** to get good marks; **he sacado un siete en matemáticas** I got seven (out of ten) in maths; **5 sacar una foto** to take a picture; **6 sacar una fotocopia** to make a photocopy; **7 sacar un libro** to publish a book; **sacar un disco** to release a record; **8 sacar la lengua** to stick your tongue out; **9** to serve (*in tennis*); **te toca a ti sacar** it's your service; **10** to kick off (*in football*).
sacarse *reflexive verb* [31]
1 sacarse una muela to have a tooth out; **2 sacarse una foto** to have one's photograph taken; **me saqué una foto frente al palacio** I had my photograph taken in front of the palace.

sacerdote *noun Masc.* priest.

saco *noun Masc.* sack; **un saco de dormir** a sleeping bag.

sacrificar *verb* [31] to sacrifice.

sacrificio *noun Masc.* sacrifice.

sacudida *noun Fem.* **1** shake; **le di una sacudida** I gave it a shake; **2 el coche iba dando sacudidas** the car was jerking along.

sacudir *verb* [19] **1** to shake; **2** to shake off; **sacudió las migas del mantel** she shook the crumbs off the tablecloth.

sacudirse *reflexive verb* [19] to shake off; **se sacudió el polvo de la chaqueta** he shook off the dust from his jacket.

sagaz *adjective* shrewd.

sagitario *noun Masc./Fem.* Sagittarius; **es sagitario** she's Sagittarius.

Sagitario *noun Masc.* Sagittarius.

sagrado/sagrada *adjective* **1** sacred; **2** holy.

sal *noun Fem.* salt; **sales de baño** bath salts.

sala *noun Fem.* **1** room; **una sala de estar** a living room; **una sala de espera** a waiting room; **2** hall; **una sala de exposiciones** an exhibition hall; **3** ward (*in a hospital*); **4 una sala de fiestas** a night club.

salado/salada *adjective* salted; **está muy salado** it's too salty; **agua salada** salt water.

salario *noun* **1** wages (*when weekly*); **2** salary (*when monthly*).

salchicha *noun Fem.* sausage.

salchichón *noun Masc.* salami sausage.

saldar *verb* [17] **1** to settle (*a debt*); **2** to sell off.

saldo *noun Masc.* **1** balance; **saldo positivo** credit balance; **saldo negativo** debit balance; **2** settlement; **3 saldos** sales; **precios de saldo** sale prices.

saldrá, **saldré**, **saldría**, **salga**, **salgo**, **etc.** *verb* SEE **salir**.

a
b
c
d
e
f
g
h
i
j
k
l
m
n
ñ
o
p
q
r
s
t
u
v
w
x
y
z

a
b
c
d
e
f
g
h
i
j
k
l
m
n
ñ
o
p
q
r
s
t
u
v
w
x
y
z

salero noun Masc. **1** salt cellar; **2 tener mucho salero** (informal) to be very funny.

salida noun Fem. exit.

salir verb [63] **1** to go out; **salen mucho por la noche** they go out a lot in the evenings; **2** to come out; **salieron uno a uno** they came out one by one; **3** to get out; **no pude salir** I couldn't get out; **4** to leave; **el vuelo sale a las cinco** the flight leaves at five; **5 salgo de casa a las ocho** I leave home at eight; **no sale nunca de su habitación** he never leaves his room; **salió de la casa corriendo** he ran out of the house; **sal de debajo de la cama** come out from under the bed; **6 salir con alguien** to go out with someone; **sale con mi hermano** she's going out with my brother; **7 salir en la televisión** to appear on television; **la noticia salió en el periódico** the news was in the paper; **8** to turn out; **las cosas salieron mal** things turned out badly; **todo salió como esperábamos** everything turned out as we expected; **9 las vacaciones nos salieron muy caras** the holidays were very expensive in the end; **si compras tres, sale más barato** it's cheaper if you buy three; **10 ¿cómo te salieron las cosas en Inglaterra?** how did things turn out for you in England?; **le sale muy bien la tortilla de patatas** he can cook a really good Spanish omelette; **el retrato te ha salido perfecto** you've done a perfect portrait; **el examen me salió fatal** I did

terribly in the exam; **11 me ha salido un grano** I've got a spot; **le están saliendo canas** his hair's starting to go grey; **le salía sangre de la nariz** his nose was bleeding.

salirse reflexive verb [63] **1** to leave; **el cantante se ha salido del grupo** the singer has left the group; **salirse del colegio** to leave school; **2** to leak; **3 el agua se salió del fregadero** the sink overflowed; **se ha salido la leche** the milk has boiled over; **4 el coche se salió de la carretera** the car went off the road.

saliva noun Fem. saliva.

salmón noun Masc. salmon; **salmón ahumado** smoked salmon.
salmón adjective salmon-pink.

salón noun Masc. **1** living room; **2** function room; **3 salón de belleza** beauty salon; **4 salón de actos** assembly hall; **5 salón de fiestas** reception room.

salpicar verb [31] to splash.

salsa noun Fem. **1** sauce; **salsa besamel** white sauce; **2** gravy; **3** salsa (music).

saltamontes noun Masc. grasshopper.

saltar verb [17] to jump; **saltar por encima de la verja** to jump over the fence; **saltar un muro** to jump over a wall; **saltar al suelo** to jump to the ground; **saltar de la cama** to jump out of bed.

saltarse reflexive verb [17] **1** to skip (a page or an appointment); **2 se saltaron un semáforo en rojo** they drove through a red light.

salto *noun Masc.* jump; **dar un salto** to jump; **ponerse de pie de un salto** to jump to your feet; **levantarse de un salto de la cama** to leap out of bed; **salto de altura** high jump.

salud *noun Fem.* health; **estar bien de salud** to be in good health. **salud** *exclamation* cheers!; **¡a tu salud!** cheers!

saludable *adjective* healthy.

saludar *verb* [17] **1** to say hello; **nos saludó con la mano** she waved hello to us; **2** '**le saluda atentamente**' 'Yours sincerely', 'Yours faithfully' (*ending a letter*).

saludo *noun Masc.* **1** greeting; **te envían sus saludos** they send their regards; **dale saludos de mi parte** give him my regards; **2 Un afectuoso saludo** Best wishes.

salvadoreño/salvadoreña *noun* Salvadorean. **salvadoreño** *adjective* Salvadorean.

salvaje *adjective* **1** savage; **2** wild. **salvaje** *noun Masc./Fem.* savage.

salvamanteles *noun Masc.* (*does not change in the plural*) table mat.

salvamento *noun Masc.* rescue; **bote de salvamento** lifeboat; **operación de salvamento** rescue operation.

salvar *verb* [17] to save. **salvarse** *reflexive verb* [17] to survive.

salvavidas *noun Masc.* (*does not change in the plural*) life jacket.

salvo¹**/salva** *adjective* safe.

salvo² *preposition, conjunction* except; **salvo que** unless. **salvo** *in phrase* **estar a salvo** to be out of danger; **ponerse a salvo** to reach safety.

San *adjective* St (*Saint*).

San Salvador *noun Masc.* San Salvador.

sanar *verb* [17] **1** to recover (*patient*); **2** to heal (*injury*).

sandalia *noun Fem.* sandal.

sandía *noun Fem.* watermelon.

sándwich *noun Masc.* sandwich.

sangrar *verb* [17] to bleed.

sangre *noun Fem.* blood; **te sale sangre** you're bleeding.

sangría *noun Fem.* sangria (*a fruit punch made with red wine and lemonade*).

sano/sana *adjective* **1** healthy; **2 sano y salvo** safe and sound.

santo¹ *noun Masc.* name day (*in Spain each day of the year is associated with the name of a saint and many people celebrate the day of the saint they are named after*).

santo²**/santa** *noun Masc./Fem.* saint; **tener la paciencia de un santo** to have the patience of a saint. **santo** *adjective* holy.

santuario *noun* shrine.

sapo *noun Masc.* toad.

saque *noun Masc.* **1** serve (*in tennis*); **2** kick-off (*in football*);

a
b
c
d
e
f
g
h
i
j
k
l
m
n
ñ
o
p
q
r
s
t
u
v
w
x
y
z

saque de banda throw in; **saque de esquina** corner kick.

sarampión noun Masc. measles.

sarcasmo noun Masc. sarcasm.

sardina noun Fem. sardine.

sargento noun Masc./Fem. sergeant.

sarpullido noun Masc. rash; **me ha salido un sarpullido** I've come out in a rash.

sartén noun Fem. frying pan.

sastre noun Masc./Fem. tailor.

satélite noun Masc. satellite.

satén noun Masc. satin.

satisfacción noun Fem. satisfaction.

satisfacer verb [7] to satisfy; **la calidad del producto no nos satisface** we are not satisfied with the quality of the product; **para satisfacer mi curiosidad** to satisfy my curiosity.

satisfacerse reflexive verb [7] to be satisfied.

satisfecho/satisfecha adjective satisfied; **estamos muy satisfechos con los resultados** we are very happy with the results.

sauce noun Masc. willow.

saxofón noun Masc. saxophone.

sazonado/sazonada adjective seasoned.

sazonar verb [17] to season.

se pronoun **1** himself/herself; **se cortó** he cut himself/she cut herself; **2** itself; **se desconecta solo** it disconnects itself; **3** themselves; **¿se han portado bien?** did they behave themselves?; **4** yourself

(polite form); **espero que no se haya hecho daño** I hope you haven't hurt yourself; **5** yourselves (polite form); **¿se han divertido ustedes?** did you enjoy yourselves?; **6** him/her; **no se lo pregunté** I didn't ask him/I didn't ask her; **7** to him/to her; **se lo mandaré** I'll send it to him/I'll send it to her; **8** them; **cuando les vea se lo preguntaré** I'll ask them when I see them; **9** to them; **cuando les vea se lo daré** I'll give it to them when I see them; **10** you (polite form); **se lo dije a usted ayer** I told you yesterday; **11** to you (polite form); **se lo di a usted ayer** I gave it to you yesterday; **12** each other; **se quieren** they love each other; **se miraron** they looked at each other; **13** (with parts of your body and personal belongings); **se lavó las manos** he washed his hands/she washed her hands; **¿se ha cortado usted el dedo?** have you cut your finger?; **se pusieron la ropa** they put their clothes on; **14** (the infinitives of many verbs in Spanish end in '-se' but are not reflexive in English) **me reí mucho** I laughed a lot; **se cayó** he fell down/she fell down; **se han peleado** they've had a fight; **se levantaron** they stood up; **15** (used in impersonal phrases) **'se vende piso'** 'flat for sale'; **se habla inglés** English spoken here; **se hace así** it is done like this; **se corta la hoja en dos** cut the sheet in two.

sé verb SEE **saber**.

secador *noun Masc.* **secador de pelo** hairdryer.

secadora *noun Fem.* dryer.

secar *verb* [31] to dry.
secarse *reflexive verb* [31] **1** to dry; **¿cuánto tarda en secarse la pintura?** how long does the paint take to dry?; **la camisa ya se ha secado** the shirt's dry already; **2** to dry yourself; **secarse el pelo** to dry your hair; **secarse las lágrimas** to dry your tears; **sécate las manos con este trapo** dry your hands with this cloth; **3** to dry up.

sección *noun Fem.* **1** section; **2** department.

seco/seca *adjective* **1** dry; **limpieza en seco** dry-cleaning; **2** dried (*flowers, for example*).

secretaría *noun Fem.* secretary's office.

secretario/secretaria *noun Masc./Fem.* secretary.

secreto[1] *noun Masc.* secret.

secreto[2]**/secreta** *adjective* secret.

secuestrador/ secuestradora *noun Masc./Fem.* **1** highjacker; **2** kidnapper.

secuestrar *verb* [17] **1** to kidnap; **2** to hijack.

secuestro *noun Masc.* **1** kidnapping; **2** hijacking.

secundario/secundaria *adjective* secondary.

sed *noun Fem.* thirst; **tenían sed** they were thirsty; **las patatas fritas me dan sed** crisps make me thirsty.

seda *noun Fem.* silk.

sedal *noun Masc.* fishing line.

sede *noun Fem.* **la sede de las Olimpiadas** the venue for the Olympics; **la sede de la compañía** the company's head office; **la sede del gobierno** the seat of government.

seguida[1] *in phrase* **en seguida** straight away; **voy en seguida** I'll be right there.

seguido[1]**/seguida**[2] *adjective* **1 tres días seguidos** three days in a row; **dan las dos películas seguidas** they show both films one after the other; **los tres autobuses vinieron seguidos** the three buses came one after the other; **2 seguido de** followed by.

seguido[2] *adverb* straight on; **vaya todo seguido** go straight on.

seguir *verb* [64] **1** to follow; **seguir a alguien** to follow somebody; **seguir una pista** to follow a trail; **seguir un consejo** to follow a piece of advice; **2** to carry on, to continue; **sigamos** let's carry on; **3 seguir haciendo** to carry on doing; **colgué el teléfono y seguí leyendo** I put down the telephone and carried on reading; **4 seguir haciendo** to be still doing; **siguen viviendo en Sevilla** they're still living in Seville; **5** to go on; **siga todo recto** go straight on; **siga por esta calle** go on down this street.

según *preposition* **1** according to; **según la ley** according to the law; **2 según parece** apparently; **3 según dijo él** from what he said.

a
b
c
d
e
f
g
h
i
j
k
l
m
n
ñ
o
p
q
r
s
t
u
v
w
x
y
z

a
b
c
d
e
f
g
h
i
j
k
l
m
n
ñ
o
p
q
r
s
t
u
v
w
x
y
z

según *adverb* '¿te interesa apuntarte?' – 'según' 'would you be interested in enrolling?' – 'it depends'.

según *conjunction* as; **según los vayas terminando** as you finish them.

segunda[1] *noun Fem.* **la segunda** second gear.

segundo[1] *noun Masc.* **1** second; **espera un segundo** wait a moment; **no tardé ni un segundo en hacerlo** it didn't take me a minute to do it; **2 el segundo** the main course.

segundo[2]/**segunda**[2] *adjective* **1** second; **segunda clase** second class; **viven en el segundo piso** they live on the second floor; **llegar en segundo lugar** to finish in second position; **2 en segundo plano** in the background.

seguridad *noun Fem.* **1** security; **seguridad nacional** national security; **2** safety; **por razones de seguridad** for safety reasons; **3** certainty; **no lo sé con seguridad** I don't know for certain; **4 seguridad social** social security.

seguro[1] *noun Masc.* **1** insurance; **hacerse un seguro** to take out insurance; **seguro a todo riesgo** comprehensive insurance; **seguro contra incendios** fire insurance; **¿tienes seguro médico?** have you got medical insurance?; **2** clasp (*of a bracelet*); **3** safety catch (*on a weapon*); **4 el Seguro Social** Security.

seguro[2]/**segura** *adjective* **1** safe; **la escalera no es muy segura** the

ladder isn't very safe; **aquí me siento seguro** I feel safe here; **2 seguro/segura de sí mismo/mismoes muy segura de sí misma** she's very self-confident; **3** sure; **¿estás seguro de que se pone así?** are you sure this is the way to put it?; **estoy completamente seguro** I'm absolutely certain; **4** definite; **no es seguro todavía** it's not definite yet; **5** reliable; **es un método muy seguro** it's a very reliable method.

seguro[3] *adverb* definitely; **irán seguro** they'll definitely go; **seguro que no están** I bet they're not there.

seis *number* **1** six; **tiene seis años** he's six (years old); **2** sixth (*in dates*); **el seis de junio** the sixth of June; **3** six (*in clock time*); **son las seis** it's six o'clock.

seiscientos/seiscientas *number* six hundred; **seiscientos dos** six hundred and two.

selección *noun Fem.* **1** selection; **2 la selección nacional** the national team.

seleccionar *verb* [17] to select.

self-service *noun Masc.* self-service restaurant.

sello *noun Masc.* **1** stamp; **2 sello discográfico** record label.

selva *noun Fem.* **1** jungle; **2** forest; **la selva tropical** the tropical rainforest.

semáforo *noun Masc.* traffic lights; **saltarse un semáforo en rojo** to go through a red light; **cuando llegue al semáforo, tuerza a la derecha**

when you get to the traffic lights, turn right.

semana *noun Fem.* week; **la próxima semana** next week; **entre semana** during the week; **Semana Santa** Easter; **en Semana Santa** at Easter.

semanal *adjective* weekly.

semanalmente *adverb* weekly.

sembrar *verb* [29] **1** to sow; **2** to plant.

semejante *adjective* similar; **semejante a** similar to.

semifinal *noun Fem.* semifinal.

semilla *noun Fem.* seed.

sémola *noun Fem.* semolina.

sencillo¹ *noun Masc.* **1** single (*record*); **2** single ticket.

sencillo²/sencilla *adjective* **1** simple; **2** modest.

senda *noun Fem.* path.

senderismo *noun Masc.* trekking.

senderista *noun Masc./Fem.* hiker.

seno *noun Masc.* **1** breast; **2** bosom.

sensación *noun Fem.* **1** feeling; **tengo la sensación de que** … I have the feeling that …; **una sensación de tristeza** a feeling of sadness; **2** sense; **una sensación de pérdida** a sense of loss; **3** sensation; **causar sensación** to cause a sensation; **su llegada causó sensación** her arrival caused a sensation.

sensacional *adjective* sensational; **una noticia sensacional** a sensational piece of news.

sensatez *noun Fem.* sense; **tener sensatez** to be sensible; **actuar con sensatez** to act sensibly.

sensato/sensata *adjective* sensible.

sensibilidad *noun Fem.* sensitivity.

sensible *adjective* **1** sensitive; **2** noticeable (*difference or change*).

sensiblemente *adverb* considerably.

sentado/sentada *adjective* **estar sentado** to be sitting; **estaban sentados cerca de la puerta** they were sitting near the door; **estábamos sentados a la mesa** we were sitting at the table; **permanezcan sentados, por favor** please remain seated.

sentar *verb* [29] **1** to sit; **senté al niño en su silla** I sat the baby on his chair; **2** to suit; **ese vestido te sienta muy bien** that dress really suits you; **el rojo me sienta fatal** red doesn't suit me at all; **3 los pimientos me sientan mal** peppers don't agree with me.
sentarse *reflexive verb* [29] to sit down.

sentido *noun Masc.* **1** sense; **sentido del deber** sense of duty; **sentido común** common sense; **2 no tiene sentido** it doesn't make sense; **en sentido literal** in the literal sense; **3** consciousness; **perder el sentido** to lose consciousness; **4** direction; **venían en sentido contrario** they were coming from the opposite direction; **en sentido de las agujas del reloj**

a
b
c
d
e
f
g
h
i
j
k
l
m
n
ñ
o
p
q
r
s
t
u
v
w
x
y
z

clockwise; **en el sentido contrario al de las agujas del reloj** anticlockwise; **5 calle de sentido único** one-way street.

sentimental *adjective*
1 sentimental; **2 ¿qué tal tu vida sentimental?** how's your love life?.

sentimiento *noun Masc.* **1** feeling; **2 te acompaño en el sentimiento** my condolences.

sentir *verb* [14] **1** to feel; **sentir dolor** to feel pain; **sentir sed** to feel thirsty; **sentir alegría** to feel happy; **2 sentir un ruido** to hear a noise; **3** (*used to express apology*) **lo siento mucho** I'm very sorry; **siento llegar tarde** sorry I'm late; **sentimos tener que comunicarle que ...** we regret to inform you that ....
sentirse *reflexive verb* [14] to feel; **¿cómo te sientes?** how do you feel?; **no se sentía bien y se fue a casa** he wasn't feeling well and he went home; **me siento un poco cansado** I feel a bit tired.

seña *noun Fem.* **1** sign; **hacer una seña** to make a sign; **me hizo señas para que entrase** he beckoned to me to come in; **2 señas** address; **¿quieres darme tus señas?** would you like to give me your address?.

señal *noun Fem.* **1** sign; **señal de tráfico** traffic sign; **2 en señal de amistad** as a token of friendship; **3** sign; **hacer una señal** to make a sign; **nos estaba haciendo señales** she was signalling to us; **4** deposit; **dar una señal** to pay a deposit.

señalar *verb* [17] **1** to point; **señaló hacia la casa** he pointed to the

house; **no es de buena educación señalar con el dedo** it's bad manners to point at people; **2** to point out; **señaló que ...** she pointed out that ...; **3** to fix (*a date or time*).
señalarse *reflexive verb* [17] **se señaló la pierna** he pointed at his leg.

señor *noun Masc.* **1** gentleman; **había un señor esperando** there was a gentleman waiting; **2** sir; **perdone señor, ¿me deja pasar?** excuse me sir, could you let me through?; **3** Mr; **el señor Puyol** Mr Puyol; **los señores López** Mr and Mrs López; (*note that sometimes 'señor' is used in Spanish before somebody's first name as a sign of respect, for example 'el señor Mateo' and also in front of titles*) **el señor presidente** the President; **4 Muy señor mío** Dear Sir (*in letters*); **5** (*for emphasis*) **no señor, eso no se hace** you mustn't do that; **si señor, es verdad** yes, that's quite right.

señora *noun Fem.* **1** lady; **una señora se me acercó** a lady came up to me; **2** madam; **perdone señora, ¿me deja pasar?** excuse me madam, could you let me through?; **3** Mrs, Ms; **la señora Frutos** Ms Frutos (*in Spain, women use their maiden name after they get married and not their husband's surname*) **Doña Ana Villa, señora de García** Mrs Ana García (*literally, Ms Ana Villa, marrried to Mr García*) (*note that sometimes 'señora' is used in Spanish before somebody's first name as a sign of respect, for example 'la señora Juana'*); **4** wife;

fui de vacaciones con mi señora I went on holiday with my wife; **5** (*for emphasis*) **no señora, no fui yo** it was not me; **sí señora, es mío** it certainly is mine.

señorita *noun Fem.* **1** young lady; **le ha llamado una señorita** a young lady has called you; **2** Miss, Ms; **la señorita García** Miss García, Ms García (*'señorita' is also used to address a teacher*) **aquí están mis deberes, señorita** here's my homework, Miss; **3** (*for emphasis*) **no señorita, no se lo dejo** I am certainly not lending it to you.

sepa, **sepan**, etc. *verb* SEE **saber**.

separación *noun Fem.* **1** gap; **2** separation.

separado/separada *adjective* **1** separated; **2 por separado** separately.

separar *verb* [17] **1** to separate; **2** to move (something) away; **separa la silla de la chimenea** move the chair away from the fire.
separarse *reflexive verb* [17] **1** to separate (*a couple*); **2 nunca nos hemos separado antes** we've never been apart before.

septiembre *noun Masc.* September; **en septiembre/en el mes de septiembre** in September.

séptimo/séptima *adjective* seventh; **el séptimo piso** the seventh floor.

sequía *noun Fem.* drought.

ser *noun Masc.* **ser humano** human being.

ser *verb* [1] **1** to be; **es muy bonito** it's very beautiful; **es soltero** he's single; **es muy simpática** she's very friendly; **soy bastante alta** I'm quite tall; **'¿quién es?' – 'soy yo'** 'who's that?' – 'it's me'; **mi madre es médico** my mother's a doctor; **estas naranjas son buenísimas** these oranges are really nice; **¿cuánto es?** how much is it?; **hoy es once** it's the eleventh today; **eran las seis y media** it was half past six; **2 ser de** to be from; **mi amiga es de Argentina** my friend is from Argentina; **3 el coche es de Juan** the car is Juan's; **era de mi hermano** it was my brother's; **4 ser de** to be made of; **es de madera** it's made of wood; **es de metal** it's made of metal; **5** (*passive use*) to be; **la propuesta ha sido rechazada** the proposal has been rejected; **6 cuando sea** whenever; **como sea** however; **donde sea** wherever; **7 lo que sea** whatever; **8 ya sea ... o ...** either ... or ...; **ya sea por carta o por teléfono** either by post or by telephone; **9 o sea, que no lo has terminado** so, you haven't finished; **dentro de una semana, o sea el próximo jueves** in a week, that is, next Thursday; **10 a no ser** unless; **a no ser que no le interese** unless he's not interested.

será, **seré**, **sería**, etc. *verb* SEE **ser**.

serie *noun Fem.* **1** series; **fabricación en serie** mass production; **2 fuera de serie** out of this world.

a
b
c
d
e
f
g
h
i
j
k
l
m
n
ñ
o
p
q
r
s
t
u
v
w
x
y
z

serio/seria *adjective* **1** serious; **ponerse serio** to have a serious expression; **un problema serio** a serious problem; **2** reliable (*a person*); **3** reputable (*a company*); **4 lo digo en serio** I mean it.

serpiente *noun Fem.* snake.

servicio *noun Masc.* **1** service; **servicios públicos** public services; **servicio incluido** service included; **servicio de atención al cliente** customer services; **2 estar de servicio** to be on duty; **3 'servicios'** 'toilets'; **4 servicio militar** military service.

servilleta *noun Fem.* serviette.

servir *verb* [57] **1** to serve; **servir la sopa** to serve the soup; **¿te sirvo más vino?** shall I pour you some more wine?; **2** to be of use; **estas herramientas ya no sirven** these tools are no good any more; **3 servir para algo** to be used for; **¿para qué sirve este interruptor?** what's this switch for?; **esto no nos sirve para abrirlo** this is no use for opening it; **4 no sirves para nada** you're useless; **yo no sirvo para camarera** I'm no good as a waitress.

servirse *reflexive verb* [57] to help yourself to; **se sirvió ensalada** she helped herself to some salad; **sírvete más** help yourself to some more.

sesenta *number* sixty; **tiene sesenta años** he's sixty (years old); **sesenta y dos** sixty-two; **los años sesenta** the sixties.

sesión *noun Fem.* **1** session; **2** performance; **la sesión de noche** the evening performance; **sesión continua** continuous performance.

seta *noun Fem.* **1** mushroom; **2** toadstool.

setecientos/setecientas *number* seven hundred; **setecientos ochenta** seven hundred and eighty.

setenta *number* seventy; **tiene setenta años** he's seventy (years old); **setenta y dos** seventy-two; **los años setenta** the seventies.

seto *noun Masc.* hedge.

severo/severa *adjective* **1** severe (*person, punishment*); **2** harsh (*climate*)

sexo *noun Masc.* sex.

sexto/sexta *adjective* sixth; **el sexto piso** the sixth floor.

sexual *adjective* sexual; **tener relaciones sexuales con alguien** to have sex with someone.

sí *adverb* yes; **sí, es cierto** yes, it's true; **'¿lo vas a comprar?' – 'sí'** 'are you going to buy it? ' – 'yes I am'; **'¿es suyo?' – 'creo que sí'** 'is it hers? ' – 'I think so'; **ellos no lo saben, pero yo sí** they don't know, but I do.

sí *pronoun* **1** himself/herself; **pensó para sí** he thought to himself/she thought to herself; **2** (*polite form*) yourself, (*polite form*) yourselves; **3** itself; **este problema es, en sí mismo** ... this problem is, in itself ...; **4** themselves; **los dos hermanos lo quieren todo para sí** both brothers want everything for themselves; **5 sí mismo** himself; **sí**

misma herself; **quiere hacerlo por sí mismo** he wants to do it by himself; **quiere hacerlo por sí misma** she wants to do it by herself; **6 sí mismo/sí misma** yourself (*polite form*); **sí mismos/sí mismas** yourselves (*polite form*); **7 sí mismo** oneself; **reírse de sí mismo** to laugh at oneself; **8 entre sí** between themselves.

si *conjunction* **1** if; **si yo estuviera en tu lugar** if I were you; **si lo hubiese sabido** ... if I had known ...; **si tuviese dinero, lo compraría** if I had the money I would buy it; **2** whether; **no sé si podré** I don't know whether I'll be able to; **tanto si quiere como si no** whether he wants to or not.

Sicilia *noun Fem.* Sicily.

sida *noun Masc.* Aids.

sidra *noun Fem.* cider.

siempre *adverb* **1** always; **casi siempre** almost always; **desde siempre** always; **2 para siempre** for ever; **¿te vas a quedar allí para siempre?** are you going to stay there for ever?; **3 como siempre** as usual; **la historia de siempre** the usual story; **4 siempre que** whenever; **siempre que puedo** whenever I can.

sienta, siento, etc. *verb* SEE **sentar, sentir.**

sierra *noun Fem.* **1** saw; **2** range of mountains; **veranean en la sierra** they spend their summer holidays in the mountains.

siesta *noun Fem.* nap; **echarse una siesta** (*informal*) to have a nap; **está durmiendo la siesta** he's having a nap.

siete *number* **1** seven; **tiene siete años** she's seven (years old); **2** seventh (*in dates*); **hoy es siete de abril** it's the seventh of April today; **3** seven (*in clock time*); **son las siete** it's seven o'clock.

siga, sigan, etc. *verb* SEE **seguir.**

siglo *noun Masc.* century; **el siglo XIII** the 13th century (*centuries are always indicated in roman numbers in Spanish*); **hace un siglo que no nos vemos** (*informal*) we haven't seen each other for ages.

significado *noun Masc.* meaning.

significar *verb* [31] to mean; **¿qué significa esta palabra?** what does this word mean?; **eso no significa nada para él** that doesn't mean anything to him.

signo *noun Masc.* **1** sign; **signo del zodiaco** star sign; **¿de qué signo eres?** what sign are you?; **2** mark; **signo de exclamación** exclamation mark; **signo de interrogación** question mark.

sigo, sigue, etc. *verb* SEE **seguir.**

siguiente *noun Masc./Fem.* **el siguiente, por favor** next, please. **siguiente** *adjective* next, following; **al día siguiente** ... the next day ....

siguió *verb* SEE **seguir.**

sílaba *noun Fem.* syllable.

silbar *verb* [17] to whistle.

silbato *noun Masc.* whistle; **tocar el silbato** to blow the whistle.

a
b
c
d
e
f
g
h
i
j
k
l
m
n
ñ
o
p
q
r
s
t
u
v
w
x
y
z

silbido *noun Masc.* whistle; **dar un silbido** to whistle.

silencio *noun Masc.* silence.

silenciosamente *adverb* quietly.

silencioso/silenciosa *adjective* quiet.

silla *noun Fem.* chair; **silla de montar** saddle (*for a horse*); **una silla de ruedas** a wheelchair.

sillín *noun Masc.* saddle (*on a bicycle*).

sillón *noun Masc.* armchair.

símbolo *noun Masc.* symbol.

similar *adjective* similar; **similar a** similar to.

similitud *noun Fem.* similarity.

simio *noun Masc./Fem.* ape.

simpático/simpática *adjective* nice; **me cae simpático** I think he's really nice.

simple *adjective* 1 simple; 2 mere; **una simple formalidad** a mere formality.

simplemente *adverb* simply.

simplificar *verb* [31] to simplify.

simular *verb* [17] 1 to feign; 2 to fake.

simultáneo/simultánea *adjective* simultaneous.

sin *preposition* 1 without; **sin esfuerzo** without effort; **lo hice sin pensar** I did it without thinking; 2 **agua mineral sin gas** still mineral water; **cerveza sin alcohol** non-alcoholic beer; 3 **está sin revisar** it hasn't been checked yet; **terminó sin amigos** he ended up with no friends; **nos quedamos sin dinero** we ran out of money; **estamos sin azúcar** we're out of sugar; 4 **sin querer** unintentionally; 5 **sin embargo** nevertheless.

sinagoga *noun Fem.* synagogue.

sinceramente *adverb* 1 sincerely; 2 quite honestly.

sinceridad *noun Fem.* sincerity.

sincero/sincera *adjective* sincere.

sindicalista *noun Masc./Fem.* trade unionist.

sindicato *noun Masc.* trade union.

singular *noun Masc.* singular; **en singular** in the singular.

siniestro¹ *noun Masc.* 1 accident; 2 disaster.

siniestro²/siniestra *adjective* sinister.

sino *conjunction* but; **no verde, sino amarillo** not green but yellow.

sinónimo *noun Masc.* synonym. **sinónimo** *adjective* synonymous.

sintético/sintética *adjective* synthetic.

sintieron, sintió, etc. *verb* SEE **sentir**.

síntoma *noun Masc.* symptom.

sintonizar *verb* [22] to tune in.

sinvergüenza *noun Masc./Fem.* 1 swine; 2 crook; 3 rascal.

siquiera *adverb* 1 at least; **dales siquiera un poco de dinero** give them at least a bit of money; 2 **ni siquiera** not even; **ni siquiera me di cuenta** I didn't even realise.

sirena *noun Fem.* **1** mermaid; **2** siren.

sistema *noun Masc.* system.

sitio *noun Masc.* **1** place; **ponlo otra vez en su sitio** put it back in its place; **2** room; **no tengo sitio en la maleta** I haven't got any room in my suitcase; **hay sitio para uno más en el coche** there's room for one more in the car; **hacer sitio** to make room; **3** seat; **hay un sitio al lado de la ventana** there's a seat by the window; **4 en cualquier sitio** anywhere; **en algún sitio** somewhere; **en ningún sitio** nowhere; **en otro sitio** somewhere else; **5** siege; **6 un sitio web** a web site.

situación *noun Fem.* **1** situation; **2** position; **la situación de la casa es buena** the house is in a good position.

situado/situada *adjective* situated.

situar *verb* [20] **1** to site (*a building*); **2** to set (*a plot in a novel*). **situarse** *reflexive verb* [20] **1** to be situated; **2 situarse en primer puesto** to reach the first position; **3 situarse bien en la vida** to do very well for yourself.

smoking *noun Masc.* dinner jacket.

sobaco *noun Masc.* armpit.

sobra *in phrase* **1 de sobra** to spare; **tenemos pan de sobra** we have plenty of bread; **hay una silla de sobra** there's a spare chair; **2 saber algo de sobra** to know something full well; **3 aquí estás de sobra** you're not wanted here;

como estaba de sobra me fui I wasn't needed, so I left.

sobrar *verb* [17] **1 nos ha sobrado vino** we had a lot of wine left over; **¿te sobró algo de papel?** did you have any paper left over?; **va a sobrar dinero** there will be money left over; **2 le sobraba una entrada** he had a spare ticket; **3 aquí sobra dinero** there is too much money here; **sobran tres sillas** there are three chairs too many; **4 nos sobraba un sitio** we'd got an extra place; **5 nos sobra tiempo** we have plenty of time.

sobras *plural noun Fem.* leftovers.

sobre *noun Masc.* envelope. **sobre** *preposition* **1** on; **lo dejó sobre la cama** he left it on the bed; **2** above; **la lámpara que está sobre el sofá** the lamp above the sofa; **sobre el nivel del mar** above sea level; **3** over; **el puente sobre el río** the bridge over the river; **4** about; **una conferencia sobre literatura** a lecture about literature; **5 sobre todo** especially.

sobredosis *noun Fem.* overdose.

sobrenatural *adjective* supernatural.

sobrepasar *verb* [17] to exceed.

sobresaliente *noun Masc.* mark between 8.5 and 10 (out of 10). **sobresaliente** *adjective* outstanding, excellent.

sobresalir *verb* [63] **1 sobresalir en algo** to excel in something; **2** to overhang; **3** to protrude.

a
b
c
d
e
f
g
h
i
j
k
l
m
n
ñ
o
p
q
r
s
t
u
v
w
x
y
z

a
b
c
d
e
f
g
h
i
j
k
l
m
n
ñ
o
p
q
r
s
t
u
v
w
x
y
z

sobresalto *noun Masc.* fright; **llevarse un sobresalto** to get a fright.

sobreviviente *noun Masc./Fem.* survivor.

sobrevivir *verb* [19] to survive; **sobrevivir a algo** to survive something.

sobrina *noun Fem.* niece.

sobrino *noun Masc.* nephew; **sobrinos** nephews, nephews and nieces.

sociable *adjective* sociable.

social *adjective* social.

socialista *noun Masc./Fem.*, **socialista** *adjective* socialist.

sociedad *noun Fem.* **1** society; **la sociedad de consumo** the consumer society; **2 sociedad anónima** public limited company.

socio/socia *noun Masc./Fem.* member; **hacerse socio de algo** to join something.

socorrer *verb* [18] to help.

socorrista *noun Masc./Fem.* lifeguard; **¿hay un socorrista en la playa?** is there a lifeguard at the beach?

socorro *noun Masc.* help; **pedir socorro** to ask for help. **socorro** *exclamation* ¡socorro! help!

sofá *noun Masc.* sofa.

sofocar *verb* [31] to put out (*a fire*). **sofocarse** *reflexive verb* [31] to get worked up.

sois *verb* SEE **ser**.

soja *noun Fem.* soya.

sol *noun Masc.* sun; **hacía sol** it was sunny; **un día de sol** a sunny day; **al ponerse el sol** at sunset; **el sol estaba saliendo** the sun was rising; **sentarse al sol** to lie in the sun.

solamente *adverb* only.

soldado *noun Masc./Fem.* soldier.

soleado/soleada *adjective* sunny.

soledad *noun Fem.* loneliness.

soler *verb* [38] **1 suele salir por las noches** he usually goes out in the evenings; **suelen verse** they usually see each other; **no suele importarle** he usually doesn't mind; **2 solía escribirme de vez en cuando** she used to write to me from time to time.

sólido/sólida *adjective* **1** solid; **2** sound.

solitario/solitaria *adjective* lonely.

solo/sola *adjective* **1** alone; **vive solo** he lives alone; **cuando me quedé solo** when I was left alone; **2** lonely; **está muy sola** she's very lonely; **sentirse solo** to feel lonely; **3** on your own; **desde que murió su madre está sola** she's been on her own since her mother died; **4** by yourself; **lo hice sola** I did it by myself; **5 con una sola mano** with one hand; **sin una sola queja** without a single complaint; **6 un café solo** a black coffee; **una ginebra sola** a straight gin.

sólo *adverb* only.

solomillo *noun Masc.* fillet steak.

252

soltar *verb* [24] **1** to let go of; **le solté la mano** I let go of his hand; **¡suéltame!** let go of me!; **2** to release (*a prisoner*); **3** to untie; **soltar un nudo** to untie a knot; **4** soltar al perro to let the dog off the lead; **5** soltar un grito to let out a cry; **soltar una carcajada** to let out a laugh; **soltar una palabrota** to come out with a swearword.
soltarse *reflexive verb* [24] **1** no te sueltes de la barandilla don't let go of the banister; **se soltó de mi mano** he let go of my hand; **2** soltarse el pelo to let your hair down; **3** to come undone (*a knot*).

soltero/soltera *noun Masc./Fem.* **1** bachelor (*male*); **2** single woman.
soltero *adjective* single.

soltura *noun Fem.* hablar español con soltura to speak Spanish fluently; **moverse con soltura** to move with ease.

soluble *adjective* soluble.

solución *noun Fem.* solution.

solucionar *verb* [17] **1** to solve; **2** to settle (*a conflict*).

sombra *noun Fem.* **1** shadow; **2** shade; **sentarse en la sombra** to sit in the shade; **dar sombra** to give shade; **3** sombra de ojos eye shadow.

sombrero *noun Masc.* hat.

sombrilla *noun Fem.* **1** parasol; **2** sunshade.

sombrío/sombría *adjective* **1** dark (*street or room*); **2** gloomy (*face or look*).

somos, son *verb* SEE ser.

sonar *verb* [24] **1** to sound; **suena a hueco** it sounds hollow; **sonó un ruido** there was a noise; **2** to ring (*a doorbell or telephone*); **3** el despertador no ha sonado the alarm clock hasn't gone off; **4** me suena mucho su cara her face is very familiar to me; **¿Carlos Ramírez? no me suena** Carlos Ramírez? it doesn't ring any bells.
sonarse *reflexive verb* [24] **sonarse la nariz** to blow one's nose.

soñar *verb* [24] to dream.

sondeo *noun Masc.* survey.

sonido *noun Masc.* sound.

sonreír *verb* [61] to smile; **me sonrió** he smiled at me.
sonreírse *reflexive verb* [61] to smile.

sonría, sonríe, sonrío, etc. *verb* SEE **sonreír**.

sonrisa *noun Fem.* smile.

sonrojarse *verb* [17] to blush.

sopa *noun Fem.* soup.

soplar *verb* [17] **1** to blow; **2** to blow off; **soplar el polvo de la mesa** to blow the dust off the table; **3** soplarle la respuesta a alguien (*informal*) to whisper the answer to someone (*in an exam*).

soportar *verb* [17] **1** to put up with (*situation*); **2** to bear (*pain or heat*); **3** no puedo soportar a Rafael I can't stand Rafael; **4** to withstand.

soporte *noun Masc.* support.

sorbete *noun Masc.* sorbet.

sorbo *noun Masc.* **1** sip; **beber a sorbos** to sip; **2** gulp; **beberse algo**

a
b
c
d
e
f
g
h
i
j
k
l
m
n
ñ
o
p
q
r
s
t
u
v
w
x
y
z

de un sorbo to drink something in one gulp.

sordo/sorda *noun Masc./Fem.* deaf person.
sordo *adjective* deaf.

sordomudo/sordomuda *noun Masc./Fem.* deaf mute.
sordomudo *adjective* deaf and dumb.

sorprendente *adjective* surprising.

sorprender *verb* [18] to surprise; **me sorprende que se retrase** I'm surprised he's late.
sorprenderse *reflexive verb* [18] to be surprised.

sorprendido/sorprendida *adjective* surprised.

sorpresa *noun Fem.* surprise.

soso/sosa *adjective* **1** dull; **2** bland.
soso *noun* bore.

sospecha *noun Fem.* suspicion; **tengo la sospecha de que ...** I have a feeling that ....

sospechar *verb* [17] to suspect.

sospechoso/sospechosa *adjective* suspicious; **me parece sospechoso** I find it suspicious.

sostén *noun Masc.* **1** support; **2** bra.

sostener *verb* [9] **1** to support (*arch, ceiling, or family*); **2** to bear (*a weight or load*).

sótano *noun Masc.* **1** basement; **2** cellar.

soy *verb* SEE **ser**.

Sr. *abbreviation* (*short for: Señor*) Mr.

Sra. *abbreviation* (*short for: Señora*) Mrs, Ms.

Sres. *abbreviation* (*short for: Señores*) Messrs.

Srta. *abbreviation* (*short for: Señorita*) Miss, Ms.

su *adjective* **1** his/her; **¿es su falda como ésta?** is her skirt like this one?; **ahí está Carlos con sus padres** there's Carlos with his parents; **2** its; **el perro duerme en su caseta** the dog sleeps in its kennel; **3** their; **mis padres viven allí y éste es su coche** my parents live there and that's their car; **4** your (*polite form*); **¿son éstos sus zapatos?** are these your shoes?

suave *adjective* **1** soft; **2** smooth; **3** gentle (*voice*); **4** mild (*weather*).

suavizante *noun Masc.* **1** fabric softener; **2** hair conditioner.

subestimar *verb* [17] underestimate.

subida *noun Fem.* **1** rise (*in temperature or price, for example*); **2** climb.

subir *verb* [19] **1** to go up; **el ascensor está subiendo** the lift is going up; **subir al tercer piso** to go up to the third floor; **la temperatura ha subido tres grados** the temperature has gone up three degrees; **2** to come up; **¡sube!** come up!; **3** to bring up; **sube estas cajas al segundo piso** bring these boxes up to the third floor; **súbeme un vaso de agua** bring a glass of water up for me; **4** to take up; **¿le subo las maletas a su habitación?** shall I take the luggage up to your room?;

suegra

5 to put up; **han vuelto a subir el precio de la gasolina** they've put up the price of petrol again; **6 subir al tren** to get on the train; **subir a un coche** to get into a car; **subir a bordo** to board; **7** to turn up (*volume*); **subió un poco la música** he turned up the music a bit; **8** to raise; **subir una persiana** to raise a blind; **9** to rise; **el nivel del agua ha subido** the water level has risen; **10** to come in (*the tide*).
subirse *reflexive verb* [19]
1 subirse al tren to get on the train; **subirse a un coche** to get into a car; **subirse a bordo** to board; **2 subirse a un árbol** to climb up a tree; **3 subirse los calcetines** to pull up your socks.

súbitamente *adverb* suddenly.

súbito/súbita *adjective* sudden.

subjuntivo *noun Masc.* subjunctive.

submarinismo *noun Masc.* scuba diving.

submarinista *noun Masc./Fem.* scuba diver.

submarino *noun Masc.* submarine.

subrayar *verb* [17] to underline.

subsidio *noun Masc.* **1** subsidy; **2 subsidio de desempleo** unemployment benefit; **subsidio de invalidez** disability allowance.

subterráneo[1] *noun Masc.* subway.

subterráneo[2]**/subterránea** *adjective* underground.

suburbio *noun Masc.* **1** slum area (*on the outskirts of a town*); **2** suburb.

subvención *noun Fem.* subsidy.

subvencionar *verb* [17] to subsidize.

suceder *verb* [18] **1** to happen; **¿qué le ha sucedido?** what's happened to him?; **sucedió todo muy rápido** it all happened very quickly; **2** to succeed (*to the throne*).

suceso *noun Masc.* **1** event; **2** incident; **'página de sucesos'** 'accidents and crimes report' (*in a newspaper*).

suciedad *noun Fem.* **1** dirt; **2** dirtiness.

sucio/sucia *adjective* **1** dirty; **tienes la cara sucia** your face is dirty; **2 primero hice el trabajo en sucio** I did the essay in rough first.

sucursal *noun Fem.* **1** branch (*of a bank*); **2** office (*of a company*).

sudadera *noun Fem.* sweatshirt.

Sudamérica *noun Fem.* South America.

sudamericano/ sudamericana *noun Masc./Fem., adjective* South American.

sudar *verb* [17] to sweat.

sudeste *noun Masc.* southeast.

sudoeste *noun Masc.* southwest.

sudor *noun Masc.* sweat.

Suecia *noun Fem.* Sweden.

sueco[1] *noun Masc.* Swedish (*the language*).

sueco[2]**/sueca** *noun Masc./Fem.* Swede.
sueco *adjective* Swedish.

suegra *noun Fem.* mother-in-law.

a
b
c
d
e
f
g
h
i
j
k
l
m
n
ñ
o
p
q
r
s
t
u
v
w
x
y
z

a
b
c
d
e
f
g
h
i
j
k
l
m
n
ñ
o
p
q
r
s
t
u
v
w
x
y
z

suegro *noun Masc.* **1** father-in-law; **2 mis suegros** my parents in law.

suela¹ *noun Fem.* sole.

suela², **suelas**, **etc.** *verb* SEE **soler.**

sueldo *noun Masc.* **1** salary; **2** wage; **3 aumento de sueldo** pay rise.

suelo¹ *noun Masc.* **1** floor; **2** ground; **tirarse al suelo** to throw yourself to the ground.

suelo² *verb* SEE **soler.**

suelta¹, **suelte**, **suelto**¹, **etc.** *verb* SEE **soltar.**

suelto² *noun Masc.* small change; **¿tienes suelto?** do you have any small change?.

suelto³/**suelta**² *adjective* **1** loose; **el tornillo está suelto** the screw is loose; **2 dinero suelto** small change.

suena, **suene**, **sueno**, **etc.** *verb* SEE **sonar.**

sueña, **sueñe**, **sueño**¹, **etc.** *verb* SEE **soñar.**

sueño² *noun Masc.* **1** dream; **2 tener sueño** to be sleepy; **tener el sueño ligero** to be a light sleeper.

suerte *noun Fem.* luck; **tener suerte** to be lucky; **traer mala suerte** to bring bad luck; **¡qué mala suerte!** what bad luck!

suéter *noun Masc.* sweater.

suficiente *noun Masc.* pass (*equivalent to 5 out of 10*). **suficiente** *adjective* enough.

sufrir *verb* [19] **1** to suffer; **sufre mucho** he's suffering a lot; **2** to have; **sufrir un accidente** to have an accident; **sufre una grave enfermedad** he has a serious illness.

sugerencia *noun Fem.* suggestion.

sugerir *verb* [14] to suggest.

sugestión *noun Fem.* suggestion.

sugiera, **sugiero**, **sugirieron**, **etc.** *verb* SEE **sugerir.**

suicidarse *reflexive verb* [17] to commit suicide.

suicidio *noun Masc.* suicide.

Suiza *noun Fem.* Switzerland.

suizo/suiza *noun Masc./Fem.*, *adjective* Swiss.

sujetador *noun Masc.* bra.

sujeto/sujeta *adjective* **1** secure; **está bien sujeto** it's really secure; **2 tener sujeto a** to have hold of; **3 estar sujeto a algo** to be subject to something.

suma *noun Fem.* **1** addition; **2 en suma** in short.

sumar *verb* [17] to add.

supe, **supiste**, **etc.** *verb* SEE **saber.**

súper, **super** *adjective* (*informal*) super.

súper *adverb* (*informal*) really; **cantan súper bien** they sing really well; **me lo pasé súper bien** I had a great time.

superar *verb* [17] **1** to overcome (*fear or a problem*); **2** to get over (*a shock*); **3** to exceed.

superficie *noun Fem.* surface.

superior *adjective* **1** superior; **es superior a los demás en calidad**

it's better quality than all the others; **2** top (*floor or layer*); **3** upper (*lip*); **4** higher (*level or class*).

supermercado *noun Masc.* supermarket.

superstición *noun Fem.* superstition.

supersticioso/ supersticiosa *adjective* superstitious.

supervisar *verb* [17] supervise.

supervisor/supervisora *noun Masc./Fem.* supervisor.

superviviente *noun Masc./Fem.* survivor.

suplementario/ suplementaria *adjective* additional.

suplemento *noun Masc.* supplement.

supondrá, **supondré**, **supondría**, **etc.** *verb* SEE **suponer**.

suponer *verb* [11] to suppose; **supongo que sí** I suppose so.

suponga, **supongo**, **etc.** *verb* SEE **suponer**.

supositorio *noun Masc.* suppository.

suprimir *verb* [19] **1** to suppress (*news*); **2** to abolish; **3** to delete.

supuesto *in phrase* **por supuesto** of course.

supuse, **supuso** *verb* SEE **suponer**.

sur *noun Masc.* south.

Suramérica *noun Fem.* South America.

suramericano/ suramericana *noun Masc./Fem.*, **suramericano** *adjective* South American.

sureste *noun Masc.* southest.

surf *noun Masc.* surfing; **practicar el surf** to go surfing.

surfista *noun Masc./Fem.* surfer (*in the sea*).

suroeste *noun Masc.* southwest.

surtido[1] *noun Masc.* **1** assortment; **2** selection.

surtido[2]**/surtida** *adjective* **1** assorted; **2** **una tienda bien surtida** a well-stocked shop.

surtidor *noun Masc.* petrol pump.

suspender *verb* [18] **1** to fail; **he suspendido la física** I've failed physics; **2** to suspend (*a payment or service*); **3** **suspender un viaje** to call off a trip.

suspense *noun Masc.* suspense; **película de suspense** thriller (*film*).

suspenso *noun Masc.* fail; **sacar un suspenso en examen** to fail an exam.

suspirar *verb* [17] to sigh.

suspiro *noun Masc.* sigh.

sustancia *noun Fem.* substance.

sustantivo *noun Masc.* noun.

sustituir *verb* [54] **1** to replace; **sustituir algo por algo** to replace something with something; **2** **sustituir a alguien** to stand in for someone (*at work*), to come on as a substitute for someone (*in football, for example*).

a b c d e f g h i j k l m n ñ o p q r **s** t u v w x y z

a
b
c
d
e
f
g
h
i
j
k
l
m
n
ñ
o
p
q
r
s
t
u
v
w
x
y
z

sustituto/sustituta noun Masc./Fem. **1** replacement; **2** substitute; **3** locum.

susto noun Masc. fright; **darle un susto a alguien** to give someone a fright; **¡qué susto me llevé!** I got such a fright!

sustraer verb [42] to subtract.

susurrar verb [17] to whisper.

sutil adjective subtle.

suyo/suya adjective **1** his/hers; (goes after the noun) **un conocido suyo** a friend of his/hers; **2** theirs; **venían con un amigo suyo** they came with a friend of theirs; **3** yours (polite form).
suyo pronoun **1** his/hers; **el suyo es gris** his/hers is grey; **las suyas son mejores** his/hers are better; **2** yours (polite form); **3** theirs; **no es el de mis hijos, el suyo es más grande** it's not my children's, theirs is bigger.

Tt

tabaco noun Masc. **1** tobacco; **2** cigarettes; **tengo que comprar tabaco** I've got to buy some cigarettes.

taberna noun Fem. bar (selling wine).

tabla noun Fem. **1** plank; **2** board; **una tabla de planchar** an ironing board; **una tabla de picar** a chopping board; **3 tabla de multiplicar** multiplication table; **4 tabla de gimnasia** circuit training; **5** pleat.

tablao noun Masc. **un tablao flamenco** a flamenco bar.

tablero noun Masc. **1** board (for a game); **un tablero de damas** a draughtboard; **2** noticeboard.

tablón noun Masc. **1** plank; **2 tablón de anuncios** noticeboard.

taburete noun Masc. stool.

tacaño/tacaña noun Masc./Fem. miser.
tacaño adjective stingy.

tachar verb [17] to cross out.

taco noun Masc. **1** cue (in billards); **2** stud (on a sports boot); **3** (informal) swearword.

tacón noun Masc. heel; **zapatos de tacón alto** high-heeled shoes; **tacón de aguja** stiletto heel.

táctica noun Fem. **1** tactic; **2** tactics.

tacto noun Masc. **1** sense of touch; **2** feel; **3** tact; **fue una falta de tacto** it was really tactless.

tal adjective **1** such; **tal cosa es imposible** such a thing is impossible; **2 tenía tal preocupación que** ... I was so worried that ...; **había tal cantidad de cajas que** ... there were so many boxes that ...; **3 en tal caso** in that case.
tal adverb **1 ¿qué tal estás?** (informal) how are you doing?; **¿qué tal van las cosas?** (informal) how are things?; **2 tal vez** maybe; **3 con tal de que** as long as; ★ **son tal para cual** one is as bad as the other.

talco noun Masc. talc; **polvos de talco** talcum powder.

talento noun Masc. talent.

TALGO abbreviation Masc. (*short for: Tren Articulado Ligero Goicoechea Oriol*) express train.

talla noun Fem. size; **¿qué talla de pantalones tienes?** what size of trousers do you take?

taller noun Masc. **1** workshop; **2** garage; **llevar el coche al taller** to take the car to the garage.

talón noun Masc. heel.

talonario noun Masc. chequebook.

tamaño noun Masc. size; **hay de todos los tamaños** they come in all sizes.

también adverb too; **ella también vive allí** she lives there too; **'tengo quince años' – 'yo también'** 'I'm fifteen' – 'so am I'; **'yo quiero tarta' – 'yo también'** 'I want some cake' – 'so do I'.

tambor noun Masc. drum.

tampoco adverb **él tampoco irá** he won't go either; **'a mí no me gusta' – 'a mí tampoco'** 'I don't like it' – 'neither do I'.

tampón noun Masc. tampon.

tan adverb **1** so; **no es tan fácil** it's not so easy; **2** such; **es una persona tan egoísta** he's such a selfish person; **3** (*in comparisons*) **es tan alto como su padre** he's as tall as his father; **no era tan caro como el otro** it wasn't as expensive as the other one; **4 ¡qué casa tan grande!** what a big house!

tanque noun Masc. tank.

tanto[1] noun Masc. **1 tanto por ciento** percentage; **gano un tanto por ciento de las ventas** I get a percentage on the sales; **2** point, goal; **marcar un tanto** to score a point, to score a goal.

tanto[2] adverb **1** so; **tanto mejor** so much the better; **no corras tanto** don't go so fast; **se enfadó tanto** he got so upset; **2** so much; **no deberías gastar tanto** you shouldn't spend so much; **3** so often; **yo no les visito tanto** I don't visit them all that often; **4** so long; **lleva tanto hacerlo** it takes so long to do; **5 pesa tanto como éste** it's as heavy as this one.

tanto[3]/**tanta** adjective **1** so much; **tanto dinero** so much money; **tanta sal** so much salt; **2** so many; **tantos libros** so many books; **tantas cajas** so many boxes; **había tanta gente que no cabíamos** there were so many people that there wasn't room for us; **3 tanto/tanta ... como ...** as much ... as ...; **no gasta tanta gasolina como el coche viejo** it doesn't use as much petrol as the old car; **4 tantos/tantas ... como ...** as many ... as ...; **no hay tantos alumnos como antes** there aren't as many students as before.

tanto pronoun **1 tanto/tanta** so much; **no hace falta tanto/tanta** we don't need so much; **2 tantos/tantas** so many; **vinieron tantos que no había sillas libres** so many came that there weren't any chairs left; **3 tanto** (*referring to time*) so long; **no tardes tanto como ayer** don't

a
b
c
d
e
f
g
h
i
j
k
l
m
n
ñ
o
p
q
r
s
t
u
v
w
x
y
z

take as long as yesterday; **'me llevará dos días hacerlo'** – **'¿tanto?'** 'it'll take me two days to do it' – 'as long as that?'; **4 por lo tanto** therefore; **5 mientras tanto** in the meantime; **entre tanto** in the meantime.

tapa *noun Fem.* **1** lid; **2** top; **tapa de rosca** screw top; **3** tapa (*a small snack chosen from a selection in a tapas bar*); **un bar de tapas** a tapas bar; **comer de tapas** to eat tapas for lunch, supper, etc.

tapar *verb* [17] **1** to cover; **2** to put the top on; **3 tapar un agujero** to fill a hole; **4** to block (*a road or door*).

tapón *noun Masc.* **1** cork; **2** top (*of a bottle*); **3** plug (*of a sink or bath*).

taquilla *noun Fem.* **1** box office; **éxito de taquilla** box office hit; **2** ticket office.

tardar *verb* [17] to take a long time; **tardó mucho en contestarme** she took a long time to answer; **¿cuánto se tarda de Sevilla a Córdoba?** how long does it take from Seville to Cordoba?; **¡no tardes!** don't be long!; **no tardes en volver** come back soon; **a las cuatro a más tardar** at four o'clock at the latest.

tarde *noun Fem.* afternoon, evening; **buenas tardes** good afternoon, good evening; **por la tarde** in the afternoon, in the evening.
tarde *adverb* late; **llegar tarde** to be late; **se hizo tarde** it got late; **tarde o temprano** sooner or later.

tarea *noun Fem.* **1** task; **2 las tareas de la casa** the housework; **3** homework.

tarifa *noun Fem.* **1** price list; **2 tarifa telefónica** telephone charges.

tarjeta *noun Fem.* card; **una tarjeta (postal)** a postcard; **una tarjeta de crédito** a credit card; **una tarjeta telefónica** a telephone card; **una tarjeta de embarque** a boarding card; **una tarjeta de cumpleaños** a birthday card; **una tarjeta de Navidad** a Christmas card; **una tarjeta de fidelidad** a loyalty card; **sacarle a alguien la tarjeta amarilla/roja** to show somebody the yellow/red card.

tarrina *noun Fem.* tub (*for food*).

tarro *noun Masc.* jar.

tarta *noun Fem.* cake; **una tarta de cumpleaños** a birthday cake; **tarta helada** ice-cream cake.

tartera *noun Fem.* sandwich box.

tasa *noun Fem.* **1** rate; **la tasa de interés** the interest rate; **la tasa de desempleo** the level of unemployment; **2** valuation; **3** tax.

tatuaje *noun Masc.* tatoo.

tauro *noun Masc./Fem.* taurus; **es tauro** he's Taurus.

Tauro *noun Masc.* Taurus.

taxi *noun Masc.* taxi.

taxista *noun Masc./Fem.* taxi driver.

taza *noun Fem.* **1** cup; **taza de café** coffee cup, cup of coffee; **2** (toilet) bowl.

tazón *noun Masc.* bowl.

te *pronoun* **1** you; **te quiero** I love you; **te vi ayer** I saw you yesterday; **2** to you; **te lo mandaré por correo** I'll post it to you; **3** (*with parts of the* *body and personal belongings)* **¿te has cortado el dedo?** have you cut your finger?; **¿quieres quitarte los zapatos?** do you want to take your shoes off?; **4** *(having things done)* **¿te has cortado el pelo?** have you had your hair cut?; **5** yourself; **cuídate mucho** look after yourself; **6 siéntate** sit down.

té *noun Masc.* tea; **voy a tomar un té** I'm going to have a cup of tea.

teatro *noun Masc.* theatre.

tebeo *noun Masc.* comic *(for children)*.

techo *noun Masc.* **1** ceiling; **2 techo corredizo/solar** sunroof; **3 sin techo** homeless.

tecla *noun Fem.* key.

teclado *noun Masc.* keyboard.

técnica[1] *noun Fem.* technique.

técnico/técnica[2] *noun Masc./ Fem.* technician.
  técnico *adjective* technical.

tecnología *noun Fem.* technology.

teja *noun Fem.* tile.

tejado *noun Masc.* roof.

tejanos *plural noun Masc.* jeans.

tejer *verb* [18] **1** to weave; **2** to knit.

tela *noun Fem.* **1** fabric; **tela de algodón** cotton fabric; **2** canvas *(for painting)*.

telaraña *noun Fem.* **1** spider's web; **2** cobweb; **3** spider diagram.

tele *noun Fem.* *(informal)* telly, TV; **ver la tele** to watch telly; **poner la tele** to switch on the telly.

telediario *noun Masc.* television news.

telefonear *verb* [17] to telephone.

telefónico/telefónica *adjective* telephone; **conversación telefónica** telephone conversation; **listín telefónico** telephone book.

teléfono *noun Masc.* telephone; **llamar por teléfono a alguien** to phone somebody; **no tengo teléfono** I'm not on the phone *(I don't have a phone)*; **contestar el teléfono** to answer the phone; **colgar el teléfono** to put down the phone; **estaba hablando por teléfono** I was on the phone; **no has colgado bien el teléfono** you've left the phone off the hook; **teléfono celular/móvil** mobile phone.

telegrama *noun Masc.* telegram.

telenovela *noun Fem.* TV series.

telescopio *noun Masc.* telescope.

televisión *noun Fem.* television; **ver la televisión** to watch television; **poner la televisión** to switch on the television; **hoy ponen una película en la televisión** there's a film on the television today.

televisor *noun Masc.* television set.

tema *noun Masc.* **1** subject; **2** topic.

temblar *verb* [29] **1** to shiver; **2** to shake; **le temblaban las manos** his hands were shaking.

temer *verb* [18] **1** to fear *(danger or punishment)*; **2 temer a alguien** to be afraid of somebody.
  temerse *reflexive verb* [18] **1** to fear; **2 me temo que no podré acudir** I'm afraid I won't be able to come.

a
b
c
d
e
f
g
h
i
j
k
l
m
n
ñ
o
p
q
r
s
t
u
v
w
x
y
z

a
temperatura *noun Fem.*
temperature; **ha bajado la**
b
temperatura the temperature has
c
dropped.

d
tempestad *noun Fem.* storm.

templado/templada *adjective*
e
1 mild (*climate*); **2** warm;
f
3 lukewarm.

temporada *noun Fem.* season;
g
fuera de temporada out of season.

h
temprano¹ *adverb* early; **llegar**
i
temprano to arrive early.

temprano²**/temprana**
j
adjective early.

k
tendencia *noun Fem.* tendency.

l
tender *verb* [36] **1 tender a** to tend
to; **tienden a molestarse** they tend
m
to get upset; **2 tender la ropa** to
hang out the washing.
n
tenderse *reflexive verb* [36] to lie
ñ
down; **tenderse al sol** to lie down in
the sun.

o
tendero/tendera *noun Masc./*
p
Fem. shopkeeper.

tendrá, tendré, tendría, etc.
q
verb SEE **tener**.

r
tenedor *noun Masc.* fork.

s
tener *verb* [9] **1** to have; **tengo dos**
hermanas I've got two sisters; **tiene**
t
los ojos marrones he's got brown
u
eyes; **tener dolor de cabeza** to have
a headache; **no tengo tiempo** I
v
haven't got the time; **¿tienes hora?**
have you got the time?; **ha tenido un**
w
niño she had a baby; **2 tener sed** to
x
be thirsty; **tener frío** to be cold; **¡qué**
calor tengo! I'm really hot!; **ten**
y
cuidado be careful; **3 tener sueño**
z
to feel sleepy; **tener envidia de**

alguien to be jealous of somebody;
4 tener que hacer to have to do; **no**
puedo, tengo que estudiar I can't,
I have to study; **tienes que**
obedecerme you must do as I tell
you; **tengo que ir a verla un día** I
must go and see her one day;
tendrían que ayudarme they would
have to help me; **tendría que ir al**
banco I should go to the bank;
5 tiene que haberse perdido he
must have got lost; **6 tener que ver**
con alguien; no tiene nada que ver
con él it has nothing to do with him;
7 lo tengo hecho I've done it; **lo**
tienen solucionado they've sorted
it out; **tenía pensado invitarlos** I'd
thought about inviting them.

tenga, tengo, etc. *verb* SEE
tener.

teniente *noun Masc./Fem.*
lieutenant.

tenis *noun Masc.* tennis; **tenis de**
mesa table tennis.

tenista *noun Masc./Fem.* tennis
player.

tensión *noun Fem.* **1** tension;
2 stress; **3** blood pressure; **tomarse**
la tensión to have your blood
pressure taken.

tentación *noun Fem.* temptation.

tentar *verb* [29] to tempt.

teñir *verb* [65] to dye.
teñirse *reflexive verb* [65] to dye;
teñirse el pelo to have your hair
dyed.

tercer *adjective* third (*see also*
'tercero/tercera').

tercero/tercera *adjective* (*note that 'tercero' becomes 'tercer' before a masculine singular noun*) third; **la tercera puerta a la derecha** the third door on the right; **el tercer piso** the third floor; **llegar en tercer lugar** to finish in third position; **el Tercer Mundo** the Third World.

terminado/terminada *adjective* finished.

terminal *noun Fem.* **1** terminal; **2** bus station.
terminal *adjective* terminal.

terminar *verb* [17] **1** to finish; **¿cuándo termina el colegio?** when does school finish; **aún no he terminado** I haven't finished yet; **no he terminado de revisarlo** I haven't finished checking it; **2 terminar con** to finish with; **¿has terminado con el libro?** have you finished with the book?; **ha terminado con su novio** she's broken up with her boyfriend; **3** to end up; **terminamos en una discoteca** we ended up in a disco; **terminó harta** she was fed up in the end; **terminaron por pelearse** they ended up having a fight; **4** to end in; **su nombre termina en 'l'** her name ends in 'l'; **termina en punta** it's pointed; **termina en una cruz** it's got a cross at the end.

terminarse *reflexive verb* [17] **1** to be over; **la clase se terminó a las cinco** the lesson was over at five; **2 se ha terminado la leche** we've run out of milk; **se me terminó la tinta del boli** my pen ran out (of ink).

termo™ *noun Masc.* Thermos™.

termómetro *noun Masc.* thermometer.

ternera¹ *noun Fem.* veal.

ternero/ternera² *noun Masc./ Fem.* calf.

terraza *noun Fem.* **1** balcony; **2** terrace (*of a café or bar*).

terremoto *noun Masc.* earthquake.

terreno *noun Masc.* **1** plot of land; **2** field; **3** land; **la casa tiene mucho terreno** the house has a lot of land; **4 terreno de juego** football pitch.

terrible *adjective* terrible.

territorio *noun Masc.* territory.

terrón *noun Masc.* lump (*of sugar, earth*).

terror *noun Masc.* terror.

terrorismo *noun Masc.* terrorism.

terrorista *noun Masc./Fem.*, **terrorista** *adjective* terrorist.

tesoro *noun Masc.* treasure.

test *noun Masc.* **1** test; **2 examen tipo test** multiple-choice exam.

testamento *noun Masc.* will; **hacer testamento** to make your will.

testigo *noun Masc./Fem.* witness.

tétano *noun Masc.* tetanus.

tetera *noun Fem.* teapot.

texto *noun Masc.* text.

ti *pronoun* **1** you; **detrás de ti** behind you; **se olvidaron de ti** they forgot about you; **a mí no me dijo nada, ¿y a ti?** he hasn't told me anything – has he told you?; **2** to you; **te lo dio**

a ti he gave it to you; **3 ¿a ti te gusta?** do you like it?; **¿a ti qué te parece?** what do you think?; **4 ti mismo/misma** yourself; **sabes cuidar de ti misma** you can look after yourself.

tía noun Fem. aunt.

tibio/tibia adjective lukewarm.

tiburón noun Masc. shark.

tiembla, tiemblo, etc. verb SEE **temblar.**

tiempo noun Masc. **1** time; **llegar a tiempo** to be on time; **tiempo libre** spare time; **ha pasado mucho tiempo desde entonces** it's been a long time since then; **hace mucho tiempo que no la veo** I haven't seen her for a long time; **¿cuánto tiempo hace que se fueron?** how long ago did they go?; **al mismo tiempo** at the same time; **la mayor parte del tiempo** most of the time; **2 ¿cada cuánto tiempo?** how often?; **cada cierto tiempo** every so often; **3 por un tiempo** for a while; **4 a su debido tiempo** in due course; **5 trabajar a tiempo completo** to work full time; **trabajar a tiempo parcial** to work part time; **6 en aquellos tiempos** in those days; **corren otros tiempos** things are different now; **7** weather; **el pronóstico del tiempo** the weather forecast; **nos hizo buen tiempo** we had nice weather; **8 el primer tiempo** the first half (of a match); **9** tense (in grammar).

tienda[1] noun Fem. **1** shop; **una tienda de discos** a record shop; **una tienda de recuerdos** a souvenir shop; **una tienda de comestibles** a grocer's; **2 una tienda de campaña** a tent.

tienda[2]**, tiendo, etc.** verb SEE **tender.**

tierno/tierna adjective **1** tender (meat); **2** affectionate.

tierra noun Fem. **1** land; **tierra adentro** inland; **viajar por tierra** to travel overland; **2** earth; **3** ground; **tierra firme** solid ground; **4 tomar tierra** to land.

tiesto noun Masc. flowerpot.

tigre noun Masc. tiger.

tijeras plural noun Fem. scissors; **un par de tijeras/unas tijeras** a pair of scissors.

timbre noun Masc. bell, doorbell; **tocar el timbre** to ring the bell.

tímido/tímida adjective shy.

tinta noun Fem. ink.

tinto noun Masc. red wine. **tinto** adjective red (wine).

tintorería noun Fem. dry cleaner's.

tiña, tiñeron, tiño, tiñó, etc. verb SEE **teñir.**

tío noun Masc. **1** uncle; **2 mis tíos** my uncles; my aunt and uncle; **3** (informal) guy.

tiovivo noun Masc. merry-go-round.

típico/típica adjective typical.

tipo noun Masc. **1** type; **2** figure, physique; **tiene buen tipo** she's got a good figure; **3 tipo de cambio** exchange rate; **tipo de interés** interest rate.

tirantes noun Masc. (plural) braces.

tirar *verb* [17] **1** to throw; **tirar algo al suelo** to throw something on the floor; **2 tirarle algo a alguien** to throw something at somebody; **tírame ese boli** throw me that pen; **3** to throw away; **no tires esos papeles** don't throw those papers away; **tirar algo a la basura** to throw something out (*that you no longer want*); **4** to pull; **tira un poco más** pull a bit more; **5 tirar de algo** to pull something; **tira de la cuerda cuando yo te diga** pull the rope when I tell you; **6 tirarle de las orejas a alguien** to tweak somebody's ear (*in Spain you do this when you wish somebody happy birthday*); **7** to shoot; **tirar una flecha** to shoot an arrow; **tirar una bomba** to drop a bomb; **8** to knock over; **tiré una silla sin querer** I accidentally knocked a chair over; **9** to knock down; **tiraron la puerta abajo** they knocked the door down. **tirarse** *reflexive verb* [17] **tirarse al suelo** to throw yourself to the ground; **tirarse al agua** to dive into the water; **tirarse en paracaídas** to parachute, to bale out.

tirita™ *noun Fem.* sticking plaster.

tiritar *verb* [17] to shiver; **tiritar de frío** to shiver with cold.

tiro *noun Masc.* **1** shot; **disparar un tiro** to fire a shot; **matar a alguien de un tiro** to shoot somebody dead; **tiro al blanco** target shooting; **2** shot (*in sport*); **un tiro a portería** a shot at goal; **un tiro libre** a free kick.

tirón *noun Masc.* pull; **dar un tirón a algo** to pull something; ★**de un tirón** (*informal*) in one go.

títere *noun Masc.* **1** puppet; **2 títeres** puppet show.

título *noun Masc.* **1** title; **2** heading; **3** degree; **título universitario** university degree; **4** certificate; **5 título nobiliario** title (*such as 'duke' or 'duchess'*).

tiza *noun Fem.* chalk; **una tiza** a piece of chalk.

toalla *noun Fem.* towel.

tobillo *noun Masc.* ankle.

tobogán *noun Masc.* slide.

tocador *noun Masc.* dressing table.

tocar *verb* [31] **1** to touch; **me tocó el hombro** he touched me on the shoulder; **toqué la escultura** I touched the sculpture; **tocar un tema** to touch on a subject; **2 tocar el timbre** to ring the bell; **3 tocar la bocina** to blow the horn; **4** to play (*an instrument*); **tocar el violín** to play the violin; **5 tocarle a alguien hacer** to be somebody's turn to do; **te toca jugar** it's your turn to play; **6 les ha tocado un viaje** they've won a trip; **nunca me ha tocado la lotería** I've never won the lottery. **tocarse** *reflexive verb* [31] to touch; **se tocó la cabeza** he touched his head; **los dos cables se están tocando** the two cables are touching.

tocino *noun Masc.* bacon.

todavía *adverb* **1** still; **todavía nos vemos** we still see each other; **2** yet; **todavía no han llegado** they haven't arrived yet; **3** even; **todavía más tarde** even later.

todo¹/toda *adjective* **1** all; **todos mis amigos** all my friends; **viajar por todo el mundo** to travel all over the world; **2** whole; **toda la semana** the whole week; **se comieron toda la caja de bombones** they ate the whole box of chocolates; **3** **todos los días** every day; **hay que revisar todas las carpetas** we have to check every folder; **4** **a toda velocidad** at top speed.

todo *pronoun* **1** everything; **se lo conté todo** I told him everything; **a pesar de todo** despite everything; **2** all; **todo o nada** all or nothing; **vinieron todos** they all came; **todos estábamos de acuerdo** we were all in agreement; **3** **ante todo** above all; **4** **con todo** even so; **5** **de todo** everything; **tienen de todo** they've got everything; **6** **sobre todo no te olvides del billete** above all, don't forget the ticket; **se divirtieron mucho, sobre todo Ana** they enjoyed themselves a lot, specially Ana.

todo *adverb* **1** all; **estaba todo nervioso** he was all nervous; **2** completely; **está todo roto** it's completely had it; **3** **seguir todo derecho** to carry straight on.

todo² *noun Masc.* **el todo** the whole.

tomar *verb* [17] **1** to take; **tomar el autobús** to take the bus; **me tomó del brazo** she took me by the arm; **2** to have; **tomar el desayuno** to have breakfast; **¿quieres tomar un café?** would you like a coffee?; **3** **toma, tu billete** here's your ticket; **4** **tomar el sol** to sunbathe; **5** **tomar el aire** to get some fresh air; **6** **tomar algo en serio** to take something seriously; **tomar algo a mal** to take something the wrong way; **tomar algo mal/bien** to take something badly/well.

tomarse *reflexive verb* [17] **1** to take; **tomarse unas vacaciones** to take some holiday; **tomarse la molestia de hacer** to take the trouble to do; **2** to have; **se tomó un helado** she had an ice cream; **3** **tomarse la tensión** to have your blood pressure taken; ★ **tomarle el pelo a alguien** (*informal*) to pull somebody's leg (*literally: to take somebody's hair*).

tomate *noun Masc.* tomato; **salsa de tomate** tomato sauce; ★ **ponerse (colorado) como un tomate** to go as red as a beetroot.

tonelada *noun Fem.* ton.

tónica *noun Fem.* tonic water.

tono *noun Masc.* **1** tone; **en tono serio** in a serious tone; **2** shade; **telas de tonos suaves** materials in soft shades; **3** **tono de marcar** dial tone; **tono de ocupado** engaged tone; ★ **fuera de tono** inappropriate (*a comment*).

tontería *noun Fem.* **vaya tontería** how silly; **no te enfades por esa tontería** don't get upset over such a silly thing; **decir tonterías** to talk nonsense.

tonto/tonta *noun Masc./Fem.* idiot; ★ **hacerse el tonto** (*informal*) to play the fool; ★ **hacer el tonto**

(*informal*) to act dumb.
tonto *adjective* silly.

topo *noun Masc.* mole (*animal*).

torbellino *noun Masc.* whirlwind.

torcer *verb* [41] **1** to turn; **tuerce a la derecha al final de la calle** turn right at the end of the road; **torcer la esquina** to turn the corner; **torcer la cabeza** to turn your head; **2** to twist.
torcerse *reflexive verb* [41] **1** to twist; **torcerse el tobillo** to twist your ankle; **2** to warp.

torcido/torcida *adjective*
1 twisted; **tiene el tobillo torcido** he's twisted his ankle; **2** crooked; **una línea torcida** a crooked line; **3** bent.

torero/torera *noun Masc./Fem.* bullfighter.

tormenta *noun Fem.* storm; **tormenta de nieve** snowstorm.

tornado *noun Masc.* tornado.

torneo *noun Masc.* tournament.

tornillo *noun Masc.* screw; ★ **le falta un tornillo** (*informal*) he's got a screw loose.

toro *noun Masc.* **1** bull; **2 los toros** bullfighting; **ir a los toros** to go to a bullfight; **¿te gustan los toros?** do you like bullfighting?.

torpe *adjective* **1** clumsy; **2** awkward.

torre *noun* **1** tower; **torre de alta tensión** pylon; **2** rook, castle (*in chess*).

torta *noun Fem.* **1** cake; **2 darle una torta a alguien** to slap somebody;

3 me pegué una torta con la farola I banged into the streetlamp (*on foot*), I crashed into the streetlamp (*in a car*); ★ **no entiendo ni torta** (*informal*) I don't understand a thing.

tortilla *noun Fem.* omelette; **tortilla francesa** French omelette; **tortilla española** Spanish omelette, tortilla.

tortuga *noun Fem.* **1** tortoise; **2** turtle.

torturar *verb* [17] to torture.

tos *noun Fem.* cough; **tener tos** to have a cough; **le dio la tos** he started coughing.

toser *verb* [18] to cough.

tostada *noun Fem.* **una tostada** a piece of toast; **tomo tostadas para desayunar** I have toast for breakfast.

tostador *noun Masc.* toaster.

tostadora *noun Fem.* toaster.

tostar *verb* [24] **1** to toast (*bread*); **2** to roast (*coffee*).
tostarse *reflexive verb* [24] to tan, to go brown.

total *noun Masc.* total; **¿cuánto es el total?** how much is the total?; **son cinco mil quinientas en total** it's five thousand five hundred in total.
total *adjective* total.

totalidad *noun Fem.* **la totalidad del colegio** the whole school; **la totalidad de los alumnos** all the pupils.

tóxico/tóxica *adjective* tóxico/tóxica; **residuos tóxicos** toxic waste.

a
b
c
d
e
f
g
h
i
j
k
l
m
n
ñ
o
p
q
r
s
t
u
v
w
x
y
z

a

b

c

trabajador/trabajadora *noun*
Masc./Fem. worker.
trabajador *adjective* hard-working.

d

e

f

g

h

trabajar *verb* [17] to work; **trabaja
de camarera** she works as a
waitress; **trabaja de canguro** she's
a babysitter; **trabajar a tiempo
completo** to work full time;
trabajar a tiempo parcial to work
part time.

i

j

k

l

m

n

ñ

trabajo *noun Masc.* **1** work; **estar
sin trabajo** to be out of work;
trabajo a tiempo completo full-
time work; **trabajo a tiempo
parcial** part-time work; **el trabajo
de la casa** the housework; **2** job;
buscar trabajo to look for a job;
quedarse sin trabajo to lose your
job; **un trabajo fijo** a steady job;
3 trabajos manuales handicrafts;
4 piece of work; **un trabajo sobre la
contaminación** an essay on
pollution.

o

tractor *noun Masc.* tractor.

p

tradición *noun Fem.* tradition.

q

tradicional *adjective* traditional.

r

traducción *noun Fem.* translation.

s

traducir *verb* [60] to translate.

t

traductor/traductora *noun*
Masc./Fem. translator.

u

v

traduje, traduzca, traduzco,
etc. *verb* SEE **traducir**.

w

x

y

z

traer *verb* [42] **1** to bring; **he traído
algo de comida** I've brought some
food; **me trae un café, por favor**
would you bring me a coffee, please?;
la traerá en coche a la estación
he'll bring her to the station in his

car; **traer buena suerte** to bring
good luck, to be lucky; **2** to carry; **la
traía en brazos** he was carrying her
in his arms.

traficante *noun Masc./Fem.* dealer;
traficante de armas arms dealer.

tráfico *noun Masc.* **1** traffic; **2** trade;
tráfico de armas arms trade;
tráfico de drogas drug dealing.

tragaperras *noun Masc./Fem.* (*does
not change in the plural*) (*informal*)
slot machine.

tragar *verb* [28] to swallow.
tragarse *reflexive verb* [28] to
swallow; **se tragó un hueso de
aceituna** he swallowed an olive
stone.

tragedia *noun Fem.* tragedy.

trágico/trágica *adjective* tragic.

traición *noun Fem.* **1** treason;
2 una traición an act of treachery.

traidor/traidora *noun Masc./Fem.*
traitor.

traiga, traigo, traje¹**, etc.** *verb*
SEE **traer**.

traje² *noun Masc.* **1** suit; **2 traje de
baño** swimsuit, swimming trunks;
3 costume; **un traje de luces** a
bullfighter's costume; **4** dress; **en
traje típico** in traditional dress.

trampa *noun Fem.* trap; **tenderle
una trampa a alguien** to set a trap
for somebody.

trampilla *noun Fem.* trapdoor.

trampolín *noun Masc.*
1 springboard, diving board;
2 trampoline; **3** ski jump.

tranquillo *noun Masc.* knack; **coger el tranquillo a algo** to get the knack of something.

tranquilo/tranquila *adjective* 1 quiet; **una calle tranquila** a quiet street; 2 relaxed; **se le ve tranquilo** he looks relaxed; **¡tranquilo!** relax!; 3 calm; **un ambiente tranquilo** a calm environment; 4 **¡déjame tranquilo!** leave me alone!; 5 **tengo la conciencia tranquila** my conscience is clear.

transbordador *noun Masc.* 1 ferry; 2 **transbordador espacial** space shuttle.

transbordar *verb* [17] 1 to transfer (*luggage or goods*); 2 to change (*trains, for example*).

transbordo *noun Masc.* change; **hacer transbordo** to change (*trains, buses*); **haz transbordo en Sol** change at Sol.

transeúnte *noun Masc./Fem.* passer-by.

transferencia *noun Fem.* transfer; **transferencia bancaria** bank transfer.

transformar *verb* [17] 1 to transform; 2 to convert; **tranformar algo en algo** to convert something into something.
transformarse *reflexive verb* [17] 1 to be transformed; 2 to be converted.

transfusión *noun Fem.* transfusion.

transmisión *noun Fem.* broadcast; **transmisión en directo** live broadcast; **transmisión en diferido** pre-recorded broadcast.

transparente *adjective* transparent.

transportar *verb* [17] to transport, to carry (*people*).

transporte *noun Masc.* transport.

tranvía *noun Masc.* tram.

trapo *noun Masc.* cloth; **un trapo del polvo** a duster; **un trapo de cocina** a tea towel.

tras *preposition* 1 behind; **tras de mí** behind me; 2 after; **hora tras hora** hour after hour; **tras despedirme, subí al coche** after saying goodbye, I got in the car.

trasero/trasera *adjective* 1 back; **la puerta trasera** the back door; 2 rear; **la rueda trasera** the rear wheel.

traslado *noun Masc.* transfer (*of an employee*).

trasnochar *verb* [17] to stay up late; **anoche trasnochamos** we had a late night last night.

trasplante *noun Masc.* transplant.

tratado *noun Masc.* treaty.

tratamiento *noun Masc.* treatment; **estar en tratamiento** to be undergoing medical treatment.

tratar *verb* [17] 1 to treat; **no me trataron bien** they didn't treat me very well; 2 **no trata sus libros con cuidado** she's not careful with her books; 3 **tratar a alguien de usted** to address somebody using the polite 'usted' form; **tratar a alguien de tú** to address somebody using the

a
b
c
d
e
f
g
h
i
j
k
l
m
n
ñ
o
p
q
r
s
t
u
v
w
x
y
z

less formal 'tú' form; **4 tratar de hacer** to try to do; **trató de impedirlo** he tried to stop it; **5 tratar de algo** to be about something; **¿de qué trata la película?** what's the film about?

tratarse *reflexive verb* [17] **1 tratarse de algo** to be about something; **2 tratarse de usted** to address each other using the polite 'usted' form; **tratarse de tú** to address each other using the less formal 'tú' form.

través *in phrase* **a través de algo** through something (*from one side to the other*), across something.

travieso/traviesa *adjective* naughty; **no seas travieso** don't be naughty.

trayecto *noun Masc.* **1** journey; **cubrir un trayecto** to make a journey; **2** road; **3 final de trayecto** end of the line (*on public transport*).

trazar *verb* [22] **1** to trace; **2** to draw (*a map*); **3** to draw up (*a plan*).

trece *number* **1** thirteen; **tiene trece años** she's thirteen (years old); **2** thirteenth (*in dates*); **el trece de mayo** the thirteenth of May.

treinta *number* **1** thirty; **tiene treinta años** she's thirty (years old); **treinta y siente** thirty-seven; **2** thirtieth (*in dates*); **el treinta de mayo** the thirtieth of May.

tremendo/tremenda *adjective* tremendous; **una tremenda victoria/derrota** a tremendous victory/defeat.

tren *noun Masc.* **1** train; **coger el tren** to catch the train; **ir en tren** to go by train; **un tren directo** a through train; **un tren de cercanías** a local train; **un tren de largo recorrido** a long-distance train; **un tren de alta velocidad** a high-speed train; **2 tren de aterrizaje** landing gear; **3 tren de montaje** assembly line.

trepar *verb* [17] to climb; **trepar a un árbol** to climb a tree.

tres *number* **1** three; **tiene tres años** she's three (years old); **2** third (*in dates*); **el tres de mayo** the third of May; **3** three (*in clock time*); **son las tres** it's three o'clock.

trescientos/trescientas *number* three hundred; **trescientos veinte** three hundred and twenty.

triángulo *noun Masc.* triangle.

tribu *noun Fem.* tribe.

tribunal *noun Masc.* **1** court; **2** tribunal.

trigo *noun Masc.* wheat.

trillizos/trillizas *plural noun Masc./Fem.* triplets.

trimestre *noun Masc.* **1** term (*in school*); **2** quarter (*three months*).

trineo *noun Masc.* sledge.

Trinidad *noun Fem.* Trinidad.

triniteño/triniteña *adjective, noun* Trinidadian.

trinitense *adjective, noun* Trinidadian.

tripa *noun Fem.* **1** (*informal*) belly; **2** gut; **3 tripas** innards.

triple *noun Masc.* **el triple del precio original** three times the original price; **es el triple de ancho**

it's three times as wide; **subió al triple** it tripled.

triple *adjective* triple.

triplicarse *reflexive verb* [31] to triple; **el precio se ha triplicado** the price has tripled.

tripulación *noun Fem.* crew.

tripulante *noun Masc./Fem.* crew member.

triste *adjective* **1** sad; **2** gloomy.

tristeza *noun Fem.* sadness.

triunfar *verb* [17] to triumph.

triunfo *noun Masc.* **1** victory; **2** triumph.

trivial *adjective* trivial.

trofeo *noun Masc.* trophy.

trombón *noun Masc.* trombone.

trompeta *noun Fem.* trumpet.

tronar *verb* [24] to thunder.

tronco *noun Masc.* **1** trunk; **2** log; ★**dormir como un tronco** to sleep like a log.

trono *noun Masc.* throne.

tropezar *verb* [25] to trip; **tropezar con algo** to trip over something. **tropezarse** *reflexive verb* [25] to trip; **tropezarse con algo** to trip over something, to come up against something (*a problem*).

tropezón *noun Masc.* stumble; **dar un tropezón** to stumble.

trópico *noun Masc.* tropic.

tropiece, tropiezo, etc. *verb* SEE **tropezar**.

trotar *verb* [17] to trot.

trozo *noun Masc.* piece; **un trozo de tela** a piece of cloth.

trucha *noun Fem.* trout.

truco *noun Masc.* trick; **el truco está en hacerlo despacio** the trick is to do it slowly.

trueno *noun Masc.* thunder.

tu *adjective* your; **tu casa** your house; **tus amigos** your friends.

tú *pronoun* **1** you; **tú no lo sabes** you don't know it; **2 tú mismo/misma** yourself; **hazlo tú mismo** do it yourself; **3 tratar a alguien de tú** to address somebody using the 'tú' form (*rather than the more formal 'usted'*).

tubo *noun Masc.* **1** tube; **2 tubo de escape** exhaust pipe.

tuerca *noun Fem.* nut.

tuerza, tuerzo, etc. *verb* SEE **torcer**.

tuesta, tueste, tuesto, etc. *verb* SEE **tostar**.

tulipán *noun Masc.* tulip.

tumba *noun Fem.* **1** grave; **2** tomb.

tumbar *verb* [17] to knock down; **tumbar a alguien de un puñetazo** to floor somebody (*with a punch*). **tumbarse** *reflexive verb* [17] to lie down; **se tumbó en el sofá** he lay down on the sofa.

tumbona *noun Fem.* deckchair.

tunecino/tunecina *noun Masc./ Fem.*, *adjective* Tunisian.

túnel *noun Masc.* tunnel.

Túnez *noun Masc.* Tunisia.

turbante *noun Masc.* turban.

turco/turca *noun Masc./Fem.*, *adjective* Turkish.

a
b
c
d
e
f
g
h
i
j
k
l
m
n
ñ
o
p
q
r
s
t
u
v
w
x
y
z

a
b
c
d
e
f
g
h
i
j
k
l
m
n
ñ
o
p
q
r
s
t
u
v
w
x
y
z

turismo *noun Masc.* **1** tourism; **oficina de turismo** tourist office; **hacer turismo** to travel around, to go sightseeing; **2** saloon car.

turista *noun Masc./Fem.* tourist.

turístico/turística *adjective* tourist.

turnarse *reflexive verb* [17] to take turns.

turno *noun Masc.* **1** turn; **tocarle el turno a alguien** to be somebody's turn; **te toca el turno a ti** it's your turn; **2** shift; **turno de noche** night shift; **hacer turnos trabajo** to work shifts.

Turquía *noun Fem.* Turkey.

turrón *noun Masc.* nougat (*a special sort traditionally eaten in Spain at Christmas*).

tutear *verb* [17] **tutear a alguien** to address somebody using the familiar 'tú' form (*rather than the more formal 'usted'*).
   tutearse *reflexive verb* [17] to address each other using the familiar 'tú' form (*see note above*).

tutor/tutora *noun Masc./Fem.* **1** tutor; **2** class teacher.

tutoría *noun Fem.* **1** study period; **2** tutorship.

tuvo, tuvieron, tuviste, etc. *verb* SEE **tener**.

tuyo/tuya *adjective* yours (*goes after the noun*); **un amigo tuyo** a friend of yours; **una vecina tuya** a neighbour of yours.
   tuyo *pronoun* yours; **el tuyo es verde** yours is green; **las tuyas son mejores** yours are better.

Uu

u *conjunction* or (*'o' becomes 'u' before words beginning with 'o-' or 'ho-'*); **uno u otro** one or the other.

Ucrania *noun Fem.* Ukraine.

ucraniano/ucraniana *noun Masc./Fem., adjective* Ukrainian.

Ud. *abbreviation* (*short for: usted*) you.

Uds. *abbreviation* (*short for: ustedes*) you.

UE *abbreviation Fem.* (*short for: Unión Europea*) EU.

úlcera *noun Fem.* ulcer.

últimamente *adverb* lately.

último/última *noun Masc./Fem.* **el último** the last one; **esta es la última que queda** this is the last one left; **coge el último del montón** take the one at the bottom of the pile.
   último *adjective* **1** last; **el último día fuimos a la playa** on the last day we went to the beach; **2** latest; **su última película** her latest film; **lo último en equipo audio** the latest in audio equipment; **3** top; **el último libro del montón** the book at the bottom of the pile.

ultramarinos *noun Masc.* (*does not change in the plural*) grocer's shop.

un/una¹ *indefinite article* **1** a, an; **un hombre** a man; **una manzana** an apple; **tiene un año** she's a year old/ one year old (*'un' is used before feminine nouns starting with stressed 'a' or 'ha'*) **un ala** a wing; **un**

hacha an axe; **2** (*plural*) **unos/unas** some, a few; **compré unos sobres** I bought some envelopes; **se quedarán unas horas** they will stay for a few hours; **3 cuesta unas tres mil euros** it costs about three thousand euros; **llevará unos treinta minutos hacerlo** it'll take about thirty minutes to do it.

único/única *noun Masc./Fem.* **el único/la única** the only one; **el único que funciona** the only one that works.
único *adjective* **1** unique; **2** only; **su único hijo** her only child; **3 talla única** one size.

unidad *noun Fem.* **1** unit; **unidad de cuidados intensivos, unidad de vigilancia intensiva** intensive care unit; **2** unity.

unido/unida *adjective* **1** united; **2** joined; **3** close; **las dos hermanas están muy unidas** the two sisters are very close.

uniforme *noun Masc.* uniform.
uniforme *adjective* **1** uniform; **2** even.

Unión Europea *noun Fem.* European Union.

unir *verb* [19] **1** to join; **2** to combine; **el diseño une la elegancia con la eficacia** the design combines elegance and efficiency; **3** to merge (*companies, for example*).
unirse *reflexive verb* [19] **1** to join together; **2** to combine; **3** to merge.

universidad *noun Fem.* university; **universidad a distancia** open university; **universidad laboral** technical college; **estar en la universidad** to be at university.

universitario/universitaria *noun Masc./Fem.* university student.
universitario *adjective* university; **profesores universitarios** university teachers.

universo *noun Masc.* universe.

uno¹**/una** *number* **1** one; **compré sólo uno** I bought only one; **hay una razón** there is one reason; **2** one (*in clock time*); **la una** one o'clock; **es la una** it's one o'clock; **llegaron a la una** they arrived at one o'clock; **3** first (*in dates*); **el uno de enero** the first of January.

uno²**/una** *pronoun* **1** one; **de uno en uno** one by one (*note that 'uno' becomes 'un' before a masculine singular noun*) ; **2 unos/unas** some; **unos saben y otros no** some know and some don't.

unos/unas SEE **un/una**¹, **uno/una**².

uña *noun Fem.* nail (*of finger, toe*); **una uña del dedo del pie** a toe nail.

urbano/urbana *adjective* urban.

urgencia *noun Fem.* **1** urgency; **2** (*in hospital*) **'urgencias'** 'accident and emergency'; **sala de urgencias** accident and emergency department.

urgente *adjective* **1** urgent; **2** express (*post*).

a
b
c
d
e
f
g
h
i
j
k
l
m
n
ñ
o
p
q
r
s
t
u
v
w
x
y
z

urgentemente *adverb* urgently;
quiere verte urgentemente she
wants to see you urgently.

Uruguay *noun Masc.* Uruguay.

uruguayo/uruguaya *noun
Masc./Fem., adjective* Uruguayan.

usado/usada *adjective* **1** used;
2 second-hand; **ropa usada** second-
hand clothes.

usar *verb* [17] **1** to use; **¿qué
champú usas?** what shampoo do
you use?; **2** to take (*clothes size*).

uso *noun Masc.* use; **instrucciones
de uso** instructions for use.

usted *pronoun* you (*the formal,
polite form: talking to one person*);
usted mismo/misma yourself.

ustedes *pronoun* you (*the formal,
polite form: talking to more than one
person*); **ustedes mismos/mismas**
yourselves.

usual *adjective* usual.

usuario/usuaria *noun Masc./Fem.*
user.

utensilio *noun Masc.* **1** tool;
2 utensil.

útil *adjective* useful.

utilizar *verb* [22] to use.

uva *noun Fem.* grape; **las uvas de la
suerte** the twelve grapes (*one for
each month of the year*) eaten
traditionally in Spain at midnight
on New Year's Eve; **tomar las uvas**
to eat grapes (*at midnight on New
Year's Eve*).

Vv

vaca *noun Fem.* cow.

vacaciones *plural noun Fem.*
holiday, holidays; **irse de
vacaciones** to go on holiday;
tomarse unas vacaciones to take a
holiday; **las vacaciones de
Navidad** the Christmas holidays;
estar de vacaciones to be on
holiday.

vaciar *verb* [32] to empty.

vacilar *verb* [17] **1** to hesitate; **sin
vacilar** without hesitating; **vacilaba
entre quedarse o no** she was
hesitating whether to stay or not;
2 to falter; **3** (*informal*) to joke;
¡deja de vacilar! stop fooling about!

vacío/vacía *adjective* empty.
vacío *noun Masc.* vacuum.

vacuna *noun Fem.* vaccine.

vacunar *verb* [17] to vaccinate.

vagabundo/vagabunda *noun
Masc./Fem.* vagrant.
vagabundo *adjective* **un perro
vagabundo** a stray dog.

vago/vaga *noun Masc./Fem.*
layabout.
vago *adjective* lazy.

vagón *noun Masc.* **1** carriage;
2 wagon.

vainilla *noun Fem.* vanilla.

valdrá, **valdré**, **valdría**, **etc.**
verb SEE **valer**.

vale *noun Masc.* **1** voucher; **2** credit
slip.
vale *exclamation* okay; **'¿vamos a**

cenar fuera?' – **'¡vale!'** 'shall we go out for dinner?' – 'okay!'.

valer *verb* [43] **1** to cost; **¿cuánto vale?** how much is it?; **vale trescientos cincuenta euros** it's three hundred and fifty euros; **2** to be worth; **vale bastante dinero** it's worth quite a lot of money; **3** **valer la pena** to be worth it; **no vale la pena** it's not worth it; **no vale la pena enfadarse por ello** it's not worth getting upset about; **vale la pena el esfuerzo** it's worth the effort; **4** to be valid (*a ticket or coupon*); **5** to be allowed; **no vale preguntar** you can't ask; **eso no vale, tú ya lo habías visto** that's not fair, you'd already seen it.

valga, **valgo**, etc. *verb* SEE **valer**.

válido/válida *adjective* valid.

valiente *adjective* brave.

valioso/valiosa *adjective* valuable.

valle *noun Masc.* valley.

valor *noun Masc.* courage.

valorar *verb* [17] to value.

vals *noun Masc.* waltz.

vamos *verb* SEE **ir**.

vandalismo *noun Masc.* hooliganism.

vanidoso/vanidosa *adjective* vain.

vano/vana *adjective* **1** futile; **2** pointless.

vapor *noun Masc.* steam; **al vapor** steamed.

vaquero *noun Masc.* jeans; **vaqueros** jeans.

variado/variada *adjective* varied.

variar *verb* [32] **1** to vary; **2** to change.

varicela *noun Fem.* chicken pox.

variedad *noun Fem.* variety.

varios/varias *pronoun, adjective* several; **varias veces** several times.

varón *noun Masc.*,
varón *adjective* male.

varonil *adjective* manly.

vasco¹ *noun Masc.* Basque (*the language*).

vasco²/vasca *noun Masc./Fem.*, *adjective* Basque.

vasija *noun Fem.* vessel.

vaso *noun Masc.* glass; **un vaso de agua** a glass of water; **un vaso de papel** a paper cup.

Vd. *abbreviation* (*short for: usted*) you.

Vds. *abbreviation* (*short for: ustedes*) you.

vecindad *noun Fem.* neighbourhood.

vecino/vecina *noun Masc./Fem.* neighbour.
vecino *adjective* neighbouring.

vegetariano/vegetariana *noun Masc./Fem.*, *adjective* vegetarian.

vehículo *noun Masc.* vehicle; **vehículo espacial** spacecraft.

veía, **veían**, etc. *verb* SEE **ver**.

veinte *number* **1** twenty; **tiene veinte años** she's twenty (years old); **veintidós** twenty-two;

a
b
c
d
e
f
g
h
i
j
k
l
m
n
ñ
o
p
q
r
s
t
u
v
w
x
y
z

2 twentieth (*in dates*); **el veinte de diciembre** the twentieth of December; **3** twenty (*in clock time*); **a las vienticinco** at twenty-five past.

vejez *noun Fem.* old age.

vela *noun Fem.* **1** candle; **2** sail; **3** sailing; **4 pasar la noche en vela**; **he pasado toda la noche en vela** I've been awake all night.

velero *noun Masc.* sailing ship, sailing boat.

velocidad *noun Fem.* **1** speed; **el coche iba a mucha velocidad** the car was going very fast; **disminuir la velocidad** to slow down; **2** gear (*in a car*); **la cuarta velocidad** fourth gear.

vena *noun Fem.* vein.

vencedor/vencedora *adjective* winning.

vencer *verb* [44] **1** to defeat; **vencer a alguien** to defeat somebody; **2** to win; **3** to overcome; **4** to expire (*a passport, for example*).

vencido/vencida *adjective* defeated.

venda *noun Fem.* bandage.

vendar *verb* [17] **1** to bandage; **2 vendar los ojos a alguien** to blindfold somebody.

vendaval *noun Masc.* gale.

vendedor/vendedora *noun* **1** shop assistant; **2** salesman/saleswoman; **3** seller; **un vendedor ambulante** a street seller.

vender *verb* [18] to sell; **le he vendido mi coche** I've sold him my car; **los venden a ciento ochenta euros** they're selling them for a hundred and eighty euros; **'se vende'** 'for sale'.

vendimia *noun Fem.* wine harvest.

vendrá, **vendré**, **vendría**, **etc.** *verb* SEE **venir**.

veneno *noun Masc.* poison, venom.

venenoso/venenosa *adjective* poisonous.

venezolano/venezolana *noun Masc./Fem., adjective* Venezuelan.

Venezuela *noun Fem.* Venezuela.

venga, **vengo**, **etc.** *verb* SEE **venir**.

venganza *noun Fem.* revenge.

vengarse *reflexive verb* [28] **vengarse de alguien** to get one's revenge on someone.

venir *verb* [15] **1** to come; **sus padres no vinieron** her parents didn't come; **ven a las siete** come at seven; **2 venir de** to come from; **viene de Italia** it comes from Italy; **3 venir a hacer** something to do; **yo vendré a buscarte** I'll come and collect you; **4 venir a por algo** to come to fetch something; **vengo a por el paquete** I've come to fetch the parcel; **venir a por alguien** to come to collect somebody; **yo vendré a buscarte** I'll come and collect you; **5** to be; **la noticia viene en la primera página** the news is on the front page; **6 venirle bien a alguien** to suit someone; **mañana no les viene bien** tomorrow doesn't suit them; **¿te viene bien quedar**

en la entrada? is it okay for you if we meet at the entrance?; **esta parada de metro me viene muy bien** this tube station's very convenient for me; **7 que viene: la semana que viene** next week; **el domingo que viene** next Sunday; **8 ¡venga!** come on!

venta *noun Fem.* sale; **estar en venta** to be for sale; **'prohibida su venta'** 'not for sale'.

ventaja *noun Fem.* advantage.

ventana *noun Fem.* window.

ventanilla *noun Fem.* **1** window (*in a train or car*); **2** box office; **3 horario de ventanilla** opening hours (*at a consulate, for example*).

ventilación *noun Fem.* ventilation.

ventilador *noun Masc.* fan.

ventisca *noun Fem.* blizzard.

ver *verb* [16] **1** to see; **los vi ayer** I saw them yesterday; **la vi cogerlo** I saw her take it; **no veo nada desde aquí** I can't see anything from here; **no veo bien de lejos** I'm shortsighted; **ya veo cuál es el problema** I can see the problem; **ya veremos lo que hacemos** we'll see what we do; **2** to watch; **ver la tele** to watch TV; **anoche vimos una película muy buena** we watched a very good film last night; **3** to think; **lo que ha hecho no lo veo bien** I don't think what he's done is right; **4 tener que ver con algo** to have something to do with something; **eso no tiene nada que ver** that has nothing to do with it; **5 a ver, ¿qué te pasa?** okay, what's the matter with you?; **'mira lo que he encontrado' – '¿a ver?'** 'look what I've found' – 'let's see'.

verse *reflexive verb* [16] **1** to see yourself; **verse en el espejo** to see yourself in the mirror; **2** to see each other; **se ven todas las semanas** they see each other every week; **3** to meet; **¿nos vemos a la entrada del cine?** shall we meet outside the cinema?; ★**verse en un aprieto** to find yourself in a tight spot.

veraneante *noun Masc./Fem.* holidaymaker.

veranear *verb* [17] **veranear en** to spend your summer holidays in; **veranean en la montaña** they spend their summer holidays in the mountains.

veras *in phrase* **¡de veras!** really!; **una moto de veras** a real motorbike.

verbena *noun Fem.* festival (*held to celebrate the Saint's Day of a town or village*); dance (*in the open air*).

verbo *noun Masc.* verb.

verdad *noun Fem.* **1** truth; **dime la verdad** tell me the truth; **la pura verdad** the absolute truth; **la verdad, no me acuerdo** I don't remember, honestly; **la verdad es que ...** the truth is that ...; **2 a decir verdad ...** to tell the truth ...; **3 de verdad** really; **de verdad que no me importa** I don't mind, really; **4 de verdad** real; **un amigo de verdad** a real friend.

verdadero/verdadera *adjective* **1** real; **su verdadero nombre** his real name; **es un verdadero idiota** he's a real idiot;

a
b
c
d
e
f
g
h
i
j
k
l
m
n
ñ
o
p
q
r
s
t
u
v
w
x
y
z

2 true; **una historia verdadera** a true story.

verde noun Masc. **1** green; **verde botella** bottle-green; **2 los Verdes** the Greens (in politics).
verde adjective **1** green; **tiene los ojos verdes** she has green eyes; **una blusa verde oscuro** a dark green blouse; **2** smutty; **un chiste verde** a dirty joke.

verdulería noun Fem. greengrocer's.

verdura noun Fem. vegetable; **cómete la verdura** eat your vegetables; **un puesto de verduras** a vegetable stall.

vergonzoso/vergonzosa adjective **1** timid; **2** shameful.

vergüenza noun Fem. **1** shame; **tener vergüenza** to be ashamed; **¡qué poca vergüenza tienes!** have you no shame at all?; **2 darle vergüenza a alguien** to be ashamed; **me da vergüenza haberme portado de esa forma** I'm ashamed of behaving the way I did; **3** embarrassment; **pasar vergüenza** to feel embarrassed; **4 me da vergüenza hablar en público** I feel embarrassed when I have to speak in public.

verruga noun Fem. **1** wart; **2** verruca.

versión noun Fem. version; **una película en versión original** a film which has not been dubbed (a foreign film, usually with subtitles).

verso noun Masc. **1** verse; **en verso** in verse; **2** poem; **3** line of a poem; **el**

tercer verso the third line of the poem.

vertical adjective **1** vertical; **2** down (in crosswords); **ocho vertical** eight down.

vertiente noun Fem. slope.

vértigo noun Masc. vertigo; **me da vértigo mirar abajo** looking down makes me dizzy.

vestíbulo noun Masc. **1** hall; **2** foyer.

vestido¹ noun Masc. dress; **un vestido de noche** an evening dress; **un vestido de novia** a wedding dress.

vestido²/vestida adjective dressed; **ir bien vestido** to be well dressed; **iba vestida con un traje azul** she was wearing a blue suit; **tenemos que ir al colegio vestidos de uniforme** we have to wear school uniform.

vestir verb [57] to dress; **vestir bien** to dress well.
vestirse reflexive verb [57] **1** to get dressed; **voy a vestirme** I'm going to get dressed; **2** to dress; **se viste a la última moda** she wears the latest fashions; **me gusta vestirme de azul** I like wearing blue.

vestuario noun Masc. **1** wardrobe; **2** changing room.

veterinario/veterinaria noun Masc./Fem. veterinary surgeon.

vez (plural **veces**) noun Fem. **1** time; **la primera vez que fui a Inglaterra** the first time I went to England; **por última vez** for the last time; **algunas veces** sometimes; **¿has**

estado alguna vez en Italia? have you ever been to Italy?; **a veces** sometimes; **tal vez** perhaps, maybe; **de vez en cuando** ocasionally, from time to time; **de vez en cuando nos manda una carta** occasionally he sends us a letter; **2 a la vez** at the same time, at once; **3 cada vez** each time; **cada vez más** more and more; **hay cada vez más turistas** there are more and more tourists; **4 cada vez menos** less and less, fewer and fewer; **5 muchas veces** often; **pocas veces** not very often; **rara vez** seldom; **6 una vez** once; **dos veces** twice; **tres veces al año** three times a year; **7 otra vez** again; **8 en vez de** instead of; **9 érase una vez** ... once upon a time ....

vía *noun Fem.* **1** track; **la vía férrea** the railway track; **2 por vía aérea** by air; **por vía marítima** by sea; **3 vía de acceso** slip road; **4 Vía Láctea** Milky Way.

viajar *verb* [17] to travel; **viajar en avión** to travel by plane.

viaje *noun Masc.* journey, trip; **estar de viaje** to be away; **hacer un viaje** to go on a journey, to go on a trip; **salir de viaje** to go on a journey, to go on a trip; **¡buen viaje!** have a good journey!; **viaje de negocios** business trip; **viaje organizado** package tour; **viaje de novios** honeymoon.

viajero/viajera *noun Masc./Fem.* **1** traveller; **2** passenger.

víbora *noun Fem.* viper.

vibrar *verb* [17] to vibrate.

vicio *noun Masc.* **1** vice; **2** bad habit; **tengo el vicio de morderme las uñas** I have the bad habit of biting my nails.

víctima *noun Fem.* victim; **el número de víctimas mortales asciende a 25** the death toll has risen to 25.

victoria *noun Fem.* victory.

vid *noun Fem.* vine.

vida *noun Fem.* life; **¡esto es vida!** this is the life!; **la vida está muy cara** the cost of living is very high; **una cuestión de vida o muerte** a matter of life or death; **llevar una vida muy ajetreada** to lead a very busy life; **ganarse la vida** to earn a living.

vídeo *noun Masc.* video; **en vídeo** on video.

videocámara *noun Fem.* video camera.

videoclub *noun Masc.* video shop.

videojuego *noun Masc.* video game.

vidrio *noun Masc.* glass.

viejo/vieja *noun Masc./Fem.* old man/old woman.
viejo *adjective* old.

viento *noun Masc.* **1** wind; **hace viento** it's windy; **2** guy rope (*of tent*).

vientre *noun Masc.* **1** belly; **2** womb.

viernes *noun Masc.* Friday; **Viernes Santo** Good Friday (*see 'domingo' for more examples*).

vigésimo/vigésima *adjective* twentieth.

a b c d e f g h i j k l m n ñ o p q r s t u v w x y z

a
b
c
d
e
f
g
h
i
j
k
l
m
n
ñ
o
p
q
r
s
t
u
v
w
x
y
z

villancico *noun Masc.* Christmas carol.

vinagre *noun Masc.* vinegar.

vine, viniste, vino, etc. *verb* SEE **venir.**

viñedo *noun Masc.* vineyard.

vino *noun Masc.* wine; **vino tinto** red wine; **vino blanco** white wine; **vino de mesa** table wine.

violar *verb* [17] to rape.

violencia *noun Fem.* violence.

violento/violenta *adjective* **1** violent; **2** embarrassing (*situation*); **3** embarrassed.

violeta *noun Fem.*, **violeta** *adjective* violet.

violín *noun Masc.* violin; **tocar el violín** to play the violin.

violoncelo, violonchelo *noun Masc.* cello.

virar *verb* [17] to swerve; **el coche viró brucamente para esquivar al perro** the car swerved sharply to avoid the dog.

virgen *noun Fem.* virgin.

virgo *noun Masc./Fem.* Virgo; **es virgo** he's Virgo.

Virgo *noun Masc.* Virgo.

virtud *noun Fem.* virtue.

virus *noun Masc.* virus; **software anti virus** anti-virus software.

visado *noun Masc.* visa.

visibilidad *noun Fem.* visibility.

visible *adjective* visible.

visión *noun Fem.* **1** vision; **2** sight; **perder la visión** to lose your sight.

visita *noun Fem.* **1** visit; **una visita al museo** a visit to the museum; **hacer una visita a alguien** to visit somebody; **2** visitor; **tienes una visita** you have a visitor; **3** hit (*on web site*).

visitar *verb* [17] to visit.

víspera *noun Fem.* **la víspera** the day before; **la víspera del partido** the day before the match.

vista¹ *noun Fem.* **1** eyesight; **tener buena vista** to have good eyesight; **perder la vista** to lose your sight; **el sol me hace daño a la vista** the sun's hurting my eyes; **conocer a alguien de vista** to know someone by sight; **2 estar a la vista** to be within sight; **no estar a la vista** to be out of sight; **3** view; **el hotel tiene unas vistas preciosas** the hotel has beautiful views; **4 con vistas a** with a view to; **5 ¡hasta la vista!** see you!

vistieron, vistió, etc. *verb* SEE **vestir.**

visto¹ *verb* SEE **ver.**

visto²/vista² *adjective* **1** clear; **está visto que ...** it's clear that ...; **2 por lo visto** apparently; **3 estar bien visto** to be acceptable; **está mal visto** it's not the done thing; **4 eso está muy visto** that's not very original.

vitamina *noun Fem.* vitamin.

viudo/viuda *noun Fem.* widow/ widower.

viva¹ *exclamation* ¡viva! hurray!; **¡viva la novia!** three cheers for the bride!

vivienda *noun Fem.* **1** housing; **el problema de la vivienda** the housing problem; **2** flat, house; **un bloque de viviendas** a block of flats.

vivir *verb* [19] to live; **vive en casa de su hermana** she lives with her sister; **vive de las traducciones** she makes her living from translation; **vive de su pensión** she lives off her pension.

vivo/viva² *adjective* **1** alive; **2** **actuación en vivo** live performance.

vocabulario *noun Masc.* vocabulary.

volante *noun Masc.* steering wheel.
volante *adjective* flying.

volar *verb* [24] **1** to fly; **2** to blow up; **volar un edificio** to blow up a building.

volcán *noun Masc.* volcano.

volcar *verb* [24] **1** to turn over; **el camión volcó** the lorry turned over; **2 volcar el contenido de algo** to empty something; **3** to knock over.
volcarse *reflexive verb* [24] **1** to turn over (*a vehicle*); **2 volcarse en algo** to throw yourself into something.

vóleibol, **voleibol** *noun Masc.* volleyball; **jugar al vóleibol** to play volleyball.

voltereta *noun Fem.* somersault.

volumen *noun Masc.* volume; **subir el volumen** to turn up the volume.

voluntad *noun Fem.* **1** will; **fuerza de voluntad** will power; **lo hice por mi propia voluntad** I did it of my own free will; **2** wish; ★ **siempre hace su santa voluntad** she always does exactly as she pleases.

voluntario/voluntaria *noun Masc./Fem.* volunteer.
voluntario *adjective* voluntary.

volver *verb* [45] **1** to turn; **volver la página** to turn the page; **volvió la cabeza** she turned her head; **al volver la esquina** ... when I turned the corner ...; **2** to come back; **aún no ha vuelto** he hasn't come back yet; **¿cuándo volverás?** when will you come back?; **3** to go back; **volver al colegio** to go back to school; **¿quieres que volvamos a casa?** do you want us to go back home?; **ha vuelto con su novia** he's gone back to his girlfriend; **4** to be back; **volveré a eso de las siete** I'll be back by about seven; **no había vuelto a Sevilla desde el verano pasado** I hadn't been back to Seville since last summer; **5** to get back; **¿cuándo volviste de tu viaje?** when did you get back from your trip?; **6 volver a hacer** to do again; **volví a revisarlo** I checked it again; **¡no lo vuelvas a hacer!** don't do it again!; **tenemos que volver a empezar** we have to start again; **7 volver loco a alguien** to drive someone mad; **me está volviendo loca con tantas preguntas** she's driving me mad with all her questions; **8 volver en sí** to come round (*recover consciousness*).
volverse *reflexive verb* [45] **1** to turn around; **me volví para mirar** I turned around to see; **2 volverse de espaldas** to turn your back; **¡no te**

a
b
c
d
e
f
g
h
i
j
k
l
m
n
ñ
o
p
q
r
s
t
u
v
w
x
y
z

vuelvas de espaldas cuando te estoy hablando! don't turn your back on me when I'm talking to you!; **3 volverse boca abajo** to turn over onto your stomach; **volverse boca arriba** to turn over onto your back; **4** to become; **se ha vuelto muy vanidosa** she's turned very vain; **la situación se ha vuelto insoportable** the situation has become unbearable; **volverse loco** to go mad.

vomitar *verb* [17] to be sick; **tener ganas de vomitar** to feel sick.

vosotros/vosotras *pronoun* you (*talking to more than one person*); **¿vosotras queréis ir?** do you want to go?; **vosotros mismos/ vosotras mismas** yourselves.

votar *verb* [17] **1** to vote on (*a measure*); **2** to vote for (*a party, a candidate*); **siempre vota a los verdes** she always votes for the Greens; **¿por quién votaste?** who did you vote for?.

voto *noun Masc.* **1** vote; **un voto a favor** a vote for; **un voto en contra** a vote against; **un voto secreto** a secret ballot; **un voto en blanco** a blank ballot paper; **un voto de censura** a vote of no confidence; **2** vow.

voy *verb* SEE **ir**.

voz (*plural* **voces**) *noun Fem.* voice; **oír voces** to hear voices; **tener la voz tomada** to be hoarse; **en voz baja** quietly; **hablar en voz alta** to speak loudly; **leer algo en voz alta** to read something out loud.

vuelo *noun Masc.* flight; **un vuelo regular** a scheduled flight.

vuelta *noun Fem.* **1** turn; **una vuelta a la derecha** a turn to the right; **2** return; **a la vuelta podemos visitar el museo** we can visit the museum on our way back; **'vuelta al colegio'** 'back to school' (*after the summer holidays*); **3 dar la vuelta a algo** to turn something; **dar la vuelta a la página** to turn the page; **dale la vuelta al cuadro** turn the picture round the other way; **dar la vuelta a un disco** to turn a record over; **4 dar la vuelta a la esquina** to turn the corner; **5 dar la vuelta al mundo** to go round the world; **dar una vuelta a la manzana** to go round the block; **6 dar una vuelta** to go for a walk; **¿te vienes a dar una vuelta?** are you coming for a walk?; **dar una vuelta en coche** to go for a drive; **7 dar una vuelta alrededor de algo** to go around something.

vuelva, vuelvo, etc. *verb* SEE **volver**.

vuestro/vuestra *adjective* your (*talking to more than one person*); **vuestra casa** your house; **un familiar vuestro** a relative of yours. **vuestro** *pronoun* yours; **la vuestra es verde** yours is green; **los vuestros están en el salón** yours are in the living room; **aquel es el vuestro** that one is yours.

vulgar *adjective* **1** vulgar; **2** common.

Ww

walkman™ *noun Masc.* personal stereo.

wáter *noun Masc.* toilet.

whisky *noun Masc.* whisky.

windsurf *noun Masc.* **hacer windsurf** to go windsurfing.

windsurf *noun Masc.* windsurfing.

Xx

xilófono *noun Masc.* xylophone.

Yy

y *conjunction* (*'y' becomes 'e' before a word beginning with 'i-' or 'hi-'*) **1** and; **Amanda y yo** Amanda and I; **2** (*with numbers and times*) **treinta y siete** thirty-seven; **3** (*with clock time*) **las dos y media** half past two; **a las diez y cinco** at five past ten; **4 ¿y a mí qué?** so what's it to me?

ya *adverb* **1** already; **ya está hecho** it's already done; **¿has comido ya?** have you already eaten?; **2** yet; **¿han llegado ya?** have they arrived yet?; **3** any more; **ya no importa** it doesn't matter any more; **4** now; **antes no quería, pero ya ha cambiado de idea** he didn't want to before but he's changed his mind now; **tenemos que decidirnos ya** we must decide now; **5** (*in the future*) **ya veremos** we'll see; **ya te contaré**

I'll tell you about it; **6** (*not translated but used to stress what you are saying*) **ya lo sé** I know; **ya entiendo** I understand; **ya era hora** it's about time too; **¡ya está!** that's it!; **¡ya estoy!** I'm ready!; **¡ya voy!** I'm just coming!; **¡ya lo creo!** you bet!; **preparados, listos, ¡ya!** ready, steady, go!; **7 'esto es de Juan' – 'ya'** 'this is Juan's' – 'I know'; **8 'yo no he sido' – 'ya, ya'** 'it wasn't me' – 'yeah, yeah!'; **9 ya que** since; **ya que vas a estar aquí** since you're going to be here.

yate *noun Masc.* yacht.

yedra *noun Fem.* ivy.

yegua *noun Fem.* mare.

yema *noun Fem.* **1** yolk; **2 la yema del dedo** the fingertip.

yerno *noun Masc.* son-in-law.

yo *pronoun* **1** I; **yo no lo sé** I don't know; **2** me; **soy yo** it's me; **3 yo mismo/misma** myself; **lo haré yo mismo** I'll do it myself.

yoga *noun Fem.* yoga.

yogur *noun Masc.* yoghurt.

yudo *noun Masc.* judo.

Yugoslavia *noun Fem.* Yugoslavia.

yugoslavo/yugoslava *noun Masc./Fem., adjective* Yugoslavian.

Zz

zanahoria *noun Fem.* carrot.

zapatería *noun Fem.* shoe shop.

a
b
c
d
e
f
g
h
i
j
k
l
m
n
ñ
o
p
q
r
s
t
u
v
w
x
y
z

a
b
c
d
e
f
g
h
i
j
k
l
m
n
ñ
o
p
q
r
s
t
u
v
w
x
y
z

zapatero/zapatera *noun Masc./ Fem.* **1** shoemaker; **2** shoe repairer's.

zapatilla *noun Fem.* **1** slipper; **2** canvas shoe; **3 zapatilla de deporte** trainer; **4 zapatilla de esparto** espadrille; **5 zapatilla de ballet** ballet shoe.

zapato *noun Masc.* shoe; **zapato de tacón** high heeled shoe; **zapato bajo** flat shoe.

zarzamora *noun Fem.* blackberry.

zarzuela *noun Fem.* Spanish light opera.

zodíaco, **zodiaca** *noun Masc.* zodiac.

zona *noun Fem.* area; **viven en la zona** they live locally; **zona peatonal** pedestrian precinct; **zona comercial** commercial district.

zoo *noun Masc.* zoo.

zoológico *noun Masc.* zoo.

zorro *noun Masc.* fox.

zueco *noun Masc.* clog.

zumo *noun Masc.* juice; **zumo de fruta** fruit juice; **zumo de naranja** orange juice.

zurdo/zurda *noun Masc./Fem.* left-handed person.

VERB TABLES AND FORMS

Spanish verb tables
The following verb tables show you how Spanish verbs are formed. They fall into three categories – main irregular verbs, the three regular verb patterns using **hablar**, **comer**, and **vivir** as models, and other irregular verbs.

Main Spanish irregular verbs (pages 286–301)
The following Spanish verbs are unlike any others – they are irregular. The way that they are formed is given in the following section. When you look up a verb in this dictionary, you will see that it has a number in square brackets ([1], [2] etc.) This number tells you which verb to look up in this section.

[1]	**ser**	to be	[9]	**tener**	to have
[2]	**estar**	to be	[10]	**poder**	to be able
[3]	**coger**	to take	[11]	**poner**	to put
[4]	**dar**	to give	[12]	**querer**	to want, to love
[5]	**decir**	to say, to tell	[13]	**saber**	to know (facts)
[6]	**haber**	to have	[14]	**sentir**	to feel
[7]	**hacer**	to make, to do	[15]	**venir**	to come
[8]	**ir**	to go	[16]	**ver**	to see

Regular Spanish verbs (pages 302–304)
All other Spanish verbs belong to verb families. These are the **-ar**, **-er**, and **-ir** verbs. The ones with regular patterns follow the ones given in full here. In this dictionary, the numbers in square brackets ([17], [18] or [19]) tell you which verb pattern to follow.

-ar verbs	[17]	**hablar**	to speak, to talk
-er verbs	[18]	**comer**	to eat
-ir verbs	[19]	**vivir**	to live

Other irregular verbs (pages 305–315)
However, some of the verbs in the **-ar**, **-er**, and **-ir** regular verb families have differences from the regular patterns. These verbs are also numbered in the dictionary to tell you where to find them in this centre section. These verbs follow the regular verb patterns, apart from the forms that are given on pages 305-315.

Reflexive verbs
Many Spanish verbs may also be used reflexively with the appropriate pronouns (**me/te/se/nos/os/se**) for each person. Remember that when a verb is used reflexively its meaning may change, so check carefully in the dictionary. A typical example is [14] **sentir** on page 299.

1

ser
to be

Gerund		**Past participle**	
siendo	being	sido	been

Present indicative

soy — I am
eres
es
somos
sois
son

Imperfect indicative

era — I was *or* I used to be
eras
era
éramos
erais
eran

Past simple indicative

fui — I was
fuiste
fue
fuimos
fuisteis
fueron

Future indicative

seré — I will be
serás
será
seremos
seréis
serán

Conditional (present)

sería — I would be
serías
sería
seríamos
seríais
serían

Present subjunctive

sea — I am
seas
sea
seamos
seáis
sean

Imperfect subjunctive

fuera — I was *or* I were
fueras
fuera
fuéramos
fuerais
fueran

Imperative

sé (tú)	be (singular)
sea (usted)	be (sing formal)
seamos (nosotros)	let us be *or* let's be
sed (vosotros)	be (plural)
sean (ustedes)	be (pl formal)

Gerund
estando   being

Past participle
estado   been

2

estar
to be

Present indicative

estoy   I am
estás
está
estamos
estáis
están

Imperfect indicative

estaba   I was *or* I used to be
estabas
estaba
estábamos
estabais
estaban

Past simple indicative

estuve   I was
estuviste
estuvo
estuvimos
estuvisteis
estuvieron

Future indicative

estaré   I will be
estarás
estará
estaremos
estaréis
estarán

Conditional (present)

estaría   I would be
estarías
estaría
estaríamos
estaríais
estarían

Present subjunctive

esté   I am
estés
esté
estemos
estéis
estén

Imperfect subjunctive

estuviera   I was *or* I were
estuvieras
estuviera
estuviéramos
estuvierais
estuvieran

Imperative

está (tú)	be (singular)
esté (usted)	be (sing formal)
estemos (nosotros)	let us be *or* let's be
estad (vosotros)	be (plural)
estén (ustedes)	be (pl formal)

3

coger
to take

Gerund
cogiendo   taking

Past participle
cogido   taken

Present indicative

cojo   I take or I am taking
coges
coge
cogemos
cogéis
cogen

Imperfect indicative

cogía   I was taking or
         I used to take
cogías
cogía
cogíamos
cogíais
cogían

Past simple indicative

cogí   I took
cogiste
cogió
cogimos
cogisteis
cogieron

Future indicative

cogeré   I will take
cogerás
cogerá
cogeremos
cogeréis
cogerán

Conditional (present)

cogería   I would take
cogerías
cogería
cogeríamos
cogeríais
cogerían

Present subjunctive

coja   I take
cojas
coja
cojamos
cojáis
cojan

Imperfect subjunctive

cogiera   I took or I were to take
cogieras
cogiera
cogiéramos
cogierais
cogieran

Imperative

coge (tú)   take (singular)
coja (usted)   take (sing formal)
cojamos   let us take or
(nosotros)   let's take
coged (vosotros)   take (plural)
cojan (ustedes)   take (pl formal)

Gerund
dando   giving

Past participle
dado   given

4

dar
to give

Present indicative

doy   I give
das
da
damos
dais
dan

Imperfect indicative

daba   I gave *or* I used to give
dabas
daba
dábamos
dabais
daban

Past simple indicative

di   I gave
diste
dio
dimos
disteis
dieron

Future indicative

daré   I will give
darás
dará
daremos
daréis
darán

Conditional (present)

daría   I would give
darías
daría
daríamos
daríais
darían

Present subjunctive

dé   I give
des
dé
demos
deis
den

Imperfect subjunctive

diera   I gave *or* I were to give
dieras
diera
diéramos
dierais
dieran

Imperative

da (tú)	give (singular)
de (usted)	give (sing formal)
demos (nosotros)	let us give *or* let's give
dad (vosotros)	give (plural)
den (ustedes)	give (pl formal)

5

decir
to say *or* to tell

Gerund
diciendo   saying

Past participle
dicho   said

Present indicative

digo   I say *or* I am saying
dices
dice
decimos
decís
dicen

Imperfect indicative

decía   I was saying *or*
         I used to say
decías
decía
decíamos
decíais
decían

Past simple indicative

dije   I said
dijiste
dijo
dijimos
dijisteis
dijeron

Future indicative

diré   I will say
dirás
dirá
diremos
diréis
dirán

Conditional (present)

diría   I would say
dirías
diría
diríamos
diríais
dirían

Present subjunctive

diga   I say
digas
diga
digamos
digáis
digan

Imperfect subjunctive

dijera   I said *or* I were to say
dijeras
dijera
dijéramos
dijerais
dijeran

Imperative

di (tú)   say (singular)
diga (usted)   say (sing formal)
digamos   let us say *or*
(nosotros)   let's say
decid (vosotros)   say (plural)
digan (ustedes)   say (pl formal)

Gerund
habiendo   having

Past participle
habido   been

6

haber
to have

Present indicative

he	I have
has	
ha	
hemos	
habéis	
han	

Imperfect indicative

había	I was having *or* I used to have
habías	
había	
habíamos	
habíais	
habían	

Past simple indicative

hube	I had
hubiste	
hubo	
hubimos	
hubisteis	
hubieron	

Future indicative

habré	I will have
habrás	
habrá	
habremos	
habréis	
habrán	

Conditional (present)

habría	I would have
habrías	
habría	
habríamos	
habríais	
habrían	

Present subjunctive

haya	I have
hayas	
haya	
hayamos	
hayáis	
hayan	

Imperfect subjunctive

hubiera	I had *or* I were to have
hubieras	
hubiera	
hubiéramos	
hubierais	
hubieran	

Imperative

he (tú)	have (singular)
haya (usted)	have (sing formal)
hayamos (nosotros)	let us have *or* let's have
habed (vosotros)	have (plural)
hayan (ustedes)	have (pl formal)

7
hacer
to make *or* to do

Gerund
haciendo
making *or* doing

Past participle
hecho
made *or* done

Present indicative

hago — I make *or* I am making *or* I do *or* I am doing
haces
hace
hacemos
hacéis
hacen

Imperfect indicative

hacía — I was making *or* I used to make *or* I was doing *or* I used to do
hacías
hacía
hacíamos
hacíais
hacían

Past simple indicative

hice — I made *or* I did
hiciste
hizo
hicimos
hicisteis
hicieron

Future indicative

haré — I will make *or* I will do
harás
hará
haremos
haréis
harán

Conditional (present)

haría — I would make *or* I would do
harías
haría
haríamos
haríais
harían

Present subjunctive

haga — I make *or* I do
hagas
haga
hagamos
hagáis
hagan

Imperfect subjunctive

hiciera — I made *or* I were to make *or* I did *or* I were to do
hicieras
hiciera
hiciéramos
hicierais
hicieran

Imperative

haz (tú)	make *or* do (singular)
haga (usted)	make *or* do (sing formal)
hagamos (nosotros)	let us make *or* let's make *or* let us do *or* let's do
haced (vosotros)	make *or* do (plural)
hagan (ustedes)	make *or* do (pl formal)

Gerund
yendo   going

Past participle
ido   gone

ir
to go

Present indicative

voy   I go or I am going
vas
va
vamos
vais
van

Imperfect indicative

iba   I was going or
          I used to go
ibas
iba
íbamos
ibais
iban

Past simple indicative

fui   I went
fuiste
fue
fuimos
fuisteis
fueron

Future indicative

iré   I will go
irás
irá
iremos
iréis
irán

Conditional (present)

iría   I would go
irías
iría
iríamos
iríais
irían

Present subjunctive

vaya   I go
vayas
vaya
vayamos
vayáis
vayan

Imperfect subjunctive

fuera   I went or I were to go
fueras
fuera
fuéramos
fuerais
fueran

Imperative

ve (tú)   go (singular)
vaya (usted)   go (sing formal)
vayamos   let us go or
(nosotros)   let's go
id (vosotros)   go (plural)
vayan (ustedes)   go (pl formal)

9
tener
to have

Gerund
teniendo
having

Past participle
tenido   had

Present indicative

tengo   I have or I am having
tienes
tiene
tenemos
tenéis
tienen

Imperfect indicative

tenía   I was having or I used to have
tenías
tenía
teníamos
teníais
tenían

Past simple indicative

tuve   I had
tuviste
tuvo
tuvimos
tuvisteis
tuvieron

Future indicative

tendré   I will have
tendrás
tendrá
tendremos
tendréis
tendrán

Conditional (present)

tendría   I would have
tendrías
tendría
tendríamos
tendríais
tendrían

Present subjunctive

tenga   I have
tengas
tenga
tengamos
tengáis
tengan

Imperfect subjunctive

tuviera   I have
tuvieras
tuviera
tuviéramos
tuvierais
tuvieran

Imperative

ten (tú)	have (singular)
tenga (usted)	have (sing formal)
tengamos (nosotros)	let us have or let's have
tened (vosotros)	have (plural)
tengan (ustedes)	have (pl formal)

Gerund
pudiendo
being able to

Past participle
podido
been able to

10

poder
to be able

Present indicative

puedo	I am able to *or* I can
puedes	
puede	
podemos	
podéis	
pueden	

Imperfect indicative

podía	I was able to *or* I used to be able to
podías	
podía	
podíamos	
podíais	
podían	

Past simple indicative

pude	I was able to to *or* I could
pudiste	
pudo	
pudimos	
pudisteis	
pudieron	

Future indicative

podré	I will be able to
podrás	
podrá	
podremos	
podréis	
podrán	

Conditional (present)

podría	I would be able to
podrías	
podría	
podríamos	
podríais	
podrían	

Present subjunctive

pueda	I am able to *or* I can
puedas	
pueda	
podamos	
podáis	
puedan	

Imperfect subjunctive

pudiera	I was able to *or* I were able to
pudieras	
pudiera	
pudiéramos	
pudierais	
pudieran	

Imperative

The imperative is not used with poder

11
poner
to put

Gerund
poniendo
putting

Past participle
puesto   put

Present indicative

pongo   I put or I am putting
pones
pone
ponemos
ponéis
ponen

Imperfect indicative

ponía   I was putting or I used to
         put
ponías
ponía
poníamos
poníais
ponían

Past simple indicative

puse   I put
pusiste
puso
pusimos
pusisteis
pusieron

Future indicative

pondré   I will put
pondrás
pondrá
pondremos
pondréis
pondrán

Conditional (present)

pondría   I would put
pondrías
pondría
pondríamos
pondríais
pondrían

Present subjunctive

ponga   I put
pongas
ponga
pongamos
pongáis
pongan

Imperfect subjunctive

pusiera   I put or I were to put
pusieras
pusiera
pusiéramos
pusierais
pusieran

Imperative

pon (tú)	put (singular)
ponga (usted)	put (sing formal)
pongamos (nosotros)	let us put or let's put
poned (vosotros)	put (plural)
pongan (ustedes)	put (pl formal)

Gerund
queriendo
wanting to or loving

Past participle
querido   loved

12

querer
to want or to love

Present indicative

quiero	I want to or I love
quieres	
quiere	
queremos	
queréis	
quieren	

Imperfect indicative

quería	I wanted to or I used to want to or I loved or I used to love
querías	
quería	
queríamos	
queríais	
querían	

Past simple indicative

quise	I wanted to or I loved
quisiste	
quiso	
quisimos	
quisisteis	
quisieron	

Future indicative

querré	I will want to or I will love
querrás	
querrá	
querremos	
querréis	
querrán	

Conditional (present)

querría	I would want to or I would love
querrías	
querría	
querríamos	
querríais	
querrían	

Present subjunctive

quiera	I want to or I love
quieras	
quiera	
queramos	
queráis	
quieran	

Imperfect subjunctive

quisiera	I wanted to or I were to want or I loved or I were to love
quisieras	
quisiera	
quisiéramos	
quisierais	
quisieran	

Imperative

quiere (tú)	want (singular)
quiera (usted)	want (sing formal)
queramos (nosotros)	let us put or let's put
quered (vosotros)	want (plural)
quieran (ustedes)	want (pl formal)

13

saber
to know

Gerund
sabiendo   knowing

Past participle
sabido   known

Present indicative
sé   I know
sabes
sabe
sabemos
sabéis
saben

Imperfect indicative
sabía   I knew *or* I used to know
sabías
sabía
sabíamos
sabíais
sabían

Past simple indicative
supe   I knew
supiste
supo
supimos
supisteis
supieron

Future indicative
sabré   I will know
sabrás
sabrá
sabremos
sabréis
sabrán

Conditional (present)
sabría   I would know
sabrías
sabría
sabríamos
sabríais
sabrían

Present subjunctive
sepa   I know
sepas
sepa
sepamos
sepáis
sepan

Imperfect subjunctive
supiera   I knew
supieras
supiera
supiéramos
supierais
supieran

Imperative
sabe (tú)	know (singular)
sepa (usted)	know (sing formal)
sepamos (nosotros)	let us know *or* let's know
sabed (vosotros)	know (plural)
sepan (ustedes)	know (pl formal)

Gerund
sintiendo   feeling

Past participle
sentido   felt

14

sentir
to feel

Present indicative

siento   I feel
sientes
siente
sentimos
sentís
sienten

Imperfect indicative

sentía   I felt or I used to feel
sentías
sentía
sentíamos
sentíais
sentían

Past simple indicative

sentí   I felt
sentiste
sintió
sentimos
sentisteis
sintieron

Future indicative

sentiré   I will feel
sentirás
sentirá
sentiremos
sentiréis
sentirán

Conditional (present)

sentiría   I would feel
sentirías
sentiría
sentiríamos
sentiríais
sentirían

Present subjunctive

sienta   I feel
sientas
sienta
sintamos
sintáis
sientan

Imperfect subjunctive

sintiera   I felt or I were to feel
sintieras
sintiera
sintiéramos
sintierais
sintieran

Imperative

siente (tú)   feel (singular)
sienta (usted)   feel (sing formal)
sintamos (nosotros)   let us feel or
                         let's feel
sentid (vosotros)   feel (plural)
sientan (ustedes)   feel (pl formal)

15
venir
to come

Gerund
viniendo
coming

Past participle
venido
come

Present indicative

vengo   I come or I am coming
vienes
viene
venimos
venís
vienen

Imperfect indicative

venía   I was coming or I used to
           come
venías
venía
veníamos
veníais
venían

Past simple indicative

vine   I came
viniste
vino
vinimos
vinisteis
vinieron

Future indicative

vendré   I will come
vendrás
vendrá
vendremos
vendréis
vendrán

Conditional (present)

vendría   I would come
vendrías
vendría
vendríamos
vendríais
vendrían

Present subjunctive

venga   I come
vengas
venga
vengamos
vengáis
vengan

Imperfect subjunctive

viniera   I came or I were to come
vinieras
viniera
viniéramos
vinierais
vinieran

Imperative

ven (tú)	come (singular)
venga (usted)	come (sing formal)
vengamos (nosotros)	let us come or let's come
venid (vosotros)	come (plural)
vengan (ustedes)	come (pl formal)

Gerund
viendo   seeing

Past participle
visto   seen

16

ver
to see

Present indicative

veo   I see or I am seeing
ves
ve
vemos
veis
ven

Conditional (present)

vería   I would see
verías
vería
veríamos
veríais
verían

Imperfect indicative

veía   I saw or I used to see
veías
veía
veíamos
veíais
veían

Present subjunctive

vea   I see
veas
vea
veamos
veáis
vean

Past simple indicative

vi   I saw
viste
vio
vimos
visteis
vieron

Imperfect subjunctive

viera   I saw or I were to see
vieras
viera
viéramos
vierais
vieran

Future indicative

veré   I will see
verás
verá
veremos
veréis
verán

Imperative

ve (tú)	see (singular)
vea (usted)	see (sing formal)
veamos (nosotros)	let us see or let's see
ved (vosotros)	see (plural)
vean (ustedes)	see (pl formal)

17

hablar
to talk *or* to speak

regular -*ar*

Gerund
hablando
speaking

Past participle
hablado
spoken

Present indicative
hablo   I speak
hablas
habla
hablamos
habláis
hablan

Imperfect indicative
hablaba   I was speaking *or* I used
              to speak
hablabas
hablaba
hablábamos
hablabais
hablaban

Past simple indicative
hablé   I spoke
hablaste
habló
hablamos
hablasteis
hablaron

Future indicative
hablaré   I will speak
hablarás
hablará
hablaremos
hablaréis
hablarán

Conditional (present)
hablaría   I would speak
hablarías
hablaría
hablaríamos
hablaríais
hablarían

Present subjunctive
hable   I speak
hables
hable
hablemos
habléis
hablen

Imperfect subjunctive
hablara   I spoke *or* I were to speak
hablaras
hablara
habláramos
hablarais
hablaran

Imperative
habla (tú)	speak (singular)
hable (usted)	speak (sing formal)
hablemos (nosotros)	let us speak *or* let's speak
hablad (vosotros)	speak (plural)
hablen (ustedes)	speak (pl formal)

Gerund
comiendo eating

Past participle
comido eaten

18

comer
to eat

regular *-er*

Present indicative

como   I eat *or* I am eating
comes
come
comemos
coméis
comen

Imperfect indicative

comía   I was eating *or* I used to eat
comías
comía
comíamos
comíais
comían

Past simple indicative

comí   I ate
comiste
comió
comimos
comisteis
comieron

Future indicative

comeré   I will eat
comerás
comerá
comeremos
comeréis
comerán

Conditional (present)

comería   I would eat
comerías
comería
comeríamos
comeríais
comerían

Present subjunctive

coma   I eat
comas
coma
comamos
comáis
coman

Imperfect subjunctive

comiera   I ate *or* I were to eat
comieras
comiera
comiéramos
comierais
comieran

Imperative

come (tú)	eat (singular)
coma (usted)	eat (sing formal)
comamos (nosotros)	let us eat *or* let's eat
comed (vosotros)	eat (plural)
coman (ustedes)	eat (pl formal)

19

vivir
to live

regular *-ir*

Gerund
viv**iendo** living

Past participle
viv**ido** lived

Present indicative

viv**o** I live *or* I am living
viv**es**
viv**e**
viv**imos**
viv**ís**
viv**en**

Imperfect indicative

viv**ía** I lived *or* I used to live
viv**ías**
viv**ía**
viv**íamos**
viv**íais**
viv**ían**

Past simple indicative

viv**í** I lived
viv**iste**
viv**ió**
viv**imos**
viv**isteis**
viv**ieron**

Future indicative

viv**iré** I will live
viv**irás**
viv**irá**
viv**iremos**
viv**iréis**
viv**irán**

Conditional (present)

viv**iría** I would live
viv**irías**
viv**iría**
viv**iríamos**
viv**iríais**
viv**irían**

Present subjunctive

viv**a** I live
viv**as**
viv**a**
viv**amos**
viv**áis**
viv**an**

Imperfect subjunctive

viv**iera** I lived *or* I were to live
viv**ieras**
viv**iera**
viv**iéramos**
viv**ierais**
viv**ieran**

Imperative

viv**e** (tú)	live (singular)
viv**a** (usted)	live (sing formal)
viv**amos** (nosotros)	let us live *or* let's live
viv**id** (vosotros)	live (plural)
viv**an** (ustedes)	live (pl formal)

20 **actuar** - like **17 hablar** except:

Present indicative	Present subjunctive
actúo	actúe
actúas	actúes
actúa	actúe
actuamos	actuemos
actuáis	actuéis
actúan	actúen

	Imperative
	actúa (tú)
	actúe (usted)
	actuemos (nosotros
	actuad (vosotros)
	actúen (ustedes)

21 **andar** - like **17 hablar** except:

Past simple indicative	Imperfect subjunctive
anduve	anduviera
anduviste	anduvieras
anduvo	anduciera
anduvimos	anduviéramos
andivisteis	anduvierais
anduvieron	anduvieran

22 **cazar** - like **17 hablar** except:

Past simple indicative	Present subjunctive
cacé	cace
cazaste	caces
cazó	cace
cazamos	cacemos
cazasteis	cacéis
cazaron	cacen

	Imperative
	caza (tú)
	cace (usted)
	cacemos (nosotros)
	cazad (vosotros)
	cacen (ustedes)

23 **colgar** - like **17 hablar** except:

Present indicative	Present subjunctive
cuelgo	cuelgue
cuelgas	cuelgues
cuelga	cuelgue
colgamos	colguemos
colgáis	colguéis
cuelgan	cuelguen

Past simple indicative	Imperative
colgué	cuelga (tú)
colgaste	cuelgue (usted)
colgó	colguemos (nosotros)
colgamos	colgad (vosotros)
colgasteis	cuelguen (ustedes)
colgaron	

24 **contar** - like **17 hablar** except:

Present indicative	Present subjunctive
cuento	cuente
cuentas	cuentes
cuenta	cuente
contamos	contemos
contáis	contéis
cuentan	cuenten

	Imperative
	cuenta (tú)
	cuente (usted)
	contemos (nosotros)
	contad (vosotros)
	cuenten (ustedes)

25 **empezar** - like **17 hablar** except:

Present indicative	Present subjunctive
empiezo	empiece
empiezas	empieces
empieza	empiece
empezamos	empecemos
empezáis	empecéis
empiezan	empiecen

Past simple indicative	Imperative
empecé	empieza (tú)
empezaste	empiece (usted)
empezó	empecemos
empezamos	(nosotros)
empezasteis	empezad (vosotros)
empezaron	empiecen (ustedes)

26 **forzar** - like **17 hablar** except:

Present indicative	Present subjunctive
fuerzo	fuerce
fuerzas	fuerces
fuerza	fuerce
forzamos	forcemos
forzáis	forcéis
fuerzan	fuercen

Past simple indicative	Imperative
forcé	fuerza (tú)
forzaste	fuerce (usted)
forzó	forcemos (nosotros
forzamos	forzad (vosotros)
forzasteis	fuercen (ustedes)
forzaron	

27 **jugar** - like **17 hablar** except:

Present indicative	Present subjunctive
juego	juegue
juegas	juegues
juega	juegue
jugamos	juguemos
jugáis	juguéis
juegan	jueguen

Past simple indicative	Imperative
jugué	juega (tú)
jugaste	juegue (usted)
jugó	juguemos (nosotros)
jugamos	jugad (vosotros)
jugasteis	jueguen (ustedes)
jugaron	

28 **pagar** - like **17 hablar** except:

Past simple indicative	Present subjunctive
pagué	pague
pagaste	pagues
pagó	pague
pagamos	paguemos
pagasteis	paguéis
pagaron	paguen

	Imperative
	paga (tú)
	pague (usted)
	paguemos (nosotros)
	pagad (vosotros)
	paguen (ustedes)

29 **pensar** - like **17 hablar** except:

Present indicative	Present subjunctive
pienso	piense
piensas	pienses
piensa	piense
pensamos	pensemos
pensáis	penséis
piensan	piensen

Imperative

piensa (tú)
piense (usted)
pensemos (nosotros)
pensad (vosotros)
piensen (ustedes)

31 **sacar** - like **17 hablar** except:

Past simple indicative	Imperative
saqué	saca (tú)
sacaste	saque (usted)
sacó	saquemos (nosotros)
sacamos	sacad (vosotros)
sacasteis	saquen (ustedes)
sacaron	

Present subjunctive

saque
saques
saque
saquemos
saquéis
saquen

30 **regar** - like **17 hablar** except:

Present indicative	Present subjunctive
riego	riegue
riegas	riegues
riega	riegue
regamos	reguemos
regáis	reguéis
riegan	rieguen

Past simple indicative	Imperative
regué	riega (tú)
regaste	riegue (usted)
regó	reguemos (nosotros)
regamos	regad (vosotros)
regasteis	rieguen (ustedes)
regaron	

32 **vaciar** - like **17 hablar** except:

Present indicative	Present subjunctive
vacío	vacíe
vacías	vacíes
vacía	vacíe
vaciamos	vaciemos
vaciáis	vaciéis
vacían	vacíen

Imperative

vacía (tú)
vacíe (usted)
vaciemos (nosotros)
vaciad (vosotros)
vacíen (ustedes)

33 **caber** - like **18 comer** except:

Present indicative	Conditional (present)
quepo	cabría
cabes	cabrías
cabe	cabría
cabemos	cabríamos
cabéis	cabríais
caben	cabrían

Past simple indicative	Present subjunctive
cupe	quepa
cupiste	quepas
cupo	quepa
cupimos	quepamos
cupisteis	quepáis
cupieron	quepan

Future indicative	Imperfect subjunctive
cabré	cupiera
cabrás	cupieras
cabrá	cupiera
cabremos	cupiéramos
cabréis	cupierais
cabrán	cupieran

Imperative
cabe (tú)
quepa (usted)
quepamos
(nosotros)
cabed (vosotros)
quepan (ustedes)

34 **caer** - like **18 comer** except:

Gerund cayendo
Past participle caído

Present indicative	Present subjunctive
caigo	caiga
caes	caigas
cae	caiga
caemos	caigamos
caéis	caigáis
caen	caigan

Past simple indicative	Imperfect subjunctive
caí	cayera
caíste	cayeras
cayó	cayera
caimos	cayéramos
caísteis	cayerais
cayeron	cayeran

Imperative
cae (tú)
caiga (usted)
caigamos (nosotros)
caed (vosotros)
caigan (ustedes)

35 **conocer** - like **18 comer** except:

Present indicative	Present subjunctive
conozco	conozca
conoces	conozcas
conoce	conozca
conocemos	conozcamos
conocéis	conozcáis
conocen	conozcan

Imperative
conoce (tú)
conozca (usted)
conozcamos
(nosotros)
conoced (vosotros)
conozcan (ustedes)

36 **entender** - like **18 comer** except:

Present indicative	Present subjunctive
entiendo	entienda
entiendes	entiendas
entiende	entienda
entendemos	entendamos
entendéis	entendáis
entienden	entiendan

Imperative
entiende (tú)
entienda (usted)
entendamos
 (nosotros)
entended (vosotros)
entiendan (ustedes)

37 **leer** - like **18 comer** except:

Gerund leyendo
Past participle leído

Past simple indicative	Imperfect subjunctive
leí	leyera
leíste	leyeras
leyó	leyera
leímos	layéramos
leísteis	leyerais
leyeron	leyeran

38 **mover** - like **18 comer** except:

Present indicative	Present subjunctive
muevo	mueva
mueves	muevas
mueve	mueva
movemos	movamos
movéis	mováis
mueven	muevan

Imperative
mueve (tú)
mueva (usted)
movamos
 (nosotros)
moved (vosotros)
muevan (ustedes)

39 **oler** - like **18 comer** except:

Present indicative	Present subjunctive
huelo	huela
hueles	huelas
huele	huela
olemos	olamos
oléis	oláis
huelen	huelan

Imperative
huele (tú)
huela (usted)
olamos (nosotros)
oled (vosotros)
huelan (ustedes)

40 **romper** - like **18 comer** except:

Past participle roto

41 **torcer** - like **18 comer** except:

Present indicative	Present subjunctive
tuerzo	tuerza
tuerces	tuerzas
tuerce	tuerza
torcemos	torzamos
torcéis	torzáis
tuercen	tuerzan

Imperative
tuerce (tú)
tuerza (usted)
torzamos (nosotros)
torced (vosotros)
tuerzan (ustedes)

42 **traer** - like **18 comer** except:

Gerund trayendo
Past participle traído

Present indicative	Imperfect subjunctive
traigo	trajera
traes	trajeras
trae	trajera
traemos	trajéramos
traéis	trajerais
traen	trajeran

Present subjunctive	Past simple indicative
traiga	traje
traigas	trajiste
traiga	trajo
traigamos	trajimos
traigáis	trajisteis
traigan	trajeron

Imperative

trae (tú)
traiga (usted)
traigamos (nosotros)
traed (vosotros)
traigan (ustedes)

43 **valer** - like **18 comer** except:

Present indicative	Present subjunctive
valgo	valga
vales	valgas
vale	valga
valemos	valgamos
valéis	valgáis
valen	valgan

Future indicative	Imperfect subjunctive
valdré	valiera
valdrás	valieras
valdrá	valiera
valdremos	valiéramos
valdréis	valierais
valdrán	valieran

Conditional (present)	Imperative
valdría	vale (tú)
valdrías	valga (usted)
valdría	valgamos (nosotro
valdríamos	valed (vosotros)
valdríais	valgan (ustedes)
valdrían	

44 **vencer** - like **18 comer** except:

Present indicative	Present subjunctive
venzo	venza
vences	venzas
vence	venza
vencemos	venzamos
vencéis	venzáis
vencen	venzan

Imperative

vence (tú)
venza (usted)
venzamos (nosotros)
venced (vosotros)
venzan (ustedes)

45 **volver** - like **18 comer** except:

Past participle vuelto

Present indicative	Present subjunctive
vuelvo	vuelva
vuelves	vuelvas
vuelve	vuelva
volvemos	volvamos
volvéis	volváis
vuelven	vuelvan

Imperative

vuelve (tú)
vuelva (usted)
volvamos (nosotros)
volved (vosotros)
vuelvan (ustedes)

46 **abrir** - like **19 vivir** except:

Past participle abierto

47 **adquirir** - like **19 vivir** except:

Present indicative	Present subjunctive
adquiero	addquiera
adquieres	adquieras
adquiere	adquiera
adquirimos	adquiramos
adquirís	adquiráis
adquieren	adquieran

	Imperative
	adquiere (tú)
	adquiera (usted)
	adquiramos (nosotros)
	adquirid (vosotros)
	adquieran (ustedes

48 **corregir** - like **19 vivir** except:

Present indicative	Present subjunctive
corrijo	corrija
corriges	corrijas
corrige	corrija
corregimos	corrijamos
corregís	corrijáis
corrigen	corrijan

Past simple indicative	Imperative
corregí	corrige (tú)
corregiste	corrija (usted)
corrigió	corrijamos (nosotros)
corrigieron	
corregisteis	corregid (vosotros)
corrigieron	corrijan (ustedes)

49 **dirigir** - like **19 vivir** except:

Present indicative	Present subjunctive
dirijo	dirija
diriges	dirijas
dirige	dirija
dirigimos	dirijamos
dirigís	dirijáis
dirigen	dirijan

	Imperative
	dirige (tú)
	dirija (usted)
	dirijamos (nosotros)
	dirigid (vosotros)
	dirijan (ustedes)

50 **distinguir** - like **19 vivir** except:

Present indicative	Present subjunctive
distingo	distinga
distingues	distingas
distingue	distinga
distinguimos	distingamos
distinguís	distingáis
distinguen	distingan

	Imperative
	distingue (tú)
	distinga (usted)
	distingamos (nosotros)
	distinguid (vosotros)
	distingan (ustedes)

51 **dormir** - like **19 vivir** except:

Gerund durmiendo
Past participle dormido

Present indicative	Past simple indicative
duermo	dormí
duermes	dormiste
duerme	dormid
dormimos	dormimos
dormís	dormisteis
duermen	durmieron

Imperfect subjunctive	Imperative
durmiera	duerme (tú)
durmieras	duerma (usted)
durmiera	durmamos
durmiéramos	(nosotros)
durmierais	dormid (vosotros)
durmieran	duerman (ustedes)

	Present subjunctive
	duerma
	duermas
	duerma
	durmamos
	durmáis
	duerman

52 **escriber** - like **19 vivir** except:

Past participle excrito

53 **freír** - like **19 vivir** except:

Gerund friendo
Past participle frito

Present indicative	Present subjunctive
frío	fría
fríes	frías
fríe	fría
freímos	friamos
freís	friáis
fríen	frían

Past simple indicative	Imperfect subjunctive
freí	friera
freíste	frieras
frió	friera
freímos	friéramos
freísteis	frierais
frieron	frieran

	Imperative
	fríe (tú)
	fría (usted)
	friamos (nosotros)
	freíd (vosotros)
	frían (ustedes)

54 **huir** - like **19 vivir** except:

Gerund huyendo
Past participle huido

Present indicative	Present subjunctive
huyo	huya
huyes	huyas
huye	huya
huimos	huyamos
huís	huyáis
huyen	huyan

Past simple indicative	Imperfect subjunctive
huí	huyera
huíste	huyeras
huyó	huyera
huimos	huyéramos
huísteis	huyerais
huyeron	huyeran

	Imperative
	huye (tú)
	huya (usted)
	huyamos (nosotros)
	huid (vosotros)
	huyan (ustedes)

55 **morir** - like **19 vivir** except:

Gerund muriendo
Past participle muerto

Present indicative	Present subjunctive
muero	muera
mueres	mueras
muere	muera
morimos	muramos
morís	muráis
mueren	mueran

Past simple indicative	Imperfect subjunctive
morí	muriera
moriste	murieras
murió	muriera
morimos	muriéramos
moristeis	murierais
murieron	murieran

56 oír - like 19 vivir except:

Gerund oyendo
Past participle oído

Present indicative	Imperfect indicative
oigo	oía
oyes	oías
oye	oía
oímos	oíamos
oís	oíais
oyen	oían

Past simple indicative	Present subjunctive
oí	oiga
oíste	oigas
oyó	oiga
oímos	oigamos
oísteis	oigáis
oyeron	oigan

Future indicative	Imperfect subjunctive
oiré	oyera
oirás	oyeras
oirá	oyera
oiremos	oyéramos
oiréis	oyerais
oirán	oyeran

Conditional (present)	Imperative
oiría	oye (tú)
oirías	oiga (usted)
oiría	oigamos (nosotros)
oiríamos	oíd (vosotros)
oiríais	oigan (ustedes)
oirían	

57 pedir - like 19 vivir except:

Present indicative	Present subjunctive
pido	pida
pides	pidas
pide	pida
pedimos	pidamos
pedís	pidáis
piden	pidan

Past simple indicative	Imperfect subjunctive
pedí	pidiera
pediste	pidieras
pidió	pidiera
pedimos	pidiéramos
pedisteis	pidierais
pidieron	pidieran

	Imperative
	pide (tú)
	pida (usted)
	pidamos (nostros)
	pedid (vosotros)
	pidan (ustedes)

58 prohibir - like 19 vivir except:

Present indicative	Present subjunctive
prohíbo	prohíba
prohíbes	prohíbas
prohíbe	prohíba
prohibimos	prohibamos
prohibís	prohibáis
prohíben	prohíban

	Imperative
	prohíbe (tú)
	prohíba (usted)
	prohibamos (nosotros)
	prohibid (vosotros)
	prohíban (ustedes)

59 **pudrir** - like **19 vivir** except:

Past participle podrido

60 **reducir** - like **19 vivir** except:

Present indicative	Present subjunctive
reduzco	reduzca
reduces	reduzcas
reduce	reduzca
reducimos	reduzcamos
reducís	reduzcáis
reducen	reduzcan

Past simple indicative	Imperfect subjunctive
reduje	redujera
redujiste	redujeras
redujo	redujera
redujimos	redujéramos
redujisteis	redujerais
redujeron	redujeran

Imperative
reduce (tú)
reduzca (usted)
reduzcamos (nosotros)
reducid (vosotros)
reduzcan (ustedes)

61 **reír** - like **19 vivir** except:

Present indicative	Conditional (present)
río	reiría
ríes	reirías
ríe	reiría
reímos	reiríamos
reís	reiríais
ríen	reirían

Imperfect indicative	Present subjunctive
reía	ría
reías	rías
reía	ría
reíamos	riamos
reíais	riáis
reían	rían

Past simple indicative	Imperfect subjunctive
reí	riera
reíste	rieras
rió	riera
reímos	riéramos
reísteis	rierais
rieron	rieran

Future indicative	Imperative
reiré	ríe (tú)
reirás	ría (usted)
reirá	riamos (nosotros)
reiremos	reíd (vosotros)
reiréis	rían (ustedes)
reirán	

62 **reunir** - like **19 vivir** except:

Present indicative	Imperative
reúno	reúne (tú)
reúnes	reúna (usted)
reúne	reunamos (nosotros)
reunimos	reunid (vosotros)
reunís	reúnan (ustedes)
reúnen	

Present subjunctive
reúna
reúnas
reúna
reunamos
reunáis
reúnan

63 salir - like 19 vivir except:

Present indicative	Present subjunctive
salgo	salga
sales	salgas
sale	salga
salimos	salgamos
salís	salgáis
salen	salgan

Future indicative	Imperfect subjunctive
saldré	saliera
saldrás	salieras
saldrá	saliera
saldremos	saliéramos
saldréis	salierais
saldrán	salieran

Conditional (present)	Imperative
saldría	sal (tú)
saldrías	salga (usted)
saldría	salgamos (nosotros)
saldríamos	salid (vosotros)
saldríais	salgan (ustedes)
saldrían	

64 seguir - like 19 vivir except:

Present indicative	Past simple indicative
sigo	seguí
sigues	seguiste
sigue	siguió
seguimos	seguimos
seguís	seguisteis
siguen	siguieron

Present subjunctive	Imperfect subjunctive
siga	siguiera
sigas	siguieras
siga	siguiera
sigamos	siguiéramos
sigáis	siguierais
sigan	siguieran

	Imperative
	sigue (tú)
	siga (usted)
	sigamos (nosotros)
	seguid (vosotros)
	sigan (ustedes)

65 teñir - like 19 vivir except:

Gerund tiñendo

Present indicative	Present subjunctive
tiño	tiña
tiñes	tiñas
tiñe	tiña
teñimos	tiñamos
teñís	tiñáis
tiñen	tiñan

Past simple indicative	Imperfect subjunctive
teñí	tiñera
teñiste	tiñeras
tiñó	tiñera
teñimos	tiñéramos
teñisteis	tiñerais
tiñeron	tiñeran

	Imperative
	tiñe (tú)
	tiña (usted)
	tiñamos (nosotros)
	teñid (vosotros)
	tiñan (ustedes)

Aa

a *indefinite article* **1** (*before a noun which is masculine in Spanish*) un; **a tree** un árbol; **2** (*before a noun which is feminine in Spanish*) una; **a table** una mesa; **3** (*before professions, occupations, etc. 'a' is not translated*) **I'm a doctor** soy médico; **4 five euros a kilo** cinco euros el kilo; **5 fifty kilometres an hour** cincuenta kilómetros por hora; **6 three times a day** tres veces al día.

abandon *verb* abandonar [17].

abbey *noun* abadía *Fem.*; **Westminster Abbey** la abadía de Westminster.

abbreviation *noun* abreviatura *Fem.*

abide *verb* **I can't abide** ... no puedo soportar ....

ability *noun* **1** capacidad *Fem.*; **the ability to do** la capacidad de hacer; **2 do it to the best of your ability** hazlo lo mejor que puedas; **I did it to the best of my ability** lo hice lo mejor que pude.

able *adjective* **to be able to do** poder [10] hacer; **she wasn't able to come** no pudo venir.

abnormal *adjective* anormal.

abolish *verb* abolir [19].

abortion *noun* aborto *Masc.*

about *preposition* **1** (*on the subject of*) sobre; **a film about Picasso** una película sobre Picasso; **2 what's it about?** ¿de qué trata?; **3** (*concerning or in relation to*) acerca de; **he wants to talk to you about your exam** quiere hablarte acerca de tu examen; **4 to talk about something** hablar de algo; **what is she talking about?** ¿de qué está hablando?; **5 to think about something/somebody** pensar en algo/alguien; **I'm thinking about you** estoy pensando en ti.

about *adverb* **1** (*approximately*) **there are about sixty people** hay unas sesenta personas; **2** (*when talking about time*) **at about three o'clock** como a las tres; **about three weeks/a month ago** hace cosa de tres semanas/de un mes; **3 to be about to do** estar a punto de hacer; **I'm (just) about to leave** estoy a punto de marcharme.

above *preposition* **1** encima de; **above the sink** encima del fregadero; **2 above all** sobre todo. **above** *adverb* de arriba; **the flat above** el piso de arriba.

abroad *adverb* **to go abroad** irse al extranjero; **to live abroad** vivir en el extranjero.

abscess *noun* flemón *Masc.*

abseiling *noun* rappel *Masc.*

absent *adjective* ausente; **to be absent from** faltar a; **he was absent from the lesson** faltó a clase; **she's often absent from meetings** falta a menudo a las reuniones; (*when referring to the present moment, 'to be absent' is translated by the present perfect*) **he's absent from school today** hoy ha faltado a clase.

a
b
c
d
e
f
g
h
i
j
k
l
m
n
o
p
q
r
s
t
u
v
w
x
y
z

absent-minded *adjective*
despistado/despistada.

absolute *adjective* absoluto/
absoluta; **an absolute disaster** un
desastre absoluto.

absolutely *adverb* **1** (*completely*)
totalmente; **I'm absolutely certain**
estoy totalmente segura;
2 (*extremely*) realmente; **it's
absolutely dreadful** es realmente
terrible; **3 you're absolutely right**
tienes toda la razón; **4 absolutely!**
¡por supuesto!

absorb *verb* absorber [18].

abuse *noun* **1 alcohol abuse**
alcoholismo *Masc.*; **drug abuse**
consumo *Masc.* de drogas; **2** (*violent
treatment of a person*) malos tratos
Masc. plural; **3** (*insults*) insultos
Masc. plural.

abuse *verb* **to abuse somebody**
maltratar [17] a alguien.

academic *adjective* académico/
académica; **the academic year** el
año académico.

accelerate *verb* acelerar [17].

accelerator *noun* acelerador *Masc.*

accent *noun* acento *Masc.*; **she has
a Spanish accent** tiene acento
español.

accept *verb* aceptar [17].

acceptable *adjective* aceptable.

access *noun* acceso *Masc.*
access *verb* **to access something**
obtener [9] acceso a algo.

accessory *noun* accesorio *Masc.*

accident *noun* **1** (*an unfortunate
happening*) accidente *Masc.*; **to have**

an accident tener [9] un accidente;
a road accident un accidente de
carretera; **a car accident** un
accidente de coche; **2** (*chance*)
casualidad *Fem.*; **it's no accident** no
es casualidad; **3 by accident** (*by
chance*) por casualidad(*without
meaning to*) sin querer; **I found it by
accident** lo encontré por
casualidad; **she broke it by
accident** lo rompió sin querer.

accidental *adjective* fortuito/
fortuita; **an accidental discovery**
un descubrimiento fortuito.

accident & emergency *noun*
urgencias *Fem. plural*.

accidentally *adverb* **1** (*without
meaning to*) sin querer; **I
accidentally knocked over his
glass** le tiré el vaso sin querer; **2** (*by
chance*) por casualidad; **I
accidentally discovered that ...**
descubrí por casualidad que ....

accommodation *noun*
alojamiento *Masc.*; **I'm looking for
accommodation** estoy buscando
alojamiento; **hotel
accommodation** alojamiento en
hotel.

accompany *verb* **to accompany
somebody** acompañar [17] a
alguien.

according *in phrase* **according to**
según; **according to Sophie** según
Sophie.

accordion *noun* acordeón *Masc.*

account *noun* **1** (*in a bank, shop,
or post office*) cuenta *Fem.*; **a bank
account** una cuenta bancaria; **to
open an account** abrir [46] una

cuenta; **I have fifty pounds in my account** tengo cincuenta libras en mi cuenta; **2** (*a description of an experience or event*) relato Masc.; **3 on account of** debido a; **the station is closed on account of the strike** la estación está cerrada debido a la huelga; **4 to take something into account** tener [9] algo en cuenta; **we will take his illness into account** tendremos en cuenta su enfermedad.

accountant *noun* contable Masc./ Fem.; **she's an accountant** es contable.

accuracy *noun* precisión Fem.

accurate *adjective* preciso/ precisa.

accurately *adverb* con precisión.

accuse *verb* acusar [17]; **to accuse somebody of something** acusar a alguien de algo; **to accuse somebody of doing something** acusar a alguien de hacer algo; **she accused me of stealing her pen** me acusó de haber robado su pluma.

accustomed to *adjective* **to be accustomed to something** estar [2] acostumbrado/acostumbrada a algo; **she's accustomed to having lots of homework** está acostumbrada a tener muchos deberes.

ace *noun* as Masc.; **the ace of hearts** el as de corazones.
ace *adjective* de primera (*informal*); **he's an ace drummer** es un batería de primera.

ache *verb* **my arm aches** me duele el brazo; **my head aches** me duele la cabeza.

achieve *verb* **1** conseguir [64]; **she's achieved a great deal** consiguió mucho; **2 to achieve an ambition** hacer [7] realidad una ambición; **3 to achieve an aim** lograr [17] un objetivo; **4 to achieve success** tener [9] éxito.

achievement *noun* **1** éxito Masc.; **it's a great achievement** es un gran éxito; **2 a sense of achievement** un sentimiento de satisfacción.

acid *noun* ácido Masc.

acid rain *noun* lluvia Fem. ácida.

acne *noun* acné Masc.

acorn *noun* bellota Fem.

acrobat *noun* acróbata Masc./Fem.

across *preposition* **1** (*over to the other side of*) **to walk across something** cruzar [22] algo; **we walked across the park** cruzamos el parque; **to run across the road** cruzar la calle corriendo; **2** (*on the other side of*) al otro lado de; **the house across the street** la casa de enfrente; **3 across from** en frente de; **she was sitting across from me** estaba sentada en frente de mí.

acrylic *noun* acrílica Fem.

act *noun* acto Masc.
act *verb* actuar [20].

acting *noun* actuación Fem.; **she wants to go into acting** quiere ser actriz.

action *noun* acción Fem.

319

a
b
c
d
e
f
g
h
i
j
k
l
m
n
o
p
q
r
s
t
u
v
w
x
y
z

action replay *noun* repetición *Fem.* de la jugada.

active *adjective* activo/activa.

activity *noun* actividad *Fem.*

activity holiday *noun* vacaciones *Fem. plural* con actividades programadas.

actor *noun* actor *Masc.*; **who's your favourite actor?** ¿quién es tu actor favorito?

actress *noun* actriz *Fem.* (*plural* actrices); **who's your favourite actress?** ¿quién es tu actriz favorita?

actual *adjective* **1** his actual words sus palabras textuales; **2** actual cases casos reales; **3** in actual fact de hecho.

actually *adverb* **1** (*in fact, as it happens*) la verdad es que; **actually, I've changed my mind** la verdad es que he cambiado de idea; **he's not actually here at the moment** la verdad es que no está aquí en este momento; **2** (*really and truly*) de verdad; **did she actually say that?** ¿dijo eso de verdad?

acupuncture *noun* acupuntura *Fem.*

acute *adjective* **1** (*pain*) agudo/aguda; **2** an acute accent un acento agudo.

ad *noun* anuncio *Masc.*; **to put an ad in the paper** poner un anuncio en el periódico; **the small ads** los anuncios por palabras.

AD d. de C. (*después de Cristo*); **in 400 AD** en el año 400 d. de C.

adapt *verb* **1** to adapt something adaptar [17] algo; **2** to adapt to

something adaptarse [17] a algo; **she's adapted to the new system** se adaptó al nuevo sistema.

adaptor *noun* adaptador *Masc.*

add *verb* añadir [19]; **add three eggs** añadir tres huevos.
- **to add something up** sumar [17] algo.

addict *noun* **1** (*drug addict*) drogadicto *Masc.*, drogadicta *Fem.*; **2** (*of television, chocolate, for example*) adicto *Masc.*, adicta *Fem.*; **she's a telly addict** es una adicta a la televisión; **3** (*of sport*) fanático *Masc.*, fanática *Fem.*; **he's a football addict** es un fanático del fútbol.

addicted *adjective* **1** (*to drugs, television, computer games, etc.*) adicto/adicta; **she's addicted to heroin** es adicta a la heroína; **he's addicted to the Net** es un adicto a Internet; **2** (*to food*) **I'm addicted to tomatoes** los tomates son mi vicio (*informal*); **3** to become addicted to something (*to drugs*) hacerse adicto a algo (*to television, chocolate*) enviciarse con algo.

addition *noun* **1** (*adding up*) suma *Fem.*; **2** in addition además; **3** in addition to además de.

additional *adjective* adicional; **additional costs** costes *Masc. plural* adicionales.

additive *noun* aditivo *Masc.*

address *noun* **1** (*of person, house, office*) dirección *Fem.*; **what's your address?** ¿cuál es tu dirección?; **2** (*on a form*) domicilio *Masc.*; **3** to change address cambiar [17] de domicilio.

address book *noun* libreta *Fem.* de direcciones.

adequate *adjective* suficiente.

adhesive *noun* pegamento *Masc.*
adhesive *adjective* adhesivo/ adhesiva; **adhesive tape** cinta *Fem.* adhesiva.

adjective *noun* adjetivo *Masc.*

adjust *verb* 1 regular [17] (*volume, temperature*), ajustar [17] (*height, width*); 2 **to adjust to something** adaptarse [17] a algo.

adjustable *adjective* regulable.

administration *noun* administración *Fem.*

admiral *noun* almirante *Masc./Fem.*

admiration *noun* admiración *Fem.*

admire *verb* admirar [17].

admission *noun* entrada *Fem.*; **'no admission'** prohibida la entrada; **'admission free'** entrada gratuita.

admit *verb* 1 (*confess*) admitir [19]; **she admits she lied** admite que mintió; 2 (*concede*) reconocer [35]; **I must admit that** ... debo reconocer que ...; 3 (*allow to enter*) dejar [17] entrar; **to admit somebody to a restaurant** dejar entrar a alguien en un restaurante.

adolescence *noun* adolescencia *Fem.*

adolescent *noun* adolescente *Masc./Fem.*

adopt *verb* adoptar [17].

adopted *adjective* adoptado/ adoptada.

adoption *noun* adopción *Fem.*

adore *verb* adorar [17].

Adriatic Sea *noun* **the Adriatic Sea** el mar Adriático.

adult *noun* adulto *Masc.*, adulta *Fem.*
adult *adjective* adulto/adulta; **the adult population** la población adulta.

Adult Education *noun* educación *Fem.* para adultos.

advance *noun* avance *Masc.*; **advances in technology** avances en tecnología.
advance *verb* avanzar [22].

advanced *adjective* avanzado/ avanzada.

advantage *noun* 1 ventaja *Fem.*; **there are several advantages** hay varias ventajas; 2 **to take advantage of something** aprovechar [17] algo; **I took advantage of the sales to buy myself some shoes** aproveché las rebajas para comprarme unos zapatos; 3 **to take advantage of somebody** (*unfairly*) aprovecharse [17] de alguien.

adventure *noun* aventura *Fem.*

adventurous *adjective* 1 (*person*) aventurero/aventurera; 2 (*design, designer, composer, etc.*) innovador/ innovadora.

adverb *noun* adverbio *Masc.*

advert, advertisement *noun* 1 (*on television, in a newspaper*) anuncio *Masc.*; 2 (*small ad in a newspaper advertising a job, an article for sale, etc.*) anuncio *Masc.* por palabras.

advertise *verb* 1 **to advertise a product** hacer [7] publicidad de un

a
b
c
d
e
f
g
h
i
j
k
l
m
n
o
p
q
r
s
t
u
v
w
x
y
z

producto; **2 to advertise something in the newspaper** anunciar [17] algo en el periódico; **I saw it advertised on telly** lo vi anunciado en la tele; **I saw a bike advertised in the paper** (*in the small ads*) vi un anuncio (*por palabras*) de una bicicleta en el periódico.

advertising *noun* publicidad *Fem*.

advice *noun* **1** consejos *Masc. plural*; **his advice is good** sus consejos son buenos; **2 a piece of advice** un consejo; **3 to give somebody advice** aconsejar [17] a alguien; **they gave me good advice** me aconsejaron bien; **4 to ask for advice about something** pedir [57] consejo sobre algo.

advise *verb* aconsejar [17]; **to advise somebody to ...** aconsejar a alguien que ... (*followed by the subjunctive*); **I advised him to study more** le aconsejé que estudiase más; **I advised her not to wait** le aconsejé que no esperase.

adviser *noun* asesor *Masc.*, asesora *Fem*.

aerial *noun* antena *Fem*.

aerobics *noun* aerobic *Masc.*; **to do aerobics** hacer [7] aerobic.

aeroplane *noun* avión *Masc*.

aerosol *noun* **an aerosol (can)** un aerosol.

affair *noun* **1** asunto *Masc.*; **international affairs** asuntos internacionales; **2 a love affair** una aventura amorosa.

affect *verb* afectar [17].

affectionate *adjective* cariñoso/cariñosa.

afford *verb* **to be able to afford to do** tener [9] dinero para hacer; **I can't afford to go out much** no tengo dinero para salir mucho; **I can't afford a new bike** no tengo dinero para una bicicleta nueva.

afraid *adjective* **1 to be afraid** tener [9] miedo; **I'm afraid** tengo miedo; **2** (*with 'of'*) **I'm afraid of dogs** me dan miedo los perros; **Dan's afraid of spiders** a Dan le dan miedo las arañas; **he's afraid of flying** le da miedo volar; **she's afraid of failing the exam** le da miedo suspender el examen; **3 I'm afraid there's no milk left** me temo que no queda leche; **I'm afraid so** me temo que sí; **I'm afraid not** me temo que no.

Africa *noun* África *Fem*.

African *noun* africano *Masc.*, africana *Fem*.
African *adjective* africano/africana.

after *preposition, adverb*
after *conjunction* **1** (*later in time*) después de; **after 10 o'clock** después de las diez en punto; **after lunch** después de comer; **after school** después del colegio; **after I've finished my homework** después de terminar mis deberes; **2 soon after** poco después; **3 the day after tomorrow** pasado mañana.

● **to run after somebody** correr [18] tras alguien.

after all *adverb* después de todo; **after all, she's only six** después de todo, sólo tiene seis años.

afternoon *noun* tarde *Fem.*; **this afternoon** esta tarde; **tomorrow afternoon** mañana por la tarde; **yesterday afternoon** ayer por la tarde; **on Saturday afternoon** el sábado por la tarde; **on Saturday afternoons** los sábados por la tarde; **at four o' clock in the afternoon** a las cuatro de la tarde; **every afternoon** todas las tardes.

afters *noun* postre *Masc.*

aftershave *noun* loción *Fem.* para después del afeitado.

afterwards *adverb* después; **shortly afterwards** poco después.

again *adverb* 1 (*one more time*) otra vez; **try again** inténtalo otra vez; **I've forgotten it again** se me ha olvidado otra vez; **you should ask again** deberías preguntar otra vez; 2 (*with a negative verb*) **I don't want to see her again** no quiero volver a verla; **don't do it again** no lo vuelvas a hacer; 3 **never again!** ¡nunca más!

against *preposition* contra; **against the wall** contra la pared; **to lean against the wall** apoyarse contra la pared; **I'm against the idea** estoy en contra de la idea; **to fight against racism** luchar contra el racismo.

age *noun* 1 edad *Fem.*; **at the age of fifteen** a la edad de quince años; **she's the same age as me** tiene mi misma edad; **to be under age** ser menor de edad; 2 **I haven't seen Johnny for ages** hace siglos que no he visto a Johnny (*informal*); **I haven't been to London for ages** hace un montón de tiempo que no voy a Londres (*informal*).

agenda *noun* agenda *Fem.*

agent *noun* agente *Masc./Fem.*

aggressive *adjective* agresivo/agresiva.

ago *adverb* **an hour ago** hace una hora; **three days ago** hace tres días; **five years ago** hace cinco años; **a long time ago** hace mucho tiempo; **not long ago** no hace mucho (tiempo); **how long ago was it?** ¿cuánto tiempo hace de eso?

agree *verb* 1 **to agree with somebody** estar [2] de acuerdo con alguien; **I agree with Laura** estoy de acuerdo con Laura; **I don't agree** no estoy de acuerdo; 2 **I agree that ...** estoy de acuerdo en que ...; **I agree that it's too late now** estoy de acuerdo en que ya es muy tarde; 3 **to agree to do** aceptar [18] hacer; **Steve's agreed to help me** Steve ha aceptado ayudarme; 4 **coffee doesn't agree with me** el café no me sienta bien.

agreement *noun* acuerdo *Masc.*

agricultural *adjective* agrícola.

agriculture *noun* agricultura *Fem.*

ahead *adverb* 1 **go ahead!** ¡adelante!; 2 **straight ahead** todo recto; **go straight ahead until you get to the crossroads** sigue todo recto hasta que llegues al cruce; 3 **our team was ten points ahead** nuestro equipo llevaba diez puntos de ventaja; **I'll go ahead** yo voy delante; **4 to be ahead of time** ir [8] adelantado.

aid *noun* **1** ayuda *Fem.*; **aid to developing countries** ayuda a los países en vías de desarrollo; **2 in aid of** en beneficio de; **in aid of the homeless** en beneficio de la gente sin hogar.

Aids *noun* sida *Masc.* (*síndrome de inmunodeficiencia adquirida*); **to have Aids** tener [9] el sida.

aim *noun* objetivo *Masc.*; **their aim is to control pollution** su objetivo es controlar la contaminación.
aim *verb* **1 to aim to do** proponerse [11] hacer; **we're aiming to finish it today** nos proponemos terminarlo hoy; **2 a campaign aimed at young people** una campaña dirigida a los jóvenes; **3 to aim a gun at somebody** apuntar [17] una pistola a alguien.

air *noun* **1** aire *Masc.*; **in the open air** al aire libre; **to go out for a breath of air** salir [8] a tomar el aire; **2 to travel by air** viajar [8] en avión.

airbag *noun* airbag *Masc.*

air-conditioned *adjective* con aire acondicionado.

air conditioning *noun* aire *Masc.* acondicionado.

air force *noun* fuerza *Fem.* aérea.

air hostess *noun* azafata *Fem.*; **she's an air hostess** es azafata.

airline *noun* compañía *Fem.* aérea.

airmail *noun* correo *Masc.* aéreo; **by airmail** por correo aéreo.

airport *noun* aeropuerto *Masc.*

aisle *noun* (*in theatre, on plane*) pasillo *Masc.*

alarm *noun* alarma *Fem.*; **a fire alarm** una alarma contra incendios; **a burglar alarm** una alarma antirrobo.

alarm clock *noun* reloj *Masc.* despertador.

album *noun* álbum *Masc.*

alcohol *noun* alcohol *Masc.*

alcoholic *noun* alcohólico *Masc.*, alcohólica *Fem.*
alcoholic *adjective* alcohólico/ alcohólica; **alcoholic drinks** bebidas alcohólicas.

alert *adjective* espabilado/ espabilada.
alert *noun* **to be on the alert** estar [2] al alerta; **be on the alert for pickpockets** hay que estar al tanto con los carteristas.

A levels *noun* selectividad *Fem.* (*Students take 'la selectividad' at the same age as A levels are taken in Britain.*) *You can explain A levels briefly as follows: Son exámenes que se realizan a dos niveles, AS y A2. Los exámenes AS se hacen después de un año de preparación, generalmente en cuatro o cinco asignaturas; los A2 abarcan un número menor de asignaturas que ya se hayan estudiado para el nivel AS. Ambos exámenes se califican desde A (nota máxima), a N (sin calificar). La calificación de los A levels se toma en cuenta para ingresar a la universidad*) SEE **selectividad**.

alibi *noun* coartada *Fem.*

alien *noun* **1** (*foreigner*) extranjero *Masc.*, extranjera *Fem.*; **2** (*from outer space*) extraterrestre *Masc./Fem.*

alike *adjective* **1** parecido/parecida; **they're all alike** son todos parecidos; **2 to look alike** parecerse [35]; **the two brothers look alike** los dos hermanos se parecen.

alive *adjective* vivo/viva.

all *adjective, pronoun* **1** todo/toda; **all the knives** todos los cuchillos; **all the cups** todas las tazas; **all the time** todo el tiempo; **all day** todo el día; **2 they've eaten it all** se lo han comido todo; **after all** después de todo; **not at all** de nada (*to somebody who's said 'thank you'*); **they're all there** están todos allí; **3 it's all I have** es todo lo que tengo; **4** (*in scores*) **three all** tres iguales.
all *adverb* completamente; **all alone** completamente solo; **she's all alone at the moment** ahora está completamente sola.

all along *adverb* desde el primer momento; **I knew it all along** lo supe desde el primer momento.

allergic *adjective* alérgico/ alérgica; **to be allergic to something** ser [13] alérgico a algo.

allergy *noun* alergia *Fem.*

alligator *noun* caimán *Masc.*

allow *verb* **1 to allow somebody to do** permitir [19] a alguien hacer; **the teacher allowed them to go out** el maestro les permitió salir; **2** (*to do*) **I'm not allowed to go out during the week** no me dejan salir durante la semana; **they are allowed to**

watch TV in the evenings les dejan ver la tele por las noches.

all right *adverb* **1** (*showing agreement*) de acuerdo, vale (*informal*); **'come round to my house around six' – 'all right'** 'ven a mi casa a eso de las seis' – 'de acuerdo', 'ven a mi casa a eso de las seis' – 'vale'; **it's all right by me** por mí de acuerdo, por mí vale (*informal*); **2** (*fine*) **is everything all right?** ¿va todo bien?; **3** (*talking about health, wellbeing*) **bien**; **are you all right?** ¿estás bien?; **she's all right now** ya está bien; **4** (*not bad*) **the meal was all right** la comida no estuvo mal; **5 is it all right to leave the door open?** ¿puedo dejar la puerta abierta?

ally *noun* aliado *Masc.*, aliada *Fem.*

almond *noun* almendra *Fem.*

almost *adverb* casi; **almost every day** casi cada día; **almost everybody** casi todo el mundo; **she's almost five** tiene casi cinco años.

alone *adjective* **1** solo/sola; **he lives alone** vive solo; **2 leave me alone!** ¡déjame en paz!; **3 leave these papers alone!** ¡deja esos papeles!

along *preposition* **1** a lo largo de; **there are trees all along the road** hay árboles a lo largo de toda la carretera; **2** (*there is often no direct translation for 'along' so the sentence has to be expressed differently*) **she lives along the street from me** vive en mi misma calle; **to go for a walk along the beach** pasear por la

a
b
c
d
e
f
g
h
i
j
k
l
m
n
o
p
q
r
s
t
u
v
w
x
y
z

a
b
c
d
e
f
g
h
i
j
k
l
m
n
o
p
q
r
s
t
u
v
w
x
y
z

playa; **a bit further along** un poco más adelante.

aloud *adverb* en voz alta; **to read something aloud** leer [37] algo en voz alta.

alphabet *noun* alfabeto *Masc.*

alphabetical *adjective* alfabético/alfabética; **in alphabetical order** por orden alfabético.

Alps *plural noun* **the Alps** los Alpes.

already *adverb* ya; **they've already left** ya han salido; **it's six o'clock already!** ¡ya son las seis!

Alsatian *noun* pastor *Masc.* alemán.

also *adverb* también; **I've also invited Karen** he invitado también a Karen.

alter *verb* cambiar [17].

alternate *adjective* **on alternate days** un día sí y otro no.

alternative *noun* alternativa *Fem.*; **we have no alternative** no tenemos alternativa.
alternative *adjective* otro/otra; **to find an alternative solution** encontrar otra solución.

alternatively *adverb* o bien; **alternatively, we could go together on Saturday** o bien podríamos ir juntos el sábado.

alternative medicine *noun* medicina *Fem.* alternativa.

although *conjunction* aunque; **although she's ill, she's willing to help us** aunque está enferma, está dispuesta a ayudarnos.

altitude *noun* altitud *Fem.*

altogether *adverb* **1** en total; **I've spent thirty pounds altogether** he gastado treinta libras en total; **2** (*completely*) totalmente; **I'm not altogether convinced** no estoy del todo convencido.

aluminium *noun* aluminio *Masc.*

always *adverb* siempre; **I always leave at five** siempre salgo a las cinco.

am *verb* SEE **be**.

a.m. *abbreviation* de la mañana; **at 8 a.m.** a las ocho de la mañana.

amateur *noun* amateur *Masc./Fem.* (*plural* amateurs); **amateur dramatics** teatro *Masc.* de amateurs.

amaze *verb* asombrar [17]; **what amazes me is** … lo que me asombra es ….

amazed *adjective* asombrado/asombrada; **I was amazed to see her** me me quedé asombrado al verla; **he'll be amazed to find out** se quedará asombrado al enterarse.

amazement *noun* asombro *Masc.*; **to my amazement she agreed** para mi gran sorpresa aceptó.

amazing *adjective* increíble; **they've got an amazing house** tienen una casa increíble; **she has an amazing number of friends** tiene un número increíble de amigos.

ambassador *noun* embajador *Masc.*, embajadora *Fem.*

ambition *noun* ambición *Fem.*

ambitious *adjective* ambicioso/ambiciosa.

ambulance *noun* ambulancia *Fem.*

ambulance driver *noun* conductor/conductora *Masc./Fem.* de ambulancia.

amenities *plural noun* servicios *Masc. plural* públicos.

America *noun* América *Fem.*

American *noun* americano *Masc.*, americana *Fem.*
American *adjective* americano/americana.

ammunition *noun* municiones *Fem. plural.*

among, amongst *preposition* entre; **I found it among my books** lo encontré entre mis libros; **you can decide amongst yourselves** podéis decidirlo entre vosotros.

amount *noun* **1** cantidad *Fem.*; **an enormous amount of bread** una enorme cantidad de pan; **a huge amount of work** una enorme cantidad de trabajo; **2** (*of money*) suma *Fem.*; **a large amount of money** una gran suma de dinero.
amount to *verb* ascender [36] a; **the bill amounts to five hundred euros** la cuenta asciende a quinientos euros.

amp *noun* **1** amperio *Masc.*; **2** (*amplifier*) amplificador *Masc.*

amplifier *noun* amplificador *Masc.*

amuse *verb* divertir [14].

amusement arcade *noun* salón *Masc.* de juegos recreativos.

amusement park *noun* parque *Masc.* de atracciones.

amusing *adjective* divertido/divertida.

an *article* SEE **a**.

anaesthetic *noun* anestesia *Fem.*

analyse *verb* analizar [22].

analysis *noun* análisis *Masc.*

ancestor *noun* antepasado *Masc.*, antepasada *Fem.*

anchor *noun* ancla *Fem.*

anchovy *noun* anchoa *Fem.*

ancient *adjective* **1** (*historic*) antiguo/antigua; **an ancient abbey** una antigua abadía; **2** (*very old*) viejísimo/viejísima; **an ancient pair of jeans** unos vaqueros viejísimos; **3** ancient Greece la Grecia antigua.

and *conjunction* **1** y; **Sean and Anna** Sean y Anna; **your shoes and socks** tus calcetines y tus zapatos (*'y' becomes 'e' before a word that starts with 'i' or 'hi'*) **Spain and Italy** España e Italia; **2** (*with numbers*) **three hundred and six** trescientos seis; **five hundred and thirty-one** quinientos treinta y uno; **3 fish and chips** pescado con patatas fritas; **4 bigger and bigger** cada vez más grande.

Andalusia *noun* Andalucía *Fem.*

Andalusian *noun* andaluz, andaluza *Masc./Fem.*
Andalusian *adjective* andaluz/andaluza.

angel *noun* ángel *Masc.*

anger *noun* ira *Fem.*

angle *noun* ángulo *Masc.*

angrily *adverb* con enfado.

a
b
c
d
e
f
g
h
i
j
k
l
m
n
o
p
q
r
s
t
u
v
w
x
y
z

a
b
c
d
e
f
g
h
i
j
k
l
m
n
o
p
q
r
s
t
u
v
w
x
y
z

angry *adjective* **to be angry** estar [2] enfadado/enfadada; **she was angry with me** estaba enfadada conmigo; **to get angry (about something)** enfadarse [17] (por algo).

animal *noun* animal *Masc.*

ankle *noun* tobillo *Masc.*; **to break your ankle** romperse [40] el tobillo.

anniversary *noun* aniversario *Masc.*; **a wedding anniversary** un aniversario de boda.

announce *verb* anunciar [17].

announcement *noun* anuncio *Masc.*

annoy *verb* **to be annoyed** estar [2] enfadado/enfadada; **to get annoyed (about something)** enfadarse [17] (por algo); **she got annoyed** se enfadó.

annoying *adjective* **1** (*person*) pesado/pesada; **2** (*noise or habit*) irritante; **3 how annoying!** ¡qué rabia!; **the whole thing's really annoying** todo es un verdadero fastidio.

annual *adjective* anual.

anorak *noun* anorak *Masc.* (*plural* anoraks).

anorexia *noun* anorexia *Fem.*

another *adjective* otro/otra; **would you like another cup of tea?** ¿quieres otra taza de té?; **another two years** otros dos años; **we need another three chairs** necesitamos otras tres sillas; **I'll come another time** vendré en otro momento.

answer *noun* **1** respuesta *Fem.*; **the right answer** la respuesta correcta; **the wrong answer** la respuesta

equivocada; **2 the answer to a problem** la solución a un problema.
answer *verb* **1** contestar [17]; **he hasn't answered our letter** no ha contestado a nuestra carta; **to answer the phone** contestar el teléfono; **2 to answer the door** abrir [46] la puerta.

answering machine *noun* contestador *Masc.* automático; **to leave a message on the answering machine** dejar [17] un mensaje en el contestador.

ant *noun* hormiga *Fem.*

Antarctic *noun* **the Antarctic** la Antártida.

anthem *noun* **the national anthem** el himno nacional.

antibiotic *noun* antibiótico *Masc.*

anticlockwise *adverb* en el sentido contrario al de las agujas del reloj; **it turns anticlockwise** gira en el sentido contrario al de las agujas del reloj.

antique *noun* **antiques** las antigüedades.
antique *adjective* antiguo/antigua; **an antique table** una mesa antigua.

antique shop *noun* tienda *Fem.* de antigüedades.

antiseptic *noun* antiséptico *Masc.*

anxious *adjective* preocupado/preocupada.

anxiously *adverb* con preocupación.

any *pronoun* **1** (*in negative sentences*) ninguno/ninguna; **I don't want any** no quiero ninguno/ninguna; **2** (*in questions*) alguno/

alguna; **do you want any?** ¿quieres alguno/alguna?

any *adjective, adverb* **1** (*when followed by a noun 'any' is not translated*) **is there any butter?** ¿hay mantequilla?; **have you got any glasses?** ¿tienes vasos?; **there isn't any flour** no hay harina; **I haven't got any glasses** no tengo vasos; **2 is there any more?** (*followed by a singular*) ¿queda más? (*followed by a plural*) ¿quedan más?; **there isn't any more butter** no me queda más mantequilla; **I haven't got any more glasses** no me quedan más vasos; **3** (*referring to time*) **I don't go there any more** ya no voy nunca; **I used to phone her but not any more** solía llamarla, pero ya no.

anybody, **anyone** *pronoun* **1** (*in questions and after 'if'*) alguien; **does anybody want some tea?** ¿alguien quiere té?; **is anybody home?** ¿hay alguien en casa?; **if anybody wants some beer, it's in the fridge** si alguien quiere cerveza, está en la nevera; **2 not ... anybody** no ... nadie; **there isn't anybody in her office** no hay nadie en su oficina; **I don't know anybody there** no conozco a nadie allí; **3** (*absolutely anybody*) cualquiera; **anybody can go** puede ir cualquiera.

anyhow *adverb* SEE **anyway**.

anyone *pronoun* SEE **anybody**.

anything *pronoun* **1** (*in questions*) algo; **is there anything I can do to help?** ¿puedo hacer algo para ayudar?; **2 not ... anything** no ... nada; **there isn't anything on the table** no hay nada en la mesa; **3** (*anything at all*) cualquier cosa; **anything could happen** puede pasar cualquier cosa.

anyway, **anyhow** *adverb* de todos modos; **anyway, I'll ring you before I leave** de todos modos te llamaré antes de salir.

anywhere *adverb* **1** (*in questions*) **have you seen my keys anywhere?** ¿has visto mis llaves por algún lado?; **are you going anywhere tomorrow?** ¿vas a algún lado mañana?; **2 not ... anywhere** por ningún lado; **I can't find my keys anywhere** no puedo encontrar mis llaves por ningún lado; **I'm not going anywhere tonight** esta noche no voy a ningún lado; **3** (*absolutely anywhere*) donde sea; **put your cases down anywhere** pon las maletas donde sea.

apart *adjective, adverb* **1** (*separate*) separado/separada; **we don't like being apart** no nos gusta estar separados; **they're too far apart** están demasiado separados; **2 to be two metres apart** estar [2] a dos metros de distancia; **3 apart from** aparte de; **apart from Judy everybody was there** aparte de Judy, todo el mundo estaba allí.

apartheid *noun* apartheid *Masc.*

apartment *noun* apartamento *Masc.*

ape *noun* simio *Masc./Fem.*

apologize *verb* **1** disculparse [17]; **he apologized for his behaviour** se disculpó por su comportamiento;

a b c d e f g h i j k l m n o p q r s t u v w x y z

2 to apologize to somebody pedirle [57] perdón a alguien; **he apologized to Tanya** le pidió perdón a Tanya.

apology noun disculpa Fem.

apostrophe noun apóstrofe Masc.

apparent adjective aparente.

apparently adverb al parecer.

appeal noun **1** (call) **an appeal for calm** un llamamiento a la calma; **2 an appeal for help** una solicitud de ayuda.

appeal verb **to appeal to somebody** atraer [42] a alguien; **horror films don't appeal to me** las películas de miedo no me atraen.

appear verb **1** aparecer [35]; **Mick appeared at the door** Mick apareció en la puerta; **2 to appear on television** salir [63] en televisión; **3** (seem) parecer [35]; **it appears that somebody has stolen the key** parece que alguien ha robado la llave; **he appears to be calm** parece que está tranquilo.

appendicitis noun apendicitis Fem.

appendix noun apéndice Masc.

appetite noun apetito Masc.; **it'll spoil your appetite** te quitará el apetito.

applaud verb aplaudir [19].

applause noun aplausos Masc. plural.

apple noun manzana Fem.

apple tree noun manzano Masc.

applicant noun candidato Masc., candidata Fem.

application noun **a job application** una solicitud de trabajo.

application form noun impreso Masc. de solicitud.

apply verb **1 to apply for a job** solicitar [17] un trabajo; **2 I've applied for the course** he solicitado que me admitan en el curso; **3 to apply to** aplicarse [31] a; **that doesn't apply to students** eso no se aplica a los estudiantes.

appointment noun cita Fem.; **to make a dental appointment** pedir [57] cita en el dentista; **I've got a hair appointment at 4 o'clock** tengo cita en la peluquería para las cuatro.

appreciate verb agradecer [35]; **I appreciate your advice** te agradezco tus consejos; **I'd appreciate it if you could tidy up afterwards** te agradecería que luego recogieses.

apprentice noun aprendiz Masc., aprendiza Fem.

apprenticeship noun aprendizaje Masc.

approach verb **1** (come near to) acercarse [31] a; **we were approaching Madrid** nos acercábamos a Madrid; **2** (tackle) abordar [17] (a problem, task).

appropriate adjective apropiado/apropiada.

approval noun aprobación Fem.

approve verb **I don't approve of her friends** me no gustan sus amigos; **I don't approve of his**

methods no estoy de acuerdo con sus métodos; **does he approve of the idea?** ¿le parece bien la idea?

approximate *adjective* aproximado/aproximada.

approximately *adverb* aproximadamente; **approximately fifty people** aproximadamente cincuenta personas.

apricot *noun* albaricoque *Masc.*

apricot tree *noun* albaricoquero *Masc.*

April *noun* abril *Masc.*; **in April** en abril.

April Fool *noun* inocente *Masc./Fem.* (*see the entry for 'April Fool's Day'*).

April Fool's Day *noun* el día de los Santos Inocentes (*the rough equivalent of April Fool's Day, but on the 28 December*).

apron *noun* delantal *Masc.*

aquarium *noun* acuario *Masc.*

Aquarius *noun* Acuario *Masc.*; **Sharon's Aquarius** Sharon es Acuario.

Arab *noun* árabe *Masc./Fem.*. **Arab** *adjective* árabe; **the Arab countries** los países árabes.

arch *noun* arco *Masc.*

archaelogist *noun* arqueólogo *Masc.*, arqueóloga *Fem.*; **she's an archeologist** es arqueóloga.

archaeology *noun* arqueología *Fem.*

archbishop *noun* arzobispo *Masc.*

architect *noun* arquitecto *Masc.*, arquitecta *Fem.*; **he's an architect** es arquitecto.

architecture *noun* arquitectura *Fem.*

Arctic *noun* **the Arctic** el Ártico.

are *verb* SEE **be**.

area *noun* **1** (*part of a town*) barrio *Masc.*; **a nice area** un buen barrio; **a rough area** un barrio peligroso; **2** (*region*) zona *Fem.*; **in the Leeds area** en la zona de Leeds; **3** (*of square, circle*) superficie *Fem.*

Argentina *noun* Argentina *Fem.*

Argentinian *noun* argentino *Masc.*, argentina *Fem.*. **Argentinian** *adjective* argentino/ argentina.

argue *verb* discutir [19]; **there's no point in arguing** no tiene sentido discutir; **to argue about something** discutir sobre algo; **they're arguing about the result** están discutiendo sobre el resultado.

argument *noun* discusión *Fem.*; **to have an argument** discutir [19].

Aries *noun* Aries *Masc.*; **Pauline's Aries** Pauline es Aries.

arithmetic *noun* aritmética *Fem.*

arm *noun* brazo *Masc.*; **he took my arm** me cogió del brazo; **to fold your arms** cruzar los brazos; **to go arm in arm** ir [8] del brazo; **to break your arm** romperse [40] el brazo.

armchair *noun* sillón *Masc.*

armed *adjective* armado/armada.

armpit *noun* axila *Fem.*

arms *plural noun* armas *Fem. plural.*

army *noun* ejército *Masc.*; **to join the army** alistarse en el ejército.

a b c d e f g h i j k l m n o p q r s t u v w x y z

a

b

c

d

e

f

g

h

i

j

k

l

m

n

o

p

q

r

s

t

u

v

w

x

y

z

around *preposition, adverb* **1** (*with time*) alrededor de; **we'll be there around ten** estaremos allí alrededor de las diez; **2** (*with amounts, age*) **we need around six kilos** necesitamos unos seis quilos; **she's around fifteen** tiene unos quince años; **3** (*surrounding*) alrededor de; **the countryside around Edinburgh** el campo de alrededor de Edinburgo; **we sat around the table** nos sentamos alrededor de la mesa; **4** (*near*) por aquí; **is there a post office around here?** ¿hay una oficina de correos por aquí?; **is Phil around?** ¿está Phil por aquí?; **5** (*wrapped around*) alrededor de; **she had a scarf around her neck** tenía una bufanda alrededor del cuello; **6 around the corner** a la vuelta de la esquina; **7 to travel around the world** viajar por el mundo.

arrange *verb* **to arrange to do** quedar [17] en hacer; **we've arranged to see a film on Saturday** quedamos en ver una película el domingo.

arrangement *noun* **1** (*of things*) disposición *Fem.*; **2** (*agreement*) acuerdo *Masc.*

arrest *noun* **he's under arrest** está detenido; **you're under arrest** queda detenido.
arrest *verb* arrestar [17].

arrival *noun* llegada *Fem.*

arrive *verb* llegar [17]; **they arrived at three** llegaron a las tres.

arrow *noun* flecha *Fem.*

art *noun* **1** arte *Masc.* (*plural* artes) (*note that the plural 'artes' is*

feminine); **modern art** arte moderno; **the arts** las artes; **2** (*school subject*) dibujo *Masc.*; **the art class** la clase de dibujo.

art school *noun* escuela *Fem.* de Bellas Artes.

artery *noun* arteria *Fem.*

art gallery *noun* (*public*) museo *Masc.* de arte.

article *noun* artículo *Masc.*

artichoke *noun* alcachofa *Fem.*

artificial *adjective* artificial.

artist *noun* artista *Masc./Fem.*; **he's an artist** es artista.

artistic *adjective* artístico/artística.

as *conjunction, adverb* **1** como; **as you know** como sabes; **as usual** como siempre; **as I told you** como te dije; **2** (*because*) como; **as there were no trains, we took the bus** como no había trenes, cogimos el autobús; **3 as … as** tan … como; **he's as tall as his brother** es tan alto como su hermano; **you must be as tired as I am** debes estar tan cansado como yo; **I did it as quickly as I could** lo hice tan rápido como pude; **4 as much … as** tanto/tanta … como; **you have as much time as I do** tienes tanto tiempo como yo; **5 as many … as** tantos/tantas … como; **we have as many problems as he does** tenemos tantos problemas como él; **6 as long as** siempre que (*followed by the subjunctive*); **we'll go tomorrow, as long as it's a nice day** iremos mañana, siempre que haga buen tiempo; **7 you can stay**

for as long as you like puedes quedarte todo el tiempo que quieras; **8 as soon as possible** lo más pronto posible; **9 to work as** trabajar [17] de; **he works as a taxi driver in the evenings** trabaja de taxista por las noches.

asbestos noun asbestos Masc.

ash noun ceniza Fem.

ashamed adjective **to be ashamed** estar [2] avergonzado; **you should be ashamed of yourself!** ¡debería darte vergüenza!

ashtray noun cenicero Masc.

Asia noun Asia Fem.

Asian noun asiático Masc., asiática Fem.

Asian adjective asiático/asiátia.

ask verb **1** (inquire) preguntar [17]; **you can ask at reception** puedes preguntar en recepción; **to ask somebody something** preguntarle algo a alguien; **I asked him where he lived** le pregunté dónde vivía; **2** (request) pedir [57]; **to ask for something** pedir algo; **I asked for three coffees** pedí tres cafés; **to ask somebody to do** pedirle a alguien que haga (note that 'que' is followed by subjunctive) **ask Danny to give you a hand** pídele a Danny que te eche una mano; **3 to ask somebody a question** hacerle una pregunta a alguien; **I asked you a question!** ¡te he hecho una pregunta!; **4** invitar [17]; **they've asked us to a party at their house** nos han invitado a una fiesta en su casa; **5 Paul's asked Janie out on Friday** Paul invitó a Janie a salir el viernes.

asleep adjective dormido/dormida; **to be asleep** estar [2] dormido; **the baby's asleep** el niño está dormido; **to fall asleep** quedarse [17] dormido.

asparagus noun espárrago Masc.

aspirin noun aspirina Fem.

assignment noun (at school, college) tarea Fem.

assist verb ayudar [17].

assistance noun ayuda Fem.

assistant noun **1** (at work) ayudante Masc./Fem.; **2 a shop assistant** un dependiente/una dependienta.

association noun asociación Fem.

assorted adjective variado/variada.

assortment noun surtido Masc.

assume verb suponer [11].

assure verb asegurar [17]; **I assure you** te lo aseguro.

asterisk noun asterísco Masc.

asthma noun asma Fem.; **she has asthma** tiene asma.

astonishing adjective asombroso/asombrosa; **her knowledge is astonishing** sus conocimientos son asombrosos.

astrologer noun astrólogo Masc., astróloga Fem.

astrology noun astrología Fem.

astronaut noun astronauta Masc./Fem.

astronomer noun astrónomo Masc., astrónoma Fem.

astronomy noun astronomía Fem.

a
b
c
d
e
f
g
h
i
j
k
l
m
n
o
p
q
r
s
t
u
v
w
x
y
z

at *preposition* **1** (*in a place*) en; **at home** en casa; **at school** en el colegio; **at my office** en mi oficina; **I'll be at work** estaré en el trabajo; **2** (*talking about the time*) a; **at eight o'clock** a las ocho; **3 at night** por la noche; **I'll be there at the weekend** estaré allí el fin de semana; **4 at Emma's house** en casa de Emma; **she's at her brother's this evening** esta noche está en casa de su hermano; **at the hairdresser's** en la peluquería; **5 at last** por fin; **he's found a job at last** por fin ha encontrado un trabajo; **6** (*in email addresses*) arroba *Fem.*; **john.smith@easycom.com** john-punto-smith-arroba-easycom-punto-com.

athlete *noun* atleta *Masc./Fem.*

athletic *adjective* atlético/atlética.

athletics *noun* atletismo *Masc.*

Atlantic *noun* **the Atlantic** el Atlántico.

atlas *noun* atlas *Masc.*

atmosphere *noun* atmósfera *Fem.*

atom *noun* átomo *Masc.*

atomic *adjective* atómico/atómica.

attach *verb* **1** (*fasten*) sujetar [17]; **2** (*tie*) atar [17]; **3** (*glue*) pegar [28].

attached *adjective* **to be attached to** (*be fond of*) tenerle cariño a.

attachment *noun* **1** (*to letter*) documento *Masc.* adjunto; **2** (*in e-mail*) archivo *Masc.* adjunto.

attack *noun* ataque *Masc.*

attack *verb* atacar [31].

attacker *noun* agresor *Masc.*, agresora *Fem.*

attempt *noun* intento *Masc.*; **at the first attempt** al primer intento.

attempt *verb* **to attempt to do** intentar [17] hacer.

attend *verb* asistir [19] a; **to attend a class** asistir a clase.

attention *noun* atención *Fem.*; **to pay attention to** prestar atención a; **I wasn't paying atttention** no estaba prestando atención.

attic *noun* desván *Masc.*

attitude *noun* actitud *Fem.*

attract *verb* atraer [42].

attraction *noun* atracción *Fem.*

attractive *adjective* atractivo/atractiva.

aubergine *noun* berenjena *Fem.*

auction *noun* subasta *Fem.*

audience *noun* público *Masc.*

August *noun* agosto *Masc.*

aunt, **auntie** *noun* tía *Fem.*

au pair *noun* au pair *Masc./Fem.*; **I'm looking for a job as an au pair** estoy buscando un trabajo de au pair.

Australia *noun* Australia *Fem.*

Australian *noun* australiano *Masc.*, australiana *Fem.*
Australian *adjective* australiano/australiana.

Austria *noun* Austria *Fem.*

Austrian *noun* austriaco *Masc.*, austriaca *Fem.*
Austrian *adjective* austriaco/austriaca.

author *noun* autor *Masc.*, autora *Fem.*

autobiography *noun* autobiografía *Fem.*

autograph *noun* autógrafo *Masc.*

automatic *adjective* automático/automática.

automatically *adverb* automáticamente.

autumn *noun* otoño *Masc.*

availability *noun* disponibilidad *Fem.*

available *adjective* disponible.

avalanche *noun* avalancha *Fem.*

avenue *noun* avenida *Fem.*

average *noun* **1** media *Fem.*; **above average** por encima de la media; **2 on average** como promedio. **average** *adjective* medio/media; **of average height** de estatura media.

avocado *noun* aguacate *Masc.*

avoid *verb* evitar [17]; **she avoided me** me evitó; **to avoid doing** evitar hacer; **I avoid speaking to him** evito hablar con él.

awake *adjective* **to be awake** estar [2] despierto/despierta; **is Lola awake?** ¿está despierta Lola?

award *noun* premio *Masc.*; **to win an award** ganar [17] un premio.

aware *adjective* **to be aware of a problem** ser [1] consciente de un problema; **to become aware of something** darse [4] cuenta de algo; **as far as I'm aware** que yo sepa; **to be aware of a noise** oír [56] un ruido.

away *adverb* **1 to be away** estar [2] fuera; **I'll be away next week** estaré fuera la próxima semana; **2 to go away** irse [8]; **Laura's gone away for a week** Laura se ha ido por una semana; **go away!** ¡vete!; **3 to run away** escaparse [17]; **the thieves ran away** los ladrones se escaparon; **4 the school is two kilometres away** el colegio está a dos kilómetros; **how far away is it?** ¿a qué distancia está?; **not far away** no muy lejos; **a long way away** muy lejos; **5 to put something away** guardar [17] algo; **I'll just put my books away** voy a guardar mis libros; **6 to give something away** regalar [17] algo; **she's given away all her tapes** ha regalado todas sus cintas.

away match *noun* partido *Masc.* fuera de casa.

awful *adjective* **1** horrible; **the film was awful!** la película era horrible; **2** (*ill*) **I feel awful** me siento fatal; **3** (*guilty*) **I feel awful about it** me siento muy culpable; **4 an awful lot of** un montón de; **5 how awful!** ¡qué horror!

awkward *adjective* **1** difícil; **it's an awkward situation** es una situación difícil; **it's a bit awkward** es un poco delicado; **an awkward child** un niño difícil; **2 an awkward question** una pregunta comprometida.

axe *noun* hacha *Fem.* (*even though 'hacha' is feminine, it takes 'el' and 'un' in the singular*).

Bb

baby *noun* bebé *Masc.*

babysit *verb* hacer [7] de canguro.

babysitter *noun* canguro *Masc./Fem.*

babysitting *noun* hacer [7] de canguro.

bachelor *noun* soltero *Masc.*

back *noun* **1** (*of a person or garment*) espalda *Fem.*; **to do something behind somebody's back** hacer [7] algo a espaldas de alguien; **2** (*of an animal*) lomo *Masc.*; **3** (*of a piece of paper or your hand*) dorso *Masc.*; **on the back** en el dorso; **4** (*of a car, a plane, or a hall*) fondo *Masc.*; **we have seats at the back** tenemos asientos al fondo; **the children are at the back of the room** los niños que están al fondo de la habitación; **5** (*of a building*) parte *Fem.* de atrás; **a garden at the back of the house** un jardín en la parte de atrás de la casa; **6** (*of a chair or sofa*) respaldo *Masc.*; **7** (*in football or hockey*) defensa *Masc.*, *Fem.*
back *adjective* **1** trasero/trasera (*a wheel or seat*); **the back seat of the car** el asiento trasero del coche; **2 the back garden** el jardín de atrás; **the back gate** la verja de atrás.
back *adverb* **1 to go back** volver [45]; **to go back to school** volver al colegio; **Lisa's gone back to London** Lisa ha vuelto a Londres; **2 to come back** volver [45]; **they've come back from Italy** han vuelto de Italia; **she's back at work** ha vuelto al trabajo; **Sue's not back yet** Sue no ha vuelto aún; **she went by bus and walked back** fue en autobús y volvió andando; **3 to phone back** volver [45] a llamar; **I'll ring back later** te volveré a llamar más tarde; **4 to give something back to somebody** devolverle [45] algo a alguien; **I gave him back his cassettes** le devolví sus cintas; **give it back!** ¡devuélvemelo!
back *verb* **1** apoyar [17] (*a candidate*); **2** apostar [24] por (*a horse*).

● **to back up** (*on a computer*) **to back up a file** hacer [7] una copia de seguridad de un archivo.

● **to back somebody up** apoyar [17] a alguien.

backache *noun* dolor *Masc.* de espalda.

backbone *noun* columna *Fem.* vertebral.

back door *noun* **1** (*of a building*) puerta *Fem.* de atrás; **2** (*of a car*) puerta *Fem.* trasera.

backfire *verb* (*turn out badly*) salir [63] mal.

background *noun* **1** (*of a person*) origen *Masc.*; **2** (*of events or a situation*) contexto *Masc.*; **3** (*in a picture or view*) fondo *Masc.*; **the trees in the background** los árboles del fondo; **4 background music** música de fondo; **background noise** ruido de fondo.

backhand *noun* revés *Masc.*

backing *noun* (*moral support*) apoyo *Masc.*

backpack *noun* mochila *Fem.*
backpack *verb* **to go**
backpacking viajar con mochila.

back seat *noun* asiento *Masc.*
trasero.

backside *noun* trasero *Masc.*

backstroke *noun* estilo *Masc.*
espalda; **to swim backstroke** nadar
a espalda.

back to front *adverb* al revés;
your jumper's back to front te has
puesto el jersey al revés.

backup *noun* **1** (*support*) apoyo
Masc.; **2** (*in computing*) **a backup
disk** un disco de seguridad.

backwards *adverb* (*to lean or fall*)
hacia atrás.

bacon *noun* bacon *Masc.*; **bacon
and eggs** huevos con bacon.

bad *adjective* **1** (*not good*) malo/
mala (*'malo' becomes 'mal' before a
masculine singular noun*) **a bad
moment** un mal momento; **it's bad
for your health** es malo para la
salud; **2** grave (*an accident, a
mistake*); **a bad accident** un
accidente grave; **3** fuerte (*a
headache, a cold*); **a bad cold** un
resfriado fuerte; **4** (*rotten*) podrido/
podrida; **a bad apple** una manzana
podrida; **to go bad** estropearse [17];
5 (*rude*) **bad language** lenguaje
grosero; **6** (*naughty*) malo/mala;
bad dog! ¡(perro) malo!; **7 to be bad
at something** dársele [4] algo mal a
alguien; **I'm bad at physics** se me
da mal la física; **8 it's not bad** no
está mal; **his new film's not bad** su
nueva película no está mal; ★**too**

bad! (*I'm sorry for you*) ¡qué rabia!,
(*I don't care*) ¡y a mí qué!

badge *noun* **1** (*pin-on*) chapa *Fem.*;
2 a policeman badge una placa de
policía.

badly *adverb* **1** mal; **he writes
badly** escribe mal; **I slept badly**
dormí mal; **my exam went badly** el
examen me fue mal; **2 badly hurt**
gravemente herido; **3 the car was
badly damaged** el coche quedó muy
estropeado.

bad-mannered *adjective*
maleducado/maleducada.

badminton *noun* bádminton *Masc.*;
to play badminton jugar al
bádminton.

bad-tempered *adjective*
1 (*answer, look*) malhumorado/
malhumorada; **2 to be bad-
tempered** (*for a while*) estar de mal
humor (*always*) tener mal genio.

bag *noun* **1** (*plastic, paper*) bolsa
Fem.; **2** (*handbag*) bolso *Masc.*

bags *plural noun* maletas *Fem.
plural*; **to pack your bags** hacer las
maletas; ★ **to have bags under your
eyes** tener ojeras.

baggage *noun* equipaje *Masc.*

baggage allowance *noun*
franquicia *Fem.* de equipaje.

baggage reclaim *noun*
recogida *Fem.* de equipaje.

bagpipes *plural noun* gaita *Fem.*;
to play the bagpipes tocar la gaita.

Bahamas *plural noun* **the
Bahamas** las Bahamas; **the
Bahama Islands** las islas Bahamas.

a
b
c
d
e
f
g
h
i
j
k
l
m
n
o
p
q
r
s
t
u
v
w
x
y
z

Bahamian *noun* bahameño *Masc.*, bahameña *Fem.*
Bahamian *adjective* bahameño/bahameña.

bake *verb* to bake a cake hacer [7] un pastel; to bake potatoes asar [17] patatas.

baked *adjective* 1 (*fruit or vegetables*) asado/asada; baked apples manzanas asadas; a baked potato una patata asada; 2 (*fish*) al horno.

baked beans *plural noun* judías *Fem. plural* en salsa de tomate.

baker *noun* panadero *Masc.*, panadera *Fem.*; to go to the baker's ir a la panadería.

bakery *noun* panadería *Fem.*

balance *noun* 1 equilibrio *Masc.*; to lose your balance perder el equilibrio; 2 (*money in your bank account*) saldo *Masc.*

balanced *adjective* equilibrado/equilibrada.

balcony *noun* balcón *Masc.*

bald *adjective* calvo/calva.

Balearic Islands *plural noun* las Islas Baleares.

ball *noun* 1 (*for tennis or golf*) pelota *Fem.*; 2 (*for football or volleyball*) balón *Masc.*; 3 (*of string or wool*) ovillo *Masc.*

ballet *noun* ballet *Masc.*

ballet dancer *noun* bailarín *Masc.* de ballet, bailarina *Fem.* de ballet.

ballet shoe *noun* zapatilla *Fem.* de ballet.

balloon *nosun* globo *Masc.*

ballot *noun* votación *Fem.*

ballpoint (pen) *noun* boli *Masc.* (*informal*), bolígrafo *Masc.*

ban *noun* prohibición *Fem.*; to put a ban on smoking prohibir fumar.
ban *verb* prohibir [58].

banana *noun* plátano *Masc.*; a banana yoghurt un yogur de plátano.

band *noun* 1 (*playing music*) grupo *Masc.*; a rock band un grupo de rock; 2 a jazz band (*big*) una orquesta de jazz, (*small*) un conjunto de jazz; 3 a brass band una banda de música; 4 a rubber band una goma elástica.

bandage *noun* venda *Fem.*
bandage *verb* vendar [17].

bang *noun* 1 (*noise*) estallido *Masc.*; 2 (*of a window*) golpe *Masc.*; 3 (*of a door*) portazo *Masc.*
bang *verb* 1 (*to hit*) golpear [17] (*a drum, for example*); he banged his fist on the table golpeó la mesa con el puño; 2 (*to knock*) dar [4] golpes a; to bang on the door dar golpes a la puerta; I banged my head on the door me di un golpe en la cabeza con la puerta; I banged into the table me choqué con la mesa; 3 to bang the door aporrear [17] la puerta.
bang *exclamation* (*like a gun*) ¡pum!

bangle *noun* pulsera *Fem.*

banister(s), bannister(s) *plural noun* barandilla *Fem.* (*singular*).

bank *noun* 1 (*for money*) banco *Masc.*; I'm going to the bank voy al banco; **2** (*of a river or lake*) orilla *Fem.*

bank account *noun* cuenta *Fem.* bancaria.

bank balance *noun* saldo *Masc.*

bank card *noun* tarjeta *Fem.* bancaria.

bank holiday *noun* día *Masc.* festivo.

banking *noun* banca *Fem.*

banknote *noun* billete *Masc.* de banco.

bank statement *noun* extracto *Masc.* de cuenta.

baptize *verb* bautizar [22].

bar *noun* **1** (*selling drinks*) bar *Masc.*; **Janet works in a bar** Janet trabaja en un bar; **2** (*the counter in a bar*) barra *Fem.*; **on the bar** en la barra; **3 a bar of chocolate** una tableta de chocolate; **4 a bar of soap** una pastilla de jabón; **5** (*made of wood or metal*) barra *Fem.*; **a metal bar** una barra de metal; **6** (*in music*) compás *Masc.*
bar *verb* (*to block physically*) bloquear [17]; **to bar someone's way** bloquear el paso a alguien.

Barbadian *noun* barbadense *Masc./Fem.*
Barbadian *adjective* barbadense.

barbecue *noun* barbacoa *Fem.*; **there's a barbecue tonight** hay una barbacoa esta noche.
barbecue *verb* **to barbecue a chicken** asar [17] un pollo a la parrilla; **barbecued chicken** pollo a la parrilla.

barbed wire *noun* alambre *Masc.* de púas.

bare *adjective* desnudo/desnuda.

barefoot *adjective* descalzo/descalza; **to be barefoot** estar descalzo/descalza.

bargain *noun* (*a good buy*) ganga *Fem.*; **I got a bargain** conseguí una ganga; **it's a bargain!** ¡es una ganga!

barge *noun* barcaza *Fem.*

bark *noun* **1** (*of a tree*) corteza *Fem.*; **2** (*of a dog*) ladrido *Masc.*
bark *verb* ladrar [17].

barley *noun* cebada *Fem.*

barmaid *noun* camarera *Fem.*

barman *noun* camarero *Masc.*

barn *noun* granero *Masc.*

barometer *noun* barómetro *Masc.*

barrel *noun* tonel *Masc.*

barrier *noun* barrera *Fem.*

base *noun* base *Fem.*

baseball *noun* baloncesto *Masc.*

based *adjective* **1 to be based on** estar basado en; **the film is based on a true story** la película está basada en una historia real; **2 to be based in** (*a company*) tener su base en, (*a person*) vivir en; **he's based in Bristol** vive en Bristol.

basement *noun* sótano *Masc.*; **in the basement** en el sótano.

bash *noun* **1** golpe *Masc.*; **it's got a bash on the bumper** tiene un golpe en el guardabarros; **2 I'll have a bash** voy a probar.
bash *verb* **I bashed my head** me di un golpe en la cabeza.

a
b
c
d
e
f
g
h
i
j
k
l
m
n
o
p
q
r
s
t
u
v
w
x
y
z

basic *adjective* 1 básico/básica; **basic knowledge** conocimientos básicos; 2 **the basic facts** los hechos fundamentales; 3 **basic salary** sueldo base; 4 (*not luxurious*) sencillo/sencilla; **the flat's a bit basic** el piso es bastante sencillo.

basically *adverb* 1 fundamentalmente; **it's basically all right** fundamentalmente está bien; 2 **basically, I don't really want to go** en pocas palabras, no quiero ir.

basics *noun* rudimentos *Masc. plural*.

basin *noun* (*washbasin*) lavabo *Masc.*

basis *noun* 1 base *Fem.*; **on the basis of** en base a; 2 **on a regular basis** regularmente.

basket *noun* 1 cesta *Fem.*; **a shopping basket** una cesta de la compra; **a linen basket** una cesta de ropa sucia; 2 **a waste-paper basket** una papelera.

basketball *noun* baloncesto *Masc.*; **to play basketball** jugar al baloncesto.

Basque *noun* 1 (*the language*) euskera *Masc.*, vasco *Masc.*; 2 (*person*) vasco *Masc.*, vasca *Fem.*
Basque *adjective* vasco/vasca; **the Basque Country** el País vasco, Euskadi *Masc.*

bass *noun* 1 bajo *Masc.*; **to play bass** tocar el bajo; 2 **a double bass** un contrabajo.

bass drum *noun* bombo *Masc.*

bass guitar *noun* bajo *Masc.*

bassoon *noun* fagot *Masc.*; **to play the bassoon** tocar el fagot.

bat *noun* 1 (*for cricket or baseball*) bate *Masc.*; 2 (*for table tennis*) paleta *Fem.*; 3 (*animal*) murciélago *Masc.*

batch *noun* lote *Masc.*; **a batch of letters** un lote de cartas.

bath *noun* 1 baño *Masc.*; **I was in the bath** estaba en el baño; 2 (*bathtub*) bañera *Fem.*; **the bath's pink** la bañera es rosa; 3 **to have a bath** bañarse [17].

bathe *verb* 1 lavar [17] (*a wound*); 2 (*go swimming*) bañarse [17].

bathroom *noun* cuarto *Masc.* de baño.

bath towel *noun* toalla *Fem.* de baño.

batter *noun* 1 (*for frying*) rebozado *Masc.*; **fish in batter** pescado rebozado; 2 (*for pancakes*) masa *Fem.*

battery *noun* 1 (*for a torch or radio, for example*) pila *Fem.*; 2 (*for a car*) batería *Fem.*

battle *noun* batalla *Fem.*

bay *noun* 1 (*on coast*) bahía *Fem.*; **the Bay of Biscay** el Golfo de Vizcaya; 2 (*for bus*) dársena *Fem.*

B.C. a.de C. (*antes de Cristo*).

be *verb* 1 (*referring to permanent characteristics*) ser [1]; **it's beautiful** es precioso; **she's very tall** es muy alta; **honey is sweet** la miel es dulce; 2 (*referring to changeable emotions and situations*) estar [2]; **she's angry** está enfadada; **I'm tired**

estoy cansada; **the soup is cold** la sopa está fría; **this cake is too sweet** este pastel está demasiado dulce; **3** (*in a place*) estar [2]; **Melanie is in the kitchen** Melanie está en la cocina; **¿where's the butter?** ¿dónde está la mantequilla?; **when we were in France** cuando estábamos en Francia; **4 there is** hay; **there are** hay; **there's more here** aquí hay más; **there are two children outside** hay dos niños fuera; **is there any problem?** ¿hay algún problema?; **5** (*with jobs and professions*) ser [1] (*note that 'a' is not translated*) **she's a teacher** es profesora; **he's a taxi driver** es taxista; **6** (*marital status*) estar [2] es [1]; **she's married** está casada; **he's single** está/es soltero; **7** (*in clock times*) ser [1]; **it's one o'clock** es la una en punto; **it's half past five** son las cinco y media; **8** (*for days of the week and dates*) ser [1]; **what day is it today?** ¿qué día es hoy?; **it's Tuesday today** hoy es martes; **it's the twentieth of May** es veinte de mayo; **9** (*talking about age*) tener [9]; **to be fifteen** tener quince años; **how old are you?** ¿cuántos años tienes?; **Samuel's two** Samuel tiene dos años; **10** (*feeling cold, hot, hungry*) **I'm hot** tengo calor; **I'm cold** tengo frío; **I'm hungry** tengo hambre; **11** (*talking about weather*) **it's cold today** hoy hace frío; **it's a nice day** hace buen día; **12** (*to a country or town*) estar [2]; **I've never been to Paris** nunca he estado en París; **have you been to Spain before?** ¿has estado en

España antes?; **13 to be loved** ser [1] amado (*but note that often the passive is translated by the third person plural*) **he has been killed** lo han matado (*literally: they have killed him*).

beach *noun* playa *Fem.*; **on the beach** en la playa.

bead *noun* cuenta *Fem.*

beak *noun* pico *Masc.*

beam *noun* **1** (*of light*) rayo *Fem.*; **2** (*for a roof*) viga *Fem.*

bean *noun* alubia *Fem.*, judía *Fem.*; **baked beans** alubias en salsa de tomate; **green beans** judías verdes.

bear *noun* oso *Masc.*
bear *verb* **1** soportar [17]; **I can't bear him** no puedo soportarlo; **I can't bear the idea** no puedo soportar la idea; **2 to bear something in mind** tener [9] algo en cuenta; **I'll bear it in mind** lo tendré en cuenta.

beard *noun* barba *Fem.*

bearded *adjective* barbudo/barbuda.

bearings *plural noun* **to get your bearings** orientarse [17].

beast *noun* **1** (*animal*) bestia *Fem.*; **2 you beast!** ¡bruto!

beat *noun* ritmo *Masc.*
beat *verb* **1** (*defeat*) ganarle a [17]; **we beat them!** ¡les hemos ganado!; **he beat me at chess** me ganó al ajedrez; **2** (*hit repeatedly*) golpear [17]; **3** batir [19]; **to beat the eggs** batir los huevos; **4 you can't beat a good meal** no hay nada mejor que una buena comida.

a
b
c
d
e
f
g
h
i
j
k
l
m
n
o
p
q
r
s
t
u
v
w
x
y
z

• **to beat somebody up** darle [4] una paliza a alguien (*informal*).

beautician *noun* esteticista *Masc./ Fem.*

beautiful *adjective* precioso/ preciosa; **a beautiful day** un día precioso; **how beautiful!** ¡qué precioso!

beautifully *adverb* maravillosamente.

beauty *noun* belleza *Fem.*

beauty spot *noun* (*for tourists*) lugar *Masc.* pintoresco.

because *conjunction* **1** porque; **because it's you** porque eres tú; **because it's cold** porque hace frío; **2 because of** a causa de; **because of the accident** a causa del accidente.

become *verb* **1** hacerse [7]; **I want to become a lawyer** quiero hacerme abogado; **she became famous** se hizo famosa; **we became friends** nos hicimos amigos; **2** (*'become' with an adjective is sometimes translated by a reflexive verb in Spanish*) **to become bored** aburrirse [19]; **to become tired** cansarse [17].

bed *noun* **1** cama *Fem.*; **a double bed** una cama de matrimonia; **in bed** en la cama; **to go to bed** ir a la cama; **2** (*flower bed*) macizo *Masc.*

bedclothes *plural noun* ropa *Fem.* de cama (*singular*).

bedding *noun* ropa *Fem.* de cama.

bedroom *noun* habitación *Fem.*; **my bedroom window** la ventana de mi habitación.

bedside table *noun* mesilla *Fem.* de noche.

bedsit, bedsitter *noun* habitación *Fem.* amueblada de aquiler.

bedspread *noun* colcha *Fem.*

bedtime *noun* **it's bedtime** es hora de acostarse.

bee *noun* abeja *Fem.*

beech *noun* haya *Fem.*

beef *noun* carne *Fem.* de vaca; **a roast of beef** un rosbif.

beefburger *noun* hamburguesa *Fem.*

beer *noun* cerveza *Fem.*; **two beers please** dos cervezas, por favor; **a beer can** una lata de cerveza.

beetle *noun* escarabajo *Masc.*

beetroot *noun* remolacha *Fem.*

before *preposition, adverb* **1** antes de; **before Monday** antes del lunes; **2 before somebody** antes que alguien; **he left before me** se fue antes que yo; **3 the day before** el día anterior; **the day before the wedding** el día anterior a la boda; **the day before yesterday** anteayer; **the week before** la semana anterior; **4** (*already*) ya; **I've seen him before somewhere** ya le he visto en algún sitio; **I had seen the film before** ya había visto la película; **she'd never tried before** nunca lo había intentado antes.

before *conjunction* **1** antes de; **before doing** antes de hacer; **I closed the windows before leaving** cerré las ventanas antes de salir; **phone before you leave**

llámame antes de salir; **2** antes de que (*followed by the subjunctive*); **phone me before they leave** llámame antes de que salgan; **oh, before I forget** ... ah, antes de que se me olvide ....

beforehand *adverb* antes; **phone beforehand** llama antes.

beg *verb* **1** (*ask for money*) mendigar [28]; **2** (*ask*) suplicarle a [31]; **she begged me not to leave** me suplicó que no me marchase; **I beg your pardon** perdone.

begin *verb* **1** empezar [25]; **the meeting begins at ten** la reunión empieza a las diez; **the words beginning with P** las palabras que empiezan con P; **2 to begin to do** empezar a hacer; **I'm beginning to understand** empiezo a comprender.

beginner *noun* principiante *Masc./Fem.*

beginning *noun* **1** principio *Masc.*; **at the beginning** al principio; **at the beginning of the holidays** al principio de las vacaciones; **2** (*with 'day', 'week', 'month', 'year'*) **at the beginning of** a principios de; **at the beginning of the month** a principios de mes.

behalf *noun* **on behalf of** en nombre de.

behave *verb* **1** portarse [17]; **he behaved badly** se portó mal; **2 to behave yourself** portarse bien; **behave yourselves!** ¡portaos bien!

behaviour *noun* comportamiento *Masc.*

behind *noun* trasero *Masc.*
behind *preposition* detrás de; **behind the sofa** detrás del sofá; **behind them** detrás de ellos.
behind *adverb* **1** detrás; **you go behind** tú vas detrás; **the car behind** el coche de detrás; **2 to leave something behind** olvidarse algo; **I've left my keys behind** me he olvidado las llaves; **to stay behind** quedarse; **3** (*not making progress*) **he's behind in class** va retrasado en clase.

beige *adjective* beige (*does not change*); **beige socks** calcetines beige.

Belgian *noun, adjective* belga *Masc./Fem.*

Belgium *noun* *Fem.* Bélgica.

belief *noun* creencia *Fem.*; **his political beliefs** sus creencias políticas.

believe *verb* **1** creer [37]; **I believe you** te creo; **they believed what I said** se creyeron lo que dije; **I don't believe you!** ¡no te creo!; **2 to believe in** creer en; **to believe in ghosts** creer en fantasmas; **to believe in God** creer en Dios.

bell *noun* **1** (*in a church*) campana *Fem.*; **2** (*on a door*) timbre *Masc.*; **ring the bell!** ¡toca el timbre!; **3** (*for a cat or toy*) cascabel *Masc.*; ★ **that name rings a bell** ese nombre me suena.

belong *verb* **1 to belong to** ser [1] de; **that belongs to Lucy** eso es de Lucy; **2 to belong to a club** pertenecer [35] a un club; **3** (*go*) ir [8]; **that chair belongs in the study** esa silla va en el estudio; **where**

a
b
c
d
e
f
g
h
i
j
k
l
m
n
o
p
q
r
s
t
u
v
w
x
y
z

a

b

c

d

e

f

g

h

i

j

k

l

m

n

o

p

q

r

s

t

u

v

w

x

y

z

does this vase belong? ¿adónde va este jarrón?

belongings *plural noun* pertenencias *Fem. plural*; **all my belongings are in London** todas mis pertenencias están en Londres.

below *preposition* debajo de; **below the window** debajo de la ventana; **the flat below yours** el piso de debajo del tuyo.
below *adverb* abajo; **shouts came from below** se oyeron gritos abajo; **the flat below** el piso de abajo.

belt *noun* cinturón *Masc.*

bench *noun* banco *Masc.*

bend *noun* (*in a road, river*) curva *Fem.*
bend *verb* **1** (*to make a bend in*) doblar [17] (*your arm or leg, or a wire*); **2** (*to curve*) (*a road or path*) torcer [41]; **the road bends to the right** la carretera tuerce a la derecha; **3 to bend down** agacharse [17]; **she bent down to look** se agachó para mirar.

beneath *preposition* bajo.

benefit *noun* **1** beneficio *Masc.*; **2 unemployment benefit** subsidio *Masc.* de desempleo.

bent *adjective* doblado/doblada.

beret *noun* boina *Fem.*

berry *noun* baya *Fem.*

berth *noun* litera *Fem.*

beside *preposition* (*next to*) al lado de; **it's beside the table** está al lado de la mesa; **she was sitting beside me** estaba sentada a mi lado; ★**that's beside the point** eso no viene al caso.

besides *adverb* además; **besides, it's too late** además, es demasiado tarde; **four dogs, and six cats besides** cuatro perros y además seis gatos.

best *adjective* **1** mejor; **it's the best** es el mejor; **that's the best car** ese coche es el mejor; **the best song of the album** la mejor canción del álbum; **she's my best friend** es mi mejor amiga; **2 she's the best at tennis** es la mejor jugando al tenis; **he's the best at English** es el mejor en inglés; **the best thing to do is to phone them** lo mejor es llamarlos por teléfono; **its the best I can do** es lo más que puedo hacer; **I did my best to help her** hice todo lo posible para ayudarla.
best *adverb* **1** mejor; **he plays best** es el que mejor juega; **best of all** lo mejor de todo; **2 I like Barcelona best** Barcelona es la ciudad que más me gusta.

best man *noun* padrino *Masc.* de boda.

bet *noun* apuesta *Fem.*
bet *verb* apostar [24]; **to bet on a horse** apostar por un caballo; **I bet you he'll forget!** ¡te apuesto algo a que se le olvida!

better *adjective* **1** mejor; **she's found a better flat** ha encontrado un piso mejor; **this road's better than the other one** esta calle es mejor que la otra; **this pen writes better** esta pluma escribe mejor; **2 even better** todavía mejor; **it's even better than before** es todavía mejor que antes; **3** (*less ill*) **to be**

better estar [2] mejor; **to feel better** sentirse [14] mejor; **I feel better** hoy me siento mejor; **4 to get better** mejorar [17]; **my Spanish is getting better** mi español está mejorando; **I hope you get better soon** espero que te mejores pronto; **5 so much the better** mucho mejor; **the sooner the better** cuanto antes mejor.

better *adverb* **you/she/etc. had better** más vale que (*followed by the subjunctive*); **you'd better phone at once** más vale que llames ahora mismo; **he'd better not go** más vale que no vaya; **I'd better go now** más vale que me vaya ahora.

better off *adjective* **1** (*richer*) **they're better off than us** tienen más dinero que nosotros; **2** (*more comfortable*) mejor; **you'd be better off in bed** estarás mejor en la cama.

between *preposition* **1** entre; **between London and Dover** entre Londres y Dover; **I'll go sometime between Monday and Friday** iré entre el lunes y el viernes; **between you and me** entre tú y yo; **2 it's closed between 2 and 5** está cerrado de dos a cinco.

beware *verb* **beware of the dog!** ¡cuidado con el perro!

beyond *preposition* **1** (*in space and time*) **beyond the border** más allá de la frontera; **2 it's beyond me!** ¡no lo entiendo!

Bible *noun* **the Bible** la Biblia.

bicycle *noun* bicicleta *Fem.*; **by bicycle** en bicicleta.

bicycle lane *noun* carril *Masc.* de bicicletas.

big *adjective* **1** grande; **a big house** una casa grande; **big cities** ciudades grandes; **it's too big for me** es demasiado grande para mí; (*'grande' becomes 'gran' when it comes before a singular noun*) **a big disappointment** una gran desilusión; **2** (*older*) mayor; **my big sister** mi hermana mayor.

bigheaded *adjective* creído/ creída; **to be bigheaded** ser un creído/una creída.

big screen *noun* pantalla *Fem.* grande.

big toe *noun* dedo *Masc.* gordo del pie.

bike 1 (*with pedals*) bici *Fem.*; **by bike** en bici; **2** (*with motor*) moto *Fem.*; **by bike** en moto.

bikini *noun* bikini *Masc.*

bilingual *adjective* bilingüe.

bill *noun* **1** (*in a restaurant*) cuenta *Fem.*; **can I have the bill, please?** ¿me trae la cuenta por favor?; **2** (*for gas, electricity, or in a hotel*) factura *Fem.*

billiards *noun* billar *Masc.*; **to play billiards** jugar al billar.

billion *noun* mil millones *Masc. plural.*

bin *noun* **1** (*dustbin*) cubo *Masc.* de la basura; **2** (*wastepaper bin*) papelera *Fem.*

binoculars *plural noun* prismáticos *Masc. plural.*

biochemistry *noun* bioquímica *Fem.*

biography *noun* biografía *Fem.*

biologist *noun* biólogo *Masc.*, bióloga *Fem.*

biology *noun* biología *Fem.*

bird *noun* **1** (*small*) pájaro *Masc.*; **2** (*large*) ave *Fem.* (*even though 'ave' is feminine, it takes 'el' and 'un' in the singular*).

birdwatching *noun* **to go birdwatching** ir [8] a observar pájaros.

Biro™ *noun* boli *Masc.* (*informal*).

birth *noun* nacimiento *Masc.*

birth certificate *noun* certificado *Masc.* de nacimiento.

birth control *noun* control *Fem.* de la natalidad.

birthday *noun* cumpleaños *Masc.* (*does not change in the plural*); **a birthday present** un regalo de cumpleaños; **happy birthday!** ¡feliz cumpleaños!

birthday party *noun* fiesta *Fem.* de cumpleaños.

biscuit *noun* galleta *Fem.*

bishop *noun* obispo *Masc.*

bit *noun* **1** (*small piece*) trozo *Masc.*; **a bit of string** un trozo de cordón; **a bit of chocolate** un trozo de chocolate; **2** (*small quantity*) **a bit of** un poco de; **a bit of sugar** un poco de azúcar; **with a bit of luck** con un poco de suerte; **to have a bit of trouble with something** tener un pequeño problema con algo; **3** (*in a book or film, for example*) trozo *Masc.*; **this bit's brilliant!** ¡este trozo es genial!; **4 to fall to bits** hacerse pedazos; **5 a bit of news** una noticia; **a bit of advice** un consejo; **6 a bit** un poco; **wait a bit!** ¡espera un poco!; **a bit hot** un poco caliente; **a bit early** un poco pronto; **7** (*for a horse*) bocado *Masc.*; ★ **bit by bit** poco a poco.

bite *noun* **1** (*snack*) bocado *Masc.*; **I'll just have a bite before I go** voy a tomar un bocado antes de irme; **2** (*from an insect*) picadura *Fem.*; **a mosquito bite** una picadura de mosquito; **3** (*from a dog*) mordisco *Masc.*; **it gave me a bite** me dio un mordisco.
bite *verb* **1** (*a person or a dog*) morder [38]; **to bite your nails** morderse las uñas; **2** (*an insect*) picar [31].

bitter *adjective* (*taste*) amargo/amarga.

black *adjective* **1** negro/negra; **my black jacket** mi chaqueta negra; **to turn black** volerse negro/negra; **2 a Black man** un negro; **a Black woman** una negra; **3 a black coffee** un café solo.

blackberry *noun* mora *Fem.*

blackbird *noun* mirlo *Masc.*

blackboard *noun* pizarra *Fem.*

blackcurrant *noun* grosella *Fem.* negra.

black eye *noun* ojo *Masc.* morado.

black pudding *noun* morcilla *Fem.*

blade *noun* hoja *Fem.*

blame *noun* **1** culpa *Fem.*; **to put the blame on somebody** echarle la culpa a alguien; **2 to take the blame for something** asumir la responsabilidad de algo.
blame *verb* culpar [17]; **to blame somebody for something** culpar a alguien de algo; **they blamed him for the accident** lo culparon por el accidente; **she is to blame for it** ella tiene la culpa; **I blame the parents!** ¡yo culpo a los padres!; **I don't blame you!** ¡no me extraña!

blank *noun* (*empty space*) espacio *Masc.* en blanco (*on a form, for instance*).
blank *adjective* **1** (*a page or piece of paper, or a cheque, or a screen*) en blanco (*a tape or disk*) virgen; **2 my mind went blank** me quedé en blanco.

blanket *noun* manta *Fem.*

blast *noun* **1** (*an explosion*) explosión *Fem.*; **2** (*of air*) ráfaga *Fem.*; **3 to play music at full blast** poner la música a todo volumen.

blaze *noun* incendio *Masc.*
blaze *verb* arder [18].

blazer *noun* blázer *Masc.*

bleach *noun* lejía *Fem.*

bleed *verb* sangrar [17]; **my nose is bleeding** me está sangrando la nariz.

blend *noun* mezcla *Fem.*
blend *verb* mezclar [17].

blender *noun* batidora *Fem.*

bless *verb* bendecir [5]; **bless you!** (*after a sneeze*) ¡Jesús!

blind *noun* (*in a window*) persiana *Fem.*
blind *adjective* ciego/ciega; **to go blind** quedarse ciego/ciega.

blindness *noun* ceguera *Fem.*

blink *verb* (*a person*) pestañear [17].

blister *noun* ampolla *Fem.*

blizzard *noun* tormenta *Fem.* de nieve.

block *noun* **1** bloque *Masc.*; **a block of flats** un bloque de pisos; **an office block** un bloque de oficinas; **2** (*a group of buildings*) manzana *Fem.*; **to run** (*or* **drive**) **round the block** dar la vuelta a la manzana.
block *verb* **1** bloquear [17] (*an exit or a road*); **2** atascar [31] (*a drain or a hole*); **the sink's blocked** el fregadero está atascado.

blond *adjective* rubio/rubia.

blood *noun* sangre *Fem.*

blood test *noun* análisis *Masc.* de sangre.

blossom *noun* flor *Fem.*; **to be in blossom** estar [2] en flor.

blot *noun* borrón *Masc.*

blouse *noun* blusa *Fem.*

blow *noun* golpe *Masc.*
blow *verb* **1** (*the wind or a person*) soplar [17]; **2 to blow off/away** salir [63] volando; **my hat blew off** mi sombrero salió volando; **3** (*in an explosion*) **the bomb blew a hole in the wall** la bomba hizo un agujero en la pared; **4 to blow your nose** sonarse [24] la nariz.
● **to blow something out** (*a candle or flames*) apagar [28] algo.
● **to blow up** (*explode*) explotar [17].

a
b
c
d
e
f
g
h
i
j
k
l
m
n
o
p
q
r
s
t
u
v
w
x
y
z

• **to blow something up** inflar [17] algo (*a balloon or tyre*), hacer [7] volar algo (*a building or car*); **they blew up the president's residence** hicieron volar la residencia del presidente.

blow-dry *noun* brushing *Masc.*; **to have a blow-dry** hacerse [7] el brushing.

blue *adjective* azul; **blue eyes** ojos azules.

bluebell *noun* jacinto *Masc.* silvestre.

blues *plural noun* (*jazz*) blues *Masc.* (*singular*).

blunder *noun* metedura *Fem.* de pata.

blunt *adjective* 1 (*a knife or scissors*) desafilado/desafilada; 2 (*a pencil*) sin punta; 3 (*a person*) directo/directa.

blurred *adjective* 1 (*vision or image*) borroso/borrosa; 2 (*photo*) movido/movida.

blush *verb* ponerse [11] colorado.

board *noun* 1 (*plank*) tabla *Fem.*; 2 (*blackboard*) pizarra *Fem.*; 3 (*notice board*) tablón *Masc.* de anuncios; 4 (*for a board game*) tablero *Masc.*; **a chess board** un tablero de ajedrez; 5 (*accommodation*) **full board** pensión completa; **half board** media pensión; **board and lodging** comida y alojamiento; 6 **on board** a bordo; **on board the ferry** a bordo del ferry.

board *verb* embarcarse [31].

boarder *noun* (*in a school*) interno *Masc.*, interna *Fem.*

board game *noun* juego *Masc.* de mesa.

boarding *noun* embarque *Masc.*

boarding card *noun* tarjeta *Fem.* de embarque.

boarding school *noun* internado *Masc.*

boast *verb* presumir [19]; **he was boasting about his new bike** estaba presumiendo de su nueva bici.

boat *noun* 1 (*in general*) barco *Masc.*; 2 (*rowing boat*) barca *Fem.*

body *noun* 1 cuerpo *Masc.*; 2 (*corpse*) cadáver *Masc.*

bodybuilding *noun* culturismo *Masc.*

bodyguard *noun* guardaespaldas *Masc./Fem.*

boil *noun* (*swelling*) furúnculo *Masc.*

boil *verb* 1 hervir [14]; **the water's boiling** el agua está hirviendo; **I'm going to boil some water** voy a hervir un poco de agua; 2 **to boil vegetables** cocer [41] verduras; **to boil an egg** cocer un huevo.

• **to boil over** salirse [63].

boiled egg *noun* huevo *Masc.* pasado por agua.

boiler *noun* 1 (*for central heating*) caldera *Fem.*; 2 (*for central heating*) calentador *Masc.*

boiling *adjective* 1 (*water*) hirviendo; 2 **it's boiling hot today!** ¡hoy hace un calor espantoso!

Bolivia *noun* Bolivia *Fem.*

Bolivian *noun* boliviano *Masc.*, boliviana *Fem.*
Bolivian *adjective* boliviano/boliviana.

bolt *noun* 1 (*large*) cerrojo *Masc.*; 2 (*small*) pestillo *Masc.*
bolt *verb* (*a door*) cerrar [29] con cerrojo.

bombing *noun* 1 (*in a war*) bombardeo *Masc.*; 2 (*a terrorist attack*) atentado *Masc.* terrorista.

bomb *noun* bomba *Fem.*
bomb *verb* bombardear [17].

bone *noun* 1 hueso *Masc.*; 2 (*of a fish*) espina *Fem.*

bonfire *noun* hoguera *Fem.*

bonnet *noun* (*of a car*) capó *Masc.*

bony *adjective* 1 (*fish*) lleno/llena de espinas; 2 (*body*) huesudo/huesuda.

boo *verb* abuchear [17]; **the crowd booed the referee** el público abucheó al árbitro.

book *noun* 1 (*that you read*) libro *Masc.*; **a book about dinosaurs** un libro sobre los dinosaurios; **a biology book** un libro de biología; 2 **an exercise book** un cuaderno; 3 **a book of tickets** un taco de billetes; **a book of stamps** un librito de sellos.
book *verb* reservar [17]; **I booked a table for 8 o'clock** reservé una mesa para las ocho.

bookcase *noun* estantería *Fem.*

booking *noun* reserva *Fem.*

booking office *noun* taquilla *Fem.*

booklet *noun* folleto *Masc.*

bookshelf *noun* estante *Masc.*

bookshop *noun* librería *Fem.*

boot *noun* 1 (*item of clothing*) bota *Fem.*; **walking boots** botas de montaña; **wellington boots** botas de agua; 2 (*short fashion boot*) botín *Masc.*; 3 (*of a car*) maletero *Masc.*

border *noun* (*between countries*) frontera *Fem.*; **we crossed the border at Irún** cruzamos la frontera en Irún.

bore *noun* 1 (*a boring person*) pesado *Masc.*, pesada *Fem.* (*informal*); 2 (*a nuisance*) **what a bore!** ¡qué rollo! (*informal*).

bored *adjective* aburrido/aburrida; **to be bored** estar aburrido; **I'm bored** estoy aburrido; **to get bored** aburrirse [19].

boring *adjective* aburrido/aburrida.

born *verb* **to be born** nacer [35]; **she was born in June** nació en junio.

borrow *verb* **can I borrow your bike?** ¿me prestas tu bici?; **to borrow something from someone** pedirle algo prestado a alguien (*literally, to ask somebody for something on loan*); **I'll borrow some money from Dad** le pediré dinero prestado a papá.

boss *noun* jefe *Masc.*, jefa *Fem.*

bossy *adjective* mandón/mandona (*informal*).

both *pronoun*, *adjective* los/las dos; **they both came** vinieron los dos; **they're both sold** los dos están vendidos; **both sisters were there** las dos hermanas estaban allí; **both**

a
b
c
d
e
f
g
h
i
j
k
l
m
n
o
p
q
r
s
t
u
v
w
x
y
z

349

a
b
c
d
e
f
g
h
i
j
k
l
m
n
o
p
q
r
s
t
u
v
w
x
y
z

my feet mis dos pies.
both *conjunction* **both ... and** tanto ... como; **both at home and at school** tanto en casa como en colegio; **both in summer and in winter** tanto en verano como en el invierno.

bother *noun* problemas *Fem. plural*; **I've had a lot of bother with the car** he tenido muchos problemas con el coche; **it's no bother** no es ningún problema; **without any bother** sin ningún problema; **it's too much bother** no merece la pena molestarse.

bother *verb* **1** (*disturb*) molestar [17]; **I'm sorry to bother you** siento molestarte; **2** (*worry*) preocuparse [17]; **that doesn't bother me at all** no me preocupa en absoluto; **don't bother about dinner** no te preocupes de la cena; **3** (*take the trouble*) molestarse [17]; **she didn't even bother to come** ni siquiera se molestó en venir; **don't bother!** ¡no te molestes!

bottle *noun* botella *Fem.*

bottle bank *noun* contenedor *Masc.* de botellas.

bottle opener *noun* abrebotellas *Masc.* (*does not change in the plural*).

bottom *noun* **1** (*of a page, a hill, a wall, or steps*) pie *Masc.*; **at the bottom of the ladder** al pie de la escalera; **at the bottom of the page** al pie de la página; **2** (*of a bag, a hole, a stretch of water, a street, or a garden*) fondo *Masc.*; **at the bottom of the lake** en el fondo del lago; **3** (*of a list*) final *Masc.*; **4** (*of a bottle*) culo

Masc.; **5** (*buttocks*) trasero *Masc.*

bottom *adjective* **1** (*lowest*) de abajo; **the bottom shelf** el estante de abajo; **2** (*a team, or place*) último/ última; **3 the bottom sheet** la sábana bajera; **the bottom flat** el piso bajo.

bounce *verb* rebotar [17].

bouncer *noun* gorila *Masc.* (*informal*).

bound *adjective* **he's bound to be late** seguro que llega tarde; **that was bound to happen** eso tenía que pasar.

boundary *noun* línea *Fem.* divisoria.

bow *noun* **1** (*in a shoelace or ribbon*) lazo *Masc.*; **2** (*for playing the violin or shooting arrows*) arco *Masc.*

bowl *noun* **1** (*for cereal*) bol *Masc.*; **2** (*larger, for mixing*) cuenco *Masc.*; **3** (*for washing up*) barreño *Masc.*; **4 a salad bowl** una ensaladera; **a fruit bowl** un frutero.
bowl *verb* lanzar [22] (*a ball*).

bowling *noun* (*tenpin*) bolos *Masc. plural*; **to go bowling** ir a jugar a los bolos.

bow tie *noun* pajarita *Fem.*

box *noun* **1** caja *Fem.*; **a box of chocolates** una caja de bombones; **a cardboard box** una caja de cartón; **2** (*of matches*) cajetilla *Fem.*; **3** (*on a form*) recuadro *Masc.*

boxer *noun* **1** (*fighter*) boxeador *Masc.*; **2** (*dog*) bóxer *Masc.*

boxer shorts *plural noun* calzoncillos *Masc. plural*.

boxing *noun* **1** boxeo *Masc.*; **2 a boxing match** un combate de boxeo.

Boxing Day *noun* fiesta del 26 de diciembre.

box office *noun* taquilla *Fem.*

boy *noun* niño *Masc.*; **a little boy** un niño pequeño.

boyfriend *noun* novio *Masc.*

bra *noun* sujetador *Masc.*

brace *noun* (*for teeth*) aparato *Masc.* de los dientes.

braces *plural noun* (*for trousers*) tirantes *Masc. plural.*

bracelet *noun* pulsera *Fem.*

bracket *noun* **in brackets** entre paréntesis.

brain *noun* cerebro *Masc.*

brainwave *noun* idea *Fem.* genial.

brake *noun* freno *Masc.*
brake *verb* frenar [17].

bramble *noun* zarzamora *Fem.*

branch *noun* **1** (*of a tree*) rama *Fem.*; **2** (*of a shop, company or bank*) sucursal *Fem.*; **our Oxford branch** nuestra sucursal de Oxford.

brand *noun* marca *Fem.*

brand new *adjective* nuevo/ nueva.

brandy *noun* coñac *Masc.*

brass *noun* **1** (*the metal*) latón *Masc.*; **a brass candlestick** un candelabro dorado; **2** (*in an orchestra*) **the brass** los metales.
brass *adjective* de latón.

brass band *noun* banda *Fem.* de música.

Brazil *noun* Brasil *Masc.*

Brazilian *noun* brasileño *Masc.*, brasileña *Fem.*
Brazilian *adjective* brasileño/ brasileña.

brave *adjective* valiente.

bread *noun* pan *Masc.*; **a slice of bread** una rebanada de pan.

break *noun* **1** (*a short rest*) descanso *Masc.*; **a fifteen-minute break** un descanso de quince minutos; **to take a break** descansar un rato; **2** (*in school*) recreo *Masc.*; **3 the Christmas break** las vacaciones de Navidad.
break *verb* **1** romper [40]; **he broke a glass** rompió un vaso; **2 to break your leg** romperse una pierna; **I broke my arm** me rompí un brazo; **3 to break your promise** romper una promesa; **to break the rules** infringir [49] las reglas; **you mustn't break the rules** no debes infringir las reglas; **4 to break a record** batir [19] un récord; **5 to break the news** dar [4] la noticia.

● **to break down** estropearse [17]; **the car broke down** el coche se estropeó.

● **to break in: the thief broke in through the window** el ladrón se metió en la casa por la ventana; **the house was broken into** entraron ladrones en la casa.

● **to break out 1** (*a fire*) declararse [17]; **2** (*a war or a storm*) estallar [17]; **3** (*a prisoner*) escaparse [17].

● **to break up 1** (*a family*) separarse [17]; **2** (*a couple*) romper [40]; **3** (*a crowd or clouds*) dispersarse [17]; **4** (*for the holidays*) **we break up on**

a **b** c d e f g h i j k l m n o p q r s t u v w x y z

a

b

c

d

e

f

g

h

i

j

k

l

m

n

o

p

q

r

s

t

u

v

w

x

y

z

Thursday empezamos las vacaciones el jueves.

breakdown *noun* **1** (*of a vehicle*) avería *Fem.*; **we had a breakdown on the motorway** tuvimos una avería en la autopista; **2** (*in talks or negotiations*) ruptura *Fem.*; **3** (*a nervous collapse*) crisis *Fem.* nerviosa; **to have a (nervous) breakdown** sufrir una crisis nerviosa.

breakdown truck *noun* grúa *Fem.* de recogiola en carretera.

breakfast *noun* desayuno *Masc.*; **to have breakfast** desayunar [17]; **we have breakfast at eight** desayunamos a las ocho.

break-in *noun* robo *Masc.*

breast *noun* **1** (*a woman's*) pecho *Masc.*; **2** (*of a chicken or other fowl*) pechuga *Fem.*

breaststroke *noun* braza *Fem.*

breath *noun* aliento *Masc.*; **out of breath** sin aliento; **to get one's breath** recobrar el aliento; **to take a deep breath** respirar hondo.

breathe *verb* respirar [17].

breathing *noun* respiración *Fem.*

breed *noun* (*of animal*) raza *Fem.* **breed** *verb* **1** criar [32] (*animals*); **2** (*to have babies*) reproducirse [60]; **rabbits breed fast** los conejos se reproducen mucho.

breeze *noun* brisa *Fem.*

brewery *noun* cervecería *Fem.*

bribe *noun* soborno *Masc.* **bribe** *verb* sobornar [17].

brick *noun* ladrillo *Masc.*; **a brick wall** una pared de ladrillo.

bride *noun* novia *Fem.*; **the bride and groom** los novios, el novio y la novia.

bridegroom *noun* novio *Masc.*

bridesmaid *noun* dama *Fem.* de honor.

bridge *noun* **1** (*over a river*) puente *Masc.*; **a bridge over the Thames** un puente sobre el Támesis; **2** (*card game*) bridge *Masc.*; **to play bridge** jugar al bridge.

bridle *noun* brida *Fem.*

brief *adjective* breve.

briefcase *noun* maletín *Masc.*

briefly *adjective* brevemente.

briefs *plural noun* calzoncillos *Masc. plural.*

bright *adjective* **1** (*star, light*) brillante; **2** (*colour*) vivo/viva; **bright green socks** calcetines de un verde vivo; **3 bright sunshine** un sol radiante; **4** (*clever*) inteligente; **she's not very bright** no es muy inteligente; ★**to look on the bright side** ver el lado bueno de las cosas.

brighten up *verb* **the weather's brightening up** el tiempo está aclarando.

brilliant *adjective* **1** (*very clever*) brillante; **a brilliant surgeon** un brillante cirujano; **he's brilliant at maths** es genial para las matemáticas; **2** (*wonderful*) fenomenal (*informal*); **the party was brilliant!** ¡la fiesta estuvo fenomenal!

bring *verb* **1** traer [42]; **they brought a present** trajeron un regalo; **bring your camera** trae tu cámara; **it brings good luck** trae buena suerte; **she's bringing all the children** trae a todos los niños; **2 to bring something back** devolver [45] algo; **3 to bring up** criar [32] (*children*); **he was brought up by his aunt** lo crió su tía.

bristle *noun* cerda *Fem.*

Britain *noun* Gran Bretaña *Fem.*

British *plural noun* **the British** los británicos.
British *adjective* británico/británica; **the British Isles** las islas británicas.

broad *adjective* (*wide*) ancho/ancha.

broad bean *noun* haba *Fem.*

broadcast *noun* emisión *Fem.*
broadcast *verb* emitir [19] (*a programme*).

broccoli *noun* brécol *Masc.*

brochure *noun* folleto *Masc.*

broke *adjective* **to be broke** (*no money*) no tener un duro (*informal*).

broken *adjective* roto/rota; **the window's broken** la ventana está rota; **to have a broken leg** tener una pierna rota.

bronchitis *noun* bronquitis *Fem.*

bronze *noun* bronce *Masc.*
bronze *adjective* de bronce.

brooch *noun* broche *Masc.*

broom *noun* **1** (*for sweeping*) escoba *Fem.*; **2** (*bush*) retama *Fem.*

brother *noun* hermano *Masc.*; **my little brother** mi hermano pequeño; **my mother's brother** el hermano de mi madre.

brother-in-law *noun* cuñado *Masc.*

brown *adjective* **1** marrón (*never changes*); **brown shoes** zapatos marrón; **2** castaño/castaña (*hair or eyes*); **3** (*tanned in the sun*) moreno/morena; **to go brown** ponerse moreno/morena.

brown bread *noun* pan *Masc.* integral.

brown sugar *noun* azúcar *Masc./Fem.* moreno/morena.

bruise *noun* **1** (*on a person*) moratón *Masc.*; **2** (*on fruit*) magulladura *Fem.*

brush *noun* **1** (*for your hair, clothes, nails, or shoes*) cepillo *Masc.*; **my hair brush** mi cepillo del pelo; **2** (*for sweeping*) escoba *Fem.*; **3** (*paintbrush*) brocha *Fem.*
brush *verb* **1** cepillar [17] (*your hair or shoes*); **to brush your hair** cepillarse el pelo; **she brushed her hair** se cepilló el pelo; **2 to brush your teeth** limpiarse [17] los dientes; **I'm going to brush my teeth** voy a limpiarme los dientes.

Brussels *noun* Bruselas *Fem.*

Brussels sprouts *noun* coles *Fem. plural* de Bruselas.

bubble *noun* burbuja *Fem.*

bubble bath *noun* gel *Masc.* de baño.

bucket *noun* cubo *Masc.*

buckle *noun* hebilla *Fem.*

a
b
c
d
e
f
g
h
i
j
k
l
m
n
o
p
q
r
s
t
u
v
w
x
y
z

bud *noun* brote *Masc.*

Buddhism *noun* budismo *Masc.*

Buddhist *noun* budista *Masc./Fem.*

budget *noun* presupuesto *Masc.*

budgie *noun* periquito *Masc.*

buffet *noun* **1** (*on train*) bar *Masc.*; **2** (*meal*) buffet *Masc.*

buffet car *noun* coche *Masc.* restaurante.

bug *noun* **1** (*insect*) bicho *Masc.* (*informal*); **2** (*virus*) virus *Masc.*; **a stomach bug** un virus en el estómago.

build *verb* construir [54].

builder *noun* albañil *Masc./Fem.*

building *noun* edificio *Masc.*

building site *noun* solar *Masc.*

building society *noun* sociedad *Fem.* de crédito hipotecario.

built-in *adjective* empotrado/ empotrada.

built-up *adjective* urbanizado/ urbanizada; **a built-up area** una zona urbanizada.

bulb *noun* **1** (*for a light*) bombilla *Fem.*; **2** (*that you plant*) bulbo *Masc.*

bulky *adjective* voluminoso/ voluminosa.

bull *noun* toro *Masc.*

bulldozer *noun* bulldozer *Masc.*

bullet *noun* bala *Fem.*

bulletin *noun* boletín *Masc.*; **a news bulletin** boletín de noticias.

bullfight *noun* corrida *Fem.* de toros.

bullfighter *noun* torero *Masc.* torera *Fem.*

bullfighting *noun* los toros; **do you like bullfighting?** ¿te gustan los toros?

bullring *noun* plaza *Fem.* de toros.

bully *noun* bravucón *Masc.*, bravucona *Fem.*; **he's a bully** es un bravucón.
bully *verb* intimidar [17].

bum *noun* (*bottom*) trasero *Masc.* (*informal*).

bump *noun* **1 a bump on the head** un chichón en la cabeza; **2 a bump in the road** un bache en la carretera; **3** (*jolt*) sacudida *Fem.*; **4** (*noise*) golpe *Masc.*
bump *verb* **1** (*bang*) darse [4] un golpe; **I bumped my head** me di un golpe en la cabeza; **2 to bump into something** chocarse [31] con algo; **I bumped into the table** me choqué con la mesa; **3 to bump into somebody** (*meet by chance*) encontrarse [24] con alguien.

bumper *noun* parachoques *Masc.* (*does not change in the plural*).

bumpy *adjective* **1** lleno/llena de baches (*road*); **2** con muchas sacudidas (*plane landing*).

bun *noun* **1** (*for a burger*) panecillo *Masc.*; **2** (*sweet*) bollo *Masc.*

bunch *noun* **1** (*of flowers*) ramo *Masc.*; **2** (*of carrots, radishes or keys*) manojo *Masc.*; **3 a bunch of grapes** un racimo de uvas.

bundle *noun* **1** (*of clothes*) fardo *Masc.*; **2** (*of papers, letters*) paquete *Masc.*

bungalow *noun* casa *Fem.* de una planta.

bunk *noun* (*on a train or boat*) litera *Fem.*

bunk beds *plural noun* literas *Fem. plural.*

bureau *noun* 1 (*agency*) agencia *Fem.*; 2 (*desk*) escritorio *Masc.*

bureau de change *noun* casa *Fem.* de cambio.

burger *noun* hamburguesa *Fem.*

burglar *noun* ladrón *Masc.*, ladrona *Fem.*

burglar alarm *noun* alarma *Fem.* antirobo.

burglary *noun* robo *Masc.*

burn *noun* quemadura *Fem.*
burn *verb* quemar [17]; **I've burned the rubbish** he quemado la basura; **she burnt herself on the grill** se quemó en la parrilla; **you'll burn your finger!** ¡te vas a quemar el dedo!; **Mum's burnt her cake** a mamá se le ha quemado el pastel; **I burn easily** (*in the sun*) me quemo fácilmente.

burnt *adjective* quemado/quemada.

burst *verb* 1 estallar [17] (*a balloon*); 2 reventar [29] (*a tyre or pipe*) **a burst tyre** una rueda con un reventón; 3 **to burst out laughing** echarse [17] a reír; **to burst into tears** echarse [17] a llorar; 4 **to burst into flames** empezar [25] a arder.

bury *verb* enterrar [29].

bus *noun* 1 (*for urban transport*) autobús *Masc.*, bus *Masc.*; **we'll take the bus** cogeremos el autobús; **we missed the bus** perdimos el autobús; **on the bus** en el autobús; **a bus ticket** un billete de autobús; 2 (*coach*) autocar *Masc.*; **to go to London by bus** ir [8] a Londres en autocar.

bus driver *noun* conductor *Masc.* de autobús, conductora *Fem.* de autobús.

bush *noun* arbusto *Masc.*

business *noun* 1 (*commercial dealings*) negocios *Masc. plural*; **he's in Leeds on business** está en Leeds de viaje de negocios; **a business letter** una carta de negocios; 2 (*firm or company*) negocio *Masc.*; **small businesses** las pequeñas empresas; 3 **mind your own business!** ¡no te metas en lo que no te importa!; **that's my business!** ¡eso es asunto mío!.

business class *noun* clase *Fem.* preferente.

businessman *noun* hombre *Masc.* de negocios.

business trip *noun* viaje *Masc.* de negocios.

businesswoman *noun* mujer *Fem.* de negocios.

bus lane *noun* carril *Masc.* bus.

bus pass *noun* abono *Masc.* de autobús.

bus route *noun* línea *Fem.* de autobús.

bus shelter *noun* marquesina *Fem.*

bus station *noun* estación *Fem.* de autobús.

a
b
c
d
e
f
g
h
i
j
k
l
m
n
o
p
q
r
s
t
u
v
w
x
y
z

bust *noun* busto *Masc.*

bus stop *noun* parada *Fem.* del autobús.

busy *adjective* **1** ocupado/ocupada (*a person*); **don't disturb him, he's busy** no lo molestes, está ocupado; **2** ajetreado/ajetreada (*a day or week*); **a very busy day** un día muy ajetreado; **3** (*full of cars or people*) muy concurrido/concurrida (*a road*); **the shops were busy** las tiendas estaban muy concurridas; **4** (*phone*) **the line's busy** está comunicando.

but *conjunction* **1** pero; **small but strong** pequeño pero fuerte; **I'll try, but it's difficult** lo intentaré, pero es difícil; **2 not ... but ...** no ... sino ...; **not Thursday but Friday** no el jueves sino el viernes.
but *preposition* **1** menos; **anything but that** cualquier cosa menos eso; **everyone but Leah** todos menos Leah; **2 the last but one** el penúltimo.

butcher *noun* carnicero *Masc.*, carnicera *Fem.*; **the butcher's** la carnicería.

butter *noun* mantequilla *Fem.*
butter *verb* untar [17] con mantequilla.

buttercup *noun* botón *Masc.* de oro.

butterfly *noun* mariposa *Fem.*

button *noun* botón *Masc.*; **the record button** el botón de grabar.

buttonhole *noun* ojal *Masc.*

buy *noun* **a good buy** una buena compra; **a bad buy** una mala compra.

buy *verb* comprar [17]; **I bought the cinema tickets** compré las entradas para el cine; **to buy something for somebody** comprarle algo a alguien; **Sarah bought him a sweater** Sarah le compró un jersey; **to buy something from someone** comprarle algo a alguien; **he bought his bike from Tim** le compré a Tom su bici.

buyer *noun* comprador *Masc.*, compradora *Fem.*

buzz *verb* (*a fly or bee*) zumbar [17].

buzzer *noun* timbre *Masc.*

by *preposition* **1** por; **by telephone** por teléfono; **the thief came in by the window** el ladrón entró por la ventana; **eaten by a dog** comido por un perro; **it's two metres by four** mide dos metros por cuatro; **by mistake** por equivocación; **they pay by the hour** pagan por hora; **written by Lorca** escrito por Lorca; **2** (*travel*) en; **to come by bus** venir en autobús; **to leave by train** salir en tren; **by bike** en bicicleta; **3** (*near*) al lado de; **by the fire** al lado del fuego; **by the sea** al lado del mar; **close by** cerca; **4** (*before*) para; **it'll be ready by Monday** estará listo para el lunes; **Kevin was back by four** Kevin estaba de vuelta para las cuatro; **5 they should have finished by now** ya deberían haber terminado; **6 by yourself** solo/sola; **I was by myself in the house** estaba solo en la casa; **she did it by herself** lo hizo sola; **7 to take somebody by the hand** coger a alguien de la mano; **8 by the way** por cierto; **9 to go by** pasar.

bye *exclamation* adiós; **bye for now!** ¡hasta luego!

bypass *noun* carretera *Fem.* de circunvalación.

Cc

cab *noun* **1** taxi *Masc.*; **to call a cab** llamar un taxi; **2** (*on a lorry*) cabina *Fem.*

cabbage *noun* repollo *Masc.*

cabin *noun* **1** (*on lorry, plane*) cabina *Fem.*; **2** (*on ship*) camarote *Masc.*

cable *noun* cable *Masc.*

cable car *noun* funicular *Masc.*

cable television *noun* televisión *Fem.* por cable.

cactus *noun* cactus *Masc.*

café *noun* cafetería *Fem.*

cage *noun* jaula *Fem.*

cagoule *noun* canguro *Masc.*

cake *noun* pastel *Masc.*; **would you like a piece of cake?** ¿quieres un trozo de pastel?

calculate *verb* calcular [17].

calculation *noun* cálculo *Masc.*

calculator *noun* calculadora *Fem.*

calendar *noun* calendario *Masc.*

calf *noun* **1** (*animal*) ternero *Masc.*, ternera *Fem.*; **2** (*of your leg*) pantorrilla *Fem.*

call *noun* (*telephone*) llamada *Fem.*; **I had several calls this morning;** he tenido varias llamadas esta mañana; **thank you for your call** gracias por llamar; **a phone call** una llamada de teléfono; **to give somebody a call** llamar [17] a alguien.

call *verb* **1** (*telephone*) llamar [17]; **to call a taxi** llamar un taxi; **to call the doctor** llamar al médico; **call this number** llama a este número; **thank you for calling** gracias por llamar; **I'll call you back later** te llamo más tarde; **2** (*name*) **they've called the baby Julie** le han puesto Julie al bebé; **3 to be called** llamarse [17]; **she has a brother called Dan** tiene un hermano que se llama Dan; **what's he called?** ¿cómo se llama?

● **to call in** pasar [17]; **I'll call in on my way back** pasaré por tu casa cuando vuelvo.

call box *noun* cabina *Fem.* telefónica.

calm *adjective* calma *Fem.* **calm** *verb* calmar [17].

● **to calm down** calmarse; **he's calmed down a bit** se ha calmado un poco.

● **to calm somebody down** calmar a alguien; **I tried to calm her down** intenté calmarla.

calmly *adverb* con calma.

calorie *noun* caloría *Fem.*

camcorder *noun* videocámara *Fem.*

camel *noun* camello *Masc.*

a
b
c
d
e
f
g
h
i
j
k
l
m
n
o
p
q
r
s
t
u
v
w
x
y
z

camera noun **1** (for photos) cámara Fem. de fotos; **2** (film or TV camera) cámara Fem.

cameraman noun cámara Masc./ Fem.

camp noun campamento Masc. **camp** verb acampar [17].

campaign noun campaña Fem.

camper noun campista Masc./Fem.

camper van noun caravana Fem.

camping noun camping Masc.; **to go camping** ir de camping; **we're going camping in Andalusia this summer** nos vamos de camping a Andalucía este verano.

campsite noun camping Masc.

can¹, **can** noun **1** lata Fem.; **a can of tomatoes** una lata de tomates; **2** (for petrol or oil) bidón Masc.

can², **can** verb **1** poder [10]; **I can't be there before ten** no puedo estar allí antes de las diez; **you can leave your bag here** puedes dejar tu bolsa aquí; **can you open the door, please?** ¿me abres la puerta por favor?; **can I help you?** ¿qué desea?; **they couldn't come** no pudieron venir; **you could ring back tomorrow** podrías volver a llamar mañana; **you could have told me** me lo podrías haber dicho; **2** (with hear, see, remember, find, 'can' is not translated) **can you hear me?** ¿me oyes?; **I can't see her** no la veo; **I can't remember** no me acuerdo; **I can't find my keys** no encuentro mis llaves; **3** (know how to) saber [13]; **she can't drive** no sabe

conducir; **can you play the piano?** ¿sabes tocar el piano?.

Canada noun Canadá Masc.

Canadian noun canadiense Masc./ Fem.
Canadian adjective canadiense.

canal noun canal Masc.

canary noun canario Masc.

Canary Islands noun **the Canary Islands** las Islas Canarias.

cancel verb cancelar [17]; **the concert's been cancelled** han cancelado el concierto.

cancer noun cáncer Masc.; **to have lung cancer** tener cáncer de pulmón.

Cancer noun Cáncer Masc.; **I'm Cancer** soy Cáncer.

candidate noun candidato Masc., candidata Fem.

candle noun vela Fem.

candlestick noun candelabro Masc.

candyfloss noun algodón Masc. de azúcar.

canned adjective en lata; **canned tomatoes** tomates en lata.

cannon noun cañón Masc.

cannot verb SEE **can**².

canoe noun piragua Fem.

canoeing noun piragüismo Masc.; **to go canoeing** hacer piragüismo; **I like canoeing** me gusta hacer piragüismo.

can-opener noun abrelatas Fem. (does not change in the plural).

canteen noun cantina Fem.

canvas noun **1** (*fabric*) lona Fem.; **2** (*painting*) lienzo Masc.

cap noun **1** (*hat*) gorro Masc.; **a baseball cap** un gorro de béisbol; **2** (*on a bottle or tube*) tapón Masc.

capable adjective capaz.

capacity noun capacidad Fem.

capital noun **1** (*city*) capital Fem.; **Madrid is the capital of Spain** Madrid es la capital de España; **2** (*letter*) mayúscula Fem.; **in capitals** en mayúsculas.

capitalism noun capitalismo Masc.

Capricorn noun Capricornio Masc.; **Linda's Capricorn** Linda es Capricornio.

captain noun **1** (*of a ship or a team*) capitán Masc., capitana Fem.; **2** (*of a plane*) comandante Masc./Fem.

captivity noun cautiverio Masc.; **to keep someone in captivity** mantener [9] a alguien en cautiverio.

capture verb capturar [17].

car noun coche Masc.; **a car crash** un accidente de coche; **to park the car** aparcar el coche; **we're going by car** vamos en coche.

caramel noun caramelo Masc.

caravan noun caravana Fem.

card noun **1** (*for a card game*) carta Fem.; **a card game** un juego de cartas; **to have a game of cards** jugar a las cartas; **2** (*greetings, phone, bank*) tarjeta Fem.; **a birthday card** una tarjeta de cumpleaños.

cardboard noun cartón Masc.

cardigan noun rebeca Fem.

cardphone noun teléfono Masc. de tarjeta.

care noun **1** cuidado Masc.; **he took care opening it** tuvo cuidado al abrirlo; **2 to take care to do** asegurarse [17] de hacer; **3 to take care of somebody** cuidar a alguien; **4 take care!** (*be careful*) ¡cuidado!, (*when saying goodbye*) ¡cuídate! **care** verb **1 to care about** preocuparse [17] por; **to care about pollution** preocuparse por la contaminación; **2 she doesn't care** a ella no le importa; **I couldn't care less!** ¡no me importa en absoluto!

career noun carrera Fem.

careful adjective **1** cuidadoso/ cuidadosa; **try to be more careful** procura ser más cuidadoso; **2 a careful driver** un conductor/una conductora prudente; **3 be careful!** ¡ten cuidado!

carefully adverb **1 read the instructions carefully** lea las instrucciones atentamente; **listen carefully** escuchad atentamente; **2** (*handle*) con cuidado; **she put the vase down carefully** colocó el jarrón con cuidado; **3 drive carefully!** ¡conduce con precaución!

careless adjective **1 he's very careless** no pone atención en lo que hace; **2 this is careless work** este trabajo está hecho sin cuidado; **a careless mistake** una falta de atención; **3 careless driving** conducción negligente.

a
b
c
d
e
f
g
h
i
j
k
l
m
n
o
p
q
r
s
t
u
v
w
x
y
z

caretaker noun (*in block of flats*) portero *Masc.*, portera *Fem.*

car ferry noun ferry *Masc.*

cargo noun carga *Fem.*

car hire noun alquiler *Masc.* de coches.

Caribbean¹ noun the Caribbean el Caribe; **the Caribbean Sea** el mar Caribe.

Caribbean² noun caribeño *Masc.*, caribeña *Fem.*
Caribbean *adjective* caribeño/caribeña.

caricature noun caricatura *Fem.*

carnation noun clavel *Masc.*

carnival noun carnaval *Masc.*

car park noun aparcamiento *Masc.*

carpenter noun carpintero *Masc.*, carpintera *Fem.*

carpentry noun carpintería *Fem.*

carpet noun 1 (*fitted*) moqueta *Fem.*; 2 (*loose*) alfombra *Fem.*

car phone noun teléfono *Masc.* de automóvil.

car radio noun radio *Masc.* de coche.

carriage noun vagón *Masc.*

carrier bag noun bolsa *Fem.*

carrot noun zanahoria *Fem.*

carry verb 1 llevar [17]; **she was carrying a parcel** llevaba un paquete; 2 (*vehicle, plane*) transportar [17]; **the coach was carrying schoolchildren** el autobús transportaba colegiales.

● **to carry on** seguir [64]; **they carried on talking** siguieron hablando.

carrycot noun cuna *Fem.* portátil.

carsick *adjective* **to be carsick** marearse [17] al viajar en coche.

cart noun carro *Masc.*

carton noun envase *Masc.*

cartoon noun 1 (*a film*) dibujos *Masc. plural* animados; 2 (*a comic strip*) tira *Fem.* cómica; 3 (*an amusing drawing*) chiste *Masc.*

cartridge noun 1 (*for a pen*) recambio *Masc.*; 2 (*for a gun*) cartucho *Masc.*

carve verb trinchar [17] (*meat*).

case¹ noun 1 (*suitcase*) maleta *Fem.*; **to pack a case** hacer una maleta; 2 (*for wine bottles for example*) caja *Fem.*; 3 (*for spectacles or small things*) estuche *Masc.*

case² noun 1 caso *Masc.*; **a case of flu** un caso de gripe; **in that case** en ese caso; **that's not the case** no se trata de eso; 2 **in case** en caso; **in case he's late** en caso de que llegue tarde; **check first, just in case** asegúrate, por si acaso; 3 **in any case** de todas formas; **in any case, it's too late** de todas formas, es demasiado tarde.

cash noun 1 (*money in general*) dinero *Masc.*; **I haven't any cash on me** no llevo dinero encima; 2 (*money rather than a cheque*) dinero *Masc.* en efectivo; **to pay in cash** pagar en efectivo; **£50 in cash** cincuenta libras en efectivo.

cash card *noun* tarjeta *Fem.* de cajero automático.

cash desk *noun* caja *Fem.*; **pay at the cash desk** pagar en caja.

cash dispenser *noun* cajero *Masc.* automático.

cashew *noun* anacardo *Masc.*

cashier *noun* cajero *Masc.*, cajera *Fem.*

cash point *noun* cajero *Masc.* automático.

cassette *noun* cinta *Fem.* de cassette.

cassette recorder *noun* cassette *Masc.*

cast *noun* los actores *Masc. plural*; **the cast were on stage** los actores estaban en el escenario.

castle *noun* **1** castillo *Masc.*; **2** (*in chess*) torre *Fem.*

casual *adjective* informal.

casualty *noun* **1** (*in an accident*) víctima *Fem.*; **2** (*hospital department*) urgencias *Fem. plural*; **he's in casualty** está en urgencias.

cat *noun* gato *Masc.*, (*female*) gata *Fem.*; ⋆ **it's raining cats and dogs** está lloviendo a cántaros (*literally: it's raining in jugfuls*).

Catalan *noun* **1** (*the language*) catalán *Masc.*; **2** (*person*) catalán *Masc.*, catalana *Fem.*
Catalan *adjective* catalán/catalana.

Catalonia *noun* Cataluña *Fem.*

catalogue *noun* catálogo *Masc.*

catastrophe *noun* catástrofe *Fem.*

catch *noun* **1** (*on a door*) pestillo *Masc.*; **2** (*a drawback*) trampa *Fem.*; **what's the catch?** ¿dónde está la trampa?
catch *verb* **1** coger [3]; **Tom caught the ball** Tom cogió la pelota; **you can't catch me!** ¡no me coges!; **can you catch hold of the branch?** ¿puedes coger la rama?; **2 to catch somebody doing** coger [3] a alguien haciendo; **he was caught stealing money** lo cogieron robando dinero; **3** coger [3] (*a bus or plane*); **did Tim catch his bus?** ¿cogió Tim el autobús?; **4** coger [3] (*an illness*); **he's caught chickenpox** ha cogido la varicela; **I've caught a cold** he cogido un resfriado; **5** (*fishing or hunting*) **to catch a fish** pescar [31] un pez; **to catch a mouse** cazar [22] un ratón; **6** oír [56] (*what somebody says*); **I didn't catch your name** no he oído tu nombre.

● **to catch up with somebody** alcanzar [22] a alguien.

category *noun* categoría *Fem.*

catering *noun* catering *Masc.*

caterpillar *noun* oruga *Fem.*

cathedral *noun* catedral *Fem.*; **Seville cathedral** la catedral de Sevilla.

Catholic *noun* católico *Masc.*, católica *Fem.*
Catholic *adjective* católico/católica.

cattle *plural noun* ganado *Masc.* (*singular*).

a
b
c
d
e
f
g
h
i
j
k
l
m
n
o
p
q
r
s
t
u
v
w
x
y
z

cauliflower *noun* coliflor *Fem.*;
cauliflower cheese coliflor con
besamel.

cause *noun* causa *Fem.*; **the cause
of the accident** la causa del
accidente; **for a good cause** por
una buena causa.
cause *verb* causar [17]; **to cause
problems** causar problemas.

caution *noun* cautela *Fem.*

cautious *adjective* cauteloso/
cautelosa.

cave *noun* cueva *Fem.*

caving *noun* espeleología *Fem.*; **to
go caving** hacer espeleología.

CD *noun* disco *Masc.* compacto, CD
Masc.

CD player *noun* compacto *Masc.*

CD-ROM *noun* CD-ROM *Masc.*

ceiling *noun* techo *Masc.*; **on the
ceiling** en el techo.

celebrate *verb* celebrar [17]; **I'm
celebrating my birthday** estoy
celebrando mi cumpleaños.

celebrity *noun* famoso *Masc.*,
famosa *Fem.*

celery *noun* apio *Masc.*

cell *noun* célula *Fem.*

cellar *noun* sótano *Masc.*

cello *noun* violonchelo *Masc.*; **to
play the cello** tocar [31] el
violonchelo.

cement *noun* cemento *Masc.*

cemetery *noun* cementerio *Masc.*

cent *noun* **1** (*in the euro system*)
céntimo *Masc.*; **2** (*in the dollar
system*) centavo *Masc.*

centenary *noun* centenario *Masc.*

centigrade *adjective* centígrado
Masc.; **ten degrees centigrade** diez
grados centígrados.

centimetre *noun* centímetro
Masc.

central *adjective* central; **central
London** el centro de Londres; **the
office is very central** la oficina está
en pleno centro.

Central America *noun* América
Fem. Central.

central heating *noun*
calefacción *Fem.* central.

centre *noun* centro *Masc.*; **in the
centre of** en el centro de; **in the
town centre** en el centro de la
ciudad; **a shopping centre** un
centro comercial.

century *noun* siglo *Masc.*; **in the
twentieth century** en el siglo
veinte; **the sixth century** el siglo
seis; **the twenty-first century** el
siglo veintiuno.

cereal *noun* **breakfast cereal**
cereales *Masc. plural* para el
desayuno; **to have cereal for
breakfast** desayunar cereales.

ceremony *noun* ceremonia *Fem.*

certain *adjective* **1** (*sure*) seguro/
segura; **are you certain of the
address?** ¿estás seguro de las
señas?; **I'm certain of it** estoy
seguro; **to be certain that** ... estar
seguro de que ...; **Nicky's certain
(that) you're wrong** Nicky está
segura de que estás equivocado;
nobody knows for certain nadie lo
sabe con seguridad; **2** (*particular*)

cierto/cierta; **a certain number of** un cierto número de.

certainly *adverb* **certainly** ¡por supuesto!; **certainly not** desde luego que no.

certificate *noun* certificado *Masc.*; **a birth certificate** un certificado de nacimiento.

chain *noun* cadena *Fem.*

chair *noun* **1** (*upright*) silla *Fem.*; **a kitchen chair** una silla de cocina; **2** (*with arms*) butaca *Fem.*

chair lift *noun* telesilla *Fem.*

chalet *noun* **1** (*in the mountains*) chalet *Masc.*; **2** (*in a holiday camp*) bungalow *Masc.*

chalk *noun* tiza *Fem.*

challenge *noun* reto *Masc.*; **the exam was a real challenge** el examen fue un verdadero reto.

champion *noun* campeón/ campeona *Masc./Fem.*; **world champion** campeón del mundo.

chance *noun* **1** (*an opportunity*) ocasión *Fem.*; **to have the chance to do** tener [9] ocasión de hacer; **if you have the chance to go to New York** si tienes ocasión de ir a Nueva York; **I haven't had the chance to write to him** no he tenido ocasión de escribirle; **2** (*likelihood*) posibilidad *Fem.*; **there's a chance that she'll pass** existe la posibilidad de que apruebe (*'de que' is followed by the subjunctive*); **there's little chance of winning** hay pocas posibilidades de ganar; **3** (*luck*) **by chance** por casualidad; **do you have her**

address, by any chance? ¿tienes sus señas por casualidad?

change *noun* **1** cambio *Masc.*; **a change of plan** un cambio de planes; **they've made some changes to the house** han hecho algunos cambios en la casa; **it makes a change from hamburgers** por lo menos, es algo distinto a las hamburguesas; **2 a change of clothes** una muda de ropa; **3** (*cash*) cambio *Masc.*; **I haven't any change** no tengo cambio; **keep the change** quédese con el cambio; **4 for a change** para variar; **for a change, let's eat out** vamos a comer fuera, para variar.

change *verb* **1** (*transform completely*) cambiar [17]; **it changed my life** cambió mi vida; **Liz never changes** Liz no cambia; **2** (*to switch from one thing to another*) cambiar [17] de; **we changed trains at Crewe** cambiamos de tren en Crewe; **she's changed her address** ha cambiado de dirección; **to change your mind** cambiar de opinión; **to change the subject** cambiar de tema; **they changed places** se cambiaron de sitio; **to change colour** cambiar de color; **3** (*to swap one for another*) cambiar [17]; **have you changed the towels?** ¿has cambiado las toallas?; **4** (*to exchange in a shop*) cambiar [17]; **can I change it for the larger size?** ¿puedo cambiarlo por una talla más grande?; **5** (*to change your clothes*) cambiarse [17]; **Mike's gone up to change** Mike ha ido a cambiarse; **I**

a
b
c
d
e
f
g
h
i
j
k
l
m
n
o
p
q
r
s
t
u
v
w
x
y
z

a
b
c
d
e
f
g
h
i
j
k
l
m
n
o
p
q
r
s
t
u
v
w
x
y
z

must change my shirt tengo que
cambiarme de camisa.

changing room noun **1** (for sport
or swimming) vestuario Masc.; **2** (in
a shop) probador Masc.

channel noun **1** (on TV) canal
Masc.; **to change channels** cambiar
[17] de canal; **2 the Channel** el
Canal de la Mancha.

Channel Tunnel noun
Eurotúnel Masc.

chaos noun caos Masc.; **it was
chaos!** ¡fue un caos!

chapel noun capilla Fem.

chapter noun capítulo Masc.; **in
chapter two** en el capítulo número
dos.

character noun **1** (personality)
carácter Masc.; **a house with a lot of
character** una casa con mucho
carácter; **2** (in a book, play, or film)
personaje Masc.; **the main
character** el personaje principal.

characteristic noun
característica Fem.

charcoal noun **1** (for burning)
carbón Masc. vegetal; **2** (for drawing)
carboncillo Masc.

charge noun **1** (what you pay)
precio Masc.; **admission charge**
precio de admisión; **there's no
charge** es gratis; **an extra charge**
un suplemento; **2 to be in charge**
ser responsable; **who's in charge?**
¿quién es el responsable?; **to be in
charge of something/somebody**
estar a cargo de algo/alguien; **who's
in charge of these children?**
¿quién está a cargo de estos niños?;

3 to be on a charge of theft estar
acusado de robo.

charge verb **1** (ask payment)
cobrar [17]; **they charge ten
pounds an hour** cobran diez libras
la hora; **how much do you charge
for one day?** ¿cuánto cobráis por un
día?; **we don't charge, it's free** no
cobramos, es gratis; **they didn't
charge me for the drinks** no me
cobraron las bebidas; **2 to charge
somebody with** acusar [17] a
alguien de (a crime).

charity noun organización Fem.
benéfica.

charm noun encanto Masc.

charming adjective encantador/
encantadora.

chart noun **1** (table) tabla Fem.;
2 the weather chart el mapa del
tiempo; **3 the charts** las listas de
éxitos; **number one in the charts**
número uno en las listas de éxitos.

charter flight noun vuelo Masc.
chárter.

chase noun persecución Fem.; **a car
chase** una persecución en coche.
chase verb perseguir [64] (a person
or animal).

chat noun charla Fem.; **to have a
chat with somebody** charlar con
alguien.

chatroom noun chat Masc.

chat show noun programa Masc.
de entrevistas.

chatter verb **1** (talk) cotorrear [17]
(informal); **2 my teeth are
chattering** me castañetean los
dientes.

cheap *adjective* barato/barata; **cheap shoes** zapatos baratos; **that's very cheap!** ¡eso es muy barato!

cheaply *adverb* **to buy/sell cheaply** comprar/vender barato; **to eat/dress cheaply** comer/vestir con poco dinero.

cheap-rate *adjective* de tarifa reducida; **a cheap-rate phone call** una llamada de teléfono de tarifa reducida.

cheat *noun* tramposo *Masc.*, tramposa *Fem.*
cheat *verb* engañar [17].

check *noun* **1** (*in a factory or at border controls*) control *Masc.*; **2** (*by a doctor*) examen *Masc.* médico; **3** (*in chess*) **check!** ¡jaque!
check *verb* (*to make sure*) comprobar [24]; **he checked the time** comprobó la hora; **check they're all back** comprueba que ya han llegado todos; **check with your father** pregunta a tu padre.
• **to check in 1** (*for a flight*) facturar [17] el equipaje; **2** (*at a hotel*) registrarse [17]; **she checked in at five o'clock** se registró a las cinco.
• **to check out** irse [17].

check-in *noun* facturación *Fem.* de equipajes.

checkout *noun* caja *Fem.*; **at the checkout** en caja.

checkup *noun* chequeo *Masc.*

cheek *noun* **1** (*part of face*) mejilla *Fem.*; **2** (*nerve*) **what a cheek!** ¡qué cara! (*informal*).

cheeky *adjective* **1** (*mischievous*) descarado/descarada; **2** (*rude*) impertinente.

cheer *noun* **1 three cheers for Tom!** ¡tres hurras por Tom!; **2** (*when you have a drink*) **cheers!** ¡salud!
cheer *verb* (*to shout hurray*) vitorear [17].
• **to cheer on** animar [17].
• **to cheer somebody up** animar [17] a alguien; **cheer up!** ¡ánimo!.

cheerful *adjective* alegre.

cheese *noun* queso *Masc.*; **blue cheese** queso azul; **a cheese sandwich** un sandwich de queso.

cheesecake *noun* tarta *Fem.* de queso.

chef *noun* chef *Masc./Fem.*

chemical *noun* producto *Masc.* químico.

chemist *noun* **1** farmacéutico *Masc.*, farmacéutica *Fem.*; **2 chemist's** farmacia *Fem.*; **at the chemist's** en la farmacia; **3** (*scientist*) químico *Masc.*, química *Fem.*

chemistry *noun* química *Fem.*

cheque *noun* cheque *Masc.*; **to pay by cheque** pagar [28] con cheque; **to write a cheque** extender [18] un cheque.

chequebook *noun* talonario *Masc.* de cheques.

cherry *noun* cereza *Fem.*

chess *noun* ajedrez *Masc.*; **to play chess** jugar [27] al ajedrez.

chessboard *noun* tablero *Masc.* de ajedrez.

a
b
c
d
e
f
g
h
i
j
k
l
m
n
o
p
q
r
s
t
u
v
w
x
y
z

chest noun **1** (*part of the body*) pecho *Masc.*; **2** (*box*) arcón *Masc.*

chestnut noun castaña *Fem.*

chestnut tree noun castaño *Masc.*

chest of drawers noun cómoda *Fem.*

chew verb masticar [31] (*food*).

chewing gum noun chicle *Masc.*

chick noun (*of a hen*) pollito *Masc.*

chicken noun pollo *Masc.*; **roast chicken** pollo asado; **chicken thighs** muslos de pollo.

chickenpox noun varicela *Fem.*

chicory noun endivia *Fem.*

chief noun jefe *Masc.*, jefa *Fem.*; **the chief of police** el jefe de policía.

child noun (*boy*) niño *Masc.*, (*girl*) niña *Fem.*; **Jenny's children** los niños de Jenny.

childish adjective infantil.

childminder noun niñero *Masc.*, niñera *Fem.*

Chile noun Chile *Masc.*

Chilean noun chileno *Masc.*, chilena *Fem.*
  Chilean adjective chileno/chilena.

chilled adjective (*drink*) frío/fría.

chilli noun chile *Masc.*

chilly adjective frío/fría (*a room or the weather*); **it's chilly today** hoy hace fresco.

chimney noun chimenea *Masc.*

chimpanzee noun chimpancé *Masc.*

chin noun barbilla *Fem.*

china noun porcelana *Fem.*; **a china plate** un plato de porcelana.

China noun China *Fem.*

Chinese noun **1 the Chinese** (*people*) los chinos; **2** (*language*) chino *Masc.*
  Chinese adjective chino/china; **a Chinese man** un chino; **a Chinese woman** una china; **a Chinese meal** una comida china.

chip noun **1** (*fried potato*) patata *Fem.* frita; **I'd like some chips** quiero unas patatas fritas; **2** (*microchip*) chip *Masc.*; **3** (*in glass or china*) desportilladura *Fem.*

chipped adjective desportillado/desportillada.

chives noun cebolletas *Fem. plural.*

chocolate noun **1** chocolate *Masc.*; **a chocolate ice-cream** un helado de chocolate; **hot chocolate** chocolate caliente; **milk chocolate** chocolate con leche; **dark chocolate** chocolate sin leche; **2 a chocolate** un bombón; **a box of chocolates** una caja de bombones.

choice noun elección *Fem.*; **freedom of choice** libertad de elección; **it was a good choice** fue una buena elección; **you have a choice of two flights** puede elegir entre dos vuelos; **I had no choice** no tuve más remedio.

choir noun coro *Masc.*

choke noun (*on a car*) estárter *Masc.*
  choke verb atragantarse [17]; **she choked on a bone** se atragantó con un hueso.

choose *verb* elegir [48]; **you chose well** elegiste bien; **Cathy chose the red one** Cathy eligió el rojo; **it's hard to choose from all these colours** es difícil elegir entre todos estos colores.

chop *noun* chuleta *Fem.*; **a lamb chop** una chuleta de cordero. **chop** *verb* **1** cortar [17] (*wood*); **2** cortar [17] en trozos pequeños (*vegetables or meat*); **3** picar [31] (*onion*).

chopstick *noun* palillo *Masc.* para comida china.

chord *noun* acorde *Masc.*

chorus *noun* **1** (*of a song*) estribillo *Masc.*; **2** (*a group of singers*) coro *Masc.*

Christ *noun* Cristo.

christening *noun* bautizo *Masc.*

Christian *noun, adjective* cristiano/cristiana.

Christianity *noun* cristianismo *Masc.*

Christian name *noun* nombre *Masc.* de pila.

Christmas *noun* Navidad *Fem.*; **at Christmas** en Navidad; **Happy Christmas!** ¡Feliz Navidad!

Christmas card *noun* tarjeta *Fem.* de Navidad.

Christmas carol *noun* villancico *Masc.*

Christmas Day *noun* día *Masc.* de Navidad.

Christmas dinner *noun* cena *Fem.* de Navidad.

Christmas Eve *noun* Nochebuena *Fem.*; **on Christmas Eve** en Nochebuena.

Christmas present *noun* regalo *Masc.* de Navidad.

Christmas tree *noun* árbol *Masc.* de Navidad.

chunk *noun* trozo *Masc.*

church *noun* iglesia *Fem.*; **to go to church** ir a la iglesia.

churchyard *noun* cementerio *Masc.*

chute *noun* (*for sliding down*) tobogán *Masc.*

cider *noun* sidra *Fem.*

cigar *noun* puro *Masc.*

cigarette *noun* cigarrillo *Masc.*; **to light a cigarette** encender un cigarrillo.

cinema *noun* cine *Masc.*; **to go to the cinema** ir al cine.

circle *noun* círculo *Masc.*; **to sit in a circle** sentarse en círculo; **to go round in circles** dar vueltas.

circuit *noun* (*racing track*) pista *Fem.*

circular *adjective* circular.

circumference *noun* circunferencia *Fem.*

circumstances *plural noun* **under the circumstances** en estas circunstancias.

circus *noun* circo *Masc.*

citizen *noun* ciudadano *Masc.*, ciudadana *Fem.*

city *noun* ciudad *Fem.*; **the city of Seville** la ciudad de Sevilla.

a
b
c
d
e
f
g
h
i
j
k
l
m
n
o
p
q
r
s
t
u
v
w
x
y
z

a
b
c
d
e
f
g
h
i
j
k
l
m
n
o
p
q
r
s
t
u
v
w
x
y
z

city centre noun centro Masc. de la ciudad; **in the city centre** en el centro de la ciudad.

civilian noun civil Masc./Fem.

civilization noun civilización Fem.

civil servant noun funcionario Masc., funcionaria Fem.; **she's a civil servant** es funcionaria.

civil service noun administración Fem. pública.

civil war noun guerra Fem. civil.

claim noun 1 (statement) afirmación Fem.; 2 (on insurance) reclamación Fem.; **to make a claim on insurance** hacer [7] una reclamación al seguro.
claim verb asegurar [17]; **he claimed to know** aseguró saberlo.

clap verb 1 aplaudir [19]; **everyone clapped** todo el mundo aplaudió; 2 **to clap your hands** dar [4] palmadas.

clapping noun aplausos Masc. plural.

clarinet noun clarinete Masc.; **to play the clarinet** tocar [31] el clarinete.

clash noun (violent incident) choque Masc.
clash verb 1 (rival groups) chocar [31]; 2 (colours) desentonar [17]; **the curtains clash with the wallpaper** las cortinas desentonan con el papel pintado.

clasp noun (of a necklace) broche Masc.

class noun clase Fem.; **she's in the same class as me** está en la misma clase que yo; **an art class** una clase de arte; **in class** en clase; **a social class** una clase social.

classic adjective clásico/clásica.

classical adjective clásico/clásica; **classical music** música clásica.

classmate noun compañero Masc. de clase, compañera Fem. de clase.

classroom noun clase Fem.

claw noun 1 (of a cat or dog) zarpa Fem.; 2 (of a crab) pinza Fem.

clay noun 1 (for modelling) arcilla Fem.; 2 **a clay court** (in tennis) una pista de tierra batida.

clean adjective 1 limpio/limpia; **a clean shirt** una camisa limpia; **my hands are clean** tengo las manos limpias; 2 (germ-free) puro/pura (air or water).
clean verb 1 limpiar [17]; **I cleaned the whole house** limpié toda la casa; 2 **to clean your teeth** lavarse [17] los dientes; **I'm going to clean my teeth** voy a lavarme los dientes.

cleaner noun 1 (in a public place) limpiador Masc., limpiadora Fem.; 2 (a cleaning lady) señora Fem. de la limpieza; 3 **a dry cleaner's** una tintorería.

cleaning noun **to do the cleaning** hacer [7] la limpieza.

cleanser noun 1 (for the house) producto Masc. de limpieza; 2 (for your face) crema Fem. limpiadora.

clear adjective 1 (that you can see through) transparente; **clear glass** cristal transparente; 2 (cloudless) despejado/despejada; 3 (easy to understand) claro/clara; **clear instructions** instrucciones claras;

is that clear? ¿está claro?; **it's clear that** ... está claro que ....

clear *verb* **1** sacar [31] (*papers, rubbish, or clothes*); **have you cleared your stuff out of your room?** ¿has sacado todas tus cosas de tu habitación?; **2** recoger [3] (*a table*); **can I clear the table?** ¿puedo recoger la mesa?; **3** despejar [17] (*a road or path*); **4** (*fog or smoke*) disiparse [17]; **and then the fog cleared** y entonces la niebla se disipó; **5 to clear your throat** aclararse [17] la voz.

● **to clear something up** recoger [3]; **I'll just clear up my books** voy a recoger mis libros.

clearly *adjective* **1** (*to think, speak, or hear*) con claridad; **2** (*obviously*) claramente; **she was clearly worried** estaba claramente preocupada.

clementine *noun* clementina *Fem.*

clever *adjective* **1** inteligente; **their children are all very clever** todos sus hijos son muy inteligentes; **2** (*ingenious*) ingenioso/ingeniosa; **a clever idea** una idea ingeniosa.

click *noun* clic *Masc.*; **a double click** un doble clic.

click *verb* hacer [7] clic en ; **click on the icon twice** haz clic dos veces en el icono.

client *noun* cliente *Masc./Fem.*

cliff *noun* acantilado *Masc.*

climate *noun* clima *Masc.*

climb *verb* **1** subir [19] (*stairs*); **2** escalar [17] (*a hill or a tree*); **we climbed Mont Blanc** escalamos el Mont Blanc.

climber *noun* alpinista *Masc./Fem.*

climbing *noun* alpinismo *Masc.*; **they go climbing in Italy** practican el alpinismo en Italia.

clinic *noun* **1** (*in a hospital*) consultorio *Masc.*; **2** (*a private hospital*) clínica *Fem.*

clip *noun* **1** (*from a film*) clip *Masc.*; **2** (*for your hair*) horquilla *Fem.*

clip *verb* **1** (*to cut*) cortar [17]; **2** (*to fasten*) sujetar [17] con un clip.

cloakroom *noun* (*for coats*) guardarropa *Masc.*

clock *noun* reloj *Masc.*; **an alarm clock** un reloj despertador; **to put the clocks forward an hour** adelantar los relojes una hora; **to put the clocks back** atrasar los relojes.

clock radio *noun* radiodespertador *Masc.*

clockwise *adverb* en el sentido de las agujas del reloj *Masc.*; **it turns clockwise** gira en el sentido de las agujas del reloj; **anticlockwise** en el sentido contrario al de las agujas del reloj.

clog *noun* zueco *Masc.*

close¹ *adjective, adverb* **1** (*result*) reñido/reñida; **2** (*relation*) cercano/cercana; **3** (*friend or relationship*) **she's a close friend of mine** es muy amiga mía; **they are very close** están muy unidos; **4** (*near*) cerca; **the station's very close** la estación está muy cerca; **she lives close by** vive cerca; **not very close** no muy cerca; **close to the cinema** cerca del cine.

a
b
c
d
e
f
g
h
i
j
k
l
m
n
o
p
q
r
s
t
u
v
w
x
y
z

close² *verb* cerrar [29]; **close your eyes!** ¡cierra los ojos!; **she closed the door** cerró la puerta; **the post office closes at six** la oficina de correos cierra a las seis.

● **to close down** (*a shop or factory*) cerrar [29].

closed *adjective* cerrado/cerrada; **'closed on Mondays'** 'cerrado los lunes'.

closely *adverb* de cerca; **to examine something closely** examinar [17] algo de cerca.

closing date *noun* fecha *Fem.* límite; **the closing date for entries** la fecha límite para inscribirse.

closing-down sale *noun* liquidación *Fem.* por cierre de negocio.

closing time *noun* hora *Fem.* de cierre.

cloth *noun* **1** (*for the floor or wiping surfaces*) bayeta *Fem.*; **2** (*for polishing*) trapo *Masc.* del polvo; **3** (*for drying up*) paño *Masc.* de cocina; **4** (*fabric by the metre*) tela *Fem.*

clothes *plural noun* ropa *Fem.* (*singular*); **to put your clothes on** ponerse [11] la ropa; **to take your clothes off** quitarse [17] la ropa; **to change your clothes** cambiarse [17] de ropa.

clothes hanger *noun* percha *Fem.*

clothes line *noun* cuerda *Fem.* de tender.

clothes peg *noun* pinza *Fem.* para tender.

cloud *noun* nube *Fem.*.

● **to cloud over** nublarse [17]; **it clouded over in the afternoon** se nubló por la tarde.

cloudy *adjective* nublado/nublada.

clove *noun* **1** clavo *Masc.*; **2 a clove of garlic** un diente de ajo.

clown *noun* payaso *Masc.*, payasa *Fem.*

club *noun* **1** (*association*) club *Masc.*; **he's in the football club** está en el club de fútbol; **2** (*in cards*) trébol; **the four of clubs** el cuatro de tréboles; **3** (*golfing iron*) palo *Masc.* de golf.

clue *noun* **1** pista *Fem.*; **they have a few clues** tienen unas cuantas pistas; ★ **I haven't a clue** no tengo ni idea; **2** (*in a crossword*) clave *Fem.*

clumsy *adjective* torpe.

clutch *noun* (*in a car*) embrague *Masc.*
clutch *verb* **to clutch something** tener [9] algo firmemente agarrado.

coach *noun* **1** (*bus*) autobús *Masc.*; **by coach** en autobús; **on the coach** en el autobús; **to travel by coach** viajar en autobús; **2** (*sports trainer*) entrenador *Masc.*, entrenadora *Fem.*; **3** (*railway carriage*) vagón *Masc.*

coach station *noun* estación *Fem.* de autobuses.

coach trip *noun* excursión *Fem.* en autobús; **to go on a coach trip** hacer una excursión en autobús.

coal *noun* carbón *Masc.*

coal mine *noun* mina *Fem.* de carbón.

coal miner *noun* minero *Masc.*, minera *Fem.*

coarse *adjective* basto/basta.

coast *noun* costa *Fem.*; **on the east coast** en la costa este.

coat *noun* **1** (*that you wear*) abrigo *Masc.*; **2 a coat of paint** una capa de pintura.

coat hanger *noun* percha *Fem.*

cobweb *noun* telaraña *Fem.*

cocaine *noun* cocaína *Fem.*

cockerel *noun* gallo *Masc.*

cocoa *noun* (*drink*) chocolate *Masc.*, (*powder*) cacao *Masc.*

coconut *noun* coco *Masc.*

cod *noun* bacalao *Masc.*

code *noun* **1** código *Masc.*; **the highway code** el código de la circulación; **2 the dialling code for Barcelona** el prefijo de Barcelona.

coffee *noun* café *Masc.*; **a cup of coffee** un café; **a black coffee, please** un café solo, por favor; **a white coffee** un café con leche.

coffee break *noun* pausa *Fem.* para el café.

coffee cup *noun* taza *Fem.* de café.

coffee machine *noun* **1** (*vending machine*) máquina *Fem.* de café; **2** (*electric*) cafetera *Fem.* eléctrica.

coffee pot *noun* cafetera *Fem.*

coffee table *noun* mesa *Fem.* de centro.

coffin *noun* ataúd *Masc.*

coin *noun* moneda *Fem.*; **a pound coin** una moneda de una libra.

coincidence *noun* coincidencia *Fem.*

Coke™ *noun* Coca-Cola™ *Fem.*; **two Cokes please** dos Coca-Colas, por favor.

colander *noun* colador *Masc.*

cold *noun* **1** (*cold weather*) frío *Masc.*; **I don't want to go out in this cold** no quiero salir con este frío; **come in out of the cold** entra, que hace frío; **she was shivering with cold** estaba temblando de frío; **2** (*illness*) resfriado *Masc.*; **to have a cold** estar resfriado/resfriada; **Carol's got a cold** Carol está resfriada; **a bad cold** un fuerte resfriado.
cold *adjective* **1** frío/fría; **your hands are cold** tienes las manos frías; **cold milk** leche fría; **2** (*weather, temperature*) **it's cold today** hoy hace frío; **it's cold in the kitchen** hace frío en la cocina; **3** (*feeling*) **I'm cold** tengo frío; **he was feeling very cold** tenía mucho frío.

cold sore *noun* calentura *Fem.*

collapse *verb* **1** (*a roof or a wall*) derrumbarse [17]; **2** (*a person*) **he collapsed in his office** sufrió un desmayo en su oficina.

collar *noun* **1** (*on a garment*) cuello *Masc.*; **2** (*for a dog*) collar *Masc.*

collarbone *noun* clavícula *Fem.*

colleague *noun* compañero *Masc.*, compañera *Fem.*

collect *verb* **1** (*as a hobby*) coleccionar [17]; **I collect stamps** colecciono sellos; **2** recoger [3] (*a person or a thing*); **she collects the**

a b c d e f g h i j k l m n o p q r s t u v w x y z

a
b
c
d
e
f
g
h
i
j
k
l
m
n
o
p
q
r
s
t
u
v
w
x
y
z

children from school ella recoge a los niños del colegio; **to collect in the exercise books** recoger los cuadernos; **3** cobrar [17] (*fares or money*); **4** reunir [62] (*data or information*).

collection *noun* **1** (*of stamps, CDs, etc.*) colección *Fem.*; **2** (*of money*) colecta *Fem.*

collector *noun* coleccionista *Masc./Fem.*

college *noun* **1** (*for higher education*) colegio *Masc.* universitario; **to go to college** ir a la universidad; **2** (*for vocational training*) escuela *Fem.* de formación profesional; **3** (*a school*) instituto *Masc.*

collie *noun* collie *Masc./Fem.*

collision *noun* choque *Masc.*

Colombia *noun* Colombia *Fem.*

Colombian *noun* colombiano *Masc.*, colombiana *Fem.*
Colombian *adjective* colombiano/colombiana.

colonel *noun* coronel *Masc.*

colour *noun* color *Masc.*; **what colour is your car?** ¿de qué color es tu coche?; **what colour is it?** ¿de qué color es?; **do you have it in a different colour?** ¿lo tiene en otros colores?
colour *verb* (*with paints or crayons*) colorear [17]; **to colour something red** colorear algo de rojo.

colour blind *adjective* daltónico/daltónica.

colour film *noun* (*for a camera*) carrete *Masc.* de color.

colourful *adjective* de colores.

colouring book *noun* libro *Masc.* para colorear.

colour supplement *noun* suplemento *Masc.* a color.

column *noun* columna *Fem.*

comb *noun* peine *Masc.*
comb *verb* **to comb your hair** peinarse [17]; **I'll just comb my hair** voy a peinarme.

combine *verb* combinar [17] (*two separate things*); **they don't combine well** no combinan bien.

combination *noun* combinación *Fem.*

come *verb* venir [15]; **come quick!** ¡ven rápido!; **come and see!** ¡ven a ver!; **Nick came by bike** Nick vino en bici; **did Jess come to school yesterday?** ¿vino Jess ayer a clase?; **can you come over for a coffee?** ¿puedes venir a tomar un café?; **the bus is coming** ya viene el autobús; **come on!** ¡venga!; **coming!** ¡ya voy!
• **to come apart** deshacerse [7]; **it came apart in my hands** se deshizo en mis manos.
• **to come back** volver [45]; **she's coming back to collect us** volverá para recogernos.
• **to come down** bajar [17] (*the stairs or the street*).
• **to come for** venir [15] a por (*a person*); **my father's coming for me** mi padre va a venir a por mí.
• **to come from** ser [1] de; **Ian comes from Scotland** Ian es de Escocia; **the wine comes from Spain** el vino es español.
• **to come in** entrar [17]; **come in!**

372

¡adelante!; **she came into the kitchen** entró en la cocina.

• **to come off 1** (*a button*) desprenderse [18], (*a handle*) soltarse [24]; **2** (*a lid*) **I can't get the lid to come off** no puedo quitar la tapa.

• **to come out** salir [63]; **they came out when I called** salieron cuando los llamé; **the CD's coming out soon** el compacto va a salir pronto; **the sun hasn't come out yet** el sol no ha salido aún.

• **to come to 1** (*get to*) llegar [28] a; **when you come to the church turn right** gira a la derecha cuando llegues a la iglesia; **2** (*add up to*) **it comes to 150 euros** suma ciento cincuenta euros.

• **to come up** subir [19]; **can you come up a moment?** ¿puedes subir un momento?.

• **to come up to somebody** acercarse [31] a alguien.

comedian *noun* cómico *Masc.*, cómica *Fem.*

comedy *noun* comedia *Fem.*

comfortable *adjective* cómodo/cómoda; **this chair's really comfortable** esta silla es muy cómoda; **to feel comfortable** (*a person*) estar cómodo/cómoda; **are you comfortable there?** ¿estás cómodo ahí?

comfortably *adverb* cómodamente.

comic *noun* (*magazine*) cómic *Masc.*

comic strip *noun* tira *Fem.* cómica.

comma *noun* coma *Fem.*

command *noun* orden *Fem.*

comment *noun* (*in a conversation*) comentario *Masc.*; **he made some rude comments about my friends** hizo unos comentarios groseros sobre mis amigos.

commentary *noun* crónica *Fem.*; **the commentary of the match** la crónica del partido.

commentator *noun* comentarista *Masc./Fem.*; **a sports commentator** un comentarista deportivo.

commercial *noun* anuncio *Masc.* de televisión.

commercial *adjective* comercial.

commit *verb* **1** cometer [18] (*a crime*); **2 to commit yourself** comprometerse [18].

committee *noun* comité *Masc.*

common *adjective* **1** corriente; **it's a common problem** es un problema corriente; **2 in common** en común; **they have nothing in common** no tienen nada en común.

common sense *noun* sentido *Masc.* común.

communicate *verb* comunicar [31].

communication *noun* **1** (*message, letter etc*) comunicación *Fem.*; **2** (*in transport*) **communications are good** las comunicaciones son buenas.

communion *noun* comunión *Fem.*

communism *noun* comunismo *Masc.*

communist *noun* comunista *Masc./Fem.*

community *noun* comunidad *Fem.*; **the European Community** la comunidad europea.

commute *verb* **to commute between Oxford and London** viajar [17] todos los días de Oxford a Londres para ir a trabajar.

commuter *noun* **trains full of commuters** trenes llenos de personas que van a trabajar (*Spanish does not have a word for 'commuters' so it has to be explained as 'people travelling to work'*).

compact disc *noun* disco *Masc.* compacto.

compact disc player *noun* compacto *Masc.*

company *noun* **1** compañía *Fem.*; **an insurance company** una compañía de seguros; **she's set up a company** ha montado una compañía; **an airline company** una compañía aérea; **a theatre company** una compañía de teatro; **2 to keep somebody company** hacer [7] compañía a alguien; **the dogs keep me company** los perros me hacen compañía.

comparatively *adverb* relativamente.

compare *verb* comparar [17]; **if you compare the Spanish with the English** si comparas los españoles con los ingleses; **our house is small compared with yours** nuestra casa es pequeña comparada con la tuya.

comparison *noun* comparación *Fem.*; **in comparison with** en comparación con.

compartment *noun* compartimento *Masc.*

compass *noun* brújula *Fem.*

compatible *adjective* (*computing*) compatible.

compensation *noun* indemnzación *Fem.*

compete *verb* **1 to compete in something** participar [17] en algo (*race, event*); **2 to compete for something** competir [57] (*jobs, places*); **thirty people are competing for the job** treinta personas compiten por el puesto.

competent *adjective* competente.

competition *noun* **1** (*in a magazine or at school*) concurso *Masc.*; **a poetry competition** un concurso de poesía; **2** (*in sports*) competición *Fem.*; **a fishing competition** una competición de pesca; **3** (*in business*) competencia *Fem.*

competitor *noun* **1** (*in sports*) participante *Masc./Fem.*; **2** (*in business*) competidor *Masc.*, competidora *Fem.*

complain *verb* quejarse [17]; **we complained about the hotel and the meals** nos quejamos del hotel y de las comidas.

complaint *noun* queja *Fem.*; **to make a complaint** presentar [17] una queja; **she made a complaint to the manager about the bad**

374

service presentó una queja al gerente por el mal servicio.

complete *adjective* completo/completa; **the complete collection** la colección completa.
complete *verb* (*to finish*) terminar [17].

completely *adverb* completamente.

complexion *noun* cutis *Masc.*

complicated *adjective* complicado/complicada.

complication *noun* complicación *Fem.*; **there were complications** hubo complicaciones.

compliment *noun* cumplido *Masc.*; **to pay somebody a compliment** hacer [7] un cumplido a alguien.

compose *verb* componer [11]; **composed of** compuesto de.

composer *noun* compositor *Masc.*, compositora *Fem.*

comprehension *noun* comprensión *Fem.*; **a comprehension test** un ejercicio de comprensión.

compulsory *adjective* obligatorio/obligatoria.

computer *noun* ordenador *Masc.*; **to work on a computer** trabajar en ordenador.

computer engineer *noun* técnico *Masc.* en informática, técnica *Fem.* en informática.

computer game *noun* juego *Masc.* de ordenador.

computer program *noun* programa *Masc.* informático.

computer programmer *noun* programador *Masc.*, programadora *Fem.*

computer science *noun* informática *Fem.*

computing *noun* informática *Fem.*

conceited *adjective* engreído/engreída.

concentrate *verb* concentrarse [17]; **I can't concentrate** no puedo concentrarme; **I was concentrating on the film** me estaba concentrando en la película.

concentration *noun* concentración *Fem.*

concern *noun* (*worry*) preocupación *Fem.*; **there is no cause for concern** no hay razón para preocuparse.
concern *verb* **1** (*to affect*) concernir [14]; **this doesn't concern you** esto no te concierne; **2 as far as I'm concerned** por mi parte.

concert *noun* **1** concierto *Masc.*; **to go to a concert** ir [8] a un concierto; **2 a concert ticket** una entrada para un concierto.

conclusion *noun* conclusión *Fem.*

concrete *noun* cemento *Masc.*; **a concrete floor** un suelo de cemento.

condemn *verb* condenar [17].

condition *noun* condición *Fem.*; **in good condition** en buenas condiciones; **weather conditions** condiciones meteorológicas; **the conditions of sale** las condiciones

a
b
c
d
e
f
g
h
i
j
k
l
m
n
o
p
q
r
s
t
u
v
w
x
y
z

de venta; **on one condition** con una condición; **on condition that you let me pay** a condición de que me dejes pagar.

conditional *noun* condicional *Masc.*

conditioner *noun* (*for your hair*) suavizante *Masc.*

condom *noun* condón *Masc.*

conduct *noun* conducta *Fem.*
conduct *verb* dirigir [49] (*an orchestra or a piece of music*).

conductor *noun* **1** (*of an orchestra*) director *Masc.* de orquesta, directora *Fem.* de orquesta; **2** (*on bus*) cobrador *Masc.*, cobradora *Fem.*

cone *noun* **1** (*for ice cream*) cucurucho *Masc.*; **2** (*for traffic*) cono *Masc.*

confectionery *noun* dulces *Fem. plural*; **she works in a confectionery shop** trabaja en una confitería.

conference *noun* conferencia *Fem.*

confess *verb* confesar [29].

confession *noun* confesión *Fem.*

confidence *noun* **1** (*self-confidence*) seguridad *Fem.* en sí mismo; **he has a lot of confidence** tiene mucha seguridad en sí mismo; **you're lacking in confidence** te falta seguridad en ti mismo; **2** (*faith in somebody else*) confianza *Fem.*; **to have confidence in somebody** tener [9] confianza en alguien.

confident *adjective* **1** (*sure of yourself*) seguro de sí mismo, segura

de sí misma; **you look very confident** pareces muy seguro de ti mismo; **she's a confident young woman** es una joven segura de sí misma; **2** (*sure that something will happen*) **to be confident that** estar [2] seguro de que; **I'm confident that it will work out all right** estoy seguro de que saldrá bien.

confirm *verb* confirmar [17]; **we'll confirm the date** confirmaremos la fecha.

confuse *verb* confundir [19]; **I confuse him with his brother** lo confundo con su hermano.

confused *adjective* **1** (*unclear*) confuso/confusa; **he gave us a confused story** contó una historia muy confusa; **2** confundido/confundida; **now I'm completely confused** ahora estoy completamente confundida; **I'm confused about the holiday dates** no estoy segura de las fechas de las vacaciones; **3 to get confused** confundirse [19]; **she got confused** se confundió.

confusing *adjective* poco claro/clara; **the instructions are confusing** las instrucciones son poco claras.

confusion *noun* confusión *Fem.*

congratulate *verb* felicitar [17]; **I congratulated Tim on his success** felicité a Tim por su éxito; **we congratulate you on winning** te felicitamos por haber ganado.

congratulations *plural noun* enhorabuena *Fem.*; **congratulations**

on the baby! ¡enhorabuena por el bebé!

conjurer *noun* mago *Masc.*, maga *Fem.*

connect *verb* (*to plug in to the mains*) conectar [17] (*a dishwasher or TV, for example*).

connection *noun* conexión *Fem.*; **a faulty connection** una conexión defectuosa; **Sally missed her connection** Sally perdió su conexión; **there's no connection between his letter and my decision** no hay relación entre su carta y mi decisión.

conscience *noun* conciencia *Fem.*; **to have a guilty conscience** no tener la conciencia tranquila.

conscious *adjective* consciente.

consequence *noun* consecuencia *Fem.*

consequently *adverb* por consiguiente.

conservation *noun* (*of nature*) protección *Fem.* del medio ambiente.

conservative *noun, adjective* conservador/conservadora.

conservatory *noun* jardín *Masc.* de invierno.

consider *verb* **1** (*to give thought to*) considerar [17] (*a suggestion or idea*); **2** (*to think you might do*) plantearse [17]; **we're considering buying a flat** estamos planteándonos comprar un piso; **3 all things considered** bien considerado.

considerable *adjective* considerable; **a considerable**

number of students un número considerable de estudiantes.

considerate *adjective* considerado/considerada (*a person*).

consideration *noun* consideración *Fem.*

considering *preposition* teniendo en cuenta; **considering her age** teniendo en cuenta su edad; **considering he did it all himself** teniendo en cuenta que lo hizo todo él solo.

consist *verb* **to consist of** consistir [19] en.

consistent *adjective* constante.

consonant *noun* consonante *Fem.*

constant *adjective* constante.

constantly *adverb* constantemente.

constipated *adjective* estreñido/estreñida.

construct *verb* construir [54].

construction *noun* construcción *Fem.*

consul *noun* cónsul *Masc.*

consulate *noun* consulado *Masc.*

consult *verb* consultar [17].

consumer *noun* consumidor *Masc.*, consumidora *Fem.*

consumption *noun* consumo *Masc.*

contact *noun* contacto *Masc.*; **to be in contact with somebody** estar en contacto con alguien; **we've lost contact** hemos perdido contacto; **Rob has contacts in the music business** Rob tiene contactos en el

a
b
c
d
e
f
g
h
i
j
k
l
m
n
o
p
q
r
s
t
u
v
w
x
y
z

a
b
c
d
e
f
g
h
i
j
k
l
m
n
o
p
q
r
s
t
u
v
w
x
y
z

mundo de la música.
contact *verb* ponerse [11] en
contacto con; **I'll contact you
tomorrow** me pondré en contacto
contigo mañana.

contact lens *noun* lentilla *Fem.*

contain *verb* contener [9].

container *noun* recipiente *Masc.*

contaminate *verb* contaminar
[17].

contemporary *adjective*
contemporáneo/contemporánea.

contents *plural noun* contenido
Masc.; **the contents of my suitcase**
el contenido de mi maleta.

contest *noun* **1** concurso *Masc.*;
2 (*in sport*) competición *Fem.*

contestant *noun* concursante
Masc./Fem.

context *noun* contexto *Masc.*

continent *noun* continente *Masc.*;
on the Continent en Europa
continental.

continental *adjective* **a
continental holiday** unas
vacaciones en Europa continental.

continue *verb* **1** continuar [20]; **we
continued our journey**
continuamos con nuestro viaje; **'to
be continued'** 'continuará'; **2 to
continue doing** seguir [64]
haciendo; **Jill continued talking**
Jill siguió hablando.

continuous *adjective* continuo/
continua; **continuous assessment**
evaluación *Fem.* continua.

contraception *noun*
anticoncepción *Fem.*

contraceptive *noun*
anticonceptivo *Masc.*

contract *noun* contrato *Masc.*

contradict *verb* contradecir [5].

contradiction *noun*
contradicción *Fem.*

contrary *noun* **the contrary** lo
contrario; **on the contrary** al
contrario.

contrast *noun* contraste *Masc.*

contribute *verb* contribuir [54]
(*money*).

contribution *noun* (*to charity or
an appeal*) contribución *Fem.*

control *noun* (*of a crowd or
animals*) control *Masc.*; **the police
have lost control** la policía ha
perdido el control; **everything's
under control** todo está bajo
control.
control *verb* **1** controlar [17] (*a
crowd, animals, or a fire, for
example*); **2 to control oneself**
controlarse [17].

controversial *adjective*
controvertido/controvertida; **a
controversial decision** una
decisión controvertida.

convenient *adjective* **1** práctico/
práctica; **frozen vegetables are
very convenient** las verduras
congeladas son muy prácticas; **2 to
be convenient for somebody**
venirle [15] bien a alguien; **if that's
convenient for you** si te va bien;
**3 the house is convenient for
shops and schools** la casa está bien
situada respecto a tiendas y
colegios.

convent *noun* convento *Masc.*

conventional *adjective*
1 convencional; **2** (*person*) tradicional.

conversation *noun* conversación *Fem.*

convert *verb* convertir [14]; **we're going to convert the garage into a workshop** vamos a convertir el garaje el un taller.

convince *verb* convencer [44]; **I'm convinced you're wrong** estoy convencido de que estás equivocado.

convincing *adjective* convincente.

cook *noun* cocinero *Masc.*, cocinera *Fem.*
cook *verb* **1** cocinar [17]; **who's cooking tonight?** ¿quién cocina esta noche?; **I like cooking** me gusta cocinar; **2** cocer [41] (*vegetables, pasta, etc*); **cook the carrots for five minutes** cuece las zanahorias durante cinco minutos; **3** hacer [7] (*a meal*); **Fran's busy cooking supper** Fran está haciendo la cena; **4** (*food*) hacerse [7]; **the sausages are cooking** las salchichas se están haciendo; **is the chicken cooked?** ¿está hecho el pollo?

cooker *noun* cocina *Fem.*; **an electric cooker** una cocina eléctrica; **a gas cooker** una cocina de gas.

cookery *noun* cocina *Fem.*

cookery book *noun* libro *Masc.* de cocina.

cooking *noun* cocina *Fem.*; **Italian cooking** la cocina italiana; **home cooking** la comida casera; **to do the cooking** cocinar [27].

cool *noun* **1** (*coldness*) fresco *Masc.*; **stay in the cool** quedarse [17] al fresco; **2** (*calm*) calma *Fem.*; **to lose one's cool** perder [36] la calma; **he kept his cool** mantuvo la calma.
cool *adjective* **1** (*cold*) fresco/fresca; **a cool drink** una bebida fresca; **it's cool inside** dentro hace fresco; **2** (*laid-back*) tranquilo/tranquila; **3 to be cool** (*a person*) estar en la onda (*informal*); **he's so cool** está muy en la onda (*informal*); **4** (*trendy*) molón/molona (*informal*) (*a car or a jacket*).
cool *verb* **to cool (down)** enfriarse [32].

cooperate *verb* cooperar [17].

cop *noun* poli *Masc./Fem.* (*informal*).

cope *verb* **1** (*to manage*) defenderse [36]; **she copes well** se defiende bien; **2 to cope with** ocuparse [17] de (*children or work*); **I'll cope with the dishes** yo me ocupo de los platos; **3** hacer [7] frente a (*problems*); **she's had a lot to cope with** ha tenido que hacer frente a muchos problemas; **he can't cope any more** ya no puede más.

copper *noun* cobre *Masc.*

copy *noun* **1** copia *Fem.*; **make ten copies of this letter** haz diez copias de esta carta; **2** (*of a book*) ejemplar *Masc.*
copy *verb* copiar [17]; **I copied (down) the address** copié las señas.

cord *noun* (*for a blind, for example*) cordón *Masc.*

cordless telephone *noun* teléfono *Masc.* inalámbrico.

core *noun* (*of an apple or a pear*) corazón *Masc.*

cork *noun* **1** (*in a bottle*) tapón *Masc.*; **2** (*material*) corcho *Masc.*

corkscrew *noun* sacacorchos *Masc.* (*does not change in the plural*).

corn *noun* **1** (*wheat*) trigo *Masc.*; **2** (*sweetcorn*) maíz *Masc.*

corner *noun* **1** (*of street or page*) esquina *Fem.*; **at the corner of the street** en la esquina de la calle; **it's just round the corner** está a la vuelta de la esquina; **in the bottom right-hand corner of the page** en la esquina inferior derecha de la página; **2** (*of room or cupboard*) rincón *Masc.*; **in a corner of the kitchen** en un rincón de la cocina; **3 out of the corner of your eye** por el rabillo del ojo; **4** (*in football*) córner *Masc.*

cornflakes *noun* copos *Masc. plural* de maíz.

Cornwall *noun* Cornualles *Masc.*

corpse *noun* cadáver *Masc.*

correct *adjective* **1** correcto/correcta; **the correct sum** la cantidad total correcta; **the correct answer** la respuesta correcta; **the correct choice** la elección adecuada; **2 yes, that's correct** sí, así es.

correct *verb* corregir [48].

correction *noun* corrección *Fem.*

correctly *adverb* correctamente; **have you filled in the form correctly?** ¿has rellenado el formulario correctamente?.

correspond *verb* corresponder [18].

corridor *noun* pasillo *Masc.*

cosmetics *plural noun* cosméticos *Masc. plural.*

cost *noun* coste *Masc.*; **the cost of a new computer** el coste de un nuevo ordenador; **the cost of living** el coste de la vida.

cost *verb* costar [24]; **how much does it cost?** ¿cuánto cuesta?; **the tickets cost ten pounds** las entradas cuestan diez libras; **it costs too much** cuesta demasiado caro.

Costa Rica *noun* Costa Rica *Fem.*

Costa Rican *noun* costarricense *Masc., Fem.*
Costa Rican *adjective* costarricense.

costume *noun* **1** (*fancy dress*) disfraz *Masc.*; **2** (*for an actor*) traje *Masc.*

cosy *adjective* (*a room*) acogedor/acogedora; **it's cosy by the fire** se está muy bien al lado del fuego.

cot *noun* cuna *Fem.*

cottage *noun* casita *Fem.* en el campo.

cotton *noun* **1** (*fabric*) algodón *Masc.*; **a cotton shirt** una camisa de algodón; **2** (*thread*) hilo *Masc.*

cotton wool *noun* algodón *Masc.* en rama.

couch *noun* sofá *Masc.*

cough *noun* tos *Fem.*; **a nasty cough** una tos mala; **to have a cough** tener [9] tos.
cough *verb* toser [18].

could *verb* **1** poder [10]; **if he could pay** si pudiese pagar; **I couldn't open it** no podía abrirlo; **they couldn't smoke there** no podían fumar allí; **she did all she could** hizo todo lo que pudo; **2** (*knew how to*) **he couldn't drive** no sabía conducir; **I couldn't swim** no sabía nadar; **3** (*with see, hear, smell, remember, or understand, 'could' is not translated*) **I could hear a police car** oí un coche de policía; **she couldn't see anything** no veía nada; **4** (*talking about a possibility*) **they could be home by now** puede que ya estén en casa; **you could be right** puede que tengas razón; **5** (*in 'if' sentences 'could' is translated by the subjunctive*) **I would buy it if I could afford it** lo compraría si pudiese; **I could have gone if I'd wanted** hubiese podido ir si hubiese querido; **6** (*asking permission or suggesting*) **could I speak to David?** ¿podría hablar con David?; **you could try telephoning** podrías intentar llamar por teléfono.

council *noun* consejo *Masc.*; **the town council** el ayuntamiento.

councillor *noun* concejal *Masc.*, concejala *Fem.*; **her uncle is a councillor** su tío es concejal.

count *verb* **1** (*reckon up*) contar [24]; **I counted my money** conté mi dinero; **thirty-five not counting the children** treinta y cinco sin contar a

los niños; **2 to count as** considerarse [17] como; **children over twelve count as adults** los niños mayores de doce años se consideran como adultos; **3** (*to be allowed*) **that doesn't count** eso no vale.

counter *noun* **1** (*in a shop*) mostrador *Masc.*; **2** (*in a café*) barra *Fem.*; **3** (*in a post office or bank*) ventanilla *Fem.*; **4** (*for board games*) ficha *Fem.*

country *noun* **1** (*Spain, Britain, etc*) país *Masc.*; **a foreign country** un país extranjero; **from another country** de otro país; **2** (*not town*) campo *Masc.*; **to live in the country** vivir en el campo; **a country walk** un paseo por el campo; **a country road** un camino rural.

country dancing *noun* baile *Masc.* folklórico.

countryside *noun* campo *Masc.*

county *noun* condado *Masc.*

couple *noun* **1** (*a pair*) pareja *Fem.*; **a married couple** una pareja de casados; **2 a couple of** un par de; **a couple of times** un par de veces; **I've got a couple of things to do** tengo que hacer un par de cosas.

courage *noun* valor *Masc.*

courgette *noun* calabacín *Masc.*

courier *noun* **1** (*on a package holiday*) guía *Masc./Fem.*; **2** (*delivery service*) mensajería *Fem.*; **by courier** por mensajería.

a
b
c
d
e
f
g
h
i
j
k
l
m
n
o
p
q
r
s
t
u
v
w
x
y
z

a

b

c

d

e

f

g

h

i

j

k

l

m

n

o

p

q

r

s

t

u

v

w

x

y

z

course noun 1 (*lessons*) curso Masc.; **a beginners' course** un curso para principiantes; **a computer course** un curso de informática; **to go on a course** asistir a un curso; 2 (*part of a meal*) plato Masc.; **the main course** el plato principal; 3 **a golf course** un campo de golf; 4 **of course** claro; **yes, of course!** ¡sí, claro!; **he's forgotten, of course** se ha olvidado, claro.

court noun 1 (*for tennis, squash, or basketball*) cancha Fem.; 2 (*of law*) tribunal Masc.

courtyard noun patio Masc.

cousin noun primo Masc., prima Fem.; **my cousin Sonia** mi prima Sonia.

cover noun 1 (*for a book*) tapa Fem.; 2 (*for a duvet or cushion*) funda Fem.; **a duvet cover** una funda de edredón.

cover verb 1 cubrir [46]; **to cover the wound** cubrir la herida; **the ground was covered with snow** el suelo estaba cubierto de nieve; **he was covered in mud** estaba cubierto de barro; 2 (*your face or eyes*) cubrirse [46]; **she covered her face** se cubrió la cara.

cow noun vaca Fem.; **mad cow disease** la enfermedad de las vacas locas.

coward noun cobarde Masc./Fem.

cowboy noun vaquero Masc.

crab noun cangrejo Masc.

crack noun 1 (*in a wall*) grieta Fem.; 2 (*in a cup or plate*) raja Fem.; 3 (*a cracking noise*) crujido Masc.

crack verb 1 (*to make a crack in*) hacer [7] una raja en (*a cup or a window*); 2 fracturar [17] (*a bone*); 3 (*break open*) cascar [31] (*a nut or an egg*); 4 (*split by itself: ice, for example*) rajarse [17]; 5 (*make a noise*) (*a twig*) crujir [19].

cracker noun (*biscuit*) galleta Fem. salada.

crackle verb crujir [19].

craft noun (*at school*) trabajos Masc. plural manuales.

crafty adjective astuto/astuta; **that was very crafty of her** eso fue muy astuto por su parte.

cramp noun calambre Masc.; **I've got cramp in my leg** tengo un calambre en la pierna.

crane noun grúa Fem.

crash noun 1 (*an accident*) accidente Masc.; **a car crash** un accidente de coche; 2 (*smashing noise*) estrépito Masc.; **a crash of broken glass** un estrépito de cristales rotos.

crash verb 1 (*a car or plane*) tener [9] un accidente; **the plane crashed** el avión tuvo un accidente; 2 **to crash into something** chocar [31] con algo; **the car crashed into a tree** el coche chocó con un árbol.

crash course noun curso Masc. intensivo.

crash helmet noun casco Masc.

crate noun 1 (*for china*) cajón Masc. para embalar; 2 (*for bottles or fruit*) caja Fem.

crawl noun (in swimming) crol Masc.
crawl verb **1** (a person, a baby) ir [8] a gatas; **2** (cars in a jam) ir [8] muy despacio; **we were crawling along** íbamos muy despacio.

crayon noun **1** (wax) pintura Fem. de cera; **2** (coloured pencil) lápiz Masc. de color.

craze noun fiebre Fem.; **the craze for computer games** la fiebre de los juegos de ordenador.

crazy adjective loco/loca; **to go crazy** volverse loco/loca; **to be crazy about someone** estar loco/loca por alguien; **he's crazy about football** le encanta el fútbol.

creak verb (a hinge) chirriar [32], (a floorboard) crujir [19].

cream noun **1** (dairy cream) nata Fem.; **strawberries and cream** fresas con nata; **2** (for hands, face, etc.) crema Fem.

cream cheese noun queso Masc. para untar.

crease noun arruga Fem.

creased adjective arrugado/arrugada.

create verb crear [17].

creative adjective creativo/creativa (a person).

creature noun criatura Fem.

creche noun guardería Fem.

credit noun crédito Masc.; **to buy something on credit** comprar algo a crédito.

credit card noun tarjeta Fem. de crédito.

crew noun **1** (on a ship or plane) tripulación Fem.; **2** (rowing or filming) equipo Masc.

crew cut noun corte Masc. de pelo al rape.

cricket noun **1** (game) críquet Masc.; **to play cricket** jugar [27] al críquet; **2** (insect) grillo Masc.

cricket bat noun bate Masc. de críquet.

crime noun **1** delito Masc.; **theft is a crime** el robo es un delito; **2** (murder) crimen Masc.; **3** (within society) crimen Masc.; **the fight against crime** la lucha contra el crimen.

criminal noun criminal Masc./Fem..
criminal adjective criminal.

crisis noun crisis Fem.

crisp noun patata Fem. frita; **a packet of (potato) crisps** un paquete de patatas fritas.
crisp adjective crujiente.

critical adjective **1** crítico/crítica (a remark or somebody's condition); **2** decisivo/decisiva (a moment).

criticism noun crítica Fem.

criticize verb criticar [31].

Croatia noun Croacia Fem.

crockery noun vajilla Fem.

crocodile noun cocodrilo Masc.

crook noun (criminal) granuja Masc./Fem.

crooked adjective torcido/torcida; **a crooked line** una línea torcida.

crop noun cosecha Fem.

cross noun cruz Fem.
cross adjective enfadado/

a
b
c
d
e
f
g
h
i
j
k
l
m
n
o
p
q
r
s
t
u
v
w
x
y
z

a
b
c
d
e
f
g
h
i
j
k
l
m
n
o
p
q
r
s
t
u
v
w
x
y
z

enfadada; **she's very cross** está muy enfadada; **I'm cross with you** estoy enfadada contigo; **to get cross** enfadarse [17].

cross *verb* **1** (*to cross over*) cruzar [22]; **to cross the road** cruzar la calle; **2 to cross your legs** cruzar las piernas; **3 to cross into Spain** pasar [17] a España; **4** (*to cross each other*) cruzarse [22]; **the two roads cross here** las dos carreteras se cruzan aquí.

● **to cross out** tachar [17] (*a word or sentence*).

cross-Channel *adjective* **a cross-Channel ferry** un ferry que cruza el Canal de la Mancha.

cross-country *noun* **1** cross *Masc.*; **2 cross-country skiing** esquí *Masc.* de fondo.

crossing *noun* **1** (*from one place to another*) travesía *Fem.*; **a Channel crossing** una travesía por el Canal de la Mancha; **2 a pedestrian crossing** un cruce de peatones; **a level crossing** un paso a nivel.

cross-legged *adjective* **to sit cross-legged** sentarse con las piernas cruzadas.

crossroads *noun* cruce *Masc.*; **at the crossroads** en el cruce.

crossword *noun* crucigrama *Masc.*; **to do the crossword** hacer el crucigrama.

crouch *verb* ponerse [11] en cuclillas.

crow *noun* cuervo *Masc.*; ★ **as the crow flies** en línea recta.
crow *verb* (*a cock*) cacarear [17].

crowd *noun* multitud *Fem.*; **in the crowd** en la multitud; **a crowd of 5,000** una multitud de cinco mil personas.

crowd *verb* **to crowd into** (or **onto**) aglomerarse [17] en (*a room or bus, for example*); **we all crowded into the train** nos aglomeramos en el tren.

crowded *adjective* lleno/llena de gente.

crown *noun* corona *Fem.*

crude *adjective* **1** (*rough and ready*) rudimentario/rudimentaria; **2** (*vulgar*) grosero/grosera.

cruel *adjective* cruel.

cruelty *noun* crueldad *Fem.*; **they were treated with great cruelty** los trataron con gran crueldad.

cruise *noun* crucero *Masc.*; **to go on a cruise** ir de crucero.

crumb *noun* miga *Fem.*

crumple *verb* arrugar [28].

crunchy *adjective* crujiente.

crush *verb* aplastar [17].

crust *noun* corteza *Fem.*

crutch *noun* muleta *Fem.*; **to be on crutches** andar con muletas.

cry *noun* grito *Masc.*
cry *verb* **1** (*weep*) llorar [17]; **2** (*call out*) gritar [17].

crystal *noun* cristal *Masc.*

cub *noun* **1** (*animal*) cachorro *Masc.*; **2** (*scout*) lobato *Masc.*

Cuba *noun* Cuba *Fem.*

Cuban *noun* cubano *Masc.*, cubana *Fem.*
Cuban *adjective* cubano/cubana.

cube *noun* cubo *Masc.*; **an ice cube** un cubito de hielo.

cubic *adjective* (*for measurements*) cúbico/cúbica; **three cubic metres** tres metros cúbicos.

cubicle *noun* **1** (*in a changing room*) vestuario *Masc.*; **2** (*in a public lavatory*) cubículo *Masc.*

cuckoo *noun* cuco *Masc.*

cucumber *noun* pepino *Masc.*

cuddle *noun* **to give somebody a cuddle** dar [4] un abrazo a alguien.
cuddle *verb* abrazar [22].

cue *noun* (*billiards, pool, snooker*) taco *Masc.*

cuff *noun* (*on a shirt*) puño *Masc.*

cul-de-sac *noun* callejón *Masc.* sin salida.

culture *noun* cultura *Fem.*

cunning *adjective* astuto/astuta.

cup *noun* **1** (*for drinking*) taza *Fem.*; **a cup of tea** una taza de té; **2** (*a trophy*) copa *Fem.*

cupboard *noun* armario *Masc.*; **in the kitchen cupboard** en el armario de la cocina.

cup tie *noun* partido *Masc.* de copa.

cure *noun* cura *Fem.*
cure *verb* curar [17].

curiosity *noun* curiosidad *Fem.*

curious *adjective* curioso/curiosa.

curl *noun* rizo *Masc.*
curl *verb* rizar [22] (*hair*).

curly *adjective* rizado/rizada.

currant *noun* pasa *Fem.* de Corinto.

currency *noun* moneda *Fem.*; **foreign currency** moneda extranjera.

current *noun* (*of electricity or water*) corriente *Fem.*
current *adjective* actual (*a situation, for example*).

current affairs *noun* sucesos *Masc. plural* de actualidad.

curriculum *noun* **1** (*national*) plan *Masc.* de estudios; **2** (*for a single course*) programa *Masc.* de estudios.

curry *noun* curry *Masc.*; **chicken curry** curry de pollo.

cursor *noun* cursor *Masc.*

curtain *noun* cortina *Fem.*

cushion *noun* cojín *Masc.*

custard *noun* **1** (*runny*) natillas *Fem.* (*plural*); **2** (*baked*) flan *Masc.*

custom *noun* costumbre *Masc.*

customer *noun* cliente *Masc.*, clienta *Fem.*; **customer services** atención al cliente.

customs *plural noun* aduana *Fem.*; **to go through customs** pasar por la aduana.

customs hall *noun* aduana *Fem.*

customs officer *noun* agente *Masc./Fem.* de aduana.

cut *noun* (*injury or haircut*) corte *Masc.*
cut *verb* **1** cortar [17]; **I've cut the bread** he cortado el pan; **you'll cut yourself!** ¡te vas a cortar!; **Kevin's**

a
b
c
d
e
f
g
h
i
j
k
l
m
n
o
p
q
r
s
t
u
v
w
x
y
z

cut his finger Kevin se ha cortado el dedo; **to cut the grass** cortar la hierba; **2 to get your hair cut** cortarse el pelo; **Ayesha's had her hair cut** Ayesha se ha cortado el pelo; **3 to cut prices** bajar [17] los precios.

● **to cut down something** cortar [17] algo (*a tree*).

● **to cut down on something: to cut down on fats** consumir [19] menos grasas.

● **to cut out something 1** recortar [17] algo (*a shape, a newspaper article*); **2** suprimir [19] algo (*sugar, fatty food, etc*).

● **to cut up something** cortar [17] algo en trocitos (*food*).

cute *adjective* mono/mona.

cutlery *noun* cubertería *Fem.*

CV *noun* currículum *Masc.* vitae.

cycle *noun* (*bike*) bicicleta *Fem.*
cycle *verb* montar [17] en bicicleta; **do you like cycling?** ¿te gusta montar en bicicleta?; **we cycle to school** vamos al colegio en bicicleta.

cycle lane *noun* carril *Masc.* de bicicletas.

cycle race *noun* carrera *Fem.* de ciclismo.

cycling *noun* ciclismo *Masc.*

cycling holiday *noun* vacaciones *Fem. plural* en bicicleta.

cyclist *noun* ciclista *Masc./Fem.*

cylinder *noun* cilindro *Masc*; **a gas cylinder** una bombona.

Dd

dad *noun* **1** (*father*) padre *Masc.*; **Anna's dad** el padre de Ana; **my dad works in a bank** mi padre trabaja en un banco; **2** (*daddy*) papá; **Dad's not home yet** papá no ha llegado a casa aún.

daffodil *noun* narciso *Masc.*

daily *adjective* diario/diaria; **his daily visit** su visita diaria.
daily *adverb* a diario; **she visits him daily** le visita a diario.

dairy products *plural noun* productos *Masc. plural* lácteos.

daisy *noun* margarita *Fem.*

dam *noun* presa *Fem.*

damage *noun* daño *Masc.*; **the damage is done** el daño ya está hecho; **there's no damage** no ha habido daños.
damage *verb* dañar [17].

damn *noun* **he doesn't give a damn** le importa un comino (*informal*).
damn *exclamation* **damn!** ¡maldita sea! (*informal*).

damp *noun* humedad *Fem.*; **because of the damp** a causa de la humedad.
damp *adjective* húmedo/húmeda.

dance *noun* baile *Masc.*; **a folk dance** un baile folklórico.
dance *verb* bailar [17]; **I like dancing** me gusta bailar.

dancer *noun* bailarín *Masc.*, bailarina *Fem.*

dancing *noun* baile *Masc.*; **I love dancing** me encanta bailar.

dancing class *noun* clase *Fem.* de baile; **to go to dancing classes** ir a clase de baile.

dandruff *noun* caspa *Fem.*

danger *noun* peligro *Masc.*; **to be in danger** estar en peligro; **out of danger** fuera de peligro.

dangerous *adjective* peligroso/peligrosa; **it's dangerous to drive so fast** es peligroso conducir tan rápido.

Danish *noun* danés *Masc.*, danesa *Fem.*
Danish *adjective* danés/danesa.

dare *verb* 1 atreverse [18]; **to dare to do** atreverse a hacer; **I didn't dare suggest it** no me atreví a sugerirlo; **how dare you!** ¡cómo te atreves!; **2 don't you dare tell her I'm here!** ¡no se te ocurra decirle que estoy aquí!; **3 I dare you!** ¡a que no te atreves! (*informal*); **I dare you to tell him!** ¡a que no te atreves a decírselo! (*informal*).

daring *adjective* osado/osada; **that was a bit daring!** ¡eso ha sido un poco osado!

dark *noun* **in the dark** en la oscuridad; **to be afraid of the dark** tener miedo de la oscuridad; **after dark** de noche.
dark *adjective* 1 (*colour or room*) oscuro/oscura; **a dark blue suit** un traje azul oscuro; **she has dark brown hair** tiene el pelo castaño oscuro; **the kitchen's a bit dark** la cocina es un poco oscura; **it's dark in here** está oscuro aquí; **2 it's dark already** ya es de noche; **to get dark**

oscurecer; **it gets dark around five** oscurece a eso de las cinco.

darkness *noun* oscuridad *Fem.*

darling *noun* querido *Masc.*, querida *Fem.*; **see you later, darling!** ¡te veo luego querido!

dart *noun* dardo *Masc.*; **to play darts** jugar a los dardos.

data *noun* información *Fem.*

database *noun* base *Fem.* de datos.

date *noun* 1 fecha *Fem.*; **the date of the meeting** la fecha de la reunión; **to fix a date for** fijar una fecha para; **2 what's the date today?** ¿qué día es hoy?; **3** (*when you go out*) **I have a date with Jerry on Sunday** he quedado para salir con Jerry el domingo; **4 out of date** (*passport, driving licence, etc*) caducado/caducada, (*technology, method, information, etc*) anticuado/anticuada; **5** (*fruit*) dátil *Masc.*

date of birth *noun* fecha *Fem.* de nacimiento.

daughter *noun* hija *Fem.*; **Tina's daughter** la hija de Tina.

daughter-in-law *noun* nuera *Fem.*

dawn *noun* amanecer *Masc.*

day *noun* 1 día *Masc.*; **three days later** tres días más tarde; **it rained all day** llovió todo el día; **it's going to be a nice day tomorrow** mañana va a hacer buen día; **2 the day after** al día siguiente; **the day after the wedding** el día después de la boda; **the day after tomorrow** pasado mañana; **my sister's arriving the day after tomorrow** mi hermana

a
b
c
d
e
f
g
h
i
j
k
l
m
n
o
p
q
r
s
t
u
v
w
x
y
z

llega pasado mañana; **3 the day before** el día anterior; **the day before the wedding** el día antes de la boda; **the day before yesterday** anteayer; **my sister arrived the day before yesterday** mi hermana llegó anteayer; **4 every day** todos los días.

day off *noun* día *Masc.* libre.

dead *adjective* muerto/muerta; **her father's dead** su padre ha muerto.
dead *adverb* (*really*) super (*informal*); **he's dead nice** es super majo; **it's dead easy** es super fácil; **it was dead good** fue genial; **you're dead right** tienes toda la razón; **she arrived dead on time** llegó justo a la hora.

dead end *noun* callejón *Masc.* sin salida.

deadline *noun* fecha *Fem.* límite.

deaf *adjective* sordo/sorda; **to go deaf** quedarse sordo/sorda.

deafening *adjective* ensordecedor/ensordecedora.

deal *noun* **1** (*involving money*) negocio *Masc.*; **it's a good deal** es un buen negocio; **2** (*pact*) trato *Masc.*; **I'll make a deal with you** voy a hacer un trato contigo; **it's a deal!** ¡trato hecho!; **3 a great deal of** mucho/mucha; **I don't have a great deal of time** no tengo mucho tiempo; **a great deal of energy** mucha energía; **4 a great deal** mucho; **it has improved a great deal** ha mejorado mucho.
deal *verb* (*in cards*) repartir [19].
• **to deal with something** ocuparse [17] de algo; **Linda deals with the**

accounts Linda se ocupa de las cuentas; **I'll deal with it as soon as possible** me ocuparé de ello tan pronto como sea posible.

dear *adjective* **1** querido/querida; **Dear Jo** Querida Jo; **2** (*expensive*) caro/cara.

death *noun* muerte *Fem.*; **after his father's death** después de la muerte de su padre; ★ **you'll frighten him to death** vas a matarlo del susto; ★ **I'm bored to death** me muero de aburrimiento; ★ **I'm sick to death of his complaining** estoy harta de sus quejas.

death penalty *noun* pena *Fem.* de muerte.

debate *noun* debate *Masc.*
debate *verb* debatir [19].

debt *noun* deuda *Fem.*; **to get into debt** endeudarse [17].

decade *noun* década *Fem.*

decaffeinated *adjective* descafeinado/descafeinada.

deceive *verb* engañar [17].

December *noun* diciembre *Masc.*

decent *adjective* decente; **a decent salary** un sueldo decente; **a decent meal** una comida decente; **he seems a decent enough guy** parece un tipo decente.

decide *verb* decidir [19]; **to decide to do** decidir hacer; **she's decided to buy a car** ha decidido comprarse un coche; **they've decided not to go on holiday** han decidido non irse de vacaciones.

decimal *adjective* decimal.

decimal point *noun* decimal *Masc.*

decision *noun* decisión *Fem.*; **the right decision** la decisión acertada; **the wrong decision** la decisión errónea; **to make a decision** tomar una decisión.

deck *noun* (*on a ship*) cubierta *Fem.*

deckchair *noun* tumbona *Fem.*

declare *verb* declarar [17].

decorate *verb* **1** adornar [17]; **to decorate the Christmas tree** adornar el árbol de Navidad; **2** (*a room*) (*with paint*) pintar [17] (*with wallpaper*) empapelar [17].

decoration *noun* **1** decoración *Fem.*; **2** (*ornament*) adorno *Masc.*

decorator *noun* pintor *Masc.*, pintora *Fem.*

decrease *noun* disminución *Fem.*; **a decrease in the number of** una disminución en el número de. **decrease** *verb* disminuir [54].

deduct *verb* deducir [60].

deep *adjective* profundo/profunda; **a deep feeling of gratitude** un profundo sentimiento de gratitud; **the river is very deep here** aquí el río es muy profundo; **how deep is the swimming pool?** ¿qué profundidad tiene la piscina?; **a hole two metres deep** un agujero de dos metros de profundidad.

deep end *noun* (*of a swimming pool*) **the deep end** la parte honda de la piscina.

deep freeze *noun* congelador *Masc.*

deeply *adverb* profundamente.

deer *noun* ciervo *Masc.*

defeat *noun* derrota *Fem.* **defeat** *verb* derrotar [17].

defect *noun* defecto *Masc.*

defence *noun* defensa *Fem.*

defend *verb* defender [36].

defender *noun* **1** (*of cause*) defensor *Masc.*, defensora *Fem.*; **2** (*in football*) defensa *Masc./Fem.*

define *verb* definir [19].

definite *adjective* **1** (*clear*) claro/clara; **a definite improvement** una clara mejora; **a definite advantage** una clara ventaja; **it's a definite possibility** es claramente una posibilidad; **2** (*certain*) seguro/segura; **it's not definite yet** aún no es seguro; **3** (*exact*) preciso/precisa; **a definite answer** una respuesta precisa; **I don't have a definite idea of what I want** no tengo una idea precisa de lo que quiero.

definite article *noun* artículo *Masc.* definido.

definitely *adverb* **1** (*when giving your opinion about something*) sin ninguna duda; **the blue one is definitely the biggest** el azul es sin ninguna duda el más grande; **your French is definitely better than mine** hablas francés mejor que yo sin ninguna duda; **'are you sure you like this one better?' – 'definitely'** ¿estás seguro de que te gusta más éste?' – 'segurísimo'; **2** (*for certain*) **she's definitely going to be there** es seguro que va a estar aquí; **I'm definitely not**

a b c d e f g h i j k l m n o p q r s t u v w x y z

a
b
going es seguro que no voy; **she definitely said she would do it** dijo que seguro que lo haría.

c
definition *noun* definición *Fem.*

d
degree *noun* **1** grado *Masc.*; **thirty degrees** treinta grados; **2 a university degree** un título universitario.

e

f

g
delay *noun* retraso *Masc.*; **a two-hour delay** un retraso de dos horas. **delay** *verb* retrasar [17]; **the flight was delayed by bad weather** el mal tiempo retrasó el vuelo; **the decision has been delayed until Thursday** retrasaron la decisión hasta el jueves.

h

i

j

k

l
deliberate *adjective* deliberado/ deliberada.

m
deliberately *adverb* a propósito; **you did it deliberately** lo hiciste a propósito; **he left it there deliberately** lo dejó allí a propósito.

n

o
delicate *adjective* delicado/ delicada.

p

q
delicatessen *noun* charcutería *Fem.*

r
delicious *adjective* delicioso/ deliciosa.

s

t
delighted *adjective* encantado/ encantada; **they're delighted with their new flat** están encantados con su nuevo piso; **I'm delighted to hear you can come** estoy encantado de saber que puedes venir.

u

v

w

x
deliver *verb* **1** (*goods*) entregar [28]; **the person who delivered the parcel** la persona que entregó el paquete; **2** (*mail*) repartir [19].

y

z

delivery *noun* entrega *Fem.*

demand *noun* petición *Fem.* **demand** *verb* exigir [49].

democracy *noun* democracia *Fem.*

democratic *adjective* democrático/democrática.

demolish *verb* destruir [54].

demonstrate *verb* **1** demostrar [24] (*a theory or a skill*); **2** hacer [7] una demostración de (*a machine, product, or technique*); **3** (*protest*) manifestarse [29]; **to demonstrate against something** manifestarse en contra de algo.

demonstration *noun* **1** (*of machine, product, technique*) demostración *Fem.*; **2** (*protest*) manifestación *Fem.*

demonstrator *noun* (*in protest*) manifestante *Masc./Fem.*

denim *noun* tela *Fem.* vaquera; **a denim jacket** una chaqueta vaquera.

Denmark *noun* Dinamarca *Fem.*

dense *adjective* denso/densa.

dent *noun* abolladura *Fem.* **dent** *verb* abollar [17].

dental *adjective* **1** dental; **dental hygiene** higiene *Fem.* dental; **2 a dental appointment** una cita con el dentista.

dental floss *noun* hilo *Masc.* dental.

dental surgeon *noun* cirujano *Masc.* dentistacirujana *Fem.* dentista.

dentist *noun* dentista *Masc./Fem.*; **my mum's a dentist** mi madre es dentista.

deny *verb* negar [30].

deodorant *noun* desodorante *Masc.*

depart *verb* salir [63].

department *noun* **1** (*in school, university*) departamento *Masc.*; **the language department** el departamento de idiomas; **2** (*in a shop*) sección *Fem.*; **the men's department** la sección de caballeros.

department store *noun* grandes almacenes *Masc. plural.*

departure *noun* salida *Fem.*

departure gate *noun* puerta *Fem.* de embarque.

departure lounge *noun* sala *Fem.* de embarque.

depend *verb* **to depend on** depender [18] de; **it depends on the price** depende del precio; **it depends on what you want** depende de lo que tú quieras (*note that 'que' is followed by the subjunctive*); **it depends** depende.

deposit *noun* **1** (*when renting, hiring, or making a booking*) depósito *Masc.*; **to pay a deposit** pagar un depósito; **2** (*when buying something*) entrada *Fem.*

depressed *adjective* deprimido/deprimida.

depressing *adjective* deprimente.

depth *noun* profundidad *Fem.*

deputy *noun* segundo *Masc.*, segunda *Fem.*

deputy head *noun* subdirector *Masc.*, subdirectora *Fem.*

descend *verb* descender [36].

describe *verb* describir [52].

description *noun* descripción *Fem.*

desert *noun* desierto *Masc.*

desert island *noun* isla *Fem.* desierta.

deserve *verb* merecer [35].

design *noun* diseño *Masc.*; **the design of the plane** el diseño del avión; **fashion design** diseño de moda; **a floral design** un diseño de flores.
design *verb* diseñar [17].

designer *noun* diseñador *Masc.*, diseñadora *Fem.*

desire *noun* deseo *Masc.*
desire *verb* desear [17].

desk *noun* **1** (*in office or at home*) escritorio *Masc.*; **2** (*pupil's*) pupitre *Masc.*; **3 the reception desk** la recepción; **the information desk** información *Fem.*

despair *noun* desesperación *Fem.*

desperate *adjective* **1** desesperado/desesperada; **a desperate attempt** un intento desesperado; **2 to be desperate to do** estar [2] deseando hacer; **I'm desperate to see you** estoy deseando verte.

despise *verb* despreciar [17].

dessert *noun* postre *Masc.*; **what's for dessert?** ¿qué hay de postre?

a
b
c
d
e
f
g
h
i
j
k
l
m
n
o
p
q
r
s
t
u
v
w
x
y
z

a **destination** *noun* destino *Masc.*

b **destroy** *verb* destruir [54].

c **destruction** *noun* destrucción *Fem.*

d **detached house** *noun* casa *Fem.* no adosada.

e **detail** *noun* detalle *Masc.*

f **detailed** *adjective* detallado/ detallada.

g **detective** *noun* 1 (*police*) agente *Masc./Fem.*; 2 a private detective un detective privado/una detective privada.

h

i **detective story** *noun* novela *Fem.* policiaca.

j **detention** *noun* (*in school*) to be in detention estar [2] castigado/ castigada.

k

l **detergent** *noun* detergente *Masc.*

m **determined** *adjective* decidido/ decidida; he's determined to leave está decidido a irse.

n

o **detour** *noun* rodeo *Masc.*

p **develop** *verb* 1 (*a film*) revelar [17]; to get a film developed revelar un carrete de fotos; 2 desarrollarse [17]; how children develop cómo se desarrollan los niños.

q

r

s

t **developing country** *noun* país *Masc.* en vías de desarrollo.

u **development** *noun* desarrollo *Masc.*

v **devil** *noun* diablo *Masc.*

w **devoted** *adjective* 1 (*couple or family*) unido/unida; 2 (*admirer*) ferviente.

x

y

z **dew** *noun* rocío *Masc.*

diabetes *noun* diabetes *Fem.*

diabetic *noun* diabético *Masc.*, diabética *Fem.*
diabetic *adjective* diabético/ diabética; to be diabetic ser diabético/diabética.

diagonal *adjective* diagonal.

diagnosis *noun* diagnóstico *Masc.*

diagram *noun* diagrama *Masc.*

dial *verb* marcar [31]; dial 00 34 for Spain marca 00 34 para España.

dialling tone *noun* tono *Masc.* de marcar.

dialogue *noun* diálogo *Masc.*

diameter *noun* diámetro *Masc.*

diamond *noun* 1 diamante *Masc.*; 2 (*in cards*) diamonds diamantes; the jack of diamonds la jota de diamantes; 3 (*shape*) rombo *Masc.*

diarrhoea *noun* diarrea *Fem.*; to have diarrhoea tener [9] diarrea.

diary *noun* 1 (*for dates*) agenda *Fem.*; I've noted the date of the meeting in my diary he anotado la fecha de la reunión en mi agenda; 2 (*personal*) diario *Masc.* íntimo; to keep a diary tener [9] un diario íntimo.

dice *noun* dado *Masc.*; to throw the dice tirar [17] los dados.

dictation *noun* dictado *Masc.*

dictionary *noun* diccionario *Masc.*; to look up a word in the dictionary buscar [31] una palabra en el diccionario.

did *verb* SEE **do**.

die *verb* 1 morir [55]; my grandmother died in January mi abuela murió en enero; 2 to be

dying to do something estar [2] deseando hacer algo; **I'm dying to see them!** ¡estoy deseando verlos!.

• **die out** desaparecer [35]; **the tradition is dying out** la tradición está desapareciendo.

diesel *noun* **1** diesel *Masc.*; **2 a diesel engine** un motor diesel; **a diesel car** un diesel.

diet *noun* **1** dieta *Fem.*; **to have a healthy diet** llevar una dieta saludable; **2** (*slimming or special*) régimen *Masc.*; **to be on a diet** estar a régimen; **to go on a diet** ponerse a régimen; **a salt-free diet** un régimen sin sal.

difference *noun* **1** diferencia *Fem.*; **I can't see any difference between the two** no puedo ver ninguna diferencia entre los dos; **what's the difference between ... ?** ¿qué diferencia hay entre ... ?; **2 it makes a difference** eso cambia las cosas; **it makes no difference** da lo mismo; **it makes no difference what I say** da lo mismo lo que yo diga.

different *adjective* distinto/distinta; **the two sisters are very different** las dos hermanas son muy distintas; **she's very different from her sister** es muy distinta a su hermana.

difficult *adjective* difícil; **it's really difficult** es muy difícil; **it's difficult to decide** es difícil decidir.

difficulty *noun* **1** dificultad *Fem.*; **2 I had difficulty finding your house** me resultó difícil encontrar tu casa.

dig *verb* cavar [17]; **to dig a hole** cavar [17] un agujero.

digestion *noun* digestión *Fem.*

digital *adjective* digital; **a digital watch** un reloj digital.

dignity *noun* dignidad *Fem.*

dim *adjective* **1** tenue; **a dim light** una luz tenue; **2 she's a bit dim** es un poco tonta (*informal*).

dimension *noun* dimensión *Fem.*

din *noun* ruido *Masc.*; **they were making a dreadful din** estaban haciendo un ruido enorme; **stop making such a din!** ¡deja de hacer tanto ruido!

dinghy *noun* **1 a sailing dinghy** un bote; **2 a rubber dinghy** un bote neumático.

dining room *noun* comedor *Masc.*; **in the dining room** en el comedor.

dinner *noun* **1** (*evening meal*) cena *Fem.*; **to have dinner** cenar [17]; **to invite somebody to dinner** invitar [17] a alguien a cenar; **2** (*midday meal*) comida *Fem.*; **to have dinner** comer [18]; **to have school dinner** comer [18] en el colegio.

dinner party *noun* cena *Fem.*

dinner time *noun* **1** (*evening*) hora *Fem.* de cenar; **2** (*midday*) hora *Fem.* de comer.

dinosaur *noun* dinosaurio *Masc.*

diploma *noun* diploma *Masc.*

direct *adjective* directo/directa; **a direct flight** un vuelo directo. **direct** *adverb* directo; **the bus goes direct to the airport** el autobús va directo al aeropuerto.

direction

a
b
c
d
e
f
g
h
i
j
k
l
m
n
o
p
q
r
s
t
u
v
w
x
y
z

direct *verb* **1** (*a programme, film, play or traffic*) dirigir [49]; **2** (*give directions to*) indicarle [31] el camino a; **I directed them to the station** les indiqué el camino a la estación.

direction *noun* **1** dirección *Fem.*; **in the direction of the church** en dirección a la iglesia; **in the other direction** en la otra dirección; **2 to ask somebody for directions** pedir a alguien que te indique el camino; **3 directions for use** instrucciones *Fem. plural* de uso.

directly *adverb* **1** (*to go, fly, deal or ask*) directamente; **2** (*at once*) inmediatamente; **3 directly afterwards** inmediatamente después.

director *noun* director *Masc.*, directora *Fem.* (*of a company, programme, film or play*).

directory *noun* guía *Fem.* telefónica; **to be ex-directory** no estar en la guía telefónica.

dirt *noun* suciedad *Fem.*

dirty *adjective* sucio/sucia; **my hands are dirty** tengo las manos sucias; **to get something dirty** ensuciar [17] algo; **I got the floor dirty** ensucié el suelo; **you'll get your dress dirty** te vas a ensuciar el vestido; **to get dirty** ensuciarse [17]; **the curtains get dirty quickly** las cortinas se ensucian rápido.

disability *noun* discapacidad *Fem.*; **does he have a disability?** ¿tiene alguna discapacidad?

disabled *adjective* discapacitado/discapacitada; **disabled people** los discapacitados.

disadvantage *noun* **1** desventaja *Fem.*; **2 to be at a disadvantage** estar en desventaja.

disagree *verb* **I disagree** no estoy de acuerdo; **I disagree with James** no estoy de acuerdo con James.

disappear *verb* desaparecer [35].

disappearance *noun* desaparición *Fem.*

disappointed *adjective* decepcionado/decepcionada; **I was disappointed with my marks** mis notas me decepcionaron.

disappointment *noun* decepción *Fem.*

disaster *noun* desastre *Masc.*; **it was a complete disaster** fue un completo desastre.

disastrous *adjective* desastroso/desastrosa.

discipline *noun* disciplina *Fem.*

disc *noun* **1 a compact disc** un disco compacto; **2 a slipped disc** una hernia de disco.

discipline *noun* disciplina *Fem.*

disc-jockey *noun* disc-jockey *Masc./Fem.*

disco *noun* **1** baile *Masc.*; **they're having a disco** tienen un baile; **2** (*club*) discoteca *Fem.*

disconnect *verb* desconectar [17]; **have you disconnected the electricity?** ¿has desconectado la electricidad?

discount *noun* descuento *Masc.*

discourage *verb* **1** (*depress*) desanimar [17]; **2 to discourage somebody from doing** convencer a alguien de que no haga (*note that 'que no' is followed by the subjunctive*); **I tried to discourage her from buying it** intenté convencerla de que no lo comprase.

discover *verb* descubrir [46].

discovery *noun* descubrimiento *Masc.*

discreet *adjective* discreto/discreta.

discrimination *noun* discriminación *Fem.*; **racial discrimination** discriminación racial.

discuss *verb* **1** (*a subject or topic*) hablar [17] de; **to discuss politics** hablar [17] de política; **I'm going to discuss it with Phil** voy a hablarlo con Phil; **2** (*a problem or plan*) discutir [19].

discussion *noun* discusión *Fem.*

disease *noun* enfermedad *Fem.*

disgraceful *adjective* vergonzoso/vergonzosa.

disguise *noun* disfraz *Masc.*; **to be in disguise** ir disfrazado.
disguise *verb* disfrazar [22]; **to disguise oneself as something** disfrazarse [22] de algo; **disguised as a woman** disfrazado de mujer.

disgust *noun* **1** (*indignation*) indignación *Fem.*; **2** (*physical revulsion*) asco *Masc.*

disgusted *adjective* **1** (*indignant*) indignado/indignada; **2** (*physically sick*) asqueado/asqueada.

disgusting *adjective* asqueroso/asquerosa.

dish *noun* **1** (*plate or food*) plato *Masc.*; **to do the dishes** lavar [17] los platos; **he cooked my favourite dish** cocinó mi plato favorito; **2** (*serving dish*) fuente *Fem.*; **a large white dish** una fuente grande blanca.

dishcloth *noun* (*for drying up*) paño *Masc.* de cocina.

dishonest *adjective* deshonesto/deshonesta.

dishonesty *noun* falta *Fem.* de honradez.

dish towel *noun* paño *Masc.* de cocina.

dishwasher *noun* lavaplatos *Masc.* (*does not change in the plural*).

disinfect *verb* desinfectar [17].

disinfectant *noun* desinfectante *Masc.*

disk *noun* disco *Masc.*; **a floppy disk** un disquete; **the hard disk** el disco duro; **the disk drive** la disquetera.

diskette *noun* disquete *Masc.*

dislike *verb* **I dislike sport** no me gusta el deporte; **he dislikes my friends** no le gustan mis amigos.

dismay *noun* consternación *Fem.*

dismiss *verb* despedir [57] (*an employee*).

disobedient *adjective* desobediente.

disobey *verb* desobedecer [35]; **she disobeyed the rules** desobedeció el reglamento.

display *noun* **1** exposición *Fem.*; **a handicrafts display** una exposición de artesanía; **to be on display** estar

a
b
c
d
e
f
g
h
i
j
k
l
m
n
o
p
q
r
s
t
u
v
w
x
y
z

a

b

c

d

e

f

g

h

i

j

k

l

m

n

o

p

q

r

s

t

u

v

w

x

y

z

expuesto; **2 a window display** un escaparate; **3 a firework display** fuegos *Masc. plural* artificiales.

display *verb* exponer [11].

disposable *adjective* desechable.

dispute *noun* **1** (*quarrel*) disputa *Fem.*; **2** (*argument*) polémica *Fem.*

disqualify *verb* descalificar [31].

dissolve *verb* disolver [45].

distance *noun* distancia *Fem.*; **from a distance** de lejos; **in the distance** a lo lejos; **it's within walking distance** se puede ir andando.

distant *adjective* distante.

distinct *adjective* claro/clara.

distinctly *adverb* **1** claramente; **2 it's distinctly odd** es realmente raro.

distract *verb* distraer [42].

distribute *verb* distribuir [54].

distribution *noun* distribución *Fem.*

district *noun* **1** (*in town*) barrio *Masc.*; **a poor district of Barcelona** un barrio pobre de Barcelona; **2** (*in the country*) región *Fem.*

disturb *verb* molestar [17]; **sorry to disturb you** perdona que te moleste; **do not disturb** se ruega no molestar.

ditch *noun* zanja *Fem.*
ditch *verb* **to ditch somebody** plantar [17] a alguien (*informal*).

dive *noun* zambullida *Fem.*
dive *verb* tirarse [17]; **to dive into the water** tirarse al agua.

diver *noun* (*deep-sea*) submarinista *Masc./Fem.*

diversion *noun* (*for traffic*) desvío *Masc.*

divide *verb* dividir [19].

diving *noun* **1** (*from a board*) saltos *Masc. plural* de trampolín; **2** (*from the surface of the water*) submarinismo *Masc.*

diving board *noun* trampolín *Masc.*

division *noun* división *Fem.*

divorce *noun* divorcio *Masc.*
divorce *verb* divorciarse [17]; **they divorced in Mexico** se divociaron en México.

divorced *adjective* divorciado/divorciada; **my parents are divorced** mis padres están divorciados.

DIY *noun* bricolaje *Masc.*; **to do DIY** hacer [7] bricolaje; **a DIY shop** una tienda de bricolaje.

dizzy *adjective* **to feel dizzy** estar [2] mareado/mareada; **I feel dizzy** estoy mareado.

DJ *noun* disc-jockey *Masc./Fem.*

do *verb* **1** hacer [7]; **what are you doing?** ¿qué estás haciendo?; **I'm doing my homework** estoy haciendo mis deberes; **what have you done with the hammer?** ¿qué has hecho con el martillo?; **2** (*in questions, 'do' is not translated*) **did Maria go to the party?** ¿fue María a la fiesta?; **do you want some strawberries?** ¿quieres fresas?; **when does it start?** ¿cuándo empieza?; **how did you open the**

door? ¿cómo has abierto la puerta?;
3 (*in negative sentences*) (*the
negative in Spanish is formed
adding 'no' before the verb*) **I don't
like this kind of music** no me gusta
este tipo de música; **Rosie doesn't
like spinach** a Rosie no le gustan
las espinacas; **you didn't shut the
door** no has cerrado la puerta; **it
doesn't matter** no importa; **4** (*when
it refers back to another verb, 'do' is
not translated*) **'do you live here?'** –
'yes, I do' '¿vives aquí?' – 'sí'; **she
has more money than I do** tiene
más dinero que yo; **'I live in Oxford'**
– **'so do I'** 'vivo en Oxford' – 'yo
también'; **'I didn't phone Gemma'** –
'neither did I' 'no he llamado a
Gemma' – 'yo tampoco'; **5 don't
you?, doesn't he?** etc. ¿no?; **you
know Helen, don't you?** conoces a
Helen, ¿no?; **she left on Thursday,
didn't she?** se marchó el jueves ,
¿no?; **6 that'll do** así basta; **it'll do
like that** así vale.

● **do with 1** tener [9] que ver con; **it
has nothing to do with him** no
tiene nada que ver con él; **2 I could
do with a rest** me vendría bien un
descanso.

● **to do something up 1** atar [17]
(*shoes*); **I did my shoes up** me até los
zapatos; **2** abrochar [17] (*cardigan,
jacket*); **do your jacket up**
abróchate la chaqueta; **3** arreglar
[17] (*house*).

● **to do without something**
arreglarse [17] sin algo; **we can do
without knives** nos arreglaremos
sin cuchillos.

doctor *noun* médico *Masc./Fem.*; **her
mother's a doctor** su madre es
médico.

document *noun* documento *Masc.*

documentary *noun* documental
Masc.

dodgems *plural noun* **the
dodgems** los cochecitos de choque.

dog *noun* perro *Masc.* perra *Fem.*.

do-it-yourself *noun* bricolage
Masc.

dole *noun* paro *Masc.*; **to be on the
dole** estar en el paro.

doll *noun* muñeca *Fem.*

dollar *noun* dólar *Masc.*

dolphin *noun* delfín *Masc.*

dominate *verb* dominar [17].

Dominican *noun* dominicano
Masc., dominicana *Fem.*
Dominican *adjective* dominicano/
dominicana.

Dominican Republic *noun*
República Dominicana *Fem.*

domino *noun* ficha *Fem.* de dominó;
to play dominoes jugar al dominó.

donation *noun* donación *Fem.*

donkey *noun* burro *Masc.*

don't SEE **do**.

door *noun* puerta *Fem.*; **to open the
door** abrir [46] la puerta; **to shut the
door** cerrar [29] la puerta.

doorbell *noun* timbre *Masc.*; **to ring
the doorbell** tocar [31] el timbre;
there's the doorbell llaman a la
puerta.

doorstep *noun* umbral *Masc.* de la
puerta.

a
b
c
d
e
f
g
h
i
j
k
l
m
n
o
p
q
r
s
t
u
v
w
x
y
z

dormitory *noun* dormitorio *Masc.*

dot *noun* **1** (*written*) punto *Masc.*;
2 (*on fabric*) lunar *Masc.*; **3 at ten on
the dot** a las diez en punto.

double *adjective, adverb* **1** doble; **a
double helping** una ración doble; **a
double whisky** un whisky doble; **a
double room** una habitación doble;
a double bed una cama de
matrimonio; **2** el doble; **double the
time** el doble de tiempo; **double the
price** el doble del precio.

double bass *noun* contrabajo
Masc.; **to play the double bass** tocar
[31] el contrabajo.

double-breasted *adjective* **a
double-breasted jacket** una
chaqueta cruzada.

double-decker bus *noun*
autobús *Masc.* de dos pisos.

double glazing *noun* doble
ventana *Fem.*

doubles *noun* (*in tennis*) dobles
Masc. plural; **to play a game of
doubles** jugar un partido de dobles.

doubt *noun* duda *Fem.*; **there's no
doubt about it** no hay ninguna duda
al respecto; **I have my doubts** tengo
mis dudas.
doubt *verb* **to doubt something**
dudar [17] algo; **I doubt it** lo dudo; **I
doubt that** dudo que (*note that 'que'
is followed by the subjunctive*); **I
doubt they'll do it** dudo que lo
hagan.

doubtful *adjective* **1 it's doubtful
that** no es seguro que (*note that 'que'
is followed by the subjunctive*); **it's
doubtful that she'll want to** no es

seguro que quiera; **2 to be doubtful
about doing** dudar [17] si hacer; **I'm
doubtful about inviting them
together** estoy dudando si
invitarlos a los dos juntos.

dough *noun* masa *Fem.*

doughnut *noun* donut *Masc.*

down *adverb, preposition* **1** abajo;
he's down in the cellar está abajo,
en el sótano; **2 down the road**
(*nearby*) un poco más allá; **there's a
chemist's just down the road** hay
una farmacia un poco más allá; **3 to
go down** bajar [17]; **I went down to
the kitchen** bajé a la cocina; **to walk
down the street** bajar la calle; **to
run down the stairs** bajar
corriendo la escalera; **4 to come
down** bajar [17]; **she came down
from her bedroom** bajó de la
habitación; **5 to sit down** sentarse
[29]; **she sat down on the sofa** se
sentó en el sofá.

downstairs *adverb* **1** abajo; **she's
downstairs in the sitting-room**
está abajo en el salón; **the dog
sleeps downstairs** el perro duerme
abajo; **2** (*after a noun*) de abajo; **the
flat downstairs** el piso de abajo; **the
people downstairs** la gente de
abajo.

doze *verb* dormitar [17].

dozen *noun* docena *Fem.*; **a dozen
eggs** una docena de huevos.

drag *noun* **what a drag!** ¡qué rollo!
(*informal*); **she's a bit of a drag** es
un poco pesada (*informal*).
drag *verb* arrastrar [17].

dragon *noun* dragón *Masc.*

a
b
c
d
e
f
g
h
i
j
k
l
m
n
o
p
q
r
s
t
u
v
w
x
y
z

drink

drain noun 1 (plughole) desagüe Masc.; 2 (in street) alcantarilla Fem. **drain** verb escurrir [19] (vegetables).

drama noun 1 (subject) arte Masc. dramático; 2 **he made a big drama about it** montó una escena por eso (informal).

dramatic adjective dramático/dramática.

draught noun corriente Fem. de aire.

draughts noun damas Fem. plural; **to play draughts** jugar a las damas.

draw noun 1 (in a match) empate Masc.; **it was a draw** fue un empate; 2 (lottery) sorteo Masc. **draw** verb 1 dibujar [17]; **I can't draw horses** no sé dibujar caballos; **she can draw really well** dibuja muy bien; 2 **to draw a picture** hacer [7] un dibujo; 3 **to draw the curtains** correr [18] las cortinas; 4 **to draw a crowd** atraer [42] a una multitud; 5 (in a match) empatar [17]; **we drew three all** empatamos a tres; 6 **to draw lots for something** echar [17] algo a suertes.

drawback noun inconveniente Masc.

drawer noun cajón Masc.

drawing noun dibujo Masc.

drawing pin noun chincheta Fem.

dreadful adjective terrible.

dreadfully adverb 1 (to sing or act) espantosamente; 2 **I'm dreadfully late** llego tardísimo; **I'm dreadfully sorry** lo siento muchísmo.

dream noun sueño Masc.; **to have a dream** tener [9] un sueño; **I had a horrible dream last night** tuve un sueño horrible anoche. **dream** verb soñar [24]; **to dream about something** soñar con algo.

drenched adjective empapado/empapada; **to get drenched** empaparse [17]; **I got drenched on the way home** me empapé yendo a casa.

dress noun vestido Masc. **dress** verb vestir [57]; **to dress a child** vestir a un niño.

• **to dress up** disfrazarse [22]; **to dress up as a vampire** disfrazarse de vampiro.

dressed adjective 1 vestido/vestida; **is Tom dressed?** ¿está Tom vestido?; **she was dressed in black trousers and a yellow shirt** iba vestida con unos pantalones negros y una blusa amarilla; 2 **to get dressed** vestirse [57].

dresser noun (for dishes) aparador Masc.

dressing gown noun bata Fem.

dressing table noun tocador Masc.

drier noun **a hair drier** un secador de pelo; **a tumble drier** una secadora.

drift noun **a snow drift** una ventisca de nieve.

drill noun 1 (tool) taladradora Fem.; 2 (in homework) ejercicio Masc.

drink noun 1 bebida Fem.; **a hot drink** una bebida caliente; **a cold drink** un refresco; 2 **would you like**

a
b
c
d
e
f
g
h
i
j
k
l
m
n
o
p
q
r
s
t
u
v
w
x
y
z

a drink? ¿te apetece beber algo?;
3 to go out for a drink salir [63] a
tomar una copa (*informal*).

drink *verb* beber [18]; **he drank a
glass of water** bebió un vaso de
agua.

drive *noun* **1 to go for a drive** ir [8]
a dar una vuelta en coche; **2** (*up to a
house*) entrada *Fem.* para coches.
drive *verb* **1** conducir [60]; **she
drives very fast** conduce muy
rápido; **to drive a car** conducir [60]
un coche; **I'd like to learn to drive**
me gustaría aprender a conducir;
can you drive? ¿sabes conducir?;
2 ir [8] en coche; **we drove to
Seville** fuimos en coche a Sevilla;
3 to drive somebody (to a place)
llevar [17] en coche a alguien (a un
sitio); **Mum drove me to the
station** mamá me llevó en coche a la
estación; **to drive somebody home**
llevar [17] a alguien a casa en coche;
★ **she drives me mad!** ¡me saca de
quicio!

driver *noun* **1** (*of a car, taxi or bus*)
conductor *Masc.*, conductora *Fem.*;
2 (*of a racing car*) piloto *Masc./Fem.*

driving instructor *noun*
instructor *Masc.* de autoescuela,
instructora *Fem.* de autoescuela.

driving lesson *noun* clase *Fem.* de
conducir.

driving licence *noun* permiso
Masc. de conducir.

driving school *noun* autoescuela
Fem.

driving test *noun* examen *Masc.* de
conducir; **to take your driving test**
presentarse [17] al examen de

conducir; **Jenny's passed her
driving test** Jenny ha aprobado el
examen de conducir.

drop *noun* gota *Fem.*
drop *verb* **1 I dropped my glasses**
se me cayeron las gafas; **careful,
don't drop it!** ¡cuidado, que no se te
caiga!; **2** (*a course, subject or topic*)
dejar [17]; **I'm going to drop history
next year** voy a dejar la historia el
próximo año; **3** dejar [17] (*a person*);
could you drop me at the station?
¿me podrías dejar en la estación?;
4 drop it! ¡déjalo ya!.

drought *noun* sequía *Fem.*

drown *verb* ahogarse [28]; **she
drowned in the lake** se ahogó en el
lago.

drug *noun* **1** (*medicine*) medicina
Fem.; **2** (*illegal*) **drugs** las drogas; **to
be on drugs** drogarse [28].

drug abuse *noun* consumo *Masc.*
de drogas.

drug addict *noun* drogadicto
Masc., drogadicta *Fem.*

drug addiction *noun*
drogadicción *Fem.*

drum *noun* **1** tambor *Masc.*; **2 drums**
batería *Fem.*; **to play drums** tocar
[31] la batería.

drum kit *noun* batería *Fem.*

drummer *noun* batería *Masc./Fem.*

drunk *noun* borracho *Masc.*,
borracha *Fem.*
drunk *adjective* borracho/
borracha.

dry *adjective* seco/seca.
dry *verb* **1** secar [31]; **to dry the
dishes** secar los platos; **2 to let**

something dry dejar que algo se seque; **it took ages to dry** tardó muchísimo en secarse; **3 to dry oneself** secarse [31]; **to dry your hair** secarse [31] el pelo; **I'm going to dry my hair** me voy a secar el pelo.

dry cleaner's *noun* tintorería *Fem.*

dryer *noun* SEE **drier**.

dual carriageway *noun* autovía *Fem.*

dubbed *adjective* **a dubbed film** una película doblada.

duck *noun* pato *Masc.*, pata *Fem.*

due *adjective, adverb* **1 to be due to do** tener [9] que hacer; **we're due to leave on Thursday** tenemos que salir el jueves; **Paul's due back soon** Paul tiene que volver pronto; **2 what time is the train due?** ¿cuándo llega el próximo tren?; **3 due to** debido a; **the match has been cancelled due to bad weather** el partido ha sido cancelado debido al mal tiempo.

duke *noun* duque *Masc.*

dull *adjective* **1 dull weather** tiempo gris; **it's a dull day today** hoy hace un día muy gris; **2** (*boring*) aburrido/aburrida.

dumb *adjective* **1** mudo/muda; **to be deaf and dumb** ser sordomudo/sordomuda; **2** (*stupid*) tonto/tonta; **he asked some dumb questions** hizo unas preguntas muy tontas.

dummy *noun* (*for a baby*) chupete *Masc.*

dump *verb* **1** tirar [17] (*rubbish*); **2** plantar [17] (*a person*) (*informal*);

she's dumped her boyfriend ha plantado a su novio.

dune *noun* duna *Fem.*

dungarees *plural noun* pantalón *Masc.* de peto.

dungeon *noun* mazmorra *Fem.*

during *preposition* durante; **during the night** durante la noche; **I saw her during the holidays** la vi durante las vacaciones.

dusk *noun* anochecer *Masc.*; **at dusk** al anochecer.

dust *noun* polvo *Masc.*
dust *verb* quitar [17] el polvo; **to dust the table** quitarle el polvo a la mesa.

dustbin *noun* cubo *Masc.* de la basura; **to put something in the dustbin** tirar [17] algo al cubo de la basura.

dustman *noun* basurero *Masc.*

dusty *adjective* cubierto/cubierta de polvo.

Dutch *noun* **1** (*language*) holandés *Masc.*; **2 the Dutch** (*people*) los holandeses.
Dutch *adjective* holandés/holandesa.

duty *noun* **1** deber *Masc.*; **to have a duty to do** tener [9] el deber de hacer; **you have a duty to inform us** tienes el deber de informarnos; **2 to be on duty** (*a nurse or doctor*) estar [2] de guardia (*a policeman*) estar [2] de servicio; **to be on night duty** tener [9] el turno de noche.

duty-free *adjective* libre de impuestos; **the duty-free shops** las tiendas libres de impuestos; **duty-**

a
b
c
d
e
f
g
h
i
j
k
l
m
n
o
p
q
r
s
t
u
v
w
x
y
z

a

b

c

d

e

f

g

h

i

j

k

l

m

n

o

p

q

r

s

t

u

v

w

x

y

z

free purchases artículos libres de impuestos.

duvet *noun* edredón *Masc.*

duvet cover *noun* funda *Fem.* de edredón.

dwarf *noun* enano *Masc.*, enana *Fem.*

dye *noun* tinte *Masc.*
dye *verb* teñir [65]; **to dye your hair** teñirse [65] el pelo; **I'm going to dye my hair pink** me voy a teñir el pelo de rosa.

dynamic *adjective* dinámico/dinámica.

dyslexia *noun* dislexia *Fem.*

dyslexic *adjective* disléxico/disléxica.

Ee

each *adjective* cada; **each time** cada vez; **curtains for each window** cortinas para cada ventana.
each *pronoun* cada uno/una; **my sisters each have a computer** mis hermanas tienen un ordenador cada una; **she gave us an apple each** nos dio una manzana a cada uno; **each of you** cada uno de vosotros; **we each bought a book** cada uno de nosotros compró un libro; **the tickets cost ten pounds each** las entradas cuestan diez libras cada una.

each other *pronoun* (*'each other' is usually translated using a reflexive pronoun*) **they love each other** se quieren; **we know each other** nos

conocemos; **do you often see each other?** ¿os veis a menudo?

eagle *noun* águila *Fem.* (*even though 'águila' is feminine, it takes 'el' and 'un' in the singular*).

ear *noun* oreja *Fem.*

earache *noun* **to have earache** tener dolor de oídos.

earlier *adverb* **1** (*a while ago*) hace un rato; **your brother phoned earlier** tu hermano llamó hace un rato; **2** (*not as late*) más temprano; **we should have started earlier** deberíamos haber empezado más temprano; **earlier in the morning** por la mañana temprano.

early *adverb* **1** (*in the morning*) temprano; **I get up early** me levanto temprano; **it's too early** es demasiado temprano; **2** (*for an appointment*) pronto; **we're early, the train doesn't leave until ten** hemos llegado pronto, el tren no sale hasta las diez; **Grandma likes to be early** a la abuela le gusta llegar pronto.
early *adjective* **1** (*one of the first*) primero/primera; **in the early months** en los primeros meses; **2 to have an early lunch** comer temprano; **Jan's having an early night** Jan se ha acostado temprano; **we're making an early start** vamos a salir temprano; **3 in the early afternoon** a primera hora de la tarde; **in the early hours** de madrugada.

earn *verb* ganar [17] (*money*);
**Richard earns four pounds an
hour** Richard gana cuatro libras por
hora.

earnings *plural noun* ingresos
Masc. plural.

earphones *plural noun*
auriculares Masc. plural.

earring *noun* pendiente Masc.

earth *noun* tierra Fem.; **life on earth**
la vida en la tierra; ★ **what on earth
are you doing?** ¿qué demonios
estás haciendo?.

earthquake *noun* terremoto Masc.

easily *adverb* **1** (*to do something*)
con facilidad; **2** (*by far*) con mucho;
he's easily the best es con mucho el
mejor.

east *noun* este Masc.; **in the east** en
el este.
east *adjective, adverb* **the east
side** el lado este; **an east wind** un
viento del este; **east of Seville** al
este de Sevilla.

Easter *noun* Semana Fem. Santa;
they're coming at Easter vienen en
Semana Santa.

Easter Day *noun* Domingo Masc.
de Pascua.

Easter egg *noun* huevo Masc. de
Pascua.

Eastern Europe *noun* Europa
Fem. del Este.

easy *adjective* fácil; **it's easy!** ¡es
fácil!; **it was easy to decide** fue
fácil decidir.

eat *verb* **1** comer [18]; **he was eating
a banana** estaba comiendo un

plátano; **we're going to have
something to eat** vamos a comer
algo; **2** tomar [17] (*a meal*); **we were
eating breakfast** estábamos
tomando el desayuno; **3 to eat out**
comer [18] fuera.

EC *noun* CE Fem., Comunidad Fem.
Europea.

echo *noun* eco Masc.
echo *verb* hacer [7] eco.

eclipse *noun* eclipse Masc.

ecological *adjective* ecológico/
ecológica.

ecologist *noun* ecologista Masc.,
ecologista Fem.

ecology *noun* ecología Fem.

economic *adjective* **1** (*relating to
economics*) económoco/económica;
2 (*profitable*) rentable.

economical *adjective*
económico/económica (*way of doing
something*); **it's more economical
to buy a big one** sale más
económico comprar uno grande.

economics *noun* economía Fem.

economy *noun* economía Fem.

Ecuador *noun* Ecuador Masc.

Ecuadorian *noun* ecuatoriano
Masc., ecuatoriana Fem.
Ecuadorian *adjectiv* ecuatoriano/
ecuatoriana.

eczema *noun* eczema Masc.

edge *noun* **1** (*of table, plate, or cliff*)
borde Masc.; **the edge of the table** el
borde de la mesa; **2** (*of river or lake*)
orilla Fem.; **at the edge of the lake**
en la orilla del lago; **3 to be on edge**
estar nervioso.

a
b
c
d
e
f
g
h
i
j
k
l
m
n
o
p
q
r
s
t
u
v
w
x
y
z

a

edible *adjective* comestible.

b

Edinburgh *noun* Edimburgo *Masc.*

c

edit *verb* editar [17].

editor *noun* (*of a newspaper*) redactor *Masc.*, redactora *Fem.*

d

educate *verb* (*a teacher*) educar [31].

e

f

education *noun* educación *Fem.*

g

educational *adjective* educativo/ educativa.

h

effect *noun* efecto *Masc.*; **the effect of the accident** el efecto del accidente; **to have an effect on** afectar [17] a; **it had a good effect on the whole family** afectó positivamente a toda la familia; **special effects** efectos especiales.

i

j

k

l

m

effective *adjective* eficaz.

n

efficient *adjective* eficiente.

o

effort *noun* esfuerzo *Masc.*; **to make an effort** hacer [7] un esfuerzo; **Jess made an effort to help us** Jess hizo un esfuerzo para ayudarnos; **he didn't even make the effort to apologize** mi sí quiera se molestó en disculparse; **it's not worth the effort** no merece la pena.

p

q

r

s

t

e.g. *abbreviation* p.ej.

u

egg *noun* huevo *Masc.*; **a dozen eggs** una docena de huevos; **a fried egg** un huevo frito; **two boiled eggs** dos huevos pasados por agua; **a hard-boiled egg** un huevo duro; **scrambled eggs** huevos revueltos.

v

w

x

egg-cup *noun* huevera *Fem.*

y

eggshell *noun* cáscara *Fem.* de huevo.

z

egg-white *noun* clara *Fem.* de huevo.

egg-yolk *noun* yema *Fem.* de huevo.

eight *number* ocho *Masc.*; **Rosie's eight** Rosie tiene ocho años; **it's eight o'clock** son las ocho.

eighteen *number* dieciocho; **Kate's eighteen** Kate tiene dieciocho años.

eighth *noun* **1** (*fraction*) **an eighth** una octava parte; **2 the eighth of July** el ocho de julio.
eighth *adjective* octavo/octava; **on the eighth floor** en la octava planta.

eighties *plural noun* **the eighties** los años ochenta; **in the eighties** en los años ochenta.

eighty *number* ochenta *Masc.*; **she's eighty** tiene ochenta años; **eighty-five** ochenta y cinco.

Eire *noun* Irlanda *Masc./Fem.*

either *pronoun* **1** (*one or the other*) **choose either (of them)** elige cualquiera (de los dos); **I don't like either (of them)** no me gusta ninguno (de los dos); **2** (*both*) **either is possible** las dos cosas son posibles.
either *conjunction* **1 either ... or** o ... o; **you either pay or return it** o pagas o lo devuelves; **I'll phone either Thursday or Friday** llamaré o el jueves o el viernes (*'o' becomes 'u' before a word starting with 'o' or 'ho'*) **either one or the other** o uno u otro; **2** (*with a negative*) **he doesn't want to go either** él tampoco quiere ir; **I don't know them either** yo tampoco los conozco.

elastic *noun* elástico *Masc.*
elastic *adjective* elástico/elástica.

elastic band *noun* goma *Fem.* elástica.

elbow *noun* codo *Masc.*

elder *adjective* mayor; **her elder brother** su hermano mayor.

elderly *adjective* **an elderly man** un anciano; **an elderly woman** una anciana; **an elderly couple** una pareja de ancianos; **the elderly** los ancianos.

eldest *adjective* mayor; **her eldest brother** su hermano mayor.

elect *verb* elegir [48]; **she has been elected** ha sido elegida.

election *noun* elecciones *Fem. plural*; **in the election** en las elecciones; **to call a general election** convocar [31] elecciones generales.

electric *adjective* eléctrico/eléctrica.

electrical *adjective* eléctrico/eléctrica.

electrician *noun* electricista *Masc./Fem.*

electricity *noun* electricidad *Fem.*; **to turn off the electricity** desconectar [17] la corriente.

electronic *adjective* electrónico/electrónica.

electronic mail *noun* correo *Masc.* electrónico.

electronics *noun* electrónica *Fem.*

elegant *adjective* elegante.

element *noun* elemento *Masc.*

elephant *noun* elefante *Masc.*

eleven *number* once *Masc.*; **Josh is eleven** Josh tiene once años; **it's eleven o'clock** son las once.

eleventh *noun* **the eleventh of May** el once de mayo.
eleventh *adjective* onceavo/onceava; **on the eleventh floor** en la onceava planta.

eliminate *verb* eliminar [17].

else *adverb* **1** (*in questions and negative sentences*) más; **who else?** ¿quién más?; **what else?** ¿qué más?; **nothing else** nada más; **I don't want anything else** no quiero nada más; **2 somebody else** otra persona; **somebody else must have done it** lo ha debido hacer otra persona; **3 something else** otra cosa; **would you like something else?** ¿quieres otra cosa?; **4 everybody else** todos los demás; **everything else** todo lo demás; **5 somewhere else** en otra parte; **6 or else** si no; **hurry up, or else we'll be late** date prisa, que si no vamos a llegar tarde.

e-mail *noun* correo *Masc.* electrónico.

embankment *noun* **1** (*by a river*) muro *Masc.* de contención; **2** (*by a railway*) terraplén *Masc.*

embarrassed *adjective* **I was terribly embarrassed** me daba mucha vergüenza; **she feels a bit embarrassed** le da un poco de vergüenza.

embarrassing *adjective* violento/violenta (*situation or silence*); **how embarrassing!** ¡qué vergüenza!

a
b
c
d
e
f
g
h
i
j
k
l
m
n
o
p
q
r
s
t
u
v
w
x
y
z

embarrassment *noun*
vergüenza *Fem.*

embassy *noun* embajada *Fem.*; **the Spanish Embassy** la embajada española.

embroider *verb* bordar [17].

embroidery *noun* bordado *Masc.*

emergency *noun* 1 emergencia *Fem.*; **in an emergency, break the glass** en caso de emergencia, rompa el cristal; **it's an emergency!** ¡es una emergencia!; 2 (*medical*) urgencia *Fem.*; **an emergency operation** una operación de urgencia.

emergency exit *noun* salida *Fem.* de emergencia.

emergency landing *noun* aterrizaje *Masc.* forzoso.

emotion *noun* emoción *Fem.*

emotional *adjective* 1 (*person*) **to be emotional** estar [2] emocionado/emocionada; **to get emotional** emocionarse [17]; **she got quite emotional** se emocionó mucho; 2 (*a speech or an occasion*) emotivo/emotiva.

emperor *noun* emperador *Masc.*

emphasis *noun* énfasis *Masc.*

emphasize *verb* recalcar [31]; **he emphasized that it wasn't compulsory** recalcó que no era obligatorio.

empire *noun* imperio *Masc.*; **the Roman Empire** el imperio romano.

employ *verb* 1 (*have in employment*) emplear [17]; 2 (*give work to*) dar [4] un trabajo a.

employee *noun* empleado *Masc.*, empleada *Fem.*

employer *noun* patrón *Masc.*, patrona *Fem.*

employment *noun* empleo *Masc.*

empress *noun* emperatriz *Fem.*

empty *adjective* vacío/vacía; **an empty bottle** una botella vacía; **the room was empty** la habitación estaba vacía.

empty *verb* vaciar [32]; **I emptied the teapot into the sink** vacié la tetera en el fregadero.

enchanting *adjective*
encantador/encantadora.

enclose *verb* (*in a letter*) adjuntar [17]; **please find enclosed a cheque** se adjunta un cheque.

encore *noun* bis *Masc.*; **encore!** ¡otra!

encourage *verb* animar [17]; **to encourage somebody to do** animar a alguien a hacer; **Mum encouraged me to try again** mamá me animó a intentarlo otra vez.

encouragement *noun* ánimo *Masc.*

encouraging *adjective*
alentador/alentadora.

encyclopedia *noun* enciclopedia *Fem.*

end *noun* 1 (*last part*) final *Masc.*; **at the end of the film** al final de la película; **by the end of the day** al final del día; **in the end I went home** al final me fui a casa; 2 **at the end of the year** a finales de año; **Sally's coming at the end of June** Sally viene a finales de junio; 3 'The

End' (*in a book or film*) 'Fin'; **4** (*of a table, garden, or stick, for example*) extremo *Masc.*; **hold the other end** sujeta el otro extremo; **5** (*of a street or road*) final *Masc.*; **at the end of the street** al final de la calle; **6** (*of a football pitch*) lado *Masc.*; **to change ends** cambiar [17] de lado.

end *verb* **1** (*put an end to*) poner [11] fin a (*an arrangement*); **they've ended the strike** han puesto fin a la huelga; **2** (*to come to an end*) terminar [17]; **the day ended with a dinner** el día terminó con una cena.

● **to end up** terminar [17]; **we ended up taking a taxi** terminamos cogiendo un taxi; **Ross ended up in San Francisco** Ross terminó en San Francisco.

endangered *adjective* en peligro; **an endangered species** una especie en en vías de extinción.

ending *noun* final *Masc.*

endless *adjective* interminable.

enemy *noun* enemigo *Masc.*, enemiga *Fem.*; **to make enemies** hacer [7] enemigos.

energetic *adjective* energético/energética.

energy *noun* energía *Fem.*

engaged *adjective* **1** (*to be married*) prometido/prometida; **they're engaged** están prometidos; **to get engaged** prometerse [18]; **2** (*a phone*) comunicando; **it's engaged, I'll ring later** está comunicando, llamaré más tarde; **3** (*a toilet*) ocupado/ocupada.

engagement *noun* (*to marry*) compromiso *Masc.*

engagement ring *noun* anillo *Masc.* de compromiso.

engine *noun* **1** (*in a car*) motor *Masc.*; **2** (*locomotive*) locomotora *Fem.*

engineer *noun* **1** (*who does repairs*) técnico *Masc./Fem.*; **2** (*who builds roads and bridges*) ingeniero *Masc.*, ingeniera *Fem.*.

England *noun* Inglaterra *Fem.*; **I'm from England** soy inglés.

English *noun* **1** (*the language*) inglés *Masc.*; **do you speak English?** ¿hablas inglés?; **he answered in English** contestó en inglés; **2** (*English people*) **the English** los ingleses.

English *adjective* **1** (*of or from England*) inglés/inglesa; **the English team** el equipo inglés; **2 an English lesson** una clase de inglés; **our English teacher** nuestro profesor de inglés.

English Channel *noun* **the English Channel** el Canal de la Mancha.

Englishman *noun* inglés *Masc.*

Englishwoman *noun* inglesa *Fem.*

enjoy *verb* **1** disfrutar [17]; **did you enjoy the party?** ¿disfrutaste de la fiesta?; **we really enjoyed the concert** disfrutamos mucho del concierto; **2 I enjoy swimming** me gusta nadar; **do you enjoy living in York?** ¿te gusta vivir en York?; **3 to enjoy youself** divertirse [14]; **we**

a
b
c
d
e
f
g
h
i
j
k
l
m
n
o
p
q
r
s
t
u
v
w
x
y
z

a
b
c
d
e
f
g
h
i
j
k
l
m
n
o
p
q
r
s
t
u
v
w
x
y
z

really enjoyed ourselves nos divertimos muchísimo; **did you enjoy yourself?** ¿te divertiste?.

enjoyable *adjective* agradable.

enlarge *verb* ampliar [32].

enlargement *noun* (*of a photo*) ampliación *Fem.*

enormous *adjective* enorme.

enough *adverb, pronoun*
1 suficiente; **there's enough for everyone** hay suficiente para todos; **is there enough bread?** ¿hay pan suficiente?; **there weren't enough books** no había libros suficientes; 2 (*with an adjective or adverb*) lo suficientemente; **big enough** lo suficientemente grande; **slowly enough** lo suficientemente despacio; 3 **that's enough** ya basta.

enquire *verb* informarse [17]; **I'm going to enquire about the trains** voy a informarme sobre los trenes.

enquiry *noun* **to make enquiries about something** pedir [57] información sobre algo.

enrol *verb* matricularse [17]; **I want to enrol on the course** quiero matricularme en el curso.

enter *verb* 1 (*go inside*) entrar [17] en (*a room or building*); **we all entered the church** todos entramos en la iglesia; 2 **to enter for** presentarse [17] a (*an exam*); tomar [17] parte en (*a race or competition*).

entertain *verb* 1 (*keep amused*) entretener [9]; **something to entertain the children** algo para entretener a los niños; 2 (*have people round*) invitar [17] a gente;

they don't entertain much no invitan a mucha gente.

entertaining *noun* **they do a lot of entertaining** invitan a mucha gente.
entertaining *adjective* entretenido/entretenida.

entertainment *noun* (*fun*) entretenimiento *Masc.*; **there wasn't much entertainment in the evenings** por las noches no había mucho entretenimiento.

enthusiasm *noun* entusiasmo *Masc.*

enthusiast *noun* **to be a rugby enthusiast** ser [1] un apasionado/ una apasionada del rugby.

enthusiastic *adjective* entusiasta.

entire *adjective* entero/entera; **the entire class** la clase entera.

entirely *adverb* completamente.

entrance *noun* entrada *Fem.*

entry *noun* (*the way in*) entrada *Fem.*; **'no entry'** 'prohibida la entrada'.

entry phone *noun* portero *Masc.* automático.

envelope *noun* sobre *Masc.*

envious *adjective* envidioso/ envidiosa; **he's envious of my exam results** tiene envidia de las notas de mis exámenes.

environment *noun* medio *Masc.* ambiente.

environmental *adjective* medioambiental.

environment-friendly . *adjective* ecológico/ecológica.

envy *noun* envidia *Fem.*

epidemic *noun* epidemia *Fem.*

epileptic *noun* epiléptico *Masc.*, epiléptica *Fem.*

episode *noun* episodio *Masc.*

equal *adjective* igual; **in equal quantities** en cantidades iguales. **equal** *verb* ser [1] igual a.

equalize *verb* empatar [17]; **they equalized in the last minute** empataron en el último minuto.

equally *adjective* (*to share*) en partes iguales; **we divided it equally** lo dividimos en partes iguales.

equality *noun* igualdad *Fem.*

equator *noun* ecuador *Masc.*

equip *verb* equipar [17]; **well equipped for the walk** bien equipado para la marcha.

equipment *noun* 1 (*for sport*) artículos *Masc. plural* deportivos; 2 (*in office or lab*) material *Masc.*

equivalent *adjective* **to be equivalent to** ser [1] equivalente a.

error *noun* 1 (*in spelling or typing*) falta *Fem.*; **a spelling error** una falta de ortografía; 2 (*in maths or on a computer*) error *Masc.*

escalator *noun* escalera *Fem.* mecánica.

escape *noun* (*from prison*) fuga *Fem.*
escape *verb* 1 (*a person*) fugarse [28]; 2 (*an animal*) escaparse [17].

escort *noun* escolta *Fem.*; **a police escort** una escolta policial.

especially *adjective* especialmente.

essay *noun* redacción *Fem.*; **an essay on pollution** una redacción sobre la contaminación.

essential *adjective* esencial; **it's essential to reply quickly** es esencial responder rápidamente.

estate *noun* 1 (*a housing estate*) urbanización *Fem.*; 2 (*a big house and grounds*) propiedad *Fem.*

estate agent's *noun* agencia *Fem.* inmobiliaria.

estate car *noun* coche *Masc.* ranchera.

estimate *noun* 1 (*a quote for work*) presupuesto *Masc.*; 2 (*a rough guess*) cálculo *Masc.* aproximado.
estimate *verb* 1 calcular [17]; 2 **the estimated time of arrival** la hora prevista de llegada.

etc. *abbreviation* etc.

ethnic *adjective* étnico/étnica; **an ethnic minority** una minoría étnica.

EU *abbreviation* EU *Fem.*, Unión *Fem.* Europea.

euro *noun* euro *Masc.*; **the euro is divided into a hundred cents** el euro se divide en cien céntimos.

Europe *noun* Europa *Fem.*

European *noun* europeo *Masc.*, europea *Fem.*
European *adjective* europeo/europea.

a
b
c
d
e
f
g
h
i
j
k
l
m
n
o
p
q
r
s
t
u
v
w
x
y
z

a
b
c
d
e
f
g
h
i
j
k
l
m
n
o
p
q
r
s
t
u
v
w
x
y
z

European Union *noun* Unión *Fem.* Europea.

eurozone *noun* eurozona *Fem.*

evaporate *verb* evaporarse [17].

eve *noun* **Christmas Eve** Nochebuena *Fem.*; **New Year's Eve** Nochevieja *Fem.*.

even[1] *adverb* **1** incluso; **even I could do it** incluso yo podría hacerlo; **2** (*in comparisons*) **even more difficult** aún más difícil; **even faster** aún más rápido; **even more than** aún más que; **I liked the song even more than their last one** la canción me gustó aún más que la anterior; **3** (*in negative sentences or after 'without'*) ni siquiera; **even Lisa didn't like it** ni siquiera a Lisa le gustó; **without even asking** sin ni siquiera preguntar; **not even** ni siquiera; **I don't like animals, not even dogs** no me gustan los animales, ni siquiera los perros; **4 even if** incluso si; **even if they arrive** incluso si llegan; **5 even so** aun así; **even so, we had a good time** aun así lo pasamos bien; **6 even though** aunque.

even[2] *adjective* **1** (*a surface or layer*) plano/plana; **2** (*a number*) par; **six is an even number** seis es un número par; **3** (*with the same score*) igualado/igualada; **Lee and Tony are even** Lee y Tony están igualados.

evening *noun* **1** (*before dark*) tarde *Fem.* (*after dark*) noche *Fem.*; **this evening** (*before dark*) esta tarde (*after dark*) esta noche; **at six o'clock in the evening** a las seis de la tarde; **at ten in the evening** a las diez de la noche; **tomorrow evening** mañana por la tarde, mañana por la noche; **on Thursday evening** el jueves por la tarde, el jueves por la noche; **the evening before** la tarde anterior, la noche anterior; **every evening** cada tarde, cada noche; **good evening** buenas tardes, buenas noches; **I work in the evening(s)** trabajo por las noches; **2 the evening meal** la cena; **3** (*event*) velada *Fem.*; **an evening with Pavarotti** una velada con Pavarotti.

evening class *noun* clase *Fem.* nocturna.

event *noun* **1** (*a happening*) acontecimiento *Masc.*; **2** (*in athletics*) prueba *Fem.*; **track events** pruebas de atletismo.

eventful *adjective* lleno de incidentes.

eventually *adverb* finalmente.

ever *adverb* **1** (*at any time*) alguna vez; **have you ever been to Spain?** ¿has estado alguna vez en España?; **have you ever noticed that?** ¿lo notaste alguna vez?; **hardly ever** casi nunca; **no-one ever came** nunca vino nadie; **more slowly than ever** más despacio que nunca; **2** (*always*) siempre; **as cheerful as ever** tan contento como siempre; **the same as ever** como siempre; **3 ever since** desde entonces; **and it's been raining ever since** y ha estado lloviendo desde entonces.

every *adjective* **1** todos/todas; **every house has a garden** todas las casas tienen jardín; **every day** todos los días; **every Monday** todos los lunes; **I've seen every one of his films** he visto todas sus películas; **2** (*repetition*) cada; **every ten kilometres** cada diez kilómetros; **every time** cada vez; **3 every now and then** de vez en cuando; **every second day** un día sí y otro no.

everybody, **everyone** *pronoun* todo el mundo; **everybody knows that** ... todo el mundo sabe que ...; **everyone else** todos los demás.

everything *pronoun* todo; **everything's ready** está todo listo; **everything's fine** está todo bien; **everything else** todo lo demás; **everything you said** todo lo que dijiste.

everywhere *adverb* **there was mud everywhere** había barro por todas partes; **everywhere she went** a todos los sitios a los que fue; **everywhere else is closed** todos los demás sitios están cerrados.

evidently *adverb* obviamente.

evil *noun* mal *Masc.*
evil *adjective* malvado/malvada.

exact *adjective* exacto/exacta; **the exact amount** la cantidad exacta; **it's the exact opposite** es exactamente lo contrario.

exactly *adverb* exactamente; **they're exactly the same age** tienen exactamente la misma edad; **yes, exactly** exacto.

exaggerate *verb* exagerar [17].

exaggeration *noun* exageración *Fem.*

exam *noun* examen *Masc.*; **a history exam** un examen de historia; **to sit an exam** presentarse [17] a un examen; **to pass an exam** aprobar [24] un examen; **to fail an exam** suspender [18] un examen.

examination *noun* examen *Masc.*

examine *verb* examinar [17].

examiner *noun* examinador *Masc.*, examinadora *Fem.*

example *noun* ejemplo *Masc.*; **for example** por ejemplo; **to set a good example** dar [4] buen ejemplo.

excellent *adjective* excelente.

except *preposition* excepto; **except in March** excepto en marzo; **except Tuesdays** excepto los martes; **except when it rains** excepto cuando llueve.

exception *noun* excepción *Fem.*; **without exception** sin excepción; **with the exception of** con la excepción de.

exchange *noun* **1** (*of information or students*) intercambio *Masc.*; **an exchange visit** un viaje de intercambio; **2 in exchange for his help** a cambio de su ayuda.
exchange *verb* cambiar [17]; **can I exchange this shirt for a smaller one?** ¿puedo cambiar esta camisa por una más pequeña?

exchange rate *noun* tipo *Masc.* de cambio.

excited *adjective* **1** (*happy*) entusiasmado/entusiasmada; **they're really excited about the idea** están entusiasmados con la idea; **2** (*noisy, boisterous*)

a
b
c
d
e
f
g
h
i
j
k
l
m
n
o
p
q
r
s
t
u
v
w
x
y
z

a
b
c
d
e
f
g
h
i
j
k
l
m
n
o
p
q
r
s
t
u
v
w
x
y
z

alborotado/alborotada; **the children were too excited** los niños estaban demasiado alborotados; **3 to get excited** (*happy*) entusiasmarse [17] (*boisterous*) alborotarse [17]; **the dogs get excited when they hear the car** los perros se alborotan cuando oyen el coche.

excitement *noun* emoción *Fem.*

exciting *adjective* emocionante; **a really exciting film** una película realmente emocionante.

exclamation mark *noun* signo *Masc.* de admiración.

excursion *noun* excursión *Fem.*

excuse *noun* excusa *Fem.*; **Gary has a good excuse** Gary tiene una buena excusa; **that's no excuse** eso no es excusa; **to make excuses** poner [11] excusas.

excuse *verb* (*apologizing*) **excuse me!** ¡perdón!

exercise *noun* ejercicio *Masc.*; **a maths exercise** un ejercicio de matemáticas; **physical exercise** ejercicio físico.

exercise book *noun* cuaderno *Masc.*; **my Spanish exercise book** mi cuaderno de español.

exhausted *adjective* agotado/agotada.

exhaust fumes *noun* gases *Masc. plural* del tubo de escape.

exhaust (pipe) *noun* tubo *Masc.* de escape.

exhibition *noun* exposición *Fem.*; **the Cézanne exhibition** la exposición de Cézanne.

exist *verb* existir [19].

exit *noun* salida *Fem.*

expect *verb* **1** esperar [17] (*guests or a baby*); **we're expecting about thirty people** esperamos unas treinta personas; **2** esperarse [17] (*something to happen*); **I didn't expect that** no me esperaba eso; **I didn't expect it at all** no me lo esperaba en absoluto; **3** (*to suppose*) suponer [11]; **I expect you're tired** supongo que estarás cansado; **I expect she'll bring her boyfriend** supongo que traerá a su novio; **yes, I expect so** supongo que sí.

expedition *noun* expedición *Fem.*

expel *verb* **to be expelled** (*from school*) ser [1] expulsado.

expenses *noun* gastos *Masc. plural.*

expensive *adjective* caro/cara; **those shoes are too expensive for me** esos zapatos son demasiado caros para mí; **the most expensive hotels** los hoteles más caros.

experience *noun* experiencia *Fem.*

experienced *adjective* con experiencia.

experiment *noun* experimento *Masc.*; **to do an experiment** hacer [7] un experimento.

expert *noun* experto *Masc.*, experta *Fem.*; **he's a computer expert** es un experto en ordenadores.

expire *verb* caducar [31].

expiry date *noun* fecha *Fem.* de caducidad.

explain *verb* explicar [31].

explanation *noun* explicación *Fem.*

explode *verb* explotar [17].

explore *verb* explorar [17].

explosion *noun* explosión *Fem.*

export *verb* exportar [17].
export *noun* exportación *Fem.*;
wool is the most important export el artículo de exportación más importante es la lana.
export *verb* exportar [17]; **Russia exports a lot of timber and oil** Rusia exporta mucha madera y petróleo.

exposure *noun* (*of a film*) exposición *Fem.*; **a 24-exposure film** un carrete de veinticuatro fotos.

express *noun* (*a train*) rápido *Masc.*
express *verb* **1** expresar [17]; **2 to express yourself** expresarse [17].

expression *noun* expresión *Fem.*

extend *verb* ampliar [32] (*a building*).

extension *noun* **1** (*to a house*) ampliación *Fem.*; **2** (*telephone*) extensión *Fem.*; **can I have extension 2347 please?** ¿me puede poner con la extensión veintitrés cuarenta y siete, por favor? (*note that in spoken Spanish telephone numbers are usually said in pairs; this also applies to long numbers*).

extension lead *noun* alargador *Masc.*

extension number *noun* número *Masc.* de extensión.

extinct *adjective* extinto/extincta;
to become extinct extinguirse [50].

extinguish *verb* apagar [28].

extinguisher *noun* (*fire extinguisher*) extintor *Masc.*

extra *adjective, adverb* **1 they gave us some extra homework** nos dieron más deberes; **2 you have to pay extra** tiene que pagar un suplemento; **to charge extra for something** cobrar [17] un suplemento por algo; **wine is extra** el vino se cobra aparte; **at no extra charge** sin coste suplementario; **3 extra hot** super picante; **extra large** super grande.

extraordinary *adjective* extraordinario/extraordinaria.

extra-special *adjective* super especial.

extra time *noun* (*in football*) prórroga *Fem.*

extravagant *adjective* derrochador/derrochadora (*a person*).

extreme *noun* extremo *Masc.*; **to go to extremes** llevar [17] las cosas al extremo.
extreme *adjective* extremo/extrema.

extremely *adverb* **extremely difficult** dificilísimo; **extremely fast** rapidísimo.

eye *noun* ojo *Masc.*; **a girl with blue eyes** una niña con ojos azules; **shut your eyes!** ¡cierra los ojos!; ★**to keep an eye on something** vigilar [17] algo; ★**to make eyes at**

a
b
c
d
e
f
g
h
i
j
k
l
m
n
o
p
q
r
s
t
u
v
w
x
y
z

somebody hacerle [7] ojitos a alguien (*informal*).

eyebrow *noun* ceja *Fem.*

eyelash *noun* pestaña *Fem.*

eyelid *noun* párpado *Masc.*

eyeliner *noun* delineador *Masc.* de ojos.

eye make-up *noun* maquillaje *Masc.* de ojos.

eye shadow *noun* sombra *Fem.* de ojos.

eyesight *noun* vista *Fem.*

Ff

fabric *noun* tela *Fem.*

fabulous *adjective* fabuloso/fabulosa.

face *noun* **1** (*of a person*) cara *Fem.*; **on your face** en la cara; **2 to pull a face** hacer [7] muecas; **3** (*of a clock or watch*) esfera *Fem.*
face *verb* **1** (*a person*) enfrentarse [17] a; **2** (*to be opposite*) estar [2] frente a; **the hotel faces the sea** el hotel está frente al mar; **3 it faces south** está orientado hacia el sur; **4 I can't face going back** no soporto la idea de volver.

face cloth *noun* toalla *Fem.* de cara.

facilities *plural noun* **1 sports facilities** instalaciones *Fem. plural* deportivas; **2 the flat has cooking facilities** el piso tiene cocina.

fact *noun* hecho *Masc.*; **in fact** de hecho; **is that a fact?** ¿es eso cierto?

factory *noun* fábrica *Fem.*

fail *verb* **1** suspender [18] (*a test or exam*); **I failed my driving test** he suspendido el examen de conducir; **three students failed** tres estudiantes suspendieron; **2 to fail to do** no hacer; **he failed to contact us** no se puso en contacto con nosotros; ★**without fail** sin falta;; **ring me without fail** llámame sin falta.

failure *noun* **1** fracaso *Masc.*; **it was a terrible failure** fue un fracaso terrible; **2 a power failure** un apagón.

faint *adjective* **1 to feel faint** sentirse [14] mareado/mareada; **2** (*slight*) ligero/ligera; **a faint smell of gas** un ligero olor a gas; **I haven't the faintest idea** no tengo ni la más remota idea; **3** (*a voice or sound*) débil.
faint *verb* desmayarse [17]; **Lisa fainted** Lisa se desmayó.

fair *noun* feria *Fem.*
fair *adjective* **1** (*not unfair*) justo/justa; **it's not fair!** ¡no es justo!; **2** (*hair*) rubio/rubia; **he's fair-haired** tiene el pelo rubio; **3** (*skin*) blanco/blanca; **4** (*fairly good*) bastante bueno/buena.

fairground *noun* parque *Masc.* de atracciones.

fairly *adverb* (*quite*) bastante; **she's fairly happy** es bastante feliz.

fairy *noun* hada *Fem.* (*even though 'hada' is feminine, it takes 'el' and 'un' in the singular*).

fairy tale *noun* cuento *Masc.* de hadas.

faith *noun* **1** (*trust*) confianza *Fem.*; **to have faith in somebody** tener confianza en alguien; **2** (*religious belief*) fe *Fem.*

faithful *adjective* fiel.

faithfully *adverb* **yours faithfully** le saluda atentamente.

fall *noun* caída *Fem.*; **to have a fall** sufrir [19] una caída.
fall *verb* **1** caerse [34]; **mind, you'll fall** cuidado, te vas a caer; **Tony fell off his bike** Tony se cayó de la bici; **she fell downstairs** se cayó por las escaleras; **my jacket fell on the floor** mi chaqueta se cayó al suelo; **2** (*the temperature or prices*) bajar [17]; **it fell to minus eleven last night** la temperatura bajó a once grados bajo cero anoche.

false *adjective* falso/falsa; **a false passport** un pasaporte falso; **a false alarm** una falsa alarma.

false teeth *plural noun* dentadura *Fem.* (*singular*) postiza.

fame *noun* fama *Fem.*

familiar *adjective* familiar; **your face is familiar** tu cara me es familiar.

family *noun* familia *Fem.*; **a family of six** una familia de seis personas; **Ben's one of the family** Ben es uno de la familia; **the Bunting family** la familia Bunting.

family name *noun* apellido *Masc.*

famous *adjective* famoso/famosa.

fan *noun* **1** (*of a pop group*) fan *Masc./Fem.* (*informal*); **Sarah's an Oasis fan** Sarah es fan de Oasis; **2** (*of a team*) hincha *Masc./Fem.*; **Martin's a Chelsea fan** Martin es hincha del Chelsea; **3** (*electric, for cooling*) ventilador *Masc.*; **4** (*that you hold in your hand*) abanico *Masc.*

fanatic *noun* fanático *Masc.*, fanática *Fem.*

fancy *noun* **the picture took his fancy** se encaprichó del cuadro. **fancy** *adjective* (*equipment*) sofisticado/sofisticada, (*hotel*) de lujo.
fancy *verb* **1** (*to want*) **do you fancy a coffee?** ¿te apetece un café?; **I don't fancy going out** no me apetece salir; **2 I really fancy him** me gusta mucho; **3 (just) fancy that!** ¡imagínate!; **fancy you being here!** ¡qué casualidad que estés aquí!.

fancy dress *noun* disfraz *Masc.*; **in fancy dress** disfrazado/disfrazada; **a fancy-dress party** una fiesta de disfraces.

fantastic *adjective* estupendo/ estupenda (*informal*); **really? that's fantastic!** ¿de verdad?¡ eso es estupendo!; **a fantastic holiday** unas vacaciones estupendas.

far *adverb, adjective* **1** lejos; **it's not far** no está lejos; **is it far to Cordoba?** ¿está muy lejos Córdoba?; **how far is it to Granada?** ¿a qué distancia está Granada?; **he took us as far as Bilbao** nos llevó hasta Bilbao; **2 by far** con mucho; **the prettiest by far** es con mucho la más bonita; **3** (*much*) mucho; **far better** mucho mejor; **far faster** mucho más rápido; **4 far too many people** demasiada gente; **far too much noise** demasiado ruido; **5 so far** hasta ahora; **so far everything's going well** hasta ahora todo va bien; **as far as I know** que yo sepa.

fare *noun* precio *Masc.* del billete; **half fare** medio billete *Masc.*; **full fare** billete *Masc.* entero; **the return fare to Barcelona** el billete de ida y vuelta a Barcelona.

Far East *noun* Lejano Oriente *Masc.*

farm *noun* granja *Fem.*

farmer *noun* agricultor *Masc.*, agricultora *Fem.*

farmhouse *noun* casa *Fem.* de labranza.

farming *noun* agricultura *Fem.*

farthest *adjective* más lejano/más lejana; **the farthest hill** la colina más lejana.
farthest *pronoun* lo más lejos; **the farthest we went** lo más lejos que fuimos aquel día.

fascinating *adjective* fascinante.

fashion *noun* moda *Fem.*; **in fashion** de moda; **out of fashion** pasado/pasada de moda.

fashionable *adjective* de moda.

fashion model *noun* modelo *Masc./Fem.*

fashion show *noun* desfile *Masc.* de modas.

fast *adjective* **1** rápido/rápida; **a fast car** un coche rápido; **2 my watch is fast** mi reloj adelanta; **you're ten minutes fast** vas diez

minutos adelantado.
fast *adverb* **1** rápido; **she swims very fast** nada muy rápido; **2 to be fast asleep** estar [2] profundamente dormido.

fast food *noun* comida *Fem.* rápida.

fat *noun* grasa *Fem.*
fat *adjective* gordo/gorda; **a fat man** un hombre gordo; **to get fat** engordar [17].

fatal *adjective* (*accident*) fatal.

father *noun* padre *Masc.*; **my father's office** la oficina de mi padre.

Father Christmas *noun* Papá *Masc.* Noel.

father-in-law *noun* suegro *Masc.*

father's day *noun* día *Masc.* del padre.

fault *noun* **1** (*responsibility*) culpa *Fem.*; **it's Steve's fault** es culpa de Steve; **it's not my fault** no es culpa mía; **2** (*in tennis*) falta *Fem.*

favour *noun* **1** (*a kindness*) favor *Masc.*; **to do somebody a favour** hacerle [7] un favor a alguien; **can you do me a favour?** ¿me haces un favor?; **to ask a favour of somebody** pedirle [57] un favor a alguien; **2 to be in favour of something** estar [2] a favor de algo.

favourite *adjective* favorito/favorita; **my favourite band** mi grupo favorito.

fax *noun* fax *Masc.*; **a fax machine** un fax.

fear *noun* miedo *Masc.*
fear *verb* temer [18].

feather *noun* pluma *Fem.*

feature *noun* **1** (*of your face*) rasgo *Masc.*; **to have delicate features** tener [9] rasgos delicados; **2** (*of a machine, product, etc.*) característica *Fem.*

February *noun* febrero *Masc.*; **in February** en febrero.

fed up *adjective* **I'm fed up** estoy harto/harta (*informal*); **I'm fed up with working every day** estoy harta de trabajar todos los días.

feed *verb* dar [4] de comer a; **have you fed the dog?** ¿has dado de comer al perro?

feel *verb* **1** sentirse [14]; **I feel tired** me siento cansada; **I don't feel well** no me siento bien; **2** sentir [14]; **I didn't feel a thing** no sentí nada; **3 to feel afraid** tener [9] miedo; **to feel cold** tener [9] frío; **to feel thirsty** tener [9] sed; **4 I feel like some chocolate** me apetece un poco de chocolate; **do you feel like a walk?** ¿te apetece dar un paseo?; **I don't feel like it** no me apetece; **5 to feel like doing** tener [9] ganas de hacer; **I feel like going to the cinema** tengo ganas de ir al cine; **6** (*touch*) tocar [31].

feeling *noun* **1** (*in your mind*) sentimiento *Masc.*; **a feeling of embarrassment** un sentimiento de vergüenza; **to show your feelings** de mostrar los sentimientos; **to hurt somebody's feelings** herir [14] los sentimientos de alguien; **2** (*in your body*) sensación *Fem.*; **a dizzy feeling** una sensación de mareo; **3** (*impression*) impresión *Fem.*; **I**

have the feeling James doesn't like me tengo la impresión de que no le caigo bien a James.

felt-tip (pen) *noun* rotulador *Masc.*

female *noun* (*animal*) hembra *Fem.*
female *adjective* **1** femenino/femenina (*person, population*); **2** hembra (*animal, insect*).

feminine *adjective* femenino/femenina.

feminist *noun, adjective* feminista *Masc./Fem.*

fence *noun* valla *Fem.*

fern *noun* helecho *Masc.*

ferry *noun* ferry *Masc.*

fetch *verb* ir [8] a por; **Tom's fetching the children** Tom ha ido a por los niños; **fetch me the other knife!** ¡vete a por el otro cuchillo!

fever *noun* fiebre *Fem.*

few *adjective, pronoun* **1** pocos/pocas; **few people think that** ... pocos piensan que ...; **2 a few** (*followed by a noun*) algunos/algunas; **a few weeks earlier** algunas semanas antes; **in a few minutes** dentro de algunos minutos; **3 a few** (*by itself*) unos cuantos/unas cuantas; **have you any tomatoes? we want a few for the salad** ¿tienes tomates? queremos unos cuantos para la ensalada; **a few more books** unos cuantos libros más; **4 quite a few** bastantes; **there were quite a few questions** hubo bastantes preguntas.

fewer *adjective* menos; **there are fewer tourists this year** hay menos

a
b
c
d
e
f
g
h
i
j
k
l
m
n
o
p
q
r
s
t
u
v
w
x
y
z

turistas este año; **fewer than six** menos de seis.

fiancé *noun* prometido *Masc.*

fiancée *noun* prometida *Fem.*

fiction *noun* ficción *Fem.*

field *noun* campo *Masc.*; **a field of wheat** un campo de trigo; **a football field** un campo de fútbol.

fifteen *number* quince *Masc.*; **Lara's fifteen** Lara tiene quince años.

fifth *noun* **1** (*fraction*) **a fifth** una quinta parte; **2 the fifth of January** el cinco de enero.
fifth *adjective* quinto/quinta; **on the fifth floor** en la quinta planta.

fifties *plural noun* **the fifties** los años cincuenta; **in the fifties** en los años cincuenta.

fifty *number* cincuenta *Masc.*; **she's fifty** tiene cincuenta años; **fifty-five** cincuenta y cinco.

fig *noun* higo *Masc.*

fight *noun* **1** (*a scuffle or in boxing*) pelea *Fem.*; **2** (*in war or against illness or poverty*) lucha *Fem.*
fight *verb* **1** (*in war or against poverty or a disease*) luchar [17]; **2** (*to quarrel*) pelear [17]; **they're always fighting** siempre se están peleando.

figure *noun* **1** (*number*) cifra *Fem.*; **a four-figure number** un número de cuatro cifras; **2** (*body shape*) figura *Fem.*; **3** (*a person*) personaje *Masc.*; **a public figure** un personaje público.

file *noun* **1** (*for records of a person or case*) archivo *Masc.*; **2** (*in computer system*) fichero *Masc.*; **3** (*ring binder*) archivador *Masc.*; **4** (*cardboard folder for documents*)

carpeta *Fem.*; **5 a nail file** una lima.
file *verb* **1** archivar [17] (*documents*); **2 to file your nails** limarse [17] las uñas.

fill *verb* llenar [17]; **she filled my glass** me llenó el vaso.
• **to fill in** rellenar [17] (*a form*).

filling *noun* **1** (*of pie*) relleno *Masc.*; **2** (*in tooth*) empaste *Masc.*

film *noun* **1** (*in a cinema*) película *Fem.*; **shall we go and see a film?** ¿vamos a ver una película?; **the new film about Picasso** la nueva película sobre Picasso; **2** (*for a camera*) carrete *Masc.* de fotos; **a 24-exposure colour film** un carrete de color de veinticuatro fotos.

film star *noun* estrella *Fem.* de cine.

filthy *adjective* asqueroso/asquerosa (*informal*).

final *noun* (*in sport*) final *Fem.*
final *adjective* **1** (*definite*) final; **the final result** el resultado final; **2** (*last*) último/última; **the final instalment** el último plazo.

finally *adverb* finalmente.

find *verb* encontrar [24]; **did you find your passport?** ¿has encontrado tu pasaporte?; **I can't find my keys** no puedo encontrar mis llaves.
• **to find out 1** (*to enquire*) informarse [17]; **I don't know, I'll find out** no lo sé, me informaré; **2 to find something out** descubrir [46] algo (*the facts or an answer*); **when Lucy found out the truth** cuando Lucy se enteró de la verdad.

fine *noun* multa *Fem.*

fine *adjective* **1** bien; **'how are you?' – 'fine, thanks'** ¿cómo estás? – 'bien, gracias'; **ten o'clock? yes, that's fine** ¿a las diez? sí, está bien; **Friday will be fine** el viernes está bien; **2** (*very good*) muy bueno/buena; **she's a fine athlete** es muy buena atleta; **3** (*weather or a day;*) bueno/buena; **if it's fine** si hace buen tiempo; **4** (*not coarse or thick*) fino/fina; **in fine wool** de lana fina.

finely *adjective* (*chopped or grated*) muy fino/fina.

finger *noun* dedo *Masc.*; ⋆ **I'll keep my fingers crossed for you** te deseo suerte.

fingernail *noun* uña *Fem.*

finish *noun* **1** (*end*) final *Masc.*; **2** (*in a race*) llegada *Fem.*

finish *verb* **1** terminar [17]; **wait, I haven't finished** espera, no he terminado; **when does school finish?** ¿cuándo termina el colegio?; **have you finished the book?** ¿has terminado el libro?; **2 to finish doing** terminar [17] de hacer; **have you finished telephoning?** ¿has terminado de llamar por teléfono?.

• **to finish with** terminar [17] con; **have you finished with the computer?** ¿has terminado con el ordenador?.

finishing line *noun* meta *Fem.*

Finland *noun* Finlandia *Fem.*

Finn *noun* Finlandés *Masc.*, Finlandesa *Fem.*

Finnish *noun* (*the language*) finlandés *Masc.*

Finnish *adjective* finlandés/finlandesa.

fire *noun* **1** (*in a grate*) fuego *Masc.*; **to light the fire** encender [36] el fuego; **2** (*accidental*) incendio *Masc.*; **3 to catch fire** prenderse [18] fuego; **to be on fire** estar [2] ardiendo.

fire *verb* (*to shoot*) disparar [17]; **to fire at somebody** disparar a alguien.

fire alarm *noun* alarma *Fem.* contra incendios.

fire brigade *noun* cuerpo *Masc.* de bomberos.

fire engine *noun* coche *Masc.* de bomberos.

fire escape *noun* escalera *Fem.* de incendios.

fire extinguisher *noun* extintor *Masc.*

firefighter *noun* bombero *Masc./Fem.*

fireplace *noun* chimenea *Fem.*

fire station *noun* estación *Fem.* de bomberos.

fireworks *plural noun* fuegos *Masc. plural* artificiales.

firm *noun* (*business*) empresa *Fem.*

firm *adjective* firme.

first *noun* **the first of May** el primero de mayo.

first *pronoun, adjective, adverb* **1** primero/primera; **Susan's the first** Susan es la primera; **the first of May** el primero de Mayo; **for the first time** por primera vez; **Christy got here first** Christy llegó aquí la primera; **Ben came first in the 200 metres** Ben llegó el primero en los

419

doscientos metros; **2** (*to begin with*) primero; **first, I'm going to make some tea** primero voy a hacer té; **first of all** en primer lugar; **3 at first** al principio; **at first he didn't want to** al principio no quería.

first aid *noun* primeros auxilios *Masc. plural*.

first aid kit *noun* botiquín *Masc.* de primeros auxilios.

first class *adjective, adverb* de primera (*a ticket, carriage, or hotel*); **a first-class compartment** un compartimento de primera; **he always travels first class** siempre viaja en primera.

first floor *noun* primera planta *Fem.*; **on the first floor** en la primera planta.

firstly *adverb* en primer lugar.

first name *noun* nombre *Masc.* de pila.

fir tree *noun* abeto *Masc.*

fish *noun* **1** (*as a meal*) pescado *Masc.*; **do you like fish?** ¿te gusta el pescado?; **2** (*in the sea*) pez *Masc.* (*plural* peces).
fish *verb* pescar [31]; **Dad was fishing for trout** papá estaba pescando truchas.

fish and chips *noun* pescado *Masc.* con patatas fritas.

fisherman *noun* pescador *Masc.*

fishing *noun* pesca *Fem.*; **fishing is my favourite sport** la pesca es mi deporte favorito; **I love fishing** me encanta pescar; **to go fishing** ir a pescar.

fishing rod *noun* caña *Fem.* de pescar.

fishing tackle *noun* aparejos *Masc. plural* de pesca.

fist *noun* puño *Masc.*

fit *noun* ataque *Masc.*; **an epileptic fit** un ataque epiléptico; **I had a fit** me dio un ataque; **your dad'll have a fit when he sees your hair!** ¡a tu padre le va a dar un ataque cuando te vea el pelo!
fit *adjective* (*healthy*) en forma; **I feel really fit** me siento muy en forma; **to keep fit** mantenerse [9] en forma.
fit *verb* **1** (*a garment or shoes*) estar [2] bien (*a person*); **this skirt doesn't fit me** esta falda no me está bien; **does it fit you okay?** ¿te está bien?; **2** (*go into*) entrar [17] en; **will my cases all fit in the car?** ¿entrarán todas mis maletas en el coche?; **3** (*install*) poner [11].

fitness *noun* estado *Masc.*, físico; **fitness training** entrenamiento *Masc.*

fitted carpet *noun* moqueta *Fem.*

five *number* cinco *Masc.*; **Oskar's five** Oskar tiene cinco años; **it's five o'clock** son las cinco.

fix *verb* **1** (*repair*) arreglar [17]; **Mum's fixed the computer** mamá ha arreglado el ordenador; **2** (*to decide on*) fijar [17]; **to fix a date** fijar [17] una fecha; **at a fixed price** a un precio fijo; **3** preparar [17] (*a meal*).

fizzy *adjective* con gas; **fizzy water** agua con gas.

flag *noun* bandera *Fem.*

flame *noun* llama *Fem.*

flan *noun* 1 (*savoury*) quiche *Masc.*; **an onion flan** un quiche de cebolla; 2 (*sweet*) tarta *Fem.*

flap *verb* (*a flag or sail*) agitarse [17].

flash *noun* 1 **a flash of lightning** un relámpago; 2 (*of light*) destello *Masc.*; 3 **to do something in a flash** hacer [7] algo a la velocidad del rayo; 4 (*on a camera*) flash *Masc.*
flash *verb* 1 (*a light*) destellar [17]; 2 **to flash by or past** pasar [17] como un rayo; 3 **to flash your headlights** hacer [7] señas con los faros del coche.

flask *n* 1 (*insulated bottle*) termo *Masc.*; 2 (*container*) frasco *Masc.*

flat *noun* piso *Masc.*; **a third-floor flat** un piso en la tercera planta.
flat *adjective* 1 plano/plana; **flat shoes** zapatos planos; **a flat surface** una superficie plana; 2 (*landscape*) llano/llana; 3 **a flat tyre** una rueda pinchada.

flatmate *noun* compañero *Masc.*, compañera *Fem.* de piso.

flavour *noun* sabor *Masc.*; **the sauce had no flavour** la salsa no tenía sabor; **what flavour of ice cream would you like?** ¿de qué sabor quieres el helado?
flavour *verb* sazonar [17]; **vanilla-flavoured** con sabor a vainilla.

flea *noun* pulga *Fem.*

fleet *n* 1 (*of ships*) flota *Fem.*; 2 (*of vehicles*) parque *Masc.* móvil.

flight *noun* 1 vuelo *Masc.*; **a charter flight** un vuelo chárter; **the flight**

from Moscow is delayed el vuelo procedente de Moscú lleva retraso; 2 **a flight of stairs** un tramo de escalera; **four flights of stairs** cuatro tramos de escalera.

flight attendant *noun* auxiliar *Masc./Fem.* de vuelo.

fling *verb* lanzar [22].

flipper *noun* (*for a swimmer*) aleta *Fem.*

flirt *verb* flirtear [17].

float *verb* flotar [17].

flood *noun* 1 (*of water*) inundación *Fem.*; **the floods in the south** las inundaciones del sur; 2 (*of letters or complaints*) avalancha *Fem.*; 3 **to be in floods of tears** estar [2] llorando a mares (*literally: to be weeping oceans*).
flood *verb* inundar [17].

floodlight *noun* foco *Masc.*

floor *noun* 1 suelo *Masc.*; **on the floor** en el suelo; **to sweep the floor** barrer [18]; 2 (*a storey*) planta *Fem.*; **on the second floor** en la segunda planta.

floppy disk *noun* disquete *Masc.*

florist *noun* florista *Masc./Fem.*

florist's *noun* floristería *Fem.*

flour *noun* harina *Fem.*

flower *noun* flor *Fem.*; **a bunch of flowers** un ramo de flores.
flower *verb* florecer [35].

flu *noun* gripe *Fem.*; **to have flu** tener [9] la gripe.

fluent *adjective* **she speaks fluent Italian** habla italiano con fluidez.

fluently *adverb* con fluidez.

a

b

c

d

e

f

g

h

i

j

k

l

m

n

o

p

q

r

s

t

u

v

w

x

y

z

fluid noun fluido Masc.

flush verb 1 (to go red) enrojecer [35]; 2 **to flush the lavatory** tirar [17] de la cadena.

flute noun flauta Fem.; **to play the flute** tocar [30] la flauta.

fly noun mosca Fem.

fly verb 1 (a bird, an insect, or a plane) volar [24]; 2 (in a plane) ir [8] en avión; **we flew to Edinburgh** fuimos en avión a Edimburgo; **we flew from Gatwick** salimos desde Gatwick; 3 hacer [7] volar (a kite); 4 (to pass quickly) (time) pasar [17] volando.

foam noun 1 (foam rubber) goma Fem. espuma; **a foam mattress** un colchón de goma espuma; 2 (on a drink) espuma Fem.

focus noun **to be in focus** estar [2] enfocado; **to be out of focus** estar [2] desenfocado.

focus verb enfocar [31] (a camera).

fog noun niebla Fem.

foggy adjective **it was foggy** había niebla; **a foggy day** un día de niebla.

foil noun (kitchen foil) papel Masc. de aluminio.

fold noun doblez Masc.

fold verb doblar [17]; **to fold something up** doblar algo.

folder noun carpeta Fem.

follow verb seguir [64]; **follow me!** ¡sígueme!; **followed by a dinner** seguido de una cena; **do you follow me?** ¿me sigues?

following adjective siguiente; **the following year** el año siguiente.

fond adjective 1 **to be fond of somebody** tenerle [9] cariño a alguien; **I'm very fond of him** le tengo mucho cariño; 2 **I'm fond of dogs** me gustan los perros.

food noun comida Fem.; **to buy food** comprar [17] comida; **I like Italian food** me gusta la comida italiana.

food poisoning n intoxicación Fem. alimenticia.

fool noun idiota Masc./Fem.

foot noun 1 pie Masc.; **he stepped on my foot** me pisó el pie; **Lucy came on foot** Lucy vino a pie; **at the foot of the stairs** al pie de las escaleras; 2 (of animal) pata Fem.

football noun 1 (the game) fútbol Masc.; **to play football** jugar [27] al fútbol; 2 (ball) balón Masc. de fútbol.

footballer noun futbolista Masc./Fem.

footpath noun sendero Masc.

for preposition 1 para; **a present for my mother** un regalo para mi madre; **petrol for the car** gasolina para el coche; **sausages for lunch** salchichas para comer; **it's for cleaning** es para limpiar; **what's it for?** ¿para qué es?; 2 (in time expressions in the past or future, 'for' is not usually translated) **I studied Spanish for four years** estudié español cuatro años; **I'll be away for four days** estaré fuera cuatro días; **I've been waiting here for an hour** llevo esperando aquí una hora; **my brother's been living in London for three years** mi hermano lleva tres años viviendo en Londres; 3 (cost or amount) por; **I sold my**

bike for fifty pounds vendí mi bicicleta por cincuenta libras; **4 what's the Spanish for 'bee'?** ¿cómo se dice 'bee' en español?.

forbid *verb* prohibir [58]; **to forbid somebody to do something** prohibir [58] a alguien hacer algo; **I forbid you to go out** te prohíbo salir.

forbidden *adjective* prohibido/ prohibida.

force *noun* fuerza *Fem.*
force *verb* forzar [26]; **to force somebody to do** forzar a alguien a hacer.

forecast *noun* (*weather forecast*) pronóstico *Masc.*

forehead *noun* frente *Fem.*

foreign *adjective* extranjero/ extranjera; **in a foreign country** en un país extranjero.

foreigner *noun* extranjero *Masc.*, extranjera *Fem.*

forest *noun* bosque *Masc.*

forever *adverb* **1** para siempre; **I'd like to stay here forever** me gustaría quedarme aquí para siempre; **2** (*non-stop*) siempre; **he's forever asking questions** siempre está preguntando.

forgery *noun* falsificación *Fem.*

forget *verb* olvidarse [17]; **I forget his name** se me ha olvidado su nombre; **we've forgotten the bread!** ¡se nos ha olvidado el pan!; **to forget to do** olvidarse [17] de hacer; **I forgot to phone** se me olvidó llamar por teléfono; **to forget about something** olvidarse [17] de algo.

forgetful *adjective* olvidadizo/ olvidadiza.

forgive *verb* perdonar [17]; **I forgave him** lo perdoné; **to forgive somebody for doing** perdonar [17] a alguien que (*followed by subjunctive*); **I forgave her for losing my ring** la perdoné por perderme el anillo.

fork *noun* tenedor *Masc.*

form *noun* **1** formulario *Masc.*; **to fill in a form** rellenar [17] un formulario; **2** (*shape or kind*) forma *Fem.*; **in the form of** bajo forma de; **3 to be on form** estar [2] en forma; **4** (*school class*) clase *Fem.*; **5** (*school year*) curso *Masc.*
form *verb* formar [17].

formal *adjective* formal (*invitation, event, complaint, etc*).

former *adjective* antiguo/antigua (*goes before the noun*); **a former pupil** un antiguo alumno.

formula *noun* fórmula *Fem.*

fortnight *noun* quince días *Masc. plural*; **we're going to Spain for a fortnight** vamos quince días a España.

fortress *noun* fortaleza *Fem.*

fortune *noun* fortuna *Fem.*; **to make a fortune** hacer [7] una fortuna.

fortunate *adjective* afortunado/ afortunada.

fortunately *adverb* afortunadamente.

forty *number* cuarenta *Masc.*; **he's forty** tiene cuarenta años; **forty-five** cuarenta y cinco.

a

forward *noun* (*in sport*) delantero *Masc./Fem.*
forward *adverb* **a seat further forward** un asiento de más adelante; **to move forward** ir [8] hacia adelante.

b

c

d

foster child *noun* hijo *Masc.* acogido, hija *Masc.* acogida.

e

f

foster family *noun* familia *Fem.* de acogida.

g

foul *noun* (*in sport*) falta *Fem.*
foul *adjective* asqueroso/asquerosa (*smell or taste*); **the weather's foul** el tiempo es horroroso.

h

i

fountain *noun* fuente *Fem.*

j

fountain pen *noun* pluma *Fem.*

k

four *number* cuatro *Masc.*; **Simon's four** Simon tiene cuatro años; **it's four o'clock** son las cuatro.

l

m

fourteen *number* catorce *Masc.*; **Susie's fourteen** Susie tiene catorce años.

n

o

fourth *noun* **1** (*fraction*) **a fourth** un cuarto; **2 the fourth of July** el cuatro de julio.
fourth *adjective* cuarto/cuarta; **on the fourth floor** en la cuarta planta.

p

q

r

fox *noun* zorro *Masc.*

s

fracture *noun* fractura *Fem.*

t

fragile *adjective* frágil.

u

frame *noun* (*of picture or photograph*) marco *Masc.*

v

France *noun* Francia *Fem.*

w

frantic *adjective* **1** (*desperate*) desesperado/desesperada (*efforts or a search*); **2** (*very upset*) **Mum was frantic with worry** mamá estaba muerta de preocupación.

x

y

z

freckle *noun* peca *Fem.*

free *adjective* **1** (*when you don't pay*) gratis; **the bus is free** el autobús es gratis; **a free ticket** un billete gratis; **2** (*not occupied*) libre; **are you free on Thursday?** ¿estás libre el jueves?; **3 sugar-free** sin azúcar; **lead-free** sin plomo.
free *verb* **1** (*a person*) poner [11] en libertad; **2** (*an animal*) soltar [24].

free kick *noun* tiro *Masc.* libre.

freedom *noun* libertad *Fem.*

free gift *noun* regalo *Masc.*

freeze *verb* **1** (*in a freezer*) congelar [17]; **frozen peas** guisantes congelados; **2** (*in cold weather*) helarse [29] (*person or ground*).

freezer *noun* congelador *Masc.*

freezing *noun* **three degrees below freezing** tres grados bajo cero.
freezing *adjective* **I'm freezing** ¡estoy helado! (*informal*); **it's freezing outside!** ¡fuera hace un frío que pela! (*informal*).

French *noun* **1** (*the language*) francés *Masc.*; **2** (*the people*) **the French** los franceses.
French *adjective* francés/francesa.

French beans *plural noun* judías *Fem. plural* verdes.

French fries *plural noun* patatas *Fem. plural* fritas.

Frenchman *noun* francés *Masc.*

French stick *noun* baguette *Fem.*

French window *noun* cristalera *Fem.*

Frenchwoman *noun* francesa *Fem.*

frequently *noun* frecuentemente, a menudo.

fresh *adjective* fresco/fresca; **fresh eggs** huevos frescos; **I'm going out for some fresh air** voy fuera a tomar un poco el aire.

Friday *noun* viernes *Masc.* (*plural* viernes); **last Friday** el pasado viernes; **on Friday** el viernes; **I'll phone you on Friday evening** te llamaré el viernes por la tarde; **on Fridays** los viernes; **closed on Fridays** cerrado los viernes; **every Friday** cada viernes; **Good Friday** Viernes Santo.

fridge *noun* nevera *Fem.*; **put it in the fridge** ponlo en la nevera.

friend *noun* amigo *Masc.*, amiga *Fem.*; **a friend of mine** un amigo mío/una amiga mía; **to make friends** hacer [7] amigos; **he made friends with Danny** se hizo amigo de Danny.

friendly *adjective* **1** (*a person*) simpático/simpática; **2** (*a letter or gesture*) amable.

friendship *noun* amistad *Fem.*

fries *plural noun* patatas *Fem. plural* fritas.

fright *noun* susto *Masc.*; **to get a fright** asustarse [17]; **to give somebody a fright** asustar [17] a alguien; **you gave me a fright!** ¡me has asustado!

frighten *verb* asustar [17].

frightened *adjective* **to be frightened** estar [2] asustado/ asustada; **I'm frightened of asking her** me da miedo preguntarle; **Martin's frightened of snakes** a Martin le dan miedo las serpientes.

frightening *adjective* espantoso/ espantosa.

fringe *noun* (*of hair*) flequillo *Masc.*.

frog *noun* rana *Fem.*

from *preposition* **1** de; **a letter from Tom** una carta de Tom; **100 metres from the cinema** a cien metros del cine; **he comes from Dublin** es de Dublín; **from seven o'clock onwards** de las siete en adelante; **2 from ... to ...** de ... a ...; **from Monday to Friday** de lunes a viernes; **the train from London to Liverpool** el tren de Londres a Liverpool; **from here to the wall** de aquí a la pared; **3** (*starting from*) desde; **tickets from ten pounds** entradas desde diez libras; **from today** desde hoy; **4 two years from now** dentro de dos años; **from then on** a partir de entonces.

front *noun* **1** (*of a car, train, envelope, or queue*) parte *Fem.* de delante; **sitting in the front** sentado en la parte de delante; **the address is on the front** las señas están en la parte de delante; **from the front** por delante; **2** (*of a building*) fachada *Fem.*; **3** (*of a garment*) delantera *Masc.*; **4 the front of the class** el frente de la clase; **5 in front of** delante de; **in front of the TV** delante de la televisión; **in front of me** delante de mí.

front *adjective* **1** delantero/ delantera; **the front seat** (*of a car*) el

a
b
c
d
e

f

g
h
i
j
k
l
m
n
o
p
q
r
s
t
u
v
w
x
y
z

asiento delantero; **2 in the front row** en la fila de delante.

front door *noun* puerta *Fem.* de la calle.

frontier *noun* frontera *Fem.*

frost *noun* helada *Fem.*

frosty *adjective* **1 it was frosty this morning** había helada esta mañana; **2** cubierto/cubierta de escarcha (*windscreen, grass, etc*).

frown *verb* fruncir [66] el ceño.

frozen *adjective* (*in a freezer*) congelado/congelada; **a frozen pizza** una pizza congelada.

fruit *noun* fruta *Fem.*; **fruit juice** zumo *Masc.* de fruta.

fruit salad *noun* macedonia *Fem.* de frutas.

frustrating *adjective* frustrante.

fry *verb* freír [53]; **we fried the fish** freímos el pescado; **a fried egg** un huevo frito.

frying pan *noun* sartén *Fem.*

fuel *noun* (*for a vehicle or plane*) combustible *Masc.*

full *adjective* **1** lleno/llena; **this glass is full** este vaso está lleno; **the train was full of tourists** el tren estaba lleno de turistas; **I'm full** estoy lleno; **2** completo/completa (*a hotel or flight*); **3** (*top*) **at full speed** a toda velocidad; **at full volume** a todo volumen; **4** (*complete*) todo/toda; **the full story** toda la historia; **5 to write your name out in full** escribir [52] su nombre completo.

full stop *noun* punto *Masc.*

full-time *adjective* a tiempo completo *Masc.*; **a full-time job** un trabajo a tiempo completo.
full time *noun* final *Masc.* de partido.

fully *adjective* completamente.

fun *noun* **to have fun** divertirse [14]; **have fun!** ¡que te diviertas!; **we had fun catching the ponies** nos divertimos atrapando a los poneys; **skiing is fun** esquiar es divertido; **I do it for fun** lo hago para divertirme; **to make fun of somebody** reírse [61] de alguien.

funds *noun* fondos *Masc. plural.*

funeral *noun* **1** (*ceremony*) funeral *Masc.*; **2** (*burial*) entierro *Masc.*

funfair *noun* feria *Fem.*

funny *adjective* **1** (*when you laugh*) gracioso/graciosa; **how funny you are!** ¡qué gracioso eres!; **a funny story** una historia graciosa; **2** (*strange*) raro; **that's funny, I'm sure I paid** qué raro, estoy seguro de que pagué; **a funny noise** un ruido raro.

fur *noun* **1** (*on an animal*) pelaje *Masc.*; **2** (*for a coat*) piel *Fem.*; **a fur coat** un abrigo de piel.

furious *adjective* furioso/furiosa; **she was furious with Steve** estaba furiosa con Steve.

furniture *noun* muebles *Masc. plural*; **to buy some furniture** comprar muebles; **a piece of furniture** un mueble.

further *adverb* **further than the station** más allá de la estación; **ten kilometres further on** diez kilómetros más adelante; **further forward** más adelante; **further back** más atrás; **further in** más adentro.

fuse *noun* fusible *Masc.*

fuss *noun* escándalo *Masc.*; **to make a fuss** montar [17] un escándalo; **to make a fuss about the bill** montar [17] un escándalo a causa de la factura.

fussy *adjective* **1** (*about how things are done*) quisquilloso/quisquillosa; **to be fussy about something** ser [1] muy quisquilloso/quisquillosa para algo; **2** (*about food*) maniático/maniática.**to be fussy about food** ser [1] muy maniático/maniática para la comida.

future *noun* futuro *Masc.*; **in the future** en el futuro; **in future** en el futuro; **in future, ask me first** en el futuro, pregúntame antes.

Gg

gadget *noun* aparato *Masc.*

gain *verb* ganar [17]; **in order to gain time** para ganar tiempo; **to gain weight** ganar peso.

gale *noun* vendaval *Masc.*

Galicia *noun* Galicia *Fem.*

Galician *noun* **1** (*the language*) gallego *Masc.*; **2** (*person*) gallego *Masc.*, gallega *Fem.*

Galician *adjective* gallego/gallega.

galaxy *noun* galaxia *Fem.*

gallery *noun* **an art gallery** (*public*) un museo de pintura (*private*) una galería de arte.

gambling *noun* juego *Masc.*

game *noun* **1** juego *Masc.*; **a board game** un juego de mesa; (*to be good at games*) **Jack's very good at games** Jack es muy buen deportista; **2 a game of** una partida de; **a game of cards** una partida de cartas; **to play cards** jugar [27] a las cartas; **3** partido *Masc.*; **a game of football** un partido de fútbol.

gang *noun* **1** panda *Fem.* (*of friends*); **all the gang were there** toda la panda estaba allí; **2** banda *Fem.* (*of criminals*).

gangster *noun* gángster *Masc./Fem.*

gap *noun* **1** (*hole*) hueco *Masc.*; **2** (*in time*) intervalo *Masc.*; **a two-year gap** un intervalo de dos años; **3 an age gap** una diferencia de edad.

gap year *noun* año *Masc.* libre antes de entrar a la universidad.

garage *noun* garaje *Masc.*

garden *noun* jardín *Masc.*

gardener *noun* jardinero *Masc.*, jardinera *Fem.*; **he's a gardener** es jardinero.

gardening *noun* jardinería *Fem.*

garlic *noun* ajo *Masc.*

garment *noun* prenda *Fem.*

gas *noun* gas *Masc.*

gas cooker *noun* cocina *Fem.* de gas.

gas fire *noun* estufa *Fem.* de gas.

a
b
c
d
e
f
g
h
i
j
k
l
m
n
o
p
q
r
s
t
u
v
w
x
y
z

a

gas meter *noun* contador *Masc.* de gas.

b

gate *noun* **1** (*garden*) verja *Fem.*; **2** (*field*) portillo *Masc.*; **3** (*at the airport*) puerta *Fem.* (de embarque).

c

d

gather *verb* **1** (*people*) juntarse [17]; **a crowd gathered** se juntó una multitud; **2** recoger [3] (*fruit, vegetables, flowers*); **3 as far as I can gather** según tengo entendido.

e

f

g

gay *adjective* gay (*homosexual*).

h

GCSEs *noun plural* (*You can explain GCSEs briefly as follows: Son exámenes que se realizan alrededor de los 16 años y abarcan hasta 12 asignaturas. Se califican desde A-star (nota máxima), a N (sin calificar). Muchos alumnos estudian para los A levels después de hacer los GCSEs*) SEE **A levels**.

i

j

k

l

m

gear *noun* **1** (*in a car*) marcha *Fem.*; **to change gear** cambiar [17] de marcha; **in third gear** en tercera; **2** (*equipment*) equipo *Masc.*; **camping gear** equipo de acampada; **3 fishing gear** aparejos *Masc. plural* de pesca; **4** (*things*) cosas *Fem. plural*; **I've left all my gear at Gary's** he dejado todas mis cosas en casa de Gary.

n

o

p

q

r

s

gear lever *noun* palanca *Fem.* de cambio.

t

u

gel *noun* gel *Masc.*; **hair gel** gel para el pelo.

v

Gemini *noun* Géminis *Masc. plural*; **Steph's Gemini** Steph es Géminis.

w

x

gender *noun* (*of a word*) género *Masc.*; **what is the gender of 'casa'?** ¿de qué género es 'casa'?

y

z

general *adjective* general; **in general** en general.
general *noun* general *Masc.*; **General Jackson** el general Jackson.

general election *noun* elecciones *Fem. plural* generales.

general knowledge *noun* cultura *Fem.* general.

generally *adverb* generalmente.

generation *noun* generación *Fem.*

generous *adjective* generoso/generosa.

genetics *noun* genética *Fem.*

genius *noun* genio *Masc.*; **Lisa, you're a genius!** Lisa, ¡eres un genio!

gentle *adjective* **1** (*person , voice or nature*) dulce; **2** (*breeze, murmur, heat*) suave.

gentleman *noun* caballero *Masc.*; **ladies and gentlemen** señoras y caballeros.

gently *adverb* **1** (*talk*) dulcemente; **2** (*touch*) suavemente; **3** (*handle*) con cuidado.

gents *noun* servicios *Masc. plural* de caballeros; (*sign*) Caballeros; **where's the gents?** ¿dónde están los servicios de caballeros?

genuine *adjective* **1** (*real*) auténtico/auténtica; **a genuine diamond** un diamante auténtico; **2** sincero/sincera (*person*); **she's very genuine** es muy sincera.

geography *noun* geografía *Fem.*

geology *noun* geología *Fem.*

geometry *noun* geometría *Fem.*

germ *noun* germen *Masc.*

German *noun* **1** alemán *Masc.*, alemana *Fem.*; **2** (*language*) alemán *Masc.*

German *adjective* alemán/alemana.

Germany *noun* Alemania *Fem.*

get *verb* **1** (*to obtain*) **I got fifteen for my maths exam** saqué un quince en el examen de matemáticas; **where did you get that jacket?** ¿de dónde has sacado esa chaqueta?; **2** (*as a present*) **I got a bike for my birthday** me regalaron una bicicleta por mi cumpleaños; **3** (*a parcel or letter*) recibir [19]; **I got your letter yesterday** recibí tu carta ayer; **4** (*a job*) conseguir [64], **Fred's got a job** Fred ha conseguido un trabajo; **5** (*fetch*) ir [8] a buscar; **go and get some bread** vete a buscar pan; **I'll get your bag for you** voy a buscar tu bolso; **6** (*to buy*) comprar [17]; **I got a nice shirt in the sales** compré una camisa muy bonita en las rebajas; **7 to have got** tener [9]; **he's got lots of money** tiene mucho dinero; **she's got long hair** tiene el pelo largo; **8 to have got to do** tener [9] que hacer; **I've got to phone before midday** tengo que llamar antes del mediodía; **9 to get to** llegar [28] a; **when we got to London** cuando llegamos a Londres; **to get here/there** llegar [28]; **we got here this morning** llegamos esta mañana; **what time did they get there?** ¿a qué hora llegaron?; **10** (*become*) **to get tired** cansarse [17]; **she was getting**

worried se estaba preocupando; **it's getting late** se está haciendo tarde; **I'm getting hungry** me está entrando hambre; **11 to get your hair cut** cortarse [17] el pelo.

● **to get back** volver [45]; **Mum gets back at six** mamá vuelve a las seis.

● **to get something back: we got the money back** nos devolvieron el dinero; **did you get your books back?** ¿te devolvieron los libros?.

● **to get into something** entrar [17] (*a vehicle*); **he got into the car** entró en el coche.

● **to get off something** bajarse [17] de; **I got off the train at Banbury** me bajé del tren en Banbury.

● **to get on: how's Amanda getting on?** ¿cómo le va a Amanda?

● **to get on something** subir [19] a (*vehicle*); **she got on the train at Reading** subió al tren en Reading.

● **to get on with somebody** llevarse [17] bien con alguien; **she doesn't get on with her brother** no se lleva bien con su hermano.

● **to get out of something** salir [63] de algo (*vehicle*); **Laura got out of the car** Laura salió del coche.

● **to get something out** sacar [31] algo; **Robert got his guitar out** Robert sacó la guitarra.

● **to get together** verse [16]; **we must get together soon** tenemos que vernos pronto.

● **to get up** levantarse [17]; **I get up at seven** me levanto a la siete.

ghost *noun* fantasma *Masc.*

giddy *adjective* mareado/mareada; **I'm feeling giddy** me siento mareado/mareada.

gift *noun* **1** regalo *Masc.*; **a Christmas gift** un regalo de Navidad; **2 to have a gift for something** estar [2] dotado/dotada para; **Jo has a real gift for languages** Jo está realmente dotada para los idiomas.

gig *noun* concierto *Masc.*

gigabyte *noun* gigabyte *Masc.*; **a fifty gigabyte hard disk** un disco duro de cincuenta gigabytes.

gin *noun* ginebra *Fem.*

ginger *noun* jengibre *Masc.*

giraffe *noun* jirafa *Fem.*

gipsy *noun* gitano *Masc.*, gitana *Fem.*.

girl *noun* **1** niña *Fem.*; **three boys and four girls** tres niños y cuatro niñas; **a little girl** una niña pequeña; **when I was a little girl** cuando yo era pequeña; **2** (*a teenager or young woman*) chica *Fem.*; **an eighteen-year-old girl** una chica de dieciocho años.

girlfriend *noun* **1** (*in relationship*) novia *Fem.*; **Darren's girlfriend** la novia de Darren; **2** (*female friend*) amiga *Fem.*; **Lizzie and her girlfriends have gone to the cinema** Lizzie y sus amigas han ido al cine.

give *verb* dar [4]; **to give something to somebody** darle [4] algo a alguien; **I'll give you my address** te daré mis señas; **give me the key** dame la llave; **I gave Sandy the books** le di los libros a Sandy; **Yasmin's dad gave her the money** el padre de Yasmin le dio el dinero.

- **to give something away** regalar [17] algo; **she's given away all her books** ha regalado todos sus libros.
- **to give something back to somebody** devolverle [45] algo a alguien; **I gave her back the keys** le devolví las llaves.
- **to give in** ceder [18]; **she gave in in the end** al final cedió.
- **to give up** rendirse [57]; **I give up!** ¡me rindo!
- **to give up doing** dejar [17] de hacer; **she's given up smoking** ha dejado de fumar.

glacier *noun* glaciar *Masc.*

glad *adjective* **to be glad to** alegrarse [17]; **I'm glad to hear he's better** me alegra saber que está mejor; **I'm glad to be back** me alegro de haber vuelto.

glamorous *adjective* **1** (*life, job*) con mucho glamour; **2** (*woman*) elegante.

glass *noun* **1** (*for drinking*) vaso *Masc.*; **a glass of water** un vaso de agua; **2** (*material*) cristal *Masc.*; **a glass table** una mesa de cristal.

glasses *plural noun* gafas *Fem. plural*; **to wear glasses** llevar [17] gafas.

global *adjective* global.

global warming *noun* calentamiento *Masc.* global.

globe *noun* globo *Masc.* terráqueo.

gloomy *adjective* **1** (*expression*) lúgubre; **2** (*weather*) gris.

glory *noun* gloria *Fem.*

glove *noun* guante *Masc.*; **a pair of gloves** un par de guantes.

glue *noun* pegamento *Masc.*

go *noun* **1** (*in a game*) **whose go is it?** ¿a quién le toca?; **it's my go** me toca a mí; **2 to have a go at doing** intentar [17] hacer; **I'll have a go at mending it for you** intentaré arreglártelo.

go *verb* **1** ir [8]; **we're going to London tomorrow** mañana vamos a Londres; **Mark's gone to the dentist's** Mark ha ido al dentista; **to go for a walk** ir [8] a dar un paseo; **to go shopping** ir [8] de compras; **2** (*with another verb*) **to go to do** ir [8] a hacer; **I'm going to make some tea** voy a hacer té; **he was going to phone me** él iba a llamarme; **3** (*leave*) irse [8]; **Pauline's already gone** Pauline ya se ha ido; **we're going on holiday tomorrow** nos vamos de vacaciones mañana; **4** (*a train or plane*) salir [63]; **the train goes at seven** el tren sale a las siete; **5** (*time*) pasar [17]; **the time goes quickly** el tiempo pasa rápido; **6** (*an event*) ir [8]; **did the party go well?** ¿qué tal fue la fiesta?; **7** (*a pain*) pasarse [17]; **my headache's gone** se me ha pasado el dolor de cabeza.

● **to go away** irse [8]; **go away!** ¡vete!

● **to go back** volver [45]; **I'm going back to Madrid in March** vuelvo a Madrid en marzo; **I'm not going back there again!** ¡no voy a volver nunca!; **I went back home** volví a casa.

● **to go down 1** bajar [17]; **she's gone down to the kitchen** ha bajado a la cocina; **to go down the stairs** bajar las escaleras; **prices have gone down** los precios han bajado; **2** (*tyre, balloon, airbed*) desinflarse [17].

● **to go in** entrar [17]; **he went in and shut the door** entró y cerró la puerta.

● **to go into** entrar [17]; **Fran went into the kitchen** Fran entró en la cocina; **this file won't go into my bag** esta carpeta no entra en mi bolsa.

● **to go off 1** (*bomb*) estallar [17]; **2** (*alarm clock*) sonar [24]; **my alarm clock went off at six** mi despertador sonó a las seis; **3** (*fire or burglar alarm*) dispararse [17]; **the fire alarm went off** la alarma contra incendios se disparó.

● **to go on 1** pasar [17]; **what's going on?** ¿qué pasa?; **2 to go on doing** seguir [64] haciendo; **she went on talking** siguió hablando; **3 to go on about something** hablar [17] de algo; **he's always going on about his dog** siempre está hablando de su perro.

● **to go out 1** salir [63]; **I'm going out tonight** voy a salir esta noche; **she went out of the kitchen** salió de la cocina; **2 to be going out with somebody** salir [63] con alguien; **she's going out with my brother** está saliendo con mi hermano; **3** (*light, fire*) apagarse [28]; **the light went out** la luz se apagó.

● **to go past something** pasar [17] por algo; **we went past your house** pasamos por tu casa.

● **to go round: to go round to somebody's house** ir [8] a casa de alguien; **I went round to Fred's last night** anoche fui a casa de Fred.

a
b
c
d
e
f
g
h
i
j
k
l
m
n
o
p
q
r
s
t
u
v
w
x
y
z

a
b
c
d
e
f
g
h
i
j
k
l
m
n
o
p
q
r
s
t
u
v
w
x
y
z

- **to go round something 1** recorrer [18] (*building, park, garden*); **2** visitar [17] (*museum, monument*).

- **to go through** pasar [17] por; **the train went through York** el tren pasó por York; **you can go through my office** puedes pasar por mi oficina.

- **to go up** subir [19]; **she's gone up to her room** ha subido a su habitación; **to go up the stairs** subir las escaleras; **the price of petrol has gone up** el precio de la gasolina ha subido.

goal *noun* gol *Masc.*; **to score a goal** marcar un gol; **to win by three goals to two** ganar [17] por tres goles a dos.

goalkeeper *noun* portero *Masc.*, portera *Fem.*

goat *noun* cabra *Fem.*; **goat's cheese** queso *Masc.* de cabra.

god *noun* dios *Masc.*

God *noun* Dios *Masc.*; **to believe in God** creer en Dios.

godchild *noun* ahijado *Masc.*, ahijada *Fem.*

goddaughter *noun* ahijada *Fem.*

goddess *noun* diosa *Fem.*

godfather *noun* padrino *Masc.*

godmother *noun* madrina *Fem.*

godparent *noun* padrino *Masc.*, madrina *Fem.*; **my godparents** mis padrinos.

godson *noun* ahijado *Masc.*

goggles *plural noun* **swimming goggles** gafas *Fem. plural* de

natación; **skiing goggles** gafas *Fem. plural* de esquí.

go-karting *noun* karting *Masc.*; **to go go-karting** hacer karting.

gold *noun* oro *Masc.*; **a gold bracelet** una pulsera de oro.

goldfish *noun* pececito *Masc.* (rojo).

golf *noun* golf *Masc.*; **to play golf** jugar [31] al golf.

golf club *noun* **1** (*place*) club *Masc.* de golf; **2** (*iron*) palo *Masc.* de golf.

golf course *noun* campo *Masc.* de golf.

golfer *noun* golfista *Masc./Fem.*

good *noun* **to do somebody good** irle [15] bien a alguien; **it will do you good** te irá bien.
good *adjective* **1** bueno/buena (*'bueno' becomes 'buen' before a masculine singular noun*) **she's a good teacher** es una buena profesora; **a good deal** un buen negocio; **be good!** ¡sé bueno!; **to feel good** sentirse [14] bien; **2 to be good for you** ser [1] bueno para la salud; **tomatoes are good for you** los tomates son muy buenos para la salud; **3 she's good at art** se la da bien el arte; **I'm good at cooking** se me da bien cocinar; **4** (*kind*) amable; **she's been very good to me** ha sido muy amable conmigo; **5** bien; **it smelled good** olía bien; **it tastes good** sabe bien; **his Spanish is very good** habla español muy bien; **good!** (*well done*) ¡muy bien!; **6 for good** para siempre; **I've stopped smoking for good** he dejado de fumar para siempre.

good afternoon *exclamation* buenas tardes.

goodbye *exclamation* adiós.

good evening *exclamation* **1** (*up to eight or nine*) buenas tardes; **2** (*from nine onwards*) buenas noches.

Good Friday *noun* Viernes *Masc.* Santo.

good-looking *adjective* guapo/ guapa; **Maya's boyfriend's really good-looking** el novio de Maya es muy guapo.

good morning *exclamation* buenos días.

goodness *exclamation* ¡Dios mío!; **for goodness sake!** ¡por Dios!

goodnight *exclamation* buenas noches.

goods *plural noun* artículos *Masc. plural.*

goods train *noun* tren *Masc.* de mercancías.

goose *noun* ganso *Masc.*

goose pimples *noun* carne *Fem.* de gallina.

gorgeous *adjective* precioso/ preciosa; **a gorgeous dress** un vestido precioso; **it's a gorgeous day** un día precioso.

gorilla *noun* gorila *Masc.*

gosh *exclamation* ¡Dios mío!

gossip *noun* **1** (*person*) cotilla *Masc./ Fem.*; **2** (*news*) cotilleo *Masc.*; **what's the latest gossip?** ¿qué hay de nuevo?
gossip *verb* cotillear [17].

government *noun* gobierno *Masc.*

grab *verb* **1** agarrar [17]; **she grabbed my arm** me agarró el brazo; **2 to grab something from somebody** arrebatarle [17] algo a alguien; **he grabbed the book from me** me arrebató el libro.

graceful *adjective* elegante.

grade *noun* (*mark*) notas *Fem. plural*; **to get good grades** sacar [31] buenas notas.

gradual *adjective* gradual.

gradually *adverb* poco a poco; **the weather got gradually better** el tiempo mejoró poco a poco.

graffiti *plural noun* grafitti *Masc. plural.*

grain *noun* grano *Masc.*

grammar *noun* gramática *Fem.*

grammar school *noun* colegio *Masc.*

grammatical *adjective* gramatical; **a grammatical error** un error gramatical.

gramme *noun* gramo *Masc.*

gran *noun* abuelita *Fem.*

grandchildren *plural noun* nietos *Masc. plural.*

granddad *noun* abuelito (*informal*) *Masc.*

granddaughter *noun* nieta *Fem.*

grandfather *noun* abuelo *Masc.*

grandma *noun* abuelita (*informal*) *Fem.*

grandmother *noun* abuela *Fem.*

grandpa *noun* abuelito (*informal*) *Masc.*

a
b
c
d
e
f
g
h
i
j
k
l
m
n
o
p
q
r
s
t
u
v
w
x
y
z

a

b **grandparents** *plural noun*
abuelos *Masc. plural*.

c **grandson** *noun* nieto *Masc. plural*.

granny *noun* abuelita (*informal*)
d *Fem.*

e **grape** *noun* **a grape** una uva; **to**
buy some grapes comprar uvas; **a**
f **bunch of grapes** un racimo de
uvas.

g **grapefruit** *noun* pomelo *Masc.*

h **graph** *noun* gráfico *Masc.*

i **graphic designer** *noun*
diseñador *Masc.* gráfico, diseñadora
Fem. gráfica.

j

k **graphics** *noun* gráficos *Masc.*
plural.

l **grass** *noun* **1** hierba *Fem.*; **he was**
sitting on the grass estaba sentado
m en la hierba; **2** (*lawn*) césped *Masc.*;
to cut the grass cortar [17] el
n césped.

o **grasshopper** *noun* saltamontes
Masc. (*plural* saltamontes).

p

grate *verb* rallar [17]; **grated**
q **cheese** queso rallado.

r **grateful** *adjective* agradecido/
agradecida.

s **grater** *noun* rallador *Masc.*

t **grave** *noun* tumba *Fem.*

u **gravel** *noun* grava *Fem.*

graveyard *noun* cementerio *Masc.*
v

gravity *noun* gravedad *Fem.*

w **gravy** *noun* salsa *Fem.* del asado.

x **grease** *noun* grasa *Fem.*

y **greasy** *adjective* **1** (*hands or*
surface) grasiento/grasienta;
z **2** (*hair, skin or food*) graso/grasa; **to**

have greasy skin tener [9] la piel
grasa; **I hate greasy food** no
soporto la comida grasa.

great *adjective* **1** gran (*plural*
grandes); **a great poet** un gran
poeta; **a great opportunity** una
gran oportunidad; **great**
expectations grandes esperanzas;
2 (*terrific*) estupendo/estupenda; **it**
was a great party! ¡fue una fiesta
estupenda!; **great!** ¡estupendo!; **3 a**
great deal of un montón de; **a great**
many muchos/muchas; **there are a**
great many things still to be done
aún quedan muchas cosas por hacer.

Great Britain *noun* Gran Bretaña
Fem.

Greece *noun* Grecia *Fem.*

greedy *adjective* (*with food*) glotón/
glotona.

Greek *noun* **1** (*person*) griego *Masc.*,
griega *Fem.*; **2** (*language*) griego
Masc.
Greek *adjective* griego/griega.

green *noun* **1** (*colour*) verde *Masc.*; **a**
pale green un verde pálido;
2 greens (*vegetables*) verduras *Fem.*
plural; **3 the Greens** (*ecologists*) los
verdes (*informal*).
green *adjective* **1** verde; **a green**
door una puerta verde; **2** ecologista;
the Green Party el partido
ecologista.

greengrocer *noun* verdulero
Masc., verdulera *Fem.*; **the**
greengrocer's la verdulería.

greenhouse *noun* invernadero
Masc.

greenhouse effect *noun* efecto *Masc.* invernadero.

greetings *plural noun* **Season's Greetings** Feliz Navidad.

greetings card *noun* tarjeta *Fem.* de felicitación.

grey *adjective* **1** gris; **a grey skirt** una falda gris; **2** (*hair*) canoso/canosa; **to have grey hair** tener el pelo canoso.

greyhound *noun* galgo *Masc.*

grid *noun* **1** (*grating*) parrilla *Fem.*; **2** (*network*) red *Fem.*

grief *noun* dolor *Masc.*

grill *noun* (*of a cooker*) grill *Masc.* **grill** *verb* **to grill something** hacer [7] algo al grill; **I grilled the sausages** hice las salchichas al grill.

grin *noun* sonrisa *Fem.* **grin** *verb* sonreír [61].

grip *verb* agarrar [17].

grit *noun* (*for roads*) arenilla *Fem.*

groan *noun* **1** (*of pain*) gemido *Masc.*; **2** (*of disgust, boredom*) gruñido *Masc.* **groan** *verb* **1** (*in pain*) gemir [57]; **2** (*in disgust, boredom*) refunfuñar [17].

grocer *noun* tendero *Masc.*, tendera *Fem.*; **my dad's a grocer** mi padre es tendero.

groceries *plural noun* cosas *Fem. plural* de comer; **to buy some groceries** comprar [17] cosas de comer.

grocer's *noun* tienda *Fem.* de comestibles.

groom *noun* (*bridegroom*) novio *Masc.*

gross *adjective* **1 a gross injustice** una flagrante injustica; **2 a gross error** un grave error; **3** (*disgusting*) repugnante; **the food was gross!** ¡la comida era repugnante!

ground *noun* **1** suelo *Masc.*; **to sit on the ground** sentarse [29] en el suelo; **to throw something on the ground** tirar [17] algo al suelo; **2** (*for sport*) campo *Masc.*; **a football ground** un campo de fútbol. **ground** *adjective* molido/molida; **ground coffee** café *Masc.* molido.

ground floor *noun* planta *Fem.* baja; **they live on the ground floor** viven en la planta baja.

group *noun* grupo *Masc.*

grow *verb* **1** (*plant, hair or person*) crecer [35]; **your hair's grown!** te ha crecido el pelo; **my little sister's grown a lot this year** mi hermana pequeña ha crecido mucho este año; **2** cultivar [17] (*fruit, vegetables*); **our neighbour grows strawberries** nuestro vecino cultiva fresas; **3 to grow a beard** dejarse [17] barba; **4 to grow old** envejecer [35].
● **to grow up** crecer [35]; **the children are growing up** los niños están creciendo; **she grew up in Scotland** creció en Escocia.

growl *verb* gruñir [65].

grown-up *noun* adulto *Masc.*, adulta *Fem.*

growth *noun* crecimiento *Masc.*

grudge *noun* **to bear a grudge against somebody** guardarle [17] rencor a alguien; **she bears me a grudge** me guarda rencor.

gruesome *adjective* horrible.

grumble *verb* refunfuñar [17]; **she's always grumbling** siempre está refunfuñando; **to grumble about something** refunfuñar por algo.

guarantee *noun* garantía *Fem.*; **a year's guarantee** una garantía de un año.
guarantee *verb* garantizar [22].

guard *noun* **1 a prison guard** un guardia de prisiones; **2** (*on a train*) jefe *Masc.* de tren, jefa *Fem.* de tren; **3 a security guard** un guardia de seguridad.
guard *verb* vigilar [17].

guard dog *noun* perro *Masc.* guardián.

guardian *noun* tutor *Masc.*, tutora *Fem.*

Guatemalan *noun* guatemalteco *Masc.*, guatemalteca *Fem.*
Guatemalan *adjective* guatemalteco/guatemalteca.

guess *noun* **have a guess!** ¡adivina!; **it's a good guess** lo has adivinado.
guess *verb* **1** adivinar [17]; **guess who I saw last night!** ¡adivina a quién vi anoche!; **you'll never guess!** ¡no lo vas a adivinar nunca!; **guess what!** ¿sabes qué?; **2** (*suppose*) suponer [11]; **I guess so** supongo que sí.

guest *noun* **1** invitado *Masc.*, invitada *Fem.*; **we've got guests coming tonight** tenemos invitados

esta noche; **2** (*in a hotel*) cliente *Masc./Fem.*; **3 a paying guest** un huésped de pago.

guide *noun* **1** (*book , girl guide*) guía *Fem.*; **2** (*person*) guía *Masc./Fem.*

guidebook *noun* guía *Fem.*

guide dog *noun* perro *Masc.* lazarillo.

guideline *noun* pauta *Fem.*

guilty *adjective* culpable; **to feel guilty** sentirse [14] culpable.

guinea pig *noun* (*pet*) cobaya *Fem.*, (*in an experiment*) conejillo *Masc.* de indias.

guitar *noun* guitarra *Fem.*; **to play the guitar** tocar [31] la guitarra; **on the guitar** a la guitarra.

guitarist *noun* guitarrista *Masc./Fem.*

gum *noun* **1** (*in mouth*) encía *Fem.*; **2** (*chewing gum*) chicle *Masc.*

gun *noun* **1** pistola *Fem.*; **2** (*rifle*) fusil *Masc.*

guy *noun* tipo *Masc.* (*informal*); **he's a nice guy** es un tipo muy majo; **a guy from Newcastle** un tipo de Newcastle.

guy rope *noun* viento *Masc.* de un tienda de campaña.

gym *noun* **1** (*gymnasium*) gimnasio *Masc.*; **to go to the gym** ir [8] al gimnasio; **2** (*gymnastics*) gimnasia *Fem.*

gymnasium *noun* gimnasio *Masc.*

gymnast *noun* gimnasta *Masc./Fem.*

gymnastics *noun* gimnasia *Fem.*

gym shoe *noun* zapatilla *Fem.* de gimnasia.

Hh

habit *noun* costumbre *Fem.*; **to have a habit of doing** tener [9] la costumbre de hacer; **it's a bad habit** es una mala costumbre.

hail *noun* granizo *Masc.*

hailstone *noun* granizo *Masc.*

hailstorm *noun* granizada *Fem.*

hair *noun* **1** pelo *Masc.*; **to have short hair** tener [9] el pelo corto; **to brush your hair** cepillarse [17] el pelo; **to wash your hair** lavarse [17] el pelo; **to have your hair cut** cortarse [17] el pelo; **she's had her hair cut** se ha cortado el pelo; **2 a hair** (*from the head*) un pelo (*from the body*) un vello.

hairbrush *noun* cepillo *Masc.* del pelo.

haircut *noun* **1** corte *Masc.* de pelo; **I like your new haircut** me gusta tu nuevo corte de pelo; **2 to have a haircut** cortarse [17] el pelo.

hairdresser *noun* peluquero *Masc.*, peluquera *Fem.*; **she's a hairdresser** es peluquera; **at the hairdresser's** en la peluquería.

hair drier *noun* secador *Masc.* de pelo.

hair gel *noun* gel *Masc.* para el cabello.

hairslide *noun* pasador *Masc.*

hairspray *noun* laca *Fem.* del pelo.

hairstyle *noun* peinado *Masc.*

hairy *adjective* peludo/peluda.

Haiti *noun* Haití *Masc.*

Haitian *noun* haitiano *Masc.*, haitiana *Fem.*
Haitian *adjective* haitiano/haitiana.

half *noun, pronoun* **1** mitad *Fem.*; **half of** la mitad de; **I gave him half of the money** le di la mitad del dinero; **2 to cut something in half** cortar algo por la mitad; **3** (*as a fraction*) medio; **three and a half** tres y medio; **she's five and a half** tiene seis años y medio; **4** (*in time*) media; **half an hour** media hora; **an hour and a half** una hora y media; **it's half past three** son las tres y media; **5 half a** medio/media; **half a litre** medio litro; **half an apple** media manzana; **6 half the people** la mitad de la gente; **half the time he's not here** la mitad del tiempo no está aquí.

half hour *noun* media hora *Fem.*; **every half hour** cada media hora.

half price *adjective, adverb* a mitad de precio; **half-price CDs** compactos a mitad de precio; **I bought it half price** lo compré a mitad de precio.

half-time *noun* descanso *Masc.*; **at half-time** en el descanso.

halfway *adverb* **1** a mitad de camino; **halfway between Madrid and Barcelona** a mitad de camino entre Madrid y Barcelona; **2 to be halfway through** ir [8] por la mitad de; **I'm halfway through my homework** voy por la mitad de los deberes.

hall *noun* **1** (*in a house*) entrada *Fem.*; **2** (*public*) salón *Masc.*; **the village**

a
b
c
d
e
f
g
h
i
j
k
l
m
n
o
p
q
r
s
t
u
v
w
x
y
z

hall el salón de actos del pueblo; **3 a concert hall** una sala de conciertos.

ham *noun* **1** (*cooked*) jamón *Masc.* de York; **2** (*cured*) jamón *Masc.* serrano.

hamburger *noun* hamburguesa *Fem.*

hammer *noun* martillo *Masc.*

hammock *noun* hamaca *Fem.*

hamster *noun* hámster *Masc.*

hand *noun* **1** mano *Fem.*; **to have something in your hand** tener [9] algo en la mano; **to be holding hands** (*two people*) ir [8] cogidos de la mano; **they were holding hands** iban cogidos de la mano; **2 to give somebody a hand** echar [17] una mano a alguien; **can you give me a hand to move the table?** ¿puedes echarme una mano para mover la mesa?; **do you need a hand?** ¿necesitas que te echen una mano?; **3 on the other hand** ... por otro lado ...; **4** (*of a watch or clock*) manecilla *Fem.*; **the hour hand** la manecilla de las horas.

hand *verb* **to hand something to somebody** pasarle [17] algo a alguien; **I handed him the keys** le pasé las llaves.

handbag *noun* bolso *Masc.*

handbrake *noun* freno *Masc.* de mano.

handcuffs *plural noun* esposas *Fem. plural.*

handful *noun* **a handful of** un puñado de.

handkerchief *noun* pañuelo *Masc.*

handicapped *adjective* disminuido/disminuida.

handle *noun* **1** (*of a door*) picaporte *Masc.*; **2** (*of a drawer*) tirador *Masc.*; **3** (*on a cup or basket*) asa *Fem.*; **4** (*of a knife, tool, or pan*) mango *Masc.*

handle *verb* **1** encargarse [28] de; **Gina handles the accounts** Gina se encarga de la contabilidad; **2 she's good at handling people** se le da muy bien tratar con la gente.

handlebars *plural noun* manillar *Masc.*

hand luggage *noun* equipaje *Masc.* de mano.

handsome *adjective* guapo; **he's a very handsome guy** es un tipo muy guapo.

handwriting *noun* letra *Fem.*

handy *adjective* **1** práctico/práctica; **this little knife's very handy** este cuchillito es muy práctico; **2** a mano; **I always keep a notebook handy** siempre guardo un cuaderno a mano.

hang *verb* colgar [23]; **we hung the mirror on the wall** colgamos el espejo en la pared; **there was a mirror hanging on the wall** había un espejo colgado en la pared.

- **to hang on** esperar [17]; **hang on a second!** ¡espera un poco!
- **to hang up** (*on the phone*) colgar [23]; **she hung up on me** me colgó.
- **to hang something up** colgar [23] algo; **you can hang your coat up in the hall** puedes colgar el abrigo en la entrada.

hangover *noun* resaca *Fem.*; **to have a hangover** tener [9] resaca.

happen *verb* **1** pasar [17]; **what's happening?** ¿qué pasa?; **what**

happened to him? ¿qué le pasó?; **it happened in June** pasó en junio; **2 what's happened to the can-opener?** ¿dónde se ha metido el abridor?; **3 if you happen to see Jill** si ves a Jill.

happily *adverb* **1** alegremente; **she smiled happily** sonrió alegremente; **2** (*willingly*) con mucho gusto; **I'll happily do it for you** lo haré por ti con mucho gusto.

happiness *noun* felicidad *Fem.*

happy *adjective* feliz; **a happy child** un niño feliz; **happy birthday!** ¡feliz cumpleaños!

harbour *noun* puerto *Masc.*

hard *adjective* **1** duro/dura; **2** (*difficult*) difícil; **a hard question** una pregunta difícil; **it's hard to know** ... es difícil saber ....
hard *adverb* mucho; **to study hard** estudiar [17] mucho; **to try hard** esforzarse [26] mucho; **to work hard** trabajar [17] duro.

hard-boiled egg *noun* huevo *Masc.* duro.

hard disk *noun* (*in a computer*) disco *Masc.* duro.

hardly *adverb* **1** apenas; **I can hardly hear him** apenas puedo oírle; **2 hardly any** casi nada; **there's hardly any milk** casi no hay nada de leche; **3 hardly ever** casi nunca; **I hardly ever see them** casi nunca los veo; **4 there was hardly anybody** no había casi nadie.

hard up *adjective* **to be hard up** estar [2] mal de dinero (*informal*).

harm *noun* **it won't do you any harm** no te va a pasar nada.
harm *verb* **to harm somebody** hacerle [7] daño a alguien; **a cup of coffee won't harm you** una taza de café no te va a hacer daño.

harvest *noun* cosecha *Fem.*; **to get the harvest in** hacer [7] la cosecha.

hat *noun* sombrero *Masc.*

hate *verb* odiar [17]; **I hate geography** odio la geografía.

hatred *noun* odio *Masc.*

haunted *adjective* embrujado/embrujada.

have *verb* **1** tener [9]; **Anna has three brothers** Anna tiene tres hermanos; **how many sisters do you have?** ¿cuántas hermanas tienes?; **2 to have got** tener [9]; **we've got a dog** tenemos un perro; **what have you got in your hand?** ¿qué tienes en la mano?; **3** (*to form past tenses, verbs in Spanish take 'haber'*) **I've finished** he terminado; **have you seen the film?** ¿has visto la película; **Rosie hasn't arrived yet** Rosie aún no ha llegado; **he had left** se había ido (*in question tags "have" is not translated*) **you've done this before, haven't you?** tú has hecho esto antes, ¿no?; **4 to have to do** tener [9] que hacer; **I have to phone my mum** tengo que llamar a mi madre; **5** tomar [17] (*food or drink*); **we had a coffee** tomamos un café; **what will you have?** ¿qué vais a tomar?; **I'll have an omelette** voy a tomar una tortilla; **6 to have a shower** ducharse [17]; **to have a bath**

a b c d e f g h i j k l m n o p q r s t u v w x y z

bañarse [17]; **7 to have lunch** comer [18]; **to have dinner** (*in the evening*) cenar [17]; **8 to have a party** dar [4] una fiesta; **9** (*for illnesses*) tener [9]; **he has cancer** tiene cáncer; **I had flu** tuve la gripe; **10** (*for aches*) **she has stomachache** le duele el estómago; **I had a terrible headache** me dolía mucho la cabeza; **11 I'm going to have my hair cut** voy a cortarme el pelo; **she's had her TV repaired** ha arreglado la tele.

hawk *noun* halcón *Masc.*

hay *noun* heno *Masc.*

hay fever *noun* fiebre *Fem.* del heno.

hazelnut *noun* avellana *Fem.*

he *pronoun* **1** (*'he', like other subject pronouns, is generally not translated in Spanish; the form of the verb tells you whether the subject of the verb is 'he/she/it, you, they', etc., so 'he' is only translated for emphasis*) **he lives in Newcastle** vive en Newcastle; **he's a student** es estudiante; **he's a very good teacher** es muy buen profesor; **here he is!** ¡aquí está!; **2** (*for emphasis*) él; **he did it** lo hizo él.

head *noun* **1** cabeza *Fem.*; **he had a cap on his head** tenía un sombrero en la cabeza; **at the head of the queue** a la cabeza de la cola; **2** (*of school*) director *Masc.*, directora *Fem.*; **3** (*when tossing a coin*) **'heads or tails?' – 'heads'** '¿cara o cruz?' – 'cara'.

● **to head for something** dirigirse [49] a; **Liz headed for the door** Liz se dirigió a la puerta.

headache *noun* **I've got a headache** me duele la cabeza.

headlight *noun* faro *Masc.*

headline *noun* titular *Masc.*; **to hit the headlines** aparecer [35] en los titulares.

headmaster *noun* director *Masc.*

headmistress *noun* directora *Fem.*

headphones *plural noun* auriculares *Masc. plural.*

headquarters *n* (*plural*) **1** (*of organization*) sede *Fem.*; **2** (*military*) cuartel *Masc.* general.

headteacher *noun* director *Masc.*, directora *Fem.*

health *noun* salud *Fem.*

health centre *noun* centro *Masc.* médico.

healthy *adjective* **1** (*person*) **to be healthy** estar [2] sano; **2 a healthy diet** una dieta sana.

heap *noun* montón *Masc.*; **I've got heaps of things to do** tengo montones de cosas que hacer.

hear *verb* oír [56]; **I can't hear you** no te oigo; **I can't hear anything** no oigo nada; **I hear you've bought a dog** he oído que te has comprado un perro.

● **to hear about something** enterarse [17] de algo; **have you heard about the concert?** ¿te has enterado de lo del concierto?

● **to hear from somebody: have you heard from Amanda?** ¿sabes algo de Amanda?; **I haven't heard from them** no sé nada de ellos.

hearing aid noun audífono Masc.

heart noun 1 corazón Masc.; 2 (in cards) **hearts** corazones Masc. plural; **the jack of hearts** la jota de corazones; ★ **to learn something by heart** aprender [18] algo de memoria.

heart attack noun ataque Masc. al corazón.

heat noun calor Masc.
heat verb 1 calentarse [29]; **the soup's heating** la sopa se está calentando; **2 to heat something** calentar [29] algo; **I'll go and heat the soup** voy a calentar la sopa.

heater noun estufa Fem.

heating noun calefacción Fem.

heaven noun cielo Masc.

heavy adjective 1 pesado/pesada; **a heavy bag** una bolsa pesada; **to be heavy** pesar [17] mucho; **my rucksack's really heavy** mi mochila pesa mucho; **2** (busy) ocupado/ocupada; **I've got a heavy day tomorrow** mañana tengo un día muy ocupado; **3 heavy rain** lluvia fuerte.

hectic adjective **a hectic day** un día muy ajetreado.

hedge noun seto Masc.

hedgehog noun erizo Masc.

heel noun 1 (of foot) talón Masc.; **2** (of shoe) tacón Masc.

height noun 1 (of a person) estatura Fem.; **2** (of a building) altura Fem.; **3** (of a mountain) altitud Fem.

helicopter noun helicóptero Masc.

hell noun infierno Masc.; **it's hell here!** ¡esto es un infierno!

hello exclamation 1 (greeting) hola; **2** (on the telephone) ¿dígame?

helmet noun casco Masc.

help noun ayuda Fem.; **do you need any help?** ¿necesitas ayuda?
help verb 1 ayudar [17]; **to help somebody to do** ayudar [17] a alguien a hacer; **can you help me move the table?** ¿me ayudas a mover la mesa?; **2 to help yourself to something** servirse [57] algo; **help yourselves to vegetables** serviros verdura; **help yourself!** ¡sírvete!; **3 help!** ¡socorro!

helping noun porción Fem.; **would you like a second helping?** ¿quieres repetir?.

hem noun dobladillo Masc.

hen noun gallina Fem.

her pronoun 1 la; **I know her** la conozco; **I saw her last week** la vi la semana pasada (with an infinitive or when telling someone to do something, 'la' joins onto the verb) **I can hear her** puedo oírla; **listen to her!** ¡escúchala!; (but when telling someone NOT to do something, 'la' comes before the verb) **don't push her!** ¡no la empujes!; **2** (to her) le; **I gave her my address** le di mis señas ('le' becomes 'se' before pronouns 'lo' or 'la') **I lent it to her** se lo dejé; **3** (after a preposition, in comparisons, or after the verb 'to be') ella; **with her** con ella; **without her** sin ella; **he's older than her** él es mayor que ella; **it was her** era ella.

her *adjective* **1** (*before a singular noun*) su; **her brother** su hermano; **her house** su casa; **2** (*before a plural noun*) sus; **her children** sus niños; **3** (*with parts of the body*) el, la, los, las; **she had a glass in her hand** tenía un vaso en la mano; **she's washing her hands** se está lavando las manos.

herb *noun* hierba *Fem.*

herd *n* **1** (*of cattle*) manada *Fem.*; **2** (*of goats*) rebaño *Masc.*

here *adverb* **1** aquí; **not far from here** no lejos de aquí; **and here they are!** ¡aquí están!; **Tom isn't here at the moment** Tom no está aquí en este momento; **2** (*giving something*) **here it is** toma; **here's my address** toma mis señas; **here you are** toma.

hero *noun* héroe *Masc.*

heroin *noun* heroína *Fem.*

heroine *noun* heroína *Fem.*

hers *pronoun* **1** (*referring to a singular noun*) el suyo/la suya; **I took my hat and she took hers** yo cogí mi sombrero y ella cogió el suyo; **I phoned my mum and Donna phoned hers** llamé a mi madre y Donna llamó a la suya; **2** (*referring to a plural noun*) los suyos/las suyas; **I've invited my parents and Karen's invited hers** yo he invitado a mis padres y Karen a los suyos; **I showed her my photos and she showed me hers** yo le enseñé mis fotos y ella me enseñó las suyas.

herself *pronoun* **1** (*as reflexive*) se; **she's hurt herself** se ha hecho daño; **she washed herself** se lavó; **2** (*for emphasis*) ella misma; **she said it herself** lo dijo ella misma; **3 she did it by herself** lo hizo ella sola.

hesitate *verb* dudar [17]; **to hesitate to do** dudar en hacer.

heterosexual *noun* heterosexual *Masc./Fem.*

hi *exclamation* hola.

hiccups *plural noun* **to have the hiccups** tener [9] hipo.

hidden *adjective* escondido/escondida.

hide *verb* **1** (*person*) esconderse [18]; **she hid behind the door** se escondió detrás de la puerta; **2 to hide something** esconder [18] algo; **who's hidden the chocolate?** ¿quién ha escondido el chocolate?

hide-and-seek *noun* **to play hide-and-seek** jugar [27] al escondite.

hi-fi *noun* equipo *Masc.* de alta fidelidad.

high *adjective* **1** alto/alta; **on a high shelf** en una estantería alta; **the wall is very high** la pared es muy alta; **how high is the wall?** ¿qué altura tiene la pared?; **the wall is two metres high** la pared tiene dos metros de altura; **2** (*number, price, temperature*) alto/alta; **food prices are very high** el precio de la comida es muy alto; **3 at high speed** a alta velocidad; **4 high winds** vientos fuertes.

Highers, Advanced Highers *noun plural* selectividad *Fem.* (*Students take 'la selectividad' at the same age as Advanced Highers* *in Scotland.) You can explain Highers and Advanced Highers briefly as follows: Son exámenes que se hacen en hasta cinco asignaturas, en el penúltimo año de la educación secundaria. Algunos alumnos también se presentan al Advanced Highers en el último años que pueden abarcar hasta tres asignaturas que ya se hayan estudiado para el nivel de los Highers)* SEE **selectividad**.

high-heeled *adjective* de tacón alto; **high-heeled shoes** zapatos de tacón alto.

high jump *noun* salto *Masc.* de altura.

hijacking *noun* secuestro *Masc.*

hiking *noun* senderismo *Masc.*

hilarious *adjective* divertidísimo/divertidísima.

hill *noun* **1** (*low*) colina *Fem.* (*higher*) montaña *Fem.*; **2** (*sloping street or road*) **to go up the hill** subir la cuesta.

him *pronoun* **1** lo; **I know him** lo conozco; **I saw him last week** lo vi la semana pasada (*with an infinitive or when telling someone to do something, 'lo' joins onto the verb*) **I can't hear him** no puedo oírlo; **listen to him!** ¡escúchalo!; (*but when telling someone NOT to do something, 'lo' comes before the verb*) **don't push him!** ¡no lo empujes!; **2** (*to him*) le; **I gave him my address** le di mis señas (*'le' becomes 'se' before pronouns 'lo' or 'la'*) **I lent it to him** se lo dejé; **3** (*after a preposition, in comparisons, or after*

the verb 'to be') él; **with him** con él; **without him** sin él; **she's older than him** ella es mayor que él; **it was him** era él.

himself *pronoun* **1** (*as a reflexive*) se; **he's hurt himself** se hizo daño; **2** (*for emphasis*) él mismo; **he said it himself** lo dijo él mismo; **3 he did it by himself** lo hizo él solo.

hip *noun* cadera *Fem.*

hire *noun* alquiler *Masc.*; **car hire** alquiler de coches; **for hire** se alquila.
hire *verb* alquilar [17]; **we're going to hire a car** vamos a alquilar un coche.

his *adjective* **1** (*before a singular noun*) su; **his brother** su hermano; **his house** su casa; **2** (*before a plural noun*) sus; **his children** sus niños; **3** (*with parts of the body*) el, la, los, las; **he had a glass in his hand** tenía un vaso en la mano; **he's washing his hands** se está lavando las manos.
his *pronoun* **1** (*referring to a singular noun*) el suyo/la suya; **I took my hat and he took his** yo cogí mi sombrero y él cogió el suyo; **I phoned my mum and Danny phoned his** llamé a mi madre y Danny llamó a la suya; **2** (*referring to a plural noun*) los suyos/las suyas; **I've invited my parents and Steve's invited his** yo he invitado a mis padres y Steve a los suyos; **I showed him my photos and he showed me his** yo le enseñé mis fotos y él me enseñó las suyas.

a
b
c
d
e
f
g
h
i
j
k
l
m
n
o
p
q
r
s
t
u
v
w
x
y
z

historic *adjective* histórico/
histórica.

history *noun* historia *Fem.*

hit *noun* (*song*) éxito *Masc.*; **their
latest hit** su último éxito; **the film is
a huge hit** la película es un gran
éxito.

hit *verb* 1 golpear [17]; **to hit the
ball** golpear la pelota; 2 **to hit your
head on something** darse [4] un
golpe en la cabeza con algo; 3 chocar
[31] con; **the car hit a tree** el coche
chocó con el árbol; 4 **she was hit by
a car** la atropelló un coche.

hitch *noun* problema *Masc.*; **there's
been a slight hitch** ha habido un
pequeño problema.

hitch *verb* **to hitch a lift** hacer [7]
dedo (*informal*).

hitchhike *verb* hacer [7] dedo
(*informal*); **we hitchhiked to
Valencia** hicimos dedo hasta
Valencia.

hitchhiker *noun* autoestopista
Masc./Fem.

hitchhiking *noun* autostop *Masc.*

HIV-negative *adjective*
seronegativo/seronegativa.

HIV-positive *adjective*
seropositivo/seropositiva.

hobby *noun* pasatiempo *Masc.*

hockey *noun* hockey *Masc.*; **to play
hockey** jugar al hockey.

hockey stick *noun* palo *Masc.* de
hockey.

hold *verb* 1 sostener [9]; **to hold
something in your hand** sostener
algo en la mano; **can you hold the
torch?** ¿puedes sostener la

linterna?; 2 (*contain*) contener [9]; **a
jug which holds a litre** una jarra
que contiene un litro; 3 **to hold a
meeting** celebrar [17] una reunión;
4 **can you hold the line, please** no
se retire, por favor; 5 **hold on!**
(*wait*) ¡un momento!, (*on telephone*)
¡no cuelgue!
● **to hold somebody up** (*delay*)
entretener [9] a alguien; **I don't
want to hold you up** no quiero
entretenerte; **I was held up at the
dentist's** me entretuve en el
dentista.
● **to hold something up** (*raise*)
levantar [17]; **he held up his glass**
levantó su vaso.

hold-up *noun* 1 (*delay*) retraso
Masc.; 2 (*traffic jam*) atasco *Masc.*;
3 (*robbery*) atraco *Masc.*

hole *noun* agujero *Masc.*

holiday *noun* 1 vacaciones *Fem.
plural*; **where are you going for
your holiday?** ¿dónde vas de
vacaciones?; **have a good holiday!**
¡que pases unas buenas vacaciones!;
to be away on holiday estarde
vacaciones; **to go on holiday** irse de
vacaciones; **the school holidays** las
vacaciones escolares; 2 **a public
holiday** un día de fiesta; **Monday's a
holiday** el lunes es fiesta.

Holland *noun* Holanda *Fem.*

hollow *adjective* hueco/hueca.

holly *noun* acebo *Masc.*

holy *adjective* santo/santa.

home *noun* casa *Fem.*; **I was at
home** estaba en casa; **to stay at
home** quedarse [17] en casa; **make
yourself at home** ponte cómodo.

home *adverb* a casa; **Susie's gone home** Susie se ha ido a casa; **I'll call in and see you on my way home** te iré a visitar de camino a mi casa; **to get home** llegar [28] a casa; **we got home at midnight** llegamos a casa a media noche.

homeless *adjective* sin hogar; **the homeless** la gente sin hogar.

homemade *adjective* casero/ casera; **homemade cakes** pasteles caseros.

home match *noun* **to play a home match** jugar [27] en casa.

homeopathic *adjective* homeopático/homeopática.

homesick *adjective* **to be homesick** tener [9] morriña.

homework *noun* deberes *Masc. plural*; **I did my homework** hice mis deberes; **my Spanish homework** mis deberes de español.

homosexual *noun, adjective* homosexual.

Honduran *noun* hondureño *Masc.*, hondureña *Fem.*
Honduran *adjective* hondureño/ hondureña.

Honduras *noun* Honduras *Fem.*

honest *adjective* **1** honrado/ honrada; **2 to be honest** ... para serte sincero ....

honestly *adverb* sinceramente.

honesty *noun* honradez *Fem.*

honey *noun* miel *Fem.*

honeymoon *noun* luna *Fem.* de miel.

honour *noun* honor *Masc.*

hood *noun* capucha *Fem.*

hook *noun* **1** (*in clothes*) corchete *Masc.*; **2** (*for fishing*) anzuelo *Masc.*; **3** (*for hanging pictures or clothes*) gancho *Masc.*; **4 to take the phone of the hook** descolgar [23] el teléfono.

hooligan *noun* gamberro *Masc.*, gamberra *Fem.*

hooray *exclamation* ¡hurra!

hoover *verb* pasar [17] la aspiradora por; **I hoovered my bedroom** pasé la aspiradora por mi habitación.

Hoover™ *noun* aspirador *Masc.*, aspiradora *Fem.*

hope *noun* esperanza *Fem.*; **to give up hope** perder [36] la esperanza. **hope** *verb* esperar [17]; **hoping to see you on Friday** esperando verte el domingo; **here's hoping!** ¡esperemos!; **I hope so** espero que sí; **I hope not** espero que no; **we hope you'll be able to come** esperamos que puedas venir (*'espero que' is followed by the subjunctive*).

hopeless *adjective* **to be hopeless at something** ser [1] un negado para algo (*informal*); **I'm hopeless at geography** soy un negado para la geografía.

horizon *noun* horizonte *Masc.*

horn *noun* **1** (*of an animal*) cuerno *Masc.*; **2** (*of a car*) bocina *Fem.*; **to sound your horn** tocar [31] la bocina; **3** (*musical instrument*) trompa *Fem.*; **to play the horn** tocar [31] trompa.

horoscope *noun* horóscopo *Masc.*

a
b
c
d
e
f
g
h
i
j
k
l
m
n
o
p
q
r
s
t
u
v
w
x
y
z

a
b
c
d
e
f
g
h
i
j
k
l
m
n
o
p
q
r
s
t
u
v
w
x
y
z

horrible *adjective* **1** horrible; **the weather was horrible** el tiempo era horrible; **she's really horrible!** ¡es realmente horrible!; **2 he was really horrible to me** me trató muy mal.

horrific *adjective* horroroso/horrorosa; **a horrific accident** un accidente horroroso.

horror *noun* horror *Masc.*

horror film *noun* película *Fem.* de terror.

horse *noun* caballo *Masc.*

horse racing *noun* carreras *Fem. plural* de caballos.

hose *noun* manguera *Fem.*

hospital *noun* hospital *Masc.*; **to be in hospital** estar [2] en el hospital; **to be taken into hospital** ser [1] hospitalizado.

hospitality *noun* hospitalidad *Fem.*

host *noun* anfitrión *Masc.*, anfitriona *Fem.*; **my host family is very nice** la familia que me hospeda es muy amable.

hostage *noun* rehén *Masc.*

hostel *noun* **youth hostel** albergue *Masc.* juvenil.

hostess *noun* azafata *Fem.*; **an air hostess** una azafata de vuelo.

hot *adjective* **1** caliente; **a hot drink** una bebida caliente; **be careful, the plates are hot!** ¡cuidado! los platos están calientes; **2** (*a person*) **to be hot** tener [9] calor; **I'm hot** tengo calor; **I'm very hot** tengo mucho calor; **I'm too hot** tengo demasiado calor; **3** (*the weather or temperature in a room*) **it's hot** hace calor; **it's hot today** hace calor hoy; **it's very hot in the kitchen** hace mucho calor en la cocina; **4 a hot climate** un clima cálido; **5** (*food: spicy*) picante; **this curry's too hot for me** este curry es demasiado picante para mí.

hot dog *noun* perrito *Masc.* caliente.

hotel *noun* hotel *Masc.*

hour *noun* hora *Fem.*; **two hours later** dos horas más tarde; **we waited for two hours** esperamos dos horas; **two hours ago** hace dos horas; **to be paid by the hour** cobrar [17] por hora; **I earn six pounds an hour** gano seis libras por hora; **every hour** cada hora; **half an hour** media hora; **a quarter of an hour** un cuarto de hora; **an hour and a half** una hora y media.

hourly *adjective* **there is an hourly bus** hay un bus que sale cada hora.

hourly *adverb* **the trains leave hourly** los trenes salen cada hora.

house *noun* casa *Fem.*; **I'm at Judy's house** estoy en casa de Judy; **I'm going to Judy's house tonight** voy a casa de Judy esta noche; **I phoned from Judy's house** llamé desde casa de Judy.

housework *noun* tareas *Fem. plural* de la casa; **to do the housework** hacer [7] las tareas de la casa.

hovercraft *noun* aerodeslizador *Masc.*

how *adverb* **1** cómo; **how did you do it?** ¿cómo lo hiciste?; **how are you?** ¿cómo estás?; **I know how to do it** sé cómo hacerlo; **2 how was the party?** ¿qué tal fue la fiesta?; **3 how much?** ¿cuánto?; **how much money do you have?** ¿cuánto dinero tienes?; **how much is it?** ¿cuánto cuesta?; **4 how many?** ¿cuántos?; **how many brothers do you have?** ¿cuántos hermanos tienes?; **5 how old are you?** ¿cuántos años tienes?; **how heavy is it?** ¿cuánto pesa?; **6 how far is it?** ¿a qué distancia está?; **how far is it to Bilbao?** ¿a qué distancia está Bilbao?; **7 how long will it take?** ¿cuánto tardará?; **how long have you known her?** ¿cuánto tiempo hace que la conoces?; **8** (*in exclamations*) qué; **how nice!** ¡qué bonito!

however *adverb* sin embargo.

hug *noun* **to give somebody a hug** darle [4] un abrazo a alguien; **she gave me a hug** me dio un abrazo.

huge *adjective* enorme.

hum *verb* tararear [17] (*a person*).

human *adjective* humano/humana.

human being *noun* ser *Masc.* humano.

humour *noun* humor *Masc.*; **to have a sense of humour** tener [9] sentido del humor.

hundred *number* **1** cien; **a hundred** cien; **about a hundred** unos/unas cien; **about a hundred people** unas cien personas; **hundreds of people** cientos de personas; **2** (*for numbers 101 to 199*) ciento; **one hundred and six** ciento seis; **3** (*for numbers 200 to 999*) **two hundred** doscientos/doscientas; **two hundred and ten** doscientos

diez; **six hundred** seiscientos/ seiscientas.

Hungary *noun* Hungría *Fem.*

hunger *noun* hambre *Fem.* (*even though 'hambre' is feminine, it takes 'el' and 'un'*).

hungry *adjective* **to be hungry** tener [9] hambre; **I'm hungry** tengo hambre.

hunt *verb* cazar [22] (*animals*).

● **hunt for** (*search for*) buscar.

hurricane *noun* huracán *Masc.*

hurry *noun* **to be in a hurry** tener [9] prisa; **I'm in a hurry** tengo prisa. **hurry** *verb* darse [4] prisa; **I must hurry** debo darme prisa; **we hurried home** nos dimos prisa para llegar a casa; **hurry up!** ¡date prisa!

hurt *verb* **1 to hurt somebody** hacer [7] daño a alguien; **you're hurting me!** me estás haciendo daño; **that hurts!** ¡eso hace daño!; **2 my back hurts** me duele la espalda; **my legs hurt** me duelen las piernas; **3 to hurt yourself** hacerse [7] daño; **did you hurt yourself?** ¿te has hecho daño?; **4 to hurt your hand** hacerse [7] daño en la mano; **I hurt my arm** me hice daño en el brazo.

husband *noun* marido *Masc.*

hymn *noun* himno *Masc.*

hypermarket *noun* hipermercado *Masc.*

hyphen *noun* guión *Masc.*

hypnotize *verb* hipnotizar [25].

a
b
c
d
e
f
g
h
i
j
k
l
m
n
o
p
q
r
s
t
u
v
w
x
y
z

a
b
c
d
e
f
g
h
i
j
k
l
m
n
o
p
q
r
s
t
u
v
w
x
y
z

Ii

I *pronoun* **1** (*like other subject pronouns, 'I' is generally not translated; in Spanish the form of the verb tells you whether the subject of the verb is 'I, we, they', etc., so 'I' is only translated for emphasis*) **I am Scottish** soy escocés; **I have two sisters** tengo dos hermanas; **2** (*for emphasis*) yo; **I did it** lo hice yo; **I went but Robert didn't** yo fui pero Robert no; **Tony and I** Tony y yo.

Iberia *noun* Iberia *Fem.*

Iberian *adjective* ibérico/ibérica.

ice *noun* hielo *Masc.*

iceberg *noun* iceberg *Masc.*

ice cream *noun* helado *Masc.*; **a chocolate ice cream** un helado de chocolate.

ice-cube *noun* cubito *Masc.* de hielo.

ice hockey *noun* hockey *Masc.* sobre hielo.

ice rink *noun* pista *Fem.* de hielo.

ice-skating *noun* patinaje *Masc.* sobre hielo; **to go ice-skating** ir [8] a patinar sobre hielo.

icing *noun* azúcar *Masc.* glaseado.

icon *noun* icono *Masc.*

icy *adjective* **1** cubierto/cubierta de hielo (*a road*); **2** (*very cold*) helado/helada; **an icy wind** un viento helado.

idea *noun* idea *Fem.*; **what a good idea!** ¡qué buena idea!; **I've no idea** no tengo ni idea.

ideal *adjective* ideal.

identical *adjective* idéntico/idéntica; **identical twins** gemelos (*male, or male and female*), gemelas (*female only*).

identity card *noun* carné *Fem.* de identidad.

idiot *noun* idiota *Masc./Fem.*

idiotic *adjective* idiota.

i.e. (*in writing*) i.e. (*in speech*) esto es.

if *conjunction* **1** si; **if Sue's there** si Sue está allí; **if it rains** si llueve; **if not** si no (*when talking about something that might or might not happen, 'si' is followed by the subjunctive*) **if I won the lottery** si ganase la lotería; **2 if only ...** ojalá ...; **if only you'd told me** ojalá me lo hubieses dicho; **3 even if** incluso si; **even if it snows** incluso si nieva; **4 if I were you ...** yo que tú ...; **if I were you, I'd forget it** yo que tú me olvidaría del asunto.

ignore *verb* **1** ignorar [17] (*a person*); **2** no hacer [7] caso de (*what somebody says*); **just ignore it** no hagas caso.

ill *adjective* enfermo/enferma; **to fall ill, to be taken ill** enfermar [17]; **to feel ill** sentirse [14] mal.

illegal *adjective* ilegal.

illness *noun* enfermedad *Fem.*

illustrated *adjective* ilustrado/ilustrada.

illustration *noun* ilustración *Fem.*

imagination *noun* imaginación *Fem.*; **to show imagination** demostrar [24] imaginación.

imaginative *adjective* imaginativo/imaginativa.

imagine *verb* imaginar [17]; **imagine that you're very rich** imagina que eres muy rico; **you can't imagine how hard it was!** ¡no puedes imaginarte lo difícil que fue!

imitate *verb* imitar [17].

imitation *noun* imitación *Fem.*

immediate *adjective* inmediato/ inmediata.

immediately *adverb* inmediatamente; **I rang them immediately** los llamé inmediatamente; **immediately before** justo antes; **immediately after** justo después.

immigrant *noun* inmigrante *Masc./ Fem.*

immigration *noun* inmigración *Fem.*

impact *noun* impacto *Masc.*

impatience *noun* impaciencia *Fem.*

impatient *adjective* **1** impaciente; **2 to get impatient with somebody** impacientarse [17] con alguien.

impatiently *adverb* con impaciencia.

imperfect *noun* (*of a verb*) imperfecto *Masc.*; **in the imperfect** en imperfecto.

import *noun* importación *Fem.* **import** *verb* importar [17].

importance *noun* importancia *Fem.*

important *adjective* importante.

impossible *adjective* imposible; **it's impossible to find a telephone** es imposible encontrar un teléfono.

impressed *adjective* impresionado/impresionada.

impression *noun* impresión *Fem.*; **to make a good impression on somebody** causar [17] una buena impresión a alguien; **I got the impression he was hiding something** me dio la impresión de que estaba ocultando algo.

improve *verb* mejorar [17]; **to improve something** mejorar [17] algo; **the weather is improving** el tiempo está mejorando.

improvement *noun* **1** (*a change for the better*) mejora *Fem.*; **2** (*gradual progress*) progreso *Masc.* (*in schoolwork, for example*).

in *preposition, adverb* **1** en; **in Spain** en España; **in Spanish** en español; **in Barcelona** en Barcelona; **in my pocket** en mi bolsillo; **in the newspaper** en el periódico; **in my class** en mi clase; **I was in the bath** estaba en el baño; **a house in the country** una casa en el campo; **in school** en el colegio; **in town** en la ciudad; **in the photo** en la foto; **2 in pencil** a lápiz; **in twos** de dos en dos; **3** (*wearing*) de; **the girl in the pink shirt** la chica de la falda rosa; **he was in a suit** llevaba un traje; **dressed in white** vestida de blanco; **4** (*with month, season, or year*) **in May** en mayo; **in 1998** en mil novecientos noventa y ocho; **in winter** en invierno; **5** (*with parts of the day*) **in the morning** por la

mañana; **in the night** por la noche;
at eight in the morning a las ocho
de la mañana; **6 I'll phone you in
ten minutes** te llamaré dentro de
diez minutos; **she did it in five
minutes** lo hizo en cinco minutos;
7 (*after superlative*) de; **the tallest
boy in the class** el chico más alto de
la clase; **the biggest city in the
world** la ciudad más grande del
mundo; **8 in time** con el tiempo; **9 in
the sun** al sol; **in the rain** bajo la
lluvia; **10 to come in** entrar [17]; **to
go in** entrar [17]; **we went into the
cinema** entramos en el cine; **to run
in** entrar [17] corriendo; **11 to be in**
(*at home, around*) estar [2]; **Mick's
not in at the moment** Mick no está
en este momento.

include *verb* incluir [54]; **dinner is
included in the price** la cena está
incluida en el precio; **service
included** servicio incluido.

including *preposition* incluido; **50
pounds including VAT** cincuenta
libras IVA incluido; **everyone,
including children** todo el mundo
incluidos los niños; **including
Sundays** incluidos los domingos;
not including Sundays sin incluir
los domingos.

income *noun* ingresos *Masc. plural*.

income tax *noun* impuesto *Masc.*
sobre la renta.

inconvenient *adjective* **1** poco
conveniente (*a place or an
arrangement*); **2** inoportuno/
inoportuna (*a time*).

increase *noun* aumento *Masc.* (*in
price, for example*).

increase *verb* aumentar [17]; **the
price has increased by ten
pounds** el precio ha aumentado diez
libras.

incredible *adjective* increíble.

incredibly *adverb* (*very*)
increíblemente; **the film's
incredibly boring** la película es
increíblemente aburrida.

indeed *adverb* **1** (*to emphasize*)
she's very pleased indeed está
contentísima; **I'm very hungry
indeed** tengo muchísima hambre;
thank you very much indeed
muchísimas gracias; **2** (*certainly*)
**'can you hear his radio?' – 'indeed
I can!'** ¿oyes su radio?' – 'ya lo creo';
'do you like it?' – 'I do indeed!' ¿te
gusta?' – 'sí, muchísimo'.

indefinite article *noun* (*in
grammar*) artículo *Masc.* indefinido.

independence *noun*
independencia *Fem.*

independent *adjective* **1** (*a
country or person*) independiente;
2 an independent school una
escuela privada.

index *noun* índice *Masc.*

index finger *noun* dedo *Masc.*
índice.

India *noun* India *Fem.*

Indian *noun* (*of India*) indio *Masc.*,
india *Fem.*
Indian *adjective* (*of India*) indio/
india.

indigestion *noun* indigestión
Fem.; **to have indigestion** tener [9]
indigestión.

indirect *adjective* indirecto/indirecta.

individual *noun* individuo *Masc.* **individual** *adjective* **1** individual (*a serving or a contribution, for example*); **2 individual tuition** clases *Fem. plural* particulares.

indoor *adjective* **an indoor swimming pool** una piscina cubierta; **an indoor plant** una planta de interior.

indoors *adverb* dentro; **it's cooler indoors** hace más fresco dentro; **to go indoors** entrar [17]; **to stay indoors** quedarse [17] dentro.

industrial *adjective* industrial.

industrial estate *noun* zona *Fem.* industrial.

industry *noun* industria *Fem.*; **the advertising industry** la industria de la publicidad.

inevitable *adjective* inevitable.

inevitably *adverb* inevitablemente.

inexperienced *adjective* inexperto/inexperta.

infected *adjective* infectado/infectada.

infection *noun* infección *Fem.*; **an eye infection** una infección de ojos; **a throat infection** anginas *Fem. plural*.

infectious *adjective* infeccioso/infecciosa.

infinitive *noun* infinitivo *Masc.*; **in the infinitive** en infinitivo.

inflation *noun* inflación *Fem.*

influence *noun* influencia *Fem.*; **to be a good influence on somebody** ser [1] una buena influencia para alguien.

inform *verb* informar [17]; **to inform somebody that** informar a alguien de que; **they informed us that there was a problem** nos informaron de que había un problema; **to inform somebody of something** informar a alguien de algo.

informal *adjective* **1** informal (*a meal or event, for example*); **2** (*language*) familiar; **an informal expression** una expresión familiar.

information *noun* información *Fem.*; **I need some information about flights to Madrid** necesito información sobre vuelos a Madrid; **a piece of information** un dato.

information desk *noun* mostrador *Masc.* de información.

information office *noun* oficina *Fem.* de información.

information technology, **IT** *noun* informática *Fem.*

infuriating *adjective* exasperante.

ingredient *noun* ingrediente *Masc.*

initials *plural noun* iniciales *Fem. plural*; **put your initials here** pon tus iniciales aquí.

injection *noun* inyección *Fem.*; **to give somebody an injection** ponerle [11] una inyección a alguien.

injure *verb* herir [14].

injured *adjective* herido/herida.

injury *noun* herida *Fem.*

a
b
c
d
e
f
g
h
i
j
k
l
m
n
o
p
q
r
s
t
u
v
w
x
y
z

a

ink *noun* tinta *Fem.*

b

in-laws *plural noun* suegros *Masc. plural.*

c

innocent *adjective* inocente.

d

insane *adjective* loco/loca.

e

inscription *noun* inscripción *Fem.*

f

insect *noun* insecto *Masc.*; **an insect bite** una picadura de insecto.

g

insert *verb* insertar [17].

h

inside *noun* interior *Masc.*; **the inside of the oven** el interior del horno.

i

inside *preposition* dentro de; **inside the cinema** dentro del cine.

j

inside *adverb* dentro; **she's inside, I think** creo que está dentro; **to go inside** entrar [17].

k

l

m

inside out *adjective, adverb* del revés; **your jumper's inside out** llevas el jersey del revés.

n

insist *verb* **1** insistir [19]; **if you insist** si insistes; **to insist on doing** insistir en hacer; **he insisted on paying** insistió en pagar; **2 to insist that** insistir en que; **Ruth insisted I was wrong** Ruth insistió en que yo estaba equivocada.

o

p

q

r

s

inspection *noun* inspección *Fem.*

t

inspector *noun* inspector *Masc.*, inspectora *Fem.*

u

inspiration *noun* inspiración *Fem.*

v

install *verb* instalar [17].

w

instalment *noun* **1** (*of a TV or radio serial*) episodio *Masc.*; **2** (*payment*) plazo *Masc.*; **to pay by instalments** pagar [28] a plazos.

x

y

instance *noun* **for instance** por ejemplo.

z

instant *noun* instante *Masc.*; **come here this instant!** ¡ven aquí ahora mismo!

instant *adjective* **1** instantáneo/instantánea (*coffee or soup*); **2** (*immediate*) inmediato/inmediata (*an effect or a success, for example*).

instead *adverb* **1 Ted couldn't go, so I went instead** Ted no pudo ir, así que fui yo en su lugar; **we didn't go to the concert, we went to Lucy's instead** no fuimos al concierto, fuimos a casa de Lucy; **2 instead of** en vez de; **instead of pudding I had cheese** en vez de dulce tomé queso; **instead of playing tennis we went swimming** en vez de jugar al tenis nos fuimos a nadar.

instinct *noun* instinto *Masc.*

instruct *verb* **to instruct somebody to do** ordenar [17] a alguien que haga (*'que' is followed by the subjunctive*); **the teacher instructed us to stay together** la profesora nos ordenó que nos quedásemos juntos.

instructions *plural noun* instrucciones *Fem. plural*; **follow the instructions on the packet** siga las instrucciones del paquete; **'instructions for use'** 'modo de empleo'.

instructor *noun* **1** monitor *Masc.*, monitora *Fem.*; **my skiing instructor** mi monitor de esquí; **2** profesor *Masc.*, profesora *Fem.*; **my driving instructor** mi profesor de conducir.

instrument *noun* instrumento Masc.; **to play an instrument** tocar [31] un instrumento.

insulin *noun* insulina Fem.

insult *noun* insulto Masc.
insult *verb* insultar [17].

insurance *noun* seguro Masc.; **travel insurance** seguro de viaje; **fire insurance** seguro contra incendios; **do you have medical insurance?** ¿tienes seguro médico?

intelligence *noun* inteligencia Fem.

intelligent *adjective* inteligente.

intend *verb* 1 querer [12]; **as I intended** como yo quería; 2 **to intend to do** tener [9] pensado hacer; **we intend to spend the night in Rome** tenemos pensado pasar la noche en Roma.

intensive *adjective* intensivo/ intensiva; **an intensive course** un curso intensivo; **in intensive care** en cuidados intensivos.

intention *noun* intención Fem.; **I have no intention of paying** no tengo ninguna intención de pagar.

interest *noun* 1 (*hobby*) afición Fem.; **what are your interests?** ¿qué aficiones tienes?; 2 (*keenness*) interés Masc.; **she showed interest** mostró interés.
interest *verb* interesar [17]; **that doesn't interest me** eso no me interesa.

interested *adjective* **Sean's very interested in cooking** a Sean le interesa mucho la cocina.

interesting *adjective* interesante.

interfere *verb* 1 **to interfere with something** (*to fiddle with it*) tocar [31] algo; **don't interfere with my computer!** ¡no toques mi ordenador!; 2 **to interfere in** entrometerse [18] en (*someone else's affairs*).

interior *adjective* interior.

interior designer *noun* interiorista Masc./Fem.

international *adjective* internacional.

Internet *noun* Internet Fem.; **on the Internet** en Internet (*'Internet' is never used with an article*).

Internet cafe *noun* cibercafé Masc.; **where is there an Internet cafe?** ¿dónde hay un cibercafé?

interpreter *noun* intérprete Masc./ Fem.

interrupt *verb* interrumpir [19].

interruption *noun* interrupción Fem.

interval *noun* intermedio Masc. (*in a play or concert*).

interview *noun* entrevista Fem.; **a job interview** una entrevista de trabajo; **a TV interview** una entrevista en la tele.
interview *verb* entrevistar [17] (*on TV, radio*).

interviewer *noun* entrevistador Masc., entrevistadora Fem.

into *preposition* 1 dentro; **I put the cat into his basket** puse al gato dentro de su cesta; 2 **to go into** entrar, entrar [17] a; **he's gone into the bank** ha entrado al banco; 3 **to get into** entrar [17] en (*car*); **we all**

got **into the car** entramos todos en el coche; **4 to go into town** ir [8] a la ciudad; **Mum's gone into town** mamá se ha ido a la ciudad; **to get into bed** meterse [18] a la cama; **5 to translate into Spanish** traducir [60] al español; **to change pounds into euros** cambiar [17] libras a euros.

introduce *verb* presentar [17]; **she introduced me to her brother** me presentó a su hermano; **can I introduce you to my mother?** ¿te puedo presentar a mi madre?

introduction *noun* (*in a book*) introducción *Fem.*

invade *verb* invadir [19].

invalid *noun* inválido *Masc.*, inválida *Fem.*

invasion *noun* invasión *Fem.*

invent *verb* inventar [17].

invention *noun* invento *Masc.*

inverted commas *plural noun* comillas *Fem. plural*; **in inverted commas** entre comillas.

investigation *noun* investigación *Fem.*; **an investigation into the fire** una investigación sobre el fuego.

invisible *adjective* invisible.

invitation *noun* invitación *Fem.*; **an invitation to dinner** una invitación a cenar.

invite *verb* invitar [17]; **Kirsty invited me to lunch** Kirsty me invitó a comer; **he's invited me out on Tuesday** me ha invitado a salir el martes.

invoice *noun* factura *Fem.*

involve *verb* **1** suponer [11]; **it involves a lot of work** supone mucho trabajo; **2** (*consist in*) **what does the job involve?** ¿en qué consiste el trabajo?; **3 to be involved in** tomar [17] parte en; **I am involved in the new project** estoy tomando parte en el nuevo proyecto.

Iran *noun* Iran *Masc.*

Iraq *noun* Irak *Masc.*

Ireland *noun* Irlanda *Fem.*; **the Republic of Ireland** la República Irlandesa.

iris *noun* lirio *Masc.*

Irish *noun* **1** (*the language*) irlandés *Masc.*; **2** (*the people*) **the Irish** los irlandeses.
Irish *adjective* irlandés/irlandesa.

Irishman *noun* irlandés.

Irish Sea *noun* mar *Masc.* de Irlanda.

Irishwoman *noun* irlandesa *Fem.*

iron *noun* **1** (*for clothes*) plancha *Fem.*; **2** (*the metal*) hierro *Masc.*
iron *verb* planchar [17].

ironing *noun* **to do the ironing** planchar [17].

ironing board *noun* tabla *Fem.* de planchar.

irregular *adjective* irregular.

irresponsible *adjective* irresponsable.

irritating *adjective* irritante.

Islam *noun* Islam *Masc.*

Islamic *adjective* islámico/islámica.

island *noun* isla *Fem.*

isolated *adjective* aislado/aislada.

Israel *noun* Israel *Masc.*

Israeli *noun* israelí *Masc./Fem.*.
Israeli *adjective* israelí.

issue *noun* **1** (*something you discuss*) tema *Masc.*; **a political issue** un tema político; **2** (*of a magazine*) número *Masc.*
issue *verb* distribuir [54].

it *pronoun* **1** (*'it' like other subject pronouns is generally not translated; in Spanish the form of the verb tells you whether the subject of the verb is 'he/she/it, we, they', etc*) **'where is my bag?' – 'it's in the kitchen'** '¿dónde está mi bolso?' – 'está en la cocina'; **read this book, it's great** lee este libro, es genial; **'how old is your car?' – 'it's five years old'** '¿cuántos años tiene tu coche?' - 'cinco'; **2** (*as the object of the verb*) lo/la; **where's my book? I've lost it** ¿dónde está mi libro? lo he perdido; **give me the suitcase, I'll carry it** dame la maleta, yo la llevo (*with a verb in the infinitive or when telling somebody to do something, 'lo' or 'la' join onto the verb*) **I've finished the letter, I only have to sign it** he terminado la carta, sólo me queda firmarla; **it's your money, take it** es tu dinero, cógelo (*but when telling somebody NOT to do something, 'lo' or 'la' goes before the verb*) **it's an expensive vase, don't break it** es un jarrón caro, no lo rompas; **3 who is it?** ¿quién es?; **it's me** soy yo; **what is it?** ¿qué es?; **4 yes, it's true** sí, es verdad; **it doesn't matter** no importa; **5 it's raining** está lloviendo; **it's a nice day** hace buen día; **it's very cold here** hace mucho frío aquí; **it's two o'clock** son las dos; **6** (*after a preposition*) **I don't want to talk about it** no quiero hablar de ello; **the box goes behind it** la caja va detrás.

IT *noun* (*short for information technology*) informática *Fem.*

Italian *noun* **1** (*the language*) italiano *Masc.*; **2** (*person*) italiano *Masc.*, italiana *Fem.*.
Italian *adjective* **1** italiano/italiana; **Italian food** la comida italiana; **2** de italiano (*a teacher or a lesson*); **my Italian class** mi clase de italiano.

italics *noun* cursiva *Fem.*; **in italics** en cursiva.

Italy *noun* Italia *Fem.*

itch *verb* **1** (*a garment*) picar [31]; **this sweater itches** este jersey pica; **2** (*a part of the body*) **my back is itching** me pica la espalda; **I'm itching all over** me pica todo el cuerpo.

item *noun* artículo *Masc.*

its *adjective* **1** (*before a singular noun*) su; **its ear** su oreja; **2** (*before a plural noun*) sus; **its toys** sus juguetes.

itself *pronoun* **1** (*as a reflexive*) se; **the cat is washing itself** el gato se está lavando; **2 by itself** solo/sola; **he left the dog by itself** dejó al perro solo.

ivory *noun* marfil *Masc.*

ivy *noun* hiedra *Fem.*

Jj

jack noun **1** (*in cards*) jota Fem.; **the jack of clubs** la jota de tréboles; **2** (*for a car*) gato Masc.

jacket noun **1** chaqueta Fem.; **2** (*casual*) americana Fem.

jagged adjective dentado/dentada.

jail noun cárcel Fem.
jail verb meter [18] en la cárcel.

jam noun **1** (*that you eat*) mermelada Fem.; **raspberry jam** mermelada de frambuesa; **2 a traffic jam** un atasco (de tráfico).

Jamaica noun Jamaica Fem.

Jamaican noun jamaicano Masc., jamaicana Fem.
Jamaican adjective jamaicano/jamaicana.

January noun enero Masc.

Japan noun Japón Masc.

Japanese noun **1** (*the language*) japonés Masc.; **2** (*person*) japonés Masc., japonesa Fem.; **the Japanese** los japoneses.
Japanese adjective japonés/japonesa.

jar noun bote Masc.; **a jar of jam** un bote de mermelada.

jazz noun jazz Masc.

jealous adjective celoso/celosa.

jealousy noun celos Masc. plural.

jeans noun vaqueros Masc. plural; **my jeans** mis vaqueros; **a pair of jeans** unos vaqueros.

jelly noun **1** (*clear jam*) jalea Fem.; **2** (*dessert*) gelatina Fem.

jellyfish noun medusa Fem.

jersey noun **1** (*sweater*) jersey Masc.; **2** (*for football*) camiseta Fem.

Jesus noun Jesús Masc.; **Jesus Christ** Jesucristo.

Jew noun judío Masc., judía Fem.

jewel noun joya Fem.

jeweller noun joyero Masc., joyera Fem.

jeweller's noun joyería Fem.

jewellery noun joyas Fem. plural.

Jewish adjective judío/judía.

jigsaw noun rompecabezas Masc. puzzle Masc.

job noun **1** (*paid work*) trabajo Masc.; **a job as a secretary** un trabajo de secretaria; **he's got a job** tiene un trabajo; **out of a job** sin trabajo; **what's your job?** ¿en qué trabajas?; **2** (*a task*) tarea Fem.; **it's not an easy job** no es una tarea fácil; **she made a good job of it** lo hizo muy bien.

jobless adjective en paro.

jog verb **to go jogging** hacer [7] footing.

join verb **1** (*become a member of*) hacerse [7] socio de; **I've joined the judo club** me he hecho socio del club de judo; **2** (*to meet up with*) **you go ahead, I'll join you later** id vosotros, yo voy más tarde; **we are going for a meal, do you want to join us?** vamos a salir a comer, ¿quieres venirte con nosotros?; **3 to join two things together** unir [19] dos cosas; **4 to join a queue** ponerse [11] a la cola.

- **to join in 1** participar [17]; **Ruth never joins in** Ruth nunca participa; **2 to join in something** tomar [17] parte en algo; **won't you join in the game?** ¿no quieres tomar parte en el juego?

joiner *noun* carpintero *Masc.*, carpintera *Fem.*

joint *noun* **1** (*of meat*) corte *Masc.*; **a joint of beef** un corte de carne; **2** (*in your body*) articulación *Fem.*; **3 the joint winner of the Nobel Prize** uno de los ganadores del Premio Nobel.

joke *noun* **1** (*a funny story*) chiste *Masc.*; **to tell a joke** contar [24] un chiste; **2** (*directed against somebody*) broma *Fem.*; **to play a joke on somebody** gastarle [17] una broma a alguien.
joke *verb* bromear [17]; **you must be joking!** ¡estás bromeando!

joker *noun* (*in cards*) comodín *Masc.*

journalism *noun* periodismo *Masc.*

journalist *noun* periodista *Masc./ Fem.*; **Sean's a journalist** Sean es periodista.

journey *noun* viaje *Masc.*; **our journey to Turkey** nuestro viaje a Turquía; **a bus journey** un viaje en autobús.

joy *noun* alegría *Fem.*

joystick *noun* (*for computer games*) mando *Masc.*

Judaism *noun* judaísmo *Masc.*

judge *noun* juez *Masc.*, jueza *Fem.*
judge *verb* juzgar [28].

judgement *noun* **1** (*sense*) juicio *Masc.*; **2** (*judge's decision*) sentencia *Fem.*

judo *noun* judo *Masc.*; **he does judo** hace judo.

jug *noun* jarra *Fem.* (*big*) jarrita *Fem.* (*small*).

juggle *verb* hacer [17] malabarismos.

juice *noun* zumo *Masc.*; **two orange juices, please** dos zumos de naranja, por favor.

juicy *adjective* jugoso/jugosa.

jukebox *noun* máquina *Fem.* de discos.

July *noun* julio *Masc.*

jumble sale *noun* mercadillo *Masc.* de beneficencia.

jumbo jet *noun* jumbo *Masc.*

jump *noun* salto *Masc.*; **a parachute jump** un salto en paracaídas.
jump *verb* saltar [17].

jumper *noun* jersey *Masc.*

junction *noun* **1** (*of roads*) cruce *Masc.*; **2** (*on railway*) empalme *Masc.*.

June *noun* junio *Masc.*

jungle *noun* selva *Fem.*

junior *adjective* **a junior school** una escuela primaria; **the juniors** los alumnos de primaria.

junk *noun* **1** (*rubbish*) basura *Fem.*; **2** (*discarded things*) trastos *Masc. plural* viejos.

junk food *noun* comida *Fem.* basura.

jury *noun* jurado *Masc.*

a
b
c
d
e
f
g
h
i
j
k
l
m
n
o
p
q
r
s
t
u
v
w
x
y
z

457

just *adverb* **1** justo; **just on time** justo a tiempo; **just after the church** justo después de misa; **it's just what I need** es justo lo que necesito; **2 to have just done** acabar [17] de hacer; **Tom has just arrived** Tom acaba de llegar; **Helen had just called** Helen acaba de llamar; **3 I'm just finishing the ironing** estoy terminando de planchar; **4** (*only*) sólo; **just for fun** sólo por pasarlo bien; **he's just a child** es sólo un niño; **there's just me and Justine** sólo estamos Justine y yo; **5 just as** igual de; **it's just as good as the other** es igual de bueno que el otro; **it's just as possible** es igualmente posible; **6 just coming!** ¡ahora mismo voy!

justice *noun* justicia *Fem.*

Kk

kangaroo *noun* canguro *Masc.*

karate *noun* kárate *Masc.*

kebab *noun* brocheta *Fem.*

keen *adjective* **1** (*enthusiastic*) **you don't look too keen** no pareces muy entusiasmado; **they were keen on the idea** estaban interesados en la idea; **he's not keen on fish** no le gusta el pescado; **2** (*committed*) **he's a keen photographer** le encanta la fotografía.

keep *verb* **1** quedarse [17] con; **I kept the letter** me quedé con la carta; **keep the change** quédese con el cambio; **2 to keep**
something for someone guardarle [17] algo a alguien; **will you keep my seat?** ¿me guardas el sitio?; **to keep a secret** guardar [17] un secreto; **3 to keep somebody waiting** hacer [7] esperar a alguien; **4** (*to store*) guardar; **I keep my bike in the garage** guardo mi bici en el garaje; **where do you keep the saucepans?** ¿dónde guardas las cacerolas?; **5 to keep on doing** seguir [64] haciendo; **she kept on talking** siguió hablando; **keep straight on** siga todo recto; **6 to keep on doing** (*time after time*) no parar de hacer; **he keeps on ringing me up** no para [17] de llamarme; **7 keep calm!** ¡no te pongas nervioso!; **keep still!** ¡estate quieto!; **keep out of the sun** no te pongas al sol; **8 to keep a promise** mantener [9] una promesa.

kerb *noun* bordillo *Masc.* de la acera.

ketchup *noun* ketchup *Masc.*

kettle *noun* hervidora *Fem.*; **to put the kettle on** enchufar la hervidora (*electric*).

key *noun* **1** (*for a lock*) llave *Fem.*; **a bunch of keys** un manojo de llaves; **2** (*on a piano or typewriter*) tecla *Fem.*

keyboard *noun* (*for a piano or a computer*) teclado *Masc.*

keyhole *noun* ojo *Masc.* de la cerradura.

kick *noun* (*from a person or a horse*) patada *Fem.*; **to give somebody a kick** darle [4] una patada a alguien; ★**to get a kick out of doing** disfrutar [17] haciendo.

kick *verb* **to kick somebody** darle [4] una patada a alguien; **to kick the ball** darle [4] una patada al balón.

● **to kick off** empezar [25].

kick-off *noun* saque *Masc.* inicial.

kid *noun* niño *Masc.*, niña *Fem.* (*child*); **Dad's looking after the kids** papá está cuidando de los niños.

kidnap *verb* secuestrar [17].

kidnapper *noun* secuestrador *Masc.*, secuestradora *Fem.*

kidney *noun* riñón *Masc.*

kill *verb* matar [17]; **she was killed in an accident** se mató en un accidente.

killer *noun* (*murderer*) asesino *Masc.*, asesina *Fem.*

kilo *noun* kilo *Masc.*; **a kilo of sugar** un kilo de azúcar; **five euros a kilo** cinco euros el kilo.

kilogramme *noun* kilogramo *Masc.*

kilometre *noun* kilómetro *Masc.*

kilt *noun* falda *Fem.* escocesa.

kind *noun* tipo *Masc.*; **it's a kind of fruit** es un tipo de fruta; **all kinds of people** todo tipo de personas.
kind *adjective* amable; **Marion was very kind to me** Marion fue muy amable conmigo.

kindness *noun* amabilidad *Fem.*

king *noun* rey *Masc.*; **King Juan Carlos** el rey Juan Carlos; **the king of hearts** el rey de corazones.

kingdom *noun* reino *Masc.*; **the United Kingdom** el Reino Unido.

kiosk *noun* **1** (*for newspapers or snacks*) quiosco *Masc.*; **2** (*for a phone*) cabina *Fem.*

kiss *noun* beso *Masc.*; **to give somebody a kiss** darle [4] un beso a alguien.
kiss *verb* besar [17]; **kiss me!** ¡bésame!; **to kiss somebody goodbye** darle [4] un beso de despedida a alguien; **we kissed each other** nos besamos.

kit *noun* **1** (*of tools*) **a tool kit** una caja de herramientas; **a first-aid kit** un botiquín; **2** (*clothes*) equipo *Masc.*; **where's my gym kit?** ¿dónde está mi equipo de gimnasia?; **3** (*for making a model, a piece of furniture, etc*) kit *Masc.*

kitchen *noun* cocina *Fem.*; **the kitchen table** la mesa de la cocina.

kitchen roll *noun* papel *Masc.* de cocina.

kite *noun* (*toy*) cometa *Fem.*; **to fly a kite** hacer [7] volar una cometa.

kitten *noun* gatito *Masc.*, gatita *Fem.*

kiwi fruit *noun* kiwi *Masc.*

knack *noun* tranquillo *Masc.*

knee *noun* rodilla *Fem.*; **to be on your knees** estar [2] de rodillas.

kneel *verb* (*to kneel down*) arrodillarse [17] (*to be on your knees*) estar [2] de rodillas.

knickers *plural noun* bragas *Fem. plural.*

knife *noun* cuchillo *Masc.*

knight *noun* (*in chess*) caballo *Masc.*

knit *verb* hacer [7] punto.

knitting *noun* punto *Masc.*

a **knocker** noun aldaba Fem.

b **knob** noun pomo Masc. (on a door);
tirador Masc. (on a drawer).

c **knock** noun golpe Masc.; **a knock
on the head** un golpe en la cabeza;
d **a knock at the door** un golpe en la
puerta.

e **knock** verb 1 (to bang) darse [4] un
f golpe; **I knocked my arm on the
table** me di un golpe en el brazo con
g la mesa; 2 **to knock at the door**
llamar [17] a la puerta.

h • **to knock down 1** (in a traffic
i accident) atropellar [17] (a person);
2 (to demolish) derribar [17] (an old
j building).

• **to knock out 1** (to make
k unconscious) dejar [17] sin sentido;
l 2 (in sport, to eliminate) eliminar
[17].

m **knot** noun nudo Masc.; **to tie a knot
n in something** hacer [7] un nudo a
algo.

o **know** verb 1 (facts) saber [13]; **do
p you know where Tim is?** ¿sabes
dónde está Tim?; **I know they've
q moved house** sé que se han
cambiado de casa; **he knows it by
r heart** se lo sabe de memoria; **yes, I
s know** sí, ya lo sé; **you never know!**
¡nunca se sabe!; 2 (be personally
t acquainted with) conocer [35] (a
person, place, book, or music, for
u example); **do you know that song?**
v ¿conoces esa canción?; **all the
people I know** toda la gente que
w conozco; **I don't know his mother**
no conozco a su madre; 3 **to know
x how to do** saber [13] hacer; **Steve
y knows how to make paella** Steve
z sabe hacer paella; 4 **to know about**

estar [2] al corriente de (the latest
news); 5 **to know about** saber [13]
de (a subject, machines); **Lindy
knows about computers** Lindy
sabe de ordenadores.

knowledge noun conocimientos
Masc. plural; **scientific knowledge**
conocimientos científicos.

knuckle noun nudillo Masc.

koala noun koala Masc.

Koran noun Corán Masc.

kosher adjective kosher.

Ll

lab noun laboratorio Masc.

label noun etiqueta Fem.

laboratory noun laboratorio Masc.

Labour noun los laboristas Masc.
plural; **to vote for Labour** votar [17]
por los laboristas; **the Labour Party**
el partido laborista.

lace noun 1 (for a shoe) cordón Masc.;
to do up your laces atarse los
cordones; 2 (fabric) encaje Masc.

lad noun chaval Masc. (informal).

ladder noun 1 (for climbing)
escalera Fem.; 2 (in your tights)
carrera Fem.

ladies noun (lavatory) servicio
Masc. de señoras; (sign) **'Ladies'**
'Señoras'.

lady noun señora Fem.; **ladies and
gentlemen** señoras y señores.

lager noun cerveza Fem. rubia.

laid-back *adjective* relajado/relajada.

lake *noun* lago *Masc.*

lamb *noun* cordero *Masc.*; **a leg of lamb** una pierna de cordero.

lamp *noun* lámpara *Fem.*

lamp-post *noun* farola *Fem.*

lampshade *noun* pantalla *Fem.*

land *noun* **1** tierra *Fem.*; **2** (*property*) **a piece of land** un terreno; **he has land** tiene tierras.
land *verb* **1** (*plane, passenger*) aterrizar [22]; **2** (*leave a ship*) desembarcar [31].

landing *noun* **1** (*on the stairs*) descansillo *Masc.*; **2** (*of a plane*) aterrizaje *Masc.*; **3** (*from a boat*) desembarco *Masc.*

landlady *noun* **1** (*of rented house*) casera *Fem.*; **2** (*of pub*) dueña *Fem.*

landlord *noun* **1** (*of rented house*) casero *Masc.*; **2** (*of pub*) dueño *Masc.*

lane *noun* **1** (*in the country*) camino *Masc.*; **2** (*of a motorway or road*) carril *Masc.*; **bus lane** carril de autobuses.

language *noun* **1** (*Spanish, Italian, etc.*) idioma *Masc.*; **a foreign language** un idioma extranjero; **2** (*way of speaking*) lenguaje *Masc.*; **scientific language** lenguaje científico; **3 bad language** palabrotas *Fem. plural*; **to use bad language** decir [5] palabrotas.

language lab *noun* laboratorio *Masc.* de idiomas.

language school *noun* academia *Fem.* de idiomas.

lap *noun* **1** (*your knees*) rodillas *Fem. plural*; **on my lap** en mis rodilla; **2** (*in races*) vuelta *Fem.*

laptop *noun* ordenador *Masc.* portátil.

laser *noun* láser *Masc.*; **a laser beam** un rayo láser; **a laser printer** una impresora láser.

last *adjective* **1** (*in final position*) (*to arrive or leave*); **Rob arrived last** Rob llegó el último; **I came last in the race** llegué en último lugar en la carrera; **2** (*most recently*) **I last saw him in May** la última vez que lo vi fue en mayo; **3 at last!** ¡por fin!
last *verb* durar [17]; **the play lasted two hours** la obra duró dos horas.

last *adjective* **1** último/última; **the last time** la última vez; **the last thing I did** lo último que hice; **2 last week** la semana pasada; **last night** (*in the evening*) ayer por la tarde; (*in the night*) anoche.

late *adjective, adverb* **1** tarde; **we're late** llegamos tarde; **they arrived late** llegaron tarde; **to be late for something** llegar [28] tarde a algo; **we were late for the film** llegamos tarde a la película; **2 to be late** (*a bus or train*) llegar [28] con retraso; **the train was an hour late** el tren llegó con una hora de retraso; **3** (*late in the day*) tarde; **we got up late** nos levantamos tarde; **it's getting late** se está haciendo tarde; **late last night** ayer por la noche ya tarde; **too late!** ¡demasiado tarde!

later *adverb* más tarde; **I'll explain to you later** te lo explicaré más tarde; **later that same day** ese

a
b
c
d
e
f
g
h
i
j
k
l
m
n
o
p
q
r
s
t
u
v
w
x
y
z

mismo día más tarde; **no later than Thursday** no más tarde del jueves; **see you later!** ¡hasta luego!

latest *adjective* último/última; **the latest news** las últimas noticias.
latest *noun* **at the latest** a más tardar; **the latest in audio equipment** lo último en equipo de audio.

Latin *noun* latín *Masc.*

Latin America *noun* América *Fem.* Latina.

Latin American *adjective* latinoamericano/latinoamericana.

laugh *noun* risa *Fem.*; **to do something for a laugh** hacer [7] algo por divertirse.
laugh *verb* **1** reírse [61]; **everybody laughed** todo el mundo se rió; **2** **to laugh at** reírse [61] de; **I tried to explain but they laughed at me** intenté explicarlo pero se rieron de mí.

laughter *noun* risas *Fem. plural.*

launch *noun* **1** (*of product, spacecraft*) lanzamiento *Masc.*; **1** (*of ship*) botadura *Fem.*
launch *verb* **1** (*product, spacecraft*) lanzar [22]; **1** (*ship*) botar [17].

launderette *noun* lavandería *Fem.*

laundry *noun* lavandería *Fem.*

lavatory *noun* servicio *Masc.*, aseo *Masc.*

lavender *noun* lavanda *Fem.*

law *noun* **1** ley *Fem.*; **it's against the law** es ilegal; **2** (*subject of study*) derecho *Masc.*

lawn *noun* césped *Masc.*

lawnmower *noun* cortacésped *Masc.*

lawyer *noun* abogado *Masc.*, abogada *Fem.*

lay *verb* poner [11]; **she laid the card on the table** puso la tarjeta en la mesa; **to lay the table** poner la mesa.

lay-by *noun* área *Fem.* de reposo (*even though 'área' is a feminine, it takes 'el' and 'un' in the singular*); **a lay-by** un área de reposo.

layer *noun* capa *Fem.*

laziness *noun* pereza *Fem.*

lazy *adjective* perezoso/perezosa.

lead *noun* **1** (*when you are ahead*) **to be in the lead** llevar [17] la delantera; **Sam's in the lead** Sam lleva la delantera; **we have a lead of three points** llevamos una ventaja de tres puntos; **2** (*electric*) cable *Masc.*; **3** (*for a dog*) correa *Fem.*; **on a lead** con correa.
lead *adjective* (*a role or a singer*) principal.
lead *verb* **1** llevar [17]; **the path leads to the sea** el sendero lleva al mar; **2** **to lead the way** ir [8] delante; **3** (*in a competition*) llevar [17] la delantera; **4** **this will lead to problems** esto traerá problemas; **to lead to an accident** causar [17] un accidente.

leader *noun* **1** (*of a gang*) cabecilla *Masc./Fem.*; **2** (*of a political party*) líder *Masc./Fem.*; **3** (*in a competition*) primero *Masc.*, primera *Fem.*.

lead-free petrol *noun* gasolina *Fem.* sin plomo.

lead singer *noun* cantante *Masc./ Fem.* principal.

leaf *noun* hoja *Fem.*

leaflet *noun* folleto *Masc.*

league *noun* (*in sport*) liga *Fem.*

lean *adjective* (*meat*) magro/magra. **lean** *verb* **1 to lean on something** apoyarse [17] en algo; **2** (*prop*) apoyar [17]; **lean the ladder against the tree** apoya la escalera en el árbol; **3** (*a person*) echarse [17]; **lean forward a bit** échate para delante un poco; **4 to lean out of the window** asomarse [17] por la ventana.

leap year *noun* año *Masc.* bisiesto.

learn *verb* aprender [18]; **to learn Russian** aprender ruso; **to learn to drive** aprender a conducir.

learner driver *noun* **she's a learner driver** está aprendiendo a conducir.

least *adverb, adjective* **least** *pronoun* **1** menos; **the least expensive hotel** el hotel menos caro; **the least expensive glasses** las gafas menos caras; **Tony has the least money** Tony es el que menos dinero tiene; **I like the blue shirt least** la camisa azul es la que menos me gusta; **2** (*slightest*) más mínimo/ más mínima; **I haven't the least idea** no tengo ni la más mínima idea; **he didn't show the least interest** no mostró el más mínimo interés; **3 at least** (*at a minimum*) por lo menos; **there must be at least twenty people** debe haber por lo menos veinte personas; **4 at least** (*at any rate*) al menos; **at least,**

that's what I think al menos eso creo.

leather *noun* cuero *Masc.*; **a leather jacket** una chaqueta de cuero.

leave *verb* **1** (*go away*) irse [8]; **they're leaving tomorrow** se van mañana; **we left at six** se fueron a las seis; **2** (*go away from*) irse [8] de; **I left the office at five** me fui de la oficina a las cinco; **3** (*go out of*) salir [63] de; **she left the cinema at ten** salió del cine a las diez; **4** (*abandon*) dejar [17] a (*family or partner*); **he left his wife** dejó a su mujer; **5** (*deposit*) dejar [17]; **you can leave your coats in the hall** podéis dejar los abrigos en la entrada; **6** (*forget*) dejarse [17]; **he left his umbrella on the train** se dejó el paraguas en el tren; **7 to leave school** dejar [17] los estudios; **Guy left school at sixteen** Guy dejó los estudios a los dieciséis años; **8 be left** quedar [17]; **there are two cakes left** quedan dos pasteles; **we have ten minutes left** nos quedan diez minutos; **I don't have any money left** no me queda dinero.

lecture *noun* **1** (*at university*) clase *Fem.*; **2** (*public*) conferencia *Fem.*

lecturer *noun* profesor *Masc.*, profesora *Fem.*

ledge *noun* **1** (*of window*) repisa *Fem.*; **2** (*on cliff*) saliente *Masc.*

leek *noun* puerro *Masc.*

left *noun* izquierda *Fem.*; **to drive on the left** conducir [60] por la izquierda; **turn left at the church** tuerce a la izquierda en la iglesia; **on my left** a mi izquierda.

a
b
c
d
e
f
g
h
i
j
k
l
m
n
o
p
q
r
s
t
u
v
w
x
y
z

a

b

c

d

e

f

g

h

i

j

k

l

m

n

o

p

q

r

s

t

u

v

w

x

y

z

left *adjective* izquierdo/izquierda; **his left foot** su pie izquierdo.

left-click *noun* clic *Masc.* con el botón izquierdo.

left-click *verb* hacer [7], clic con el botón izquierdo; **left-click the icon** haz clic en el icono con el botón izquierdo.

left-hand *noun* **the left-hand side** la parte izquierda.

left-handed *adjective* zurdo/ zurda.

left luggage office *noun* consigna *Fem.*

leftovers *plural noun* sobras *Fem. plural.*

leg *noun* **1** (*of a person*) pierna *Fem.*; **my left leg** mi pierna izquierda; **to break your leg** romperse [40] una pierna; **2** (*of a table, chair, or animal*) pata *Fem.*; **3** (*in cooking*) **a leg of chicken** un muslo de pollo; **a leg of lamb** una pierna de cordero; ★ **to pull somebody's leg** tomarle [17] el pelo a alguien (*literally: to take somebody's hair*).

legal *adjective* legal.

legend *noun* **1** (*story*) leyenda *Fem.*; **2** (*star, personality*) leyenda *Fem.*

leggings *plural noun* leggings *Masc. plural.*

leisure *noun* tiempo *Masc.* libre; **in my leisure time** en mi tiempo libre.

leisure centre *noun* polideportivo *Masc.*

lemon *noun* limón *Masc.*; **a lemon yoghurt** un yogur de limón.

lemonade *noun* **1** (*made with lemons*) limonada *Fem.*; **2** (*fizzy drink*) gaseosa *Fem.*

lemon juice *noun* zumo *Masc.* de limón.

lend *verb* dejar [17]; **to lend something to somebody** dejarle algo a alguien; **I lent Judy my bike** le dejé mi bici a Judy; **will you lend it to me?** ¿me lo dejas?

length *noun* **1** (*of fabric, board, etc.*) largo *Masc.*; **2** (*of film, play*) duración *Fem.*; **3** (*of book, list*) extensión *Fem.*

lens *noun* **1** (*in a camera*) lente *Fem.*; **2** (*in spectacles*) cristal *Masc.*; **3 contact lenses** lentillas *Fem. plural.*

Lent *noun* Cuaresma *Fem.*

lentil *noun* lenteja *Fem.*

Leo *noun* Leo *Masc.*; **I'm Leo** soy Leo.

leotard *noun* malla *Fem.*

lesbian *noun* lesbiana *Fem.*

less *pronoun, adjective* **less** *adverb* **1** menos; **Richard eats less** Richard come menos; **less time** menos tiempo; **less interesting** menos interesante; **less quickly than us** menos rápido que nosotros; **2 less than** menos de; **less than a kilo** menos de un kilo; **less than three hours** menos de tres horas; **3 less than** (*in comparisons*) menos que; **you spend less than me** gastas menos que yo.

lesson *noun* clase *Fem.*; **the history lesson** la clase de historia; **a driving lesson** una clase de conducir; **to take tennis lessons** tomar [17] clases de tenis.

let¹ *verb* **1** (*allow*) dejar [17]; **will you let me go alone?** ¿me dejas ir sola?; **the police let us through** la policía me dejó pasar; **let me help you** déjame que te ayude; **she lets me borrow her bike** me deja que coja su bici prestada; **let me see** (*show me*) déjame ver; **2** (*as a suggestion or a command*) **let's go!** ¡vámonos!; **let's not talk about it** no hablemos de ello; **let's see, if Tuesday is the third** ... vamos a ver, si el martes es el tres ...; **let's eat out** vamos a comer fuera.

● **to let off 1** tirar [17] (*fireworks*); **2** hacer [7] estallar (*a bomb*); **3** (*to excuse from*) perdonar [17] (*homework or task*); **I'll let you off doing the dishes** te perdono que no laves los platos.

let² *verb* (*to rent out*) alquilar [17]; **'flat to let'** 'se alquila apartamento'.

lethal *adjective* mortal.

letter *noun* **1** carta *Fem.*; **a letter for you from Delia** una carta de Delia para ti; **2** (*of alphabet*) letra *Fem.*; **M is the letter after L** M es la letra que viene depués de L.

letterbox *noun* buzón *Masc.*

lettuce *noun* lechuga *Fem.*

leukaemia *noun* leucemia *Fem.*

level *noun* nivel *Masc.*; **at street level** a nivel de la calle.
level *adjective* **1** plano/plana (*a shelf or floor*); **2** llano/llana (*ground*).

level crossing *noun* paso *Masc.* a nivel.

lever *noun* palanca *Fem.*

liar *noun* mentiroso *Masc.*, mentirosa *Fem.*

liberal *adjective* liberal; **the Liberal Democrats** los demócratas liberales.

liberty *noun* libertad *Fem.*

Libra *noun* Libra *Fem.*; **Sean's Libra** Sean es Libra.

librarian *noun* bibliotecario *Masc.*, bibliotecaria *Fem.*; **Mark's a librarian** Mark es bibliotecario.

library *noun* biblioteca *Fem.*; **the public library** la biblioteca pública.

licence *noun* **1** (*for driving or fishing*) permiso *Masc.*; **a driving licence** un permiso de conducir; **2** (*for a TV*) licencia *Fem.*

lick *verb* lamer [18].

lid *noun* tapa *Fem.*; **she took the lid off** quitó la tapa.

lie *noun* mentira *Fem.*; **to tell lies** decir [5] mentiras.
lie *verb* **1** (*to be stretched out*) estar [2] tumbado; **Jimmy was lying on the bed** Jimmy estaba tumbado en la cama; **2 to lie down** tumbarse [17] (*for a little while*); **come and lie down in the sun** ven y a tumbarte al sol; **3** (*object*) estar [2]; **my coat lay on the bed** mi abrigo estaba sobre la cama; **4** (*not to tell the truth*) mentir [14].

lieutenant *noun* teniente *Masc./ Fem.*

life *noun* vida *Fem.*; **all her life** toda su vida; **full of life** lleno/llena de vida; **that's life!** ¡así es la vida!

lifebelt *noun* salvavidas *Masc.* (*does not change in the plural*).

a
b
c
d
e
f
g
h
i
j
k
l
m
n
o
p
q
r
s
t
u
v
w
x
y
z

a

b

c

d

e

f

g

h

i

j

k

l

m

n

o

p

q

r

s

t

u

v

w

x

y

z

lifeboat *noun* bote *Masc.* salvavidas.

lifeguard *noun* socorrista *Masc./Fem.*; **is there a lifeguard at the pool?** ¿hay un socorrista en la piscina?

life jacket *noun* chaleco *Masc.* salvavidas.

life-style *noun* estilo *Masc.* de vida.

lift *noun* **1** ascensor *Masc.*; **let's take the lift** vamos a coger el ascensor; **2** (*a ride*) **to give somebody a lift to the station** llevar [17] a alguien a la estación; **Tom gave me a lift home** Tom me llevó a casa; **can you give me a lift?** ¿me puedes llevar?
lift *verb* levantar [17].

light *noun* **1** (*electric*) luz *Fem.*; **can you turn the light on?** ¿puedes encender la luz?; **to turn off the light** apagar la luz; **are your lights on?** (*on a car*) ¿tienes las luces encendidas?; **2** (*streetlight*) farola *Fem.*; **3** (*on a machine*) piloto *Masc.*; **4 traffic lights** semáforo *Masc.*; **the lights were green** el semáforo estaba en verde; **5 have you got a light?** ¿tienes fuego?
light *adjective* **1** (*in colour*) claro/clara; **light blue eyes** ojos azul claro; **2** (*not night*) **it gets light at six** se hace de día a las seis; **3** (*not heavy*) ligero/ligera; **a light sweater** un jersey fino.
light *verb* encender [36] (*the oven, the fire, a match, or a cigarette*); **we lit a fire** encendimos un fuego.

light bulb *noun* bombilla *Fem.*

lighter *noun* encendedor *Masc.*

lightning *noun* relámpago *Masc.*; **a flash of lightning** un relámpago;

the tree was struck by lightning cayó un rayo en el árbol.

light switch *noun* interruptor *Masc.* de la luz.

like¹ *preposition, conjunction* **1** como; **like me** como yo; **like this** como esto; **like a duck** como un pato; **like I said** como dije (yo); **what's it like?** ¿cómo es?; **what was the weather like?** ¿qué tiempo hizo?; **2 to look like** parecerse [35] a; **Cindy looks like her father** Cindy se parece a su padre.

like² *verb* **1 I like fish** me gusta el pescado; **I don't like dogs** no me gustan los perros; **Mum likes travelling** a mamá le gusta viajar; **she likes my brother** le gusta mi hermano; **I like Picasso best** el que más me gusta es Picasso; **2 I would like** quiero; **would you like a coffee?** ¿quieres un café?; **what would you like to eat?** ¿qué quieres comer?; **yes, if you like** sí, si tú quieres.

likely *adjective* probable; **it's not very likely** no es muy probable; **she's likely to phone** es probable que llame.

lime *noun* lima *Fem.* (*fruit*).

limit *noun* límite *Masc.*; **the speed limit** el límite de velocidad.

line *noun* **1** línea *Fem.*; **a straight line** una línea recta; **to draw a line** trazar [22] una línea; **2 a railway line** (*from one place to another*) una línea de ferrocarril; **on the railway line** (*the track*) en la vía férrea; **3** (*queue*) cola *Fem.*; **to stand in line** hacer [7] cola; **4** (*telephone*) línea

Fem.; **the line's bad** no se oye bien; **hold the line, please** no cuelgue, por favor.

linen *noun* lino *Masc.*; **a linen jacket** una chaqueta de lino.

link *noun* conexión *Fem.*; **what's the link between the two?** ¿qué conexión hay entre los dos? **link** *verb* conectar [17] (*two places*); **the terminals are linked by a shuttle service** las terminales están conectadas por un servicio de enlace.

lion *noun* león *Masc.*

lip *noun* labio *Masc.*

lip-read *verb* leer [37] los labios.

lipstick *noun* lápiz *Masc.* de labios.

liquid *noun* líquido *Masc.* **liquid** *adjective* líquido/líquida.

liquidizer *noun* licuadora *Fem.*

list *noun* lista *Fem.*

listen *verb* escuchar [17]; **I wasn't listening** no estaba escuchando; **to listen to** escuchar [17]; **listen to the music** escucha la música; **you're not listening to me** no me estás escuchando.

literature *noun* literatura *Fem.*

litre *noun* litro *Masc.*; **a litre of milk** un litro de leche.

litter *noun* (*rubbish*) basura *Fem.*

litter bin *noun* papelera *Fem.*

little *adjective, pronoun* **1** (*small*) pequeño/pequeña; **a little boy** un niño pequeño; **a little break** una pequeña pausa; **2** (*not much*) poco/poca; **we have very little time** tenemos muy poco tiempo; **3 a little**

un poco; **we have a little money** tenemos un poco de dinero; **just a little, please** sólo un poco, por favor; **it's a little late** es un poco tarde; **a little more** un poco más; **a little less** un poco menos; ★ **little by little** poco a poco.

live¹ *verb* vivir [19]; **Susan lives in York** Susan vive en York; **they live at number 57** viven en el número cincuenta y siete; **they live together** viven juntos.

live² *adjective* **1** en directo (*a broadcast*); **a live concert** un concierto en directo; **2** (*alive*) vivo/viva.

liver *noun* hígado *Masc.*

living *noun* **to earn a living** ganarse [17] la vida.

living room *noun* salón *Masc.*

load *noun* **1** (*on a lorry*) cargamento *Masc.*; **2 a bus-load of tourists** un autobús lleno de turistas; **3 loads of** un montón de (*informal*); **loads of people** un montón de gente; **they've got loads of money** tienen un montón de dinero. **load** *verb* cargar [28].

loaf *noun* **a loaf of bread** un pan; **a loaf of wholemeal bread** un pan integral.

loan *noun* préstamo *Masc.* **loan** *verb* prestar [17].

lobster *noun* langosta *Fem.*

local *noun* **1** (*a pub*) **our local** el bar de nuestro barrio; **2 the locals** (*people*) la gente del lugar. **local** *adjective* **the local library** la

a
b
c
d
e
f
g
h
i
j
k
l
m
n
o
p
q
r
s
t
u
v
w
x
y
z

biblioteca del barrio; **the local newspaper** el periódico local.

locally *adverb* en la zona.

lock *noun* **1** (*with a key*) cerradura *Fem.*; **2** (*on a canal*) esclusa *Fem.*
lock *verb* **to lock the door** cerrar [29] la puerta con llave; **the door was locked** la puerta estaba cerrada con llave.

locker *noun* armario *Masc.*

locker room *noun* vestuario *Masc.*

lodger *noun* inquilino *Masc.*, inquilina *Fem.*

loft *noun* desván *Masc.*

log *noun* tronco *Masc.*

logical *adjective* lógico/lógica.

lollipop *noun* piruleta *Fem.*

London *noun* Londres *Masc.*; **to London** a Londres; **the London streets** las calles de Londres.

Londoner *noun* londinense *Masc./Fem.*

loneliness *noun* soledad *Fem.*

lonely *adjective* **1** solitario/solitaria; **she has a lonely life** tiene una vida solitaria; **2 to feel lonely** sentirse solo.

long *adjective, adverb* **1** largo/larga; **a long film** una película larga; **a long illness** una enfermedad larga; **it's five metres long** mide cinco metros de largo; **how long is the corridor?** ¿cuánto mide el pasillo de largo?; **how long is the play?** ¿cuánto dura la obra?; **it's been a long day** ha sido un día muy largo; **2 a long time** mucho tiempo; **he stayed for a long time** se quedó

mucho tiempo; **it's an hour long** dura una hora; **I've been here for a long time** he pasado mucho tiempo aquí; **a long time ago** hace mucho tiempo; **this won't take long** esto no llevará mucho tiempo; **I won't be long** no tardo mucho; **3 how long?** ¿cuánto tiempo?; **how long have you been here?** ¿cuánto tiempo llevas aquí?; **4 a long way** muy lejos; **we're a long way from the cinema** estamos muy lejos del cine; **5 all night long** toda la noche.
long *verb* **to long to do** anhelar [17] hacer; **I'm longing to see you** anhelo verte.

longer *adverb* **no longer** ya no; **he doesn't work here any longer** ya no trabaja aquí; **I no longer know** ya no lo sé; **they no longer live here** ya no viven aquí.

long jump *noun* salto *Masc.* de longitud.

longlife milk *noun* leche *Fem.* uperizada.

loo *noun* váter *Masc.* (*informal*).

look *noun* **1** (*a glance*) mirada *Fem.*; **to have a look at something** mirar [17] algo; **2 to have a look round the town** visitar [17] la ciudad; **to have a look round the shops** ver [16] tiendas; **3 to have a look for** buscar [31] (*something you've lost*).
look *verb* **1** mirar [17]; **I wasn't looking** no estaba mirando; **to look out of the window** mirar por la ventana; **2 to look at** mirar [17]; **Andy was looking at the photos** Andy estaba mirando las fotos; **3** (*to seem*) parecer [35]; **Melanie looked**

pleased Melanie parecía contenta; **you look well** tienes buen aspecto; **he looks ill** tiene mal aspecto; **the salad looks delicious** la ensalada tiene un aspecto delicioso; **4 to look like** parecerse [35] a; **Sally looks like her aunt** Sally se parece a su tía; **they look like each other** se parecen; **it looks like rain** parece que va a llover; **5 what does the house look like?** ¿cómo es la casa?

● **to look after** cuidar [17]; **Dad's looking after the baby** papá está cuidando del niño; **I'll look after your luggage** yo te cuido el equipaje.

● **to look for** buscar [31]; **I'm looking for the keys** estoy buscando las llaves.

● **to look forward to something: I'm looking forward to the holidays** estoy deseando que lleguen las vacaciones; **she's looking forward to the trip** está deseando ir de viaje.

● **to look out** (*to be careful*) tener [9] cuidado; **look out, it's hot!** ¡cuidado, está caliente!

● **to look something up** buscar [17] algo (*in a dictionary or directory*); **you can look it up in the dictionary** puedes buscarlo en el diccionario.

loose *adjective* **1** (*a screw or knot*) flojo/floja; **2** (*a garment*) amplio/amplia; **3 loose change** cambio *Masc.*; ★ **I'm at a loose end** no sé qué hacer.

lorry *noun* camión *Masc.*

lorry driver *noun* camionero *Masc.*, camionera *Fem.*

lose *verb* **1** perder [36]; **we lost** perdimos; **we lost the match** perdimos el partido; **Sam's lost his watch** Sam ha perdido su reloj; **2 to get lost** perderse [36]; **we got lost in the woods** nos perdimos en el bosque.

loss *noun* pérdida *Fem.*

lost *adjective* perdido/perdida; **I'm lost** me he perdido; **are you lost?** ¿te has perdido?

lost property *noun* objetos *Masc. plural* perdidos.

lot *noun* **1 a lot** mucho; **Jason eats a lot** Jason come mucho; **I spent a lot** gasté mucho; **your house is a lot bigger than ours** tu casa es mucho más grande que la nuestra; **2 a lot of** mucho/mucha (*plural* muchos/ muchas); **a lot of coffee** mucho café; **lots of people** mucha gente; **a lot of books** muchos libros; **'what are you doing tonight?' – 'not a lot'** ¿qué haces esta noche?' – 'no mucho'.

lottery *noun* lotería *Fem.*; **to win the lottery** ganar [17] la lotería.

loud *adjective* **1** fuerte; **a loud banging** unos golpes fuertes; **a loud shout** un grito fuerte; **the radio is very loud** la radio está muy fuerte; **2 in a loud voice** en voz alta; **to say something out loud** decir algo en voz alta.

loudspeaker *noun* altavoz *Masc.*

lounge *noun* **1** (*in a house or hotel*) salón *Masc.*; **2** (*in an airport*) **the departure lounge** la sala de embarque.

a
b
c
d
e
f
g
h
i
j
k
l
m
n
o
p
q
r
s
t
u
v
w
x
y
z

love *noun* **1** amor *Masc.*; **to be in love with somebody** estar [2] enamorado de alguien; **she's in love with Jake** está enamorada de Jake; **2 Gina sends her love** Gina manda recuerdos; **3 with love from Charlie** con cariño de Charlie; **lots of love, Ann** con mucho cariño: Ann; **4** (*in tennis*) cero *Masc.*
love *verb* **1** querer [12] (*a person*) **I love you** te quiero; **2 she loves London** le encanta Londres; **I'd love to come** me encantaría venir; **I love dancing** me encanta bailar; **Wayne loves seafood** a Wayne le encanta el marisco.

lovely *adjective* **1** (*to look at*) precioso/preciosa; **a lovely house** una casa preciosa; **2 it's a lovely day** hace un día muy bueno; **we had lovely weather** tuvimos un tiempo muy bueno; **3 I had a lovely time at their house** lo pasé muy bien en su casa; **4 it's lovely to see you!** ¡qué alegría verte!; **5** (*food, meal*) riquísimo/riquísima.

lover *noun* amante *Masc./Fem.*

low *adjective* bajo/baja; **a low table** una mesa baja; **at a low price** a un precio bajo; **in a low voice** en voz baja.

lower *adjective* (*not as high*) inferior.

loyalty *noun* lealtad *Fem.*; **a loyalty card** una tarjeta de fidelidad.

luck *noun* suerte *Fem.*; **good luck!** ¡buena suerte!; **bad luck!** ¡qué mala suerte!; **with a bit of luck** con un poco de suerte.

luckily *adverb* afortunadamente; **luckily for them** afortunadamente para ellos.

lucky *adjective* **1 to be lucky** (*a person*) tener [9] suerte; **we were lucky** tuvimos suerte; **2 to be lucky** (*bringing luck*) traer [42] suerte; **it's supposed to be lucky** se supone que trae suerte; **my lucky number** mi número de la suerte.

luggage *noun* equipaje *Masc.*

lump *noun* **1** bulto *Masc.* (*on the body*); **2** terrón *Masc.* (*of sugar*); **3** trozo *Masc.* (*of cheese*).

lunch *noun* comida *Fem.*; **to have lunch** comer [18]; **we had lunch in Oxford** comimos en Oxford.

lunch break *noun* descanso *Masc.* para comer.

lunch hour, lunch time *noun* hora *Fem.* de comer.

Luxembourg *noun* Luxemburgo *Masc.*

luxurious *adjective* lujoso/lujosa.

luxury *noun* lujo *Masc.*; **a luxury hotel** un hotel de lujo.

lyrics *plural noun* letra *Fem.*

Mm

macaroni *noun* macarrones *Masc. plural.*

machine *noun* máquina *Fem.*

machinery *noun* maquinaria *Fem.*

mad *adjective* **1** loco/loca; **she's completely mad!** ¡está completamente loca!; **2** (*angry*) enfadado/enfadada; **to be mad with somebody** estar enfadado/enfadada con alguien; **my mum will be mad!** ¡mamá se pondrá hecha una furia! (*informal*); **3 she's mad about horses** le encantan los caballos.

madam *noun* señora *Fem.*

madness *noun* locura *Fem.*

magazine *noun* revista *Fem.*

maggot *noun* gusano *Masc.*

magic *noun* magia *Fem.*
magic *adjective* **1** mágico/mágica; **a magic wand** una varita mágica; **2** (*great*) fantástico/fantástica.

magician *noun* mago *Masc.*, maga *Fem.*

magnet *noun* imán *Masc.*

magnifying glass *noun* lupa *Fem.*

maid *noun* criada *Fem.*; **is there a maid service?** ¿ha asistenta?.

maiden name *noun* nombre *Masc.* de soltera.

mail *noun* correo *Masc.*; **e-mail** (*electronic mail*) correo *Masc.* electrónico.

mail order *noun* **to buy something by mail order** comprar [17] algo por correo; **a mail order catalogue** un catálogo de venta por correo.

main *adjective* principal; **the main entrance** la entrada principal.

main course *noun* plato *Masc.* principal, segundo plato *Masc.*

mainly *adverb* principalmente.

main road *noun* carretera *Fem.* principal.

major *adjective* muy importante; **a major problem** un problema muy importante.
major *noun* comandante *Masc./Fem.*

Majorca *noun* Mallorca *Fem.*

majority *noun* mayoría *Fem.*

make *noun* marca *Fem.*; **what make is your bike?** ¿de qué marca es tu bici?
make *verb* **1** hacer [7]; **I made an omelette** hice una tortilla; **she made her bed** hizo su cama; **he made me wait** me hizo esperar; **she makes me laugh** me hace reír; **to make a phone call** hacer una llamada de teléfono; **I have to make a few phone calls** tengo que hacer varias llamadas de teléfono; **2** fabricar [31]; **they make computers** fabrican ordenadores; **'made in Spain'** 'fabricado en España'; **3 that makes me hungry** eso me da hambre; **it made me sleepy** me dio sueño; **4** (*sad, happy*) **to make somebody sad** poner [11] triste a alguien; **it made me sad** me puso triste; **to make somebody happy** hacer [7] feliz a alguien; **it made him really annoyed** le dio mucha rabia; **it makes me so angry** me da tanta rabia; **5** ganar [17] (*money*); **he makes forty pounds a day** gana cuarenta libras al día; **to make a living** ganarse [17] la vida; **6** (*force*) **to make somebody do ...** obligar [28] a alguien a hacer ...; **she made him**

a
b
c
d
e
f
g
h
i
j
k
l
m
n
o
p
q
r
s
t
u
v
w
x
y
z

471

give the money back le obligó a devolver el dinero; **7 to make a meal** preparar [17] una comida; **8** (*add up to*) sumar [17]; **two and three make five** dos y tres suman cinco; **9 I can't make it tonight** no puedo venir esta noche.

● **to make something up**
1 inventarse [17] algo; **she made up an excuse** se inventó una excusa; **2 to make it up** (*after a quarrel*) hacer [7] las paces; **they've made it up now** han hecho las paces ahora.

make-up *noun* maquillaje *Masc.*; **to put on your make-up** ponerse [11] el maquillaje; **Jo's putting on her make-up** Jo se está poniendo el maquillaje; **I don't wear make-up** yo no uso maquillaje.

male *adjective* **1** (*animal*) macho; **a male rat** una rata macho; **2** (*of a man*) masculino/masculina; **a male voice** una voz masculina; **3** (*sex : on a form*) varón.

male chauvinist *noun* machista *Masc.*

mall *noun* centro *Masc.* comercial.

mammal *noun* mamífero *Masc.*

man *noun* hombre *Masc.*; **modern man is taller than his ancestors** el hombre moderno es más alto que sus antepasados.

manage *verb* **1** dirigir [49] (*business, team*); **she manages a travel agency** ella dirige una agencia de viajes; **2** (*cope*) arreglárselas [17]; **I can manage** puedo arreglármelas; **3 to manage to do** conseguir [64] hacer; **I didn't manage to get in touch with her**

no conseguí ponerme en contacto con ella.

management *noun* **1** dirección *Fem.*; **the management of the company** la dirección de la empresa; **2** (*management staff*) directivos *Masc. plural.*

manager *noun* **1** (*of a company or a bank*) director *Masc.*, directora *Fem.*; **2** (*of a shop or restaurant*) encargado *Masc.*, encargada *Fem.*; **3** (*in sport and entertainment*) manager *Masc./Fem.*

manageress *noun* encargada *Fem.*

managing director *noun* consejero *Masc.*delegado, consejera *Fem.* delegada.

mango *noun* mango *Masc.*

maniac *noun* loco *Masc.*, loca *Fem.*; **she drives like a maniac** conduce como una loca.

mankind *noun* humanidad *Fem.*

manner *noun* **1 in a manner of speaking** por así decirlo; **2 to have good manners** tener [9] buena educación; **it's bad manners to talk like that** no es de es buena educación hablar así.

mansion *noun* mansión *Fem.*

mantelpiece *noun* repisa *Fem.* de la chimenea.

manual *noun* manual *Masc.*

manufacture *verb* fabricar [31].

manufacturer *noun* fabricante *Masc.*

many *adjective, pronoun* **1** muchos/ muchas; **does she have many**

472

friends? ¿tiene muchos amigos?; **there aren't many onions left** no quedan muchas cebollas; **not many** no muchos/muchas; **many of them forgot** muchos de ellos se olvidaron; **many people** mucha gente; **2 very many** muchos/muchas; **there aren't very many glasses** no hay muchos vasos; **3 so many** tantos/tantas; **I have so many things to do!** ¡tengo tantas cosas que hacer!; **I've never eaten so many cakes** nunca he comido tantos pasteles; **4 as many as** todos los que/todas las que; **you can take as many as you like** puedes llevarte todos los que quieras; **5 too many** demasiados/demasiadas; **I've got too many things to do** tengo demasiadas cosas que hacer; **that's far too many!** ¡ésos son demasiados!; **there were too many people** había demasiada gente; **6 how many?** ¿cuántos?/¿cuántas?; **how many are there?** ¿cuántos hay?; **how many sisters have you got?** ¿cuántas hermanas tienes?; **how many are there left?** ¿cuántos quedan?; **7 as many as** tantos/tantas como; **there aren't as many as before** no hay tantos como antes; **she got as many points as I did** consiguió tantos puntos como yo.

map noun **1** mapa Masc.; **a road map** un mapa de carreteras; **2** (of a town) plano Masc.

marathon noun maratón Masc./Fem.

marble noun **1** mármol Masc.; **a marble fireplace** una chimenea de mármol; **2** canica Fem.; **to play marbles** jugar [27] a las canicas.

March noun marzo Masc.

march noun (demonstration) manifestación Fem.
march verb (demonstrators) manifestarse [29].

mare noun yegua Fem.

margarine noun margarina Fem.

margin noun margen Masc.

marijuana noun marihuana Fem.

mark noun **1** (at school) nota Fem.; **I got a good mark for my Spanish homework** he sacado una buena nota en los deberes de español; **what mark did you get for Spanish?** ¿que nota sacaste en español?; **2** (stain) mancha Fem.
mark verb (correct) corregir [48].

market noun mercado Masc.

marketing noun marketing Masc.

marmalade noun mermelada Fem. de naranja.

marriage noun matrimonio Masc. (relationship).

married adjective casado/casada; **to be married** estar [2] casado/casada; **he's married** está casado; **they've been married for twenty years** llevan casados veinte años; **a married couple** un matrimonio.

marry verb **1 to marry somebody** casarse [17] con alguien; **she married a Spaniard** se casó con un español; **2 to get married** casarse [17]; **they got married in July** se casaron en julio.

a
b
c
d
e
f
g
h
i
j
k
l
m
n
o
p
q
r
s
t
u
v
w
x
y
z

a
b
c
d
e
f
g
h
i
j
k
l
m
n
o
p
q
r
s
t
u
v
w
x
y
z

marvellous *adjective*
maravilloso/maravillosa; **the weather's marvellous** el tiempo es maravilloso; **how marvellous!** ¡qué maravilla!

marzipan *noun* mazapán *Masc.*

mascara *noun* rímel *Masc.*

masculine *noun* (*in Spanish and other grammars*) masculino *Masc.*; **in the masculine** en masculino.

mash *verb* triturar [17] (*vegetables*).

mashed potatoes *noun* puré *Masc.* de patatas.

mask *noun* máscara *Fem.*

mass *noun* **1 a mass of** un montón de; **2 masses of** un montón de; **they've got masses of money** tienen un montón de dinero; **there's masses left over** queda un montón; **3** (*religious*) misa *Fem.*; **to go to mass** ir [8] a misa.

massacre *noun* matanza *Fem.*

massage *noun* masaje *Masc.*

massive *adjective* enorme.

mat *noun* **1** (*doormat*) felpudo *Masc.*; **2** (*bathmat*) alfombrilla *Fem.*; **3** (*for hot dish*) salvamanteles *Masc.* (*does not change in the plural*).

match *noun* **1** cerilla *Fem.*; **a box of matches** una caja de cerillas; **2** (*sports*) partido *Masc.*; **a football match** un partido de fútbol; **to watch the match** ver [16] el partido; **to win the match** ganar [17] el partido; **to lose the match** perder [36] el partido.

match *verb* hacer [7] juego con; **the jacket matches the skirt** la chaqueta hace juego con la falda.

mate *noun* amigo *Masc.*, amiga *Fem.*; **I'm going out with my mates tonight** voy a salir esta noche con mis amigos.

material *noun* **1** (*fabric*) tela *Fem.*; **2** (*information*) material *Masc.*; **teaching materials** material educativo; **3** (*substance*) materia *Fem.*; **raw materials** materias primas.

mathematics *noun* matemáticas *Fem. plural.*

maths *noun* matemáticas *Fem. plural*; **I like maths** me gustan las matemáticas; **Anna's good at maths** a Anna se le dan bien las matemáticas.

matter *noun* **what's the matter?** ¿qué pasa?
matter *verb* **1** importar [17]; **the things that matter** lo que importa; **it matters a lot to me** me importa mucho; **2 it doesn't matter** no importa; **it doesn't matter if it rains** no importa que llueva; **3 it doesn't matter** (*whether one thing or another*) da lo mismo; **you can write it in Spanish or French, it doesn't matter** puedes escribirlo en español o en francés, da lo mismo.

mattress *noun* colchón *Masc.*

maximum *noun* máximo *Masc.*
maximum *adjective* máximo/máxima.

May *noun* mayo *Masc.*

may *verb* **1 she may be ill** puede que esté enferma; **we may go to Spain** puede que vayamos a España; **2** (*asking permission*) **may I close the door?** ¿puedo cerrar la puerta?

maybe *adverb* quizás; **maybe not** quizás no; **maybe he's forgotten** quizás se ha olvidado; **maybe they've got lost** quizás se han perdido.

mayonnaise *noun* mayonesa *Fem.*

mayor *noun* alcalde *Masc.*, alcaldesa *Fem.*

mayoress *noun* alcaldesa *Fem.*

me *pronoun* **1** me; **she knows me** me conoce; **she gave me the documents** me dio los documentos; **2** (*with an infinitive or when telling someone to do something, 'me' joins onto the verb*) **can you help me, please?** ¿puedes ayudarme por favor?; **listen to me!** ¡escúchame!; **wait for me!** ¡espérame!; (*but when telling someone NOT to do something, 'me' comes before the verb*) **don't push me!** ¡no me empujes!; **3** (*after a preposition*) mí; **behind me** detrás de mí; **they left without me** se fueron sin mí; **with me** conmigo; **I took her with me** la traje conmigo; **4** (*in comparisons or after the verb 'to be'*) yo; **she's older than me** es mayor que yo; **it's me** soy yo; **me too!** ¡yo también!; **5 excuse me!** ¡perdona!

meadow *noun* prado *Masc.*

meal *noun* comida *Fem.*; **they have three meals a day** hacen tres comidas al día.

mean *verb* **1** querer [12] decir; **what do you mean?** ¿qué quieres decir?; **what does that mean?** ¿qué quiere decir eso?; **that's not what I meant** eso no es lo que quería decir; **2** (*imply*) suponer [11]; **that means that I'll have to do it again** eso supone que voy a tener que hacerlo otra vez; **3 to mean to do** tener [9] la intención de; **I meant to phone my mother** tenía la intención de llamar a mi madre; **4 she was meant to be here at six** se supone que ella tenía que estar aquí a las seis; **this is meant to be easy** se supone que esto es fácil.

mean *adjective* **1** (*with money*) tacaño/tacaña; **2** (*nasty*) **she's really mean to her brother** trata muy mal a su hermano; **what a mean thing to do!** ¡qué maldad!

meaning *noun* significado *Masc.*

means *noun* **1** medio *Masc.*; **a means of transport** un medio de transporte; **by means of** por medio de; **2 a means of doing** una forma de hacer; **we have no means of contacting him** no tenemos forma de contactar con él; **3 by all means** por supuesto.

meantime *adverb* **for the meantime** por ahora; **in the meantime** mientras tanto.

meanwhile *adverb* mientras tanto; **meanwhile she was waiting at the station** mientras tanto ella estaba esperando en la estación.

measles *noun* sarampión *Masc.*

measure *verb* medir [57].

measurements *plural noun* **1** (*of a room or an object*) medidas *Fem. plural*; **the measurements of the room** las medidas de la habitación; **2** (*of a person*) medida *Fem.*; **my waist measurement** mi medida de cintura.

a b c d e f g h i j k l **m** n o p q r s t u v w x y z

meat *noun* carne *Fem.*

Mecca *noun* La Meca *Fem.*

mechanic *noun* mecánico *Masc.*, mecánica *Fem.*; **he's a mechanic** es mecánico.

medal *noun* medalla *Fem.*; **the gold medal** la medalla de oro.

media *noun* **the media** los medios de comunicación.

medical *noun* revisión *Fem.* médica; **to have a medical** someterse [18] a una revisión médica.

medical *adjective* médico/médica; **on medical grounds** por razones de salud.

medicine *noun* **1** medicamento *Masc.*; **2** (*science*) medicina *Fem.*; **she's studying medicine** está estudiando medicina; **alternative medicine** medicina alternativa.

medieval *adjective* medieval.

Mediterranean *noun* **the Mediterranean** el Mediterráneo.

medium *adjective* mediano/mediana.

medium-sized *adjective* de tamaño mediano.

meet *verb* **1** (*by chance*) encontrarse [24] con; **I met Rosie outside the baker's** me encontré con Rosie en la puerta de la panadería; **2** (*by appointment*) haber [6] quedado (con); **we're meeting at six** hemos quedado a las seis; **I'm meeting him at the museum** he quedado con él en el museo; **shall we meet after work?** ¿quedamos después del trabajo?; **3** (*get to know*) conocer [35]

a; **I met a Spanish girl last week** conocí a una chica española la semana pasada; **have you met Oskar?** ¿conoces a Oskar?; **4 Tom, meet Ann** Tom, te presento a Ann; **pleased to meet you!** ¡encantado/encantada!; **5** (*off a train, bus, plane*) recoger [3]; **my dad's meeting me at the station** mi padre va a ir a recogerme a la estación.

meeting *noun* reunión *Fem.*; **there's a meeting a ten o'clock** hay una reunión a las diez; **she's in a meeting** está en una reunión.

megabyte *noun* megabyte *Masc.*

melon *noun* melón *Masc.*

melt *verb* **1** (*snow, butter, ice cream*) derretirse [57]; **it melts in your mouth** se derrite en la boca; **2 to melt something** derretir [57] algo; **melt the butter in a saucepan** derretir la mantequilla en una sartén.

member *noun* **1** (*of party or committee*) miembro *Masc./Fem.*; **she's a member of the Labour Party** es miembro del partido laborista; **2** (*of club*) socio *Masc.*, socia *Fem.*

Member of Parliament *noun* diputado *Masc.*, diputada *Fem.*

memorial *noun* monumento *Masc.*; **a war memorial** un monumento a los caídos.

memorize *verb* **to memorize something** aprender [18] algo de memoria.

memory *noun* **1** (*of a person or computer*) memoria *Fem.*; **you have**

a good memory! ¡tienes buena memoria!; **I have a bad memory** tengo mala memoria; **2** (*of the past*) recuerdo *Masc.*; **I have good memories of my stay in Spain** tengo buenos recuerdos de mi estancia en España.

mend *verb* arreglar [17].

mental *adjective* mental; **a mental illness** una enfermedad mental; **a mental hospital** un hospital psiquiátrico.

mention *verb* mencionar [17].

menu *noun* **1** (*in restaurant*) carta *Fem.*, menú *Masc.*; **what's on on the menu?** ¿qué hay en la carta?; **have you got a set menu?** ¿tienen un menú del día?; **2** (*in computer program*) menú *Masc.*

merge *verb* **1** (*documents*) fusionar [17]; **2** (*roads*) confluir [54].

meringue *noun* merengue *Masc.*

merit *noun* mérito *Masc.*

merry *adjective* **1** alegre; **Merry Christmas** Feliz Navidad; **2** (*from drinking*) achispado/achispada (*informal*).

merry-go-round *noun* tiovivo *Masc.*

mess *noun* desorden *Masc.*; **my papers are in a mess** mis papeles están desordenados; **don't make a mess!** ¡no desordenes nada!; **what a mess!** ¡qué desastre! (*informal*).

● **to mess about** hacer [7] el tonto; **stop messing about!** ¡deja de hacer el tonto!.

● **to mess about with something** jugar [27] con algo; **it's dangerous to mess about with matches** es peligroso jugar con cerillas.

● **to mess something up** desordenar [17] algo; **you've messed up all my papers** ¡me has desordenado todos mis papeles!.

message *noun* mensaje *Masc.*; **a telephone message** un recado.

messenger *noun* mensajero *Masc.*, mensajera *Fem.*

messy *adjective* **1** it's a messy job es un trabajo sucio; **2** he's a messy eater se ensucia mucho comiendo; **her writing's really messy** escribe sin poner cuidado.

metal *noun* metal *Masc.*

meter *noun* **1** (*electricity, gas, taxi*) contador *Masc.*; **to read the meter** leer [37] el contador; **2** a parking meter un parquímetro.

method *noun* método *Masc.*

Methodist *noun* metodista *Masc./Fem.*; **I'm a Methodist** soy metodista.

metre *noun* metro *Masc.*

metric *adjective* métrico/métrica.

Mexico *noun* Méjico *Masc.*

Mexican *noun* mexicano *Masc.*, mexicana *Fem.*
Mexican *adjective* mexicano/mexicana.

microchip *noun* microchip *Masc.*

microphone *noun* micrófono *Masc.*

microscope *noun* microscopio *Masc.*

microwave oven *noun* microondas *Masc.* (*does not change in the plural*).

a
b
c
d
e
f
g
h
i
j
k
l
m
n
o
p
q
r
s
t
u
v
w
x
y
z

midday *noun* mediodía *Masc.*; **at midday** al mediodía.

middle *noun* **1** medio *Masc.*; **in the middle of the room** en medio de la habitación; **2 in the middle of the night** en mitad de la noche; **in the middle of the day** alrededor del mediodía; **in the middle of the year** a mediados de año; **3 to be in the middle of doing** estar [2] haciendo; **when she phoned I was in the middle of washing my hair** cuando llamó estaba lavándome el pelo.

middle-aged *adjective* de mediana edad; **a middle-aged woman** una mujer de mediana edad.

middle-class *adjective* de clase media; **a middle-class family** una familia de clase media.

Middle-East *noun* Oriente *Masc.* Medio.

middle finger *noun* dedo *Masc.* corazón.

midge *noun* mosquito *Masc.* pequeño.

midnight *noun* medianoche *Fem.*; **at midnight** a medianoche.

Midsummer's Day *noun* la noche de San Juan.

midwife *noun* comadrona *Fem.*

might *verb* **I might invite Jo** puede que invite a Jo; **Amanda might know** puede que Amanda lo sepa; **he might have forgotten** puede que se haya olvidado; **'are you going to phone him?' – 'I might'** '¿vas a llamarlo?' – 'quizás'.

migraine *noun* jaqueca *Fem.*

mike *noun* micro *Masc.* (*informal*).

mild *adjective* **1** suave (*soap or cheese*); **2** templado/templada (*climate*); **it's quite mild today** hoy no hace frío.

mile *noun* **1** milla *Fem.* (*in Spain distances are measured in kilometres; to convert miles roughly to kilometres, multiply by 8 and divide by 5*) **the village is ten miles from Oxford** el pueblo está a dieciseis kilómetros de Oxford; **2 it's miles better!** ¡es mil veces mejor! (*informal*).

mileage *noun* distancia *Fem.* en millas; **what's the mileage on your car?**¿cuántas millas ha hecho tu coche?

milk *noun* leche *Fem.*; **full-cream milk** leche entera; **skimmed milk** leche desnatada; **semi-skimmed milk** leche semidesnatada.
milk *verb* ordeñar [17].

milk chocolate *noun* chocolate *Masc.* con leche.

milkman *noun* lechero *Masc.*

milkshake *noun* batido *Masc.*

millennium *noun* milenio *Masc.*

millimetre *noun* milímetro *Masc.*

million *noun* millón *Masc.*; **a million people** un millón de personas; **two million people** dos millones de personas.

millionaire *noun* millonario *Masc.*, millonaria *Fem.*

mince *noun* carne *Fem.* picada.

mind *noun* **1** mente *Fem.*; **a logical mind** una mente lógica; **2 it crossed my mind that ...** se me pasó por la cabeza que ...; **3 to change your**

mind cambiar [17] de opinión; **I've changed my mind** he cambiado de opinión; **4 to make up your mind** decidirse [19]; **I can't make up my mind** no puedo decidirme.

mind *verb* **1** cuidar [17]; **can you mind my bag for me?** ¿me cuidas el bolso?; **could you mind the baby for ten minutes?** ¿puedes cuidar del niño diez minutos?; **2 do you mind if ...?** ¿te importa que ...?; **do you mind if I close the door?** ¿te importa que cierre la puerta?; **I don't mind** no me importa; **never mind!** ¡no importa!; **3 I don't mind the heat** no me molesta el calor; **4 mind the step!** ¡cuidado con el escalón!.

mine¹ *noun* mina *Fem.*; **a coal mine** una mina de carbón.

mine² *pronoun* **1** (*referring to a singular noun*) el mío/la mía; **she took her hat and I took mine** ella cogió su sombrero y yo cogí el mío; **Tessa phoned her mum and I phoned mine** Tessa llamó a su madre y yo llamé a la mía; **2** (*referring to a plural noun*) los míos/las mías; **Karen's invited her parents and I've invited mine** Karen ha invitado a sus padres y yo a los míos; **she showed me her photos and I showed her mine** ella me enseñó sus fotos y yo le enseñé las mías.

miner *noun* minero *Masc.*, minera *Fem.*

mineral water *noun* agua *Fem.* mineral.

minibus *noun* microbús *Masc.*

minimum *noun* mínimo *Masc.* minimum *adjective* mínimo/mínima; **the minimum age** la edad mínima.

miniskirt *noun* minifalda *Fem.*

minister *noun* **1** (*in government*) ministro *Masc.*, ministra *Fem.*; **2** (*of a church*) pastor *Masc.*, pastora *Fem.*.

minor *adjective* menor.

minority *noun* minoría *Fem.*

mint *noun* **1** (*herb*) menta *Fem.*; **2** (*sweet*) caramelo *Masc.* de menta.

minus *preposition* **1** menos; **seven minus three is four** siete menos tres es cuatro; **2 it was minus ten this morning** esta mañana hacía diez grados bajo cero.

minute *noun* minuto *Masc.*; **it's five minutes' walk from here** está a cinco minutos andando de aquí; **I'll be ready in two minutes** en dos minutos estoy lista; **just a minute!** ¡un momento!

miracle *noun* milagro *Masc.*

mirror *noun* **1** espejo *Masc.*; **I looked at myself in the mirror** me miré al espejo; **2** (*rearview mirror in a car*) retrovisor *Masc.*

misbehave *verb* portarse [17] mal.

mischief *noun* **to get up to mischief** hacer [7] travesuras.

mischievous *adjective* travieso/traviesa.

miser *noun* avaro/avara.

miserable *adjective* **1** triste; **he was miserable without her** estaba triste sin ella; **I feel really miserable today** hoy tengo el

a
b
c
d
e
f
g
h
i
j
k
l
m
n
o
p
q
r
s
t
u
v
w
x
y
z

a
b
c
d
e
f
g
h
i
j
k
l
m
n
o
p
q
r
s
t
u
v
w
x
y
z

ánimo por los suelos; **2 it's miserable weather** un tiempo deprimente; **3 she gets paid a miserable wage** le pagan un sueldo miserable.

misery *noun* miseria *Fem.*; **he was in misery** estaba muy triste.

miss *verb* **1** perder [36]; **she missed her train** perdió el tren; **I missed the film** me perdí la película; **to miss an opportunity** perder una oportunidad; **2 the ball missed the goal** la pelota no entró en la portería; **you missed!** ¡fallaste!; **3** faltar [17] a; **he's missed several classes** ha faltado a varias clases; **4 I miss you** te echo de menos; **she's missing her sister** echa de menos a su hermana; **I miss Madrid** echo de menos Madrid.

Miss *noun* señorita *Fem.* (*usually abbreviated to 'Srta'*); **Miss Jones** la señorita Jones.

missile *noun* misil *Masc.*

missing *adjective* **1 the missing piece** la pieza que falta; **the missing documents** los documentos que faltan; **the missing link** el eslabón perdido; **2** faltar [17]; **there's a plate missing** falta un plato; **there are three forks missing** faltan tres tenedores; **is there anybody missing?** ¿falta alguien?; **3 to go missing** desaparecer [35]; **several things have gone missing lately** han desaparecido varias cosas últimamente; **three people have gone missing** han desaparecido tres personas.

mist *noun* neblina *Fem.*

mistake *noun* **1** error *Masc.*; **by mistake** por error; **it was my mistake** fue un error mío; **2** falta *Fem.*; **a spelling mistake** una falta de ortografía; **you've made lots of mistakes** has cometido muchas faltas; **3 to make a mistake** (*be mistaken*) cometer [18] un error; **sorry, I made a mistake** perdona, he cometido un error.
mistake *verb* confundir [19]; **I mistook you for your brother** te confundí con tu hermano.

mistaken *adjective* **to be mistaken** estar [2] equivocado/equivocada; **you're mistaken** estás equivocado.

mistletoe *noun* muérdago *Masc.*

misunderstand *verb* entender [36] mal; **I misunderstood** lo entendí mal.

misunderstanding *noun* malentendido *Masc.*; **there's been a misunderstanding** hay un malentendido.

mix *noun* **1** mezcla *Fem.*; **a good mix of people** una buena mezcla de gente; **2 a cake mix** un preparado para hacer un pastel.
mix *verb* **1** mezclar [17]; **mix all the ingredients together** mezclar todos los ingredientes; **2 to mix with** tratarse [17] con; **she mixes with lots of interesting people** se trata con mucha gente interesante.
● **to mix up 1** desordenar [17]; **you've mixed up all my papers** has desordenado todos mis papeles; **2** (*confuse*) confundir [19] (*confuse*) **I**

480

get him mixed up with his brother lo confundo con su hermano; **you've got it all mixed up!** ¡te has confundido!.

mixed *adjective* variado/variada; **a mixed programme** un programa variado.

mixed salad *noun* ensalada *Fem.* mixta.

mixer *noun* batidora *Fem.*

mixture *noun* mezcla *Fem.*; **it's a mixture of jazz and rock** es una mezcla de jazz y rock.

moan *verb* (*complain*) quejarse [17]; **stop moaning!** ¡deja de quejarte!

mobile home *noun* caravana *Fem.* fija.

mobile phone *noun* teléfono *Masc.* móvil, móvil *Masc.*

mock *noun* (*mock exam*) examen *Masc.* de práctica.
mock *verb* burlarse [17] de; **stop mocking me!** ¡deja de burlarte de mí!

model *noun* **1** (*type*) modelo *Masc.*; **the latest model** el último modelo; **2** (*fashion model*) modelo *Masc./Fem.*; **she's a model** es modelo; **3** (*of a plane, car, etc.*) maqueta *Fem.*; **he makes models** construye maquetas; **a model of Westminster Abbey** una maqueta de la abadía de Westminster.

model aeroplane *noun* aeromodelo *Masc.*

model railway *noun* ferrocarril *Masc.* de juguete.

modem *noun* módem *Masc.*

moderate *adjective* moderado/moderada.

modern *adjective* moderno/moderna.

modern languages *noun* lenguas *Fem. plural* modernas.

modernize *verb* modernizar [22].

moisturizer *noun* **1** (*lotion*) loción *Fem.* hidratante; **2** (*cream*) crema *Fem.* hidratante.

mole *noun* **1** (*animal*) topo *Masc.*; **2** (*on skin*) lunar *Masc.*

moment *noun* momento *Masc.*; **he'll be here in a moment** llegará en cualquier momento; **at any moment** en cualquier momento; **at the moment** en este momento; **at the right moment** en el momento preciso; **for the moment** de momento.

monarchy *noun* monarquía *Fem.*

Monday *noun* lunes *Masc.* (*does not change in the plural*); **on Monday** el lunes; **I'm going out on Monday** voy a salir el lunes; **see you on Monday!** ¡te veo el lunes!; **on Mondays** los lunes; **the museum is closed on Mondays** el museo cierra los lunes; **every Monday** todos los lunes; **last Monday** el lunes pasado; **next Monday** el próximo lunes.

money *noun* dinero *Masc.*; **I don't have enough money** no tengo suficiente dinero; **to make money** hacer [7] dinero; **they gave me my money back** (*in a shop*) me devolvieron el dinero.

money box *noun* hucha *Fem.*

a

mongrel noun chucho Masc. (informal).

b

monitor noun (on computer) monitor Masc.

c

d

monkey noun **1** mono Masc.; **2 you little monkey!** ¡diablillo! (informal).

e

monster noun monstruo Masc.

f

g

h

i

j

k

month noun mes Masc.; **in the month of May** en el mes de mayo; **this month** este mes; **next month** el próximo mes; **we're leaving next month** nos vamos el próximo mes; **last month** el mes pasado; **every month** todos los meses; **in two months' time** dentro de dos meses; **at the end of the month** a final de mes.

l

m

monthly adjective mensual; **a monthly payment** una mensualidad.

n

monument noun monumento Masc.

o

p

q

mood noun humor Masc.; **to be in a good mood** estar [2] de buen humor; **to be in a bad mood** estar [2] de mal humor; **I'm not in the mood** no estoy de humor.

r

moody adjective temperamental.

s

t

u

moon noun luna Fem.; **by the light of the moon** a la luz de la luna; ★ **to be over the moon** estar loco/loca de contento (literally: to be mad with happiness).

v

w

moonlight noun luz Fem. de la luna; **by moonlight** a la luz de la luna.

moped noun ciclomotor Masc.

x

y

moral noun moraleja Fem.; **the moral of the story** la moraleja de la historia.

z

moral adjective moral.

morals plural noun moralidad Fem.

more adverb, adjective
more pronoun **1** más; **more interesting** más interesante; **more easily** más fácilmente; **a little more milk** un poco más de leche; **a few more glasses** unos cuantos vasos más; **would you like some more cake?** ¿quieres más pastel?; **we need three more** necesitamos tres más; **2 more ... than** más ... que; **the book's more interesting than the film** el libro es más interesante que la película; **he eats more than me** come más que yo; **3 more and more** cada vez más; **books are getting more and more expensive** los libros están cada vez más caros; **it takes more and more time** lleva cada vez más tiempo; **4 more or less** más o menos; **it's more or less finished** está más o menos terminado; **5 any more** más; **I don't want any more** no quiero más; **I don't like it any more** ya no me gusta.

morning noun mañana Fem.; **this morning** esta mañana; **tomorrow morning** mañana por la mañana; **yesterday morning** ayer por la mañana; **in the morning** por la mañana; **she doesn't work in the morning** no trabaja por las mañanas; **on Friday mornings** los viernes por la mañana; **at six o'clock in the morning** a las seis de la mañana; **I spent the whole morning doing the washing-up** me pasé toda la mañana lavando los platos.

Morocco *noun* Marruecos *Masc.*

mortgage *noun* hipoteca *Fem.*

Moscow *noun* Moscú *Masc.*

Moslem *noun* musulmán *Masc.*, musulmana *Fem.*

mosque *noun* mezquita *Fem.*

mosquito *noun* mosquito *Masc.*; **a mosquito bite** una picadura de mosquito.

most *adjective, adverb, pronoun* **1** (*followed by a plural noun*) la mayoría de; **most children like chocolate** a la mayoría de los niños les gusta el chocolate; **most of my friends** la mayoría de mis amigos; **2** (*followed by a singular noun*) casi todo; **they've eaten most of the chocolate** se han comido casi todo el chocolate; **3** most of the time la mayor parte del tiempo; **most of it is clear** la mayor parte está claro; **4** the most (*followed by adjective*) más; **the most interesting film** la película más interesante; **the most exciting story** la historia más emocionante; **the most boring books** los libros más aburridos; **5** the most (*followed by noun*); **I've got the most time** soy el que más tiempo tiene; **6** (*after averb*) what I hate most is the noise lo que más odio es el ruido.

mother *noun* madre *Fem.*; **my mother** mi madre; **Kate's mother** la madre de Kate.

mother-in-law *noun* suegra *Fem.*

Mother's Day *noun* día *Masc.* de la Madre (*in Spain, the first Sunday in May*).

motivated *adjective* motivado/motivada.

motivation *noun* motivo *Masc.*

motor *noun* motor *Masc.*

motorbike *noun* motocicleta *Fem.*

motorboat *noun* motora *Fem.*

motorcyclist *noun* motociclista *Masc./Fem.*

motorist *noun* automovilista *Masc./Fem.*

motor racing *noun* carreras *Fem. plural* de coches.

motorway *noun* autopista *Fem.*

mouldy *adjective* mohoso/mohosa.

mountain *noun* montaña *Fem.*; **in the mountains** en las montañas.

mountain bike *noun* bicicleta *Fem.* de montaña.

mountaineer *noun* montañero *Masc.*, montañera *Fem.*

mountaineering *noun* montañismo *Masc.*; **to go mountaineering** hacer [7] montañismo.

mountainous *adjective* montañoso/montañosa.

mouse *noun* ratón *Masc.* (*both the animal and for a computer*).

mousse *noun* mousse *Fem.*; **chocolate mousse** mousse de chocolate.

moustache *noun* bigote *Masc.*

mouth *noun* boca *Fem.*

a
b
c
d
e
f
g
h
i
j
k
l
m
n
o
p
q
r
s
t
u
v
w
x
y
z

mouthful *noun* bocado *Masc.* (*of food*) trago *Masc.* (*of drink*).

mouth organ *noun* armónica *Fem.*; **to play the mouth organ** tocar [31] la armónica.

move *noun* **1** (*to a different house*) mudanza *Fem.*; **2** (*in a game*) **your move!** ¡tu turno!
move *verb* **1** moverse [38]; **she didn't move** no se movió; **2 move up a bit** córrete un poco; **3** (*an object*) cambiar [17] de sitio; **you've moved the picture** has cambiado el cuadro de sitio; **can you move your bag, please?** ¿puedes correr tu bolsa, por favor?; **4** mover [38] (*an object or part of the body*); **she moved her hand** movió la mano; **5** (*car, traffic*) avanzar [22]; **the traffic was moving slowly** el tráfico avanzaba lentamente; **6 to move forward** avanzar [22]; **he moved forward a step** avanzó un paso; **7** (*move house*) mudarse [17]; **we're moving on Tuesday** nos mudamos el martes; **they've moved house** se han mudado de casa; **they've moved to Spain** se han ido a vivir en España; **8** (*emotionally*) conmover [38]; **it really moved me** me conmovió de verdad; **to be moved** estar [2] conmovido/conmovida.

● **to move in** mudarse [17]; **when are you moving in?** ¿cuándo se mudan.

● **to move out** mudarse [17]; **I'm moving out at the end of the month** me mudo a finales del mes.

movie *noun* película *Fem.*; **to go to the movies** ir [8] al cine.

moving *adjective* **1** en marcha; **a moving vehicle** un vehículo en marcha; **2** (*emotionally*) conmovedor/conmovedora; **it's a very moving film** es una película muy conmovedora.

MP *noun* diputado *Masc.*, diputada *Fem.*; **she's an MP** es diputada.

Mr *noun* Señor (*usually abbreviated to 'Sr.'*); **Mr Angus Brown** el Sr. Angus Brown.

Mrs *noun* Señora (*usually abbreviated to 'Sra.'*); **Mrs Mary Hendry** la Sra. Mary Hendry.

Ms *noun* Señora (*usually abbreviated to 'Sra.'; note that there is no direct equivalent to 'Ms' in Spanish, but 'Señora' may be used whether a woman is married or not*).

much *adverb, pronoun, adjective* **1** mucho; **she doesn't eat much** no come mucho; **we don't go out much** no salimos mucho; **much more** mucho más; **much shorter** mucho más bajo; **2** (*followed by a noun*) mucho/mucha; **we don't have much time** no tenemos mucho tiempo; **there isn't much butter left** no queda mucha mantequilla; **3 very much** mucho; **I don't watch television very much** no veo mucho la tele; **thank you very much** muchas gracias; **4 very much** (*followed by a noun*) mucho/mucha; **there isn't very much milk** no queda mucha leche; **5 not much** (*referring to a verb*) no mucho; **'do you go out?' – 'not much'** '¿sales?' – 'no mucho'; **6 not much** (*referring to a noun*) no mucho/no mucha; **'did**

you add salt?' – 'yes, but not
much' '¿has puesto sal?' – 'sí, pero
no mucha'; **7 so much** tanto; **we
liked it so much!** ¡nos gustó tanto!; **I
have so much to do!** ¡tengo tanto
que hacer!; **you shouldn't have
given me so much** no deberías
haberme dado tanto; **8 as much as**
tanto como; **you can take as much
as you like** puedes coger tanto como
quieras; **9 too much** demasiado;
that's far too much! ¡eso es
demasiado!; **10 too much** (*followed
by noun*) demasiado/demasiada; **too
much ink** demasiada tinta; **11 how
much?** ¿cuánto?; **how much is it?**
¿cuánto cuesta?; **how much do you
want?** ¿cuánto quieres?; **12 how
much?** (*followed by a noun*)
¿cuánto?/¿cuánta?; **how much milk
do you want?** ¿cuánta leche
quieres?

mud *noun* barro *Masc.*

muddle *noun* desorden *Masc.*; **to be
in a muddle** estar [2] todo
desordenado.

muddy *adjective* lleno de barro/
llena de barro; **your boots are all
muddy** tus botas están llenas de
barro; **a muddy road** una carretera
llena de barro.

mug *noun* taza *Fem.* alta; **a mug of
coffee** una taza alta de café.
mug *verb* **to mug somebody**
atracar [31] a alguien; **my brother
was mugged in the park** atracaron
a mi hermano en el parque.

mugging *noun* atraco *Masc.*

multiplication *noun*
multiplicación *Fem.*

multiply *verb* multiplicar [31]; **to
multiply six by four** multiplicar
seis por cuatro.

mum, mummy *noun* **1** madre
Fem.; **Tom's mum** la madre de Tom;
I'll ask my mum preguntaré a mi
madre; **2** (*within the family or as a
name*) mamá *Fem.*; **Mum's not back
yet** mamá no ha vuelto todavía.

mumps *noun* paperas *Fem. plural.*

murder *noun* asesinato *Masc.*
murder *verb* asesinar [17].

murderer *noun* asesino *Masc.*,
asesina *Fem.*

muscle *noun* músculo *Masc.*

museum *noun* museo *Masc.*; **to go
to the museum** ir [8] al museo.

mushroom *noun* champiñón *Masc.*

music *noun* música *Fem.*; **pop
music** música pop; **classical music**
música clásica.

musical *noun* musical *Masc.*
musical *adjective* **1 a musical
instrument** un instrumento
musical; **2 they're a very musical
family** toda la familia tiene dotes
para la música.

musician *noun* músico *Masc.*,
música *Fem.*

Muslim *noun* musulmán *Masc.*,
musulmana *Fem.*

mussel *noun* mejillón *Masc.*

must *verb* **1** (*expressing obligation*)
tener [9] que (*stronger*) deber [18];
you must be there at eight tienes
que estar allí a las ocho, debes estar
allí a las ocho; **2** (*expressing
probability*) deber [18]; **you must be**

a
b
c
d
e
f
g
h
i
j
k
l
m
n
o
p
q
r
s
t
u
v
w
x
y
z

tired debes estar cansado; **it must be five o'clock** deben ser las cinco en punto; **he must have forgotten** debe haberse olvidado.

mustard *noun* mostaza *Fem.*

my *adjective* 1 (*before a singular noun*) mi; **my book** mi libro; **my sister** mi hermana; 2 (*before a plural noun*) mis; **my children** mis hijos; 3 (*with parts of the body*) el/la/los/las; **I had a glass in my hand** tenía un vaso en la mano; **I'm washing my hands** me estoy lavando las manos.

myself *pronoun* 1 (*as a reflexive*) me; **I've hurt myself** me he hecho daño; 2 **I said it myself** lo dije yo mismo; 3 (*for emphasis*) yo; **by myself** yo solo/yo sola; **I did it by myself** lo hice yo solo/yo sola.

mysterious *adjective* misterioso/misteriosa.

mystery *noun* 1 misterio *Masc.*; 2 (*book*) novela *Fem.* de misterio.

Nn

nail *noun* 1 (*on finger or toe*) uña *Fem.*; **to bite your nails** morderse [38] las uñas; 2 (*metal*) clavo *Masc.*

nailbrush *noun* cepillo *Masc.* de uñas.

nailfile *noun* lima *Fem.* de uñas.

nail scissors *noun* tijeras *Fem. plural* de uñas.

nail varnish *noun* esmalte *Masc.* de uñas.

nail varnish remover *noun* quitaesmalte *Masc.*

name *noun* 1 nombre *Masc.*; **I've forgotten her name** se me ha olvidado su nombre; **what's your name?** ¿cómo te llamas?; **my name's Lily** me llamo Lily; 2 (*of a book or film*) título *Masc.*

nanny *noun* niñera *Fem.*

napkin *noun* servilleta *Fem.*

nappy *noun* pañal *Masc.*

narrow *adjective* estrecho/estrecha; **a narrow street** una calle estrecha.

nasty *adjective* 1 (*mean*) cruel; **they were nasty to him** fueron crueles con él; **that was a nasty thing to do** eso fue una crueldad; 2 (*unpleasant*) desagradable; **that's a nasty job** ese es un trabajo desagradable; 3 (*bad*) repugnante; **a nasty smell** un olor repugnante.

nation *noun* nación *Fem.*

national *adjective* nacional.

national anthem *noun* himno *Masc.* nacional.

nationality *noun* nacionalidad *Fem.*

national park *noun* parque *Masc.* nacional.

Nativity scene *noun* belén *Masc.*

natural *adjective* natural.

naturally *adverb* naturalmente.

nature *noun* naturaleza *Fem.*

nature reserve *noun* reserva *Fem.* natural.

naughty *adjective* malo/mala.

nausea *noun* náuseas *Fem. plural*.

navel *noun* ombligo *Masc.*

navigate *verb* navegar [28].

navy *noun* marina *Fem.*; **my uncle's in the navy** mi tío está en la marina.

navy-blue *adjective* azul marino; **navy-blue gloves** guantes azul marino.

near *adjective* cercano/cercana; **the nearest shop** la tienda más cercana.
near *adverb, preposition* **1** cerca; **they live quite near** viven bastante cerca; **to come nearer** acercarse [31]; **2 near (to)** cerca de; **near the station** cerca de la estación.

nearby *adverb* cerca; **there's a park nearby** hay un parque cerca.

nearly *adverb* casi; **nearly empty** casi vacío; **we're nearly there** ya casi hemos llegado.

neat *adjective* **1** (*well-organized*) ordenado/ordenada; **a neat desk** un pupitre ordenado; **2** arreglado/arreglada (*your clothes, or the way you look*); **she always looks very neat** siempre va muy arreglada; **3** muy cuidado/muy cuidada (*a garden*).

necessarily *adverb* **not necessarily** no necesariamente.

necessary *adjective* necesario/necesaria; **if necessary** si es necesario.

neck *noun* cuello *Masc.* (*of a person or garment*).

necklace *noun* collar *Masc.*

nectarine *noun* nectarina *Fem.*

need *noun* necesidad *Fem.*; **there's no need, I've done it already** no hay necesidad, ya lo he hecho; **there's no need to wait** no hay necesidad de esperar.
need *verb* **1** necesitar [17]; **we need bread** necesitamos pan; **they need help** necesitan ayuda; **everything you need** todo lo que necesites; **2** (*to have to*) tener [9] que; **I need to drop in at the bank** tengo que pasarme por el banco; **she'll need to check** tendrá que comprobarlo; **3 you needn't decide today** no hace falta que decidas hoy; **you needn't wait** no hace falta que esperes.

needle *noun* aguja *Fem.*

negative *noun* (*of a photo*) negativo *Masc.*

neglected *adjective* descuidado/descuidada.

neighbour *noun* vecino *Masc.*, vecina *Fem.*; **we're going round to the neighbours'** vamos a casa de los vecinos.

neighbourhood *noun* barrio *Masc.*; **a nice neighbourhood** un barrio agradable.

neither *conjunction* **1 neither ... nor** ni ... ni; **I have neither the time nor the money** no tengo ni tiempo ni dinero; **2 neither do I** yo tampoco; **'I didn't go' – 'neither did I'** 'no fui' – 'yo tampoco'; **3** (*with*

a
b
c
d
e
f
g
h
i
j
k
l
m
n
o
p
q
r
s
t
u
v
w
x
y
z

'gustar') **'I don't like fish'** – **'neither do I'** 'no me gusta el pescado' – 'ni a mí tampoco'; **'I didn't like the film'** – **'neither did Kirsty'** 'no me gustó la película' – 'ni a Kirsty tampoco'; **'which do you like?'** – **'neither'** '¿cuál te gusta?' – 'ninguno'.

nephew *noun* sobrino *Masc.*

nerve *noun* **1** (*in the body*) nervio *Masc.*; **2 to lose one's nerve** perder [36] el valor; **3 you've got a nerve!** ¡vaya cara que tienes! (*informal*); ★ **he gets on my nerves** me pone los nervios de punta (*informal*).

nervous *adjective* nervioso/ nerviosa; **to feel nervous** (*before a performance or an exam*) estar nervioso.

nervous breakdown *noun* crisis *Fem.* nerviosa.

nest *noun* nido *Masc.*

net *noun* red *Fem.*

Netherlands *noun* **the Netherlands** los Países Bajos.

nettle *noun* ortiga *Fem.*

network *noun* red *Fem.*

neutral *noun* (*in a gearbox*) punto *Masc.* muerto; **to be in neutral** estar [2] en punto muerto.
neutral *adjective* **1** (*impartial*) neutral; **2** (*colour*) neutro.

never *adjective* **1** nunca; **Ben never smokes** Ben no fuma nunca; **I've never seen the film** no he visto nunca la película; **'have you ever been to Spain?'** – **'no, never'** ¿has estado alguna vez en España?' – 'no, nunca'; **2 never again!** ¡nunca jamás!; **3 never mind** no importa.

nevertheless *adverb* sin embargo.

new *adjective* nuevo/nueva; **have you seen their new house?** ¿has visto su casa nueva?; **Debbie's new boyfriend** el nuevo novio de Debbie; **it's a new car** es un coche nuevo.

news *plural noun* **1** (*everyday gossip*) noticia *Fem.*; **a piece of good news** una buena noticia; **have your heard the news?** ¿te has enterado de la noticia?; **any news?** ¿hay alguna noticia?; **2** (*on TV or radio*) noticias *Fem. plural*; **the midday news** las noticias del mediodía.

newsagent *noun* vendedor *Masc.* de periódicos vendedora *Fem.* de periódicos; **at the newsagent's** en la tienda de periódicos.

newspaper *noun* periódico *Masc.*

newsreader *noun* presentador *Masc.*, presentadora *Fem.*

New Year *noun* Año *Masc.* Nuevo; **Happy New Year!** ¡Feliz Año Nuevo!

New Year's Day *noun* día *Masc.* de Año Nuevo.

New Year's Eve *noun* Nochevieja *Fem.*

New Zealand *noun* Nueva Zelanda *Fem.*

New Zealander *noun* neozelandés *Masc.*, neozelandesa *Fem.*

next *adjective* **1** próximo/próxima; **the next train is at ten** el próximo tren sale a las diez; **next week** la próxima semana; **next Thursday** el próximo jueves; **next year** el próximo año; **the next time I see**

you la próxima vez que te vea;
2 (*following*) siguiente; **the next
day** el día siguiente; **at the next
stop** en la siguiente parada; **3** (*next-
door*) **in the next room** en la
habitación de al lado.

next *adverb* **1** (*afterwards*) luego;
what did he say next? ¿qué dijo
luego?; **2** (*now*) ahora; **what shall
we do next?** ¿qué hacemos ahora?;
3 next to al lado de; **the girl next to
Pat** la chica que está al lado de Pat;
it's next to the baker's está al lado
de la panadería.

next door *adverb* al lado; **they live
next door** viven al lado; **the girl
next door** la chica de al lado.

Nicaraguan *noun* nicaragüense
Masc./Fem.
Nicaraguan *adjective*
nicaragüense.

nice *adjective* **1** (*pleasant*)
agradable; **we had a very nice
evening** pasamos una tarde muy
agradable; **Brighton's a very nice
town** Brighton es una ciudad muy
agradable; **have a nice time!** ¡que lo
pases bien!; **2** (*attractive to look at*)
bonito/bonita (*an object or place*);
that's a nice dress ese vestido es
bonito; **3** (*attractive to look at*)
guapo/guapa (*a person*); **you look
nice in that dress** estás muy guapa
con ese vestido; **4** (*kind, friendly*)
majo/maja (*informal*); **she's really
nice** es muy maja (*informal*); **5 to
be nice to somebody** ser [1] bueno/
buena con alguien; **she's been very
nice to me** ha sido muy buena
conmigo; **6** (*tasting good*) rico/rica;
the food was really nice la comida

estaba muy rica; **7** (*weather*) bueno/
buena; **it's a nice day** hace buen día;
we had nice weather tuvimos buen
tiempo.

nick *verb* (*steal*) mangar [28]
(*informal*).

nickname *noun* apodo *Masc.*

niece *noun* sobrina *Fem.*

night *noun* noche *Fem.*; **what are
you doing tonight?** ¿qué haces esta
noche?; **see you tonight!** ¡hasta esta
noche!; **I saw Greg last night**
anoche vi a Greg; **it's cold at night**
hace frío por la noche; **to stay the
night with somebody** pasar [17] la
noche con alguien.

night club *noun* club *Masc.*
nocturno.

nightie *noun* camisón *Masc.*

nightmare *noun* pesadilla *Fem.*; **to
have a nightmare** tener [9] una
pesadilla.

night-time *noun* noche *Fem.*

nil *noun* cero *Masc.*; **they won four-nil**
ganaron cuatro a cero.

nine *number* nueve *Masc.*; **Jake's
nine** Jake tiene nueve años; **it's nine
o'clock** son las nueve.

nineteen *number* diecinueve *Masc.*;
Jonny's nineteen Jonny tiene
diecinueve años.

nineties *plural noun* **the nineties**
los años noventa; **in the nineties** en
los años noventa.

ninety *number* noventa *Masc.*; **he's
ninety** tiene noventa años; **ninety-
five** noventa y cinco.

a
b
c
d
e
f
g
h
i
j
k
l
m
n
o
p
q
r
s
t
u
v
w
x
y
z

ninth *noun* **1** (*fraction*) **a ninth** una novena parte; **2 the ninth of June** el nueve de junio.
ninth *adjective* noveno/novena; **on the ninth floor** en la novena planta.

nitrogen *noun* nitrógeno *Masc.*

no *adverb* no; **I said no** he dicho que no; **no thank you** no, gracias.
no *adjective* **1 we've got no bread** no tenemos pan; **no problem!** ¡sin problema!; **2** (*on a notice*) **'no smoking'** 'prohibido fumar'; **'no parking'** 'prohibido aparcar'.

nobody *pronoun* nadie; **'who's there?' – 'nobody'** ¿quién está ahí? – 'nadie'; **there's nobody in the kitchen** no hay nadie en la cocina; **nobody knows me** nadie me conoce; **nobody answered** no contestó nadie.

nod *verb* (*to say yes*) asentir [14] con la cabeza; **he nodded** asintió con la cabeza.

noise *noun* ruido *Masc.*; **to make a noise** hacer [7] ruido.

noisy *adjective* ruidoso/ruidosa.

none *pronoun* **1** (*not one*) niguno/ninguna; **'how many students failed the exam?' – 'none'** '¿cuántos estudiantes suspendieron?' – 'ninguno'; **none of the girls knows him** ninguna de las chicas lo conoce; **2 there's none left** no queda nada; **there are none left** no queda ninguno/ninguna.

nonsense *noun* tonterías *Fem.* plural; **to talk nonsense** decir [5] tonterías; **nonsense! she's at least thirty** ¡tonterías! tiene por lo menos treinta años.

non-smoker *noun* no fumador *Masc.*, no fumadora *Fem.*

non-stop *adjective* directo/directa (*a train or flight*).
non-stop *adverb* **she talks non-stop** habla sin parar.

noodles *plural noun* fideos *Masc. plural.*

noon *noun* mediodía *Masc.*; **at (twelve) noon** a mediodía.

no-one *pronoun* nadie; **'who's there?' – 'no-one'** ¿quién está ahí? – 'nadie'; **there's no-one in the kitchen** no hay nadie en la cocina; **no-one knows me** nadie me conoce; **no-one answered** nadie contestó.

nor *conjunction* **1 neither ... nor** ni ... ni; **I have neither the time nor the money** no tengo ni tiempo ni dinero; **2 nor do I** yo tampoco; **'I didn't go' – 'nor did I'** 'no fui' – 'yo tampoco'; **3** (*with 'gustar'*) **'I don't like fish' – 'nor do I'** 'no me gusta el pescado' – 'ni a mí tampoco'; **'I didn't like the film' – 'nor did Kirsty'** 'no me gustó la película' – 'ni a Kirsty tampoco'.

normal *adjective* normal.

normally *adverb* normalmente.

north *noun* norte *Masc.*; **in the north** en el norte.
north *adjective, adverb* norte (*never changes*); **the north side** la parte norte; **a north wind** un viento del norte; **north of Madrid** al norte de Madrid.

North America *noun* Norteamérica *Fem.*

North American *noun* norteamericano *Masc.*,

norteamericana *Fem.*
North American *adjective*
norteamericano/norteamericana.

northeast *noun* noreste *Masc.*
northeast *adjective* **in northeast England** en el noreste de Inglaterra.

Northern Ireland *noun* Irlanda *Fem.* del Norte.

North Pole *noun* Polo *Masc.* Norte.

North Sea *noun* **the North Sea** el mar del Norte.

northwest *noun* noroeste *Masc.*
northwest *adjective* **in northwest England** en el noroeste de Inglaterra.

Norway *noun* Noruega *Fem.*

Norwegian *noun* 1 (*person*) noruego *Masc.*, noruega *Fem.*;
2 (*language*) noruego *Masc.*
Norwegian *adjective* noruego/noruega.

nose *noun* nariz *Fem.*; **to blow your nose** sonarse [24] la nariz.

nosebleed *noun* **to have a nosebleed** tener [9] una hemorragia nasal.

nostril *noun* fosa *Fem.* nasal.

not *adverb* 1 no; **not on Saturdays** los sábados no; **not all alone!** ¡completamente solo no!; **it's not bad** no está mal; **not at all** (*in no way*) en absoluto (*after somebody says 'thank you'*) de nada; **not yet** todavía no; **of course not!** ¡por supuesto que no!; 2 (*when used with a verb*) no; **it's not my car** no es mi coche; **I don't know** no sé; **Sam didn't phone** Sam no llamó; **we**

decided not to wait decidimos no esperar; 3 **I hope not** espero que no.

note *noun* 1 (*a short letter*) nota *Fem.*; **she left me a note** me dejó una nota; 2 **to take notes** tomar [17] apuntes; 3 (*a banknote*) billete *Masc.*; **a ten-pound note** un billete de diez libras; 4 (*in music*) nota *Fem.*

notebook *noun* cuaderno *Masc.*

notepad *noun* bloc *Masc.*

nothing *pronoun* 1 nada; **'what did you say?' – 'nothing'** ¿qué has dicho? – 'nada'; **nothing new** nada nuevo; **nothing special** nada especial; 2 (*when used with a verb*) no ... nada; **she knows nothing** no sabe nada; **but there was nothing there** pero no había nada allí; **I saw nothing** no vi nada; **there's nothing happening** no está pasando nada; **there's nothing new** no hay nada nuevo; 3 **they do nothing but fight** no hacen más que pelearse.

notice *noun* 1 (*a sign*) letrero *Masc.*; 2 **don't take any notice of her!** ¡no le hagas caso!; 3 **to do something at short notice** hacer [7] algo con poca antelación.
notice *verb* notar [17]; **I didn't notice anything** no noté nada.

notice board *noun* tablón *Masc.* de anuncios.

nought *noun* cero *Masc.*

noun *noun* nombre *Masc.*

novel *noun* novela *Fem.*

novelist *noun* novelista *Masc./Fem.*

November *noun* noviembre *Masc.*

now *adverb* 1 ahora; **where is he now?** ¿dónde está ahora?; **they live**

a
b
c
d
e
f
g
h
i
j
k
l
m
n
o
p
q
r
s
t
u
v
w
x
y
z

in the country now ahora viven en el campo; **2 he's busy just now** está ocupado en este momento; **I saw her just now in the corridor** acabo de verla en el pasillo; **3 do it right now!** ¡hazlo ahora mismo!; **4 now and then** de vez en cuando; **from now on** de ahora en adelante.

nowadays *adverb* hoy en día; **nowadays they are quite common** hoy en día son bastante comunes.

nowhere *adjective* **1** ninguna parte; **nowhere in Spain** en ninguna parte de España; **'where did she go after work?'** – **'nowhere'** '¿dónde fue después del trabajo?' – 'a ninguna parte'; **2 there's nowhere to park** no hay sitio donde aparcar.

nuclear *adjective* nuclear; **a nuclear power station** una central nuclear.

nuisance *noun* **1** (*a person*) pesado/pesada; **he's a real nuisance** es un verdadero pesado; **2 it's a nuisance** es un fastidio.

numb *adjective* entumecido/ entumecida; **my fingers are numb with cold** tengo los dedos entumecidos del frío.

number *noun* número *Masc.*; **I live at number thirty-one** vivo en el número treinta y uno; **my new phone number** mi nuevo número de teléfono; **a large number of visitors** un gran número de visitantes; **the third number is a 7** el tercer número es un siete.

number plate *noun* matrícula *Fem.*

nun *noun* monja *Fem.*

nurse *noun* enfermero *Masc.*, enfermera *Fem.*; **Janet's a nurse** Janet es enfermera.

nursery *noun* **1** (*for children*) guardería *Fem.*; **2** (*for plants*) vivero *Masc.*

nursery school *noun* jardín *Masc.* de infancia.

nursing *noun* enfermería *Fem.*

nut *noun* **1** (*walnut*) nuez *Fem.*; **2** (*almond*) almendra *Fem.*; **3** (*peanut*) cacahuete *Masc.*; **4** (*for a bolt*) tuerca *Fem.*

nylon *noun* nylon *Masc.*

Oo

oak *noun* roble *Masc.*

oar *noun* remo *Masc.*

oasis *noun* oasis *Masc.*

obedient *adjective* obediente.

obey *verb* obedecer [35] (*a person*); **to obey the rules** respetar [17] las reglas.

object *noun* objeto *Masc.* **object** *verb* oponerse [11]; **if you don't object** si no te opones.

objection *noun* objeción *Fem.*

oboe *noun* oboe *Masc.*; **to play the oboe** tocar [31] el oboe.

obsessed *adjective* obsesionado/ obsesionada; **she's obsessed with her diet** está obsesionada con su dieta.

obsession *noun* obsesión *Fem.*; **he has an obsession with cleanliness** tiene obsesión con la limpieza.

obvious *adjective* obvio/obvia.

obviously *adverb* evidentemente; **the house is obviously empty** evidentemente la casa está vacía; **'do you want to come too?' – 'obviously, but it's a bit difficult'** '¿tú quieres venir también?' – 'evidentemente, pero es un poco difícil'.

occasion *noun* ocasión *Fem.*; **a special occasion** una ocasión especial.

occasional *adjective* **he sends us the occasional letter** de vez en cuando nos manda una carta.

occasionally *adverb* de vez en cuando.

occupation *noun* ocupación *Fem.*

occupied *adjective* ocupado/ocupada.

occur *verb* ocurrir [19]; **the accident occurred on Monday** el accidente ocurrió el lunes; **it never occurred to me** nunca se me había ocurrido.

ocean *noun* océano *Masc.*

o'clock *adverb* **at ten o'clock** a las diez; **it's three o'clock** son las tres; **exactly five o'clock** exactamente las cinco en punto.

October *noun* octubre *Masc.*

odd *adjective* 1 (*strange*) raro/rara; **that's odd, I'm sure I heard the phone** qué raro, estoy seguro de que he oído el teléfono; 2 (*number*)

impar; **three is an odd number** el tres es un número impar.

odds and ends *plural noun* cachivaches *Masc. plural.*

of *preposition* 1 de (*note that 'de+el' becomes 'del'*); **a kilo of tomatoes** un kilo de tomates; **the end of my work** el final de mi trabajo; **the beginning of the concert** el principio del concierto; **the name of the flower** el nombre de la flor; **the sixth of June** el seis de junio; **a cup of tea** una taza de té; 2 Ray has four horses but he's selling three of them Ray tiene cuatro caballos, pero va a vender tres; **we ate a lot of it** comimos mucho; **a lot of them** muchos/muchas; **some of them** algunos/algunas; **3 two of us** dos de nosotros; **there are two of us** somos dos; **a friend of mine** un amigo mío; **4 a bracelet made of silver** una pulsera de plata.

off *adverb, adjective*
off *preposition* 1 (*switched off*) apagado/apagada; **is the telly off?** ¿está apagada la tele?; **to turn off the lights** apagar [28] la luz; 2 (*tap, water, gas*) cerrado/cerrada; **to turn off the tap** cerrar [29] el grifo; **3 to be off** (*to leave*) irse [8]; **I'm off** me voy; **4 a day off** un día libre; **Caro took three days off work** Caro se tomó tres días libres en el trabajo; **Maya's off school today** Maya no ha venido al colegio hoy; **5 he's off sick** no ha venido al trabajo porque está enfermo; 6 (*cancelled*) suspendido/suspendida; **the match is off** el partido se ha suspendido; **7 to be off** (*meat or fish*) estar malo/

a
b
c
d
e
f
g
h
i
j
k
l
m
n
o
p
q
r
s
t
u
v
w
x
y
z

mala; **the milk's off** la leche está
cortada.

offence *noun* **1** (*crime*) delito *Masc.*;
2 to take offence ofenderse [18]; **he
takes offence easily** se ofende
fácilmente.

offer *noun* **1** oferta *Fem.*; **a job offer**
una oferta de trabajo; **2 'on
(special) offer'** 'de oferta
(especial)'.

offer *verb* **1** ofrecer [35] (*a present, a
reward, or a job*) **he offered her a
chair** le ofreció una silla; **2 to offer
to do** ofrecerse [35] a hacer; **Mike
offered to drive me to the station**
Mike se ofreció a llevarme a la
estación.

office *noun* oficina *Fem.*; **he's still
at the office** aún está en la oficina.

office block *noun* bloque *Masc.* de
oficinas.

officer *noun* oficial *Masc./Fem.*

official *adjective* oficial; **the
official version** la versión oficial.

off-licence *noun* tienda *Fem.* de
vinos y licores.

offside *adverb* fuera de juego.

often *adverb* **1** a menudo; **he's
often late** a menudo llega tarde; **I'd
like to see Eric more often** me
gustaría ver a Eric más a menudo;
do you go often? ¿vas a menudo?;
2 how often? ¿con qué frecuencia?;
how often do you see Rosie? ¿con
qué frecuencia ves a Rosie?

oil *noun* aceite *Masc.*; **olive oil** aceite
de oliva; **suntan oil** aceite
bronceador.

oil painting *noun* óleo *Masc.*
(*picture*).

ointment *noun* pomada *Fem.*

okay *adjective* **1** (*showing
agreement*) vale; **okay, tomorrow at
ten** vale, mañana a las diez;
2 (*asking or giving permission*) **is it
okay to use the phone?** ¿puedo
usar el teléfono?; **is it okay with you
if I don't come till Friday?** ¿te va
bien si no vengo hasta el viernes?;
it's okay if you don't want to do it
no pasa nada si no quieres hacerlo;
3 (*person*) majo/maja (*informal*);
Daisy's okay Daisy es maja;
4 (*nothing special*) **the film was
okay** la película no estuvo mal;
5 (*not ill*) **are you okay?** ¿estás
bien?; **I've been ill but I'm okay
now** he estado enferma, pero ahora
estoy bien.

old *adjective* **1** (*not young, not new*)
viejo/vieja; **an old man** un hombre
viejo; **an old lady** una señora vieja;
bring some old clothes trae ropa
vieja; **an old friend of mine** un viejo
amigo mío; **old people** los ancianos;
2 (*previous*) antiguo/antigua; **our
old car was a Rover** su antiguo
coche era un Rover; **their old
address** su antigua dirección;
3 (*talking about age*) **how old are
you?** ¿cuántos años tienes?; **James
is ten years old** James tiene diez
años; **a three-year-old child** un
niño de tres años; **4 my older sister**
mi hermana mayor; **she's older
than me** es mayor que yo; **he's a
year older than me** es un año
mayor que yo.

old age *noun* vejez *Fem.*

old age pensioner *noun* pensionista *Masc./Fem.*

old-fashioned *noun* **1** (*clothes, music, style*) pasado de moda/pasada de moda; **2** (*a person*) anticuado/anticuada; **my parents are so old-fashioned** mis padres son tan anticuados.

olive *noun* aceituna *Fem.*

olive oil *noun* aceite *Fem.* de oliva.

Olympic Games, **Olympics** *plural noun* Juegos *Masc. plural* Olímpicos.

ombudsman *noun* **the ombudsman** el defensor/la defensora del pueblo *Masc./Fem.*

omelette *noun* tortilla *Fem.*; **a cheese omelette** una tortilla de queso.

omit *verb* omitir [19].

on *preposition* **1** en; **on the desk** en el escritorio; **on the road** en la carretera; **on the beach** en la playa; **2** (*in expressions of time*) **on March 21st** el 21 de marzo; **he's arriving on Tuesday** llega el martes; **it's shut on Saturdays** cierra los sábados; **on rainy days** los días de lluvia; **3** (*for buses, trains, etc.*) **she arrived on the bus** llegó en autobús; **I met Jackie on the bus** me encontré con Jackie en el autobús; **I slept on the plane** dormí en el avión; **let's go on our bikes!** ¡vayamos en las bicis!; **4 on TV** en la tele; **on the radio** en la radio; **on video** en vídeo; **5 on holiday** de vacaciones; **on strike** de huelga.

on *adjective* **1** (*TV, light, oven, radio*) **to be on** estar [2] encendido/encendida; **all the lights were on** todas las luces estaban encendidas; **is the radio on?** ¿está encendida la radio?; **I've put the oven on** he encendido el horno; **2** (*machine*) estar en marcha; **the dishwasher's on** el lavaplatos está en marcha; **3** (*happening*) **what's on TV?** ¿qué ponen en la tele?; **what's on this week at the cinema?** ¿qué ponen en el cine esta semana?

once *adverb* **1** una vez; **I've tried once already** ya lo he intentado una vez; **try once more** inténtalo una vez más; **once a day** una vez al día; **more than once** más de una vez; **once upon a time** érase una vez; **2 at once** (*immediately*) inmediatamente; **the doctor came at once** el médico vino inmediatamente; **3 at once** (*at the same time*) a la vez; **I can't do two things at once** no puedo hacer dos cosas a la vez.

one *number* **1** uno/una; **one apple** una manzana; (*note that 'uno' becomes 'un' before a masculine singular noun*) **one son** un hijo; **2 it's one o'clock** es la una. **one** *pronoun* **1** uno/una; **if you want a pen I've got one** si quieres un boli yo tengo uno; **one of us** uno de nosotros; **one of my friends** uno de mis amigos; **you never know** uno nunca sabe; **2 this one** éste/ésta; **I like that jumper, but this one's cheaper** me gusta ese jersey, pero éste es más barato; **do you want this red tie or this one?** ¿quieres esta corbata roja o ésta otra?; **3 that one** ése/ésa; **'which video?'** – **'that one'** '¿qué vídeo?' – 'ése'; **4 which one?** ¿cuál?; **'my foot's hurting'** – **'which one?'** 'me duele el pie' – '¿cuál?'; **5 another one** otro/otra; **I've already had a coffee, but I'll have another one** ya he tomado un café pero voy a tomar otro; **I liked the shirt so much that I bought another one** me gustó tanto la camisa que compré otra.

one's *adjective* **to pay for one's car** pagar su coche; **to wash one's hands** lavarse las manos.

oneself *pronoun* **1** (*as a reflexive*) se; **to wash oneself** lavarse; **to hurt oneself** hacerse daño; **2** (*for emphasis*) uno mismo/una misma; **one has to do everything oneself** lo tiene que hacer todo uno mismo.

one-way street *noun* calle *Fem.* de sentido único.

onion *noun* cebolla *Fem.*

only *adjective* único/única; **the only free seat** el único sitio libre; **the only thing to do** lo único que se puede hacer; **I am an only child** soy hijo único.

only *adverb, conjunction* **1** (*with a verb*) sólo; **they've only got two bedrooms** sólo tienen dos habitaciones; **Anne's only free on Fridays** Anne sólo tiene libres los viernes; **there are only three left** sólo quedan tres; **'how long did they stay?'** – **'only two days'** '¿cuánto tiempo se quedaron?' – 'sólo dos días'; **2** (*but*) pero; **I'd walk, only it's raining** iría andando, pero

está lloviendo; **3 I've only just seen it** acabo de verlo.

onto *preposition* sobre.

open *noun* **in the open** al aire libre. **open** *adjective* **1** (*not shut*) abierto/ abierta; **the door's open** la puerta está abierta; **the baker's isn't open** la panadería no está abierta; **2 in the open air** al aire libre.
open *verb* **1** abrir [46]; **can you open the door for me?** ¿me puedes abrir la puerta?; **Sam opened his eyes** Sam abrió los ojos; **the banks open at nine** los bancos abren a las nueve; **2** (*by itself*) abrirse [46]; **the door opened slowly** la puerta se abrió lentamente.

open-air *adjective* al aire libre; **an open-air swimming pool** una piscina al aire libre.

opener *noun* abridor *Masc.*

opening *noun* **1** (*space*) abertura *Fem.*; **2** (*opportunity*) oportunidad *Fem.*

opera *noun* ópera *Fem.*

operate *verb* **1** (*a machine*) manejar [17]; **2** (*on a patient, organ*) operar [17]; **will they have to operate** ¿tendrán que operarlo?

operation *noun* operación *Fem.*; **she's had an operation** le han operado.

opinion *noun* opinión *Fem.*; **in my opinion** en mi opinión.

opinion poll *noun* encuesta *Fem.* de opinión.

opponent *noun* oponente *Masc./ Fem.*

opportunity *noun* oportunidad *Fem.*; **to have the opportunity of doing** tener [9] la oportunidad de hacer; **I took the opportunity to visit the museum** aproveché la oportunidad para visitar el museo.

opposed *adjective* **to be opposed to something** oponerse [11] a algo; **they are opposed to any change in the rules** se oponen a cualquier cambio de las reglas.

opposite *noun* **the opposite** lo contrario; **no, quite the opposite** no, todo lo contrario.
opposite *adjective* **1** opuesto/ opuesta (*a direction, side, or view, for example*); **she went off in the opposite direction** se fue en la dirección opuesta; **2** (*facing*) de enfrente; **in the house opposite** en la casa de enfrente.
opposite *adverb* enfrente; **they live opposite** viven enfrente.
opposite *preposition* enfrente de; **opposite the station** enfrente de la estación.

opposition *noun* oposición *Fem.*

optician *noun* oculista *Masc./Fem.*

optimistic *adjective* optimista.

or *conjunction* **1** o (*note that 'o' becomes 'u' before a word starting with 'o-' or 'ho-'*); **English or Spanish?** ¿inglés o español?; **yesterday or today?** ¿ayer u hoy?; **2** (*in negatives*) **I don't have a cat or a dog** no tengo ni un gato ni un perro; **not in June or July** ni en junio ni en julio; **3** (*or else*) si no; **phone Mum, or she'll worry** llama a mamá, si no se va a preocupar.

oral *noun* (*an exam*) oral *Masc.*; **the Spanish oral** el oral de español.

orange *noun* (*the fruit*) naranja *Fem.*; **an orange juice** un zumo de naranja.
orange *adjective* naranja (*never changes*); **my orange socks** mis calcetines naranja.

orchard *noun* huerto *Fem.*

orchestra *noun* orquesta *Fem.*

order *noun* **1** (*arrangement*) orden *Masc.*; **in the right order** ordenado/ ordenada; **the books are in the right order** los libros estan ordenados; **in the wrong order** desordenado/desordenada; **in alphabetical order** en orden alfabético; **2** (*command*) orden *Fem.*; **that's an order** es una orden; **3** (*in a restaurant or café*) **can I take your orders?** ¿les tomo la nota?; **4** **'out of order'** 'no funciona'; **5** **in order to do** para hacer; **we hurried in order to be on time** nos dimos prisa para llegar a tiempo.
order *verb* **1** (*in a restaurant or a shop*) pedir [57]; **we ordered steaks** pedimos filetes; **2** llamar [17] a (*a taxi*).

ordinary *adjective* normal.

organ *noun* (*the instrument*) órgano *Masc.*; **to play the organ** tocar [31] el órgano.

organic *adjective* biológico/ biológica (*food*).

organization *noun* organización *Fem.*

organize *verb* organizar [22].

a
b
c
d
e
f
g
h
i
j
k
l
m
n
o
p
q
r
s
t
u
v
w
x
y
z

a
b
c
d
e
f
g
h
i
j
k
l
m
o
p
q
r
s
t
u
v
w
x
y
z

original *adjective* original; **the original version was better** la versión original era mejor; **it's a really original novel** es una novela realmente original.

originally *adverb* al principio; **originally we wanted to take the car** al principio queríamos llevar el coche.

Orkneys *plural noun* **the Orkneys** las Órcadas *Fem. plural*.

ornament *noun* adorno *Masc.*

orphan *noun* huérfano *Masc.*, huérfana *Fem.*

other *adjective* **1** (*before a singular noun*) otro/otra; **the other day** el otro día; **we took the other road** cogimos la otra carretera; **the other one** el otro/la otra; **I don't like this book, give me the other one** no me gusta este libro, dame el otro; **2 the others** los otros/las otras; **where are the others?** ¿dónde están los otros?; **the other two cars** los otros dos coches; **3 every other week** una semana sí y otra no; **4 somebody or other** alguien; **something or other** algo; **somewhere or other** en algún sitio.

otherwise *adverb* (*in other ways*) aparte de eso; **the flat's a bit small but otherwise it's lovely** el piso es pequeño, pero aparte de eso es precioso.

otherwise *conjunction* (*or else*) si no; **I'll phone home, otherwise they'll worry** voy a llamar a casa, si no van a preocuparse.

ought *verb* deber [18] (*'ought' is translated by the conditional tense of 'deber'*); **I ought to go now** debería irme ahora; **they ought to know the address** deberían saber las señas; **you oughtn't to have any problems** no deberías tener ningún problema.

our *adjective* **1** (*before a singular noun*) nuestro/nuestra; **our house** nuestra casa; **2** (*before a plural noun*) nuestros/nuestras; **our parents** nuestros padres; **our address** nuestras señas; **3** (*with parts of the body*) el/la/los/las; **we'll go and wash our hands** vamos a lavarnos las manos.

ours *pronoun* **1** (*referring to a singular noun*) el nuestro/la nuestra; **their garden's bigger than ours** su jardín es más grande que el nuestro; **their house is smaller than ours** su casa es más pequeña que la nuestra; **2** (*referring to a plural noun*) los nuestros/las nuestras; **they've invited their friends and we've invited ours** han invitado a sus amigos y nosotros a los nuestros; **they showed us their photos and we showed them ours** ellos nos enseñaron sus fotos y nosotros les enseñamos las nuestras.

ourselves *pronoun* **1** (*as a reflexive*) nos; **we introduced ourselves** nos presentamos; **2** (*for emphasis*) nosotros solos/nosotras solas; **in the end we did it ourselves** al final lo hicimos nosotros solos.

out *adverb* **1** (*outside*) fuera; **it's cold out there** hace frío ahí fuera; **out in**

the rain bajo la lluvia; **they're out in the garden** están en el jardín; **2 to go out** salir [63]; **he went out of the room** salió de la habitación; **are you going out this evening?** ¿vas a salir esta noche?; **Alison's going out with Danny at the moment** Alison está saliendo ahora con Danny; **he's asked me out** me ha pedido que salga con él; **3 to be out** (*absent*) no estar [2]; **my mum's out** mi madre no está; **when they were out** cuando ellos no estaban; **4** (*light, fire*) apagado/apagada; **are all the lights out?** ¿están todas las luces apagadas?; **the fire was out** el fuego estaba apagado; **5 he threw it out of the window** lo tiró por la ventana; **to drink out of a glass** beber [18] de un vaso; **she took the photo out of her bag** sacó la foto del bolso.

outing *noun* excursión *Fem.*; **to go on an outing** ir [8] de excursión.

outline *noun* (*of an object*) contorno *Masc.*

out-of-date *adjective* **1** (*no longer valid*) caducado/caducada; **my passport's out of date** mi pasaporte está caducado; **2** (*old-fashioned*) pasado/pasada de moda; **they played out-of-date music** tocaron música pasada de moda.

outside *noun* parte *Fem.* de fuera; **it's blue on the outside** la parte de fuera es azul.
  outside *adjective* exterior.
  outside *adverb* fuera; **it's cold outside** hace frío fuera.
  outside *preposition* fuera de; **I'll**

meet you outside the cinema te veo fuera del cine.

outskirts *noun* afueras *Fem. plural*; **on the outskirts of York** en las afueras de York.

outstanding *adjective* excepcional.

oven *noun* horno *Masc.*; **I've put it in the oven** lo he puesto en el horno.

over *preposition, adverb* **1** (*above*) encima de; **there's a mirror over the sideboard** hay un espejo encima del aparador; **2** (*involving movement*) por encima de; **she jumped over the fence** saltó por encima de la valla; **he threw the ball over the wall** tiró la pelota por encima del muro; **3 over here** aquí; **the drinks are over here** las bebidas están aquí; **4 over there** allí; **she's over there talking to Julian** está allí, hablando con Julián; **5** (*more than*) más de; **it will cost over a hundred pounds** costará más de cien libras; **he's over sixty** tiene más de sesenta años; **6** (*during*) durante; **over the weekend** durante el fin de semana; **over Christmas** durante las Navidades; **7** (*finished*) **when the meeting's over** cuando la reunión haya acabado; **it's all over now** ahora todo ha acabado; **8 over the phone** por teléfono; **9 to ask someone over** invitar [17] a alguien; **can you come over on Saturday?** ¿puedes venir el sábado?; **10 all over the place** por todas partes; **all over the house** por toda la casa.

overcast *adjective* nublado/nublada.

overcrowded *adjective* abarrotado/abarrotada.

overdose *noun* sobredosis *Fem.*

overdraft *noun* descubierto *Masc.*

overflow *verb* 1 (*water*) derramarse [17]; 2 (*river*) desbordarse [17].

overseas *adverb* en el extranjero; **Dave works overseas** Dave trabaja en el extranjero.

overtake *verb* adelantar [17] (*another car*).

overtime *noun* horas *Fem. plural* extras; **to work overtime** trabajar [17] horas extras.

owe *verb* deber [18]; **I owe Rick ten pounds** le debo diez libras a Rick.

owing *adjective* 1 (*to pay*) a pagar; **there's five pounds owing** quedan cinco libras a pagar; 2 **owing to** debido a; **owing to the snow** debido a la nieve.

owl *noun* búho *Masc.*

own *adjective* 1 propio/propia (*goes before the noun*); **my own computer** mi propio ordenador; **I've got my own room** tengo mi propia habitación; 2 **on your own** solo/sola; **Annie did it on her own** Annie lo hizo sola.
own *verb* tener [9].

owner *noun* dueño *Masc.*, dueña *Fem.*

oxygen *noun* oxígeno *Masc.*

oyster *noun* ostra *Fem.*

ozone layer *noun* capa *Fem.* de ozono.

Pp

Pacific *noun* **the Pacific Ocean** el océano *Masc.* Pacífico.

pack *noun* 1 paquete *Masc.*; 2 **a pack of cards** baraja *Fem.*.
pack *verb* 1 hacer [7] las maletas; 2 **I'll pack my case tonight** voy a hacer la maleta esta noche.

package *noun* paquete *Masc.*

package holiday, **package tour** *noun* viaje *Masc.* organizado.

packed lunch *noun* comida *Fem.* preparada desde casa.

packet *noun* 1 paquete *Masc.*; **a packet of biscuits** un paquete de galletas; 2 (*bag*) bolsa *Fem.*; **a packet of crisps** una bolsa de patatas.

packing *noun* **to do your packing** hacer [7] las maletas.

pad *noun* (*of paper*) bloc *Masc.*

padlock *noun* cercado *Masc.*

page *noun* página *Fem.*; **on page seven** en la página siete.

pain *noun* dolor *Masc.*; **to be in pain** tener [9] dolor; **I've got a pain in my leg** me duele la pierna; ★ **Eric's a real pain (in the neck)** Eric es un verdadero pesado.

painkiller *noun* analgésico *Masc.*

paint *noun* pintura *Fem.*; **'wet paint'** 'recién pintado'.
paint *verb* pintar [17]; **to paint something pink** pintar algo de rosa.

paintbrush *noun* **1** (*for painting pictures*) pincel *Masc.*; **2** (*for decorating*) brocha *Fem.*

painter *noun* pintor *Masc.*, pintora *Fem.*

painting *noun* (*picture*) cuadro *Masc.*; **a painting by Monet** un cuadro de Monet.

pair *noun* **1** par *Masc.*; **a pair of socks** un par de calcetines; **a pair of shoes** un par de zapatos; **a pair of jeans** unos vaqueros; **a pair of trousers** unos pantalones; **a pair of knickers** unas bragas; **a pair of scissors** unas tijeras; **2** (*of people*) pareja *Fem.*; **to work in pairs** trabajar [17] en parejas.

Pakistan *noun* Pakistán *Masc.*

Pakistani *noun* pakistaní *Masc./Fem.*
Pakistani *adjective* pakistaní.

palace *noun* palacio *Masc.*

pale *adjective* pálido/pálida; **pale green** verde pálido (*never changes*); **pale green curtains** cortinas verde pálido; **to turn pale** palidecer [35].

palm *noun* **1** (*of your hand*) palma *Fem.*; **2** (*a palm tree*) palmera *Fem.*

pan *noun* **1** (*saucepan*) cacerola *Fem.*; **a pan of water** una cacerola de agua; **2** (*frying-pan*) sartén *Fem.*

pancake *noun* crepe *Masc.*

panel *noun* **1** (*on radio or TV*) (*for a discussion*) panel *Masc.* (*for a quiz show*) equipo *Masc.*; **2** (*for a wall or a bath, for example*) panel *Masc.*

panel game *noun* concurso *Masc.* por equipos.

panic *noun* pánico *Masc.*
panic *verb* dejarse [17] llevar por el pánico; **don't panic!** ¡no pierdas la calma!

panties *plural noun* bragas *Fem. plural.*

pantomime *noun* pantomima *Fem.*

pants *plural noun* calzoncillos *Masc. plural.*

paper *noun* **1** papel *Masc.*; **a sheet of paper** una hoja de papel; **2 a paper hanky** un pañuelo de papel; **3** (*newspaper*) periódico *Masc.*; **it was in the paper** salió en el periódico.

paperback *noun* libro *Masc.* en rústica.

paperclip *noun* clip *Masc.*

paper towel *noun* toalla *Fem.* de papel.

parachute *noun* paracaídas *Masc.* (*does not change in the plural*).

parade *noun* desfile *Masc.*

paradise *noun* paraíso *Masc.*

paragraph *noun* párrafo *Masc.*; **'new paragraph'** 'punto y aparte'.

Paraguayan *noun* paraguayo *Masc.*, paraguaya *Fem.*
Paraguayan *adjective* paraguayo/paraguaya.

parallel *adjective* paralelo/paralela.

Paralympics *plural noun* **the Paralympic Games** los Juegos Paralímpicos.

paralysed *adjective* paralizado/paralizada.

a
b
c
d
e
f
g
h
i
j
k
l
m
n
o
p
q
r
s
t
u
v
w
x
y
z

a **parcel** *noun* paquete *Masc.*

b **pardon** *noun* **I beg your pardon** (*to someone you know*) perdón (*to show respect*) perdone; **pardon?** (*to someone you know*) ¿cómo dices? (*to show respect*) ¿cómo dice?

c

d

e **parents** *noun* **my parents** mis padres; **a parents' evening** una reunión de padres.

f

g **park** *noun* **1** parque *Masc.*; **a theme park** un parque temático; **2 a car park** un aparcamiento.
park *verb* **1** aparcar [31]; **you can park outside the house** puedes aparcar fuera de la casa; **2 to park a car** aparcar [31] un coche; **where did you park the car?** ¿dónde has aparcado el coche?

h

i

j

k **parking** *noun* aparcamiento *Masc.*; **'no parking'** 'no aparcar'.

l

m **parking meter** *noun* parquímetro *Masc.*

n **parking space** *noun* sitio *Masc.* para aparcar.

o

p **parking ticket** *noun* multa *Fem.*

q **parliament** *noun* parlamento *Masc.*

r

s **parrot** *noun* loro *Masc.*

parsley *noun* perejil *Masc.*

t **part** *noun* **1** parte *Fem.*; **part of the garden** parte del jardín; **the last part of the concert** la última parte del concierto; **that's part of your job** eso es parte de tu trabajo; **2 to take part in something** participar [17] en algo; **3** (*in a play*) papel *Masc.*

u

v

w

x

y **particular** *adjective* particular; **nothing in particular** nada en particular.

z

particularly *adverb* especialmente; **not particularly interesting** no especialmente interesante.

partly *adverb* en parte.

partner *noun* **1** (*in a game*) pareja *Fem.*; **2** (*the person you live with*) compañero *Masc.*, compañera *Fem.*; **3** (*in business*) socio *Masc.*, socia *Fem*

partridge *noun* perdiz *Fem.*

part-time *adjective, adverb* a tiempo parcial; **part-time work** trabajo a tiempo parcial; **to work part-time** trabajar [17] a tiempo parcial.

party *noun* **1** fiesta *Fem.*; **a Christmas party** una fiesta de Navidad; **to have a birthday party** celebrar [17] una fiesta de cumpleaños; **we've been invited to a party at the Smiths' house** estamos invitados a una fiesta en casa de los Smith; **2** (*group*) grupo *Masc.*; **a party of schoolchildren** un grupo de colegiales; **a rescue party** un equipo de rescate; **3** (*in politics*) partido *Masc.*; **the Labour party** el partido laborista.

pass *noun* **1** (*to let you in*) pase *Masc.* **2 a bus pass** un abono de autobús; **3** (*a mountain pass*) paso *Masc.*; **4** (*in an exam*) aprobado *Masc.*; **to get a pass in history** sacar [31] un aprobado en historia.
pass *verb* **1** (*go past*) pasar [17] por (*a place or building*); **we passed your house** pasamos por tu casa; **2** (*to overtake*) adelantar [17] (*a car*) **3** (*give*) pasar [17]; **could you pass me the paper please?** ¿me pasas el

papel, por favor?; **4** (*time*) pasar [17]; **the time passed slowly** el tiempo pasaba lentamente; **5** (*in an exam*) aprobar [24]; **did you pass?** ¿aprobaste?; **to pass an exam** aprobar un examen.

passenger *noun* pasajero *Masc.*, pasajera *Fem.*

passion *noun* pasión *Fem.*

passionate *adjective* apasionado/apasionada.

passive *noun* voz *Fem.* pasiva.
passive *adjective* pasivo/pasiva.

Passover *noun* Pascua *Fem.* judía.

passport *noun* pasaporte *Masc.*; **an EU passport** un pasaporte de la Comunidad Europea.

password *noun* contraseña *Fem.*

past *noun* pasado *Masc.*; **in the past** en el pasado.
past *adjective* **1** (*recent*) último/última (*goes before the noun*); **in the past few weeks** en las últimas semanas; **2** (*over*) **winter is past** ya ha pasado el invierno.
past *preposition, adverb* **1 to walk or drive past something** pasar [17] por delante de algo; **we went past the school** pasamos por delante del colegio; **Ray went past in his new car** Ray pasó en su coche nuevo; **2** (*the other side of*) pasado/pasada; **it's just past the post office** está justo pasada la oficina de correos; **3** (*talking about time*) **ten past six** las seis y diez; **half past four** las cuatro y media; **a quarter past two** las dos y cuarto.

pasta *noun* pasta *Fem.*; **I don't like pasta** no me gusta la pasta.

pasteurized *adjective* pasteurizado/pasteurizada.

pastry *noun* masa *Fem.*

patch *noun* **1** (*of colour*) mancha *Fem.*; **2** (*for repairs*) parche *Masc.*

path *noun* camino *Masc.* (*very narrow*) sendero *Masc.*

patience *noun* **1** paciencia *Fem.*; **2** (*card game*) solitario *Masc.*

patient *noun* paciente *Masc./Fem.*.
patient *adjective* paciente.

patiently *adverb* pacientemente.

patio *noun* patio *Masc.*

patrol *noun* patrulla *Fem.*

patrol car *noun* coche *Masc.* patrulla.

pattern *noun* **1** (*on wallpaper or fabric*) diseño *Masc.*; **2** (*dressmaking*) patrón *Masc.*; **3** (*knittting*) modelo *Masc.*

pavement *noun* acera *Fem.*; **on the pavement** en la acera.

paw *noun* pata *Fem.*

pawn *noun* peón *Masc.*

pay *noun* sueldo *Masc.*
pay *verb* **1** pagar [28]; **I'm paying** yo pago; **to pay cash** pagar al contado; **2 to pay for something** pagar [28] algo; **Tony paid for the drinks** Tony pagó las bebidas; **it's all paid for** está todo pagado; **3 to pay by credit card** pagar [28] con tarjeta de crédito; **to pay by cheque** pagar [28] con cheque; **4 to pay somebody back** (*money*) devolverle [45] dinero a alguien; **5 to pay attention**

a
b
c
d
e
f
g
h
i
j
k
l
m
n
o
p
q
r
s
t
u
v
w
x
y
z

prestar [17] atención; **6 to pay a visit to somebody** hacer [7] una visita a alguien.

payment noun pago Masc.

pay phone noun teléfono Masc. público.

PC noun (computer) PC Masc.

pea noun guisante Masc.

peace noun paz Fem.

peaceful adjective tranquilo/tranquila (day, scene).

peach noun melocotón Masc.

peacock noun pavo Masc. real.

peak noun (of a mountain) pico Masc.

peak period (for holidays) temporada Fem. alta.

peak rate noun (for phoning) tarifa Fem. máxima.

peak time noun (for traffic) hora Fem. punta.

peanut noun cacahuete Masc.

peanut butter noun mantequilla Fem. de cacahuete.

pear noun pera Fem.

pearl noun perla Fem.

peasant noun campesino Masc., campesina Fem.

pebble noun guijarro Masc.

pedal noun pedal Masc.
pedal verb pedalear [17].

pedestrian noun peatón Masc., peatona Fem.

pedestrian crossing noun paso Masc. peatonal.

pedestrian precinct noun zona Fem. peatonal.

pee noun **to have a pee** hacer [7] pis (informal).

peel noun **1** (of an apple) piel Fem.; **2** (of an orange) cáscara Fem.
peel verb pelar [17] (fruit, vegetables).

peg noun **1** (hook) gancho Masc.; **2 a clothes peg** una pinza de la ropa; **3 a tent peg** una piqueta.

pen noun **1** bolígrafo Masc., boli Masc. (informal); **2** (fountain pen) pluma Fem.; **3 a felt pen** un rotulador.

penalty noun **1** (a fine) multa Fem.; **2** (in football or rugby) penalty Masc.

penalty area noun área Fem. de castigo (even though 'area' is feminine it takes 'el' and 'un').

pence plural noun peniques Masc. plural.

pencil noun lápiz Masc.; **to write in pencil** escribir [52] a lápiz.

pencil case noun estuche Masc. para lápices.

pencil sharpener noun sacapuntas Masc. (does not change in the plural).

pendant noun colgante Masc.

penfriend noun amigo Masc. por correspondencia, amiga Fem. por correspondencia; **my Spanish pen-friend is called Cristina** mi amiga, por correspondencia española se llama Cristina.

penis noun pene Masc.

penknife noun navaja Fem.

penny noun penique Masc.

pension noun pensión Fem.

pensioner *noun* pensionista *Masc./Fem.*

people *plural noun* **1** gente *Fem.* (*singular*); **people round here** la gente de por aquí; **nice people** gente simpática; **people say he's very rich** la gente dice que es muy rico; **2** (*when you're counting them*) persona *Fem.*; **ten people** diez personas; **several people** varias personas; **how many people have you asked?** ¿a cuántas personas has preguntado?

pepper *noun* **1** (*spice*) pimienta *Fem.*; **2** (*pepper*) pimiento *Masc.*; **a green pepper** un pimiento verde.

peppermill *noun* pimentero *Masc.*

peppermint *noun* menta *Fem.*; **peppermint tea** infusión *Fem.* de menta.

per *preposition* por; **ten pounds per person** diez libras por persona.

per cent *adverb* por ciento; **sixty per cent of the students** el sesenta por ciento de los estudiantes.

percentage *noun* porcentaje *Masc.*

percussion *noun* percusión *Fem.*; **to play percussion** tocar [31] la percusión.

perfect *adjective* **1** perfecto/perfecta; **she speaks perfect English** habla un inglés perfecto; **2** (*ideal*) ideal; **the perfect place for a picnic** el sitio ideal para un picnic.

perfectly *adverb* perfectamente.

perform *verb* **1** interpretar [17] (*a piece of music or a role*);

2 representar [17] (*a play*); **3** cantar [17] (*a song*).

performance *noun* **1** (*playing or acting*) interpretación *Fem.*; **a wonderful performance of Macbeth** una maravillosa interpretación de Macbeth; **2** (*show*) espectáculo *Masc.*; **the performance starts at eight** el espectáculo empieza a las ocho; **3** (*the results of a team or company*) actuación *Fem.*

performer *noun* artista *Masc./Fem.*

perfume *noun* perfume *Masc.*

perhaps *adverb* quizás; **perhaps it's in the drawer?** ¿a lo mejor está el cajón?; **perhaps he's missed the train** quizás ha perdido el tren.

period *noun* **1** periodo *Masc.*; **a two-year period** un periodo de dos años; **2** (*in school*) clase *Fem.*; **a forty-five-minute period** una clase de cuarenta y cinco minutos; **3** (*menstruation*) periodo *Masc.*; **to have your period** tener [9] el periodo.

perm *noun* permanente *Fem.*

permanent *adjective* permanente.

permanently *adverb* permanentemente.

permission *noun* permiso *Masc.*; **to get permission to do** conseguir [64] permiso para hacer.

permit *noun* permiso *Masc.* **permit** *verb* permitir [19]; **to permit somebody to do** permitir [19] a alguien hacer; **smoking is not permitted** está prohibido fumar; **weather permitting** si el tiempo lo permite.

a
b
c
d
e
f
g
h
i
j
k
l
m
n
o
p
q
r
s
t
u
v
w
x
y
z

a
b
c
d
e
f
g
h
i
j
k
l
m
n
o
p
q
r
s
t
u
v
w
x
y
z

person *noun* persona *Fem.*; **there's room for one more person** hay sitio para una persona más; **in person** en persona.

personal *adjective* personal.

personality *noun* personalidad *Fem.*

personally *adverb* personalmente; **personally, I'm against it** personalmente, estoy en contra.

personal stereo *noun* walkman™ *Masc.*

perspiration *noun* sudor *Masc.*

persuade *verb* convencer [44]; **to persuade somebody to do** convencer a alguien para que haga (*note that 'para que' is followed by the subjunctive*); **we persuaded Tim to wait a bit** convencimos a Tim para que esperara un poco.

peseta *noun* peseta *Fem.* (*former Spanish currency replaced by the euro; 500 pesetas = 3.00 euros*).

pessimistic *adjective* pesimista.

pest *noun* **1** (*greenfly for example*) plaga *Fem.*; **2** (*annoying person*) pesado *Masc.*, pesada *Fem.*

pester *verb* fastidiar [17].

pet *noun* **1** animal *Masc.* de compañía; **do you have a pet?** ¿tienes un animal de compañía?; **a pet dog** un perro de compañía; **2** (*favourite person*) favorito *Masc.*, favorita *Fem.*; **Julie is teacher's pet** Julie es la favorita de la maestra.

petal *noun* pétalo *Masc.*

pet name *noun* apodo *Masc.* cariñoso.

petrol *noun* gasolina *Fem.*; **to fill up with petrol** llenar [17] de gasolina; **to run out of petrol** quedarse [17] sin gasolina.

petrol station *noun* gasolinera *Fem.*

petticoat *noun* enagua *Fem.*

pharmacist *noun* farmacéutico *Masc.*, farmacéutica *Fem.*

pharmacy *noun* farmacia *Fem.*

pheasant *noun* faisán *Masc.*

philosophy *noun* filosofía *Fem.*

phone *noun* teléfono *Masc.*; **she's on the phone** está hablando por teléfono; **I was on the phone to Sophie** estaba hablando por teléfono con Sophie; **you can book by phone** puedes reservar por teléfono.

phone *verb* **1** llamar [17] por teléfono; **while I was phoning** mientras llamaba por teléfono; **2 to phone somebody** llamar [17] a alguien; **I'll phone you tonight** te llamaré esta noche.

phone book *noun* guía *Fem.* telefónica.

phone box *noun* cabina *Fem.* telefónica.

phone call *noun* llamada *Fem.* telefónica; **phone calls are free** las llamadas telefónicas son gratis; **to make a phone call** hacer [7] una llamada (telefónica).

phone card *noun* tarjeta *Fem.* telefónica.

phone number noun número Masc. de teléfono.

photo noun foto Fem.; **to take a photo** hacer [7] una foto; **to take a photo of somebody** hacerle [7] una foto a alguien; **I took a photo of their house** hice una foto de su casa.

photocopier noun fotocopiadora Fem.

photocopy noun fotocopia Fem.
photocopy verb fotocopiar [17].

photograph noun fotografía Fem.; **to take a photograph** hacer [7] una fotografía; **to take a photograph of somebody** hacerle [7] una fotografía a alguien.
photograph verb fotografiar [32].

photographer noun fotógrafo Masc., fotógrafa Fem.

photography noun fotografía Fem.

phrase noun frase Fem.

phrase-book noun manual Masc. de conversación.

physicist noun físico Masc., física Fem.

physics noun física Fem.

physiotherapist noun fisioterapeuta Masc./Fem.

physiotherapy noun fisioterapia Fem.

pianist noun pianista Masc./Fem.

piano noun piano Masc.; **to play the piano** tocar [31] el piano; **Steve played it on the piano** Steve lo tocó al piano; **a piano lesson** una clase de piano.

pick noun **take your pick!** ¡escoge!
pick verb **1** (to choose) escoge [3]; **pick a card** escoger una carta; **2** (for a team) seleccionar [17]; **I've been picked for Saturday** me han seleccionado para el sábado; **3** recoger [3] (fruit); **4** coger [3] (flowers).

● **to pick up 1** (lift) coger [3]; **he picked up the papers and went out** cogió los papeles y salió; **to pick up the phone** coger el teléfono; **2** (from the floor) recoger [3]; **pick up that piece of paper** recoge ese papel; **3** (collect together) recoger [3]; **I'll pick up the toys** voy a recoger los juguetes; **4** (to collect) recoger [3]; **I'll pick you up at six** te recogeré a las seis; **I'll pick up the keys tomorrow** recogeré las llaves mañana; **5** (learn) aprender [18]; **you'll soon pick it up** lo aprenderás pronto.

picnic noun picnic Masc.; **to have a picnic** hacer [7] un picnic.

pickpocket noun carterista Masc./Fem.

picture noun **1** (a painting) cuadro Masc.; **a picture by Picasso** un cuadro de Picasso; **he painted a picture of a horse** pintó un caballo; **2** (a drawing) dibujo Masc.; **draw me a picture of your house** hazme un dibujo de tu casa; **3** (in a book) ilustración Fem.; **a book with lots of pictures** un libro con muchas ilustraciones; **4 the pictures** el cine; **to go to the pictures** ir [8] al cine.

a
b
c
d
e
f
g
h
i
j
k
l
m
n
o
p
q
r
s
t
u
v
w
x
y
z

pie *noun* **1** (*sweet*) pastel *Masc.*; **an apple pie** un pastel de manzana; **2** (*savoury*) empanada *Fem.*; **a meat pie** una empanada de carne.

piece *noun* **1** (*a bit*) trozo *Masc.*; **a big piece of cheese** un trozo grande de queso; **2** (*that you fit together*) pieza *Fem.*; **the pieces of a jigsaw** las piezas de un rompecabezas; **to take something to pieces** desmontar [17] algo; **3 a piece of furniture** un mueble; **four pieces of luggage** cuatro maletas; **a piece of information** un dato; **that's a piece of luck!** ¡qué suerte!; **4** (*coin*) moneda *Fem.*; **a 10p piece** una moneda de diez peniques.

pierced *adjective* **to have pierced ears** tener [9] agujeros en las orejas.

pig *noun* cerdo *Masc.*, cerda *Fem.*

pigeon *noun* paloma *Fem.*

piggy bank *noun* hucha *Fem.*

pigsty *noun* pocilga *Fem.*; **your room is a pigsty** tu habitación está hecha una pocilga.

pigtail *noun* trenza *Fem.*

pile *noun* **1** (*a neat stack*) pila *Fem.*; **a pile of plates** una pila de platos; **2** (*a heap*) montón *Masc.*; **a pile of dirty shirts** un montón de camisas sucias.

● **to pile something up** (*neatly*) apilar [17] algo, (*in a heap*) amontonar [17] algo.

pilgrimage *noun* peregrinación *Fem.*; **to go on a pilgrimage** irse [8] de peregrinación.

pill *noun* pastilla *Fem.*; **the pill** (*contraceptive*) la píldora.

pillow *noun* almohada *Fem.*

pillow case *noun* almohadón *Masc.*

pilot *noun* piloto *Masc./Fem.*

pimple *noun* grano *Masc.*

pin *noun* **1** (*for sewing*) alfiler *Masc.*; **2 a three-pin plug** un enchufe de tres clavijas.

● **to pin up 1** prender [18] con alfileres (*a hem*); **2** poner [11] (*a notice*).

PIN *noun* (*personal identification number*) PIN *Masc.*

pinball *noun* flipper *Masc.*; **to play pinball** jugar [27] al flipper; **a pinball machine** un flipper.

pinch *noun* (*of salt, for example*) pellizco *Masc.*

pinch *verb* **1** (*steal*) mangar [28] (*informal*); **somebody's pinched my bike** alguien me ha robado la bici; **2 to pinch somebody** pellizcar [31] a alguien.

pine *noun* pino *Masc.*; **a pine table** una mesa de pino.

pineapple *noun* piña *Fem.*

pine cone *noun* piña *Fem.*

ping-pong *noun* ping-pong *Masc.*; **to play ping-pong** jugar [27] al ping-pong.

pink *adjective* rosa (*never changes*); **my pink dress** mi vestido rosa; **pink socks** calcetines rosa.

pint *noun* pinta *Fem.*

pip *noun* pepita *Fem.*

pipe *noun* **1** (*for gas or water*) tubería *Fem.*; **2** (*to smoke*) pipa *Fem.*; **he smokes a pipe** fuma en pipa.

a b c d e f g h i j k l m n o p q r s t u v w x y z

Pisces noun Piscis Masc.;
Amanda's Pisces Amanda es
Piscis.

pistachio noun pistacho Masc.

pit noun foso Masc.

pitch noun campo Masc.; **a football
pitch** un campo de fútbol.
pitch verb **to pitch a tent** montar
[17] una tienda.

pity noun **1** lástima Fem.; **what a
pity!** ¡qué lástima!; **it would be a
pity to miss the beginning** sería
una lástima perderse el principio;
2 (for a person) piedad Fem.;
pity verb **to pity somebody**
compadecer [35] a alguien.

pizza noun pizza Fem.

place noun **1** sitio Masc.; **in a warm
place** en un sitio caliente; **Rome is
a wonderful place** Roma es un
lugar maravilloso; **all over the
place** por todos sitios; **a place for
the car** un sitio para el coche; **will
you keep my place?** ¿me guardas el
sitio?; **to change places** cambiarse
[17] de sitio; **2** (in a race) lugar Masc.;
in first place en primer lugar; **3 at
your place** et tu casa; **we'll go
round to Zafir's place** iremos a
casa de Zafir; **4 to take place** tener
[9] lugar; **the competition will take
place at four** la competición tendrá
lugar a las cuatro; **5 if I was in your
place** ... si yo estuviese en tu lugar
....
place verb poner [11]; **he placed
his cup on the table** puso su taza en
la mesa.

plain adjective **1** sencillo/sencilla;
plain cooking la cocina sencilla;

2 (unflavoured) natural; **a plain
yoghurt** yogur natural; **3 plain
chocolate** chocolate sin leche;
4 (not patterned) liso/lisa; **plain
curtains** cortinas lisas.

plait noun trenza Fem.

plan noun **1** plan Masc.; **what are
your plans for this summer?** ¿qué
planes tienes para este verano?; **to
go according to plan** salir [63]
según el plan; **everything went
according to plan** todo salió según
el plan; **2** (a map) plano Masc.
plan verb **1** planear [17]; **Ricky's
planning a trip to Italy** Ricky está
planeando un viaje a Italia; **to plan
to do** planear [17] hacer; **we're
planning to leave at eight**
planeamos salir a las ocho;
2 (organize) organizar [22]; **I'm
planning my day** estoy
organizándome el día; **3** (to design)
diseñar [17] (a house or garden) **a
well-planned kitchen** una cocina
bien diseñada.

plane noun avión Masc.; **we went by
plane** fuimos en avión.

planet noun planeta Masc.

plant noun planta Fem.; **a house
plant** una planta de interior.
plant verb plantar [17].

plaster noun **1** (sticking plaster)
tirita™ Fem.; **2** (for walls) yeso Masc.;
3 to have your leg in plaster tener
[9] una pierna escayolada.

plastic noun plástico Masc.; **a
plastic bag** una bolsa de plástico.

plate noun plato Masc.

a
b
c
d
e
f
g
h
i
j
k
l
m
n
o
p
q
r
s
t
u
v
w
x
y
z

a
b
c
d
e
f
g
h
i
j
k
l
m
n
o
p
q
r
s
t
u
v
w
x
y
z

platform *noun* **1** (*in a station*) andén *Masc.*; **the train arriving at platform six** el tren que llega al andén número seis; **2** (*for lecturing or performing*) estrado *Masc.*

play *noun* obra *Fem.*; **a play by Shakespeare** una obra de Shakespeare; **our school is putting on a play** nuestro colegio está preparando una obra.

play *verb* **1** jugar [27]; **the children were playing with a ball** los niños estaban jugando con una pelota; **to play tennis** jugar al tenis; **they were playing cards** estaban jugando a las cartas; **2** (*music or an instrument*) tocar [31]; **Helen plays the violin** Helen toca el violín; **they play all kinds of music** tocan todo tipo de música; **3** poner [11] (*a tape, CD, or record*) **play me your new CD** ponme tu nuevo compacto; **4 who's playing Hamlet?** ¿quién hace el papel de Hamlet?

player *noun* **1** (*in sport*) jugador *Masc.*, jugadora *Fem.*; **a football player** un jugador de fútbol; **2** (*musician*) músico *Masc.*, música *Fem.*

playground *noun* patio *Masc.* de recreo.

playing card *noun* naipe *Masc.*

playing field *noun* campo *Masc.* de juego.

playroom *noun* cuarto *Masc.* de los juguetes.

pleasant *adjective* agradable.

please *adverb* por favor; **two coffees, please** dos cafés, por favor;

could you turn the TV off, please? ¿puedes apagar la tele, por favor?

pleased *adjective* contento/ contenta; **I'm very pleased** estoy muy contento (*in the past tense 'ponerse' is used in place of 'estar'*); **I was really pleased!** ¡me puse muy contento!; **she was pleased with her present** se puso muy contenta con su regalo; **pleased to meet you!** ¡encantado de conocerte!

pleasure *noun* placer *Masc.*

plenty *pronoun* **1** (*lots*) mucho/ mucha; **there's plenty of bread** hay mucho pan; **he's got plenty of experience** tiene mucha experiencia; **2** (*with a plural noun*) muchos/muchas; **there are plenty of cases** hay muchos casos; **she's got plenty of ideas** tiene muchas ideas; **there were plenty of them** había muchos; **3** (*quite enough*) más que suficiente; **we've got plenty of time for a coffee** tenemos tiempo más que suficiente para tomar un café; **thank you, that's plenty!** gracias, esto es más que suficiente.

pliers *plural noun* alicates *Masc. plural.*

plug *noun* **1** (*electrical*) enchufe *Masc.*; **2** (*in a bath or sink*) tapón *Masc.*; **to pull out the plug** quitar [17] el tapón.

• **to plug something in** enchufar [17] algo.

plum *noun* ciruela *Fem.*; **a plum tart** una tarta de ciruelas.

plumber *noun* fontanero *Masc.*, fontanera *Fem.*; **he's a plumber** es fontanero.

plump *adjective* regordete/
regordeta.

plural *noun* plural *Masc.*; **in the
plural** en plural.

plus *preposition* más; **three
children plus the baby** tres niños
más el bebé.

p.m. *adverb* (*Spanish people usually
use 'de la tarde', for times up to
approximately 8 p.m. and 'de la
noche' for times approximately after
8 p.m.*) **at two p.m.** a las dos de la
tarde; **at nine p.m.** a las nueve de la
noche.

poached egg *noun* huevo *Masc.*
escalfado.

pocket *noun* bolsillo *Masc.*

pocket money *noun* **1** (*for
children*) paga *Fem.*; **2** (*for minor
purchases*) dinero *Masc.* para gastos
personales.

poem *noun* poema *Masc.*

poet *noun* poeta *Masc./Fem.*

poetry *noun* poesía *Fem.*

point *noun* **1** (*tip*) punta *Fem.*; **the
point of a nail** la punta de un clavo;
2 (*in time*) momento *Masc.*; **at that
point the police arrived** en ese
momento llegó la policía; **3 to get
the point** entender [36]; **I don't get
the point** no lo entiendo; **4 what's
the point of waiting?** ¿qué sentido
tiene esperar?; **there's no point
phoning, he's out** no tiene sentido
llamar, ha salido; **that's not the
point** no se trata de eso; **5 that's a
good point!** ¡es verdad!; **6 from my
point of view** desde mi punto de
vista; **7 her strong point** su punto

fuerte; **8** (*in scoring*) punto *Masc.*;
fifteen points to eleven quince
puntos a once; **9** (*in decimals*) (*in
Spanish, a comma is used for the
decimal point, so 6.4 = 6.4, said*) **6
point 4** seis coma cuatro.

point *verb* **1** señalar [17]; **a notice
pointing to the station** un cartel
señalando hacia la estación; **James
pointed out the cathedral** James
señaló la catedral; **he pointed at
one of the children** señaló a uno de
los niños; **2 I'd like to point out
that I'm paying** quisiera dejar claro
que pago yo.

poison *noun* veneno *Masc.*
poison *verb* envenenar [17].

poisonous *adjective* venenoso/
venenosa.

poker *noun* **1** (*for fire*) atizador
Masc.; **2** (*card game*) póker *Masc.*

Poland *noun* Polonia *Fem.*

polar bear *noun* oso *Masc.* polar.

pole 1 (*for a tent*) mástil *Masc.*; **2 the
North Pole** el Polo Norte.

Pole *noun* (*a Polish person*) polaco
Masc., polaca *Fem.*

police *noun* **the police** la policía;
the police are coming ya viene la
policía (*note that a singular verb is
used with 'la policía'*).
police *verb* patrullar [17] (*the
streets*).

police car *noun* coche *Masc.* de
policía.

policeman *noun* policía *Masc.*

police station *noun* comisaría
Fem.

a **policewoman** noun mujer Fem. policía.

b **policy** noun 1 (plan of action) política Fem.; 2 (document) póliza Fem.

c **polish** noun 1 (for furniture) cera Fem.; 2 (for shoes) betún Masc.
polish verb sacar [31] brillo a (shoes or furniture).

d **Polish** noun 1 (language) polaco Masc.; 2 (people) the Polish los polacos (plural).
Polish adjective polaco/polaca.

e **polite** adjective educado/educada; **to be polite to somebody** ser [1] educado/educada con alguien.

f **political** adjective político/ política.

g **politician** noun político Masc., política Fem.

h **politics** noun política Fem.

i **polluted** adjective contaminado/ contaminada.

j **pollution** noun contaminación Fem.

k **polo-necked** adjective de cuello alto; **a polo-necked jumper** un jersey de cuello alto.

l **polythene bag** noun bolsa Fem. de plástico.

m **pond** noun 1 (natural) laguna Fem.; 2 (man-made) estanque Masc.

n **pony** noun poni Masc.

o **ponytail** noun cola Fem. de caballo.

p **poodle** noun caniche Masc.

q **pool** noun 1 (swimming pool) piscina Fem.; 2 (in the country) alberca Fem.; 3 (puddle) charco

Masc.; 4 (game) billar Masc. americano; **to have a game of pool** jugar [27] al billar americano; 5 **the football pools** las quinielas; **to do the pools** hacer [7] las quinielas.

poor adjective 1 pobre; **a poor area** un zona pobre; **a poor family** una familia pobre; **poor Tanya's failed her exam** la pobre Tanya suspendió el examen; 2 (bad) malo/mala; **this is poor quality** esto es de mala calidad; **the weather was pretty poor** el tiempo fue bastante malo.

pop noun pop Masc.; **a pop concert** un concierto de pop; **a pop star** una estrella del pop; **a pop song** una canción de pop.

• **to pop into** entrar [17] un momento a; **I'll just pop into the bank** voy a entrar un momento en el banco.

popcorn noun palomitas Fem. plural de maíz.

pope noun papa Masc.

poppy noun amapola Fem.

popular adjective popular.

population noun población Fem.

porch noun porche Masc.

pork noun cerdo Masc.; **a pork chop** una chuleta de cerdo.

porridge noun gachas Fem. plural.

port noun 1 (for ships) puerto Masc.; 2 (wine) oporto Masc.

portable computer noun (ordenador) portátil Masc.

porter noun 1 (at a station or airport) mozo Masc. de las maletas; 2 (in a hotel) portero Masc.

portion noun (of food) ración Fem.

portrait *noun* retrato *Masc.*

Portugal *noun* Portugal *Masc.*

Portuguese *noun* **1** (*language*) portugués *Masc.*; **2** (*a person*) portugués *Masc.*, portuguesa *Fem.*
Portuguese *adjective* portugués/portuguesa.

posh *adjective* elegante; **a posh house** una casa elegante.

position *noun* posición *Fem.*

positive *adjective* **1** (*sure*) seguro/segura; **I'm positive he's left** estoy seguro de que se ha ido;
2 (*enthusiastic*) positivo/positiva; **her reaction was very positive** su reacción fue muy positiva; **try to be more positive** intenta tener una actitud más positiva.

possessions *plural noun* pertenencias *Fem. plural*; **all my possessions are in the flat** todas mis pertenencias están en el piso.

possibility *noun* posibilidad *Fem.*

possible *adjective* posible; **it's possible** es posible; **if possible** si es posible; **as quickly as possible** tan rápidamente como sea posible.

possibly *adverb* **1** (*maybe*) posiblemente; **'will you be at home at midday?' – 'possibly'** ¿estarás en casa a mediodía?' – 'posiblemente'; **2** (*for emphasis*) **how can you possibly believe that?** pero, ¿cómo puedes creerte eso?; **I can't possibly arrive before Thursday** no puedo llegar antes del jueves de ninguna manera.

post *noun* **1** correo *Masc.*; **to send something by post** mandar [17] algo por correo; **2** (*letters*) **is there any post for me?** ¿hay alguna carta para mí?; **3** (*a pole*) poste *Masc.*; **4** (*a job*) puesto *Masc.*
post *verb* **to post a letter** echar [17] una carta al correo; **to post something to somebody** mandarle [17] algo a alguien.

postbox *noun* buzón *Masc.*

postcard *noun* postal *Fem.*

postcode *noun* código *Masc.* postal.

poster *noun* **1** (*for decoration*) póster *Masc.*; **I've bought an Oasis poster** he comprado un póster de Oasis; **2** (*advertising*) cartel *Masc.*; **I saw a poster for the concert** vi un cartel del concierto.

postman *noun* cartero *Masc.*; **has the postman been?** ¿ha venido el cartero?

post office *noun* oficina *Fem.* de correos.

postpone *verb* **to postpone something** posponer [11] algo.

postwoman *noun* cartera *Fem.*

pot *noun* **1** (*jar*) tarro *Masc.*; **a pot of honey** un tarro de miel; **2** (*teapot*) tetera *Fem.*; **I'll make a pot of tea** voy ha hacer té; **3 the pots and pans** los cacharros; ★**to take pot luck** probar [24] suerte.

potato *noun* patata *Fem.*; **fried potatoes** patatas fritas; **mashed potatoes** puré de patatas.

potato crisps *plural noun* patatas *Fem. plural* fritas de bolsa.

pottery *noun* cerámica *Fem.*

a

b

c

d

e

f

g

h

i

j

k

l

m

n

o

p

q

r

s

t

u

v

w

x

y

z

pound *noun* **1** (*money*) libra *Fem.*;
fourteen pounds catorce libras;
how much is that in pounds?
¿cuánto es eso en libras?; **2** (*in
weight*) libra *Fem.*; **a pound of
apples** una libra de manzanas.

pour *verb* **1** echar [17] (*liquid*); **he
poured the milk into the pan** echó
la leche en la cacerola; **2** servir [57]
(*a drink*); **to pour the tea** servir el
té; **I poured him a drink** le serví una
bebida; ★ **it's pouring down** (*with
rain*) está lloviendo a cántaros
(*literally: it's raining jugfuls*).

poverty *noun* pobreza *Fem.*

powder *noun* polvo *Masc.*

power *noun* **1** (*electricity*) corriente
Fem. eléctrica; **2** (*energy*) energía
Fem.; **nuclear power** energía
nuclear; **3** (*over other people*) poder
Masc.; **to be in power** estar en el
poder.

power cut *noun* apagón *Masc.*

powerful *adjective* poderoso/
poderosa.

power point *noun* enchufe *Masc.*

power station *noun* central *Fem.*
eléctrica.

practical *adjective* práctico/
práctica.

practical joke *noun* broma *Fem.*
pesada.

practice *noun* **1** (*for sport*)
entrenamiento *Masc.*; **hockey
practice** entrenamiento de hockey;
2 (*for an instrument*) **to do your
piano practice** hacer [7] los
ejercicios de piano; **3 to be out of
practice** (*for a sport*) estar

desentrenado/desentrenada; **4 in
practice** en la práctica.

practise *verb* **1** practicar [31]
(*music, language, etc*); **a week in
Granada to practise my Spanish**
una semana en Granada para
practicar mi español; **2** (*in a sport*)
entrenar [17]; **the team practises
on Wednesdays** el equipo entrena
los miércoles.

praise *verb* **to praise somebody
for something** elogiar [17] a alguien
por algo.

pram *noun* cochecito *Masc.* de bebé.

prawn *noun* gamba *Fem.*

pray *verb* rezar [22].

prayer *noun* oración *Fem.*

precious *adjective* precioso/
preciosa.

precise *adjective* preciso/precisa.

prefer *verb* preferir [14]; **I prefer
coffee to tea** prefiero el café al té;
he'd prefer not to see them
preferiría no verlos.

pregnant *adjective* embarazada.

pregnancy *noun* embarazo *Masc.*

prejudice *noun* prejuicio *Masc.*; **a
prejudice** un prejuicio; **to fight
against racial prejudice** luchar [17]
contra los prejuicios raciales.

prejudiced *adjective* **to be
prejudiced** tener [9] prejuicios.

premiere *noun* estreno *Masc.* (*of a
play or film*).

prep *noun* deberes *Masc. plural*; **my
English prep** mis deberes de inglés.

preparation *noun* **1** preparación *Fem.*; **2 the preparations for** los preparativos para.

prepare *verb* **1 to prepare for something** prepararse para algo; **2** preparar [17]; **to prepare somebody for** preparar [17] a alguien para (*a surprise or shock*); **to be prepared for the worst** estar [2] preparado para lo peor.

prepared *adjective* dispuesto/dispuesta; **I'm prepared to pay half** estoy dispuesta a pagar la mitad.

preposition *noun* preposición *Fem.*

prescribe *verb* recetar [17].

prescription *noun* receta *Fem.*; **on prescription** con receta.

present *noun* **1** (*a gift*) regalo *Masc.*; **to give somebody a present** regalarle [17] algo a alguien; **2** (*the time now*) presente *Masc.*; **in the present (tense)** en presente; **that's all for the present** eso es todo por ahora.
present *adjective* **1** (*attending*) presente; **is Tracy present?** ¿está Tracy presente?; **to be present at** asistir [19] a; **fifty people were present at the funeral** cincuenta personas asistieron al funeral; **2** (*existing now*) actual; **the present situation** la situación actual; **3 at the present time** en este momento.
present *verb* **1** entregar [28] (*a prize*); **2** (*introduce*) presentar [17].

presenter *noun* (*on TV*) presentador *Masc.*, presentadora *Fem.*

president *noun* presidente *Masc.*, presidenta *Fem.*

press *noun* **the press** la prensa. **press** *verb* **1** (*to push*) empujar [17]; **press here to open** para abrir, empuje aquí; **2** apretar [29] (*a button or doorbell*); **she pressed the button** apretó el botón.

press conference *noun* conferencia *Fem.* de prensa.

pressure *noun* presión *Fem.*

pressure gauge *noun* manómetro *Masc.*

pressure group *noun* grupo *Masc.* de presión.

pretend *verb* **to pretend to do** fingir [49] hacer; **he's pretending not to hear** está fingiendo no oír.

pretty *adjective* bonito/bonita; **a pretty dress** un vestido bonito.
pretty *adverb* bastante; **it was pretty embarrassing** fue bastante vergonzoso.

prevent *verb* **1** evitar [17] (*a war or disaster*); **2 to prevent somebody from doing** impedir [57] a alguien hacer; **there's nothing to prevent you from leaving** no hay nada que te impida irte.

previous *adjective* anterior.

previously *adverb* antes.

price *noun* precio *Masc.*; **the price per kilo** el precio por kilo; **CDs have gone up in price** los compactos han subido de precio.

price list *noun* lista *Fem.* de precios.

a
b
c
d
e
f
g
h
i
j
k
l
m
n
o
p
q
r
s
t
u
v
w
x
y
z

515

a
b
c
d
e
f
g
h
i
j
k
l
m
n
o
p
q
r
s
t
u
v
w
x
y
z

price ticket *noun* etiqueta *Fem.* del precio.

pride *noun* orgullo *Masc.*

priest *noun* sacerdote *Masc.*

primary school *noun* escuela *Fem.* primaria.

prime minister *noun* primer ministro *Masc.*, primera ministra *Fem.*

prince *noun* príncipe *Masc.*; **Prince Charles** el príncipe Carlos.

princess *noun* princesa *Fem.*; **Princess Anne** la Princesa Ana.

principal *noun* (*of a college*) rector *Masc.*, rectora *Fem.*
principal *adjective* (*main*) principal.

print *noun* 1 (*letters*) letra *Fem.*; **in small print** en letra pequeña; **2** (*a photo*) copia *Fem.*; **a colour print** una copia a color.

printer *noun* (*machine*) impresora *Fem.*

print-out *noun* copia *Fem.* en papel.

prison *noun* cárcel *Fem.*; **in prison** en la cárcel.

prisoner *noun* preso *Masc.*, presa *Fem.*

private *adjective* 1 privado/ privada; **a private school** una escuela privada; **'private property'** 'propiedad privada'; **2** particular (*lesson*); **to have private lessons** tener [9] clases particulares.

prize *noun* premio *Masc.*; **to win a prize** ganar [17] un premio.

prize-giving *noun* entrega *Fem.* de premios.

prizewinner *noun* ganador *Masc.*, ganadora *Fem.*

probable *adjective* probable.

probably *adverb* probablemente.

problem *noun* problema *Masc.*; **it's a serious problem** es un problema grave; **no problem!** ¡no hay problema!

procession *noun* 1 (*at religious festival*) procesión *Fem.*; **2** (*parade*) desfile *Masc.*

produce *noun* (*food*) productos *Masc. plural.*
produce *verb* 1 producir [60]; **it produces a lot of heat** produce mucho calor; **2** (*show*) presentar [17]; **I produced my passport** presenté mi pasaporte.

producer *noun* (*of a film or programme*) productor *Masc.*, productora *Fem.*

product *noun* producto *Masc.*

production *noun* 1 (*of a film*) producción *Fem.*; **2** (*of a play or opera*) puesta *Fem.* en escena; **a new production of Hamlet** una nueva puesta en escena de Hamlet; **3** (*by a factory*) producción *Fem.*

profession *noun* profesión *Fem.*

professional *noun* profesional *Masc./Fem.*; **he's a professional** es un profesional.
professional *adjective* profesional; **she's a professional singer** es cantante profesional.

professor *noun* catedrático *Masc.*, catedrática *Fem.*

profit *noun* beneficios *Masc. plural.*

profitable *adjective* rentable.

program *noun* **a computer program** un programa de ordenador.

programme *noun* programa *Masc.*

programmer *noun* programador *Masc.*, programadora *Fem.*

progress *noun* **1** progreso *Masc.*; **to make progress** (*in your work*) hacer [7] progresos; **2 to be in progress** estar [2] en curso.

project *noun* **1** (*at school*) trabajo *Masc.*; **2** (*a plan*) proyecto *Masc.*; **a project to build a bridge** un proyecto para construir un puente.

projector *noun* proyector *Masc.*

promise *noun* promesa *Fem.*; **to make a promise** hacer [7] una promesa; **to break a promise** romper [40] una promesa; **it's a promise!** ¡lo prometo!
promise *verb* **to promise to do** prometer [18] hacer; **I've promised to be home by ten** he prometido estar en casa a las diez.

promote *verb* ascender [36]; **she's been promoted** la han ascendido.

promotion *noun* ascenso *Masc.*

prompt *adjective* pronto/pronta; **a prompt reply** una pronta respuesta.

pronoun *noun* pronombre *Masc.*

pronounce *verb* pronunciar [17]; **it's hard to pronounce** es difícil de pronunciar.

pronunciation *noun* pronunciación *Fem.*

proof *noun* pruebas *Fem. plural*; **they've got proof** tienen pruebas;

there's no proof that ... no hay pruebas de que ....

propaganda *noun* propaganda *Fem.*

propeller *noun* hélice *Fem.*

proper *adjective* **1** (*real, genuine*) de verdad; **a proper doctor** un médico titulado; **I need a proper meal** necesito una comida de verdad; **2** (*correct*) adecuado/adecuada; **the proper tool** la herramienta adecuada; **3 in its proper place** en su sitio.

properly *adverb* bien; **hold it properly** sujétalo bien; **is it properly wrapped?** ¿está bien envuelto?

property *noun* (*your belongings*) propiedad *Fem.*; **'private property'** 'propiedad privada'.

propose *verb* **1** (*suggest*) proponer [11]; **2** (*marriage*) **he proposed to her** le pidió que se casara con él.

prostitute *noun* prostituta *Fem.*

protect *verb* proteger [3].

protection *noun* protección *Fem.*

protein *noun* proteína *Fem.*

protest *noun* protesta *Fem.*; **in spite of their protests** a pesar de sus protestas.
protest *verb* **1** (*to grumble*) protestar [17]; **he protested, but** ... él protestó, pero ...; **2** (*demonstrate*) manifestarse [29].

Protestant *noun, adjective* protestante *Masc./Fem.*

protester *noun* manifestante *Masc./Fem.*

protest march *noun*
manifestación *Fem.*

proud *adjective* orgulloso/
orgullosa.

prove *verb* probar [24].

proverb *noun* refrán *Masc.*

provide *verb* proveer [37].

provided *conjunction* siempre que;
provided you do it now siempre
que tú lo hagas (*note that 'que' is
followed by the subjunctive*).

province *noun* provincia *Fem.*

prune *noun* ciruela *Fem.* pasa.

PS *abbreviation* (*in letter*) PD.

psychiatrist *noun* psiquiatra
Masc./Fem.; **he's a psychiatrist** es
psiquiatra.

psychological *adjective*
psicológico/psicológica.

psychologist *noun* psicólogo
Masc., psicóloga *Fem.*; **she's a
psychologist** es psicóloga.

psychology *noun* psicología *Fem.*

PTO *abbreviation* sigue al dorso.

pub *noun* bar *Masc.*

public *noun* **the public** el público;
in public en público.
public *adjective* **1** público/pública;
2 the public library la biblioteca
pública.

public address system *noun*
sistema *Masc.* de megafonía.

public holiday *noun* día *Masc.* de
fiesta; **the first of January is a
public holiday** el uno de enero es
fiesta.

publicity *noun* publicidad *Fem.*

public school *noun* colegio *Masc.*
privado.

public transport *noun*
transporte *Masc.* público.

publish *verb* publicar [31].

publisher *noun* **1** (*person*) editor
Masc., editora *Fem.*; **2** (*company*)
editorial *Fem.*

pudding *noun* (*dessert*) postre
Masc.; **for pudding we've got
strawberries** de postre tenemos
fresas.

puddle *noun* charco *Masc.*

Puerto Rican *noun*
puertorriqueño *Masc.*,
puertorriqueña *Fem.*
Puerto Rican *adjective*
puertorriqueño/puertorriqueña.

puff pastry *noun* hojaldre *Masc.*

pull *verb* tirar [17]; **pull hard!** ¡tira
fuerte!; **to pull a rope** tirar de una
cuerda; ★**you're pulling my leg!**
¡me estás tomando el pelo! (*literally:
you are taking my hair*).
● **to pull down** bajar [17] (*a blind*).
● **to pull in** (*at the roadside*) parar
[17].
● **to pull something out** sacar [31]
algo; **he pulled a letter out of his
pocket** sacó una carta del bolsillo.

pullover *noun* jersey *Masc.*

pulse *noun* pulso *Masc.*; **the doctor
took my pulse** el médico me tomó el
pulso.

pump *noun* **1** bomba *Fem.*; **a bicycle
pump** una bomba de bicicleta; **2 a
petrol pump** un surtidor de
gasolina.
pump *verb* bombear [17]; **they**

were pumping the water out of the cellar estaban bombeando el agua del sótano.

● **to pump up** inflar [17] (*a tyre*).

punch *noun* **1** (*in boxing*) puñetazo *Masc.*; **2** (*drink*) ponche *Masc.*

punch *verb* **1 to punch somebody** darle [4] un puñetazo a alguien; **he punched me** me dio un puñetazo; **2** picar [31] (*a ticket*).

punctual *adjective* puntual.

punctuation *noun* puntuación *Fem.*

punctuation mark *noun* signo *Masc.* de puntuación.

puncture *noun* pinchazo *Masc.*; **we had a puncture on the way** tuvimos un pinchazo en el camino.

punish *verb* castigar [28].

punishment *noun* castigo *Masc.*

pupil *noun* alumno *Masc.*, alumna *Fem.*

puppet *noun* títere *Masc.*

puppy *noun* cachorro *Masc.* (*female*) cachorra *Fem.*; **a labrador puppy** un cachorro de labrador.

pure *adjective* puro/pura.

purple *adjective* morado/morada.

purpose *noun* **1** propósito *Masc.*; **what was the purpose of her call?** ¿qué propósito tenía su llamada?; **2 on purpose** a propósito; **she did it on purpose** lo hizo a propósito.

purr *verb* ronronear [17].

purse *noun* monedero *Masc.*

push *noun* empujón *Masc.*; **to give something a push** dar [4] un empujón a alguien.

push *verb* **1** empujar [17]; **he pushed me** me empujó; **2** (*to press*) apretar [29] (*a bell or button*); **3 to push somebody to do** presionar [17] a alguien para que haga (*note that 'que' is followed by the subjunctive*) **his teacher is pushing him to sit the exam** su profesor le está presionando para que se presente al examen.

● **to push something away** apartar [17] algo; **she pushed her plate away** apartó su plato.

pushchair *noun* sillita *Fem.* de niño.

put *verb* **1** poner [11]; **you can put the cream in the fridge** puedes poner la nata en la nevera; **where did you put my bag?** ¿dónde has puesto mi bolso?; **put your suitcase here** pon tu maleta aquí; **put your address here** pon tus señas aquí; **2** (*put inside*) meter [18]; **I put it in the drawer** lo metí en el cajón.

● **to put away** guardar [17]; **I'll put the shopping away** voy a guardar la compra.

● **to put back 1** volver [45] a poner; **I put it back in the drawer** lo volví a poner en el cajón; **2** (*postpone*) aplazar [22]; **the meeting has been put back until Thursday** han aplazado la reunión hasta el jueves.

● **to put down** poner [11]; **she put the vase down on the table** puso el jarrón en la mesa.

● **to put off 1** (*postpone*) aplazar [22]; **he's put off my lesson till Thursday** ha aplazado mi clase hasta el jueves; **2 it put me off Chinese food!** ¡hizo que se me quitaran las ganas de tomar comida china!; **3 to be put off** (*doing something*) desanimarse [17]; **don't be put off!** ¡no te desanimes!

● **to put on 1** ponerse [11] (*clothing, make-up*); **I'll just put my shoes on** voy a ponerme los zapatos; **2** poner [11] (*TV, radio*); **shall we put on the telly?** ¿ponemos la tele?; **he's put on Oasis** ha puesto a Oasis; **3** (*switch on*) encender [36] (*a light or heating*); **could you put the lamp on?** ¿puedes encender la lámpara?; **4** montar [17] (*a play*); **we're putting on a Spanish play** estamos montando una obra española.

● **to put out 1** (*put outside*) sacar [31]; **have you put the rubbish out?** ¿has sacado la basura?; **2** apagar [28] (*a fire, light, or cigarette*); **I've put the lights out** he apagado las luces; **3 to put out your hand** extender [36] la mano.

● **to put through** pasar [17] con; **I'll put you through to the manager** le paso con el gerente.

● **to put up 1** levantar [17] (*your hand*); **I put up my hand** levanté la mano; **2** poner [11] (*picture*); **I've put up some photos in my room** he puesto algunas fotos en mi habitacion; **3** colgar [23] (*a notice*); **4** subir [19] (*the price*); **they've put up the price of the tickets** han subido el precio de las entradas; **5** (*for the night*) **can you put me up on Friday?** ¿puedo quedarme a dormir en tu casa el viernes?

● **to put up with something** aguantar [17] algo; **I don't know**

how she puts up with it no sé cómo lo aguanta.

puzzle *noun* (*jigsaw*) rompecabezas *Masc.*, puzzle *Masc.*

puzzled *adjective* confuso/confusa.

pyjamas *plural noun* pijama *Masc.*; **a pair of pyjamas** un pijama; **where are my pyjamas?** ¿dónde está mi pijama?

pylon *noun* torre *Fem.* de alta tensión.

Pyrenees *noun* **the Pyrenees** los Pirineos.

Qq

quail *noun* codorniz *Fem.*

qualification *noun* **1** título *Masc.* (*certificate, exam, degree*); **2 qualifications** titulación *Fem.*; **vocational qualifications** titulación profesional.

qualified *adjective* **1** cualificado/cualificada; **she's a qualified ski instructor** es una monitora de esquí cualificada; **2** (*having a degree or a diploma*) titulado/titulada; **a qualified architect** un arquitecto titulado.

qualify *verb* **1** (*to be eligible*) tener [9] derecho a; **we don't qualify for a reduction** no tenemos derecho a una reducción; **2** (*in sport*) clasificarse [31].

quality *noun* calidad *Fem.*; **good quality vegetables** verduras de buena calidad.

quantity *noun* cantidad *Fem.*

quarantine *noun* cuarentena *Fem.*

quarrel *noun* pelea *Fem.*; **to have a quarrel** tener [9] una pelea. **quarrel** *verb* pelearse [17]; **they're always quarrelling** siempre se están peleando.

quarry *noun* cantera *Fem.*

quarter *noun* **1** cuarta parte *Fem.*; **a quarter of the class** una cuarta parte de la clase; **three quarters of the class** tres cuartas partes de la clase; **2** (*telling the time*) cuarto *Masc.*; **a quarter past ten** las diez y cuarto; **a quarter to ten** las diez menos cuarto; **a quarter of an hour** un cuarto de hora; **three quarters of an hour** tres cuartos de hora; **an hour and a quarter** una hora y cuarto.

quarter finals *plural noun* cuartos *Masc. plural* de final.

quartet *noun* cuarteto *Masc.*; **a jazz quartet** un cuarteto de jazz.

quay *noun* muelle *Masc.*

queen *noun* reina *Fem.*; **Queen Elizabeth** la reina Isabel; **the Queen Mother** la reina madre.

query *noun* duda *Fem.*; **are there any queries?** ¿hay alguna duda?

question *noun* **1** pregunta *Fem.*; **to ask a question** hacer [7] una pregunta; **I asked her a question** le hice una pregunta; **2 it's a question of time** es una cuestión de tiempo; **it's out of the question!** ¡es completamente imposible! **question** *verb* interrogar [28].

question mark *noun* signo *Masc.* de interrogación.

questionnaire *noun* cuestionario *Masc.*; **to fill in a questionnaire** rellenar [17] un cuestionario.

queue *noun* **1** (*of people*) cola *Fem.*; **to stand in a queue** estar [2] en la cola; **2** (*of cars*) fila *Fem.* **queue** *verb* hacer [7] cola; **we were queueing for check-in** estábamos haciendo cola para facturar.

quick *adjective* **1** rápido/rápida; **a quick lunch** una comida rápida; **it's quicker on the motorway** es más rápido por la autopista; **to have a quick look at something** echarle [17] un vistazo rápido a algo; **2 quick! there's the bus!** ¡de prisa, que viene el autobús!; **be quick!** ¡date prisa!

quickly *adverb* rápidamente; **I'll just quickly phone my mother** voy a llamar rápidamente a mi madre.

quiet *adjective* **1** (*silent*) silencioso/silenciosa; **the children are very quiet** los niños están muy silenciosos; **2 to keep quiet** no hablar [17]; **please keep quiet** por favor, no hablen; **3** (*gentle*) suave; **some quiet music** una música suave; **in a quiet voice** en voz baja; **4** (*peaceful*) tranquilo/tranquila; **a quiet street** una calle tranquila; **a quiet day at home** un día tranquilo en casa.

quietly *adverb* **1** (*to move*) sin hacer ruido; **he got up quietly** se levantó sin hacer ruido; **2** (*speak*) en voz baja; **3** (*read or play*) en silencio.

a
b
c
d
e
f
g
h
i
j
k
l
m
n
o
p
q
r
s
t
u
v
w
x
y
z

a

quilt *noun* edredón *Masc.*

b

quite *adverb* **1** bastante; **it's quite cold outside** hace bastante frío fuera; **that's quite a good idea** es una idea bastante buena; **he sings quite well** canta bastante bien; **quite often** bastante a menudo; **2 not quite** no ... todavía; **the meat's not quite cooked** la carne no está hecha todavía; **3 quite a lot of** bastante; **quite a lot of money** bastante dinero; **quite a few people** bastante gente; **4 quite a lot of** (*with a plural noun*) bastantes; **I've got quite a lot of friends here** tengo bastantes amigos aquí.

c
d
e
f
g
h
i

j

quiz *noun* concurso *Masc.*

k

quotation *noun* (*from a book*) cita *Fem.*

l
m

quotation marks *plural noun* comillas *Fem. plural*; **in quotation marks** entre comillas.

n
o

quote *noun* **1** (*from a book*) cita *Fem.*; **2** (*estimate*) presupuesto *Masc.*; **3 in quotes** entre comillas.
quote *verb* citar [17].

p

q

r

s
t

Rr

u

rabbi *noun* rabino *Masc.*, rabina *Fem.*

v

rabbit *noun* conejo *Masc.*

w

race *noun* **1** (*a sports event*) carrera *Fem.*; **a cycle race** una carrera de bicicletas; **to have a race** echar [17] una carrera; **2** (*an ethnic group*) raza *Fem.*

x
y
z

racer *noun* (*bike*) bicicleta *Fem.* de carreras.

racetrack *noun* **1** (*for horses*) pista *Fem.* de carreras; **2** (*for cars*) circuito *Masc.*; **3** (*for cycles*) velódromo *Masc.*

racing *noun* carreras *Fem. plural.*

racing car *noun* coche *Masc.* de carreras.

racing driver *noun* piloto *Masc./Fem.* de carreras.

racial *adjective* racial; **racial discrimination** discriminación racial.

racism *noun* racismo *Masc.*

racist *noun*, racista *Masc./Fem.*.
racist *adjective* racista.

racket *noun* **1** (*for tennis*) raqueta *Fem.*; **2** (*noise*) jaleo *Masc.*; **what a racket!** ¡qué jaleo!.

radar *noun* radar *Masc.*

radiator *noun* radiador *Masc.*

radio *noun* radio *Fem.*; **to listen to the radio** escuchar [17] la radio; **to hear something on the radio** oír [56] algo en la radio.

radio station *noun* emisora *Fem.* de radio.

radish *noun* rabanito *Masc.*

radius *noun* radio *Masc.*

raffle *noun* rifa *Fem.*

raft *noun* balsa *Fem.*

rag *noun* trapo *Masc.*

rage *noun* furia *Fem.*; **she's in a rage** está furiosa; ★ **it's all the rage** hace furor (*informal*).

rail *noun* **1** (*the railway*) **to go by rail** ir [8] en tren; **2** (*on a balcony or bridge*) baranda *Fem.*; **3** (*on stairs*) pasamanos *Masc.*; **4** (*for a train*) raíl *Masc.*

rail strike *noun* huelga *Fem.* de trenes.

railings *noun* verja *Fem.*

railway *noun* **1** (*the system*) ferrocarril *Masc.*; **the railways** el ferrocarril; **2 a railway line** una línea de ferrocarril (*from one place to another*); **3 on the railway line** en la vía férrea (*the rails*).

railway carriage *noun* vagón *Masc.* de tren.

railway station *noun* estación *Fem.* de tren; **opposite the railway station** enfrente de la estación de tren.

rain *noun* lluvia *Fem.*; **in the rain** bajo la lluvia.
rain *verb* llover [38]; **it's raining** está lloviendo; **it's going to rain** va a llover.

rainbow *noun* arco *Masc.* iris.

raincoat *noun* impermeable *Masc.*

rainfall *noun* precipitaciones *Fem. plural.*

rainy *adjective* lluvioso/lluviosa.

raise *verb* **1** (*lift up*) levantar [17]; **she raised her head** levantó la cabeza; **2** (*increase*) subir [19] (*a price or a salary*); **3 to raise money for something** recaudar [17] dinero para algo; **4 to raise the alarm** dar [4] la alarma; **5 to raise somebody's spirits** animar [17] a alguien.

raisin *noun* pasa *Fem.*

rally *noun* **1** (*a meeting*) concentración *Fem.*; **2** (*for sport*) rally *Masc.*; **3** (*in tennis*) peloteo *Masc.*

rambler *noun* excursionista *Masc./Fem.*

rambling *noun* **to go rambling** ir [8] de excursión.

ramp *noun* (*for a wheelchair, for example*) rampa *Fem.*

range *noun* **1** (*a choice*) gama *Fem.*; **in a wide range of colours** en una amplia gama de colores; **2** (*of mountains*) cordillera *Fem.*

rap *noun* rap *Masc.* (*music*).

rape *noun* violación *Fem.*
rape *verb* violar [17].

rare *adjective* **1** poco común; **a rare bird** un pájaro poco común; **2** poco hecho (*a steak*); **medium-rare** un filete poco hecho.

raspberry *noun* frambuesa *Fem.*; **raspberry jam** mermelada de frambuesa; **a raspberry tart** una tarta de frambuesas.

rat *noun* rata *Fem.*

rate *noun* **1** (*a charge*) tarifa *Fem.*; **what are the rates for children?** ¿cuáles son las tarifas para niños?; **reduced rates** tarifas reducidas; **2 at any rate** en todo caso.

rather *adverb* **1** bastante; **I'm rather busy** estoy bastante ocupado; **2 rather a lot of** bastante; **I've got rather a lot of work** tengo bastante trabajo; **3 rather a lot of** (*with a plural noun*) bastantes; **there are rather a lot of mistakes** hay bastantes errores; **4 rather than** en

a
b
c
d
e
f
g
h
i
j
k
l
m
n
o
p
q
r
s
t
u
v
w
x
y
z

a
b
c
d
e
f
g
h
i
j
k
l
m
n
o
p
q
r
s
t
u
v
w
x
y
z

vez de; **in summer rather than winter** en verano más que en invierno; **5 I'd rather wait** preferiría esperar; **they'd rather come on Thursday** preferirían venir el jueves.

raw *adjective* crudo/cruda.

ray *noun* rayo *Masc.*

razor *noun* máquina *Fem.* de afeitar (*safety*).

razor blade *noun* cuchilla *Fem.*

RE *noun* religión *Fem.*

reach *noun* alcance *Masc.*; **out of my reach** fuera de mi alcance; **within reach** (*of your hand*) al alcance; **within easy reach of the sea** cerca del mar.
reach *verb* llegar [28]; **when you reach the church** cuando llegues a la iglesia; **to reach the final** llegar [28] a la final.

read *verb* leer [37]; **what are you reading at the moment?** ¿qué estás leyendo en este momento?; **I'm reading a detective novel** estoy leyendo una novela policiaca; **he read out the list** leyó la lista.

reading *noun* lectura *Fem.*; **I don't much like reading** no me gusta mucho la lectura; **some easy reading for the beach** lectura fácil para la playa.

ready *adjective* **1** preparado/ preparada; **supper's not ready yet** la cena aún no está preparada; **2** (*person*) listo/lista; **are you ready to leave?** ¿estás listo para salir?; **3 to get ready** (*meal or things*) preparar [17]; **I'll get your room ready** voy a preparar tu habitación; **4 to get ready** (*a person*) prepararse [17]; **I'm getting ready to go out** me estoy preparando para salir; **I was getting ready for bed** estaba preparándome para irme a la cama.

real *adjective* verdadero/verdadera; **is that his real name?** ¿es ése su verdadero nombre?; **her real father is dead** su verdadero padre está muerto; **he's a real bore** es un verdadero pesado; **it's a real diamond** es un diamante de verdad.

realize *verb* darse [4] cuenta; **I hadn't realized** no me había dado cuenta; **to realize (that)** ... darse cuenta de que ...; **I didn't realize (that) he was French** no me di cuenta de que era francés; **do you realize what time it is?** ¿te das cuenta de la hora que es?

really *adverb* **1** (*truly*) **is it really midnight?** ¿de verdad son las doce de la noche?; **really?** ¿de verdad?; **not really** la verdad es que no; **2 I really don't know** realmente no lo sé; **3** (*extremely*) (*Spanish uses the superlative of the adjective to express this sense*) **the film was really good** la película fue buenísima.

reason *noun* razón *Fem.*; **the reason for the delay** la razón del retraso; **the reason why I phoned** la razón por la que llamé.

reasonable *adjective* razonable.

rebel *noun* rebelde *Masc./Fem.*

rebellion *noun* rebelión *Fem.*

receipt *noun* recibo *Masc.*

receive *verb* recibir [19].

receiver *noun* auricular *Masc.*; **to pick up the receiver** descolgar [23] el teléfono.

recent *adjective* reciente; **a recent change** un cambio reciente.

recently *adverb* recientemente.

reception *noun* **1** recepción *Fem.*; **he's waiting at reception** está esperando en recepción; **a big wedding reception** un gran banqueté de bodas; **2 to get a good reception** tener [9] buena acogida.

receptionist *noun* recepcionista *Masc./Fem.*

recipe *noun* receta *Fem.*; **can I have the recipe for your salad?** ¿me puedes dar tu receta de la ensalada?

reckon *verb* creer [37]; **I reckon it's a good idea** creo que es una buena idea.

recognize *verb* reconocer [35].

recommend *verb* recomendar [29]; **can you recommend a dentist?** ¿puedes recomendarme un dentista?; **I recommend the fish soup** recomiendo la sopa de pescado.

recommendation *noun* recomendación *Fem.*

record *noun* **1** récord *Masc.*; **it's a world record** es un récord mundial; **record sales** récord de ventas; **the hottest summer on record** el verano más caluroso del que se tienen datos; **2 to keep a record of something** llevar [17] un registro de algo; **3** (*music*) disco *Masc.*; **a Miles Davis record** un disco de Miles Davis; **4** (*office files*) archivo *Masc.*; **I'll just check your records** voy a mirar tu ficha; **5** (*of attendance*) registro *Masc.*

record *verb* (*on tape or CD*) grabar [17]; **they're recording a new album** están grabando un nuevo álbum.

recorder *noun* **1** flauta *Fem.* dulce; **to play the recorder** tocar [31] la flauta dulce; **2 a cassette recorder** un cassette; **a video recorder** una cámara de vídeo.

recording *noun* grabación *Fem.*

record player *noun* tocadiscos *Masc.* (*does not change in the plural*).

recover *verb* recuperarse [17]; **she's recovered now** ya se ha recuperado.

recovery *noun* (*from an illness*) recuperación *Fem.*

recovery vehicle *noun* grúa *Fem.*

rectangle *noun* rectángulo *Masc.*

rectangular *adjective* rectangular.

recycle *verb* reciclar [17].

red *adjective* **1** rojo/roja; **a red shirt** una camisa roja; **a bright red car** un coche rojo vivo; **2 to go red** ponerse [11] colorado; **3** (*hair*) **to have red hair** ser [1] pelirrojo.

Red Cross *noun* **the Red Cross** la Cruz Roja.

redcurrant *noun* grosella *Fem.*; **redcurrant jelly** jalea de grosellas.

a
b
c
d
e
f
g
h
i
j
k
l
m
n
o
p
q
r
s
t
u
v
w
x
y
z

a
b
c
d
e
f
g
h
i
j
k
l
m
n
o
p
q
r
s
t
u
v
w
x
y
z

reduce *verb* reducir [60]; **they've reduced the price** han reducido el precio.

reduction *noun* rebaja *Fem.* (*in price*).

redundant *adjective* **he was made redundant** lo despidieron por reducción de plantilla.

refer to *verb* referirse [14] a; **she's referring to you** se refiere a ti.

referee *noun* (*in sport*) árbitro *Masc./Fem.*

reference *noun* referencia *Fem.* (*for a job*); **she gave me a good reference** me dio una buena referencia.

referendum *noun* referendum *Masc.*

refill *noun* **1** (*for pen*) recambio *Masc.*; **2** (*for lighter*) carga *Fem.*

reflect *verb* reflejar [17].

reflection *noun* **1** (*in a mirror*) reflejo *Masc.*; **2** (*thought*) reflexión *Fem.*; **on reflection** pensándolo bien.

reflexive *adjective* **a reflexive verb** un verbo reflexivo.

refreshing *adjective* refrescante.

refreshment *noun* refresco *Masc.*

refrigerator *noun* nevera *Fem.*

refuge *noun* refugio *Masc.*; **a mountain refuge** un refugio (de montaña); **to take refuge in** refugiarse [17] en.

refugee *noun* refugiado *Masc.*, refugiada *Fem.*

refund *noun* reembolso *Masc.*
refund *verb* reembolsar [17].

refuse *noun* (*rubbish*) desperdicios *Masc. plural.*
refuse *verb* negarse [30]; **I refused** me negué; **he refuses to help** se niega a ayudar.

regards *plural noun* recuerdos *Masc. plural*; **'regards to your parents'** 'recuerdos a tus padres'; **Nat sends his regards** Nat manda recuerdos.

reggae *noun* reggae *Masc.*

region *noun* región *Fem.*

regional *adjective* regional.

register *noun* (*in school*) lista *Fem.*
register *verb* inscribirse [52].

registered letter *noun* carta *Fem.* certificada.

registration number *noun* número *Masc.* de matrícula (*of a vehicle*).

regret *verb* **to regret something** arrepentirse [14] de algo.

regular *adjective* **1 regular visits** visitas frecuentes; **2** habitual (*customer*).

regularly *adverb* regularmente.

regulation *noun* norma *Fem.*

rehearsal *noun* ensayo *Masc.*

rehearse *verb* ensayar [17].

reign *noun* reinado *Masc.*

rein *noun* rienda *Fem.*

reject *verb* rechazar [22].

related *adjective* **1** relacionado/ relacionada (*subject or ideas*);

2 we're not related no somos parientes.

relation *noun* pariente *Masc./Fem.*; **my relations** mis parientes.

relationship *noun* relación *Fem.*; **we have a good relationship** tenemos una buena relación.

relative *noun* pariente *Masc./Fem.*; **all my relatives** todos mis parientes.

relax *verb* relajarse [17]; **I'm going to relax and watch telly tonight** esta noche voy a relajarme y ver la tele.

relaxation *noun* esparcimiento *Masc.*; **tennis is her relaxation** el tenis es su esparcimiento.

relaxed *adjective* relajado/relajada.

relaxing *adjective* relajante.

relay race *noun* carrera *Fem.* de relevos.

release *noun* **1** estreno *Masc.*; **this week's new releases** los estrenos de esta semana; **2** (*of a prisoner or hostage*) puesta *Fem.* en libertad. **release** *verb* **1** sacar [31] (*a record or a video*); **2** estrenar [17] (*a film*); **3** poner [11] en libertad (*a person*).

reliable *adjective* **1** responsable (*person*); **2** fidedigno/fidedigna (*information*).

relief *noun* alivio *Masc.*; **what a relief!** ¡qué alivio!

relieved *adjective* aliviado/aliviada; **I was relieved to hear you'd arrived** fue un alivio oír que habías llegado.

religion *noun* religión *Fem.*

religious *adjective* religioso/religiosa; **Jane's not religious** Jane no es religiosa.

reluctant *adjective* reacio/reacia; **he's reluctant to go** se muestra reacio a ir.

rely *verb* **to rely on somebody** contar [24] con alguien; **I'm relying on you for Saturday** cuento contigo el para sábado.

remain *verb* permanecer [35].

remark *noun* comentario *Masc.*; **to make remarks about** hacer [7] comentarios sobre.

remember *verb* **1** acordarse [24]; **I don't remember** no me acuerdo; **2 to remember something** acordarse de algo; **I can't remember the number** no me acuerdo del número; **3 to remember to do** acordarse de hacer; **remember to shut the door!** ¡acuérdate de cerrar la puerta!; **I remembered to bring the CDs** me acordé de traer los compactos.

remind *verb* **1** recordar [24]; **to remind somebody to do** recordarle a alguien que haga (*note that 'que' is followed by the subjunctive*) **remind your mother to pick me up** recuérdale a tu madre que me recoja; **2 it reminds me of Paris** me recuerda a París; **he reminds me of Frank** me recuerda a Frank; **oh, that reminds me** ... ¡ah!, por cierto ....

remove *verb* quitar [17]; **he removed his jacket** se quitó la chaqueta; **the chairs had all been**

removed habían quitado todas las sillas.

renew *verb* renovar [24] (*a passport or licence*).

rent *noun* alquiler *Masc.*
rent *verb* alquilar [17]; **Simon's rented a flat** Simon ha alquilado un piso.

repair *noun* reparación *Fem.*
repair *verb* arreglar [17]; **to get something repaired** arreglar [17] algo; **we've had the television repaired** hemos arreglado la televisión.

repay *verb* devolver [45]; **he repaid me the money he owed me** me devolvió el dinero que me debía.

repeat *noun* repetición *Fem.* (*of a programme*).
repeat *verb* repetir [57].

replacement *noun* **1** (*person*) sustituto *Masc.*, sustituta *Fem.*; **2** (*thing*); **when can you find me a replacement?** ¿para cuándo me puedes encontrar otro?

reply *noun* contestación *Fem.*; **I didn't get a reply to my letter** no recibí contestación a mi carta; **there's no reply** no contestan (*on the telephone*).
reply *verb* contestar [17]; **I still haven't replied to the letter** aún no he contestado a la carta.

report *noun* **1** (*of an event*) informe *Masc.*; **2** (*school report*) boletín *Masc.* de notas.
report *verb* **1** informar [17] sobre (*a problem or accident*); **2** denunciar [17] (*a crime*); **we've reported the theft** hemos denunciado sobre el

robo; **3** presentarse [17]; **I had to report to reception** tuve que presentarme en recepción.

reporter *noun* periodista *Masc./Fem.*

representative *noun* representante *Masc./Fem.*

reproach *noun* reproche *Masc.*
reproach *verb* reprochar [17].

republic *noun* república *Fem.*

reputation *noun* **1** reputación *Fem.*; **a good reputation** una buena reputación; **2 to have a reputation for something** tener [9] fama de algo; **she has a reputation for honesty** tiene fama de honesta.

request *noun* petición *Fem.*; **on request** a solicitud.
request *verb* pedir [57].

rescue *noun* **1** rescate *Masc.*; **2 to come to somebody's rescue** acudir [19] en auxilio de alguien.
rescue *verb* rescatar [17]; **they rescued the dog** rescataron al perro.

rescue party *noun* equipo *Masc.* de rescate.

rescue worker *noun* socorrista *Masc./Fem.*

research *noun* investigación *Fem.*; **for research into Aids** para la investigación sobre el sida; **to do research** investigar [28].
research *verb* **to research into** investigar [28] sobre; **a well-researched programme** un programa bien documentado.

resemble *verb* parecerse [35] a; **she looks like her aunt** se parece a su tía.

reservation *noun* (*a booking*) reserva *Fem.*; **to make a reservation** hacer [7] una reserva.

reserve *noun* **1** reserva *Fem.*; **we have some in reserve** tener [9] algo de reserva; **2 a nature reserve** una reserva natural; **3** (*for a match*) reserva *Masc./Fem.*
reserve *verb* reservar [17]; **this table is reserved** la mesa está reservada.

resident *noun* residente *Masc./Fem.*

residential *adjective* residencial; **a residential area** un área residencial.

resign *verb* dimitir [19].

resignation *noun* (*from a post*) dimisión *Fem.*

resist *verb* resistir [19] (*an offer or temptation*); **I can't resist!** ¡no puedo resistirlo!

resit *verb* **to resit an exam** volver [45] a presentarse a un examen.

resort *noun* **1** (*for holidays*) **a holiday resort** un c entro turístico; **a ski resort** una estación de esquí; **a seaside resort** un centro turístico costero; **2 as a last resort** como último recurso.

respect *noun* respeto *Masc.*
respect *verb* respetar [17].

respectable *adjective* respetable.

respectful *adjective* respetuoso/respetuosa.

responsibility *noun* responsabilidad *Fem.*

responsible *adjective* responsable; **he's responsible for the delay** él es el responsable del retraso; **I'm responsible for booking the rooms** soy responsable de reservar las habitaciones; **he's not very responsible** no es muy responsable.

rest *noun* **1 the rest** el resto; **the rest of the day** el resto del día; **the rest of the bread** el resto del pan; **2** (*the others*) los otros; **the rest have gone home** los otros se han ido a casa; **3** descanso *Masc.*; **ten days' complete rest** diez días de completo descanso; **to have a rest** descansar [17]; **4** (*a short break*) **to stop for a rest** parar [17] para descansar.
rest *verb* (*have a rest*) descansar [17].

restaurant *noun* restaurante *Masc.*

restore *verb* restaurar [17].

result *noun* **1** resultado *Masc.*; **the exam results** los resultados del examen; **2 as a result** como consecuencia de ello; **as a result we missed the ferry** como consecuencia de ello perdimos el ferry.

retire *verb* (*from work*) jubilarse [17]; **she retires in June** se jubila en junio; **for retired people** para los jubilados.

retirement *noun* jubilación *Fem.*

return *noun* **1** vuelta *Fem.*; **the return journey** el viaje de vuelta; **by**

a

b

c

d

e

f

g

h

i

j

k

l

m

n

o

p

q

r

s

t

u

v

w

x

y

z

return of post a vuelta de correo;
2 in return a cambio; **in return for
his help** a cambio de su ayuda;
★ **many happy returns!** ¡muchas
felicidades!
return *verb* **1** (*come back or get
home*) volver [45]; **he returned ten
minutes later** volvió diez minutos
más tarde; **to return from holiday**
volver de vacaciones; **I'll ask her to
phone as soon as she returns** le
diré que te llame en cuanto vuelva;
2 (*to give back*) devolver [45];
**Gemma's never returned the
video** Gemma no devolvió nunca el
vídeo.

return fare *noun* precio *Masc.* del
billete de ida y vuelta.

return ticket *noun* billete *Masc.*
de ida y vuelta.

reunion *noun* reunión *Fem.*; **a class
reunion** una reunión de ex
compañeros de clase.

revenge *noun* venganza *Fem.*; **to
get one's revenge on someone**
vengarse [28] de alguien.

reverse *noun* **1** (*of coin*) anverso
Masc.; **2** (*gear*) marcha *Fem.* atrás;
3 (*of page*) dorso *Masc.*; **4** (*opposite*)
the reverse is true es al contrario.
reverse *verb* **1** (*in a car*) dar [4]
marcha atrás; **2 to reverse the
charges** llamar [17] a cobro
revertido.

review *noun* (*of a book, play, or
film*) crítica *Fem.*
review *verb* escribir [52] la crítica
de; **the film was well reviewed** la
película recibió buenas críticas.

revise *verb* repasar [17]; **Tessa's
busy revising for her exams** Tessa
está muy ocupada repasando para
los exámenes.

revision *noun* repaso *Masc.*

revolting *adjective* asqueroso/
asquerosa; **the sausages are
revolting** las salchichas están
asquerosas.

revolution *noun* revolución *Fem.*;
the Fench Revolution la
Revolución Francesa.

reward *noun* recompensa *Fem.*; **a
£100 reward** una recompensa de
cien libras.
reward *verb* recompensar [17].

rewarding *adjective* gratificante.

rhubarb *noun* ruibarbo *Masc.*

rhyme *noun* rima *Fem.*

rhythm *noun* ritmo *Masc.*

rib *noun* costilla *Fem.*

ribbon *noun* cinta *Fem.*

rice *noun* arroz *Masc.*; **chicken and
rice** pollo y arroz; **rice pudding**
arroz con leche.

rich *adjective* rico/rica; **we're not
very rich** no somos muy ricos; **the
rich and the poor** los ricos y los
pobres.

rid *adjective* **to get rid of something**
deshacerse [7] de algo; **we got rid of
the car** nos deshicimos del coche.

riddle *noun* adivinanza *Fem.*

ride *noun* **to go for a ride (on a
bike)** ir [8] a montar en bicicleta; **to
go for a ride (on a horse)** ir [8] a
montar a caballo.
ride *verb* **1 to learn to ride a bike**

aprender [18] a montar en bicicleta; **can you ride a bike?** ¿sabes montar en bicicleta?; **2 to learn to ride (a horse)** aprender [18] a montar a caballo; **I've never ridden a horse** nunca he montado a caballo.

rider noun **1** (of horse) jinete Masc., amazona Fem.; **2** (of bicycle) ciclista Masc./Fem.; **3** (of motorbike) motorista Masc./Fem.

ridiculous adjective ridículo/ridícula.

riding noun equitación Fem.; **to go riding** hacer [7] equitación.

riding school noun escuela Fem. de equitación.

rifle noun rifle Masc.

right noun **1** (not left) derecha Fem.; **on the right** a la derecha; **on my right** a mi derecha; **2** (to do something) derecho Masc.; **the right to strike** el derecho a hacer huelga; **you have no right to say that** no tienes derecho a decir eso.
right adjective **1** (not left) derecho/derecha; **my right hand** mi mano derecha; **2** (correct) correcto/correcta; **the right answer** la respuesta correcta; **the right telephone number** el teléfono correcto; **is this the right address?** ¿son éstas las señas?; **3 to be right** (a person) tener [9] razón; **you see, I was right** ¿ves? tenía yo razón; **4 you were right to stay at home** hiciste bien en quedarte en casa; **he was right not to say anything** hizo bien en no decir nada; **5 it's not right to talk like that** no está bien hablar así.

right adverb **1** (direction) derecha; **turn right at the lights** gira a la derecha en el semáforo; **2** (correctly) bien; **you're not doing it right** no lo estás haciendo bien; **3** (completely) **right at the bottom** al fondo del todo; **right now** ahora mismo; **right at the beginning** justo al principio; **right in the middle** justo en medio; **4** (okay) vale; **right, let's go** vale, vamos.

right click noun clic Masc. con el botón derecho del ratón.

right-hand adjective **on the right-hand side** a mano derecha.

right-handed adjective diestro/diestra.

ring noun **1** (on the phone) **to give somebody a ring** llamar [17] a alguien; **2** (for your finger) anillo Masc.; **3** (circle) círculo Masc.; **4 there was a ring at the door** llamaron a la puerta.
ring verb **1** (a bell or phone) sonar [24]; **the phone rang** sonó el teléfono; **2** (to phone) llamar [17]; **I'll ring you tomorrow** te llamaré mañana; **could you ring for a taxi?** ¿podrías llamar un taxi?.

● **to ring back** volver [45] a llamar; **I'll ring you back later** te volveré a llamar más tarde.

● **to ring off** colgar [23].

rinse verb enjuagar [28].

ripe adjective maduro/madura; **are the tomatoes ripe?** ¿están maduros los tomates?

rip-off noun **it's a rip-off!** ¡es una estafa!

rise *noun* **1** subida *Fem.*; **a rise in price** una subida de precio; **2 a pay rise** un aumento de sueldo.

rise *verb* **1** (*the sun*) salir [63]; **when the sun rose** cuando salió el sol; **2** (*prices*) subir [19].

risk *noun* riesgo *Masc.*; **to take risks** arriesgarse [28].

risk *verb* arriesgar [28] (*your life or reputation*); **she risked her life** arriesgó su vida.

rival *noun* rival *Masc./Fem.*

river *noun* río *Masc.*

road *noun* **1** carretera *Fem.*; **the road to London** la carretera de Londres; **2** (*in a town*) calle *Fem.*; **on the other side of the road** al otro lado de la calle; **3 across the road** enfrente; **they live across the road from us** viven enfrente de nosotros.

road accident *noun* accidente *Masc.* de carretera.

road map *noun* mapa *Masc.* de carreteras.

roadside *noun* **by the roadside** al borde de la carretera.

road sign *noun* señal *Fem.* de tráfico.

roadworks *plural noun* obras *Fem. plural.*

roast *noun* asado *Masc.*

roast *adjective* asado/asada; **roast potatoes** patatas asadas; **roast beef** rosbif *Masc.*

rob *verb* **1** robar [17] (*a person*); **2** atracar [31] (*a bank*).

robber *noun* **bank robber** atracador/atracadora *Masc./Fem..*

robbery *noun* atraco *Masc.*; **a bank robbery** un atraco a un banco.

rock *noun* **1** (*a big stone*) roca *Fem.*; **she was sitting on a rock** estaba sentada en una roca; **2** (*the material*) piedra *Fem.*; **3** (*music*) rock *Masc.*; **a rock band** un grupo de rock; **to dance rock and roll** bailar [17] rock and roll.

rock climbing *noun* escalada *Fem.* en roca; **to go rock climbing** hacer [7] escalada.

rock star *noun* estrella *Fem.* de rock.

rocket *noun* cohete *Masc.*

rocking horse *noun* caballito *Masc.* de balancín.

rocky *adjective* rocoso/rocosa.

rod *noun* **a fishing rod** una caña de pescar.

role *noun* papel *Masc.*; **to play the role of** interpretar [17] el papel de.

roll *noun* **1** rollo *Masc.*; **a roll of fabric** un rollo de tela; **a toilet roll** un rollo de papel higiénico; **2 a bread roll** un panecillo.

● **to roll something up** (*a carpet*) enrollar [17] algo; **he rolled up his sleeves** se remangó las mangas.

rollerblades™ *plural noun* patines *Masc. plural* en línea.

rollercoaster *noun* montaña *Fem.* rusa (*literally: Russian mountain*).

roller skates *plural noun* patines *Masc. plural.*

Roman Catholic *noun* católico *Masc.*, católica *Fem.*

Roman Catholic *adjective* católico/católica.

romantic *adjective* romántico/romántica.

roof *noun* tejado *Masc.*

roof rack *noun* baca *Fem.*

rook *noun* 1 (*in chess*) torre *Fem.*; 2 (*bird*) grajo *Masc.*

room *noun* 1 habitación *Fem.*; **she's in the other room** está en la otra habitación; **it's the biggest room in the house** es la habitación más grande de la casa; **a three-room flat** un piso de tres habitaciones; 2 (*a bedroom*) habitación *Masc.*; **Lola's in her room** Lola está en su habitación; 3 (*space*) sitio *Masc.*; **enough room for two** sitio suficiente para dos; **very little room** muy poco sitio.

root *noun* raíz *Fem.*

rope *noun* cuerda *Fem.*

rose *noun* rosa *Fem.*

rosebush *noun* rosal *Masc.*

rot *verb* pudrirse [59].

rota *noun* lista *Fem.* de turnos.

rotten *adjective* podrido/podrida.

rough *adjective* 1 (*scratchy*) áspero/áspera; 2 (*vague*) aproximado/aproximada; **a rough idea** una idea aproximada; 3 (*stormy*) **a rough sea** un mar agitado; 4 (*difficult*) **to have a rough time** pasarlo [17] mal; 5 **to sleep rough** dormir [51] a la intemperie.

roughly *adjective* (*approximately*) aproximadamente; **roughly ten per cent** aproximadamente el diez por ciento; **it takes roughly three hours** lleva aproximadamente tres horas.

round *noun* 1 (*in a tournament*) vuelta *Fem.*; 2 (*of cards*) partida *Fem.*; 3 **a round of drinks** una ronda de bebidas; **it's my round** esta ronda la pago yo.

round *adjective* redondo/redonda; **a round table** una mesa redonda.

round *preposition* 1 alrededor de; **round the city** alrededor de la ciudad; **round my arm** alrededor de mi brazo; **they were sitting round the table** estaban sentados alrededor de la mesa; 2 **to go round the shops** ir [8] de tiendas; **to go round a museum** visitar [17] un museo; **it's just round the corner** está a la vuelta de la esquina.

round *adverb* 1 **to go round to somebody's house** ir [8] a casa de alguien; **we invited Sally round for lunch** invitamos a Sally a comer; 2 **all the year round** todo el año.

roundabout *noun* 1 (*for traffic*) rotonda *Fem.*; 2 (*in a fairground*) tiovivo *Masc.*

route *noun* 1 (*that you plan*) ruta *Fem.*; **the best route is via Leeds** la mejor ruta es pasando por Leeds; 2 **a bus route** el recorrido de un autobús.

row¹ *noun* 1 fila *Fem.* (*of seats*); **in the front row** en la primera fila; **in the back row** en la última fila; 2 hilera *Fem.*; **a row of huts** un hilera de cabañas; 3 **four times in a row** cuatro veces seguidas.

a
b
c
d
e
f
g
h
i
j
k
l
m
n
o
p
q
r
s
t
u
v
w
x
y
z

row² *verb* (*in a boat*) remar [17]; **it's your turn to row** te toca remar; **we rowed across the lake** cruzamos el lago remando.

row³ *noun* **1** (*a quarrel*) pelea *Fem.*; **to have a row** pelearse [17]; **they've had a row** se han peleado; **I had a row with my parents** me peleé con mis padres; **2** (*noise*) ruido *Masc.*; **they are making a terrible row!** ¡están haciendo un ruido terrible!

rowing *noun* remo *Masc.*; **to go rowing** practicar [31] el remo.

rowing boat *noun* bote *Masc.* de remos.

royal *adjective* real; **the royal family** la familia real.

rub *verb* frotar [17]; **to rub your eyes** frotarse los ojos.
• **to rub something out** borrar [17] algo.

rubber *noun* **1** (*an eraser*) goma *Fem.* de borrar; **2** (*material*) goma *Fem.*; **rubber soles** suelas de goma.

rubber band *noun* goma *Fem.* elástica.

rubbish *noun* **1** (*for the bin*) basura *Fem.*; **2** (*nonsense*) estupideces *Fem. plural*; **you're talking rubbish!** ¡estás diciendo estupideces!
rubbish *adjective* **the film was rubbish** la película fue una porquería; **they're a rubbish band** es una porquería de grupo.

rubbish bin *noun* cubo *Masc.* de la basura.

rucksack *noun* mochila *Fem.*

rude *adjective* **1** maleducado/ maleducada (*a person*); **2** **that's**

rude eso es de mala educación; **3 a rude joke** una broma grosera; **a rude word** una palabrota.

rug *noun* **1** alfombra *Fem.*; **2** (*a blanket*) manta *Fem.* de viaje.

rugby *noun* rugby *Masc.*; **to play rugby** jugar [27] al rugby; **a rugby match** un partido de rugby.

ruin *noun* ruina *Fem.*; **in ruins** en ruinas.
ruin *verb* **1** estropear [17]; **you'll ruin your jacket** vas a estropear tu chaqueta; **2** fastidiar [17] (*informal*) (*day, holiday*); **it ruined my holiday** me fastidió las vacaciones.

rule *noun* **1** regla *Fem.*; **the rules of the game** las reglas del juego; **2 the school rules** el reglamento del colegio; **3 as a rule** como norma.

ruler *noun* regla *Fem.*; **I've lost my ruler** he perdido mi regla.

rumour *noun* rumor *Masc.*

run *noun* **1 to go for a run** ir [8] a correr; **2** (*in cricket*) carrera *Fem.*; **3 in the long run** a la larga.
run *verb* **1** correr [18]; **I ran ten kilometres** corrí diez kilómetros; **he ran across the pitch** cruzó el campo corriendo; **Kitty ran for the bus** Kitty corrió para coger el autobús; **2** (*organize*) organizar [22]; **who's running this concert?** ¿quién organiza el concierto?; **3** dirigir [49] (*a business*); **he ran the firm for forty years** dirigió la compañía durante cuarenta años; **4** (*a train or bus*) circular [17]; **the buses don't run on Sundays** los autobuses no circulan los domingos;

5 (*to operate*) hacer [7] funcionar; **to run a bath** preparar [17] un baño.

● **to run away** huir [54].

● **to run into** chocar [31] con; **the car ran into a tree** el coche chocó con un árbol.

● **to run out of something I'm running out of money** se me está acabando el dinero.

● **to run somebody over** atropellar [17] a alguien; **you'll get run over!** ¡te van a atropellar!.

runner-up *noun* segundo *Masc.*, segunda *Fem.*

running *noun* **running is good exercise** correr es un buen ejercicio.

runway *noun* pista *Fem.*

rush *noun* (*a hurry*) **to be in a rush** tener [9] prisa; **sorry, I'm in a rush** perdona, tengo prisa.
rush *verb* **1** (*hurry*) darse [4] prisa; **I must rush!** ¡tengo que darme prisa!; **2** (*run*) **she rushed into the street** salió corriendo a la calle; **I rushed into the room** entré corriendo en la habitación; **3** **Louise was rushed to hospital** llevaron a Louise corriendo al hospital.

rush hour *noun* hora *Fem.* punta; **in the rush hour** a la hora punta.

Russia *noun* Rusia *Fem.*

Russian *noun* **1** (*a person*) ruso *Masc.*, rusa *Fem.*; **2** (*the language*) ruso *Masc.*
Russian *adjective* ruso/rusa.

rye *noun* centeno *Masc.*

Ss

Sabbath *noun* **1** (*Jewish*) sábado *Masc.*; **2** (*Christian*) domingo *Masc.*

sack *noun* **1** saco *Masc.*; **2 he got the sack** le despidieron.
sack *verb* **to sack somebody** despedir [57] a alguien.

sacred *adjective* sagrado/sagrada.

sacrifice *noun* sacrificio *Masc.*

sad *adjective* triste.

saddle *noun* silla *Fem.* de montar.

saddlebag *noun* alforja *Fem.* (*on bike*).

safe *adjective* **1** (*out of danger*) seguro/segura; **to feel safe** sentirse [14] seguro/segura; **2** (*not dangerous*) seguro/segura; **the path is safe** el camino es seguro; **it's not safe** no es seguro; **3** (*unharmed*) **to be safe** estar [2] sano y salvo.

safety *noun* seguridad *Fem.*

safety belt *noun* cinturón *Masc.* de seguridad.

safety pin *noun* imperdible *Masc.*

Sagittarius *noun* Sagitario *Masc.*; **Kylie's Sagittarius** Kylie es Sagitario.

sail *noun* vela *Fem.*

sailing *noun* vela *Fem.*; **to go sailing** ir [8] a hacer vela; **she does a lot of sailing** practica mucho la vela.

sailing boat *noun* bote *Masc.* de vela.

sailor *noun* marinero *Masc.*

saint *noun* santo *Masc.*, santa *Fem.*

sake *noun* **1** for your mother's sake por tu madre; **2** for heaven's sake! ¡por el amor de Dios!

salad *noun* ensalada *Fem.*; a tomato salad una ensalada de tomate.

salad dressing *noun* aliño *Masc.* para la ensalada.

salary *noun* sueldo *Masc.*

sale *noun* **1** (*selling*) venta *Fem.*; the sale of the house la venta de la casa; **'for sale'** 'se vende'; **2** the sales las rebajas; I bought it in the sales lo compré en las rebajas.

sales assistant *noun* dependiente *Masc.*, dependienta *Fem.*

salesman *noun* representante *Masc.*; he's a salesman es representante.

saleswoman *noun* representante *Fem.*

saliva *noun* saliva *Fem.*

salmon *noun* salmón *Masc.*

salt *noun* sal *Fem.*

salty *adjective* salado/salada.

Salvadorean *noun* salvadoreño *Masc.*, salvadoreña *Fem.* **Salvadorean** *adjective* salvadoreño/salvadoreña.

Salvation Army *noun* Ejército *Masc.* de Salvación.

same *adjective* **1** mismo/misma; she said the same thing ella dijo lo mismo; her birthday's the same day as mine su cumpleaños es el mismo día que el mío; at the same time al mismo tiempo; their car's the same as ours su coche es el mismo que el nuestro; **2** (*with a plural noun*) mismos/mismas; they were wearing the same shoes llevaban los mismos zapatos; **3** to look the same parecer [35] iguales; they all look the same to me a mí todos me parecen iguales.
same *pronoun* the same lo mismo; it's not the same no es lo mismo; it's always the same siempre pasa lo mismo.

sample *noun* muestra *Fem.*; a free sample una muestra gratuita.

sand *noun* arena *Fem.*

sandal *noun* sandalia *Fem.*; a pair of sandals un par de sandalias.

sand castle *noun* castillo *Masc.* de arena.

sandpaper *noun* papel *Masc.* de lija.

sandwich *noun* sándwich *Masc.*; a ham sandwich un sándwich de jamón.

sanitary towel *noun* compresa *Fem.*

Santa Claus *noun* Papá *Masc.* Noel.

sarcasm *noun* sarcasmo *Masc.*

sarcastic *adjective* sarcástico/sarcástica.

sardine *noun* sardina *Fem.*

SARS *noun* síndrome *Masc.* respiratorio agudo severo.

satchel *noun* cartera *Fem.*

satellite *noun* satélite *Masc.*

satellite dish *noun* antena *Fem.* parabólica.

satellite television *noun* televisión *Fem.* por vía satélite.

satisfactory *adjective* satisfactorio/satisfactoria.

satisfied *adjective* satisfecho/satisfecha.

satisfy *verb* satisfacer [7].

satisfying *adjective* **1** (*pleasing*) satisfactorio/satisfactoria; **2 a satisfying meal** una comida que llena.

Saturday *noun* sábado *Masc.*; **on Saturday** el sábado; **I'm going out on Saturday** voy a salir el sábado; **see you on Saturday!** ¡te veo el sábado!; **on Saturdays** los sábados; **the museum is closed on Saturdays** el museo cierra los sábados; **every Saturday** todos los sábados; **last Saturday** el sábado pasado; **next Saturday** el próximo sábado; **to have a Saturday job** trabajar [17] los sábados.

sauce *noun* salsa *Fem.*

saucepan *noun* cazo *Masc.*

saucer *noun* platillo *Masc.*

sausage *noun* **1** salchicha *Fem.*; **2** (*salami*) salchichón *Masc.*

savage *noun* salvaje *Masc./Fem.*

save *verb* **1** (*rescue*) salvar [17]; **to save somebody's life** salvarle la vida a alguien; **the doctors saved his life** los médicos le salvaron la vida; **2** ahorrar [17] (*money or energy*); **I've saved £60** he ahorrado sesenta libras; **try to save electricity** intenta ahorrar electricidad; **3** (*put aside*) guardar [17] (*food*); **save the cake for later** guarda el pastel para luego; **4** (*avoid spending*) no gastar [17]; **I walk to school to save money** voy andando al colegio para no gastar dinero; **5 to save time** ahorrar [17] tiempo; **we'll take a taxi to save time** cogeremos un taxi para ahorrar tiempo; **6** (*on a computer*) guardar [17].

● **to save up** ahorrar [17]; **I'm saving up to go to Spain** estoy ahorrando para ir a España.

savings *plural noun* ahorros *Masc. plural*; **I've spent all my savings** me he gastado todos los ahorros.

savoury *adjective* salado/salada; **I prefer savoury things to sweet things** prefiero lo salado a lo dulce.

saw *noun* sierra *Fem.*

saxophone *noun* saxofón *Masc.*; **to play the saxophone** tocar [31] el saxofón.

say *verb* **1** decir [5]; **what did you say?** ¿qué has dicho?; **she says she's tired** dice que está cansada; **he said to wait here** dijo que esperásemos aquí; **as they say** como se suele decir; **that goes without saying** eso no hace falta ni decirlo; **2 to say something again** repetir [57] algo.

saying *noun* refrán *Masc.*; **as the saying goes** como dice el refrán.

scab *noun* costra *Fem.*

scale *noun* **1** (*size*) escala *Fem.*; **on a large scale** en gran escala; **the scale of the disaster** la escala del desastre; **2** (*in music*) escala *Fem.*; **3** (*of a fish*) escama *Fem.*

scales *noun* **1** balanza *Fem.*; **kitchen scales** una balanza de a cocina; **2 bathroom scales** una báscula de baño.

scalp noun cuero Masc. cabelludo.

scandal noun **1** escándalo Masc.; **2** (gossip) chismorreo Masc.

Scandinavia noun Escandinavia Fem.

Scandinavian adjective escandinavo/escandinava.

scanner noun escáner Masc.

scar noun cicatriz Fem.

scarce adjective escaso/escasa.

scarcely adverb apenas; **I could scarcely see it** apenas lo veía.

scare noun **1** susto Masc.; **to give somebody a scare** darle [4] un susto a alguien; **2 a bomb scare** una amenaza de bomba.
scare verb **to scare somebody** asustar [17] a alguien; **you scared me!** ¡me has asustado!

scarecrow noun espantapájaros Masc. (does not change in the plural).

scared adjective **to be scared** estar [2] asustado/asustada; **I'm scared!** estoy asustado; **to be scared of** tenerle [9] miedo a; **he's scared of dogs** le tiene miedo a los perros.

scarf noun **1** (long, warm) bufanda Fem.; **2** (silky) foulard Masc.

scary adjective de miedo (book or film).

scene noun **1** (of an incident or a crime) escena Fem.; **the scene of the crime** la escena del crimen; **2** (world) mundo Masc.; **the music scene** el mundo de la música; **3 scenes of violence** escenas

violentas; **4 to make a scene** montar [17] un número (informal).

scenery noun **1** (landscape) paisaje Masc.; **2** (theatrical) decorado Masc.

schedule noun programa Masc.

scheduled flight noun vuelo Masc. regular.

scheme noun plan Masc.

scholarship noun beca Fem.

school noun colegio Masc.; **to go to school** ir [8] al colegio; **she's still at school** todavía va al colegio.

schoolbook noun libro Masc. de texto.

schoolboy noun colegial Masc.

schoolchildren plural noun colegiales Masc. plural.

schoolfriend noun amigo Masc., amiga Fem. del colegio.

schoolgirl noun colegiala Fem.

science noun ciencia Fem.; **I like science** me gustan las ciencias; **the science teacher** el profesor de ciencias.

science fiction noun ciencia Fem. ficción.

scientific adjective científico/científica.

scientist noun científico Masc., científica Fem.

scissors plural noun tijeras Fem. plural; **a pair of scissors** unas tijeras.

scoop noun **1** (of ice-cream) bola Fem.; **how many scoops would you like?** ¿cuántas bolas quieres?; **2** (in newspaper) primicia Fem.

score *noun* (*in game*) resultado *Masc.*; **the score was three two** el resultado fue tres a dos; **what's the score?** ¿a cómo van?
score *verb* **1** (*goal*) marcar [31]; **Lenny scored a goal** Lenny marcó un gol; **2** (*points*) **I scored three points** conseguí tres puntos; **3** (*keep score*) llevar [17] la puntuación; **4** (*in test or card game*) puntuación *Fem.*

Scorpio *noun* Escorpio *Masc.*; **Jess is Scorpio** Jess es Escorpio.

Scot *noun* escocés *Masc.*, escocesa *Fem.*; **the Scots** los escoceses.

Scotland *noun* Escocia *Fem.*; **in Scotland** en Escocia; **Pauline's from Scotland** Pauline es de Escocia.

Scots *adjective* escocés/escocesa; **a Scots accent** un acento escocés.

Scotsman *noun* escocés *Masc.*

Scotswoman *noun* escocesa *Fem.*

Scottish *adjective* escocés/escocesa; **a Scottish accent** un acento escocés.

scout *noun* explorador *Masc.*, exploradora *Fem.*

scrambled eggs *noun* huevos *Masc. plural* revueltos.

scrap *noun* **a scrap of paper** un trocito de papel.

scrape *verb* rayar [17].

scratch *noun* **1** (*on your skin*) arañazo *Masc.*; **2** (*on a surface*) rayón *Masc.*; ★**to start from scratch** empezar [25] de cero.
scratch *verb* (*scratch yourself*) rascarse [31]; **to scratch your head** rascarse [31] la cabeza.

scream *noun* grito *Masc.*
scream *verb* gritar [17].

screen *noun* pantalla *Fem.*; **on the screen** en la pantalla.

screw *noun* tornillo *Masc.*
screw *verb* atornillar [17].

screwdriver *noun* destornillador *Masc.*

scribble *verb* garabatear [17].

scrub *verb* **1** fregar [30] (*a saucepan*); **2 to scrub your nails** cepillarse [17] las uñas.

scuba diving *noun* submarinismo *Masc.*

sculpture *noun* escultura *Fem.*

sculptor *noun* escultor *Masc.*, escultora *Fem.*; **Frazer's a sculptor** Frazer es escultor.

sea *noun* mar *Masc.*

seafood *noun* marisco *Masc.*

seagull *noun* gaviota *Fem.*

seal *noun* (*animal*) foca *Fem.*
seal *verb* cerrar [29] (*envelope*).

seaman *noun* marinero *Masc.*

search *noun* **1** búsqueda *Fem.*
search *verb* **1** (*to look for*) buscar [31]; **I've searched my desk but I can't find the letter** he buscado en mi escritorio pero no encuentro la carta; **to search for something** buscar [31] algo; **I've been searching everywhere for the scissors** he buscado las tijeras por todas partes; **2** (*a building, a person*) registrar [17]; **the police searched the house** la policía registró la casa.

seashell *noun* concha *Fem.* de mar.

a
b
c
d
e
f
g
h
i
j
k
l
m
n
o
p
q
r
s
t
u
v
w
x
y
z

a
b
c
d
e
f
g
h
i
j
k
l
m
n
o
p
q
r
s
t
u
v
w
x
y
z

seasick *adjective* **to be seasick** estar [2] mareado/mareada; **to get seasick** marearse [17].

seaside *noun* costa *Fem.*; **at the seaside** en la costa.

season *noun* temporada *Fem.*; **the rugby season** la temporada de rugby; **strawberries are not in season at the moment** ahora no es temporada de fresas; **off-season prices** billetes de fuera de temporada.

season ticket *noun* abono *Masc.* de temporada.

seat *noun* **1** asiento *Masc.*; **the front seat** (*in a car*) el asiento delantero; **the back seat** el asiento trasero; **take a seat** (*in a cinema, theatre, etc.*) localidad *Fem.*; **to book a seat** reservar [17] una localidad; **3 can you keep my seat?** ¿puedes guardarme el sitio?

seatbelt *noun* cinturón *Masc.* de seguridad.

second *noun* **1** (*time unit*) segundo *Masc.*; **can you wait a second?** ¿puedes esperar un segundo?; **2 the second of July** el dos de julio.
second *adjective* segundo/ segunda; **for the second time** por segunda vez; **on the second floor** en la segunda planta.

second class *adjective* de segunda clase (*a ticket, hotel*); **a second class team** un equipo de segunda clase.

secondary school *noun* colegio *Masc.* de enseñanza secundaria.

secondhand *adjective, adverb* de segunda mano; **a secondhand bike** una bicicleta de segunda mano; **I bought it secondhand** lo compré de segunda mano.

secondly *adverb* en segundo lugar.

secret *noun* secreto *Masc.*; **to keep a secret** guardar [17] un secreto; **in secret** en secreto.
secret *adjective* secreto/secreta; **a secret plan** un plan secreto.

secretarial college *noun* escuela *Fem.* de secretariado.

secretary *noun* secretario *Masc.*, secretaria *Fem.*; **she's a secretary** es secretaria; **the secretary's office** la secretaría.

secretly *adverb* en secreto.

sect *noun* secta *Fem.*

section *noun* sección *Fem.*

security *noun* seguridad *Fem.*

security guard *noun* guarda *Masc.* jurado; guarda *Fem.* jurada; **he's a security guard** es guarda jurado.

see *verb* **1** ver [16]; **I saw Lindy yesterday** vi a Lindy ayer; **have you seen the film?** ¿has visto la película?; **I haven't seen her for ages** hace años que no la veo; **I'll see what I can do** veré lo que puedo hacer; **let's see** a ver; **2 to be able to see** ver [16]; **I can't see anything** no veo nada; **3 see you!** ¡hasta luego!; **see you on Saturday!** ¡hasta el sábado!; **see you soon!** ¡hasta pronto!; **see you tomorrow!** ¡hasta mañana!; **4 to see**

somebody home acompañar [17] a alguien a casa.

- **to see to something** ocuparse [17] de algo; **Jo's seeing to the drinks** Jo se está ocupando de las bebidas.

seed *noun* semilla *Fem.*; **to plant seeds** plantar [17] semillas.

seem *verb* parecer [35]; **it seems odd to me** me parece raro; **it seems she's left** parece que se ha ido; **he seems a bit shy** parece un poco tímido; **the museum seems to be closed** parece que el museo está cerrado.

seesaw *noun* balancín *Masc.*

select *verb* seleccionar [17].

selection *noun* selección *Fem.*

self-confidence *noun* confianza *Fem.* en sí mismo; **I don't have much self-confidence** no tengo mucha confianza en mí misma.

self-confident *adjective* seguro/ segura de sí mismo/misma.

self-conscious *adjective* cohibido/cohibida.

self-employed *noun* autónomo *Masc.*, autónoma *Fem.*; **the self-employed** los autónomos. **self-employed** *adjective* autónomo/autónoma; **to be self-employed** ser [1] autónomo.

selfish *adjective* egoísta.

self-service *adjective* **a self-service restaurant** un autoservicio.

sell *verb* vender [18]; **to sell something to somebody** venderle algo a alguien; **I sold him my bike** le vendí mi bici; **the house has been**

sold la casa se ha vendido; **the concert's sold out** se han agotado las localidades para el concierto.

sell-by date *noun* fecha *Fem.* límite de venta.

seller *noun* vendedor *Masc.*, vendedora *Fem.*

Sellotape™ *noun* celo™ *Masc.*

semi *noun* casa *Fem.* adosada; **we live in a semi** vivimos en una casa adosada.

semicircle *noun* semicírculo *Masc.*

semicolon *noun* punto *Masc.* y coma.

semi-detached house *noun* casa *Fem.* adosada.

semi-final *noun* semifinal *Fem.*

semi-skimmed milk *noun* leche *Fem.* semidesnatada.

send *verb* mandar [17]; **to send something to somebody** mandarle algo a alguien; **I sent her a present for her birthday** le mandé un regalo por su cumpleaños.

- **to send somebody back** hacer [7] volver a alguien.
- **to send something back** devolver [45] algo.

senior citizen *noun* persona *Fem.* de la tercera edad.

sensation *noun* **1** (*feeling*) sensibilidad *Fem.*; **she had no sensation in her fingers** no tenía sensibilidad en los dedos; **2** (*impact*) sensación *Fem.*; **she caused a sensation** causó sensación.

sensational *adjective* sensacional.

a
b
c
d
e
f
g
h
i
j
k
l
m
n
o
p
q
r
s
t
u
v
w
x
y
z

541

a
b
c
d
e
f
g
h
i
j
k
l
m
n
o
p
q
r
s
t
u
v
w
x
y
z

sense *noun* **1** sentido *Masc.*; **common sense** sentido común; **it doesn't make sense** no tiene sentido; **it makes sense** tiene sentido; **to have a sense of humour** tener [9] sentido del humor; **she has no sense of humour** no tiene sentido del humor; **2 the sense of smell** el olfato; **the sense of touch** el tacto.

sensible *adjective* sensato/sensata; **she's very sensible** es muy sensata; **it's a sensible decision** es una decisión sensata.

sensitive *adjective* sensible; **for sensitive skin** para pieles sensibles.

sentence *noun* **1** frase *Fem.*; **write a sentence in Spanish** escribe una frase en español; **2** (*by judge*) sentencia *Fem.*
sentence *verb* condenar [17].

sentimental *adjective* sentimental.

separate *adjective* **1** aparte; **in a separate pile** en un montón aparte; **on a separate sheet of paper** en una hoja de papel aparte; **2** (*different*) distinto/distinta; **that's a separate problem** ese es un problema distinto; **3** (*individual*) separado/separada; **they have separate rooms** tienen habitaciones separadas.
separate *verb* **1** separar [17]; **2** (*a couple*) separarse [17].

separately *adverb* por separado.

separation *noun* separación *Fem.*

September *noun* septiembre *Masc.*

sequel *noun* continuación *Fem.*

serial *noun* serie *Fem.*

series *noun* serie *Fem.*; **a television series** una serie de televisión.

serious *adjective* **1** serio/seria; **a serious discussion** una discusión seria; **are you serious?** ¿lo dices en serio?; **2** grave (*illness, injury, mistake, problem*); **we have a serious problem** tenemos un problema grave.

seriously *adverb* **1** en serio; **seriously, I have to go now** en serio, tengo que irme; **seriously?** ¿en serio?; **2 to take somebody seriously** tomarse [17] en serio a alguien; **3** gravemente (*ill, injured*).

servant *noun* criado *Masc.*, criada *Fem.*

serve *noun* (*in tennis*) saque *Masc.*; **it's my serve** me toca sacar.
serve *verb* **1** servir [57]; **can you serve the vegetables, please?** ¿puedes servir la verdura, por favor?; **2 are you being served?** ¿le atienden?; **3** (*in tennis*) sacar [31]; ★**it serves him right** lo tiene bien merecido.

service *noun* **1** (*in a restaurant, from a company, etc.*) servicio *Masc.*; **the service is very slow** el servicio es muy lento; **service is included** el servicio está incluido; **2 the emergency services** los servicios de emergencia; **3** (*church*) oficio *Masc.* religioso; **4** (*of a car or machine*) revisión *Fem.*
service *verb* hacerle [7] una revisión a (*a car or a machine*).

service charge *noun* servicio *Masc.*; **what's the service charge?** ¿cuánto se cobra por el servicio?

service station *noun* estación *Fem.* de servicio.

serviette *noun* servilleta *Fem.*

session *noun* sesión *Fem.*

set *noun* **1** (*for playing a game*) juego *Masc.*; **a chess set** un juego de ajedrez; **2** (*of keys, tools, etc.*) juego *Masc.*; **3 a train set** un tren de juguete; **4** (*in tennis*) set *Masc.*
set *adjective* **at a set time** a una hora determinada; **a set menu** un menú del día; **a set price** un precio fijo.
set *verb* **1** fijar [17] (*date, time*); **2** establecer [35] (*record*); **3 to set the table** poner [11] la mesa; **to set the alarm clock** poner [11] el despertador; **I've set my alarm for seven** he puesto el despertador para las siete; **4 to set a watch** poner [11] el reloj en hora; **5** (*the sun*) ponerse [11].
● **to set off** salir [63]; **we're setting off at ten** salimos a las diez; **they set off for Barcelona yesterday** salieron ayer para Barcelona.
● **to set off something 1** tirar [17] (*firework*); **2** hacer [7] sonar (*alarm*).
● **to set out** salir [63]; **they set out for Seville yesterday** salieron ayer para Sevilla.

settee *noun* sofá *Masc.*

settle *verb* **1** (*a bill*) pagar [28]; **2** (*a problem*) solucionar [17].

seven *number* siete *Masc.*; **Khalil's seven** Khalil tiene siete años; **it's seven o'clock** son las siete.

seventeen *number* diecisiete *Masc.*; **Jason's seventeen** Jason tiene diecisiete años.

seventh *noun* **1** (*fraction*) **a seventh** una séptima parte; **2 the seventh of July** el siete de julio.
seventh *adjective* séptimo/ séptima; **on the seventh floor** en la séptima planta.

seventies *plural noun* **the seventies** los años setenta; **in the seventies** en los años setenta.

seventy *number* setenta *Masc.*; **he's seventy** tiene setenta años; **seventy-five** setenta y cinco.

several *adjective, pronoun* varios/ varias; **I've seen her several times** la he visto varias veces; **I've read several of her novels** he leído varias novelas suyas; **he took several** cogió varios.

severe *adjective* **1** (*person*) severo/ severa; **2** (*weather*) malo/mala; **3** (*injury*) grave.

Seville *noun* Sevilla *Fem.*

sew *verb* coser [18].

sewer *noun* alcantarilla *Fem.*

sewing *noun* costura *Fem.*; **I like sewing** me gusta la costura.

sewing machine *noun* máquina *Fem.* de coser.

sex *noun* **1** (*gender*) sexo *Masc.*; **2** (*intercourse*) relaciones *Fem. plural* sexuales; **to have sex with someone** tener [9] relaciones sexuales con alguien.

sex education *noun* educación *Fem.* sexual.

a
b
c
d
e
f
g
h
i
j
k
l
m
n
o
p
q
r
s
t
u
v
w
x
y
z

a

sexism *noun* sexismo *Masc.*

b

sexist *adjective* sexista; **sexist remarks** comentarios sexistas.

c

sexual *adjective* sexual.

d

sexual harassment *noun* acoso *Masc.* sexual.

e

sexuality *noun* sexualidad *Fem.*

f

sexy *adjective* sexy.

g

shabby *adjective* gastado/gastada.

h

shade *noun* **1** (*of a colour*) tono *Masc.*; **a pretty shade of green** un bonito tono verde; **2 in the shade** en la sombra.

i

j

shadow *noun* sombra *Fem.*

k

shake *verb* **1** (*tremble*) temblar [29]; **my hands are shaking** me tiemblan las manos; **2 to shake something** agitar [17] algo; **3 to shake hands with somebody** estrecharle [17] la mano a alguien; **she shook hands with me** me dio la mano; **we shook hands** nos estrechamos la mano; **4 to shake your head** (*meaning no*) negar [30] con la cabeza.

l

m

n

o

p

shall *verb* **shall I come with you?** ¿voy contigo?; **shall we stop now?** ¿paramos ya?

q

r

s

shallow *adjective* poco profundo/ poco profunda; **the water's very shallow here** el agua es muy poco profunda aquí.

t

u

v

shallow end *noun* (*of a swimming pool*) **the shallow end** la parte poco profunda de la piscina.

w

x

shambles *noun* caos *Masc.*; **it was a total shambles!** ¡fue un caos total!

y

shame *noun* **1** vergüenza *Fem.*; **shame on you!** ¡debería darte

z

vergüenza!; **2 what a shame!** ¡qué pena!; **it's a shame she can't come** ¡qué pena que no pueda venir! (*note that 'que' is followed by the subjunctive*).

shampoo *noun* champú *Masc.*; **I bought some shampoo** compré champú.

shamrock *noun* trébol *Masc.*

shandy *noun* clara *Fem.*; **a shandy** una clara.

shape *noun* forma *Fem.*; **to be in good shape** estar [2] en buena forma.

share *noun* **1** parte *Fem.*; **your share of the money** tu parte del dinero; **2** (*in a company*) acción *Fem.* **share** *verb* compartir [19]; **I'm sharing a room with Emma** comparto una habitación con Emma.

• **to share out** repartir [19].

sharp *adjective* **1** (*knife*) afilado/ afilada; **this knife isn't very sharp** este cuchillo no está muy afilado; **2 a sharp pencil** un lápiz con mucha punta; **3 a sharp bend** una curva cerrada; **4** (*clever*) agudo/ aguda.

sharpen *verb* **1** sacarle [31] punta a (*a pencil*); **2** afilar [17] (*a knife*).

sharpener *noun* sacapuntas *Masc. plural.*

shave *verb* **1** (*have a shave*) afeitarse [17]; **he's shaving** se está afeitando; **2 to shave your legs** afeitarse [17] las piernas; **to shave off your beard** afeitarse [17] la barba.

shaving cream *noun* crema *Fem.* de afeitar.

shaving foam *noun* espuma *Fem.* de afeitar.

she *pronoun* **1** (*'she' like other subject pronouns is generally not translated; in Spanish the form of the verb tells you whether the subject of the verb is 'he/she/it, you', they', etc., so 'she' is only translated for emphasis*) **she's in her room** está en su cuarto; **she's a student** es estudiante; **she's a very good teacher** es muy buena profesora; **here she is!** ¡aquí está!; **2** (*for emphasis*) ella; **she did it** lo hizo ella.

shed *noun* **1** cabaña *Fem.*; **2** (*in garden*) cobertizo *Masc.*

sheep *noun* oveja *Fem.*

sheepdog *noun* perro *Masc.* pastor.

sheet *noun* **1** (*for a bed*) sábana *Fem.*; **2 a sheet of paper** una hoja de papel; **a blank sheet** una hoja en blanco; **3** (*of glass or metal*) plancha *Fem.*; ★**to be as white as a sheet** estar [2] blanco como el papel.

shelf *noun* **1** (*in the home*) estante *Masc.*; **a set of shelves** una estantería *Fem.*; **2** (*in a shop or a fridge*) balda *Fem.*

shell *noun* **1** (*of an egg or a nut*) cáscara *Fem.*; **2** (*seashell*) concha *Fem.*; **3** (*explosive*) proyectil *Masc.*

shellfish *noun* marisco *Masc.*

shelter *noun* **1** refugio *Masc.*; **to take shelter from the rain** refugiarse [17] de la lluvia; **in the** **shelter of** al abrigo de; **2 a bus shelter** una marquesina.

sherry *noun* jerez *Masc.*

Shetland Islands *noun* islas *Fem. plural* Shetland.

shield *noun* escudo *Masc.*

shift *noun* turno *Masc.*; **the night shift** el turno de noche; **to be on night shift** hacer [7] el turno de noche.

shift *verb* **to shift something** mover [38] algo.

shin *noun* espinilla *Fem.*

shine *verb* brillar [17].

shiny *adjective* brillante.

ship *noun* **1** barco *Masc.*; **a passenger ship** un barco de pasajeros; **2 a sailing ship** un velero.

shirt *noun* camisa *Fem.*

shiver *verb* temblar [29].

shock *noun* **1** shock *Masc.*; **it was a shock** fue un shock; **it gave me a shock** me llevé un shock; **in a state of shock** en estado de shock; **2 an electric shock** una descarga eléctrica; **I got an electric shock** me dio una descarga eléctrica.

shock *verb* horrorizar [22].

shocked *adjective* horrorizado/horrorizada.

shocking *adjective* espantoso/espantosa.

shoe *noun* zapato *Masc.*; **a pair of shoes** un par de zapatos.

shoelace *noun* cordón *Masc.* de zapato.

shoe polish *noun* betún *Masc.*

a **shoe shop** noun zapatería Fem.

b **shoot** verb 1 (fire) disparar [17]; **to shoot at somebody** disparar a alguien; **she shot him in the leg** le disparó en la pierna; **he was shot in the arm** le dispararon en el brazo; 2 (kill) matar [17] a tiros; **he was shot by terrorists** los terroristas lo mataron a tiros; 3 (execute) fusilar [17]; 4 (in football, hockey) lanzar [22]; 5 **to shoot a film** rodar [24] una película.

shooting noun tiro Masc. al blanco.

shop noun tienda Fem.; **a record shop** una tienda de discos; **a shoe shop** una zapatería; **to go round the shops** ir [8] de tiendas.

shop assistant noun dependiente Masc., dependienta Fem.; **Brad's a shop assistant** Brad trabaja de dependiente.

shopkeeper noun tendero Masc., tendera Fem.

shoplifter noun ladrón Masc., ladrona Fem.

shoplifting noun hurto Masc. en las tiendas.

shopping noun compras Fem. plural; **can you put the shopping away?** ¿puedes guardar las compras?; **I've got a lot of shopping to do** tengo muchas cosas que comprar; **to go shopping** ir [8] a hacer la compra; (for fun, to buy clothes or presents) ir [8] de compras.

shopping centre noun centro Masc. comercial.

shop window noun escaparate Masc.

shore noun orilla Fem. del mar.

short adjective 1 corto/corta; **a short dress** un vestido corto; **she has short hair** tiene el pelo corto; 2 (person) bajo/baja (in height); **he's quite short** es bastante bajo; 3 **a short break** un descanso corto; **a short visit** una visita corta; **to go for a short walk** ir [8] a dar un pequeño paseo; **it's a short walk from the station** es un pequeño paseo desde la estación; 4 **a short time ago** hace poco tiempo; 5 **to be short of** no tener mucho; **we're a bit short of money at the moment** no tenemos mucho dinero en este momento; **we're getting short of time** se nos está acabando el tiempo.

shortage noun escasez Fem.

shortbread noun galleta Fem. de mantequilla.

shortcrust pastry noun pasta Fem. quebrada.

short cut noun atajo Masc.; **we took a short cut** tomamos un atajo.

shorten verb acortar [17].

shortly adverb dentro de poco.

shorts plural noun shorts Masc. plural; **a pair of shorts** unos shorts; **my red shorts** mis shorts rojos.

short-sighted adjective miope; **I'm short-sighted** soy miope.

shotgun noun escopeta Fem.

should verb 1 deber [18] ('should' is translated by the conditional tense of 'deber'); **you should ask Simon** deberías preguntárselo a Simon; **the potatoes should be cooked now** las patatas deberían estar hechas ya;

2 (*'should have' is translated by the past conditional tense of 'deber'*) **you should have told me** deberías habérmelo dicho; **I shouldn't have stayed** no deberías haberte quedado; **3** (*'should' meaning 'would' is translated by the conditional tense of the appropriate verb*) **I should forget it if I were you** yo en tu lugar me olvidaría del asunto; **4 I should think** yo diría; **I should think he's forgotten** yo diría que se ha olvidado.

shoulder *noun* hombro *Masc.*

shoulder bag *noun* bolso *Masc.*

shout *noun* grito *Masc.*
shout *verb* gritar [17]; **stop shouting!** ¡deja de gritar!; **they shouted at us to come back** nos gritaron que volviésemos.

shovel *noun* pala *Fem.*

show *noun* **1** (*on stage*) espectáculo *Masc.*; **we went to see a show** fuimos a ver un espectáculo; **2** (*on TV*) programa *Masc.*; **he has a TV show** tiene un programa en la tele; **3** (*exhibition*) salón *Masc.*; **the motor show** el salón del automóvil.
show *verb* **1** enseñar [17]; **to show something to somebody** enseñar a alguien algo; **I'll show you my photos** te enseñaré mis fotos; **to show somebody how to do** enseñar algo a alguien cómo hacer; **he showed me how to make pancakes** me enseñó cómo hacer crepes; **2 it shows!** ¡ya se ve!
● **to show off** (*be quiet*) presumir [19]; **stop showing off!** ¡déjate de hacer fanfarronadas!

shower *noun* **1** (*in a bathroom*) ducha *Fem.*; **to have a shower** ducharse [17]; **2** (*of rain*) chaparrón *Masc.*

show-off *noun* fanfarrón *Masc.*, fanfarrona *Fem.*

shriek *verb* gritar [17].

shrimp *noun* camarón *Masc.*

shrine *noun* santuario *Masc.*

shrink *verb* encoger [3].

Shrove Tuesday *noun* martes *Masc.* de Carnaval.

shrug *verb* **to shrug your shoulders** encogerse [3] de hombros.

shuffle *verb* **to shuffle the cards** barajar [17] las cartas.

shut *adjective* cerrado/cerrada; **the shops are shut** las tiendas están cerradas.
shut *verb* cerrar [29]; **can you shut the door please?** ¿puedes cerrar la puerta por favor?; **the shops shut at six** las tiendas cierran a las seis.
● **to shut up** (*be quiet*) callarse [17]; **shut up!** ¡cállate!.

shuttlecock *noun* volante *Masc.*

shy *adjective* tímido/tímida.

shyness *noun* timidez *Fem.*

Sicily *noun* Sicilia *Fem.*

sick *adjective* **1** (*ill*) enfermo/enferma; **2 to be sick** (*vomit*) devolver [45]; **I was sick several times** devolví varias veces; **to feel sick** tener [9] ganas de devolver; **3 a sick joke** una broma de mal gusto; **4 to be sick of something** estar [2] harto/harta de algo; **I'm sick of**

a
b
c
d
e
f
g
h
i
j
k
l
m
n
o
p
q
r
s
t
u
v
w
x
y
z

staying at home every night estoy harto de quedarme en casa todas las noches.

sickness *noun* enfermedad *Fem.*

side *noun* **1** lado *Masc.*; **on the other side of the street** al otro lado de la calle; **on the wrong side** en el lado equivocado; **I'm on your side** (*I agree with you*) estoy de tu lado; **2** (*edge*) borde *Masc.*; **at the side of the road** al borde de la carretera; **by the side of the pool** al borde de la piscina; **by the side of the river** a la orilla del río; **3** (*team*) equipo *Masc.*; **she plays on our side** juega en nuestro equipo; **4 to take sides** tomar [17] partido; **5 side by side** uno al lado del otro.

sideboard *noun* aparador *Masc.*

siege *noun* sitio *Masc.*

sieve *noun* tamiz *Masc.*

sigh *noun* suspiro *Masc.*
sigh *verb* suspirar [17].

sight *noun* **1** espectáculo *Masc.*; **it was a marvellous sight** era un espectáculo maravilloso; **2 at the sight of** a la vista de; **at first sight** a primera vista; **3** (*eyesight*) vista *Fem.*; **to have poor sight** tener [9] mala vista; **to know somebody by sight** conocer [35] a alguien de vista; **I'd lost sight of them** los había perdido de vista; **4 to see the sights** visitar [17] los lugares de interés.

sightseeing *noun* **to do some sightseeing** visitar [17] los lugares de interés.

sign *noun* **1** (*notice*) letrero *Masc.*; **there's a sign on the door** hay un letrero en la puerta; **2** (*trace, indication*) señal *Fem.*; **3** (*of the Zodiac*) signo *Masc.*; **what sign are you?** ¿de qué signo eres?
sign *verb* **1** firmar [17]; **to sign a cheque** firmar un cheque; **2** (*using sign language*) comunicarse [31] por señas.

● **to sign on** (*as unemployed*) inscribirse [17] al paro.

signal *noun* señal *Fem.*

signature *noun* firma *Fem.*

significance *noun* importancia *Fem.*

significant *adjective* importante.

sign language *noun* lenguaje *Masc.* de gestos.

signpost *noun* señal *Fem.*

silence *noun* silencio *Masc.*

silent *adjective* silencioso/silenciosa.

silk *noun* seda *Fem.*
silk *adjective* de seda; **a silk shirt** una blusa de seda.

silky *adjective* sedoso/sedosa.

silly *adjective* tonto/tonta; **it was a really silly thing to do** hacer eso fue una verdadera tontería.

silver *noun* plata *Fem.*
silver *adjective* de plata; **a silver spoon** una cuchara de plata.

similar *adjective* parecido/parecida.

similarity *noun* parecido *Masc.*

simple *adjective* sencillo/sencilla.

simplify *verb* simplificar [31].

simply *adverb* sencillamente.

sin *noun* pecado *Masc.*

since *preposition, adverb*
since *conjunction* **1** desde (*notice that Spanish uses the present tense where English uses 'have done' or 'have been doing'*) **I've been in Madrid since Saturday** llevo en Madrid desde el sábado; **I've been learning Spanish since last year** estoy aprendiendo español desde el año pasado; **2** desde que (*the same thing happens with tenses here as above*) **since I have known her** desde que la conozco; **since I've been learning Spanish** desde que estoy aprendiendo español; **3 I haven't seen her since** no la he visto desde entonces; **I haven't seen her since Monday** no la he visto desde el lunes; **since when?** ¿desde cuándo?; **4** (*because*) como; **since it was raining, the match was cancelled** como estaba lloviendo, cancelaron el partido.

sincere *adjective* sincero/sincera.

sincerely *adverb* **Yours sincerely** Atentamente.

sing *verb* cantar [17].

singer *noun* cantante *Masc./Fem.*

singing *noun* **1** canto *Masc.*; **a singing lesson** una lección de canto; **2 I like singing** me gusta cantar.

single *noun* (*ticket*) billete *Masc.* de ida; **a single to Barcelona** un billete de ida para Barcelona.
single *adjective* **1** (*not married*) soltero/soltera; **2 a single room** una habitación individual; **a single bed** una cama individual; **3 not a single** ... ni un solo/ni una sola ...; **I haven't had a single reply** no he tenido ni una sola respuesta; **4 every single day** todos los días; **every single morning** todas las mañanas.

single parent *noun* **she's a single parent** es madre soltera; **a single-parent family** una familia monoparental.

singular *noun* singular *Masc.*; **in the singular** en singular.

sink *noun* **1** (*in kitchen*) fregadero *Masc.*; **2** (*in bathroom*) lavabo *Masc.*
sink *verb* hundirse [19].

sir *noun* señor *Masc.*; **yes, sir** sí, señor.

sister *noun* hermana *Fem.*; **my sister's ten** mi hermana tiene diez años.

sister-in-law *noun* cuñada *Fem.*

sit *verb* **1** sentarse [29]; **you can sit on the sofa** puedes sentarte en el sofá; **I can sit on the floor** me puedo sentar en el suelo; **2 to be sitting** estar [2] sentado; **Leila was sitting on the sofa** Leila estaba sentada en el sofá; **3 to sit an exam** presentarse [17] a un examen; **she's sitting her driving test on Thursday** se presenta al examen de conducir el jueves.

- **to sit down** sentarse [29]; **he sat down on a chair** se sentó en una silla; **do sit down** siéntate.

site *noun* **1 a building site** una obra; **2 a camping site** un camping.

sitting room *noun* salón *Masc.*

situation *noun* situación *Fem*.

six *number* seis *Masc*.; **Tom's six** Tom tiene seis años; **it's six o'clock** son las seis.

sixteen *number* dieciséis *Masc*.; **Hannah's sixteen** Hannah tiene dieciséis años.

sixth *noun* 1 (*fraction*) **a sixth** una sexta parte; 2 **the sixth of July** el seis de julio.
sixth *adjective* sexto/sexta; **on the sixth floor** en el sexto piso.

sixties *plural noun* **the sixties** los años sesenta; **in the sixties** en los años sesenta.

sixty *number* sesenta *Masc*.; **she's sixty** tiene sesenta años; **sixty-five** sesenta y cinco.

size *noun* 1 tamaño *Masc*.; **it depends on the size of the house** depende del tamaño de la casa; 2 (*precise measurements*) medidas *Fem. plural*; **what size is the window?** ¿qué medidas tiene la ventana?; 3 (*in clothes*) talla *Fem*.; **what size do you take?** ¿qué talla usas?; 4 (*of shoes*) número *Masc*.; **I take a size thirty-eight** calzo el número treinta y ocho.

skate *noun* 1 **an ice skate** un patín de hielo; 2 **a roller skate** un patín de ruedas.
skate *verb* 1 (*ice-skate*) hacer [7] patinaje sobre hielo; 2 (*roller-skate*) hacer [7] patinaje sobre ruedas.

skateboard *noun* monopatín *Masc*.

skateboarding *noun* **to go skateboarding** patinar [17] con el monopatín.

skater *noun* patinador *Masc*., patinadora *Fem*.

skating *noun* 1 (*ice*) patinaje *Masc*. sobre hielo; **to go skating** ir [8] a patinar sobre hielo; 2 **roller-skating** patinaje *Masc*. sobre ruedas; **to go roller-skating** ir [8] a patinar sobre ruedas.

skating rink *noun* pista *Fem*. de patinaje.

sketch *noun* 1 (*drawing*) boceto *Masc*.; 2 (*comedy routine*) sketch *Masc*.

ski *noun* esquí *Masc*.
ski *verb* esquiar [32].

ski boot *noun* bota *Fem*. de esquí.

skid *verb* derrapar [17]; **the car skidded** el coche derrapó.

skier *noun* esquiador *Masc*., esquiadora *Fem*.

skiing *noun* esquí *Masc*.; **to go skiing** ir [8] a esquiar.

skilful *noun* habilidoso/habilidosa.

skill *noun* habilidad *Fem*.

ski lift *noun* telesquí *Masc*.

skill *noun* habilidad *Fem*.; **it's not one of my skills** no es una de mis habilidades.

skimmed milk *noun* leche *Fem*. desnatada.

skin *noun* piel *Fem*.

skinhead *noun* cabeza *Masc*. rapada, cabeza *Fem*. rapada.

skinny *adjective* flaco/flaca.

skip noun (for rubbish) contenedor Masc.

skip verb **1** saltarse [17] (a meal, part of a book); **I skipped a few chapters** me salté algunos capítulos; **2 to skip a lesson** hacer [7] pellas de una clase (informal).

ski pants noun pantalones Masc. plural de esquí.

skipping rope noun comba Fem.

ski suit noun traje Masc. de esquí.

skirt noun falda Fem.; **a long skirt** una falda larga; **a straight skirt** una falda de tubo; **a mini-skirt** una minifalda.

sky noun cielo Masc.

skyscraper noun rascacielos Masc. (does not change in the plural).

slam verb cerrar [29] de un portazo; **she slammed the door** cerró la puerta de un portazo.

slang noun argot Masc.

slap noun **1** (on the face) bofetada Fem.; **2** (on the leg, bottom) azote Masc.

slap verb **to slap somebody** (on the face) dar [4] una bofetada a alguien (on the leg or bottom) dar [4] un azote a alguien.

slate noun pizarra Fem.

slave noun esclavo Masc., esclava Fem.

sledge noun trineo Masc.

sledging noun **to go sledging** ir [8] en trineo.

sleep noun sueño Masc.; **six hours' sleep** seis horas de sueño; **I had a good sleep** dormí bien; **to go to**

sleep dormirse [51].

sleep verb dormir [51]; **she's sleeping** está durmiendo.

sleeping bag noun saco Masc. de dormir.

sleeping pill noun somnífero Masc.

sleepy adjective **to be sleepy** tener [9] sueño; **I feel sleepy** tengo sueño; **I was getting sleepy** me estaba entrando sueño.

sleeve noun manga Fem.; **a long-sleeved jumper** un jersey de manga larga; **a short-sleeved shirt** una camisa de manga corta; **to roll up your sleeves** arremangarse [28].

slice noun **1** (of bread, cheese) rebanada Fem.; **2** (of meat) loncha Fem.; **a slice of ham** una loncha de jamón; **3** (of cake) trozo Masc.; **4** (a round slice: of lemon, tomato, etc.) rodaja Fem.

slice verb **to slice something** cortar [17] algo en rebanadas (or 'lonchas', 'trozos', etc, depending on what you are slicing: see noun translations above).

slide noun **1** (photo) diapositiva Fem.; **2** (hairslide) pasador Masc.; **3** (for sliding down) tobogán Masc.

slight adjective ligero/ligera; **there's a slight problem** hay un pequeño problema.

slightly adverb ligeramente.

slim adjective delgado/delgada. **slim** verb adelgazar [22]; **I'm slimming** estoy adelgazando.

slip noun **1** (mistake) error Masc.; **2** (petticoat) combinación Fem.

a
b
c
d
e
f
g
h
i
j
k
l
m
n
o
p
q
r
s
t
u
v
w
x
y
z

slip *verb* **1** (*slide*) resbalarse [17]; **2 the jar slipped out of my hands** el frasco se me resbaló de las manos; **3 it slipped my mind** se me olvidó completamente.

slipper *noun* zapatilla *Fem.*

slippery *adjective* resbaladizo/resbaladiza.

slope *noun* cuesta *Fem.*

slow *adjective* **1** lento/lenta; **the service is a bit slow** el servicio es un poco lento; **2 my watch is slow** mi reloj está atrasado.
● **to slow down** reducir [60] la velocidad (*a car*).

slowly *adverb* despacio; **he got up slowly** se levantó despacio; **can you speak more slowly, please?** ¿puedes hablar más despacio, por favor?

slum *noun* barrio *Masc.* bajo.

smack *noun* **1** (*on the face*) bofetada *Fem.*; **2** (*on the leg or bottom*) azote *Masc.*
smack *verb* **to smack somebody** (*on the face*) dar [4] una bofetada a alguien; (*on the leg or bottom*) dar [4] un azote a alguien.

small *adjective* pequeño/pequeña; **a small dog** un perro pequeño.

smart *adjective* **1** (*well-dressed, posh*) elegante; **a smart restaurant** un restaurante elegante; **2** (*clever*) inteligente.

smash *verb* romper [40]; **they smashed the window** rompieron la ventana.

smashing *adjective* fantástico/fantástica.

smell *noun* olor *Masc.*; **a nasty smell** un mal olor; **there's a smell of burning** huele a quemado.
smell *verb* **1** oler [39]; **I can't smell anything** no huelo nada; **I can smell lavender** huele a lavanda; **2** (*smell bad*) oler [39] mal; **the drains smell** las alcantarillas huelen mal.

smelly *adjective* apestoso/apestosa.

smile *noun* sonrisa *Fem.*
smile *verb* sonreír [61].

smoke *noun* humo *Masc.*
smoke *verb* fumar [17]; **she doesn't smoke** no fuma; **he smokes a pipe** fuma en pipa.

smoked *adjective* ahumado/ahumada; **smoked salmon** salmón ahumado.

smoker *noun* fumador *Masc.*, fumadora *Fem.*

smoking *noun* 'no smoking' 'prohibido fumar'; **to give up smoking** dejar [17] de fumar.

smooth *adjective* **1** (*stone or surface*) liso/lisa; **a smooth surface** una superficie lisa; **2** (*skin*) suave.

SMS *noun* SMS *Masc.*; **an SMS message** un mensaje SMS.

smuggle *verb* **to smuggle something** pasar [17] algo de contrabando.

smuggler *noun* **1** contrabandista *Masc./Fem.*; **2 a drugs smuggler** un/una traficante de drogas.

smuggling *noun* **1** contrabando *Masc.*; **2 drugs smuggling** tráfico *Masc.* de drogas; **arms smuggling** tráfico *Masc.* de armas.

snack *noun* tentempié *Masc.*

snack bar noun cafetería Fem., bocatería Fem.

snail noun caracol Masc.

snake noun serpiente Fem.

snap verb 1 (break) romperse [40]; **2 to snap your fingers** chasquear [17] los dedos.

snatch verb 1 arrebatar [17]; **to snatch something from somebody** arrebatar algo a alguien; **he snatched my book** me arrebató el libro; **2** (steal) robar [17]; **she had her bag snatched** le robaron el bolso.

sneak verb **to sneak in** entrar [17] a escondidas; **to sneak out** salir [63] a escondidas; **he sneaked up on me** se acercó a mí sin que yo me diese cuenta.

sneeze noun estornudo Masc.
sneeze verb estornudar [17].

sniff verb olisquear [17].

snob noun esnob Masc./Fem.

snobbery noun esnobismo Masc.

snooker noun snooker Masc.; **to play snooker** jugar [27] al snooker.

snore verb roncar [31].

snow noun nieve Fem.
snow verb nevar [29]; **it's snowing** está nevando; **it's going to snow** va a nevar.

snowball noun bola Fem. de nieve.

snow drift noun montón Masc. de nieve.

snowman noun muñeco Masc. de nieve.

snowy adjective **it was very snowy** hubo mucha nieve.

so conjunction, adverb **1** tan; **he's so lazy** es tan vago; **the coffee's so hot I can't drink it** este café está tan caliente que no puedo beberlo; **2 not so** no tan; **our house is like yours, but not so big** nuestra casa es parecida a la tuya pero no tan grande; **3 so much** (after a verb) tanto; **I hate it so much!** ¡lo odio tanto!; **4 so much** (before a noun) tanto/tanta; **I have so much work to do** tengo tanto trabajo que hacer; **5 so many** (before a noun) tantos/tantas; **we've got so many problems** tenemos tantos problemas; **6** (therefore) así que; **he got up late so he missed his train** se levantó tarde así que perdió el tren; **7** (starting a sentence: there is no direct translation) **so what's your name?** ¿y cómo te llamas?; **so what shall we do?** ¿y entonces qué hacemos?; **so what?** ¿y qué?; **8 so do I, so did I** yo también; **'I live in Leeds' – 'so do I'** 'vivo en Leeds' – 'yo también'; **so am I, so was I** yo también; **so do we, so did we** nosotros también; **'I have a headache' – 'so do I'** 'me duele la cabeza' – 'a mí también'; **'I like Miró' – 'so do I'** 'me gusta Miró' – 'a mí tambien'; **9 I think so** creo que sí; **I hope so** espero que sí.

soap noun **1** jabón Masc.; **a cake of soap** una pastilla de jabón; **2** (soap opera: on TV) telenovela Fem.

soap powder noun jabón Masc. en polvo.

sober adjective **to be sober** estar [2] sobrio/sobria.

a

b **soccer** noun fútbol Masc.; **to play soccer** jugar (27) al fútbol.

c **social** adjective social.

socialism noun socialismo Masc.

d **socialist** noun, socialista Masc./
Fem.

e **socialist** adjective socialista.

f **social security** noun
1 asistencia Fem. social; **to be on
social security** recibir [19]

g asistencia social; **2 the social
security** (the system) la seguridad

h social.

i **social worker** noun asistente
Masc./Fem. social; **she's a social

j worker** es asistente social.

k **society** noun sociedad Fem.

sociology noun sociología Fem.

l
sock noun calcetín Masc.; **a pair of

m socks** un par de calcetines.

sofa noun sofá Masc.

n
sofa bed noun sofá-cama Masc.

o
soft adjective suave; ★ **to have a soft

p spot for somebody** tener [9]
debilidad por alguien.

q
soft drink noun refresco Masc.

r
software noun software Masc.

s
soft toy noun muñeco Masc. de

t peluche.

u **soil** noun tierra Fem.

v **solar energy** noun energía Fem.
solar.

w
soldier noun soldado Masc./Fem.

x
solicitor noun abogado Masc.,

y abogada Fem.; **she's a solicitor** es
abogada.

z

solid adjective **1** macizo/maciza; **a
table made of solid pine** una mesa
de pino macizo; **a solid gold ring** un
anillo de oro macizo; **solid silver**
plata maciza; **2** (not flimsy) sólido/
sólida; **a solid structure** una
estructura sólida.

solo noun solo Masc.; **a guitar solo**
un solo de guitarra.
solo adjective, adverb en solitario; **a
solo album** un álbum en solitario;
to play solo tocar [31] en solitario.

soloist noun solista Masc./Fem.

some adjective, adverb **1** (with a
singular noun) un poco de; **would
you like some butter?** ¿quieres un
poco de mantequilla?; **may I have
some salad?** ¿puedo tomar un poco
de ensalada?; **can you lend me
some money?** ¿puedes prestarme
un poco de dinero?; **2** (with a plural
noun) unos/unas; **I've bought some
apples** he comprado unas
manzanas; **we picked some
flowers** cogimos unas flores;
3 (referring to something that has
already been mentioned, 'some' is not
translated) **'would you like butter?'
– 'thanks, I've got some'** ¿quieres
mantequilla?' – 'gracias ya tengo';
he's eaten some of it ya ha comido
un poco; **4** (certain) algunos/
algunas; **some people think he's
wrong** algunas personas piensan
que él no tiene razón; **5 some day**
algún día.

somebody, **someone** pronoun
alguien; **there's somebody in the
garden** hay alguien en el jardín.

somehow *adverb* **1** de alguna forma; **I've got to finish this essay somehow** tengo que terminar esta composición de alguna forma; **2 I somehow think they won't come** no sé por qué, pero creo que no van a venir.

somersault *noun* voltereta *Fem*.

something *pronoun* algo; **I've got something to tell you** tengo algo que decirte; **something pretty** algo bonito; **something interesting** algo interesante; **there's something wrong** algo va mal; **their house is really something!** ¡su casa es increíble!; **a guy called Colin something or other** un tipo llamado Colin, o algo así.

sometime *adverb* un día de estos; **give me a ring sometime** llámame un día de estos; **I'll ring you sometime next week** te llamaré un día de la semana que viene.

sometimes *adverb* a veces; **I sometimes take the train** a veces cojo el tren.

somewhere *adverb* en algún sitio; **I've put my bag down somewhere** he puesto mi bolso en algún sitio; **I've met you somewhere before** te he conocido antes en algún sitio.

son *noun* hijo *Masc*.

song *noun* canción *Fem*.

son-in-law *noun* yerno *Masc*.

soon *adverb* **1** pronto; **it will soon be the holidays** pronto llegarán las vacaciones; **see you soon!** ¡hasta pronto!; **it's too soon** es demasiado pronto; **2 as soon as** tan pronto como; **as soon as she arrives** tan pronto como llegue; **as soon as possible** tan pronto como sea posible.

sooner *adverb* **1** antes; **we should have started sooner** deberíamos haber empezado antes; **2 I'd sooner wait** prefiero esperar; **★ sooner or later** tarde o temprano.

soprano *noun* soprano *Masc./Fem*.

sore *noun* llaga *Fem*.
sore *adjective* he has a sore leg le duele la pierna; **my arm's sore** me duele el brazo; **★ it's a sore point** es un tema delicado.

sorry *adjective* **1 I'm really sorry** lo siento mucho; **I'm sorry I forgot your birthday** siento haberme olvidado de tu cumpleaños; **2 sorry to disturb you** perdona que te moleste; **3 sorry!** ¡perdón!; **4 sorry?** ¿cómo?; **5 to feel sorry for somebody** compadecer [35] a alguien; **6 to say you're sorry** pedir [57] perdón.

sort *noun* tipo *Masc*.; **what sort of music do you like?** ¿qué tipo de música te gusta?; **all sorts of** todo tipo de; **for all sorts of reasons** por todo tipo de razones.

● **to sort something out 1** ordenar [17] algo (*room, desk, papers, possessions*); **I must sort out my room tonight** tengo que ordenar mi habitación esta noche; **2** solucionar [17] (*problem, arrangement*); **Liz is sorting it out** Liz se está ocupando de ello.

a
b
c
d
e
f
g
h
i
j
k
l
m
n
o
p
q
r
s
t
u
v
w
x
y
z

soul *noun* **1** alma *Fem.* (*even though 'alma' is feminine, it takes 'el' and 'un' in the singular*) **the soul** el alma; **2** (*music*) soul *Masc.*

sound *noun* **1** (*noise*) ruido *Masc.*; **the sound of voices** el ruido de voces; **2** (*volume*) volumen *Masc.*; **to turn down the sound** bajar el volumen.
sound *verb* **it sounds easy** parece fácil; **it sounds as if she's happy** parece que está contenta.

sound asleep *adjective* profundamente dormido/dormida.

sound effect *noun* efecto *Masc.* sonoro.

soundtrack *noun* banda *Fem.* sonora.

soup *noun* **1** (*clear*) consomé *Masc.*; **2** (*thick*) sopa *Fem.*; **3** (*pureed*) crema *Fem.*; **mushroom soup** crema de champiñones.

soup plate *noun* plato *Masc.* de sopa.

soup spoon *noun* cuchara *Fem.* de sopera.

sour *adjective* **1** (*taste*) agrio/agria; **2 the milk's gone sour** la leche se ha cortado.

south *noun* sur *Masc.*; **in the south** en el sur.
south *adjective, adverb* sur (*never changes*); **the south side** la parte sur; **a south wind** un viento del sur; **south of Paris** al sur de París.

South Africa *noun* Sudáfrica *Fem.*

South America *noun* Sudamérica *Fem.*

South American *noun* suramericano *Masc.*, suramericana *Fem.*
South American *adjective* suramericano/suramericana.

southeast *noun* sureste *Masc.*
southeast *adjective* sureste (*never changes*); **in southeast England** en el sureste de Inglaterra.

South Pole *noun* Polo *Masc.* Sur.

southwest *noun* suroeste *Masc.*
southwest *adjective* suroeste (*never changes*); **in southwest England** en el suroeste de Inglaterra.

souvenir *noun* recuerdo *Masc.*

soya *noun* soja *Fem.*

space *noun* **1** (*room*) sitio *Masc.*; **is there enough space?** ¿hay sitio suficiente?; **there's enough space for two** hay sitio suficiente para dos; **2** (*gap*) espacio *Masc.*; **leave a space** deja un espacio; **3** (*outer space*) espacio *Masc.*; **in space** en el espacio.

spacecraft *noun* nave *Fem.* espacial.

spade *noun* **1** pala *Fem.*; **2** (*in cards*) pica *Fem.*; **the queen of spades** la reina de picas.

spaghetti *noun* espaguetis *Masc. plural.*

Spain *noun* España *Fem.*

Spaniard *noun* español *Masc.*, española *Fem.*

spaniel *noun* spaniel *Masc.*

Spanish *noun* **1** (*language*) español *Masc.*; **to speak Spanish** hablar [17] español; **say it in**

Spanish dilo en español; **I'm learning Spanish** estoy aprendiendo español; **2 the Spanish** (*people*) los españoles *Masc. plural*.
Spanish *adjective* **1** español/española; **Pedro's Spanish** Pedro es español; **2** de español (*a teacher or lesson*); **the Spanish class** la clase de español.

spanner *noun* llave *Fem.* inglesa.

spare *adjective* **1** (*part, battery*) de repuesto; **a spare battery** una batería de repuesto; **2** (*extra*) de más; **we have a spare ticket** tenemos una entrada de más.
spare *verb* **I can't spare the time** no tengo tiempo para eso; **can you spare a moment?** ¿tienes un momento libre?; **I don't have any money to spare** no me sobra el dinero.

spare room *noun* habitación *Fem.* de invitados.

spare time *noun* tiempo *Masc.* libre; **in my spare time** en mi tiempo libre.

spare wheel *noun* rueda *Fem.* de repuesto.

sparrow *noun* gorrión *Masc.*

speak *verb* **1** hablar [17]; **do you speak Spanish?** ¿hablas español?; **spoken Spanish** el español hablado; **'Spanish spoken here'** 'aquí se habla español'; **2 to speak to somebody** hablar [17] con alguien; **she's speaking to Mike** está hablando con Mike; **I've never spoken to her** nunca he hablado con ella; **I'll speak to him about it**

hablaré sobre ello con él; **3 who's speaking?** (*on the phone*) ¿quién es?; **Mike speaking** soy Mike.

speaker *noun* **1** (*on a music system*) altavoz *Masc.*; **2** (*at a public lecture*) conferenciante *Masc./Fem.*; **3** (*of a language*) **a Spanish speaker** un hablante de español; **an English speaker** un hablante de inglés.

spear *noun* lanza *Fem.*

special *adjective* especial.

specialist *noun* especialista *Masc./Fem.*

specialize *verb* **to specialize in** especializarse [22] en.

specially *adverb* especialmente; **not specially** no especialmente; **the poems have been specially chosen for small children** los poemas han sido escogidos especialmente para niños pequeños; **I came specially in order to see you** vine especialmente para verte.

spectacles *noun* gafas *Fem. plural*.

spectacular *adjective* espectacular.

spectator *noun* espectador *Masc.*, espectadora *Fem.*

speech *noun* discurso *Masc.*; **to make a speech** dar [4] un discurso.

speechless *adjective* **1** sin habla; **I was speechless** me quedé sin habla; **2 to be speechless with rage** quedarse [17] mudo de cólera.

speed *noun* velocidad *Fem.*; **what speed was he doing?** ¿a qué

a b c d e f g h i j k l m n o p q r s t u v w x y z

a
b

velocidad iba?; **a twelve-speed bike** una bici de doce marchas.
• **to speed up** acelerar [17].

c
d
e

speeding *noun* **he was fined for speeding** le multaron por exceso de velocidad.

speed limit *noun* límite *Masc.* de velocidad.

f
g
h
i
j
k
l
m

spell *noun* **1** (*of time*) periodo *Masc.*; **2** (*talking about weather*) **a cold spell** una ola de frío; **sunny spells** intervalos de sol.
spell *verb* **1** (*in writing*) escribir [52]; **how do you spell it?** ¿cómo se escribe?; **how do you spell your surname?** ¿cómo se escribe tu apellido?; **2** (*out loud*) deletrear [17]; **shall I spell it for you?** ¿se lo deletreo?

n
o

spelling *noun* ortografía *Fem.*; **a spelling mistake** una falta de ortografía.

p
q

spelling checker *noun* corrector *Masc.* ortográfico.

r
s
t
u
v

spend *verb* **1** gastar [17] (*money*); **I've spent all my money** me he gastado todo el dinero; **2** pasar [17] (*time*); **we spent three days in Barcelona** pasamos tres días en Barcelona; **she spends her time writing letters** pasa el tiempo escribiendo cartas.

w

spice *noun* especia *Fem.*

x
y

spicy *adjective* picante; **I don't like spicy food** no me gustan los platos picantes.

z

spider *noun* araña *Fem.*

spill *verb* derramar [17]; **I've spilled my wine on the carpet** he derramado vino en la alfombra.

spinach *noun* espinacas *Fem. plural*; **do you like spinach?** ¿te gustan las espinacas?

spire *noun* aguja *Fem.*

spirit *noun* **1** (*energy*) brío *Masc.*; **2 to get into the spirit of the occasion** entrar [17] en el ambiente.

spirits *noun* **1** (*alcohol*) bebidas *Fem. plural* alcohólicas; **2 to be in good spirits** estar [2] de buen humor.

spit *verb* escupir [19]; **to spit something out** escupir algo.

spite *noun* **1 in spite of** a pesar de; **we decided to go in spite of the rain** decidimos ir a pesar de la lluvia; **2** (*nastiness*) maldad *Fem.*; **to do something out of spite** hacer [7] algo por maldad.

spiteful *adjective* **1** (*person*) malo/ mala; **2** (*comment*) malicioso/ maliciosa.

splash *noun* **1** (*noise*) **we heard a splash** oímos el ruido de algo que caía al agua; **2 a splash of colour** un toque de color.
splash *verb* salpicar [31].

splendid *adjective* espléndido/ espléndida.

splinter *noun* astilla *Fem.*

split *verb* **1** (*with an axe or a knife*) partir [19]; **to split a piece of wood** partir un trozo de madera; **2** (*come apart*) rajarse [17]; **the lining has split** el forro se ha rajado; **3** (*divide up*) dividirse [19]; **they split the**

money between them se dividieron el dinero entre ellos.

● **to split up 1** (*a married couple or group*) separarse [17]; **2 she's split up with her boyfriend** ha roto con su novio.

spoil *verb* **1** arruinar [17]; **it completely spoiled the evening** arruinó la tarde completamente; **to spoil the surprise** arruinar la sorpresa; **2** malcriar [32] (*a child*).

spoiled *adjective* malcriado/malcriada; **a spoiled child** un niño malcriado.

spoilsport *noun* aguafiestas *Masc./Fem.* (*does not change in the plural*).

spokesperson *noun* portavoz *Masc./Fem.*

sponge *noun* esponja *Fem.*

sponge cake *noun* bizcocho *Masc.*

sponsor *noun* patrocinador *Masc.*, patrocinadora *Fem.*
sponsor *verb* patrocinar [17].

spooky *adjective* espeluznante.

spoon *noun* cuchara *Fem.*; **a soup spoon** una cuchara sopera; **a teaspoon** una cucharilla.

spoonful *noun* (*large*) cucharada *Fem.*; (*small*) cucharadita *Fem.*

sport *noun* deporte *Masc.*; **to be good at sport** tener [9] facilidad para los deportes; **my favourite sport** mi deporte favorito.

sports bag *noun* bolsa *Fem.* de deportes.

sports car *noun* coche *Masc.* deportivo.

sports centre *noun* polideportivo *Masc.*

sports club *noun* club *Masc.* deportivo.

sportsman *noun* deportista *Masc.*

sportswear *noun* ropa *Fem.* de deporte.

sportswoman *noun* deportista *Fem.*

spot *noun* **1** (*in fabric*) lunar *Masc.*; **a red tie with black spots** una corbata roja con lunares negros; **2** (*on your skin*) grano *Masc.*; **I've got spots** tengo granos; **to be covered in spots** estar [2] cubierto de granos; **3** (*stain*) mancha *Fem.*; **4** (*place*) sitio *Masc.*; **a beautiful spot** un sitio precioso; **5** (*spotlight*) foco *Masc.*; (*in the home*) luz *Fem.* direccional.
spot *verb* **1** divisar [17] (*a person or object*); **I spotted her in the crowd** la divisé entre la multitud; **2** encontrar [24] (*an error*).

spotlight *noun* **1** foco *Masc.*; **2** (*in the home*) luz *Fem.* direccional.

spotty *adjective* (*pimply*) lleno de granos/llena de granos.

sprain *noun* esguince *Masc.*
sprain *verb* **to sprain your ankle** hacerse [7] un esguince en el tobillo.

spray *noun* (*spray can*) espray *Masc.*

spread *verb* **1** (*news or a disease*) propagarse [28]; **2** extender [36] (*butter, jam, cement, glue, etc*).

spring *noun* **1** (*the season*) primavera *Fem.*; **in the spring** en primavera; **spring flowers** flores de primavera; **2** (*made of metal*) muelle

a
b
c
d
e
f
g
h
i
j
k
l
m
n
o
p
q
r
s
t
u
v
w
x
y
z

Masc.; **3** (*providing water*) manantial *Masc.*

springtime *noun* primavera *Fem.*; **in springtime** en primavera.

spring water *noun* agua *Fem.* de manantial.

sprint *noun* esprint *Masc.*
sprint *verb* correr [18] a toda velocidad.

sprout *noun* (*Brussels sprout*) col *Fem.* de Bruselas.

spy *noun* espía *Masc./Fem.*
spy *verb* **to spy on somebody** espiar [32] a alguien.

spying *noun* espionaje *Masc.*

square *noun* **1** (*shape*) cuadrado *Masc.*; **2** (*in a town or village*) plaza *Fem.*; **the village square** la plaza del pueblo; ★ **to go back to square one** volver [45] a empezar de cero.

square *adjective* cuadrado/cuadrada; **a square box** una caja cuadrada; **three square metres** tres metros cuadrados; **the room is four metres square** la habitación tiene cuatro metros cuadrados.

squash *noun* **1** (*drink*) **lemon squash** limonada *Fem.*; **orange squash** naranjada *Fem.*; **2** (*sport*) squash *Masc.*; **to play squash** jugar [27] al squash.

squeak *verb* **1** (*door, hinge*) chirriar [32]; **2** (*person, animal*) chillar [17].

squeeze *verb* **1** apretar [29] (*somebody's arm, hand or a toothpaste tube*); **2** exprimir [19] (*a lemon or an orange*).

squid *noun* calamar *Masc.*

squirrel *noun* ardilla *Fem.*

stab *verb* apuñalar [17].

stable *noun* cuadra *Fem.*
stable *adjective* estable.

stack *noun* **1** (*pile*) montón *Masc.*; **2 stacks of** montones de; **she's got stacks of CDs** tiene montones de compactos.

stadium *noun* estadio *Masc.*

staff *noun* **1** (*of a company*) personal *Masc.*; **2** (*in a school*) profesorado *Masc.*

stage *noun* **1** (*for a performance*) escenario *Masc.*; **on stage** en el escenario; **2** (*phase*) etapa *Fem.*; **the earlier stages of the project** las primeras etapas del proyecto; **3 at this stage it's hard to know** a estas alturas es difícil saberlo.

stain *noun* mancha *Fem.*
stain *verb* manchar [17].

stainless steel *noun* acero *Masc.* inoxidable; **a stainless steel sink** un fregadero de acero inoxidable.

stair *noun* **1** (*step*) escalón *Masc.*; **2 stairs** escaleras *Fem. plural*; **I met her on the stairs** me la encontré en las escaleras.

staircase *noun* escaleras *Fem. plural*.

stale *adjective* (*bread*) correoso/correosa.

stalemate *noun* (*in chess*) tablas *Fem. plural*.

stall *noun* **1** (*at a market or fair*) puesto *Masc.*; **2 the stalls** (*in a theatre*) patio *Masc.* de butacas.

a
b
c
d
e
f
g
h
i
j
k
l
m
n
o
p
q
r
s
t
u
v
w
x
y
z

stamp *noun* sello *Masc.*
stamp *verb* **1** poner [11] sello(s) a (*a letter*); **2 to stamp your foot** dar [4] una patada en el suelo.

stamp album *noun* álbum *Masc.* de sellos.

stamp collection *noun* colección *Fem.* de sellos.

stand *verb* **1** estar [2] de pie; **several people were standing** varias personas estaban de pie; **2** (*when you say somebody is standing somewhere, 'standing' is not usually translated*) **we were standing outside the cinema** estábamos delante del cine; **I'm standing here waiting for you** estoy aquí esperándote; **3 to stand on something** pisar [17] algo; **4** (*bear*) soportar [17]; **I can't stand her** no la soporto; **I can't stand waiting** no soporto esperar.
● **to stand for something** (*be short for*) significar [31]; **what does 'plc' stand for?** ¿qué significa 'plc'?.
● **stand up** levantarse [17]; **everybody stood up** todo el mundo se levantó.

standard *noun* nivel *Masc.*; **the standard of living** el nivel de vida.
standard *adjective* estándar; **the standard price** el precio estándar.

standard grades *noun plural* (*You can explain Standard grades as follows: Son exámenes que se realizan alrededor de los 16 años y pueden abarcar hasta 7 asignaturas. Se califican desde 1 (nota máxima) hasta 7 (por haber terminado el curso). Muchos alumnos continúan*

estudiando para los Highers y Advanced Highers después de hacer los Standard grades.) SEE **Highers**.

stands *noun* (*in a stadium*) tribuna *Fem.*

staple *noun* grapa *Fem.*
staple *verb* grapar [17]; **to staple the pages together** grapar las hojas.

stapler *noun* grapadora *Fem.*

star *noun* (*in the sky or rock star, etc*) estrella *Fem.*; **he's a film star** es una estrella de cine.
star *verb* **to star in a film** protagonizar [22] una película.

stare *verb* mirar [17] fijamente; **he was staring at me** me estaba mirando fijamente; **what are you staring at?** ¿qué miras?

star sign *noun* signo *Masc.* del zodíaco; **what star sign are you?** ¿de qué signo eres?.

start *noun* **1** principio *Masc.*; **at the start** al principio; **at the start of the book** al principio del libro; **from the start** desde el principio; **we knew from the start that it was dangerous** sabíamos desde el principio que era peligroso; **2 to make a start on something** empezar [25] algo; **I've made a start on my homework** he empezado mis deberes; **3** (*of a race*) salida *Fem.*
start *verb* **1** empezar [25]; **the film starts at eight** la película empieza a las ocho; **I've started the book** he empezado el libro; **2 to start doing** empezar [25] a hacer; **I've started learning Spanish** he empezado a aprender español; **3 to start a**

a b c d e f g h i j k l m n o p q r s t u v w x y z

business montar [17] un negocio; **4 to start a car** arrancar [31] un coche; **she started the car** arrancó el coche; **the car wouldn't start** el coche no arrancaba.

starter noun (*in a meal*) entrante *Masc.*; **what would you like as a starter?** ¿qué quieres de entrante?

starve verb morirse [55] de hambre; **I'm starving!** ¡me muero de hambre!

state noun 1 estado *Masc.*; **the house is in a very bad state** la casa está en muy mal estado; 2 (*administrative*) estado *Masc.*; **the state el estado; 3 the States** (los) Estados Unidos; **they live in the States** viven en Estados Unidos.
state verb 1 declarar [17] (*intention, opinion*); 2 indicar [31] (*address, income, occupation, reason, etc*).

statement noun declaración *Fem.*

station noun 1 estación *Fem.*; **the railway station** la estación de trenes; **the bus station** la estación de autobuses; **2 the police station** la comisaría; **3 a radio station** una emisora de radio; **a TV station** un canal de televisión.

stationary adjective estacionario/estacionaria.

stationer's noun papelería *Fem.*

stationery noun artículos *Masc. plural* de papelería.

statistics noun 1 (*subject*) estadística *Fem.*; **2 the statistics** (*figures*) las estadísticas.

statue noun estatua *Fem.*

status noun estatus *Masc.*

stay noun estancia *Fem.*; **our stay in Paris** nuestra estancia en París; **enjoy your stay!** ¡que disfruten de su estancia!
stay verb 1 quedarse [17]; **I'll stay here** me quedaré aquí; **how long are you staying?** ¿cuánto tiempo te quedas?; 2 (*with time*) **we're going to stay in Berlin for three days** vamos a pasar tres días en Berlín; 3 (*at somebody's house*) **to stay with somebody** quedarse [17] con alguien; **I'm going to stay with my sister this weekend** me voy a quedar con mi hermana este fin de semana; 4 (*be temporarily lodged*) hospedarse [17]; **where are you staying?** ¿dónde te hospedas?
● **to stay in** no salir [63]; **I'm staying in tonight** esta noche no salgo.

steady adjective 1 estable; **a steady job** un trabajo estable; 2 constante; **a steady increase** un incremento constante; 3 (*hand, voice*) firme; **4 to hold something steady** sostener [9] algo firmemente.

steak noun filete *Masc.*; **steak and chips** filete con patatas fritas.

steal verb robar [17].

steam noun vapor *Masc.*

steam engine noun locomotora *Fem.* de vapor.

steam iron noun plancha *Fem.* a vapor.

steel noun acero *Masc.*

steep adjective empinado/empinada; **a steep slope** una cuesta empinada.

steeple *noun* **1** (*spire*) aguja *Fem.*; **2** (*bell tower*) campanario *Masc.*

steering wheel *noun* volante *Masc.*

step *noun* **1** paso *Masc.*; **to take a step forwards** dar [4] un paso hacia adelante; **2** (*stair*) escalón *Masc.*; **'mind the step'** 'cuidado con el escalón'.
• **to step back** retroceder [18].
• **to step forward** avanzar [22].
• **to step into** entrar [17] en (*a lift*).

stepbrother *noun* hermanastro *Masc.*

stepdaughter *noun* hijastra *Fem.*

stepfather *noun* padrastro *Masc.*

stepladder *noun* escalera *Fem.* de mano.

stepmother *noun* madrastra *Fem.*

stepsister *noun* hermanastra *Fem.*

stepson *noun* hijastro *Masc.*

stereo *noun* estéreo *Masc.*

sterling *noun* libra *Fem.* esterlina; **in sterling** en libras esterlinas.

stew *noun* estofado *Masc.*

steward *noun* camarero *Masc.*

stewardess *noun* camarera *Fem.*

stick *noun* **1** palo *Masc.*; **2 a walking stick** un bastón; **3 a hockey stick** un palo de hockey.
stick *verb* **1** (*with glue*) pegar [28]; **2** (*put*) poner [11]; **stick them on my desk** ponlos en mi mesa.

sticker *noun* pegatina *Fem.*

sticky *adjective* **1** pegajoso/ pegajosa; **my hands are sticky** tengo las manos pegajosas;

2 adhesivo/adhesiva; **sticky paper** papel *Masc.* adhesivo.

sticky tape *noun* cinta *Fem.* adhesiva.

stiff *adjective* **to feel stiff** estar [2] entumecido; **to have stiff legs** tener [9] las piernas entumecidas; **to have a stiff neck** tener [9] tortícolis; ★ **to be bored stiff** estar más aburrido que una ostra (*literally: to be more bored than an oyster*); ★ **to be scared stiff** estar muerto de miedo (*literally: to be dead from fear*).

still *adjective* **1** quieto/quieta; **sit still!** ¡siéntate quieto!; **keep still!** ¡estate quieto!; **2 still mineral water** agua *Fem.* mineral sin gas.
still *adverb* **1** todavía, aún; **do you still live in London?** ¿vives todavía en Londres?, ¿vives aún en Londres?; **I've still not finished** todavía no he terminado, aún no he terminado; **he's still working** está trabajando todavía; **there's still a lot of beer left** todavía queda mucha cerveza; **2 better still** todavía mejor, aún mejor.

sting *noun* aguijón *Masc.*; **a wasp sting** un aguijón de avispa.
sting *verb* picar [31]; **I was stung by a bee** me picó una abeja.

stink *noun* peste *Fem.*; **what a stink!** ¡qué peste!
stink *verb* apestar [17]; **it stinks of cigarette smoke in here** aquí apesta a tabaco.

stir *verb* remover [38].

stitch *noun* **1** (*in sewing*) puntada *Fem.*; **2** (*in knitting*) punto *Masc.*; **3** (*surgical*) punto *Masc.* de sutura.

a
b
c
d
e
f
g
h
i
j
k
l
m
n
o
p
q
r
s
t
u
v
w
x
y
z

a
b
c
d
e

stock *noun* **1** (*in a shop*) estock *Masc.*; **to have something in stock** tener [9] algo en estock; **2** (*supply*) reserva *Fem.*; **I always have a stock of pencils** siempre tengo una reserva de lápices; **3** (*for cooking*) caldo *Masc.*; **chicken stock** caldo de pollo.

f

stock *verb* (*in a shop*) vender [18]; **they don't stock dictionaries** no venden diccionarios.

g

h

stock cube *noun* pastilla *Fem.* de caldo.

i

stock exchange *noun* bolsa *Fem.* de valores.

j

k

stocking *noun* media *Fem.* (de liguero).

l

stomach *noun* estómago *Masc.*

m

n

stomachache *noun* dolor *Masc.* de estómago; **to have stomachache** tener [9] dolor de estómago.

o

p

stone *noun* **1** piedra *Fem.*; **a stone wall** una pared de piedra; **to throw a stone** tirar [17] una piedra; **2** (*in fruit*) hueso *Masc.*

q

stool *noun* taburete *Masc.*

r

s

t

stop *noun* parada *Fem.*; **the bus stop** la parada del autobús.
stop *verb* **1** (*person or vehicle*) parar [17]; **he stopped in front of the shop** paró enfrente de la tienda; **does the train stop in Cordoba?** ¿para el tren en Córdoba?; **the music stopped** la música paró; **2** (*engine or machine*) pararse [17]; **3 to stop something/somebody** parar [17] algo/a alguien; **she stopped me in the street** me paró en la calle; **4 to stop doing** dejar [17] de hacer; **he's stopped**

u

v

w

x

y

z

smoking ha dejado de fumar; **she never stops asking questions** nunca deja de hacer preguntas; **5 to stop somebody doing** impedir [57] a alguien hacer; **there's nothing to stop you going on your own** nada te impide ir solo.

stopwatch *noun* cronómetro *Masc.*

store *noun* (*shop*) tienda *Fem.*
store *verb* **1** guardar [17]; **2** (*on a computer*) almacenar [17].

storey *noun* piso *Masc.*; **a three-storey house** una casa de tres pisos.

stork *noun* cigüeña *Fem.*

storm *noun* tormenta *Fem.*; **a snowstorm** una tormenta de nieve; **a rainstorm** una tormenta de lluvia.

stormy *adjective* de tormenta.

story *noun* **1** historia *Fem.*; **to tell a story** contar [24] una historia; **2** (*tale*) cuento *Masc.*

stove *noun* (*cooker*) cocina *Fem.*

straight *adjective* **1** recto/recta; **a straight line** una línea recta; **2 to have straight hair** tener [9] el pelo liso; **3** (*not crooked*) derecho/derecha; **the candle's not straight** la vela no está derecha.
straight *adverb* **1** (*in direction*) recto; **go straight ahead** sigue todo recto; **2** (*in time*) directamente; **he went straight to the doctor's** fue directamente al médico; **3 straight away** en seguida.

strain *verb* **1** colar [17] (*vegetables, rice*); **2** hacerse [7] un esguince en (*a muscle*).
strain *noun* tensión *Fem.*

strange *adjective* extraño/extraña; **a strange situation** una situación extraña.

stranger *noun* desconocido *Masc.*, desconocida *Fem.*

strangle *verb* estrangular [17].

strap *noun* 1 (*on camera or watch*) correa *Fem.*; **a watchstrap** una correa de reloj; 2 (*on case or bag*) asa *Fem.*; 3 (*on a garment*) tirante *Masc.*; 4 (*on a shoe*) tira *Fem.*

straw *noun* paja *Fem.* (*both the material and for drinking with*); **a straw hat** un sombrero de paja.

strawberry *noun* fresa *Fem.*; **strawberry jam** mermelada de fresa.

stream *noun* (*small river*) arroyo *Masc.*

street *noun* calle *Fem.*; **I met Simon in the street** me encontré con Simon en la calle.

streetlamp *noun* farol *Masc.*

street map *noun* plano *Masc.* de la ciudad.

streetwise *adjective* avispado/avispada.

strength *noun* fuerza *Fem.*

stress *noun* tensión *Fem.*; 2 (*in a word*) acento *Masc.*
stress *verb* (*emphasize*) recalcar [31]; **to stress the importance of something** recalcar la importancia de algo.

stretch *verb* (*garment or shoes*) dar [4] de sí; **this jumper has stretched** este jersey ha dado de sí.

strict *adjective* estricto/estricta.

strike *noun* huelga *Fem.*; **to go on strike** ponerse [11] en huelga; **to be on strike** estar [2] en huelga.
strike *verb* 1 (*hit*) golpear [17] (*a person*); 2 (*clock*) dar [4]; **the clock struck six** el reloj dio las seis; 3 (*go on strike*) ponerse [11] en huelga.

striker *noun* 1 (*in football*) delantero *Masc.*, delantera *Fem.*; 2 (*person on strike*) huelguista *Masc./Fem.*

string *noun* 1 (*for tying*) cordel *Masc.*; 2 (*for a musical instrument*) cuerda *Fem.*

strip *noun* tira *Fem.*
strip *verb* (*undress*) desnudarse [17].

strip cartoon *noun* tira *Fem.* cómica.

stripe *noun* raya *Fem.*

striped *adjective* de rayas.

stroke *noun* 1 (*in swimming*) brazada *Fem.*; 2 (*medical*) derrame *Masc.* cerebral; **to have a stroke** sufrir [19] un derrame cerebral; ⋆**a stroke of luck** un golpe de suerte.
stroke *verb* acariciar [17].

strong *adjective* 1 (*person, drink, smell, taste, or feeling*) fuerte; 2 (*material*) resistente; 3 (*accent*) marcado.

struggle *noun* 1 lucha *Fem.*; **the struggle for independence** la lucha por la independencia; **a power struggle** una lucha por el poder; 2 **it's been a struggle** ha sido muy difícil.
struggle *verb* 1 (*to obtain something*) luchar [17]; **they have**

a
b
c
d
e
f
g
h
i
j
k
l
m
n
o
p
q
r
s
t
u
v
w
x
y
z

struggled to survive han luchado para sobrevivir; **2** (*physically, in order to escape or get something*) forcejear [17]; **3** (*have difficulty in doing*) **I'm struggling to finish my homework** me está costando terminar mis deberes.

stubborn *adjective* terco/terca.

stuck *adjective* (*jammed*) atascado/atascada; **the drawer's stuck** el cajón está atascado.

stud *noun* **1** (*on a belt or jacket*) tachuela *Fem.*; **2** (*on a boot*) taco *Masc.*; **3** (*earring*) pendiente *Masc.* de bolita.

student *noun* estudiante *Masc./Fem.*

studio *noun* estudio *Masc.*

studio flat *noun* estudio *Masc.*

study *verb* estudiar [17]; **he's busy studying for his exams** está muy ocupado estudiando para los exámenes; **she's studying medicine** estudia medicina.

stuff *noun* **1** (*things*) cosas *Fem. plural*; **we can put all that stuff in the attic** podemos poner todas estas cosas en el ático; **you can leave your stuff at my house** puedes dejar tus cosas en mi casa; **2** (*substance*) cosa *Fem.*
stuff *verb* **1** (*shove*) meter [18]; **she stuffed some things into a suitcase** metió algunas cosas en una maleta; **2** rellenar [17] (*chicken, turkey, vegetables*); **stuffed aubergines** berenjenas rellenas.

stuffing *noun* (*for cooking*) relleno *Masc.*

stuffy *adjective* viciado/viciada; **it's very stuffy in here** aquí dentro falta aire.

stunned *adjective* (*amazed*) atónito/atónita.

stunning *adjective* sensacional.

stunt *noun* (*in a film*) escena *Fem.* peligrosa.

stupid *adjective* estúpido/estúpida; **a stupid man** un hombre estupido; **that was really stupid** eso fue una verdadera estupidez; **to do something stupid** hacer [7] una estupidez.

stutter *noun* **to have a stutter** tartamudear [17].
stutter *verb* tartamudear [17].

style *noun* **1** estilo *Masc.*; **a style of living** un estilo de vida; **he has his own style** tiene su propio estilo; **2** (*fashion*) moda *Fem.*; **it's the latest style** es la última moda.

subject *noun* **1** tema *Masc.*; **the subject of my talk** el tema de mi charla; **2** (*at school*) asignatura *Fem.*; **my favourite subject is biology** mi asignatura favorita es la biología.

submarine *noun* submarino *Masc.*

subscription *noun* suscripción *Fem.*; **to take out a subscription to** suscribirse [52] a.

subsidy *noun* subvención *Fem.*

substance *noun* sustancia *Fem.*

substitute *noun* (*person*) sustituto *Masc.*, sustituta *Fem.*
substitute *verb* sustituir [54].

subtitled *adjective* (*film*) subtitulado/subtitulada.

subtitles *plural noun* subtítulos *Masc. plural*.

subtract *verb* restar [17].

suburb *noun* barrio *Masc.* residencial de las afueras; **a suburb of Edinburgh** un barrio residencial de las afueras de Edimburgo; **in the suburbs of London** en los barrios residenciales de las afueras de Londres.

subway *noun* (*underpass*) paso *Masc.* subterráneo.

succeed *verb* **1** lograr [17]; **to succeed in doing** lograr hacer; **we've succeeded in contacting her** hemos logrado contactar con ella; **2** (*be successful*) tener [9] éxito; **to succeed in business** tener éxito en los negocios.

success *noun* éxito *Masc.*; **a great success** un gran éxito.

successful *adjective* **1** de éxito; **he's a successful writer** es un escritor de éxito; **2 to be successful in doing** lograr [17] hacer.

successfully *adverb* satisfactoriamente.

such *adjective, adverb* **1** tan; **they're such nice people!** ¡son gente tan agradable!; **I've had such a busy day!** ¡he tenido un día tan ocupado!; **it's such a long way** está tan lejos; **it's such a pity** es una verdadera lástima; **2 such a lot of** tantos/ tantas; **I've got such a lot of things to tell you!** ¡tengo tantas cosas que contarte!; **3 such as** como; **in big cities such as Glasgow** en ciudades grandes como Glasgow;

4 there's no such thing eso no existe.

sudden *adjective* repentino/ repentina; ★ **all of a sudden** de repente.

suddenly *adverb* de repente; **he suddenly started to laugh** de repente empezó a reír; **suddenly the light went out** de repente se apagó la luz; **to die suddenly** morir [55] de repente.

suede *noun* ante *Masc.*; **a suede jacket** una chaqueta de ante.

suffer *verb* sufrir [19].

sugar *noun* azúcar *Masc. or Fem.*; **would you like sugar?** ¿quieres azúcar?; **brown sugar** azúcar morena.

suggest *verb* sugerir [14]; **he suggested I should speak to you about it** sugirió que hablase contigo acerca de ello.

suggestion *noun* sugerencia *Fem.*; **to make a suggestion** hacer [7] una sugerencia.

suicide *noun* suicidio *Masc.*; **to commit suicide** suicidarse [17].

suit *noun* **1** (*man's*) traje *Masc.*; **2** (*woman's*) traje *Masc.* de chaqueta.

suitable *adjective* **1** adecuado/ adecuada; **a suitable hotel** un hotel adecuado; **to be suitable for** ser [1] adecuado para; **2** (*clothing*) apropiado/apropiada; **I don't have any suitable shoes** no tengo zapatos apropiados.

suitcase *noun* maleta *Fem.*

sulk *verb* enfurruñarse [17].

a
b
c
d
e
f
g
h
i
j
k
l
m
n
o
p
q
r
s
t
u
v
w
x
y
z

sum *noun* **1** cantidad *Fem.*; **a sum of money** una cantidad de dinero; **a large sum** una cantidad grande; **2** (*calculation*) suma *Fem.*

● **to sum up** resumir [19].

summarize *verb* resumir [19].

summary *noun* resumen *Masc.*

summer *noun* verano *Masc.*; **in summer** en verano; **summer clothes** ropa *Fem.* de verano; **the summer holidays** las vacaciones de verano.

summertime *noun* verano *Masc.*; **in summertime** en verano.

summit *noun* cumbre *Fem.*

sun *noun* sol *Masc.*; **in the sun** en el sol.

sunbathe *verb* tomar [17] el sol.

sunblock *noun* filtro *Masc.* solar.

sunburn *noun* quemadura *Fem.* solar.

sunburned *adjective* **1** (*tanned*) moreno/morena; **2 to get sunburned** (*burned*) quemarse [17].

Sunday *noun* domingo *Masc.*; **on Sunday** el domingo; **I'm going out on Sunday** voy a salir el domingo; **see you on Sunday!** ¡hasta el domingo!; **on Sundays** los domingos; **the museum is closed on Sundays** el museo cierra los domingos; **every Sunday** todos los domingos; **last Sunday** el domingo pasado; **next Sunday** el próximo domingo.

sunflower *noun* girasol *Masc.*; **sunflower oil** aceite *Masc.* de girasol.

sunglasses *plural noun* gafas *Fem. plural* de sol.

sunlight *noun* luz *Fem.* del sol.

sunny *adjective* **1** **it's a sunny day** hace sol; **it's going to be sunny** va a hacer sol; **2** (*place*) soleado/soleada; **in a sunny corner of the garden** una esquina soleada del jardín.

sunrise *noun* salida *Fem.* del sol; **at sunrise** al amanecer.

sunroof *noun* techo *Masc.* solar.

sunset *noun* puesta *Fem.* de sol; **at sunset** al atardecer.

sunshine *noun* sol *Masc.*

sunstroke *noun* insolación *Fem.*; **to get sunstroke** coger [3] una insolación.

suntan *noun* bronceado *Masc.*; **to get a suntan** broncearse [17].

suntan lotion *noun* loción *Fem.* bronceadora.

suntan oil *noun* aceite *Masc.* bronceador.

super *adjective* genial; **we had a super time!** ¡lo pasamos genial!

supermarket *noun* supermercado *Masc.*

supernatural *adjective* supernatural.

superstitious *adjective* supersticioso/supersticiosa.

supervise *verb* supervisar [17].

supervisor *noun* supervisor *Masc.*, supervisora *Fem.*

supper *noun* cena *Fem.*; **I had supper at Sandy's** cené en casa de Sandy.

supplement *noun* suplemento *Masc.*

supplies *plural noun* (*of food*) provisiones *Fem. plural.*

supply *noun* **1** (*stock*) reservas *Fem. plural*; **2 to be in short supply** escasear [17].

supply *verb* suministrar [17]; **the school supplies the paper** el colegio suministra el papel; **to supply somebody with something** suministrar algo a alguien.

supply teacher *noun* profesor *Masc.* suplente, profesora *Fem.* suplente.

support *noun* apoyo *Masc.*; **he has a lot of support** tiene mucho apoyo. **support** *verb* **1** (*back up*) apoyar [17]; **her teachers have really supported her** sus profesoras la han apoyado mucho; **2** ser [1] hincha de (*a team*); **Graeme supports Liverpool** Graeme es hincha del Liverpool; **3** (*financially*) **to support a family** mantener [9] una familia.

supporter *noun* hincha *Masc./Fem.*; **an Arsenal supporter** un hincha del Arsenal.

suppose *verb* suponer [11]; **I suppose she's forgotten** supongo que se ha olvidado.

supposed *adjective* **to be supposed to do** tener [9] que; **you're supposed to wear a helmet** tienes que usar casco; **he was supposed to be here at six** tenía que estar aquí a las seis.

sure *adjective* **1** seguro/segura; **are you sure?** ¿estás seguro?; **are you sure you've had enough to eat?** ¿seguro que has comido suficiente?; **are you sure you saw her?** ¿estás seguro de que la viste?; **2 sure!** ¡claro!; **'can you shut the door?' – 'sure!'** '¿puedes cerrar la puerta?' – '¡por supuesto!'

surely *adverb* **surely she couldn't have forgotten!** ¡no es posible que se haya olvidado! (*note that 'que' is followed by the subjunctive*).

surf *noun* rompiente *Masc.* **surf** *verb* **1** (*in the sea*) hacer [7] surfing; **2** (*on the Net*) navegar [28].

surface *noun* superficie *Fem.*

surfboard *noun* tabla *Fem.* de surf.

surfer *noun* **1** (*in the sea*) surfista *Masc./Fem.*; **2** (*on the Net*) internauta *Masc./Fem.*

surfing *noun* surfing *Masc.*; **to go surfing** hacer [7] surfing.

surgeon *noun* cirujano *Masc.*, cirujana *Fem.*; **she's a surgeon** es cirujana.

surgery *noun* **1** (*treatment*) cirugía *Fem.*; **laser surgery** cirugía láser; **to have surgery** operarse [17]; **2** (*doctor's*) consultorio *Masc.*; **the dentist's surgery** la consulta del dentista.

surname *noun* apellido *Masc.*

surprise *noun* sorpresa *Fem.*; **what a surprise!** ¡qué sorpresa!

surprised *adjective* sorprendido/sorprendida; **I was surprised to see her** me sorprendió verla.

surprising *adjective* sorprendente.

a
b
c
d
e
f
g
h
i
j
k
l
m
n
o
p
q
r
s
t
u
v
w
x
y
z

surrender noun rendición Fem.
surrender verb 1 (to give up) rendirse [57]; 2 entregar [28] (a castle, town).

surround verb 1 rodear [17]; 2 to be surrounded by estar [2] rodeado de; she's surrounded by friends está rodeada de amigos.

survive verb sobrevivir [19].

survivor noun superviviente Masc./Fem.

suspect noun sospechoso Masc., sospechosa Fem.
suspect adjective sospechoso/sospechosa.
suspect verb sospechar [17].

suspend verb 1 (hang) suspender [18]; 2 to be suspended (from school) ser [1] expulsado.

suspense noun suspense Masc.

suspicious adjective sospechoso/sospechosa; to be suspicious of sospechar [17] de; a suspicious parcel un paquete sospechoso; a suspicious-looking individual un individuo de apariencia sospechosa.

swallow noun (bird) golondrina Fem.
swallow verb tragar [28].

swamp noun pantano Masc.

swan noun cisne Masc.

swap verb 1 cambiar [17]; do you want to swap? ¿quieres que cambiemos?; he's swapped his bike for a computer ha cambiado su bici por un ordenador; 2 to swap seats with somebody cambiarse [17] de sitio con alguien.

swear verb (use bad language) decir [5] palabrotas; he swears a lot dice muchas palabrotas.

swearword noun palabrota Fem.

sweat noun sudor Masc.
sweat verb sudar [17].

sweater noun suéter Masc.

sweatshirt noun sudadera Fem.

Swede noun sueco Masc., sueca Fem.

Sweden noun Suecia Fem.

Swedish noun (language) sueco Masc.
Swedish adjective sueco/sueca.

sweep verb barrer [18].

sweet noun 1 caramelo Masc.; I bought her some sweets le he comprado unos caramelos; 2 (dessert) postre Masc.
sweet adjective 1 (food or smile) dulce; I try not to eat sweet things intento no comer cosas dulces; 2 (kind) encantador/encantadora; she's a really sweet person es realmente encantadora; it was really sweet of him ha sido un detalle encantador; 3 (cute) rico/rica; he looks really sweet in that hat! ¡está muy rico con ese sombrero!

sweetcorn noun maíz Masc. tierno.

swelling noun hinchazón Fem.

swerve verb virar [17] bruscamente; the car swerved to avoid the dog el coche viró bruscamente para esquivar al perro.

swim noun to go for a swim ir [8] a nadar.

swim *verb* nadar [17]; **can he swim?** ¿sabe nadar?; **to swim across something** cruzar [22] algo a nado.

swimmer *noun* nadador *Masc.*, nadadora *Fem.*; **she's a strong swimmer** es muy buena nadadora.

swimming *noun* natación *Fem.*; **to go swimming** ir [8] a nadar.

swimming cap *noun* gorro *Masc.* de baño.

swimming pool *noun* piscina *Fem.*

swimming trunks *noun* bañador *Masc.*

swimsuit *noun* traje *Masc.* de baño.

swindle *noun* estafa *Fem.*; **what a swindle!** ¡qué estafa!

swing *noun* columpio *Masc.*

Swiss *noun* (*person*) suizo *Masc.*, suiza *Fem.*; **the Swiss** los suizos. **Swiss** *adjective* suizo/suiza.

switch *noun* interruptor *Masc.* **switch** *verb* (*change*) cambiar [17]; **to switch places** cambiar de sitio.
● **to switch something off** apagar [28] algo.
● **to switch something on** encender [36] algo.

Switzerland *noun* Suiza *Fem.*

swollen *adjective* hinchado/hinchada.

swop *verb* SEE **swap**.

sword *noun* espada *Fem.*

swordfish *noun* pez *Masc.* espada.

syllabus *noun* programa *Masc.*; **to be on the syllabus** estar [2] en el programa.

sympathetic *adjective* comprensivo/comprensiva.

sympathize *verb* **to sympathize with somebody** compadecer [35] a alguien; **I sympathize with her** la compadezco.

sympathy *noun* compasión *Fem.*

symphony *noun* sinfonía *Fem.*

symphony orchestra *noun* orquesta *Fem.* sinfónica.

symptom *noun* síntoma *Masc.*

synagogue *noun* sinagoga *Fem.*

synthesizer *noun* sintetizador *Masc.*

synthetic *adjective* sintético/sintética.

syringe *noun* jeringa *Fem.*

system *noun* sistema *Masc.*

Tt

table *noun* mesa *Fem.*; **on the table** en la mesa; **to set the table** poner [11] la mesa; **to clear the table** quitar [17] la mesa.

tablecloth *noun* mantel *Masc.*

table football *noun* futbolín *Masc.*

table mat *noun* salvamanteles *Masc.* (*doesn't change in the plural*).

tablespoon *noun* cuchara *Fem.* de servir; (*in recipes*) **a tablespoon of flour** una cucharada grande de harina.

tablet *noun* pastilla *Fem.*

a
b
c
d
e
f
g
h
i
j
k
l
m
n
o
p
q
r
s
t
u
v
w
x
y
z

a
b
c
d
e
f
g
h
i
j
k
l
m
n
o
p
q
r
s
t
u
v
w
x
y
z

table tennis noun ping-pong Masc.; **to play table tennis** jugar [27] al ping-pong.

tackle noun 1 (in football) entrada Fem.; 2 (in rugby) placaje Masc. **tackle** verb 1 (in football or hockey) entrarle [17] a; 2 abordar [17] (a job or problem).

tact noun tacto Masc.

tactful adjective diplomático/diplomática; **that wasn't very tactful** eso no ha sido muy diplomático.

tactic noun táctica Fem.

tadpole noun renacuajo Masc.

tail noun 1 (of dog, cat) rabo Masc.; 2 (of horse, fish, bird) cola Fem.; 3 'heads or tails?' – 'tails' '¿cara o cruz?' – 'cruz'.

tailor noun sastre Masc.

take verb 1 coger [3]; **he took a chocolate** cogió un bombón; **take my hand** cógeme la mano; **I took the bus** cogí el autobús; **who's taken my keys?** ¿quién ha cogido mis llaves?; **to take a holiday** cogerse [3] unas vacaciones; 2 (person or car) llevar [17]; **I'm taking Jake to the doctor's** voy a llevar a Jake al médico; **I must take the car to the garage** debo llevar el coche al garaje; 3 (carry away) llevar [17]; **I'll take my camera with me** me llevaré la cámara; **4 to take something up(stairs)** subir [19] algo; **could you take these towels up?** ¿puedes subir estas toallas?; **5 to take something down(stairs)** bajar [17] algo; **Cheryl's taken the cups down**

Cheryl ha bajado las tazas; 6 (time: for a task or job) llevar [17]; **it takes two hours** lleva dos horas; 7 (food or medicine) tomar [17]; **do you take sugar?** ¿tomas azúcar?; 8 aceptar [17] (a credit card or a cheque) **do you take cheques?** ¿aceptan cheques?; 9 hacer [7] (an exam); **she's taking her driving test tomorrow** va a hacer el examen de conducir mañana; **10 what size do you take?** ¿qué talla usas?

● **to take something apart** desmontar [17] algo.

● **to take something back** devolver [45] algo.

● **to take off 1** (a plane) despegar [28]; 2 quitarse [17] (clothes or shoes); **he took off his shirt** se quitó la camisa; 3 rebajar [17] (money); **he took five pounds off the price** rebajó cinco libras del precio.

● **to take out 1** (from a bag or pocket) sacar [31]; **Eric took out his wallet** Eric sacó su cartera; 2 **he's taking me out to lunch** me ha invitado a comer fuera; **she took me out to the theatre** me invitó a ir al teatro.

takeaway noun 1 (a meal) comida Fem. para llevar; **an Indian takeaway** comida india para llevar; 2 (where you buy it) restaurante Masc. que hace comida para llevar.

tale noun historia Fem.

talent noun talento Masc.; **to have a talent for something** estar [2] dotado/dotada para algo.

talented adjective **he's really talented** tiene mucho talento.

alk noun **1** (*a chat*) conversación Fem.; **after our talk** después de nuestra conversación; **I had a talk with Rob about it** hablé con Rob acerca de ello; **2** (*lecture*) charla Fem.; **she's giving a talk on Hungary** va a dar una charla sobre Hungría.

talk verb hablar [17]; **I was talking to Jeevan about football** estuve hablando con Jeevan sobre fútbol; **what's he talking about?** ¿de qué está hablando?; **we'll talk about it later** hablaremos de ello más tarde.

talkative adjective hablador/habladora; **he's not very talkative!** ¡no es muy hablador!

tall adjective alto/alta; **she's very tall** es muy alta; **I'm 1.7 metres tall** mido un metro setenta; **how tall is she?** ¿cuánto mide?; **the tallest buildings in the city** los edificios más altos de la ciudad.

tambourine noun pandereta Fem.

tame adjective domesticado/domesticada (*an animal*).

tampon noun tampón Masc.

tan noun bronceado Masc.; **to get a tan** broncearse [17].
tan verb broncearse [17]; **I tan easily** me bronceo fácilmente.

tangerine noun mandarina Fem.

tank noun **1** (*for petrol or water*) depósito Masc.; **2 a fish tank** una pecera; **3** (*military*) tanque Masc.

tanker noun **1** (*ship*) petrolero Masc.; **2** (*on road*) camión Masc. cisterna.

tanned adjective bronceado/bronceada.

tap noun **1** grifo Masc.; **to turn on the tap** abrir [46] el grifo; **to turn off the tap** cerrar [29] el grifo; **the hot tap** el grifo del agua caliente; **2** (*a pat*) golpecito Masc.
tap verb dar [4] golpecitos.

tap-dancing noun claqué Masc.; **to do tap-dancing** hacer [7] claqué.

tape noun **1** cinta Fem.; **my tape of the Stones** mi cinta de los Stones; **I've got it on tape** lo tengo en cinta; **2 sticky tape** cinta Fem. adhesiva.
tape verb grabar [17]; **I want to tape the film** quiero grabar la película.

tape measure noun cinta Fem. métrica.

tar noun alquitrán Masc.

target noun objetivo Masc.

tart noun tarta Fem.; **a raspberry tart** una tarta de frambuesas.

tartan adjective escocés/escocesa; **a tartan skirt** una falda escocesa.

task noun tarea Fem.

taste noun **1** (*flavour*) sabor Masc.; **the taste of onions** el sabor a cebolla; **2** (*judgement*) gusto Masc.; **she has good taste** tiene buen gusto; **in bad taste** de mal gusto.
taste verb **1** saber [13]; **the soup tastes horrible** la sopa sabe fatal; **to taste of** saber a; **it tastes of strawberries** sabe a fresas; **2 do you want to taste?** ¿quieres probarlo?

tasty adjective sabroso/sabrosa.

a
b
c
d
e
f
g
h
i
j
k
l
m
n
o
p
q
r
s
t
u
v
w
x
y
z

a
b
c
d
e
f
g
h
i
j
k
l
m
n
o
p
q
r
s
t
u
v
w
x
y
z

tattoo *noun* tatuaje *Masc.*; **he's got a tattoo on his arm** tiene un tatuaje en el brazo.

Taurus *noun* Tauro *Masc.*; **Jo's Taurus** Jo es Tauro.

tax *noun* impuesto *Masc.*

taxi *noun* taxi *Masc.*; **by taxi** en taxi; **to take a taxi** coger [3] un taxi.

taxi driver *noun* taxista *Masc./Fem.*

taxi rank *noun* parada *Fem.* de taxis.

TB *noun* tuberculosis *Fem.*

tea *noun* **1** té *Masc.*; **a cup of tea** una taza de té; **to have tea** tomar [17] té; **a herbal tea** una infusión; **2** (*evening meal*) cena *Fem.*

teabag *noun* bolsita *Fem.* de té.

teach *verb* **1** enseñar [17]; **she's teaching me Italian** me está enseñando italiano; **that'll teach you!** ¡así aprenderás!; **2** (*working as a teacher*) dar [4] clases de; **her mum teaches maths** su madre da clases de matemáticas; **3 to teach yourself something** aprender [18] algo por su cuenta; **Anne taught herself Italian** Anne ha aprendido italiano por su cuenta.

teacher *noun* **1** (*in a secondary school*) profesor *Masc.*, profesora *Fem.*; **my mother's a teacher** mi madre es profesora; **our biology teacher** nuestra profesora de biología; **2** (*in primary school*) maestro *Masc.*, maestra *Fem.*; **she's a primary school teacher** es maestra.

teaching *noun* enseñanza *Fem.*

team *noun* equipo *Masc.*; **a football team** un equipo de fútbol; **our team won** nuestro equipo ganó.

teapot *noun* tetera *Fem.*

tear¹ *noun* (*a rip*) roto *Masc.*; **I've got a tear in my jeans** tengo un roto en los vaqueros.
tear *verb* **1** romper [40]; **you've torn your shirt** te has roto la camisa; **she tore up my letter** rompió mi carta; **2** romperse [40]; **be careful, it tears easily** cuidado, se rompe fácilmente.
● **to tear off 1** (*carefully*) recortar [17]; **2** (*violently*) arrancar [31].
● **to tear open 1** (*carefully*) abrir [46]; **2** (*violently*) rasgar [28].

tear² *noun* (*when you cry*) lágrima *Fem.*; **to be in tears** estar [2] llorando; **to burst into tears** ponerse [11] a llorar.

teaspoon *noun* cucharita *Fem.*; (*in recipes*) **a teaspoonful of** ... una cucharadita de ....

teatime *noun* hora *Fem.* merendar.

tea towel *noun* paño *Masc.* de cocina.

technical *adjective* técnico/ técnica.

technical college *noun* escuela *Fem.* politécnica.

technician *noun* técnico *Masc.*, técnica *Fem.*

technological *adjective* tecnológico/tecnológica.

technology *noun* tecnología *Fem.*; **information technology** informática *Fem.*

teddy bear *noun* osito *Masc.* de peluche.

teenage *adjective* **1** adolescente; **they have a teenage son** tienen un hijo adolescente; **2** *(films, magazines, etc.)* para adolescentes; **a teenage magazine** una revista para adolescentes.

teenager *noun* adolescente *Masc./ Fem.*; **a group of teenagers** un grupo de adolescentes.

teens *plural noun* adolescencia *Fem.*; **he's in his teens** es un adolescente.

tee-shirt *noun* camiseta *Fem.*

telegraph pole *noun* poste *Masc.* telegráfico.

telephone *noun* teléfono *Masc.*; **on the telephone** al teléfono.
telephone *verb* llamar [17] por teléfono; **I'll telephone the bank** llamaré al banco por teléfono.

telephone box *noun* cabina *Fem.* telefónica.

telephone call *noun* llamada *Fem.* de teléfono.

telephone card *noun* carta *Fem.* telefónica.

telephone directory *noun* guía *Fem.* telefónica.

telephone number *noun* número *Masc.* de teléfono.

television *noun* televisión *Fem.*; **she was watching television** estaba viendo la televisión; **I saw it on television** lo vi en televisión.

television programme *noun* programa *Masc.* de televisión.

tell *verb* **1 to tell somebody something** decirle [5] algo a alguien; **that's what she told me** eso es lo que ella me dijo; **I told him it was silly** le dije que era una tontería; **have you told Sara?** ¿se lo has dicho a Sara?; **I didn't tell anyone** no se lo dije a nadie; **2 to tell somebody to do** decirle [5] a alguien que haga (*note that 'que' is followed by the subjunctive*) **he told me to do it myself** me dijo que lo hiciese solo; **she told me not to wait** me dijo que no esperase; **3** *(explain)* decir [5]; **can you tell me how to do it?** ¿puedes decirme cómo hacerlo?; **4** contar [24] *(a story)*; **tell me about your holiday** cuéntame qué tal tus vacaciones; **5** *(to see)* notar [17]; **to tell the difference** notar la diferencia; **you can tell ...** se nota ...; **you can tell it's old** se nota que es viejo; **you can tell she's cross** se nota que está enfadada; **I can't tell them apart** no puedo distinguirlos.

telly *noun* tele *Fem.* *(informal)*; **to watch telly** ver [16] la tele; **I saw her on telly** la vi en la tele.

temper *noun* **to be in a temper** estar [2] de mal humor; **to lose your temper** perder [36] los estribos.

temperature *noun* **1** temperatura *Fem.*; **the oven temperature** la temperatura del horno; **2 to have a temperature** tener [9] fiebre *Fem.*

temporary *adjective* temporal.

temptation *noun* tentación *Fem.*

a b c d e f g h i j k l m n o p q r s t u v w x y z

tempted *adjective* tentado/
tentada; **I'm really tempted to go**
estoy realmente tentado de ir.

tempting *adjective* tentador/
tentadora.

ten *number* diez *Masc.*; **Harry's ten**
Harry tiene diez años; **it's ten
o'clock** son las diez.

tend *verb* **to tend to do** tender [36] a
hacer; **he tends to talk a lot** tiende
a hablar mucho.

tendency *noun* tendencia *Fem.*

tennis *noun* tenis *Masc.*; **to play
tennis** jugar [27] al tenis.

tennis ball *noun* pelota *Fem.* de
tenis.

tennis court *noun* cancha *Fem.* de
tenis.

tennis player *noun* jugador/
jugadora *Masc./Fem.* de tenis.

tennis racket *noun* raqueta *Fem.*
de tenis.

tenor *noun* tenor *Masc.*

tenpin bowling *noun* bolos *Masc.
plural*; **to go tenpin bowling** jugar
[27] a los bolos.

tense *noun* **the present tense** el
presente; **in the future tense** en
futuro.
tense *adjective* tenso/tensa.

tent *noun* tienda *Fem.*

tenth *noun* **1** (*fraction*) **a tenth** una
décima parte; **2 the tenth of April** el
diez de abril.
tenth *adjective* décimo/décima; **on
the tenth floor** en la décima planta.

term *noun* **1** (*in school*) trimestre
Masc.; **2 to be on good terms with**

somebody llevarse [17] bien con
alguien.

terminal *noun* terminal *Fem.*;
terminal two la terminal dos; **a
computer terminal** una terminal de
ordenador.

terrace *noun* **1** (*of a house or hotel*)
terraza *Fem.*; **2 the terraces** (*at a
stadium*) las gradas.

terrible *adjective* espantoso/
espantosa; **the weather was
terrible** el tiempo fue espantoso.

terribly *adverb* **1** (*very*) muy; **not
terribly clean** no muy limpio que
digamos; **2** (*badly*) fatal; **I played
terribly** jugué fatal.

terrific *adjective* **1** increíble; **at a
terrific speed** a una velocidad
increíble; **a terrific amount** una
cantidad increíble; **2 terrific!**
¡fenomenal!

terrified *adjective* aterrorizado/
aterrorizada.

terrify *verb* aterrar [17].

territory *noun* territorio *Masc.*

terrorism *noun* terrorismo *Masc.*

terrorist *noun* terrorista *Masc./Fem.*

test *noun* **1** (*in school*) examen *Masc.*;
we've got a maths test tomorrow
tenemos un examen de matemáticas
mañana; **2** (*of your skills or patience*)
prueba *Fem.*; **3** (*medical*) análisis
Masc.; **a blood test** un análisis de
sangre; **4 a driving test** un examen
de conducir; **she's sitting her
driving test on Friday** va a hacer el
exámen de conducir mañana; **he
passed his driving test** ha
aprobado el examen de conducir.

test *verb* **1** (*in school*) examinarse [17]; **2 to test something out** probar [24] algo.

text *noun* texto *Masc.*

text *verb* mandar [17] un mensaje de texto a; **I'll text you tomorrow** te mandaré un mensaje (de texto) mañana.

textbook *noun* libro *Masc.* de texto.

text message *noun* mensaje *Masc.* de texto.

Thames *noun* **the Thames** el Támesis.

than *preposition, conjunction* **1** que; **their new album's better than the last one** su nuevo álbum es mejor que el último; **they have more money than we do** tienen más dinero que nosotros; **2** (*for quantities*) de; **more than forty** más de cuarenta; **more than thirty years** más de treinta años.

thank *verb* dar [4] las gracias a.

thanks *plural noun* **1** gracias *Fem. plural*; **no thanks** no gracias; **thanks a lot** muchas gracias; **thanks for your letter** gracias por tu carta; **2 thanks to** gracias a; **it was thanks to Micky** fue gracias a Micky.

thank you *exclamation* gracias; **thank you very much for the cheque** muchas gracias por el cheque; **no thank you** no, gracias; **a thank-you letter** un carta de agradecimiento.

that *adjective* **1** (*before a masculine noun*) ese; **that dog** ese perro; **that blue car** ese coche azul; **2** (*before a feminine noun*) esa; **that woman** esa mujer; **3 that one** (*referring to a masculine noun*) ese, ése; (*referring to a feminine noun*) esa, ésa; **'which cake would you like?' – 'that one, please'** ¿qué pastel quieres? – 'ese, por favor'; **I like all the skirts but I'm going to buy that one** me gustan todas las faldas pero voy a comprar esa.

that *adverb* **it's not that funny** no es tan divertido; **their house isn't that big** su casa no es tan grande.

that *pronoun* **1** (*referring to a masculine noun*) ese, ése; (*referring to a masculine noun*) esa, ésa; **that's not his car** ese no es su coche; **that's my bedroom** esa es mi habitación; **2** eso; **that's not what you told me** eso no es lo que tú me dijiste; **that's not true** eso no es cierto; **did you see that?** ¿has visto eso?; **what's that?** ¿qué es eso?; **who's that?** ¿quién es?; **where's that?** ¿dónde está?; **3** que; **the book that's on the table** el libro que está en la mesa; **the girl that I saw** la chica que yo vi; **4** (*when the verb is followed by a preposition*) (*referring to a masculine noun*) el que; (*referring to a feminine noun*) la que; **the drawer that I put it in** el cajón en el que lo metí.

that *conjunction* que; **I knew that he was wrong** sabía que no tenía razón.

thaw *noun* deshielo *Masc.*

the *definite article* **1** (*before a masculine noun*) el; **the cat** el gato; **the tree** el árbol (*when 'el' follows 'de', they join to become 'del'*); **the branches of the tree** las ramas del

a
b
c
d
e
f
g
h
i
j
k
l
m
n
o
p
q
r
s
t
u
v
w
x
y
z

árbol; *(when 'el' follows 'a' they join to become 'al')* **we went to the park** fuimos al parque; **2** *(before a feminine noun)* la; **the table** la mesa; **the orange** la naranja; **3** *(before masculine plural nouns)* los; **the plates** los platos; **4** *(before feminine plural nouns)* las; **the windows** las ventanas.

theatre *noun* teatro *Masc.*; **to go to the theatre** ir [8] al teatro.

theft *noun* robo *Masc.*

their *adjective* **1** *(before a singular noun)* su; **their flat** su piso; **their mother** su madre; **2** *(before a plural noun)* sus; **their presents** sus regalos; **3** *(with parts of the body)* el, la, los, las; **they had tatoos on their arms** tenían tatuajes en los brazos; **they're washing their hands** se están lavando las manos.

theirs *pronoun* **1** *(when referring to a singular noun)* el suyo/la suya; **our garden's smaller than theirs** nuestro jardín es más pequeño que el suyo; **our house is bigger than theirs** nuestra casa es más grande que la suya; **2** *(when referring to a plural noun)* los suyos/las suyas; **our shoes were newer than theirs** nuestros zapatos eran más nuevos que los suyos; **our photos were better that theirs** nuestras fotos eran mejores que las suyas.

them *pronoun* **1** los/las; **she's got two brothers, but I don't know them** tiene dos hermanos, pero no los conozco; **remember Ann and Lisa? I saw them last week** ¿te acuerdas de Ann y Lisa? las vi la

semana pasada; **2** *(with an infinitive or when telling somebody to do something 'los'/'las' join onto the verb)* **I don't want to see them** no quiero verlos; **listen to them!** ¡escúchalos!; *(but when telling someone NOT to do something, 'los' or 'las' comes before the verb)* **don't push them!** ¡no los empujes!; **3** *(to them)* les; **I gave them my address** les di mis señas *('les' becomes 'se' before pronouns 'lo' or 'la')* **I lent it to them** se lo dejé; *(when giving an order 'se' joins the verb)* **give it back to them** ¡devuélveselo!; **4** *(after a preposition, in comparisons, or after the verb 'to be')* ellos/ellas; **I'll go with them** iré con ellos/ellas; **without them** sin ellos/sin ellas; **she's older than them** es mayor que ellos; **it's them!** ¡son ellos!/¡son ellas!

theme park *noun* parque *Masc.* temático.

themselves *pronoun* **1** *(as a reflexive)* se; **they've helped themselves** se sirvieron; **2** *(for emphasis)* ellos mismos/ellas mismas; **the boys can do it themselves** los chicos pueden hacerlo ellos mismos; **the girls will tell you themselves** las chicas te lo dirán ellas mismas; **3 by themselves** ellos solos/ellas solas.

then *adverb* **1** *(next)* luego; **have a shower and then make your bed** dúchate y luego haz la cama; **I went to the post office and then the bank** fui a Correos y luego al banco; **2** *(at that time)* entonces; **we were living in York then** entonces vivíamos en York; **3** (*in that case*) entonces; **then why worry?** entonces ¿para qué preocuparse?; **that's all right then** entonces vale; **4 by then** para entonces; **by then it was too late** para entonces era demasiado tarde.

theory *noun* teoría *Fem.*; **in theory** en teoría.

there *adverb* **1** ahí; (*further away*) allí; **put it there** ponlo ahí; (*further away*) ponlo allí; **stand there** ponte ahí; **they're in there** están ahí dentro; **look up there!** ¡mira ahí arriba!; **2 over there** ahí; (*further away*) allí; **she's over there talking to Mark** está ahí hablando con Mark; (*further away*) está allí hablando con Mark; **3 down there** ahí abajo; (*further away*) allí abajo; **up there** ahí arriba; (*further away*) allí arriba; **4** (*when there stands for something already mentioned, it is usually not translated*) **I've seen photos of Oxford but I've never been there** he visto fotos de Oxford, pero nunca he estado; **yes, I'm going there on Tuesday** sí, voy a ir el martes; **5 there is/there are** hay; **there's a cat in the garden** hay un gato en el jardín; **there was no bread** no había pan; **yes, there's enough** sí, hay suficiente; **there are plenty of seats** hay muchos asientos; **6 there they are!** ¡ahí están!; **there she is!** ¡ahí está!; **there's the bus coming!** ¡ahí viene el autobús!

thermometer *noun* termómetro *Masc.*

these *adjective* **1** (*with a masculine noun*) estos; **these envelopes** estos sobres; **2** (*with a feminine noun*) estas; **these postcards** estas postales.

they *pronoun* **1** (*like other subject pronouns 'they' is generally not translated; in Spanish the form of the verb tells you whether the subject of the verb is 'we, you, they', etc., so 'they' is only translated for emphasis*) **'where are the knives?' – 'they're in the drawer'** ¿dónde están los cuchillos? – 'están en el cajón'; **I bought some apples but they're not very nice** compré unas manzanas pero no están muy buenas; **2** (*for emphasis*) ellos/ellas; **they did it** lo hicieron ellos.

thick *adjective* **1** grueso/gruesa; **a thick layer of butter** una capa gruesa de mantequilla; **2** denso/densa (*fog, fumes*).

thickness *noun* **1** (*of wall, paper*) espesor *Masc.*; **2** (*of fog*) densidad *Fem.*

thief *noun* ladrón *Masc.*, ladrona *Fem.*

thigh *noun* muslo *Masc.*

thin *adjective* **1** delgado/delgada (*a person*); **to get thin** adelgazar [22]; **2** fino/fina (*a slice*); **3** (*too thin, skinny*) flaco/flaca; **she's very thin** está muy flaca.

thing *noun* **1** (*an object*) cosa *Fem.*; **shops full of pretty things** tiendas llenas de cosas preciosas; **she told me some surprising things** me dijo algunas cosas sorprendentes; **2** (*a whatsit*) chisme *Masc.* (*informal*); **you can use that thing to open it**

a
b
c
d
e
f
g
h
i
j
k
l
m
n
o
p
q
r
s
t
u
v
w
x
y
z

a
b
c
d
e
f
g
h
i
j
k
l
m
n
o
p
q
r
s
t
u
v
w
x
y
z

puedes usar ese chisme para abrirlo;
3 things (*belongings*) cosas *Fem.
plural*; **you can put your things in
my room** puedes poner tus cosas en
mi habitación; **4 the best thing to
do is ...** lo mejor es ...; **the thing is,
I've lost her address** la cuestión es
que he perdido sus señas; **5 how are
things with you?** ¿qué tal te van las
cosas?

think *verb* **1** pensar [29]; **I'm
thinking about you** estoy pensando
en ti; **Tony thinks it's silly** Tony
piensa que es una tontería; **what do
you think of my new jacket?** ¿qué
piensas de mi chaqueta nueva?;
what do you think of that? ¿qué
piensas de eso?; **he thought for a
moment** pensó un momento; **she's
thinking of studying medicine** está
pensando estudiar medicina;
2 (*believe*) creer [37]; **do you think
they'll come?** ¿crees que vendrán?;
no, I don't think so no, creo que no;
I think he's already left creo que ya
se ha ido; **3** (*imagine*) imaginar [17];
**I never thought it would be like
this!** ¡nunca imaginé que sería así!;
just think! we'll soon be in Spain!
¡imagínate! ¡pronto estaremos en
España!

third *noun* **1** (*fraction*) **a third** un
tercio; **2 the third of March** el tres
de marzo.
third *adjective* tercero/tercera; **on
the third floor** en la tercera planta.

thirdly *adverb* en tercer lugar.

Third World *noun* **the Third
World** el Tercer Mundo.

thirst *noun* sed *Fem.*

thirsty *adjective* **to be thirsty** tener
[9] sed; **I'm thirsty** tengo sed; **we
were all thirsty** todos teníamos sed.

thirteen *number* trece *Masc.*;
Ahmed's thirteen Ahmed tiene
trece años.

thirty *number* treinta *Masc.*; **she's
thirty** tiene treinta años; **thirty-five**
treinta y cinco.

this *adjective* **1** este (*before a
masculine noun*); esta (*before a
feminine noun*); **this paintbrush**
este pincel; **this tree** este árbol; **this
cup** esta taza; **this morning** esta
mañana; **2 this one** (*referring to a
masculine noun*) este, éste; (*referring
to a feminine noun*) esta, ésta; **if you
need a pen you can use this one** si
necesitas un boli puedes usar este; **if
you want a lamp you can borrow
this one** si quieres una lámpara
puedes coger esta.
this *pronoun* **1** (*referring to a
masculine noun*) este, éste; **this is
my car** este es mi coche; **2** (*referring
to a feminine noun*) esta, ésta; **this is
the best photo** esta es la mejor foto;
3 esto; **can you hold this for a
moment?** ¿puedes sostener esto un
momento?; **what's this?** ¿qué es
esto?; **4 this is Tracy speaking** (*on
the phone*) soy Tracy; **5** (*in
introductions*) **this is my sister
Carla** te presento a mi hermana
Carla.

thistle *noun* cardo *Masc.*

thorough *adjective* **1** (*search*) a
fondo; **2** (*person*) concienzudo/
concienzuda.

those *adjective* (*before a masculine noun*) esos; (*before a feminine noun*) esas; **those books** esos libros; **those cups** esas tazas.
those *pronoun* (*referring to a masculine noun*) esos, ésos; (*referring to a feminine noun*) esas, ésas; **if you want some knives you can take those** si quieres cuchillos puedes coger esos; **if you want some cups you can take those** si quieres tazas puedes coger esas.

though *conjunction* **1** aunque; **though it's cold** aunque hace calor; **though he's older than she is** aunque es mayor que ella; **2 it was a good idea, though** aun así era una buena idea.

thought *noun* pensamiento *Masc.*

thoughtful *adjective* **1** (*considerate*) amable; **it was really thoughtful of you** fue muy amable de tu parte; **2** (*deep in thought*) pensativo/pensativa.

thoughtless *adjective* desconsiderado/desconsiderada.

thousand *number* **1** mil *Masc.*; **a thousand** mil; **a thousand euros** mil euros; **three thousand** tres mil; **2 thousands of** miles de; **there were thousands of tourists in Barcelona** había miles de turistas en Barcelona.

thread *noun* hilo *Masc.*
thread *verb* enhebrar [17] (*a needle*).

threat *noun* amenaza *Fem.*

threaten *verb* amenazar [22]; **to threaten to do** amenazar con hacer.

three *number* tres *Masc.*; **Lily's three** Lily tiene tres años.

three-quarters *noun* tres cuartos *Masc. plural*.

thrilled *adjective* encantado/encantada; **I was thrilled to hear from you** me encantó tener noticias tuyas.

thriller *noun* **1** (*book*) novela *Fem.* de suspense; **2** (*film*) película *Fem.* de suspense.

thrilling *adjective* emocionante.

throat *noun* garganta *Fem.*; **to have a sore throat** tener [9] dolor de garganta.

through *preposition* **1** (*across*) a través de; **a path through the forest** un camino a través del bosque; **to go through something** atravesar [29] algo; **we went through the park** atravesamos el parque; **2** (*by way of*) por; **the train went through Leeds** el tren fue por Leeds; **through the window** por la ventana; **3 to go through customs** pasar [17] la aduana.
through *adjective* directo/directa (*a train or flight*).

throughout *preposition* **throughout the match** durante todo el partido; **throughout the world** por todo mundo.

throw *verb* tirar [17]; **I threw the letter into the bin** tiré la carta a la basura; **he threw the book on the floor** tiró el libro al suelo; **throw me the ball!** ¡tírame la pelota!; **we were throwing snowballs** estábamos tirando bolas de nieve.
• **to throw something away** tirar

[17] algo; **I've thrown away the old newspapers** he tirado los periódicos viejos.

● **to throw somebody out** echar [17] a alguien.

● **to throw something out** tirar [17] algo (*rubbish*).

● **to throw up** devolver [45].

thumb *noun* pulgar *Masc.*

thunder *noun* truenos *Masc. plural*; **a peal of thunder** un trueno.

thunderstorm *noun* tormenta *Fem.* eléctrica.

Thursday *noun* jueves *Masc.*; **on Thursday** el jueves; **I'm going out on Thursday** voy a salir el jueves; **see you on Thursday!** ¡hasta el jueves!; **on Thursdays** los jueves; **the museum is closed on Thursdays** el museo cierra los jueves; **every Thursday** todos los jueves; **last Thursday** el jueves pasado; **next Thursday** el próximo jueves.

tick *verb* **1** (*clocks*) hacer [7] tictac; **2** (*on paper*) marcar [31].

ticket *noun* **1** entrada *Fem.* (*for an exhibition, a theatre or cinema*) **two tickets for the concert** dos entradas para el concierto; **2** (*for a plane, a train, a bus or the underground*) billete *Masc.*; **a bus ticket** un billete de autobús; **3** (*for left luggage*) ticket *Masc.*; **4 a parking ticket** una multa.

ticket inspector *noun* revisor *Masc.*, revisora *Fem.*

ticket office *noun* **1** (*at a station*) mostrador *Masc.* de venta de billetes; **2** (*at a cinema*) taquilla *Fem.*

tickle *verb* hacer [7] cosquillas.

tide *noun* marea *Fem.*; **at high tide** cuando la marea está alta; **the tide is out** la marea está baja.

tidy *adjective* **1** ordenado/ordenada (*a room*); **2** bien escrito/bien escrita (*homework*); **3** bien arreglado/bien arreglada (*a person*).
tidy *verb* ordenar [17].

tie *noun* **1** corbata *Fem.*; **a red tie** una corbata roja; **2** (*in a match*) empate *Masc.*
tie *verb* **1** atar [17]; **to tie your shoelaces** atarse los zapatos; **2 to tie a knot in something** hacer [7] un nudo a algo; **3** (*in a match*) **we tied two all** empatamos a dos.

tiger *noun* tigre *Masc.*

tight *adjective* **1 to be tight** apretar [29]; **the skirt's a bit tight** la falda aprieta un poco; **these shoes are too tight** estos zapatos aprietan mucho; **2** (*close-fitting*) ceñido/ceñida; **she was wearing a tight dress** llevaba un vestido ceñido.

tighten *verb* apretar [29].

tightly *adverb* fuerte; **hold it tightly** agárralo fuerte.

tights *plural noun* medias *Fem. plural*; **a pair of purple tights** un par de medias moradas.

tile *noun* **1** (*on a floor or wall*) azulejo *Masc.*; **2** (*on a roof*) teja *Fem.*

till¹ *preposition* hasta; **they're here till Sunday** están aquí hasta el domingo; **till then** hasta entonces; **till now** hasta ahora; **she won't be back till ten** no volverá hasta las diez.

till[2] *noun* caja *Fem.*; **pay at the till** pase a pagar por caja.

time *noun* **1** (*on the clock*) hora *Fem.*; **what time is it?** ¿qué hora es?; **it's time for lunch** es hora de comer; **ten o'clock Spanish time** las diez hora española; **on time** a la hora; **2** (*an amount of time*) tiempo *Masc.*; **we've got lots of time** tenemos mucho tiempo; **there's not much time left** no queda mucho tiempo; **he talked for a long time** habló durante mucho tiempo; **she hasn't called me for a long time** hace mucho que no me llama; **3** (*moment*) momento *Masc.*; **is this a good time to phone?** ¿es buen momento para llamar?; **at any time** en cualquier momento; **4 from time to time** de vez en cuando; **at times** a veces; **for the time being** por ahora; **5** (*in a series*) vez *Fem.* (*plural* veces); **six times** seis veces; **the first time** la primera vez; **the first time I saw you** la primera vez que te vi; **three times a year** tres veces al año; **6** (*multiplying*) **three times two is six** tres por dos son seis; **7 to have a good time** pasárselo [17] bien; **we had a really good time** nos lo pasamos muy bien; **have a good time!** ¡pásatelo bien!

time off *noun* **1** (*free time*) tiempo *Masc.* libre; **2** (*leave*) días *Masc. plural* libres.

timetable *noun* horario *Masc.*; **the bus timetable** el horario de los autobuses.

tin *noun* lata *Fem.*; **a tin of tomatoes** una lata de tomates.

tin foil *noun* papel *Masc.* aluminio.

tinned *adjective* en lata; **tinned peas** guisantes en lata.

tin opener *noun* abrelatas *Masc.* (*does not change in the plural*).

tiny *adjective* diminuto/diminuta.

tip *noun* **1** (*the end*) punta *Fem.*; **the tip of my finger** la punta de mi dedo; **2** (*money*) propina *Fem.*; **3** (*a useful hint*) consejo *Masc.*
tip *verb* **1** (*to give money to*) darle [4] una propina a; **we tipped the waiter** le dimos una propina al camarero; **2** tirar [17] (*liquid*).

tiptoe *noun* **on tiptoe** de puntillas.

tired *adjective* **1** cansado/cansada; **I'm tired** estoy cansado; **you look tired** pareces cansado; **2 to be tired of** estar [2] harto de/harta de; **he's tired of London** está harto de Londres; **she says she's tired of watching TV** dice que está harta de ver la tele.

tiring *adjective* cansado/cansada.

tissue *noun* (*a paper hanky*) pañuelo *Masc.* de papel; **do you have a tissue?** ¿tienes un pañuelo de papel?

title *noun* título *Masc.*

to *preposition* **1** (*to a place*) a; **to London** a Londres; **to Spain** a España; **she's gone to the office** se ha ido a la oficina; **to Paul's house** a casa de Paul; **from Monday to Friday** de lunes a viernes; (*when 'el' follows 'a' they join to become 'al'*) **I'm going to school** voy al colegio; **I'm going to the dentist's tomorrow** voy al dentista mañana;

a
b
c
d
e
f
g
h
i
j
k
l
m
n
o
p
q
r
s
t
u
v
w
x
y
z

a
b
c
d
e
f
g
h
i
j
k
l
m
n
o
p
q
r
s
t
u
v
w
x
y
z

2 (*to a person*) a; **give the book to Leila** dale el libro a Leila; **who did you give it to?** ¿a quién se lo diste?; **to talk to somebody** hablar [17] con alguien; **he didn't talk to me** no habló conmigo; **I was nice to them** fui amable con ellos; **3 we're ready to go** estamos listos para irnos; **it's easy to do** es fácil de hacer; **I have nothing to do** no tengo nada que hacer; **I have a lot of homework to do** tengo muchos deberes que hacer; **4** (*talking about the time*) **it's ten to nine** son las nueve menos diez; **it's twenty to** son menos veinte; **5** (*in order to*) para; **he gave me some money to buy a sandwich** me dio dinero para comprar un sandwich.

toast *noun* **1** pan *Masc.* tostado; **a piece of toast** una tostada; **two slices of toast** dos tostadas; **2** (*to your health*) brindis *Masc.*; **to drink a toast to the future** brindar [17] por el futuro.

toaster *noun* tostador *Masc.*

tobacco *noun* tabaco *Masc.*

tobacconist's *noun* estanco *Masc.*

today *adverb, noun* hoy; **today's her birthday** hoy es su cumpleaños.

toe *noun* dedo *Masc.* del pie; **my big toe** mi dedo gordo del pie.

toenail *noun* uña *Fem.* de un dedo del pie.

toffee *noun* toffee *Masc.*

together *adverb* juntos/juntas; **Kate and Lindy arrived together** Kate y Lindy llegaron juntas; **they all left together** se fueron todos juntos.

toilet *noun* **1** (*in a house*) baño *Masc.*; **she's gone to the toilet** ha ido al baño; **2** (*in a public place*) servicio *Masc.*; **where's the toilet?** ¿dónde está el servicio?; **3 toilets** (*in a public place*) servicios *Masc. plural*; **where are the toilets?** ¿dónde están los servicios.

toilet paper *noun* papel *Masc.* higiénico.

toilet roll *noun* rollo *Masc.* de papel higiénico.

token *noun* **1** (*for a machine or game*) ficha *Fem.*; **2** (*as a present*) cheque *Masc.* regalo; **a record token** un cheque regalo para un disco.

toll *noun* **1** (*on motorway*) peaje *Masc.*; **2** (*number*) número *Masc.*; **the death toll is 25** el número de víctimas mortales asciende a 25.

tomato *noun* tomate *Masc.*; **a tomato salad** una ensalada de tomate; **tomato sauce** salsa *Fem.* de tomate.

tomorrow *adverb* mañana; **I'll do it tomorrow** lo haré mañana; **tomorrow afternoon** mañana por la tarde; **tomorrow morning** mañana por la mañana; **tomorrow night** mañana por la noche; **the day after tomorrow** pasado mañana.

ton *noun* tonelada *Fem.*; **she gets tons of letters** recibe montones de cartas.

tongue *noun* lengua *Fem.*; **to stick your tongue out** sacar [31] la lengua; ★ **it's on the tip of my**

tongue lo tengo en la punta de la lengua.

tonic *noun* tónica *Fem.*; **a gin and tonic** un gin tonic.

tonight *adverb* esta noche; **I'm going out with my mates tonight** esta noche voy a salir con mis amigos.

tonsillitis *noun* anginas *Fem. plural*.

too *adverb* 1 demasiado; **it's too expensive** es demasiado caro; **the tickets are too expensive** los billetes son demasiado caros; **too often** demasiado a menudo; 2 **too much** (*before a masculine noun*) demasiado; (*before a feminine noun*) demasiada; **it takes too much time** lleva demasiado tiempo; **I watch too much TV** veo demasiada televisión; 3 **too much** (*before verb*) demasiado; **he eats too much** come demasiado; 4 **too many** (*before a masculine noun*) demasiados; (*before a feminine noun*) demasiadas; **there are too many accidents** hay demasiados accidentes; 5 (*as well*) también; **Karen's coming too** Karen también viene; **me too!** ¡yo también!; 6 (*very*) muy; **I'm not too convinced** no estoy muy convencida.

tool *noun* herramienta *Fem.*

tool kit *noun* juego *Masc.* de herramientas.

tooth *noun* 1 diente *Masc.*; **to brush your teeth** cepillarse [17] los dientes; 2 (*back tooth*) muela *Fem.*

toothache *noun* dolor *Masc.* de muelas; **to have toothache** tener [9] dolor de muelas.

toothbrush *noun* cepillo *Masc.* de dientes.

toothpaste *noun* pasta *Fem.* de dientes.

top *noun* 1 alto *Masc.* (*of a ladder, or stairs*); **at the top of the stairs** en lo alto de las escaleras; 2 (*of a page, container or box*) parte *Fem.* superior; **the top of the box is red** la parte superior de la caja es roja; 3 **on top of** (*a table, wardrobe, etc*) encima de; **it's on top of the chest-of-drawers** está encima de la cómoda; 4 (*of a mountain*) cima *Fem.*; 5 (*a lid, cap*) (*of a bottle*) tapón *Masc.* (*of a pan or jar*) tapa *Fem.* (*of a pen*) capuchón *Masc.*; 6 **to be at the top of the list** encabezar [22] una lista.
top *adjective* 1 (*a step or floor*) último/última; **it's on the top floor** está en el último piso; 2 de arriba (*a bunk, drawer or shelf*); 3 **in the top left-hand corner** en la esquina superior izquierda; ⋆ **and on top of all that** y para colmo; ⋆ **it was a bit over the top** fue un poco excesivo.

topic *noun* tema *Masc.*

topping *noun* guarnición *Fem.*; **which topping do you want?** ¿qué guarnición quieres?

torch *noun* linterna *Fem.*

torn *adjective* roto/rota.

tornado *noun* tornado *Masc.*

tortoise *noun* tortuga *Fem.*

a
b
c
d
e
f
g
h
i
j
k
l
m
n
o
p
q
r
s
t
u
v
w
x
y
z

a
b
c
d
e
f
g
h
i
j
k
l
m
n
o
p
q
r
s
t
u
v
w
x
y
z

torture noun tortura Fem.
torture verb torturar [17].

Tory noun conservador Masc., conservadora Fem.

total noun total Masc.
total adjective total.

totally adverb totalmente.

touch noun 1 (contact) to get in touch with somebody contactar [17] con alguien; to stay in touch with somebody mantenerse [9] en contacto con alguien; we've lost touch hemos perdido el contacto; 2 (a little bit) poco Masc.; a touch of vanilla un poco de vainilla; it was a touch embarrassing fue un poco embarazoso.
touch verb 1 tocar [31]; 2 (emotionally) conmover [38].

tough adjective 1 duro/dura; the meat's a bit tough la carne está un poco dura; a tough guy un tipo duro; you need to be tough to survive tienes que ser duro para sobrevivir; 2 (severe) severo/severa; 3 (fabric) resistente; 4 (question, problem or job) difícil; things are a bit tough at the moment las cosas están un poco difíciles en este momento; 5 tough luck! ¡mala suerte!

tour noun 1 visita Fem.; we did the tour of the castle hicimos la visita al castillo; a tour of the city una visita a la ciudad; 2 a package tour un viaje organizado; 3 (by a band or theatre group) gira Fem.; to go on tour ir [8] de gira.

tourism noun turismo Masc.

tourist noun turista Masc./Fem.

tourist information office noun oficina Fem. de información y turismo.

towards adverb hacia; she went off towards the lake se fue hacia el lago.

towel noun toalla Fem.

tower noun torre Fem.; the Eiffel Tower la torre Eiffel.

tower block noun bloque Masc. de apartamentos.

town noun ciudad Fem.; to go into town ir [8] a la ciudad; (to the centre) ir [8] al centro.

town centre noun centro Masc. de la ciudad.

town hall noun ayuntamiento Masc.

toxic adjective tóxico/tóxica.

toy noun juguete Masc.

trace noun rastro Masc.; there is no trace of it no hay rastro de ello.
trace verb 1 (on paper) calcar [31]; 2 (a missing person) localizar [22].

tracing paper noun papel Masc. de calco.

track noun 1 (for sport) pista Fem.; a track event una prueba de atletismo; a racing track (for cars) un circuito; 2 (a path) sendero Masc. 3 (song) tema Masc.; this is my favourite track es mi tema favorito

track suit noun chandal Masc.

tractor noun tractor Masc.

trade noun (a profession) oficio Masc.

trade mark *noun* marca *Fem.* comercial; **a registered trade mark** una marca registrada.

trade union *noun* sindicato *Masc.*

tradition *noun* tradición *Fem.*

traditional *adjective* tradicional.

traffic *noun* tráfico *Masc.*

traffic jam *noun* embotellamiento *Masc.*

traffic lights *plural noun* semáforo *Masc.*

traffic warden *noun* guardia *Masc./Fem.* municipal.

tragedy *noun* tragedia *Fem.*

tragic *adjective* trágico/trágica.

trail *noun* (*a path*) sendero *Masc.*; **a nature trail** un sendero ecológico.

trailer *noun* remolque *Masc.*

train *noun* tren *Masc.*; **he's coming by train** viene en tren; **I met her off the train** fui a recogerla en la estación; **the train for York** el tren para York.

train *verb* **1** estudiar [17] (*a student*); **2 to train to be something** estudiar para algo; **he's training to be a nurse** está estudiando para ser enfermero; **3** (*in sport*) entrenar [17]; **the team trains on Saturdays** el equipo entrena los sábados.

train ticket *noun* billete *Masc.* de tren.

train timetable *noun* horario *Masc.* de trenes.

trainer *noun* **1** (*of an athlete or a horse*) entrenador *Masc.*, entrenadora *Fem.*; **2** (*shoe*) zapatilla

Fem. de deporte; **my new trainers** mis zapatillas de deporte nuevas.

training *noun* **1** (*for a career*) formación *Fem.*; **2** (*for sport*) entrenamiento *Masc.*

tram *noun* tranvía *Masc.*

trampoline *noun* cama *Fem.* elástica.

transfer *noun* **1** (*of money*) transferencia *Fem.*; **2** (*to new post*) traslado *Masc.*; **3** (*sticker*) calcomanía *Fem.*

translate *verb* traducir [60]; **to translate something into Spanish** traducir algo al español.

translation *noun* traducción *Fem.*

translator *noun* traductor *Masc.*, traductora *Fem.*; **I'd like to be a translator** me gustaría ser traductora.

transparent *adjective* transparente.

transplant *noun* trasplante *Masc.*

transport *noun* transporte *Masc.*; **air transport** transporte aéreo; **public transport** transporte público.

trap *noun* trampa *Fem.*

travel *noun* viajes *Masc. plural*; **foreign travel** viajes al extranjero; **a travel brochure** un folleto de viajes.

travel *verb* viajar [17].

travel agency *noun* agencia *Fem.* de viajes.

travel agent *noun* agente *Masc.* de viajes.

a
b
c
d
e
f
g
h
i
j
k
l
m
n
o
p
q
r
s
t
u
v
w
x
y
z

traveller noun 1 viajero Masc., viajera Fem.; 2 (gypsy) gitano Masc., gitana Fem.

traveller's cheque noun cheque Masc. de viaje.

travelling noun I like travelling me gusta viajar.

travel-sick noun to be/get travel-sick marearse [17] en los viajes.

tray noun bandeja Fem.

tread verb to tread on something pisar [17] algo.

treasure noun tesoro Masc.

treat noun 1 capricho Masc.; to give yourself a treat darse [4] un capricho; it's a little treat es un caprichito; 2 I took them to the circus as a treat les llevé al circo como algo especial.
treat verb 1 tratar [17]; he treats his dog well trata bien a su perro; the doctor who treated you el médico que te trató; 2 to treat somebody to something invitar [17] a alguien a algo; I'll treat you to a drink te invito a una copa; 3 I treated myself to a new dress me compré un vestido para darme un capricho.

treatment noun tratamiento Masc. (medical).

treaty noun tratado Masc.

tree noun árbol Masc.

tree trunk noun tronco Masc.

tremendous adjective tremendo/tremenda; a tremendous victory/defeat una tremenda victoria/derrota.

trend noun 1 (a fashion) moda Fem.; 2 (a tendency) tendencia Fem.

trendy adjective de moda.

trial noun juicio Masc. (legal).

triangle noun triángulo Masc.

trick noun 1 (card or conjuring trick, knack) truco Masc.; a card trick un truco con las cartas; it doesn't work, there must be a trick to it no funciona, debe tener truco; 2 (a joke) broma Fem.; to play a trick on somebody gastarle [17] una broma a alguien.
trick verb engañar [17]; he tricked me! me engañó!

tricky adjective delicado/delicada; it's a tricky situation es una situación delicada.

tricycle noun triciclo Masc.

tribe noun tribu Fem.

tribute noun homenaje Masc.

Trinidad noun Trinidad Fem.

Trinidadian noun trinitense Masc., Fem.
Trinidadian adjective trinitense.

trip noun viaje Masc.; a trip to Florida un viaje a Florida; he's on a business trip está en viaje de negocios; a day trip to France un viaje de un día a Francia.
trip verb (to stumble) tropezar [25]; Nicky tripped over a stone Nicky tropezó con una piedra.

triple verb triplicar [31]; the price has tripled el precio se ha triplicado.

trolley noun carro Masc.

trombone *noun* trombón *Masc.*; **to play the trombone** tocar [31] el trombón.

trophy *noun* trofeo *Masc.*

trouble *noun* **1** problemas *Masc. plural*; **we had trouble with the car** tuvimos problemas con el coche; **Steve's in trouble** Steve tiene problemas; **to get into trouble** meterse [18] en problemas; **2 what's the trouble?** ¿cuál es el problema?; **3** (*difficulty*) **I had trouble finding a seat** me costó encontrar un sitio; **it's not worth the trouble** no vale la pena; **the trouble is, I've forgotten the number** el problema es que he olvidado el número; **it's no trouble!** ¡no es ningún problema!

trousers *plural noun* pantalones *Masc. plural*; **a new pair of trousers** unos pantalones nuevos, un nuevo par de pantalones.

trout *noun* trucha *Fem.*

truant *noun* estudiante *Masc./Fem.* que falta a clase sin autorización; **she's playing truant** está haciendo novillos.

truck *noun* camión *Masc.*

true *adjective* **a true story** una historia verídica; **to be true** ser [1] verdad; **is that true?** ¿es eso verdad?; **it's true she's absent-minded** es verdad que es despistada.

truly *adverb* de veras.

trump *noun* triunfo *Masc.*; **spades are trumps** las picas son triunfo.

trumpet *noun* trompeta *Fem.*; **to play the trumpet** tocar [31] la trompeta.

trunk *noun* **1** (*of a tree*) tronco *Masc.*; **2** (*of an elephant*) trompa *Fem.*; **3** (*a suitcase*) baúl *Masc.*

trunks *plural noun* **swimming trunks** bañador *Masc.*

trust *noun* confianza *Fem.* **trust** *verb* confiar [32]; **I trust her** confío en ella.

truth *noun* verdad *Fem.*; **to tell the truth, I'd completely forgottten** si quieres que te diga la verdad, me he olvidado completamente.

try *noun* intento *Masc.*; **it's my first try** es mi primer intento; **to have a try** intentar [17]; **you should give it a try** deberías intentarlo.
try *verb* **1** intentar [17]; **to try to do** intentar hacer; **I'm trying to open the door** estoy intentando abrir la puerta; **2** (*taste*) probar [24]; **try this sauce** prueba esta salsa; **to try hard to do** esforzarse [26] por hacer.
• **to try something on** probarse [26] algo (*a garment*).

T-shirt *noun* camiseta *Fem.*

tub *noun* **1** (*food container*) tarrina *Fem.*; **2** (*bath*) bañera *Fem.*

tube *noun* **1** tubo *Masc.*; **2 the tube** (*London underground*) (*informal*) el metro.

tuberculosis *noun* tuberculosis *Fem.*

Tuesday *noun* martes *Masc.*; **on Tuesday** el martes; **I'm going out on Tuesday** voy a salir el martes; **see you on Tuesday!** ¡hasta el martes!; **on Tuesdays** los martes; **the museum is closed on Tuesdays** el museo cierra los

a
b
c
d
e
f
g
h
i
j
k
l
m
n
o
p
q
r
s
t
u
v
w
x
y
z

martes; **every Tuesday** todos los martes; **last Tuesday** el martes pasado; **next Tuesday** el próximo martes.

tuition *noun* clases *Fem. plural*; **piano tuition** clases de piano; **private tuition** clases particulares.

tulip *noun* tulipán *Masc.*

tumble-drier *noun* secadora *Fem.*

tummy *noun* barriga *Fem.*

tuna *noun* atún *Masc.*

tune *noun* melodía *Fem.*

tunnel *noun* túnel *Masc.*; **the Channel Tunnel** el Eurotúnel.

turban *noun* turbante *Masc.*

turkey *noun* pavo *Masc.*

Turkey *noun* Turquía *Fem.*

Turkish *noun* turco *Masc.* (*language*).
Turkish *adjective* turco/turca.

turn *noun* 1 (*in a game*) turno *Masc.*; **it's your turn** es tu turno; **whose turn is it?** ¿a quién le toca?; **it's Jane's turn to play** es el turno de Jane; **to take turns driving** turnarse [17] para conducir; **2** (*in a road*) curva *Fem.*
turn *verb* 1 girar [17]; **turn your chair round** gira la silla; **turn left at the next set of lights** gira a la izquierda en el próximo semáforo; **2** dar [4] la vuelta a (*a page or mattress*); **3** (*become*) ponerse [11]; **she turned red** se puso roja.
● **to turn back** volverse [45]; **we turned back** nos volvimos.
● **to turn off 1** (*from a road*) girar [17]; **2** (*switch off*) apagar [28] (*a light, an oven, a TV, or radio*); cerrar [29] (*gas, electricity or a tap*).
● **to turn on** encender [36] (*a light, an oven, a TV, or radio*), abrir [46] (*a tap*).
● **to turn out: 1 to turn out well/badly** salir [63] bien/mal; **it all turned out well in the end** todo salió bien al final; **the holiday turned out badly** las vacaciones salieron mal; **2 it turned out that I was wrong** resultó que estaba equivocado.
● **to turn over 1** (*roll over*) darse [4] la vuelta; **2** dar [4] la vuelta a (*a page*).
● **to turn up 1** (*to arrive*) presentarse [17]; **they turned up an hour late** se presentaron con una hora de retraso; **2** abrir [46] más (*the gas*); **3** subir [19] (*the heating or volume*); **can you turn up the volume?** ¿puedes subir el volumen?

turning *noun* bocacalle *Fem.*; **take the first turning on the right/left** toma la primera bocacalle a la derecha/izquierda.

turnip *noun* nabo *Masc.*

turquoise *adjective* turquesa.

turtle *noun* tortuga *Fem.*

TV *noun* tele *Fem.*; **I saw her on TV** la vi en la tele.

tweezers *noun* pinzas *Fem. plural.*

twelfth *noun* **the twelfth of May** el doce de mayo.
twelfth *adjective* doceavo/doceava; **on the twelfth floor** en la planta duodécima.

twelve *number* doce *Masc.*; **Tara's twelve** Tara tiene doce años; **it's twelve o'clock** (*midday*) son las doce de la mañana, (*midnight*) son las doce de la noche.

twenty *number* veinte; **Marie's twenty** Marie tiene veinte años; **twenty-one** veintiuno; **twenty-five** veinticinco.

twice *adverb* **1** dos veces; **I've asked him twice** le he preguntado dos veces; **2 twice as much** el doble.

twig *noun* ramita *Fem.*

twilight *noun* anochecer *Masc.*

twin *noun* gemelo *Masc.*, gemela *Fem.*; **Helen and Tim are twins** Helen y Tim son gemelos; **her twin sister** su hermana gemela.
twin *verb* **Oxford is twinned with León** Oxford está hermanado con León.

twist *verb* girar [17] (*knob or cap of bottle*).

two *number* dos *Masc.*; **Ben's two** Ben tiene dos años; **two by two** dos por dos.

type *noun* tipo *Masc.*; **what type of computer is it?** ¿qué tipo de ordenador es?
type *verb* (*on a typewriter*) escribir [52] a máquina; **I'm learning to type** estoy aprendiendo a escribir a máquina; **I was busy typing some letters** estaba ocupada escribiendo unas cartas a máquina.

typewriter *noun* máquina *Fem.* de escribir.

typical *adjective* típico/típica.

typing *noun* mecanografía *Fem.*; **her typing is awful** escribe muy mal a máquina.

tyre *noun* neumático *Masc.*

Uu

UFO *noun* ovni *Masc.*

ugly *adjective* feo/fea.

UK *noun* Reino *Masc.* Unido.

Ulster *noun* el Ulster.

ulcer *noun* úlcera *Fem.*

umbrella *noun* paraguas *Masc.* (*does not change in the plural*).

umpire *noun* árbitro *Masc.*, árbitra *Fem.*

UN *noun* ONU *Fem.* (*short for 'Organización de las Naciones Unidas'*).

unable *adjective* **to be unable to do** no poder [10] hacer; **he's unable to come** no puede venir.

unavoidable *adjective* inevitable.

unbearable *adjective* insoportable.

unbelievable *adjective* increíble.

uncertain *adjective* incierto/ incierta, no seguro/no segura; **I'm uncertain whether they are coming** no estoy seguro/segura si vienen o no.

uncle *noun* tío *Masc.*; **my Uncle Tom** mi tío Tom.

uncomfortable *adjective* incómodo/incómoda.

unconscious *adjective* (*out cold*) sin sentido; **Tessa's still unconscious** Tessa está todavía sin sentido.

a b c d e f g h i j k l m n o p q r s t u v w x y z

a

b

c

d

e

f

g

h

i

j

k

l

m

n

o

p

q

r

s

t

u

v

w

x

y

z

under *preposition* **1** (*underneath*) debajo de; **under the bed** debajo de la cama; **perhaps it's under there** quizás está ahí debajo; **to go under something** pasar por debajo de algo; **2** (*less than*) menos de; **under £20** menos de veinte libras; **3 children under five** niños menores de cinco años.

under-age *noun* **to be under-age** ser [1] menor de edad.

underground *noun* (*a railway*) metro *Masc.*; **shall we go by underground?** ¿vamos en metro? **underground** *adjective* subterráneo/subterránea; **an underground carpark** un parking subterráneo.

underline *verb* subrayar [17].

underneath *preposition* debajo de; **it's underneath these papers** está debajo de esos papeles. **underneath** *adverb* debajo; **look underneath** mira debajo.

underpants *plural noun* calzoncillos *Masc. plural*; **my underpants** mis calzoncillos; **a pair of underpants** unos calzoncillos.

underpass *noun* **1** (*pedestrian*) paso *Masc.* subterráneo; **2** (*for traffic*) paso *Masc.* inferior.

understand *verb* entender [36]; **I don't understand** no entiendo; **I couldn't understand what he was saying** no entendí lo que estaba diciendo.

understandable *adjective* comprensible; **that's understandable** eso es comprensible.

underwear *noun* ropa *Fem.* interior.

undo *verb* **1** desabrochar [17] (*a button or a garment*); **2** desatar [17] (*shoelaces*); **3** deshacer [7] (*a parcel or knot*).

undone *adjective* **to come undone** desabrocharse [17] (*a button*) desatarse [17] (*shoelaces*).

undress *verb* **to get undressed** desvestirse [57]; **I got undressed** me desvestí.

unemployed *noun* **the unemployed** los parados. **unemployed** *adjective* parado/parada; **she's unemployed** está parada.

unemployment *noun* paro *Masc.*

uneven *adjective* irregular.

unexpected *adjective* inesperado/inesperada.

unexpectedly *adverb* (*to happen, arrive*) de improviso.

unfair *adjective* injusto/injusta; **it's unfair to young people** es injusto para la gente joven.

unfasten *verb* desabrochar [17].

unfold *verb* desdoblar [17].

unforgettable *adjective* inolvidable.

unfortunate *adjective* desgraciado/desgraciada.

unfortunately *adverb* desgraciadamente.

unfriendly *adjective* antipático/antipática.

ungrateful *adjective* desagradecido/desagradecida.

592

unhappy *adjective* **1** infeliz; **an unhappy childhood** una infancia infeliz; **2** (*discontented*) **to be unhappy** no estar [2] contento/contenta.

unhurt *adjective* ileso/ilesa.

uniform *noun* uniforme *Masc.*; **in school uniform** con el uniforme del colegio.

uninhabited *adjective* desierto/desierta.

union *noun* (*a trade union*) sindicato *Masc.*

Union Jack *noun* **the Union Jack** la bandera del Reino Unido.

unique *adjective* único/única.

unit *noun* **1** (*for measuring, for example*) unidad *Fem.*; **2** (*in a kitchen*) módulo *Masc.*; **3** (*a hospital department*) servicio *Masc.*

United Kingdom *noun* Reino *Masc.* Unido.

United Nations *noun* Naciones *Fem. plural* Unidas.

United States (of America) *plural noun* Estados *Masc. plural* Unidos (de América).

universe *noun* universo *Masc.*

university *noun* universidad *Fem.*; **to go to university** ir [8] a la universidad.

unjust *adjective* injusto/injusta.

unkind *adjective* poco amable.

unknown *adjective* desconocido/desconocida.

unleaded petrol *noun* gasolina *Fem.* sin plomo.

unless *conjunction* a no ser que (*followed by subjunctive*); **unless he does it** a no ser que él lo haga; **unless you tell her** a no ser que tú se lo digas.

unlikely *adjective* poco probable; **it's unlikely** es poco probable.

unload *verb* descargar [28].

unlock *verb* **to unlock a door** abrir [46] una puerta; **the car's unlocked** el coche está abierto; **the door was unlocked** la puerta no estaba cerrada con llave.

unlucky *adjective* **1** (*a person*) **to be unlucky** no tener [9] suerte; **I was unlucky, it was shut** no tuve suerte, estaba cerrado; **2 thirteen is an unlucky number** el trece trae mala suerte.

unmarried *adjective* soltero/soltera.

unnatural *adjective* poco natural.

unnecessary *adjective* no necesario; **it's unnecessary to book** no es necesario reservar.

unpack *verb* **I unpacked my rucksack** saqué las cosas de mi mochila; **I'll just unpack and then come down** voy a deshacer las maletas y bajo.

unpaid *adjective* **1** sin pagar (*a bill*); **2** no remunerado (*work*).

unpleasant *adjective* desagradable.

unpopular *adjective* poco popular.

unrealistic *adjective* poco realista.

a
b
c
d
e
f
g
h
i
j
k
l
m
n
o
p
q
r
s
t
u
v
w
x
y
z

a
b
c
d
e
f
g
h
i
j
k
l
m
n
o
p
q
r
s
t
u
v
w
x
y
z

unreasonable *adjective* poco razonable; **he's being really unreasonable** no está siendo nada razonable.

unreliable *adjective* **1** poco fidedigno (*information*); **2 this computer is unreliable** no te puedes fiar de este ordenador; **3** informal (*person*); **he's unreliable** es informal.

unroll *verb* desenrrollar [17].

unsafe *adjective* peligroso/peligrosa (*wiring, for instance*).

unscrew *verb* destornillar [17].

unsuccessful *adjective* **to be unsuccessful** fracasar [17]; **I tried, but I was unsuccessful** lo intenté pero fracasé; **an unsuccessful attempt** un intento fallido.

untidy *adjective* desordenado/desordenada; **the house is always untidy** la casa siempre está desordenada.

untie *verb* desatar [17].

until *preposition* **1** hasta; **until Monday** hasta el lunes; **until the tenth** hasta el diez; **until now** hasta ahora; **until then** hasta entonces; **2 not until** no hasta; **not until September** no hasta septiembre; **it won't be finished until Friday** no estará terminado hasta el viernes.

unusual *adjective* poco corriente; **an unusual beetle** un escarabajo poco corriente; **storms are unusual in June** las tormentas son poco corrientes en junio.

unwilling *adjective* **to be unwilling to do** no estar [2] dispuesto a hacer; **he's unwilling to wait** no está dispuesto a esperar.

unwrap *verb* desenvolver [45].

up *preposition, adverb* **1** (*higher up*) arriba; **hands up!** ¡manos arriba!; **up here** aquí arriba; **up there** ahí arriba; **it's just up the road** está en esta calle un poco más arriba; **up on the roof** en el tejado; **up in Glasgow** en Glasgow; **2 to go up** subir [19] (*stairs or road*); **we went up the street** subimos la calle; **I ran up the street** subí la calle corriendo; **I'll go up to Glasgow this weekend** iré a Glasgow este fin de semana; **3** (*out of bed*) **to be up** estar [2] levantado; **Liz isn't up yet** Liz aún no está levantada; **to get up** levantarse [17]; **we got up at six** nos levantamos a las seis; **I was up late last night** me acosté tarde anoche; **she was up all night** no se acostó en toda la noche; **4** (*wrong*) **what's up?** ¿qué pasa?; **what's up with him?** ¿qué le pasa?; **5 up to** hasta; **up to here** hasta aquí; **up to fifty people** hasta cincuenta personas; **she came up to me** se acercó a mí; **6 what's she up to?** ¿qué está haciendo?; **it's up to you (to decide)** tú tienes que decidir; ★**time's up!** ¡se acabó el tiempo!

uphill *adverb* cuesta arriba.

upright *adjective* derecho/derecha; **put it upright** ponlo derecho; **to stand upright** estar [2] derecho.

upset *noun* **a stomach upset** un dolor de estómago.
upset *adjective* disgustado/disgustada; **he's upset** está disgustado.

upset *verb* to upset somebody disgustar [17] a alguien.

upside down *adjective* boca abajo.

upstairs *adverb* arriba; **Mum's upstairs** mamá está arriba; **to go upstairs** subir [19].

up-to-date *adjective* **1** (*in fashion*) moderno/moderna; **2** (*information*) actualizado/actualizada.

urgent *adjective* urgente.

urgently *adverb* urgentemente; **she wants to see you urgently** quiere verte urgentemente.

us *pronoun* **1** nos; **she knows us** nos conoce; **they saw us** nos vieron; **he gave us a cheque** nos dio un cheque (*when there are two pronouns, 'nos' comes first*) **they lent it to us** nos lo dejaron; **2** (*with an infinitive or when telling someone to do something, 'nos' joins onto the verb*) **can you help us, please?** ¿puedes ayudarnos por favor?, ¿nos puedes ayudar, por favor?; **listen to us!** ¡escúchanos!; **wait for us!** ¡espéranos!; (*but when telling someone NOT to do something, 'nos' comes before the verb*) **don't push us!** ¡no nos empujes!; **3** (*after a preposition, in comparisons, or after the verb 'to be'*) nosotros/nosotras; **behind us** detrás de nosotros/nosotras; **they left without us** se fueron sin nosotros/nosotras; **with us** con nosotros/nosotras; **she's older than us** es mayor que nosotros/nosotras; **it's us!** ¡somos nosotros/nosotras!

US, USA *noun* EE.UU *Masc.* (*short for Estados Unidos*).

use *noun* **1** uso *Masc.*; **instructions for use** instrucciones de uso; **2 it's no use** no sirve de nada; **it's no use phoning** no sirve de nada llamar. **use** *verb* usar [17]; **we use the dictionary** usamos el diccionario; **to use something to do** usar [17] algo para hacer; **I used a knife to open the parcel** usé un cuchillo para abrir el paquete.

● **to use up 1** consumir [19] todo (*food*); **2** gastar [17] todo (*money or petrol*).

used *adjective* **1 to be used to something** estar [2] acostumbrado/acostumbrada a algo; **I'm not used to cats** no estoy acostumbrado a los gatos; **I'm not used to it** no estoy acostumbrado; **I'm not used to eating in restaurants** no estoy acostumbrado a comer en restaurantes; **2 to get used to** acostumbrarse [17] a; **I've got used to living here** me he acostumbrado a vivir aquí; **you'll get used to it!** ¡ya te acostumbrarás! **used** *verb* **they used to live in the country** vivían en el campo; **she used to smoke** antes fumaba.

useful *adjective* útil.

useless *adjective* **1** inútil (*person*); **you're completely useless!** ¡eres un completo inútil!; **2 this knife is useless** este cuchillo no sirve para nada.

user *noun* usuario *Masc.*, usuaria *Fem.*

user-friendly *adjective* fácil de usar.

usual *adjective, adverb* **1** (*time, place, problem*) de siempre; **it's the usual problem** es el problema de siempre; **2** (*method*) habitual; **3 as usual** como siempre; **4 it's colder than usual** hace más frío de lo normal.

usually *adverb* normalmente; **I usually leave at eight** normalmente salgo a las ocho.

utensil *noun* utensillo *Masc.*

Vv

vacancy *noun* **1** (*in a hotel*) **'vacancies'** 'habitaciones libres'; **'no vacancies'** 'completo'; **2 a job vacancy** una oferta de trabajo.

vacant *adjective* libre (*room or seat*).

vaccinate *verb* vacunar [17].

vaccination *noun* vacuna *Fem.*

vacuum *noun* vacío *Masc.*
vacuum *verb* pasar [17] la aspiradora; **I'm going to vacuum my room** voy a pasar la aspiradora por mi habitación.

vacuum cleaner *noun* aspiradora *Fem.*

vagina *noun* vagina *Fem.*

vague *adjective* poco preciso/poco precisa.

vaguely *adverb* vagamente.

vain *adjective* vano/vana (*attempt*); **in vain** en vano.

valentine card *noun* tarjeta *Fem.* que se envía el día de los enamorados.

Valentine's Day *noun* día *Masc.* de San Valentín.

valid *adjective* válido/válida.

valley *noun* valle *Masc.*

valuable *adjective* valioso/valiosa; **to be valuable** ser [1] valioso/valiosa; **that watch is very valuable** este reloj es muy valioso; **he gave us some valuable information** nos dio información muy valiosa.

value *noun* valor *Masc.*
value *verb* valorar [17] (*somebody's help, opinion, or friendship*).

van *noun* furgoneta *Fem.*

vandal *noun* gamberro *Masc.*, gamberra *Fem.*

vandalism *noun* gamberrismo *Masc.*

vandalize *verb* destrozar [22].

vanilla *noun* vainilla *Fem.*; **a vanilla ice cream** un helado de vainilla.

vanish *verb* desaparecer [35].

variety *noun* variedad *Fem.*

various *adjective* varios/varias (*always goes before the noun*); **there are various ways of doing it** hay varias formas de hacerlo.

vary *verb* variar [32]; **it varies a lot** varía mucho.

vase *noun* jarrón *Masc.*

VAT *noun* IVA *Masc.*

a
b
c
d
e
f
g
h
i
j
k
l
m
n
o
p
q
r
s
t
u
v
w
x
y
z

VCR noun cámara Fem. de vídeo.

VDU noun monitor Masc.

veal noun ternera Fem.

vegetable noun verdura Fem.

vegetarian noun vegetariano Masc., vegetariana Fem.
vegetarian adjective vegetariano/vegetariana; **he's vegetarian** es vegetariano.

vehicle noun vehículo Masc.

vein noun vena Fem.

velvet noun terciopelo Masc.

vending machine noun máquina Fem. expendedora.

ventilation noun ventilación Fem.

verb noun verbo Masc.

verdict noun veredicto Masc.

verge noun 1 (the roadside) arcén Masc.; 2 **to be on the verge of doing** estar [2] a punto de hacer; **I was on the verge of leaving** estaba a punto de irme.

version noun versión Fem.

versus preposition contra; **Arsenal versus Chelsea** Arsenal contra Chelsea.

vertical adjective vertical.

vertigo noun vértigo Masc.

very adverb 1 muy; **it's very difficult** es muy difícil; **very well** muy bien; 2 **very much** mucho; **I like it very much** me gusta mucho.
very adjective 1 **the very person I need!** ¡justo la persona que necesito!; **the very thing he was looking for** justo lo que estaba buscando; 2 **in the very middle** justo en medio; **at the very end** justo al final; **at the very front** justo delante.

vest noun camiseta Fem.

vet noun veterinario Masc., veterinaria Fem.; **she's a vet** es veterinaria.

via preposition **to go via** ir [8] por; **we're going via Dover** vamos por Dover; **we'll go via the bank** pasaremos por el banco.

vicar noun párroco Masc.

vicious adjective 1 fiero/fiera (a dog); 2 feroz (an attack).

victim noun víctima Fem.

victory noun victoria Fem.

video noun 1 (film) vídeo Masc.; **to watch a video** ver [16] un vídeo; **I've got it on video** lo tengo en vídeo; 2 (cassette) cinta Fem. de vídeo; **I bought a video** he comprado una cinta de vídeo; 3 (video recorder) vídeo Masc.
video verb grabar [17]; **I'll video it for you** yo te lo grabo.

video cassette noun cinta Fem. de vídeo.

video game noun videojuego Masc.

video recorder noun vídeo Masc.

video shop noun tienda Fem. de vídeos.

view noun 1 vista Fem.; **a room with a view of the lake** una habitación con vista al lago; 2 (opinion) opinión Fem.; **in my view** en mi opinión; **a point of view** una opinión.

viewer noun (of TV) televidente Masc./Fem.

viewpoint *noun* punto *Masc.* de vista.

vile *adjective* horrible.

villa *noun* chalet *Masc.*

village *noun* pueblo *Masc.*

villager *noun* habitante *Masc./Fem.* de un pueblo.

vine *noun* vid *Fem.*

vinegar *noun* vinagre *Masc.*

vineyard *noun* viñedo *Masc.*

violence *noun* violencia *Fem.*

violent *adjective* violento/violenta.

violin *noun* violín *Masc.*; **to play the violin** tocar [31] el violín.

violinist *noun* violinista *Masc./Fem.*

virgin *noun* virgen *Fem.*

Virgo *noun* Virgo *Masc.*; **Robert's Virgo** Robert es virgo.

virtual reality *noun* realidad *Fem.* virtual.

virus *noun* virus *Masc.*; **anti-virus software** software anti virus.

visa *noun* visado *Masc.*

visible *adjective* visible.

visit *noun* visita *Fem.*
visit *verb* visitar [17]; **we visited Auntie Pat at Christmas** visitamos a la tía Pat en Navidad.

visitor *noun* **1** visita *Fem.*; **we've got visitors tonight** hoy tenemos visita; **2** (*a tourist*) visitante *Masc./Fem.*

visual *adjective* visual.

vital *adjective* muy importante; **it's vital to book** es muy importante reservar.

vitamin *noun* vitamina *Fem.*

vivid *adjective* **1** (*colour or imagination*) vivo/viva; **to have a vivid imagination** tener una imaginación muy viva; **2** (*memory or dream*) vívido/vívida.

vocabulary *noun* vocabulario *Masc.*

vocational *adjective* vocacional.

vodka *noun* vodka *Masc.*

voice *noun* voz *Fem.*

volcano *noun* volcán *Masc.*

volleyball *noun* vóleibol *Masc.*; **to play volleyball** jugar [27] al vóleibol.

volume *noun* volumen *Masc.*; **could you turn down the volume?** ¿puedes bajar el volumen?

voluntary *adjective* **1** (*not compulsory*) voluntario/voluntaria **2** **to do voluntary work** trabajar [17] de voluntario.

volunteer *noun* voluntario *Masc.*, voluntaria *Fem.*

vomit *verb* vomitar [17].

vote *noun* voto *Masc.*
vote *verb* votar [17]; **she always votes for the Greens** siempre vota a los verdes.

voucher *noun* vale *Masc.*

vowel *noun* vocal *Fem.*

voyage *noun* viaje *Masc.*

vulgar *adjective* grosero/grosera (*person or speech*).

Ww

waffle *noun* (*to eat*) gofre *Masc.*

wage(s) (*plural*) *noun* sueldo *Masc.*

wagon *noun* vagón *Masc.*

waist *noun* cintura *Fem.*

waistcoat *noun* chaleco *Masc.*

waist measurement *noun* medida *Fem.* de cintura.

wait *noun* espera *Fem.*; **an hour's wait** una espera de una hora. **wait** *verb* 1 esperar [17]; **they're waiting in the car** están esperando en el coche; **she kept me waiting** me tuvo esperando; **2 to wait for** esperar algo; **wait for me!** ¡espérame!; **wait for the signal** espera la señal; **3 I can't wait to open it!** ¡estoy deseando abrirlo!

waiter *noun* camarero *Masc.*

waiting list *noun* lista *Fem.* de espera.

waiting room *noun* sala *Fem.* de espera.

waitress *noun* camarera *Fem.*

wake *verb* 1 despertar [29] (*somebody else*); **Jess woke me at six** Jess me despertó a las seis; **2** despertarse [29]; **I woke (up) at six** me desperté a las seis; **wake up!** ¡despiértate!

Wales *noun* País *Masc.* de Gales.

walk *noun* paseo *Masc.*; **to go for a walk** ir [8] a dar un paseo; **we went for a walk in the woods** fuimos a dar un paseo por el bosque; **we'll go for a little walk round the village**

daremos un paseo por el pueblo; **to take the dog for a walk** sacar [31] a pasear al perro; **it's about five minutes' walk from here** está a unos cinco minutos de aquí a pie. **walk** *verb* 1 andar [21]; **I like walking on sand** me gusta andar sobre la arena; **2** (*on foot rather than by car or bus*) ir [8] andando; **it's not far, we can walk** no está lejos, podemos ir andando.

● **to walk around** dar [4] una vuelta por; **we walked around the old town** dimos una vuelta por la parte vieja de la ciudad.

● **to walk with somebody** acompañar a alguien; **I'll walk to the bus stop with you** te acompaño hasta la parada del autobús.

walking *noun* (*hiking*) hacer [7] senderismo; **we're going walking in Scotland** vamos a hacer senderismo en Escocia.

walking distance *noun* **it's within walking distance of the sea** se puede ir andando hasta la playa.

walking stick *noun* bastón *Masc.*

walkman™ *noun* walkman™ *Masc.*

wall *noun* 1 (*of a house*) pared *Fem.*; **2** (*of a city*) muralla *Fem.*; **the Great Wall of China** la Gran Muralla de China.

wallet *noun* cartera *Fem.*

wallpaper *noun* papel *Masc.* pintado.

walnut *noun* nuez *Fem.*

a
b
c
d
e
f
g
h
i
j
k
l
m
n
o
p
q
r
s
t
u
v
w
x
y
z

wander *verb* to wander around town pasear [17] por la ciudad; **to wander off** alejarse [17].

want *noun* all our wants todo lo que necesitamos.

want *verb* querer [12]; **do you want some coffee?** ¿quieres café?; **what do you want to do?** ¿qué quieres hacer?; **I don't want to bother him** no quiero molestarlo; **I want them to help me** quiero que me ayuden (*note that 'querer que' is followed by the subjunctive*).

war *noun* guerra *Fem.*

ward *noun* sala *Fem.* (*in a hospital*).

wardrobe *noun* **1** (*piece of furniture*) armario *Masc.*; **2** (*clothes*) vestuario *Masc.*

warehouse *noun* almacén *Masc.*

warm *adjective* **1** (*water*) templado/templada (*not very hot*); **2** (*breeze*) cálido/cálida; **3** (*hot*) caliente; **a warm drink** una bebida caliente; **I'll keep your dinner warm** te tendré la comida caliente; **a warm bath** un baño caliente; **4 it's warm today** hoy hace calorcito; **I'm warm** tengo calor; **are you warm enough?** ¿tienes frío?; **5** (*friendly*) caluroso/calurosa; **a warm welcome** una bienvenida calurosa; **a warm person** una persona cariñosa.

warm *verb* calentar [29]; **to warm the plates** calentar los platos.

• **to warm up 1** (*the weather*) **it's warming up** está empezando a hacer más calor; **2** (*an athlete*) entrar [17] en calor; **3** (*to heat up*) calentar [29] (*food*); **I'll warm up** some soup for you te calentaré un poco de sopa.

warmth *noun* calor *Masc.*

warn *verb* advertir [14]; **I warn you it's expensive** te lo advierto, es caro; **to warn somebody to do** advertir a alguien que haga (*note that 'que' is followed by the subjunctive*); **he warned me to lock the car** me advirtió que cerrase el coche.

warning *noun* advertencia *Fem.*

wart *noun* verruga *Fem.*

wash *noun* to give something a wash lavar [17] algo; **to have a wash** lavarse.

wash *verb* lavar [17]; **I've washed your jeans** he lavado tus vaqueros; **to wash your hands** lavarse las manos; **I washed my hands** me he lavado las manos; **to wash your hair** lavarse la cabeza; **I have to wash my hair** tengo que lavarme la cabeza; **to get washed** lavarse; **to wash the dishes** lavar los platos.

• **to wash up** lavar los platos.

washbasin *noun* lavabo *Masc.*

washing *noun* **1** (*dirty*) ropa *Fem.* sucia; **2** (*clean*) ropa *Fem.* limpia.

washing machine *noun* lavadora *Fem.*

washing powder *noun* detergente *Masc.*

washing-up *noun* platos *Fem.* sucios; **to do the washing-up** lavar [17] los platos.

washing-up liquid *noun* lavavajillas *Masc.* (*does not change in the plural*).

wasp noun avispa Fem.

waste noun 1 (of food, money, paper) desperdicio Masc.; 2 (of time) **it's a waste of time** es una pérdida de tiempo.

waste verb 1 desperdiciar [17] (food, money, paper); 2 perder [36] (time); **you're wasting your time** estás perdiendo el tiempo.

waste-bin noun papelera Fem.

wastepaper-basket noun papelera Fem.

watch noun reloj Masc.; **my watch is fast** mi reloj está adelantado; **my watch is slow** mi reloj está atrasado.

watch verb 1 (to look at) mirar [17]; **I was watching TV** estaba viendo la televisión; 2 **to watch a film** ver [16] una película; 3 (keep a check on) **watch the time** estate atento al reloj; **could you watch the baby for a while?** ¿puedes cuidar al niño un rato?; 4 (suspect) vigilar [17]; 5 (to be careful) **watch you don't spill it** ten cuidado de no tirarlo; **watch out for nettles** cuidado con las ortigas; **watch out!** ¡cuidado!

water noun agua Fem. (even though 'agua' is feminine, it takes 'el' in the singular)

water verb regar [30]; **to water the plants** regar las plantas.

watercolours plural noun acuarelas Fem. plural.

waterfall noun cascada Fem.

watering can noun regadera Fem.

water melon noun sandía Fem.

waterproof adjective impermeable.

water-skiing noun esquí Masc. acuático; **to go water-skiing** hacer [7] esquí acuático.

water sports plural noun deportes Masc. náuticos.

wave noun 1 (in the sea) ola Fem.; 2 (with your hand) (to say hello) saludo Masc.; (to say goodbye) adiós Masc.; **she gave him a wave from the bus** le saludó con la mano desde el autobús; (to say goodbye) le dijo adiós con la mano desde el autobús. **wave** verb 1 (with your hand) (to say hello) saludar [17]; (to say goodbye) decir [5] adiós; 2 (flap) agitar [17] (your ticket or the newspaper, for example).

wax noun cera Fem.

way noun 1 (a route or road) camino Masc.; **the way to town** el camino a la ciudad; **we asked the way to the station** preguntamos el camino a la estación; **on the way back** en el camino de vuelta; **on the way** en camino; **'way in'** 'entrada'; **'way out'** 'salida'; 2 (direction) dirección Fem.; **which way did he go?** ¿en qué dirección se fue?; **come this way** ven por aquí; **to be in the way** estorbar [17]; 3 **put it the right way up** ponlo bien; **the wrong way up** boca abajo; **your jumper is the wrong way round** tu jersey está al revés; 4 (distance) **it's a long way** está muy lejos; **Terry went all the way to York** Terry fue hasta York; 5 (manner) manera Fem.; **a way of talking** una manera de hablar; **he**

a
b
c
d
e
f
g
h
i
j
k
l
m
n
o
p
q
r
s
t
u
v
w
x
y
z

a
b
c
d
e
f
g
h
i
j
k
l
m
n
o
p
q
r
s
t
u
v
w
x
y
z

does it his way lo hace a su manera;
I did it the wrong way lo hice mal;
that's not the way to do it no se
hace así; **either way, she's wrong**
sea como sea, está equivocada; **do it
this way** hazlo de esta manera; **6 no
way!** ¡ni hablar!; **7 by the way** por
cierto.

way in *noun* entrada *Fem.*

way out *noun* salida *Fem.*

we *pronoun* **1** *('we' like other subject
pronouns is generally not translated;
in Spanish the form of the verb tells
you whether the subject of the verb is
'we', 'you', 'they', etc., so 'we' is only
translated for emphasis*) **we live in
Carlisle** vivimos en Carlisle; **we're
going to the cinema tonight** vamos
a ir al cine esta noche; **2** (*for
emphasis*) nosotros/nosotras; **we
did it** lo hicimos nosotros.

weak *adjective* **1** (*feeble*) débil; **her
voice was weak** su voz era débil;
2 poco cargado/poco cargada (*coffee
or tea*).

wealth *noun* riqueza *Fem.*

wealthy *adjective* rico/rica.

weapon *noun* arma *Fem.*

wear *noun* **children's wear** ropa
Fem. de niños; **sports wear** ropa de
deporte.
wear *verb* llevar [17]; **Tamsin's
wearing her trainers** Tamsin lleva
sus zapatillas de deporte; **he was
wearing black trousers** llevaba
pantalones negros; **she often wears
red** a menudo viste de rojo; **to wear
make-up** llevar maquillaje.

weather *noun* tiempo *Masc.*; **what
the weather like?** ¿qué tiempo
hace?; **in fine weather** cuando hace
buen tiempo; **the weather was col**
hacía frío; **the weather here is
terrible** aquí hace un tiempo
horrible.

weather forecast *noun*
pronóstico *Masc.* del tiempo; **the
weather forecast says it will rain**
el pronóstico del tiempo dice que va
a llover.

web *noun* **1** (*spider's*) telaraña *Fem.*
2 (*Internet*) **the Web** la Web.

web site *noun* sitio *Masc.* web.

wedding *noun* boda *Fem.*

Wednesday *noun* miércoles *Masc*
(*does not change in the plural*); **on
Wednesday** el miércoles; **I'm going
out on Wednesday** voy a salir el
miércoles; **see you on Wednesday**
¡hasta el miércoles!; **on
Wednesdays** los miércoles; **the
museum is closed on
Wednesdays** el museo cierra los
miércoles; **every Wednesday** cada
miércoles; **last Wednesday** el
miércoles pasado; **next Wednesday**
el próximo miércoles.

weed *noun* mala hierba *Fem.*

week *noun* semana *Fem.*; **last week**
la semana pasada; **next week** la
próxima semana; **this week** esta
semana; **for weeks** durante
semanas; **a week today** una semana
a partir de hoy.

weekday *noun* **on weekdays**
entre semana.

weekend *noun* fin *Masc.* de semana; **last weekend** el fin de semana pasado; **next weekend** el próximo fin de semana; **they're coming for the weekend** vienen a pasar el fin de semana; **I'll do it at the weekend** lo haré durante el fin de semana; **have a nice weekend!** ¡que pases un buen fin de semana!

weekly *adverb* semanalmente, cada semana; **I see her weekly** la veo cada semana.

weekly *adjective* semanal; **a weekly magazine** una revista semanal.

weigh *verb* pesar [17]; **to weigh something** pesar algo; **how much do you weigh?** ¿cuánto pesas?; **I weigh 50 kilos** peso cincuenta kilos; **to weigh yourself** pesarse [17].

weight *noun* peso *Masc.*; **to put on weight** engordar [17]; **to lose weight** adelgazar [22].

weird *adjective* extraño/extraña.

welcome *noun* bienvenida *Fem.*; **they gave us a warm welcome** nos dieron una calurosa bienvenida. **welcome** *adjective* **1** bienvenido/bienvenida; **you're welcome any time** siempre eres bienvenido; **welcome to Oxford!** ¡bienvenido a Oxford!; **2** 'thank you!' – 'you're welcome!' 'gracias'– 'de nada'. **welcome** *verb* dar [4] la bienvenida a.

well¹ *noun* (*for water*) pozo *Masc.*

well² *adverb* **1** bien; **to feel well** sentirse [14] bien; **I'm very well, thank you** estoy muy bien, gracias;

2 bien; **Terry played well** Terry jugó bien; **the operation went well** la operación salió bien; **well done!** ¡bien hecho!; **3** as well también; **Kevin's coming as well** Kevin también viene; **4** as well as además de; **5** well then, what's the problem? entonces, ¿cuál es el problema?; **6** very well then, you can go muy bien, entonces ya puedes irte.

well-behaved *adjective* **a well behaved child** un niño que se porta bien; **be well-behaved** pórtate bien.

well-done *adjective* muy hecho/muy hecha (*a steak*).

wellington (boot) *noun* catiusca *Fem.*

well-known *adjective* conocido/bien conocida.

well-off *adjective* acomodado/acomodada.

Welsh *noun* **1** the **Welsh** (*people*) los galeses; **2** (*language*) galés *Masc.* **Welsh** *adjective* galés/galesa.

Welshman *noun* galés *Masc.*

Welshwoman *noun* galesa *Fem.*

west *noun* oeste *Masc.*; **in the west** al oeste. **west** *adjective, adverb* (*does not change*) **the west side** la parte oeste; **a west wind** un viento del oeste; **west of Paris** al oeste de París.

western *noun* (*a film*) película *Fem.* de vaqueros.

West Indian *noun* afroantillano *Masc.*, afroantillana *Fem.*

a
b
c
d
e
f
g
h
i
j
k
l
m
n
o
p
q
r
s
t
u
v
w
x
y
z

West Indian *adjective*
afroantillano/afroantillana.

West Indies *plural noun* Antillas
Fem.; **in the West Indies** en las
Antillas.

wet *adjective* **1** (*damp*) húmedo/
húmeda; **the grass is wet** la hierba
está húmeda; **to get wet** mojarse
[17]; **we got wet** nos mojamos; **2 a
wet day** un día lluvioso.

whale *noun* ballena *Fem.*

what *pronoun, adjective* **1** qué (*in
questions*); **what did you say?** ¿qué
has dicho?; **what's she doing?** ¿qué
está haciendo?; **what did you buy?**
¿qué has comprado?; **what is it?**
¿qué es?; **what's the matter?** ¿qué
pasa?; **what's happening?** ¿qué está
pasando?; **2 what's your address?**
¿cuál es su dirección?; **what
country is it in?** ¿en qué país está?;
what colour is it? ¿de qué color es?;
what make is it? ¿de qué marca es?;
3 what's her name? ¿cómo se
llama?; **what?** ¿cómo?; **what's it
like?** ¿cómo es?; **4 what for?** ¿para
qué?; **what's it for?** ¿para qué
sirve?; **what did you buy it for?**
¿para qué lo has comprado?; **5** lo
que; **tell me what you bought** dime
lo que has comprado; **she told me
what had happened** me dijo lo que
había pasado; **what I want is a car**
lo que quiero es un coche.

wheat *noun* trigo *Masc.*

wheel *noun* rueda *Fem.*; **the spare
wheel** la rueda de repuesto; **the
steering wheel** el volante.

wheelbarrow *noun* carretilla
Fem.

wheelchair *noun* silla *Fem.* de
ruedas.

when *adverb* cuándo; **when's she
arriving?** ¿cuándo llega?; **when's
your birthday?** ¿cuándo es tu
cumpleaños?; **ask when the next
train is leaving** pregunta cuándo
sale el próximo tren.
when *conjunction* cuando; **it was
raining when I went out** estaba
lloviendo cuando salí.

whenever *adverb* **1** (*any time*)
cuando; **come whenever you like**
ven cuando quieras; **2** (*each time*)
siempre que; **whenever we go out,
we lock the door** siempre que
salimos, cerramos la puerta con
llave.

where *adverb* dónde; **where are
the plates?** ¿dónde están los
platos?; **where do you live?** ¿dónde
vives?; **where are you going?**
¿dónde vas?; **I don't know where
they live** no sé donde viven.
where *pronoun* donde; **the place
where I live** el lugar dónde vivo.
where *conjunction* donde; **this is
where I left it** ahí es donde lo dejé.

whether *conjunction* si; **I don't
know whether he's back or not** no
sé si ha vuelto o no.

which *adjective* qué; **which CD did
you buy?** ¿qué compacto
compraste?; **which drawer did you
put it in?** ¿en qué cajón lo metiste?;
which one cuál; **'I saw your
brother' – 'which one?'** 'ví a tu
hermano' –'¿a cuál?'.
which *pronoun* **1** (*in questions*)
which of these jackets is yours?

¿cuál de estas chaquetas es la tuya?;
2 (*relative pronoun*) que; **the lamp
which is on the table** la lámpara
que está en la mesa; **the book which
you chose** el libro que escogiste;
the film which I told you about el
libro del que te hablé.

while *noun* **for a while** (*long time*)
durante un tiempo; (*short time*)
durante un rato; **she worked here
for a while** trabajó allí durante un
tiempo; **I read for a while** leí
durante un rato; **after a while** (*long
time*) después de un tiempo; (*short
time*) después de un rato.
while *conjunction* mientras; **you
can make some tea while I'm
finishing my homework** puedes
hacer un té mientras termino los
deberes.

whip *noun* (*for a horse*) látigo *Masc.*
whip *verb* montar [17] (*cream*);
whipped cream nata *Fem.* montada.

whirlpool *noun* remolino *Masc.*

whiskers *plural noun* bigotes *Masc.
plural.*

whisky *noun* whisky *Masc.*

whisper *noun* susurro *Masc.*; **to
speak in a whisper** hablar [17] en
susurros.
whisper *verb* susurrar [17].

whistle *noun* **1** (*sound*) silbido
Masc.; **2** (*instrument*) silbato *Masc.*
whistle *verb* silbar [17].

white *noun* **1** (*colour*) blanco *Masc.*;
2 an egg white una clara de huevo.
white *adjective* blanco/blanca; **a
white shirt** una camisa blanca.

white coffee *noun* café *Masc.* con
leche.

Whitsun *noun* Pentecostés *Masc.*

who *pronoun* **1** (*in questions*) quién;
who wants some sweets? ¿quién
quiere caramelos?; **2** (*relative
pronoun as subject of the verb*) que;
my friend who lives in Madrid el
amigo mío que vive en Madrid; **3** (*as
object of the verb: referring to one
person*) el que/la que; **the girl who I
gave it to** la chica a la que se lo di;
4 (*as object of the verb: referring to
more than one person*) los que/las
que; **the friends who we invited** los
amigos a los que hemos invitado.

whole *noun* **the whole of the class**
toda la clase; **on the whole** en
general.
whole *adjective* todo/toda; **the
whole family** toda la familia; **the
whole morning** toda la mañana; **the
whole time** todo el tiempo; **the
whole world** todo el mundo.

wholemeal *adjective* integral;
wholemeal bread pan integral.

whom *pronoun* **1** (*in questions*)
quién; **whom did you see?** ¿a quién
viste?; **2** (*as relative pronoun*) que;
the person whom I saw la persona
que vi; **3** (*after a preposition:
referring to one person*) el que/la
que; **the person to whom I wrote** la
persona a la que escribí; **4** (*after a
preposition: referring to more than
one person*) los que/las que; **the
people to whom I wrote** las
personas a las que escribí.

whose *pronoun, adjective* **1** de
quién; **whose is this jacket?** ¿de

a
b
c
d
e
f
g
h
i
j
k
l
m
n
o
p
q
r
s
t
u
v
w
x
y
z

quién es esta chaqueta?; **whose shoes are these?** ¿de quién son estos zapatos?; **whose is it?** ¿de quién es?; **I know whose it is** sé de quién es; **2** (*as relative: before a singular noun*) cuyo/cuya (*agree with the noun that follows*); **the man whose car has been stolen** el hombre cuyo coche había sido robado; **3** (*as relative; before a plural noun*) cuyos/cuyas (*agree with the noun that follows*); **the people whose names are on the list** las personas cuyos nombres están en la lista; **a friend whose children I give lessons to** un amigo a cuyos hijos doy clase.

why *adverb* por qué; **why did she phone?** ¿por qué llamó?; **nobody knows why he did it** nadie sabe por qué lo hizo.

wicked *adjective* **1** (*bad*) malvado/malvada; **2** (*brilliant*) genial.

wide *adjective* **1** ancho/ancha; **the Thames is very wide here** el Támesis es muy ancho por aquí; **a piece of paper 20 cm wide** un trozo de papel de veinte centímetros de ancho; **how wide is it?** ¿cuánto mide de ancho?; **2 a wide range** una amplia gama.
wide *adverb* **the door was wide open** la puerta estaba abierta de par en par.

wide awake *adjective* completamente despierto/despierta.

widen *verb* ensanchar [17].

widow *noun* viuda *Fem.*

widower *noun* viudo *Masc.*

width *noun* ancho *Masc.*

wife *noun* mujer *Fem.*

wig *noun* peluca *Fem.*

wild *adjective* **1** (*an animal*) salvaje, (*plant*) silvestre; **2** (*idea*) disparatado/disparatada; **3** (*party*) desenfrenado/desenfrenada; **4** (*person*) loco/loca; **5 to be wild about something** estar [2] loco por algo.

wildlife *noun* **a programme on wildlife in Africa** un programa sobre la flora y la fauna de África.

wildlife park *noun* reserva *Fem.* natural.

will *verb* **1** (*if you are unsure of the future tense of a Spanish verb, you can check it in the dictionary's verb tables*) **I will/I'll see you soon** te veré pronto; **he'll be pleased to see you** estará contento de verte; **it won't rain** no lloverá; **there won't be a problem** no habrá problemas; **2** ir [8] a hacer (*can be used for the immediate future*); **I'll phone them at once** voy a llamarlos ahora mismo; **3** (*in questions and requests*) **'will you write to me?'** – **'of course I will!'** ¿me escribirás? – 'claro que sí'; **will you have a drink?** ¿quieres beber algo?; **will you help me?** ¿me ayudas?; **4 he won't open the door** no quiere abrir la puerta; **the car won't start** el coche no arranca; **the drawer won't open** el cajón no abre.

willing *adjective* **to be willing to do** estar [2] dispuesto/dispuesta a hacer; **I'm willing to pay half** estoy dispuesta a pagar la mitad.

willingly *adverb* con gusto.

willow *noun* sauce Masc.; **a weeping willow** un sauce llorón.

win *noun* victoria Fem.; **our win over Everton** nuestra victoria sobre Everton.
win *verb* ganar [17]; **we won!** ¡hemos ganado!; **Rovers won by two goals** Rovers ganó por dos goles.

wind¹ *noun* viento Masc.; **the North wind** el viento del norte.

wind² *verb* **1** enrollar [17] (*a wire or a rope, for example*); **2** dar [4] cuerda a (*a clock*).

wind farm *noun* parque Masc. aeólico.

wind instrument *noun* instrumento Masc. de viento.

window *noun* **1** (*in a building*) ventana Fem.; **to look out of the window** mirar [17] por la ventana; **2** (*in a car, bus, train*) ventanilla Fem.

windscreen *noun* parabrisas Masc. (*doesn't change in the plural*).

windscreen wipers *plural noun* limpiaparabrisas Masc. plural (*doesn't change in the plural*).

windsurfing *noun* windsurf Masc.; **to go windsurfing** hacer [7] windsurf.

windy *adjective* **1** con mucho viento (*a place*); **2** de viento (*a day*); **3 it's windy today** hoy hace viento.

wine *noun* vino Masc.; **a glass of white wine** una copa de vino blanco.

wing *noun* **1** ala Fem. (*even though 'ala' is feminine, it takes 'el' and 'un' in the singular*); **the wing** el ala; **2** (*in sport*) alero Masc./Fem.

wink *verb* **to wink at somebody** guiñar [17] el ojo a alguien.

winner *noun* ganador Masc., ganadora Fem.

winning *adjective* ganador (*team for example*).

winnings *plural noun* ganancias Fem. plural.

winter *noun* invierno Masc.; **in winter** en invierno.

wipe *verb* limpiar [17]; **I'll just wipe the table** voy a limpiar la mesa; **to wipe your nose** limpiarse [17] la nariz.
• **to wipe up** (*dishes*) secar [17].

wire *noun* alambre Masc.; **an electric wire** un cable.

wire netting *noun* red Fem. de alambre.

wise *adjective* sabio/sabia.

wish *noun* **1** deseo Masc.; **make a wish!** ¡piensa un deseo!; **2 best wishes on your birthday** nuestros mejores deseos en tu cumpleaños; **'best wishes, Ann'** 'saludos de: Ann' (*in letters*).
wish *verb* **1 I wish he were here** ojalá estuviese aquí (*note that 'ojalá' is followed by the subjunctive*); **2 I wished him happy birthday** le deseé un feliz cumpleaños.

wit *noun* ingenio Masc.

witch *noun* bruja Fem.

with *preposition* **1** con; **with James** con James; **with me** conmigo; **with them** con ellos; **with pleasure** con gusto; **beat the eggs with a fork** bate los huevos con un tenedor; **he took his umbrella with him** se llevó

a
b
c
d
e
f
g
h
i
j
k
l
m
n
o
p
q
r
s
t
u
v
w
x
y
z

a el paraguas; **2** (*at the house of*) **we're staying the night with Frank** nos quedamos a dormir en casa de Frank; **3** (*in descriptions*) **a man with blue eyes** un hombre de ojos azules; **the boy with the broken arm** el chico con el brazo roto; **4** de; **filled with water** lleno de agua; **covered with mud** cubierto de barro; **red with rage** rojo de ira.

without *preposition* sin; **without you** sin ti; **without sugar** sin azúcar; **without a sweater** sin un jersey; **without looking** sin mirar.

witness *noun* testigo *Masc./Fem.*

witty *adjective* ingenioso/ ingeniosa.

wizard *noun* brujo *Masc.*

wolf *noun* lobo *Masc.*

woman *noun* mujer *Fem.*; **a woman friend** una amiga.

wonder *noun* **1** maravilla *Fem.*; **2 it's no wonder you're tired** no es extraño que estés cansado.
wonder *verb* preguntarse [17]; **I wonder why** me pregunto por qué; **I wonder where Jack is** me pregunto dónde está Jack.

wonderful *adjective* maravilloso/ maravillosa.

wood *noun* madera *Fem.*; **the lamp is made of wood** la lámpara está hecha de madera.

wooden *adjective* de madera.

woodwork *noun* carpintería *Fem.*

wool *noun* lana *Fem.*

woollen *adjective* de lana.

word *noun* **1** palabra *Fem.*; **a long word** una palabra larga; **what's the French word for 'window'?** ¿cómo se dice 'ventana' en francés?; **in other words** en otras palabras; **to have a word with somebody** hablar [17] con alguien; **2** (*promise*) **to give somebody your word** prometer [18] algo a alguien; **he broke his word** rompió su promesa; **3 the words of a song** la letra de una canción.

word processing *noun* tratamiento *Masc.* de textos.

word processor *noun* procesador *Masc.* de textos.

work *noun* **1** trabajo *Masc.*; **Mum's at work** mamá está en el trabajo; **I've got some work to do** tengo trabajo que hacer; **he's out of work** está sin trabajo; **Ben's off work** (*sick*) Ben no ha ido a trabajar porque está enfermo; **2 to be hard work** ser [1] difícil; **it's hard work to understand it** es difícil entenderlo.
work *verb* **1** trabajar [17]; **she works in an office** trabaja en una oficina; **Dad works at home** papá trabaja en la casa; **Ruth works in advertising** Ruth trabaja en publicidad; **he works nights** trabaja por las noches; **2** (*to operate*) hacer [7] funcionar; **can you work the video?** ¿sabes hacer funcionar el vídeo?; **3** (*function*) funcionar [17]; **the dishwasher's not working** el lavavajillas no funciona; **that worked really well!** ¡eso ha funcionado muy bien!

b
c
d
e
f
g
h
i
j
k
l
m
n
o
p
q
r
s
t
u
v
w
x
y
z

- **to work out 1** (*understand*) entender [36]; **I can't work out why** no entiendo por qué; **2** (*exercise*) hacer [7] ejercicio; **3** (*to go well*) (*a plan*) salir [63] bien; **4** (*calculate*) calcular [17]; **I'll work out how much it would cost** calcularé cuánto puede costar.

worked up *adjective* **to get worked up** ponerse [11] nervioso/ nerviosa.

worker *noun* **1** (*in a factory*) trabajador *Masc.*, trabajadora *Fem.*; **2** (*in an office or bank*) empleado *Masc.*, empleada *Fem.*

work experience *noun* prácticas *Fem. plural* de trabajo; **to do work experience** hacer [7] prácticas; **to be on work experience** estar [2] haciendo prácticas.

working-class *adjective* clase *Fem.* obrera; **a working-class background** un ambiente de clase obrera.

work of art *noun* obra *Fem.* de arte.

workshop *noun* taller *Masc.*

workstation *noun* (*computer*) terminal *Fem.* de trabajo.

world *noun* mundo *Masc.*; **the best in the world** lo mejor del mundo; **the Western world** el mundo occidental.

World Cup *noun* **the World Cup** el Mundial.

world war *noun* guerra *Fem.* mundial; **the Second World War** la segunda Guerra Mundial.

worm *noun* gusano *Masc.*

worn out *adjective* **1** (*a person*) agotado/agotada; **2** (*clothes or shoes*) muy gastado/muy gastada.

worried *adjective* preocupado/ preocupada; **they're worried** están preocupados; **to be worried about** estar [2] preocupado/preocupada por; **we're worried about Susan** estamos preocupados por Susan.

worry *noun* preocupación *Fem.* **worry** *verb* preocuparse [17]; **don't worry!** ¡no te preocupes!; **there's nothing to worry about** no hay razón para preocuparse.

worrying *adjective* preocupante.

worse *adjective* peor; **it was even worse than the last time** fue aún peor que la última vez; **to get worse** empeorar [17]; **the weather's getting worse** el tiempo está empeorando; **things are getting worse and worse** las cosas van cada vez peor.

worst *adjective* **the worst** el peor; **it was the worst day of my life** fue el peor día de mi vida; **if the worst comes to the worst** en el peor de los casos.

worth *adjective* **1 to be worth** valer [43]; **how much is it worth?** ¿cuánto vale?; **2 to be worth doing** merecer [35] la pena hacer; **it's worth trying** merece la pena intentarlo; **it's not worth it** no merece la pena.

would *verb* **1** (*if you are unsure of the conditional tense of a Spanish verb, you can check it in the dictionray's verb tables*) **that would be a good idea** eso sería una buena

a
b
c
d
e
f
g
h
i
j
k
l
m
n
o
p
q
r
s
t
u
v
w
x
y
z

a
b
c
d
e
f
g
h
i
j
k
l
m
n
o
p
q
r
s
t
u
v
w
x
y
z

idea; **if we asked her she would help us** si la preguntásemos, nos ayudaría; **2** (*expressing wishes*) **I'd like to go to the cinema** me gustaría ir al cine; **I would like an omelette** quisiera una tortilla (*the subjunctive is used when ordering something*); **3 would you like … ?** ¿quieres … ?; **would you like something to eat?** ¿quieres comer algo?; **4 would you mind … ?** ¿te importaría … ?; **would you mind closing the window?** ¿te importaría cerrar la ventana?; **5 he wouldn't answer** no contestaba; **the car wouldn't start** el coche no arrancaba.

wound *noun* herida *Fem.*
wound *verb* herir [14].

wrap *verb* envolver [45]; **I'm going to wrap (up) my presents** voy a envolver mis regalos; **could you wrap it for me please?** ¿me lo envuelve, por favor?

wrapping paper *noun* papel *Masc.* de envolver.

wreck *noun* **I feel a wreck!** ¡estoy hecho/hecha polvo!
wreck *verb* **1** destrozar [22] (*an object, a car*); **2** arruinar [17] (*plans, occasion*); **it completely wrecked my evening!** ¡me arruinó la tarde!

wrestler *noun* luchador *Masc.*, luchadora *Fem.*

wrestling *noun* lucha *Fem.*

wrinkle *noun* arruga *Fem.*

wrinkled *adjective* arrugado/arrugada.

wrist *noun* muñeca *Fem.*

write *verb* **1** escribir [52] (*a letter or a story*); **I'll write her a letter** le escribiré una carta; **to write to somebody** escribirle a alguien; **I wrote to Jean yesterday** ayer le escribí a Jean; **2 to write somebody a cheque** extenderle [36] un cheque a alguien.

● **to write down** anotar [17]; **I wrote down her name** anoté su nombre.

writer *noun* escritor *Masc.*, escritora *Fem.*

writing *noun* escritura *Fem.*

wrong *adjective* **1** (*not correct*) equivocado/equivocada; **the wrong answer** la respuesta equivocada; **I've brought the wrong file** he traído la carpeta equivocada; **it's the wrong address** no son las señas correctas; **2 to be wrong** (*mistaken*) equivocarse [31]; **I was wrong** me equivoqué; **I was wrong when I said it was finished** me equivoqué cuando dije que estaba terminado; **3 what's wrong?** ¿qué pasa?; **what's wrong with her?** ¿qué le pasa?; **something's wrong** pasa algo; **4** (*false*) incorrecto/incorrecta; **the information was wrong** la información era incorrecta.

Xx

xerox™ *noun* fotocopia *Fem.*
xerox™ *verb* fotocopiar [17].

X-ray *noun* radiografía *Fem.*; **I saw the X-rays** vi las radiografías.

X-ray *verb* hacer [7] una radiografía de; **they X-rayed her ankle** le hicieron una radiografía del tobillo.

Yy

yacht *noun* **1** (*sailing boat*) velero *Masc.*; **2** (*large luxury boat*) yate *Masc.*

yawn *verb* bostezar [22].

year *noun* año *Masc.*; **six years ago** hace seis años; **the whole year** todo el año; **they lived in Moscow for years** vivieron en Moscú durante años; **he's seventeen years old** tiene diecisiete años; **a two-year-old child** un niño de dos años.

yearly *adverb* anualmente, cada año.
yearly *adjective* anual; **a yearly event** un acontecimiento anual.

yell *verb* gritar [17].

yellow *adjective* amarillo/amarilla.

yes *adverb* **1** sí; **yes, I know** sí, ya lo sé; **'is Tom in his room?' – 'yes, he is'** '¿está Tom en su habitación?' – 'sí'; **2** (*answering a negative*) que sí; **'you don't want to go, do you?' – ' yes I do!'** 'no quieres ir, ¿verdad?' – 'que sí quiero'; **'you haven't finished, have you?' – 'yes, I have'** 'no has terminado, ¿verdad?' – 'que sí'.

yesterday *adverb* ayer; **I saw her yesterday** la vi ayer; **yesterday afternoon** ayer por la tarde; **yesterday morning** ayer por la

mañana; **the day before yesterday** anteayer.

yet *adverb* **1** (*with a negative*) aún; **not yet** aún no; **it's not ready yet** no está listo aún; **2** (*in a question*) ya; **have you finished yet?** ¿has terminado ya?

yoga *noun* yoga *Fem.*

yoghurt *noun* yogur *Masc.*; **a banana yoghurt** un yogur de plátano.

yolk *noun* yema *Fem.*

you *pronoun* **1** (*'you' like other subject pronouns is generally not translated; in Spanish the form of the verb tells you whether the subject of the verb is 'you', 'we, they', etc., so 'you' is only translated for emphasis*) **do you want to go to the cinema tonight?** (*talking to one person*) ¿quieres ir al cine esta noche?; (*talking to more than one person*) ¿quereis ir al cine esta noche?; **2** (*when emphasizing 'you'*) (*talking to one person*) tú; (*talking to more than one person*) vosotros/vosotras; **you said it!** ¡tú lo dijiste!; **you all saw it!** ¡todos vosotros lo vísteis!; **3** (*although 'tú', 'vosotros', and 'vosotras' are now commonly used in most situations, there are the formal translations of 'you', which you use in a job interview and other formal situations*) (*talking to one person*) usted; (*talking to more than one person*) ustedes; **are you our new teacher?** ¿es usted nuestro nuevo profesor?; **excuse me, are you Mr and Mrs Lawrence?** perdonen, ¿son ustedes los señores Lawrence?;

a
b
c
d
e
f
g
h
i
j
k
l
m
n
o
p
q
r
s
t
u
v
w
x
y
z

4 (*when used as the direct or indirect object of the verb*) (*talking to one person*) te; (*talking to more than one person*) os; **I'll lend you my bike** te presto mi bici; **I'll write to you both** os escribiré a los dos; **5** (*in formal situations*) (*talking to one person*) le; (*talking to more than one person*) les; **I shall send you the document** le mandaré el documento; **Dear Mr and Mrs Jones, I am sending you the information you requested** Estimados señor y señora Jones, les mando la información que solicitaron; (*when used with another pronoun, 'le' and 'les' become 'se'*) **I shall send it to you on Monday** se lo mandaré el lunes; **6** (*in comparisons*) tú; (*more than one person*) vosotros/vosotras; **he's older than you** es mayor que tú, mayor que vosotros/vosotras; **7 for you** para ti (*more than one person*) para vosotros/vosotras; **I'll go with you** iré contigo; **8** (*in formal situations: after a preposition or in comparisons*) usted; (*talking to more than one person*) ustedes; **for you** para usted, para ustedes.

young *adjective* joven; **he's younger than me** es más joven que yo; **Tessa's two years younger than me** Tessa tiene dos años menos que yo; **young people** la gente joven.

your *adjective* **1** (*talking to one person*) (*with a singular noun*) tu, (*with a plural noun*) tus; **I like your skirt** me gusta tu falda; **you've forgotten your CDs!** ¡te has olvidado tus compactos!; **2** (*talking

to more than one person*) (*with a singular noun*) vuestro/vuestra; (*with a plural noun*) vuestros/vuestras; **your Spanish test is on Friday** vuestro examen de español es el viernes; **your rucksacks are in the dining room** vuestras mochilas están en el comedor; **3** (*although 'tu', vuestro', 'vuestra' are now commonly used in most situations, there are formal translations of 'your' which you use in a job interview or other formal situation*) (*with a singular noun*) su; (*with a plural noun*) sus; **thank you for your hospitality** gracias por su hospitalidad; **4** (*with parts of the body or clothing*) (*with a singular noun*) el/la; (*with a plural noun*) los/las; **do you want to take your coat off?** ¿quieres quitarte el abrigo?; **wash your hands** lávate las manos.

yours *pronoun* **1** (*talking to one person*) (*referring to a singular noun*) el tuyo/la tuya, (*referring to a plural noun*) los tuyos/las tuyas; **my brother's younger than yours** mi hermano es más joven que el tuyo; **these aren't my glasses – are they yours?** estas gafas no son mías – ¿son tuyas?; **yours are better** los tuyos/las tuyas son mejores; **a friend of yours** un amigo tuyo/una amiga tuya; **2** (*talking to more than one person*) (*referring to a singular noun*) el vuestro/la vuestra; (*referring to a plural noun*) los vuestros/las vuestras; **our house is smaller than yours** nuestra casa es más pequeña que la vuestra; **our car is smaller than yours** nuestro coche es más pequeño que el vuestro; **our children are older than yours** nuestros hijos son mayores que los vuestros; **a friend of yours** un amigo vuestro/una amiga vuestra; **3** (*as with 'you' and 'your' there are formal translations for formal situations*) (*referring to a singular noun*) el suyo/la suya; (*referring to a plural noun*) los suyos/las suyas (*note that here the translation is the same whether you are talking to one person or to more than one person*) **excuse me, is this book yours?** ¿perdone, es suyo este libro?; **excuse me, are these books yours?** ¿perdone, son suyos estos libros?

yourself *pronoun* **1** te; **you'll hurt yourself** te vas a hacer daño; **2** (*for emphasis*) tú mismo/tú misma; **did you do it yourself?** ¿lo hiciste tú mismo?/¿lo hiciste tú misma?; **by yourself** solo/sola; **3** (*like 'you' and 'your' there are formal translations for 'yourself' for formal situations*) se, (*for emphasis*) usted mismo/usted misma; **as you yourself will understand** como usted mismo comprenderá.

yourselves *pronoun* **1** os; **when you have washed yourselves** cuando os hayáis lavado (*when used with a verb in the infinitive or in commands, 'os' is joined to the verb*) **help yourselves** servidos; **by yourselves** solos/solas; **2** (*for emphasis*) vosotros mismos/vosotras mismas; **did you do it yourselves?** ¿lo hicisteis vosotros mismos?/¿lo hicisteis vosotras

mismas?; **3** (*like 'you' and 'your' there are formal translations for 'yourself' for formal situations*) se (*when used with a verb in the infinitive or in commands, 'se' is joined to the verb*) **please, help yourselves** sírvanse, por favor; (*for emphasis*) ustedes mismos/ustedes mismas; **did you do it yourselves?** ¿lo hicieron ustedes mismos?/¿lo hicieron ustedes mismas?

youth *noun* **1** (*stage of life*) juventud *Fem.*; **2** (*young people*) juventud *Fem.*; **today's youth** la juventud de hoy, los jóvenes de hoy; **3** (*young male*) joven *Masc.*

youth hostel *noun* albergue *Masc.* juvenil.

Yugoslavia *noun* Yugoslavia *Fem.*

Zz

zany *adjective* chiflado/chiflada (*informal*).

zebra *noun* cebra *Fem.*

zebra crossing *noun* paso *Masc.* de cebra.

zero *noun* cero *Masc.*

zigzag *verb* zigzaguear [17].

zip *noun* cremallera *Fem.*

zodiac *noun* zodiaco *Masc.*; **the signs of the zodiac** los signos del zodiaco.

zone *noun* zona *Fem.*

zoo *noun* zoo *Masc.*

zoom lens *noun* lente *Fem.* de zoom.

a
b
c
d
e
f
g
h
i
j
k
l
m
n
o
p
q
r
s
t
u
v
w
x
y
z

SPANISH LIFE AND CULTURE

At school

Spanish	English
Voy al colegio a pie.	I walk to school.
Estoy en el primero de ESO.	I'm in year 8.
Hay 25 alumnos en mi curso.	There are 25 pupils in my class.
Los lunes, a las nueve, tengo matemáticas.	On Mondays, at 9 o'clock, I have maths.
Hago inglés y español.	I do English and Spanish.
Soy fuerte en/Voy bien en...	I'm good at...
Soy débil en...	I'm not very good at...
Estoy estudiando para el examen de...	I'm studying for the ... exam.
Tenemos muchos deberes.	We have a lot of homework.
Al mediodía, como en la cantina.	At midday, I have lunch in the canteen.

Spanish	English
¡Pasa!	Come in! (to one pupil)
¡Entrad!	Come in! (to two or more pupils)
Sacad vuestros cuadernos.	Take out your exercise books.
Abrid vuestro libros a la página 23.	Open your books at page 23.
En silencio por favor.	Quietly, please.
Escuchad bien.	Listen carefully.
Escuchad y repetid.	Listen and repeat.
Trabaja con una pareja.	Work with a partner.
Leed el primer párrafo.	Read the first paragraph.
Escribid una descripción de...	Write a description of...
Buscad las palabras en un diccionario.	Look up the words in a dictionary.

Necesito...
I need...

Spanish	English	Spanish	English
un libro de texto.	a textbook.	*una goma.*	a rubber.
un cuaderno.	an exercise book.	*un sacapuntas.*	a pencil sharpener.
un lápiz.	a pencil.	*unas tijeras.*	scissors.
un bolígrafo.	a ballpoint pen.	*una calculadora.*	a calculator.
un rotulador.	a felt-tip pen.		
una regla.	a ruler.		

Mi asignatura preferida es...
My favourite subject is...

el alemán.	German.	*la geografía.*	geography.
la biología.	biology.	*la historia.*	history.
las ciencias.	science.	*la informática.*	ICT.
el diseño.	art.	*el inglés.*	English.
el español.	Spanish.	*las mates.*	maths.
la educación física.	PE.	*la música.*	music.
la física.	physics.	*la química.*	chemistry.
el francés.	French.	*la tecnología.*	technology.

Más tarde, quisiera...
Later on I'd like to...

ir a la universidad.	go to university.	*hacer un aprendizaje.*	do an apprenticeship.
estudiar.	study.	*encontrar un empleo.*	find a job.
hacer un diploma.	do a diploma.	*viajar al extranjero.*	go abroad.

Did you know...?

- that Spanish compulsory secondary school (*ESO*) is for young people between 12 and 16, while 16 to 18 year olds study for the Baccalaureate (*Bachillerato*).
- that pupils in state schools in Spain do not wear uniforms, but in many countries in Latin America pupils have to wear a uniform.
- that in Spain and most Latin American countries, parents have to pay for their children's school books and other learning materials.
- that the main school holidays in most Latin American countries are from Christmas to February?

At home

En mi familia, somos cinco.	There are five of us in my family.
Tengo un hermano/una hermana.	I have a brother/a sister.
un hermanastro/una hermanastra	a half-brother/a half-sister
un mellizo/una melliza	a twin brother/a twin sister
Soy hijo único.	I'm an only child *(boy speaking)*.
Soy hija única.	I'm an only child *(girl speaking)*.

Vivo en...
I live in...

una casa.	a house.	*en la segunda/ cuarta planta.*	on the second/ fourth floor.
un apartamento.	a flat.	*en la planta baja.*	on the ground floor.

Hay...
There is...

una cocina.	a kitchen.	*un WC.*	a toilet.
una sala de estar.	a living room.	*un estudio.*	a study/an office.
un comedor.	a dining room.	*un garaje.*	a garage.
un dormitorio.	a bedroom.	*un jardín.*	a garden.
un cuarto de baño.	a bathroom.		

Mi pasatiempo preferido es...
My favourite pastime is...

salir con amigos.	going out with friends.
ir al centro (de la ciudad).	going into town.
ir de compras.	going shopping.
ir a un concierto.	going to concerts.
la lectura.	reading.
escuchar la música.	listening to music.
ver la tele.	watching TV.
jugar a la consola.	playing on a games console.
ir de fiestas/ir de discotecas.	going to parties/discos.
ir a montar en bici.	going cycling.

¿Qué programas hay en la tele?	What's on the telly ?

Mi programa/serie preferida es...
My favourite programme/series is...

un programa de deporte.	a sports programme.	*un concurso.*	a game show.
un culebrón.	a soap.	*las noticias/el noticiero.*	the news.

Tengo...
I've got...

un televisor (pantalla grande).	a (wide screen) TV.
una consola de juegos.	a games console.
una cámara digital.	a digital camera.
un iPod®.	an iPod®.
un (telefono) móvil.	a mobile phone.

On the computer

el ordenador	computer
el sitio web, el web	website
el blog, la bitácora	blog
la webcam, la cámara	webcam

Con el ordenador...
On my computer I...

nevego en Internet.	surf the Web.	*busco algo en Internet.*	look something up on the Internet.
mando mails a mis amigos.	email friends.	*tuiteo.*	tweet.
descargo música.	download music.	*entro en redes sociales.*	go on social network sites.
veo DVDs.	watch DVDs.		
hago los deberes.	do homework.	*visito chats.*	visit chatrooms.

Email

un correo electrónico, un email	an email
una dirección de correo electrónico	an email address
enviar un correo electrónico, un email	to send an email
recibir un correo electrónico, un email	to get an email
borrar un mensaje	to delete a message
correo basura	spam
responder	to reply
reenviar	to forward
hacer click (en)	to click (on)
copiar y pegar	to cut and paste
un archivo	a file

On the phone

¡Diga!	Hello!
¿Puedo hablar con?	Can I speak to...?
¿Quien llama?	Who's calling?
No cuelgas.	Hold on.
¿Puedo dejar un mensaje?	Can I leave a message?
Volveré a llamar más tarde.	I'll call back later.
un mensaje de texto, un SMS	a text
mandar un mensaje de texto	to send a text
mandar un mensaje de texto a alguien	to text someone

Did you know...?
- that in email addresses, @ is called *arroba* and dot is *punto*.

Food and eating out

¿Que desea?	What would you like?
Me gustaría tomar... I'd like...	
un zumo de naranja.	an orange juice.
¿Tiene usted helado de vainilla?	Have you got vanilla ice cream?

Para comenzar/como entrada deme... For a starter I'll have...	
una sopa de cebolla.	onion soup.
la crema de champiñones.	mushroom soup.
Como plato fuerte/principal deme... For my main course I'll have...	
el pollo asado	roast chicken
una hamburguesa	a burger
con... with...	
patatas fritas.	chips.
una ensalada de tomate.	tomato salad.
una ensalada de mixta.	mixed salad.
De postre me gustaría For dessert I'd like...	
el mousse de chocolate.	chocolate mousse.
la tarta de pera.	pear tart.
helado de fresa.	strawberry ice cream.
Para beber... To drink I'll have...	
agua mineral.	mineral water.
una Coca-Cola.	a Coke.
un zumo de fruta.	a fruit juice.

Tengo hambre.	I'm hungry.
Tengo sed.	I'm thirsty.
Tengo alergia.	I have an allergy.

Did you know...?
- that shops in Spain and some Latin American countries are often closed (*cerrado*) from about 2 p.m. to 4.30 p.m., but are open (*abierto*) late into the evening?
- that lunch in Spain (*la comida*) is usually taken after 2 p.m. and dinner (*la cena*) from about 10 p.m.?

Meals

el desayuno	breakfast
el almuerzo/la comida	lunch
la cena	dinner

Food and drink

agua	If you order bottled water in a restaurant in Spain, you will be asked if you want *agua con gas* (sparkling), or *agua sin gas* (still). A *gaseosa* is like bottled lemonade, whereas *limonada*, more common in Latin America, is made with fresh lemons and is not fizzy.
antojitos	In Mexico, *antojitos* (little snacks) are often served before a meal. This might be *guacamole* with *nachos* (tortilla chips), or it might be a variety of delicious small appetizers typical of the region.
bocadillo	This is the word in Spain for a sandwich made from French bread. In Mexico it is usually called a *torta*, and in other countries in Latin America a *sándwich*. In Spain a *sándwich* is always made from sliced bread (*pan de molde*).
café	Latin America produces some of the best quality coffee in the world, and it is drunk everywhere. In Colombia, a *tinto* is a small black coffee, and in Mexico *café de olla* is prepared on the stove, with spices and sugar. In Spain, *café con leche* is white coffee, usually half milk; *café cortado* is a black coffee with a dash of milk; and *café solo* is black coffee.
chorizo	A cured salami-shaped sausage, often eaten in Spain in *bocadillos*, as *tapas*, etc. They are always made with paprika, and may also contain chilli.

churrasco	This is steak and Argentina is famous for its beef. It is usually chargrilled, and often served with *chimichurri*, a hot sauce made with chilli, garlic, and vinegar.
dulce de coco or *cocada*	A popular sweet all over the Spanish Caribbean, made by boiling grated coconut with brown sugar and water.
empanadas	These small pies are a popular snack in most Spanish Caribbean countries. They are usually filled with meat, but other fillings such as shrimp or chicken can also be used.
enchiladas	These are wheat *tortillas* filled with meat or cheese and often served in Mexico in a spicy tomato sauce. *Tacos* are thinner *tortillas* made of maize and served with a variety of fillings.
frijoles or *frijoles*	These are beans, which are an essential part of most meals in many Spanish Caribbean and Latin American countries. Often served with rice.
guacamole	A salad made of mashed avocados, seasoned with diced onions, chilli, and sometimes tomatoes. In Mexico it is often eaten as a snack with *nachos*, or tortilla chips.
helados	Ice cream, flavours include *chocolate* (chocolate), *fresa* (strawberry), *pistacho* (pistachio), *vainilla* (vanilla), and many others.
horchata (de chufa)	A thick, creamy, chilled drink made in Spain, particularly around Valencia, from tiger nuts. Often sold in summer in open-air cafes.
jugos or *zumos (de fruta)*	The word *jugo* is more common in Latin America, and *zumo* in Spain. In Latin America many juices (*jugos*) are made from tropical fruits like mango, *guayaba* (guava), *papaya*, and *piña* (pineapple).
maíz	Maize, or corn, is very important in most Latin American countries, as it forms the basis of the diet. In Mexico and Central America it is usually eaten in the form of *tortillas*, but in other countries it is prepared in different ways.
pan	*Pan* is used to mean both 'bread' and 'loaf'. The most common kind is *una barra*. The narrower variety is called a *baguette* and rolls are *panecillos*. A British-style loaf is *un pan de molde*. A *panadería* (baker's) also sells *croissants*, *bollos* (buns), and *roscos* (a kind of doughnut).

patatas or *papas*	These are potatoes. The word *patatas* is used in Spain, except in the Canary Islands, and *papas* everywhere in Latin America. Chips or French fries are *patatas/papas fritas*.
tamales	A popular Latin American dish found in many countries between Mexico and Peru, made from a corn-based dough stuffed with a spicy filling made of meat, together with carrots, onions, olives, or other ingredients. It is then cut into squares, wrapped in banana leaves, and boiled.
tapas	Small snacks served in bars and cafes in Spain; the selection can be very varied.
tortilla	In Spain a *tortilla* is an omelette: a plain omelette is a *tortilla francesa*, and a potato omelette is a *tortilla española*. In Mexico and Central America, a *tortilla* is made of maize or wheat and is wrapped around fillings of various kinds.

Healthy living

Para mantenerse en forma, hay que...	To keep healthy, you have to...
levantarse temprano	get up early
acostarse temprano	go to bed early
hacer deporte	take exercise
ir a pie/caminar	walk
Es saludable/sano.	It's healthy.
No es saludable/sano.	It's unhealthy.
Hay que evitar...	You must avoid...
beber	drinking
fumar	smoking
todo los días	every day
una vez a la/por semana	once a week
de vez en cuando	now and then
nunca	never
siempre	always

Soy/Es...	I am/He/She is...
deportisa.	sporty.
Estoy/Está...	I am/He/She is...
lesionada/lesionada.	injured.
bien.	well.

Me gusta...
I like...

Me gustan...
I like... (+plural)

No me gusta...
I don't like...

No me gustan...
I don't like... (+plural)

la gaseosa.	fizzy drinks.	*los dulces/*	sweets.
el zumo de fruta.	fruit juice.	*caramelos.*	
el café.	coffee.	*la verdura.*	vegetables.
la leche.	milk.	*la carne.*	meat.
la fruta.	fruit.	*el pescado.*	fish.

Shopping

hacer las compras ...
to go shopping (for food) ...

en la pastelería	at the cake shop	*en la charcutería*	at the
en la panadería	at the baker's		delicatessen
en la carnicería	at the butcher's	*en el mercado*	at the market
		en el	at the
		supermercado	supermarket

Quisiera...
I'd like...

un pan de molde.	a loaf of bread.	*un kilo de*	a kilo of
quattros	four rolls.	*manzanas.*	apples.
panecillos.			

| *¿Cuanto cuesta?* | How much is it? |

625

On holiday

El verano pasado, fui a España.   Last summer, I went to Spain.
El próximo verano, voy a ir a Francia.   Next summer, I'm going to France.

Fuimos... We travelled...			
en avión.	by plane.	*en barco.*	by ship.
en coche.	by car.	*en autocar.*	by coach.
en tren.	by train.	*en bici.*	by bike.

Did you know...?
- that in Spain you can buy stamps in a tobacconist's shop (*un estanco*)?

Did you know...?
- that football is the most popular sport throughout Latin America, except in some Caribbean countries like Cuba, the Dominican Republic, and Venezuela, where baseball is preferred?
- that basketball is very popular in Spain, second only to football?
- that FC Barcelona (nicknamed *Barça*) is one of Europe's biggest football clubs? *Barça's* home is the huge Camp Nou stadium.
- that *Real Madrid* is one of Europe's biggest football clubs and that they play at the huge Santiago Bernabéu stadium?
- that Spain's most important road cycle race is called the *Vuelta Ciclista a España*, and that cycling is very popular in Spain?

Places of interest in Spain

Alhambra The famous fortified Moorish palace which dominates Granada.

Asturias Northern Spain. A beautiful mountainous area where it is traditional to drink cider rather than wine, and where some people play the bagpipes.

Baleares or **las Islas Baleares** Mediterranean islands of Mallorca, Menorca, Ibiza, and Formentera, popular holiday resorts.

Canarias or **las Islas Canarias** A group of islands off the coast of West Africa including Tenerife, Gran Canaria, Lanzarote, and La Palma. They are popular holiday resorts.

Catalunya The Catalan name for Catalonia, or *Cataluña* in Spanish. Barcelona is its capital and the majority of people speak Catalan as their first language.

Costa The Spanish for 'coast'. Some of the famous tourist areas are *la Costa Brava* in the northeast, *la Costa Blanca* in the southeast, and *la Costa del Sol* on the southern coast.

Cuevas de Altamira These caves in northern Spain are famous for their prehistoric paintings (18,000 BC), discovered in 1869.

Euzkadi The Basque name for the Basque country, or *el País Vasco* in Spanish. A green, rainy area with the industrial city of Bilbao, famous for the Guggenheim Museum of modern art, and the resort of San Sebastián, known for the most elaborate *tapas* in Spain.

Galicia The north-western part of Spain, famous for its wet climate, beautiful coast, excellent seafood, and Celtic culture. The language is *gallego*.

Museo del Prado This museum in Madrid is one of the finest art galleries in the world.

Palacio de la Zarzuela The official residence of the royal family in Madrid.

Puerta del Sol A square in the old part of Madrid. Road distances from the capital are calculated from here.

las Ramblas A tree-lined avenue in Barcelona famous for the variety of street stalls, entertainers, cafes, and strollers.

Sagrada Familia This church in Barcelona is the unfinished masterpiece of the Catalan Art Nouveau architect, Gaudí.

Did you know...?

- that Spain's highest mountain is *Teide* (3710 m), on the island of Tenerife, and that the highest mainland mountain is *Mulhacén* (3482m), in the Sierra Nevada south of Granada?

- that there are about 400 million speakers of Spanish, which makes it the third most spoken language in the world?

- that as well as Spanish, Galician, Catalan, and Basque are important languages in Spain?

Places of interest in Latin America

The Amazon   This great river passes through Peru and Colombia before entering Brazil, forming by far the largest area of tropical rainforest left in the world. Many groups of Indian peoples still live a traditional lifestyle.

Iguazú falls   Spectacular and world-famous series of waterfalls on the Iguazú river, on the border between Argentina, Brazil, and Paraguay, set in a unique tropical forest full of birds and butterflies.

las Islas Galapagos Small islands off the coast of Ecuador famous for their unique animals, including giant tortoises, iguanas, and many species of birds. Charles Darwin visited in the 19th century, and his study of the wildlife helped him to develop his theory of evolution.

Macchu Picchu   These ruins in the mountains of Peru, rediscovered in 1911, are one of the most beautiful and mysterious ancient sites in the world. The Inca people built the city near the top of a mountain in the early fifteenth century, and it contained palaces, baths, temples, and about 150 houses. There are many other Inca remains in Peru, and also in Ecuador and Bolivia.

Mayan culture   In the south of Mexico (especially the Yucatán peninsula) and Guatemala, there are many relics of the Mayan civilization which existed before the Spanish conquest. These include palaces and great pyramids, often very well-preserved, like the ones at Chichén Itza and Tikal.

Salto del Angel   The highest waterfall in the world at 970m, the Salto del Angel (Angel Falls) is in the far south of Venezuela, close to the Amazon basin, and falls from a huge flat-topped mountain onto the plains far below.

Did you know...?

- that the highest mountain in South America, *Aconcagua*, is the highest in the world outside the Himalayas?
- that *Quechua*, the language of the Incas, is still spoken by 13 million people, and is an official language in Peru?
- that Mexico City has a population of over 20 million people and is the second largest city in the world?
- that the Amazon river system contains over 20% of all the world's fresh water?
- that the three countries in the world with the greatest biodiversity are all in Latin America—Brazil, Colombia, and Mexico?
- that most of the population of Paraguay speak *guaraní*, an Indian language, as well as Spanish?

Festivals and celebrations

Año Nuevo	New Year's Day. A public holiday throughout Spain and Latin America.
Carnaval	Carnival is celebrated the week before Lent. People often dress up in elaborate costumes, and there are usually processions.
Día de los Inocentes	28 December, the equivalent of April Fool's Day. People play tricks on each other called *inocentadas*, while saying the words *Mariposa Inocente*.
Día de los Muertos	Day of the Dead, 1 November. Known as *Día de Todos los Santos* outside Mexico, this is celebrated throughout Spain and Latin America, but is particularly important in Mexico, most famously in the city of Oaxaca.
Día del Trabajo	1 May, Labour Day is a public holiday in Spain and many countries in Latin America.
Inti Raymi or Fiesta del Sol	24 June, the Festival of the Sun, the most important feast of the Incas, is still celebrated in Peru.
Local holidays	Many cities and towns in Spain and Latin America celebrate local holidays, for example, 15 May in Madrid, and 24 September in Barcelona. These are usually associated with the patron saint of the city or town.

Navidades	Christmas Day is a holiday in Spain and Latin America, but is not as important as it is in Britain or the USA. In Spain the word *navidades* is used to refer to the period around Christmas when people are on holiday.
Nochebuena	Christmas Eve, and many people go to Midnight Mass, the *misa del gallo*. In most Spanish-speaking countries, this is also the night of a big family meal.
Nochevieja	New Year's Eve when people see the New Year in with parties, and in Spain twelve grapes are eaten (one for each month of the new year) at midnight. In Ecuador in South America, it is traditional to make figures, making fun of people who have been in the news in the previous year. These are then burnt.
Reyes (Fiesta de los Reyes Magos)	Feast of the Three Kings: 6th January. Traditionally Spaniards and Latin Americans exchange gifts on this day. Nowadays many people also give each other presents on Christmas Day.
Semana Santa	Holy Week, which precedes Easter, is a very important holiday in Spain and Latin America. Many cities and towns stage religious processions during *Semana Santa*, the most famous being in Seville in Spain.

Dates

el primero de enero	the 1st of January	*duodécimo*	12th
		decimotercero	13th
segundo (2º)	2nd	*decimocuarto*	14th
tercero (3º)	3rd	*decimoquinto*	15th
cuarto (4º)	4th	*dicimosexto*	16th
quinto	5th	*decimoséptimo*	17th
sexto	6th	*decimoctavo*	18th
séptimo	7th	*dicimonoveno*	19th
octavo	8th	*vigésimo*	20th
noveno	9th	*vigésimo primero*	21st
décimo	10th	*trigésimo*	30th
undécimo	11th		

Mi cumpleaños es en febrero.	My birthday is in February.
Se fue en marzo.	She left in March.
Llegamos el 11 de noviembre.	We're arriving on 11th November.
Ricardo nació el 2 de agosto.	Richard was born on 2nd August.
en el año 2006 (dos mil seis)	in 2006

Days

lunes	Monday	*viernes*	Friday
martes	Tuesday	*sábado*	Saturday
miércoles	Wednesday	*domingo*	Sunday
jueves	Thursday		

Months

enero	January	*julio*	July
febrero	Febuary	*agosto*	August
marzo	March	*septiembre*	September
abril	April	*octubre*	October
mayo	May	*noviembre*	November
junio	June	*diciembre*	December

Seasons

la primavera	spring	*el otoño*	autumn
el verano	summer	*el invierno*	winter

Time

¿Que hora es?
What time is it?

Es la una.	It's one o'clock.
Son las cuatro y media.	It's half past four.
Son las seis y cuarto.	It's quarter past six.
Son las seis menos cuarto.	It's quarter to six.
Son las nueve y diez.	It's ten past nine.
Son las nueve menos diez.	It's ten to nine.
Es el mediodía.	It's midday.
Es la media noche.	It's midnight.
Son las diecinueve horas.	It's 7 pm (19.00).
Son las trece horas y quince minutos.	It's 1.15 pm (13.15).

Numbers

cero	0
uno	1
dos	2
tres	3
cuatro	4
cinco	5
seis	6
siete	7
ocho	8
nueve	9
diez	10
once	11
doce	12
trece	13
catorce	14
quince	15
dieciséis	16
diecisiete	17
dieciocho	18
diecinueve	19
veinte	20
veintiuno	21
veintidós	22
veintitrés	23
veinticuatro	24
veinticinco	25
veintiséis	26
veintisiete	27
veintiocho	28
veintinueve	29
treinta	30

cuarenta	40
cincuenta	50
sesenta	60
setenta	70
ochenta	80
noventa	90
cien	100

mil	1000
un millón	1 000 000